W9-DCZ-650

Evaluating Practice

EVALUATING PRACTICE

Guidelines for the Accountable Professional

FOURTH EDITION

Martin Bloom
University of Connecticut

Joel Fischer
University of Hawaii, Manoa

John G. Orme
University of Tennessee, Knoxville

Boston   New York   San Francisco
Mexico City   Montreal   Toronto   London   Madrid   Munich   Paris
Hong Kong   Singapore   Tokyo   Cape Town   Sydney

Series Editor: Patricia Quinlin
Editorial Assistant: Annemarie Kennedy
Marketing Manager: Taryn Wahlquist
Editorial-Production Service: Omegatype Typography, Inc.
Composition and Prepress Buyer: Linda Cox
Manufacturing Buyer: JoAnne Sweeney
Cover Administrator: Linda Knowles
Electronic Composition: Omegatype Typography, Inc.

For related titles and support materials, visit our online catalog at www.ablongman.com.

Between the time Website information is gathered and published, some sites may have closed.
Also, the transcription of URLs can result in typographical errors. The publisher would
appreciate notification where these occur so that they may be corrected in subsequent editions.

To obtain permission(s) to use material from this work, please submit a written request to Allyn and
Bacon, Permissions Department, 75 Arlington Street, Boston, MA 02116, or fax your request to 617-848-7320.

Library of Congress Cataloging-in-Publication Data
Bloom, Martin
    Evaluating practice : guidelines for the accountable professional /
Joel Fischer, Martin Bloom, John Orme.–4th ed.
     p.   cm.
  Includes bibliographical references and index.
   ISBN 0-205-34261-2
  1. Social service–Evaluation. 2. Evaluation research (Social action
programs) I. Fischer, Joel. II. Orme, John G. III. Title.
  HV41 .B4498   2003
  361'.0068–dc21

                            2002016310

Printed in the United States of America
10 9 8 7 6 5 4 3 2 1 RRD-VA 07 06 05 04 03 02

To the readers of our book,
we dedicate this dream of scientific practice–
To be both sensitive and humane,
and to be systematic and rigorous,
at the same time, all of the time.

CONTENTS

Preface   xiii

Prologue   1

PART I
WHAT ARE YOU GETTING INTO?   33

1 ■ **Integrating Evaluation and Practice**   35

Introduction to Single-System Designs   *36*
What Are Single-System Designs?   *37*
Single-System Designs and Classical Research: The Knowledge-Building Context   *43*
Single-System Evaluation, Qualitative Research, and Quantitative Research   *48*
Advantages of Using Single-System Designs in Practice   *50*
A Walk through the Evaluation Process   *51*
Summary   *54*

PART II
CONCEPTUALIZING AND MEASURING TARGETS AND OBJECTIVES/GOALS   55

2 ■ **Basic Principles of Conceptualization and Measurement**   57

Introduction   *58*
What Is Measurement?   *58*
Definition as a First Step in Measurement   *60*
Can Everything Be Measured?   *61*
Key Characteristics of All Measures   *62*
Summary   *84*

3 ▦ Specifying Problems and Goals 86

Introduction: From General Problems to Specific Targets of Intervention *87*
Specifying Client Concerns: Identifying and Clarifying Problems and Potentials *88*
Specifying Goals and Objectives *97*
Using Goal Attainment Scaling (GAS) to Establish Goals *102*
Setting Goals in Groups *105*
Problems and Issues in Setting Goals *107*
Summary *114*

4 ▦ Developing a Measurement and Recording Plan 116

Introduction *117*
Steps in Developing a Recording Plan *118*
Charting: Putting Your Information on Graphs *126*
Problem-Oriented Records (POR) *134*
Computerized Recording *137*
Summary *138*

▦ COMPUTER ASSISTED SOCIAL SERVICES (CASS): A USER'S GUIDE 139
APPENDIX: INSTALLING CASS 156

5 ▦ Behavioral Observation 163

Introduction *164*
General Guidelines for Behavioral Observation *166*
Sampling Behaviors *168*
Instruments for Recording Behaviors *173*
Ensuring Accurate Observations *175*
Methods of Recording Behavior *179*
Analog Situations *189*
Recording Behavior in Groups *191*
Summary *193*

6 ▦ Individualized Rating Scales 194

Introduction *194*
Uses of Individualized Rating Scales *196*
Constructing and Using Individualized Rating Scales *199*
Summary *210*

7 ▦ Standardized Questionnaires 211

Introduction *212*
What Are Standardized Questionnaires? *212*
Selecting a Standardized Questionnaire *216*
Administering a Standardized Questionnaire *225*
Some Available Standardized Self-Report Questionnaires *228*
Some Available Standardized Questionnaires for Practitioners *254*
Some Available Standardized Questionnaires for Relevant Others *257*
Some Available Standardized Questionnaires for Independent Observers *261*
Do-It-Yourself Questionnaires *261*
Using Standardized Questionnaires in Groups *262*
Computer Management of Standardized Questionnaires *263*

Summary   *264*
Appendix   *265*

COMPUTER ASSISTED ASSESSMENT PACKAGE (CAAP): A USER'S GUIDE   267

8   Logs   277

Introduction   *277*
Types of Client Logs   *278*
Putting Qualitative and Quantitative Information Together   *288*
Introducing Clients to Logs   *291*
Practitioner Logs   *292*
Maximizing and Verifying the Reliability and Validity of Logs   *293*
Summary   *295*

9   Reactivity and Nonreactive Measures   296

Introduction   *296*
Reactivity of Measures   *298*
Unobtrusive (Nonreactive) Measures   *302*
Summary   *311*

10   Selecting a Measure   312

Introduction   *312*
Considerations in Deciding on a Measure   *313*
Use of Multiple Measures   *317*
Selecting a Measure   *322*
Summary   *322*

PART III
EVALUATION DESIGNS   325

11   Basic Principles of Single-System Designs   327

Introduction   *328*
An Example Connecting Practice and Evaluation Designs   *328*
Purposes of Single-System Designs   *330*
Unique Characteristics of Single-System Designs   *331*
Causality in Single-System Designs   *347*
External Validity and Generalizability   *353*
Overview of Single-System Designs   *360*
Summary   *363*

12   Baselining   364

Introduction   *364*
Purposes of the Baseline   *365*
Types of Baselines   *367*
How Long Should Baselining Continue?   *368*
When Are Baselines Not Necessary?   *374*

Issues Regarding Baselining   *375*
Summary   *379*

13 ▨ From the Case Study to the Basic Single-System Design: *A-B*   380

Introduction   *380*
Case Studies or Predesigns   *381*
Design *A-B:* The Basic Single-System Design   *386*
Summary   *399*

14 ▨ The Experimental Single-System Designs: *A-B-A, A-B-A-B, B-A-B*   400

Introduction   *401*
Basic Experimental Designs   *404*
Summary   *427*

15 ▨ Multiple Designs for Single Systems   428

Introduction   *429*
Multiple-Baseline Designs: Across Problems, Clients, or Settings   *429*
Multiple-Target Designs   *452*
Variations on Multiple Designs   *454*
Summary   *456*

16 ▨ Changing Intensity Designs and Successive Intervention Designs   458

Introduction   *458*
Changing Intensity Designs: $A\text{-}B^1\text{-}B^2\text{-}B^3$ *459*
Successive Intervention Designs: *A-B-C, A-B-A-C, A-B-A-C-A*   *470*
Summary   *480*

17 ▨ Complex and Combined Designs   481

Introduction   *481*
Alternating Intervention Design: *A-B/C-(B* or *C)*   *482*
Interaction Design: *A-B-A-B-BC-B-BC*   *489*
Summary   *495*

18 ▨ Selecting a Design   496

Introduction   *496*
Framework for Selecting a Design   *496*
Needed: A Design for All Seasons   *499*
Creativity in Single-System Designs: Making Your Own Designs   *499*
Evaluation in Minimal-Contact Situations   *501*
Single-System Designs in Managed Care: The Stretch Design   *506*
Trouble-Shooting: "Okay, I Understand Everything That You Said,
    but My Case Is Different."   *507*
Summary   *511*

PART IV
ANALYZING YOUR RESULTS   513

19 ■ **Basic Principles of Analysis**   515

Introduction   *516*
Distinguishing Effort, Effectiveness, and Efficiency   *516*
Significance–Practical, Statistical, and Theoretical   *518*
Evaluating Goal Achievement   *524*
Issues in Analysis of Data   *525*
Computer Analysis of Data for Single-System Designs   *531*
The Issue of Autocorrelation   *532*
Tools in Analysis of Data   *538*
Summary   *552*

20 ■ **Visual Analysis of Single-System Design Data**   554

Introduction   *554*
Definition of Terms   *554*
Basic Patterns and Implications   *557*
Visual Inspection of Raw Data   *562*
Interpreting Ambiguous Patterns   *564*
Problems of Visual Inspection   *566*
Creating a Chart with SINGWIN   *568*
Summary   *568*

21 ■ **Descriptive Statistics**   569

Introduction   *569*
Measures of Central Tendency   *570*
Measures of Variation   *574*
Computing and Graphing Measures of Central Tendency and Variation
    with SINGWIN   *576*
Measures of Trend   *576*
Measures of Effect Size   *581*
Optimal Uses and Cautions for Specific Descriptive Statistics   *592*
Summary   *594*

22 ■ **Tests of Statistical Significance for Single-System Designs**   595

Introduction   *595*
Proportion/Frequency Approach   *596*
Three-Standard-Deviation-Band Approach (X-Moving Range-Chart)   *600*
Chi-Square   *605*
t-Test   *609*
General Considerations in Using Tests of Statistical Significance   *610*
Optimal Uses and Cautions for Specific Analytic Procedures   *612*
Summary   *613*

23 ■ Computer Analysis of Single-System Design Data   614

Chapter Overview   *615*
Starting SINGWIN   *616*
Exiting SINGWIN   *616*
Getting the Big Picture   *617*
Using Specific Procedures   *618*
Appendix: Installing SINGWIN   *646*
Summary   *650*

24 ■ Selecting a Procedure for Analyzing Data   651

Introduction   *651*
Framework for Selecting a Procedure for Analyzing Data   *651*
Other Statistical Considerations   *653*
Nonstatistical Considerations   *655*
Limitations   *655*
Summary   *656*

PART V
THE CHALLENGE OF SINGLE-SYSTEM DESIGNS   657

25 ■ Not for Practitioners Alone   659

Introduction   *660*
Special Applications of Single-System Designs   *660*
Recent Criticisms of Single-System Evaluation   *665*
For the Client   *674*
For the Administrator   *680*
For Educators and Students   *686*
Summary   *688*

References   689

Name Index   713

Subject Index   719

PREFACE

I appeal to you. . . . Measure, evaluate, estimate, appraise your results, in some form, in any terms that rest on something beyond faith, assertion, and "illustrative case."

State your objectives and how far you have reached them. . . . Let time enough elapse so that there may be some reasonable hope of permanence in the results which you state.

The greatest value [of evaluation of practice] will be . . . an evaluation of one method against another, or one's present work with one's past and one's hope for the future. Out of such evaluations will come, I believe, better service to the client. [We will be able to deliver better services to clients] by getting attention focused on at least a fair proportion of attainable goals and by finding better means of knowing when we are off the track that we meant to follow.

There are few human service professionals who would deny the importance of the message contained in the above quotation. But how long will it take for the concept of accountability to visibly influence our thoughts, our attitudes, and our behavior? Take another look at that quotation. These remarks were made over 70 years ago by Dr. Richard Cabot (1931) in a presidential address to a helping profession. It

sometimes takes an incredibly long time before good ideas have much impact.

Today there is an increasing sense of urgency about being accountable as the government, managed care systems, our clients and consumers, and colleagues all point to the need to evaluate our practice and to provide evidence of the effectiveness of our work. Yet even with this increased pressure, some of us in the helping professions have not yet been successful in building systematic evaluation into our practice. We believe that part of the reason for this is that the tools for such evaluations have not been widely available to professionals.

This book addresses that need. The purpose of *Evaluating Practice: Guidelines for the Accountable Professional* is to make available to students and practitioners in all of the helping professions–including social work, psychology, psychiatry, education, medicine and health, and counseling–the knowledge, skills, and specific procedures to evaluate their own practices. The primary tools for achieving this are called *single-system designs,* which are systematic ways of going about analyzing, measuring, and evaluating practice. Single-system designs involve approaches and procedures that show how evaluation and practice can be integrated, thus offering an excellent opportunity for practitioners to demonstrate their accountability. Moreover, as we shall discuss in detail later, single-system designs provide a number of specific advantages for practice—ways that we believe will actually help you enhance the effectiveness and efficiency of your services.

We have tried to make this book as practical as possible. You can connect to the evaluation procedures presented whatever theories or approaches to practice you ordinarily use. Each step of the evaluation process is thoroughly discussed with many examples presented from a wide variety of professions and fields of practice. Also, because single-system designs can be used to evaluate practice across all levels of intervention from micro- to macro-level practice (i.e., from work with individuals to work with communities), we have provided examples, especially in Part III, of evaluation of practice at all those levels, including several examples of macro-level practice and evaluation. We've also provided a number of references so that you can explore topics of interest in greater depth. We have tried to discover what you need in order to use evaluation in the problems and tasks you face in everyday practice. Thus, we have included guidelines for selecting the best measures, designs, and analytic procedures. We even suggest ways by which you can introduce evaluation procedures to your clients.

We provide the background for all of the steps in the evaluation process—measurement, design, and analysis—but the accent is on helping you to translate these ideas into concrete actions to help make your practice more effective. Indeed, the heart of this book involves three main components: *conceptualizing and measuring client and client/system targets and goals,* including those of individuals, families, groups, communities, and institutions; *designing an evaluation* that is appropriate to the task but sensitive to the needs of the client or client/system; and *analyzing the ongoing data so as to supply corrective feedback to practice* in order to more effectively achieve client and client/system goals.

While there are ways to deal with accountability other than by evaluation, and while there are ways to evaluate other than by single-system designs, we strongly suggest that monitoring and evaluating our practice using single-system designs is an important step on the way to demonstrating our accountability. Moreover, single-system designs offer an extremely helpful set of methods for beginning to translate our commitment to evaluation into visible actions.

It has been over 20 years since the publication of the first edition of this book. During the interim, the field of single-system designs has exploded with new knowledge. We have tried to capture that new knowledge in this edition of the book and have done our best to try to translate it into something approximating English because the field is becoming increasingly technical, even about what is intended to be a rapid and approximate evaluation method. But we still hope this will be *useful* knowledge, not merely new knowledge for the sake of new knowledge.

As you begin to read the book you will see that we are strong advocates of a holistic approach to scientific practice. That is, we believe that every practice situation requires an integration of intervention, ethical and evaluation principles, and procedures. This book, of course, focuses largely on the evaluation component, but evaluation without practice and ethics or practice without ethics and evaluation are hollow endeavors at best. As you also will see from the Prologue, the practiceethics/evaluation process often is not perfect or particularly smooth. Sometimes, we must use approximations of ideal models. But using a systematic, holistic approach to scientific practice—wherein each practice, ethical, or evaluation situation is treated much like an experiment with hypotheses to be examined—can be very rewarding for all parties involved.

In this book we have attempted to provide an integration of both quantitative and qualitative approaches to evaluation. We believe that both perspectives have a place in evaluation and reject the idea that only one or the other should dominate.

This edition also continues to make changes and additions in the area of analysis for single-system designs as new approaches are developed. Some of these are a little more complicated than the procedures we described in the first edition–although we also have retained many of those procedures–but we have tried to describe them in ways that will be both comprehensible and useful.

Finally, one of the major features of this book is the description of two personal computer programs using the Windows operating system, including step-by-step guidelines for their use. Knowledge about and use of computers is increasingly a priority in the helping professions, and we hope the inclusion of this material will be a boon to readers. One of the programs is called SINGWIN; it was developed specifically for this book, and it is our hope that it will make calculation of some of the analytic methods less dreary and time consuming. Computer Assisted Social Services (CASS), the other program, will help you manage caseloads, administer measures, and even graph your results. These programs can help simplify the occasionally tedious part of evaluation practice and enhance your efficiency overall. We believe it will be well worth your while to learn how to use these new tools for evaluation, not just for this book but for the whole of your professional career in the twenty-first century. In this edition, both of these computer programs are included on an easy-to-use CD-ROM.

This edition is partly a result of feedback we received from a number of users of the book, based on a survey we took of those users. We have tried to make the improvements that were suggested to us and to keep the strengths that were highlighted for us by the people kind enough to provide feedback.

We believe this book can be used in a variety of educational arrangements–in a course on evaluation, in a course on practice, or in an integrated course combining practice and evaluation. In fact, we have available for our faculty colleagues an *Instructor's Manual* that can be ordered from the publisher. This manual contains some notes on our educational philosophy, chapter summaries, suggested exercises for each chapter, and a test bank of questions that can be used for quizzes or examinations.

We invite you to visit the *Evaluating Practice* website created by John Orme and Mary Ellen Cox (**http://utcmhsrc.csw.utk.edu/ evaluatingpractice/**). This site contains a list of Frequently Asked Questions (FAQ), Power-Point presentation downloads that cover most of this book and that can be viewed or downloaded, links to related sites, a discussion of problems with use of the computer programs accompanying this book, and numerous other features. The site will act as a clearinghouse for information about evaluating practice. Those readers willing to share course syllabi, data, exercises, and so on can send them to John Orme (jorme@utk.edu) to be posted on the web page. The main website for this book is **http:// www.ablongman.com/bloom**. On this site you can find information on downloading the programs included with this book, technical support, links to other sites, and other information related to the book.

When all is said and done, more than anything else, we hope this book will provide some stimulating ideas for you, will challenge you to do your best in your practice efforts with clients and consumers, and will help you to meet the challenges of accountable practice in the twenty-first century.

ACKNOWLEDGMENTS

No book is ever a product of the authors alone. Over the years we have been aided by many colleagues and students who contributed to this book through critical discussions with some of us, or in providing case illustrations. Thank you Art Vandalay, David Patterson, Jim Post, Mary Ellen Cox, Bradley Huitema, Patrick Onghena, Nina Heller, Gail Phillips, Deborah Siegel, Fredric Reamer, Bill Nugent, Vaughn DeCoster, Wallace Gingerich, David Gillespie, Walter Hudson, Siri Jayaratne, William Reid, Waldo Klein, Ingred Beremus, Helen Reinhart, J. Leydon, Richie Greene, Amy Willbrand, and the Icelandic Workshop group–25 social work instructors who came together to study single-system designs with Martin Bloom in Scandinavia in 1989. Hisae Tachi, LeeAnn Killion, and Cathy Greenburg provided fantastic secretarial support as always.

We also want to express special appreciation to the late Walter Hudson for his permission to include the Computer Assisted Social Services material. Walter's death was a great loss to the field and to us personally. We would like to thank Walter's wife, Myrna Hudson, of Walmyr Publishing Company, for her continuing support of our work. We also want to express our deep appreciation to Charles Auerbach, David Schnall, and Heidi Heft Laporte for developing SINGWIN for this book. We would also like to thank the reviewers of this edition: Mary Collins, Boston University; Wanda M. Spaid, Brigham Young University; and Dr. Ellen Whipple, Michigan State University.

Most of all, to our families, we want to express our love and appreciation: Lynn Bloom; Bard and Vicki Bloom; Laird, Sara, Paul Alexander, and Elizabeth Anna Bloom; Renee H. Furuyama; Schmoopie Fischer; Tom, Nikki, and Christy Kelly; and Terri Combs Orme and Charlie Combs Orme. "How do we love thee? Let us count the ways."

Martin Bloom
Joel Fischer
John G. Orme

PROLOGUE
The Whole Story—Briefly

PART I. STARTING SCIENTIFIC PRACTICE

I.A.1., I.B.1, and I.C.1: Establishing the Practice, Ethical, and Evaluation Contexts

Welcome to what may be for you a new way of looking at the world, as a scientific practitioner. We assume that you are (or want to become) a practitioner first and foremost, but also that you want to be as effective and sensitive a practitioner as possible. What we offer in this book is a step toward those goals, but an unusual step in that we want to present an integrated experience that involves all of the major components of scientific practice. There are five components, as follows.

The *practice component* is touched on briefly, as your professional school will provide many classes in this area. Here, we emphasize that practice is a problem-solving process in which the practitioner makes contact with the client so as to understand what problems and strengths are present in the situation, uses the-

ory and its empirically supported evidence to guide practice, gets into and out of ethical problems involved in practice, and ultimately makes sense of all this through a carefully planned evaluation.

The *practice theory and its research-based evidence* is a vital component that involves using the best available information to determine what guiding models you choose to direct your practice. There is a considerable body of empirically informed theory. We present some guidelines for connecting abstract theory/research to concrete practice as part of the ongoing search for new and more effective ways to serve consumers. This involves the skills, attitudes, and the commitment to keep learning from others as well as from our own experience.

Every human interaction involves *ethical choices,* and the helping professional has to negotiate these choices with great care, for all of the people directly and indirectly involved in the case situation. The helping professions have a commitment in words and deeds to the values of a democratic society where there is care and concern for the well-being, rights, and

1

dignity of clients and consumers. We will raise these issues in this Prologue and offer a specific code of ethics for evaluators near the end of the book (Chapter 25).

Evaluation of one's own practice is the focus of this book, and in this Prologue we want to illustrate why evaluation is such a critically important feature of scientific practice. Evaluation, and especially its systematic monitoring, essentially tells us where the client starts, how the client is doing during the helping process, and whether the client gets to where he or she wants to go. We believe that if practitioners can answer at least these questions, then they will be doing the task society has set for professional helping practice. If not, then we all are going to be in trouble–the consumers, the profession, and society.

There is one more ingredient in scientific practice: *you, the person who is providing the professional help.* By including you in the equation, we want to recognize how much the helping person brings to scientific practice. It is your motivation to help, your intelligence to make sense of challenging information, your sensitivity to the cultural and value nuances of the situation, and your energy to bring all of the pieces together that in fact make scientific practice a reality. One reason we have introduced portions of this evaluation text on CD-ROM and refer to numerous Internet sites is to encourage you to interact with this material and to feel comfortable using it in field situations.

Now the question is how to present an integrated perspective on practice methods, theories and research studies, ethics, and evaluation of your own practice? It is difficult to do all of these at the same time, and most textbooks (let alone classes) focus on one or another, and essentially leave it up to the student to make the integration. We believe this is a major mistake, and so we have tried to avoid it by integrating these components in this Prologue, although the rest of this book will focus mainly on the evaluation component. Here is a preview of coming attractions.

Imagine yourself in a three-dimensional space. In front of you is your client (or client-system, like fam-

ilies, neighborhood associations, etc.; we'll use the word *client* to refer to any client/system). Keep your eye steadily on the client.

On your left hand is a body of theoretical information and a smaller portion of it that is supported by empirical research. You will use this general information to make sense of the specific problems your individual client is facing.

On your right hand is a body of ethical information, useful in keeping clearly on the professional path toward helping the client if you can, but if you can't, then doing no harm (a brief restatement of the Hippocratic code of ethics).

And backing you up are the ideas and processes for evaluating your own practice.

There you are, moving through this space and time with your client, but always in contact with evidence-based theory, professional ethical principles, and reasonably objective evaluation of your own practice so you know where your client started, where the client wants to go, where the client is currently headed, and when the client reaches the goal. As you are close enough to shake hands with your client, so too, you are close enough to lay your hands on theoretical ideas and empirical evidence, on guiding ethical principles, and on the relatively simple tools to evaluate your practice. All within your hands' reach, all at the same time. This is the space of scientific practice (see Figure P.1).

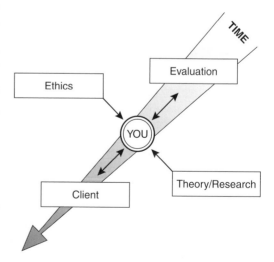

FIGURE P.1   The space of scientific practice.

INTRODUCING MRS. ABBOTT AND THE "ROARING NINETIES" CLUB

Why is it that programs that teach various forms of social and human services expect the students to put everything together from the 15 to 20 classes and field experiences they might have? We'll tell you why: because many teachers have trouble teaching it. Each student practitioner has to struggle to complete this multidimensional puzzle for himself or herself. Most teachers are more comfortable teaching one piece of the whole, but that is not how reality is. What is real is that there is a client or a client/system in front of you, with some problems and some resources, and you have to help that client/system solve a problem or achieve some desired goal. Any human action is automatically a system of moral relationships, so that you and the clients have to consider what the ethical issues are in taking or not taking some particular course of action. The clients probably have exhausted other sources of advice and, finding them lacking, have turned to you. This often is true even when clients are legally mandated.

Why? The clients don't know you from Adam or Eve, but they do know that you have some professional training that sets you apart from their buddies, or parents, or the local bartender. And they believe—or hope—that you literally will reach into your professional bag and pull out some theory and research that will let you facilitate their solving the challenges facing them. They also believe that you will do this with all due confidentiality for their private affairs. Fortunately, you do have some behavioral science theory and research as part of your training, and you have considered how to use your profession's code of ethics, so you can in fact do something like what they fantasize. More than that, you are now about to learn how to evaluate your professional actions as they influence the client and his or her environment, a bonus for the client and for the society that is ultimately paying the bill.

Now, the task of this Prologue is to see if we can put all these elements together in a way that will help you put similar ingredients together as you begin your scientific practice. To do this, we can't present a linear progression of facts and instructions. We have to tell a story. Granted, storytelling is a bit fuzzy, but so is life. Now sit back and enjoy a holistic experience about scientific practice in which you can imagine that you are one of the principal actors. Of course, this is just a brief sketch; more of the evaluation details will be found in this book, and other details in your other textbooks on practice, theory, research, and ethics. The flowchart on pages 4–5 (Exhibit P.1) is your road map, and the numbers and letters in the text that follows refer to that chart. Keep one thing in mind throughout this Prologue—you are moving through that scientific practice space, and the client, theory and research, ethical guidelines, and the evaluation of your ongoing practice are all within your reach.

PART II. DEVELOPING A GOOD SOCIAL RELATIONSHIP, IDENTIFYING CLIENT PROBLEMS AND STRENGTHS, IDENTIFYING CLIENT GOALS AND OBJECTIVES, AND ASSESSMENT

II.A.2. Rapport-Building for a Trusting Relationship: Getting a Feeling for the Presenting Situation

Come meet Mrs. Abbott, a widow in her early 90s, who lives at the Wintergreen Senior Citizens' Residence. I'll tell you about her as we go in. It's a fairly nice building, set back a ways from a major boulevard and located about three miles from the heart of downtown. This is the main entrance. I will nod to the receptionist (who will recognize me as a social work student intern, and I introduce you to her as a student in community psychology who is looking into some group projects among the elderly), and then we head for the rear second floor suite of Mrs. Abbott. You notice the public calendar of activities at the Residence and seem amazed at how many activities a person might engage in this month (October). "That's pretty typical," I observe, having seen a notebook of prior calendars. We pass the dining

Exhibit P.1 Flow Diagram for Evaluating Practice

*Read down one step; then read across for concurrent activities.

The Flow of Scientific Practice	A — The Practice Context	B — Contexts of Theory and Ethical Concerns	C — The Evaluation Context
Part I, Starting Scientific Practice	A.1. Establishing the Practice Context	B.1. Establishing Ethical and Conceptual Contexts	C.1. Establishing the Evaluation Context (Ch. 1)
Part II, Developing a Good Relationship, Assessment	A.2. Rapport-Building	B.2. Developing a Working Theory through Conceptualization	C.2. Rapport-Building for Evaluation
	A.3. Presenting Problems and Strengths		C.3. Conceptualization: Basis for Measurement (Ch. 2)
		B.3. Exercising the Working Theory: Finding Unrecognized Events	C.4. Redefining Problems and Strengths (Ch. 3)
	A.4. Presenting Goals and Objectives	B.4. Ethical Review: "Act, if you can, but do no harm"	C.5. Reconceptualization and Measurement: Planning for Evaluation (Ch. 4)
	A.5. Assessment: Matching Client and Practitioner Perceptions of the Whole Situation; Connections with Intervention	B.5. Ethical Assessment: Matching Client and Practitioner Ethical Perceptions of the Whole Situation	C.6. Measurement a. Behavioral Observations (Ch. 5) b. Individualized Rating Scales (Ch. 6) c. Standardized Questionnaires (Ch. 7) d. Logs (Ch. 8) e. Reactivity and Nonreactive Measures (Ch. 9) f. Selecting a Measure (Ch. 10)
Part III, Designs for Informed and Ethical Practice and Evaluation	A.6. Selecting and Implementing Interventions: Practice Designs a. Primary Prevention b. Treatment c. Rehabilitation d. Palliative Care	B.6. Ethical Designs: Review and Modification of Practice Plans	C.7. Single-System Evaluation: Basic Principles of Design (Chs. 11 and 12)
			C.8. Baselining (Ch. 12)
	A.7. Contracting: Who Does What with Whom under What Circumstances?	B.7. Practice Hypotheses: What Specific Ways Will the Client and/or Situations Change for the Better? What Are the Risks the Situation Will Change for the Worse?	C.9. Evaluation Designs a. Case Study to A-B (Ch. 13) b. Experimental Designs (Ch. 14) c. Multiple Designs (Ch. 15) d. Changing Intensity and Successive Intervention Designs (Ch. 16) e. Complex and Combined Designs (Ch. 17) f. Selecting a Design (Ch. 18)

Exhibit P.1 Flow Diagram for Evaluating Practice (*continued*)

The Flow of Scientific Practice	**A** *The Practice Context*	**B** *Contexts of Theory and Ethical Concerns*	**C** *The Evaluation Context*

Part IV, Analysis of Data, Monitoring Change, Decision Making, Maintenance Planning, and Termination and Follow-Up	A.8. Monitoring the Data: Modifying the Intervention as Needed
	
	A.9. Comparing Goals and Outcomes: Using Your Results to Test Your Practice Hypotheses
	
	A.10. Decision Making: Combining Evaluation with Values and Practice Wisdom
	  a. Acting on the Basis of Empirically Supported Evidence
	  b. Planning to Maintain Positive Results after Intervention
	  c. Termination
	  d. Follow-up (with possible need for "booster shots")
		B.8. The Ethics of Changing Events
		
		B.9. Client Bill of Rights (Ch. 25)
		
		B.10. Informed Consent (Ch. 25)
			C.10. Analysis (Ch. 19)
			  a. Visual Analysis (Ch. 20)
			  b. Descriptive Statistics (Ch. 21)
			  c. Tests of Statistical Significance (Ch. 22)
			  d. Computer Analysis (Ch. 23)
			  e. Selecting a Procedure (Ch. 24)

Part V, Scientific Practice in the Community: The Challenge	A.11. Report to the Agency:
	  a. Adding to Practice Wisdom and Personal Practice Repertoire
		B.11. Report to the Community
		  a. Innovations for Managed Care (Ch. 25)
		  b. Innovations for Primary Prevention (Ch. 25)
		  c. Ethical Accountability and Cost-Benefit Analyses
			C.11. Report to the Profession
			  a. Critical Issues in Single-System Design (Ch. 25)

area, which looks quite gracious, with tables seating six, comfortable chairs with arms, and large windows facing the terrace and lawn. "They serve three meals a day, seven days a week," I mention. We go by some game rooms, a craft hall, a medical area where a visiting physician sees residents several times a week. "There are also several nurses here, around the clock," I report. And we noticed something new, a computer room—an addition to the old library.

On the way up, I tell you a bit about Mrs. Abbott. She's a former school teacher and later principal, a widow, no children, and some family who live all over the country but not here. The pictures on the wall are from her many favorite pupils over the years. The Residence Administrator (RA) called my agency and indicated that Mrs. Abbott was acting in a moody and unsettled way—which was unusual for her—and she didn't seem to be coming down to meals regularly, which also was unusual. The RA asked her whether she had any health problems, and she said no, nothing to speak of. But something is going on. Could we do something, please? That happened just as my practicum instructor was looking for cases for me. And so, here I am.

I ring the bell, and in a few moments an attractive, gray-haired woman comes to the door, smiles in recognition, but then sighs, and motions us in. We walk past a tiny alcove that houses the kitchenette, and go into the living room, which is quite cheery with a big picture window overlooking an expanse of lawn and trees in the distance, and several pieces of comfortable, if worn, furniture, a TV, a desk, lots of pictures of children in a cluster of frames on the wall and a patterned Indian rug that covers a bit of the institutional red tile throughout the apartment. On the other side of the room is a short hallway leading to the bedroom, a walk-in closet, and the bathroom.

I introduce you and we sit down to talk. "How have you been, Mrs. Abbott?" I ask. "Oh, about the same, not so good. I just don't seem to have energy to do anything, and the worst thing is, I don't seem to care," she says in a rather weak voice.

I summarize the events to date, partly for your sake, but mainly to put things into perspective for Mrs. Abbott. "Mr. Johnston, the Residence Administrator, was concerned about you and asked our family agency to see if there was something we might do to help. The first time we met, you were telling me about your friends, many of whom seem to have had problems that occurred about the same time. I think they were all members of your card group, what was the name? Oh, yes, the "Roaring Nineties" Club.

"Yes, that's right," Mrs. Abbott replies. "We were just going into our 90s and were pretty feisty when we started our club four years ago. Oh, everyone had a few aches and pains, but we were all bright-eyed and bushy-tailed. But now, Mrs. Bennet is back at the Residence after a fall that broke her hip, and she's having trouble getting up and around. She's afraid she might have to go to a nursing home. And about a year ago, Miss Carol had a stroke that left her paralyzed on her left side, and she's getting lots of medical rehabilitation. But she thinks it is only a matter of time before all the other things catch up with her and overwhelm her, and she'll have to go live with her daughter and son-in-law somewhere out west. She's a wonderful friend and I'd hate to see her go. Poor David Dunn died; he was such a cheerful man; made us all laugh. His wife, Dorothy, is doing quite well physically, but she is still in mourning and doesn't seem to want to come out of her shell. Say, is there something you can do for her?"

"I'll check on that with my supervisor; thanks for mentioning it," I say. Mrs. Abbott goes on about a few of her other friends at the Wintergreen who were having problems, and how she feels about the situation. (I'll say more about this part of the conversation later.) When she finishes I ask, "Are you and your friends still playing cards together?"

"No, we hardly get together nowadays." She pulls out her desk calendar and points to the few occasions when her card group met. Then she continues: "We used to meet a lot, maybe several times a week when we could reserve one of the card rooms downstairs. But now, when we do meet, we don't even pick up the cards. We just talk and commiserate. But that's important for some of them," she notes, with a bit of defensiveness in her voice. I say that I agree with her about that. We talk about her other friends at the Wintergreen who played cards with the Roaring Nineties group on occasion, but it seems that everyone had her or his own problems, and not much was happening among residents, even with all the movies, crafts, outings to local stores, exercise classes, and such that were part of life at this well-run residence.

You summarize the conversation quite well when you say to Mrs. Abbott, "It sounds to me as if these past few months have been very hard on all of you, for different reasons, but that you are still trying to maintain what goal you and your friends all share in common: being here at the Wintergreen and enjoying each other's company in the best way you can. And it's distressing because there's no good solution that's apparent."

"Yes," she says, "yes, that's it in a nutshell."

As we say our goodbyes for this session, Mrs. Abbott insists on taking us over to the photo gallery and telling us about her favorite pupils of long ago. She laughs, in spite of herself, at memories of some of the jokes they shared. She clearly enjoys laughing when there was something to laugh about.

II.A.3. Identifying the Presenting Problems and Strengths of the Client

We sit down in the staff cafeteria and think about this case. You get out a legal sized notepad and begin to make some jottings, including both the presenting risks or limitations *and* the presenting strengths, for both Mrs. Abbott and this supportive setting. Then you pause, pencil in midair, "I suddenly realize," you say, "that I never actually talked with someone over 90 before, and I was amazed at her vocabulary and her physical energy, even though you said she had slowed down lately. Yet I feel uneasy. Maybe I am just afraid of introducing any change in her fragile life."

"I had a similar reaction when I first met Mrs. Abbott," I reply, "but she seems quite re-silient and was able to set limits on what I was suggesting at first. Maybe some of the other residents are more fragile, so it is good to keep sensitive to working with the very old. My field instructor suggested I read some books about older persons, and maybe this would be helpful for you too. I liked Betty Friedan's *The Fountains of Age* (1993), but there are lots of good books out there in gerontology.

"Mrs. Abbott is what they call the *new old,* an older person with a good education, pretty good health, and an adequate income. She's also a great example of the strengths perspective," I add, "and a great antidote to all of the focus on pathology in the literature and at school. (See Cowger, 1994; Saleebey, 1997.) Let's see now: what do we have?"

With regard to personal limitations or circumstances that posed risks for her, we both agree that Mrs. Abbott looked weak, had low levels of energy, and seemed to be dwelling on problems among her friends; she spent most of our time together talking about her friends' problems. We recall that we weren't able to get her to articulate any specific happy objectives in her immediate future. Her apartment seemed much less tidy than I recalled from my earlier visits. In addition, she didn't have any nearby relatives and most of her friends were either in residences like hers, or living with family. You are especially concerned about that, but I point out that she has a lot of friends among the other residents and staff of this residence.

On the strengths side, we realize that we have to distinguish factors more carefully. Even though she had low energy, she was doing all of her own housework—slowly—and that was fine. It seemed to give her a sense of accomplishment. We also recognize that Mrs. Abbott herself seemed to be free of any illness or chronic condition, and that while she was much involved with the ills of her friends, this could be viewed positively as reflecting her care and concern for her friends. She is clearly mentally alert, has a good sense of humor, and commands a lot of respect among staff and friends at the Wintergreen. The Residence itself should be counted among her resources because, in fact, it has a lot to offer, including a new computer room where residents can e-mail their friends and relatives. "I can't believe that these ninety-year-olds are going to start using computers," you mutter. "But we passed the computer center on the way down here, and it was filled with residents. So I guess I had better believe it." (I see your stereotypes about the elderly collapsing, one by one, just as mine did a few weeks earlier.)

II.A.4. Identifying the Presenting Goals and Objectives

"What has Mrs. Abbott said about her needs and goals?" you ask, after we had gone through the inventory of her strengths and limitations.

"About the first thing she said to me, after we met, was that she wanted to stay here at the Wintergreen, that it was truly a home for her that provided all of the basic supports that she ever wanted—good friends, comfort, stimulation, and a good deal of security now that she was getting older," I report. "It is sort of like Maslow's (1968) discussion of the hierarchy of needs. Let's see. First, there are physiological needs like food and such. Then, safety needs, like a safe shelter in a safe environment. Then there are the needs to belong to a loving group, and this is one of the critical points in her life at this time. She gets plenty of esteem (the next hierarchical need), but that means nothing if she doesn't belong to a loving group. I think the self-actualization needs are next."

"What are they?" you ask.

"It means, at least in my terms, being all you can be and being happy about it," I reply, smiling as I realize that I inadvertently quoted the U.S. Army recruiting slogan. "I think each person formulates his or her own version of being self-actualized or fulfilled. For Mrs. Abbott, this has meant service to others. She was a dedicated teacher and administrator, and that photographic display shows her success in that endeavor."

"So you're saying that our job is to help her achieve her goal to belong to and maintain a loving group," you summarize. "And she has pretty well worked through the other goals, but she needs to reaffirm that belongingness goal. This makes sense as a guide for our working on

keeping her support group together at the Wintergreen as long as feasible, and not let irrelevant issues break up the old gang."

"You've got it!" I exclaim. "And of course there are a lot of intervening tasks to accomplish before we can hope to reach any one person's long-term goal, let alone goals common to the group. From the way Mrs. Abbott was speaking, each of the others had quite different problems, from physical to emotional, and yet I got the sense that all of them relished their Roaring Nineties group. So, all we have to do is to add the sum of individual goals and get a group goal. Right?"

"Well," you say, "not exactly. Some group goals, like morale or satisfaction with the group, are dependent on the interaction of the whole group, and aren't just the sum of individual ideas or feelings on that topic. It is like something new emerges when people continually interact together. No one person has group morale; rather, it is something that floats in their collective atmosphere, so to speak, and is shared by each of them. Group morale is something apart from the specific feelings of any member. We know it exists because we can measure its effects on members, keeping them attracted to the group, like Mrs. Abbott is, for example."

II.B.1. Establishing an Ethical Context

II.B.2. Developing a Working Theory through Conceptualization

After we had listed all of the problems or limitations with Mrs. Abbott and her living situation, plus all of the strengths and resources she had available, we just sit there thinking about these points. How are we to go about helping Mrs. Abbott and do it well? It is hard to describe what happened, but for me, it seems that, as I think about those key words over and over, certain general ideas come up that seem to summarize the whole lot of them. Ah, so these particular human events are instances of the abstract and general concepts—just what my instructor was saying in that theory class last semester. I realize that I just generalized

Mrs. Abbott's comments and my observations of her into an abstract and summarizing term, a concept. I am rather pleased with myself for having made this conceptual connection, until you ask me to explain how I did it.

I try to retrace my steps. I had many observations that came to me about the same time, but I especially noticed the affective tone in Mrs. Abbott's conversations and movements. She seemed unhappy and unsettled. It was as if she was thinking about and grappling with a lot of things and was not able to come to any resolution. It was easy to see the sources of her distress, the various states of ill health of her friends who constituted her closest friendship group. And she, who had been so good at organizing events to help people, didn't see any solution to these existential issues. It got her down. She walked more slowly, had less energy for doing other things, and it showed up in how she was fulfilling her own basic needs, including having no appetite to eat regularly, or to plan for pleasant future objectives. In a word, or rather, a concept, I thought Mrs. Abbott was depressed. *This seems to be a major dimension in the ethical context for our work with Mrs. Abbott: Can we help? Or, at least, can we make sure we do no harm?*

You think about that for a moment, nod your head in agreement, and say, "I think you may have a good idea, even though depression could be either a strictly personal concept (like when you say 'the individual feels very unhappy') or it could be a person:environment (P:E) concept (Germain & Bloom, 1999); that is, the individual is inseparable from her environment; both must be considered in any assessment—like saying that in this depressing context, the person's unhappy feelings get magnified."

"Why does it matter whether it is a personal, or a P:E concept?" I ask, and you say it influences how we are supposed to direct our energies to make suitable changes, to the person alone, or necessarily to both the person and the context. "Ah ha!" I say. "Then I would definitely go with the P:E interpretation. We have more options on how to direct our energies. For example, this P:E interpretation would lead us to check out things we didn't

currently know about, like the medications she is taking (a personal factor) in interaction with the social atmosphere of the dining hall (an environmental factor). Both factors might influence her level of nutrition. We'll have to check into those things. Anyway, that concept (P:E depression) was quite an eye-opener. But I guess that is what concepts are supposed to do."

You must have been doing the same abstracting because you are sort of muttering to yourself, "strong, a real survivor, a person with lots of strengths." As we talk about these observations, we both arrive at another concept at about the same time. This concept (strengths) seems to summarize a lot of the other traits we had observed in Mrs. Abbott. So now we have two concepts to work with, depression and strength. It also seems that as we define our concepts, we are also clarifying the ethical context within which we have to work—to try to decrease the former, while increasing the latter, without damaging any other ethical relationships.

"Concepts don't stand alone," I pontificate. "Where there's smoke, there's fire. Where there are concepts, there must be a theory." You look a bit glazed and comment that I must have been studying too hard, but yes, you agree that we ought to consider theories because they not only describe situations and offer explanations for what's going on, but also they predict future events and thus allow us to interrupt those events so as to attain a better outcome, one that the client prefers. We first start to think about the concept, depression. What theories would be useful here that have the concept *depression* as a key term or that analyze the condition?

There is a moment of silence, and I offer several possibilities. "I think psychoanalytic theory says something about depression, and the cognitive-behavioral model does too. I believe there is some biological thinking about depression as genetic or inherited. And I was reading something about the existential position and dread; maybe that's like depression."

"So, what evidence do we know about any of these theories?" you ask. Neither of us can think of any supporting evidence for the psychoanalytic model (Ford & Urban, 2000), and besides, we can't hope to use techniques involving the unconscious to produce changes in people with our level of training. I mention the cognitive-behavioral theory and say I had read some books that presented a lot of evidence supporting that idea (Beck, 1976; Clark, Beck, & Alford, 1999). You mention the existentialist notion of dread (Frankl, 1962). Maybe Mrs. Abbott was fearing death, which she was seeing in bits and pieces in all her friends. We can't disregard that idea, but there doesn't seem to be any research evidence that we know. As for biological models, or maybe basic physiological development in very elderly people, we realize that we don't have much information. Maybe there was something about Mrs. Abbott's health or nutrition that was involved. We would have to check with her records at the Residence, and we agree to check out the other theories at the university library information retrieval center. But, for the moment, we think the cognitive-behavioral approach has the most to offer in this situation. We'll call this our working theory—to see whether it works for guiding us to see the whole picture, including some new ideas we may have overlooked.

I don't want to brag, but I studied so hard for that theory exam last year that I even remember some of what I learned. As I recall, the main concepts and propositions of the cognitive-behavioral model are these:

People are complex cognitive/affective/behavioral beings. A significant proportion of our mental distress (and delight) comes from how we understand the world around us. Some of these areas of mental distress are well justified (friends do die, senseless discrimination does exist), but others are distress that we create for ourselves. We may, for example, expect or desire the impossible—to be perfect in every way on all occasions before all people. And when we inevitably recognize that we are not perfect, this may become distressing. However, it is possible to dispute this senseless belief and reframe our thoughts to view the world in more adaptive terms—we would prefer to be well liked, but in reality, not everyone is going to like us, no matter what we do. It may take learning new skills to restructure our thinking in less harmful ways, and to actively work on performing them. This might include relaxation exercises, problem-solving training, self-instructional skills, among others (Clark et al., 1999; Meichenbaum, 1985). Moreover, the model also examines the relationship between environmental events and how they affect peoples' perceptions and other cognitions. Thus, interventions also could be targeted to changing those environmental events so that changes in cognitions will follow.

II.B.3. Exercising the Working Theory: Finding Unrecognized Events to Give a More Complete Understanding of the Client/Situation

You get up to get another glass of orange juice. "This thinking requires more energy," you announce. And while you are gone, I am thinking about cognitive-behavioral theory in relationship to Mrs. Abbott, and wonder, did we forget anything? Does the theory tell us to look for something we haven't considered yet? The people who publish well-constructed theories probably had a lot of experience with the topic, and may have considered events that we hadn't. I am thinking about this when you bring back two glasses. "Here," you order. "You need it too." This prompts me to think that maybe Mrs. Abbott might need more food for her energy, but I decide to hold that idea and check it out later. You can't do everything at once.

We sit there silently, staring at the notepad and thinking. Suddenly, you say, "Wait a minute. If Mrs. Abbott is really depressed, why isn't she thoroughly and consistently depressed? She seems to go in and out of acting like she's depressed, and yet there is nothing specifically about her personal health that should make her depressed. At times, she looks and acts spritely; other times, she looks really down. Shouldn't people be consistently depressed, if they are really depressed?"

"Good question," I observe, "and I don't know the answer. But thinking about Beck's cognitive theory itself, I would say that people can look at some situations as depressing and respond to those with their own depressed behaviors. And at other times, they can look at pleasant or neutral situations, and see the world as relatively pleasant or neutral."

"So, it depends on how a person views the situation that in effect contributes to his or her depression?" you ask. "Then, all we have to do is to change how they view those situations, which also means trying to change those situations?"

"I guess so," I say, and immediately add (since I know you would say it anyway), "but guessing isn't the best way to run a practice. So we had better find out. But at least this insight gives us something to think about and something for which to use the information retrieval services to find a specific answer." Silence.

II.B.4. Ethical Review: "Help, if you can, but do no harm"

You frown. "What's the matter?" I ask.

"It's just that this theory is leading us to do things *to* Mrs. Abbott, like change her cognitive frame of reference, and I wonder if that is ethical to do? Are we such great experts that we can impose our solution on her? I mean, how do we know it wouldn't do more harm than good?" you lament.

I reply, "I don't know if anyone is an expert with someone else's life. All we can do is offer hopefully enlightened suggestions relevant to client goals. Remember that the Hippocratic Oath says first to help if you can, and then it says to do no harm. I think that the least harmful and least intrusive way to help should give us the greatest helping effect. Yet, we better check our plans of action to see if they fulfill ethical guidelines while also meeting client goals." Warming to this topic, I go on: "At minimum, I think we have to believe that we have something to offer in this situation, namely, our theories and the practice suggestions based on them. We have to begin with Mrs. Abbott and discuss these ideas and the direction in which they are leading us. She might have some other ideas that would change the direction, as she knows her own feelings and the context a lot better than we do.

"Sharing our ideas on practice between the client and the practitioner is like informed consent applied to the practice situation, rather than informed consent in research terms. The client knows exactly what the plans are and in fact has contributed her ideas and directions to them. And she would likely be more motivated to participate if she had a full part in the discussion and decisions."

Just then, Mrs. Hill and Mike Breen come up to our table—she's a practicum instructor at the Residence and some other places where students are placed, and he's my classmate and a real nag. I'll tell you about him in a minute, but we do get into an interesting discussion with Mrs. Hill that I want to note because this is why I think having a practicum in the field is such a great idea—one gets some very important practice wisdom conveyed immediately and in the context of one's own clients. We exchange greetings and invite them to join us at the table. Then we talk about our field placement and our idea for a group and individual intervention project. Our excitement must have sparked an interest in Mrs. Hill because she asks us to give her more details. Happily we reconstruct our ideas of the goals and objectives, and some of our other ideas. When we stop, we look at Mrs. Hill and wait for a response. There is a long silence, and then she says, "Interesting."

We are not going to take that lying down, and so we ask her to give us some early warning feedback, and this is what she says:

"I don't know Mrs. Abbott personally, but I wonder if there is more going on in her life than what you have said—or even what you know. After all, you have only been with her two or three times, and you can't expect a client to give you the whole story of her situation in that amount of time. She may be depressed, but it may also be that she is exhibiting some depressed feelings for good reasons as you were saying. Either idea is a reasonable hypothesis to explore. But she also has some unique strengths that you aren't employing directly, and if you look at the whole person in the whole context, then you probably should consider her 'adopted family,' her friends at this residence, and even the children she taught and their children. It seems to me that she has some real leadership skills and personal skills. How can you use that part of her strength in your overall planning? She belongs to several domains in her life here, and you might want to consider all or most of them in your planning, since they are all tied together. Your intervention plan has to account for all of these."

We listen attentively to Mrs. Hill, and nod in agreement that we should explore other aspects of Mrs. Abbott's life situation. In fact, we were discussing strengths just as Mrs. Hill and Mike came to our table. Maybe the pieces would come together in a larger plan. But I am fascinated at the way Mrs. Hill brought pieces of information together and created new ways of looking at the situation. You and I had those pieces of information at hand too, but we didn't see the connections. This is perhaps a matter of experience in developing practice wisdom. In class, our teacher had pointed out that practice wisdom involves the balanced interactions among theory and its supporting research, direct contact with clients, and our generalizations from this practice. These generalizations become concepts made about the client situation, but they also link us with concepts from theories that provide additional options on further aspects of practice (Klein & Bloom, 1995).

Another observation I make on Mrs. Hill's comments was the intrinsic connection between any action we might take with regard to Mrs. Abbott and the ethical stances we were necessarily taking. To interact professionally is to take an ethical stance. When these ethical positions are pointed out, we realize that taking professional action automatically involves operating within our codes of ethics.

Mrs. Hill looks at her watch and says she has to be moving to another agency to talk with students in practicum. We all say goodbye.

II.C.2. Building Rapport with the Client for Evaluating the Practice Situation

As we are talking about ethics and practice, we are both surprised to realize how much vocabulary we are using from theory and research classes we had taken—informed consent, client participation with the process of helping, our own critiques of theories and concepts. It all seems to flow together when we begin to think about what we are doing. But we get stuck on one thing: How do we know whether the interventions we want to do with Mrs. Abbott, even with her full understanding and participation, will be effective?

"Won't this be obvious?" you ask eagerly.

"Maybe so or maybe not," I reply. "I'm just as eager as you and she would be to have a successful outcome, and that may be the problem—a little bit too much bias in our own favor. The real proof of the pudding in terms of effective outcomes will come in how others (who don't share our biases that stem from working toward these goals) see Mrs. Abbott and her friends behaving in the ordinary world. Somehow, we have to tap into their opinions and observations to see if what we are planning to do has the desired effects we all eagerly (too eagerly?) want to happen."

"Okay. I can go along with that," you say. "Now, how should we get this evaluation started? Is it something different from all the other things we will have to do in the practice procedures? I'm not sure I can handle a whole lot more things to do as an intern."

"I hear you," I say, nodding in agreement, "but do we intend to think clearly about what the targets are in this case situation? Do we intend to be careful in observing what is happening as we continue our interventions? Do we expect to be sensitive to the feedback from our observations that will lead us to make corrections in the way we are proceeding with our work? What my practice teacher said about all this is that if we want to have this kind of practice, then inevitably how we conduct our practice actions will constitute a good part of how we evaluate. We define terms clearly. We observe the ongoing process carefully. And we consider honestly what these data tell us about how the intervention is going and whether we might need to make some adjustments to get to where we all want to go."

"I'd like to see that in action," you say. "How do we begin?"

"According to this point of view, we have begun evaluation in the very process of being clear about practice. The one point we have to consider is helping the client to see that evaluation is an intrinsic part of practice. It is like a social thermometer that takes readings on the major components of the client's problems and goals. Even a social thermometer can be intrusive, so we have to be careful to emphasize the positive. For example, we might not want to have the client help in measuring how many depressive thoughts he or she was having–because it emphasizes thinking about being depressed. However, we would want to get equivalent but opposite information, such as how much of the time this person was involved in pleasant and socially useful activities. You ordinarily can't be thinking about the former (how depressed you are) while doing the latter (being involved in fun activities)."

"Let's talk specifically about Mrs. Abbott," you suggest. "She probably will be a cooperative participant in evaluation because she will be able to see the value of taking readings, as you said. In fact, being as sharp as she is, she might positively enjoy participating in the evaluation as well as the practice. But how should we introduce this topic to her?"

"Let's see. First, we have to be sure she trusts us, and that she knows we really care about helping her. We also want her to know that we are doing our best to understand her and her feelings. Once we've accomplished that, I think we might begin discussing evaluation, but only after we agreed on our plans for the intervention. We might start by talking about the need for accurate information, as feedback to fine-tune our intervention, but also because we need to have clear evidence of the effectiveness of our work for the agency."

"And for the taxpayers and charity contributors who underwrite a large portion of our agency's activities," you add. "I think that is a reasonable beginning plan."

II.C.3. Conceptualization: Basis for Measurement (Chapter 2)

"Let me be clear about what we've been saying," you start anew. "I need to put some substantive content in our abstract thinking so far. Let's start with the concept of depression from a cognitive-behavioral perspective. This implies that we should look at the social situation at the Residence and how Mrs. Abbott views this as affecting her unhappy feelings and her decreased energy level. Once we understand how she views this complex situation, then we can plan with her some possible interventions and observe, or actually measure, the changes that occur, both in the environment and in her views of these changes.

"As I see it," you go on, "these possible interventions have to include working with Mrs. Abbott's strengths and the other positive resources in her environment. After all, it is these strengths and resources that we want to focus on; they are the substance of our intervention."

"Good points," I respond. "Let's get specific. At least four of the mainstays of her card club have gotten sick or lost a spouse in the past year, and they all need help of one sort or another in order to function on their own at the Residence. If they go, they all lose out on what was a wonderful support group. What do they need to stay here? None of them seems to have figured out an answer, and they are all in mourning for their dying friendship (or at least their immediate proximity friendship). They are all sort of depressed about this."

"But I still come back to the fact that these seem to be basically bright and mentally healthy individuals who have one kind or another of some physical problem," you add.

"Don't forget Mrs. Dunn, a widow who has not been able to get back her functioning since the death of her spouse," I remark. "She needs someone who can be there more to get her involved with other activities than those associated with caring for a sick spouse."

II.A.5. Part 1. Assessment: Matching Practitioner and Client Perceptions of the Whole Situation; Connections with Interventions

II.B.5. Ethical Assessment

I see Mrs. Abbott coming back from lunch, one day, and I walk back with her to her apartment. We talk about nothing in particular, but when we get to her door, she raises the point about the still gloomy atmosphere hanging over her group of friends. "What do you mean?" I ask.

"I can't express it exactly, but it is as if we're spinning our wheels and getting nowhere, while inevitably things are occurring that are going to drive us apart and drive some people away from the Wintergreen. It's like we are in mourning for the old gang, even though we are still the old gang.

"So, you're saying that you and your friends haven't been able to solve this tough problem that seems to have so many ramifications, and you're all feeling rather blue," I say.

"Yes," she replies. "It really does have a lot of ramifications, and each one adds something depressing to the others. It seems like there would be some kinds of solutions, but I think our brain power is being used up with daily crises, and we're not seeing the bigger picture. And I am especially frustrated with myself because I can't seem to step away to see the larger picture." Mrs. Abbott then enumerates all the problems she sees in her friends' situations, first one point, then another, then another in regard to one friend. Then, again, with another friend . . . . She really does see many particulars in their situations, and they are quite varied, from ill health to psychological depression, from family pressures to leave, to doubts about where they might go.

"I know that it's hard to step outside yourself when you are so close to this situation," I console. "Maybe I can be of some help, as I come to understand what you and your friends are facing. I think I understand everything that you've been saying about these matters, so far. I'd like to think about them and then meet with you; maybe I could suggest some new possibilities."

She looks at me a minute, and then says, "Maybe so." We make plans to meet early next week.

The next day, you and I are talking by telephone: You begin to speculate, "How can the people in the Roaring Nineties group attain their individual objectives, and thereby increase chances of obtaining their overall common goal? They can't afford full-time help, you said, right?"

"Yes."

"And yet they all have some part-time help now, I assume."

"Yes," I answer, "but they are not always pleased with their helpers. When someone calls in sick, their own planned schedules are shot, since there aren't any substitutes, apparently. Or, Mrs. Abbott hasn't mentioned any. But she did mention that she wished they had full-time, well-trained aides, but no one could afford such a person."

"What if they went in together and hired one, no, maybe two well-trained aides full-time, since they all live in the same residence? Then the aides could move among apartments as needed, and with two aides, there would be some safety in case one couldn't make it sometime," you suggest. "There are an increasing number of home aide agencies in the community and good standards of training and service are being developed."

"That sounds interesting," I reply, brightening up at this good suggestion. "And you know what, Mrs. Abbott might play some part in arranging for these aides, and sort of managing the situation. That would give her some role in all this, and she might reframe her view of the situation now that she was contributing to and promoting the general health and welfare of all of her friends. I think that is what cognitive-behavioral theory might suggest—getting some new ideas about the situation, helping the residents to see things in a new way, and then facilitating their growth by assisting in whatever ways we can to make an environmental change in this situation."

Several days later, I meet with Mrs. Abbott myself. She greets me with her usual warmth and a bit more energy than previously, and so I decide to continue explorations of her feelings and ideas about her situation. Her small friendship group had gotten together over meals several days in a row, and they even played a game of cards.

"I'm glad to hear that everyone is getting along well," I say. "Maybe it is the beautiful weather we have been having."

"No," says Mrs. Abbott, "it's not that. I think it is just a chance event where everyone's helpers were on the job. Shows what can happen when that occurs. If we could only make it happen more often," she muses.

Sensing an opening, I say, "It certainly would be a good thing to have a more consistent group of helpers. Have you and your friends given any thought to the idea that if you all went in together, you all could probably afford to hire maybe two full-time aides, and you could take turns employing them? Emergencies would come first, but everyone would have the satisfaction of having a well-trained aide who would be backed up by the agency in case one of them got sick. This one action might help deal with a lot of different ramifications that we were talking about the other day."

Mrs. Abbott listens without saying anything, but it is clear that gears were whirring in her mind. "Say," she says. "That reminds me. I was talking with a guest speaker the other day—I think she was the director of a social agency—and she was talking about just the kind of aides you were describing. And all I did was to say to myself, 'too bad my friends couldn't get an aide like that.' But I think you're right; if we all chipped in, we might just make a go of such an arrangement."

"Oh?" I said. "So what are you going to do next?"

"Why, I am going to call my friends, as soon as we are finished talking, and suggest the idea. If they agree, I'll call that speaker and see if we can work something out. I'll probably have to handle the details. That is something I was pretty good at when I was working. So I think I just might be able to handle this new project. And if it works, why, my old gang can hang around the Wintergreen until they have to carry us out feet first. I'd love that, sticking around the Wintergreen, that is. Why, thank you, my dear. That was a great idea. It's like Popeye and a can of spinach. Do you know Popeye, the sailor?" she asks.

"I've heard of Popeye, but I don't think I ever saw any comic strips," I reply.

"Too bad," she says. "You're a wee bit too young, but this cartoon character was popular when I was your age, and just when Popeye was getting into some terrible situation, he would pop open a can of spinach, swallow it

down, and energy would surge into his body and he would carry the day. That's how I felt just now. My dear, if you wouldn't mind calling it a day, I have some work to do."

II.A.5. Part 2. Reassessing the Situation: Change Is Inevitable

I call on Mrs. Abbott several days later after I was finished with another client, and Mrs. Abbott sounds decidedly unhappy. "What happened?" I ask. "You were so happy the other day with the idea of organizing home aides for you and your friends."

"It's my dear friend, Joanne Carol," Mrs. Abbott said. "She had another stroke two days ago, and I think she is still in intensive care. It does not look good, and we are all sick to death about it. Her daughter flew into town and has been making plans to have her put into a nursing home. Joanne's roommate, Amanda, has been keeping us informed, and we all cry together. It is so sad."

"I'm very sorry to hear this; it must be very distressing for you all."

"Yes," replies Mrs. Abbott, "but it also is interesting. As soon as Joanne went to the hospital, a number of other residents came forward and comforted us. And now, through this sad experience, we seem to have gained more friends than we had before. I guess every cloud has a silver lining."

"I think times of crisis bring out the best in many people, and this is one of those special times when everyone shares the same hopes and fears, and it does pull people together. Do you see these new people as becoming a part of the Roaring Nineties group?" I ask as lightly as possible.

"Maybe," she replies. "We haven't talked about that, but I think it is inevitable that new folks will come in as . . . as other folks leave." We are both silent for a moment. I take her hand and she looks so grateful. There is a sisterhood, even across ages, I think. Maybe she thinks the same thing, because we both give each other a big hug.

I call Mrs. Abbott after the weekend, and she matter of factly tells me that Miss Carol has died. The old gang does not appear to be greatly distressed at this news; they did their mourning as best they could when she had her stroke. But there is a somber air about the Wintergreen, as original members of the Roaring Nineties plan a commemorative at the Residence. They discuss music and short readings and such, and make arrangements with the management. (Mrs. Abbott made the arrangements.) And I am able to be there for the service. It has a quiet dignity, but it is poignant to watch the original Nineties and the new Nineties (who were hardly into their eighties) working together.

II.C.4. Redefining Problems and Strengths (Chapter 3)

Matters were changing, and we had to change our thinking about them, too. Miss Carol's death had put a new urgency in our work, but the way the residents responded to the death showed greater sources of strength than we had previously recognized. I observe little clusters of residents talking in earnest around the building, as if they are trying to process these events and connect them with their own lives. I believe that the death actually was bringing the residents closer together, as though people were helping each other deal with this shared experience. I can see that we might tap into this reservoir of shared feeling in order to introduce the idea of shared helpers. The question is how?

II.C.5 Reconceptualization and Measurement: Planning for Evaluating through the Many Ways of Collecting Data (Chapter 4)

"I was trying to reconstruct what we were talking about the other day," you say as we walked into the lunch room of the Wintergreen early one morning. "I think we had better write down these brainstorms before the weather clears up. As a general goal, we are thinking about helping the club members to stay at the Residence as long as they want and are able to do so. For specific intermediary objectives (or short-term goals), the members' states of health

have to be at least at some minimum level to stay at this residence, since it doesn't provide ongoing nursing care. Also, they have to be able to manage their apartments up to some level of acceptability. Then there is the question of bringing new members into the Roaring Nineties group."

"Let's focus on two objectives: health and managing their apartments," I suggest, "as being essential steps toward the general goal of staying at the Wintergreen. How would we measure levels of health and managing apartments? This is what researchers call *operationalizing* objectives. I know there are some simple measures of the activities of daily living that probably represent the lower levels of functioning, such as the ability to get up from a chair, dress oneself, feed oneself, and the like. These are easily observed and yet provide important danger signals to deteriorating levels of functioning. With managing apartments, I suppose a weekly visit to apartments would enable us to estimate orderliness and cleanliness."

You agree, but add, "We better connect our project with each participant's physician to get clear directions if something special is needed."

Then Mike comes bounding up. I have a feeling about what he is going to say, and he says it. "So, how's your client doing? Making any progress?" Mike is our local expert in research, and for him everything needs to be evaluated. At first, I resented these questions, but I finally got used to them—especially when I started asking these same questions myself— and Mike was a great resource. He is interning at a Head Start program and is involved in a project to link people at the Wintergreen with preschoolers, for their mutual benefit. But he wanted to hear about us. "We're just starting out, so nothing to report," I say, and immediately regret saying that.

"What do you mean, 'nothing to report'? What about your baseline?" he asks.

You look a bit perplexed until I explain that a baseline is a starting point in any case situation, a kind of point of reference in order to know if what you instigated in the case had any effect.

II.C.6. Measurement (Chapters 5–10)

"So, tell me what your plans are for measuring your baseline," he repeats.

"Well, look, Mike, we really are just starting, and we have a hunch that there is some depression in our client. We've both noticed some behaviors that seem to indicate depression. Yeah, yeah, I know. Behaviors are behaviors and what we make of them by imposing a concept like depression goes beyond sheer behavioral observation. But we really do see concrete behaviors, like low energy, flat expression in her voice, disinterest in ordinary daily activities, and from what we remember from the literature, these and others may be related to depression," I state with a bit more firmness than I feel. "And I think we can reliably measure how often these behaviors occur."

"Okay, I hear you," Mike says, but then he goes on. "You ought to consider the wide array of ways you can measure what is happening in your clients. Behavioral observations that you just spoke of are fine (see Chapter 5), but do you remember those discussions of the other ways of evaluating, such as creating individualized rating scales (see Chapter 6), or using standardized questionnaires (see Chapter 7)? And don't forget client logs about what is happening in their lives (see Chapter 8). And above all, don't forget about reactivity—how the act of measurement itself can change client behaviors; to overcome that, we try to use unobtrusive (nonreactive) measures (see Chapter 9)."

"What is he talking about?" you ask, and I try to explain briefly about each of those ways of measuring. They're not particularly difficult, one by one when you study them in class, but presented this way, you just have to take my word for it that we will be able to look at all of the situations we've talked about and use some appropriate ways to get the data we need to see how well our intervention is working.

You look at Mike; then you look at me, and say, "Okay, I'll suspend judgment for the time being, until I study those methods of measuring."

PART III. DESIGNS FOR INFORMED AND ETHICAL PRACTICE AND EVALUATION

III.A.6. Selecting Interventions and Practice Designs

We decide that we have enough information at this point to identify what our interventions will be. We all agree that our ongoing meetings with Mrs. Abbott will be one intervention, and that the home aide plan will be the second one. However, as the three of us talk together over the course of this semester, we realize that we each have different practice preferences, for primary prevention, treatment, or rehabilitation. And, in the course of our conversations, we each try to persuade the others of the centrality of his or her favorite practice. What actually happens is that we all become better informed about these three modes of practice, whatever we think about our favorite. Mrs. Hill, the practicum instructor, also meets with us from time to time and argues for a better understanding of palliative care.

"I don't understand why you want to go into treatment when you can prevent some problems from occurring in the first place," you argue. "Help people stay healthy and also try to enhance their desired objectives, isn't that what professional practice is all about?"

"But there are so many people needing treatment," I argue. "We have to take care of them here and now. Some problems just don't cure themselves. That is where real practice takes place."

"I don't know about that," says Mike. "After all, you have to rehabilitate people back into their ordinary world after any treatment. It would be inexcusable to stop before the real job was finished."

Mrs. Hill says, "You're all correct. Professional helping has many aspects and they are all equally important, especially to the clients involved." Then she excuses herself, as she has to give a talk to a community group on the provision of palliative care to the terminally ill. "This is where professional practice is greatly needed, and sadly neglected," she says as she leaves. Mike has the audacity to ask, after she is out of earshot, what she meant by "where professional practice" really was—in trying to make changes in the community, or in the lives of individual ill clients, or in impressionable students?

So you say, "They're all correct, Mike."

"I recall one of my practice teachers saying that 'what we do in practice *is* our practice design,'" I said.

"What does that mean?" Mike asks.

"I think it means that the whole package of our thoughts and actions over time constitutes whatever it is we do in practice," I respond. "We may intend to be ever so subtle and brilliant, but there are some times we say and do things that don't quite match our plans. So, we may say we are using a cognitive-behavioral model in practice, but if we do things that are more than, or less than, the model calls for, then it is what we *do,* not what we say we are planning to do, that is our practice design."

"I have another take on that," you say. "I think practice designs are the larger structures of our actions. So, if we act before some problem emerges, we are doing preventive practice. If we act after a problem surfaces, we are doing treatment. And if we act after treatment has gone as far as it can, then we are following a rehabilitative model."

"But I can see a situation where we might be doing all three of these at once," Mike says. "For example, say you have a delinquent teenager who has been sent back to his home. The father is steaming mad at his son, and that is going to require some judicious rehabilitation work for the whole family to get reconciled. And the son himself is getting counseling for his substance use problems. That would be treatment of an existing problem. But say there is also a younger brother in the family; the very fact that the counselor is there (doing rehabilitation and treatment) may mean that the younger brother may be diverted from starting on the same path as his older sibling. That would be prevention" (Alexander, Robbins, & Sexton, 2000).

"I don't see any contradiction between what you both just said," you say. "I mean the whole package of our specific actions within a preventive or treatment or rehabilitative context

are just the opposite sides of the same three-sided coin. Together they make up a practice design, especially when it is all *planned,* because, after all, *planning is what makes it a design.*"

Mike mutters something about three-sided coins, but I nod in agreement. "Yeah, I like that," I say.

"But once you have a practice design that you use with evaluation, doesn't this lead to some ethical problems?" you ask. "For example, I would imagine that doing evaluation takes time away from the actual helping practice. Doesn't it?"

"Yes and no," I remark with all the wisdom of one research course under my belt. "Yes, it takes time to learn in the first place, but remember that evaluation is an intrinsic part of practice. All practice methods take time to learn. And with evaluation, you get important feedback about how practice itself is going. If you don't take the time to evaluate as you go along, it will catch up with you when something goes wrong that you weren't expecting. Maybe ongoing monitoring would have given you some advanced warning."

"I see what you are saying," you reply, "but really aren't we just doing all this to pass our research requirements? I mean, isn't evaluation nothing more than disguised research?"

I can see Mike turning three shades of red, but fortunately, he is quite restrained as he says, "Not exactly. Research has an entirely different purpose—the creation of new knowledge or the validation of old knowledge—whereas evaluation seeks to provide feedback for practice situations, so as to make that practice more helpful to the client. Evaluation is more practice oriented, whereas research is more science oriented."

"Well," you go on, "all this talk of objective measures of subtle human problems leaves me a bit cold. I mean, if the social construction theorists are correct, then there is no hard reality out there; everything we see or do is influenced by our own way of viewing the world, including what researchers—I mean evaluators, sorry—do with their clients. Talk about self-fulfilling prophecies, just look at what we are doing."

Mike and I look at each other and are speechless.

"Sorry, guys, I was just kidding," you go on. "I just had a philosophy class the other day, and this is one of those paradigmatic situations that lead to questions about everything. I know this point of view is no way to run a scientific practice, but it certainly gives one pause on how strongly to believe in the objectivity of everything we do."

III.A.7. Contracting: Who Does What with Whom under What Circumstances?

You continue, "Something else is bothering me. There seems to be a lot of work not only in conducting but also in evaluating practice. Who's going to do all this work? We've got lots of people involved in this project, and potentially we will be doing a million things all at the same time. I'm dedicating my life to human services, but I didn't think that meant every minute in every twenty-four hours."

"Calm down," Mike says. "We don't have to do it all ourselves. It's sort of like conducting an orchestra. You contract with different people to perform as part of a team, and you wave your arms and make beautiful music."

"What Mike means," I say, "is that we do the planning and then figure out who is the natural person to do the various aspects of the project. The Residence nutritionist ordinarily keeps tabs on who is or is not coming to meals, and we just collect that information from time to time. Same thing with the ordinary records on use of the lounge for group activities. Mrs. Abbott could be asked to keep a log book of her state of contentment at the end of each day, for example. And again we would collect this information once a week and plot the data, along with all the other data, to see if we could make sense of the patterns. That's essentially our evaluation task, which we would integrate with our practice activities, like asking Mrs. Abbott how it has been going for the past week. Contracting means figuring out who is to do what with whom under what conditions, both for practice and evaluation activities."

"What she means," Mike says, "is that many hands make light work."

It is getting late, and we agree to get together at the library next Saturday morning to do some of the information retrieval searches, and to talk some more about this case situation. In the meantime, I will be seeing Mrs. Abbott to assess some of the basic ideas we had considered.

III.B.6. Ethical Designs: Review of Practice Plans

It is you who, once again, brings us back to the recognition that we are working with ninety-year-old people, and that we had better be extremely careful in making plans that might cause harm, even as we intend them to cause good. "What are the risks involved in our intervention plan?" you ask. "For example, is there any downside of having agency-based home aides on a regular basis? The costs per person should be about the same as they are currently paying for irregular nonagency services, and if anything, the risk of theft is probably smaller among trained workers. Certainly, the level of personal service (and resident–employee relationships) should be higher because of their training in sensitivity, although the cleaning services might be at about the same level."

We can't think of any ethical downside, which doesn't mean there won't be any. We have to be attentive to the comments of our clients about their home aides. We also speculate about the effects of maintaining the Roaring Nineties group longer. Maybe it will become the Roaring Centenarians? But eventually we all will die. Are we setting them up for a more difficult reaction because they have been together longer? We realize we haven't a clue about how the very old reacted to death among their own, except for the quiet and somber period that occurred at the death of Miss Carol. Perhaps we have more to learn about dying and our reactions to death than did the Roaring Nineties group.

We realize that we aren't very successful in this ethical review. We agree to talk about it with our practicum supervisors on a personal basis. Maybe we can get a better handle on these difficult matters, especially when our practice gets too close for comfort to our lives. And maybe that is the essence of an ethical design for practice—realizing how much what we do affects not only clients but also ourselves. That is why ethical clarity is needed—to keep the focus of helping on the client (see Loewenberg & Dolgoff, 1996; Reamer, 1995).

II.B.7. Practice Hypotheses

You and Mike and I are sitting in the staff lounge again, on an orange juice break. We have been talking about our work at the Wintergreen, especially on those cases where our work overlapped. Mike says that since Mrs. Abbott is my direct client, I should call the shots on what specific practice hypotheses we make. What exactly do we intend to happen as a result of our intervention involving the home aide arrangement as organized by Mrs. Abbott? So, as team leader, I construct the following practice hypotheses, first for the group as a whole, and later, for my individual clients. You and Mike construct your own for your own clients.

First, for the Roaring Nineties group:

Hypothesis I: The presence of a dependable, well-trained, and economical home aide service would increase the probability of group members staying at the Wintergreen Residence and maintaining their friendship and support group, compared to the time before the arrival of this service. Specifically, we would observe a significant improvement in sign-ups for group get-togethers in the Wintergreen card rooms, representing one important way this group of people supplies mutual support for one another.

Second, for my individual client:

Hypothesis II-A (Abbott/Nutrition): Mrs. Abbott would participate in regularly planned residence meals at a higher level after the introduction of the home aide service than before. Specifically, we would examine the Residence dietician's records of attendance at meals during the time before and after the introduction of the home aide service, attendance being a prerequisite indicator for obtaining proper nutrition defined as the average daily caloric intake for a person her age.

Hypothesis II-B (Abbott/Level of Energy): Mrs. Abbott would demonstrate a higher level of energy in engaging in social activities of everyday life after she maintained regular eating patterns than before. Specifically, we would examine nursing records that originally identified lower energy levels and compare that period of time before with the time during her regular meal-partaking behavior.

Hypothesis II-C (Abbott/Depression): Mrs. Abbott would demonstrate a more contented and less depressed emotional pattern, comparing the time before the introduction of the home aide service and her regular attendance at meals with the time during. Specifically, (1) we would introduce at least one standardized measure of depression to be used once a week with the goal of reducing depression to below the clinical cutoff score; (2) we would also simultaneously collect practitioner observations of her behavior, including a standard probe, "How are you feeling today?" to be used at each regularly scheduled meeting; (3) we would ask permission to use the nursing staff summary evaluations of all residents on affective states. (This was the original source of concern over Mrs. Abbott's affective state.)

We also identify different objectives for the other clients, but we won't go into them here. Mike does note that what we are driving at, with these various hypotheses, is to attain a kind of practical significance, something that makes a practical difference in the world that the clients experience. Our statistical tests would tell us about statistical significance, whether the changes we observed could have happened by chance or not. Both are important, but they are different, as is the idea of theoretical significance, regardless of whether what we observe happening is what our guiding theory led us to believe would happen. These three kinds of significance are the three dimensions of scientific efficacy (see Chapter 19).

III.C.7. Single-System Evaluation: Basic Principles of Design (Chapter 11)

But one day, Mike comes into the staff cafeteria where we are meeting, and he has his hands on his hips and is glaring at us. "What's up, Mike?" I venture.

"If the three of us are going to cooperate on working with the Roaring Nineties group, then we really had better start collecting our baseline data," he declares. "There's a lot at stake in this, you know."

"You're feeling a little anxious, are you Mike?" you ask.

"Do you believe that you are going to flunk out of school because of your two lazy colleagues?" I ask, and we both snicker.

"Now, cut that out, you two. This is serious." Mike looks a bit redder than usual. "Do you know how late it is in the semester?"

"Actually, yes, we do. We were looking at the calendar in the Resident Administrator's office just before you got here, and we recorded some interesting data. Look here." I show him the rough sketch of the data on sign-ups for card rooms by Mrs. Abbott or any of the group of 'Roaring Nineties' over the last several months. Mike's mouth dropped open and then he smiled.

III.C.8. Baselining (Chapter 12)

"Ah, baselining! Now you're talking my language," he responds.

"We talked about these ideas before, that when the group met in the card room after dinner, it could be a simple but nonreactive indicator that the group was getting together and enjoying each other's company," you say. "Even when they didn't play cards much, just about the time we were called in, there is still a rough indication that they are getting together and providing whatever mutual support they can. It isn't a perfect indicator by any means, but it's simple to collect and it goes right to the heart of the matter. So, we recorded the number of weekly sign-ups by Mrs. Abbott or any of the group. We were plotting these numbers on some graph paper just as you (Mike) came charging up.

"Moreover, I also went to the dietician and got some other records of Mrs. Abbott's meal-eating pattern. I was just in time; she was going to toss out some old records, so I have data for about three months before I started interning

here. I'll plot these data on nutrition as soon as I can."

"What about those several measures of depression you were thinking about?" Mike asks.

"We're making some progress on these too. But it took a bit of persuasion from my practicum instructor to get to use records from the Residence, since I needed some reliability checks as part of my research class project," you add.

III.C.9. Evaluation Designs

It was several days after the memorial service for Miss Carol that I asked Mrs. Abbott how the home aide arrangement was working, and she said all of the details had been ironed out among the various residents, herself, and the agency. And the home aides were set to come in Mondays. More residents were involved than Mrs. Abbott had expected, and some were on a waiting list, to see if there would be enough home aides to help them. But Mrs. Abbott seemed to rise to the occasion and got all the agreements in place. I asked to see what the plans looked like and how the residents were going to decide whether the program was a success. Mrs. Abbott said she had given a lot of thought to that, since there were so many people involved. First, she was going to circulate a little survey every so often to see if people were satisfied with their agency home aide services, compared to what help they were getting before. Then, she was going to find out what her close friends needed (she herself had put in some extra money in order to get the home aide to do some housework for her) and whether they thought that particular work was being done adequately. She paused and said that she should probably check in with her friends on these points reasonably often because things change so suddenly around the Residence.

"Brilliant, Mrs. Abbott," I thought. "You just passed the first exam in my research class with flying colors. An attitude survey and an impressionistic behavioral study, using a kind of *A-B* design (that is, a before and during intervention design) with multiple data collection points" (see Chapter 13). I volunteered to assist her in designing the questionnaire and in being a bit more systematic in the behavioral study, and she readily agreed.

I am musing this over in the cafeteria when you and Mike come in. I proudly tell you about Mrs. Abbott's evaluation plans being the basic evaluation design we had studied last semester, and Mike frowns.

"Something wrong, Mike?" you ask.

"No, not really," he replies. "It's just that the *A-B* design tells us only part of the story, whether or not there is change in the target events. But it takes a stronger design to help us infer that what we did had a part in causing those changes. So long as we are doing the evaluation, we should probably try to use the strongest design that is suitable to this setting, and get both change information and causal information on whether we influenced that change."

Unfortunately, you ask Mike what those stronger designs were, but I glance at my watch. Mike takes the cue and says that it's too long a story to tell now, but that he is sure you would enjoy the various evaluation designs (see Chapters 14–18) when you got to them. "To set up the most powerful and yet least intrusive design is really the artistic part of the whole evaluation process," Mike muses.

"And the most ethical as well," I add. "We have to be very careful about being intrusive, but let's face it, to serve people can be somewhat intrusive. So, let's make the most of the time we have available with clients to get the best possible information to help them reach their goals and objectives."

PART IV. ANALYZING AND USING YOUR RESULTS: MAKING PRACTICE DECISIONS BASED ON EVALUATED PRACTICE IN THE CONTEXT OF THEORY AND ETHICS

IV.A.8. Monitoring Progress, Annotating Graphs, and Modifying the Intervention

One of the big surprises for me was watching the data as they came in, and trying to make

sense of the patterns that were emerging. Our theories told us what to expect; this was, of course, the basis for our particular practice decisions. But nothing quite prepared us for monitoring progress. It must be a little like watching the stock market go up and down each day, which must be nerve-racking for compulsive investors. We learned to be a little patient and watch for patterns over time. We had the luxury of being patient because there were no life-threatening conditions that we were addressing. And when anything unusual appeared on the charts, we annotated those data. That is, we made notes on the graph paper of events that may account for the observed changes (e.g., see Figure P.2). So we continued our work and carefully watched the data for a number of weeks.

The point is, numbers tell a story—if we will listen. How does one become sensitive to these numbers that keep coming in, week after week? This was a new experience for us, and we spend some time discussing this. Mike, as usual, has some ideas:

"Let's look at the nutrition data," Mike says (see Figure P.2). "We have reconstructed the baseline from the dietician's records of the number of meals Mrs. Abbott had for the past three months before we arrived. We could have had more, but the dietician said that Mrs. Abbott's pattern of eating was very constant, as were the patterns of most residents—a very high level of coming to every meal. But that began to change about three months ago, and we transcribed those data onto our graphs as reconstructed baseline data."

"What does reconstructed data mean?" you ask.

I pipe in that most baseline data are collected concurrently with the targeted event we are studying, but sometimes that is impossible—for example, when no one ever thought about using standardized measures of depression when Mrs. Abbott wasn't having any problems. Fortunately for us, the nurses routinely collect information about all of the residents at Wintergreen, one portion of which is close to our understanding of depressed behavior. Because of this, we decide to use this nursing information as a rough indicator of depression to

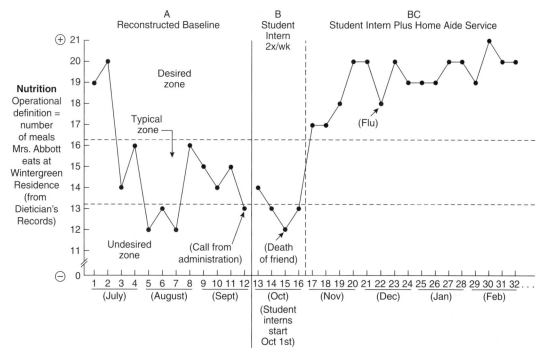

FIGURE P.2   Change in nutrition over several months.

give us a ballpark picture of what Mrs. Abbott was like during that time. That is, we reconstruct information collected for one purpose for use in another (our) purpose. It was the best we had at the time.

"Okay," you say. "Now what? I see that you have combined the two interventions: B is our regular two times a week meeting with our clients, and C is the home aide service. I presume you did that since they mostly occurred concurrently. Right?"

"Yes," Mike says.

"And looking at the data," you go on, "it looks like things continued to get worse in the first four weeks we were here—so much for our impact. Then, after the home aide service was set up, Mrs. Abbott seems to have had a major turnaround. Just look at those data!"

"Yes, very encouraging," Mike says, "until week 22 when all of a sudden Mrs. Abbott's attendence at meals went down sharply. I began to wonder if something had gone wrong with the home aide service. I looked again at the data and then I noticed that you had annotated the graph that she got the flu that week and I interpreted this to mean that she didn't feel much like eating in the dining hall."

"More than that, Mike," I say. "I saw those data too, and I alerted the nurses, who then tried to persuade her to eat as much as she could, even in her room. Monitoring data often helps keep the intervention on course, or to make vital corrections."

"But how do you see meaning in data, especially when data keep coming in on a regular basis? I sort of got stuck seeing nice positive data, and I missed the downturn," you say.

Mike goes into his professorial posture and we listen attentively. "The first principle is just to pay attention to the numbers. We have in mind what we want to happen, namely, that Mrs. Abbott will eat more regularly to keep up her health and energy. Then, any time something different occurs during intervention, pay attention and see if you can figure out why. Annotating concurrent events helps a lot. But sometimes, people just get tired of doing something one way and decide to do it another way, and those times are hard to figure out, unless we ask the client directly, of course."

"Another way to keep attentive to the data as they come in," I chime in, "is to involve the client in the data record. Clients are probably more interested in their own data, or rather, their own lives, than we can ever be, and so they might know something about their life situations that can account for the data whatever they may be. If you have to discuss the way things are going with your client, this also is an incentive to keep up with the data monitoring and use it as part of your conversations with clients. And they enjoy seeing progress—who wouldn't?"

"The one corrective I would add," you say, "is that I wouldn't rush to change any major part of a carefully thought-out plan of intervention, just because of a blip in the record. I guess that is another point in which annotations can be helpful."

"Straight on!" Mike says.

"It's 'right on,' Mike," you say with a small smirk.

IV.B.8, IV.B.9, and IV.B.10: The Ethics of Changing Events, Client Bill of Rights, and Informed Consent (Chapter 25)

"I couldn't help overhear what you were talking about," says Mrs. Hill. (I hadn't realized how loudly we were talking.) "And I thought it would be an appropriate time to ask about what kind of informed consent you obtained from your clients. After all, it would be in their best interests to be well informed about any plans that affected their lives."

Mike is uncharacteristically quiet, and I manage to say that we didn't have any signed informed consent forms because I thought that this was just for big research projects.

"It's true that federal grants usually require informed consent forms, but even when we discussed the client bill of rights (Chapter 25) in class, we have to honor the ideas of our professional code of ethics, even if the government doesn't require us to do so. Our profession does," she said.

"Events were moving so fast that I don't think we even thought about this," you explain, and Mrs. Hill nods in understanding.

"All the more reason to keep the issue in the middle of all your planning for helping," she says gently. Point taken.

IV.C.10. Analysis (Chapter 19)

Frankly, even though I really wanted to do this evaluation, I was a little overwhelmed with all of the different options for analysis. Then I went back to the text and got some reassurance in keeping my eye on the big picture—what had to be analyzed—and then thinking logically as to the best way to do this, given a few possible ways of approaching it. I decided to start most simply with visual analysis, and then look at other options as the need arose. I checked my thinking with Mike and you, and you both thought this was a reasonable start.

IV.C.10.a. Visual Analysis (Chapter 20)

You laugh. "What's that for?" I ask.

"Well, I was just looking at these charts, as far as we have collected information, and I must say that they look pretty skimpy for all the work that went into them," you comment.

Mike is aghast. "But that's the whole point," he sputters. "We want to simplify some very complex situations into some relatively simple indicators of what is happening, so we can read the simple stuff as a clue to the complex whole.

We know that isn't the whole story, but life is too short to spend collecting every possible relevant fact. So be happy for these simple graphs."

"Yes, but only if we selected the right simple graphs to use," I add. "You know, it may be that we are way off on one or another of these indicators and that we are not getting useful information at all."

"That's bad," you say. "So how do you protect yourself against choosing the wrong indicator?"

"I can think of one way," Mike says. "Remember, we have a whole set of factors, and they are expected to react with each other in predictable ways, according to our theory. One is supposed to go up, another down, and so forth. If one of these factors doesn't respond as expected, then we should examine it carefully to see if it is measuring the wrong thing."

"Is this what you mean by analysis of the data?" you ask.

"Essentially, yes," I say. "Analysis means looking at the pattern the data take and comparing it to something. Either standard norms, if we have any; or against some idealized goal; or just comparing the patterns of change from before to during or after intervention."

"That doesn't sound hard," you say.

"Well, no one can guarantee that," Mike confesses. "We can go in stages of analysis. Whatever else we do, we should just start by looking at the pattern of data as they appear on the graph. Here, look at Figure P.2. What do you see?"

"Wiggly lines," you report, too honestly.

"Yeah, yeah, but beyond that. What patterns?" Mike asks.

"Looks like things are getting worse during baseline," you observe.

"Right!" Mike says. "That's exactly so. And that is the reason that we became involved in the first place. Things were getting worse and there was no easy explanation or solution."

"Then things continue to get worse after we started working here," you observe.

"Let's not dwell on that," I request uncomfortably. "Let's say this is a kind of training period. We were trying to get Mrs. Abbott and the others used to the fact that we were here

and that we would be offering some ideas to them to facilitate changes."

"Moreover, you can see this is also the time when Miss Carol died, and Mrs. Abbott was quite upset about that, which may also account for why she didn't go to meals as often as she had before," Mike notes.

"Then, in the fourth week Mrs. Abbott starts to improve," you suggest.

"Maybe," Mike says. "That improvement could have been due to chance factors in the fourth week, but look at the data after that. Big changes and relatively steady improvement. That's what we like to see. That is also when the home aide service started, taking a big burden off Mrs. Abbott's mind."

"It is sort of like you guys are reading a sheet of notes and making beautiful music from it," you say.

"Sometimes the music isn't as harmonious as it is here," Mike comments. "In fact, it is sometimes hard to tell what is really an important change and what isn't. Statistical analysis may help us find the answers."

IV.C.10.b. Descriptive Statistics (Chapter 21)

Mike says, "Notice that we are going to need some basic arithmetic in order to analyze these data. Can you calculate means? Or proportions? We'll need proportions when it comes time to do one kind of analysis; it's called the proportion/frequency approach. Like, how many times did the behaviors appear in the desired behavior zone, as compared with the total number of observation times during that period? To get a proportion, you just divide the big number into the little number, like 9 divided by 12 is, ah, ..."

".75," you say. "I went as far as calculus in college."

"Sorry," Mike blushes. "I was just asking."

IV.C.10.c. Tests of Statistical Significance (Chapter 22)

"The real payoff of analysis," Mike quickly goes on, "is to find out how likely a given set of outcomes could have happened by chance alone. When some outcome is very unlikely to occur by chance alone, and when we tried to make that kind of outcome occur, then we can test for statistical significance–that is, how common or how rare a given finding is. After that, we can make some interpretations about what that significance level means."

"That sounds hard," you admit.

"Not really," I say. "Once you get into a few good habits, it is quite easy to do. Mike is a computer buff, and he says he can do the same things much faster and more accurately using a computer analysis program in our textbook (Chapter 23). But it may be useful to learn the basics by hand, and then try your hand at the computer."

"Okay," you say, somewhat doubtfully. "Let's do the analysis on the nutrition data and see if the interventions caused Mrs. Abbott to eat more regular meals."

Mike and I look at each other. "Well, not so fast," I say gently. "This simple before and during evaluation design (A-B) is not strong enough to tell us whether the intervention *caused* the outcomes, or whether other factors that we didn't measure in fact caused the outcomes. All we can tell from this design is whether the problem really has changed. That's why we talked some time ago about different kinds of evaluation designs; some were more limited and others were stronger and thus able to provide causal information–whether what we did through the intervention in fact is the likely cause of some perceived outcome."

Mike takes it from there. "Look at the data on nutrition again." Mike then explains briefly the proportion/frequency approach to analysis. He describes the approach as if one were superimposing a normal curve over the data on the vertical line, and finding the middle two-thirds of the data points as representing the "typical" pattern of problematic behavior during the baseline period of 12 weeks. Then, by projecting those typical lines into the future (the intervention period), in effect we predict what will happen if nothing is changed. But of course, something is changed, namely, we intervened, and so we can look for patterns of change and see whether there is statistically significant improvement, including the chance

that matters may grow significantly worse. Mike shows you some models in the text (Chapter 13), and you seemed to get the idea that if the pattern of data during intervention is "better" than the typical pattern of problem behavior in baseline, then we can claim real improvement. However, the simple A-B design that we are using can't permit us to infer causality–that we caused the positive results.

You look a bit puzzled when Mike starts pointing to the tables that he says tell us about statistical significance, but I suggest that you wait until you come to that chapter in the text to understand what Mike is saying. "It seems so easy when you do it," you say, and we agree. It really is easy once you get the hang of it.

IV.C.10.d. Computer Analysis (Chapter 23)

You and I wander back through the halls on the way out, and happen past the computer room. No one is there. "Say," you mention, "how about if we do some data analysis here with the various tables?"

I respond, "We can't do them here, because we would have to enter the program into a computer, and I don't know if there is enough capacity with these computers. They are primarily dedicated to e-mail and writing. But we could stop off at the university computer center and run some of these data."

Later, at the computer center, I bring up the program. "Then, all you do," I explain, "is to follow the instructions on the screen, and the computer does all the work for you. Here, let me enter some data and then get a printout of the computer analysis."

"That looks like fun," you observe. "Where did you say I could read more about this?"

"In several chapters in the textbook," I reply. "And this same program can generate the graphs we drew by hand, and it can also construct the trend lines that we'll need as we analyze our data."

"Then, I'll bet I could use my laptop to do all of this at the Wintergreen on an ongoing basis," you suggest.

"Absolutely," I reply.

IV.C.10.e. Selecting a Procedure for Analyzing Data

Later, at school, we are looking at some printouts and begin to compare them with the work involved in visual analysis and the use of the tables of significance. "When you are all set up and have the data in the computer, the computer analysis makes a lot of sense," you say, "especially if you need to be formal about results for your instructor or for publication. But if you don't have that program available, especially on the spot at the Wintergreen, then it is useful just to do a quick visual analysis for clues on whether it is worth going further. The hand analysis using the tables seems reasonable, once you get used to the procedures. I am glad that the instructions are specified in the titles of those tables. So, I guess each method of analysis has its uses in certain places."

"Awesome," I exclaim. "You are a fast learner."

IV. A.9. Comparing Goals and Objectives: Using Results to Test Practice Hypotheses

The weeks went by with incredible speed; we were busy every moment and often exhilarated with field work and its outcomes. But the semester was coming to an end, and we had to pull all of our work together for the final evaluation/practice joint project.

You say, "I sure wish I had some models of how evaluation reports should be written." And Mike replies that there are hundreds of references to reports in the text. I happen to have some photocopies of a couple that I loaned you, including Jason & Brackshaw (1999); Staat, van Leeuwen, & Wit (2000); Kastner, Tingstrom, & Edwards (2000), and Austin, Alvero, & Olson (1998).

I'll tell you what I did, as an example. First, I went back to the practice hypotheses, which described in advance what we expected to happen. Our group hypothesis stated that the home aide service would increase the probability that the group could stay together at the Wintergreen, and thus maintain their friendship and support of one another. We chose to use a simple, nonobtrusive indicator of the mutual support group being together, the sign-up sheets for the card room.

Looking at Figure P.3, which uses a proportion/frequency approach with the Mutual Support meetings, we observe that there was a statistically significant change in the attendance during the intervention period, compared with the projected pattern stemming from the baseline pattern. In statistical language, we can say, based on these data, that the improved attendance we observed could not have happened by chance alone, except 5 times in 100 occasions ($P < .05$).

I had two hypotheses specifically for Mrs. Abbott. The first was that her nutrition would improve, as indicated by her attendance at regularly scheduled meals in the dining room of the Wintergreen. We analyzed those data using the proportion/frequency model, and found a sharp improvement as compared with the baseline condition, enough to claim there was a statistically significant difference at the $P < .05$ level (see Figure P.2). But again, because of the limited logical properties of the design, we cannot assert that we caused this strong positive change with the intervention, and, of course, we really cannot distinguish the effects of the two interventions that we combined–the home aide service and our direct work as interns.

The second hypothesis for Mrs. Abbott concerned her signs of depression, as indicated in three ways. First, we used a standardized depression scale, which we could obtain only after we started interning at the Wintergreen. So we had no baseline, but we did have the norms of the scale in general, compared to the scores Mrs. Abbott got. There we observed positive change, comparing her scores with the norms for people who had scores indicating clinical depression.

Then, we also continued to use the monthly nursing rating of all residents, which included one indicator item that we used as our operational definition of depression, namely, level of social functioning, as interpreted on a five-point scale, with 1 meaning very poor, and 5 meaning very good. These were the only baseline data we had, and since we adapted them

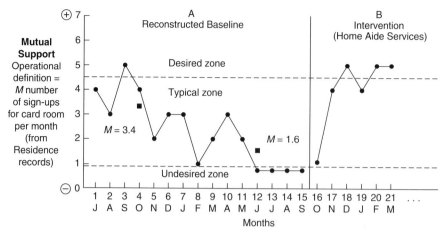

Proportion of events in desired zone in the baseline = .06 or .05 using
"conservative rule" (1 out of 15; Table 19.2)

Number of positive events in intervention period = 3 (3 out of 6)

Number of events needed in desired zone in the intervention period to
constitute statistical significance at the $P < .05 = 2$ (Table 19.2)
$P < .01 = 3$ (Table 19.3)

•• Graph shows significant change at the $P < .05$ level and $P < .01$ level

■ = Monthly intern data

FIGURE P.3   Mutual support.

from other original uses, we took them as a rough reconstructed baseline on Mrs. Abbott's state of mind. It showed reasonably high levels of functioning until a few months before we started at the Wintergreen, when she began to exhibit the behaviors that eventually led to a call to our agency for help. After the joint intervention of both of us (the interns, B, on the chart) and home aide services, C, we observe some improvements.

Finally, we also made some observational ratings twice each week as part of our regular meetings with clients (bottom graph in Figure P.4). These ratings were averaged weekly. The weekly ratings showed some improvements, but since no other data were collected weekly, we had to average these weekly data over a month-long period to be able to compare them with other depression data. Look at the middle graph in Figure P.4 where we added (with small boxes) the constructed monthly intern data to compare those data with the monthly

nursing data. We can see some closely correlated findings, but we always saw the client as lower in social functioning, that is, as more nearly depressed, than did the nurses. We don't know how to interpret such a discrepancy; it may be that we are simply less experienced than the nurses in the ranges of functioning of very old persons.

When we compare all three sets of depression data in Figure P.4, we find a general common pattern of improvement after the home aide services began. This is a useful finding as it suggests that as long as these basic needs are met, then the group probably can continue to function as a mutual support group. However, because of the advanced ages of its members, we encouraged them to admit a few more members to their ranks as insurance against the inevitable.

Overall, especially when we look at the pattern of positive changes across all three charts, we can show evidence of some real improve-

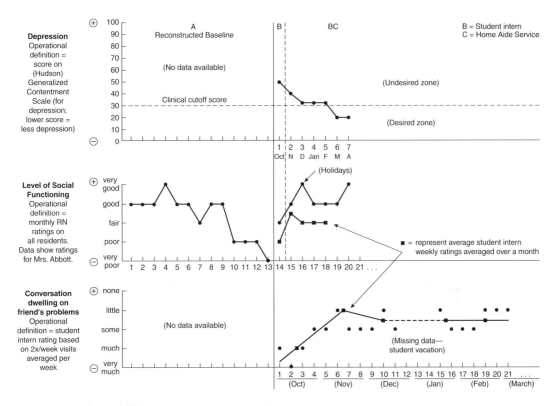

FIGURE P.4   Charts of different perspectives on depression.

ments in outcomes over the baseline period (including reconstructed baselines). Not perfect, but we speculated that nothing would be perfect in an imperfect world. We are pretty pleased with ourselves, I must admit.

IV.A.10. Decision Making: Combining Evaluation with Values and Practice Wisdom

In the second semester, we were assigned other cases, including Mrs. Dunn, who continued to be morose after the death of her husband; our field instructor urged us to look at the data on Mrs. Abbott and our practice goals, and decide when we should terminate services. We recognized that the home aide service, especially with Mrs. Abbott monitoring it from the Wintergreen, was an ongoing service. From the

records, Mrs. Abbott was eating regularly; the dietician told us this was the norm for her, from her memory of Mrs. Abbott before the records we had gotten from her. And the Roaring Nineties (now with a number of younger 80-year-olds included) met almost every night, even if not all members met that regularly. It proved to be a self-sustaining group as well.

What we realize in this review of the cases was that we were acting on the basis of some empirical information. It may not have been the strongest empirical information, but it was reasonable, given the time and energy we had to put into it. "That's what single-system designs are all about," Mike almost shouted.

"Okay, so what's next?" you ask. "Are we going to drop Mrs. Abbott and the others just like that? According to my instructors, we should be planning some maintenance phase where we help her to maintain these successes after we are no longer in the picture."

I agree, except in this situation, we will be working in the same building and can check on how things are going in a variety of ways. If need be, we might have some other contacts with Mrs. Abbott and the others to offer them encouragement or new ideas.

"That's like booster sessions," Mike says. "But at least we should make clear to Mrs. Abbott that we—or others at our agency—would be ready to step in again, if need be."

So, regretfully, we terminated service with Mrs. Abbott and her friends, as we took up new tasks with others at the Wintergreen. Mrs. Abbott had seen practitioners come and go over the years, and while we had a very good relationship, she was quite able to say good-bye. In fact, she was almost too busy with events and services at the Wintergreen to squeeze in time for me.

I realized too late that I hadn't made a regular follow-up plan, so I made it a point to drop in and see Mrs. Abbott frequently on my rounds at the Wintergreen. I did look at the nurse's reports on her and the others and was pleased to see that their progress was sustained.

PART V. SCIENTIFIC PRACTICE IN THE COMMUNITY: THE CHALLENGE (CHAPTER 25)

V.A.11. Report to the Agency: Adding to Practice Wisdom and to Our Personal Practice Repertoire

As part of our intern service, we were required to write up a report of our services to Mrs. Abbott and the group. This turned out to be quite easy because we had our field progress notes and also the graphs of the several variables we were following, especially with the annotations we had made that added flesh to the skeleton of events. We included the graphs and explanations, and received positive affirmation from agency personnel.

Whether or not we changed the world—or even the world at the Wintergreen—we cannot say. We did show the empirically based evidence that it appears that people's lives can change; we hope that our services and the home aides contributed to it. People we served seemed more satisfied; maybe we should have collected satisfaction measures to document this point. But we noted with our own satisfaction that many more residents of the Wintergreen were using home aides when we left the agency in the spring.

V.B.11. Report to the Community: Ethical Accountability and Cost-Benefits

There is a network of senior residences in our city, and we did make a presentation at the annual meeting, describing our work and its effects. The questions that we were asked were interesting. They began as accusations that we were imposing our plan onto the group, until we explained our process in greater detail. Funny, these were the same kinds of questions that you had raised in our team long before. Fortunately we had some reasonable answers.

However, the network seemed more interested in the cost figures we were able to present. Briefly, these involved the costs for supporting interns in general, plus the extra money needed to purchase home aide services when particular residents were not able to do so. These costs were to be compared with the benefits, tangible and intangible, from the project. First, more long-term residents were enabled to stay longer periods of time, which was very important to them and to the reputation of the Residence. They appeared to be healthier (until late in their lives) and much happier. This contentment with life at the Wintergreen became a prized possession in advertising for future residents, and a long waiting list was generated. We came away from this experience recognizing how applicable the single-system evaluation process was for a variety of concerns, as well as how alive and well were the many critical issues raised about this form of evaluation.

V.C.11. Report to the Profession: Adding to Applied Social Science Knowledge

The three of us did get our act together long enough to submit a proposal at the state National Association of Social Workers chapter conference to present a poster session, and it was accepted. So, about a year later, we three went to the conference and presented what we had done to a small group of interested people (mainly from nursing homes and senior residences). That was very stimulating. I am sure that we learned far more in constructing our presentation than most of the audience got in that short period of time. But it gave us a taste of what contributing to our professions could be like.

ADIOS, MRS. ABBOTT: TILL WE MEET AGAIN

I must tell you that when I was about to terminate with Mrs. Abbott, she was about to terminate with me. She was so busy with new projects. A Mrs. Alvarez was coming to the Residence, and she spoke almost no English. Mrs. Abbott met her when she came for an exploratory visit, and they got along very well—in hand signs. So, naturally, Mrs. Abbott started to learn Spanish. Adios, Mrs. Abbott. You have taught me much about human nature and have made me proud to be a helping professional.

PART I

WHAT ARE YOU GETTING INTO?

In the first, it is ridiculed;
in the second, it is resisted;
in the third, it is considered self-evident.
—Schopenhauer, 1788–1860

You've chosen to enter one of the helping professions in order to help people, not to do research. So what are you doing in a class or in an agency in which you are expected to evaluate your own practice? The brief answer is that learning how to evaluate your practice will help you to practice both more sensitively and more effectively. The long answer requires further study—the purpose of this book.

As you saw in the Prologue, and as we want to reemphasize in Chapter 1, there are close parallels between the problem-solving steps in good practice and the basic steps in evaluation. (For example, both good practice and good evaluation begin with a clear definition of the problems and goals. We can't start helping or evaluating our clients until we know their problems and their objectives.) We will outline in Chapter 1 the ways in which monitoring client behavior can tell us when we are on- or off-target, so that we can take corrective action. We will describe briefly how to analyze the overall outcome of the service program—were there changes in the client's problems or not? We will conclude Chapter 1 with a flowchart showing the evaluation process—measurement, design, analysis, and decision making—indicating where in the book you can find each component.

Most of all, we are hoping that you will come to recognize that the evaluation of practice is feasible and potentially very helpful. The basic principles of evaluation are remarkably simple; the applications can be adapted to almost any situation in which you might be called on to practice—and to evaluate. By the conclusion of this book, we hope that you will be able to evaluate your own practice, provide social accountability for your profession, and enjoy the process of being a more effective and humane practitioner.

1 INTEGRATING EVALUATION AND PRACTICE
Introduction to Single-System Designs

PURPOSE: This chapter presents an introduction to single-system designs (SSDs), a method used by helping professionals to evaluate practice. In this chapter we present the basic characteristics of single-system designs; we compare this evaluation method with the classical research methods; and we summarize the entire evaluation process with a flowchart showing which chapters will discuss which portions of the whole process. Our main purpose in this chapter is to encourage you to recognize the feasibility and the desirability of evaluating your own professional services—in whatever community setting you may work and using whatever theory guides your practice. This is a goal that we will identify as scientific practice, the combination of a sensitive and caring practitioner with the logical and empirical strengths of the applied social scientist. ■

Introduction to Single-System Designs

What Are Single-System Designs?

Basic Characteristics of Single-System Designs

Specifying the Target (Problem or Objective/Goal)

Measuring the Target by Forming Its Operational Definition

Baseline and Intervention Phases

Repeated Measures

Practice Designs

Evaluation Designs

Analysis of the Data

Decision Making on the Basis of Findings

Practice as Evaluation, Evaluation as Practice

Single-System Designs and Classical Research: The Knowledge-Building Context

Single-System Evaluation, Qualitative Research, and Quantitative Research

Advantages of Using Single-System Designs in Practice

A Walk Through the Evaluation Process

Summary

INTRODUCTION TO SINGLE-SYSTEM DESIGNS

The title of this book, *Evaluating Practice,* says it all: Everything we present in this text is intended to facilitate the evaluation of practice–that is, the systematic, ongoing, and more or less objective determination of whether we are obtaining the objectives and goals of practice that we set with our clients. This is a critical function of practice, especially as it is going to be conducted in this age of managed care that demands tangible evidence of effectiveness (Corcoran & Gingerich, 1994). In fact, the accrediting body of schools of social work requires that all students be taught how to evaluate their own practices (Council on Social Work Education, 1994), and the Code of Ethics of the social work profession requires evaluation of all intervention programs and services (NASW, 1996). The twenty-first century will likely see evaluation of practice in field settings as just as integral to professional helping as were good communication skills in the twentieth century.

Single-system designs essentially involve continuing observation of one client/system before, during, and after some intervention. By *client/system* we mean one or more persons or groups being assisted by a helping professional to accomplish some goal. These goals may involve preventive, protective, promotive (the three aspects of primary prevention), interventive, or rehabilitative practices. And these practices may be delivered by social workers; by psychologists; by people in nursing, medicine, or the allied health fields; or by professionals in education or other helping professions. For simplicity of discussion, we will use the term *client* to refer to individuals, groups, or other collectives, as the context will make clear. And we will use the term *practitioner* to refer to any helping professional. The term *treatment,* although widely used, is problematic since it is a medically oriented word that assumes a medical model of disease causation that isn't suitable to a wide range of social concerns. So, we will mainly use the term *intervention* for discussions of practice that may include medical treatment, social services, psychotherapy, community change effort, educational methods,

and the like. The context of our discussion will determine what practice term we use.

As we illustrated in the case presented in the Prologue, using single-system evaluation, you can learn what the client's problems and potentials were before the intervention. You can identify the client's objectives and goals. From this understanding of problems and goals, you can specify a target or targets for intervention. We will use the word *target* to refer to clients' problems or objectives that have been clearly specified as the focus of our interventive efforts. Combining this knowledge of the client's situation both with our theories of human behavior and behavior change and with the relevant research base, you can construct and implement a workable intervention plan.

Then we *monitor* the interventive process; that is, we check progress against the client's objectives in order to know whether to change our intervention. Should we do more than, the same as, or less than we are doing, or should we do something completely different from before? This is the heart of the evaluation process, making use of the rapid feedback of information for present and future helping.

Finally, we can determine whether the overall outcome was successful in terms of the client's objectives and goals in the social context. We will use the term *evaluation* to refer to this special analysis of outcomes, in contrast to *monitoring* the process of intervention.

There are a number of simple conventions for graphing the flow of events with regard to a particular client problem. We often obtain a reference point (or more likely, a pattern of points), called a *baseline,* of a given problem before any intervention occurs. We can then compare changes in the target against the baseline during and after intervention. We repeat these same measures on a regular basis, using a *chart* or *graph* to examine client change. Using certain conventions described in this book, we can determine for the ongoing intervention whether there is significant change occurring–in either the desired or undesired directions–in order to make suitable adaptations in the intervention. We also can have an empirical and rational basis for termination: when statistical significance is aligned with clinically or socially meaningful changes in the client's situation, as predicted by one's practice theory. This process is the essence of scientific practice–a more or less objective guide to sensitive practice changes and outcomes. As you saw in the Prologue, this is not a lock-step approach to practice and evaluation, but one that does require considerable thought and flexibility.

And that's it! The basic principles of single-system designs actually are few and simple. The principles can be combined in numerous ways to fit the needs of a given case or situation. The information obtained can be reasonably objective, and the sense of knowing how matters are proceeding is positively exhilarating. That's the fun part, assuming that the case is going well. If it isn't, then you need to know about this as soon as possible, so you can change intervention techniques or directions. Now, let us turn to a discussion of the major characteristics of single-system designs.

WHAT ARE SINGLE-SYSTEM DESIGNS?

For many years helping professionals dreamed about integrating theory, research, and practice in the belief that the more clearly their theories could be stated and tested in the real world, the better their practice would be. Unfortunately, it has been difficult to create this integration, primarily because the technologies needed were not available. The global concepts used in some theories were difficult to define in concrete terms. In classical, experimental/control group research designs, immediate feedback was almost impossible to achieve. Thus, when reasonably objective but relatively easy methods of evaluation, such as single-system designs, were developed, the helping professions had the tools for which they had long hoped.

Basic Characteristics of Single-System Designs

The phrase *single-system designs* refers to a set of empirical procedures used to observe changes in an identified target (a specified problem or objective of the client) that is measured repeatedly over time. This new evaluation technology

has been described using a number of terms, all of which are about equivalent for our purposes. These terms include intensive or idiographic research, single N or $N = 1$ research, single-subject research or single-subject design, single case-study design, time-series research, single-organism research, single-case experimental design, and the term we will use in this book, single-system designs. The term *single-system designs* emphasizes the person in the environment as a useful perspective for scientific practice. A given system–one person alone, but often one or more persons and/or groups interacting in ordinary life situations–is the object of intervention. Changes are sought in either the person or persons involved, and the relevant social or physical environments. Thus, single-*system* designs refer to evaluating practice with the relevant parts of a whole system, which could range from an individual to a family to a group to a community to any size system.

Explicit interventions should be guided by a practice theory or by specific principles of practice; consequently we learn what intervention techniques work well under what conditions. However, there are no particular intervention models (like behavior therapy) that alone are suited for single-system designs. Single-system designs are not attached to any particular theory of intervention; the single-system design model is "theory free" in this sense (i.e., it can be used with just about any intervention theory or approach). Single-system designs have been used by psychoanalytically oriented practitioners (Dean & Reinherz, 1986); practitioners working with groups (Edleson, Miller, Stone, & Chapman, 1985) and families (Bentley, 1990); communications theorists (Nelsen, 1981); practitioners using systemic, problem-solving approaches (Slonim-Nevo & Vosler, 1991); cognitive psychologists (McCullough, 1984); practitioners using paradoxical intention (Kolko & Milan, 1983), among others. In fact, we will use examples from a variety of theoretical orientations throughout this book.

Usually, but not always, single-system designs employ a before/during and/or a before/during/after approach to compare the patterns of two states of one client/system. The before-intervention state (baseline) is used as a frame of reference for changes occurring in the during-intervention or after-intervention state. Because the same party is involved throughout the service period, the practitioner looks for differences in that party's target events and tries to determine whether his or her efforts produced these differences.

Now let's examine the basic characteristics of all single-system designs. You can refer to the Prologue to see how those characteristics can be implemented in actual practice.

Specifying the Target (Problem or Objective/Goal). A fundamental rule of any professional practice requires that you identify the problem: What are we going to try to change? In practice, this often involves client and practitioner interactions that define the problems and objectives in the given situation, as well as the strengths and resources with which they have to work.

Something important goes on when clients and practitioners discuss the presenting problems and objectives and goals (what we hope to accomplish). The clients express their concerns, and practitioners simultaneously conceptualize and empathize. Practitioners conceptualize when they abstract and generalize the patterns of client behaviors (thoughts, feelings, and actions), which are given some label (a concept) representing that class of experiences (Bloom, 1975). For example, the practitioner sees a client's head slumped to the chest and the teary eyes, and hears the client talk of not sleeping well and losing interest in food and sex. The practitioner forms an initial hunch that the client may be depressed, which directs the practitioner to look for and test additional factors known to be associated with depression. Thus, concepts act as the building blocks of theory, or at least of some general principles, which in turn serve as guides to practice. It is essential to be clear about how you conceptualize because the class labels you identify lead you to bodies of information that in turn guide your practice. A fuzzy concept can lead you in unfruitful directions. Accurate conceptualizing represents the practitioner's first contribution to the helping process.

Simultaneously with conceptualizing, practitioners also empathize; they actively listen to clients, cognitively and emotionally attempting to understand the meanings of these problems and objectives, and then reflect this understanding to the clients with warmth and genuineness. Fischer (1978b) terms these the core skills for any helping practice. Scientific practice involves sensitive, empathic awareness of client problems and strengths, which constitute the practitioner's second contribution to the helping process. Both conceptualization and empathy help the practitioner to specify what is happening in the client situation.

It is important to note that no finite list of problems or objectives will ever be a comprehensive picture of the whole person or group involved. Instead, a few specified targets are chosen and represent indicators of the whole, as a compromise between feasibility and comprehensiveness. Schön (1983) describes presenting problems as "indeterminate messes"–complex, changing, fluid experiences that constitute the human condition. While case situations are often messy in this way, the practitioner tries to impose some order onto them to make the problems amenable to change. In effect, the practitioner is a problem constructor, assembling and recombining elements of the "mess" with the client until both share a common perception of the problem and how to solve it. As this process of problem construction continues, the mess may become more manageable (Witkin & Gottschalk, 1988). The client and practitioner may see progress–in part because they have agreed on ways of talking about or identifying problems and strengths in the client situation. This is a critical step in problem solving.

Measuring the Target by Forming Its Operational Definition. By means of the problem construction process just described, the broad problem and/or objective can be changed into a specific target that the practitioner will seek to influence when it is restated as an operational definition. By specifying what operations or measurement procedures we will use to define the target–how often it occurs, in what intensity, and so on–both client and practitioner can be clear about what they are dealing with. These actual procedures of measurement are called the operational definition. Changes in this target will provide feedback to the practitioner and client regarding progress toward problem resolution.

We discuss the details of the measurement process in Part II (and gave some examples in the Prologue), but we want to emphasize that the measurement procedures used in single-system designs are generally quite simple, and they are used only to the extent that they can help the practitioner make decisions about happenings in the client situation. Moreover, there are formal scales or do-it-yourself procedures available to measure just about every possible target, no matter what the practitioner's theoretical orientation. We present many case examples illustrating the range of measures throughout this book; specific discussions of the different types of measures available are the focus of Chapters 5 through 10.

Baseline and Intervention Phases. A phase is a time period during which a particular practice activity occurs. In general, there are two types of phases, baseline phases and intervention phases. The targets are measured in both phases, but during a baseline phase, no target-focused intervention is implemented, whereas during an intervention phase, one or more target-focused helping practices are introduced.

The baseline phase involves the planned, systematic collection of information regarding the target before a given intervention is begun. Usually, you collect such information at the very beginning of the case as you are trying to understand the nature and extent of the problems and strengths in the client's situation. You also may return to baseline conditions during the course of service, such as when one intervention appears not to be working well, and the practitioners need a fresh perspective in identifying changes in the client's situation (see Chapter 12). These baseline or nonintervention phases constitute the core of single-system evaluation; changes in the pattern of data between baseline and intervention phases provide the key evaluation information.

Students and practitioners frequently ask whether any baseline situation can ever be free of some intervention. The answer requires that the distinction be made clearly between the

relationship-building interactions that are not precisely structured in a way to bring about specific changes and the interventions that are intended to change specific aspects of the client situation. Practitioners rightly believe that they are providing a useful service while they are building a trusting relationship with the client. But this trust or rapport generally is a means to an end, which is problem resolution; rapport is not necessarily an end in itself. This vital relationship often provides the basis for implementing an intervention and for helping the client to make changes in his or her life; it may also provide sensitive information whereby the environment may be changed to benefit the client (see Bohart & Greenberg, 1997).

Formal interventions, on the other hand, are *planned* changes in which practitioners perform certain actions with regard to their clients, to other people, or in situations in order to achieve specified objectives. Thus, we expect changes that occur as a result of these formal interventions to be far greater than those that would occur in the baseline phase, since these planned interventions are *added* to the rapport-building and relationship-building activities in the baseline.

Repeated Measures. The heart of single-system evaluation is the collection of repeated information on the target problems or objectives. This is what is meant by a time-series design. Either the practitioner, the clients, or relevant others observe the same target problem over regular units of time (such as every day or every week–whatever is appropriate to the given problem) to see whether any changes are taking place before (the baseline phase), during (the intervention phase), and after (the follow-up phase) the intervention. This is the basis of monitoring progress to determine whether changes are needed in the intervention program, a process that is critical to good practice decisions (see Part III). Again, as you saw in the Prologue, there are any number of ways that you can creatively measure your targets for intervention.

Practice Designs. Whatever practice methods and theories are used, they should be clearly described. Thus, if the overall results are positive, you would know what exact services were delivered and under what conditions those results were produced. In this way, you would be able to build a repertoire of effective methods as well as communicate clearly with others who might wish to use these same methods. Equally important, it is useful to know what does not work with a given kind of client in a given situation, so that we won't repeat our less effective methods.

There should also be clear conceptual linkages between the identified targets and the specific interventions chosen to effect them. For example, if one were dealing with depression—a cognitive and affective state with certain typical associated behaviors, often correlated with various kinds of environmental factors—then one's intervention approach would need to take account of these cognitive, affective, behavioral, and environmental factors. A given intervention approach need not directly act on all of these factors, but it should have a rationale for what it does direct the practitioner to act on, and how it presumes those factors on which there is no planned action would be influenced (cf. Gordon & Ledray, 1985).

A practice design is the sum of systematic and planned interventions chosen to deal with a particular set of targets to achieve identified objectives and goals. Such a design may be a translation of an existing theory or set of principles of behavior change into the context of a given client, or it may be newly constructed by the practitioner. Note that the actual implementation of this design may be only an approximation of the design itself, so that you should try to implement as much as possible of what the practice design calls for (cf. McMahon, 1987; Nelsen, 1985).

Evaluation Designs.   In general, research designs are arrangements for making or structuring observations about a situation in order to identify lawful relationships (e.g., that a certain variable seems to vary consistently with another variable). *Evaluation* designs are research designs applied to the evaluation of practice outcomes. Single-system designs, as one type of evaluation design, involve arrange-

ments in which repeated observations before, during, and/or after intervention are compared to monitor the progress and assess the outcome of that service, as described in the Prologue. All single-system designs permit analysis of patterns of change in client problems; some of the more complex designs also allow you to infer whether the practitioner's efforts are causally responsible for the identified changes. (Part III discusses these two categories of evaluation designs.)

Analysis of the Data.   Unlike other forms of research, single-system designs rely on several unique types of analysis. First, a simple visual analysis of changes in the data on the chart (e.g., from baseline to intervention periods) may indicate improvement, deterioration, or even no change, providing feedback as to whether the intervention should be maintained or revised; this is the monitoring function of single-system designs. Also, a visual analysis of the data that reveals marked positive differences between baseline and intervention is sometimes used as the basis of overall accountability in the case; this is the evaluation function of single-system designs. Statistical analyses also may be used for more precise statements of outcome, and in some cases, computers can facilitate statistical analyses. (Part IV will discuss these matters more fully.)

Decision Making on the Basis of Findings. The ultimate purpose of doing single-system evaluations is to be able to make more effective and humane decisions about resolving problems or promoting desired objectives. That means that we will consider the visual and the statistical analyses of the intervention, along with an analysis of the social or clinical import of these events. A decision in human affairs involves more than the "facts" of the matter; it involves the values that are activated by these events. Single-system analyses offer ways to test hypotheses about portions of the client situation in order to receive rapid feedback. We assume as an axiom of practice that the better the information you have about the case, the more likely you are to make better service decisions (see Part V).

And there you have it. These basic points are simple, but there are plenty of variations and complications, as you will read in the rest of this book. Single-system designs are approximate methods to determine whether certain practice objectives have been achieved. In exchange for the relative simplicity of methods and the rapidity of feedback, we give up some of the power that can be attained in classical research designs. However, by use of more powerful single-system designs, it is possible to do some sophisticated and rigorous evaluation. We are advocating that everyone learn to use the basic designs, even with their limitations. We also hope to motivate some to use more sophisticated designs because of their power, and because sometimes we need to know whether we caused certain events to occur, information that the more sophisticated designs can provide.

Evaluation is simply part of good practice that informs the practitioner about how well the intervention is proceeding relative to the original objectives. But evaluation also encourages the practitioner to be clear about the targets of intervention, as well as about the helping activities themselves.

Because evaluation seems to imply research, statistics, mathematics, and computer science technology, it does raise ghosts that are fearful to some practitioners and students. But this misses the point, because it is the *logic* of clear thinking and acting that is essential to evaluation, not a bunch of difficult and esoteric technologies. Good practitioners carefully observe and subjectively evaluate their own practice. This may be why they are good practitioners—they benefit from this precise observation and accurate feedback as they monitor the progress of their clients. *The single-system methodology provides everyone with a common language and more or less objective procedures for doing what good practitioners have long done.*

As we illustrated in the Prologue, good practice is holistic practice. It involves a systematic framework for conducting the actual steps of intervention; consideration of the role of theory and ethics; and a way to measure, monitor, and evaluate outcomes. We have tried to be as honest and as accurate as possible by presenting in the Prologue an account of how new students proceed (and sometimes stumble) through that process. There are, indeed, complex issues that must be worked out with each and every case. That is one of the great challenges of scientific practice.

But we want to assure you, based on our own practice and the practice of our students and colleagues, that with experience comes greater expertise, and with greater expertise comes enhanced competence in wending your way through some of the obstacles to humane and effective scientific practice.

Practice as Evaluation, Evaluation as Practice

The essence of successful practice is to help resolve client problems and to attain client objectives, without creating problems for others or new problems for the client. Probably the most clear and socially accountable way of determining whether our practice is successful is through systematized, more or less objective evaluation methods that can be replicated (repeated) by others. This is the science of practice, professional action that is informed by the best available information, guided by techniques of demonstrated effectiveness, and combined with objective evaluation components, all within the context of professional values (Bloom, 1975; Fischer, 1978b, 1981).

Yet this focus on scientific practice, which is a central theme of this book, is not intended to rule out other crucial aspects of practice. The art and creativity of practice, and the values and philosophy undergirding practice that make it humane and caring, are combined with the empirical orientation to produce what we call a *scientific practitioner*. We illustrated many characteristics of scientific practitioners in the Prologue. Here we would like to offer our definition of the scientific practitioner. The scientific practitioner combines the following elements in his or her practice:

1. Using the results of research and evaluation to the extent possible to select intervention techniques and other procedures that have evidence of effectiveness, and

use of techniques without such evidence, only with caution;

2. Systematic monitoring and evaluation of his or her practice with each and every case, particularly through use of single-system designs;

3. Having the skills and attitudes–the commitment–to keep learning, to keep searching for new and more effective ways to serve consumers;

4. Conducting practice as a problem-solving experiment, a project in which little or nothing is assumed as known or given, with the core task of the practitioner being investigation and discovery; and, above all,

5. Maintaining a commitment in words and deeds to the ethics and values of the helping professions, a sensitivity, care, and concern for the well-being, rights, and dignity of clients and consumers.

In other words, the scientific practitioner is a person who is strongly concerned with humane helping that is provided in the most effective manner possible. Each element–the scientific, the ethical, and the practice–clarifies and reinforces each other. None can be minimized in favor of the other without detriment to the whole.

We believe that one way of enhancing this combination of science and practice is through the use of single-system designs. These designs actually allow us to view the parallels between practice and evaluation, as we did in the Prologue, especially the testing of hunches regarding the effectiveness of interventions over time. Many good practitioners have long been integrating the logical thinking of evaluation with the art of practice (Wood, 1979). But with the emergence of single-system designs, literally every practitioner has the opportunity to connect systematic and objective evaluation with his or her practice so as to benefit from corrective feedback and public accountability. We are entering a new age of professional helping, one that will be characterized by scientific practice. Clients deserve no less; the public demands as much.

Now, obviously, scientific practice involves a complicated and broad set of commitments, including evaluation, practice, and ethics and values. While we have argued the importance of integrating all of these components, this book is not directly about the whole enterprise of scientific practice. This book largely is about the *evaluation* component of scientific practice as it interacts with and, we hope, actually enhances practice. If one is to engage in scientific practice, or any practice for that matter, it is probably obvious that one must evaluate that practice to provide a foundation for any claims to effectiveness. Thus, this book is intended to be complementary to the large, available literature regarding effective practice interventions (e.g., Acierno et al., 1994; Chambless et al., 1996; Chambless et al., 1998; Cone, 2001; Dobson & Craig, 1998; Fischer, 1993; Fraser et al., 1997; Mash & Barkely, 1999; Myers & Thyer, 1997; Nathan & Gorman, 1998; Pikoff, 1996; Reid, 1997a; Roth & Fonagy, 1996; Sanderson & Woody, 1995; Seligman, 1999; Thyer & Wodarski, 1998; Wodarski & Thyer, 1998; and Woody & Sanderson, 1998; see also the Campbell Collaboration at **http://campbell.gse.openn.edu** for occasional reviews of the effects of social and behavioral interventions and the Cochrane Collaboration at **http://www.cochrane.org** for systematic reviews of the effects of health care interventions).

We have argued the parallel or dual nature of evaluation and practice, as seen in the case in the Prologue. What we want to emphasize is the similarity in problem-solving steps for both practice and evaluation. Clearly, practice is the dominant partner; we perform evaluation as an aid to clear feedback and documented outcome, in other words, as an aid to practice. We believe that thinking about evaluation during the course of practice will help to sharpen the thinking of practitioners and offer insights that cannot easily be attained in other ways.

However, there may be occasions when the procedures of evaluation interfere with some specific practice objective. In such cases, our ethics tell us there is no choice but to put practice concerns first. We should do nothing (in the name of research or evaluation) that harms clients or their chances for successful service.

Since the goal of evaluation is to improve practice, we do not believe in sacrificing the meaning and relevance of practice on the altar of scientific rigor. We believe, however, that occasions involving serious conflicts between practice and evaluation are rare. As we will endeavor to show in this book, in the great majority of situations, evaluation will help us to think clearly and act effectively and humanely on behalf of our clients.

SINGLE-SYSTEM DESIGNS AND CLASSICAL RESEARCH: THE KNOWLEDGE-BUILDING CONTEXT

The focus of this book is almost exclusively on single-system designs. Many readers have probably had some exposure to research methods, but this exposure is more likely to have involved what is called "classical" methods, in which experimental groups are compared with control groups in laboratories or field settings, or where surveys are conducted. Typically, these methods depend on the aggregation of data from groups of people—for example, one would find the mean of the group rather than look at any one person's scores. Then comparisons are made between different groups of persons; for example, the average score of one group that received an intervention is compared with the average score of another group that did not. These methods frequently use a variety of mathematical and statistical devices and computer equipment to process the large amounts of data collected from the subjects of the research.

Such classical methods are extremely powerful and useful, particularly in generalizing research results to similar populations, one of the vital functions of science. The classical group designs are also effective in ruling out alternative explanations of results (e.g., Cook & Campbell, 1979; we discuss the same issues as they apply to single-system designs in Chapter 11 of this book). In fact, most program evaluations are conducted using classical research methods, providing absolutely critical information to practitioners about the effectiveness of different intervention programs (see the new book by Cone [2001] for an excellent overview of the methods and issues in evaluating practice outcomes).

However, these classical designs are not useful for many of the situations with which most practitioners are *immediately* concerned. In fact, as Gibbs (1991) suggests, strong single-system designs may tell more about the effects of an intervention than weak group designs because the more sophisticated single-system designs rule out alternative explanations more effectively. We have summarized the similarities and differences between these models of research and evaluation—the classical experimental/control group design on the one hand, and the single-system design on the other—in Table 1.1. We also have drawn the classical and the single-system designs in Figure 1.1 (page 47), comparing their basic ingredients (from Bloom, 1990). By following the research and the evaluation processes from left to right, and then from the top to the bottom of Figure 1.1, you can see the parallels and the differences that are also described in a different form in Table 1.1.

In general, there are different roles for each of these approaches: Single-system designs are best used to monitor and evaluate practice in field situations, whereas the results of experimental/control group research are best used as the basis for selecting interventions based on demonstrated evidence of the effectiveness of the program or technique studied. From a different perspective, single-system designs are more useful for formative program evaluation (research focused on evaluating and improving a specific program) whereas classical research is more useful in summative evaluation (research focused on knowledge that can be generalized to apply to decision making in other programs or situations) (Weiss, 1972). Single-system designs can be used to suggest hypotheses to be tested in classical research. Indeed, some authors suggest combining both methods in the same study to benefit from each type of strength (Jayaratne, 1977; Nugent, 1987, 1988, 1991b).

In particular, the classical methods aggregate data to produce descriptions about group characteristics—what the average person is

Table 1.1 Comparison of single-system designs and experimental/control group designs.

Characteristic	Single-System Designs	Experimental/Control Group Designs
1. Number of clients involved	One individual, group, or collectivity.	At least two groups involved. Ideally, these groups are randomly selected from a common population and randomly assigned to groups to control between-group variability.
2. Number of attributes measured	Limited to a number feasibly collected by the client, practitioner, or others. Usually a large number of issues are assessed before selecting the specific targets, few in number.	Variable, depending on purpose of the study. Usually a medium to large number of items is asked of a large number of persons by research interviewers or others.
3. Number of measures used for each attribute	Variable. Ideally, multiple measures of the same attribute would be used (cf. Cook & Campbell, 1976, 1979).	Variable. Ideally, multiple measures of the same attribute would be used (cf. Campbell & Fiske, 1959).
4. Number of times measures are repeated	Data are collected frequently in regular intervals before, during, and sometimes after (follow-ups) the intervention. Assumes variability in behavior across time (cf. Chassan, 1979).	Data are collected only a few times, usually once before and once after intervention, and one follow-up. Assumes relatively static state of human behavior, which may be representatively sampled in research.
5. Duration of research	Variable, depending on whether time-limited services are provided wherein the duration is fixed, or whether an open-ended service is given; depends on needs of client.	Fixed time periods are usually used.
6. Choice of goals of research	Goals usually chosen by the client and agreed to and made operationally clear by the practitioner.	Goals often chosen by the researcher, occasionally in consultation with funding agency, practitioner, or community representatives.
7. Choice of research design and its review by others for ethical suitability	The practitioner usually selects the particular design and has no professional review except by the practice supervisor, if that.	The researcher chooses the design, but usually has to submit the design and instrumentation to peer review (e.g., Human Subjects Review Committee).
8. Feedback	Feedback is a vital ingredient of single-system designs; it is immediately forthcoming as progress is monitored, and the service program may be modified accordingly. This permits the study of process as well as outcome. Systematic recording opportunities are present.	There is almost no feedback in the group design until the entire project is completed, lest such information influence events under study. Little information is given about process in studies of outcome.
9. Changes in research design	Changes are permitted. Any set of interventions can be described as a "design," but some designs are logically stronger than others. Flexibility of design is a major characteristic of single-system designs.	Changes in research design are not permitted. Fixed methods are used as exactly as possible across subjects. Standardized instruments and trained interviewers are often employed.
10. Use of theory as guide to practice	Variable. In ideal form, some clear conceptual rationale is used to give meaning to the set of operational procedures.	Variable. In ideal form, some clear hypotheses are derived from a theory that gives direction to the entire project.

(continued)

Table 1.1 Comparison of single-system designs and experimental/control group designs (continued).

Characteristic	Single-System Designs	Experimental/Control Group Designs
11. Use of comparison groups in arriving at the evaluation	The relatively stable baseline period would have continued, it is assumed, had not the intervention been made. Therefore, the single-system design uses its "own control" by comparing outcomes from the intervention period with the preintervention baseline.	Ideally, a control or contrast group is randomly selected from a common population and randomly assigned on the assumption that it will represent what likely would have occurred to the experimental group had the intervention not been made.
12. Reliability	Usually achieved through having a second observer make ratings where possible. Internal consistency used with standardized measures, along with conventional methods of measuring reliability where necessary.	All the basic methods of measuring reliability can be used: reliability of tests (test-retest, alternative forms, split-half) and interobserver agreement.
13. Validity	The closeness of the measures, especially direct measures, to the ultimate outcome criteria increases the opportunity for validity, while various pressures toward distortion in reporting decrease that opportunity.	All basic methods of measuring validity can be used: face validity, content validity, criterion-related validity, and construct validity.
14. Utility of findings for intervention	Direct and immediate. May include involvement of client as well as practitioner in collecting and interpreting data and modifying intervention.	Indirect. Probably will not affect subjects of the present project, but may be useful for the class of subjects (or problems) involved.
15. Targets of intervention and measurement	Ideally, should be important life events, but single-system designs are susceptible to trivialization in choice of targets. Emphasis is on knowledge-for-use, but some efforts concern knowledge-building issues.	Variable, depending on the purpose of the study. Can include important life events or targets of theoretical interest (and low practice utility). Emphasis is more likely to be on knowledge for knowledge-building, but with some efforts on knowledge-for-use.
16. Kinds of data obtained	a. Descriptive data on the system in question, providing norms for that system b. Change for that individual system c. If the design permits, inferences of causal or functional relationships between independent and dependent variables, but susceptible to many alternative explanations for given outcomes.	a. Descriptive data, providing normative information b. Change scores, grouped or averaged, thus masking individual patterns of change (Chassan, 1979) c. Experimental designs provide strong logical bases for inference of causality and generalizability (cf. Campbell & Stanley, 1963; Cook & Campbell, 1976, 1979).
17. Costs	Relatively low. A small amount of time and energy must be expended in designing the evaluation and carrying it out, but this may be routinized as part of the empirically guided practice itself. Essentially a do-it-yourself operation.	Relatively high. Most group designs require research specialists separate from the practitioners involved, as well as expenses for data collection, analysis, and report writing. Computers typically are used.
18. Role of values in the research	Clients' values are incorporated in the choice of targets and goal-setting procedures. Practitioners remain "agents of society" in accepting or modifying	Researchers or funders generally control the values expressed in the research—the goals, instruments, designs, and interpretations.

(continued)

Table 1.1 Comparison of single-system designs and experimental/control group designs (continued).

Characteristic	Single-System Designs	Experimental/Control Group Designs
	these goals and in helping client/systems to attain them.	
19. Limitations	Statistical and logical considerations and limitations (such as generalizability of results) are not yet well explicated; indeed, there are many differences of opinion among specialists in the field. There is an increasingly large body of exemplars that can be modeled available to practitioners from all theoretical orientations. Ethical issues abound, e.g., use of baselines vs. immediate practice.	Problems remain concerning practitioners reading, understanding, and using scientific information stemming from group designs. Ethical issues (e.g., withholding treatment from controls) still not resolved among practitioners. Resistance to large-scale research by minorities increasing. Therapeutic effectiveness studies involving group designs are in a state of ambiguous disarray.
20. Prospects	Optimistic. The literature on single-system designs is expanding rapidly. Freedom from major funding needs and the relative simplicity of the task—and the teaching of the task—may stimulate more practice research and evaluation with single-system designs. It is now potentially possible for every practitioner to evaluate every case on every occasion.	Optimistic. Greater care in selecting populations and problems seems likely. Funding of large-scale research suffers in times of economic scarcity. New research journals should stimulate communication of current research.

like. Aggregate methods provide little or no information about single clients or specific groups of clients, which often are of greatest interest to the practitioner. In fact, variability of effects in group studies (e.g., some clients doing better while other clients doing worse) is often hidden in average scores. Changes in specific people are rarely presented, and so it seems that for many practitioners, the individual client or treatment group gets lost in the shuffle.

Classical studies usually involve measures at the beginning and end of long time periods, with no information about changes in the interim. Typically, many variables are measured at the same time, although not necessarily the ones that fit any particular client. The eventual outcomes may come too late to affect the participants in the study, although the knowledge so derived may help others in the future. There is still some question about whether the classical studies in the helping professions have

demonstrated convincingly the effectiveness of practice (e.g., see Fischer, 1978a, 1993; Garfield & Bergin, 1986; Hogarty, 1989; Reid & Hanrahan, 1982; Videka-Sherman, 1988). In part this is because classical studies and associated statistical procedures are complicated and make different assumptions about which persons of knowledge and good will disagree. Moreover, evidence is clear that social workers, psychotherapists, and other professionals infrequently use the existing research literature to enhance their practice, even though they are ethically committed to using the best available information in serving their clients (Cohen, Sargent, & Sechrest, 1986; Kirk, 1990; Morrow-Bradley & Elliott, 1986).

On the other hand, we know of few practitioners who do not claim to be effective at least some of the time. What they may be seeking is a method to demonstrate their claims for effectiveness and sensitivity. We believe that the single-system approach may be one

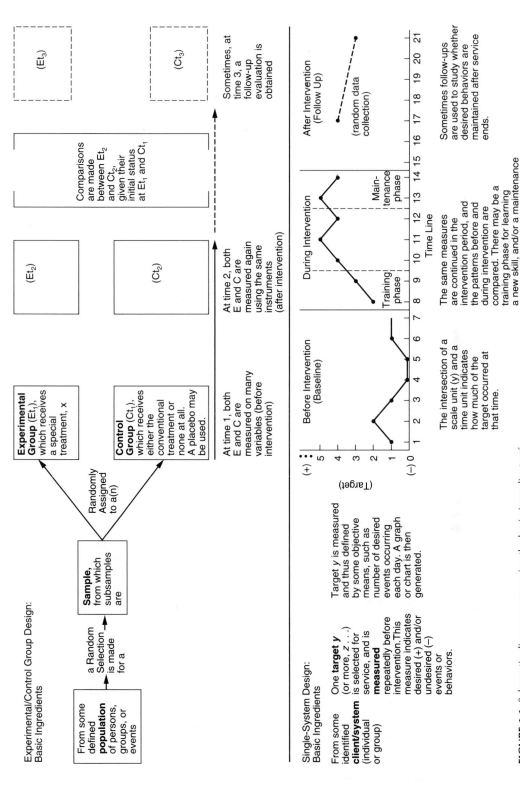

FIGURE 1.1 Schematic diagrams comparing the basic ingredients of experimental/control group designs and single-system designs.

answer to their search because these relatively easy methods are so directly and immediately useful to practice, and yet provide some objective basis for measuring the efficacy of their interventions and for making corrections in practice to improve their efficacy.

SINGLE-SYSTEM EVALUATION, QUALITATIVE RESEARCH, AND QUANTITATIVE RESEARCH

With the recent renewed interest in qualitative research, as contrasted with the traditional quantitative research, the questions arise: What is single-system evaluation? Is it more like qualitative or quantitative research, or is it different from both of them (but for different reasons)? Our answer: Yes, to all of the above. To explain this paradoxical response, let us first define terms.

Unfortunately, it is not easy to define "qualitative research." An anthology by Sherman & Reid (1994), containing over forty discussions or examples of qualitative research, reveals enormous differences of opinion even among respected qualitative researchers. The following working definition, therefore, is a sympathetic interpretation of the discussions in Sherman and Reid's anthology: *Qualitative research,* at its core, is a set of philosophical ideas and empirical methods for identifying and describing some human experience, based on spoken or written words, and/or observable behaviors *alone*–that is, without forcing a preconceived theoretical position or set of values onto the experience. Instead, the observer tries to be as sensitive as possible to the client's experience– in spite of the cultural and psychosocial differences that may stand between them–and to report this experience as fully as possible so that others who haven't had the same experience may understand. This means that units of analysis–what one pays attention to–will differ according to the observer; there are few traditional "laws of research" operating, unless it is to understand the situation as fully as possible as it is lived by the persons involved.

From this naturalistic experience of the person-in-situation, qualitative researchers de-velop subjective themes, categories, classifications, and topologies that verbalize their understanding, a rich and "thick description" (cf. Laird, 1994, pp. 175–189) of the many layers and textures of the experience. This holistic description can then be used to contribute to a kind of empirical understanding of a more nearly realistic human experience. This qualitative knowledge, or heuristic approach (Tyson, 1994, pp. 89–112), then can be used by applied social scientists for a more nearly valid description of human concerns, and eventually as a guide to resolving human problems and concerns. Qualitative research is too new to have cumulated a large body of such outcome studies, but the Sherman and Reid anthology, among others, begins to identify such studies.

Some researchers in the qualitative community sharply criticize certain aspects of quantitative research–its assumption that the methods of the natural sciences are superior to all others and should be used in the social sciences (Heineman-Pieper, 1994, pp. 71–88; Tyson, 1994, pp. 88–89); its putting research values above treatment values, which harms the helping process (Heineman-Pieper, 1994, p. 73); its inevitable intrusiveness in the helping process (Heineman-Pieper, 1994, p. 72); its foolhardy attempt to separate all values and biases from the human enterprise of research and to assume we can have independent, objective knowledge of any human situation (Heineman-Pieper, 1994, p. 75); and its erroneous seeking of universal truths, while disregarding as pesky annoyances the contexts of human actions (Heineman-Pieper, 1994, p. 80)–to name only a very few criticisms. Single-system designs are designated as a kind of quantitative research, according to Heineman-Pieper, and thus are heir to all of these criticisms.

In contrast, there are more than enough definitions of quantitative research. We offer our own equally sympathetic interpretation: *Quantitative research,* at its core, is a set of philosophical ideas and empirical methods for identifying and describing some human experience, based on spoken or written words, and/or observable behaviors, by using the cumulative understanding and common language of prior researchers. By adhering as closely as possible to shared procedures–such as defining terms in operational definitions, using clearly defined hypotheses to test implications of existing theory, and presenting results in standardized numeric and statistical terms–the results of investigation will be open to common understanding (by suitably trained persons) and replication. From this standardized experience of some specific portion of the person-in-situation, quantitative researchers develop more or less objective pieces of information that can be combined to create larger networks of understanding, codified in revised theories and new hypotheses for further testing. Thus, there emerges a knowledge base that can be used by applied social scientists for solving human problems and concerns. There is a large number of quantitative studies, which have been used by helping professionals for many years as the basis for selecting a guiding practice theory and a substantiated method of practice.

Quantitative researchers, being in the catbird seat, have responded to the barbs of qualitative critics more than they have offered full-blown critical analyses of this heuristic approach. However, quantitative researchers do ask critical questions such as these: If qualitative research is so good, show us the results in tangible effects that have helped clients; if you can't clearly (i.e., operationally) define the nature of a problem, it may not exist for any practical purpose of trying to resolve that problem (Hudson, 1982a); if qualitative research relies so heavily on individualizing people and situations, how does it avoid biases and how can results be corroborated, cumulated, and/or generalized?

As you can see, the vital differences between the definitions of qualitative and quantitative research lie in what the researcher brings to the experience, and what the researcher takes from the experience. The quantitative researcher brings cumulated shared understandings and standardized procedures, and takes away numerical and statistical information that is interpreted in terms of abstract theories and value assumptions. The qualitative researcher brings as few preconceptions as possible, and takes away a richer, more subjective interpretation of what the human experience is all about, some of which may be summarized in numerical and statistical forms. What they both share is the *research* component, a knowledge-building perspective using certain kinds of ideas and methods. Neither approach *requires* that the obtained knowledge be used in human affairs.

We now can ask the question: What is single-system evaluation, with reference to making connections to either qualitative or quantitative research, or both, or neither? We proposed earlier that single-system evaluation was all of the above. Now, we can explain. First, we emphasize that evaluation is very different from research, even though it shares some of the same methods and ideas. The differences make all the difference. Evaluation largely is obtaining information for use by practitioners to modify their practices so as to more nearly move in the direction of enhancing client goal attainment. Building knowledge is not its primary goal; however, it may help to build practice knowledge, and may contribute to forming research hypotheses that require testing using research methods. So, let us give a sympathetic definition, parallel to the issues discussed above.

Evaluation–and particularly *single-system evaluation*–is a set of philosophical ideas and empirical methods for working with clients in identifying and describing some human experience–a problem or concern that is important (valuable) to the client–based on direct observations in client–practitioner interactions, and/or spoken or written words, using both the practitioner's own human experience and past training in the language and methodology of practice. By being a sensitive human being and a trained observer–these seem to be quintessential for the qualitative researcher–the practitioner can enter a situation and form a trusting relationship with a client. With the client, the practitioner can then identify and prioritize problems and concerns (that is, the preferences or values of the client), and can begin to formulate professional ways to address them (based on past experiences and training). As part of good practice, the practitioner will engage the client to participate in as many aspects of the helping process as possible, including the monitoring of targeted concerns, so as to have corrective feedback on developments. This monitoring will involve operational procedures and numbers—important for the quantitative researcher. From this interchange over time, the client and practitioner hope to move toward problem resolution, along with training of the client for self-maintenance and empowerment after the direct intervention period has ended. The practitioner also may reflect on the intervention process for what other information it suggests, with the possibility of building an efficacious repertoire of practices for use with other clients.

Thus, single-system evaluation partakes of both qualitative and quantitative research, and yet it is different in important ways from both of them. Perhaps the most useful way to characterize these similarities and differences is by reference to Lang's (1994, pp. 265–278) insightful analysis on ways of distinguishing qualitative research and practice. Briefly, Lang distinguishes an action, or *knowledge-using,* approach from a pure-science, or *knowledge-building,* approach. The data processing cycle for *knowledge-using* involves abstracting and then generalizing from the concrete data of practice, so as to match the given case to some existing practice theory. Then the practitioner uses the logical predictions from the theory as strategies for guidance back in the concrete world. The *knowledge-building* cycle is longer; it incorporates the abstracting and generalizing steps, but then goes on to categorize and eventually conceptualize—which is the building of new theory, the goal for the *knowledge-building* approach. It does not cycle back to the real world to influence the events from which it began.

Although we accept this general model distinguishing knowledge building from practice, we submit that single-system evaluation applies to both. Yes, the action, or *knowledge-using* cycle does operate, but it doesn't merely stop back at the concrete world. It may, under some structured conditions, provide a broader perspective on what has been attained in terms of categorizing and eventually conceptualizing these events into a revised practice theory that can be cycled back for use with

new clients. Single-system evaluation procedures comprise one such set of structured conditions that encourages practitioners to build efficacious repertoires of practice and the practice theory ideas needed to apply them. However, all practitioners are not obliged to build new practice theory; it is simply an option if they wish to contribute to the knowledge development of the helping professions. Therefore, we hold that single-system designs are partly qualitative and partly quantitative enterprises, but more importantly, they are knowledge-using enterprises.

ADVANTAGES OF USING SINGLE-SYSTEM DESIGNS IN PRACTICE

Many characteristics of single-system designs will assist you to practice more effectively and humanely. Here, we summarize some of these points, noting also that these characteristics address—and we think overcome—many of the problems practitioners see regarding practice applications of traditional, classical, practice research.

1. Single-system designs can be built into almost every practice situation, usually without disrupting the intervention, because these designs emphasize good practice characteristics such as clear identification of the presenting problems.

2. Single-system designs provide more or less objective and systematic information for monitoring changes in client conditions over time so that you, the practitioner, can adapt appropriately. Important targets and special factors (placed on charts) don't get lost in the shuffle because they are all there on the graphs. This continuous record differs considerably from traditional pre- and posttest group designs.

3. Single-system designs focus on the individual client or system, mirroring the unique changes in the practice situation, rather than reflecting average scores from

group research designs. This is truly client-focused evaluation, permitting both relative objectivity in data gathering and close involvement with the unique case.

4. Single-system designs are practitioner oriented in the here-and-now situation. They provide vital feedback on what the practitioner needs to know to move the case in desired directions. They are flexible designs, capable of changing as new events occur in the client's circumstances, including allowing new targets. Traditional group designs cannot be changed once the study has begun.

5. Single-system designs can be used to assess the case or situation by clarifying what seem to be the relevant factors in the problem. This, in turn, will lead to the selection of more appropriate interventions.

6. Single-system designs can be used to test hypotheses or ideas regarding the relationship between specific intervention procedures and client changes, ruling out some alternative explanations and allowing an inference regarding causality: Was your intervention program responsible for the change in the target problem?

7. Single-system designs are essentially theory free—or, more accurately, theory neutral—in the sense that they are usable by practitioners adhering to just about any practice theory. They can be applied to the practice of any practitioner who can be reasonably clear about what targets and what interventions are being used, and who is willing to obtain continuing measures on these targets.

8. Single-system designs are relatively easy to use and to understand. They can be applied within the same time frame that you are currently using in seeing clients. (Sometimes, you can share your charts with clients as motivators of continuing progress or clarification of the nature of the problems.) Once you understand the basics, there is relatively little time spent on the mechanics of single-system de-

signs. (Students have reported a threshold effect; it takes some initial effort to learn about single-system designs and to implement them at first, but once you cross that threshold, it is much easier thereafter.)

9. The use of single-system evaluations in entire agencies largely can avoid the imposition of outside researchers coming to evaluate your work. Because clients and others are intrinsically involved in constructing and implementing single-system designs, there is a high level of intellectual and professional honesty in their use. The closeness of the measures to the client's problems produces a type of validity that cannot be matched in group designs.

10. Single-system designs provide a model for demonstrating our accountability to ourselves, our clients and consumers, our funding sources, and our communities. Use of these evaluation methods with numbers of clients can lead to new practice hypotheses that can further the knowledge base of the profession (Jayaratne, Tripodi, & Talsma, 1988).

A WALK THROUGH THE EVALUATION PROCESS

Our ultimate goal in this book is to convince you of the value of single-system designs in furthering your practice, for yourself, your clients, and society. We hope to show you how to integrate the steps of this evaluation process into your practice so that it is an automatic reaction to think clearly about the presenting problem, to ascertain more or less objectively the extent of that problem, to consider possible causal factors, and to plan specific interventions that have some chance of making the changes the client desires. All of this is part of both good practice and good evaluation. Just as you are learning or have learned how to practice well, so we hope you will learn how to evaluate well in connection with whatever type of practice you are using.

We presented the case example in the Prologue within the context of the problem-solving approach, as it is probably the most general structure by which practice methods of all sorts are described. Thinking about and working with this problem-solving process will become second nature after you study this material in the classroom or in the field. Likewise, evaluation will become second nature–and closely identified with your practice steps–once this material is carefully studied.

The problem-solving process will never fit exactly in all your cases, but it will be a point of departure in thinking systematically about the situation. Evaluation also will help you to think clearly and systematically because it raises the very questions that make for clear thinking: Specifically, what are the scope and nature of the presenting problem? What exact interventions should be tried with it? What concomitant changes are occurring when the intervention is present or absent.? Has the problem been resolved effectively and humanely? These are questions of evaluation, but they are also vital questions that practitioners ask about practice. Indeed, good practice will inevitably include good evaluation.

One way to visualize this sequence of practice and evaluation is through the flowchart, a graphic presentation of the actions, decisions, and exchanges of information in a given process. Use of this flowchart is not intended to present a rigid sequence of events. There will be occasions when we go back to an earlier step to consider new problems or new ways of measuring problems. But the general flow will help to provide a sense of direction and purpose amid all the ebbs and flows of the client's life.

Figure 1.2 is a flowchart of the evaluation process as contained in this book. Each of the three main components of the evaluation process– conceptualization and measurement, design, and analysis and decision making–plus an introduction (evaluation context) and a conclusion (challenges) is a major block in the flowchart. Each block represents one of the parts of this book, and most of the subunits, as noted, reflect either a complete chapter or a section of a chapter. Note that there are some commonalities across the three major evaluation blocks: Each part is introduced by a

"basic principles" chapter. Then other chapters follow and provide specific applications of these basic principles. Each part is concluded by a chapter on how to select from among the alternative applications.

The first major component of the evaluation process involves conceptualization and measurement. Before you can begin to measure a problem, you need some understanding of the basic principles of measurement. This is provided in Chapter 2. In Chapter 3 we discuss one of the major bridges connecting evaluation and practice–specification of problems and goals. In this chapter we describe how to move from the often vague and nebulous problems with which we are initially faced in practice to clearer, more precise statements regarding both the nature of the problem and the goals we are aiming for with each client/system.

In Chapter 4 we discuss the preliminary steps you should take in developing a recording plan, including who should do the recording, when and where the recording should take place, and deciding how many problems to record. We also present an introduction to recording and to managing cases with computers, using the computer program called CASS that is included with this book.

The next five chapters describe five major categories of measures; that is, each chapter provides information on how to select and use a different set of procedures for measuring (or observing) the target problem. This measurement is at the heart of the evaluation process. In Chapter 5 we describe methods involving direct observations–how to count and record behaviors. Chapter 6 presents individualized rating scales that you and the client can develop together to measure a given problem. Chapter 7 describes the use of standardized questionnaires and how computer programs like the CASS program in this book can help you use those measures. In Chapter 8 we discuss the use of client and practitioner logs. And in Chapter 9 we describe a number of unobtrusive measures–methods of observation and measurement that can be used without producing any changes in the problem being observed by the act of measurement.

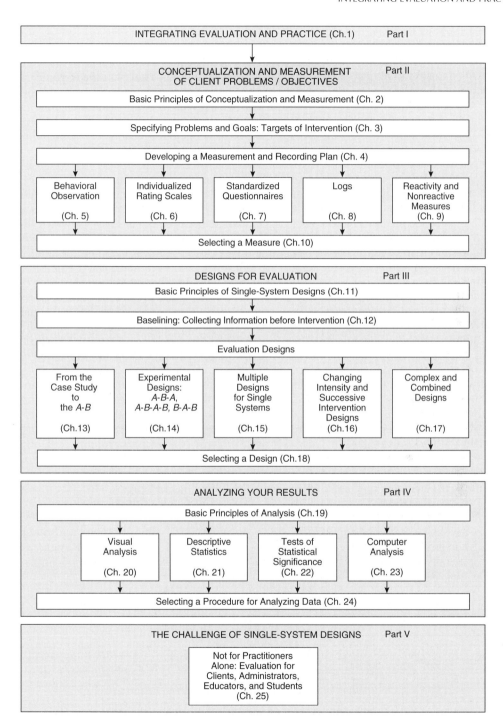

FIGURE 1.2   Flowchart showing the organization of this book.

The last chapter in the measurement section, Chapter 10, summarizes all of these measures and provides a framework for helping you decide which to select. We also talk about the importance of the use of more than one measure whenever possible.

The second major component of the evaluation process, described in Part III, involves the actual designs themselves. Chapter 11 presents an overview of basic principles of single-system designs to show just how the different variations of the designs can be used to answer different questions. Chapter 12 presents the baselining process–collecting information prior to the onset of intervention. The baseline is the first phase in just about all of the single-system designs we will describe (there are a couple of exceptions that will be noted).

The next four chapters describe the key designs available for use in your own practice. In Chapter 13 we describe the relationship between case studies and the foundation of all the single-system designs–the *A-B* design. In Chapter 14 we look at several variations of experimental single-system designs. Chapter 15 looks at multiple-baseline designs, multiple-target designs, and crossover and constant series designs. In Chapter 16 we describe changing intensity and successive intervention designs. In Chapter 17 we describe some of the more complex and combined designs that may be applicable in a limited range of situations. The last chapter in Part III, Chapter 18, presents a framework for selecting a design depending on the type of problem you are dealing with and the kind of question you want answered.

The last major component of the evaluation process is the analysis–determining the practical and statistical importance of the results achieved. This is Part IV of the book. The first chapter in this part, Chapter 19, presents basic principles of analysis. Here you are introduced to the concepts of practical, theoretical, and statistical significance; the distinction among effort, effect, effectiveness, and efficiency; and some basic concepts regarding how long information should be collected and when you should change and/or terminate interventions depending on the results achieved.

The next three chapters present different sets of methods of analysis. Chapter 20 presents a key analytic method, visual analysis, which involves looking at different patterns and trends that appear in the data. In Chapters 21 and 22 we describe a number of statistical methods for analyzing data. In Chapter 23, we present procedures for easily calculating the data analysis procedures in this book with SINGWIN, the other computer program included with the book. Part IV concludes in Chapter 24 with a framework for helping you decide which one of the analytic procedures to select, depending again on the type of question you want answered and the level of rigor desired.

It might seem as though this ends the evaluation process, and in fact, Part IV technically does conclude the actual evaluation. However, there are several challenges in the use of single-system designs. In Chapter 25 we discuss the following challenges: what single-system designs may mean for clients, for administrators, for educators, and for students. We also present a discussion of ethical and other issues in the use of single-system designs as well as some special applications of single-system designs.

SUMMARY

This chapter provided an overview of and introduction to the topic of this book–integrating evaluation and practice through the use of single-system designs. The chapter began with a brief overview of basic characteristics of single-system evaluation methods. This was followed by a comparison of single-system evaluation methods with the methods of classical research. We then examined the issue of qualitative and quantitative methods in single-system design. We then summarized the many advantages for practice of single-system designs. The chapter concluded with a flowchart of the entire evaluation process, as presented in this book, to be used as an introduction to and overview of the rest of the chapters.

PART II

CONCEPTUALIZING AND MEASURING TARGETS AND OBJECTIVES/GOALS

The heart of single-system designs is the repeated measurement of the client concerns that become the targets for your interventions. The importance of clearly and sensitively defining targets, setting objectives and goals, and finding accurate ways to measure and record them cannot be overstated. This process is useful for assessment and intervention planning. But beyond this, it is the measurement activities, conducted on a repeated basis, that allow you to monitor your outcome and evaluate your progress, to make changes if your intervention is not proceeding successfully, and to determine whether your client has made significant gains. This, in turn, may provide the basis for establishing your own accountability—to yourself, your clients, your agency, and your community. Without repeated measurement, there can be no single-system designs.

In Part II of this book, we provide a number of approaches for measuring your client's targets. We start in Chapter 2 by presenting some of the basic principles of measurement, such as reliability and validity. Understanding the key aspects of these principles can affect the measures you eventually select. In Chapter 3 we present a discussion of how to define problems and goals clearly, specifically, and sensitively. This is a crucial link between practice and research.

In Chapter 4 we discuss how to set up a recording plan, who should do the recording, how to put your information on charts, use of computers to manage case records, and a number of critical issues regarding recording.

Most single methods of measurement both fail to measure a target in its entirety and are influenced by factors other than the target. Also, different methods of measurement are suitable under different circumstances. Therefore, multiple methods are necessary to achieve adequate measurement of client targets. In Chapters 5–9 we present different methods of measurement including their relative advantages and disadvantages. These chapters describe the range of different types of strategies to measure just about any target you are likely to run up against in practice. In all cases the measurement strategies discussed in this book can be used to monitor progress over the course of the intervention.

The different measures are organized as follows: Chapter 5 discusses the observation of overt and covert behavior by clients (i.e., self-monitoring) and the observation of overt behaviors by other observers (i.e., direct observation). Chapter 6 instructs you on how to construct individually tailored scales to elicit information from clients, practitioners, relevant others, and independent evaluators. Chapter 7 discusses standardized questionnaires that elicit information from these same sources. Chapter 8 discusses another type of individualized measurement strategy, the log, which is useful for obtaining ongoing qualitative and quantitative information from clients and practitioners. Chapter 9 presents measurement strategies that help to minimize the influence that the measurement process itself has on the client's behavior.

We realize that there is overlap among the different measurement methods presented in Chapters 5 through 9 because different methods (e.g., behavioral observation or logs) can be used to measure the same target. But we believe it is most helpful to organize the chapters the way we did, rather than in other ways, say by the type of target measured. Although any categorization would have had its own problems, the one we used seemed to lead to the clearest prescriptions for how to select, and when necessary develop, a measurement strategy for a client.

We've left one type of measure out of our discussion. This involves electro-mechanical or physiological measures such as electroencephalograms (EEGs), electrocardiograms (EKGs), plethysmographs, and so on. This is because they are usually very expensive and/or complicated, generally not available to practitioners, and frequently difficult to use in an open or uncontrolled setting. In addition, there are relatively few references to which you could turn if you wanted to pursue these methods (see Kallman & Feuerstein, 1986; Rugh, Gable, & Lemke, 1986, for a review of the uses of physiological measures and instrumentation). However, we do not wish to rule out these devices as measures in special situations.

The final chapter in this part, Chapter 10, is intended to help you select a measure. We know that the numbers and types of measures available have different strengths and limitations, so in this chapter we present a set of guidelines to help you select the ones that will be the most appropriate for any given time or situation.

2 BASIC PRINCIPLES OF CONCEPTUALIZATION AND MEASUREMENT

PURPOSE: The purpose of this chapter is to introduce you to the key characteristics of measurement tools and to help you evaluate them for use in your own practice. This chapter also connects single-system designs to the larger body of social science research by indicating how this set of evaluation procedures uses the basic tools of conceptualization and measurement in practice situations. ■

Introduction
What Is Measurement?
Levels of Measurement
  Nominal Level
  Ordinal Level
  Interval Level
  Ratio Level
Advantages of Measurement
Definition as a First Step in Measurement
Can Everything Be Measured?
Key Characteristics of All Measures
Measurement Error
  Random Measurement Error
  Systematic Measurement Error
  Importance of Measurement Error
Reliability
  Test-Retest Reliability
  Alternate-Forms Reliability
  Internal-Consistency Reliability
  Interobserver Reliability
  Standard Error of Measurement (SEM)

What Is "High" Reliability?
Which Type of Reliability Should You Use?
Validity
  Face Validity
  Content Validity
  Criterion Validity
  Construct Validity
  Which Type of Validity Should You Use?
The Relationship between Reliability and Validity
Factors Influencing Reliability and Validity
  Administration Procedures
  Populations
Additional Considerations in the Selection and
  Development of Measures
  Directness
  Is There a Place for Indirect Measures?
  Ease of Use
  Accessibility
  Relevance to Intervention Planning
Summary

INTRODUCTION

Since the purpose of this book is to illustrate the usefulness of evaluation in practice, we want to avoid a lot of traditional research jargon. Most research books seem to be written with the belief that the potential readers are primarily other researchers instead of people whose callings may be oriented toward other pursuits, such as practice.

However, there are a number of principles that are important for you to understand in order to use evaluation methods effectively in practice. Many of these principles have to do with the measurement processes that we describe in the next several chapters. The repeated measurement of the client concerns that are the targets of our interventions is at the heart of single-system evaluation, and, therefore, it is important to know how to select the most accurate and practical measures from the measurement tools we'll be presenting. This is important because, as we argued in Chapter 1, the better the information, the more likely it is that the service will be effective and humane.

This chapter presents a review of the key considerations that should underlie your selection and use of every measurement procedure. First, we define measurement. Next we discuss the importance of identifying what we intend to measure. We then tackle the rather thorny question: Can everything be measured? Finally, we move to a review of the basic characteristics of measurement tools, that is, actual guidelines for selecting a measure and interpreting the results of that measure.

Many of the principles of single-system evaluation that we describe in this chapter are the same for more traditional research methods as well. We will, however, try to point out where the applications are different.

In all, we hope to provide you with enough information in this chapter to (a) understand our use of these terms in subsequent chapters and (b) encourage you to employ these principles in selecting and using the measurement tools we present. As you make decisions regarding which measures to use in practice, we hope you will evaluate these measures according to the guidelines we present in this chapter.

WHAT IS MEASUREMENT?

Measurement is generally thought of as the process of assigning labels to certain characteristics of things according to a set of rules. The "things" may be people (especially their thoughts, feelings, or actions relevant to the practice situation), objects, or events. The most common type of labels are numbers. In some circumstances, such as with young children or developmentally disabled persons, suitable innovations are used—such as pictures of faces to indicate how one is feeling—and these choices of faces would then be translated into numbers for analysis.

The measurement "rules" refer to steps for assigning labels in an explicit and consistent manner. For example, you can make a rule to count every occurrence of a certain behavior in a given time period, or to ask a client to indicate how often a target occurs by selecting one of the following categories:

1 = Rarely or never
2 = Some or a little of the time
3 = Occasionally or a moderate amount of the time
4 = Most or all of the time

Levels of Measurement

There are four different levels of measurement; each provides a different type of information. You need to understand the information conveyed by each level in order to interpret measurements correctly and analyze the results of single-system designs (e.g., some statistics are designed to be used only with certain levels of measurement). These levels of measurement are termed nominal, ordinal, interval, and ratio.

Nominal Level. Nominal-level measures provide information about whether one observation is qualitatively different from another or a person is in one category or another, for example, male or female. These categories, by definition, are mutually exclusive. For example, a person might be a Democrat or Republican or Independent but not a little of each. Or a person might be married at one time and single at another time, and different numbers could be assigned to the person depending on his or her marital status (e.g., 1 = single, 2 = married). Diagnostic systems (e.g., the fourth edition of the *Diagnostic and Statistical Manual of Mental Disorders,* DSM-IV) (American Psychiatric Association, 1994) that assign individuals to diagnostic categories are another example of nominal-level measurement. In any case, if a person has different values at different times for a nominal-level variable, it indicates a change (e.g., a different marital or diagnostic status), but not that the person has more or less of some characteristic (e.g., a value of 2 would not indicate a greater marital status than a value of 1). Many statistics commonly used in the social sciences–those requiring means and standard deviations–cannot be used with nominal (or ordinal) variables. However, special types of statistics are available for use with nominal and ordinal variables. One of these, called the *chi-square,* will be described in Chapter 22.

Ordinal Level. Ordinal-level measures provide the same information as nominal-level measures, *plus* information about the relative amount of one observation compared with another. Basically, the categories are rank-ordered on a scale from more to less for some target. For example, each week the number of marital arguments for a couple might be classified into one of the following categories:

1 = Rarely or never
2 = Some or a little of the time
3 = Occasionally or a moderate amount of the time
4 = Most or all of the time

If the frequency of arguments was assigned a "4" one week, and a "3" the next, this would indicate that the frequency was different from one week to the next, and that the frequency was less during the second week. However, the change from 4 to 3 would not necessarily be the same as a change from 3 to 2 or from 2 to 1, because for ordinal-level measures the adjacent intervals are not necessarily equal; this excludes many common statistics from use with ordinal measures.

Interval Level. Interval-level measures provide the same information as ordinal-level measures, *plus* the adjacent intervals are equal so it's possible to determine *how much* more of some characteristic is possessed by a person. The Fahrenheit scale for measuring temperature is an example of an interval measure because the difference between 0 and 1 degree is the same as the difference between 50 and 51 degrees. Examples of true interval measures are difficult to find in social work and the social sciences, although often it's reasonable to use standardized questionnaires and other measures with the assumption that they are interval-level measures. Among other things, this allows more sophisticated data analyses, including many of the most commonly used statistical procedures (described in Chapter 22). Often it is reasonable to treat variables with 11 or more categories as interval-level variables (Hunnaly, 1978).

Ratio Level. Ratio-level measures provide the same information as interval-level measures, *plus* they have a defined zero point that has some intrinsic meaning. In contrast to ratio measures, a score of zero on a standardized questionnaire that one assumes provides an *interval-level* measurement usually does not indicate the complete absence of some characteristic such as depression, problem-solving ability, or marital satisfaction. Examples of ratio measures include the amount of time spent caring for an elderly parent, the number of times a child is out of his or her seat inappropriately in class, the number of days hospitalized, number of years married, age, and so on.

Advantages of Measurement

In a way measurement is just a more formalized way of clarifying the observations that you make every day in practice, no matter what level of measurement is used. After all, before beginning an intervention program you need to decide whether a problem exists. You want to know when it is appropriate to modify an intervention during the course of providing the service. And before terminating an intervention program you need to decide whether the problem is resolved to an acceptable degree.

When you make these decisions you are measuring whether a problem is present or absent, and (in a rough way) perhaps the severity of the problem. Practitioners who make qualitative judgments about clients are in fact using a type of measurement (nominal level). What we are suggesting is that practitioners use the most accurate and informative practical measurement strategies available.

Measurement has several advantages, but these all stem from the fact that it requires you to develop explicit criteria or *rules* for determining the status of a target (e.g., its existence, intensity, frequency). Some of the advantages are: (a) The criteria provide clear guidelines for helping you evaluate where you are going with your intervention programs and to monitor changes to provide feedback on success or even failure. Indeed, using measurement will reduce the chances that you will fool yourself into thinking that things are going better than they really are, which can happen because of the often observed human tendency to avoid signs of failure. (b) You will need to talk with your clients about their targets and goals in detail in order to develop criteria for assessing change. This exchange can increase the chances of a successful intervention because it can lead to active client involvement and agreement on targets and goals over time. (c) Having criteria for determining the status of a target will put you in a better position to get consultation from your colleagues because it will be easier to give them accurate information about client targets.

The value of measurement is that it allows you to be more precise and systematic in evaluating what you are doing. (This assumes that before you decide how you will measure a problem, you are specific in defining it, the topic of the next chapter.) Measurement allows you to classify events, observing them to know when, how often, how intense or how long, or even whether they are occurring. Measurement aids you in being clear in describing and communicating to others what you are doing. Measurement, in other words, to the extent that it makes your practice more objective, and to the extent that it does indeed increase the precision of what you do, is a key to enhancing the effectiveness and efficiency of your practice efforts.

As we've only hinted above, a number of considerations enter into the measurement process. We will discuss many of these in relation to the specific measurement procedures we provide in Part II. At this point, however, it's important to note that depending on how you deal with some of these considerations, you can actually enhance the measurement process by providing more accurate measures, or distort the process by providing biased measures. Your job as a scientific practitioner is to conceptualize problems clearly, select "good" measurement methods (accurate, sensitive to such factors as the client's gender and ethnic background), and then use the measures in ways that will provide the most useful evaluation. The bulk of this chapter is devoted to taking a look at guidelines that you can use to evaluate measures for your practice, and the following chapter will be devoted to the process of specifying targets and goals. Before we discuss these guidelines, however, it's necessary to introduce the process of conceptualization.

DEFINITION AS A FIRST STEP IN MEASUREMENT

To measure something we first need to define what it is we're trying to measure. As noted in Chapter 1, two types of definitions are important: conceptual and operational definitions. A *conceptual definition* (sometimes called a nominal definition) is found in a dictionary, defining a concept by using one set of words–like synonyms–to define another word or set of words. For example, you might conceptually define "child neglect" (following Polansky, Chalmers, Buttenweisser, & Williams, 1981, p. 15) in this way:

Child neglect may be defined as a condition in which a caretaker responsible for the child either deliberately or by extraordinary inattentiveness permits the child to experience avoidable present suffering and/or fails to provide one or more of the ingredients generally deemed essential for developing a person's physical, intellectual, and emotional capacities.

However, how do you know whether child neglect occurred and, if it occurred, to what extent? For this you need an *operational definition*. An operational definition is one that assigns meaning to a concept (e.g., child neglect) in terms of the activities or operations necessary to measure it. Operational definitions are the "working definitions" of what you are trying to measure. An operational definition of child neglect might involve asking a client or someone familiar with the client the following questions, assigning a value of 0 to each "no" response and a value of 1 to each "yes" response, and then summing the response values across questions (Combs-Orme & Orme, 1986) to provide an overall measure–the operational definition–of child neglect, as in the following example:

1. Have you sometimes left young children under 6 years old home alone while you were out shopping or doing anything else?

2. Have there been times when a neighbor fed a child (of yours/you were caring for) because you didn't get around to shopping for food or cooking, or kept your child overnight because no one was taking care of him/her at home?

3. Has a nurse or social worker or teacher ever said that any child (of yours/you were caring for) wasn't being given enough to eat or wasn't being kept clean enough or wasn't getting medical care when it was needed?

The fit between our conceptual and operational definitions usually won't be perfect. For example, you can probably think of additional questions that should be asked to measure child neglect. You can probably also think of reasons why answers to the above three questions might be inaccurate. No matter how you operationalize and measure child neglect, or anything else for that matter, your operationalization will never be a complete and perfect representation of your conceptual definition–it will always contain some error. It's important to understand the different types of measurement errors that can occur so that you can avoid them or reduce them whenever possible, or minimize these errors when you select measures and when you interpret the results of your measures. Before we discuss measurement error, though, let's think about an even more fundamental question: Can everything be measured?

CAN EVERYTHING BE MEASURED?

Many years ago, the psychologist Robert Thorndike said that if something exists, it exists in some quantity; if it exists in some quantity, then it can be measured. A little more recently, Hudson (1978a) proposed what he calls the "first axioms of treatment." These are: (a) If you cannot measure the client's problem, it does not exist, and (b) if a problem doesn't exist, that is, if you cannot measure the client's problem, you cannot treat it. Hudson stated these as universal propositions, then challenged readers to refute them by citing only one concrete exception.

We are not going to address here a number of philosophical implications of these arguments, such as how indirect an indicator of a problem can we accept as measuring the real problem. But, the practice implications of Hudson's axioms are directly relevant. We view these arguments as appropriate challenges to professional practice, especially with regard to the need to clarify and specify (operationalize) the targets of our interventions.

However, the argument might run, isn't it possible that many of the problems with which we deal in practice are just too subtle or too complex and changeable to measure? We challenge you on this one. Try this exercise. List as many problems as you can that you think you can't measure. Then, after you've finished reading Part II of this book, describing everything from how to specify problems to how to measure them, go over that list and see how many of those "unmeasurable" problems are in fact measurable with one of the procedures we describe. We think you'll be happily surprised.

Our point of view on this is that if a problem is too subtle or complex to measure, it just may be too subtle or complex to work with in practice. If a problem is meaningful to the client, then you have to have some means of grasping what it is the client is facing and for what he or she needs help. Otherwise, there will be no way of knowing how well you're doing with your intervention program or the extent to which you have reached your client's goals.

However, if you're saying that it's *difficult* to measure many of the problems with which you're working, that's something else. Certainly, many problems are rather complex or even vague to begin with. But if a problem exists, it can be measured. That is the crux of the situation. Part of your job as practitioner is to identify the measurable components of a problem. This is part and parcel of practice no matter what your theoretical orientation. Although we present detailed guidelines on how to go about doing this in the next chapter, let's take a closer look at this issue right now.

Since many clients present their concerns in rather vague and amorphous terms, your job is to help clients clarify and specify their concerns. One way of doing this is to identify those parts of the problem that can serve as measurable *indicators* of the problem, so that you can measure them to gather feedback on the success of your interventions. These "measurable indicators" should be real parts of the problem, significant to the client and not selected only because they're measurable. Thus, the key step in the process of measuring anything that exists is finding indicators of the problem that are typical or representative of the problem and accessible to measurement.

Part of the discomfort with the assertion "anything that exists can be measured" is the concern among some practitioners about what the term *measurable* means. *Measurable* doesn't refer just to observing overt behaviors. As we indicated in Chapter 1, there are a number of measurement tools available to measure the whole gamut of problems you may be faced with in practice–everything from feelings to thoughts to behaviors to community activities and situations. Once you see the range, potential, and flexibility of these procedures, we think you'll agree by the end of Part II that all

of the problems that you're likely to face in your practice are, indeed, measurable.

So we would argue that if a problem exists, the problem, or reasonably close indicators of it, can be measured. However, we recognize that some problems are difficult to measure. The important question for the practitioner is how to measure them in the best possible way.

KEY CHARACTERISTICS OF ALL MEASURES

When a practitioner makes a judgment about the problems of a client, how does the practitioner know he or she is "reading" the problem consistently from one time to the next, or is reading the problem accurately, or the extent to which he or she is talking about the problem that truly is troubling the client? Most of us develop a number of devices to double-check by looking for external, independent confirmation to assure consistency. The point is that there are direct analogies between what you do in practice to ascertain that you are being accurate and consistent, and what you do in evaluation, particularly with single-system designs. This is to say once again that what makes for good practice also makes for good evaluation.

In the remainder of this chapter, we discuss a number of the key characteristics that you would want to address in selecting or developing a measurement procedure. As we noted above, it is probably impossible to cover every characteristic of measurement devices in just this chapter. So we've attempted to select those which should be most helpful for you, and which you can actually use in deciding which measure to select. The characteristics that we discuss are reliability, validity, directness, ease of use, accessibility, relevance to intervention planning, and characteristics of the client; these characteristics are actually strategies, or ways of telling just how good a measure is at indicating the target or concept. Thus, if you can meet these criteria to a high degree, you can be confident that you are providing measurement that is as free from distortions and error as possible.

Measurement Error

A client's score on a measurement instrument can result from different things. It might result just from the real or true amount of whatever it is you are trying to measure (e.g., the amount of child neglect, the amount of marital satisfaction). This is what you would like, and it's easy to assume that this is the whole story. Unfortunately, there are other plausible explanations for why a client might get a particular score. It's useful to think about two categories of alternative explanations.

Random Measurement Error. Most measures have an element of random error. Random, in this sense, means haphazard or by chance. Unfortunately, this is a little different from the use of the term *random* that you probably are familiar with, such as in random selection and random assignment where *random* refers to a systematic and scientifically based process. Let's take an example. Suppose that you're using a questionnaire to measure parents' knowledge of children's abilities, and one of the questions is, "On the average how old are children when they can ride a bicycle?" It might not be clear whether the question refers to a two-wheeler with training wheels, a two-wheeler without training wheels, or even a tricycle. On one occasion a parent might guess (i.e., mentally flip a coin) one meaning of the question; on another occasion the parent might choose another. In this case the parent's answer and, hence, score wouldn't necessarily result from whether he or she knew the correct answer to the question, because a poorly worded question contributed to the answer. Thus, random error refers to the possibility that responses to some measurement tools could be affected by chance or haphazard occurrences.

Systematic Measurement Error. Systematic error is a tendency to err in a particular way. Suppose that you ask clients a series of questions designed to measure the degree to which they neglect their children and one of the questions is, "Has a nurse or social worker or teacher ever said that any child of yours

wasn't being given enough to eat?" The client might realize that you would be critical of not giving a child enough to eat. Therefore, the client might not feel comfortable answering this question accurately, and would answer "no" to this question no matter what. The errors in clients' answers to this question are systematically biased in the sense that few people would admit to a socially reprehensible action.

Importance of Measurement Error. Why should we care about the extent to which a measure has random or systematic measurement error? The answer is that we would like to know how much measured or observed change in a client's problem is due to actual change in the problem. To the extent that change or a lack of change is due to extraneous factors such as measurement error, the results of your measures are difficult to interpret and to use in planning and evaluating your interventions. *The basic issue is that measurement error can lead to erroneous practice decisions.* Suppose that it appeared that a problem remained the same, when in fact it had gotten better or worse, or vice versa. Can you see how much this could distort or misdirect your practice?

So how do you know the extent to which a measure has random and systematic measurement error? The *reliability* of a measure indicates the extent to which a measure contains random measurement error, and the *validity* of a measure indicates the extent to which a measure contains systematic measurement error. Reliability and validity are two of the most important criteria by which the adequacy of measures are judged. To understand how to select and use measures you need to understand these concepts, and you need to know how reliability and validity are determined and interpreted. Figure 2.1 shows the different methods used to determine reliability and validity, and we'll now turn to these different methods.

Reliability

Random measurement error will lead to inconsistencies in measuring things. For example, two people observing the same event might report that different things occurred. The same

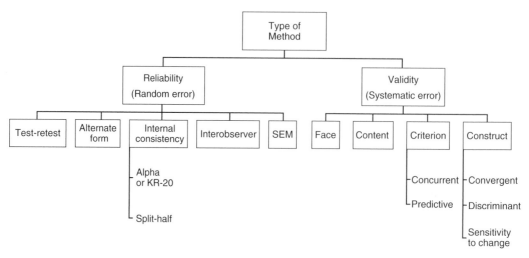

FIGURE 2.1   Methods to determine measurement error.

question asked of the same person on two different occasions might elicit two different answers. Phrasing two questions about the same thing in slightly different ways might result in different responses from the same person.

The word *reliability* is a general term for the *consistency* of measurements, and unreliability basically means inconsistency due to random measurement errors (American Psychological Association et al., 1985; Anastasi, 1988; Nunnally, 1978). In general we find out if a measurement is consistent by repeatedly and independently measuring the same people (or sometimes things) under the same circumstances. To determine the consistency of measurements the same event might be observed by two observers, the same question might be asked of the same person on two different occasions, or the same question might be asked in two slightly different ways.

A test of reliability requires first that observations be independent and second that they be made under the same circumstances, so it's necessary to have some understanding of these two requirements. *Independence* simply means that one measurement doesn't influence another measurement. For example, if two observers talked about what they observed before they decided what to record, the measurements wouldn't be independent. If people remem-

bered their answer to a question asked at one time, and this first answer influenced their answer to the same question at a second time, the measurements wouldn't be independent. The phrase *under the same circumstances* just means that the measurement is made under the same conditions. For example, if we had a client complete a depression scale in a crowded, noisy, waiting room and then in a quiet, private, comfortable office, the circumstances clearly wouldn't be the same. Therefore, there are degrees of "independence" and "sameness" of circumstances, and those examining reliability should seek to attain the highest levels of each, as circumstances permit.

Different types of measurement inconsistencies exist (e.g., between observers, between times, between questions), and therefore different types of reliability have been distinguished. In addition, a measurement strategy might be consistent (i.e., reliable) in one way but not in another. Therefore, it's actually best to think of the reliabil*ies* of a measure. For example, two observers might not agree about the frequency of a child's prosocial behavior observed in a videotape, but each observer might be consistent over time in the frequency of prosocial behavior recorded. When it comes time for you to select a standardized questionnaire to evaluate a client's progress, you should look at the reliability information available from research on the measure as one basis for selecting the measure for your client. The different types of reliability that we'll discuss include test-retest reliability, alternate-forms reliability, internal-consistency reliability, interobserver reliability, and the standard error of measurement (SEM). However, before discussing these types of reliability and validity, we must discuss the correlation coefficient, the statistic usually used to quantify and report the reliability and validity of measures.

A *correlation* tells us whether and how two variables are related. For example, if parents' knowledge of child development increases with the number of children they have, then child development knowledge and number of children are said to be positively correlated. A positive correlation means that people with high values on one variable (e.g., number of children) tend to have high values on another variable (e.g., scores on a measure of child development knowledge). Two variables also can be negatively (or inversely) correlated. For example, if parent–child conflicts decrease as parents' knowledge increases, then parent–child conflicts and child development knowledge are negatively correlated. A negative correlation means that people with low values on one variable tend to have high values on another variable. Finally, two variables might be uncorrelated. If two variables are uncorrelated, values on one variable are not related to values on another variable. For example, if parents with few children are just as knowledgeable about child development as parents with many children, then the number of children variable tells nothing about how knowledgeable parents will be about child development.

A correlation can range from −1.0 (negative correlation) to +1.0 (positive correlation). The sign of a correlation indicates whether the variables are positively or negatively correlated, and a correlation of 0 means there's no relationship at all between two variables. The absolute value of a correlation (i.e., the actual number, ignoring the plus or minus sign) indicates the strength of the relationship–the larger the absolute value, the stronger the relationship. Therefore, a correlation of −.80 indicates a stronger relationship than a correlation of +.50 because the sign of the correlation is ignored when determining the strength of the relationship.

Test-Retest Reliability. Test-retest reliability is determined by independently measuring the same group of people (or things) with the same measure on two different occasions under the same circumstances. The correlation between the first and second administration of the measure indicates the test-retest reliability or the *stability* of a measure.

What does an estimate of test-retest reliability tell? A high value tells us that the measure provides consistent results over a certain time period–for example, those who have high scores the first time are likely to have high scores the second time. Another way of thinking about high test-retest reliability is that it indicates that the measure is not very susceptible to random changes in individuals from one time to the other (e.g., changes due to fatigue, emotional strain, worry, illness, recent pleasant or unpleasant experiences), or to the measurement environment (e.g., changes due to who is present in the environment, or to noise, room temperature, or other distractions).

Test-retest reliability is particularly important for single-system evaluation because you will be administering your measures or making your observations several times over the course of assessment and intervention ("repeated measures"). If your measurement or observation tool is not stable, changes that come about may be a result of changes in the measurement tool itself. With a stable measure you can be more confident that you are recording real changes in the behavior, feelings, attitudes, and so forth, that are being measured.

There are some things that can make the test-retest reliability of a measure appear higher or lower than it really is, and you need to remember these things when interpreting the test-retest reliability of a measure. First, reliability is determined from *independent* repeated observations of the same subjects under the same circumstances. Sometimes the process of retesting violates the requirement of independence, that is, that the second measurement not be affected by the first. Individuals may be less interested, motivated, or anxious during the second measurement because they're already familiar with the measurement procedure. If the time interval between test and retest is fairly short, people might remember their initial responses and simply repeat many of the same responses they gave the first time. Finally, the initial measurement may change the response. For example, a questionnaire assessing marital satisfaction may raise questions people never thought about before, which might heighten their interest in certain issues and stimulate the development of definite opinions; consequently, a "Don't Know" response on the first questionnaire may be replaced by a "Definitely Agree" response on the second.

A second possible problem with test-retest reliability has to do with the requirement that the measurements are made under the same circumstances. One important way that circumstances can change is for genuine change to occur in whatever is being measured (i.e., change due to influences unrelated to the measurement). For example, administration of a depression inventory on two occasions separated by a 1-month interval may result in low test-retest reliability because the depression, in fact, lessened.

The test-retest reliability of any measurement strategy could be determined using many different time intervals between test and retest. Most often you will want to be assured that the measure is reliable over the time interval in which you are interested for your particular case. In general, though, the shorter the test-retest interval, the more likely it is that the first measurement will have an effect on the second one; the longer the interval, the more likely it is that real change will have occurred. Unfortunately, it's often difficult to know whether two measurements are independent, and typically the best you can do is to try to arrange conditions to maximize the chances that they're independent. In general, the time interval should be long enough for the effects of the first measurement to wear off, but not long enough for a significant amount of real change to occur. For example, it's reasonable to expect marital satisfaction, depression, self-esteem,

and other similar concepts to remain stable over relatively short periods of time (e.g., 1 or 2 weeks), but not long periods of time (e.g., 1 or 2 years). In contrast, it's reasonable to expect different types of aptitudes (e.g., general intelligence, artistic ability) and other similar constructs to remain stable over relatively longer periods of time. Therefore, overall, there's no one time interval that is best, because some things change faster than others, and some things are forgotten more easily than others, but desirable test-retest intervals typically range from 2 to 14 days (Streiner & Norman, 1989).

Usually the test-retest reliability of a measure is determined by a researcher using groups of people, and the results are reported in terms of the correlation between the scores obtained at different times. Your own evaluation of an individual client also can provide some evidence of the test-retest reliability or stability of a measure as used with your particular client. This just involves visually examining the pattern of results over time for a given client. If a relatively "flat" pattern of observations is obtained during a phase (e.g., baseline), this would provide some evidence for the test-retest reliability or stability of the measure, if it's reasonable to assume that the observations are independent. However, if a "flat" pattern is not found, don't automatically fault the measure, because it might be that real change occurred in the target, or the circumstances changed under which the measurements were made. But a fluctuating baseline at least should make you stop and think about the reliability of your measure.

Alternate-Forms Reliability.   Alternate-forms reliability, and internal-consistency reliability, which will be discussed next, are primarily concerned with the consistency with which we measure concepts. Concepts are abstract and generalized terms about classes of events, and many client problems are reframed as concepts (e.g., child neglect, depression, problem-solving ability, marital satisfaction, antisocial behavior). For example, consider the following selected items designed to measure the concept of marital satisfaction (Hudson, 1981):

1. I feel that my partner is affectionate enough.
2. I feel that my partner and I get along very well together.
3. I feel that my partner is a comfort to me.

Each item is taken to be an indicator of the concept of marital satisfaction, and we hypothesize that someone who answers affirmatively to one will probably answer affirmatively to the others. However, no single item would be sufficient to measure the concept, just as no single person will represent a group of people, because marital satisfaction is a complex and multidimensional phenomenon. So to measure concepts we need to find a sufficient number of indicators that are typical or representative of the array of events described by the concept.

Alternate-forms reliability involves the administration of two forms of a measure that are constructed according to the same specifications (e.g., they have the same number of items, items expressed in a similar form, items of equal difficulty, and comparable instructions, format, illustrative examples, and time limits), but the actual content of the items is different. The reason for doing this is to see whether the two sets of items designed to measure the same concept actually do measure the same concept. A high correlation between alternate forms tells us that people respond consistently to the different forms of the measure (i.e., different sets of indicators), suggesting that the different forms of the measure do measure the same concept. Thus, the measure is said to be consistent (reliable) because both forms agree regarding measurement of the concept.

Internal-Consistency Reliability.   It is also possible to examine the extent to which the same results would be obtained with different samples of items without having to devise and administer two versions of a measure. Methods for doing this involve the administration of a single set of items to a group of people, and an examination of the extent to which people respond consistently to the different items contained in the measure. This type of reliability is called internal consistency reliability, and it basically refers to the extent to which parts of a measure (items or even entire halves of the measure) are homogeneous or measure the same thing. There are two types of internal-consistency reliability that you're likely to see reported–split-half reliability and coefficient alpha.

Split-half reliability is determined by dividing the items in a measure into two groups containing an equal number of items (most often the even-numbered items are used for one half and the odd-numbered items for the other half, so this is sometimes called "odd-even reliability"), computing a score for each person on each half of the measure, and determining the correlation between scores on the two halves of the measure. The correlation between the two halves only indicates the reliability of one half of the measure, and so a correction formula is applied to this correlation to provide the reliability of the whole measure, and this corrected correlation is the split-half reliability of the measure. A high split-half value indicates that people respond consistently to both halves of the measure (hence the term "internal-consistency"), indicating that the different halves of the instrument measure the same concept.

Coefficient alpha is a statistic used to quantify internal-consistency reliability. Essentially, alpha is just the average intercorrelation among a set of items, weighted by the number of items (coefficient alpha is sometimes called Cronbach's alpha after its developer, or KR-20, which is a specialized version of coefficient alpha). Coefficient alpha provides more information about internal consistency than split-half reliability, so in general it is the more useful of the two. Like split-half reliability, a high value of coefficient alpha suggests that the results obtained with a measure don't depend on the particular items used. A high value of coefficient alpha also indicates that a person responds fairly consistently to all of the items in a measure (i.e., those who have high scores on one item are likely to have high scores on other items), and this in turn suggests that the items all measure the same concept, that is, they're homogeneous. The *homogeneity* of a set of items is important because most measures are designed to measure a single concept (e.g., family cohesion, depression), and coefficient alpha provides one indication of the extent to which this is accomplished.

Interobserver Reliability. The different types of reliability discussed so far are important to understand in order to select measures that already are available, and in order to understand and avoid different types of measurement error (e.g., inconsistency over time due to changes in the measurement conditions). Interobserver reliability (or, as it's sometimes called, *interrater* reliability) refers to the extent to which two or more observers are consistent with each other when they independently observe or judge the same thing. The consistency with which two or more people observe or make judgments about a client's behavior is actually something you likely will test yourself when you use single-system designs, so it's important to understand in some detail.

Interobserver reliability has been used most extensively to determine the extent to which two observers agree in their observations about whether, how often, or how long overt behaviors occur. For example, two observers (say, husband and wife) might record the amount of time their child spent doing homework, the number of parent–child arguments, or the amount of time the family spends together. The degree of agreement between the husband and wife could then be determined as one method of assessing the adequacy of the information collected.

In general, interobserver reliability is quantified using either a correlation coefficient, which we discussed earlier, or some measure of agreement such as percentage of agreement or kappa. *Percentage of agreement* refers to the percentage of times both observers agree with each other in their observations–for example, that a given behavior occurred five times in an hour. (*Kappa* and other such measures of agreement are statistics that correct for agreement that would be expected just by chance; Fleiss, 1981; Siegel & Castellan, 1988.) In any case, a high value of interobserver reliability indicates a high degree of consistency between observers. In Chapter 5 we provide detailed instructions on how to compute interobserver reliability, and how to enhance interobserver reliability by carefully giving clear instructions and training to observers.

Correlations or different indexes of agreement provide precise estimates of interobserver reliability. A less precise but still useful way to examine the extent to which two or more observers provide comparable information over time is to graph the information from the different observers on the same chart, and visually determine whether the information is comparable. For example, suppose that a husband and wife seek help because they are dissatisfied with their marriage, and one of their major complaints is that they don't spend enough time in mutually satisfying activities. You ask them to independently record the amount of time spent in mutually satisfying activities each day. Two weeks of baseline information is collected, and then an intervention designed to increase the amount of mutually satisfying time spent together is implemented. The day-to-day pattern of results shown in Figure 2.2 shows a high degree of correspondence in husband–wife reports of the amount of time spent in mutually satisfying activities, indicating that this information is reported reliably by each member of this couple.

We recognize that it's not always realistic for you to find two observers in order to do this reliability check. If the client and a relevant other are both available and willing to record (the secondary recorder only in certain situations), that would be great. But in other circumstances, no one else might be available. Then, the second recorder might be you. You might make home visits, once in the baseline period and once in the intervention, and do some recording yourself. Then your recording could form the basis for the reliability check. Or, you could set up a situation in the office in which you and the client role-play and record (we discuss this in more detail in Chapter 5).

Standard Error of Measurement (SEM). A problem might appear to change over time to some extent because of unreliability in the measurement of the problem. The standard error of measurement provides an indication of the measure's reliability by directly estimating the amount of error in the instrument;

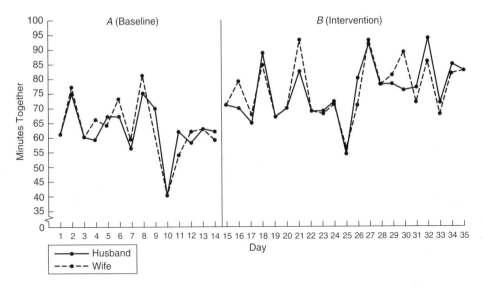

FIGURE 2.2   Interobserver reliability in measuring satisfying time together.

more importantly, the SEM provides a basis for deciding whether change in a problem is due just to unreliability in the measure. Since some of the standardized questionnaires we discuss in Chapter 7 do report the SEM, you could use this reliability index as an additional way of evaluating how useful those measures will be to you.

Let's suppose that a client got a score of 30 on a depression inventory whose SEM equals 5. If scores on that measure changed from, say, 55 to 51 from one administration to the next, this change likely is due to error in the instrument. The SEM gives us an estimate of the range of values in which the client's "true" score probably falls; in general, the smaller the SEM, the more reliable the measure.*

What use is it to know that a person's true score probably falls somewhere within a range of values? Sometimes, certain scores on measures are used as cutoff points for decision making (e.g., to help determine whether intervention with a problem is necessary). Let's say that a measure has a cutoff score of 30, an SEM of 5, and a client gets a score of 28 on the mea-

sure. You might be inclined to say that the client was below the cutoff, but a consideration of the client's score in conjunction with the SEM indicates that the client's true score actually might be 30 or above (i.e., it could be from 23 to 33). Thus, you might decide to keep the intervention in effect until the score goes below 25.

Another use for the SEM is to determine whether a change in scores may be due to unreliability or actual change. For example, let's think about our measure with the SEM of 5 and our client with the score of 28. If, upon readministration of our measure, the client's score decreased from 28 to 25 (i.e., 3 points, less than the SEM of 5), this change probably is due to error in the measuring instrument. If on the other hand the score declined from 28 to 23 or lower (i.e., one or more times the SEM) this would suggest "real" change (i.e., change due to something other than unreliability). Thus, in a way, the use of the SEM to help interpret a client's score helps us avoid placing too much emphasis on a particular score or on small changes in a client's score.

*The SEM is calculated simply by multiplying the standard deviation by the square root of 1 minus the reliability coefficient ($SD \times \sqrt{1 - rel}$).

The SEM usually should not be used to compare the adequacy of different measures. This is because the SEM is in part determined by the scale range of the measure, and therefore you can't directly compare the SEM from different measures unless they have the same range of scores, or unless you convert scores into a percentage (by dividing the SEM by the score range and multiplying by 100). But in general, if you want to compare the reliability of different measures, we use other reliability coefficients, although the SEM is useful for interpreting individual scores.

What Is "High" Reliability? As we mentioned earlier, reliability figures are generally presented either as correlations or as percentage of agreements (with the exception of the SEM). In either case a 0 indicates a totally unreliable measure, and a 1 indicates a perfectly reliable measure. Reliability estimates based on correlations can fall in the range from –1.00 to 0, but it is very unusual for this to happen, and when it does it simply indicates that the measure is unreliable.

There's fairly general agreement as to what constitutes "high" reliability. Reliability of .80 or better, or 80% agreement if percentage of agreement is used, is generally considered good or high reliability (again, with the exception of the SEM). Some researchers suggest that correlations of .70 or percentage of agreements of 70% are satisfactory. We would not necessarily dispute that, since this is a relatively small difference and an instrument with 70% reliability can be useful. It simply is that the higher the reliability the better, and the standard of .80 or 80% should be a clear and useful guideline for you to use in selecting instruments, or as a goal to shoot for in training two observers.

What Type of Reliability Should You Use? Given these several types of reliability, how do you know which one to use to evaluate a measure? Sometimes you will be able to examine the interobserver reliability of the measures you use, but typically you won't be in a position to examine other types of reliability. Therefore, when you select existing measures for use with your clients you should determine whether evidence exists in the literature for the reliability of the measures. It's important to look for existing evidence of short-term test-retest reliability (stability) for most types of measures, especially for use with single-system designs, and interobserver reliability for measures based on direct observations. You should look for estimates of internal consistency reliability for standardized questionnaires, and especially for estimates of coefficient alpha (or KR-20), although estimates of split-half reliability also can be useful. Finally, if you intend to use two or more forms of a measure (and this is rare in the conduct of single-system designs), you should look for evidence of alternate-forms reliability.

Validity

The reliability of a measure indicates only whether something is being measured consistently, but that "something" may or may not be the variable we're trying to measure. The validity of a measure indicates whether and how well it measures what is intended. For example, consider again the question "Has a nurse or social worker or teacher ever said that any child of yours wasn't being given enough to eat?" Even if the correct answer for a client is yes, the client might be very consistent (i.e., reliable) in answering no to this question on different occasions, or no to a series of similar questions designed to measure neglect. What you're measuring would be measured reliably or consistently (the unwillingness to admit to neglect when it occurs), but you wouldn't be measuring what you intended (child neglect).

Validity is perhaps the most important measurement consideration of all because validity involves knowing whether a measurement procedure actually does what it's supposed to. Does it measure what it's supposed to measure? Does it predict what it's supposed to predict? Does a measure really accomplish its aims? These are the key questions one would ask in evaluating a measure for possible use. While both reliability and validity are important, without being sure that a measure indicates what we want it to indicate, it's almost irrelevant whether the measure is consistent. That is, validity is a crucial guideline that you will want to look for when choosing an instrument. So we believe it's important to review some of the ways you might assess the validity of a measure.

It's probably obvious that different measures have different purposes. Since this is so, it also seems logical to assume that the purpose of the measure would determine the type of method needed for establishing its validity. For some measures, it's relatively easy to establish validity. For example, asking a client his age to the nearest birthday generally produces an answer that seems apparently valid, at least on the face of it. But presenting a client with a scale to measure depression or family conflict may be a different matter altogether.

As a general rule, if the problem or event you're seeking to measure can be observed directly or has a clear, observable indicator, it's easier to validate (Hudson, 1981). On the other hand, if the measure represents a more abstract construct, or if you're interpreting a score or event as representing some other event, then the task for establishing validity becomes more difficult. To use Hudson's (1981) example, pulse and respiration rates are excellent indicators of level of physiological activity, but are they good (valid) indicators of anxiety or fear?

There are several different ways researchers have gone about establishing validity. Some of these involve fairly precise methods, for example, statistical procedures correlating one measure with another. Others require you (or the original researcher) to make judgments. For these, the level of precision becomes more variable, so there's more room for differences of opinions. Indeed, in large part, validating a measure is related to the specific purpose of the measure. Therefore, one of several different methods of validation may be more appropriate than others. In addition, any given type of validation may be limited to a certain validation group. We therefore agree with Andrulis (1977) that few, if any, measures can be valid in the abstract. Instead, the key questions about validity should be "Valid for whom?" and "Valid for what?"

As we mentioned above, there are several different methods for assessing validity. Unfortunately, these terms are sometimes used in slightly different ways by different researchers. What we'll try to do here is present some working ideas for you to use and outline a few of the basic terms and methods that you can look for when trying to make a decision on a measure to use in your own practice.

Face Validity. The first method of determining validity, face validity, refers to the opinion by the developer of a measure, by some expert, or by you that an instrument measures what it intends to measure. For example, take a look back at the three questions designed to measure marital satisfaction. In your judgment do they look like they measure marital satisfaction? If so, you would say the measure has face validity.

There's no standard method for determining face validity, no way to quantify it, and no standard against which to determine how much of it we should have. For these reasons, face validity is sometimes called "faith" validity because it requires us to place considerable faith in the person who decides whether a measure has validity.

In some cases you might not even want to use a measure that has only face validity (e.g., a set of subtle questions measuring alcohol and drug use might be labeled a Health Practices Questionnaire; Sisco & Pearson, 1994). The argument here is that if clients or perhaps even observers know what is being measured, they can distort their responses more easily. On the other hand, face validity cannot be dismissed entirely because it implies that, on the "face" of it, you or someone else has made a judgment that some instrument appears to be measuring what it purports to. After all, if you ask clients to complete a questionnaire or record certain behaviors or events in their lives, and if these requests don't seem to the clients to be related to the problem for which they're seeking help, the clients might be reluctant to cooperate.

Content Validity. Content validity refers to the extent to which the questions or behaviors selected for measurement are representative or are a biased or limited sample of what you intend to measure. For example, look back at the three child-neglect questions, and suppose that you used these questions to measure child maltreatment in general (i.e., neglect and abuse). These questions represent too limited a sample of questions concerning child maltreatment because they don't include questions concerning important aspects of child maltreatment. For example, questions about physical and sexual abuse aren't included, and this exclusion would introduce a systematic source of error (i.e., invalidity) into the measurement of child maltreatment. However, although these questions might not be valid for measuring child maltreatment, they might be valid for other purposes—that is, measuring child neglect.

Content validity refers to how adequately content is sampled, but so do alternate-forms and internal-consistency reliability. What is the difference? Reliability refers to the extent to which measurement is due to *random* error (i.e., inconsistency), and validity refers to the extent to which measurement is due to *systematic* error. Unreliability due to content sampling refers to random errors in the selection of the questions asked or the behaviors observed. Invalidity due to content sampling refers to systematic errors in obtaining information about the system of events in question, as opposed to some other set of events. For example, the three questions on child neglect mentioned previously very well might consistently measure something (e.g., child neglect), but not what is intended (i.e., child maltreatment). People might respond consistently (i.e., reliably) to the three questions (e.g., those who answer yes to one question might answer yes to the other two questions—and therefore coefficient alpha would be high), and they might respond consistently over time. What is being measured consistently, though, is not child maltreatment but perhaps just child neglect, because of a systematic error (i.e., a biased sample resulting from the exclusion of questions concerning physical and sexual abuse).

Issues of content validity arise in the construction and selection of a measure supposedly addressing a system of events you have in mind (like "child abuse"). So content validity is an important consideration for you to apply with many of the measures we'll be presenting. If you observe a type of behavior (e.g., the frequency with which a family can successfully resolve family problems), you would want to make sure that you're adequately sampling the range of family problems, locations or situations in which problems occur, or times during which the problems may be occurring, in other words, that the sample of events is representative of the range of possible events. (We'll discuss this point in more detail in Chapter 5.) In evaluating a standardized questionnaire (Chapter 7), you would want to evaluate whether the items on that questionnaire appear representative of all the items and issues that could reasonably be included. Will the scores on that measure provide you with information about the individual's problems or capabilities in one area or more than one, with sufficient detail on which to make a decision, and in relation to relevant kinds of situations? Similarly, in using individualized rating scales (Chapter 6) and logs (Chapter 8), you want to be sure that the scales or logs you construct with your client are really tapping the range of problems, locations, and times during which the problem might occur.

When selecting or developing a measure, first establish the definition and essential features of the concept to determine the content validity of a measure (e.g., a measure of parenting knowledge might include subsets of questions concerning child health and safety, discipline, and child development). You won't know whether the measurement operations include the essential features of a concept and exclude irrelevant features if you don't have a definition against which to judge the measurement operations.

Content validity also is determined in other ways. Frequently experts in the particular area are asked to provide feedback on the content validity of a measure during its development (e.g., a measure of knowledge of normative child development may be sent to developmental psychologists). This approach is often useful, but remember that experts are fallible and don't always provide perfect advice.

Content validation involves a more systematic approach to the conceptual and operational definition of a concept than does face validity, but still there are no standard procedures for determining content validity or quantifying it, and no standard against which to determine how much of it you should have. In fact, content validation for the most part is based on judgments by the person constructing the measure or by you as a potential user about the definition of the concept measured, the enumeration of the questions or behaviors, and the selection of a representative set of questions or behaviors. Ultimately the validity of a measure must be empirically tested and demonstrated. Now we turn to this issue.

Criterion Validity. The criterion validity of a measure refers to its ability to predict an individual's performance or status on certain outcomes (APA et al., 1985; Anastasi, 1988). The performance or outcome that a measure is designed to predict is called a criterion, and the validity of the criterion must already be established because it is the standard against which the measure is validated. (We have to assume some nonempirical starting point to get the empirical part of science moving; this is as true of criterion validity as it was for content validity.)

Criterion validity (which is sometimes called *empirical validity*) is usually determined by collecting scores on the measure being validated and on the criterion, and determining the correlation between the measure and the criterion. The higher the correlation between the measure and the criterion, the better the criterion validity. There are two types of criterion validity, concurrent and predictive.

Concurrent validity refers to the ability of a measure to predict an individual's current performance or status. Concurrent validity can be determined in several different ways depending on the purpose of the measure being validated. One way is to examine the correlation between an existing validated measure (i.e., the criterion) and another measure of the same concept that was developed as a simpler, quicker, or less expensive substitute for the available measure. For example, suppose that a brief questionnaire measure of child behavior problems is developed as a substitute for an existing questionnaire measure of child be-

havior problems that has established validity. The existing measure could serve as a standard against which the validity of the new measure is judged. Both measures would be administered at about the same time to the same group of children, and the correlation between the two measures would be determined. A high correlation between the two measures would provide evidence of the concurrent validity of the new measure.

Another way concurrent validity is determined is by examining the extent to which a measure predicts current performance in a criterion situation. This is important if the measure is intended as a substitute for direct measurement of the actual criterion situation. For example, suppose that our questionnaire measure of child behavior problems was developed not as a simpler, quicker, or less expensive substitute for an available questionnaire measure, but rather to predict existing observable behavior problems in a classroom situation. The questionnaire might be completed by the children's teachers, and classroom observers might observe the behavior problems. A high correlation between the questionnaire and observational measures would provide evidence of the concurrent validity of the questionnaire measure.

A final way concurrent validity is determined is to examine whether a measure distinguishes between groups known to have different amounts of whatever is supposedly measured. This type of concurrent validity is sometimes called *known-groups* validity. (It's also sometimes called *discriminant validity,* but we use this term in a different way in the following section.) For example, our behavior problem questionnaire could be used with children in special classes for those with behavior problems and with children in regular classrooms. If the results indicated that the average behavior problem score for students in special classes was significantly higher than the average score for children in regular classrooms, the concurrent validity of the questionnaire would be supported. One particular reason known-groups validity is important is because a measure that is sensitive to a known-groups contrast also should be sensitive to intervention effects comparable to the difference between the groups (Lipsey, 1990, p. 104).

Usually the concurrent validity of a measure is determined by a researcher using groups of people, and the results are reported in terms of the correlation between the measure being validated and the criterion. Your own evaluation of an individual client also can provide some evidence of the concurrent validity of a measure used with your particular client (Hayes, Nelson, & Jarrett, 1986; Jayaratne, 1982; Jayaratne & Daniels, 1981), although this approach has its limitations (Hudson, 1982a). Let's look at an example of this.

Suppose that a mother and father seek help because their son is doing poorly in school. One major problem seems to be that he doesn't complete his homework, and this becomes a target of intervention. Each school day he has a homework assignment in each of six subjects, and you ask him to record the number of completed homework assignments each day. You're concerned about the accuracy of his self-reports, so you check with the boy's teachers on randomly selected days (because it would be too difficult for everyone concerned to do this every day), and the teacher reports are used as the criterion against which the accuracy of the self-reports is judged. Three weeks of baseline information is collected, and then an intervention is implemented that is designed to increase the number of completed homework assignments. As shown in Figure 2.3, there was perfect agreement between self-reports and teacher reports for 10 of the 13 checks ($10/13 \times 100 = 77\%$ agreement), and this provides support for the concurrent validity of the self-reports.

Predictive validity refers to the ability of a measure to predict or forecast some future criterion–for example, performance on another measure, prognostic reaction to an intervention program, performance in some task of daily living, grades in school, suicide attempts, and so on. The key here is to determine how useful your measure will be in predicting some future characteristic or behavior of an individual. Such predictive knowledge might allow you to identify those at high risk for certain problems, and you might then work to prevent the problems

(e.g., a child's risk of entry into foster care [Magura, Moses, & Jones, 1987], a child's risk of being physically abused [Milner, 1986; Milner, Gold, & Wimberley, 1986], an adolescent's risk of discontinuing oral contraception [Balassone, 1991]). The simplest way to determine predictive validity would be to correlate results on a measure at one time with the criterion information collected at a later time.

As an example of predictive validity, suppose that your questionnaire measure of child behavior problems was developed to predict the development of future child behavior problems. The questionnaire might be administered at the beginning of the school year, and the number of behavioral problems might be determined at the end of the school year by examining various school records (e.g., number of suspensions, calls to parents). A high correlation between the measure and the criterion would provide evidence of the predictive validity of the measure.

Construct Validity. Just because the name given to a measure suggests that it measures a particular concept (e.g., "marital satisfaction" "child maltreatment," etc.) doesn't necessarily mean that it does. Remember that a particular measure is an operational definition of a concept, and the operations (questions, observations, etc.) might not adequately represent the intended meaning. In general, there are two ways in which this can happen: Either the measure doesn't measure all that it's supposed to measure (e.g., a measure of child maltreatment that fails to measure sexual abuse), or it measures something that it's not supposed to measure (e.g., a questionnaire measure of marital satisfaction whose scores depend in part upon how well the respondent can read, and therefore, in part measures the ability to read) (Cook & Campbell, 1979).

Construct validity refers to the extent to which empirically observed relationships between measures of concepts agree with the interrelationships among concepts predicted by theories. In developing or testing a measure, a researcher uses the theory underlying the concept being measured to set up hypotheses regarding the behavior of persons with high or

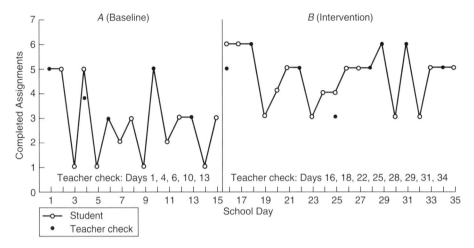

FIGURE 2.3   Concurrent validity of self-reported homework completion.

low scores on the measure (Anastasi, 1988; Wainer & Braun, 1988). The hypotheses are then tested to see whether the validity of the measure is supported. An examination of the construct validity of a measure assumes that there are well-developed theories or hypotheses about the relationships of the concept being measured to other concepts.

Three different types of construct validity hypotheses are usually tested, and these correspond to three different types of construct validity. These include an examination of whether a measure (a) correlates in a predicted manner (i.e., either positively or negatively) with variables that theoretically it should correlate with (*convergent validity*), (b) does *not* correlate significantly with variables that theoretically it should not correlate with (*discriminant validity*), or (c) changes in a predicted manner (i.e., increases or decreases) in response to an experimental intervention (*sensitivity to change*) (Anastasi, 1988).

If a measure is highly correlated with another measure of the same concept, it is said to have *convergent validity* (Anastasi, 1988; Campbell & Fiske, 1959). For example, a new self-report measure of household safety precautions for children (e.g., the installation of smoke alarms and locks on medicine cabinets) should be positively correlated with ex-

isting measures of household safety precautions. Convergent validity evidence based on correlations between measures using different measurement methods (e.g., self-reports and independent observations) is especially important. For example, a correlation between a new self-report measure of parental safety precautions and an independent observer's observation of these precautions would provide stronger evidence of convergent validity than a correlation with an existing self-report measure. The reason for this is that measures using the same method might be correlated because they measure related concepts, *or* because they use the same method. For example, two different self-report measures might be correlated because they both measure a parent's ability or willingness to report the implementation of safety precautions, not because they both measure the actual implementation of safety precautions.

Convergent validity is demonstrated not just by correlations between different measures of the same concept. More generally it's demonstrated if a measure is correlated in a predicted manner with variables with which it theoretically should correlate. For example, a parental self-report measure of household safety precautions for children should be correlated negatively with the number of child injuries that have occurred in the home, and positively with parental knowledge of accident risks and prevention strategies (Fickling, 1993).

Evidence concerning whether a measure is correlated with related variables, or changes in response to an intervention, is not sufficient to demonstrate the construct validity of a measure. It's also necessary to have evidence that a measure is not correlated significantly with variables with which it theoretically should not be correlated, and this type of evidence provides support for what is known as the *discriminant validity* (sometimes called divergent validity) of a measure (Anastasi, 1988; Campbell & Fiske, 1959). For example, if a self-report measure of safety precautions is highly correlated with a measure of self-esteem, responses might depend partially on a person's self-esteem instead of just on safety precautions. That is, self esteem and safety precautions theoretically should not be correlated.

Discriminant validity is not just demonstrated by the absence of a correlation between a measure and other variables, though, but is also demonstrated if the magnitude of the correlation suggests that the measure is measuring a distinct concept. For example, the implementation of safety precautions should be correlated with parental education, but if the correlation between a measure of safety precautions and parental education was too high, it would suggest the failure to measure a distinct concept.

When you select or design a measure for your practice, be especially skeptical in thinking about its discriminant validity. You should consider the extent to which the scores on a measure are determined by the amount of the intended concept (e.g., the actual safety precautions implemented) or by other extraneous variables (e.g., reading ability, a desire to present oneself in a socially desirable light). These extraneous variables present threats to the discriminant validity of a measure, and measures that are sensitive to the influence of extraneous variables are undesirable because they don't just measure what is intended. It would be safe to say that all measures are influenced by extraneous variables (i.e., variables other than the one supposedly measured) to some extent.

The issue is the extent to which this occurs, and the effect this has.

There are a variety of extraneous variables that present possible threats to the construct validity of measures, and an understanding of these will help you make better decisions in the selection and use of measurement strategies. For example, some types of self-reports are biased by the desire to present oneself in a socially desirable manner. Some types of observations are biased by observers' expectations about what is observed (e.g., expectations based on client characteristics such as race, age, gender, social status). To some extent these possible threats are specific to particular methods of measurement (e.g., self-reports, observation), and in our discussion of particular measurement methods we'll highlight these possible threats.

Reactivity is an example of one such possible threat. Reactive measures are those about which the client is aware and to which the client "reacts." Reactivity simply means changes that come about in the client or in the problem due to the act of measurement itself (Webb, Campbell, Schwartz, Sechrest, & Grove, 1981). When a reactive measure is used, the observation or monitoring process leads to change in the target even if an intervention doesn't occur or doesn't have any effect. Conversely, a nonreactive measure does not by itself bring about change in what you are measuring. If a target changes simply because it's measured, you obviously would have a difficult time separating the effects of an intervention from the measurement of the target.

There are a number of types of reactivity, as well as ways of overcoming or diminishing reactivity. Since this is a very important topic, we've devoted Chapter 9 to ways of overcoming reactivity and to the range of measures that could be considered nonreactive. For now, in selecting a measure, when everything else is equal (which, of course it rarely is), try to use the least reactive measure possible. That is, try to use nonreactive measures when you can, or if you're using more than one measure, try to include at least one nonreactive measure.

Construct validity also is demonstrated if a measure changes in a predicted manner in response to an intervention (Anastasi, 1988; Lipsey, 1990). Such changes provide evidence that a measure is *sensitive to change,* and in the selection of a measure to evaluate client change this is especially important. The point here is that if changes really do occur in a target, you want to be sure that your measure will be able to pick them up. An insensitive measure, by definition, is one that won't indicate change even though actual changes have come about. Of what value is a measure that will not be responsive (sensitive) to changes that occur?

It's not always possible to know in advance whether a measure will be sensitive to change, although with standardized questionnaires, such information sometimes is available from studies that have used the measure to evaluate interventions similar to the one you plan to evaluate (e.g., Lambert, Hatch, Kingston, & Edward, 1986, reviewed research comparing the relative sensitivity of the Beck Depression Inventory [BDI], the Hamilton Rating Scale for Depression [HRS-D], and the Zung Rating Scale for Depression and found that the Hamilton scale appears most sensitive to change). Measures that have shown change in previous research and evaluations in a sense have proved themselves sensitive to some change, but you should do what you can to try to obtain a sensitive measure. For example, if you have a choice between counting behaviors that occur often and those that occur rarely, all other matters being equal, use the one that occurs more often. It will be more sensitive to changes, and hence, a more accurate representation of what is occurring. This is because a high-frequency behavior is likely to be more responsive to small changes and can both increase or decrease, while a low-frequency behavior largely can only increase and may be responsive only to major changes. In some ways, determining the sensitivity of a measure could be reflected in the absence of any changes in the measure during baseline, even though the client reports major events occurring in his or her life. Then, it might be a matter of finding another measure during the baseline period that will more accurately represent what is taking place.

Usually the construct validity of a measure is determined by a researcher using groups of people, and the results are reported in terms of the correlation between different measures of theoretically related and unrelated (or less related) concepts, or in terms of change in a group of people in response to an intervention. Your own evaluation of an individual client also can provide some evidence of the construct validity of a measure as used with your particular client (Hayes et al., 1986).

As an example, suppose that a client seeks help because he is depressed and he is dissatisfied with his marriage. You decide to measure depression using the Beck Depression Inventory (Beck, Ward, Mendelson, Mock, & Erbaugh, 1961; Moran & Lambert, 1983), which is a self-report depression scale, and the Hamilton Rating Scale for Depression (Hamilton, 1960, 1967; Moran & Lambert, 1983), which is a practitioner-completed depression scale. For both depression measures, higher scores indicate greater depression. You measure marital satisfaction using the Index of Marital Satisfaction (IMS) (Hudson, 1982b, 1992), a self-report measure for which higher scores indicate greater *dis*satisfaction. Each measure is completed weekly. After a 3-week baseline, a 7-week intervention designed to ameliorate depression is implemented, and this is followed by a 7-week intervention designed to ameliorate marital distress. Results are shown in Figure 2.4, and the following patterns provide evidence of construct validity (an open circle represents IMS scores, a square represents BDI scores, and a solid circle represents HRS-D scores):

1. The week-to-week pattern of change in depression is similar for the BDI and the HRS-D; when BDI scores go up, HRS-D scores also go up; and when BDI scores go down, HRS-D scores also go down. Therefore, the BDI and the HRS-D appear correlated over time, suggesting that they measure the same thing and providing support for the convergent validity of the two measures. This evaluation doesn't provide evidence of the convergent validity of the IMS because only one

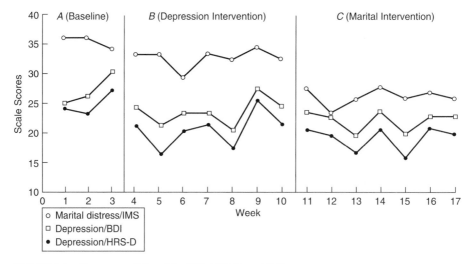

FIGURE 2.4   Construct validity of the BDI, HRS-D, and IMS.

measure of marital satisfaction was used, but it would be possible to obtain such evidence if another method of measuring marital satisfaction was included (e.g., practitioner judgment of the client's marital satisfaction).

2. The week-to-week pattern of change in IMS scores doesn't follow exactly the same pattern as BDI and HRS-D scores, but IMS scores do appear somewhat related, as would be expected. The fact that the IMS pattern is somewhat different suggests that it measures something different from either the BDI or the HRS-D, and this provides support for the discriminant validity of the BDI, HRS-D, and IMS. That is, if the week-to-week pattern of change was the same for each measure, this would suggest that they all measure the same problem (e.g., perhaps just generalized distress), instead of distinct problems.

3. The BDI, HRS-D, and IMS scores decrease when the intervention designed to ameliorate depression is implemented (i.e., the *B* phase), but the decrease in BDI and HRS-D scores is larger than the decrease in IMS scores. When the inter-

vention designed to ameliorate marital distress is implemented (i.e., the *C* phase), BDI, HRS-D, and IMS scores decrease further, but the largest decrease occurs for the IMS scores. This pattern of change between phases suggests that the BDI, HRS-D, and IMS change in a theoretically predicted manner in response to an intervention, which in turn suggests that they're sensitive to "real" change in the problems they attempt to measure.

Which Type of Validity Should You Use?
Given these several types of validity, how do you know which one to use to evaluate an instrument? In the first place, we've presented them in a rough order of increasing importance. Thus, if a measure has high predictive validity, that would be much more important to know than whether a measure has face validity. Evidence concerning construct validity may make a measure even more useful because it will be related to a specific theoretical framework.

Perhaps a more basic guideline is this: In evaluating the validity of a measure for possible selection, one can probably place most confidence in the measure that has information about all the forms of validity. The measure obviously will be most useful if one is certain it has high face and content validity and that it can be safely used to make accurate predictions about the performance of an individual at the present time or in the future. However, remember that a measure usually is not completely valid or invalid in general, but rather more or less valid for a particular purpose (e.g., a self-report depression scale may provide a valid measure of depression for adults but not children). So, the purpose of the measure should be considered in deciding what type of validity is relevant and the extent to which that validity pertains.

The Relationship between Reliability and Validity

First, you need to decide whether something is being measured consistently before you try to discover what it is that is being measured. If something isn't being measured consistently, it doesn't really make any sense to try to discover what that something is. So if a measure isn't reliable, don't spend your time deciding whether it's valid. An unreliable measure will have little or no validity. If the scores on a measure are due just to chance events (i.e., random measurement error–unreliability) that are unrelated to what you're trying to measure, the measure cannot be correlated with anything, cannot show change in response to an intervention, and so cannot be a valid measure of anything. For example, if you flipped a coin to "measure" whether a client had a problem or you rolled a die to "measure" the degree of the problem on a 6-point scale, you wouldn't expect these "measures" to be correlated with anything, and you wouldn't expect them to be sensitive to any changes brought about by an intervention.

On the other hand, there is a continuum of reliability; most measures are not absolutely reliable or absolutely unreliable. Some measures have low or moderate reliability. As a general rule, though, any lack of reliability in a measure tends to lessen its validity.

Even if a measure is reliable, it may or may not be valid. Don't make the mistake of thinking that because a measure is reliable it will be valid. Think back to the example of the use of the neglect questions to measure child mal-

treatment. Reliability is necessary but not sufficient for validity.

If the criterion and construct validity of a measure are demonstrated, you can assume that it is to some extent reliable; if it contained too much random measurement error, it probably would not show such consistent relationships (Anastasi, 1988). Therefore, if one can demonstrate that a measure has good validity, its reliability can be assumed and becomes a secondary issue. So why are researchers concerned with reliability? The reliability of a measure is relatively easier to determine than its validity, and if you find that a measure has very low reliability there's no need to examine its validity: An unreliable measure cannot be valid. Conversely, if a measure has very poor validity, it is irrelevant that it may have high reliability.

Factors Influencing Reliability and Validity

We've mentioned a variety of factors that influence the reliability and validity of measures (e.g., the adequacy with which behaviors or questionnaire items are sampled, consistency in the domain from which behaviors or questionnaire items are sampled, reactivity), and in the following chapters in Part II we discuss other factors specific to particular measurement methods. However, there are two additional factors that can influence the reliability and validity of most measures: the procedures for administering a measure and the population for which estimates of reliability and validity are obtained.

Administration Procedures. Any condition that's irrelevant to the purpose of a measure can potentially introduce random or systematic measurement error. Therefore, to the extent possible, try to structure measurement conditions that reduce measurement error, and try to maintain uniform measurement conditions.

Various types of ambiguities and distractions can produce random measurement error and reduce the reliability of a measure. For example, asking clients or observers to report information under uncomfortable, chaotic, noisy, distracting conditions can reduce reliability. Ambiguity in the instructions provided to clients or observers also can reduce reliability. Therefore, give clients or observers careful and well-planned instructions for the use of measures, and make the conditions under which measurements are obtained as conducive to accurate measurement as possible.

The conditions of measurement also can decrease validity. For example, a questionnaire designed to elicit information about alcohol consumption, or some other highly sensitive type of information, might be valid when administered under certain conditions (e.g., individually, with guarantees of confidentiality), but it might not be valid when administered under other conditions (e.g., in the presence of a family member) (D'Onofrio, 1989). Under the first condition the questionnaire might be a valid measure of alcohol consumption, but under the latter condition the questionnaire might just measure the degree to which someone is willing to disclose sensitive information in the presence of family members.

Systematic changes in measurement conditions also can introduce systematic measurement error and reduce the validity of a measure. For example, suppose that during baseline a client rated her depression each evening, but after the beginning of intervention the client rated her depression each morning. Suppose further that the client was more depressed in the evening than in the morning. This would make it look like the intervention had a positive effect even if it didn't. Therefore, in order to make valid comparisons across repeated measurements, the measures ideally should be obtained under similar conditions (e.g., in terms of time, place, instructions, assessor). In particular, avoid change in the conditions of measurement that coincide with the introduction of an intervention, because it will be difficult to tell whether the change in the measurement conditions or the introduction of the intervention caused any observed change.

Populations.   The validity with which a target is measured can differ depending on the race, cultural background, gender, age, sexual orientation and socioeconomic status of a client

(e.g., Anastasi, 1988; Davis & Proctor, 1989). The extent to which a measurement procedure is equally valid for clients with different social or cultural characteristics might be considered its "social validity." For example, some measures may be more valid with males then females (e.g., Gilligan, 1982; Kohlberg, 1983); with adults than children (e.g., Coddington, 1972; Holmes & Rahe, 1967); and with whites than people of color (e.g., Cardenas & First, 1985; Slaughter & Epps, 1987). Sometimes, though, research may be available indicating whether a measurement procedure or instrument is equally valid for different types of people, such as the clientele at your agency.

The social validity of a measurement strategy can be compromised in a variety of different ways. For example, results from a study by Newmann (1987) suggest that different measures may be needed to measure depression in men versus women, because of socialization differences in the expression of depressive symptoms. Davis and Proctor (1989, p. 163) note that many measures designed to measure stress emphasize individual determinants of stress rather than the broader social, cultural, and economic sources of stress, and this could result in an underestimate of stress for a client experiencing these broader environmental stressors. Other actions that can compromise the social validity of a measurement procedure include clients not providing extensive and accurate information to practitioners of a different race (e.g., Davis & Proctor, 1989, pp. 42–43), and practitioners judging lower socioeconomic clients as more pathological, even when their symptoms and problems are the same as higher socioeconomic clients (e.g., Davis & Proctor, 1989, pp. 278–282).

Another way the social validity of a measurement procedure can be compromised is when a standardized questionnaire or behavioral measure is used to compare the score of an individual client to some group average or normative standard (e.g., a "clinical or cutoff score," above which a client is judged to have a significant problem). Depending on the purpose of the measurement, the comparison might be with a general population norm, a subgroup norm based on people with comparable relevant backgrounds, or the individual's own previous score or behavior (Anastasi, 1988). The selection of an inappropriate comparison group can result in an incorrect decision about the magnitude of a client's problems.

The fact that the validity of a measurement procedure can vary depending on a variety of client characteristics argues for the importance of practitioner knowledge about and sensitivity to client diversity in a whole range of areas. These areas include, for example, client values and preferences in child-rearing practices, care of the elderly, religious beliefs, sexual orientation, willingness to disclose intimate information to and receive help from professionals, and, of course, ethnic and cultural differences. It also argues for the importance of using multiple measurement methods and multiple sources of information to measure a client's targets, and for the importance of verifying the validity of the measurement strategies used with a particular client whenever this is possible and practical.

These issues also require the ultimate in sensitivity from the practitioner. First, you have to be careful to find measures that are specific to the client's concerns or that have been used with people from the client's group. In this way, you can use the measures with confidence in this application, knowing they're valid and appropriate. Second, if this is not possible, you have to try to find, or construct, measures that are appropriate for the client. (We provide some guidelines in subsequent chapters for doing just that.) Finally, if the first two suggestions are impossible to implement, you may have to go ahead and use one or more measures about which you don't have total confidence in this particular application, and use them and interpret them with sensitivity, and due caution about their possibly inappropriate interpretation.

Additional Considerations in the Selection and Development of Measures

Reliability and validity are important criteria by which to judge the accuracy of a measurement strategy. However, these are not the only criteria that are important, especially when selecting

and using measurement tools for single-system evaluation. The directness of a measure, the ease with which it's used, its accessibility, and its relevance to intervention planning are also important considerations. Thus, once reliability and validity have been assessed, there are still a number of additional considerations, all of which have to do with the *utility* of a measure.

Directness. When you consider whether to use direct or indirect measures to evaluate your practice, you are really reconsidering the issues of validity, this time from a slightly different perspective. The question becomes, if we have measures that appear to deal with the client target you are concerned with, and if some of the measures are more or less direct and some are more or less indirect, which one(s) should we choose?

Direct measures clearly approximate, accurately represent, or actually are the real situation, problem, or behavior of concern. The observer or practitioner can use them by making minimal or no inferences about the target. The observations or measurements are viewed as samples of that which is being observed. The observations or measurements are said to be directly representative of how the person actually feels or behaves or thinks. Thus, intervention planning would involve developing a program that has a one-to-one relationship between assessment and intervention. The nature of the observations allows one to use them as "direct" targets of intervention.

Direct measures would be most easily seen as those involving observation of individuals in their natural environments (e.g., observing actual behaviors as they occur). Direct measures might also involve setting up an analog situation when it's impossible to study behaviors in the natural environment (e.g., a role-playing test to demonstrate assertive skills). Finally, the client's self-reports about thoughts and feelings also could be used as direct measures (Barlow & Hersen, 1984). That is, one can get a "direct" measure of a target by simply asking the client to report on it. We discuss numerous methods for doing this in the following chapters.

Indirect measures generally require inferences by the observer or practitioner in order to interpret results. Rather than being a direct sample of the target or set of behaviors, the measures are assumed to be *signs* of the behavior in that an inference is made that the performance is an indirect or symbolic manifestation of some other characteristic (Goldfried, 1977). Thus, a person's score on a personality inventory or test might be viewed as a sign of more enduring personality traits or dispositions. This would make for a less direct relationship between the specific assessment or measurement procedure and the actual intervention. Projective tests such as the Rorschach, Thematic Apperception Test (TAT), and Draw-a-Figure Test are examples of indirect measures, as are many standardized tests such as personality inventories–the Minnesota Multiphasic Personality Inventory (MMPI) and the California Psychological Inventory.

Sometimes, the line between a direct and indirect measure can be blurred. For example, we note that self-report measures are, or can be, direct measures. But many, if not most, indirect measures are also self-reports. The distinction here is in how much of an inference needs to be made and how close a measure comes to actually tapping the dimension in question. Thus, a self-report measure of depression in which you construct a 9-point scale (see Chapter 6) is a more direct measure than a subscale of a standardized personality inventory or the responses to a projective test in which the answers require the scorer to make an inference about whether the client is depressed.

The main issue here is to try to evaluate specific measures for their utility to the practitioner. Some practitioners prefer–or believe in–direct over indirect measures, or vice versa, for reasons other than those we describe here. In those situations, they make their selection on those bases. We are not trying to deny that one's theoretical orientation, philosophy, or ideology plays a part in making such decisions. The best we can hope for is that the criteria for selection are as explicit as possible so that you can be as clear as possible in evaluating what measures to use.

There are several factors to consider in deciding whether to use direct or indirect measures. Most of these have been comprehensively reviewed by Barlow and Hersen (1984),

so only a brief summary of their findings need be reported here.

The first consideration has to do with the validity of indirect versus direct measures, especially criterion-related or predictive validity. By and large, predictions made on the basis of direct measures are generally equal or superior to those made on the basis of indirect measures scored and interpreted by testing "experts."

Second, there appears to be a fair amount of research demonstrating that results from indirect measures often are less an accurate picture of underlying traits than they are a result of the situations under which they are taken (e.g., characteristics of the tester). This problem, called experimenter or examiner bias, appears to be much more widespread than was recognized some years ago.

The third consideration, which has two parts to it, deals with the relative practical advantages of direct versus indirect measures. It's important to evaluate measures in terms of their applicability to single-system evaluations. The first concern in this area is that the relationship between assessment and intervention is unclear when using indirect measures, so the immediate payoff also may be unclear (Barlow & Hersen, 1984). Direct measures by their nature tend to have clearer implications for intervention because they are an immediate indicator of the target and hence can be worked with directly.

The second concern suggested by Barlow and Hersen (1984) relates specifically to the nature of single-system designs. A key characteristic of this type of evaluation is the use of repeated measures, regular observations of the client's target, repeated over time, often daily. Most indirect measures are not suitable for repeated measures. Thus, direct measures tend to be more rapid, easier to administer and score, and less costly. Certainly, as the term implies, they're also more "direct" observations of the target and therefore more related to the behaviors, activities, and events we try to change during the intervention period (Barlow & Hersen, 1984).

In all, then, it appears that the use of direct measures, whenever possible, holds greater advantages than indirect measures for use in single-system evaluation. They approach more closely than indirect methods the client's version of his or her concerns, especially with regard to thoughts or feelings. They obviously approach the real situation of the client much more closely than indirect measures when actual overt behaviors are being observed.

It is probably obvious that while there's a broad range of direct measures, some are "more direct" than others (e.g., an overt behavior is more direct than a self-report about a behavior). Thus, as one guideline for selection of a measure, we recommend that the more direct the measure, the better.

To some extent, this principle is guided by our belief that the most, but certainly not the only, important type of change concerns the actual functioning of the client–any client. We say this because extensive research with a variety of samples indicates that a substantial portion of our clients define their concerns in terms of problems in actual functioning (Beck & Jones, 1973; Gurin, Veroff, & Feld, 1960; Lambert, Shapiro, & Bergin, 1986; Mayer & Timms, 1969). Thus, it appears that changes in functioning–in what people and organizations actually *do*–is most meaningful and relevant to our clients. Changes in functioning frequently are also readily adaptable into outcome measures. In fact, they particularly lend themselves to direct measures of change.

Thus, the more a measure approximates or actually is a measure of actual functioning, the more useful it is to you and your clients. Direct measures tend to be more related than indirect measures to actual functioning (what clients actually do) than indirect measures.

Is There a Place for Indirect Measures?   It's important to note that we're not trying to rule out the use of indirect measures. We are suggesting, though, that there may be priorities in selecting measures, and that for all the reasons described above, direct measures deserve a higher priority than indirect measures. But indirect measures may be the measures of choice (a) when direct measures are not available, (b) when the client is unable or unwilling to use them and no one else is available for direct observation, or (c) when other reasons prevent the use of direct measures.

The point is, we are not trying to argue against the use of indirect measures. Standardized questionnaires, for example, largely tend to be indirect measures, but many have high reliability and validity and have clear relevance for the assessment and evaluation process. Further, many standardized questionnaires are useful as repeated measures for single-system evaluation. A number of these measures and guidelines for their selection and utilization are discussed in Chapter 7.

Another way of looking at indirect measures is to consider them as proxy measures. *Proxy measures* are defined by Gottman and Leiblum (1974) as those that trace progress toward objectives without being as direct an assessment of progress as we would like. Just as the physician uses the thermometer as a crude index of overall health, so you can use proxy measures if more direct measures are unavailable.

Many of the measures we actually end up using are proxies. That is, if it's not a clear, overt measure of actual functioning, the measure will be a proxy to aid us in assessing functioning. Most standardized questionnaires are proxies. But even behaviors can be proxies in some situations. For example, if your key concern is to improve a client's self-esteem, you can observe the number of behaviors the client engages in that may be related to an increase in self-esteem (e.g., by bringing the client "positive strokes" from his environment).

Direct, in other words, refers not so much to behaviors (although often behavioral measures are the most direct), but to coming as close as possible to measuring the actual event you want to change.

Now, we want to be clear that we're not arguing the relative value of changes in behavior and changes in internal states. Instead, the issue here, whether the concern is behavioral changes or changes in internal functioning, is: What are the best ways of measuring what you want to change? In fact, we agree with Lambert et al. (1986) that changes in both behavior and internal functioning are important and probably both should be measured in many instances, at least in clinical practice. Our addition to this would be that both behavior and internal functioning would be more profitably assessed by use of direct measures.

Ease of Use.   Single-system designs require the repeated measurement of client targets over time. Therefore, the ease with which a measure is used becomes an important consideration. The question here is whether the client, practitioner, relevant other, or independent evaluator will be able and willing to use a given measure.

There are several considerations in deciding the ease with which a measure can be used. These include the time it takes to administer, score, and interpret the measure, and characteristics of the client. For example, clients might be irritated, overwhelmed, or bored with the repeated completion of standardized questionnaires, or they may be unable to read or understand the questionnaire. Practitioners or other observers might get worn out or bored with making certain types of observations, or a standardized questionnaire might be time-consuming for a practitioner to score and interpret.

There has been an increasing recognition of the importance of the ease with which measures can be used in practice. This recognition has led to the development and dissemination of an amazing number of measures that can be used relatively easily on a repeated basis (e.g., Corcoran & Fischer, 1987; Corcoran & Fischer, 2000a, 2000b; Fischer & Corcoran, 1994a, 1994b; Fredman & Sherman, 1987; Grotevant & Carlson, 1989; Hersen & Bellack, 1988; Hudson, 1996c; Jacob & Tennenbaum, 1988; Kestenbaum & Williams, 1988; McCubbin & Thompson, 1987; McCubbin et al., 1996; Sawin & Harrigan, 1994; Touliatos, Perlmutter, & Straus, 1990; see the Appendix to Chapter 7 for a complete list of books on measurement).

Accessibility. The accessibility of a measure is also an important criterion. Some measures are difficult to obtain. For example, they might be expensive. They might not be available for use by some professionals (e.g., some measures are only available to psychologists with appropriate training). It might be difficult and time consuming to locate and obtain copies of the measures.

Again, fortunately, there are an increasing number of source books that describe a wide variety of different types of measures and in some cases even provide copies of the measures. We provide a list and brief description of these source books and a list of publishers who specialize in measurement in Chapter 7.

Relevance to Intervention Planning. The most basic reason for measuring client targets is to improve client outcomes. Accurate measurement is not an end in and of itself. The ultimate consideration in selecting a measure is how useful it will be to the success of the intervention. Therefore, the extent to which a measure increases the chances that a client problem will be resolved should be considered an important criterion for the selection and use of a measure. In the selection of a measure you might ask yourself the following questions to determine how a measure facilitates intervention decisions:

1. Does the measure help in deciding whether a client has a particular problem or the extent to which the problem exists?
2. Does the measure help in deciding what may be affecting or maintaining the problem?
3. Does the measure help in selecting the most effective intervention strategy?
4. Does the measure help in deciding whether a target is improving or deteriorating, so that any necessary modifications in the intervention plan can be undertaken?

In most cases a single measure won't meet all of these criteria, but a measure should meet at least one of these needs or its use in practice would be hard to justify.

SUMMARY

This chapter began by introducing you to the general notion of conceptualization and measurement. We argued that although all practitioners might not rely on measurement in a formal sense, all practitioners do engage in a wide variety of measurement-like activities. The question isn't whether you will rely on measurement in your practice, but whether you will rely on the best possible measurement strategies. Therefore, the bulk of this chapter focused on key characteristics of measures—principles that you can use as guidelines to select the best possible measures for your own practice. The following criteria were discussed: reliability, validity, directness, ease of use, accessibility, and relevance to intervention planning.

If you develop a measure, or if you, the client, or some other observer observes a client's behavior or the products of a client's behavior (e.g., an adolescent's completed homework assignments), it's important that you try to determine the reliability and validity of your measurements. There are several ways to do this:

1. Examine the interobserver reliability of your measure by obtaining observations from a second observer (if only on a random spot-check basis) and determine the degree of agreement between the two observers.

2. Examine the test-retest reliability (stability) of your measure by examining the pattern of baseline change over time for your measurements; a relatively flat baseline pattern suggests that the measure probably has reasonable test-retest reliability.

3. Examine the content validity of your measure by considering whether the questions or behaviors provide a sufficiently representative and comprehensive sample to measure the target.

4. Examine the concurrent-criterion validity of your measure if it's used as a simpler, quicker, or less expensive substitute for a more valid measure (e.g., student reports of completed homework assignments used as a substitute for teacher reports); you can do this by collecting some data using the more valid measure (if only on a random spot-check basis) and determining the degree of agreement between your measure and the criterion.

5. Examine the convergent validity of your measure by using two different methods to measure a particular target when it's feasible (if only on a random spot-check basis), and determine whether the two methods show approximately the same pattern of change over time.

6. Examine the discriminant validity of your measure, when two or more targets are measured, by determining whether measures of different targets show at least somewhat different patterns of change over time.

If you select an existing measure to evaluate your client you should critically examine the evidence of the reliability and validity of the measure. Figure 2.1 provides you with an overview of the possible information that you should look for to judge the adequacy of the measure, although given your purpose in using a measure it might not be necessary to have information on each of these different types of reliability and validity (e.g., alternate-forms reliability isn't necessary unless alternate forms are required; predictive validity isn't necessary unless you plan to use the measure to make predictions). In addition to considering the reliability and validity of the measure, you should consider whether the measure was tested with people who are similar to your client, and whether the measure is feasible for your use.

Using an existing measure with established reliability and validity can provide considerable confidence that a target is measured reliably and validly. However, even if you decide to use an existing measure with established reliability and validity, it's useful to examine how reliable and valid it is with your particular client. The reason this is useful is that the circumstances under which the reliability and validity of measures are typically determined is different in important ways from the way a measure is used in practice.

3 SPECIFYING PROBLEMS AND GOALS
Targets of Intervention

PURPOSE: This chapter presents guidelines on how to develop clear and specific targets of intervention. This process usually involves moving from a client's concerns, which often are described vaguely although deeply felt, to operationally defining problems, then objectives and goals. We use the term *target* to refer to these specifically defined objects of preventive or interventive services. We also discuss setting goals in groups, the use of statistics to set goals, and Goal Attainment Scaling as a method of establishing goals. ■

Introduction: From General Problems to Specific Targets of Intervention

Specifying Client Concerns: Identifying and Clarifying Problems and Potentials

Preliminary Steps in Identifying Targets

Survey Client Concerns: Starting Where the Client Is

Select a Target

Prioritize Targets

Guidelines for Going from the Vague to the Specific: Operational Definition of the Target of Intervention

Clarity

Countability

Verifying Sources

Dereify

Increasing and Decreasing

Measurability

Case Illustrations of Operationalized Targets

Specifying Goals and Objectives

Definition of Terms: Goals and Objectives

Components of Specific Goal Statements

Who?

Will Do What?

To What Extent?

Under What Conditions?

Using Statistics to Set Goals

Using Goal Attainment Scaling (GAS) to Establish Goals

Basic Guidelines for Using GAS

Collecting Information

Designation of Problem Areas

Predictions for Each Problem Area

Follow-Up "Interview"

Setting Goals in Groups

Problems and Issues in Setting Goals

Anticipate Negative Outcomes

Who Sets the Goals?

Anticipate Impediments

Case Illustrations of Goals in the Context of Problems and Interventions

Summary

INTRODUCTION: FROM GENERAL PROBLEMS TO SPECIFIC TARGETS OF INTERVENTION

There is a profound truth in the saying that "well defined is half solved" in that if we can clearly identify what our problem is, we have taken a major step toward its solution. This saying strongly applies to practice and the evaluation of practice because all forms of professional service begin with the questions: *What client problems need to be resolved and what goals need to be achieved?*

We don't mean to imply that specifying the problem is necessarily the most important aspect of practice, only that it is the essential beginning step. Obviously, if a practitioner did not have effective intervention skills, specifying problems from now until doomsday would be useless. But experience with many groups of students and practitioners inform us that the identification and clarification of client problems and goals are difficult because of the many ways one might try to get hold of these complex human events. Our purpose in this chapter is to help you identify specific targets of intervention from the sometimes confusing mass of client concerns. This specification will not only help practice; it will also facilitate the use of the evaluation methods we describe in this book.

We use the term *target* to refer to the specific object of preventive or interventive services that is relevant in a given situation. We have chosen this neutral term because there are several ways to think about what aspects of the client's life situation we want to influence. We will distinguish among client problems, goals, objectives, and targets. We also will discuss the process of operationalization. When you state problems or goals in specific, measurable terms, you are operationalizing a target of intervention. Operationalizing (or constructing an operational definition) means that you clearly specify the actions you would go through in order to observe or measure the client's problem.

Let's begin with an example. A client tells the practitioner that she "feels depressed all the time." She recognizes that some events in

her life are going to be difficult and resistive to change, but she would prefer not to be depressed so much of the time. Note that you can begin to identify a problem (the depressed feelings), and following from this, you can also tentatively identify a goal (her preference not to be so depressed, or expressed in the positive, to be happier than she currently is much of the time). Her problematic experience does not demonstrate the intensity of these feelings or under what circumstances they occur. Indeed, while the client keenly feels her depression, she is somewhat vague about its nature as well as what goals she would like to attain. The practitioner needs more specific information on which to formulate a target of intervention.

So you might operationalize this target of intervention by asking the client to take a standardized test that measures the extent and intensity of depression. Or you might unobtrusively record the number of times the client cries during the interview hour, where crying is seen as an indicator of depression. Or you might ask her to record in a log not only the times she feels depressed during the coming week, but also what events occurred before, during, and after the times she felt depressed. These and other ways to measure client problems are discussed in Chapters 5 through 9. The point here is that there are many ways to specify measurable operations that indicate the nature and extent of the target, in this case, depression. Which ones you select depend on the nature of the case, but they become the operational meanings of the term *depression* throughout the period of service.

It is difficult to deal with global problems, and practitioners may feel overwhelmed or frustrated in the attempt. Being clear and specific about the problems and goals lends itself to selection of both specific intervention procedures and specific measures related to these identified problems and goals. By repeating such measures, you can know explicitly what changes are occurring in the target, and adopt suitable responses. This chapter discusses how you can get to a reasonable, sensitive, and accurate specification of the problems on which you might be working in a particular case.

In suggesting that practitioners should be specific, we are not suggesting that you ignore complex problems or goals. Rather, we urge you to be as clear and precise as possible in specifying what those problems and goals are and in finding ways that they can be measured or observed. This may mean breaking down a complex problem into component parts if possible. As each component is changed, the entire complex of problems becomes modified.

Likewise, by encouraging the specification of problems, we do not suggest that meaning be sacrificed for rigor, for example, by setting up irrelevant or trivial goals merely because they are easy to measure. A goal that is irrelevant or trivial to the client's situation is equally unimportant to evaluate. Indeed, we believe that specifying problems and goals can be very relevant to practitioners and clients because it leads to more precise selection of intervention methods and related procedures, clearer evaluation of results, and, we hope, more effective services.

SPECIFYING CLIENT CONCERNS: IDENTIFYING AND CLARIFYING PROBLEMS AND POTENTIALS

In this section, we focus on client's problems and potentials that will ultimately be the target of our intervention. Our task will be to move from an area of concern felt by the client as problematic to a target on which client and practitioner can agree to work. This target may involve interventive action to decrease a given set of events, to build on strengths, or both. There is no one right way to do this; rather, keep your eye on the approach that we are proposing. It will serve you in a wide variety of contexts.

We again want to emphasize that when we discuss problems, we mean concerns and issues in the life of the client or client/system that can be turned into targets for intervention. That includes identifying strengths and potentials that can be built upon. In fact, we hope you will do everything possible to focus on the strengths of the client or system you are trying to help. This means several things: (1) accentuating the positive when selecting targets (e.g.,

focusing on regular school attendance rather than truancy so as not to emphasize or reinforce dysfunctional behavior); (2) looking at measuring strengths to be increased by your interventions rather than problems to be decreased; and (3) overall, it means identifying specific strengths in a person or situation as a focus for your measurement, intervention, and evaluation efforts. Thus, a high measurement priority is to look for the strengths in people in difficult situations and attempt to build on them rather than focusing on a person's weaknesses and limitations.

Preliminary Steps in Identifying Targets

There are several steps you might take in the process of specifying a problem. We will review these here, with the understanding that we are obviously not attempting to deal with the entire assessment phase of practice or even with all of the implications of early contacts with clients. We are only carving out a chunk of the process—identifying and specifying problems.

Survey Client Concerns: Starting Where the Client Is. The first step on the path toward specifying problems begins when you attempt to review all the matters of concern to the client, referring agency, and/or relevant others. This is not the assessment proper; rather, it is a preliminary survey of problems and a discussion with those concerned, involved, or affected about how they perceive these problems. We suggest making a written list of all the concerns, perhaps adding any that you yourself might observe.

It might be useful at this initial stage to use a checklist to help the client identify problems. The checklist is simply a preset list of problems that a client can check off if he or she has a concern about one or more of them. There are numerous checklists already available in the literature (see Brown & Brown, 1977, chap. 3; Cautela, 1977; Haynes & Wilson, 1979; Sundel & Sundel, 1975; and, for an example of a checklist administered by personal computer, see Fowler, Finkelstein, Penk, Bell, & Itzig, 1987). In addition, you or your agency may want to develop your own checklist for conducting a preliminary survey of client problems. There are several ways to do this. First, you could simply list many of the problems commonly seen in your agency and ask the client to check off whether he or she wants help with them (see Figures 3.1, 3.2, and 3.3 for abbreviated examples of such a form for clinical, consultative, and community work).

Another type of checklist—actually, one that could be combined with the above checklists—simply lists relevant others and asks the client to check those with whom he or she may have special concerns, as in the abbreviated example in Figure 3.4.

Finally, your initial problem survey form could simply consist of open spaces in which you ask the client to list the problems or people with whom they are having the most difficulty, as in Figure 3.5.

Remember, you are still doing a preliminary survey of problems, so at this point it is not necessary to go into too much detail about each concern. At the end of this part of the session go over the list with the client to ensure that it is complete.

Select a Target. Unless you are lucky enough to be meeting with an individual or group that has presented only one problem for

---

Name _____   Date _____

Yes   No   Do you want help with:

_____   _____   Managing your money?

_____   _____   Being less anxious?

_____   _____   Having more friends?

_____   _____   Feeling better about yourself?

_____   _____   Controlling your anger?

FIGURE 3.1   Example of problem checklist for clinical practice.

Name _____   Date _____

Yes   No   Do you want help with:

_____   _____   Understanding family dynamics?

_____   _____   Specifying the problems?

_____   _____   Developing an intervention plan?

_____   _____   Overcoming client resistance?

FIGURE 3.2   Example of problem checklist for use in consultation.

Name		Date
Yes	No	Does your organization need help with:
_____	_____	Increasing participation?
_____	_____	Getting new members?
_____	_____	Running meetings?
_____	_____	Securing funds?

FIGURE 3.3   Example of problem checklist for community work.

Name   Date

Put a check in front of any of the relationships that seem to bother you. Circle the checks for those which bother you the most.

_____ Mother	_____ Child	_____ Friend (same sex)
_____ Father	_____ Employer	_____ Friend (opposite sex)
_____ Spouse	_____ Co-Worker	_____ Neighbor

FIGURE 3.4   Example of checklist for problem relationships.

you to work on, it is likely that you will have to make some initial selections from among several concerns presented earlier by the client. The importance of this cannot be overstated. It has been our observation that one of the greatest roadblocks to effective practice is the failure of some practitioners to partialize problems–that is, to focus on one problem and attempt to be as specific as possible in defining it. Often problems are stated vaguely or globally, leaving the practitioner and client with a feeling of tremendous frustration as they attempt to manage a problem that, as the client defines it, is essentially unmanageable.

Although selecting a problem generally comes rather early in the overall assessment process, it is important to note that this is not the only place in the process where problem selection may go. This may be largely a matter of your personal preference, theoretical orientation, or approach to practice. Some practitioners prefer to select a problem after a more comprehensive assessment has been conducted on the grounds that only after the assessment has been completed can they make an intelligent judgment as to priorities. Other practitioners prefer to select a problem prior to the formal assessment process on the grounds that this problem selection then provides clear and specific guides regarding what to assess. Either way some selection and priority-determining process must be conducted. It's up to you to decide at what point you will engage in this activity.

Name _____   Date _____

Please list below the problems or people that most concern you. Try to give one or two specific examples of the problem for each.

Problem 1: _____

_____

Example: _____

_____

Problem 2: _____

_____

Example: _____

_____

FIGURE 3.5   Example of open problem list.

Essentially, problem selection involves two steps: (a) determining the priorities within the problem/situation (which we consider to be a preliminary step), and (b) specifying the problem per se, or moving from the vague to the specific, which will take up a large section of this chapter.

As we mentioned earlier, we view problems simply as areas about which the client is concerned. Thus, the "problem" may be something the client wants to decrease (e.g., an undesired behavior or lack of cooperation of community agencies) or an asset or strength that the client wants to build on or increase (e.g., a desired behavior or the number of community members participating in meetings). In some instances you may have the option of defining a concern from either viewpoint—a problem involving decreasing lack of support for an activity is also one involving increasing support. As a general strategy, we recommend focusing on strengths or assets when possible and attempting to increase or build on these strengths or assets, rather than trying to decrease deficits. There are three basic reasons

for this: (a) It is generally easier (and more effective) to build on strengths and increase behaviors than it is to decrease negative or undesired behaviors; (b) by focusing on increasing positive behaviors, you will be more likely to marshall support from the client and others, since trying to decrease negative behaviors often produces concomitant negative emotional reactions; and (c) philosophically, for the helping professions, it is more compatible with our values to take a strength or positive perspective than a problem or negative perspective.

Prioritize Targets.   The first step in selecting a problem or area of concern on which to work is to review the written list of concerns that you developed earlier with the client. The task then becomes one of negotiating with the concerned parties regarding what concern(s) to work on. The point here is not to select one concern only for the sake of selection, but to select one concern because this is the best way to marshall resources. If you and the client have the time, energy, and resources, more than one problem may be attacked at the same time. Whether in a clinical, organizational, or community context, we suggest that you attempt to negotiate to work first with the problem that meets as many of the following criteria as possible (Brager & Specht, 1973; Sundel & Sundel, 1975): (a) It is one that clients prefer to start with or about which they are most concerned; (b) it has the greatest likelihood of being changed; (c) it is relatively concrete and specific; (d) it can be readily worked with, given your resources; (e) it has the greatest chance of producing the most negative consequences if not handled; (f) it has to be handled before other problems can be tackled; and (g) changes in the problem will result in tangible, observable changes for those involved, thereby perhaps increasing the participants' motivation to work on other problems.

Once the problem (or problems) is selected, the next step is to define the problem as specifically as possible in terms that make it measurable and clearly susceptible to change. This topic is discussed in detail in the following section.

Guidelines for Going from the Vague to the Specific: Operational Definition of the Target of Intervention

In initial contacts with clients, practitioners often hear problems such as, "My son is immature"; "I don't know what to do with my life"; "My husband and I don't communicate"; "Something's wrong but I'm not sure what"; "I'm pretty shy." Very few clients spell out their specific problems precisely in clear, observable terms. Instead, most often people apply labels to themselves or others, talk about general characteristics, or simply use vague, hard-to-decipher terms.

The task of the practitioner in situations such as this is to help the client operationalize problems, that is, redefine them in more precise, measurable (observable) terms. This will aid in assessing the problem to see what factors may be affecting it. It will also help the client and practitioner have a clearer understanding of and agreement about the nature and occur-

rence of the problem so that they can take action on it and so that they will agree on what is to be changed. Furthermore, stating the problem in observable terms means the client and practitioner will be able to evaluate their progress. Thus, the problem becomes operationalized as the *target* of intervention.

Obviously all problems can't easily be concretely and succinctly specified, as though they occurred in a few minutes' time with a discrete beginning and end. Even so, use of this model will at least help you identify those situations, and also help clarify some of the conditions that may be affecting particular occurrences of the problem—for example, what antecedents may elicit it, what consequences may follow it.

There are a number of guidelines to use in stating problems more specifically and precisely in order to convert them into targets. We suggest you consider each of these as a way of thinking about how to add more precision to your definition of problems.

Clarity. Most clients have a great deal of difficulty being clear about describing the problem or about describing where, when, or how often it occurs. The job of the practitioner in these cases is to help translate vague or even inaccurate descriptions into specific and accurate ones.

Think of how often you've heard the terms *hostile, suspicious, immature, anxious, aggressive.* What do you do with those terms?

First, ask the client to give concrete examples of the occurrence of the problem. For example, if a teacher describes Jane as being immature, he or she may mean one or more of several things: She talks too much, she talks out of turn, she doesn't talk enough, she gets out of her seat without permission, she doesn't get out of her seat when asked to, she fights with other children, she doesn't fight back when attacked. Asking the client for concrete examples (e.g., "What does Jane do when she is acting immature?"), thereby operationalizing the problem, will give both the practitioner and the client a clearer idea of what the problem actually is.

Second, the practitioner can ask the client to try to identify when and where the problem occurs, perhaps to actually observe and record its occurrence. This can be done through a combination of simply trying to recall its occurrence, or better yet (because of its greater objectivity), through recording the problem using any of the measures described in subsequent chapters, or by asking the client to keep a log (see Chapter 8).

Third, you might consider doing a functional analysis of the relationship between the problem and personal, interpersonal, or environmental events that could be affecting (or controlling) the occurrence of the problem. We call this the *A-B-C* model. *A* refers to antecedents of the problem. Ask the client what happened just before the occurrence of the problem, who was there, and what he or she said and did. These antecedents could include the client's thoughts about the occurrence of some event; these thoughts might lead the client to perceive the event as positive or negative and could lead to the next step in the functional analysis.

B refers to the behavior or the actual occurrence of the problem. What actually happened? What did the client or others do or say that led to the definition of *B* as a problem? You and the client might even role-play the situation so that you would have a clearer picture of the problem.

C refers to consequences. Here you ask the client to identify what happened as a result of the occurrence of *B*. What did the client and others do or say? Were there environmental factors that could have reinforced the client for the occurrence of the problem so that its occurrence would actually be strengthened?

Not only will an *A-B-C* analysis help you clarify the problem, it may give you some preliminary ideas about intervention. For example, if certain circumstances (*A*) consistently elicit the problem (*B*), or consistently reinforce it (*C*), you will have some ideas that could direct you to make changes in those antecedents or consequences.

Countability. Gottman and Leiblum (1974, p. 53) state, "Anything that occurs, occurs with some frequency and can therefore be *counted.*" If you think of counting simply as checking over or keeping track of each occurrence of some problem, you'll see how this can be helpful in specifying problems. When you think in terms of counting, you will begin to start thinking in terms of how often does the problem occur, and for how long does it occur. Answers to questions such as these will provide specific referents for the problem, turning vague, global statements into specifics and helping you pinpoint the problem. The focus in counting is on what the client (or person or organization with which the client is concerned) actually does. The focus is on "how long," "how often," "what," and "when" issues rather than only on "why" issues which are generally interpretive, subjective, and/or difficult to answer.

This process helps to focus on specific occurrences rather than on generalizations or motives. The husband who complains that his wife doesn't care about what goes on around the house may really mean "She doesn't help with the dishes after dinner." The parent concerned that the child is not living up to his or her potential may really mean, "He doesn't accurately complete all his math homework."

Verifying Sources. One way of thinking about specification is to try to establish a *verifying source*–a way of knowing, when possible, that the problem does in fact exist, and a way for documenting when, where, and how often it occurs. This could mean asking the spouse to observe the client's behavior, using agency records to verify impressions with regard to service load, or using school records to document a child's attendance or grades. If there are no specific verifying sources available, think of the use of this guideline in this way: If there *were* people available who could act as verifying sources, would they be able to document the existence and occurrence of the problem? In other words, think of the problem in terms of the possibility of two or more people being able to agree on its occurrence. Although this is not possible for all problems (e.g., private thoughts), when it is possible and when agreement between client and practitioner is reached, you should have a more precise idea of the nature of the problem. If not, the problem may be too vaguely defined.

Dereify. One major impediment to defining problems in specific terms and with real-world referents is called *reification,* which refers to the treating of abstractions or constructs as though they were real things.

Any number of concepts that we commonly use to explain problems are examples of reification and often keep us from both specifying the problem and taking action on it. Consider the following examples (Hudson, 1976):

"Mrs. Johnson's problems arise from a deficient ego."

"Ethel hallucinates because she is psychotic."

"Julie became pregnant because she is promiscuous."

"John rocks back and forth because he is autistic."

"Bill abandoned his family because he is an inadequate father."

"Sam hit her because he is hostile."

"Marie socked her brother because she is aggressive."

In all of these examples problems were described and explained by labels (constructs) that actually did not have real-world referents. This suggests circular reasoning: Ethel hallucinates because she is psychotic and she is psychotic because she hallucinates. In none of the above examples could you actually intervene with the presumed explanation. On the other hand, you could intervene if you were to focus on the specific problem or behavior contained or implied in the statements.

There is a simple way to do this. If you are having difficulty specifying problems, check whether you are reifying them. See if you really are simply treating an abstraction as though it were an actual thing. If you are, then you really cannot take action on it. (How does one intervene with an abstraction?) And if you are, try this: Simply convert the abstraction into an adjective. Instead of saying, "Marie is aggressive," try something like, "Marie demonstrates aggressive *behaviors.*" Instead of saying, "Billy is immature," say, "Billy demonstrates immature *behaviors.*" The next step is to identify what those behaviors are and then to describe the situation in which the behavior occurs (Gottman & Leiblum, 1974). Then you will be on your way.

Increasing and Decreasing. One way for helping you specify problems is to think of them in terms of concerns to be increased or decreased. This is related to the idea that you would want to decrease undesired situations, while you would want to increase desired ones (i.e., build on strengths). Thinking of what needs to be increased and decreased almost automatically helps you pinpoint and specify problems. Such an orientation can help guide you toward being specific, because it requires answers to the questions: "What specific strength should we increase?" and "What specific problem should we decrease?" The more global or vague the problem definition, the more difficult it is to answer those questions. Defining problems in terms of increasing or decreasing them is also valuable as a guide to selection of intervention techniques, since a number of techniques have been developed and described in terms of their focus on increasing or decreasing behaviors, thoughts, or feelings (e.g., see Fischer, 1978b, chap. 9).

Measurability. Our final suggestion involves simply taking a perspective on how to think about problems. That is, begin to consider different ways a given problem can be, or has been, measured. When we discuss defining problems in observable or measurable terms (we use these words synonymously), we are not only speaking about overt behaviors. Many problems are simply not overt behaviors. But there has to be some way to keep track of the occurrence of the problem. Thus, one of the key guidelines to think about when helping clients define their problems is how these might be sensitively, but more or less objectively, measured including how other practitioners have measured them sensitively in the past. We emphasize that we want measures that are sensitive to the reality of the client's problems; never sacrifice meaning for the sake of measurement. But try to be as objective as possible under the circumstances. And we suggest you think of measurability in terms of the measurement ideas presented in Chapters 5 through 9.

For example, if Ben's problem is that he is feeling depressed because he and hundreds of his teaching colleagues were dismissed because state funds for education were reduced, then the measurement of those feelings of depression will be limited to what the client observes and reports. Yet there are, as we will describe in detail in the next five chapters, a number of ways that the problem can be measured. The client could count negative (depressive) thoughts (see Chapter 5), or more positively, he could count the nondepressed intervals between negative thoughts. (The interventive emphasis here then might be on expanding such nondepressed intervals, a positive-oriented target, as well as increasing reality-oriented efforts at reemployment.) Or, the practitioner might devise an individualized rating scale with the client to keep track of these nondepressed intervals (see Chapter 6). Or there are standardized measures to help Ben and his practitioner keep an accurate track of the extent and nature of Ben's depressed feelings (see Chapter 7). Or a client log could be kept to indicate where the nondepressed (and the depressed) behaviors occur; when they occur most frequently (or least frequently); how often they occur on a given day; who is present when they occur; and what happens just before, during, and after the nondepressed (and the depressed) intervals occur (see Chapter 8). This set of questions represents the kinds of issues that measurability seeks to identify.

Case Illustrations of Operationalized Targets

In this section, we present some operational definitions of problems that some students and practitioners have selected for their cases. Along the way, we suggest some variations in how these targets might have been operationalized for different kinds of contexts. The point of this section is to present some real examples of targets–operationalized problems on which client and practitioner could work.

Angelica (a second-year graduate social work student) had a practicum at a senior citizen center, where a problem emerged regarding serving the noon meal. Volunteers were only too happy to get trays of food for older persons who came in for lunch, but the agency staff thought this fostered an unhealthy dependence, since most of these diners could get the trays themselves. Also, the seniors complained of long waits in line. Therefore, the intervention involved calling a table at a time to come through the lunch line. (Volunteers helped those who truly couldn't manage for themselves.) The first operationalized target constituted the numbers of elderly persons who went through the lines themselves on a given day, compared to the number of able elderly persons. Two weeks before intervention, the nutritionist for the agency counted the number of elderly persons who carried their own trays. She continued to do this during the intervention period. The second target was the satisfaction level of the participants in the luncheon program. This was measured once a week by a short survey of the elderly as they were leaving the dining area: (a) How was the food today? ("very good," "good," "adequate," "not so good," "poor"). (b) Was waiting in line for food a problem today? (ranging from "yes, very much," through three steps to "no, not at all"). (c) Did you enjoy being with your friends today during lunch? ("yes, very much," through three steps to "no, not at all"). The proportion of satisfied customers (the average of "satisfied" responses on the three questions for each individual summed over all lunch eaters) was noted on the charts before and during the intervention period.

Barbara (an undergraduate social work student) was working with the parents of a severely developmentally disabled child who were frustrated at his inability to get dressed and ready for school on time. The problem of dressing correctly was operationalized to mean putting on in the correct order all of the clothes the parents had laid out the night before in a line on the bedroom floor. The parents were simply to observe their child and note the number of clothes not put on or put on in the wrong order, and record this on a chart each day. The second problem, the parents' frustration, was operationalized by the number of times either of them yelled at their son in the morning regarding his being on time for the school bus. This too was recorded by both parents independently (to determine interrater reliability); the data were brought in to the practitioner once a week when they met to discuss the problems. (The parents could also have kept a diary of their feelings of frustration, but this may have required more cooperation than the parents were thought to be willing to give.)

Francis was a counselor at an alcoholic recovery center run by the city. A young man was referred to this center for his alcohol abuse problems that were combined with his abusive behavior toward his girlfriend. When he was sober, he was not abusive toward her, but sometimes, when he had too much to drink, she reported that he exhibited behaviors that she found very unpleasant to the point where she tried to break up with him. At that time, although sober, he was very upset and became abusive. She called the police and events escalated to the point where he was placed under court order to stay away from her, and to go through the alcohol control program at this center on a daily basis for 6 weeks.

The counselor saw need for several measures (operational definitions). First, on his drinking, she obtained his self-report. This was not considered to be a completely satisfactory indicator of his true behavior, so he was required to take a breathalyzer test each time he came to the session. Note that these two measures of alcohol use serve several functions; the breathalyzer is taken as the most nearly objective measure of alcohol in his blood, while the self-report is taken partly at least as an indicator of validity in reporting his own behavior. Eventually, the daily breathalyzer test will be stopped, while the self-reports will be continued; there will be random breathalyzer tests to ascertain his continued valid reporting. This is also an example of how the criterion validity of self-reported alcohol use could be examined, as described in Chapter 2.

The counselor also was concerned about the abusive behavior, but since the client was ordered to stay away from his former girlfriend, the counselor decided to measure the client's thoughts about abusing her. The measure was a list of questions that the client answered before

the session at the alcohol center. It asked whether he had thought about his girlfriend in the time since the last session and, if so, whether he thought about being abusive toward her. (This report was confirmed indirectly by analysis of the content of the therapeutic session in which the client's feelings were discussed in several different ways. The therapeutic discussion was seen as the best available indicator of the validity of the client's self-reports.)

George was a graduate student in a research class and kept records on himself as client. He admitted being very anxious about being in a research class, so much so that he thought it interfered with his doing his schoolwork effectively. He decided to operationalize anxiety by a self-anchored scale that ran from "bouncing butterflies in stomach, very uncomfortable feelings about self as adequate student in research class," to "fluttering butterflies in stomach, somewhat uncomfortable about self as adequate student in research class," to "no butterflies in stomach, feeling reasonably comfortable with self as adequate research student." He also turned in weekly homework, and recorded his grades as a measure of his actual competence at a given research assignment. (This student did very well in class, partly, he noted, because he was watching not only his level of anxiety, but also his grades at corresponding times. He learned that his anxiety was generally in excess of his actual quality of work in class.)

Irene was a practitioner in a rural mental health agency. Her task was to document that the special bus service for the elderly was working adequately to maintain the service. What "adequate" meant became something of a political football because the county administrators who made this decision were never able to give her an exact figure of the minimum needed to continue the service. Irene reviewed the bus censuses for the past few years and estimated that at least 40 customers a week would be necessary because, when fewer took the special buses, there were complaints from the administrators. Thus, 40 customers a week became the operational definition of "adequate." Then it was a simple matter to try some interventions, such as information campaigns, to get at least that minimum number. She was able to increase ridership, and apparently 40 was about the right number, since the county administrators voted to sustain the bus service another year.

Jack is a social work student who interned at a hospital for the mentally ill. Within a few days of his arrival, several residents at the hospital died, and there was a pervasive sadness in the facility. Jack wondered how this chance event affected the other residents so he developed a small evaluation project, which he cleared with the appropriate staff. He did some checking into the literature and found a standardized scale designed to measure a respondent's anxiety about death (Lonetto & Templer, 1983, as cited in Corcoran & Fischer, 1987, pp. 141–142). He found that this scale had norms for psychiatric patients as well as "normal" adults, so he could compare his results against those of known groups. He also noted that the reliability of this instrument was good (a 3-week test-retest correlation of .83), and that validity was fair (correlating .74 with the Fear of Death Scale, another well-studied instrument). He compared a sample of older residents with a group of patients who were admitted after the rash of deaths, and found marked differences–the older residents were more anxious than the newly admitted residents. This led the hospital staff to intensify discussions of death with older residents rather than ignoring the unpleasant subject.

These examples can be multiplied in great numbers, but they all share some basic characteristics in how they operationalized the problem: First, whatever measures were used had to reflect a commonsense view on the nature of that problem. That is, all of these measures were indicators of the problem, and to be successful, they had to be as close as possible to the problem without being burdensome for anyone to use.

Second, the measures involved thoughts, feelings, and actions of individuals, as well as collective actions of groups or clusters of people. When there was any reasonable doubt, the practitioner attempted to verify both the validity of the measure and its reliability or consistency. It would make no sense to measure

something if what was measured and how it was measured were in doubt.

Third, as we see in greater detail in Chapters 5 through 10, these practitioners had to be careful about whom they asked to collect the data. Sometimes they did it themselves, but more often they involved the clients or others in the situation. Some data had to be collected by the client, as no other person could accurately report about feeling states, for example. But other times, there were options on who could do the measuring, and the choice was made on the basis of available resources and the willingness of participants.

Fourth, no miracles were performed in selecting these measures, and most were reasonable, homemade varieties. Of course, already available standardized measures will sometimes fit the measurement needs of a case, as we illustrated. But the point of this section is to emphasize that every practitioner can come up with some reasonable and innovative measures customized to the situation at hand. It does take thought, but this is the same type of thinking that goes into the overall assessment of case problems and goals.

SPECIFYING GOALS AND OBJECTIVES

Goals usually emerge from discussions about client problems, but it is important to keep these two ideas distinct. Problems involve what currently hurts or disturbs the client; goals are preferences about the future. Goals indicate what the client would prefer to happen, to do, or to be, when the intervention is completed.

Goals specify what kinds of changes are desired and, thus, in what direction the intervention should move. Perhaps most importantly, goals provide the standard or frame of reference for evaluating whether the client is moving, and whether the destination is met. Thus, goals provide the opportunity for ongoing feedback during the process of intervention, as well as the reference point for deciding whether the end has been attained.

Unfortunately, goals are frequently stated in abstract or vague terms, what Mager (1972) calls *fuzzies.* They may point in the direction of the desired outcomes, but they don't tell us "how to know one when you see one." Here are some familiar fuzzies: "to communicate clearly within the family," "to develop an awareness of oneself," "to feel a sense of accomplishment in one's activities," and so on. These are all perhaps desirable characteristics, but we really can't tell when they have been accomplished. Thus, we need to clarify how goals can be used in evaluating practice.

Definition of Terms: Goals and Objectives

Previously, we briefly defined *goals* as statements about what the client and relevant others (family, peers, friends, the practitioner) would like to happen, or to do, or to be when the intervention is completed. This definition of goals is taken in the sense of an ultimate end of action, against which the results of the intervention are to be compared. Thus, we could view these as *ultimate goals,* or goals related to ultimate *outcomes* for the *client* (Rosen, 1993).

Most of the time, though, it is not possible to go directly from a problem to the ultimate goal. Rather, it is necessary to move first through a sequence of manageable steps or subgoals. Rather than moving from *A* to *Z*, we move from *A* to *B* to *C* and so on. We use the terms *intermediate goals, objectives,* or *outcome objectives,* to refer to these subgoals or intermediate goals. Outcome objectives simply are limited or intermediate versions of the ultimate goal and are defined in exactly the same terms as goals. For example, a goal might be to increase the initiation of communication by 50% over a period of 2 months, while the objective might be to increase the initiation of communication by 25% over a 1-month period. Also, it should be clear that goals and objectives are relative terms. What may be an objective for one client may be a goal for another.

In accord with the vast bulk of literature, when we use the terms *objectives* or *goals,* we are referring to outcomes for the *client* rather than interventive activities or tasks in which you as practitioner will be engaged. That is, all goal and objective statements refer to client or client/system attainments; interventive tasks, activities, and steps can be specified in a separate statement.

An important guideline in goal selection is that you should have some logical reason to expect that the intervention will have an effect on the selected targets. For example, if knowledge of child injury risk is selected as a target for a child welfare client (e.g., Jacobs, 1989), there should be some reason to believe that your intervention will increase this knowledge. It is not very efficient to measure something that isn't really the focus of, or is unlikely to change due to, your intervention efforts. More important though, targets that aren't the focus of an intervention will not be valid indicators of the effectiveness of that intervention, and so they can give a misleading impression of the effectiveness of the intervention. In particular, a target that isn't the focus of an intervention is unlikely to improve in response to that intervention, and this can give the misleading impression that the intervention is ineffective.

The remainder of this chapter focuses on how to establish specific client objectives and goals. We first describe the components of specific goal statements and then briefly discuss how to use statistics and other procedures such as Goal Attainment Scaling to establish goals. The chapter concludes with a review of some of the problems and issues involved in goal setting.

We should point out here that, as with selection of problems, there may be a number of different points in the assessment/intervention process at which you would logically establish goals. Some practitioners do this early in their contacts with the client, especially when the goals are reasonably clear, and then keep their assessment focused on the specific area of the goal statement. Other practitioners prefer to wait until after the assessment and baselining periods are completed in order to have more precise information about the factors affecting the problem (and, hence, the goal).

By placing "goals" in the same chapter as "problems," we do not mean that selecting goals is necessarily the next step in the process. What we are suggesting though is that goals are directly related to the problem and should reflect that relationship.

We also recognize that setting goals can be a more complicated process than what we describe here. There can be numerous pressures and points of view intruding on the goal-setting process, such as the client's, the practitioner's, the agency's, and, in some cases such as mandated service, the community's. We will discuss this later in this chapter in the section on "Problems and Issues." For now, we would mainly like to emphasize the idea that it is part of the role of the practitioner to balance these different pressures in a way that makes the most sense in any given situation and in a way that will enhance services and outcomes for the client.

Components of Specific Goal Statements

With many clients you probably will be able to arrive at some general or global goal statement relatively easily. For example, the program administrator may want to make his agency more effective, the woman may want her husband to be more sexually responsive, the father may want his son to be less obnoxious. The first step with general statements such as these is to specify just what the problem is. Once that is accomplished, the practitioner's task is to develop some clear and specific outcome objectives and goals that can serve to guide the rest of the intervention process.

Such goals and objectives should have at least four components (Gottman & Leiblum, 1974; Brown & Brown, 1977). They should specify *who, will do what, to what extent,* and *under what conditions.* Try to develop specific outcome goals for each problem encountered. Thus, you may need multiple goals for one general problem area. For example, school problems could lead to specific goals in relation to studying, attendance, peers, or relationships with teachers. Each would contain all four of the following components.

Who? Objectives and goals should be stated in terms of intermediate and ultimate outcomes for the *client.* One problem we sometimes run into is goals stated in terms of what the *practitioner* will do. These are not appropri-

ate as outcome goals. However, the practitioner's procedural steps may be appropriate intervention methods–that is, what the practitioner hopes to do or establish in order to facilitate outcome. At the least the practitioner should be able to distinguish between procedural interventive steps and outcome goals and be aware that outcome goals should be stated in terms of what the client will do or be like when intervention is completed. That is, it would not be an appropriate goal statement to say, "I will provide supportive therapy to decrease the client's depression." Decreasing the depression might be an excellent goal, but providing therapy designed to decrease a component of the depression is part of the intervention plan, not the goal for the client.

Will Do What? A most important part of establishing goals is to attempt to state them in performance terms (Mager, 1972; Brown & Brown, 1977). In other words, attempt to state what clients actually will be *doing* to show that they have achieved the goal.

The key point here is that this performance should be stated in measurable terms. If the goal cannot be observed in some way–whether by counting the actual behaviors involved or by use of a scale or other instrument–then it will be impossible to evaluate the success of the intervention, that is, whether the goal was achieved.

Again, when we talk about "measurable performance," we are not saying all performances must be overt behaviors. Some "performances" are overt, and some are covert (e.g., cognitive activities, such as remembering the names of acquaintances at the senior citizen center).

It may be best to think in terms of *indicators* when trying to decide whether a goal involves a performance or an abstraction. As discussed in Chapter 2, an indicator refers to the idea that you have some *direct way* that will indicate the presence of the alleged performance (Mager, 1972). This direct way then becomes the key measurement indicator and could involve actual observation of an overt behavior, a score on a standardized test, or a self-report on an individualized rating scale.

It might be helpful once again to think in terms of increasing or decreasing the targeted problem. This might give you a handle on stating the goal in terms of what the client will be doing (or thinking or feeling), linking interventions with this goal, and suggesting ways of measuring outcome. For example, a client believes that she is a poor socializer, and has not been able to meet eligible men. Her goal is to become a reasonable socializer to increase the possibility of finding an appropriate mate. The phrase *reasonable socializer* is her own term, so the practitioner requested that she provide some indicators of when she would feel she is a reasonable socializer. She worked out with the practitioner several indicators: when she would be able to initiate a conversation with a stranger, sustain it for at least 10 minutes, and then terminate it with the possibility of continuing at some later time. These specifications of the phrase *reasonable socializer* helped the practitioner formulate some interventions directed at initiating, sustaining, and terminating conversations. The measurement of these indicators included the client's self-report of social activities at parties, whether she initiated conversations with strangers, how long they lasted, and whether she defined these relationships as ones in which she could reinitiate conversations later. The set of these three actions formed an operational definition of "reasonable socializer." Even though these indicators are very subjective, they are clearly reportable, if the client is willing and able to provide the information.

Try to state your goals in positive rather than negative terms. This gives the client a positive mind-set, identifying a goal in terms of something attainable so that each step forward is itself reinforcing the client's constructive efforts. This point is especially important for clients with problems that are socially disapproved, such as child abuse, alcohol abuse, drug abuse, and so on. Instead of asking how many times the parent hit the child, or how many drinks a person had that day, you might ask, How many minutes did you and your child spend together having fun today? or, How many times did you call an AA buddy when you felt the urge to take a drink? Mea-

sured objectives such as these clearly reinforce some possible interventive plans while at the same time obtain useful information measuring process and outcome.

To What Extent?   The purpose here is to attempt to establish how well and how often the target event occurs. In other words, you will want to establish a level of performance—called a criterion level—that will be acceptable (Brown & Brown, 1977; Gottman & Leiblum, 1974). Without this you may never know whether the goal was achieved to anyone's satisfaction. For example, the criterion level might be to lose 30 pounds, to answer 80% of the questions successfully, or to maintain a conversation with your spouse for 15 minutes.

This is one place where taking a baseline is particularly important. The baseline establishes the level of occurrence of the target event prior to intervention and is used for comparison with changes in the target during the intervention program. The criterion level or desired level of performance can be set in comparison with the baseline level. Or it can be set in terms of some other standard, for example, weight within a "normal" range, a passing test score, and so on.

It is here, too, that the notion of outcome objectives (subgoals or intermediate outcomes) is probably most important. The key question regarding criterion level is, Can the client achieve the goal (do the activity, perform the behavior, and so forth)? In evaluating this it is important to set interim objectives that the client will be able to achieve. Make sure the first objective is realistically achievable. If you err, err on the side of setting the first objectives too low rather than too high. Achievement of these objectives will then serve as additional reinforcement or motivation for continuing on to the next step. Indeed, under most circumstances, the objective will be defined as exactly the same as the goal, but in smaller quantities.

For example, if the ultimate goal is the one in the example above involving a young woman's social skills and her engaging in conversation with a man, the first objective might be to say hello to a man in passing, the next to ask a man for directions, and so on for progressively increasing periods of time. Or, if the ultimate goal is to score 30 on a depression scale where higher scores mean more depression, the objective for the second week might be to score 75 (reduced from 90 at baseline) and the objective for the fourth week might be to score 50.

These objectives or intermediate outcomes should be set in ways that are as close to achieving the goal as possible but that are comfortable and realistic for the client (Gambrill, 1977). Furthermore, all of the objectives do not have to be set in advance at the same time, since success or failure in achieving one objective can provide information on what the next objective should be.

Under What Conditions? The fourth component of goal setting is to specify the conditions and situations under which the desired behavior or activities will occur. You may find that the desired behavior will occur (or should occur) only in specific situations (e.g., at school, but not at home). You should try to set up as clearly as possible under what occasions it *should* occur. If it does not occur in all the desired situations, then you can make its occurrence in other situations intermediate objectives to the final goal of occurrence in all relevant situations. Thus, an ultimate goal (outcome) might be for arguing to be eliminated under all circumstances, and the intermediate objectives might be for arguing to be decreased or eliminated in a sequential way in each setting in which it occurred.

When you are thinking about conditions for the behavior to occur, consider at least the following three: Where would it occur, when should it occur, and with whom? This specificity will greatly aid in developing clear and achievable goals.

Using Statistics to Set Goals

One of the frustrating choices for a practitioner intent on being specific in setting goals is deciding where to set the criterion for success. It's generally a good idea, when possible, to be precise in identifying what you are shooting for in terms of an actual target. Sometimes this is easy.

For example, in a weight-loss program, you can pretty much aim at losing a specific number of pounds. In other situations you might know exactly what you're after (having 20% of the community attend each meeting, no wetting of the bed at night, ability to maintain an erection for at least 5 minutes during intercourse, etc.). If you are using standardized measures, some actually have a cutoff or "cutting point," so that when the score gets to that point, in comparison with other people who have taken the test (norms), you have some degree of assurance that the problem has diminished.

In all of the above situations it would be possible to select a specific goal with a specific criterion level (lose 15 pounds, 0 wet nights, score of 30 or less on a questionnaire).

But sometimes this isn't so easy. In many situations it's very difficult to go beyond saying, "I want to increase participation" or "I want to decrease her depression" or "I want to see that they 'communicate more.'" What recourse do you have for being more specific under these circumstances?

In these situations we recommend the use of statistics. Now don't panic. We don't mean anything horrendous or complicated. In Part IV we provide you with some simple procedures for analyzing your data to see if a change is statistically significant—that is, if there is a mathematical difference between the preintervention data and the intervention data. Our point in this chapter is simply to inform you about this possibility, and to explain what it means with regard to goals.

When we say that these statistical procedures can help you set goals, we mean something quite specific. Goal setting is usually done in the context of client and societal values or physical realities. For example, you may not be allowed to keep your child if you exceed some social standards for permissible disciplinary actions, and you won't be allowed to become a pilot if your vision isn't good enough.

However, sometimes there are no natural markers and social values are not clear—for example, how many arguments between spouses are "too many?" What intensity of feeling between two intimates constitutes "love?" What level of morale must exist for the agency to have a "good working environment?" The practitioner has to make decisions based on the events in the situation even when social values are not clear.

Statistics provide one way of making decisions. In effect, we connect a statistical difference (such as change in the intervention period of some amount from that in the baseline period) with a practical or social difference, that the (desired) change could not have happened by chance alone and therefore we should pay attention to changes of this magnitude.

We are not saying that the amount of difference between baseline and intervention that is in the desired direction is the value we wish to achieve per se, only that this clearly definable change is in the right direction and, let us assume, could not have happened by chance alone. Whether it is a meaningful change in the everyday world when no other norms or rules are available is another question, calling for feedback from participants. For example, if the spouses mentioned above argue only half as much as they used to before intervention, is this meaningful? So statistics provide only a partial handle to hold when other methods come up short.

Here's the way the statistics we describe in Part IV can be used to establish goals. With some statistics you can compute just from the baseline data how much change would have to take place in order for the change to be statistically significant. With these procedures, you use the baseline information to set a level for the intervention phase at which the change will be statistically significant. Then when you get data from the intervention phase of your program, you just plot it on your chart and see whether it is significant. (There are simple procedures for doing this, some not much more complicated than drawing a line.) If the data do reach significance, you can conclude that your goal has been met. Thus, you would set a goal at baseline of achieving a statistically significant change in the target.

We realize that there is more to life than statistical significance, and that the practical significance of the change can be much more important. (We discuss this in detail in Part IV.) But as a shorthand guide, you might want to use statistics to establish goals. Examples of such goals might be a statistically significant increase in participation or a statistically significant decrease in depression score. This would minimize the problem of having to use some arbitrary goal-setting procedure.

USING GOAL ATTAINMENT SCALING (GAS) TO ESTABLISH GOALS

One very widely used method for establishing and tracking goals is called Goal Attainment Scaling. Goal Attainment Scaling (GAS) is a system devised by Kiresuk and Sherman (1968) to assist in goal definition and goal measurement. GAS was originally developed as an assessment approach for individual clients. Since its inception, however, it has been applied to goal-setting activities not only for individuals but for organizations as well in a broad range of human service agencies (Beidel, 1988; Kagle, 1991; Kiresuk & Garwick, 1979; Kiresuk et al., 1993). The approach has been used by members of many of the helping professions including psychologists, social workers, counselors, psychiatrists, and nurses.

The basic GAS procedures involve identifying client problems, assigning individualized weights to those problems, estimating the client's expected outcome (the "goals") for each problem area, obtaining follow-up scores on actual outcomes for each problem area, and averaging outcomes across all problems for each client or all clients within a given program.

The following sections attempt only to highlight the basic procedural guides for using GAS to supplement the previous material and as a way of helping you specify goals. More detailed information addressing issues and problems for each of the steps is available in the references, and a comprehensive review of research on the GAS, including reliability, validity, and other issues, is available in Mintz and Kiesler (1982).

Basic Guidelines for Using GAS

Four basic steps for GAS have been described by Kiresuk and Garwick (1979): (a) collection of information about the person or organization for which goals will be scaled, (b) designation of the major areas where changes would be feasible and helpful, (c) development of specific predictions for a series of outcome levels for each major area, and (d) scoring of outcomes at follow-up.

Collecting Information. This step of the process varies by practitioner, setting, and type of problem with which you may be working. Standard sources of assessment information are used (GAS does not prescribe any specific methodologies), including interviews, direct observation, questionnaires, reports from those in the environment, and/or any methods of data collection prescribed by a particular agency.

Designation of Problem Areas. Once assessment data are collected, the GAS format suggests you break these down into a series of "problem areas." Using the methods for specifying problems described in this chapter, you would identify those positive areas or strengths that should be increased and those undesired areas that should be decreased. All of the problems are listed and priorities set along the lines described earlier.

Your agency may wish to specify in advance a list of problem areas. For example, Benedict (1978) lists some 21 problem areas appropriate for a family service agency. Some of these are interpersonal conflicts, reactive emotional distress, problem solving, problems of role transition, human sexuality, child rearing/child care, and so on. Each of these is described and then examples are provided of possible specific program goals. For example, for reactive emotional distress, a specific measure might be number of days per week client reports having no thoughts fearing end of marriage; for problem solving, percentage of mutually agreed upon decisions that client takes some actions on; for problems in role transition, number of times that mother does not "hassle" daughter for spending time with friends on weekend.

For each problem area, a continuum or scale of behaviors is developed. This scale is placed on a form called the Goal Attainment Follow-Up Guide in which each vertical scale represents a scale of outcomes related to a problem area for a client (Kiresuk & Garwick, 1979). Figure 3.6 presents a blank Goal Attainment Follow-Up Guide. Room also could be left at the bottom of the page for comments on verifying sources (who would verify reports of success), time limits, presenting problems, and intervention plan.

Any number of scales or problems can be used. Each problem area is given a title, which may be relatively general (e.g., "employment"). The problem can then be described in more specific but brief terms under the title at the top of each scale. However, the remainder of the information on each scale should be as specific and objective as possible.

Since the client's problems have been prioritized, it is possible also to weight each one in the space next to the title (weight$_1$=___). Any one- or two-digit number can be used here, with a higher number indicating a more significant problem. It is sometimes helpful to imagine a scale of 1 to 20, with 20 being the most significant. Without the weights, each scale or problem is seen as equally relevant.

Predictions for Each Problem Area. The GAS framework is intended to operate within a time limit. Thus, a specific follow-up point (which can be determined for each case and in accord with agency standards) should be set for each scale or problem area. Then, a series of predictions is made for each scale. These predictions actually are the goals for each scale. For each scale, it is likely that a number of variables are applicable as indicators of change. The purpose here is to select the one that is most desirable to be used as a measure—it is most directly representative of the problem, easy to measure, and its measurements can be reliable. Any of the measures described in this book can be selected for this variable—for example, a specific behavior or scores on a scale.

As should be clear, for each one of these variables, a range of outcomes is possible—from very negative to very positive. The goal here is to try to make predictions about this variable in line with the statements along the left edge of the Follow-Up Guide. Thus, each variable, or goal, is described according to "the most favorable outcome likely," "more than expected level of outcome," "expected level of

Goal Attainment Follow-Up Guide					
	Scale Headings and Scale Weights				
Levels of Predicted Attainments	**Scale 1:**_____ (weight$_1$ =)	**Scale 2:**_____ (weight$_2$ =)	**Scale 3:**_____ (weight$_3$ =)	**Scale 4:**_____ (weight$_4$ =)	**Scale 5:**_____ (weight$_5$ =)
Most unfavorable outcome thought likely					
Less than expected success					
Expected level of success					
More than expected success					
Most favorable outcome thought likely					

FIGURE 3.6   Basic goal attainment follow-up guide.

outcome," "less than expected level of outcome" to "the most unfavorable outcome thought likely." Figure 3.7 presents a completely filled-in Goal Attainment Follow-Up Guide with weights on a scale from 1 to 20.

The most important point on the scale is the midpoint or "expected level." This is intended to be the most realistic prediction of outcome based on the expected date at which that goal can be reached. This is the part of the scale that is developed first, since it is the "most likely" outcome. The other outcome levels are developed after the expected level.

This part of the process–ranging from operationalizing the problem to making predictions– is really the trickiest part of using GAS, although with experience at doing this for each case or situation, most practitioners can become rather adept. Kiresuk and Garwick (1979) suggest that with practice, the guide can be constructed in 15 to 30 minutes.

The operationalized variables that make up each of the scales have potential for use in single-system evaluation. That is, since each of the problem areas is supposed to be opera-

tionalized according to specific, observable measures, one or more of these can be used to collect data for a baseline, placed on a chart, and used for regular feedback to help guide your intervention. Thus, GAS can be used as a context to help establish goal statements, and the results of the repeated collections of data on the target problem can be used for regular monitoring, between the point when the guide is constructed and the follow-up actually conducted.

Follow-Up "Interview."   The last part of the process is the evaluation of outcome. This can be done by the practitioner with the client, by other agency staff members, or by others in the environment. Since the expected length of intervention is preset, this part of the process should come as no surprise to anyone involved. However, since this evaluation may involve an interview by someone unfamiliar with the case or by someone very involved with the case, care should be taken to train the interviewer to do whatever is possible to avoid overly subjective or biased evaluations.

Goal Attainment Follow-Up Guide					
	Scale Headings and Scale Weights				
Levels of Predicted Attainments	**Scale 1: School Attendance** (weight$_1$ = 20)	**Scale 2: Anxiety; Scores on S-A Scale** (weight$_2$ = 12)	**Scale 3: Self-Esteem Scores on Scale** (weight$_3$ = 10)	**Scale 4: Family Agreements** (weight$_4$ = 15)	**Scale 5: Suicide** (weight$_5$ = 20)
Most unfavorable outcome thought likely	0%	Daily average rating of 9 on 9 point scale	Weekly score of 80–100 on 100 point scale	0 agreements	Client commits suicide
Less than expected success	25%	Average rating of 7 or 8	Score of 70–79	1 agreement	Client acts on at least 1 suicidal impulse
Expected level of success	50%	Average rating of 5 or 6	Score of 51–69	2–3 agreements	Client has suicidal ideas 3 or more times per day
More than expected success	75%	Average rating of 3 or 4	Score of 31–50	4 agreements	Client has suicidal ideas 1 or 2 times per day
Most favorable outcome thought likely	100%	Average rating of 1 or 2	Weekly score of 30 or below (clinical cutting point)	5 or more family agreements	Client has no suicidal ideation

FIGURE 3.7   Basic goal attainment follow-up guide as illustrated by an adolescent client at a family service agency.

To record the level of success achieved, a check or an asterisk can be inserted in the appropriate box of the follow-up guide. For example, if the "expected level of success" is achieved on a self-esteem scale, a check mark can be placed in that square on the scale.

It is here that the use of single-system designs and other procedures can have important cross-validating purposes. That is, you will have a built-in check on the results obtained on your Goal Attainment Follow-Up Guide. In fact, if the problem areas are broken down into more or less objective, or highly specific, variables, outcome will be relatively easy to determine and distortion kept to a minimum.

One of the problems with GAS is it contains no built-in systems for regular feedback, a serious potential problem if GAS is to be used with single-system designs (see Seaberg & Gillespie, 1977, for a comprehensive critique of GAS). Thus, although few practitioners would wait until the "follow-up interview" to secure feedback, GAS does not present an organized framework for collecting such data. Thus, the use of repeated measures on at least one of the target problems, in a single-system design fashion, will provide ongoing feedback as to whether the problem is indeed changing.

SETTING GOALS IN GROUPS

Throughout this book, we allude to the fact that many practitioners use single-system designs with groups; indeed, we try to illustrate these designs with individuals, groups, families, neighborhoods, work organizations, and even larger communities. The underlying principles are the same for any client/system but experience has taught us that we must provide some additional observations on using these evaluation designs with groups for both conceptual and procedural reasons.

It is difficult to identify and operationalize goals for any client, but when group goals are at stake, it seems to be even more difficult. This may be because fewer practitioners have been trained to think about groups as groups, or about the problems or objectives of groups, whether formally or informally organized. Even when some group-level objective can be conceived of, there may be additional problems in operationalizing it because the actions of several people are involved all at once.

These are real difficulties, but they are manageable to some degree. The following discussion pulls together some of the thinking and research from the literature on establishing goals and objectives with groups.

First, we should distinguish true group problems and objectives from the individual problems and objectives of people who may be seen in groups. A true group problem might include a divorcing family when the legal action of divorce will affect each member of the group as roles are changed within that family. It would also affect each person's feelings, thoughts, and actions. But as a family group, there would be targets reflecting the set of interrelationships of "the family," in addition to targets reflecting the feelings of the husband and the wife, as well as of any children. "Staying married" would be one such collective target; "number of arguments between spouses," "amount of free time spent in satisfying family activities," "proportion of assigned chores completed by each member of the household" could be others. There is nothing mysterious about these group (or family) factors; they are natural to the family in the sense that they are part of ordinary family life and functioning. Some set of such factors would constitute "family life," and their breakdown might indicate the nature and extent of problems that had to be dealt with in considering divorce counseling.

Other types of groups, such as family life education groups, disseminate information and render skills training. Each participant in a family life education meeting might have his or her own objectives, and the distance they progress might also be measured. As a group, it would be possible to take the average score from some standardized scale administered to all the participants. These are somewhat arbitrary choices the practitioner makes, seeking always to reflect as fully and faithfully as possible the nature of the group being evaluated.

Multiple indicators of success in residential youth care and treatment have been described by Whittaker, Overstreet, Grasso, Tripodi, and Boylan (1988). Their proposals are interesting for several reasons: (a) They view success as occurring at different stages of the service cycle, from intake to post-discharge placement, and (b) they propose a variety of perspectives on residential services. Table 3.1 is adapted from their paper. While individuals are necessarily involved, the use of rates or percentages indicates a collective phenomenon to which individual behaviors contribute, but which reflect how the entire group is reacting to the entire service experience. These indicators are simply the sum of individual scores.

Other indicators can be truly reflective of the group and are probably greater than the sum of individual scores. For example, group morale can be viewed as some multiple score based on the interactions of members with one another, not just the sum of each member's liking to be in the group. It might also be useful to keep track of communication patterns, who talks to whom and how much, as these patterns may also shift as the group begins to form its own structure.

Still another example of a group goal would be when a recreational group is formed to include one or two predelinquent youths who will be exposed to positive peer norms. The general behavior patterns in the group reflect the dominant norms, and comparisons might be made as to how closely individuals identify with those norms over time with the goal being higher group scores (closer identification) on the measure of those norms.

In general, we are proposing that, where possible, the group objectives and goals be identified and operationalized. In addition, it may be very useful to collect individual scores on related topics so that the relative status of each individual may be compared with the group as a whole (cf. Benbenishty, 1989). If group norms are related to individual behavior in enjoyable ways but without putting an individual in serious conflict with the group, then an individual's score that shows a discrepancy

Table 3.1 Indicators of success in residential services.

Stage	Criterion of Success	Operational Indicators
Intake	Placement in a less restricted environment	Percent of clients diverted from more restricted settings (e.g., jail)
Treatment	Decrease in violent acting out Acquisition of prosocial skills	Rate of assaults in the facility (Average) life skills progress from baseline to highest level attained by each individual
Discharge	Planned discharge occurred	Percent of clients who have completed the program without premature termination
Postplacement	No recidivism	Percent of clients who remain in less restrictive environment in community Percent of clients adjudicated

with the norm may suggest the need for extra counseling or enhanced group efforts to help this particular individual. An interesting example from a student case involved the establishment of a senior citizen support group at a new high-rise building where no one felt "at home." A measure of the cohesion of the group was the number in attendance at any given weekly meeting. Individual measures of discontent with the housing situation were obtained from standardized questions asked of the residents in weekly interviews with the student. Thus, two different phenomena were observed–cohesion and discontent–but positive changes in the former were observed to precede positive changes in the latter, as the student hypothesized.

PROBLEMS AND ISSUES IN SETTING GOALS

There are several problems and issues in establishing objectives and goals that could impede progress. You should be prepared to deal with these in negotiating goals with your client.

Anticipate Negative Outcomes

You will want to help the client anticipate the impact of achieving his or her goals. You and the client will have to evaluate the effects that changes in the client are likely to have on others in his or her environment. Have others actually received some form of reinforcement or gratification from the client's undesired behavior? Is it possible that the changes in the client will lead to some negative occurrence for the client (e.g., will being more assertive lead to being fired)? Say an agency director wants to increase the number of minority clients in his or her agency's case load. Is the staff trained and prepared to deal with a changing case load? The point of all this is to attempt to anticipate results and to examine them with clients or others in their environment. In this way, either negative impacts may be minimized, or at least clients will be prepared to deal with them.

Who Sets the Goals?

Since goal setting is largely a value judgment–a statement of what is desired–whenever possible the client should have the major, if not the sole, say in setting goals. This is not to say the practitioner does not have an important role in setting the goals–for example, in helping the client be more specific about just what he or she wants. Furthermore, this influence is likely to be greatly increased when the client is confused, unsure, incapable of speaking for himself or herself (e.g., an infant), or simply unable to decide. Indeed, the client may even have a specific goal in mind at initial contact, but the practitioner's expertise in collecting assessment information may broaden the client's perspective and even lead to a negotiated revision in goals. In addition, agencies or even communities may have their priorities, and these priorities may be evident in the goal-setting process.

Perhaps the key principle here is that *whenever possible* the client should have the predominant say in establishing goals. When this is not completely possible, it is the practitioner's responsibility to be sensitive to the client's interests and desires and to balance them against other pressures. At the least the practitioner can try to see that those interests are kept uppermost in any decision about goals. This is particularly true when there is pressure being put on the client or practitioner by outside sources (e.g., from relevant others or referring sources) to develop goals that conform to their needs or wishes.

A related issue has to do with being sure the goals are acceptable to both client and practitioner and perhaps the agency (Brown & Brown, 1977). Self-defeating, destructive, or illegal behaviors may all be put on the table for discussion and negotiation. This can occur not only when the practitioner is dealing with a client who may have been referred from another source or who is a mandated client (e.g., in a prison, school, or hospital), but also in a situation in which the client simply appears to be making poor choices. At the least it is the practitioner's responsibility to provide as accurate and as honest information as possible in evaluating how workable the goal is.

Anticipate Impediments

Since a number of issues can arise during the goal-setting process, it's always a good idea to try to anticipate problems. In reviewing this section, a number of questions, in part modified from Gambrill (1977, p. 175), could be useful as a checklist to see whether the major conditions of establishing specific goals have been set:

1. Have specific behaviors, thoughts, feelings, or activities been identified?

2. Have initial intermediate objectives been set?

3. Are objectives and goals attainable?

4. Is it clear who will be changing?

5. Could two or more people agree on whether a task has been accomplished?

6. Is it clear under what conditions the desired activities will be performed?

7. Are the goals stated in positive terms and not in terms of what the client won't be doing?

8. Are performance criteria identified? (Will it be clear when a goal or objective has been accomplished?)

9. Is there any way the goal or objective could be satisfied in an unsatisfactory way (e.g., completing homework by copying someone else's)?

10. Are there any possible negative consequences to achieving the goal?

11. Are the goals and objectives stated as client outcomes rather than in terms of what you (the practitioner) will do?

12. Is the goal acceptable to you, the client, relevant others?

Case Illustrations of Goals in the Context of Problems and Interventions

It would be impossible to list all of the possible problems and goals clients present. Instead, we have presented a framework for specifying problems and goals as a means of understanding where the client is and of seeking to help the client resolve problems and thereby attain the desired goals.

In addition, it may be instructive to consider the following sketches of cases, summarized in Table 3.2. We have combined many of the elements of scientific practice, a translation of the client's concerns into a more or less objectively definable problem (target) with its verifying source, and the goals or objectives we seek to attain in the resolution of that problem. Interventions are suggested that are clearly connected with the targeted problem. (These examples are taken from student cases and simplified for exposition.)

Table 3.2   Case illustrations of client concerns, operationalized problems, goals, and interventions.

Client Concerns	The Problem/Goals Operationally Defined	Verifying Source	The Goal of the Intervention	Intervention Methods as Linked to Problem
1a. Joe's parents are concerned that he is skipping school. The truancy officer has issued a formal warning to Joe and his family.	1a. The number of days per week that Joe does not attend school when he should be present.	1a. School records.	1a. Joe to attend school 5 full days a week as appropriate	1a. Arrange that Joe walk to school with 3 friends, eat lunch with them, and walk home together (peer support).
1b. Joe has been getting failing grades in his major subjects.	1b. The number of F-grades Joe gets in English, math, history, and science.	1b. Teacher's grade book.	1b. Joe to get passing grades in every major subject (D or better).	1b. Arrange for Joe to study with his friends. Parents permit Joe extra late hours on weekend for each passing grade.
1c. Joe is unhappy because he can't get any girls from school to go out with him.	1c. The number of dates Joe has with girls in his class per month.	1c. Client's report.	1c. Joe would like to have at least two dates a month.	1c. Joe enters interpersonal skills training group related to social skills.
2a. A family agency has gradually had a reduction in numbers of clients, which threatens the continuation of the agency.	2a. The number of active cases per month, as compared with the previous 5 years' client census.	2a. Agency statistics.	2a(1). Increase the number of referrals from other agencies by 50% per month. 2a(2). Increase agency visibility through a community health fair. 2a(3). Initiate new program where there is an identified need for which staff has qualifications.	2a(1). Send brochures of agency programs to practitioners in likely referring agencies. 2a(2). Publicize and run a health fair at local high schools. 2a(3). Do needs survey in the community and design a helping project according to results.
2b. Agency staff morale has been poor.	2b(1). The number of practitioners leaving the agency per month. 2b(2). The practitioners completed a self-report (anonymous) measure of morale once a month.	2b(1). Agency records. 2b(2). Agency records.	2b. Reduce practitioner turnover by 50%.	2b. Involve practitioners in agency policy and program making.

(continued)

Table 3.2 Case illustrations of client concerns, operationalized problems, goals, and interventions (continued).

Client Concerns	The Problem/Goals Operationally Defined	Verifying Source	The Goal of the Intervention	Intervention Methods as Linked to Problem
3a. Mary feels depressed.	3a. Mary's score on a standardized depression test.	3a. The practitioner scores the test.	3a. Mary's scores should decrease to below the clinical cutoff.	3a and 3b. Family therapy session dealing with mother–daughter relationship and how to problem-solve so as to keep disagreements under control. (Mother also takes course on Parent Effectiveness Training.)
3b. Mary and her mother get into a lot of arguments about her rights and responsibilities.	3b. The number of times Mary and her mother argue each week.	3b. They bring in a score sheet to the weekly appointment.	3b. Mary and her mother will try to reduce the number of arguments per week by half, to the point of no arguments.	
4a. Drugs are becoming a major problem in the neighborhood, as connected with several break-ins (to steal money for drugs).	4a. Number of drug-related thefts in the neighborhood.	4a. Police records.	4a. Reduce theft to zero.	4a. Neighborhood patrols (groups of citizens walking the neighborhood by shifts day and night, reporting suspicious events to police).
4b. The elderly residents express fears of leaving their homes at night.	4b. Attendance at regular neighborhood (evening) functions.	4b. Minutes of the neighborhood council.	4b. Increase involvement of neighbors in weekly activities.	4b. Each resident to bring one plan to encourage neighbors to attend social functions. Others to patrol the streets protecting homes.
5a. Miss E (age 90) has stopped coming down for (obligatory) meals at Senior House. She appears to be incoherent at times. Staff and friends are concerned.	5a. Number of meals taken at dining hall per week indicating measure of nutritional health. 5b. Number of times she is overheard by staff to be speaking incoherently.	5a. Census taken by director of Senior House each night, at dinner. 5b. Report by director while chatting with residents at dinnertime.	5a. Miss E to eat a balanced diet. 5b. Miss E to be as coherent as she is capable of being.	5a(1). Appear at Miss E's door with small gifts and short conversations in order to build rapport and gain her trust. 5a(2). Then invite her to tea and have conversations about diet, etc. Try to reinterest Miss E in eating with a new set of friends.

(continued)

Table 3.2 Case illustrations of client concerns, operationalized problems, goals, and interventions (continued).

Client Concerns	The Problem/Goals Operationally Defined	Verifying Source	The Goal of the Intervention	Intervention Methods as Linked to Problem
				5b(1). Try to make sure Miss E has balanced diet. If incoherence continues, arrange for medical contact. 5b(2). Physician to examine Miss E to ascertain extent of physiological/medical problems and to provide treatment.
6a. Bill and Elaine are going to a family life education program to learn effective parenting skills for when their baby gets older.	6a. Number of times they use rational explanations as appropriate responses to family stimulus situations, rather than ordering responses.	6a. Each spouse keeps score on self and other spouse, and records results.	6a. Bill and Elaine want to make rational responding a natural part of their child-rearing patterns—at least 80% of the time.	6a. Each spouse will positively reinforce the other for correct response, and merely indicate (without censure) incorrect responses.
6b. Elaine also wants to learn some stress-management skills, as her law position demands long hours and heavy duties.	6b. Number of times Elaine completes the appropriate number of muscle-relaxing and deep-breathing exercises at her office per day.	6b. Self-report.	6b. Elaine wants to be able to relieve work-related stress any time it occurs at the office or home, even though the workload itself probably won't be lightened for some time.	6b. Every time Elaine feels strain in her neck or back she will do relaxation exercises.
7a. P.S. 99 wants to create a drug-free school environment for the junior and senior high students.	7a. Number of students observed smoking cigarettes on campus.	7a. Faculty or maintenance personnel observation.	7a. Increase the number of students who selected allowable alternative highs to feel great in socially acceptable ways.	7a. Sponsor group activities in which allowable alternative highs are encouraged, which are antagonistic to and inhibitory of the antisocial highs.

(continued)

Table 3.2   Case illustrations of client concerns, operationalized problems, goals, and interventions (continued).

Client Concerns	The Problem/Goals Operationally Defined	Verifying Source	The Goal of the Intervention	Intervention Methods as Linked to Problem
	7b. Number of students observed to be high on drugs (dazed look, slurred speech, etc.).	7b. Faculty or nursing staff observation.	7b. Increase knowledge of problems associated with substance abuse.	7b. Conduct small group seminars and activities related to substance abuse education.
	7c. Number of students observed to be drunk while at school.	7c. Faculty or nursing staff observation.		
	7d. Number of students affirming that they have not used drugs in the past week.	7d. Self-report.		
	7e. Number of students affirming that they have had an allowable alternative high—from sports, art, religion, etc.—in the past week.	7e. Self-report.		

Note that in some of these examples, there is a one-to-one listing of concern/problem/ goal. In others, there may be several goals or objectives for one problem, or there may be several problems for one general concern. The point is to capture the meaning of the situation so that the set of problems represents a fair and full sense of the client. We can never measure everything about the client's problems or goals, but we can hope to sample these so that our intervention deals with representative indicators of the client's problems and hopes. If desired outcomes occur under these conditions, then there should be some socially significant changes occurring to the client and/or the situation—even though not everything may be resolved.

Another way to represent goals and objectives specifically is illustrated in Figures 3.8 through 3.11. On these charts are represented four targeted problems. The valued objectives or client preferences are reflected in the way the chart is constructed. Figure 3.8 presents the objective of maintaining a certain range of weight; the lines indicating the upper and lower limits of this range represent the values of the client. Figure 3.9 uses a clinical cutoff, a line separating persons whose scores are like those with known problematic conditions from persons who do not show these problems. This approach applies norms developed on large numbers of persons to setting goals in the given case.

Figure 3.10 indicates one of many statistical approaches to establishing preferred behaviors with the goal of getting as many observations below the dotted line as possible. This approach is illustrated in other chapters and described in Chapter 21, but here the point is that we make a rough estimate from what we know about the

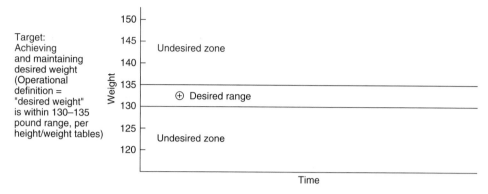

FIGURE 3.8   Goals of service indicated by reference to preestablished norms. Weights above or below the desired range are considered undesirable.

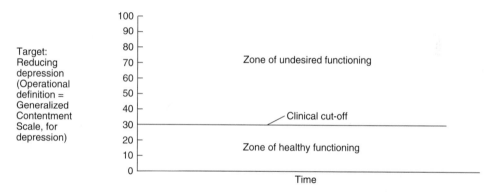

FIGURE 3.9   Goals of service indicated by reference to measures on standardized test or scale. In this case, the clinical cutoff is an empirically derived line indicating the separation of problematic and nonproblematic functioning.

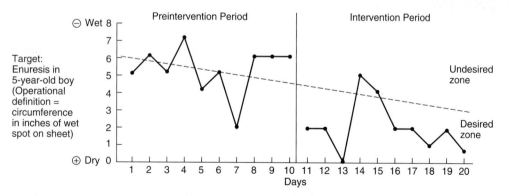

FIGURE 3.10   Goals of service established by a statistical procedure (described in Chapter 21) by which the preintervention data are compared with the intervention data.

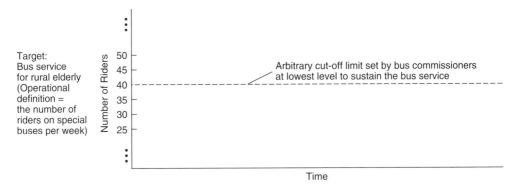

FIGURE 3.11 Goals of service established by arbitrary rules. The number of riders set as a cutoff has nothing to do with cost recovery: The bus operation is heavily subsidized. Rather, this decision seems to have been political. Nonetheless, it is a real limit in terms of practical decisions.

client's current behavior to what patterns of change must occur to exhibit improvements over the problematic behavior. This is a statistical way to construct preferences–that is, improvements over the current problematic situation.

Figure 3.11 represents the weakest approach to indicating preferences, objectives we aim for in order to claim some improvement over the preintervention situation. In effect, we make a good guess of what we should aim to achieve as a goal in a given situation. We might rationalize this choice in various ways, but because we don't have any objective basis for the choice, it is simply a plausible but arbitrary objective. This is better than nothing because it gives us something to aim at, but it would be preferable to have a sounder basis for selecting our objectives and goals.

SUMMARY

Being specific in identifying problems and goals is a crucial link among assessment, intervention, and evaluation activities. In this chapter, we started with client concerns–both those that are undesired and should be decreased and those that are desired and should be increased. Then we reviewed the rationale for being more precise and specific about defining problems and, later, establishing goals and objectives. We stated our belief that unless you can measure a problem, you cannot objectively evaluate how well you are resolving it. Focusing first on being specific in defining problems, we suggested several guidelines for using more precise problem definitions. Included in these were clarity, use of verifying sources, counting, dereification, focus on increasing and decreasing problems, and measurability. We also presented some examples of specific problems drawn from actual cases.

In the section on developing objectives and goals, we distinguished between problems ("what is") and goals ("what we prefer"). We also discussed the differences between goals (as ultimate outcomes) and objectives (intermediate outcomes). We clarified that outcome objectives are the actual stepping-stones to the ultimate goals. We then discussed the key components of goal statements as including who, will do what, to what extent, under what conditions.

We described how to use statistics to define goals and how to set goals in groups, and we presented a brief review of Goal Attainment Scaling (GAS), a widely used method of establishing goals. We then concluded the chapter by describing some problems in goal setting, with a checklist to anticipate those problems. The final illustrations of cases combined client concerns, operationally defined problems as targets of intervention, the verifying sources of these targets, goals and objectives, and the interventions used. It is important to note that one can get to specific targets of intervention or prevention from either problems or goals. Table 3.3 summarizes these two ways in which targets may be specified.

The third question in Table 3.3 brings the two paths of inquiry together and moves the discussion to an evaluative frame of reference, for which single-system designs become an appropriate tool for answering the question. The single-system design includes both a conceptual statement (the naming of the target variable) and an empirical component (the operational definition of that target). Either path, or both together, can help you identify some specific target and its operational definition.

Table 3.3   The specification of targets of intervention from an analysis of client problems and/or goals and objectives.

Professional Service Begins with the Question, How Can We Help the Client? *The Answer Involves Exploring Two Paths Regarding Client Concerns:*	
PROBLEMS as One Origin Point in Constructing Targets of Intervention	*GOALS as Another Origin Point in Constructing Targets of Intervention*
1a. What are the client's general areas of concern for which professional services were sought (survey the problem area)? "What are the difficulties you (the client) are experiencing?"	2a. What are the client's general and long-range goals (relative to the issues that brought the client and the practitioner together)? What would the client like to change? "What would you (the client) be doing, thinking, or feeling differently at that time?"
1b. Select one general concern and describe all of the topics within it, or representative types of problems within that domain.	2b. What are the short-term intervening steps or objectives that may lead to the goal? What has to get done first? Then what second? Third? And so on.
1c. Take one illustrative problem—the highest priority problem—and indicate: * Who? (what client or relevant other) * Does what? (more or less of some specific activity) * To what extent? (specify how much more or less of the problem behaviors are involved) * Under what conditions? (Where? In what settings?)	2c. In order to achieve a given goal or objective, indicate: * Who? (what client or relevant other) * Does what? (more or less of some specific activity) * To what extent? (specify what criterion levels are to be used) * Under what conditions? (Where? In what settings?)
3. How will you know whether the target (either a specified problem or a specified objective/goal) changes in the desired direction?	

DEVELOPING A MEASUREMENT AND RECORDING PLAN

PURPOSE: This chapter provides guidelines for developing a plan to measure client problems after the targets have been selected using the guidelines provided in Chapter 3. A measurement plan involves deciding who, where, when, and how to measure targets, and a good plan makes it more likely that all of the measurement bases are covered. This chapter also provides guidelines for developing a plan to record the information generated by the measurement plan, including introduction to use of a personal computer program called Computer Assisted Social Services (CASS) to help you in recording and managing your caseload. The recording plan also involves graphing the information you collect on an ongoing basis in order to document, communicate, and monitor client progress so that you can make any needed changes in your intervention in a timely fashion. ■

Introduction
Advantages of a Systematic Recording Plan
Steps in Developing a Recording Plan
Select a Method of Measurement
Decide Who Should Collect Data
   Client
   Practitioner
   Independent Evaluators
   Relevant Others
   Enhancing Cooperation in Recording
Decide When and Where to Collect Data
Decide How Often Data Should Be Collected
Decide How Many Targets to Record
Standardize Recording Procedures
Begin Collecting Baseline Information
Charting: Putting Your Information on Graphs
Presenting Data on the Chart
Phases

Problem-Oriented Records (POR)
Basic Guidelines for Using the POR
   Database
   Complete Problem List
   Initial Plans
   Monitoring Progress
Computerized Recording
   Some Advantages and Disadvantages
   of Using Computers
Summary
Computer Assisted Social Services (CASS):
  A User's Guide
Appendix: Installing Cass

INTRODUCTION

After targets have been selected using the guidelines provided in Chapter 3, it's necessary to develop a plan for their measurement. A measurement plan involves deciding *who* (e.g., the practitioner or the client), *where* (e.g., the agency or in the client's natural environment), *when* (e.g., once a day or once a week), and *how* (e.g., a standardized questionnaire or the observation of behavior) to measure targets. These decisions are important because they influence the adequacy with which targets are measured. Some people are in a better position than others to provide information about some targets (e.g., a teacher might be in a better position than a practitioner to provide information about the way a child interacts with his or her peers). Some times and places provide a more representative picture of a target than others (e.g., the observation of a child's interaction with her peers at school might provide a more representative picture of her social skills than role-playing in the practitioner's office). Some methods provide a better picture of a target than others (e.g., a client's rating of his self-esteem might provide a better picture of self-esteem than an observation of his overt behavior).

Even if a good measurement plan is carried out, to make the best use of the information, it must be recorded in a way that allows it to be used to document (e.g., to funding sources), communicate (e.g., to supervisors and consultants), and monitor client progress in a way that will let you make needed and timely changes in your intervention. Usually this just involves charting the information on a graph as we've illustrated in earlier chapters, and as we discuss in more detail in this chapter. However, there are also exciting developments using personal computers not only to graph the results of single-system designs, but also to easily store, retrieve, and manipulate recorded information in ways that are useful to practitioners and administrators. We'll discuss some of these developments.

As you probably know from your own practice, it's possible to successfully help someone without developing a plan for measuring and recording his or her concerns. If that's true,

then why go through all the bother of setting up such a plan? Isn't the measurement and recording process an unnecessary intrusion into the practitioner and client relationship? Aren't records just a form of mechanical busywork?

We believe that setting up systematic recording plans is a useful and accurate way of establishing the effectiveness and efficiency of interventions. We recognize that the ethics of professional practice require accountability. You therefore must document the success of your interventions and even provide evidence about possible negative results that arise after your interventions. Data obtained from recordings serve this need for documentation.

To be sure, there are alternatives to systematic record keeping. Mainly, these involve less structured impressions of the practitioner and the client that changes did come about. Indeed, in some situations these impressions may be the only data available. But they also have their limitations. First, they tend to be imprecise; they may fail to measure a slow but steady change. Second, they are often inaccurate; there are too many possible distortions of the information when vague, subjective impressions are relied upon as the sole source of outcome information.

Advantages of a Systematic Recording Plan

It's advantageous to use a systematic recording plan for several reasons:

1. It enhances assessment and intervention planning, particularly by providing a focus on specific targets and goals.
2. It allows the practitioner to determine client progress and to record plateaus or regression.
3. It can alert the practitioner to the need for changes in the intervention program.
4. It can motivate the client and practitioner as they see the results of their work.
5. It can keep track of small but steady changes that might be overlooked.
6. It can provide data that can be analyzed to determine the range of effective interventions for different clients.

7. It can provide evidence about the effectiveness of your practice.
8. It allows you to demonstrate your accountability.

The remainder of this chapter focuses on the steps you would take in setting up a recording plan, shows you how to chart the data from your recording plan, and includes a brief discussion of recording using a method called the Problem-Oriented Record and computerized recording. The chapter concludes with an overview of computerized recording followed by instructions on how to use the CASS computer program included with this book.

STEPS IN DEVELOPING A RECORDING PLAN

The whole process of recording should be built into the procedural guidelines that you ordinarily use as you collect and assess various sources of information about the client and target, starting prior to intervention. In other words, we suggest that the recording methods we describe should be as much an integral part of your preintervention activities as any of the activities that you typically engage in before your intervention plan is formulated. Thus, recording is an integral part of practice.

The recording plan grows out of your initial assessment of a client's targets, your hunches and the client's wishes about what needs to be done, and your preliminary review of the situation using the guidelines in Chapter 3.

Select a Method of Measurement

Once the target or situation is specified adequately, the next step is to decide how it is to be observed and to select a method of measuring it. As we have suggested, it's best to try to use at least two different methods to measure a target whenever possible. For example, you might want to observe target behaviors (Chapter 5) and have the client evaluate the more subjective nature of the targets using an individualized rating scale (Chapter 6). (The range of possible measurement methods is dis-

cussed in the following chapters. Each chapter focuses on a particular set of measurement methods. Guidelines for selecting from among them are presented in Chapter 10.) Of course, selecting a method of measurement is also based on who is available to record. Thus, these two steps—selecting a method and deciding who will use it—actually occur at roughly the same point in the process.

Decide Who Should Collect Data

An important consideration in setting up a baseline and recording plan is deciding just who should collect data. This can be the client, the practitioner, an independent professional such as a colleague or a trained observer, someone else in the client's environment, or some combination of these (e.g., the practitioner using unobtrusive measures of changes in the client's target as described in Chapter 9, while the client collects his or her own self-report data). A key question you should always ask yourself in making this decision is whether the person can and will provide accurate information.

Client. There are a number of advantages to having clients report about their own situation, and we present information on such measures in the following chapters. Clients, whether they're individuals or members of groups or families, obviously are present when the problem is occurring, so they are in a uniquely favorable position to observe their own behavior. In fact, in some instances only the client can record target information (e.g., his or her own thoughts or feelings, or private behaviors that occur when a client is alone). Also, the client may be highly motivated to change the target and therefore may be willing to do the necessary recording. Finally, with the exception of behaviors that are illegal and consequently defined as problems independently of the client, the client defines whether a problem exists, and so the client's perspective is especially important.

Client reports also have some potential limitations and disadvantages. First, the client, perhaps out of a long-term habit, may not be aware of the occurrence of the target, and even your best efforts to help the client become aware (perhaps through role-playing of the target to increase awareness) may not succeed. Second, clients may not be able to provide the needed information because they are too disabled or too young. Third, the client simply may not want to provide information, or may wittingly or unwittingly provide inaccurate information; clients might tell you what they think you want to hear, especially in situations in which you are in a position to give or withhold valued social sanctions and the client's reports might influence your decisions (e.g., a parent may not admit abusing a child to a child protective services worker, knowing that the worker is legally mandated to report this information). You may do your best to motivate the client (see the final section of this chapter), but that also may fail.

Finally, as we noted in Chapter 2, clients' recording of their own target may have a reactive effect so that the target might change during the baseline simply due to the effects of recording. Although one way to handle this is to extend the period of time over which baseline data are collected, this may not always be possible (see Chapter 9).

In some cases the client may be the only source of information about a target (e.g., if the target is a cognition or private event), and the client may not want to systematically collect baseline information on the target. For example, the client may be under stress and might be impatient to initiate intervention and go about the business of addressing his or her concerns (this impatience is often shared by the practitioner). Yet interventions that are plunged into without adequate preparation may be doomed to failure. Thus, as part of that preparation, recording in general, and baseline recording in particular, provides some of the foundation for enhancing your potential for more effective intervention.

Even though we all might agree on this principle, we still might have difficulty in persuading the client. It's our belief, however, that recording is important enough in most instances to be viewed as a prerequisite of intervention. This means that the practitioner should strive to involve the client or relevant others in collecting data.

The success or failure of recording may very well depend on the way the practitioner

presents it to the client. First, the practitioner should not throw the baselining and recording tasks at the client (or whoever is to collect the data) before some rapport has developed in the relationship and the client and practitioner begin to develop mutual trust. This is true whether the "client" is an individual, a small group, or a large agency. Too many projects have failed because the practitioner forced recording tasks on the client prematurely.

Second, recording should be explained as integral to intervention; that is, it should be clear to the client that effective assessment and intervention rely heavily on the collection of data.

Third, the procedure should be explained as clearly and precisely as possible. Of utmost importance is the amount of certainty and confidence the practitioner expresses in regard to baselining and recording in general. It would be hard for any of us to accept the task of recording (or any other task for that matter) from someone who appears uncertain about its usefulness.

Fourth, the practitioner can motivate the client to participate in any number of ways, including providing encouragement and support for the client's participation, conveying warmth and appreciation for efforts at cooperation, displaying empathy for the realistic constraints and concerns that the client expresses about recording, and by doing whatever is possible to remove any obstacles so as to facilitate recording (see Fischer & Gochros, 1975, Chapter 9, for a number of other suggestions).

Finally, if the target that is selected for recording is particularly annoying to the client, he or she may be more motivated to change it. It's important to be as certain as possible that the target is also amenable to change (so that the client won't get discouraged), and that above all, the method of recording is not aversive and perhaps even is enjoyable.

There are two other options a practitioner has if the client won't cooperate and collect information. The first is to go ahead and begin intervention anyway. This assumes, at a minimum, that assessment information collected from other sources is adequate to select the appropriate intervention and that an alternative method of evaluating success is also available.

The second option, when all else has been tried to include the client in the program, including exploration with the client of possible barriers to recording, is to terminate the relationship and possibly refer the client elsewhere. Although this option is not widely used in the helping professions and is not a popular choice, it nevertheless must be considered by the practitioner who is interested in effective and efficient use of time. This might be the option selected when not obtaining information will so obviously interfere with the assessment and intervention program that even normally effective results could not be expected. Under these conditions, when it would not be possible to expect that the client can be helped, it seems unreasonable and unfair to both client and practitioner to continue the relationship. For example, parents whose child has severe behavior problems may be unwilling to record their interactions with the child, making it impossible to assess the reasons for the child's problems, and therefore making it impossible to develop an adequate intervention.

Practitioner. Practitioners also can collect and record useful information about clients. In a way practitioners are in a unique position to observe and understand clients because of their professional training and experience, familiarity with the client, and the ease of recording unobtrusively. Therefore, we present information on data collection methods for practitioners in the following chapters.

There are potential problems and limitations of practitioners' reports. The validity of the data may vary with how the practitioner perceives the information will be used (e.g., for evaluating progress for accountability purposes). The data may be biased because of the practitioner's desire to succeed (e.g., the bias might be a function of how much time and effort were expended with a given client). In addition, the practitioner might not always be present when the problem occurs, since most problems obviously don't occur only or mainly during office or home visits.

Independent Evaluators. Other professionals, such as your colleagues, supervisor, or outside consultants, can sometimes provide valuable assessments of your clients. For example, you might have a colleague review a random sample of audiotapes or videotapes of your sessions with a client, or even interview your client. Independent evaluators have the advantage that they are less personally invested in a client and so they might be able to provide a more accurate, less biased assessment. Some evaluators may even receive special training in recording procedures. However, the fact that independent evaluators are less involved with a client also can be a disadvantage because they are less familiar with the client. Also, in busy agencies it simply might not be possible to have your colleagues provide independent assessments of your clients except on a limited basis.

Relevant Others. There are numerous people in a client's environment who interact with the client on a day-to-day basis and who might be able to provide valuable information about a client: *in homes*–parents, spouse, children, siblings, other members of an extended family such as grandparents; *in the schools*–teachers, aides, parents, volunteers, classmates, recreation workers, cafeteria workers, school counselors, or social workers; *in institutions and hospitals*–houseparents, psychiatrists or other physicians, psychologists, nurses, aides, secretaries, occupational and other specialty therapists, volunteers, social workers, other residents of the institution, other nonprofessional staff such as cafeteria workers.

There are a number of advantages to having relevant others provide information about a client. First, the ultimate goal of your intervention efforts is to improve the way clients function in their day-to-day environment, and relevant others oftentimes are in a unique position to provide information about clients' real-world functioning. Second, some interventions are interpersonally based (e.g., in treatment of couples and families), and so the perspective of other involved parties is especially pertinent in judging the success of an intervention. Third, it may be possible for others to observe the target as it "naturally" occurs, unobtrusively, without producing a reactive effect. Finally, someone in the environment may be extremely motivated to collect data because the target is especially distressing to him or her. (See Fischer & Gochros, 1975, Chapter 9, for guidelines for helping select, motivate, and train someone from the client's environment to do the recording.)

Information from relevant others can be valuable, but there are some potential problems and limitations with using relevant others to record. First, some clients simply don't have relevant others, or they may not want you to collect information from relevant others. Second, relevant others may be unwilling to cooperate, or they may "fudge" their recording depending on how they see its use. Third, the reason that makes relevant others so useful a data source—their day-to-day relationship with the client—also might bias their responses. Fourth, relevant others simply might not know enough about a particular client's target to provide adequate information (e.g., a relevant other might know that a client who abuses alcohol still drinks, but not how much). Fifth, sometimes it can be time-consuming and otherwise expensive to collect information from relevant others. Finally, if the client has access to information provided by relevant others it can prove embarrassing and even harmful to the client's relationship with relevant others (e.g., asking a person to collect information about the extent to which a neighbor abused his or her children).

In all, then, you sometimes have to weigh the pros and cons of all the factors, use whoever is available and willing to record, and try to minimize the negatives and maximize the positives as described above. Also, typically, no individual is a perfect source of information, so it's best to collect information from various sources. If the bulk of the information from different sources is consistent, you can have greater confidence in the information; if the bulk of the information isn't consistent, at least you'll know that you have to proceed with some caution in making decisions from your information.

Enhancing Cooperation in Recording. There are several additional criteria you might use in deciding who should do the recording (Fischer & Gochros, 1975):

1. Be certain the recorder understands the value and purpose of recording.
2. Be certain the recorder accepts the value and purpose of recording.
3. Be certain the recorder will be present when the target occurs.
4. Be certain the recorder clearly understands just *what* is to be recorded. (If not, this means the practitioner must train the recorder in observing the target.)
5. Be certain the recorder knows how to record. (This again always necessitates training.)
6. Be certain the recorder has the necessary equipment available.
7. Be certain the recorder is motivated and/or willing to record. (If not, the practitioner's task is to develop a situation in which the necessary motivation can be produced, whether this is through support and encouragement by the practitioner or others, or through the development of a mini-intervention program to see that the recorder is reinforced for his or her efforts.)

We cannot overemphasize how important it is to adequately prepare the person who will be doing the recording, no matter which of the methods from Chapters 5 through 9 you select. We strongly recommend that you work to establish rapport and trust with that person. Don't ram the recording task down his or her throat. Once rapport is established, present the task clearly and confidently as an integral part of the overall program. The more uncomfortable you appear with the recording assignments, the more likely it is that someone else will be reluctant to take the responsibility for recording.

Explain the relevance of the information you're requesting. You might want to say that you need a baseline to evaluate what you do, just as a physician needs blood pressure, heart rate, and other readings before starting a treatment program (Schwartz & Goldiamond, 1975). If the information you're asking for doesn't seem relevant, it might be difficult to convince recorders that the client will be better off if they provide accurate reports. Don't ask for information that isn't relevant, but make sure its relevance is understood by the person being asked for information.

Explain the importance of recording confidently, matter-of-factly, and as clearly and precisely as possible. Don't make it seem like a heavy burden, and be sure it isn't. Be certain that the recorder understands that the success or failure of the intervention may depend on collecting baseline information and information after intervention has begun. The confidence with which you request information may influence the accuracy of the information. Sometimes practitioners who aren't experienced in the use of measures in practice request this information in an uncertain, embarrassed, and apologetic fashion. This might suggest to the recorder that the task really isn't all that important or that it's indeed unreasonable to ask for the information; the recorder might act accordingly and provide less than complete or accurate information. If you believe that the information you're requesting is important, convey this to the recorder; if you don't believe it's important, don't ask for it.

A client, relevant other, or even an independent evaluator might want to provide complete and accurate information but might be reluctant to do so because he or she doesn't know who will have access to the potentially embarrassing information that was requested. Therefore, it's important to provide assurances that the information will be kept confidential to the limit of the law (cf. Albert, 1986). However, don't inadvertently deceive the person by implying that such information is completely confidential (e.g., the client might have access to information provided by a relevant other). Numerous exceptions exist to the privilege of confidentiality and you need to be careful to not promise a greater degree of confidentiality than you can guarantee (Kagle, 1983, 1984a; Wilson, 1978).

Even if someone is willing and motivated to provide requested information, he or she might not have the necessary information. For example, under the right circumstances a client seeking help with alcoholism might be willing to tell you how much alcohol he consumed on most days in the previous month, but it's quite likely also that he or she might not be able to remember. A mother being investi-

gated for child neglect might be willing to tell you when her child achieved certain developmental milestones, but often a parent doesn't remember this information. Therefore, the accuracy of information depends upon whether the recorder has what you need. You should ask yourself, and the recorder, whether he or she is able to provide the needed information. After all, if you ask a person for information that he or she doesn't have, you might get an answer, but it might be an inaccurate guess.

Try to emphasize how important it is that the recording doesn't interfere with the "natural occurrence" of the target (the reactive effect). Be certain that the recorder attempts to be as unobtrusive as possible; give suggestions about how to do that (several suggestions are described in subsequent chapters). Emphasize the importance of the recorder being honest and accurate. Be certain that the recorder–whether the client or someone else–doesn't think that he or she can "help" the program by being a trifle "overgenerous" with how he or she views the target. (Recall the idea of validity of observations as we described it in Chapter 2.)

Your reaction to the information provided by a client is another factor that can influence the accuracy of the information. For example, you might subtly show surprise or disapproval in response to a client's report, and consequently the client might subsequently provide less accurate information. You also want to avoid subtly but inadvertently encouraging a client to report improvement even when it doesn't occur. You should be careful not to suggest possible replies, although you should reinforce the recorder for his or her thoroughness and effort.

Finally, make sure the recorder is adequately prepared to collect data. Take the time to explain the task, and be sure that the recorder understands the instructions. When appropriate you might ask the recorder to restate the instructions as a means of gauging understanding. In any case, encourage the recorder to ask questions whenever something isn't clear, and be sure not to give the recorder the impression that you're hurrying, because this might discourage him or her from asking much needed questions. Also, you need to be sure that you're knowledgeable about the measurement task and prepared for any question the recorder could ask you. You might even want to develop a list to go over with the recorder before he or she begins. This list could include all the items that should be checked before recording begins (Gelfand & Hartmann, 1975). An example of such a checklist is provided in Figure 4.1, but you can make changes or add items to suit the needs of your own situation. If "no" is checked for any item, you would then go back and see that the item is accomplished.

Decide When and Where to Collect Data

In the best of all possible practice worlds, practitioners would be able to have informa-tion on all their clients' targets all of the time. In some instances (e.g., total institutions) this may indeed be possible; in many other in-stances this is highly unlikely. Often it's either impractical or simply impossible to collect in-formation about the occurrence of a target every time it occurs. But a decision about this issue should be made *before* the actual record-ing begins.

The first guideline with regard to when to record is to try to record when and where the action occurs. If you're recording actual be-haviors, this is perhaps obvious. With other forms of measurement you can work to see that whatever the recording device or instru-ment used, the measures are recorded as close to the actual occurrence of the problem as

---

Recorder's Name

_____

Practitioner's Name   Date _____

_____

Client's Name

_____

		Yes	No
1. Is the target problem clearly defined?		_____	_____
2. Has the recorder practiced observing the problem?		_____	_____
3. Is the recorder accurate in his or her observations?		_____	_____
4. Is all data collection equipment available?		_____	_____
5. Are the sheets for collecting data properly dated and labeled?		_____	_____
6. Does the recorder know where to collect data?		_____	_____
7. Does the recorder know when to collect data?		_____	_____
8. Does the recorder have any unanswered questions or problems about collecting data?		_____	_____
9. Does the recorder know how and where to contact the practitioner if problems arise?		_____	_____

FIGURE 4.1   Data collection checklist.

possible. That is, try to avoid a long delay between the occurrence of a problem and its recording (e.g., don't ask a parent to record child misbehaviors at the end of the day). The goal here is to try to minimize possible distortions of memory (e.g., Farmer & Nelson-Gray, 1990).

Deciding when to record depends mainly on the nature of the target and the measure you're using; therefore, in each of the chapters dealing with the different measurement procedures we describe specific information about how to decide when to use that particular measure. However, as a preliminary guideline, try to get as clear and representative a picture of the target problem as possible.

The key is the term *representative*. You don't want to collect information on a problem that would misrepresent how often or how intensely it occurs. For example, when recording behaviors, you would want to make sure that you understand the full range of occurrences of the problem, and that you're not underestimating it because you have decided to collect information only in one location or at one time. Similarly, if you're asking the client to note feelings of loneliness, you have to decide whether the client should record several times a day or only once a day—say, in the evening; this could give a distorted view of his or her feelings if that particular time of day has been identified as a particularly lonely time. (A more detailed discussion of how to take a sample from a range of behaviors is provided in Chapter 5.)

Decide How Often Data Should Be Collected

As a general guideline, data should be collected as often as possible without becoming tiresome, boring, aversive, or overwhelming to whomever is collecting the data. Care should be taken to see that you're not putting too much of a burden on the record keeper, that the repeated collection of information is not producing a reactive effect on the target, and that the recorder isn't changing the way he or she records or views the target halfway into the project.

Repeated measures, as we said earlier, are part of the essence of what single-system designs are all about, because you can establish and track *over time* the range and level of occurrence of a target. This gives you the clearest and best picture of what is happening to that target. These repeated measures should be collected prior to and during intervention and, we hope, at some follow-up period selected by you and the client.

Repeated measurement during baseline, intervention, and follow-up may not be possible all of the time, although we believe that it's possible most of the time. There are times when complications arise that affect your ability to measure a target repeatedly during baseline, intervention, or follow-up (e.g., a life-threatening situation arises during baseline, such as the physical abuse of a child, that requires immediate intervention and therefore precludes the prospective measurement of the target during baseline). Under such conditions we suggest that you do whatever you can to get as much of an accurate picture of the client's problems as possible. You should try to at least measure the target once prior to intervention so you have a rough preintervention estimate of the target, once at or near the end of intervention so you have a rough estimate of whether the criterion for termination is met, and once at follow-up so you have a rough estimate of whether change was maintained. At best such *single-point measures* provide suggestive information, but we definitely do not recommend them as the methods of choice, because they don't provide sufficient information to evaluate an intervention or to assess or monitor targets in order to make needed and timely changes in an intervention.

While you should try to do the best you can with the resources available, we believe the tremendous utility of repeated measures makes them the key priority for single-system evaluations. As we said before, repeated measures will give you the clearest picture of what is happening to the client problem(s).

No matter how often data are collected, you should select regular predesignated times or conditions for the data to be recorded, and you should make it clear to the person who is to record the data just exactly when and under what conditions data are to be recorded. For example, you should make it clear whether a client should rate anxiety at regular intervals (e.g., each day), at preselected times (e.g., before going to sleep in the evening), or when faced with selected critical incidents (e.g., prior to having a job interview).

Decide How Many Targets to Record

The basic guideline for all recording is to try to keep the whole procedure simple. You don't want to overburden the recorder (your client, you, a relevant other) with the task. This is particularly true when it is the recorder's first attempt at recording. You don't want to create confusion or frustration by making the process too complicated.

A rule for selecting the number of targets to be recorded is: When in doubt, do less. It would be unreasonable to ask anyone to record more than two or three separate targets at most, unless perhaps there are existing records (e.g., in a school) that would make such recording manageable. In most situations it is probably best to focus on one problem area at a time. This also allows the practitioner to develop a thorough intervention plan focused on one area at a time.

Of course, one problem area (say, marital discord) may encompass several specific targets (e.g., communication, sex, finances). Thus, it may be possible to record more than one aspect of the same problem. For example, you might ask the client to record both the number of positive thoughts he or she has about himself or herself and the number of negative thoughts. Or you might ask the client to record the number of angry feelings and to evaluate the intensity of the anger on a separate scale (see Chapter 6). Similarly, if the target involves a configuration of factors dealing with interpersonal skills and anxiety, you might ask the client to record the number of contacts he or she has with someone of the opposite sex, to rate the intensity of the anxiety he or she experi-

enced, and to evaluate the negative or positive thoughts he or she experienced with each contact. Such recording, all focused on one problem, would still provide information on several targets: overt behaviors, feelings, and thoughts.

Another example of collecting data on several aspects of one problem is not only to record the occurrence of some problem but also to note when it occurred and under what circumstances in order to assess controlling conditions. (Examples of this type of recording will be provided in Chapter 8.)

If there's still some doubt as to what target to focus on for recording, try to pick one that may be representative of the others. That is, if the target you select seems to give a clear picture of the entire configuration, or at least typifies it, you probably made a good choice. If you do decide to record only one target, select one that: (a) has the most practical advantages, (b) is relatively amenable to the recording process, (c) is clear and readily identifiable, and (d) is most direct and objective.

Focusing on recording only one target shouldn't limit you. You might want to select several measures of that target, for example, behavioral observation (Chapter 5), an individualized rating scale (Chapter 6), and a standardized questionnaire (Chapter 7) to get a clear picture of the target.

We know that the realities of practice are such that in most cases you're confronted with a host of targets. Indeed, you are probably usually working with several targets at the same time. It may be possible to record information for each of those, perhaps using a different person to collect data on each. On the other hand, the best you can do may be to work with several targets, but only record one of them. If this is the case, then we suggest you use some of the above guidelines in selecting which one to record (e.g., representativeness, availability of resources for recording). Thus, in some situations the main criteria regarding how many targets to record may involve practicality: willingness and availability of people to record; time and energy of the recorders; complexity of the target (e.g., ability to clearly identify a recording method); and the time and energy you have to devote to the task of setting up recording methods.

Standardize Recording Procedures

The time (e.g., morning or evening), place (e.g., client's home or the practitioner's office), and method (e.g., self-administered or practitioner-administered questionnaire) you use to measure a client's targets can influence your results. Therefore, if the time, place, or method used changes over time, it becomes difficult to disentangle these changes from real changes in the problem. Therefore, ideally you should use the same time, place, and method to measure a particular client's targets over time.

It's especially important that you avoid changes in the time, place, or method of measurement that coincide with a change in treatment conditions (e.g., change from baseline to intervention). When measurement procedures change at the same time that treatment conditions change, it's difficult to determine the effect of the change in treatment conditions. For example, during baseline a client might rate his or her depression in the late afternoon, a time when he or she feels especially upset. If for some reason when the intervention is implemented he or she begins to rate depression in the morning, a time when he or she feels much better, any improvement observed in the problem after the intervention begins might be due either to the intervention, or to the change in the time of rating.

Sometimes it isn't possible to use the same time, place, and method of measurement over time for a client. Clients, relevant others, and sometimes even busy practitioners, forget to complete self-administered questionnaires at appointed times, or they complete them in different settings. Computers sometimes don't work, requiring the substitution of the tried-and-true paper-and-pencil method of data collection. When such changes occur you should note the differences and try to take them into account when interpreting results. You'll just have to make a judgment concerning the extent to which a pattern of results over time was due to real changes or to changes in the time, place, or method of measurement.

Begin Collecting Baseline Information

Once you have completed the preceding steps, you're ready to begin collecting baseline information. (This is described in detail in Chapter 12.) Many of the decisions and issues that we have described may seem overwhelming at first and may indeed prove to be overwhelming the first one or two times you try collecting data. However, we're confident that with experience both the decisions and the actual act of recording information will grow to be less complicated and more rewarding.

We hope you are already convinced of the advantages of recording during the baseline and intervention periods. Once you try recording with a client and continue to use it with subsequent clients, we hope you not only will become convinced of the ultimate practicality of recording, but will also build it into your practice with every client. Hence, the last steps are to start baselining, continue to record once your intervention program begins, and start to enjoy the fruits of your labor—more precise assessments, clearer evaluations, and the potential for enhancing your effectiveness.

CHARTING: PUTTING YOUR INFORMATION ON GRAPHS

The information that you collect for the baseline and subsequent intervention periods, as we mentioned earlier, could be collected and tabulated in any number of ways, ranging from records of agency intakes, to a client's scores on a questionnaire, to a family's count of communications. Yet in this more or less raw form (e.g., just a bunch of scores or tallies on a 3" × 5" card) these data may not be helpful because they may be too complicated or jumbled. Furthermore, it seems desirable to have a standardized system for recording and checking changes for a variety of quite different forms of information.

Charting is probably the most convenient and desirable way to make the data you collect both useful and standardized. Now, if you're not one for statistics or mathematics, and the notion of charting conjures up all sorts of fears, don't stop reading. Charting–or graphing as it's sometimes called–is a convenient, simple, helpful way for you and your client to make some sense out of the data you collect.

The most important guideline for recording is to make sure the data will be *used*. Charting is perhaps the best method to help you attain that goal, since charting involves a pictorial representation of changes in the target from the onset of baselining to the termination of intervention. But charting also helps the assessment process, as changes in the data reveal patterns in factors that may affect the target.

Charting has another value. It can serve as feedback to the client and to the practitioner. This feedback can help motivate, support, and reinforce efforts to change, maintain willingness to participate in the program, and generally encourage the involvement of those concerned. The chart also can be a constant reminder of the goals and objectives of intervention.

Charting generally involves transferring the data you collect onto a piece of paper (preferably lined graph paper because it makes the charting process easier and more precise) and then displaying the chart in a prominent place (perhaps chosen by the client) so that it can be seen often. If your client is collecting data and placing this information on a chart at home, the chart might be placed on a refrigerator or some other area that people walk by frequently. If the data are for an organization, you can put the chart on the main bulletin board. Don't skimp on the space you use on the piece of charting paper. Spread the chart out along the width of the entire paper. (Remember to use these same guidelines if you're teaching your client how to record and chart.)

Graphs of client targets are easy to draw by hand, but a variety of easy-to-use personal computer programs also are available and will generate and easily update high-quality single-system design-type graphs even faster than you can draw them by hand. Harvard Graphics is an example of a personal computer program that generates single-system design-type graphs in addition to other types of graphs (e.g., cumulative charts, which we discuss below).

Some personal computer programs generate graphs and do other single-system design tasks. The Computer Assisted Social Services (CASS) system (Hudson, 1990a; 1990b; Nurius & Hudson, 1993), which is described in this book, is a good example, and we discuss it in more detail later in this chapter and in Chapter 7. Among other things, CASS administers standardized scales to clients, scores these scales, and graphs the results in a single-system design format. As another example, many agencies now have spreadsheet programs such as Excel. These programs generate single-system design-type graphs and perform statistical analyses, among other things. Spreadsheet programs will not automatically compute many of the statistics used to analyze single-system design results, but they can be programmed to conduct such analyses (Alter & Evens, 1990; Benbenishty, 1989; Benbenishty & Ben-Zaken, 1988; Bronson & Blythe, 1987).

Presenting Data on the Chart

There are standardized methods for use of charts, so all charts can be interpreted roughly in the same terms (e.g., Sanders, 1978; Zelanzny, 1985).

First, draw two straight lines at right angles, one horizontal and one vertical, joined at the lower left corner. There are some conventions as to what these lines represent, and we suggest following these conventions. The horizontal line or axis (sometimes called the abscissa) always refers to time elements. The time elements always begin on the left and move to the right. The period of time you use depends on how often you collect data. The most typical time unit is days. But if you collect a great deal of information (e.g., about organizations), you might want to average the data over some period of time, say, a week. Similarly, if the target doesn't occur frequently, you might want to count all the occurrences of the target that week and use the week as the basic unit for your horizontal axis. Each unit on the timeline is considered a "point"; thus, a baseline of 15 days has 15 points. Several charts illustrating different time elements are displayed in Figure 4.2.

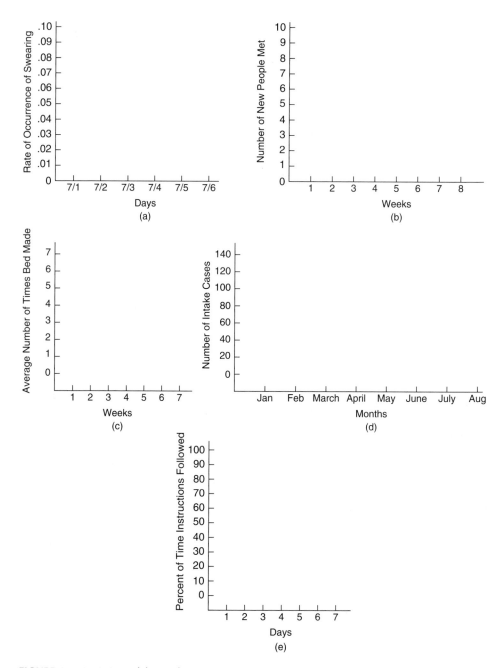

FIGURE 4.2   Variations of data and time units as presented on charts.

If you do decide to average or group data, you must be aware that you may be hiding factors that can help your assessment. It's much more difficult to investigate factors that are re-lated to daily changes in a behavior when you average or group the data over a week. On the other hand, if the baseline data are extremely variable, grouping the data can produce a more stable baseline, making the data more amenable to analysis. Furthermore, if you group data, you will probably need to extend the baseline so that you can achieve more than the minimal number of data points (requirements for the length and stability of the baseline will be discussed in Chapter 12).

Figure 4.2 illustrates two charts (4.2 a & e) using days as the time unit. (The days can be numbered or the actual dates can be placed on the chart.) Note that each time unit is denoted by a hatch mark on the horizontal axis, and the marks are equidistant. The time unit you select should be written under the line.

The vertical axis (sometimes called the ordinate) represents the target. The hatch marks on this axis also should be equidistant. The label you use for the target should be entered to the left of the axis. If you're dealing with large numbers, your increments on the vertical axis should vary accordingly (see Figure 4.2). Ordinarily the "0" (indicating no occurrences of the target) is placed on the vertical axis, where it intersects the horizontal axis, as in Figure 4.2 a & b. However, it's also possible to place the 0 above the horizontal axis using the first hatch mark on the vertical axis, as in Figure 4.2 c–e; it sometimes presents a clearer picture, since the data then don't run into the horizontal axis.

The key question at this point is what form of data to use. You have several choices: absolute numbers (e.g., number of days of school attended, number of practitioner/client contacts); percentages (e.g., percentage of time an entire family spends together); rates (when the time periods for collection of data vary [to be described in Chapter 5]); or scores (e.g., scores on a problem-solving questionnaire from 0 to 100). The method of plotting information on the chart represents the way you define the target and how you actually collect the data. Several variations of data and time units are presented in Figure 4.2.

The last step in using the chart is to plot the data. Over each number on the horizontal axis (time), put a dot next to the appropriate number on the vertical axis (target). You will be placing the dot alongside the value (e.g., the number of times the target occurred, the scale

score for that time period, etc.) for the target recorded during that time period. This continues until there's a dot for all time periods. The dots are then connected by a line so that the patterns can be more readily seen. This is depicted in Figure 4.3.

What if the client is sometimes not able to record (or even forgets)? These data should still be plotted on the chart, and they're represented either by omitting the lines between the time periods before and after data *were* recorded or by connecting the dots with a dotted rather than solid line. Of course, with days missing, you should use a little more caution in interpreting any patterns on the chart, since it would be difficult to know whether those days would have continued the pattern. This process is depicted in Figure 4.4 with Days 3 and 6 missing.

If the target could not possibly have occurred at all (e.g., disruptive behavior in the schools could not occur on weekends), those days are not entered on the chart (see Figure 4.5).

In some situations, though, you might want more than one chart to depict different parts of the same target. For example, if the goal of the program is to increase a client's number of positive self-references and to decrease the number of negative self-references, you might want to depict each of these on separate charts.

Under some circumstances you might want to depict two or sometimes three different measures on the same chart. This is useful to determine whether the different measures "vary

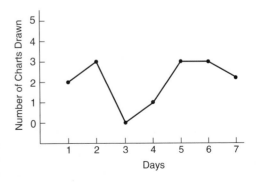

FIGURE 4.3 Chart illustrating the complete labeling and plotting process.

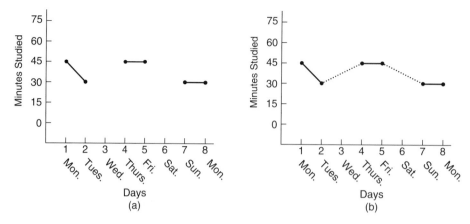

FIGURE 4.4   Two methods of recording missing data: (a) missing data—lines omitted; (b) missing data—dotted line.

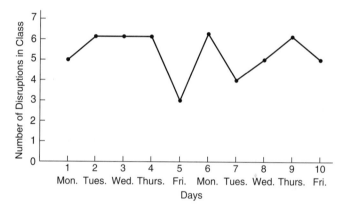

FIGURE 4.5   Chart illustrating number of disruptions in class with weekends omitted.

together" over time, as was discussed and illustrated in Chapter 2. As a hypothetical example, suppose that a Task-Centered approach (Fortune, 1985; Reid, 1978) is used with a client who is dissatisfied with his or her job, but whose goal is to keep the job and increase job satisfaction. Each week the client and practitioner jointly select a task for the client to undertake at work to improve job satisfaction (e.g., discussing job assignments with the supervisor), and the client is asked to rate the success in carrying out the week's task on the following Task Achievement Scale (Reid, 1977, p. 289; Reid & Hanrahan, 1988): (1) not

achieved or minimally achieved; (2) partially achieved; (3) substantially achieved; (4) completely achieved. Also, each week the client is asked to rate job satisfaction on the following 5-point scale: (1) not at all satisfied; (2) somewhat satisfied; (3) moderately satisfied; (4) very satisfied; (5) extremely satisfied. The objective was to at least "substantially" achieve the tasks (i.e., a rating of 3 or greater), and the ultimate goal was to have a job satisfaction rating of at least 4.

Results of this example are shown in Figure 4.6, and they show that as task achievement increases during the intervention phase job satis-

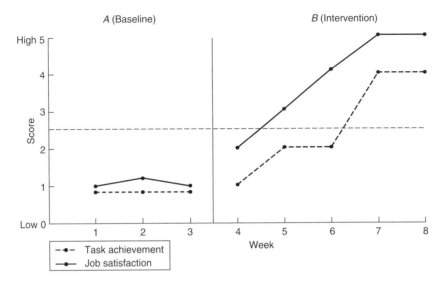

FIGURE 4.6 Task achievement and job satisfaction.

faction also increases. They also show that for Weeks 7 and 8 both the objective and ultimate goals were achieved.

The results shown in Figure 4.6 also illustrate what is called *concomitant variation*. Concomitant variation exists if two or more events change together: if they consistently increase or decrease at the same time (i.e., they're positively correlated), or one consistently increases while the other decreases (i.e., they're negatively correlated). Concomitant variation is important because it can suggest causal connections between events. For example, the results shown in Figure 4.6 suggest that task achievement increases job satisfaction. However, *it's risky to assume that one event causes another just because the events are correlated.* It might be, for example, that the more satisfied the client is with his or her job, the more likely he or she is to complete tasks, or it might be that some other factor is causing task achievement and job satisfaction to change (e.g., increased marital satisfaction).

If two or more measures are depicted on the same chart, and the scales for the two measures are about the same (e.g., a 4-point scale for one measure and a 5-point scale for the other measure), it's reasonable to use just one vertical

axis to represent the scale, as illustrated in Figure 4.6. If the scales for the different measures are very different, it's useful to use separate vertical axes to represent the different measures. Suppose that in the example just discussed job satisfaction was measured using a standardized questionnaire with a range of values from 0 to 100. In this situation it would be best to use two vertical axes to depict the different measures. An example of how this could be done is shown in Figure 4.7.

Although most charts you will use and see in the literature present the data as they occur in each time period—say, giving the number of times a target occurs each day or how long it occurs—another possibility for charting is to use *cumulative charting*. Cumulative charting involves adding each time period's recorded data to the data of the periods before it. This is a good method to use when you wish to emphasize progress, because the trend of the data is always upward (you're adding each time period's total to the total of the time periods before it). In this case you can evaluate change by looking at the slope of the line; the steeper the slope, the higher the occurrence of whatever you've targeted for change. Figure 4.8, adapted from Fischer and Gochros' (1975), illustrates a

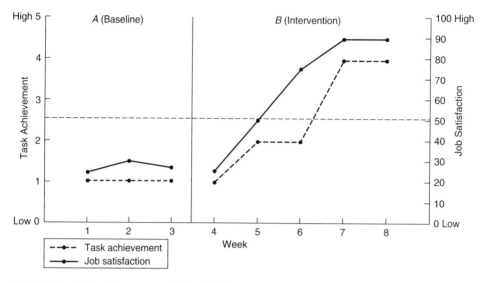

FIGURE 4.7   Task achievement and job satisfaction.

cumulative chart of cleanup activities (for another good example, see Rzepnicki, 1985). The first week involved 10 hours of cleanup activities. The second week involved 7 hours of cleanup activities, and this number was added to the first week's activities. The third week's cleanup activities involved some 5 hours, and

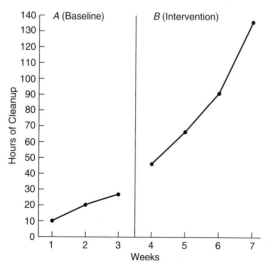

FIGURE 4.8   Cumulative hours of cleanup activities by Blue Cottage during the cleanup campaign.

this number was added to the first 2 weeks' sum for a total of 22 hours of cleanup activities during the first 3 weeks. This total is the baseline. As the figure shows, there was a dramatic change in the slope of the line once intervention started.

Another way of displaying data on the charts is the bar graph, This is most typically used in group situations—for example, where group averages or aggregate data are reported. Figure 4.9 illustrates a bar graph concerned with a class's weekly average score on a test for the first 5 weeks of the semester.

Phases

One advantage of charts is that they can help you clearly identify the different aspects of your total intervention program virtually from your first involvement with the client. The chart necessitates that you distinguish among various phases of your contact with the client. A *phase* refers to any relatively distinct part of the client's overall program from first to last contact. The most commonly used distinction between phases is between baseline and intervention. However, phases also can refer to the onset and termination of different types of interventions with the same client.

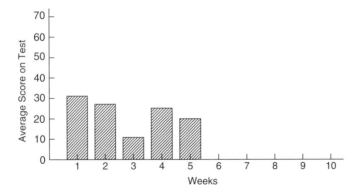

FIGURE 4.9   Bar graph of class weekly average score on a test.

Phases are usually separated on the chart by a vertical line. They also should be labeled in the appropriate section of the chart. It's customary to use a letter to designate different phases of intervention. The importance of this will become more clear in Part III, when we describe different designs that you can use to evaluate your programs. Conventional notation for designating phases is that *A* always stands for baseline, and subsequent letters of the alphabet (*B, C,* and so on) each stand for different but specific interven-

tions. Combining two earlier interventions simply calls for using both of the earlier letters. These could consist of separate intervention techniques or several techniques integrated into a package.

Let's say you conduct a baseline (*A*) and then begin your intervention (*B*). Feedback from your chart indicates that it's not working. You switch to a new intervention (*C*). Then you decide to combine the two interventions in an attempt to enhance overall effects (*B-C*). This process is charted in Figure 4.10.

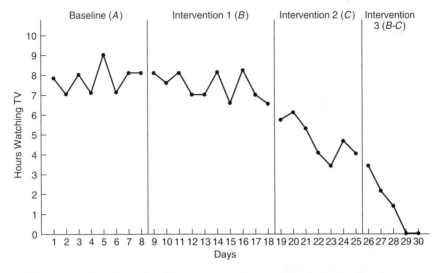

FIGURE 4.10   Chart illustrating different phases of a program including baseline (*A*), intervention 1 (*B*), intervention 2 (*C*), and a combination of interventions 1 and 2 (*B-C*).

In some articles in the literature, you will see subscripts used along with letters (e.g., A_1-B_1-A_2-B_2). These subscripts only refer to the first or second (and so on) implementation of exactly the same phase. Thus, A_1 is the first baseline and A_2 is the second, while B_1 is implementation of the intervention the first time and B_2 is implementation of exactly the same intervention the second time.

Another variation in notation is the use of *superscripts* (e.g., A-B^1-B^2). Superscripts refer to changes in the *intensity* of either the intervention or the goals. We will discuss designs using superscripts in Chapter 16.

Although we use the letter A to denote baseline and subsequent letters of the alphabet to indicate interventions, there's another system of labeling that we'll briefly describe in case you come across it in the literature. This is the system used by Campbell and Stanley (1966) and Cook and Campbell (1979) in which they label repeated observations or measurements O and interventions X. Thus, a design incorporating baseline and intervention periods $(A$-$B)$ might be labeled $OOO\ X\ OOO$ or $O_1O_2O_3O_4\ X\ O_5O_6O_7O_8$. Similarly, an A-B-A-B design (baseline-intervention-baseline-intervention) might be labeled $OOO\ X_1\ OOO\ X_2$ or simply $O\ X_1\ O\ X_2$.

These are the basics of the notation system; we elaborate on the issues involved in this use of notation, especially with regard to intervention techniques, packages, and programs, in Chapter 11.

PROBLEM-ORIENTED RECORDS (POR)

One of the great values of recording for single-system designs is precisely that these records can be used with just about any type of agency recording format. In fact, we believe use of the recording methods we describe here will actually make your other recording jobs easier. This is because you will have clearly specified targets and goals and regularly collected information on changes in targets throughout your contact with the client, both during your assessment (during which the baseline occurs) and intervention.

For example, one recording format that is commonly used in many organizations is the Problem-Oriented Record (POR); it sometimes is called the Problem-Oriented Log or POL (Burrill, 1976; Grant & Maletzky, 1972; Kagle, 1991; Kane, 1974; Martens & Holmstrup, 1974; Ryback, 1974; Sheafor, Horejsi, Horejsi, 1991; Weed, 1968). Originally developed in an attempt to systematize and reform medical records, the POR has been widely adopted in a number of human service organizations. Hence, we provide a description of the POR and the way it can be used to supplement single-system designs.

The basic purpose of the POR is to provide in a standardized format information that is directly related to the problem being dealt with by the practitioner. It's therefore thought to be helpful in the attempt to document and evaluate services. The POR basically requires that (a) client problems be specified clearly, (b) an intervention plan be specified, and (c) progress be monitored and recorded at regular intervals.

Basic Guidelines for Using the POR

The POR is composed of four major parts: (a) database, (b) complete problem list, (c) initial plans, and (d) monitoring progress.

Database. The database essentially is the information that you collect as part of the assessment. This, of course, is standard operating procedure for all professions. The POR, however, focuses on an important requirement in the development of a database: The types of data to be collected must be clearly defined in advance, based on the typical range of problems and needs and requirements of your agency or practice setting. This is an attempt to ensure that the database meets uniform minimum standards of the quality and quantity of information needed in order to produce a sound assessment. This can then lead to a sound decision regarding intervention plans (Martens & Holmstrup, 1974).

The database, because it's defined in advance, necessitates systematic collection of information. However, each agency or organization has to decide what kind of database would be most productive to further its aims and to enhance its selection of interventive methods. Obviously, an agency specializing in foster care arrangements would need a database different from the kind used by an agency specializing in cases of sexual abuse.

Similarly, the theoretical orientation of the practitioner might dictate collection of a different set of data to constitute the data base. Thus, the database could include everything from practitioner observations to reports of individuals in the client's environment to checklists and inventories.

The database can and should be added to as the evaluation proceeds. Care must be taken to ensure that it is clearly defined, not overinterpreted (i.e., that impressions don't stray too far from observations), complete, representative of actual problem occurrences, and representative of observations of all members of the professional team (if a team is involved), and that plans are specified to continue to collect data if the database is incomplete.

Because the database is developed prior to intervention, it can be used to provide suggestions for selecting one or more of the problems for more intensive and repeated observations, and for charting on a graph for evaluation using single-system designs.

Complete Problem List. The next step in use of the POR is to develop a complete problem list. This problem list is based on the information obtained from the database. Each problem should be numbered and that number can be used to refer to the problem throughout the rest of the record. The numbered problem list becomes the first page and table of contents of the record. Highlighting the problem list in this way keeps problems from being overlooked as intervention proceeds.

The problem list is constructed on the basis of what you and the client have agreed should be focused on; the items are recorded in order of priority. The problem list should include all problems that the practitioner and client can identify. No problems should be eliminated or dropped by erasure; instead, a line can be drawn through the original problem with an arrow followed by the modified problem or the term *dropped* or *resolved*. It is probably best not to note problems in terms of diagnosis, since this may lead to confusion, labeling, or different perceptions by different practitioners. Instead, the problem should be defined as precisely and specifically as possible, using guidelines such as those in Chapter 3.

The problem list can be constructed in different ways depending on the needs and priorities of the given agency. It is probably best, though, to include, at a minimum, a problem number, the name of the active problem, the date it was defined (when the practitioner found out about it), the inactive status (resolved or improved), and the date the problem was resolved.

Initial Plans. Once problems are listed, all subsequent notes should refer to a specific, numbered problem. You should also record the basis for all subsequent information and for all decisions.

There are three basic components to the plans. The first is further assessment. In this part of the record, new or additional information (and its source) that bears on the specific problem under consideration is listed. This could include elaboration of the conditions causing or maintaining the problem. It might even include an example of the problem, when and where it occurred, who was present, and so on.

The second component is a clear statement of the goal plus a statement of the system you will use to monitor progress. Remember, simply stating the problem (lack of sleep) may not have anything to do with the goal (e.g., to diminish a client's anxiety over a job interview so that he or she will be able to sleep). Actually, almost any of the material in this book–ranging from goal selection to measurement to design options–can be used to monitor progress.

The third component involves establishing an intervention plan. For each problem, a specific plan is developed. The intervention plan should include who will intervene, for how long, what intervention techniques will be used, what role the practitioner will be functioning in, and what tasks the client must undertake. The notes may even indicate the basis for the selection of those particular intervention techniques (e.g., reference to articles in the literature demonstrating effective use of those techniques with the particular problem under concern).

The initial plans also may include other categories, such as anticipated time limits, resources, potential barriers to effective intervention and plans for overcoming those barriers, and so on.

Monitoring Progress. The final component of POR is the notes that one takes as progress is monitored. As with other parts of the POR system, these notes should be dated, numbered, and titled.

A suggested POR format for these progress notes is known by the acronym SOAP.

The first component is **S**ubjective data. These are statements of the problem from the point of view of the client, practitioner, and others, including thoughts, feelings, and concerns. These data are subjective in that they're difficult or impossible to verify.

The second component is **O**bjective data. These are all important objective data related to a particular problem. These objective data could include observations (what was observed, not interpretations of the observations), test results, attendance reports, demographic data related to the problem, medications taken, and so on.

The third component of the progress notes is **A**ssessment. This is the synthesis and analysis of the subjective and objective data as related to a particular problem. The assessment is also intended to identify and evaluate new obstacles or resources as they may affect intervention. The assessment obviously is ongoing and is intended to provide information to bolster or, if need be, change the intervention plan.

The fourth component of the notes is progress with the intervention **P**lan. Here, continued use or changes in the intervention procedures are identified as the case proceeds, and specific dates and plans to review progress are identified. If there are no changes in the

overall plan, the practitioner would note this. This section, however, also would include short-range plans–for example, what is to be done in the next week.

An example (from Kane, 1974, p. 416) of a progress note for a child (John) whose problem has been identified as "uncontrollable at home," would be:

Subjective: Mrs. X states that she feels more relaxed about John, and John reports less quarreling at home. He claims he doesn't feel as "uptight."

Objective: Mrs. X has been attending a parents' group at the Q Agency since May 1. Her attendance has been perfect, and the group leader reports that she has been actively involved. The worker has observed her using the new ideas she has learned in discussing a problem with John.

Assessment: The problem seems much diminished.

Plan: (1) No further direct intervention after the group ends in two weeks, (2) review in a month to determine if the summer vacation brings new stress, (3) evaluate at that time for removal to inactive list.

An additional component of the progress notes would be the termination summary. This would follow the same format as above but would also include the final evaluation of the extent to which the goal was achieved, the reason for termination, and follow-up and maintenance plans.

While there are few data on the reliability of the POR, it appears to be a good example of the attempt to systematize recording beyond the methods used in many organizations. Single-system designs can be used in complementary ways with the POR, especially with regard to providing a system for monitoring progress to provide the basis for the more or less objective data needed in order to evaluate change with the POR (i.e., the O in the SOAP) model.

POR is used in many agencies in an integrated fashion with other procedures. One of the best examples of this is the Lutheran Social Services of Wisconsin and Upper Michigan (W. Benedict, personal communication, 1986). This agency uses a program called "Evalutreat," which actually integrates the POR and Goal Attainment Scaling (GAS) and other evaluation techniques. Evalutreat combines an agency's case recording and program evaluation functions into a unified process in a way that can satisfy most case recording requirements.

COMPUTERIZED RECORDING

As the prices of personal computers continue to drop, and programs for their use become more accessible and easy to use, it is inevitable that practitioners in the human services will come to rely on personal computers to help manage and enhance their practice. To that end, we offer in this book two basic computer programs, Computer Assisted Social Services (CASS) and SINGWIN, to help you in the management of your caseload and analysis of data. We also want to encourage you to explore the World Wide Web and to take advantage of the vast resources available there. To begin, open the Internet browser program on your computer, such as Netscape or Microsoft Internet Explorer, and type in the following address in the top window: **http://www.ablongman.com/bloom** and then hit <enter>. This will bring you to the website for this book. It will provide you with an overview of the book, allow you to connect directly with sites devoted to CASS and CAAP, provide you with links to other interesting sites, and, if you click on "Technical Support," will provide you with technical information about SINGWIN and an email address where you can get technical support for this program.

Another tremendous resource on the Internet is called the World Wide Web Resources for Social Workers (W3RSW) developed by Gary Holden. Periodically updated with verified links and addresses, this site contains links and information pertinent to all human service professionals on topics including government, measurement, psychology, reference, social cognitive theory, social science, and many more. There are well over 50,000 links on this site. All you have to do is type the following address into your browser and hit <enter> and you'll be there: **http://www.nyu.edu/socialwork/wwwrsw/.** You can also subscribe to a new, free, Internet-based information service for human service professionals called Information for Practice by sending a blank e-mail message to *join-information-for-practice@forums.nyu. edu.*

Personal computer programs are available not only to graph the results of single-system designs, but also to store, retrieve, organize, communicate, disseminate, and analyze recorded information easily for practitioners, supervisors, and administrators (e.g., Baskin, 1990; Benbenishty, 1989; Corcoran & Gingerich, 1994; Mutschler, 1987; Newman, Consoli, & Taylor, 1997; Patterson, 2000). However, because there are so many, it's impossible to describe all the different computer programs for the management of client data. (A recent review of the use of computers in assessment and treatment of clinical disorders is available in Newman et al., 1997.) This is a rapidly growing area, so you should also look for current developments in journals such as *Computers in Human Services, Social Science Computer Review,* and *Computers in Psychiatry/Psychology;* in reference books such as *Personal Computer Applications in the Social Services* (Patterson, 2000), *Computer Use in Psychology: A Directory of Software* (Stoloff & Couch, 1992), *Psychware Sourcebook* (Krug, 1993), and *The 12th Mental Measurements Yearbook* (Conoley & Kramer, 1995); and on the Web in such places as "CUSSnet" (**http://www.uta.edu/cussn/cussn.html**), Computers in Mental Health (**http:// www.ex.ac.uk/cimh/welcome.htm**), Social Work Search (**http://www.socialwork-search. com**), and New Technology in the Human Services (**http://www.fz.hse.nl/causa/swbib/sw_keyw.htm**); and in software review sections of professional journals. However, to provide you with a concrete example of one of the best, most versatile, and well-developed assessment systems, we've included detailed instructions for installing and using the Computer Assisted Social Services Program CD-ROM included with this book (CASS; Nugent, Sieppert, & Hudson, 2001; Hudson, 1996a, 1996b; Nurius & Hudson, 1993).

 There is an extensive CASS User's Guide beginning on page 139.

Some Advantages and Disadvantages of Using Computers

There are some concerns raised by the use of personal computers to manage client data (e.g.,

Moreland, 1987; Siegel, 1990). Computers require start-up time in learning the operation of the computer and the particular software program. They also require a financial investment in the computer equipment and software. In addition, eliciting information via computer may seem intimidating and impersonal to some clients, and there are some clients who won't be able to use some of these systems (e.g., those who can't read). Extra care needs to be taken to ensure that clients understand the task at hand and are able to respond appropriately.

The personal computer management of client data does have some important benefits, as suggested by the following description of CASS and other related personal computer software (see also Butcher, 1987; Hudson, 1990b; Nurius & Hudson, 1993). Computers can increase the speed and efficiency with which information is managed, and this can free up time to deliver services. They also can increase the accuracy with which measures are administered and scored. Even the most conscientious practitioner can make mistakes in scoring measures, and these mistakes can lead to incorrect practice and evaluation decisions; computers don't make such errors if properly used. Finally, there's some evidence that clients are more willing to reveal sensitive personal information (e.g., alcohol abuse, sexual behaviors) to a computer than to a practitioner or on a pencil-and-paper questionnaire (e.g., Malcolm, Sturgis, Anton, & Williams, 1989; Millstein & Irwin, 1983). Therefore, in some cases using the personal computer to elicit information directly from clients might provide more valid client information.

Finally, there are three new books that are excellent resources for finding sites on the Internet that can be helpful to professionals: *The Insider's Guide to Mental Health Resources Online* (Grohol, 2000), *Social Work and the Web* (Vernon & Lynch, 2000), and *A Quick Guide to the Internet for Social Workers* (Yaffe & Gotthoffer, 2000). These books describe sites that provide everything from information on new interventions to self-help and consumer/client education. For online updates to the Grohol book, visit the site http://www.insidemh.com.

SUMMARY

This chapter presented the basic principles involved in developing a measurement and recording plan. We first discussed how to decide who, where, when, and how to measure targets. Then we discussed guidelines for developing a plan to record the information generated by the measurement plan. The recording plan involves charting the information you collect on an ongoing basis in order to document, communicate, and monitor client progress to permit any needed changes in your intervention in a timely fashion. Also, we discussed the use of the Problem-Oriented Record, a commonly used recording device that can be used along with single-system designs. Finally, we briefly described computerized recording in general, and one of the programs that is included with this book, CASS, in particular. The CASS User's Guide begins on the following page.

COMPUTER ASSISTED SOCIAL SERVICES (CASS): A USER'S GUIDE

CASS was developed for human service practitioners, and it provides a good example of a comprehensive, easy-to-use, personal computer program that simplifies and enhances the recording, storage, retrieval, and organization of client data. CASS is the general name of this program, but there is another program included with CASS named CAAP (Computer Assisted Assessment Package). It's important to distinguish between CASS and CAAP and their different functions at the outset.

CAAP is used by *clients* to:

- Complete scales
- View scale scores
- View graphed scale scores

CASS is used by *practitioners* to:

- Manage client files (e.g., create, edit, and read files)
- Manage scales completed by clients using CAAP (e.g., view and graph scale scores)
- Manage scales completed by clients by hand (e.g., input and score scale data)
- Manage service tasks for individual clients and overall for an agency or group of practitioners who use CASS (e.g., define and redefine tasks, monitor task completion)
- Manage client casenotes (e.g., create, edit, and read casenotes)
- Manage how information is presented to clients using CAAP (e.g., edit menus of scales presented, add new scales)

CAAP administers almost any type of standardized scale or test to your clients, and it automatically scores it, charts the results in a single-system design format, updates the information for a client each time a measure is completed so you can monitor client progress over time using CASS, and stores the information in the computer. An especially notable feature is that, although CAAP comes with ready-to-use scales, you can add an almost unlimited number of additional scales, including ones constructed by you or your agency. Therefore, it's possible to use CASS to construct a tailor-made package of computer-administered instruments for use in your practice.

Essentially, CASS automatically retrieves, organizes, and saves client-completed scale data from CAAP, and it lets you view and manipulate (e.g., graph) this information. Furthermore, CASS lets you enter and otherwise manage other client information such as service tasks and casenotes.

A notable feature of CASS and CAAP is that information is stored so that only you or someone you designate can access the program and client information. Clients and practitioners are assigned unique passwords that must be used to enter the system, and scale scores and other information are encrypted so that only you or someone you designate will have access to the information.

CASS is designed to be used by practitioners with minimal knowledge of personal computers, and CAAP is designed to be used by clients with minimal knowledge of personal computers and with minimal instruction from you. To this end CASS and CAAP are Windows-based systems with on-screen menus that walk you and your clients through the program. (A computer menu is just a set of choices from which users select what they want to do.) Also, CASS and CAAP have extensive on-line, context-sensitive help that can be read on screen or printed.

We'll have more to say about CAAP in Chapter 7. Here we would like to introduce you to CASS and its numerous features. **However, before you can work through the exercises here and in Chapter 7, you need to install CASS and CAAP. The installation procedure is described in the Appendix at the end of this User's Guide.**

We assume that you know very little about computers, and we apologize in advance if this isn't the case. There are a few things that you need to know at the outset, but if you've used Windows before you probably already know these.

Before starting, first be sure to familiarize yourself with the basic operations of your computer (e.g., location of your A drive, "Enter" key, Ctrl key, and ←↑→↓ keys). In particular, find out what version of Windows your computer uses (e.g., 95, 98, 2000, ME); CASS probably installs best on computers running Windows 95 and 98).

Also, you'll need to know the following terms to install and use this software:

- **"Click"** means use your mouse to move the arrow you see on your screen to a certain word or place on the screen, and then click the *left* mouse button once.

- **"Right-click"** means use your mouse to move the arrow you see on your screen to a certain word or place on the screen, and then click the *right* mouse button once.

- **"Double-click"** means use your mouse to move the arrow you see on your screen to a certain word or place on the screen, and then click the *left* mouse button *twice quickly.*

WARNING: If CASS does not run according to the following instructions, as a last resort you might have to reinstall the program, as shown in the Appendix at the end of this user's guide. The authors' website for this book, **http://utcmhsrc.csw.utk.edu/evaluatingpractice/,** contains discussion of some of the problems with CASS. We hope your questions can be answered there.

STARTING CASS

▶ Double click the CASSWIN icon (the city scene) on your desktop.

▶ When the following window appears, enter ***walmyr*** for the User ID, press the Tab key, and enter ***scales*** for the password. (When you type scales it will appear as ******.) Note that the User ID and password must be entered using all lower case letters.

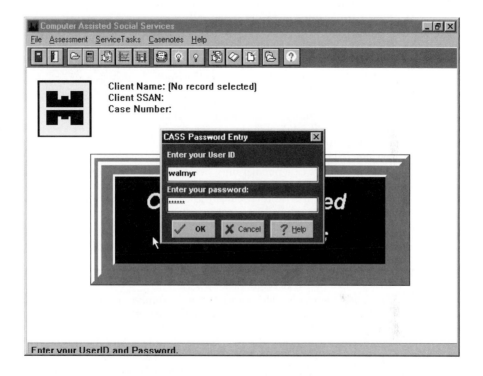

▶ After you've entered the User ID and password, click "OK" and the "Password Entry" window will disappear. We'll refer to the resulting screen (not shown) as the start screen.

Notice the menu bar items at the top of the above screen (i.e., "File," "Assessment," "Service Tasks," "Casenotes," and "Help"). You can click any of these items and menus will be displayed. We'll discuss these menu bar items and menus below. Also, note the buttons below the menu bar. These give you another way of doing the same things you can do with the menus. When you move the arrow to one of these buttons, in a moment a note appears describing its purpose.

CREATING A NEW CLIENT RECORD

▶ Click "File" and "Create New Client Record."

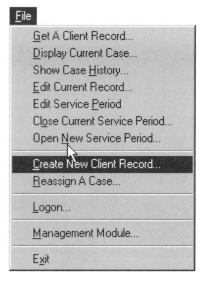

The "Add a New Client Record" window will appear, but the boxes will be empty. In our example, we entered the information in the boxes; here are the conventions used to enter this information (if you click "Help" on the window below you'll also get essentially this same information):

- **Case Number.** *The case number you assign to a new client record must be unique.* If you enter a case number that already exists you will obtain a "Key Violation" message. *Note:* If you ever get a "Key Violation" message, click on the "OK" button to remove the key violation message and then click on the "Cancel" button. Once you have entered the case number, press the Tab key to move to the next field.

  Note: The client's case number must begin with a number or a letter, it cannot exceed 15 characters in length, and no other symbols are allowed. You also must plan your case numbering system with great care. Once you enter a new case number into the database, it is difficult to change.

- **Honorific.** Type into this field the honorific title you wish to use for the client. The most frequently used honorific titles are Mr., Ms., Mrs., and Dr., but you may enter any other honorific title.

- **Client's Name.** Enter the client's first, middle, and last name in the designated data entry fields.

- **SSAN.** The client's Social Security Account Number, or SSAN, is a critically important identifier and it must be entered using the dash separator. Please always use the form, 000-00-0000 (e.g., 123-45-6789).

- **Birth Date.** Always enter the client's date of birth as Mo/Da/Year (e.g., 04/25/1944). Always use *four-digit years* with CASS.

- **Gender.** Always use the gender codes of *Male* or *Female*. You can click the down arrow in the drop-down combo box for gender and then click on the correct choice. That will ensure correct spelling and coding.

- **Ethnicity.** When entering the client's Ethnicity always enter *White, Black, Hispanic, Asian, Native American,* or *Other.* You can click the down arrow in the drop-down combo box for Ethnicity and then click on the correct choice. That will ensure correct spelling and coding.

- **Education.** Enter the number of years of school that were completed by the client. For example, a client who completed high school and four years of college would typically have completed a total of 16 years of schooling. In that case you would enter the number 16.

- **Income.** The income field should always contain the *total annual gross family income in thousands* of dollars. For example, a family with a total annual gross income of $47,834.00 would be entered as 47,834. Do not enter the dollar sign. (Entering the income in thousands means moving the decimal point three places to the left.)

- **Marital Status.** When entering the client's marital status, always enter *Never married, Married, Divorced, Separated, Widowed,* or *Other.* You can click the down arrow in the drop-down combo box for marital status and then click on the correct choice. That will ensure correct spelling and coding.

- **Number of Times Married.** Enter the number of times the client has married. Enter 0 if the client has never married.
- **Years with Spouse or Partner.** Enter the number of years the client has resided with a current spouse or partner. Enter the number 0 if the client is not currently residing with a spouse or partner.
- **Children in the Home.** Enter the number of children who are residing in the client's home.
- **Household Size.** Enter the total number of persons residing in the client's home or apartment, including the client.
- **Worker EN.** Enter the employee number of the practitioner to whom this case will be assigned. For our purposes here you can make up any number you like.
- **Supervisor EN.** Enter the employee number of the supervisor to whom this case will be assigned. For our purposes here you can make up any number you like.
- **Client Password.** Enter the password that you will give to the client for use with the Computer Assisted Assessment Package (CAAP) program.

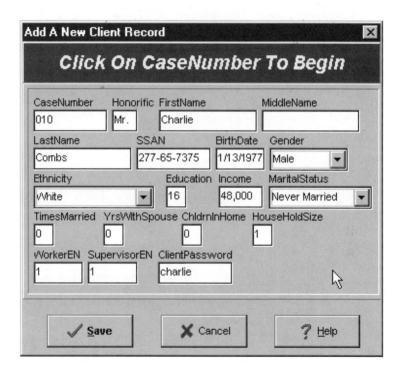

▶ Click "Save" when you're finished entering the client's information and the following window appears.

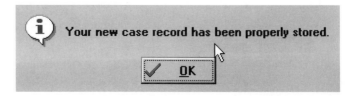

▶ Click "OK" and the "Service Code" window will appear with the client's name and case number, but "Primary," "Secondary," and "Tertiary" service will be blank.

Be sure that the first time you create a new client record you click "Help" on the window below and carefully read the instructions for selecting a service code. After doing this, enter a service code or codes. We clicked "Depression" and then "Problems at Work."

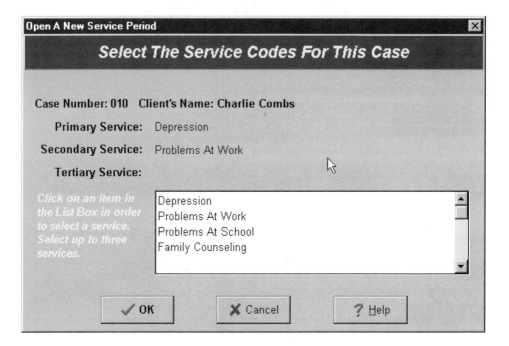

▶ Click "OK" and a verifying window will appear.

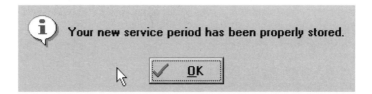

▶ Click "OK" and the "Service Task" window will again appear, except now "Enter Task Here" and "Date Due" will be entered in the boxes.

Be sure that the first time you create a new client record you click "Help" on the window below and carefully read the instructions for entering a service task. After doing this, enter a service task and date. We entered "Reduce workload," moved the arrow to "Date Due," and entered 1/31/2003 for the date. (Be sure you use the full year for the date, i.e., "2003" rather than "03.")

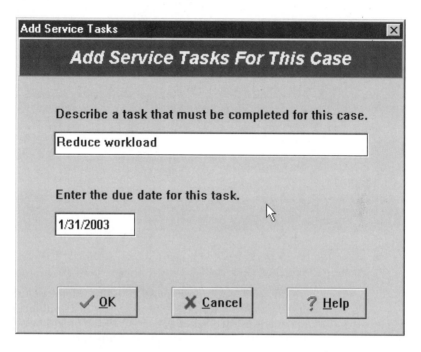

▶ Click "OK" and you'll be returned to the start screen.

GETTING A CLIENT RECORD

One of the first things you'll need to do when you use CASS is to get a client record. Here's how you do this.

▶ Click "File" and "Get A Client Record."

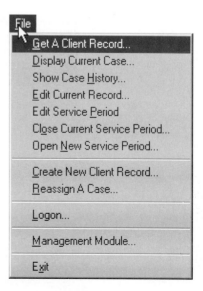

The list of client records will appear (SAMPLE1 and SAMPLE2 come with the program).

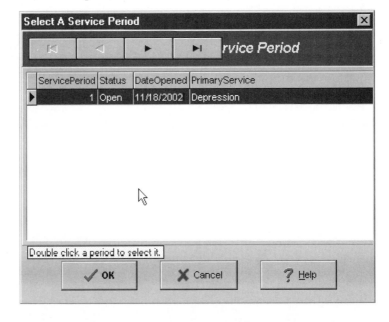

▶ Move the arrow to the row with listing Case Number "010" and double-click, or click once and then click "OK."

The service period list will appear. (You also can click "Help" on the window anytime you see a "Help" button on a window. This provides help with the task at hand. One exception to this rule is in the "Select A Service Period" window.) If you try to return to the service period and receive a message that it is currently in use, try the steps on page 149 (If Locked Out). Also see page 153; you can click on "Utilities" and "Unlock Client Record" for help.

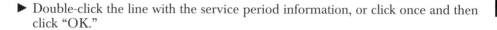

► Double-click the line with the service period information, or click once and then click "OK."

This service period will be selected and you'll be returned to the start screen. Basic client information now is listed on this screen.

> **Client Name: Mr. Charlie Combs**
> **Client SSAN: 277-65-7375**
> **Case Number: 010 Service Period: 11/18/2002**

WARNING: When creating client records or opening service periods, be sure that all dates are *past* dates, that is, prior to the date you actually enter this information on the computer.

GETTING CLIENT CASE INFORMATION

After you get a client record, but before you use it, we think it best to check to make sure that you're using the correct record. Here's how you do this.

► Click "File" and "Display Current Case."

The table of case information will appear. Click "Close" to return to the start screen.

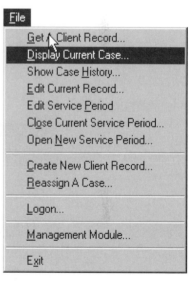

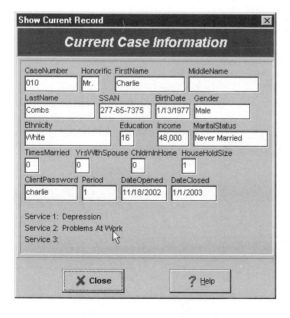

CASENOTES

Often you'll need to write, edit, and print casenotes for clients. It's possible to do this with CASS using the "Casenotes" menu.

▶ Click "Casenotes" and "Create New Casenote." (We assume that you have opened the record for Charlie.)

You can start typing your casenotes in the window that appears.

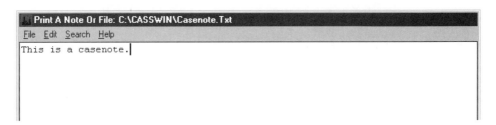

▶ Click "Edit" to do various editing tasks.

▶ Click "Search" to find or replace information in this casenote.

▶ Finally, when you're finished click "File" to save, exit, or print your casenotes.

▶ After you have created and saved a casenote for a client you can then click "Casenotes" and edit or read that casenote, or edit it using any word processor.

CASS USER'S GUIDE

Returning to Casenotes

Saving Casenotes

1. Click "File."
2. Click "Save As."
3. In "Save As" window, enter the file name for the casenote (e.g., "MaryTest" for SAMPE1).
4. Click "OK."

WARNING: You can only write one casenote per case per day because the notes are tracked by date.

Retrieving and Editing Casenotes

1. Open the client record.
2. Click "Casenotes" (at top).
3. Click "Edit Casenote."
4. The next window is "Select a Service Period." Click on service period, then click "OK." The casenote you click on will appear.
5. Make your corrections, then click "File" and "Save."
6. Click "File," then "Exit."
7. "Store a Finished Casenote" window will appear.
8. Enter the title of your casenote (e.g., MaryTest), then click "OK."
9. Click "Store It."

If Locked Out (e.g., "Case Record in Use" message)

1. Click "File."
2. Click "Management Module."
3. Click "Utilities."
4. Click option to "Unlock A Client Record."
5. Click "Unlock" on "Unlock A Client Record" window.

TASK MANAGEMENT

Practitioners often ask clients to do "homework." CASS lets you specify and track these service tasks. This is a very important feature of CASS because it adds to every practitioner's accountability.

▶ Click "Service Tasks" and "Task Completion Review."

The "All Tasks For This Case" list appears.

▶ Click "Close" to return to the start screen.

▶ Click "Service Tasks" and "Task Analysis."

The "Task Analysis For This Case" information appears.

We encourage you to try all aspects of this task management function of CASS. It will add to your pleasure of discovery and accomplishment while giving you additional tools to help you become an accountable professional.

▶ Click "Close" to return to the start screen.

Note: If you click on "Add New Service Tasks" when you want to add a new activity, be sure to use the full year when CASS requires the date (e.g., "2003," "03.")

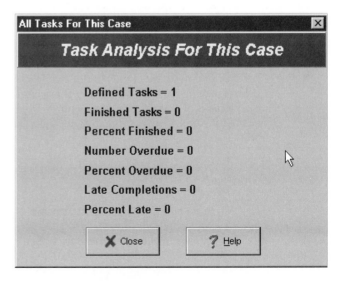

WARNING: Once an open service period is closed, you cannot change any of the information in it. You can review the information, but you cannot change it. Be sure to check all information in an open service period for correctness and accuracy before closing it.

ON-LINE HELP

On-line, context-sensitive help is available at many places in CASS, as you've already seen. Also, it's possible to get help with a wide range of topics and to print this information.

▶ Click "Help" and "CASS Help."

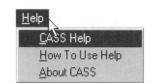

The table of contents appears.

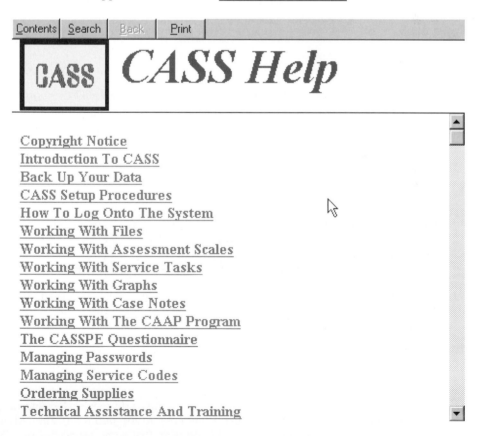

We urge you to open these help files and read at least the first six topics before attempting to use the CASS program. You will find most of the procedures explained and your questions answered in advance. This will greatly facilitate your use of CASS.

CASS USER'S GUIDE

When you locate a "Help" topic, move the arrow to it, click, and more detailed information about that topic appears. For example, click "Back Up Your Data" and the following window appears.

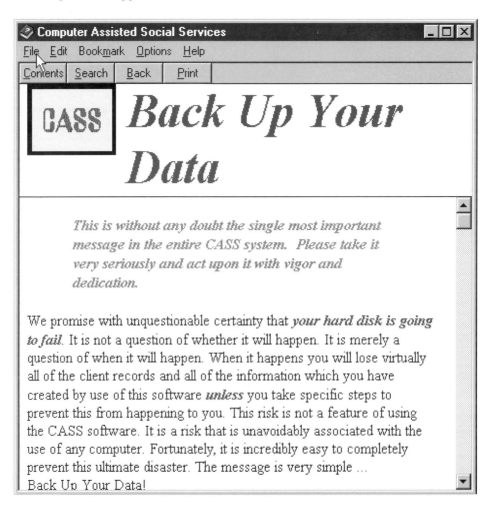

▶ Click "Print" if you want to print this information. Click "Contents" if you want to return to the table of contents. Click "Search" if you want to search for a particular topic. Click the X in the upper right hand corner when you're ready to return to the start screen.

USING THE MANAGEMENT MODULE

CASS lets you change the appearance of scale menus, add new scales, and prepare different types of order forms and correspondence to the publisher. The "Management Module" is used for these tasks. (Please note that some aspects of the "Management Module" were not functioning at the time of publication.)

► Click "File" and "Management Module."

The "Manager's Module" screen (not shown) appears.

► Click "Scales" and a menu appears.

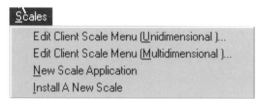

This menu is used to edit scale menus (which we'll discuss in Chapter 7) and to add new scales.

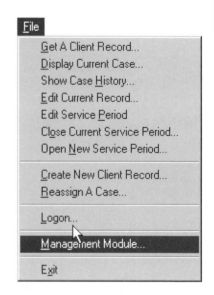

► Click "Utilities" and another menu appears.

This menu is used to write a letter to the publisher, show a list of people in your agency permitted to use this software, define and keep track of the types and frequency of services provided to clients, define and manage the service tasks used (e.g., homework assignments), and unlock closed client records.

► Click "Supplies" and a menu appears.

To use CAAP to administer a scale to a client, and to use CASS to score this scale, you must purchase a "scoring credit" from the publisher. However, the program comes with some scoring credits for a selected number of scales. When you order additional scoring credits, use CASS to prepare the order form. Then mail or fax that order form to the publisher, WALMYR (the address is in the Appendix to this guide). They will then send you an unlocking code. This menu is used to determine the number of available credits, to order credits, to get a list of available scales and their costs, to install the credits, and to keep track of all of this. (Note: At the time of publication of this edition, these credits were not available. Hopefully, they will be available in the future.)

▶ Click "Supplies" and "Display Scale Scoring Credits" to get a list of the available scales and the number of existing scoring credits for each scale.

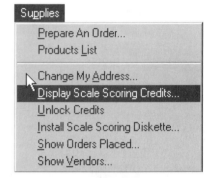

▶ Click the down (▼) and up (▲) arrows on the window to scroll through this list.

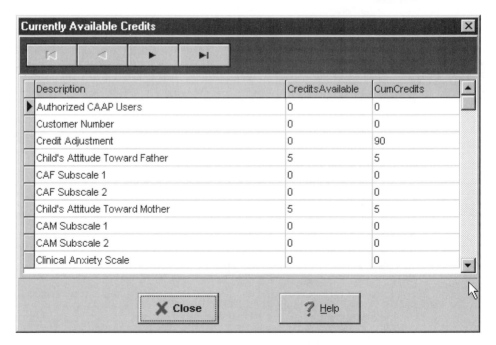

▶ Click "Close" to close this window and return to the "Manager's Module" window (not shown).

▶ Click "Exit" to return to the start screen.

EXITING CASS

▶ Click "File" and "Exit" to exit the program.

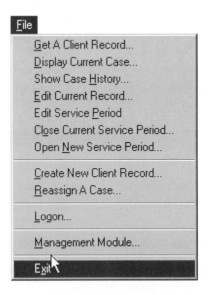

■ APPENDIX: INSTALLING CASS

The easiest way to install CASS and CAAP is to use the CD-ROM that comes with this book. However, you can also download and install these programs from the Web, especially if you encounter any problems installing them from your CD.

DOWNLOADING CASS/CAAP FROM THE WEB

CASS and CAAP also can be downloaded from the Web at two sites. The first is from the site for this book. Follow these steps.

1. Go to **http://www.ablongman.com/bloom/cass.html**.
2. Click on "CASS."
3. In the first window, click on the "New Folder" icon on the tool bar.
4. Click on "Open" in the next window.
5. Follow the instructions for downloading.
6. Repeat for CAAP.
7. Install both programs. Follow the installation instructions on the computer.

The second site is the site of the publishers of CASS (WALMYR), **http://www. walmyr.com**. You can follow the instruction there.

> **WARNING:** Once you have installed the CASS software you should never re-install it. To do so will wipe out all of your client data because a full re-install will replace all of your data tables with the ones supplied by the software.

INSTALLING CASS/CAAP FROM YOUR CD-ROM

▶ Turn your computer and monitor on.

► Insert the CD that came with the book. Wait until the following window appears, then click "Install CASS."

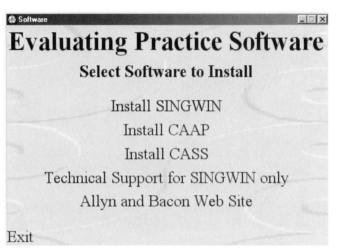

► Click "Yes" in response to the confirmation question.

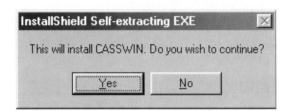

► Click "Next" at each of the subsequent windows until you reach the "User Information" window. Enter your name and company (or school or agency) in the appropriate boxes and then click "Next."

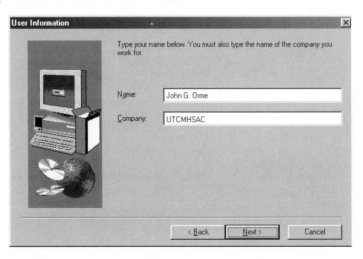

▶ Click "Next" at each subsequent window until you reach the "Setup Complete" window. Click "Finish" on this window.

▶ Move the cursor to "CASSWIN." Hold down the left mouse button and drag the icon (the night scene) to your desktop. This will create a shortcut on your desktop for easy access to CASS. Then click the X in the top right corner of the screen.

▶ To install CAAP, repeat the steps above but click "Install CAAP" in place of "Install CASS." You also can drag the CAAP icon (the clasped hands) to your desktop.

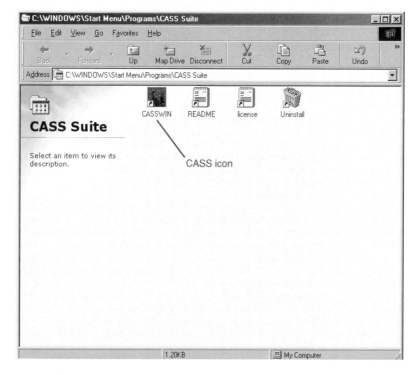

INTRODUCTION TO USING CASS (Reprinted from CASS)

Urgent! Read This Entire File Before Using CASS

1. WELCOME TO CASS
2. COPYRIGHT NOTICE
3. LEGAL NOTICE
4. SOFTWARE AND FILES LOCATIONS
5. LOADING THE SHARE.EXE PROGRAM
6. SETTING UP THE CASS SOFTWARE
7. NEXT STEPS
8. TRAINING MATERIALS
9. YOUR LOGON PASSWORD
10. NETWORK INSTALLATION

1. WELCOME TO CASS

When you install and begin using The Computer Assisted Social Services or CASS software, we believe you will then have the world's premier computer-based case management, quality assurance, and applied measurement package at your fingertips.

This version of the CASS software is provided to you without fee in order to help you get the most out of the client assessment scales that you purchase from our company.

You can order assessment scales or ask questions at the following address:

WALMYR PUBLISHING CO.
P.O. Box 12217
Tallahasee, FL 32317-2217
Voice: (850) 383-0045
Fax: (850) 383-0970
E-mail: Scales@Walmyr.com
Internet: http://www.walmyr.com

Scoring Assessment Scales

The CASS software will enable you to score our commercial assessment scales and store the results in your client records. A number of these scales are included in the program for several trial uses. However, in order to continue to use these features of the system, you must purchase additional commercial assessment scales that you wish to use with your clients. It is illegal to copy or reproduce copyrighted commercial assessment scales.

When you purchase the assessment scales which are available for use with the CASS software we will send you FREE assessment scale scoring credits so that you can use your purchased assessment scales with the CASS software. However, as of the date of publication of this edition, these scoring credits were not available.

Please Note: The CASS software will not score any of the included assessment scales if you have not purchased them.

2. COPYRIGHT NOTICE

The Computer Assisted Social Services (also known as the CASS software) is copyrighted, produced, and distributed by the WALMYR Publishing Company. You may copy and distribute this version of the software provided you make exact copies of the original distribution diskettes, you do not sell the software, you do not charge any fees for its use, and you do not make any changes of any kind to the software or its documentation. You may not copy or distribute any upgrade diskettes that are later sent to you by the publisher.

The Computer Assisted Social Services or CASS software is owned and copyrighted by the WALMYR Publishing Company, all rights are reserved, and use of the software does not imply ownership in any manner or kind.

The WALMYR Publishing Company reserves the right to deny use and to refuse continued support of the software to any and all who do not abide by the terms and conditions of its use.

3. LEGAL NOTICE

Any attempt to install or use scale scoring credits without prior purchase of the appropriate assessment scales will constitute an injury to our company and a violation of copyright law. Such violations will result in immediate termination of all rights to use the CASS software and will expose the violator to the pursuit of legal damages through civil and criminal remedies.

4. SOFTWARE AND FILES LOCATIONS

An important feature of the CASS software is that you can use it on a free-standing personal computer and you can it use on a Local Area Network or LAN system. This copy of the software is designed for use on a free-standing personal computer. Please call or write Walmyr Publishing Company if you wish to install and use the CASS software on a Local Area Network.

Where Things Are Stored

Once you install the CASS software, it is important for you to know where it will be stored on your computer. The CASS installation procedure will create a new directory on your hard disk, and it will be named \CASSWIN. All of the CASS software will be placed inside the \CASSWIN directory and any necessary subdirectories.

Although the installation program permits you to use a different directory, we strongly urge you to use \CASSWIN. It can lead to considerable additional work, errors, and frustration on your part if you do not use the defaults supplied by the publisher.

5. SETTING UP THE CASS SOFTWARE

Once you have installed the CASS software on your computer system, it is ready for use. However, there is some important setup work to be done for your agency or

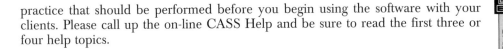

practice that should be performed before you begin using the software with your clients. Please call up the on-line CASS Help and be sure to read the first three or four help topics.

6. NEXT STEPS

If you have not yet installed the CASS software on your computer system, by all means do so now. Once you complete the installation of the software it will be ready for use by you and your colleagues. You will quickly discover how easy it is to use any of the major features of the system. However, every new software tool is a confrontation of new mysteries about how to best use it. We offer the following as suggestions for solving those mysteries.

7. TRAINING MATERIALS

The minimum training materials needed to learn how to use the CASS software are now available to you. They consist of this file and the CASS on-line Help system. However, if you or your employees are not familiar with our assessment scales or have not previously used standardized assessment tools in practice, your training needs will be much larger. We recommend that you acquire a copy of each of the following documents for yourself and your trainers. Once you and your trainers have read and evaluated them, you can decide which of them should be provided to each employee.

Hudson, W. W., & Faul, A. C. (1998). *The WALMYR Assessment System*. Tallahassee, FL: WALMYR Publishing Co. This text may be ordered directly from within the supplies option of the CASS Manager's Module.

Nugent, W. R., Sieppert, J. D., & Hudson, W. W. (2001). *Practice Evaluation for the 21st Century*. Belmont, CA: Brooks/Cole Publishing Co.

Nurius, P. S., & Hudson, W. W. (1993). *Human Services Practice, Evaluation and Computers: A Practical Guide For Today and Beyond*. Pacific Grove, CA: Brooks/Cole Publishing Co. This text may be acquired by calling (800) 354-0092 or (408) 373-0728.

The MPSI Technical Manual. (1990). Tempe, AZ: The WALMYR Publishing Co. This manual may be ordered directly from within the supplies option of the CASS Manager's Module.

The FASI Technical Manual. (1990). Tempe, AZ: The WALMYR Publishing Co. This manual may be ordered directly from within the supplies option of the CASS Manager's Module.

WALMYR Assessment Scale Scoring Manual. (1990). Tempe, AZ: The WALMYR Publishing Co. This manual may be ordered directly from within the supplies option of the CASS Manager's Module.

You should also know that the initial database that is provided when you install the CASS software contains two sample cases; their case numbers are SAMPLE1 and SAMPLE2. These two cases can be used for demonstrations and training and to test the performance of the software.

We suggest you call the SAMPLE1 case, select the open service period (Period 3), and then explore that case. For example, if you graph the ICS scores for Susan Test, you will see a nice single-system design graph.

8. YOUR LOGON PASSWORD

When you call up the CASS program you will be asked to enter your User ID and Password. These are "walmyr" and "scales," respectively (don't enter the quotes). The User ID and password must be entered as all lowercase letters.

9. NETWORK INSTALLATION

Instructions for installing CASS on a local area network can be found in the file named CASSNET.TXT. Please read and print that file if you wish to install the software on your network.

5 BEHAVIORAL OBSERVATION

PURPOSE: The purpose of this chapter is to teach you how to observe and record overt and covert behaviors using direct observation (i.e., observation by practitioners, relevant others, or independent observers) and self-monitoring (i.e., a person's observation of his or her own behavior). We describe some general guidelines and methods for both types of behavioral observation, and show you how to ensure that the observations are valid and reliable. We also discuss in detail methods of recording behavior—particularly frequency, duration, and interval recording. Because the observation of behavior is often the most direct and valid measure of a target, it should be given high priority as a measurement method. ■

Introduction
Behavioral Observation
General Guidelines for Behavioral Observation
Sampling Behaviors
Continuous Recording
Recording Samples
   Time Samples
   Client Samples
   Situation Samples
Rates
Instruments for Recording Behaviors
Principles for Selecting Instruments
Some Instruments for Your Use
Ensuring Accurate Observations
Maximizing the Reliability and Validity of Observations
Verifying Reliability
Verifying Validity

Methods of Recording Behavior
Frequency Recording
   Establishing Reliability
Duration Recording
   Establishing Reliability
Interval Recording
   Establishing Reliability
Additional Considerations with Interobserver Reliability
Analog Situations
Recording Behavior in Groups
Summary

INTRODUCTION

Most practitioners in human services hope to achieve through their efforts a change in someone's behavior, either directly or indirectly. Few are satisfied if the changes achieved fail to include changes in the actual functioning of people or organizations. The range of behaviors practitioners try to change in their diverse practices is immense—from rather specific, easily observable behaviors such as the amount of time family members spend together or the number of times a child is disciplined in school, to more complex ones such as "communication" between spouses; "positive," "self-deprecating," or "irrational" thoughts; unfulfilled urges to talk; the way an administrator "relates" to his or her staff; or the amount of "quality" time a couple spends together.

Yet many times when practitioners go about evaluating how successful their programs are, they fail to measure carefully whether the behaviors with which they are concerned actually do change. Sometimes this is because, while they hope for behavioral change, much of their practice is not focused on behaviors. They often don't specifically intervene with behaviors, so that behavioral change becomes more a by-product of intervention than a direct focus of intervention. Other times, they don't measure behavioral change because it's too complicated, too time-consuming, or too difficult, or because they haven't been able to observe or record the behavior accurately. However, measuring behavior is one of the most important ways of evaluating whether targets really do change. It also can be one of the best indicators of success.

What we really are talking about here are some of the ideas discussed in Chapter 2: validity, reliability, and directness of measures. The observation of behavior usually is the most valid method you can use because behaviors typically are the most direct expression of a client's concerns. Once these target behaviors are changed and no other target behaviors emerge to take their place, the practitioner and client have the best, most direct way of assessing their success. It would be difficult indeed to consider a case successfully terminated if other dimensions of a target appear to be changed, but the problematic target behaviors still exist. Since behavioral observation ideally occurs in the setting in which change ultimately is desired, the client's natural environment, it is indeed a direct method.

Similarly, behaviors used as outcome measures have a particularly good chance of being recorded accurately because they lend themselves well to clear, precise, and specific definitions. Therefore, the use of behavioral observation ranks highly on a hierarchy of potential methods because behaviors can be our most *accurate* indicators of success.

In addition to their value as potentially accurate indicators of outcome, the use of behaviors has special advantages for practice. Since behaviors lend themselves well to precise definition, they have particular advantages for assessment. Clearly pinpointing a behavior as a target for change allows easier determination of possible factors affecting the target. It becomes easier to pinpoint what occurs before and after the target problem occurs and to examine any controlling effects these occurrences have on the target. Once a behavior is specifically defined, it becomes easier to determine information about the who, what, when, and where, conditions of the occurrence of the target, all of which are necessary for a complete assessment.

To be sure, many types of changes are important, and there are other ways of measuring success besides behaviors. In fact, we've devoted the bulk of the chapters in Part II to these methods. But, in line with our discussion in Chapter 2, three of the important guidelines for the selection of outcome measures are: How direct an indicator of the target is the measure, how reliably can it be measured, and how valid is it? We believe that, in many instances, the use of behaviors can meet all of these criteria. Add to this some of the advantages for assessment, and we therefore would suggest that the first method you should consider in evaluating practice is the observation of behaviors.

If all of this sounds a little bit too "behavioral," read on. We think that the way we define behavior will ease some of the suspicions you may have that when we're talking about behaviors, we're being so concrete, narrow, or specific that we're ruling out a good deal of relevant human activity. Perhaps you might even feel that this perspective is linked to only certain theoretical orientations such as behavior modification and therapy. This is not what we're trying to do. In fact, in the sense in which we use the term behavior, we believe that it is directly relevant to practitioners across the whole range of theoretical orientations and approaches to practice.

Behavioral Observation

We use the word *behavior* to refer to a wide range of human activities that are typically characterized as relatively discrete events. Behaviors, in other words, include virtually everything that people *do*. These of course include *overt* events—events that can be observed by others (at least theoretically)—such as the amount of time a client spends with his or her spouse or children, the number of times a client has sexual intercourse, the number of completed intervention tasks, the amount of time nursing home residents spend interacting with one another, the number of times a parent compliments his or her child, the number of office, home, or telephone contacts with clients. But behaviors also include *covert* events—events that occur within the individual and therefore cannot be observed by others, at least directly—such as the number of self-deprecating thoughts; the amount of time spent feeling anxious, under stress, or overwhelmed; or the amount of time spent ruminating about some concern. Therefore, *behavior* includes just about all human activities, among which should be a sufficiently broad range of behaviors to suit practitioners from just about every theoretical orientation. The key is, to be considered a behavior, it must be observable by someone, whether that be the client (e.g., with thoughts) or an external observer.

Another aspect of behavioral observation has to do with who observes and records the behavior. People can observe their own behavior whether it's overt or covert. When a person observes and records his or her own

behavior it's called *self-monitoring* (e.g., Bornstein, Hamilton, & Bornstein, 1986; Kopp, 1988). Outside observers (e.g., independent observers, relevant others, practitioners) can only observe overt behaviors directly. Observation by outside observers usually is called *direct observation* (e.g., Foster & Cone, 1986). Many of the principles and practices of behavioral observation apply to both direct observation and self-monitoring, but some don't, and we'll draw distinctions between these two methods where applicable.

Whether a behavior is overt or covert, or whether direct observation or self-monitoring is used, behavioral observation most often relies on counting behaviors. Therefore, in this chapter we talk quite a bit about counting. By *counting* we mean simply adding up the total amount of behavior. Again, we prefer a broad definition of counting to include how often some behavior occurs (its *frequency*), or how long it occurs (its *duration*). These are two important ways of counting behaviors that we describe later in this chapter, along with a way of counting the relative frequency and duration of behaviors (called *interval* recording).

For now, we hope you have the idea that the types of behavior to which we're referring and the ways of counting and recording them include a broad range of human functioning and practice interests. Behavioral observation need not be at all mechanistic or unduly restrictive. In fact, behavioral observation can be a fruitful strategy for evaluating practice.

Behavioral observation is not without problems. A host of issues can arise when considering whether to observe behaviors, particularly when direct observation is used in the "natural environment" (as opposed to, say, a closed or controlled environment like a hospital ward). Some of these issues have been discussed by Nay (1986) and Foster and Cone (1986). First, it's possible that an outside observer's presence may affect the situation in some way, thereby producing an invalid sample of behavior (i.e., by changing the typical sequence of events). This is the reactive effect, which we will discuss in Chapter 9. For example, a parent is less likely to use harsh discipline with his or her child in the presence of a social worker.

Second, in an open setting, with clients moving about freely, it's often difficult to observe accurately, which has led some practitioners to resort to artificial restrictions on the behavior of the people they're observing. Third, observing behaviors in the natural environment may be both costly and impractical. Finally, since the observer (hypothetically) has no control over the environment, a whole host of temporary events may have some effect on the behavior so that the conditions of data collection could vary across observations. This would mean that it might be necessary to collect data many times to obtain clear, accurate, and consistent measures of the target.

Self-monitoring avoids some of the problems of direct observation. However, self-monitoring is not without its own problems. Some of these issues have been discussed by Bornstein et al. (1986) and Kopp (1988). In particular, the act of self-monitoring can lead to changes in the behavior being monitored, that is, like behavior observation by others, self-monitoring also can be reactive. Also, sometimes clients are unwilling or unable to monitor their own behaviors accurately. Finally, it's difficult to verify the reliability with which covert behaviors or private overt behaviors (e.g., sexual behaviors) are self-monitored. The direct observation of publicly observable overt behaviors makes it easier to determine the reliability of the observations (e.g., two or more observers can observe the behaviors and their agreement can be determined). However, we don't believe that goals should be selected only because they can be reliably measured, ignoring whether they're the most relevant goals for the client's functioning. As long as it can be observed somehow, any behavior can be considered a potential focus of intervention.

On the other hand, we believe that these problems can be minimized by taking the precautions we suggest in this chapter, by using the resources of the natural environment, and by keeping the observational process as simple as possible. Furthermore, we have a number of suggestions in Chapter 9 for ways to overcome the possible reactive effects of behavioral observation in general, and self-monitoring in particular. Putting all these suggestions together, we believe that you should place a high priority on behavioral observation to evaluate your practice.

GENERAL GUIDELINES FOR BEHAVIORAL OBSERVATION

If you've already read the preceding four chapters, you're well on your way toward understanding behavioral observation. Many of the general guidelines for observation and recording described in these chapters apply directly to behavioral observation as well as to all the other methods of measurement. If you haven't read these chapters, we suggest you do so before you read this chapter. Briefly, as a review, there are several steps to follow in developing your behavioral observation plan:

1. *Conduct a preliminary assessment.* Review the client's concerns. Gather enough information to give you a feel for the range of targets with which the client may wish to work. Begin helping the client focus on a workable area.

2. *Specify targets.* This is a most crucial concern in observing behaviors. Use the guidelines in Chapter 3. Try to identify discrete indicators for the target. For example, if the client states a concern in terms of vague attributes, motives, or other conditions, try to translate this into discrete events (what is he doing when he is acting "strange"?). Think about each target in terms of pinpointing it into "units of behavior" that can be observed and counted. In order to facilitate an accurate count, each of these behavioral units can be defined as a cycle that has a beginning and an end. Be as specific as possible. Each behavior unit can be defined in terms of either how often it occurs (its frequency) or how long it occurs (its duration). (We describe these types of recording methods in more detail later in this chapter.) Think about each target in terms of who is doing what, to what extent, and under what conditions. Remember, though, you're still

defining the target. You may not develop the goal until much later in the process–for example, after baseline data are collected. However, generally, goals are closely related to targets–for example, feelings of depression might be the target, and the reduction of these feelings the goal.

3. *Decide how many behaviors to record.* Keep the procedure simple. You don't want to frustrate or confuse whoever is doing the recording. As a general guideline, don't expect people to record more than one or two behaviors, especially when the recorders are clients or relevant others. Of course, a person may record several aspects of some behavior. For example, a husband may record not only how many times he loses his temper, but also with whom he loses his temper, when, where, and so on.

4. *Decide who should collect the data.* Essentially, you have four choices here: the client, yourself, a relevant other, or an independent observer. Follow the guidelines in Chapter 4. Each of the choices has clear advantages and disadvantages. The primary guideline perhaps is that the observer must be *able* to record; he or she must be present when the behavior occurs and be able to observe it. Sometimes only one person meets this criterion (e.g., the client must record his or her own covert behaviors), and then your decision is clear.

5. *Decide when and where to record.* You have two choices here, continuous recording or sampling. Continuous recording involves observing each occurrence of a target every time it occurs. Sampling involves observing target behaviors for a sample of clients, situations, or times, depending on the information you need. The key principle of sampling is to try to get a representative picture of the occurrence of the behavior. Whatever type of sample is collected, though, you should try to standardize the time, place, and method used to observe, or it will be difficult to evaluate change over time. Establish clear and consistent guidelines regarding who, what, when, and where behavior is observed. (We discuss sampling issues in more detail in the following sections.)

6. *Train the observer.* It would make little sense to go through all these elaborate preparations if the person who is to do the recording is not trained sufficiently. Make sure the behavior is clearly defined for the observer, and that the observer knows whose behavior is to be recorded, how it's to be recorded, when, where, and for how long. For example, a teacher who is recording a sample of disruptive behavior by a student should be certain to arrange to observe the child clearly (in order to ascertain who is shouting), what behaviors are considered disruptive (e.g., shouting, hitting other children), where to observe (in the classroom and halls only), and for how long (9:00 A.M. to 10:00 A.M.).

If possible, try to role-play or practice making the observations until the observer is comfortable and accurate. Try to develop one or two trial observation sessions in which the observer attempts to record the actual behavior. Then the observer can discuss with you any necessary revisions in the observational system, and the necessary revisions can be made. To make sure you've covered all the necessary points with the observer, go over the Data Collection Checklist (Figure 4.1) in Chapter 4 with the observer.

7. *View behavior broadly.* To make this a more systematic process, build into your recording system methods for recording when and where a target behavior occurs and what happens after it occurs. (These are the antecedents and consequences that we describe in Chapter 4 as the *A-B-C* model). This will allow you to evaluate environmental factors that might be affecting the target. Several of the forms in Chapter 8, which deals with logs, a particular method of self-monitoring, have spaces for recording antecedents and consequences; these can be modified for use by observers other than the client. Similarly, on whatever

form you do decide to use to record information, you can simply add extra columns to record the behavior, what happened right before, and what happened right after as in Figure 5.1. (Pinkston & Linsk, 1984, also provide some good examples of such forms.) Most word processing programs allow you to easily create such forms. Be sure you give clear instructions as to what is to be placed in those columns, especially that the recording be brief and that it include what happens immediately before and after the behavior occurs (Gambrill, 1977). Finally, increasingly, personal computer programs are available for the direct observation of behaviors and their antecedents and consequences (e.g., the EMPIRICIST [Ironwood Development Systems, 258 Harvard St., Suite 203, Brookline, MA 02146], ABC [Plan Software, Thomassenstraat 19, 3472 KG, Utrecht, the Netherlands], and Behavior Evaluation Strategies and Taxonomies [BEST], available from Sage Publications in Thousand Oaks, CA [for a free demonstration, go to www.scolari.com and enter "BEST" in the search space]), and we'll discuss one such program in more detail below (i.e., *The Assistant,* Human Technologies, Inc., 300 Third Ave., North, St. Petersburg, FL 33701).

8. *Collect baseline data.* Once all of the above steps have been completed, you're ready to begin collecting preintervention or baseline information. This will give you a basis for comparison with data collected during and after intervention to evaluate effectiveness. It will be crucial also for assessment because the actual level of occurrence of behavior as well as where and when it occurs will become clear. This will then allow you to develop a clear and specific goal statement.

SAMPLING BEHAVIORS

As we indicated in the previous section, it may not be possible to observe a behavior every time it occurs in every situation. This is espe-

Observer _____		Client _____	
Behavior to Be Observed _____			
Date _____	What Happened Before	Behavior	What Happened After
Time _____			

FIGURE 5.1 Form for recording behaviors, antecedents, and consequences.

cially true with direct observation, although it can be problematic with self-monitoring also. Therefore, you will have to modify your measurement plan to meet the demands of the target and situation. There are two general types of recording that focus on when to collect data—*continuous* recording and recording involving *samples*. We discuss each of these briefly in this section, as well as what to do when the observation times or, more generally, the number of opportunities for a behavior to occur vary—the use of rates.

Continuous Recording

Continuous recording involves recording every occurrence of a target behavior every time it occurs. Continuous recording as we define it implies that you already have selected what behavior (presumably from among more than one option) to observe. (We're using the term *continuous recording* in a way that's slightly different from the way it's used in some of the behavioral literature [e.g., Foster & Cone, 1986]. In the behavioral literature, recording all instances of a preselected behavior often is called "event sampling," and continuous recording in that literature actually means that literally all behaviors are observed, a difficult if not impossible task.) Continuous recording can be used when the observer is willing and available to record every occurrence of a behavior, and when the target doesn't occur so frequently that it would be impossible to record every occurrence.

It's virtually impossible not to preselect target events for recording (the alternative would be to record everything a client did, problematic or not, all the time). Therefore we assume that all methods of behavioral observation start with the selection of the behaviors to be observed. Thus, continuous recording requires the selection of specific target behaviors to observe. In essence, you are almost always either observing samples of the client's behaviors (e.g., just the communication aspect of a more complex marital problem and just certain times or types of communication at that) or taking samples of other events or targets that may be related to what you and the client identify as the pri-

mary target. In addition, examining only selected occurrences of targets may help you determine which target to focus on first. For example, if you're attempting to assess the program of an agency, you might start by observing a large number of different events, but eventually select only those that provide the most useful information (Haynes, 1978).

A number of examples of continuous recording by clients, others in the environment, or practitioners have been collected by Gambrill (1977). Examples of continuously recorded behaviors, recorded by *clients,* include all pages of schoolwork, all homosexual contacts, all times a bronchometer was used for asthmatic attacks, and all times clients failed to talk when they wished to. Examples of behaviors continuously recorded by *relevant others* include bed-wetting incidents, whines and shouts, and compliance with requests. Examples of behaviors continuously recorded by *practitioners* include who appeared at group meetings, aggressive statements, greeting responses, and verbal reinforcements between a man and a woman as counted from an audiotape.

Recording Samples

The second type of recording involves sampling times, people or clients, or situations. The key assumption here is that the sample of behavior will accurately represent all behavior that would have been recorded if the observations weren't limited (Haynes, 1978). The two basic reasons to sample behavior are because (a) it's more efficient than recording all behaviors; and (b) the observers, clients, or targets are not available or the behaviors don't occur all the time. An excellent overview of material on sampling behaviors is available in Haynes (1978, chapter 3), and we briefly summarize some key points here.

Time Samples. The most frequently used type of sampling is time sampling. In time samples, the target is observed for only portions of time, at fixed or random times selected to collect representative information about the target (Gambrill, 1977). Time samples can be used when the observer doesn't have time to record all instances of a target, when continuous recording is simply too difficult (e.g., when the target occurs over a long period of time), when the target doesn't have a clear beginning or end (e.g., a good or bad mood), or when the target lasts for varying periods of time (e.g., wearing glasses) (Gambrill, 1977).

There are two types of time sampling. The first involves preselecting time periods and then observing whether the target is occurring at all. If it is, the observer simply records that the behavior occurred during that time period. The observer would not have to record all instances of the occurrence of the target, since this may be impractical or impossible. This type of time sampling sometimes is called *spot-check recording* (Polster & Collins, 1988) or *momentary time sampling* (Foster & Cone, 1986).

Some examples of *client-recorded* spot-check time samples (from Gambrill, 1977), all of which occurred too frequently for continuous recording, are recording intensity of pain every half hour, recording the occurrence of positive self-thoughts every two hours, and recording obsessive thoughts that occur regularly by noting their presence (or absence) every hour. With this method, only selected occurrences are reported (e.g., if any at all occur during a 2-hour period, a check could be placed on a piece of paper that is divided up into 2-hour time periods). An example of a *relevant other* spot-check time sample would be a parent recording a child's studying during selected periods of time. An example of a *practitioner* spot-check time sample involves making a certain number of observations on each patient in a hospital per day to see if some target or behavior is occurring at all, say, in a situation where the target occurred frequently enough that it would be impossible to count all instances of its occurrence. An example of a form for time-sample recording, on which a check is placed in the appropriate box if the behavior is occurring during each observation interval, is presented in Figure 5.2.

When spot-check recording is used, the most desirable method is to preselect times during which the target will be observed and then simply check on a sheet of paper that is divided up into those time periods whether it was occurring

during the observation. It might also be possible for the client to just jot down on a sheet of paper or 3" × 5" card the occurrence of a behavior when he or she remembers to do so, but this would pose a problem in determining just how representative such recollections would be. In such a case an electronic beeper (a remote control device that signals its wearer when activated by a caller) might be useful, if one is available, to prompt a client to observe and record at specific times. If you, a relevant other, or an independent observer is observing a client, it's important that the observation schedule not be obvious to the client. This is important so that the client doesn't specifically perform or not perform the behavior only during the observation periods. (We discuss in detail a more rigorous type of time sampling, called "interval recording," later in this chapter.)

The second type of time sampling involves recording all instances of a target but only for selected periods during each day. This actually combines time sampling with continuous recording. This form of continuous recording can be used when the target occurs so frequently that it is possible to record only during selected periods of time (when the target occurs, or occurs with its greatest frequency), only during selected periods (e.g., only during the dinner hour, only in one classroom, only with one person), or when the observer is only available during selected periods.

The key issue in using only selected periods of time for recording is to try to ensure that the period of time will produce a *representative* picture of the target. If the target occurs often and regularly, then you would need fewer periods during the day in order to be reasonably certain that what you observe is indeed representative of the total occurrence of the behavior. However, if the target occurs in more than one situation, those situations should be included in the periods of time you select for recording. Try to make the periods you do select similar in subsequent observations (e.g., succeeding days) so that you will have consistent opportunities to observe the target as it occurs. You can imagine the difficulties in making a reasonable and reliable assessment of the occurrence of a target if, for example, a client haphazardly

Client's Name _____   Recorder's Name _____

Behaviors to Be Observed:

A. _____

B. _____

C. _____

Length of Observation Interval: _____

Time Period Between Observations: _____

Time Sample

Behavior	1	2	3	4	5	6	7	8	9	10
A										
B										
C										

FIGURE 5.2 Sample form for time-sample recording.

self-monitors his or her frequency of self-deprecating thoughts at breakfast the first day, for an hour at school the next day, and watching television at night the following day.

Similarly, being aware of the need for representativeness in the periods you select can be helpful when you use the baseline observations to develop your assessment of the target and relate it to the situations in which it occurs. For example, if a client self-monitored the frequency of his or her self-deprecating thoughts only at home, you would have information only about the frequency of these thoughts in one setting. If the client monitored these thoughts in more than one setting–say, at home, at work, and on the way home from work–you might discover that the thoughts are related to a particular setting, and this in turn might suggest strategies for intervention.

Client Samples. This type of sampling is used when you work with a large number of clients (e.g., a ward or classroom). Using client sampling, you would select only a sample of clients for direct observation or self-monitoring observation at any given time. This is particularly useful for efficiently assessing an environment or program that may affect many people. Also, sometimes such information about a group of clients can be used as a basis against which the behavior of an individual client can be compared (e.g., whether an individual child actually is out of his or her seat or off-task more than his or her classmates).

The assumption here is that the people you do select are representative of the others. You do this by randomly selecting certain people for observation across the entire period of the baseline and intervention periods, or by rotating the people whom you observe so that all people in the group are systematically observed at one period of time or another. Spreadsheet programs such as Excel can be used for this and other types of randomization (Patterson, 2000).

Situation Samples. The last type of sampling involves the location of sampling–observing clients only in those situations where a target behavior will most likely occur, and being sure that the major possible locations are included in the recording plan. This is more of an issue in direct observation than self-monitoring, but in either case, situation samples are more efficient for the observation of environmental factors that might be affecting targets, and changes in the occurrence of those targets once intervention occurs.

Thus, in assessing, monitoring, or evaluating the effects of intervention on a target, you would be observing only during those situations where the target could be expected to occur relatively frequently. Obviously, it would be highly inefficient to observe, say, targets in marital communication in a place where such communication is unlikely to take place (e.g., a movie). It would be much more efficient and useful to observe those targets in such situations as mealtime, when a communication problem is more likely to occur.

On the other hand, you want to be sure to include the range of locations in which the target event might take place. Use of an ecological-systems approach to behavior would suggest the importance of examining the different settings and locations in which a target might occur. If you aren't careful to do this, a number of problems could result (Foster & Cone, 1986; Nay, 1986). First, focusing on only one location (we mentioned earlier the problem of having a client self-monitor self-deprecating thoughts only at home) could produce a sample of behavior that is unrepresentative. If you find that the behavior occurs differently in different situations, you may need to tailor your intervention strategies for each of those different situations. Second, characteristics of any given location could change over time, leading to changes in the target behavior. This could produce the mistaken assumption that the intervention program was responsible for the changes. Third, since you know that a behavior can change simply as a function of changing the setting, sampling from several locations will provide evidence as to whether behavior change has really generalized when you compare the baseline data from multiple settings with the intervention phase data from multiple settings.

Rates

It may be that the logical period of time for observing a target varies from observation time to observation time. Let's say that a mother wants help with her son's uncontrolled behavior when riding in the family car. Such rides, of course, vary in length from day to day and even throughout the day. In such cases, you should compute the rate of occurrence of the target to ensure that you have equal bases for comparing the target's occurrence over time. For example, suppose that the mother drove her son for 2 hours the first day, 1 hour the next day, and 30 minutes the third day. If you plotted the raw data for each day–say, the number of times the son yelled during the car trip–the differences across time would be due in part to the differences in length of the car trips, not to actual changes in the behavior.

Rates are used when the periods of time in which data are collected differ between observation times. Rates indicate the amount of behavior that occurs per unit of time, such as minutes or hours (e.g., the number of times per hour the son yelled). They can be used to compare the occurrence of targets over time for the same person, or the same target among different people when the target is observed for different periods of time.

Rates are computed simply by dividing the number of occurrences of the target or the duration of the target (i.e., how long it lasted) by the period of time (hours or minutes) the target is observed. Thus, if the client records seven angry thoughts while driving during the rush hour for 70 minutes, the rate of occurrence per minute would be 7/70, or .10 (.10 could be multiplied by 60, the number of minutes in an hour, to get the rate per hour, which would be 6). Rates can be plotted on a chart to provide a common index for observing the daily occurrence of a target. Table 5.1 (redrawn from Fischer & Gochros, 1975) and Figure 5.3 provide examples of rates as they were collected, computed, and then charted.

Rates also sometimes are computed by dividing the number of times a behavior occurs

Table 5.1   Rate of put-downs per minute made by Alan and Laurie.

Child	Number of Put-Downs	Period Covered	Number of Minutes	Rate per Minute
Laurie				
Monday	⫽⫽⫽ ⫽⫽⫽ ∣∣∣∣ (14)	6:30–9:30	180	0.08
Tuesday	⫽⫽⫽ ⫽⫽⫽ ∣∣ (12)	7:00–8:45	105	0.11
Wednesday	⫽⫽⫽ ∣∣∣ (8)	7:00–9:00	120	0.07
Thursday	∣∣ (2)	6:45–8:30	105	0.02
Friday	∣∣∣∣ (4)	7:00–9:30	150	0.03
Alan				
Monday	∣∣ (2)	6:30–9:30	180	0.01
Tuesday	⫽⫽⫽ (5)	7:00–8:45	105	0.05
Wednesday	∣∣ (2)	7:00–9:00	120	0.01
Thursday	(0)	6:45–8:30	105	0
Friday	(0)	7:00–9:30	150	0

by the number of opportunities for it to be observed. For example, if you checked a client on the ward 14 times on Monday to see if he or she was interacting with other clients (i.e., the number of opportunities for the behavior to be observed), and found the client to be interacting four times, the rate for Monday would be 4/14, or .29. Other slightly different examples include the number of completed "homework" tasks assigned to clients divided by the total number of assigned tasks (Rose, 1989, p. 127), or the number of times a child complies with a parental request divided by the total number of parental requests. In any case, the resulting rates could be graphed rather than the actual

number of target behaviors, since the latter could be purely a result of the number of opportunities for the behavior to be observed.

INSTRUMENTS FOR RECORDING BEHAVIORS

We strongly believe that recording shouldn't become an end in itself. It's crucial for you as the practitioner to try to come up with a recording system that is not aversive (perhaps it might even become pleasant) to those who will do the recording. Otherwise your observer may balk at participating because of a complex

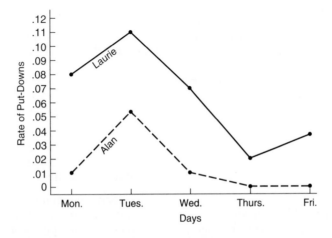

FIGURE 5.3   Rate of put-downs as plotted on a chart.

or cumbersome recording system. Try to make sure the recording system is as uncomplicated as possible. Ultimately, you want recording to be a rather simple process that enhances the intervention program by increasing rather than decreasing the motivation of those involved.

Once the behavior is recorded, it will be placed on charts, as suggested in Chapter 4, so that you can easily and clearly inspect progress visually. But before you put the data on the chart, you have to set up a system for collecting the information. Perhaps the simplest way is to use forms for recording the behavior. Forms are simple checklists that you give the observer or help the observer develop. They have spaces or boxes for checking off whether for how long a behavior occurs. We present some forms such as these for your use later in this chapter, and in Chapter 8 we describe forms for collecting more elaborate and detailed information on events surrounding the target behavior.

Sometimes forms cannot be used to record behavior, especially when the observer wishes to be unobtrusive. Imagine walking around carrying a form making check marks in front of an individual or group whose behavior you don't wish to disturb, or having a client do this at work while self-monitoring. In these situations, you want a less obtrusive or more accessible type of recording instrument. Data could be recorded on this instrument and then either placed on the checklist or form where it can be tallied up before being transferred onto the chart, or placed directly on the chart from the recording instrument.

Some interesting behavioral software can be found at the following website: **http://www. scolari.com/**. When you get the web page, enter "BEST" in the search space and click "Go." That will take you to the page describing the software. Finally, consider using Personal Digital Assistants (PDAs), such as Palm and Handspring Visor, for developing new and creative approaches to collecting data.

Principles for Selecting Instruments

Several principles should be considered when choosing an instrument to use (Fischer & Gochros, 1975). Selection depends on the na-

ture of the target, the capabilities and motivation of the observer, and the complexity of the situation:

1. Is the method portable enough to be easily used where the behavior occurs? (Many times, a small 3" × 5" card will suffice, rather than a large clipboard or pad of paper.)

2. Is the method unobtrusive enough that it won't be distracting or embarrassing to those whose behavior is being recorded?

3. Is the method *likely* to be used? (No recording method is of much value if it won't be used.)

4. Is the method pleasant or enjoyable to use? (It's worth the time to sit down with the observer and try to come up with imaginative or pleasant ways of recording data.)

Some Instruments for Your Use

If you expect some exciting or mysterious instruments for recording, you may be disappointed. Just about all of the methods we mention are probably right at hand around your house or at work, and that's why we suggest them. Each has been used successfully to count behaviors. Most of these focus on simply determining whether behaviors do occur (frequency). If you plan to record duration, you'll also need a watch or clock.

There are a number of simple but quite effective instruments for recording behaviors (Fischer & Gochros, 1975) (for a review of more expensive and sophisticated instrumentation, see Rugh et al., 1986):

1. Coins can be moved from one pocket to another or from one compartment in a purse to another every time a specified behavior occurs.

2. Poker chips can be used to keep track of behaviors around the house or in an institutional setting.

3. Inexpensive golf score counters worn on the wrist are useful for counting behaviors by inconspicuously "clicking off" behaviors on the knob.

4. Knitting stitch counters also can be used to count behaviors–for example, a parent recording the number of times a child says or does something.

5. Small pieces of masking tape can be taped to the wrist, and checks can be made with a pen each time a behavior occurs. This inexpensive recording "device" can be used when other instruments are not practical.

6. Soap or a large pencil eraser can be kept in a pocket or purse and an indentation made using a fingernail each time a specified behavior occurs. Then, the indentations can simply be totaled up at a later time.

7. Necklaces or bracelets made of lanyards or rawhide with beads tightly strung on them can be used by simply moving one of the beads each time a behavior occurs.

8. Small cards kept in a pocket or purse can be used to collect data on a variety of behaviors. You can tuck one of these cards into the back of a pack of cigarettes to count the number of cigarettes smoked each day.

9. If you can afford it or your agency has one available, you might even use a small portable cassette tape recorder or even a video camera to record incidents of behavior as they occur. One or more observers can then examine the tapes as often as necessary at convenient times, and determine the frequency or duration of selected behaviors.

As you can see, you're limited in your use of recording devices only by your imagination; most instruments are accessible, inexpensive, and easy to use. In addition to the simple instruments described above, though, there also is an increasing array of powerful computer technology available for the direct observation and analysis of behavior. In many cases this technology is not all that expensive and not all that difficult to use (e.g., Repp, Harman, Felce, Van Acker, & Karsh, 1989). Typically this technology includes a specially designed hand-held keyboard or a small laptop computer, and the observer simply presses different keys to record the observation of different behaviors. Usually the time the behavior is entered is recorded automatically, making it possible to examine the sequence of events, and oftentimes it's also possible to record the duration and frequency of the same behavior. The raw observational data can be printed or transferred to a personal computer to be charted and analyzed.

The Assistant (a device mentioned previously on page 68 in the section on General Guidelines, along with the address where it can be obtained) is a good example of computer technology available for behavioral observation. The Assistant is a small, battery-operated, hand-held computer, about the size of a hand-held calculator. The observer can use it to record the frequency and duration of up to 10 different behaviors by simply pressing the appropriate keys. The Assistant can be plugged into a conventional personal computer printer to get a printed record of the observations, or the information can be transferred easily to a personal computer for storage and analysis. A personal computer program (*The Analyst*) is available for use with the Assistant, and this program will analyze and summarize observations made with the Assistant (e.g., it will determine the frequency, duration, and rate for individual behaviors or combinations of behaviors, and it will determine the extent to which one or more behaviors are contingent on other behaviors). This computer program also will compute five different widely used estimates of interobserver reliability when two observers have used the Assistant to simultaneously record their observations.

ENSURING ACCURATE OBSERVATIONS

Accuracy, as we noted in Chapter 2, is really a combination of two factors–the reliability and validity of the data. Just as with any measurement method, there are a number of ways that the reliability and validity of behavioral observations can be compromised (e.g., Foster & Cone, 1986; Hayes et al., 1986). The definition of the behavior might be vague or incomplete or perhaps even too complex. The behavior might be difficult to observe because of problems or distractions in the observational situation. A client's behavior might change as a result of being self-monitored or observed by someone else—the observations might be "reactive." The observer might be biased, perhaps expecting certain behaviors from the person being observed because of assumptions regarding how he or she "should" behave (this is especially likely when observers are asked to make global or subjective evaluations of behavior). The instruments for collecting data might be cumbersome or poorly designed. Observers may change over time in their understanding of just what should be observed.

When the reliability or validity of your observations is compromised, it's difficult or impossible to know just what the client's actual performance was, and whether any recorded change in behavior resulted from real change or from some change in the recording of the behavior (e.g., the observer's way of viewing the behavior). All of these things can affect not only the reliability and validity of your observations, but your entire intervention program. It's therefore crucial that you try to prevent these problems from occurring, to the extent possible, and that you attempt to evaluate whether the data are being recorded reliably and validly. The following guidelines will help to maximize the reliability and validity with which behavioral observations are made.

Maximizing the Reliability and Validity of Observations

From the beginning, you should try to maximize the reliability and validity of your observations. There's no foolproof method for doing this, but using some or all of the following strategies may go a long way toward helping you collect reliable and valid observations (Bornstein et al., 1986; Foster & Cone, 1986; Kopp, 1988; Marafiote, 1985, pp. 220–222):

1. Make sure, in consultation with the client and other relevant parties, that the behavior appears to be the target of interest (i.e., it has face validity).

2. Make sure that the behaviors selected, and the times and situations selected for their observation, give a representative picture of the target (i.e., the content validity of the observations is sufficient). Don't select behaviors, times, and situations just because they are convenient.

3. Make sure the target behavior is clearly and specifically defined, and that the observer has clear cues regarding when or where the behavior is likely to occur.

4. Train and retrain the observers. Make sure the observers understand what behaviors to record and how to recognize them if they occur. Familiarize the observers with the recording instruments before they start using them. Set up trial periods, say, through role-playing, where the observers get a chance to practice. Give the observers continued training sessions, especially if the intervention program is a long one, to ensure a continuing understanding of the behaviors to be observed (to avoid "observer drift").

5. Monitor observers. Check the observers' data as soon as possible after they are recorded. Any disagreements or problems should be corrected as soon as possible. If you can (i.e., for publicly observable behaviors), conduct frequent unannounced reliability checks on a random basis by having a second person independently observe and record at the same time as your regular observer (e.g., both parents could collect data on a child's behavior; a student may be assigned to collect data along with a teacher; a nurse may make a reliability check to assess the consistency of a ward attendant's data; you as the practitioner may do a reliability probe, for example, by making a home visit and collecting data at the same time as the client). Such checks are important because evidence shows that they increase the reliability of observations. Observers who know that such unannounced checks can occur may be more vigilant.

6. If more than one observer is to be used, make sure the actions of one will not influence the other. If possible, place them in areas where they cannot view each other.

7. Make sure the recording procedure itself–the data-gathering instrument–is accessible, portable, and easy to use. If the system is too complex (e.g., too many different types of behaviors are observed), the reliability and validity of the observations can be affected. In general, try not to set up a recording procedure that will be aversive to the observer.

8. Make sure the observers don't have to work so hard or so long at collecting data that they become fatigued and begin collecting inaccurate data.

9. See that the behavior is recorded immediately after its occurrence. Delays can lead to incomplete or distorted data.

10. Try to make record keeping a routine. Make sure the observer has incentives to record. Be encouraging and supportive, and offer a good deal of praise for recording efforts.

11. Make sure the data are used. Can you imagine the observer's frustration if some clear and specific use of the data is not made? If the data are not used, you can be sure your observer will lose interest in recording.

12. Try to make observers as inconspicuous as possible in order to minimize reactivity.

13. Don't inform relevant others or independent observers of expected changes in clients' behavior, if at all possible. This precaution will minimize the chances that observations will be distorted because of observers' expectations about change.

Verifying Reliability

A range of strategies for verifying reliability were discussed in Chapter 2. In particular,

when publicly observable events are targeted you will want to verify the consistency with which different observers observe the same behavior (i.e., interobserver reliability). In order to verify that behavior is being observed consistently, different observers should independently observe and record the same behaviors (e.g., as described in the last point above) when practical. Then, once the behavior is recorded by each observer, the interobserver reliability is computed. Interobserver reliability is usually reported in terms of some type of percentage of agreement. As we noted in Chapter 2, there's some consensus that agreement of roughly 80% (or .80 if not converted to percentages) or more indicates good reliability. A lower figure suggests that perhaps too much error may be influencing the observer, and suggests the need to clarify the definition of the behavior or to provide additional training.

The procedure for estimating reliability depends on the method used for recording. Later in this chapter we provide a specific method for estimating reliability for each type of recording. These methods provide a reasonable estimate of reliability without being unduly complex; they're quite simple and require no more skill than simple multiplication and division. More accurate methods of estimating reliability are available, but these also are more complicated (see, e.g., Foster & Cone, 1986; Page & Iwata, 1986; Suen, Ary & Ary, 1986).

Don't be too put off when you see the "numbers." We promise you that each computation is simple and that you'll be able to master it with very little practice. This all should become clear later in this chapter, where we give examples for use with each of the three key methods for recording behavior–frequency, duration, and interval recording.

Verifying Validity

Several strategies for verifying validity also were discussed in Chapter 2, and it's possible to use some of these methods to verify the validity of behavioral observations. In general this can be done by comparing the observations to some standard (i.e., criterion validity) or to other measured, predicted variables (construct validity). As an example of criterion validity, in Chapter 2 (Figure 2.3) we cited the example of comparing a student's reported frequency of completed homework assignments with the teacher's records of completed homework. As an example of construct validity, you could compare a student's reported study time with changes in grades (assuming that study time and grades are positively related), or you could compare changes in study time and grades in response to an intervention designed to increase these outcomes. Figure 5.4 shows hypothetical results that support the construct validity of a student's weekly reported study time; as reported study time increases, average weekly grades increase (the two results converge). Moreover, in the intervention phase (B) you see that reported study time and grades increase following the implementation of an intervention designed to increase these outcomes (the outcome is sensitive to change).

The results shown in Figure 5.4 also provide another example of concomitant variation. When study time goes up, grades go up; when study time goes down, grades go down. This suggests the importance of study time in improving grades, although there might be other explanations for the relationship. For example, it might be that the quality of the student's relationships with his or her family, parents, or peers causes the changes in study time and grades. Therefore, this concomitant variation is useful for suggesting causal connections for intervention purposes, but you should think critically about alternative explanations for such concomitant variation before drawing conclusions about causes.

In sum, when you collect information about different though related outcomes from different observers, and when this information fits in a theoretically logical and predicted pattern, you are in a better position to conclude that the observations are valid. This is especially important when having someone self-monitor covert behaviors because of the impossibility of checking interobserver reliability. In any case, though, the measurement of multiple behaviors using multiple observers puts you in a better position to draw valid conclusions about events that influence client targets, and this in-

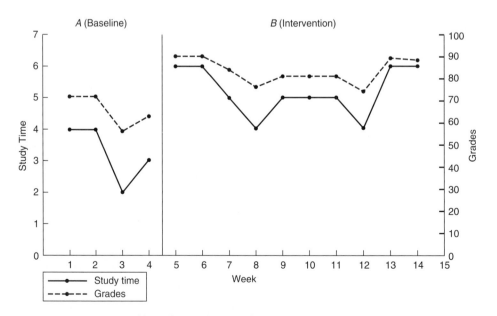

FIGURE 5.4 Average weekly study time (hours) and grades (percents).

formation can be used to select, develop, and implement more effective intervention strategies. In this way, a good single-system design is a study in validity.

METHODS OF RECORDING BEHAVIOR

There are several ways that the observation of behaviors can take place. Behavior can be measured (a) by counting the *frequency* with which it occurs (i.e., how often it occurs), (b) in terms of its *duration* (how long it lasts), or (c) by *intervals,* which provide an indication of the relative frequency and duration of behaviors. A fourth way of measuring behavior is in terms of its *magnitude* or *intensity.* Intensity is often evaluated by electromechanical devices that are not readily available to most practitioners, or that are simply too expensive or too complicated or inappropriate for naturalistic observation. Kallman and Feuerstein (1986) and Rugh et al. (1986) provide overviews of these methods. In Chapter 6 we provide a discussion of individualized rating scales (IRSs), a simple and practical way to measure intensity. All practitioners can use individualized rating scales, and we suggest you review that chapter for a description of how to use them to evaluate the intensity of a behavior.

Whatever attribute of behavior you choose to record, many behavioral observations proceed by the use of *codes.* Codes are symbols or two- or three-letter phrases that are used to represent specific categories of frequently occurring behavior or events that are being observed (Haynes, 1978). Either these codes are entered on forms as the behavior occurs or the forms can be prepared in advance with code categories already on them, so that all the observer has to do is check off whether that category exists. Almost anything can be used as a code; for example, "+" for praise, "−" for punishment, "M" for mother, "E" for eating, and so on.

Codes are valuable for several reasons (Haynes, 1978): (a) They allow the analysis of a large number of behavior categories; (b) they're adaptable to many situations, populations, and

behaviors; (c) they allow analysis of relationships among behaviors, and between behaviors and environmental events; (d) they make it easier to observe more people at the same time (e.g., in a group setting).

There are a variety of existing coding schemes for the observation of numerous different types of behaviors. Haynes (1978) provides references to 25 existing coding systems (pp. 119–120) designed for the observation of children, families, classroom behaviors, social interaction, staff and patient behavior in institutions, and so on. Hersen and Bellack (1988) and Markman and Notarius (1989) provide more recent discussions of existing coding systems. However, sometimes preexisting coding systems require extensive training, they may not always be relevant to the idiosyncratic targets presented by clients, and they may be more appropriate for direct observation than for self-monitoring. Nevertheless, preexisting coding schemes might be relevant for your clients, and they might save you the time involved in developing a coding scheme from scratch. Also, when you use a coding system that has been used before, it might be possible to compare your evaluation with previous evaluations that used the same coding scheme.

Frequency Recording

Frequency recording (also sometimes called event recording) simply involves counting the number of times a behavior occurs during a given period of time, ignoring the duration of the behavior. Frequency recording is probably the most commonly used recording procedure because of its many advantages (Brown & Brown, 1977; Kazdin, 1975). It's relatively simple to use. Usually no special equipment is necessary, but when it is, it's easy to use (e.g., a wrist counter). The number of times a behavior occurs often is especially sensitive to changes over time, so that such changes provide a clear and direct measure of change. In addition, the number of times a target occurs is often the most important characteristic to both clients and practitioners.

Frequency counts are used when a target behavior occurs too often and needs to be decreased (e.g., arguing), or doesn't occur often enough and needs to be increased (e.g., initiating communication). Therefore, if the goal of intervention is to change how often a behavior occurs, the obvious focus of measurement should be on recording its frequency. For example, Pinkston and Linsk (1984, p. 63) reported a case in which the goal was to increase the social contacts of an isolated elderly woman, and two of the measured behaviors included the number of times someone visited her at her apartment and the number of times she talked on the telephone.

A frequency count requires that the observed behavior has two characteristics. First, it should have a clear beginning and end so that separate occurrences of the behavior can be distinguished. It also should last for approximately the same amount of time each time it occurs, so that the units counted are roughly equal (Kazdin, 1975). If the behavior is ongoing (e.g., sleeping, studying, ruminative thoughts, interaction with a child), it would be inappropriate to use frequency recording. For example, if a person studied 1 hour one day and 5 minutes the next, each would be considered, using a frequency count, as only one occurrence, and a great deal of information would be lost. But if the behavior has a clear beginning and end and is fairly constant, frequency recording would probably be your best bet. Of course, the same category of behavior in different individuals may lend itself to frequency counts in some people and not in others. Crying that occurs frequently but lasts only 10–15 seconds may be appropriate for a frequency count, whereas crying that occurs infrequently and lasts for periods of 20–30 minutes would not be, and a duration count might be more appropriate.

Frequency counts are usually taken as a simple tally of how many times a behavior occurs. Once the behavior is clearly defined, the observer merely checks (or clicks) off whether a behavior occurs using either a simple form for counting or any of the instruments described earlier. (A simple all-purpose form for recording the frequency of occurrence of a behavior is displayed in Figure 5.5.) A period of time is designated in advance, although this is more important for direct observation than self-

monitoring because the client is always present to self-monitor (although self-monitoring may be more practical in some situations than in others). If the behavior occurs frequently, the time period would be shorter (imagine sitting for 4 hours recording every occurrence of a behavior that occurs 30 times per hour), while longer periods of observation are necessary for infrequently occurring behaviors to be sure you have an accurate picture of their occurrence. At the end of each observation period or at the end of the day, the total occurrences of the behavior are tallied and simply placed on a chart.

As discussed above, frequency counts can be expressed in terms of the number of times a behavior occurs, or in terms of rates. If the length of the observation time is the same each time, the number of occurrences can be used. If the length of observation times varies from day to day, you should use rates. Rates are computed by dividing the number of times a behavior occurs by the total observation time, or by the number of opportunities for it to occur if the behavior involves a response to some event or stimulus. (If, for example, an adolescent client is recording how often he or she uses a contraceptive during intercourse, the number of times he or she has intercourse may vary each week. Therefore, you would calculate the number of times he or she uses a contraceptive per times he or she has intercourse. The client may have intercourse once the first week and use a contraceptive on that occasion–for a rate of 1.00, or 100%–and he or she may have intercourse twice the second week and only use a contraceptive one of those two times–for a rate of .50, or 50%.) A form for frequency recording during varying periods of time (using rates) is displayed in Figure 5.6 (page 182).

There are some circumstances under which frequency recording is difficult. One of these, as we already mentioned, is when the behavior has no clear beginning and ending. Another is when a behavior is occurring so quickly that it's difficult to count. Finally, if a behavior occurs infrequently, it might be difficult to have observers other than the client record it because they may become bored with

Client's Name		Recorder's Name	
_____		_____	
Behaviors to Be Observed: _____			
_____			
Time Period (Hours/Day): _____			

Date	Number of Times Behavior Occurred	Additional Comments
_____	_____	_____
_____	_____	_____
_____	_____	_____
_____	_____	_____
_____	_____	_____
_____	_____	_____
_____	_____	_____
_____	_____	_____
_____	_____	_____
_____	_____	_____
_____	_____	_____

FIGURE 5.5   Sample form for recording frequency of occurrence of behavior.

the observation task and miss occurrences of the behavior (Foster & Cone, 1986).

Many behaviors have been assessed using frequency counts, including behavior by individuals, families, groups, and communities. Some of these behaviors include the following: number of occasions on which an adolescent used contraceptives, number of times an adolescent expressed refusal to risk pregnancy, number of links with community resources, number of practitioner–client contacts, number of "homework" tasks completed by a client, number of negative thoughts, number of positive self-statements, number of mistakes or errors made in completing an employment ap-

plication form, number of times a spouse initiates conversation, number of chores completed, number of times one child hits another, number of times a child gets out of his or her seat without permission, number of greetings to staff made by patients on a ward, number of aggressive phrases used, number of times an individual attends a meeting, number of fights during recess, number of times each group member speaks, and so on. The range of behaviors appropriate for frequency recording is immense.

Establishing Reliability.   Interobserver reliability in measuring the frequency of covert

Client's Name			**Recorder's Name**		
_____			_____		
Behaviors to Be Observed: _____					
_____					

Date	Frequency	Total	Time	Rate	Additional Comments
9/1	⫴⫴ ‖	7	20 minutes	.35	
9/1	‖‖	3	10 minutes	.30	

FIGURE 5.6   Form for frequency recording during varying periods of time (rates).

behaviors (e.g., thoughts) cannot be established, but for publicly observable behaviors, two observers can be used to establish the reliability of frequency recording. Each observer records the number of times a behavior occurs during the same time period. At the end of this period, their observations are compared to see whether they recorded the same number of behaviors. A percentage of agreement is determined—the interobserver reliability. We discussed the basic procedure of determining interobserver reliability earlier, and promised to show you a simple way of calculating it. Here's how to do it.

If both observers have exactly the same number of observations tallied, there's no problem. Their agreement (the reliability) is 100%. More typically though, one will have more behaviors checked than the other. Simply divide the larger number of behaviors into the smaller and multiply by 100. The result will be the interobserver reliability.

Let's say in a 1-hour period, Observer 1 checks off 10 occurrences of behavior and Observer 2 checks off 12. Divide 10 by 12 and multiply by 100 ([10/12] $\times$ 100 = 83%). (Sometimes you might see the reliability reported as .83, which simply means the results of the division weren't multiplied by 100.) Simple, wasn't it? Looking for at least 80% agreement, you'd conclude that in this case the interobserver reliability of 83% was satisfactory.

There's a problem with this procedure for computing reliability. The 83% means that the two observers agree on total frequency, not that they necessarily agree 83% of the time on the same behaviors. It may be that one observer recorded 12 occurrences of the behavior and the other observer recorded 10 different occurrences. Thus, the reliability figure should be interpreted cautiously because the two observers might not be observing the same behavior. This problem can be overcome when observers record their observations using computers that are synchronized according to time (e.g., the Assistant described above), although typically such equipment is not available. Of course, the problem of recording different behaviors will be decreased in direct proportion to how clearly the problem is defined–the clearer the definition of the problem, the more likely it is that observers will record the same event.

Duration Recording

There are many behaviors for which frequency recording would not be useful. These are behaviors where the major concern is time–the behavior either lasts too long or not long enough, or it occurs too soon or not soon enough after some event or other behavior. In such situations, where the goal is to increase or decrease the *length of time* some behavior is performed, or the amount of time that elapses before a behavior occurs, duration recording can be used.

Duration recording usually involves recording the length of time some behavior occurs. For example, a group leader might audiotape group sessions and later record the duration of on-task behavior for the group as a whole (cf. Rose, 1989, p. 126), a father and mother might record the amount of time spent reading to or talking with their children, spouses might record the amount of enjoyable leisure time they spend together, or a practitioner might record the amount of time spent with a client.

Another type of duration recording involves measuring the amount of time that elapses between an event and the occurrence of a behavior (e.g., the amount of time that elapses between a parent asking a child to go to bed and the time the child gets in bed). This latter type of duration recording usually is referred to as *latency recording.*

Another variation of duration recording, *interresponse interval recording,* is similar to latency recording. It involves recording the amount of time that elapses between different behaviors– for example, the amount of time between completing two different tasks or between having two different thoughts (Foster & Cone, 1986).

Duration recording is relatively simple to use, since it involves determining only the length of time between the beginning and end of a behavior, or the amount of time between one event or response and the occurrence of a behavior. You will need some form of timepiece; stopwatches or inexpensive runners' chronographs are useful and practical because they're relatively precise, but any watch or clock, preferably with a second hand, can be used. The observer must note the time a behavior begins and the time it ends, or the amount of time between one event or response and the occurrence of a behavior. A simple, all-purpose form for recording duration counts is displayed in Figure 5.7.

As discussed above, if different observation periods are of equal length, duration can be expressed in terms of the actual amount of time that a behavior lasts during an observation period. When observation periods are not equal, duration should be expressed as a rate, the proportion of time during an observation period that a behavior occurs. This is similar to the way that rates are determined for frequencies.

For latency or interresponse interval recording, the average latency or interresponse interval for an episode of behavior is computed. For example, suppose that the target involves reducing the amount of time between a father's request and the time the son complies with the request. On the first day of observation the father makes five requests and the elapsed times are 15, 10, 25, 5, and 10 minutes. The average latency for that day is computed by adding these times together and dividing by the number of episodes of behavior, which in this case is the number of requests by the father (i.e., $15 + 10 + 25 + 5 + 10 = 65/5 = 13$ minutes).

Duration recording, as well as frequency recording, requires that the beginning and end of the behavior be defined clearly. However, with duration recording be particularly careful that observers agree when a behavior begins and ends. Kazdin (1975) uses the example of attempting to record the duration of a tantrum where a child may cry continuously for several minutes, whimper for short periods, stop all noise for a few seconds, begin intense crying again, and so on. Thus, with duration

Client's Name		Recorder's Name	

Behaviors to Be Observed: _____

Time Period for Observation: _____

Date	Length of Time Behavior Occurred (e.g., minutes)	Total Time (minutes)	Additional Comments

FIGURE 5.7   Form for recording duration of behavior.

recording, one must be clear, and have agreement among observers, about how to handle these changes (e.g., periods of silence, changes from crying to whimpering) so that recording is consistent.

Any number of behaviors are appropriate for duration recording (Haynes, 1978), such as studying, exercise, time spent in obsessive thinking, insomnia, asthma attacks, tension and migraine headaches, tantrums, crying, length of meetings, maintenance of penile erections, time spent cleaning up before dinner, periods of feeling depressed, and so on.

Establishing Reliability.   Interobserver reliability is computed for duration recording in practically the same way as for frequency recording, but again, this is not applicable for covert behaviors. Two observers record the be-

havior during the same time period. Then, the smaller duration is divided by the larger duration, and the result is multiplied by 100.

Let's say Observer 1 recorded the behavior as occurring for 20 minutes and Observer 2 recorded the duration of the behavior as 25 minutes. Divide 20 by 25 and multiply by 100 ($[20/25] \times 100$) and you get 80% as your percentage of agreement estimate of interobserver reliability. Our standard suggests that this is an acceptable figure, although just barely.

The key to ensuring observer agreement for duration recording is to be certain that both observers begin and end at the same time so that each will be observing for the same period of time. Also, as with frequency recording, you should interpret this type of reliability estimate with caution, because even with high agreement you cannot be absolutely certain that the same behaviors were being observed. However, as with frequency recording, this problem can be overcome by clear definition of the behavior to be observed or when observers record their observations using computers that are synchronized according to time (e.g., the Assistant described above).

Interval Recording

There are times when it may be difficult to use frequency or duration recording. For example, a behavior such as speaking might not only be difficult to break into discrete units for frequency recording, but may be ongoing for long periods, making duration recording (just sitting and watching from beginning to end) difficult and impractical. In these situations, where frequency or duration recording is not quite appropriate, a variation of time sampling called interval recording can be used, although for the most part interval recording is much more feasible for direct observation than for self-monitoring.

In interval recording, a period of observation is selected (e.g., 30 minutes) and then divided into equal blocks of time (intervals), usually of rather short duration (e.g., 10–15 seconds). The behavior is then recorded as either occurring or not occurring for each interval.

There are three slightly different ways to determine whether to record a behavior as having occurred during an interval. An observer can record a behavior as having occurred (a) if the behavior occurred at all, or during a specified portion of the interval (this is called *partial-interval sampling*); (b) if the behavior occurred throughout the entire interval (this is called *whole-interval sampling*); or (c) if the behavior occurred at a particular time during the interval, such as at the beginning or end of the interval (this is called *momentary-interval sampling*, and it is similar to time sampling except that with time sampling the time between intervals is usually longer) (Foster & Cone, 1986). A review of research on the relative accuracy of these three methods indicates that momentary-interval sampling provides the most accurate estimates (Foster & Cone, 1986).

The basic process of interval recording involves the observer watching the client for the interval (called the "observation interval"), then marking his or her observation sheet (the "recording interval" period), then observing for the next interval, and so on. This method can be used with individual clients, families, or groups. For example, when observing clients receiving group-based assertiveness training, every 10 seconds the initials of the person speaking could be recorded (Rose, 1989, p. 124). One way this is done is for the observer to have a miniature tape recorder with an earphone and a tape on which a tone has been recorded at preset intervals (e.g., 10 seconds). For longer intervals a simple kitchen timer or stopwatch could be used. In any case, the observer records whether the behavior was occurring at the sound of the tone. This allows the observer time to record whether the behavior occurred and then refocus attention on the person being observed.

There are some distinct advantages to using interval recording (Kazdin, 1975). First, it's flexible, since the presence or absence of a behavior during some time period can be observed for almost any type of behavior. It doesn't matter whether the behavior is discrete or continuous.

Second, interval recording can be used to record a number of different behaviors at the same time, because you don't have to see every occurrence of the behavior, and you can alternate behaviors (e.g., watching behavior A for 10 seconds and then recording, watching behavior B for 10 seconds and then recording). Similarly, interval recording can be used to observe different people, because you don't have to see every occurrence of the behavior and you can alternate observing different people (e.g., watching the first person for 10 seconds and then recording, watching the second person for 10 seconds and then recording).

A third advantage of interval recording is that the results can be converted easily into rates. This is done by dividing the number of intervals during which the behavior occurred by the total number of intervals observed. For example, if a behavior occurs in 25 out of 100 intervals the resulting rate of .25 shows that the behavior occurs a specific proportion of time. As with frequency and duration rates, rates from interval recording are often expressed as percentages, but this just involves multiplying the proportion by 100 (i.e., .25 x 100 = 25%).

There are some problems with interval recording. First and foremost, it requires the undivided attention of the observer to both the time interval and whether the behavior occurs. Thus, it's a demanding form of recording. Therefore, interval recording is probably not suitable for most clients or relevant others. It requires higher levels of skill and training than frequency or duration recording.

Second, interval recording provides an estimate of the frequency or duration of behavior, not a direct determination of frequency or duration. That is, with interval recording, you can tell the number of intervals in which the behavior occurred, but you cannot tell how many times or for how long the behavior occurred overall. The reason for this is that you're only recording *whether* it occurred in each interval; the behavior actually might have occurred five times in one interval but only is recorded as having occurred once. Furthermore, a review of research on the accuracy of interval recording in estimating the frequency and duration of behaviors indicates that in general it doesn't provide accurate estimates of frequency, although it provides better estimates of duration (Foster & Cone, 1986). Interval recording does, however, provide an indication of the relative changes in the frequency or duration of behavior over time (e.g., changes in the proportion of intervals the behavior was observed to occur), and this is probably how it's best used (Alessi, 1988). However, some promising, but complex and relatively untested, procedures can be used to improve the estimates of frequency and duration obtained from interval recording (e.g., Quera, 1990; Suen & Ary 1989), and so eventually such estimates might be improved sufficiently.

Third, it's sometimes difficult to decide the duration of the interval. There is simply no unequivocal answer as to how long an interval should be, since intervals from 5 seconds to several minutes have been reported in the literature. As a general rule, research indicates that intervals longer than 10 seconds may produce inaccurate results, but intervals of 5 seconds or less are hard to score reliably (Foster & Cone, 1986). Therefore, as a general rule 10-second intervals seem to provide fairly accurate results.

Once the behavior is clearly defined, the duration of the interval is established, and the length of the overall observation period is set, the observer simply jots down on a preset recording sheet whether a behavior occurs. There are several ways to do this. The observer can write yes or no in a blank box, or simply put a check or hash mark in the box if it occurs, or circle some preset symbol such as a plus sign if the behavior occurs, or a minus sign if it doesn't. We recommend the latter method because it demands less of the observer. We also recommend that the observer record something in each interval whether or not the behavior occurs (e.g., a "+" if it does and a "–" if it doesn't). In that way, there will be no question later whether blank intervals were left blank because the observer forgot to record.

Interval-recording forms should have the intervals represented across the top and the periods of observation down the side. If a group is to be observed, instead of having the observation periods down the left side of the sheet, each of these could represent a different individual in the group. Thus, the first individual could be observed for a 10-second interval, then the second individual for a 10-second interval, and so on. This would continue until each individual has been observed for one interval, and then the entire process is repeated. A basic form for use in interval recording is displayed in Figure 5.8. (An alternative form would be one in which the spaces are left blank and a check mark is simply placed in the box if the behavior occurs; see Figure 5.9 on page 188.)

Any number of different behaviors have been measured using interval recording (e.g., Feldman, Caplinger, & Wodarski, 1983; Kazdin, 1975; Gambrill, 1977), including social responses of psychiatric patients; student behavior such as paying attention, sitting in seats, and working quietly; appropriate mealtime be-

Client's Name

Recorder's Name

_____   _____

Behaviors to Be Observed: _____

_____

Time Period (Length of Total Observation Period): _____

Duration of Each Interval: _____

Minutes	Interval									
	1	2	3	4	5	6	7	8	9	10
1	+ −	+ −	+ −	+ −	+ −	+ −	+ −	+ −	+ −	+ −
2	+ −	+ −	+ −	+ −	+ −	+ −	+ −	+ −	+ −	+ −
3	+ −	+ −	+ −	+ −	+ −	+ −	+ −	+ −	+ −	+ −
4	+ −	+ −	+ −	+ −	+ −	+ −	+ −	+ −	+ −	+ −
5	+ −	+ −	+ −	+ −	+ −	+ −	+ −	+ −	+ −	+ −
6	+ −	+ −	+ −	+ −	+ −	+ −	+ −	+ −	+ −	+ −
7	+ −	+ −	+ −	+ −	+ −	+ −	+ −	+ −	+ −	+ −
8	+ −	+ −	+ −	+ −	+ −	+ −	+ −	+ −	+ −	+ −
9	+ −	+ −	+ −	+ −	+ −	+ −	+ −	+ −	+ −	+ −
10	+ −	+ −	+ −	+ −	+ −	+ −	+ −	+ −	+ −	+ −

+ = Target behavior occurred
− = Target behavior did not occur

FIGURE 5.8   Form for interval recording.

havior; behavior of withdrawn or uncooperative children; verbalizations of children; prosocial, antisocial, and nonsocial group behavior; and so on.

Establishing Reliability.   The same basic principles described above are followed for determining interobserver reliability, but there are a few differences. For interval recording, reliability is determined by comparing the proportion of intervals that two observers agree on the occurrence and nonoccurrence of the behavior. This is the most frequently used method for determining reliability for interval recording. In this method, each interval in which the observers agree that a behavior did or did not occur is termed an agreement, and each interval in which only one observer scored a behavior (i.e., where different events are recorded) is considered a disagreement.

Client's Name						Recorder's Name					

Behaviors to Be Observed:

A. _____

B. _____

C. _____

Time Period:_____

Duration of Each Interval: _____

Interval

Minute	Behavior	1	2	3	4	5	6	7	8	9	10
1	A										
	B										
	C										
2	A										
	B										
	C										
3	A										
	B										
	C										
4	A										
	B										
	C										
5	A										
	B										
	C										

FIGURE 5.9   Form for interval recording of more than one behavior.

Then, reliability is determined by dividing the number of intervals in which the observers agreed by the number of agreements *plus* disagreements (i.e., the total number of observations) and multiplying by 100.

$$\frac{\text{Agreements}}{\text{Agreements} + \text{Disagreements}} \times 100$$

Let's say the observers recorded behavior for 60 10-second intervals, and the observers agreed that the behavior did occur in 20 intervals and also agreed that the behavior *did not* occur in 30 intervals. In the remaining 10 intervals they disagreed, with only one or the other observer recording the behavior as having occurred. The interobserver reliability would be calculated, as in the equation, by adding the agreements (20 + 30) and dividing by the agreements plus the disagreements (20 + 30 + 10). The resulting figure would be multiplied by 100. The reliability figure then would be 83% ([50/60] × 100).

$$\frac{20 + 30}{20 + 30 + 10} = \frac{50}{60} \times 100 = 83\%$$

A critical consideration in determining the interobserver reliability of interval recording is whether the observers start and stop their intervals at the same time. If not, the results may be meaningless. This is usually accomplished by having some type of device that alerts the observers to the beginning and end of intervals (e.g., a tape-recorded tone, a flash of light on a video screen).

Additional Considerations with Interobserver Reliability

There are a couple of problems with using the percentage of agreement between observers, described earlier in this chapter, to measure interobserver reliability. A major problem is that this method is affected by how often the behavior occurs, with more frequently occurring behaviors tending to have higher reliabilities. It also tends to be inflated by chance agreement between observers. But there are ways of computing reliability that are not subject to these limitations (Foster & Cone, 1986; Page & Iwata, 1986; Suen, 1988; Suen et al., 1986).

Kappa is a widely used measure of agreement that is useful for quantifying interobserver reliability in a way that corrects for chance agreements (e.g., Cohen, 1960; Fleiss, 1981; Foster & Cone, 1986). Because you might see kappa discussed in the literature, we'll briefly describe it here. Kappa equals 1 when perfect agreement occurs, 0 when observed agreement equals chance agreement, and less than 0 when observed agreement is less than chance agreement. Most of the time kappa will be lower than the percentage of observed agreement because it subtracts out that part of agreement that is due to chance. Therefore, the standards for adequate reliability when kappa is used are lower than for percentage agreement. A kappa in the range from .75 to 1.00 is considered good, a kappa between .60 and .74 is fair, and a kappa below .60 is poor (Cicchetti & Sparrow, 1981; Fleiss, 1981). Kappa can be computed using a simple calculator. Unfortunately, the computer program that comes with this book cannot be used.

Selecting and computing the most appropriate measure of interobserver reliability isn't the only problem in determining interobserver reliability. We also recognize that it's not always realistic for you to find two observers to do this reliability check. If the client and a relevant other are both available and willing to record (the secondary recorder only in certain situations), that would be great. But in other circumstances, no one else might be available. Then, the second recorder might be you. You might make home visits, once in the baseline period and once in the intervention and do some recording yourself. Then your recording could form the basis for the reliability check. Or, you could set up an analogue situation in the office in which you and the client role-play and record (we discuss this in more detail in the next section).

Obviously, the more you remove the behavior from its real circumstances—you in the home, a role-play in your office—the more likely it is that the validity of the behavior will be affected; that is, what you are recording might not be the real target behaviors. Thus, you would interpret reliability figures from circumstances such as these with caution. On the other hand, no reliability information on the recorded behaviors may mean that you don't really know whether changes are real or due to measurement error. Thus, without any reliability checks, you must be even more cautious in your interpretations.

ANALOG SITUATIONS

Ideally behavior should be observed in the environment in which it naturally occurs, because that is where you want behavior change to occur. However, sometimes it's not possible or practical to observe behavior in the natural environment, especially when using direct observation. The behavior might be too difficult to observe accurately in the natural environment, or observation by you, a relevant other, or an independent observer might be too time-consuming or otherwise costly. Oftentimes irrelevant and changing conditions in the natural environment are difficult to control, making it impossible to make observations under standardized conditions. Some behaviors occur so infrequently or at such unpredictable times that they are difficult if not impossible for you or an independent observer to measure (e.g., asthma attacks). In these situations we recommend that you consider the use of *analog* situations.

Analog situations are constructed situations that are designed to elicit a sample of behavior that ideally will be representative of behavior that occurs in the natural environment (Nay, 1986; Shapiro & Kratochwill, 1988). For example, a child welfare worker may ask a parent and child to play in a room full of toys so that he or she can observe them through a two-way mirror. Another example would be you and the client role-playing a job interview to observe the client's skills. Frequency, duration, or interval recording (or measures of magnitude and intensity as described in the next chapter) can be used to measure different aspects of the behavior as it occurs in the analog situation.

Nay (1986) identified several types of analogs: paper-and-pencil, audiotape, videotape, role-playing, and enactment. Clients typically are asked to respond to these analogs as they ordinarily would in the natural environment, although sometimes, in order to determine the client's goals, a practitioner may ask the client to behave the way he or she would like to ideally. A basic assumption underlying the use of analog situations is that the closer the analog situation resembles the natural environment, the more likely it is that the observed behavior will be representative of that in the natural environment. These different types of analogs are reviewed briefly, in ascending order of their sim-

ilarity to the natural environment, and we also provide some examples of their use.

With *paper-and-pencil* analogs a client is asked to respond orally or in writing to a situation that is presented in written form. (A variation of this type of analog involves the use of a personal computer to present the analog situation, and record, summarize, and store the client's responses [e.g., Gettinger, 1988].) For example, Whiteman, Fanshel, and Grundy (1987), in examining the effects of an intervention designed to reduce the risk of child abuse by reducing parental anger, asked parents to respond to a written list of eight situations that involved a child acting in a way that was likely to provoke parental anger.

Audiotape and *videotape* analogs are similar to the paper-and-pencil analog, except the client hears, or hears and sees, the stimulus situation. Then the client is asked either to describe or to actually act out how he or she would respond, and these responses are observed and recorded. For example, Berlin (1985) audiotaped descriptions of 12 different situations that were designed to elicit self-critical responses. For each audiotaped situation clients were instructed to listen to the description of the situation, imagine that it was really occurring, and orally describe their reaction to the situation. Clients' descriptions were audiotaped, and based on these audiotaped responses, observers recorded the frequency of "self-critical responses," and "positive coping responses," and the length of time between the end of the recorded situation and the beginning of the client's response (i.e., response latency).

In the *role-playing* analog, the client is asked to visualize a situation in the natural environment and his or her response to it, or to act out situations with the practitioner, other staff, or other clients (e.g., in group therapy) portraying people relevant to the situation. For example, Blythe, Gilchrist, and Schinke (1981) and Schinke, Blythe, and Gilchrist (1981), in examining the effect of pregnancy prevention groups for adolescents, had opposite-sex adolescents role-play their responses to stressful interpersonal situations related to sexuality (e.g., a discussion of contraception with a girlfriend or boyfriend). These role-plays were videotaped, and observers later recorded such behaviors as the frequency with which unreasonable requests were refused by an adolescent.

In the *enactment* analog the client interacts in the agency or clinical setting with people or objects that he or she has difficulty interacting with in the natural environment. For example, oftentimes husbands and wives are given a communication task to perform in a clinic setting (e.g., select, discuss, and resolve a family problem), and different dimensions of their communication behavior are observed or recorded for later observation (e.g., Markman & Notarius, 1989; O'Leary, 1987). Similar procedures also are used to observe interactions among parents and children (e.g., Mash, 1987; Shapiro & Kratochwill, 1988).

In all of the analog situations you will want to collect structured information on the observed behaviors. You can do this in at least two ways, particularly in the enactment and role-playing analogs. First, you can use a checklist. Depending on the situation, you can develop a list of behaviors that you consider to be optimal in a given situation, (for example, maintaining good eye contact). These behaviors can be transferred onto a checklist, and you simply check off whether or not the behavior occurred during an observation session. Second, you can develop a simple scale to rate the degree to which desired behaviors were performed, say from zero (none of the behaviors) to seven or higher equaling all desired behaviors. We'll present more details about how to construct these rating scales in Chapter 6. Both the number of behaviors checked on the checklist and the scores on the scale can be plotted as points on the chart.

In each analog situation the practitioner structures the activity to which the client will respond. Suggestions for material that can be used are available in the above references.

All of this makes analog measures sound quite viable. You might even be wondering, Why bother to measure behavior in the natural environment? The problem is that it isn't always certain that behaviors elicited in analog situations predict behaviors in the natural en-

vironment (i.e., there is contradictory evidence of the concurrent validity of analogs) (Nay, 1986; Shapiro & Kratochwill, 1988). Therefore, when analogs are used, it's a good idea whenever possible to try to collect some information concerning the concurrent validity of the analog data. This might involve having the client, a relevant other, or even an independent observer make periodic observations in the natural environment.

In addition to periodic checks on the concurrent validity of analog observations, it also is important to determine interobserver reliability, just as it is when behaviors are observed in the natural environment. Similarly, just as in the natural environment, oftentimes it's useful to examine the construct validity of the behavioral observations by using different methods to measure the target, and by examining how different measures vary together over time in a predictable way for a given client (Nay, 1986).

RECORDING BEHAVIOR IN GROUPS

Since many practitioners spend a substantial part of their practice time with families and small groups, we'd like to discuss how some of the principles covered so far apply in those situations. In fact, just about all the methods described in this and preceding chapters, plus those explored in succeeding chapters can be used in family and group situations. Thus, role-plays and analogs can be used (especially easily with groups), as can frequency, duration, and interval recording (e.g., see Rose, 1989, and the references cited in Rose, 1988).

The key here, though, is distinguishing between recording an individual's target in the context of a group, and recording information on the group as a whole. For example, you might be working with a family and ask each family member to keep track of some behavior (or fill out some standardized questionnaire like a measure evaluating the strength of family relationships). You would then have information from each individual for each measure. While, under some circumstances, these can be pooled (e.g., the total number of times family members recorded feeling "put down" by other family members), often these are simply individual measures in the *context* of a group. And while they can provide very valuable information, they may not provide information on changes in the group as a whole.

Under some circumstances, you may very well wish to record behaviors of all members of a family or group at the same time. This might involve students in a class, members of a psychotherapy group, or residents of a nursing home interacting with one another. These behaviors can be recorded using frequency, duration, or interval methods as described earlier in this chapter. While there may be some advantages to using interval recording (every person doesn't have to be watched all the time), any of the methods can be used.

First, it's decided just who will do the recording. Relevant others, caretakers like teachers or nurses, other practitioners functioning as observers, or even designated members of the group could do the recording.

Then, a checklist of behaviors to be observed should be developed. This would allow the observer to simply note in columns next to each behavior who in the group engaged in that behavior. A variation of this method is to list the names of all members of the group in the left-hand column, and along the top of the form, note what behaviors will be observed. Then only a check needs to be placed in the relevant place if the behavior occurs (see Figure 5.10).

The last condition is to make sure that the observer(s) are well trained, the behaviors clearly defined, and all observers know when they're to start and stop recording. If the recording times do vary, than rates of behavior can be used.

One widely used method of observing and recording group interactions is called SYMLOG (Systematic Multiple Level Observation of Groups; Bales, Cohen, & Williamson, 1979). Though somewhat complicated to use, this approach can analyze both overt and covert behaviors and interactions of group participants. SYMLOG uses a three-dimensional diagram based on coded observations of group interactions; it can be used to evaluate change in a number of variables at the same time including targets that range from emotional problems of group members to their behaviors in engaging in group tasks.

An interesting approach that seems especially useful with children is the "freeze technique" (Rose & Tolman, 1985), in which a timer is set off at irregular intervals and the group members are asked to "freeze" in place. Then, whatever behavior the group member is engaging in can be noted, and if this technique

Name	Behavior to Be Observed			Date _____ Time _____
	Initiates Verbal Request	**Responds Verbally to Question**	**Cries**	**Laughs**
Harvey				
Rodney				
Irving				
Sam				
Duke				
Larry				

FIGURE 5.10 Form for group recording.

is used in an intervention phase, interventions such as reinforcement can be applied.

Results of group recording can be cumulated and placed on a chart using the same methods you would for individual clients. In fact, those charts can be placed in easily observed locations and can act as a real stimulus for development of group morale, and an aid to facilitative group and family processes. When the entire group sees changes (or lack of changes) in the chart, group processes can be utilized to examine this information and develop strategies to move the group more readily toward its goal.

These group data can be used to increase or decrease the frequency or duration of certain group behaviors ranging from social amenities to number of chores completed. They also can be used to determine which group members might be most or least likely to exhibit some specific behavior, as simple as whether (or how) they are participating in the group. This information can be particularly useful in highlighting the need for selective interventions within a group. (For an innovative approach to data visualization for the evaluation of group treatment, see Patterson & Basham, in press).

SUMMARY

Behavioral observation can be one of the most useful forms of measurement because of its potentially high validity and reliability, and because it can be especially useful for assessment purposes. We defined behaviors as relatively discrete events, including both overt and covert activities. We noted that self-observation is typically called "self-monitoring," and observation by an outside observer oftentimes is called "direct observation." We then presented some general guidelines for both types of behavioral observation. This was followed by a review of a number of different methods for observing behavior as well as some principles for selecting those methods.

We emphasized methods for ensuring that your behavioral observations are accurate. We briefly reviewed the validity of behavioral observations, emphasizing their generally high face validity and the fact that behaviors often tend to be the most direct and clearest form of a target. We also discussed the importance of establishing the reliability of behavioral observations, and suggested a number of ways of preventing unreliable observations with an emphasis on the necessity for regularly checking interobserver reliability.

The last part of the chapter focused on three main methods of behavioral recording: frequency, duration, and interval recording. Each of these methods was defined and described in terms of how it can be used. We also gave examples of typical behaviors that might be measured by each, and a form for recording each type of measure. Some simple formulas for calculating interobserver reliability also were presented. Finally this chapter looked at the way behaviors can be observed in analog situations and in families and small groups.

In essence, selection of a method of behavioral observation depends on two key conditions. One is the type of behavior selected for observation. Frequency recording should be used when the goal is to increase or decrease the number of times a behavior occurs, and the behavior is relatively constant and has a clear beginning and end. Duration recording should be used when the goal is to increase or decrease the length of time a behavior occurs, or the length of time between events, and the behavior has a clear beginning and end. Interval recording should be used when the goal is to increase or decrease the relative frequency or duration of behavior and frequency or duration recording are impractical (e.g., when the beginning and end of the behavior are difficult to discern or when multiple clients or behaviors are observed simultaneously). A second consideration has to do with the practicality of the recording method and the resources available. If one recording method is not convenient, easy to use, accessible, and clear, then it is wiser to switch to another method or instrument that would more readily meet these criteria.

6 INDIVIDUALIZED RATING SCALES

PURPOSE: This chapter will show you how you can easily construct practical scales that are tailor-made to measure the intensity of the unique targets presented by your clients. It also will show you how these scales can be developed for and used by practitioners, relevant others, and independent evaluators, to provide important information about change in the specific targets presented by your particular clients. ■

Introduction
A Case Example
Uses of Individualized Rating Scales
Constructing and Using Individualized Rating Scales
Steps in Construction
  Prepare the Client
  Select Rating Dimensions
  Select the Number of Response Categories

  Create Equidistant Response Categories
  Select Rating Scale Anchors
  Construct Overall Summary Scores
Select Who, When, and Where to Collect Data
  Select Respondent(s)
  Decide When to Collect Target Information
  Decide Where to Collect Target Information
Summary

INTRODUCTION

Roger had been a practitioner for almost 7 years. From reading the literature he was aware of the desirability of monitoring his practice more systematically, but he was also uncomfortable about the idea. Roger believed that most of his clients' problems involved how they felt about themselves or others. Therefore, he thought that behavioral observation might not be appropriate, and that it could even interfere in some way with the type of relationship and insight-oriented therapy he offered. But he was still left with the dilemma of wanting to evaluate how well he was doing in his practice.

Many practitioners, like Roger, feel that since they don't define every one of their clients' targets as discrete behaviors, single-system evaluation has little to offer them. Part of this feeling may be related to the myth that only an out-and-out behaviorist can use single-system evaluation.

There are other realities involved when a practitioner and client define their goals and objectives, only one of which has to do with the way the practitioner tends to conceptualize practice. The most important of these realities has to do with the nature of the client's targets.

We strongly recommended the use of behavioral measures, broadly defined, whenever applicable for all the reasons described in Chapter 5. But the key words here are *whenever applicable*. It may be that in many practice situations, it's difficult, impossible, or undesirable to count behaviors. This may be because a target really doesn't involve behaviors; because the behaviors are too difficult, imprecise, or infrequent to count; or because of the unavailability or inability of someone to count them.

So assume that you've tried to define one of your client's targets in behavioral terms, but for one of the above reasons you couldn't. You can still measure your client's target(s). In fact, you can do it in a way that is so flexible that you can probably apply it to almost all of your cases as a secondary measure and to many of them—where appropriate—as a primary measure. Essentially, this procedure consists of actually developing your own scale to measure whatever targets you and your client have identified.

The type of measure we're talking about has been called a "target complaint scale" (e.g., Battle et al., 1966; Mintz & Kiesler, 1982), a "self-anchored scale" (Bloom & Fischer, 1982), or an "individual problem rating scale" (Gillespie & Seaberg, 1977). We call this type of measure an *Individualized Rating Scale,* or IRS for short, and in this chapter we discuss the structure and workings of IRSs. We already illustrated a variety of these scales in previous chapters (e.g., ratings of an AIDS client's suicidal ideation by his social worker; ratings of satisfaction with participation in a luncheon program by elderly clients; ratings of task achievement and job satisfaction by a client). But before we discuss the details of these scales, let's take a more detailed look at another example of when and how you could construct an IRS.

A Case Example

Douglas interned at a residential treatment center for emotionally disturbed adolescent boys. The program provides 24-hour care, including an in-house school staffed by special education teachers; individual and group counseling provided by three social workers; and a sports and craft program conducted by lay volunteers. One major focus of the program is on the development of appropriate communication skills and conflict–resolution skills. Douglas led the conflict–resolution skills groups each weekday, as well as having individual counseling sessions with four youths.

As part of the conflict–resolution group, Douglas had the six members write homework cards involving a problem (conflict) they had in the center's school the day before. They were to describe that problem, rate its difficulty on a 5-point scale, describe what they did about it, and rate the success of their efforts in resolving that problem (also on a 5-point scale). The problem scale included the following five steps:

Given the problem _____, it was:

1. A minor irritation to me. No one knew about it but me.
2. A minor disagreement or annoying situation. The other person knew about it, but it passed without an incident.
3. A major disagreement or annoying situation. The other person knew about it, and it left some bad feelings.
4. A minor argument that involved strong feelings on both sides and a threat of a physical fight.
5. A major argument that involved strong feelings on both sides and some physical fighting.

The resolution scale included these five steps:

1. I handled the problem and myself perfectly.
2. I handled the problem and myself pretty well, but I could have done some things better.
3. I got through the conflict, but there were many things I could have handled better.
4. I barely got through the conflict without making a mess of things.
5. I blew it; I made a mess of the whole thing.

In the group session, the youths talked among themselves about how a given person might have handled the problem better. There were two other aspects of the group session that should be noted. Sometimes, both conflicting youths were in the same group session and had two perspectives on the same conflict. In addition, the special education teachers, who generally were aware of the conflicts, were asked to rate both parties on similar problem and resolution scales. The teachers rated the target conflict according to the following scale:

1. Minor irritation. Both boys were annoyed, but neither said or did anything to the other. The irritation did not seem to last long.
2. Minor disagreement. Both boys were engaged in the disagreement that lasted only a brief moment (under one minute). No apparent lasting ill will between them.
3. Major disagreement. Both boys were engaged in the disagreement that lasted between 1 and 5 minutes. Some lasting ill will remained after the argument.
4. Minor argument. Both boys were engaged in the argument that involved strong feelings, harsh words, and the threat of a fight, but no fighting occurred.
5. Major argument. Both boys were arguing, showing strong feelings, and fighting.

Figure 6.1 shows an example of conflict ratings made by a client and a teacher. This also illustrates how eliciting target ratings from different perspectives can provide information about the accuracy of these ratings. As shown in this figure, the client and teacher agreed about the magnitude of the conflict in that they were in complete agreement on 15 of the 20 days (i.e., 75%). However, for 4 of the 5 days on which disagreement occurred, the teacher rated the conflict as being more severe than did the client. These results might be interpreted as a tendency on the part of the client to underestimate the magnitude of the conflict, if we assume the accuracy of the teacher ratings. Finally, the ultimate goal of the intervention was to reduce the severity of conflicts to two ("minor disagreements") or less, and as shown in Figure 6.1, on 11 of the 15 days (73%) during intervention, this goal was achieved.

USES OF INDIVIDUALIZED RATING SCALES

As illustrated in this example, IRSs are tailor-made for each client and situation as the need arises, to measure whatever has been identified as important targets, along whatever dimen-

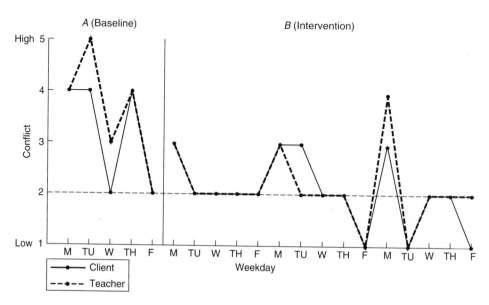

FIGURE 6.1 Client/teacher ratings of client conflict.

sion seems most appropriate to a particular target. Not only can these scales be used with individual clients, but they also can be used with groups and families to evaluate an individual's feelings about other members of the group or family. More generally, depending on the situation and type of target, IRSs can be used to obtain information from the four different perspectives discussed in Chapter 4: (a) *Clients* may rate themselves, and these are called *self-rating scales* (sometimes, *self-anchored scales*); (b) a professional *practitioner* may rate clients; (c) some *relevant other* party to the situation may rate a client (e.g., Douglas might have asked boys who got into arguments to make ratings according to how they thought the other combatant might have seen the argument or fight); and (d) *independent evaluators* may rate the client (e.g., the teacher). IRSs completed by practitioners, relevant others, or independent evaluators knowledgeable about a client's targets are usually called *observer rating scales.*

The use of IRSs to operationalize and measure client outcomes has many advantages, and this type of measure has been repeatedly recommended in major reviews of outcome measures (Lambert, Shapiro, & Bergin, 1986; Waskow & Parloff, 1975). In fact, these scales are so flexible that you can probably use them with almost all of your clients or case situations; because of their inherent flexibility and the range of situations with which they can be used, this type of measure has been called an "all-purpose measurement procedure" (Bloom, 1975). IRSs allow a lot of flexibility in the type of targets that can be measured and in who provides information about the targets. Therefore, they can be used with many different types of clients. Another advantage of IRSs is that they don't require much time to administer and score. In a way, they require little more than the systematic collection of information routinely collected in a less formal way in practice. In fact, in your practice your use of these scales is limited only by the nature of your client's targets and your own creativity in developing scales to measure those targets.

There are some times, however, when IRSs might not be the measure of choice. Your first choice should always be a measure that will give you the *best* information. We've defined best in Chapter 2 as that measure that provides the most valid, reliable, and direct information. Oftentimes behavioral observations are more valid, reliable, and direct, and hence you might first assess whether or not there are any behavioral indicators of the client's actual social functioning that you could identify and measure.

Second, you might want to examine whether any standardized questionnaires, such as those described in Chapter 7, or other measures described in succeeding chapters, are available and may be better measures of the target. Third, you should evaluate the client's willingness to use any of these measures and perhaps select the one or two measures that are most compatible with the client's willingness or ability to use them. Implicitly you also will be basing part of your decision on your own philosophy and/or orientation to practice. These may guide you in specific directions (e.g., toward or away from overt behaviors to measures that focus more on internal responding).

Finally, even if one of the above measures is available, you still might want to use an individualized rating scale as one of the measures in a measurement package designed for a specific client. There are several reasons for this, and these reasons go to the heart of the use of IRSs.

First, individualized rating scales may get at targets that no other measure can. In particular, individualized rating scales can be used to measure the intensity of targets. (Chapter 5 promised a way to measure intensity other than by the use of electromechanical devices. Well, this is it.) One obvious example would be the measurement of the intensity of pain. Another example would be the intensity of feelings of anxiety, guilt, and so on. Unless you're using biofeedback or other electromechanical devices (e.g., Kallman & Feuerstein, 1986; Rugh et al., 1986), most of which are expensive, complicated, or at least not commonly used, an individualized rating scale may be the best way to measure the intensity of a problem. For example, a colleague of one of the authors devised a simple 10-point scale to measure the intensity of migraine headache pain with one of his clients. The scale ranged from 1 (no pain) to 10 (severe, debilitating pain).

Second, individualized rating scales can be used to evaluate internal thoughts and feelings, or the intensity of those thoughts or feelings, that other measures cannot tap. Thus, thoughts and feelings such as fears, sexual excitement, depression, self-concept, any particular situation-related feeling, existential feelings (such as feeling trapped or feeling that life has no meaning), or satisfaction with relationships, abilities, resources, or services can be evaluated. One practitioner used a 5-point scale to evaluate the intensity of a client's positive thoughts about himself, with 1 being "low intensity, positive thoughts almost not there" to 5 being "high intensity, positive thoughts there most of the time." Similarly, another clinician devised a 9-point scale to measure the extent to which a woman felt satisfied with her marriage and in her role as a homemaker, where 1 equaled "not satisfied at all," and 9 equaled "feel completely satisfied."

Third, IRSs can be used to rate client change over time. Two commonly used formats involve ratings of the severity of discomfort or ratings of the degree of improvement itself. With the former type of rating, improvement is determined by the amount of change in severity. Both discomfort and improvement ratings typically use broad categories such as "much worse," "worse," "no change," "better," and "much better." Used this way, the IRS is typically called a Target Complaint Scale (Mintz & Kiesler, 1982).

Fourth, another use of individualized rating scales is related to the material in Chapter 5 where we discussed *analog measures.* There we suggested use of a scale for the practitioner to use to rate the degree to which certain behaviors were performed during a role play. All you would have to do would be to develop a list of client behaviors that you and the client would like to increase. Then, in role playing sessions, say once a week, you would simply rate the extent to which the client demonstrated those behaviors. These data could then be plotted on a chart. An example of such a scale is shown in Figure 6.2.

Fifth, IRSs often have high face validity. In other words, they may be measuring things that only the client can report on, and so they represent his or her most accurate portrayal of the circumstances, thoughts, or feelings. In fact, recent research shows that IRSs can provide data with validity that is comparable to that provided by standardized measures with excellent psychometric characteristics (Nugent, 1992a), although this may not be the case uniformly (Nugent, 1993). Of course, there's a possibility for high reactivity (as we will describe in Chapter 9) using these scales. This is especially so for self-ratings, and less so for observer ratings. For example, the client who rates his or her feelings of being satisfied may begin to feel more satisfied just as a result of completing the measure on a regular basis.

On the other hand, as Thomas (1974) and Cautela and Upper (1975) note with regard to self-report measures in general, there are two important factors to consider. First, these self-reports are behaviors in and of themselves and may in fact be the primary behaviors of interest. Second, there's little evidence that self-reports are any more or less reliable or valid than many other forms of measurement, with some studies showing low validity for self-report instruments and others showing quite high validity. More specifically, for IRSs, there is evidence of acceptable test-retest reliability (e.g., Battle et al., 1966; Morrison, Libow, Smith, & Becker, 1978), interobserver reliability (Reid, 1977, 1978), predictive validity (Liberman et al., 1972), concurrent validity

---

Extent to which client demonstrates desired behaviors (e.g., skills in initiating conversations)

0	1	2	3	4	5	6	7	8
Demonstrates none of the goal behaviors		Demonstrates some of the goal behaviors		Demonstrates half of the goal behaviors		Demonstrates most goal behaviors		Demonstrates all goal behaviors

FIGURE 6.2 Example of an analog measure.

(Rosen & Zytowski, 1977), and construct validity of IRS's (Battle et al., 1966; Bond, Bloch, & Yalom, 1979; Dasberg, van der Kleijn, Guelen, & van Praag, 1974; Mintz, Luborsky, & Christoph, 1979; Nugent, 1992b).

Sixth, IRSs are very compatible with single-system designs because they're sensitive to change. The sensitivity of clients' ratings of individualized targets has been demonstrated by the fact that they have shown improvement over the course of task-centered practice (e.g., Reid, 1977, 1978), behavior therapy (Cross, Sheehan, & Kahn, 1980, 1982), insight-oriented therapy (Cross et al., 1980, 1982; Mutschler & Rosen, 1979), psychoanalytically oriented psychotherapy (Mintz et al., 1979), group therapy (Bond et al., 1979; Johnson, 1976; Lieberman, Solow, Bond, & Reibstein, 1979; Morrison et al., 1978; Yalom, Bloch, Bond, Zimmerman, & Qualls, 1978), drug therapy (Dasberg et al., 1974; Hesbacher, Rickels, & Weise, 1968), and, various general forms of psychotherapy (Klonoff & Cox, 1975; Rosen & Zytowski, 1977; Sirles, 1982).

Seventh, IRSs can be used daily or as many times as you need to in a day and then averaged to get a single score for a day. This single score is then directly transferable to a chart, as in Figure 6.1, with the scores from the IRS being the numbers on the vertical axis. Thus, IRSs don't require any additional instrumentation or permission from copyright holders as some standardized questionnaires might.

Finally, the case for using such "subjective" measures has been made by the noted behaviorist Wolf (1978). He suggests that it is both philosophically and ethically important, and perhaps technically necessary as well, to develop systems that allow consumers to provide practitioners with feedback about how their work with clients relates to their life situations and their values. Wolf sees this as an evolution in the development of behavior modification, and he quotes from the work of Levi and Anderson (1975) on adding subjective measures to objective indicators:

We believe that each individual can be assumed to be the best judge of his own situation and state of well-being. The alternative is some type of "big brother" who makes the evaluation.

In all then, we believe that IRSs are of particular value given some of the cautions described above. They can be used as primary measures if no other measures are available or if they best tap the dimensions or targets of interest. They can be used in conjunction with other measures, such as a client log (see Chapter 8), to keep a running record of events in the client's life and his or her reactions to them (with the intensity of the reactions measured on an individualized rating scale). Finally, they can be used as secondary measures to supplement other information—for example, to tap a parent's feelings about his or her particular abilities as a parent when the primary target is the elimination of the parent's maltreatment of his or her child.

We should point out that we're assuming that when these scales are actually used to evaluate the effects of intervention, as with all other measures, there will be some logical reason to expect the intervention to have an effect on the measured target. That is, if the individualized rating scale you develop deals with a parent's satisfaction with parenting, the intervention program should be concerned with enhancing the client's satisfaction with parenting. It's not sensible to use an evaluation instrument to measure some specific behavior, thought, or feeling when the intervention program is not directly or indirectly designed to change the measured target.

CONSTRUCTING AND USING INDIVIDUALIZED RATING SCALES

Basically, all types of IRSs are constructed the same way. Figure 6.3 illustrates the general model of an individualized rating scale. As we describe below, IRSs use a single dimension (i.e., one scale per problem), usually arranged in a horizontal format, with several (and, if possible, all) of the scale points anchored by some description of the degree of the problem being measured. Typically, 5 to 11 scale points are used. IRSs require the development of an individualized list of client targets and scales for rating the targets. They also require the selection of one or, if possible and appropriate, more respondents to rate the targets, and the

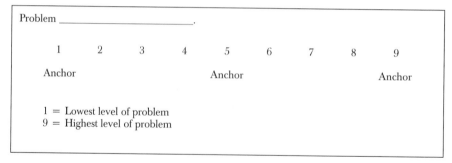

FIGURE 6.3   General model for individualized rating scale.

places and times during which the information is collected. First we discuss general guidelines involved in constructing rating scales for individualized targets (see Aday, 1989; Babbie, 1990; Judd, Smith, & Kidder, 1991; Sudman & Bradburn, 1982, for more detailed descriptions of different types of scales and ways of constructing them), and then we turn to a discussion of the guidelines for selecting who, when, and where to collect this information.

Steps in Construction

Prepare the Client.   Begin, as always, by working with the client to identify, conceptualize, and develop operational definitions of targets, as discussed in Chapter 3. The guidelines presented in Chapter 3 can be used to enumerate the targets that form the basis for IRSs. After you move from a survey of areas of concern to the client, to operationally defining targets on which you and the client agree to work, the next step in constructing an IRS is to construct scales for rating the targets.

IRSs are constructed especially for a given client, so their relevance to the client will usually be more apparent than predesigned standardized behavioral coding schemes or standardized questionnaires. Still, you should explain the reason for using an IRS. You might use something like the following, because most people have experience with assessment procedures used by physicians (the rationale, of course, would be modified depending on whether it's provided to a client, relevant other, or independent evaluator); and

you could even use the analogy to a thermometer for detecting fever, with the IRS as a sort of social or psychological thermometer:

A physician needs a lot of information about a patient to help understand his or her particular needs before prescribing treatment, and a physician also needs some way of finding out whether treatment is working. I also need ongoing information about a client's particular concerns to ensure that I thoroughly understand these concerns and that we're making progress in resolving them. You're in a unique position to provide information that's important to the success of our helping effort, and so it's important that you give me the most accurate information you can, although I know that some of this information might be personal and embarrassing. Even if the problem seems to be getting worse after we start working on it, it's important that I know this if I'm going to be of help.

Select Rating Dimensions.   A wide variety of different characteristics or dimensions of individualized targets can be rated. For example, the seriousness, intensity, importance, or frequency of a target might be rated. Also, when a client has more than one target, the different targets can be ranked along a particular dimension. For example, if a client has three targets, they might be ranked in terms of priority from most to least important. A wide variety of rating dimensions and different scales are illustrated in Table 6.1.

Whatever dimension of a target is rated, try to measure only one dimension (Gingerich, 1979). You may at times feel like using a different dimension at each end of the scale (e.g., happy at one end and sad at the other). How-

Table 6.1 Examples of individualized rating scales.

1. Intensity of cognitions of sadness.

1	2	3	4	5	6	7	8	9
No sad thoughts ("I'm not thinking about anything sad.")				Moderate number of sad thoughts				Extremely high number of sad thoughts ("All I do is think sad thoughts.")

2. Severity of feelings of anger toward authors of research books.

1	2	3	4	5	6	7	8	9
Not at all angry ("The book is fine.")				Moderately angry				Furious ("I want to throw the book away.")

3. Extent to which client feels she can express her feelings to her husband.

1	2	3	4	5	6	7	8	9
Can't express feelings at all ("Don't talk to spouse at all; feel all choked up.")				Express some feelings				Can easily express feelings ("Tell him exactly how I feel without feeling scared.")

4. Feelings of self-confidence.

1	2	3	4	5	6	7	8	9
Don't feel at all confident ("I'll never get the job.")				Moderately self-confident				Feel completely confident in everything I do ("I'm sure they'll want to hire me.")

5. Extent of feelings of anger about child.

1	2	3	4	5	6	7	8	9
Never angry at him ("He's an angel.")				Angry half of the time				Feel angry at him all the time ("I want to scream and clobber him.")

6. Extent to which client feels he/she can be honest in group.

1	2	3	4	5	6	7	8	9
Can never be honest				Can sometimes be honest				Can always be completely honest

7. Intensity of anxiety.

1	2	3	4	5	6	7	8	9
Very low anxiety ("I feel absolutely calm.")				Moderate anxiety				Extremely high anxiety (Palms sweaty, heart racing, "I feel terribly scared.")

ever, people often experience two seemingly contradictory feelings at the same time, so it's more accurate and clearer in the long run to use each scale to measure only one dimension at a time (e.g., a scale measuring degrees of sadness rather than including happiness and sadness in one scale). As discussed in Chapter 3, whenever possible try to conceptualize the target and its measurement in a way that emphasizes that the client is working toward something positive rather than just trying to eliminate something undesirable.

In some cases it might be useful to rate a target along more than one dimension. For example, in some cases it might be desirable to rate the seriousness and relative importance of targets because both of these dimensions are necessary for a complete picture of a target (e.g., Berlin, 1985). However, when it's desirable to rate the same target on more than one dimension you should construct separate rating scales to rate each dimension.

Select the Number of Response Categories. A response category is a point on a rating scale that the respondent can select to represent the degree of target seriousness, importance, frequency, or whatever dimension is being rated. As many as 100 response categories have been used to rate individualized targets, but it's possible to use as few as two categories (e.g., not serious/serious, not important/important). The number of response categories is important because it influences the reliability and validity with which a target is measured (Light, Singer, & Willett, 1990). Too few or too many response categories can lead to inaccurate measurement.

If you use too few response categories to rate a target, the rating scale will be insensitive to important differences or changes. For example, suppose that the seriousness of a target is rated using two response categories, with 0 indicating "not serious" and 1 indicating "serious." This would be like judging all temperatures under 32°F as "cold," and all at or over 32°F as "hot" (Bailey, 1982, p. 135). There's an important difference between a temperature of 100°F and one of 32°F, but both would be judged as hot. Similarly, if a target is rated as "not serious" or "serious" it's not possible to detect important differences in degree. Consequently, the seriousness of the target might change dramatically over the course of an intervention, but you wouldn't be able to detect these changes because too few response categories were used.

Too few response categories is a problem, but so is too many response categories. The number of response categories can be so large that it's difficult for a rater to distinguish among response categories. When this happens you get haphazard responses that will introduce imprecision into your measure. For example, target ratings on scales with up to 100

points have been used to rate individualized targets, but it's hard to see how a rater could make such fine distinctions. For example, can you expect a rater to distinguish accurately between a target severity rating of 38 and 39 on a 100-point scale?

The number of response categories should be large enough to detect important differences or changes in a target, but not so large that it's difficult to distinguish accurately among different categories. There's some disagreement about the optimal number of response categories. The available research suggests that in general from five to seven response categories is best (Gable, 1986, p. 45; Streiner & Norman, 1989, p. 27), but when the focus is on individual targets it might be useful to use more categories (Nunnally, 1978).

Within a certain range (e.g., 5 to 11 response categories) the number you select should depend upon the ability of the rater to distinguish among the different categories and your ability to anchor each response category. As a step toward simplification, we recommend use of 9-point scales with the midpoint, 5, being either "moderate" (since 5 is halfway between the low and high point) or, depending on the scale, "neither one way nor the other" or "neutral." For example, if a 1 on the scale is low intensity and a 9 is high intensity, the midpoint, 5, would be moderate intensity. However, even the use of a 9-point scale may not be effective for some clients. If you realize, in helping the client describe how he or she feels at each point of the scale, that he or she can't tell the difference among so many points (e.g., discriminate feelings), you might want to use seven or fewer points. A 7-point scale can be useful and would be your next best bet, but fewer than four points may limit the client's ability to discriminate or would not be sensitive enough to discriminate meaningful differences among scale points.

Finally, there's a question about whether to use an odd or even number of response categories. In general there doesn't seem to be any practical difference in the accuracy of the results obtained when an odd or an even number of response categories is used (Gable, 1986; Streiner & Norman, 1989). However, the use of an odd number of response categories lets you set a clear midpoint for a "moderate," "neutral," or "undecided" category.

Create Equidistant Response Categories.
Whatever the number of response categories you select, it's best to try to construct the response categories so that the intervals between them are equal. Equal intervals are important because they facilitate the visual and statistical analysis of change in targets. For example, suppose that in using a 5-point scale to rate the seriousness of a target, you make the difference between points 4 and 5 greater than the difference between points 3 and 4. When change in the target over time is graphed, a change from 3 to 4 will appear the same as a change from 4 to 5 despite the difference in the actual magnitude of the change.

To ensure that the intervals between response categories are equal, suggest that the person completing the scale view the scale as a thermometer, and that the steps on the "thermometer" are of equal intervals. Thus, the high point will be highest intensity (like the presence of a fever on a thermometer, and the bottom will be the lowest intensity (like the absence of fever). Each step on the scale is supposed to be equidistant from the one next to it in terms of the client's feelings. That is, you would not want a bigger jump in intensity between points 1 and 2 than you have between points 7 and 8.

Select Rating Scale Anchors.
The degree of target seriousness, importance, frequency or whatever you are rating is represented by numbers. These numbers represent gradations that are designed to quantify some dimension or characteristic of a target. In a way they are similar to the gradations on a ruler or yardstick. Almost everyone knows from experience what an inch, a foot, or a yard is, but the numbers on a rating scale almost always require some definition. These numbers are defined by providing brief explicit labels, descriptions, or examples of what the numbers represent, called *anchors*. These anchors consist of the behaviors, thoughts, and feelings that a client would be experiencing at each point on the scale. In other words, a client who is feeling that way or an observer who sees those things knows exactly what number on the scale to use.

Anchors are important because they define the meaning of the numbers on a rating scale. Without adequate anchors it's difficult for a rater to provide a reliable and valid judgment of the level at which a particular target should be rated. Also, without adequate anchors it's difficult to interpret and communicate ratings of individualized targets. Therefore, all of the points on a rating scale ideally should be labeled with clear, precise, and explicit anchors. At a minimum, the ends and the midpoint on the continuum should be anchored, though whenever possible, for clarity and accuracy, all points should be anchored. (For an excellent discussion of the use of anchored and unanchored scales, see Coulton & Solomon, 1977.)

Anchors can be tailored to individual clients and client targets. For example, you might help your client come up with word pictures, thoughts, and behaviors to use as anchors. Begin by asking your client to anchor one end of the scale. For a depressed client ask the client to imagine being severely depressed and to note in behaviors or word pictures what would be happening or how the client would feel when that level of intensity occurs (Gingerich, 1979). Ask the client to consider specifically behaviors, thoughts, and feelings to cover as many components of the problem as possible. The depressed client might characterize himself or herself as being the most depressed (level 9 on the scale) when he or she can't sleep, can't work, and has suicidal thoughts. Thus, when these conditions occur, the client would know to rate himself or herself at level 9. Then ask the client to anchor the other end of the scale. The depressed client may be least depressed, level 1, when he or she feels like going out, wants to eat a large meal, and really enjoys being with friends. Then, you and the client can fill in all the gradations between each end of the scale, and practice using the scale. If the client cannot immediately provide anchors, you can offer suggestions about possible anchors (e.g., "When you're extremely depressed, do you feel . . . ?"). But be sure to check out their accuracy with the client, encouraging modification to fit the client's specific situation.

In addition to using individually tailored anchors, you can use more general anchors; some of these are illustrated in Table 6.2 for self-rating scales, Table 6.3A and B for two different sets of observer rating scales (set B provides several variations for evaluating one target problem–depression), and Figure 6.4 for different formats for client rating of target complaints (adapted from Mintz & Kiesler, 1982; see also Gable, 1986, Table 3-3). In a way, general anchors are easier to use because the same anchors can be applied to a wide variety of targets and clients (Coulton & Solomon, 1977). This has several advantages. When you apply the same rating dimension and anchors to different targets, and you use the same number of response categories, it's easier to compare different targets. For example, suppose that an adolescent girl separately rated the seriousness of arguments with her mother and father using a 9-point scale. It would be easy to compare the seriousness of the arguments with her mother to those with her father by recording ratings of both targets on a single graph, as illustrated in Figure 6.5. As shown

in this figure, the girl's arguments with her father were more serious, but on days when a more serious argument did occur with either parent, it also tended to occur with the other parent.

Another advantage of using the same rating dimension, scale anchors, and number of response categories with all of a client's targets is that this makes it possible to compute an average rating across targets for that client. For example, the average seriousness rating for the adolescent's ratings on Monday would be the sum of her ratings of the seriousness of her arguments with her mother and father, divided by the number of targets rated ($[4 + 7]/2 = 5.5$). These average seriousness ratings also are shown in Figure 6.5.

On the other hand, individually tailored anchors do have some advantages over more general anchors. Individually tailored anchors developed for a particular client probably are more relevant and meaningful to that client. Also, individually tailored anchors generally are less ambiguous and more precise because they're developed by and for a particular client and target (Coulton & Solomon, 1977). Overall, in line with our comments throughout

Table 6.2   Examples of general scale anchors for self-rating scales.

1. Amount of anxiety you feel.

1	2	3	4	5
Little or no anxiety	Some anxiety	Moderate anxiety	Strong anxiety	Intense anxiety

2. Feelings of depression.

1	2	3	4	5	6	7	8	9
Not depressed		Slightly depressed		Moderately depressed		Strongly depressed		Severely depressed

3. How often are you depressed?

1	2	3	4	5	6	7
Rarely, if ever	Very infrequently	Infrequently	Neutral	Frequently	Very frequently	All the time

4. I feel very depressed today.

1	2	3	4	5
Strongly disagree	Disagree	Not sure	Agree	Strongly agree

5. Compared to how depressed you were last week, how would you say you are feeling now?

1	2	3	4	5	6	7
Much less depressed		Less depressed		About the same		More depressed		Much more depressed

Table 6.3 Two sets of examples of general scale anchors for observer rating scales.

A. Different Targets

1. Extent to which the client seems motivated for treatment.

1	2	3	4	5	6	7	8	9
Seems very unmotivated (Never shows up for appointment, or won't speak during the hour)				Neutral (Neither motivated nor unmotivated)				Seems extremely motivated (Always on time; very verbal about problem)

2. Extent to which family members appear to care about each other.

1	2	3	4	5	6	7	8	9
Don't appear to care at all (I see no affection between them)				Appear to care moderately				Appear to care a great deal (Lots of touching, hugging, and/or discussion between them)

3. Extent to which client appears to get flustered under stress.

1	2	3	4	5	6	7	8	9
Not flustered at all				Neither flustered nor unflustered				Extremely flustered

4. Ease with which a group member's feelings are hurt.

1	2	3	4	5	6	7	8	9
Easily hurt (Looks like he or she will cry)				Moderate				Seems impossible to hurt (Never flinches even when confronted; no change in expression)

5. Extent to which client engages in appropriate interactions with others in group.

1	2	3	4	5	6	7	8	9
Never engages in appropriate interactions (Doesn't speak to or look at anyone)				Moderate (Speaks to others but doesn't look at them)				Engages continuously in appropriate interactions (Speaks freely and easily with appropriate expression and eye contact)

B. Different (Observer Rating) Formats for Depression

1. How depressed does the client appear?

1	2	3	4	5	6	7	8	9
Not at all depressed	Slightly depressed			Moderately depressed		Strongly depressed		Severely depressed

2. The client appears depressed.

1	2	3	4	5	6	7
Strongly disagree	Disagree		Not sure		Agree	Strongly agree

3. What percentage of the time does the client appear depressed?

1	2	3	4	5
0–20%	21–40%	41–60%	61–80%	81–100%

4. How often does the client appear depressed?

1	2	3	4	5	6
Rarely, if ever	Very infrequently	Infrequently	Frequently	Very frequently	All the time

5. Compared to how depressed the client appeared last week, how would you say the client appears now?

1	2	3	4	5	6	7
Much less depressed	Less depressed		About the same		More depressed	Much more depressed

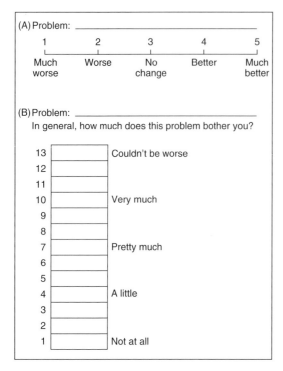

(A) Problem: _____

1	2	3	4	5
Much worse	Worse	No change	Better	Much better

(B) Problem: _____
In general, how much does this problem bother you?

13		
12		Couldn't be worse
11		
10		Very much
9		
8		
7		Pretty much
6		
5		
4		A little
3		
2		
1		Not at all

FIGURE 6.4   Alternative formats for target complaint scales.

the book, the most useful types of scales will probably be those that contain the most precise information. Thus, some of the more general anchors just described are likely to be somewhat less useful for a given client than the more specific ones. Nevertheless, given your awareness of these issues, there still may be times when general anchors are useful and appropriate.

Whatever anchors you select, arrange the anchors and numbers on a rating scale so that higher numbers represent more of whatever is being measured. For example, for rating the seriousness of a target, higher numbers should indicate greater seriousness. Scales aren't always constructed this way, but in general it's a useful convention because higher numbers would then correspond to greater intensity. In any case, whether you construct a scale or use a scale constructed by someone else, it's important to be clear about the meaning of higher (or lower) scale scores. For example, suppose that a 9-point scale is used to rate the seriousness of a target. During baseline the average rating is 8, and during intervention the average rating is 3. Unless you know that higher scores indicate greater seriousness,

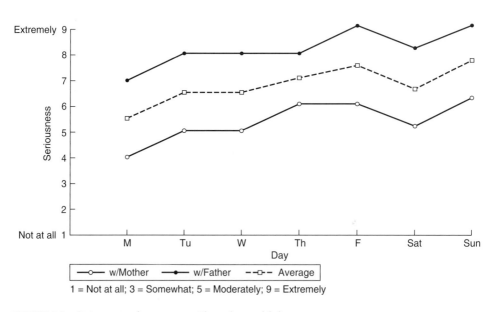

1 = Not at all; 3 = Somewhat; 5 = Moderately; 9 = Extremely

FIGURE 6.5   Seriousness of arguments with mother and father.

you'll have trouble interpreting the change from baseline to intervention.

Construct Overall Summary Scores. In addition to examining the ratings of individual targets, it is sometimes useful to compute an overall summary score for several targets. For example, an average target rating might be computed for a client by adding the ratings of the client's targets and dividing this total by the number of targets (e.g., Battle et al., 1966; Bond et al., 1979; Klonoff & Cox, 1975; Rosen & Zytowski, 1977). If you compute such a summary score, though, you should use the same response categories to rate each target (e.g., rate each target using a 9-point scale with the following anchors: 1 = Not at all serious; 3 = Somewhat serious; 5 = Moderately serious; 7 = Very serious; 9 Extremely serious).

Overall summary scores have some advantages. One advantage is that they provide an overall picture of the state of a client's targets. Another is that they are often more reliable than ratings of individual targets. Summary scores are often more reliable because some of the measurement errors associated with ratings of individual targets will be positive and some negative, and when you add the ratings of individual targets these positive and negative errors will tend to cancel each other out. However, when you add the ratings of individual targets, the component of each target that is measured reliably will be maintained and increased (Kidder & Judd, 1986, pp. 210–211).

You need to know the potential range of values to interpret almost any score, and therefore it's important to know how to determine the potential range of values for an average target rating. For example, a severity rating of 10 will mean something different if the smallest possible value for a score is 1 and the largest is 10, than if the smallest possible value is 1 and the largest is 100. When an average target rating is computed for a client, the lowest and highest possible scores for the average target rating are the same as the lowest and highest possible scores for a particular target (assuming the same response categories are used to rate each target). For example, suppose that a client has three targets and the severity of each target is

rated on a 9-point scale ranging from 1 to 9. The lowest possible average rating is 1, and this occurs if all targets are rated as 1 (i.e., [1 + 1 + 1]/3 = 1). The highest possible average rating is 9, and this occurs if all targets are rated as 9 (i.e., [9 + 9 + 9]/3 = 9).

Most often when summary scores are computed for IRSs an average target rating is computed. However, you might encounter more complex methods of computing overall summary scores (Berlin, 1985; Orme, Gillespie, & Fortune, 1983). For example, some summary scores combine ratings of both seriousness and relative importance into a single score. Many of these more complex summary scores have characteristics that make them undesirable such as problems in interpretation, and therefore they should be used with caution, if at all.

Select Who, When, and Where to Collect Data

So far we've discussed how to elicit target information. Now we'll turn to who, when, and where to collect this information.

Select Respondent(s). Target information can be obtained from several different vantage points. (We discussed the advantages and disadvantages of collecting information from different perspectives in Chapter 4.) In most cases the conceptualization and selection of targets will be the province of you and the client. For example, as discussed in Chapter 3, oftentimes you and the client will negotiate a mutually agreed upon set of targets, and these will be the focus of your intervention efforts. In some situations relevant others might even be involved in the formulation of targets. For example, a teacher might work with a school social worker and a student to formulate targets for the student. Family members might jointly formulate targets for the entire family. However, independent evaluators usually won't be involved in the formulation of targets, although sometimes this is done in research (e.g., Bloch, Bond, Qualls, Yalom, & Zimmerman, 1977).

You and your clients usually are also in a good position to rate whatever client targets are formulated, although some targets (like feeling states) can be judged directly only by clients. Also, a given set of targets could be regularly rated by relevant others or even an independent evaluator, provided that the rater has good firsthand knowledge about the targets, and that the scales are designed so that they can be used by one person to rate another–that is, to rate some externally observable behavior or activity. For example, you and the client might negotiate a target list, and then you and the client, relevant others, and an independent evaluator could rate each target regularly.

If more than one rater is used, different raters should independently rate the targets. All we mean by this is that the raters shouldn't discuss their ratings before they make them. The reason is simple. The purpose of asking different people to rate a client's targets is to get different perspectives, but if raters discuss their ratings before they make them, they might influence each other, in which case you won't end up with different perspectives.

In all cases, you should try to prepare the forms with the client or other rater, and give them all the forms they will need before they leave the office. It would even be possible to prepare a single form that can be used daily, to record ratings at multiple times on more than one target, as illustrated in Figure 6.6. Also, you should make certain that the rater knows how to make the ratings, and role playing is often one useful strategy for making sure of this.

Decide When to Collect Target Information. These scales are designed to be used over time to keep track of changes in targets before, during, and (we hope) after intervention. They're intended to monitor progress. You or the client can keep track of the client's ratings and place them on a chart for easy visual inspection of changes.

IRSs should be completed often enough to detect significant changes in targets, but not so often that they become a burden for the re-

| Client Name _____ |
| Date _____ |
| First Target _____ |
| Second Target _____ |
| Third Target _____ |

Time	Target	Rating Scale							Comments
		Anchor		Anchor		Anchor			
8 a.m.	1	1	2	3	4	5	6	7	_____
8 a.m.	2	1	2	3	4	5	6	7	_____
8 a.m.	3	1	2	3	4	5	6	7	_____
2 p.m.	1	1	2	3	4	5	6	7	_____
2 p.m.	2	1	2	3	4	5	6	7	_____
2 p.m.	3	1	2	3	4	5	6	7	_____
8 p.m.	1	1	2	3	4	5	6	7	_____
8 p.m.	2	1	2	3	4	5	6	7	_____
8 p.m.	3	1	2	3	4	5	6	7	_____

Target 1 Average = _____ Target 2 Average = _____ Target 3 Average = _____

FIGURE 6.6 Daily IRS form.

spondent or intrude on the intervention efforts. A major advantage of IRSs, though, is that they are so easy to use and can be used as often as they need to be (several times a day if necessary), with all scores then averaged to get a single score for the day. After all, rating several targets should take only a matter of seconds, although it's more time-consuming to formulate and if necessary reformulate a set of targets. However, the formulation and reformulation of targets are generally part of the normal course of events and therefore shouldn't be much of an additional burden. In short, IRSs are relatively easy to complete, administer, score, and interpret repeatedly.

No matter how often a respondent is asked to provide target information you should select regular, predesignated times or conditions for respondents to provide the information. Also, you should make it clear to respondents just exactly when they're supposed to provide the information and the importance of providing it at the agreed-upon times. For example, you should make it clear whether a client should rate targets at regular intervals (e.g., each day), at preselected times (e.g., before going to sleep in the evening), or when faced with selected critical incidents (i.e., anytime the client feels or is confronted by the problem, for example, rating oneself on an anxiety scale prior to having a job interview).

The predesignated times or conditions selected for providing target information will in part determine the time frame for the target ratings (e.g., the state of a target during a particular moment, day, or week). For example, if a client is asked to rate the severity of targets at the end of each day, the severity ratings should refer to the severity of the targets on the day the ratings are made. In any case, you should provide respondents with a time frame for ratings, or it won't be clear to the rater, or to anyone examining the resulting ratings, whether the ratings refer to the state of the targets at that moment, that day, the previous week, in general, or during some other time frame.

A final aspect of the timing of the collection of target information has to do with when this information should be elicited in relation to the provision of services. For example, if the client is to provide ratings at each treatment session, as a general rule it's probably best to elicit the ratings before a treatment session begins, with the exception of the intake interview. If the information is elicited at the end of a session, it might not represent the way the client typically views his or her problems, because it's distorted by the effect of the treatment session. However, for intake interviews it's best to collect target information from a client toward the end of the interview, so you and the client will have a clearer understanding of the targets.

Decide Where to Collect Target Information. Target information can be elicited in different types of settings. For example, you can ask a client to provide target information in the setting in which services are provided. If this is done you'll be available to answer questions about the procedure and you'll be available to give immediate feedback to the client concerning the self-reported target information. Also, if you meet with a client regularly to provide services, having the client provide target information in the service setting ensures that the information will be provided on a regular basis and in a consistent setting.

In most cases it won't be practical to have a relevant other provide target information in the setting in which services are provided unless he or she also is receiving services. If a relevant other isn't receiving services, one option is to do an interview at home by telephone on a regular, predesignated basis. Similarly, if you want a client to report target information between appointments, the client could be interviewed at home by telephone.

You also can have a relevant other or client complete an IRS at home on a regular, predesignated basis and then mail the IRS to you when it's completed or bring it in at the next appointment. This has the advantage that the respondent can complete the questionnaire without the potential of feeling watched or pressured for time and in the situation where the problem may occur, as it occurs. In any case, if you decide to have the IRS mailed to you, be sure to provide more than enough blank forms and preaddressed stamped envelopes for returning the completed questionnaires.

SUMMARY

This chapter described how you can construct scales that measure the unique targets presented by your clients along such dimensions as their intensity, seriousness, or severity. It also described how oftentimes these scales can be developed for and used by practitioners, relevant others, and independent evaluators to provide important information about change in the unique targets presented by your particular clients. Guidelines for constructing these scales were presented, as were indications for their use. We also presented a number of examples of these scales to help you develop your own scales.

7 STANDARDIZED QUESTIONNAIRES

PURPOSE: This chapter describes standardized questionnaires, how to locate them, how to select them, and how to use them for single-system evaluation. The chapter also describes a number of specific standardized questionnaires for completion by clients, practitioners, relevant others, and independent observers, and it provides a list of references for locating information about additional standardized questionnaires. The use of personal computers to administer, score, interpret, store, and manage standardized questionnaires is discussed, and one such program—CAAP—is illustrated. Finally, the construction of standardized questionnaires for particular agency needs is described briefly. ▲

Introduction
What Are Standardized Questionnaires?
Advantages of Standardized Questionnaires
    and Cautions in Their Selection
Selecting a Standardized Questionnaire
Purpose
Directness
Relevance to Intervention Planning
Reliability
Validity
Ease of Use
Accessibility
Administering a Standardized Questionnaire
Maximizing the Accuracy
    of the Information
Selecting the Administration Setting
Selecting the Timing and Frequency of
    Administration
Some Available Standardized Self-Report
    Questionnaires

WALMYR Assessment Scales (WAS)
    Scoring
    Interpretation
Some Limitations of Standardized Self-Report
    Questionnaires
Some Available Standardized Questionnaires for
    Practitioners
Some Available Standardized Questionnaires for
    Relevant Others
Some Available Standardized Questionnaires for
    Independent Observers
Do-It-Yourself Questionnaires
Using Standardized Questionnaires in Groups
Computer Management of Standardized
    Questionnaires
Summary
Appendix
Reference Books for Tests and Measurements
Computer Assisted Assessment Package (CAAP):
    A USER'S GUIDE

INTRODUCTION

Wouldn't it be nice to be able to meet a new client, get a preliminary understanding of his or her concerns, and then pull out of a drawer a questionnaire that you could easily use to measure repeatedly the targets identified for intervention? Wouldn't it be nice if you knew the reliability and validity of the questionnaire in advance?

Is it really possible to do all this? In fact, in some special situations it is indeed possible to find a questionnaire that's already available, that does do all of these things, and that you know has been used successfully before.

There's a general term for such a tool—it's called a *standardized questionnaire*. Because there are so many standardized questionnaires available—literally thousands of them—the focus of this chapter is largely on helping you select one or more for your use. However, we also recommend and describe some specific standardized questionnaires. But because your range of targets may be great, we want to enable you to select questionnaires that meet your own needs.

WHAT ARE STANDARDIZED QUESTIONNAIRES?

Standardization refers to uniformity of procedures when administering and scoring a measure, and it implies the availability of existing data concerning the validity and reliability of the measure. Thus, a standardized questionnaire is a measure that involves the administration of the same questionnaire items (or other stimuli such as statements) to different people using the same administration and scoring procedures. It typically also involves the collection of information concerning the validity and reliability of the questionnaire during its development. Suggested by the idea of standardization is the fact that standardized questionnaires measure targets in terms of concepts with some general relevance to different clients (e.g., marital satisfaction, depression). This is in contrast to individualized rating scales and, in most cases, behavioral observations, which are

developed on a client-by-client basis according to unique client needs.

Standardized questionnaires, as we use the term, oftentimes are called standardized *scales* or *indexes*. In addition, what we have in mind is not the detailed, multipaged assessment questionnaires that may be given once to a client at intake to collect data about life history, in-depth information about marital or family relations, and so on, but rather standardized questionnaires that can be used for assessment in single-system evaluation. Detailed, multi-paged assessment questionnaires definitely have their purpose in helping provide data on client functioning and for initial assessments, but they're not useful or practical for ongoing monitoring of client functioning. Rather, we're talking about briefer questionnaires that can be used in single-system evaluation as repeated measures, and that yield quantifiable information about client targets.

Standardized questionnaires can be described in terms of six characteristics: (1) what they measure, (2) how well they measure it (i.e., their validity and reliability), (3) how they're structured, (4) how many dimensions they measure, (5) from whom they elicit information, and (6) how much time and other resources are required for their use.

Standardized questionnaires are available for measuring almost every conceivable area of human functioning. In general, standardized questionnaires can be used to measure behaviors, feelings, cognitions, and attitudes. There are standardized questionnaires that measure mental health (e.g., Ciarlo, Brown, Edwards, Kiresuk, & Newman, 1986; Thompson, 1989b; van Riezen & Segal, 1988; Wetzler, 1989), environments (e.g., Moos, 1987, 1988, 1990), families (e.g., Corcoran & Fischer, 2000a, 2000b; Sawin & Harrigan, 1994; Schutte & Malouff, 1995), and a wide variety of other areas (e.g., Conoley & Kramer, 1989; Corcoran & Fischer, 1987; Fischer & Corcoran, 1994a, 1994b). Also, there are standardized questionnaires that measure almost every conceivable specific target area—ranging from alcoholism and anxiety to sexual satisfaction and suicide potential. In essence, questionnaires dealing with almost any area in which you might be working have been designed and already are available. In an Appendix at the end of this chapter is a list of books that reference, describe, evaluate, and, in many cases, include copies of such standardized questionnaires.

Standardized questionnaires differ quite a bit in terms of their demonstrated validity and reliability. Extensive research evidence is available documenting different aspects of the validity and reliability of some standardized questionnaires. For other standardized questionnaires, only minimal evidence is available. (The absence of information on a topic—most commonly on validity, especially with newly developed instruments—does not mean the measure is not standardized. It does mean, though, that you interpret the results with more caution.) Fortunately, there's an increasing number of good reference books that you can use to get critical summaries of research concerning the validity and reliability of standardized questionnaires (e.g., Ciarlo et al., 1986; Conoley & Kramer, 1989, 1995; Corcoran & Fischer, 1987; Corcoran & Fischer, 2000a, 2000b; Fischer & Corcoran, 1994a, 1994b; Grotevant & Carlson, 1989; Hammill, Brown, & Bryant, 1989; Hersen & Bellack, 1988; Jacob & Tennenbaum, 1988; Keyser & Sweetland, 1984–1991; McDowell & Newell, 1996; Sawin & Harrigan, 1994; Schutte & Malouff, 1995; Thompson, 1989b; Touliatos et al., 1990; van Riezen & Segal, 1988; Wetzler, 1989).

Standardized questionnaires also differ in terms of their structure. They vary from projective tests (usually focused on global personality constructs and requiring a good deal of practitioner training to interpret) to more discrete or direct targets requiring minimal inference by the practitioner. Typically, though, standardized questionnaires contain multiple questions, statements, or some other type of item rated along some dimension (e.g., a 7-point scale ranging from "strongly disagree" to "strongly agree"), items that require the selection of one option from several available options (e.g., multiple choice), or items that require some form of a yes or no response.

Standardized questionnaires also differ in terms of the number of concepts they measure. Some standardized questionnaires measure one concept, and the responses to all items are combined to provide a measure of that concept (e.g., marital satisfaction). Typically these are called *unidimensional* measures. Other standardized questionnaires measure more than one concept by combining responses from different subsets of items into separate measures of distinct concepts that often are related (e.g., satisfaction in relationships with coworkers, friends, and children). Typically these are called *multidimensional* measures, and the measures of different concepts are typically called *subscales*. Oftentimes multidimensional standardized questionnaires provide both measures of distinct but related concepts, and a measure of an overall concept thought to unify the distinct concepts measured by the subscales (e.g., overall satisfaction in interpersonal relationships).

Another dimension on which standardized questionnaires differ is the perspective of the respondent. Standardized questionnaires span the range of possible perspectives introduced in Chapter 4, and further discussed in Chapters 5 and 6. A primary perspective is the client (this is called a *client self-report questionnaire*). Other perspectives around which numerous questionnaires have been developed include the practitioner, relevant others, and independent observers.

Finally, standardized questionnaires differ in terms of the time, effort, and training needed to administer, score, and interpret them. Many standardized questionnaires are time-consuming, or require extensive specialized training. Many of these traditionally have been the province of clinical psychologists (e.g., the MMPI). This chapter, however, focuses on the numerous standardized questionnaires that are relatively brief; can be administered, scored, and interpreted without much time and effort; and can be used by professionals without extensive training in their use. These types of standardized questionnaires have been called Rapid Assessment Instruments (RAIs) (Levitt & Reid, 1981) when they rely on client self-reports, but they also can be viewed as encompassing other perspectives. In any case, the use of standardized questionnaires can be simplified greatly by using personal computers, and so in a later section, we discuss the use of personal computers in the management of standardized questionnaires.

Advantages of Standardized Questionnaires and Cautions in Their Selection

Standardized questionnaires have important advantages. A major advantage is that they are usually pretested for validity, reliability, or both. Therefore, you'll have some basis for judging the psychometric characteristics of a standardized questionnaire, and often you'll have some basis for comparing the results you obtain with a client with the results obtained in previous research with relevant groups (i.e., norms might be available).

Another advantage of standardized questionnaires, in contrast to an unstructured interview, for example, is that, at their best, standardized questionnaires are structured to systematically and comprehensively elicit the information necessary to measure a target. This structure imposed by a standardized questionnaire can increase the chance that the information necessary to measure a target will be collected.

Another advantage of standardized questionnaires is their efficiency. Many questionnaires are rather simple to use. They're inexpensive, readily available, generally take very little time or energy on the part of either practitioner or client, and can be easy to administer and score. Further, they often provide a good deal of information about a variety of topics that are important to assessing and evaluating practice.

Standardized questionnaires have some compelling advantages, including the ease with which they can be used, the wide range of available questionnaires to measure numerous concepts, and the increasing ease with which these measures can be located using reference texts such as the ones listed in the Appendix to this chapter.

Despite their advantages, standardized questionnaires should not be used to measure every target, nor should their results be accepted uncritically. One area for caution is that the name given to a standardized questionnaire indicates the concept the author *intended* to measure, or otherwise believes the questionnaire measures.

Just because a measure is called a measure of "family functioning," "depression," "marital satisfaction," or "self-esteem" doesn't necessarily mean that that's what it measures. Also, just because two or more standardized questionnaires claim to measure the same concept doesn't necessarily mean that they're interchangeable. For example, Thompson (1989a) reported considerable differences among seven different measures of "depression" in the percentage of items measuring different dimensions of depression (e.g., motor, social, cognitive), and Brugha (1989) enumerated similar differences among "social support" measures. Evidence of the reliability and especially the validity of a standardized questionnaire is necessary to determine whether it measures what is intended, how well it does so, and the extent to which it measures the same concept as other measures.

Another issue is the fact that in many, if not most, cases you won't know all that you'd like to know about the reliability and validity of a particular standardized questionnaire (or for that matter any measurement method). For example, you might find a standardized questionnaire that seems perfect–designed exactly for the kind of target you're dealing with–with high test-retest (stability), and high internal consistency reliability. However, you might also find that only one or two types of validity issues have been dealt with, or perhaps that there is no validity information, or that the questionnaire is fairly new, so research on its properties is not completed (e.g., its sensitivity to change, its utility with clients similar to your own). In such cases you should be cautious in your interpretation of the results you get with the questionnaire, and your caution should be in proportion to the existing amount of information concerning validity and reliability.

Even if you find a standardized questionnaire with comprehensive evidence of validity and reliability, remember that the research conducted on such questionnaires is always done on large groups, under circumstances that are different in important ways from practice, and sometimes with people who are different from your clients in important ways (e.g., race, gender, age, education, etc.). Typically, subjects employed in research on standardized questionnaires don't have an ongoing relationship with the researcher; they don't complete the questionnaire more than once or at most twice; and their scores don't have a bearing on their receipt of services (Rubin & Babbie, 1997). Thus, with an individual client there's always a chance for error–the group data may not apply. It may even be that on a particular day, something else that occurs distorts the client's or rater's perceptions so that the scores that day are off. Some of this may be overcome by the instructions you give in administering the questionnaire and in conducting reliability checks, and so on. But the point is, no measure is foolproof. Don't uncritically accept the results of standardized questionnaires; indeed, the validity of the results may vary from day to day and from client to client.

Another thing you should be cautious of is the fact that standardized questionnaires measure targets in terms of general concepts that are assumed to be relevant to different clients, but they might not correspond to the unique realities of a particular client. (In a way they're like ready-to-wear clothing instead of custom-made clothing.) One apparent solution to this problem is for you to add or delete items from a standardized questionnaire in an attempt to tailor it to a particular client. However, such ad hoc modifications in a standardized questionnaire might compromise the validity and reliability of the questionnaire in unknown ways and might compromise your ability to compare the results of the questionnaire with results from previous research. Also, in some cases standardized questionnaires are copyrighted with the provision that they be used intact without modifications, and to do otherwise would be a violation of copyright law. Therefore, in general we don't think it advisable to try to tailor standardized questionnaires to particular clients. If you can't find a standardized questionnaire suited to a particular client target, you should consider the direct observation or self-monitoring of client-specific behaviors (Chapter 5), the construction and use of individualized rating scales (Chapter 6) or logs (Chapter 8), or the use of nonreactive measures selected especially for a particular client target (Chapter 9). You also might consider developing a new standardized questionnaire,

which we discuss later in this chapter. However, you're not required to use a standardized questionnaire for each and every case (or any other measurement method for that matter). In some cases there might not be a suitable standardized questionnaire available, or other methods of measurement might be more consistent with the conceptualization of the target. Remember, *the goal is to fit the measurement method to the client's target, not to fit the client's target to a convenient measurement method.*

Related to the fact that standardized questionnaires measure targets in terms of concepts is the fact that some of these concepts are relatively general, and as such are relatively indirect measures of targets. For example, general measures of social adjustment, such as Weissman's Social Adjustment Scale (e.g., Weissman, 1990; Weissman & Bothwell, 1976; Weissman, Prusoff, Thompson, Harding, & Myers, 1978), measure adjustment in multiple areas of functioning (e.g., work, social and leisure, extended family, marital, parental, family unit, economic). The overall scores from such measures might be useful for providing a multidimensional, well-rounded picture of client change, but such overall scores might be relatively insensitive to client change in delimited areas of social functioning targeted for intervention. That is, if your intervention program is not targeted to change in all of the measured areas, you might not expect the measure to register much change in overall social adjustment over time, although it might register change in specific areas of social adjustment. Therefore, subscales of such measures might be useful as repeated measures, but the entire measure might be useful only prior to intervention to determine areas in need of intervention, and after intervention to examine the generality of change.

A final thing you should be cautious of in using standardized questionnaires is the use of too many questionnaires with a client. Because standardized questionnaires tend to be easy to use, some practitioners combine them in a sort of test battery, and routinely administer them to all their clients. Of course, if the questionnaires don't specifically apply to the client's target or situation, this is simply wasted effort. Also, the client may be overwhelmed or simply not take his or her responses seriously. In that case you may lose the client or lose meaningful results from the questionnaires.

SELECTING A STANDARDIZED QUESTIONNAIRE

The guidelines we've provided so far suggest only certain cautions in the selection of standardized questionnaires. You still need more specific guidelines to judge the adequacy of individual questionnaires, and to make comparisons of different questionnaires designed to measure the same target. For example, there are numerous standardized questionnaire measures of self-esteem (e.g., Chiu, 1988), depression (e.g., Lambert, Hatch, Kingston, & Edwards, 1986; Thompson, 1989a; Wetzler & van Praag, 1989), and marital distress (e.g., Touliatos et al., 1990), to name just a few, and oftentimes you'll be faced with having to decide among different standardized questionnaires designed to measure the same target. The purpose of this section is to help you make these judgments.

There are several guidelines that you can use to help you choose specific questionnaires. These guidelines are based on the more general material described in Chapter 2 regarding basic measurement principles, as well as on more practice-oriented criteria, all of which are applied here specifically to standardized questionnaires. We should probably start by saying that it's unlikely that you will ever find "the perfect measure." Few measures will have all the characteristics or meet all the criteria described below. Thus, you will have to try to find measures that meet as many of these criteria as possible.

While we suggest caution in using and interpreting any standardized questionnaire, for those that don't meet all the criteria, we urge that you be extra cautious. At the least, be clear about what criteria are not met, and try to estimate just how that might affect your use of the questionnaire. For example, you might find that a standardized questionnaire measure of alcohol abuse has been tested with men but not women. If your client is a woman and you suspect that women are more likely to under-

report alcohol-related problems, you might take very seriously any hint of alcohol problems from a woman's responses (Sisco & Pearson, 1994). Following, then, is a brief description of several guidelines you can use to select specific standardized questionnaires for your practice, and Table 7.1 is a suggested outline for evaluating a standardized questionnaire (see also American Psychological Association et al., 1985; and Ciarlo et al., 1986).

Purpose

The first and most obvious consideration in selecting a standardized questionnaire is to determine its purpose. For what kinds of targets was it designed? For what kinds of client groups has it been used? Does the questionnaire appear suitable to help you make an assessment or evaluation for your client with his or her unique background and experiences?

Find out if the previous research has been conducted on targets or clients like your own, and if norms for comparison purposes with your client's scores have been established. Often, norms for standardized questionnaires are developed using white, middle class college students as subjects. If your client differs substantially from the norm group (e.g., in race, ethnicity, or income), the norms may not be applicable. If you still use the questionnaire, you must interpret the results with due caution.

You may also find that a particular score serves as a "cutting point," a score that serves as a boundary separating scores that indicate serious problems from scores that suggest the absence of such problems. Thus, a score on one side of the clinical cutting point suggests the existence of problems that may require professional services, while a score on the other side of the clinical cutting point suggests the absence of problems needing attention. (We'll provide an example of such a "cutting point" later in this chapter.)

Directness

In searching for a standardized questionnaire to measure a target, try to select one that is as direct a measure of the target as possible. The

Table 7.1   Outline for evaluating standardized questionnaires.

A. General Information
   Title of questionnaire (including edition and forms if applicable)
   Author(s)
   Publisher, date of publication
   Time required to administer
   Format (booklets, answer sheets, other test materials, available scoring services)
B. Brief Description of Purpose, Nature of Questionnaire
   General type of questionnaire (e.g., individual or group, checklist)
   Population for which designed (age range, type of person)
   Nature of content (e.g., verbal, numerical)
   Subtests and separate scores
   Types of items
C. Directness
D. Relevance to Intervention Planning
   Utility for determining improvement or deterioration
   Utility for determining the presence of a condition
   Utility for determining conditions affecting or maintaining a condition
   Utility for selecting an effective intervention
E. Technical Evaluation
   1. Norms
      Type (e.g., percentiles, standard scores)
      Standardization sample: nature, size, representativeness, procedures fol-
      lowed in obtaining sample, availability of subgroup norms (e.g., age, sex,
      education, occupation, religion, ethnicity)
   2. Reliability
      Types and procedure (e.g., test-retest, alternate-form, internal consistency)
      including size and nature of samples employed
   3. Validity
      Types and validation procedures (content, criterion, construct) including
      size and nature of samples employed
   4. Sensitivity to change
F. Ease of Use
   Qualitative features of questionnaire materials (e.g., design of questionnaire
   booklet, editorial quality of content, attractiveness, durability, appropriateness
   for clients)
   Clarity of directions
   Scoring procedures
   Practicality
   Potential for repeated administration
G. Accessibility
   Practitioner qualifications and training
   Cost
   Copyright protection
H. Reviewer Comments
   Critical evaluation from formal reviews such as *The 12th Mental
   Measurements Yearbook* (Conoley & Kramer, 1995), *Test Critiques*
   (Keyser & Sweetland, 1991), and other sources
I. Summary Evaluation
   Major strengths and weaknesses of the measure cutting across all parts
   of the outline

Adapted from *Psychological Testing,* 4th ed. (pp. 676–677) by A. Anastasi, 1988, New York:
Macmillan.

more direct the questionnaire, the more likely it is to register any changes that occur in the target, and the more likely it is to be meaningful and useful in general to you and your client. There are two ways in which standardized questionnaires are sometimes used indirectly in place of more direct standardized questionnaires, and you should be cautious of such uses.

One indirect use of a standardized questionnaire is in measuring a general concept, in place of using a measure of a specific dimension of that concept targeted for intervention. For example, if your intervention is designed to improve the quality of a parent's child-discipline skills, it would be better to use a measure of the quality of those particular skills instead of a general measure of parenting skills or knowledge. Or if your intervention is designed to provide a client with tangible resources (e.g., food or clothing), it would be better to use a measure of the amount and quality of tangible resources instead of a general measure of social support. Finally, if your intervention is designed to eliminate a husband's physical abuse of his wife, it would be better to use a measure of physical abuse instead of a general measure of marital satisfaction.

Although, in general, standardized questionnaires that provide direct measures of targets are preferable to those that are more general and less direct, more general multidimensional standardized questionnaires do have a place in single-system evaluations. Such questionnaires can be used for initial screening to determine the presence of specific targets for intervention, and they can be administered periodically to determine the generality of change, including a determination of improvement or deterioration in unanticipated areas. For example, the Multi-Problem Screening Inventory (MPSI) (Hudson, 1996b; Nurius & Hudson, 1993) includes 27 different subscales measuring a wide variety of targets (e.g., depression, alcohol abuse, school problems). In some cases the MPSI might be useful for screening and for determining the generality of change, but it would be inefficient to administer such a measure frequently in a case with a delimited number of targets.

Another indirect use of standardized questionnaires that you should try to avoid is the use of a standardized questionnaire designed to measure one target as an indicator of another target that is the direct focus of intervention. For example, if your intervention is designed to increase parenting skills, don't measure the quality of the parent–child relationship and assume that this provides a sufficient indication of parenting skills. Or if your intervention is designed to enhance the quality of an adolescent's relationships with his or her peers, don't measure the adolescent's self-esteem and assume that this provides a sufficient indication of the peer relationships. The direct target of the intervention should be measured (i.e., parenting skills in the first example and peer relationships in the second) because it's unlikely that one target will represent perfectly another target.

Relevance to Intervention Planning

In the selection of a standardized questionnaire, or any measurement method for that matter, there should be reason to believe that it will enhance the intervention process in some way. Will it help determine whether a target is improving or deteriorating, so that any necessary modifications in the intervention plan can be undertaken? Will it help to determine whether a client is in need of intervention in a particular area? Will it help determine what may be affecting or maintaining the target? Will it help select the most effective intervention strategy? In most cases a single standardized questionnaire won't help answer all of these questions, but if the answer to most or all of these questions is no, you should probably rethink the use of that particular questionnaire.

Reliability

You should look to previous research to get an idea of the reliability of a standardized questionnaire, as discussed in Chapter 2. You should look for evidence of the internal consistency of the questionnaire items by looking for evidence of "split-half" or "odd-even" reliability or "coefficient alpha." If the questionnaire is designed for use by practitioners, relevant others, or independent observers, or for obtaining information from clients about publicly observable events, you should look for evidence of interobserver reliability (the consistency with which information is provided by different observers). Finally, you should look for evidence of the test-retest reliability of the questionnaire, the stability or consistency of the responses to the questionnaire over time, a criterion that is particularly important in single-system designs because of repeated use of measurement tools over the course of baseline and intervention periods. In each case, the higher the reliability the better, and as a general rule, if the reliability is .80 or better, you have reasonably good reliability.

In addition to looking for existing evidence of the reliability of a standardized questionnaire, there are some things that you can do to get some idea of the interobserver or test-retest reliability (but not internal consistency reliability) of a questionnaire as used with a particular client. If relevant and practical, you can have two different people provide information about a client, even if only on a spot-check basis, and you can examine the agreement between observers (e.g., using visual examination of a graph, or some more precise statistical index such as kappa or a correlation coefficient, described in Chapter 2). If two observers regularly complete the same standardized questionnaire, the reports can be examined individually or they can be averaged and the average examined.

Suppose, for example, that in working with the parents of an 8-year-old girl one target for intervention is the child's behavior problems in the home. You decide to measure these problems using the subscale of the Daily Child Behavior Checklist (DCBC), which is a 28-item parent-report checklist that measures displeasing child behaviors in the previous 24 hours (Furey & Forehand, 1983). This scale has a potential range of values from 0 to 28, and higher scores indicate more displeasing behaviors. Suppose that both parents completed the DCBC and the results shown in Figure 7.1a were obtained. As shown in this figure, the observations are correlated over time but they're in less than perfect agreement. Figure 7.1b illustrates the average of these observers' scores. The advantage of such an average is that it will

be more reliable than the observations of the individual observers (Fleiss, 1986), and it will make it easier to discern trends. However, some information is lost in computing an average, and so it seems best to consider the scores of individual observers before averaging scores. It might be, for example, that one observer tends to have higher scores than the other, or that there are large differences between observers on some days that, when discussed with the observers, provides useful information for treatment.

You also can get some idea about the test-retest reliability of a standardized questionnaire by examining the pattern of scores during baseline. If the scores are relatively stable during baseline you can be more confident of the test-retest reliability than if the responses are variable. In a way this is the single-system design version of test-retest reliability. Suppose, for example, that one target of intervention in working with a family is resolving problems around a fourth-grade boy's homework problems. You decide to measure these homework problems using the Homework Problem Checklist (HPC) (Anesko, Schoiock, Ramirez, & Levine, 1987), a 20-item parent-report measure of homework problems. The HPC has a potential range of scores from 0 to 60, with higher scores indicating greater problems; the average HPC score for fourth-grade boys is 11.84. You could be more confident of the test-retest reliability of the HPC if you obtained the stable HPC scores shown in Figure 7.2 than if you obtained the variable scores.

If the scores are variable, it might be due to inadequate test-retest reliability or to actual changes in homework problems. In either case, though, such variable scores can be transformed in an attempt to get a clearer picture of the pattern of results. One way to do this is to compute the average of the scores for the first and second time periods and plot this average for the first time period, average the scores for the second and third time periods, plot this average for the second time period, and so on. This is an example of a "moving average," and we will describe it in more detail in Chapter 19. The moving average for the variable HPC scores is shown in Figure 7.2. Notice that the moving average is much more stable than

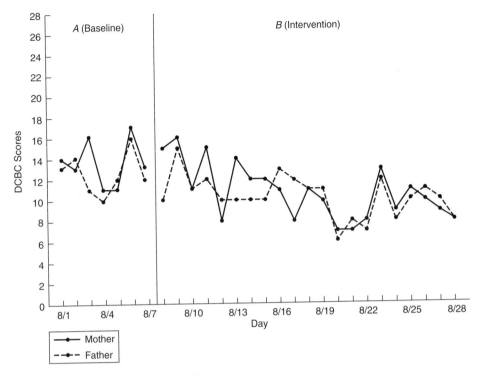

FIGURE 7.1a   Mother's and father's DCBC scores.

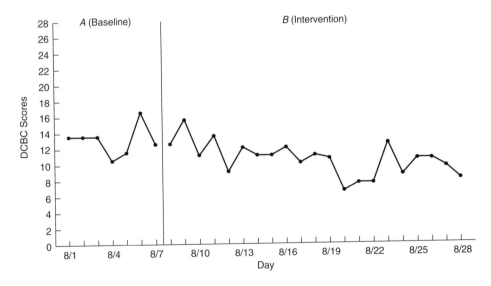

FIGURE 7.1b   Average DCBC score.

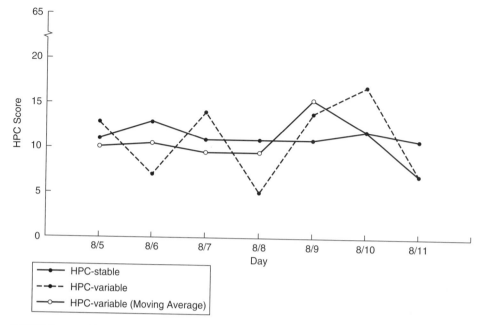

FIGURE 7.2   Stable, variable, and transformed HPC scores.

the untransformed, variable HPC scores. Also, such an average has the advantage of being more reliable than the separate data points (Fleiss, 1986), although it can obscure information. Thus, it's best to examine both untransformed and transformed scores (e.g., an unusually high score on one day and an unusually low score on another day might suggest important determinants of the target, but when scores from the 2 days are averaged they will produce a relatively typical score).

Most standardized questionnaires haven't been developed for repeated administration over time, and they haven't been tested for stability under these conditions. Therefore, in selecting a standardized questionnaire you should look for existing evidence of test-retest reliability, but you should also examine your data for particular clients for signs of stability or instability over time, especially during baseline phases when an intervention is not operating to produce change in whatever is being measured. And you should try to use baselines that are as long as practical (see Chapter 12).

Validity

Of course, you want to know whether a standardized questionnaire really measures what its name implies. Use the guidelines we presented in Chapter 2. Does it appear valid "on its face"? That is, do the items on the questionnaire appear to be "getting at" what they should? (Face validity is the least rigorous kind of validity, but a type that can be important in convincing a client of the relevance of the measure.) Check to see if other types of validity are addressed. Do the items in the questionnaire seem to represent all the areas that should have been included (content validity)? Is there any mention of criterion (concurrent or predictive) validity? If so, you should be able to evaluate how well your questionnaire compares or correlates with other measures that are considered to be valid measures of the target in question. The higher the correlation, the better. Further, you want to know whether your measure allows you to make predictions—for instance, to forecast whether people with certain scores on your questionnaire are more or less likely to be a certain way or do a certain thing in the future. Similarly, you want to know whether your questionnaire can distinguish between people who purportedly have a problem and those who don't. For example, if you're interested in a measure of psychological adjustment, you would need to know whether a measure can distinguish between people who say they have psychological problems and those who say they don't.

You also would want to see whether a questionnaire has construct validity. Has previous research on the questionnaire shown that an interpretation of the instrument as a measure of a theoretical variable has been substantiated? If so, the questionnaire you're reviewing should provide information on how many studies were conducted, how strong the associations were, and what studies might contradict this conclusion.

One aspect of construct validity for which you should be especially alert is evidence that a standardized questionnaire is *sensitive to change* (i.e., when actual change occurs, the questionnaire registers the change). If a questionnaire hasn't demonstrated sensitivity to change in previous research, you can't be sure that it will show change even if your client really changes. This in itself is difficult to demonstrate, but if your questionnaire has been used in previous research, and has shown sensitivity to change with those clients, then you do have some basis for concluding that it might pick up changes with your clients as well. This information should be supplied by the researcher about his or her questionnaire. For example, Lambert et al. (1986) reviewed research comparing the relative sensitivity of the Beck Depression Inventory, the Hamilton Rating Scale for Depression, and the Zung Rating Scale for Depression, and found that the Hamilton scale appears most sensitive to change.

Many questionnaires don't provide information on all these forms of validity. But you would be on safer grounds using a questionnaire that contains more information on validity (say, including criterion-related or construct validity) than less of it (say, just face validity). Many questionnaires in early stages of development have little information on validity

(e.g., studies relating this questionnaire to others that already have established validity). In those situations, face validity (plus all the other criteria) might be all you have to go with. Then, you simply will have to be more cautious in interpreting results.

In addition to relying on existing evidence of the validity of standardized questionnaires, your own evaluation of an individual client also can provide some evidence of the validity of standardized questionnaires as used with your particular client (Hayes et al., 1986; Proctor, 1990). Let's take an example of this.

Suppose that a client seeks help because she feels overwhelmed with the burden of caring for her elderly mother, and she wants to improve her relationship with her adolescent daughter. She believes, and you agree, that a lack of support from her family in the care of her mother is a major cause of her feeling overwhelmed. You select the following measures for your evaluation:

1. The Caregiver Burden Scale (CBS) is selected to measure the client's feelings about her role as a caregiver to her elderly mother (Zarit, Reever, & Bach-Peterson, 1980). The CBS is a 29-item self-report scale that has a potential range of values from 0 to 84, and higher scores indicate more burdens.

2. The Perceived Social Support–Family Scale (PSS-Fa) is selected to measure family social support (Procidano & Heller, 1983). The PSS-Fa is a 20-item self-report scale with a potential range of values from 0 to 20, and *lower* scores indicate *more* support. (Actually, with the author's original scoring procedure, higher scores indicate more support, but the direction of the scores was reversed for this example to make it easier to interpret the relationship between this scale and the other two scales in the example.)

3. The Parent–Child Areas of Change Questionnaire (PC-ACQ) (Jacob & Seilhamer, 1985) is selected to measure the amount of change in the adolescent perceived as necessary by the mother. It's a

34-item self-report scale with a potential range of values from –102 to +102, and higher scores indicate that more change is seen as necessary.

Each questionnaire is completed weekly. After a 3-week baseline, a 7-week intervention designed to increase family social support and decrease the mother's feelings of being burdened is implemented, and this is followed by a 7-week intervention designed to reduce the amount of change in the adolescent perceived as necessary by the mother. Results are shown in Figure 7.3 with scores on all scales ranging from 5 to 35, and the following patterns provide evidence of validity:

1. The week-to-week pattern of change in burden and social support is similar—when PSS scores go up (i.e., support decreases), CBS scores also rise (i.e., perceived burden increases), and when PSS scores go down, CBS scores also decrease. Therefore, the PSS and the CBS appear correlated over time, and this provides support for the construct validity of these two questionnaires.

2. The week-to-week pattern of change in PSS, CBS, and PC-ACQ scores are similar, but they don't follow exactly the same pattern (e.g., they're not perfectly correlated). The fact that these patterns are somewhat different suggests that to some extent the three questionnaires measure different targets, and this provides further support for their construct validity. If the week-to-week pattern of change were the same for each questionnaire, it would suggest that they all measure the same target (e.g., perhaps just generalized distress), instead of distinct targets.

3. The PSS, the CBS, and the PC-ACQ decrease when the intervention designed to enhance family social support is implemented (i.e., phase *B*), but the decrease in PSS and CBS scores is larger than the decrease in PC-ACQ scores. When the intervention designed to reduce the amount of change in the adolescent perceived as necessary by the mother is implemented (i.e., phase *C*), there's a further decrease in the PSS and the CBS, but the largest decrease occurs for the PC-ACQ scores. This pattern of change between phases

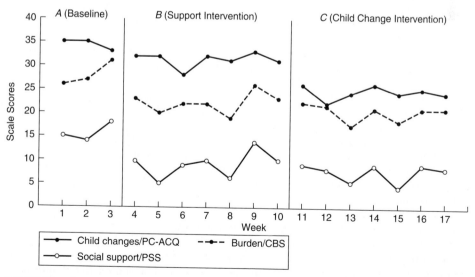

FIGURE 7.3 Construct validity of the CBS, PSS, and PC-ACQ.

suggests that the PSS, the CBS, and the PC-ACQ change in a theoretically predicted manner in response to intervention, which in turn suggests that they're sensitive to "real" change in the problems they attempt to measure. (In Chapter 19, we call this convergence "theoretical significance.")

Other measures also might be useful in the evaluation of this case, and these would let you further examine the validity of the measures. For example, the mother could be asked to self-monitor the amount of time spent caring for her elderly mother, and other family members might be asked to do the same. Individualized rating scales could be constructed to measure idiosyncratic caregiving responsibilities, mother–daughter conflicts, or aspects of family social supports of concern that weren't measured by the standardized questionnaires. In any case, though, such information and the patterns of results among the different measures can provide evidence for the validity of the measures, or raise questions about their validity that might otherwise be overlooked.

Ease of Use

Single-system designs require the repeated measurement of client targets over time. Therefore, the ease with which a questionnaire is used is an important consideration. A client or an observer might be "turned off," irritated, or bored when asked to fill out the same questionnaire week after week. Although this is not just a problem of standardized questionnaires (any measurement method may become aversive), the fact that a standardized questionnaire never changes, requires some time and energy, and may not be all that interesting after the first few times one fills it out, adds to the general problem. In part, this may be an issue regarding how much time the questionnaire takes, how clearly it is written, and how much effort it requires. Try to find standardized questionnaires that are reasonably brief, take no more than 5 to 15 minutes to complete, and don't require too much energy to fill out.

The time it takes to score and interpret a standardized questionnaire is another consideration in determining the ease with which it can be used. Most standardized questionnaires are relatively easy to score by hand or with an inexpensive calculator, and they're relatively easy to interpret. On the other hand, some standardized questionnaires are complicated to score, some even requiring computer scoring, and their interpretation requires considerable time and training.

The characteristics of the person asked to complete a standardized questionnaire also should be considered in determining ease of use. The person must be able to understand the questionnaire. Reports of standardized questionnaires increasingly include information about the reading level necessary to understand a standardized questionnaire, and you should try to match this with what you know about your client's education and abilities.

Finally, if training in the use of the questionnaire is necessary, the person must be able and willing to be trained. Don't select standardized questionnaires that are beyond the ability of clients or observers asked to complete the questionnaires.

Fortunately, there has been an increasing recognition of the importance of the ease with which measures can be used in practice. This recognition has led to the development and dissemination of a large number of standardized questionnaires that can be used relatively easily on a repeated basis (e.g., Corcoran & Fischer, 1987, 2000a, 2000b; Fischer & Corcoran, 1994a, 1994b; Fredman & Sherman, 1987; Grotevant & Carlson, 1989; Hersen & Bellack, 1988; Hudson & Faul, 1998; Jacob & Tennenbaum, 1988; Kestenbaum & Williams, 1988; Levitt & Reid, 1981; McCubbin & Thompson, 1987; McCubbin et al., 1996; McDowell & Newell, 1996; Sawin & Harrigan, 1994; Schutte & Malouff, 1995; Touliatos et al., 1990); see the Appendix to this chapter for a list of books devoted almost exclusively to standardized measures.

Accessibility

Accessibility is also an important consideration in the selection of a standardized questionnaire. Some standardized questionnaires are difficult to obtain. For example, some standardized questionnaires need to be purchased from their authors or from companies that own the questionnaires. In some cases these costs might be unacceptable. Some standardized questionnaires are copyrighted, and you need permission to use the questionnaire. Some standardized questionnaires are not available for use by some professionals (e.g., some questionnaires are available only to psychologists), or are not available to professionals without documentation of special training (e.g., courses in psychometrics and test interpretation).

ADMINISTERING A STANDARDIZED QUESTIONNAIRE

Once you've selected your questionnaire or questionnaires for use with a particular client or target, you are still faced with the task of enabling someone to complete it. This may not be an easy matter. Whether you ask the client, a relevant other, or some other helping professional to fill out a questionnaire, you may run into trouble. The way you involve someone in completing the questionnaire is probably as important as selecting just the right questionnaire for him or her to fill out.

It's likely that in your practice you mainly will be focusing on using standardized questionnaires completed by your client, that is, self-reports. There are, of course, many instances when you may be using standardized questionnaires completed by relevant others or other professionals, depending on the target or situation (e.g., a parent providing regular ratings of a child's behavior, a teacher filling out a checklist for a student, etc.). But the bulk of use of standardized questionnaires appears to be directly with clients. For that reason, this section of the chapter focuses on the use of standardized questionnaires directly with clients, though many of the principles (e.g., with regard to explaining the purpose of the instrument, etc.) apply no matter who is completing the questionnaire. Actually, many of the principles described in Chapter 5 on teaching clients or others to count behaviors (e.g., carefully defining the behavior, adequate training in observation, and achieving satisfactory interobserver reliability) apply here too. This is

especially so when you're asking a relevant other to fill out a rating scale or behavior checklist.

Ideally, no single measurement method should be used to assess and monitor a client's targets, regardless of whether it's a standardized self-report questionnaire or some other type of measurement method. In general, as we detail in Chapter 10, we think you should use more than one measurement method if possible, because no single measurement method will provide a comprehensive and completely accurate picture of a client. Different methods of measuring the same target will provide a more accurate picture of the target than a single method, although even multiple measures may not provide a completely accurate picture.

In some situations the sole use of a standardized self-report questionnaire is the only feasible option. For example, the client might refuse to use another measurement method, or information about the target of intervention is only directly available to the client (e.g., thoughts, feelings, or private behaviors).

Maximizing the Accuracy of the Information

Once you decide that a standardized questionnaire is appropriate, it's crucial to attend to how you go about involving the client in its use. As we suggest for other measurement methods, present the questionnaire with confidence and certainty about its usefulness. Sometimes practitioners with no experience in the use of measures in practice request this information in an uncertain, embarrassed, and apologetic fashion. This might suggest to the client that the task isn't important, or that it's indeed unreasonable to ask for the information, and the client might act accordingly and provide less than complete or accurate information. If you believe that the information you are requesting is important, convey this to the client; if you don't believe it's important, maybe you shouldn't ask for it!

Another way to increase the accuracy of the information collected using standardized self-report questionnaires is to give clients incentives for accuracy. A key incentive is the prospect of the successful resolution or prevention of target problems. After all, the information you are requesting is (or should be) for the client's benefit. It will be used to plan the intervention and to monitor its success so that any necessary modifications can be made to achieve a successful outcome. Oftentimes this point can be made by using the medical analogy presented in Chapter 6 (i.e., "just as a doctor uses a thermometer to monitor progress, we, too, have to have some method for checking our progress"), because most people have experience with "tests" used by physicians.

If the information you're asking for doesn't seem relevant to the client, it might be difficult to persuade the client that he or she will be better off to provide accurate reports. Therefore, the degree to which the requested information seems relevant to the client might also influence the accuracy of the client's reports. People will be more willing to provide complete and accurate reports if they understand the need for the information than if the information doesn't seem relevant. So obviously you shouldn't ask for irrelevant information, but make sure the client understands the relevance of the information you do request.

Even if a client wants to provide complete and accurate information, ambiguous instructions can reduce the reliability of the reports because clients are left guessing about just what it is they are supposed to do or report. So you can increase the chances of getting accurate information by giving the client clear instructions. Take the time to explain the task, and be sure that the client understands the instructions. When appropriate, you might ask clients to restate the instructions as a means of gauging whether they understand. In any case, encourage clients to ask questions whenever something is unclear, and be sure to give them the impression that you have the time to answer their questions, because this might encourage clients to ask much-needed questions. Also, make sure that you're knowledgeable about the measurement task and are prepared for questions.

Clients might want to provide complete and accurate information, but they might be reluctant because they don't know who has access to the potentially embarrassing information they're asked to provide. Therefore, another way to increase the accuracy of self-reports is by assuring the client of confidentiality. However, don't inadvertently deceive the client by implying that such information is completely confidential. Numerous exceptions exist to the privilege of confidentiality, and you need to be careful not to promise a greater degree of confidentiality than you can guarantee (Albert, 1986; Bloom & Orme, 1993).

Your reaction to the information provided by a client is another factor that can influence the accuracy of the information. For example, you might subtly show surprise or disapproval in response to a client's report, and consequently the client might subsequently provide less accurate information. For example, a practitioner might inadvertently encourage a client to report improvement even when it doesn't occur. You should be careful not to suggest possible responses.

Remember that self-reports are limited not only by what a client is *willing* to tell you, but also by what they're *able* to tell you. For example, under the right circumstances a client seeking help with alcohol abuse problems might be willing to tell you the average daily amount of alcohol consumed in the previous month but unable to remember this information. A parent might be willing to report, but unable to remember, the number of arguments with his or her adolescent in the previous 2 weeks. Therefore, the accuracy of self-report information depends upon whether the client has the information you request. You should ask yourself, and the client, whether the client is able to provide the needed information even if he or she is willing to do so. After all, you may get inaccurate information.

To ensure the accuracy of the information, try to be as sensitive as possible to the educational, social, and cultural background of the client, especially when there are differences between you and the client (such as age, gender, ethnicity, or sexual orientation). There is no substitute for cultural (and social) competence when requesting others to provide information. Some people may be so afraid of or uncomfortable with the questionnaire for any number of reasons that, unless you give them an opportunity to express themselves, they may simply throw away the questionnaire, not return it, or answer in an incorrect or distorted way. You may even want to read all of the questions aloud with clients just to make sure all of the terms are understood, and perhaps help them answer the first few questions to ensure that they do understand them. In fact, if clients have trouble reading or understanding the questionnaire, one option may be to read the items aloud and have clients respond orally rather than in writing. However, many clients won't tell you directly that they can't read, so you need to look for signs of this and provide these clients with a face-saving "excuse" for your reading the questions to them (e.g., the questionnaire is complicated). When you read items and ask the client to respond orally rather than in writing, interpret your results with caution since such changes may compromise the validity of the measure.

Self-report questionnaires often are subject to problems such as *response bias* (the client responds to each item on a questionnaire in the same or a patterned way—for example, all 2s on a 5-point scale)—and *social desirability response set* (the client's responses to some items are based more on what the client thinks he or she "should" say than on what he or she actually thinks or feels). Some questionnaires have built-in ways to solve these problems. For example, some try to control response bias by varying the directionality of items so that a 2 on one item might indicate something positive and a 2 on another something negative. Others may try to control social desirability by carefully wording items so that they don't obviously reflect social values. One of the most effective ways to control these problems is in how you present the questionnaire to the client, urging the client to be completely honest because that is the only way you can plan the optimal intervention program. In addition, encourage the client to try to respond to each item independently—that is, not in a pattern. If you do find a patterned response, you should use the resulting data cautiously, if at all, and you should talk with the client (or observer) to try to determine the reason for the responses and to try to increase the accuracy of the responses to the questionnaire.

Selecting the Administration Setting

You have at least two options for where your client completes the questionnaire: in your office or elsewhere—for example, in the client's home. If the questionnaire is relatively brief, you may have the client fill it out at the office just before coming in to see you or even during the first few minutes of the interview. The advantage is that you can be relatively sure it will be completed, it will be completed at about the same time on a regular basis, you will be available to answer questions, and you can give immediate feedback to the client.

On the other hand, if the client is able and willing to fill out the questionnaire at home, it could serve as a sort of "homework" task that can help structure your at-home intervention program (if you're working on one). Similarly, if the client fills out the questionnaire at home, he or she can do so without the potential pressure of feeling "watched," and perhaps the act of filling out the questionnaire will provide more material for you and the client to work on in your next meeting.

Another thing to keep in mind about the setting is that the client should have a private, quiet, physically comfortable place to complete the questionnaire. Privacy is important because asking a client to provide personal information when other people are around can be embarrassing and may lead to biased reports. For example, reports elicited from an adolescent might differ depending upon whether they're elicited in private or in the presence of parents. A quiet, comfortable environment is important because asking clients to report information under uncomfortable, chaotic, noisy, or otherwise distracting conditions also can reduce the accuracy of the report.

A final consideration is that the client should complete the questionnaire at the same time and in the same place each time. For example, if the client is filling out the questionnaire every week, try to see that he or she fills it out under generally the same conditions—for example, at the same time (say, after dinner) and in the same place (say, in the kitchen). The purpose of this is to try to minimize the chance that the client's responses will be determined or affected by the situation. If conditions do vary, try to take this into account when scoring and interpreting the results.

Selecting the Timing and Frequency of Administration

Finally, you have to make a decision about how often to fill out the questionnaire. This depends on four things. The first is instructions accompanying the questionnaire. If the questionnaire has built-in requirements for how often it should be administered, you probably don't have to worry too much about this issue. Second, the length of the questionnaire and the time and energy it takes probably are related to how often you have the client fill it out. A general rule would be the longer the questionnaire and the more time it takes, the less often you would ask someone to fill it out. Third, the willingness or ability of the client to fill out your questionnaire plays a key role in determining how often you ask him or her to fill it out. If the client indicates he or she is getting bored or annoyed with the questionnaire, it's a good sign that you should ask him or her to fill it out less frequently. This is something that should be checked each time the client returns a questionnaire to you. Finally, the reason for using the questionnaire, as well as the type of questionnaire, should have a bearing on how often you use it. As a general rule, the more you rely on a standardized questionnaire as your primary measure for assessment and evaluation, the more often you should administer it.

We generally recommend that self-report questionnaires be filled out approximately once a week, unless they are extremely brief (say, under 10 items) and have very good test-retest reliability that shows they will be stable when used repeatedly. This will give you some indication of changes in the target over time as well as a sense of the extent or magnitude of the target at any given time. On the other hand, once-a-week administration does place some limitations on the utility of the informa-

tion because it doesn't allow day-to-day tracking of changes. More precise behavior checklists and rating scales—for example, those filled out by relevant others—can be used more frequently, on an "as needed" basis, daily if necessary. Of course, it's up to you to make adjustments if the questionnaire is being used incorrectly. You may have to increase or decrease its use based on feedback from each person using it.

Once you begin to collect data from a questionnaire, and assuming this can be translated into some quantity such as a total score or subscale scores, you can chart this information just as you would any other type of data you collect. This chart can serve as a clear source of feedback to the client about his or her scores on the questionnaire and can also be used as a starting point for further work. For example, Figure 7.4 illustrates baseline and intervention information for a depression scale in which higher scores indicate greater or more depression.

SOME AVAILABLE STANDARDIZED SELF-REPORT QUESTIONNAIRES

So far the thrust of this chapter has been to try to help you evaluate and select standardized questionnaires. One of the primary reasons for this focus is that there are so many standardized questionnaires (literally thousands, as we've mentioned), and such a huge range of practitioners, targets, and settings, that it would be extremely difficult if not impossible to identify standardized questionnaires that would be suitable for all people in all settings at all times. Thus, we believe the more productive strategy is to provide guidelines for you to use to select your own questionnaires.

However, we would like to take this one step further. There are some standardized questionnaires that we can suggest just to illustrate the types and range of instruments that are available. In this and the following sections we provide some examples of standardized questionnaires to be completed by: (a) clients (i.e., self-reports), (b) practitioners, (c) relevant others, and (d) independent observers. Of course, we are not trying to present all possible

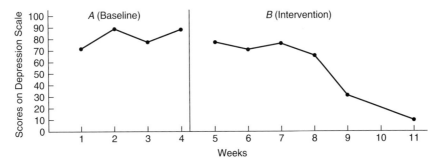

FIGURE 7.4   Scores on a depression scale for baseline and intervention period.

available instruments. For example, in the area of client self-report questionnaires, two new books by Corcoran and Fischer (2000a, 2000b) describe and reproduce hundreds of measures. Thus, we are providing only a sample of available measures in each area. The Appendix to this chapter lists a number of references for locating other measures.

WALMYR Assessment Scales (WAS)

One of the encouraging innovations in measurement for single-system evaluation in clinical practice has been the development of a set of standardized scales by Hudson and his coworkers—the WALMYR Assessment Scales (WAS) (Hudson & Faul, 1998). Most of these questionnaires were designed specifically for single-system evaluation to monitor and evaluate the magnitude (extent, degree, intensity) of a client's problem through periodic administration of the same questionnaires to the client.

To date, over 35 scales have been developed for the WAS package, based on an assessment of the types of personal, interpersonal, and social dysfunctions that appear to take up a large portion of practitioners' time. These scales are listed and described briefly in Table 7.2; 18 of the actual scales (Figures 7.5 to 7.22) are reprinted with permission of Dr. Walter Hudson.*

Of course, as indicated previously, there are hundreds of other self-report scales that are appropriate for use with single-system designs. We hope our description of the WAS package won't discourage you from using the references we provide in the Appendix and exploring and using other instruments.

The major reasons we are presenting this set of scales, as an example of available questionnaires, is that it's one of the few—perhaps the only—package of scales designed to be used as repeated measures expressly with single-system designs. Most of the scales are short (usually 25 items), easy to administer, easy to interpret, and easy to complete and score. Each one takes about 3 to 5 minutes to complete and about the same time to score. Also, all of the WAS questionnaires can be administered and scored using the CAAP computer program described later in this chapter.

In addition to being feasible for use with single-system designs, most of the scales in the WAS package have internal consistency reliabilities of .90 or better, which is very high. Similarly, for the questionnaires for which test-retest reliability (stability) has been examined, these reliabilities have been very good. Further, these questionnaires all have excellent

(text continues on page 250)

*The scales should not be reproduced directly from the book. Additional information about all of these scales and order forms for purchasing them can be obtained from WALMYR Publishing Co., PO Box 12217, Tallahassee, FL, 32317. Voice: (850) 383-0045; fax: (850) 383-0970; E-mail: Scales@walmyr.com. Also, a Web site is available to provide information about these scales: http://www.walmyr.com.

Table 7.2 The WALMYR assessment scales package.

Personal Adjustment Scales

Generalized Contentment Scale (GCS). The GCS is designed to measure the severity of nonpsychotic depression.

Index of Self-Esteem (ISE). The ISE is designed to measure the severity of problems with self-esteem.

Index of Clinical Stress (ICS). The ICS is designed to measure the severity of problems with personal stress.

Clinical Anxiety Scale (CAS). The CAS is designed to measure the severity of problems with phobic anxiety.

Index of Peer Relations (IPR). The IPR is designed to measure the severity of problems in peer relationships.

Index of Alcohol Involvement (IAI). The IAI is designed to measure the severity of problems with alcohol abuse.

Index of Drug Involvement (IDI). The IDI is designed to measure the severity of problems with drug abuse.

Sexual Attitude Scale (SAS). The SAS is designed to measure a liberal or conservative orientation toward human sexual expression.

Index of Homophobia (IHP). The IHP is designed to measure the level of homophobia.

Dyadic Adjustment Scales

Index of Marital Satisfaction (IMS). The IMS is designed to measure the severity of problems in a dyadic relationship.

Index of Sexual Satisfaction (ISS). The ISS is designed to measure the severity of problems in the sexual component of a dyadic relationship.

Partner Abuse Scale: Non-Physical (PASNP). The PASNP is completed by the abuse victim and is designed to measure the severity of problems with nonphysical abuse in a dyadic relationship.

Partner Abuse Scale: Physical (PASPH). The PASPH is completed by the abuse victim and is designed to measure the severity of problems with physical abuse in a dyadic relationship.

Non-Physical Abuse of Partner Scale (NPAPS). The NPAPS is completed by the abuser and is designed to measure the severity of problems with nonphysical abuse in a dyadic relationship.

Physical Abuse of Partner Scale (PAPS). The PAPS is completed by the abuser and is designed to measure the severity of problems with physical abuse in a dyadic relationship.

Family Adjustment Scales

Index of Family Relations (IFR). The IFR is designed to measure the severity of family relationship problems as seen by the respondent.

Index of Parental Attitudes (IPA). The IPA is designed to measure the severity of problems in a parent–child relationship as seen by the parent.

Child's Attitude toward Mother (CAM) and

Child's Attitude toward Father (CAF). The CAM and CAF scales are designed to measure the severity of problems in a parent–child relationship as seen by the child.

Index of Brother Relations (IBR). The IBR is designed to measure the severity of problems with brother relationships as seen by a sibling.

Index of Sister Relations (ISR). The ISR is designed to measure the severity of problems with sister relationships as seen by a sibling.

Children's Behavior Rating Scale (CBRS). The CBRS is designed for use by a parent or guardian as a scaled checklist to reflect the type and degree of behavioral problems that are exhibited by a child.

Organizational Assessment Scales

Index of Sexual Harassment (ISH). The ISH is designed to measure the severity of sexual harassment as seen by the respondent.

Client Satisfaction Inventory (CSI). The CSI is designed to measure the degree of satisfaction experienced by clients with respect to services.

Index of Managerial Effectiveness (IME). The IME scale is designed to measure the severity of problems in managerial ability as seen by the respondent.

Index of Job Satisfaction (IJS). The IJS scale is designed to measure the degree of satisfaction an employee feels in relationship to her or his current employment situation.

Educational Assessment Scales

Classroom Teacher Evaluation Scale (CTES). The CTES is used to evaluate teacher performance in the classroom.

Practicum Instructors Evaluation Form (PIEF). The PIEF is used to evaluate field practicum instructor performance as a teacher.

Multidimensional Assessment Scales

Brief Adult Assessment Scale (BAAS). The BAAS is a self-report measure that helps you to better assess and understand the severity or magnitude of adult client problems across 16 different areas of personal and social functioning: depression, self-esteem problems, partner problems, sexual discord, problems with a child, personal stress, problems with friends, aggression, problems with work associates, family problems, suicide, nonphysical abuse, physical abuse, problems at work, alcohol abuse, and drug use.

Brief Family Assessment Scale (BFAS). The BFAS is a self-report measure that helps you to better assess and understand the severity or magnitude of seven different family problems: personal stress, family supports for members, familial economic stress, family member aggressive behavior, problems with children, drug use in the family, alcohol use in the family.

Family Assessment Screening Inventory (FASI). The FASI scale is a multidimensional self-report measure that helps you to better assess and understand the severity or magnitude of family problems across 25 different areas of personal and social functioning.

Gate Control Pain Management Scale (GC-PMI). The GC-PMI scale is a multidimensional self-report measure that is designed for use in the assessment and management of chronic pain.

Inner Interaction Scale of Social Functioning (IISSF). The IISSF scale is a multidimensional self-report measure that helps you to better assess and understand the severity or magnitude of social functioning problems across three different areas of social functioning, namely achievement, satisfaction, expectation, and three areas of social dysfunctioning, namely frustration, stress, and helplessness.

Multidimensional Adolescent Adjustment Scale (MAAS). The MAAS scale is a self-report measure that helps you to better assess and understand the severity or magnitude of adolescent client problems across 16 different areas of personal and social functioning: depression, self-esteem problems, problems with mother, problems with father, personal stress, problems with friends, problems with school, aggression, family problems, suicide, guilt, confused thinking, disturbing thoughts, memory loss, alcohol abuse, and drug use.

Multi-Problem Screening Inventory (MPSI). The MPSI scale is a multidimensional self-report measure that helps you to better assess and understand the severity or magnitude of client problems across 27 different areas of personal and social functioning.

Multi-Problem Screening Questionnaire (MPSQ). The MPSQ scale is a brief multidimensional self-report measure that gives you rapid client assessment across eight areas of personal and social functioning with the use of only 65 items.

GENERALIZED CONTENTMENT SCALE (GCS)

Name: _____ Today's Date: _____

This questionnaire is designed to measure the way you feel about your life and surroundings. It is not a test, so there are no right or wrong answers. Answer each item as carefully and as accurately as you can by placing a number beside each one as follows.

    1 = None of the time
    2 = Very rarely
    3 = A little of the time
    4 = Some of the time
    5 = A good part of the time
    6 = Most of the time
    7 = All of the time

1. ___ I feel powerless to do anything about my life.
2. ___ I feel blue.
3. ___ I think about ending my life.
4. ___ I have crying spells.
5. ___ It is easy for me to enjoy myself.
6. ___ I have a hard time getting started on things that I need to do.
7. ___ I get very depressed.
8. ___ I feel there is always someone I can depend on when things get tough.
9. ___ I feel that the future looks bright for me.
10. ___ I feel downhearted.
11. ___ I feel that I am needed.
12. ___ I feel that I am appreciated by others.
13. ___ I enjoy being active and busy.
14. ___ I feel that others would be better off without me.
15. ___ I enjoy being with other people.
16. ___ I feel that it is easy for me to make decisions.
17. ___ I feel downtrodden.
18. ___ I feel terribly lonely.
19. ___ I get upset easily.
20. ___ I feel that nobody really cares about me.
21. ___ I have a full life.
22. ___ I feel that people really care about me.
23. ___ I have a great deal of fun.
24. ___ I feel great in the morning.
25. ___ I feel that my situation is hopeless.

5. 8, 9, 11, 12, 13, 15, 16, 21, 22, 23, 24.

FIGURE 7.5 Generalized Contentment Scale.

INDEX OF SELF-ESTEEM (ISE)

Name: _____ Today's Date: _____

This questionnaire is designed to measure how you see yourself. It is not a test, so there are no right or wrong answers. Please answer each item as carefully and as accurately as you can by placing a number beside each one as follows.

    1 = None of the time
    2 = Very rarely
    3 = A little of the time
    4 = Some of the time
    5 = A good part of the time
    6 = Most of the time
    7 = All of the time

1. ___ I feel that people would not like me if they really knew me well.
2. ___ I feel that others get along much better than I do.
3. ___ I feel that I am a beautiful person.
4. ___ When I am with others I feel they are glad I am with them.
5. ___ I feel that people really like to talk with me.
6. ___ I feel that I am a very competent person.
7. ___ I think I make a good impression on others.
8. ___ I feel that I need more self-confidence.
9. ___ When I am with strangers I am very nervous.
10. ___ I think that I am a dull person.
11. ___ I feel ugly.
12. ___ I feel that others have more fun than I do.
13. ___ I feel that I bore people.
14. ___ I think my friends find me interesting.
15. ___ I think I have a good sense of humor.
16. ___ I feel very self-conscious when I am with strangers.
17. ___ I feel that if I could be more like other people I would have it made.
18. ___ I feel that people have a good time when they are with me.
19. ___ I feel like a wallflower when I go out.
20. ___ I feel I get pushed around more than others.
21. ___ I think I am a rather nice person.
22. ___ I feel that people really like me very much.
23. ___ I feel that I am a likeable person.
24. ___ I am afraid I will appear foolish to others.
25. ___ My friends think very highly of me.

3, 4, 5, 6, 7, 14, 15, 18, 21, 22, 23, 25.

FIGURE 7.6 Index of Self-Esteem.

INDEX OF CLINICAL STRESS (ICS)

Name: _____   Today's Date: _____

This questionnaire is designed to measure the way you feel about the amount of personal stress that you experience. It is not a test, so there are no right or wrong answers. Answer each item as carefully and as accurately as you can by placing a number beside each one as follows.

1 = None of the time
2 = Very rarely
3 = A little of the time
4 = Some of the time
5 = A good part of the time
6 = Most of the time
7 = All of the time

1. ___ I feel extremely tense.
2. ___ I feel very jittery.
3. ___ I feel like I want to scream.
4. ___ I feel overwhelmed.
5. ___ I feel very relaxed.
6. ___ I feel so anxious I want to cry.
7. ___ I feel so stressed that I'd like to hit something.
8. ___ I feel very calm and peaceful.
9. ___ I feel like I am stretched to the breaking point.
10. ___ It is very hard for me to relax.
11. ___ It is very easy for me to fall asleep at night.
12. ___ I feel an enormous sense of pressure on me.
13. ___ I feel like my life is going very smoothly.
14. ___ I feel very panicked.
15. ___ I feel like I am on the verge of a total collapse.
16. ___ I feel that I am losing control of my life.
17. ___ I feel that I am near a breaking point.
18. ___ I feel wound up like a coiled spring.
19. ___ I feel that I can't keep up with all the demands on me.
20. ___ I feel very much behind in my work.
21. ___ I feel tense and angry with those around me.
22. ___ I feel I must race from one task to the next.
23. ___ I feel that I just can't keep up with everything.
24. ___ I feel as tight as a drum.
25. ___ I feel very much on edge.

5, 8, 11, 13.

FIGURE 7.7   Index of Clinical Stress.

CLINICAL ANXIETY SCALE (CAS)

Name: _____ Today's Date: _____

This questionnaire is designed to measure how much anxiety you are currently feeling. It is not a test, so there are no right or wrong answers. Answer each item as carefully and as accurately as you can by placing a number beside each one as follows.

      1 Rarely or none of the time
      2 A little of the time
      3 Some of the time
      4 A good part of the time
      5 Most or all of the time

1. ___ I feel calm.
2. ___ I feel tense.
3. ___ I feel suddenly scared for no reason.
4. ___ I feel nervous.
5. ___ I use tranquilizers or antidepressants to cope with my anxiety.
6. ___ I feel confident about the future.
7. ___ I am free from senseless or unpleasant thoughts.
8. ___ I feel afraid to go out of my house alone.
9. ___ I feel relaxed and in control of myself.
10. ___ I have spells of terror or panic.
11. ___ I feel afraid in open spaces or in the streets.
12. ___ I feel afraid I will faint in public.
13. ___ I am comfortable traveling on buses, subways or trains.
14. ___ I feel nervousness or shakiness inside.
15. ___ I feel comfortable in crowds, such as shopping or at a movie.
16. ___ I feel comfortable when I am left alone.
17. ___ I feel afraid without good reason.
18. ___ Due to my fears, I unreasonably avoid certain animals, objects or situations.
19. ___ I get upset easily or feel panicky unexpectedly.
20. ___ My hands, arms or legs shake or tremble.
21. ___ Due to my fears, I avoid social situations, whenever possible.
22. ___ I experience sudden attacks of panic which catch me by surprise.
23. ___ I feel generally anxious.
24. ___ I am bothered by dizzy spells.
25. ___ Due to my fears, I avoid being alone, whenever possible.

1, 6, 7, 9, 13, 15, 16

FIGURE 7.8 Clinical Anxiety Scale.

INDEX OF ALCOHOL INVOLVEMENT (IAI)

Name: _____ Today's Date: _____

This questionnaire is designed to measure your use of alcohol. It is not a test, so there are no right or wrong answers. Answer each item as carefully and as accurately as you can by placing a number beside each one as follows.

1 = Never
2 = Very rarely
3 = A little of the time
4 = Some of the time
5 = A good part of the time
6 = Most of the time
7 = Always

1. ___ When I have a drink with friends, I usually drink more than they do.
2. ___ My family or friends tell me I drink too much.
3. ___ I feel that I drink too much alcohol.
4. ___ After I've had one or two drinks, it is difficult for me to stop drinking.
5. ___ When I am drinking, I have three or fewer drinks.
6. ___ I feel guilty about what happened when I have been drinking.
7. ___ When I go drinking, I get into fights.
8. ___ My drinking causes problems with my family or friends.
9. ___ My drinking causes problems with my work.
10. ___ After I have been drinking, I cannot remember things that happened when I think about them the next day.
11. ___ After I have been drinking, I get the shakes.
12. ___ My friends think I have a drinking problem.
13. ___ I drink to calm my nerves or make me feel better.
14. ___ I drink when I am alone.
15. ___ I drink until I go to sleep or pass out.
16. ___ My drinking interferes with obligations to my family or friends.
17. ___ I have one or more drinks when things are not going well for me.
18. ___ It is hard for me to stop drinking when I want to.
19. ___ I have one or more drinks before noon.
20. ___ My friends think my level of drinking is acceptable.
21. ___ I get mean and angry when I drink.
22. ___ My friends avoid me when I am drinking.
23. ___ I avoid drinking to excess.
24. ___ My personal life gets very troublesome when I drink.
25. ___ I drink 3 to 4 times a week.

5, 20, 23.

FIGURE 7.9   Index of Alcohol Involvement.

INDEX OF PEER RELATIONS (IPR)

Name: _____ Today's Date: _____

PEER GROUP _____

This questionnaire is designed to measure the way you feel about the people you work, play, or associate with most of the time; your peer group. It is not a test, so there are no right or wrong answers. Place the name of your peer group at the top of the page in the space provided. Then answer each item as carefully and as accurately as you can by placing a number beside each one as follows.

    1 = None of the time
    2 = Very rarely
    3 = A little of the time
    4 = Some of the time
    5 = A good part of the time
    6 = Most of the time
    7 = All of the time

---

1. ___ I get along very well with my peers.
2. ___ My peers act like they don't care about me.
3. ___ My peers treat me badly.
4. ___ My peers really seem to respect me.
5. ___ I don't feel like am "part of the group."
6. ___ My peers are a bunch of snobs.
7. ___ My peers understand me.
8. ___ My peers seem to like me very much.
9. ___ I really feel "left out" of my peer group.
10. ___ I hate my present peer group.
11. ___ My peers seem to like having me around.
12. ___ I really like my present peer group.
13. ___ I really feel like I am disliked by my peers.
14. ___ I wish I had a different peer group.
15. ___ My peers are very nice to me.
16. ___ My peers seem to look up to me.
17. ___ My peers think I am important to them.
18. ___ My peers are a real source of pleasure to me.
19. ___ My peers don't seem to even notice me.
20. ___ I wish I were not part of this peer group.
21. ___ My peers regard my ideas and opinions very highly.
22. ___ I feel like I am an important member of my peer group.
23. ___ I can't stand to be around my peer group.
24. ___ My peers seem to look down on me.
25. ___ My peers really do not interest me.

1, 4, 7, 8, 11, 12, 15, 16, 17, 18, 21, 22.

FIGURE 7.10   Index of Peer Relations.

INDEX OF MARITAL SATISFACTION (IMS)

Name: _____ Today's Date: _____

This questionnaire is designed to measure the degree of satisfaction you have with your present marriage. It is not a test, so there are no right or wrong answers. Answer each item as carefully and as accurately as you can by placing a number beside each one as follows.

1 = None of the time
2 = Very rarely
3 = A little of the time
4 = Some of the time
5 = A good part of the time
6 = Most of the time
7 = All of the time

1. ___ My partner is affectionate enough.
2. ___ My partner treats me badly.
3. ___ My partner really cares for me.
4. ___ I feel that I would not choose the same partner if I had it to do over again.
5. ___ I feel that I can trust my partner.
6. ___ I feel that our relationship is breaking up.
7. ___ My partner really doesn't understand me.
8. ___ I feel that our relationship is a good one.
9. ___ Ours is a very happy relationship.
10. ___ Our life together is dull.
11. ___ We have a lot of fun together.
12. ___ My partner does not confide in me.
13. ___ Ours is a very close relationship.
14. ___ I feel that I cannot rely on my partner.
15. ___ I feel that we do not have enough interests in common.
16. ___ We manage arguments and disagreements very well.
17. ___ We do a good job of managing our finances.
18. ___ I feel that I should never have married my partner.
19. ___ My partner and I get along very well together.
20. ___ Our relationship is very stable.
21. ___ My partner is a real comfort to me.
22. ___ I feel that I no longer care for my partner.
23. ___ I feel that the future looks bright for our relationship.
24. ___ I feel that our relationship is empty.
25. ___ I feel there is no excitement in our relationship.

1, 3, 5, 8, 9, 11, 13, 16, 17, 19, 20, 21, 23.

FIGURE 7.11 Index of Marital Satisfaction.

INDEX OF SEXUAL SATISFACTION (ISS)

Name: _____   Today's Date: _____

This questionnaire is designed to measure the degree of satisfaction you have in the sexual relationship with your partner. It is not a test, so there are no right or wrong answers. Answer each item as carefully and as accurately as you can by placing a number beside each one as follows.

1 = None of the time
2 = Very rarely
3 = A little of the time
4 = Some of the time
5 = A good part of the time
6 = Most of the time
7 = All of the time

1. ___ I feel that my partner enjoys our sex life.
2. ___ Our sex life is very exciting.
3. ___ Sex is fun for my partner and me.
4. ___ Sex with my partner has become a chore for me.
5. ___ I feel that our sex is dirty and disgusting.
6. ___ Our sex life is monotonous.
7. ___ When we have sex it is too rushed and hurriedly completed.
8. ___ I feel that my sex life is lacking in quality.
9. ___ My partner is sexually very exciting.
10. ___ I enjoy the sex techniques that my partner likes or uses.
11. ___ I feel that my partner wants too much sex from me.
12. ___ I think that our sex is wonderful.
13. ___ My partner dwells on sex too much.
14. ___ I try to avoid sexual contact with my partner.
15. ___ My partner is too rough or brutal when we have sex.
16. ___ My partner is a wonderful sex mate.
17. ___ I feel that sex is a normal function of our relationship.
18. ___ My partner does not want sex when I do.
19. ___ I feel that our sex life really adds a lot to our relationship.
20. ___ My partner seems to avoid sexual contact with me.
21. ___ It is easy for me to get sexually excited by my partner.
22. ___ I feel that my partner is sexually pleased with me.
23. ___ My partner is very sensitive to my sexual needs and desires.
24. ___ My partner does not satisfy me sexually.
25. ___ I feel that my sex life is boring.

1, 2, 3, 9, 10, 12, 16, 17, 19, 21, 22, 23.

FIGURE 7.12 Index of Sexual Satisfaction.

PARTNER ABUSE SCALE: Non-physical (PASNP)

Name: _____ Today's Date: _____

This questionnaire is designed to measure the non-physical abuse you have experienced in your relationship with your partner. It is not a test, so there are no right or wrong answers. Answer each item as carefully and as accurately as you can by placing a number beside each one as follows:

1 = None of the time
2 = Very rarely
3 = A little of the time
4 = Some of the time
5 = A good part of the time
6 = Most of the time
7 = All of the time

1. ___ My partner belittles me.
2. ___ My partner demands obedience to his or her whims.
3. ___ My partner becomes surly and angry if I say he or she is drinking too much.
4. ___ My partner demands that I perform sex acts that I do not enjoy or like.
5. ___ My partner becomes very upset if my work is not done when he or she thinks it should be.
6. ___ My partner does not want me to have any male friends.
7. ___ My partner tells me I am ugly and unattractive.
8. ___ My partner tells me I couldn't manage or take care of myself without him or her.
9. ___ My partner acts like I am his or her personal servant.
10. ___ My partner insults or shames me in front of others.
11. ___ My partner becomes very angry if I disagree with his or her point of view.
12. ___ My partner is stingy in giving me money.
13. ___ My partner belittles me intellectually.
14. ___ My partner demands that I stay home.
15. ___ My partner feels that I should not work or go to school.
16. ___ My partner does not want me to socialize with my female friends.
17. ___ My partner demands sex whether I want it or not.
18. ___ My partner screams and yells at me.
19. ___ My partner shouts and screams at me when he or she drinks.
20. ___ My partner orders me around.
21. ___ My partner has no respect for my feelings.
22. ___ My partner acts like a bully towards me.
23. ___ My partner frightens me.
24. ___ My partner treats me like a dunce.
25. ___ My partner is surly and rude to me.

FIGURE 7.13   Partner Abuse Scale: Non-physical.

PARTNER ABUSE SCALE: Physical (PASPH)

Name: _____   Today's Date: _____

This questionnaire is designed to measure the physical abuse you have experienced in your relationship with your partner. It is not a test, so there are no right or wrong answers. Answer each item as carefully and as accurately as you can by placing a number beside each one as follows:

1 = None of the time
2 = Very rarely
3 = A little of the time
4 = Some of the time
5 = A good part of the time
6 = Most of the time
7 = All of the time

1. ___ My partner physically forces me to have sex.
2. ___ My partner pushes and shoves me around violently.
3. ___ My partner hits and punches my arms and body.
4. ___ My partner threatens me with a weapon.
5. ___ My partner beats me so hard I must seek medical help.
6. ___ My partner slaps me around my face and head.
7. ___ My partner beats me when he or she drinks.
8. ___ My partner makes me afraid for my life.
9. ___ My partner physically throws me around the room.
10. ___ My partner hits and punches my face and head.
11. ___ My partner beats me in the face so badly that I am ashamed to be seen in public.
12. ___ My partner acts like he or she would like to kill me.
13. ___ My partner threatens to cut or stab me with a knife or other sharp object.
14. ___ My partner tries to choke or strangle me.
15. ___ My partner knocks me down and then kicks or stomps me.
16. ___ My partner twists my fingers, arms or legs.
17. ___ My partner throws dangerous objects at me.
18. ___ My partner bites or scratches me so badly that I bleed or have bruises.
19. ___ My partner violently pinches or twists my skin.
20. ___ My partner badly hurts me while we are having sex.
21. ___ My partner injures my breasts or genitals.
22. ___ My partner tries to suffocate me with pillows, towels or other objects.
23. ___ My partner pokes or jabs me with pointed objects.
24. ___ My partner has broken one or more my bones.
25. ___ My partner kicks my face and head.

FIGURE 7.14   Partner Abuse Scale: Physical.

NON-PHYSICAL ABUSE
OF PARTNER SCALE (NPAPS)

Name: _____ Today's Date: _____

This questionnaire is designed to measure the non-physical abuse you have delivered upon your partner. It is not a test, so there are no right or wrong answers. Answer each item as carefully and as accurately as you can by placing a number beside each one as follows.

    1 = Never
    2 = Very rarely
    3 = A little of the time
    4 = Some of the time
    5 = A good part of the time
    6 = Very frequently
    7 = All of the time

1. ___ I make fun of my partner's ability to do things.
2. ___ I expect my partner to obey.
3. ___ I become very upset and angry if my partner says that I have been drinking too much.
4. ___ I demand my partner to perform sex acts that he or she does not enjoy or like.
5. ___ I become very upset if my partner's work is not done when I think it should be.
6. ___ I don't want my partner to have any male friends.
7. ___ I tell my partner he or she is ugly and unattractive.
8. ___ I tell my partner that he or she really couldn't manage without me.
9. ___ I expect my partner to hop to it when I give him or her an order.
10. ___ I insult or shame my partner in front of others.
11. ___ I become angry if my partner disagrees with my point of view.
12. ___ I carefully control the money I give my partner.
13. ___ I tell my partner that he or she is dumb or stupid.
14. ___ I demand that my partner stay home.
15. ___ I don't want my partner to work or go to school.
16. ___ I don't want my partner socializing with his or her female friends.
17. ___ I demand sex whether my partner wants it or not.
18. ___ I scream and yell at my partner.
19. ___ I shout and scream at my partner when I'm drinking.
20. ___ I order my partner around.
21. ___ I have no respect for my partner's feelings.
22. ___ I act like a bully towards my partner.
23. ___ I frighten my partner.
24. ___ I treat my partner like he or she is a dimwit.
25. ___ I'm rude to my partner.

Copyright © 1992, James W. Garner & Walter W. Hudson

Illegal to Photocopy or Otherwise Reproduce

FIGURE 7.15   Non-Physical Abuse of Partner Scale.

PHYSICAL ABUSE OF PARTNER SCALE (PAPS)

Name: _____ Today's Date: _____

This questionnaire is designed to measure the physical abuse you have delivered upon your partner. It is not a test, so there are no right or wrong answers. Answer each item as carefully and as accurately as you can by placing a number beside each one as follows.

1 = Never
2 = Very rarely
3 = A little of the time
4 = Some of the time
5 = A good part of the time
6 = Very frequently
7 = All of the time

1. ___ I physically force my partner to have sex.
2. ___ I push and shove my partner around violently.
3. ___ I hit and punch my partner's arms and body.
4. ___ I threaten my partner with a weapon.
5. ___ I beat my partner so hard he or she must seek medical help.
6. ___ I slap my partner around his or her face and head.
7. ___ I beat my partner when I'm drinking.
8. ___ I make my partner afraid for his or her life.
9. ___ I physically throw my partner around the room.
10. ___ I hit and punch my partner's face and head.
11. ___ I beat my partner in the face so that he or she is ashamed to be seen in public.
12. ___ I act like I would like to kill my partner.
13. ___ I threaten to cut or stab my partner with a knife or other sharp object.
14. ___ I try to choke or strangle my partner.
15. ___ I knock my partner down and then kick or stomp him or her.
16. ___ I twist my partner's fingers, arms or legs.
17. ___ I throw dangerous objects at my partner.
18. ___ I bite or scratch my partner so badly that he or she bleeds or has bruises.
19. ___ I violently pinch or twist my partner's skin.
20. ___ I hurt my partner while we are having sex.
21. ___ I injure my partner's breasts or genitals.
22. ___ I try to suffocate my partner with pillows, towels or other objects.
23. ___ I poke or jab my partner with pointed objects.
24. ___ I have broken one or more of my partner's bones.
25. ___ I kick my partner's face and head.

FIGURE 7.16 Physical Abuse of Partner Scale.

INDEX OF PARENTAL ATTITUDES (IPA)

Name: _____ Today's Date: _____

This questionnaire is designed to measure the degree of contentment you have in your relationship with your child. It is not a test, so there are no right or wrong answers. Answer each item as carefully and as accurately as you can by placing a number beside each one as follows.

1 = None of the time
2 = Very rarely
3 = A little of the time
4 = Some of the time
5 = A good part of the time
6 = Most of the time
7 = All of the time

1. ___ My child gets on my nerves.
2. ___ I get along well with my child.
3. ___ I feel that I can really trust my child.
4. ___ I dislike my child.
5. ___ My child is well behaved.
6. ___ My child is too demanding.
7. ___ I wish I did not have this child.
8. ___ I really enjoy my child.
9. ___ I have a hard time controlling my child.
10. ___ My child interferes with my activities.
11. ___ I resent my child.
12. ___ I think my child is terrific.
13. ___ I hate my child.
14. ___ I am very patient with my child.
15. ___ I really like my child.
16. ___ I like being with my child.
17. ___ I feel like I do not love my child.
18. ___ My child is irritating.
19. ___ I feel very angry toward my child.
20. ___ I feel violent toward my child.
21. ___ I feel very proud of my child.
22. ___ I wish my child was more like others I know.
23. ___ I just do not understand my child.
24. ___ My child is a real joy to me.
25. ___ I feel ashamed of my child.

2, 3, 5, 8, 12, 14, 15, 16, 21, 24.

FIGURE 7.17 Index of Parental Attitudes.

CHILD'S ATTITUDE TOWARD MOTHER (CAM)

Name: _____ Today's Date: _____

This questionnaire is designed to measure the degree of contentment you have in your relationship with your mother. It is not a test, so there are no right or wrong answers. Answer each item as carefully and as accurately as you can by placing a number beside each one as follows.

1 = None of the time
2 = Very rarely
3 = A little of the time
4 = Some of the time
5 = A good part of the time
6 = Most of the time
7 = All of the time

1. ___ My mother gets on my nerves.
2. ___ I get along well with my mother.
3. ___ I feel that I can really trust my mother.
4. ___ I dislike my mother.
5. ___ My mother's behavior embarrasses me.
6. ___ My mother is too demanding.
7. ___ I wish I had a different mother.
8. ___ I really enjoy my mother.
9. ___ My mother puts too many limits on me.
10. ___ My mother interferes with my activities.
11. ___ I resent my mother.
12. ___ I think my mother is terrific.
13. ___ I hate my mother.
14. ___ My mother is very patient with me.
15. ___ I really like my mother.
16. ___ I like being with my mother.
17. ___ I feel like I do not love my mother.
18. ___ My mother is very irritating.
19. ___ I feel very angry toward my mother.
20. ___ I feel violent toward my mother.
21. ___ I feel proud of my mother.
22. ___ I wish my mother was more like others I know.
23. ___ My mother does not understand me.
24. ___ I can really depend on my mother.
25. ___ I feel ashamed of my mother.

2, 3, 8, 12, 14, 15, 16, 21, 24.

FIGURE 7.18   Child's Attitude toward Mother.

CHILD'S ATTITUDE TOWARD FATHER (CAF)

Name: _____ Today's Date: _____

This questionnaire is designed to measure the degree of contentment you have in your relationship with your father. It is not a test, so there are no right or wrong answers. Answer each item as carefully and as accurately as you can by placing a number beside each one as follows.

        1 = None of the time
        2 = Very rarely
        3 = A little of the time
        4 = Some of the time
        5 = A good part of the time
        6 = Most of the time
        7 = All of the time

1. ___ My father gets on my nerves.
2. ___ I get along well with my father.
3. ___ I feel that I can really trust my father.
4. ___ I dislike my father.
5. ___ My father's behavior embarrasses me.
6. ___ My father is too demanding.
7. ___ I wish I had a different father.
8. ___ I really enjoy my father.
9. ___ My father puts too many limits on me.
10. ___ My father interferes with my activities.
11. ___ I resent my father.
12. ___ I think my father is terrific.
13. ___ I hate my father.
14. ___ My father is very patient with me.
15. ___ I really like my father.
16. ___ I like being with my father.
17. ___ I feel like I do not love my father.
18. ___ My father is very irritating.
19. ___ I feel very angry toward my father.
20. ___ I feel violent toward my father.
21. ___ I feel proud of my father.
22. ___ I wish my father was more like others I know.
23. ___ My father does not understand me.
24. ___ I can really depend on my father.
25. ___ I feel ashamed of my father.

2, 3, & 12, 14, 15, 16, 21, 24.

FIGURE 7.19   Child's Attitude toward Father.

INDEX OF BROTHER RELATIONS (IBR)

Name: _____ Today's Date: _____

This questionnaire is designed to measure the way you feel about your brother. It is not a test, so there are no right or wrong answers. Answer each item as carefully and as accurately as you can by placing a number beside each one as follows.

> 1 = None of the time
> 2 = Very rarely
> 3 = A little of the time
> 4 = Some of the time
> 5 = A good part of the time
> 6 = Most of the time
> 7 = All of the time

1. ___ I get along very well with my brother.
2. ___ My brother acts like he doesn't care about me.
3. ___ My brother treats me badly.
4. ___ My brother really seems to respect me.
5. ___ I can really trust my brother.
6. ___ My brother seems to dislike me.
7. ___ My brother really understands me.
8. ___ My brother seems to like me very much.
9. ___ My brother and I get along well together.
10. ___ I hate my brother.
11. ___ My brother seems to like having me around.
12. ___ I really like my brother.
13. ___ I really feel that I am disliked by my brother.
14. ___ I wish I had a different brother.
15. ___ My brother is very nice to me.
16. ___ My brother seems to respect me.
17. ___ My brother thinks I am important to him.
18. ___ My brother is a real source of pleasure to me.
19. ___ My brother doesn't seem to even notice me.
20. ___ I wish my brother was dead.
21. ___ My brother regards my ideas and opinions very highly.
22. ___ My brother is a real "jerk."
23. ___ I can't stand to be around my brother.
24. ___ My brother seems to look down on me.
25. ___ I enjoy being with my brother.

1, 4, 5, 7, 8, 9, 11, 12, 15, 16, 17, 18, 21, 25.

FIGURE 7.20 Index of Brother Relations.

INDEX OF SISTER RELATIONS (ISR)

Name: _____ Today's Date: _____

This questionnaire is designed to measure the way you feel about your sister. It is not a test, so there are no right or wrong answers. Answer each item as carefully and as accurately as you can by placing a number beside each one as follows.

1 = None of the above
2 = Very rarely
3 = A little of the time
4 = Some of the time
5 = A good part of the time
6 = Most of the time
7 = All of the time

1. ___ I get along very well with my sister.
2. ___ My sister acts like she doesn't care about me.
3. ___ My sister treats me badly.
4. ___ My sister really seems to respect me.
5. ___ I can really trust my sister.
6. ___ My sister seems to dislike me.
7. ___ My sister really understands me.
8. ___ My sister seems to like me very much.
9. ___ My sister and I get along well together.
10. ___ I hate my sister.
11. ___ My sister seems to like having me around.
12. ___ I really like my sister.
13. ___ I really feel that I am disliked by my sister.
14. ___ I wish I had a different sister.
15. ___ My sister is very nice to me.
16. ___ My sister seems to respect me.
17. ___ My sister thinks I am important to her.
18. ___ My sister is a real source of pleasure to me.
19. ___ My sister doesn't seem to even notice me.
20. ___ I wish my sister was dead.
21. ___ My sister regards my ideas and opinions very highly.
22. ___ My sister is a real "jerk."
23. ___ I can't stand to be around my sister.
24. ___ My sister seems to look down on me.
25. ___ I enjoy being with my sister.

1, 4, 5, 7, 8, 9, 11, 12, 15, 16, 17, 18, 21, 25.

FIGURE 7.21 Index of Sister Relations.

INDEX OF FAMILY RELATIONS (IFR)

Name: _____ Today's Date: _____

This questionnaire is designed to measure the way you feel about your family as a whole. It is not a test, so there are no right or wrong answers. Answer each item as carefully and as accurately as you can by placing a number beside each one as follows.

1 = None of the time
2 = Very rarely
3 = A little of the time
4 = Some of the time
5 = A good part of the time
6 = Most of the time
7 = All of the time

1. ___ The members of my family really care about each other.
2. ___ I think my family is terrific.
3. ___ My family gets on my nerves.
4. ___ I really enjoy my family.
5. ___ I can really depend on my family.
6. ___ I really do not care to be around my family.
7. ___ I wish I was not part of this family.
8. ___ I get along well with my family.
9. ___ Members of my family argue too much.
10. ___ There is no sense of closeness in my family.
11. ___ I feel like a stranger in my family.
12. ___ My family does not understand me.
13. ___ There is too much hatred in my family.
14. ___ Members of my family are really good to one another.
15. ___ My family is well respected by those who know us.
16. ___ There seems to be a lot of friction in my family.
17. ___ There is a lot of love in my family.
18. ___ Member of my family get along well together.
19. ___ Life in my family is generally unpleasant.
20. ___ My family is a great joy to me.
21. ___ I feel proud of my family.
22. ___ Other families seem to get along better than ours.
23. ___ My family is a real source of comfort to me.
24. ___ I feel left out of my family.
25. ___ My family is an unhappy one.

1, 2, 4, 5, 8, 14, 15, 17, 18, 20, 21, 23.

FIGURE 7.22   Index of Family Relations.

face, concurrent, and construct validity. They have good ability to discriminate between people known or admitting to having problems and people who claim or are known not to have problems in each area. In other words, the scales appear to measure what they're intended to measure.

Scoring. For most of the WAS package clients are asked to rate each item on a 7-point scale ranging from 1, "none of the time," to 7, "all of the time." (For some of the scales a 5-point scale is used.) For each scale the lowest possible total score is 0, the highest is 100, and higher scores indicate greater magnitude of a problem.

A distinct advantage of these scales is that they are all scored in the same way. To minimize response set bias, all of the scales contain some "reverse-scored" items, and the first step in scoring each of these questionnaires is to reverse-score these items (the particular item numbers to be reverse-scored are listed at the bottom of each scale). For example, for a questionnaire that uses a 7-point scale, a score of 7 is rescored as 1, a score of 6 is rescored as 2, a score of 5 is rescored as 3, a score of 4 is left unchanged, a score of 3 is rescored as 5, a score of 2 is rescored as 6, and a score of 1 is rescored as 7. The easiest way to do this is to first circle the reverse-scored item responses, cross out the original responses, and either use the rescoring method described earlier in this paragraph or use the following formula to get the reverse-scored item response (note that this formula produces the same results as the reverse-scoring process described above and also can be used to reverse-score any items on any questionnaires) (Hudson, 1992):

$$Y = K + 1 - X$$

where: Y = the reverse-scored item response
K = the largest possible value for an item response (i.e., 5 or 7)
X = the original item response

Thus, if an item to be reverse-scored is given a 5 by a client and K = 7, then Y = 7 + 1 − 5 = 3.

After reverse-scoring the appropriate items for a scale, the total score for that scale is computed by using the following formula (Hudson & Faul, 1998):

$$S = \frac{(\text{Sum } [Y] - N)(100)}{(N)(K - 1)}$$

where: S = the total score
Sum (Y) = the sum of the item responses (i.e., add all item responses after reverse-scoring)
N = the number of items that were properly completed
K = the largest possible value for an item response (i.e., 5 or 7)

In other words, add up all scores after reverse-scoring, subtract the number of items properly completed, multiply that by 100, and divide that by the number of items properly completed multiplied by the largest possible value for an item response minus 1.

Any item that is left blank or given a score outside the scoring range is assigned a score of 0. Incidentally, if your client does happen to omit some items, you should check with the client to see why this happened. It may be that the client did not understand the item. It also could be that the client is particularly sensitive about, or has a problem dealing with, the issue raised by that question. Indeed, these omissions could serve as a clue to other problems that could help you in developing a more well-rounded intervention program. However, if the client completes fewer than 80% of the items for a scale, we suggest that particular scale not be used, since its validity might be affected.

As an example, suppose on the Generalized Contentment Scale (a measure of the degree of nonpsychotic depression, with higher scores indicating greater depression) a client reports the scores listed in Table 7.3.

To score the scales, follow these steps:

1. *Reverse-score all the items noted at the bottom of each scale.* For this scale, reverse-score items 5, 8, 9, 11, 12, 13, 15, 16, 21, 22, 23, 24. This is done in the third column of the table.

2. *Add up all the items you reverse-scored.* The total at the bottom of the third column is 48.

3. *Add up all the items you did not reverse score.* In the second column, these scores (with the items you reverse-scored deleted) total 33.
4. *Add these two sums together* $(48 + 33) = 81$. This completes the first step, the sum of all scores after reverse-scoring.
5. *Subtract the number of properly completed items, which in this case is 25.* $(81 - 25) = 56$.
6. *Multiply this figure by 100* $(100 \times 56 = 5600)$.
7. *Divide this number by the number of items completed times 6 (if the items are answered on a 7-point scale and 4 if they are answered on a 5-point scale.)*

$$\frac{5600}{(25)(6)} = \frac{5600}{150} = 37.3, \text{ or } 37$$

8. The final number 37 is the client's score on the scale (in this case, the GCS or depression scale) *developed to range from 0 to 100.*

Table 7.3 Example of Generalized Contentment Scale.

Items	Score	Reverse Score $(K - Y + 1)$	
1	3		
2	1		
3	3		
4	4		
⑤	6̸	2	$(7 - 6 + 1)$
6	5		
7	1		
⑧	2̸	6	$(7 - 2 + 1)$
⑨	3̸	5	$(7 - 3 + 1)$
10	1		
⑪	1̸	7	$(7 - 1 + 1)$
⑫	4̸	4	$(7 - 4 + 1)$
⑬	6̸	2	$(7 - 6 + 1)$
14	2		
⑮	5̸	3	$(7 - 5 + 1)$
⑯	4̸	4	$(7 - 4 + 1)$
17	2		
18	5		
19	2		
20	2		
㉑	7̸	1	$(7 - 7 + 1)$
㉒	1̸	7	$(7 - 1 + 1)$
㉓	5̸	3	$(7 - 5 + 1)$
㉔	4̸	4	$(7 - 4 + 1)$
25	2		
	33	48	

Interpretation. On all scales of the WAS, the higher the score, the greater the magnitude of the problem. How high does a score have to be to indicate a significant problem, though? Most of the WAS questionnaires have a "clinical cutting or cutoff score" of approximately 30. The exact score varies a little depending on the particular questionnaire. The idea here is that people who score over 30 generally have been found to have problems in the area being measured, while people who score below 30 have been found not to. Therefore, the cutting score provides a rough diagnostic indicator and a useful standard against which to judge the success of an intervention.

The cutting score should be used with caution and further research is needed to completely validate it. At present it's probably best to use a score of 30 as a rough guide to the presence or absence of problems. It would be better still to consider a range of values from 25 to 35 as a gray area that indicates the cutting point regarding the possible presence or absence of a problem. This particular gray area is based on the fact that the standard error of measurement (described in Chapter 2) for these scales is approximately 5 (the exact value varies depending on the particular scale). If a score falls within this gray area ±1 SEM, it's best to get additional supporting evidence before concluding that the client does or doesn't have a significant problem in the area being assessed. Scores below 25 probably indicate the absence of a problem, and scores above 35 probably indicate the presence of a problem. However, even a score of 24 doesn't absolutely indicate the absence of a problem, and a score of 36 doesn't absolutely indicate the presence of a problem. The point is that higher scores should be seen as deserving of attention, with the goal of intervention being to reduce those scores to at least below 30.

Despite the high reliability of each scale, there will still be some degree of inaccuracy in the change indicated by these questionnaires from one administration to the next. None of these scales—or any other instrument—is perfect. The standard error of measurement gives us an estimate of the range of values in which the client's "true" score probably falls. For example, with an SEM of 5, there's a 68% chance that someone with a score of 30 would have a true score that falls between ±1 SEM of the obtained score (i.e., 25 to 35), and there's a 95% chance that someone with this score has a true score that falls between approximately ±2 SEMs of the obtained score (i.e., 20 to 40). Since the standard error of measurement for these scales is approximately 5, as a rough guide assume that changes of 5 points or fewer over repeated administrations may be a result of error, and that changes of more than 5 points in either direction probably represent real changes in the client's problem. If you want to be even more certain (i.e., 95%), assume that changes of 10 points or fewer over repeated administrations may be a result of error, and that changes of more than 10 points in either direction represent real changes in the client's problem.

While these scales are intended to be used to measure the severity, intensity, degree, or magnitude of a problem, they were not designed to determine the source or origin of the client's problem. Thus, to that extent, they don't provide all the diagnostic or assessment information that is necessary prior to beginning an intervention program. Information

about the nature, source, origin, or type of problem should be obtained from the client, relatives, co-workers, friends of the client, and your own assessment.

The periodic administration of the same questionnaire to marital partners or family members can provide useful information for planning and evaluating an intervention. For example, the Index of Marital Satisfaction (another WAS measure) might be administered periodically and independently to a husband and wife. Each spouse might be asked to rate his or her own satisfaction, and to estimate the partner's satisfaction. This might enhance the detection of misperceptions and facilitate communication, in addition to providing a basis for monitoring change over time. Ideally, an intervention designed to enhance communication would reduce dissatisfaction, and would increase the extent to which the husband and wife understand each other's level of satisfaction.

Figure 7.23, for example, shows a husband's self-ratings of marital dissatisfaction as measured using the Index of Marital Satisfaction (IMS) (higher scores indicate greater dissatisfaction), and his wife's estimates of his dissatisfaction. Figure 7.24 shows comparable data for

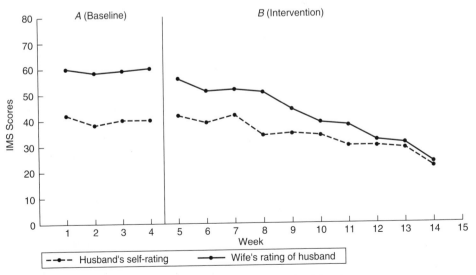

FIGURE 7.23   Index of Marital Satisfaction (IMS): husband's and wife's ratings.

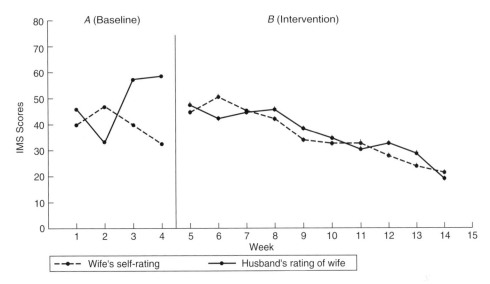

FIGURE 7.24 Index of Marital Satisfaction (IMS): wife's and husband's ratings.

the wife. Figure 7.23 shows that during baseline and intervention the wife overestimated her husband's level of dissatisfaction, although after the onset of intervention the overestimation was gradually reduced. Figure 7.24 shows that during baseline there was no relationship between the wife's self-rating of satisfaction and her husband's estimates of her satisfaction, although after the onset of intervention there was a high degree of agreement between the self-ratings and the husband's estimates. Finally, both Figure 7.23 and 7.24 indicate that the degree of dissatisfaction for both partners was steadily reduced over the course of intervention.

There are some precautions in using the WAS questionnaires. The scales are not recommended for children under the age of 12. Also, they should not be self-administered to clients with poor literacy skills. Similarly, all of the scales should be used with extreme caution with any clients who may need to demonstrate positive change in order to qualify for a change in legal status–for example, prison inmates or patients in mental hospitals seeking release. You have to discuss their use even more carefully with such clients and attempt to evaluate whether the data are reasonably accurate be-

fore you can be relatively certain of their clinical or evaluation value in such situations.

Some Limitations of Standardized Self-Report Questionnaires

Standardized client self-report questionnaires, whether administered by computer or done using paper and pencil, have some potential limitations and disadvantages. First, the client, perhaps out of a long-term habit, may not be aware of the occurrence of the target, and even your best efforts to help the client become aware (perhaps through role-playing the target to increase awareness) may not succeed. Second, clients may not be able to provide the needed information because they are too disabled or too young. Third, the client may simply not want to provide information, or may wittingly or unwittingly provide inaccurate information. Clients might tell you what they think you want to hear, especially when you're in a position to give or withhold valued social sanctions and the client's reports might influence your decisions (e.g., a parent may not admit abusing a child to a child protective services worker, knowing that the worker is legally mandated to report this information).

Clients might unwittingly report more change than actually occurred to justify their investment of time, money, and effort. You may do your best to motivate the client, but that also may fail.

Finally, as we noted in Chapter 2, a client's recording of his or her own target may have a reactive effect so that the target might change during the baseline simply due to the effects of recording. However, a study by Applegate (1992) showed no reactive effect (regarding outcome or dropout) from use of standardized questionnaires. One way to handle any possible reactivity is to extend the period of time over which baseline data are collected, but this often may not be possible (we discuss reactivity in more detail in Chapter 9).

In some cases the client may be the only source of information about a target (e.g., if the target is a cognition or other private event), and the client may not want to systematically collect baseline information on the target. For example, the client may be under stress and might be impatient to initiate intervention and go about the business of changing the target. (This impatience is often shared by the practitioner.) Yet ill-prepared interventions may be doomed to failure. Thus, as part of that preparation, recording in general, and baseline recording in particular, provide some of the foundation for enhancing your potential for more effective intervention.

SOME AVAILABLE STANDARDIZED QUESTIONNAIRES FOR PRACTITIONERS

There are a number of standardized questionnaires that can be completed by practitioners to assess client functioning. Examples are shown in Table 7.4, along with a brief description of each measure, the original reference for each measure, and information about current review(s) of the measure where available.

There are potential advantages and disadvantages to practitioner reports, just as there are with self-reports or any other type of reports (e.g., Bostwick & Bostwick, 1987; Ciarlo et al., 1986; Lambert et al., 1986; Newman, 1983;

Reid & Smith, 1989; Wittenborn, 1984). Practitioner reports can be valuable because the practitioner is in a unique position to observe and understand clients because of his or her professional training and experience, familiarity with the clients, and the ease of recording unobtrusively. However, the validity of practitioner reports may vary with how the practitioner perceives that the information will be used (e.g., by the practitioner or for administrative use). The data may be biased because of the practitioner's desire to succeed, or because of the need to justify the time and effort expended with a client. In addition, the practitioner might not always be present when the problem occurs, since most problems obviously don't occur only or mainly during office or home visits. Finally, personal biases might influence a practitioner's assessment of some types of clients (e.g., clients of lower socioeconomic status, clients of a different race or cultural background, clients with a different sexual orientation).

Most standardized questionnaires, whether they are used by clients, practitioners, or relevant others, contain multiple items that are combined into a total score or subscale scores to measure a particular concept. There are, though, several single-item standardized questionnaires developed for practitioners and independent observers that are useful for the overall assessment of client functioning. These include (a) the Global Assessment of Functioning (GAF) scale, based on Axis V of the DSM-IV (A.P.A., 2000) and shown in Figure 7.25 (there is also a variant of the GAF called the Global Assessment Scale by Endicott, Spitzer, Fleiss, & Cohen, 1975, reviewed in Ciarlo et al., 1986, p. 225, Thompson, 1989b, p. 76, and van Riezen and Segal, 1988, p. 88); (b) the Children's Global Assessment Schedule (CGAS) (Bird, Canino, Rubio-Stipeo, & Ribera, 1987; Shaffer et al., 1983), shown in Figure 7.26 and reviewed in Thompson (1989b, p. 274); and (c) the Global Assessment–Geriatric Subjects (GAGS) (van Riezen & Segal, 1988, p. 91), shown in Figure 7.27.

Global single-item ratings such as those provided by the GAF, CGAS, and the GAGS have a number of advantages (Ciarlo et al., 1986; Kazdin, 1992). They allow practitioners

Table 7.4   Examples of standardized questionnaires for practitioners.

- *Montgomery-Asberg Depression Rating Scale (MADS):* This 10-item scale yields a total score that measures depression. It is a subscale of the Comprehensive Psychiatric Rating Scale (CPRS), described below. The MADS was developed for completion by a psychiatrist or other appropriately trained mental health professional upon completion of a clinical interview with a client. It is reproduced in the original Montgomery and Asberg (1979) article, reviewed and the items listed in van Riezen and Segal (1988, p. 130), and reviewed in Thompson (1989b, p. 98).
  Montgomery, S. A., & Asberg, M. (1979). A new depression scale designed to be sensitive to change. *British Journal of Psychiatry, 134,* 382–389.

- *Scale for Suicide Ideation (SSI):* This 19-item scale yields a total score that measures the intensity of suicidal intent. It was developed for use by the mental health professional upon completion of a clinical interview with a client. The items are listed in the original Beck, Kovacs, and Weissman (1979) article, and it is reviewed in Thompson (1989b, p. 198).
  Beck, A. T., Kovacs, M., & Weissman, A. (1979). Assessment of suicidal intention: The Scale for Suicide Ideation. *Journal of Consulting and Clinical Psychology, 47,* 343–352.

- *Hamilton Anxiety Scale (HAS):* This 14-item scale yields a total score that measures overall anxiety, and subscale scores that measure the following specific dimensions of this concept: (a) "somatic" anxiety and (b) "psychic" anxiety. It was developed for use by a trained mental health professional upon completion of a clinical interview with a client. It is reviewed and the items listed in van Riezan and Segal (1988, p. 229), and it is reviewed in Thompson (1989b, p. 129).
  Hamilton, M. (1959). The assessment of anxiety states by rating. *British Journal of Medical Psychology, 32,* 50–55.

- *Comprehensive Psychiatric Rating Scale (CPRS):* This 65-item scale yields a total score that measures global psychiatric symptom severity, and subscale scores that measure depressive and schizophrenia symptoms (the depression subscale is the Montgomery-Asberg Depression Rating Scale described above). It was developed for use by a psychiatrist or other appropriately trained mental health professional upon completion of a clinical interview with a client. It is reviewed and the items listed in van Riezen and Segal (1988, p. 19).
  Montgomery, S., Perris, C., Schalling, D., & Sedvall, G. (1978). A comprehensive psychopathological rating scale. *Acta Psychiatrica Scandinavica, Supplement 272.*

- *Brief Psychiatric Rating Scale (BPRS):* This 18-item scale yields a total score that measures global psychiatric symptom severity, and subscale scores that measure the following specific dimensions: (a) "anxious depression," (b) "thinking disturbance," (c) "withdrawal-retardation," (d) "hostile suspiciousness," and (e) "tension-excitement." It was developed for use by a psychiatrist or other appropriately trained mental health professional upon completion of a clinical interview with a client. It is reproduced in Hargreaves, Attkisson, and Ochberg (1977, p. 286), reviewed and the items listed in van Riezen and Segal (1988, p. 17), and reviewed in Thompson (1989b, p. 66) and Ciarlo, Brown, Edwards, Kiresuk, and Newman (1986, p. 106).
  Overall, J. E., & Gorham, D. R. (1962). The Brief Psychiatric Rating Scale. *Psychological Reports, 10,* 799–812.

- *Nurse's Brief Psychiatric Rating Scale (N-BPRS):* This is a 26-item adaptation of the Brief Psychiatric Rating Scale that yields a total score that measures global psychiatric symptom severity. It was developed for use by nurses and ward aides to rate psychiatric inpatients. It is reviewed and the items listed in van Riezen and Segal (1988, p. 45).

- *Nurse's Assessment of Global Symptomatology—Depression (NAGS-D):* This 20-item questionnaire yields a total score that measures depression. It was developed for use by nurses to measure the depression of inpatients. It is reviewed and the items listed in van Riezen and Segal (1988, p. 143).
  Burdock, E. I., Hakerem, G., Hardesty, A. S., & Zubin, J. (1960). A ward behavior rating scale for mental hospital patients. *Journal of Clinical Psychology, 16,* 246–247.
  Raskin, A., Schulterbrandt, J. G., Reatig, N., & McKeon, J. J. (1969). Replication of factors of psycho-pathology in interview, ward behavior, and self-report ratings of hospitalized depressives. *Journal of Nervous and Mental Diseases, 148,* 87–98.

- *MACC Behavioral Adjustment Scale:* This 16-item scale yields a total score that measures the severity of social adjustment problems in areas where schizophrenics often have difficulties, and subscale scores that measure the following specific dimensions of this concept: (a) mood, (b) cooperation, (c) communication, and (d) social contact. It was developed for use by someone familiar with the client, including practitioners and relevant others. It is reviewed and the items listed in van Riezen and Segal (1988, p. 300).
  Ellsworth, R. B. (1971). *The MACC Behavioral Adjustment Scale Manual.* Los Angeles, CA: Western Psychological Services.
  Lyerly, S. B. (1973). *Handbook of psychiatric rating scales* (2nd ed.). Rockville, MD: National Institute of Mental Health.

(continued)

Table 7.4   (continued)

- *Community Adjustment Scale (CAS):* This 38-item scale yields a total score that measures social functioning of noninstitutionalized elderly clients, and subscale scores that measure the following specific dimensions of this concept: (a) "dependent-confusion," (b) "agitation-depression," (c) "friendship skills," (d) "unacceptable behavior," (e) "organization-participation," and (f) "employment." It was developed for use by social workers or by a client's relatives. It is reviewed and the items listed in van Riezen and Segal (1988, p. 415).

  Ellsworth, R. B., Foster, L., Childers, B., Arthur, G., & Kroeker, D. (1968). Hospital and community adjustment as perceived by psychiatric patients, their families and staff. *Journal of Consulting and Clinical Psychology Monograph, 32,* 1–41.

- *London Psychogeriatric Rating Scale (LPRS):* This 36-item scale yields a total score that measures impairment in the elderly, and subscale scores that measure the following specific dimensions of this concept: (a) mental disorganization, (b) physical disability, (c) socially irritating behavior, and (d) social disengagement. It is reviewed and the items listed in van Riezen and Segal (1988, p. 403).

  Hersch, E. L., Kalman, M. A., & Csapo, K. G. *London Psychogeriatric Rating Scale Manual.* Department of Psychology, London Psychiatric Hospital, POB 2532 Terminal A, London, Ontario, N6A 4HI, Canada.

- *Family Risk Scales (FRS):* This 26-item scale yields a total score that measures a child's risk of entering foster care, and subscale scores that measure the following specific dimensions of this concept: (a) "parent-centered risk," (b) "child-centered risk," and (c) "economic risk." It was developed for completion by a service provider, usually a social worker. It is reproduced in the original Magura, Moses, and Jones (1987) monograph.

  Magura, S., Moses, B. S., & Jones, M. A. (1987). *Assessing risk and measuring change in families: The Family Risk Scales.* Washington, DC: Child Welfare League of America.

- *Session Evaluation Questionnaire (SEQ):* This 24-item questionnaire is a measure of the impact of a particular psychotherapy session. It yields subscale scores that measure the following dimensions of session impact: (a) "depth" (power, value), (b) "smoothness" (comfort, safety), (c) "positive mood," and (d) "arousal." It was developed for use by practitioners and clients subsequent to a psychotherapy session, or by independent evaluators based on a recording of a psychotherapy session.

  Stiles, W. B. (1980). Measurement of the impact of psychotherapy sessions. *Journal of Consulting and Clinical Psychology, 48,* 176–185.

  Dill-Standiford, T. J., Stiles, W. B., & Rorer, L. (1988). Counselor–client agreement on session impact. *Journal of Counseling Psychology, 35,* 47–55.

  Stiles, W. B., Shapiro, D. A., & Firth-Cozens, J. A. (1990). Correlations of session evaluations with treatment outcome. *British Journal of Clinical Psychology, 29,* 13–21.

---

to use their professional judgment to measure client functioning in a holistic fashion; the practitioner can take all of the known relevant information into account, weigh it, and make a judgment about client functioning in its entirety. Also, they're easy to use, accessible, and relevant for use with a wide range of clients.

Professional judgment and discretion and the measurement of global functioning do have potential disadvantages (Ciarlo et al., 1986a; Kazdin, 1992). Measures of global functioning don't provide a basis for determining the degree of change in specific areas targeted for intervention. Also, the exercise of professional judgment and discretion in the measurement of global concepts allows considerable room for the introduction of idiosyncratic practitioner biases. However, the detailed an-

chors that accompany the GAS, CGAS, and the GAGS do help to reduce this problem, relative to other global measures with less detailed anchors (see Ciarlo et al., 1986, for an assessment of such measures), or those that are constructed on an individual basis such as the individualized rating scales described in Chapter 6. Indeed, there's evidence that acceptable interrater reliability can be achieved in the use of the GAS and the CGAS, but not under all circumstances, and there's support for the concurrent and construct validity of the GAS and CGAS (for an overview of the psychometric properties of the GAS see Ciarlo et al., 1986, and for the CGAS, see Thompson, 1989b). To our knowledge, psychometric information concerning the GAGS is not available.

Single-item global measures of client functioning completed by practitioners can be effi-

Global Assessment of Functioning (GAF) Scale

Consider psychological, social, and occupational functioning on a hypothetical continuum of mental health–illness. Do not include impairment in functioning due to physical (or environmental) limitations.

Code   (Note: Use intermediate codes when appropriate, e.g., 45, 68, 72.)

100   Superior functioning in a wide range of activities; life's problems never seem to get out of hand; is
| sought out by others because of his or her many positive qualities. No symptoms.
91

90   Absent or minimal symptoms (e.g., mild anxiety before an exam), good functioning in all areas,
| interested and involved in a wide range of activities, socially effective, generally satisfied with life,
81   no more than everyday problems or concerns (e.g., an occasional argument with family members).

80   If symptoms are present, they are transient and expectable reactions to psychosocial stressors (e.g.,
| difficulty concentrating after family argument); no more than light impairment in social,
71   occupational, or school functioning (e.g., temporarily falling behind in schoolwork.)

70   Some mild symptoms (e.g., depressed mood and mild insomnia) *or* some difficulty in social,
| occupational, or school functioning (e.g., occasional truancy or theft within the household), but
61   generally functioning pretty well; has some meaningful interpersonal relationships.

60   Moderate symptoms (e.g., flat affect and circumstantial speech, occasional panic attacks) *or*
| moderate difficulty in social, occupational, or school functioning (e.g., few friends, conflicts with
51   peers or co-workers).

50   Serious symptoms (e.g., suicidal ideation, severe obsessional rituals, frequent shoplifting) *or* any
| serious impairment in social, occupational, or school functioning (e.g., no friends, unable to
41   keep a job).

40   Some impairment in reality testing or communication (e.g., speech is at times illogical, obscure, or
| irrelevant) *or* major impairment in several areas, such as work or school, family relations, judgment,
31   thinking, or mood (e.g., depressed man avoids friends, neglects family, and is unable to work; child
   frequently beats up younger children, is defiant at home, and is failing at school).

30   Behavior is considerably influenced by delusions or hallucinations *or* serious impairment in
| communication or judgment (e.g., sometimes incoherent, acts grossly inappropriately, suicidal
21   preoccupation) *or* inability to function in almost all areas (e.g., stays in bed all day; no job, home,
   or friends).

20   Some danger of hurting self or others (e.g., suicide attempts without clear expectation of death;
| frequently violent; manic excitement) *or* occasionally fails to maintain minimal personal hygiene
11   (e.g., smears feces) *or* gross impairment in communication (e.g., largely incoherent or mute).

10   Persistent danger of severely hurting self or others (e.g., recurrent violence) *or* persistent inability to
| maintain minimal personal hygiene *or* serious suicide act with clear expectation of death.
1

0   Inadequate information.

FIGURE 7.25   Description of Global Assessment of Functioning Scale. (Adapted from American Psychiatric Association, 2000. Reprinted with permission.)

cient and useful in the repeated measurement of client functioning. However, they should not be used as the sole basis for measuring client outcome because of their potential for bias and the fact that they often don't provide information about specific areas targeted for intervention.

SOME AVAILABLE STANDARDIZED QUESTIONNAIRES FOR RELEVANT OTHERS

There are a number of standardized questionnaires that can be completed by relevant others

Children's Global Assessment Schedule (CGAS)

Rate the client's most impaired level of general functioning for the specified period by selecting the lowest level that describes his or her functioning on a hypothetical continuum of health–illness. Use intermediary levels (e.g., 35, 58, 62).

Rate actual functioning regardless of treatment or prognosis. The examples of behavior provided are only illustrative and are not required for a particular rating.

Specified Period: 1 mo

91–100   *Superior functioning in all areas* (at home, at school, and with peers); involved in a wide range of activities and has many interests (e.g., has hobbies or participates in extracurricular activities or belongs to an organized group such as Scouts, etc.); likeable; confident; "everyday" worries never get out of hand; doing well in school; no symptoms.

81–90   *Good functioning in all areas;* secure in family, school, and with peers; there may be transient difficulties and everyday worries that occasionally get out of hand (e.g., mild anxiety associated with an important examination, occasional "blowups" with siblings, parents, or peers).

71–80   *No more than slight impairment in functioning* at home, at school, or with peers; some disturbance of behavior or emotional distress may be present in response to life stresses (e.g., parental separations, deaths, birth of a sibling), but these are brief, and interference with functioning is transient; such children are only minimally disturbing to others and are not considered deviant by those who know them.

61–70   *Some difficulty in a single area, but generally functioning pretty well* (e.g., sporadic or isolated antisocial acts, such as occasional hooky or petty theft; consistent minor difficulties with school work; mood changes of brief duration; fears and anxieties that do not lead to gross avoidance behavior; self-doubts); has some meaningful interpersonal relationships; most people who do not know the child well would not consider him or her deviant, but those who do know him or her well might express concern.

51–60   *Variable functioning with sporadic difficulties or symptoms in several but not all social areas;* disturbance would be apparent to those who encounter the child in a dysfunctional setting or time but not to those who see the child in other settings.

41–50   *Moderate degree of interference in functioning in most social areas or severe impairment of functioning in one area,* such as might result from, for example, suicidal preoccupations and ruminations, school refusal and other forms of anxiety, obsessive rituals, major conversion symptoms, frequent anxiety attacks, poor or inappropriate social skills, frequent episodes of aggressive or other antisocial behavior, with some preservation of meaningful social relationships.

31–40   *Major impairment in functioning in several areas and unable to function in one of these areas,* i.e., disturbed at home, at school, with peers, or in society at large, e.g., persistent aggression without clear instigation; markedly withdrawn and isolated behavior due to either mood or thought disturbance; suicidal attempts with clear lethal intent; such children are likely to require special schooling and/or hospitalization or withdrawal from school (but this is not a sufficient criterion for inclusion in this category).

21–30   *Unable to function in almost all areas,* e.g., stays at home, in ward, or in bed all day without taking part in social activities or severe impairment in reality testing or serious impairment in communication (e.g., sometimes incoherent or inappropriate).

11–20   *Needs considerable supervision* to prevent hurting others or self (e.g., frequently violent, repeated suicide attempts) or to maintain personal hygiene or gross impairment in all forms of communication (e.g., severe abnormalities in verbal and gestural communication, marked social aloofness, stupor).

1–10   *Needs constant supervision* (24-hour care) due to severely aggressive or self-destructive behavior or gross impairment in reality testing, communication, cognition, affect, or personal hygiene.

FIGURE 7.26   Children's Global Assessment Schedule (CGAS). (Adapted from Bird et al., 1987.)

Global Assessment—Geriatric Subjects (GAGS)

The GAGS is a modification of the GAS to make it more suitable for use in geriatric patients. Data about sensitivity to drug treatment are not yet available.

The severity scale of the GAGS is reproduced below:

81–100   *Superior functioning*
Bright and alert, functions well, communicates excellently. No observable indications of cognitive or psychic disturbances. No complaints.

61–80   *Independent functioning*
Fairly alert and responsive, functions quite reasonably with only occasional problems in unusual situations. Normal communication, but occasionally has problems of understanding. Admits to mild loss of memory or mild psychic disturbance which only occasionally leads to problems or complaints. Neurotic symptoms which interfere, only slightly, with day to day functioning.

41–60   *Needs support and direction to function*
Reduction of cognitive competence and occasional periods of confusion. Functions with some difficulty in familiar surroundings and is clearly deficient in unusual situations. Cognitive impairment interferes with communication and daily activities, or spontaneous complaints of psychic symptoms and/or psychiatric signs/symptoms which can easily be elicited during interviewing and which interfere with functioning. Narrowing of social contacts. Can respond appropriately to instructions, able to work only in sheltered environment.

21–40   *Needs help to function*
Marked impairment of cognitive functioning, judgment and/or orientation which is clearly observable during interviewing and interferes strongly with activities of daily living, or moderate to severe psychic symptoms/signs which are clearly observable and interfere with functioning. Cannot respond to direction alone. Needs help and supervision. Communication is impaired and restricted.

0–20   *Completely dependent, unable to function*
Severe functional impairment, almost completely incapacitated. Communication severely impaired or impossible. Totally dependent, needs constant supervision.

FIGURE 7.27   Global Assessment—Geriatric Subjects (GAGS). (Adapted from van Riezen & Siegel, 1988.)

Note: Forms can be obtained from the author: Dr. H. van Riezen, Medical Unit, Scientific Development Group, Organon International B.V., Oss, The Netherlands.

to assess client functioning. Examples are shown in Table 7.5, along with a brief description of each measure, the original reference for each measure, and information about current review(s) of the measure where available.

There are many advantages to having relevant others provide information about a client (e.g., Bostwick & Bostwick, 1987; Ciarlo et al., 1986; Davidson & Davidson, 1983; Lambert et al., 1986; Reid & Smith, 1989; Wittenborn, 1984). First, the ultimate goal of our intervention efforts is to improve the way clients function in their day-to-day environment, and rel-

evant others often are in a unique position to provide information about clients' real-world functioning. Second, some interventions are interpersonally based (e.g., treatment of couples and families), and so the perspective of other involved parties is necessary to judge the success of an intervention. Third, it may be possible for others to observe the target as it "naturally" occurs, unobtrusively, without producing a reactive effect. Finally, someone in the environment may be extremely motivated to collect data because the target is especially distressing to him or her.

Table 7.5   Examples of standardized questionnaires for relevant others.

- *MACC Behavioral Adjustment Scale:* See Table 7.4.
- *Community Adjustment Scale (CAS):* See Table 7.4.
- *Physical Self-Maintenance Scale (PSMS):* This 6-item scale yields a total score that measures competence to live independently in mildly impaired elderly clients. It was developed for use by a variety of staff members (e.g., nurses). It is reproduced and reviewed in McDowell and Newell (1996) and reviewed and the items listed in van Riezen and Segal (1988, p. 424).
  Lawton, M. P., & Brody, E. M. (1969). Assessment of older people: Self-maintaining and instrumental activities of daily living. *Gerontologist, 9,* 179–186.
- *Rapid Disability Rating Scale—2 (RDRS-2):* This 18-item scale yields a total score that measures self-care independence in hospitalized or otherwise hospitalized geriatric patients. It was developed for use by nursing staff or someone familiar with the client. It is reproduced and reviewed in McDowell and Newell (1996).
  Linn, M. W., & Linn, B. S. (1982). The Rapid Disability Rating Scale—2. *Journal of the American Geriatrics Society, 30,* 378–382.
- *Nurse's Assessment of Global Symptomatology—Depression (NAGS-D):* This 20-item questionnaire yields a total score that measures depression. It was developed for use by nurses to measure the depression of inpatients. It is reviewed and the items listed in van Riezen and Segal (1988, p. 143).
  Burdock, E. I., Hakerem, G., Hardesty, A. S., & Zubin, S. (1960). A ward behavior rating scale for mental hospital patients. *Journal of Clinical Psychology, 16,* 246–247.
  Raskin, A., Schulterbrandt, J. G., Reatig, N., & McKeon, J. J. (1969). Replication of factors of psychopathology in intervention, ward behavior, and self-report ratings of hospitalized depressives. *Journal of Nervous and Mental Diseases, 148,* 87–98.
- *Social Adjustment Scale—Self-Report/Significant Other Report (SAS-SR):* This 54-item scale yields a total score that measures social adjustment, and subscale scores that measure social adjustment in the following areas: (a) work, (b) social and leisure, (c) extended family, (d) marital, (e) parental, (f) family unit, and (g) economic. It can be completed either by a client (i.e., self-report) or by a client's relevant other(s). It is reproduced in Weissman (1990a) and reviewed in Ciarlo et al. (1986).
  Weissman, M. M. (1990a). *Information on the Social Adjustment Scale—Self-report (SAS-SR).* Unpublished manuscript. Columbia University, College of Physicians and Surgeons.
  Weissman, M. M. (1990b). *Social Adjustment Scale: Reference to publications using the various versions of the scale and information on translations.* Unpublished manuscript. Columbia University, College of Physicians and Surgeons.
  Weissman, M., & Bothwell, S. (1976). Assessment of social adjustment by patient self-report. *Archives of General Psychiatry, 33,* 1111–1115.
- *Conners Parent Rating Scale—Revised (CPRS-R):* This 48-item scale yields a total score that measures conduct problems in children from 3 to 17 years old. It was developed for use by a child's parent(s). It is reviewed in Rutter, Tuma, and Lann (1988, p. 118) and Thompson (1989b, p. 285).
  Goyette, C. H., Conners, C. K., & Ulrich, R. F. (1978). Normative data on Revised Conners Parent and Teacher Rating Scales. *Journal of Abnormal Child Psychology, 6,* 221–236.
- *Conners Teacher Rating Scale (CTRS):* This 39-item scale yields a total score that measures conduct problems in children from 3 to 17 years old. It was developed for completion by a child's teacher(s). It is reproduced in Hargreaves et al. (1977, p. 335) and reviewed by Rutter et al. (1988, p. 129) and Thompson (1989b, p. 285).
  Conners, C. K. (1969). A teacher rating scale for use in drug studies with children. *American Journal of Psychiatry, 126,* 884–888.
- *Homework Problem Checklist (HPC):* This 20-item checklist yields a total score that measures the frequency and intensity of children's homework problems. It was developed for completion by a child's teacher(s). It is reproduced in Anesko, Schoiock, Ramirez, and Levine (1987).
  Anesko, K. M., Schoiock, G., Ramirez, R., & Levine, F. M. (1987). The Homework Problem Checklist: Assessing children's homework difficulties, *Behavioral Assessment, 9,* 179–185.
- *Self-Control Rating Scale (SCRC):* This 33-item measure yields a total score that measures self-control in children. It was developed for completion by a child's parent(s) and/or teacher(s). The items are listed in Kendall and Wilcox (1979) and it is reviewed in Rutter et al. (1988, p. 143).
  Kendall, P. C., & Wilcox, L. W. (1979). Self-control in children: Development of a rating scale. *Journal of Consulting and Clinical Psychology, 47,* 1020–1029.

Information from relevant others can be valuable, but there are some potential problems and limitations with using relevant others to record. First, some clients simply don't have relevant others, or they may not want you to collect information from relevant others. Second, relevant others may be unwilling to cooperate at all, or they may "fudge" their recording depending on how they see its use. Third, the reason that makes relevant others so useful a data source—their day-to-day relationship with the client—also might bias their responses. Fourth, relevant others might not know enough about a particular client target to provide adequate information (e.g., a relevant other might know that an alcoholic client still drinks, but not how much). Fifth, sometimes it can be time-consuming and otherwise expensive to collect information from relevant others. Finally, if the client has access to information provided by relevant others it can prove embarrassing and even harmful to the client's relationship with relevant others (e.g., asking a person to assess the extent to which a neighbor maltreats his or her children).

SOME AVAILABLE STANDARDIZED QUESTIONNAIRES FOR INDEPENDENT OBSERVERS

Many of the standardized questionnaires listed in Table 7.4 can be used by independent observers and practitioners, as can the assessment measures described in Table 7.5. Independent observers, such as your colleagues, supervisor, or outside consultants, can provide valuable assessments of your clients (e.g., Auerbach, 1983; Bostwick & Bostwick, 1987; Lambert, Shapiro, & Bergin, 1986; Reid & Smith, 1989; Wittenborn, 1984). For example, you might have a colleague review a random sample of audiotapes or videotapes of your sessions with a client, or even interview your client. Independent observers have the advantage that they're less personally invested in a client and so they might be able to provide a more accurate, less biased assessment. However, the fact that independent observers are less involved with a client also can be a disadvantage because they will be less familiar with the client. Also, in busy agencies it might not be possible to have your colleagues provide independent assessments of your clients except on a limited basis.

DO-IT-YOURSELF QUESTIONNAIRES

There are so many standardized questionnaires appropriate for practice that it hardly seems necessary to develop your own in most instances. However, if you can't find anything at all in your area of interest, you may feel you must devise your own. Developing your own standardized questionnaire is no easy matter. It requires a good deal of time, effort, and energy. Almost every major research text has a section on developing and testing questionnaires (e.g., Aday, 1989; Babbie, 1998; Bloom, 1986; Judd et al., 1991; Kerlinger, 1986; Monette, Sullivan, & DeJong, 1990; Reid & Smith, 1989; Rubin & Babbie, 1997). Also, there are numerous specialized texts on questionnaire development (e.g., DeVellis, 1991; Gable, 1986; Labaw, 1985; Osterlind, 1989; Streiner & Norman, 1989; Sudman & Bradburn, 1982), and we recommend you use one or more of these to guide your efforts.

If you do take on the task of developing a standardized questionnaire for your clients, you should try to determine its validity and reliability. Otherwise, you run the risk of collecting information that is of no use or that is misleading and possibly even harmful. Developing and testing a standardized questionnaire are rather technical tasks, but not impossible. There are a variety of good books on this subject, as mentioned, and numerous examples of measurement development and testing for you to draw upon (see the Appendix at the end of this chapter). Also, you might try to (a) enlist a colleague with expertise in measurement if you don't have this expertise yourself, (b) collaborate with a university-based measurement expert, or (c) interest doctoral students with some expertise in such projects as part of their dissertation research. You might find collaborators more easily than you imagine because of your ready access to the client population on which to test the measure.

In general, the procedures for testing the reliability and validity of your questionnaire should follow the guidelines discussed in Chapter 2. If your questionnaire is administered repeatedly to clients you might be able to examine its test-retest reliability. Also, you might be able to examine its internal consistency reliability (e.g., coefficient alpha) and the adequacy of specific questions or items (e.g., using item-analysis). In addition, you might be able to examine the criterion validity of your questionnaire by examining the extent to which it: (a) predicts certain outcomes (e.g., premature termination of treatment, child abuse or neglect, placement of a child in foster care); (b) correlates with other known measures of the concept your questionnaire was designed to measure; or (c) differentiates groups known to have more or less of the concept supposedly measured by your questionnaire. Finally, if your agency routinely administers measures of other concepts along with your questionnaire, you might be able to examine the extent to which these other measures relate to your questionnaire in a theoretically predicted manner; that is, you could examine the construct validity of your questionnaire.

Testing the validity and reliability of a standardized questionnaire with any sizable number of clients requires the use of computer programs to compute the necessary statistics (e.g., coefficient alpha, correlations among measures). There are a number of personal computer programs available for this (e.g., the personal computer versions of SPSS or SAS), and there are some specialized programs for this that are relatively inexpensive (e.g., Hays & Hayashi, 1990). MicroCAT, although not inexpensive, is a good example of a personal computer program that integrates the ability to monitor the validity, reliability, and normative values of standardized questionnaires on an ongoing basis, with the ability to construct, administer, score, and otherwise manage such questionnaires.* (For a review of this program, see Patience, 1990). You can use MicroCAT to construct and administer a wide range of different types of items and questionnaires (e.g., it can administer "adaptive" tests, that is, ones where the assessment is tailored to each indi-

vidual, and it can administer questionnaire items that include graphics and digitized images, in addition to text). You also can use MicroCAT to analyze different properties of your questionnaires. For example, MicroCAT can compute coefficient alpha, traditional item-analyses, item-response theory analyses, basic descriptive statistics, and multiple regression. Therefore, this program could be used to administer, score, manage, and analyze the results of existing standardized questionnaires, or questionnaires you construct for particular clients in your particular agency.

USING STANDARDIZED QUESTIONNAIRES IN GROUPS

Many of the standardized measures described in this chapter can be used to evaluate change in groups as well as with individual clients in groups. However, there also are several self-report standardized measures that were developed specifically to be used with groups.

One of the most widely used self-report, standardized questionnaires is the Yalom Curative Factors Scale (Lieberman, Yalom, & Miller, 1973; Stone et al., 1994). This scale is comprised of 14 items that evaluate 12 dimensions in therapeutic groups. These dimensions are: (1) altruism, (2) catharsis, (3) cohesiveness, (4) existentiality, (5) guidance, (6) hope, (7) identification, (8) family reenactment, (9) self-understanding, (10) interpersonal input, (11) interpersonal output, and (12) universality.

The Group Atmosphere Scale (GAS; Silbergeld et al., 1975) and the Hemphill Index of Group Dimensions (Hemphill, 1956) examine different aspects of group functioning, though both measures are rather long. The GAS consists of 120 true-false items with 12 subscales examining such aspects of group environment as aggression, support, autonomy, and involvement. The Hemphill Index consists of 150 items on 5-point scales and measures 13 characteristics of groups including such dimensions as autonomy, control, participation, and stability.

---

*Assessment Systems Corporation, 2233 University Avenue, Suite 440, St. Paul, MN 55114

Finally, the widely used Hill Interaction Matrix (Hill, 1977) is a measure that uses group members, leaders, and/or observers to respond to 72 items on group process. This measure can be used to distinguish between group interactions that occur on two dimensions–the content that is discussed and levels and type of activity that take place in the group.

COMPUTER MANAGEMENT OF STANDARDIZED QUESTIONNAIRES

Personal computers are being used increasingly in the administration, scoring, interpretation, storage, analysis, and general management of standardized questionnaires (e.g., Benbenishty, 1989; Corcoran & Gingerich, 1994; Grasso, Epstein, & Tripodi, 1989; Grohol, 2000; Nurius & Hudson, 1993; Patterson, 2000; see Newman et al., 1997, for a review of the use of computers in assessment). However, just as there are too many standardized questionnaires to describe here, it's also impossible to detail the many different computer programs for the management of standardized questionnaires. In addition, computerized assessment is a rapidly growing area, and it's therefore best for you to look for current developments in such journals as *Computers in Human Services, Social Science Computer Review,* and *Computers in Psychiatry/Psychology*; in reference books such as *Personal Computer Applications in the Social Services* (Patterson, 2000), *Computer Use in Psychology: A Directory of Software* (Stoloff & Couch, 1992), *Psychware Sourcebook* (Krug, 1993), and *The 12th Mental Measurements Yearbook* (Conoley & Kramer, 1995); and on the Web in such places as "CUSSnet" (http://www.uta.edu/cussn/cussn.html), Computers in Mental Health (http://www.ex. ac.uk/ cimh/welcome.htm), a site to locate information about thousands of standardized measures (http://ericae.net/testcol.htm#trev), and New Technology in the Human Services (http://www.fz.hse.nl/causa/swbib/sw_keyw. htm); and in software review sections of professional journals. However, to give you some idea of the potential and workings of such a program, we describe one such system devel-

oped for human service practitioners, the Computer Assisted Assesment Package (CAAP; Hudson, 1996a, 1996b; Nugent et al., 2001; Nurius & Hudson, 1993) introduced in Chapter 4.

 The CAAP user's guide begins on page 267.

CASS is a general-purpose personal computer program for, among other things, through CAAP, managing standardized questionnaires. In addition to such general-purpose personal computer programs, there also are a variety of specialized programs available for the management of standardized questionnaires (e.g., Butcher, 1987; Krug, 1988; Stoloff & Couch, 1988; see Newman et al., 1997 for a review of research on this topic). There are programs available for the administration, scoring, and interpretation of particular measures such as the Brief Symptom Inventory, the Piers-Harris Children's Self-Concept Scale, and the Suicide Probability Scale, to name a few (Krug, 1988). Some of these programs not only score the questionnaires, but also generate extensive narrative explanations of the scores. There also are programs known as "shells" into which you can enter existing standardized questionnaires or questionnaires developed by you or your agency, and these programs then will administer, score, and otherwise manage the measures. In addition to personal computer programs that operate solely on your on-site personal computer equipment, there also are a number of companies to which you can mail your questionnaires for scoring and interpretation, or to which you can transmit your questionnaire data by telephone via an on-site computer terminal and modem. Mail and teleprocessing are most likely to be useful to practitioners who administer lengthy standardized questionnaires that require extensive interpretation.

There are some concerns raised by the use of personal computers to manage standardized questionnaires and other types of measures (e.g., Moreland, 1987; Siegel, 1990). They require start-up time in learning the operation of the computer and the particular software program, in addition to training in the proper use and interpretation of the measures. They also require a financial investment in the computer equipment and software. In addition, computer administration of measures may seem intimidating and impersonal to some clients, and there are some clients (e.g., those who can't read) who won't be able to use some of these systems. Extra care needs to be taken to ensure that clients understand the task at hand and are able to respond appropriately. Finally, computerized measures, just like their paper-and-pencil counterparts, shouldn't be accepted uncritically. They still must have demonstrated validity and reliability, in addition to being direct, relatively easy to use, accessible, and relevant to intervention planning. Just because such measures are computerized and seemingly scientific doesn't mean that they're accurate and useful.

The personal computer management of standardized questionnaires and other measures does have some important benefits, as suggested by this brief description of CAAP and other related personal computer software (e.g., Butcher, 1987; Hudson, 1990b; Nurius &

Hudson, 1988; 1993). They can increase the speed and efficiency with which standardized questionnaires are managed, and this can free up time to deliver services. They also can increase the accuracy with which standardized questionnaires and other measures are administered and scored. Even the most conscientious practitioner can make mistakes in scoring measures, and these mistakes can lead to incorrect practice and evaluation decisions; computers don't make such errors if properly used. Also, some programs, including CAAP, check client responses to make sure that they fall in the range of requested values (e.g., a client might enter an "8" when the measure calls for a response that ranges from 1 to 7). Finally, there's some evidence that clients may be more willing to reveal sensitive personal information (e.g., alcohol abuse, sexual behaviors) to a computer than to a practitioner or on a pencil-and-paper questionnaire (e.g., Malcom et al., 1989; Millstein & Irwin, 1983). Therefore, in some cases, the personal computer administration of standardized questionnaires might provide more valid client information.

SUMMARY

Standardized questionnaires involve the uniform administration and the uniform scoring of items to provide a quantitative measure of some concept. A hallmark of standardized questionnaires is that data usually exist concerning their validity and reliability, although standardized questionnaires differ considerably in the amount and quality of such information. Standardized questionnaires are available to elicit information from clients, practitioners, relevant others, and independent observers, although most are self-report measures. Examples of questionnaires for eliciting information from different perspectives were provided, along with a list of references for locating information about additional standardized questionnaires. Advantages as well as problems in using standardized questionnaires were described. Essentially, these measures are efficient and readily available, but there's a danger in using them without appropriate cautions. Specific criteria were described to help you select a standardized questionnaire from the many that are available, and some general guidelines for administering these questionnaires were provided. The use of personal computers to administer, score, interpret, store, and in general manage standardized questionnaires was discussed, and one such program, CAAP, was noted and is described in detail in the User's Guide at the end of this chapter. Finally, the construction of standardized questionnaires for particular agency needs was described briefly.

APPENDIX

REFERENCE BOOKS
FOR TESTS AND MEASUREMENTS

AIKEN, L. R. (1985). *Psychological testing and assessment.* Rockleigh, NJ: Allyn & Bacon.

ANASTASI, A. (1988). *Psychological testing* (6th ed.). New York: Macmillan.

ANDRULIS, R. S. (1977). *Adult assessment: A source book of tests and measures of human behavior.* Springfield, IL: Chas. C Thomas.

BEERE, C. A. (1990). *Sex and gender issues: A handbook of tests and measures.* New York: Greenwood Press.

BONJEAN, C. M., HILL, R. J., & MCLEMORE, S. D. (1967). *Sociological measurement: An inventory of scales and indices.* San Francisco: Chandler.

BRODSKY, S. L., & SMITHERMAN, H. O. (1983). *Handbook of scales for research in crime and delinquency.* New York: Plenum Press.

BUROS, O. K. (ED.). (1968). *Reading tests and reviews.* Highland Park, NJ: Gryphon Press.

CAUTELA, J. R. (1981). *Behavior analysis forms for clinical intervention* (Vol. 2). Champaign, IL: Research Press.

CHUN, K., COBB, S., & FRENCH, J. R.P., JR. (1975). *Measures for psychological assessment: A guide to 3,000 original sources and their applications.* Ann Arbor, MI: Institute for Social Research.

CIARLO, J. A., BROWN, T. R., EDWARDS, D. W., KIRESUK, T. J., & NEWMAN, F. L. (1986). *Assessing mental health treatment outcome measurement techniques.* Rockville, MD: National Institute of Mental Health (DHHS Publication No. (ADM) 86–1301).

COMREY, A., BARKER, T., & GLASER, E. (1975). *A sourcebook for mental health measures.* Los Angeles: Human Interaction Research Institute.

CONOLEY, J. C., & KRAMER, J. J. (1989). *The l0th mental measurements yearbook.* Lincoln, NE: Buros Institute of Mental Measurements.

CONOLEY, J. C., & KRAMER, J. J. (1995). *The 12th mental measurements yearbook.* Lincoln, NE: Buros Institute of Mental Measurements.

CORCORAN, K., & FISCHER, J. (1987). *Measures for clinical practice.* New York: Free Press.

CORCORAN, K., & FISCHER, J. (2000a). *Measures for clinical practice: Vol. 1. Couples, families, children* (3rd ed.). New York: Free Press.

CORCORAN, K., & FISCHER, J. (2000b). *Measures for clinical practice. Vol. 2. Adults* (3rd ed.). New York: Free Press.

FILLENBAUM, G. G. (1988). *Multidimensional functional assessment of older adults: The Duke Older American Resources and Services Procedures.* Hillsdale, NJ: Erlbaum.

FISCHER, J., & CORCORAN K. (1994A). *Measures for clinical practice: Vol. 1. Couples, families, children.* (2nd ed.) New York: Free Press.

FISCHER, J., & CORCORAN, K. (1994B). *Measures for clinical practice: Vol 2. Adults.* (2nd ed.) New York: Free Press.

FREDMAN, N., & SHERMAN, R. (1987). *Handbook of measurements for marriage and family therapy.* New York: Brunner/Mazel.

GOLDMAN, B. A., & BUSCH, J. C. (1978). *Directory of unpublished experimental mental measures* (Vol. 2). New York: Human Sciences Press.

GOLDMAN, B. A., & BUSCH, J. C. (1981). *Directory of unpublished experimental mental measures* (Vol. 3). New York: Human Sciences Press.

GOLDMAN, B. A., & SAUNDERS, J. L. (1974). *Directory of unpublished experimental mental measures* (Vol. 1). New York: Human Sciences Press.

GROTEVANT, H. D., & CARLSON, C. I. (EDS.). (1989). *Family assessment: A guide to methods and measures.* New York: Guilford Press.

HAMMILL, D. D., BROWN, L., & BRYANT, B. R. (1989). *A consumer's guide to tests in print.* Austin, TX: Pro-Ed.

HARGREAVES, W. A., ATTKISSON, C. C., & SORENSEN, J. E. (EDS.). (1977). *Resource materials for community mental health program evaluation.* Rockville, MD: U.S. Department of Health, Education, and Welfare.

HARRINGTON, R. G. (ED.). (1986). *Testing adolescents: A reference guide for comprehensive psychological assessments.* Austin, TX: Pro-Ed.

HERSEN, M., & BELLACK, A. S. (EDS.). (1988). *Dictionary of behavioral assessment techniques.* Elmsford, NY: Pergamon Press.

HOLMAN, A. M. (1983). *Family assessment: Tools for understanding and intervention.* Beverly Hills, CA: Sage.

HUDSON, W. W. (1982). *The clinical measurement package: A field manual.* Homewood, IL: Dorsey Press.

HUDSON, W. W. (1992). *The WALMYR assessment scales scoring manual.* Tempe, AZ: WALMYR.

HUNT, T., & LINDLEY, C. (EDS.). (1989). *Testing older adults.* Austin, TX: Pro-Ed.

JACOB, T., & TENNENBAUM, D. L. (1988). *Family assessment: Rationale, methods, and future directions.* New York: Plenum Press.

JOHNSON, O. G. (1976). *Tests and measurements in child development* (Vols. 1, 2). San Francisco: Jossey-Bass.

KAMPHAS, R. W., & FRICK, P. J. (1996). *Clinical assessment of child and adolescent personality and behavior.* Boston: Allyn & Bacon.

KELLERMAN, H., & BURRY, A. (1997). *Handbook of psychodiagnostic testing.* Boston: Allyn & Bacon.

KESTENBAUM, C. J., & WILLIAMS, D. T. (EDS.). (1988). *Handbook of clinical assessment of children and adolescents.* Austin, TX: Pro-Ed.

KEYSER, D. J., & SWEETLAND, R. C. (EDS.). (1984–1991). *Test critiques* (Vols. 1–8). Austin, TX: Pro-Ed.

KRUG, S. E. (ED.). (1988). *Psychware sourcebook: 1988–1989* (3rd ed.). Austin, TX: Pro-Ed.

LAKE, D. G., MILES, M. B., & EARLE, R. B., JR. (1973). *Measuring human behavior: Tools for the assessment of social functioning.* New York: Teachers College Press.

MAGURA, S., & MOSES, B. S. (1987). *Outcome measures for child welfare services.* Washington, DC: Child Welfare League of America.

MCCUBBIN, H. I., & THOMPSON, A. I. (EDS.). (1987). *Family assessment inventories for research and practice.* Madison: University of Wisconsin–Madison.

MCCUBBIN, H. I., THOMPSON, A. I., & MCCUBBIN, M. A. (1996). *Family assessment: Resiliency, coping and adaptation.* Madison: University of Wisconsin Press.

MCDOWELL, I., & NEWELL, C. (1996). *Measuring health: A guide to rating scales and questionnaires.* New York: Oxford University Press.

MITCHELL, J. (1983). *Tests in print III.* Lincoln, NE: Buros Institute of Mental Measurements.

MITCHELL, J. V. (ED.). (1985). *The ninth mental measurements yearbook.* Lincoln: University of Nebraska Press.

MUELLER, D. J. (1986). *Measuring social attitudes: A handbook for researchers and practitioners.* New York: Teachers College Press.

OGLES, B. M., & MASTERS, K. S. (1996). *Assessing outcome in clinical practice.* Boston: Allyn & Bacon.

OLLENDICK, T. H., & HERSEN, M. (1992). *Handbook of child and adolescent assessment.* Des Moines, IA: Allyn & Bacon.

ORVASCHEL, H., SHOLMSKAS, D., & WEISSMAN, M. M. (1980). *The assessment of psychopathology and behavioral problems in children: A review of scales suitable for epidemiological and clinical research (1967–1979).* Rockville, MD: National Institute of Mental Health.

ORVASCHEL, H., & WALSH, G. (1984). *The assessment of adaptive functioning in children: A review of existing measures suitable for epidemiological and clinical services research.* Rockville, MD: National Institute of Mental Health.

PECORA, P. *et al.* (1995). *Evaluating family-based services.* Hawthorne, NY: Aldine de Gruyter.

REYNOLDS, C. R., & KAMPHAUS, R. W. (EDS.). (1990). *Handbook of psychological and educational assessment of children.* New York: Guilford Press.

ROBINSON, J. P., ATHANASION, R., & HEAD, K. (1973). *Measures of occupational attitudes and occupational characteristics* (rev. ed.). Ann Arbor, MI: Institute for Social Research.

ROBINSON, J. P., RUSK, J. G., & HEAD, K. B. (1968). *Measures of political attitudes.* Ann Arbor, MI: Institute for Social Research.

ROBINSON, J. P., & SHAVER, P. R. (1973). *Measures of social psychological attitudes* (rev. ed.). Ann Arbor, MI: Institute for Social Research.

RUTTER, M., TUMA, A. H., & LANN, I. S. (EDS.). (1988). *Assessment and diagnosis in child psychopathology.* New York: Guilford Press.

SATTLER, J. M. (1988). *Assessment of children* (3rd ed.). Brandon, VT: Clinical Psychology Publishing Co.

SAWIN, K. J., & HARRIGAN, M. (1994). *Measures of family functioning for research and practice.* New York: Springer.

SCHOLL, G., & SCHNUR, R. (1976). *Measures of psychological, vocational and educational functioning in the blind and visually handicapped.* New York: American Foundation for the Blind.

SCHUTTE, N. S., & MALOUFF, J. M. (1995). *Sourcebook of adult assessment strategies.* New York: Plenum.

SEDERER, L. I., & DICKEY, B. (EDS.). (1996). *Outcomes assessment in clinical practice.* Baltimore: Williams & Wilkins.

SHAW, M. E., & WRIGHT, J. M. (1967). *Scales for the measurement of attitudes.* New York: McGraw-Hill.

SOUTHWORTH, L. E., BURR, R. L., & COX, A. E. (1981). *Screening and evaluating the young infant: A handbook of instruments to use from infancy to six years.* Springfield, IL: Chas. C Thomas.

STRAUSS, M., & BROWN, B. W. (1978). *Family measurement techniques: Abstracts of published instruments, 1935–1974* (rev. ed.). Chicago: Rand-McNally.

SUZUKI, L. A., MELLER, P. J., & PONTEROTTO, J. G. (EDS.). (1996). *Handbook of multicultural assessment: Clinical, psychological and educational applications.* San Francisco: Jossey-Bass.

SWEETLAND, R. C., & KEYSER, D. J. (1991). *Tests: A comprehensive reference* (3rd ed.). Austin, TX: Pro-Ed.

SWIERCINSKY, D. P. (ED.). (1985). *Testing adults: A reference guide for special psychodiagnostic assessments.* Austin, TX: Pro-Ed.

THOMPSON, C. (ED.). (1989). *The instruments of psychiatric research.* New York: Wiley.

TOULIATOS, J., PERLMUTTER, B. F., & STRAUS, M. A. (EDS.). (1990). *Handbook of family measurement techniques.* Newbury Park, CA: Sage.

VANCE, B. H. (ED.). (1997). *Psychological assessment of children.* New York: John Wiley.

VAN RIEZEN, H., & SEGAL, M. (1988). *Comparative evaluation of rating scales for clinical psychopharmacology.* New York: Elsevier.

WALKER, D. K. (1973). *Socioemotional measures for preschool and kindergarten children.* San Francisco: Jossey-Bass.

WARD, J. J., & LINDEMAN, C. A. (1978). *Instruments for measuring nursing practice and other health care variables* (Vol. 2). Washington, DC: Department of Health, Education and Welfare (DHEW Publication No. HRA 78–54).

WASKOW, I. E., & PARLOFF, M. B. (EDS.). (1975). *Psychotherapy change measures.* Rockville, MD: National Institute of Mental Health.

WEAVER, S. J. (ED.). (1984). *Testing children: A reference guide for effective clinical and psychoeducational assessments.* Austin, TX: Pro-Ed.

WETZLER, S. (ED.). (1989). *Measuring mental illness: Psychometric assessment for clinicians.* Washington, DC: American Psychiatric Press.

WILLIS, D. J., & CULBERTSON, J. L. (EDS.). (1989). *Testing young children.* Austin, TX: Pro-Ed.

WOODY, R. H. (1980). *Encyclopedia of clinical assessment* (2 vols.). San Francisco: Jossey-Bass.

COMPUTER ASSISTED ASSESSMENT PACKAGE (CAAP): A USER'S GUIDE

CASS was developed for human service practitioners, and it provides a good example of a comprehensive, easy-to-use, personal computer program that simplifies and enhances the recording, storage, retrieval, and organization of client data. As discussed in Chapter 4, CASS is the general name of this program, but there is another program included with CASS named CAAP (Computer Assisted Assessment Package).

CAAP is used by clients and, as described in Chapter 4, the resulting client information is available to you through your use of CASS. CAAP administers almost any type of standardized scale or test to your clients, and it automatically scores it, charts the results in a single-system design format, updates the information for a client each time a measure is completed so you can monitor client progress over time, and stores the information in the computer. In particular, CAAP will administer the WALMYR Assessment Scales (WAS) package (described earlier) to your clients, reverse-score the necessary items, compute the total score, graph the results in a single-system design format of your choice, and automatically update a client's file each time a scale is completed so you can monitor the client's progress over time.

An especially notable feature of CAAP is that although it comes with ready-to-use scales, you can add an almost unlimited number of additional scales, including ones constructed by you or your agency. Therefore, it's possible to use CASS to construct a tailor-made package of computer-administered instruments for use in your practice.

To use CAAP, a client needs to have some familiarity with your computer keyboard and must be able to read, but that's about all. However, before you use CASS with a client, you should use CAAP as if you were a client, and you should walk each client through CAAP at least once before you ask him or her to use it independently. For the most part, though, on-screen menus guide the client through CAAP. We'll walk you through what a client will see in this process. *(First, though, you need to create a client record. Go to Chapter 4 and follow the steps to do this if you haven't already. Also, be sure that you read the CASS section in Chapter 4 before working through these exercises.)* Finally, after we walk you through what a client will see when he or she completes a scale using CAAP, we will show you how to exit CAAP, return to CASS, and view and graph the resulting scale scores.

We assume that you know very little about computers, and we apologize in advance if this isn't the case. There are a few things that you need to know at the outset, but if you've used Windows before you probably already know these.

Before starting, first be sure to familiarize yourself with the basic operations of your computer (e.g., location of your A drive, "Enter" key, Ctrl key, and ←↑→↓ keys). In particular, find out what version of Windows is installed on your computer.

Also, you'll need to know the following terms to install and use this software:

- **"Click"** means use your mouse to move the arrow you see on your screen to a certain word or place on the screen, and then click the *left* mouse button once.
- **"Right-click"** means use your mouse to move the arrow you see on your screen to a certain word or place on the screen, and then click the *right* mouse button once.
- **"Double-click"** means use your mouse to move the arrow you see on your screen to a certain word or place on the screen, and then click the *left* mouse button *twice quickly.*

WARNING: If the program does not run according to the following instructions, as a last resort you might have to reinstall the program, as shown in the Appendix at the end of Chapter 4.

STARTING CAAP

▶ Double click the CAAP icon (clasped hands) on your desktop screen.

CAAP

▶ When the following window appears, enter the client case number (e.g., "010" for the case we showed you how to create in Chapter 4), press the TAB key, and enter the client password (e.g., "charlie" for this case). *Remember, you cannot use CAAP without first creating a case in CASS.* When you type the password it will appear as ******. You need to enter the client case number and password exactly as you entered them when you created the case (i.e., the same combination of upper and lower case letters).

If you forget the case number or password you can use CASS to get them by clicking "Get a Client Record" from the "File" menu and then, after basic client information is established on the start screen as described in Chapter 4, clicking "Displaying Current Case" from the "File" menu. (First, though, you'll need to exit CAAP, as shown below.)

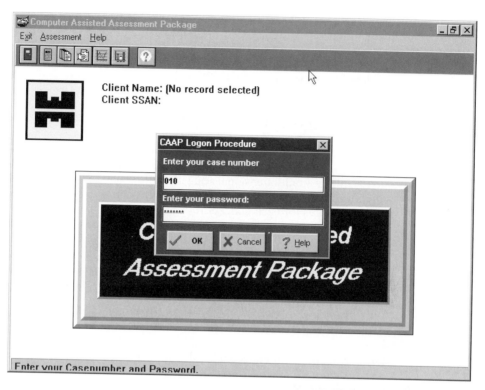

▶ After you've entered the case number and password, click "OK" and the "CAAP Logon" window will appear. Click "OK" and the window will disappear. We'll refer to the resulting screen (not shown) as the start screen.

Notice the menu bar items at the top of the above screen (i.e., "Exit," "Assessment," and "Help"). You can click any of these items and menus will be displayed. We'll discuss these menu bar items and menus next. Also, note the buttons below the menu bar. These give you another way of doing the same things you can do with the menus. When you move the arrow to one of these buttons in a moment a note appears describing its purpose.

COMPLETING A SCALE

CAAP is used to administer scales to clients, score and graph these scale scores, and automatically transfer and update this information so you can access it using CASS. To see how this is done, pretend you are a client and work through the following exercise. Note that the version of CAAP you have only lets you administer a limited number of certain scales. (You can get a list of the available scales–over 100 of them–and determine the number of "scale credits" for each by selecting "Display Scale Scoring Credits" from the "Supplies" menu in the CASS "Management Module," as shown in Chapter 4.)

CAAP USER'S GUIDE

▶ Click "Assessment," and move the arrow to "Complete An Assessment Scale" and "Unidimensional Client Record." (Note that CASS also lets you score assessment scales. Click on "Assessment" in CASS, then on "Score Assessment Scale." This option lets you enter item scores for completed scales–e.g., those completed by hand–and CASS will then automatically score and store this information just as if the client had completed it using CAAP.)

▶ Click "Unidimensional Client Record."

(Unidimensional scales measure one concept, and multidimensional scales measure more than one concept. For example, the Generalized Contentment Scale [GCS], illustrated below, is a unidimensional scale measuring depression. A multidimensional measure of psychological disorders might measure depression, anxiety, etc., and provide separate scores for each concept.)

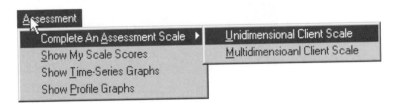

The list of available unidimensional scales appears.

▶ Click the down (▼) and up (▲) arrows on the window to scroll through this list and view the available unidimensional scales.

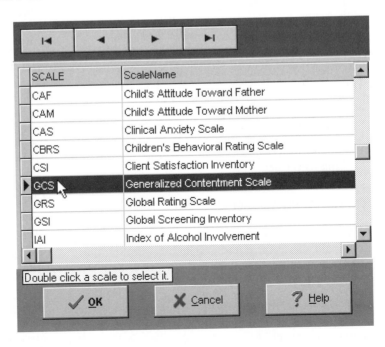

▶ Move the arrow to GCS and double-click, or click once and then click "OK." The following window appears.

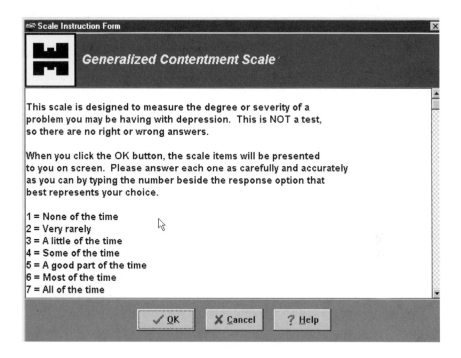

▶ Read the instructions, click "OK," and the "Please Answer All Items" window appears.

► Complete the scale as if you were a client. Use the arrow keys on your keyboard (↑↓) to move up and down. If you make a mistake, move to it and type over it. When you are finished, click "Score It" and the following window appears. (The score will be different depending on your responses to the items.)

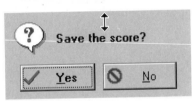

► Click "OK" and the "Save the Score?" window appears.

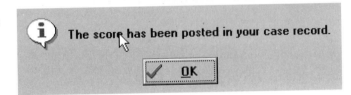

► Click "Yes" and the "Confirmation" window appears.

► Click "OK" and the start screen (not shown) appears.

VIEWING SCALE SCORES

It's possible for you and/or a client to view and graph the client's scale scores from within CAAP. (You can also do this in CASS by following roughly the same steps described here for graphing scale scores while in CAAP. While in CASS, you can enter each of the client's scores individually to view and graph them.) Here's how to do it.

► Click "Assessment" and "Show My Scale Scores."

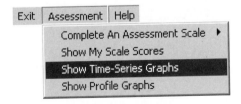

A table with client scale and item scores will appear. The client (you in this case) completed the Generalized Contentment Scale (GCS). This is a measure of nonpsychotic depression. Note that you can move your arrow to one of the arrows on this and similar screens, and click to see additional information.

► Click "Close" to return to the start screen.

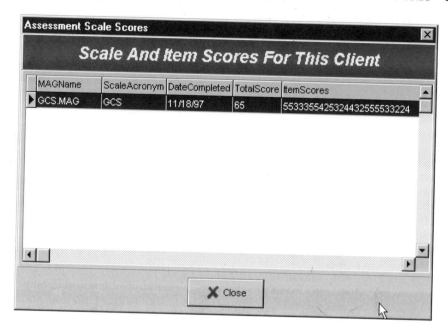

GRAPHING SCALE SCORES

CAAP creates single-system graphs of scale scores that are updated automatically each time a client completes a scale. You can edit these graphs and print them.

▶ Click "Assessment" and "Show My Time-Series Graphs." A list of scales that can be graphed appears.

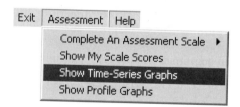

▶ Click the down (▼) and up (▲) arrows on the window to scroll through this list and view the available unidimensional scales.

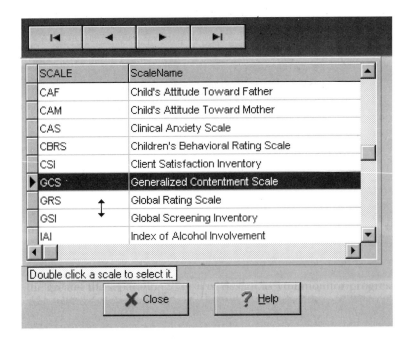

▶ Since the client completed the GCS, move the arrow to GCS and double-click. The following table appears, listing when the client completed the GCS and the resulting total scale score(s).

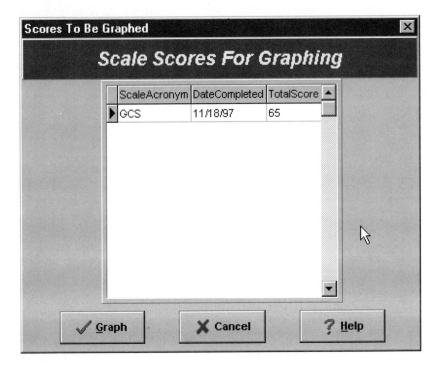

▶ Click the "GCS" line to highlight it, then click "Graph" to get the following graph. Of course, this isn't much of a graph because the scale was completed only once.

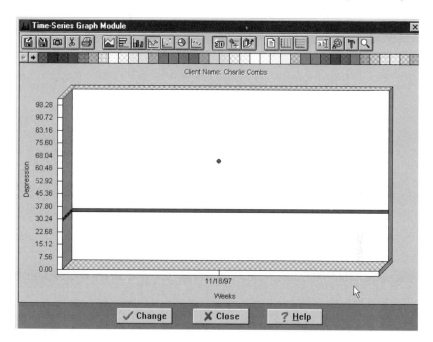

▶ If you don't like this three-dimensional graph, click the "3D" button and the following graph will appear.

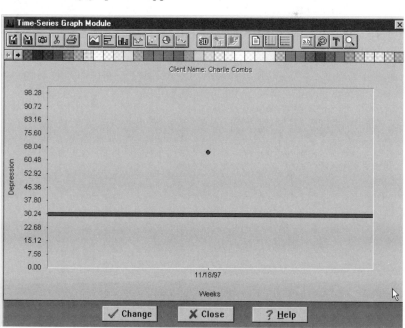

You can change this graph in a number of ways (e.g., edit titles). You can explore ways this graph can be changed by moving the arrow to any button on the tool bar line, and *holding the right* mouse button.

▶ For example, clicking the "Printer" button will print the graph.

▶ Clicking the "Edit Titles" button will let you change the chart title
   and the X and Y axes titles.

▶ Click "Close" to return to the start screen.

ONLINE HELP

Online, context-sensitive help is available at many places in CAAP, as you've already seen. Also, it's possible for the client to get help with a wide range of topics and to print this information. To do this use the CAAP "Help" menu in the same way as the CASS "Help" menu described in Chapter 4.

EXITING CAAP

▶ Click "Exit."

8 LOGS

PURPOSE: This chapter describes the use of logs or journals kept by a client to record the unique qualitative circumstances surrounding his or her problems, and to record quantitative dimensions of his or her problems, such as intensity and frequency. The use of logs to pinpoint and define targets, generate individualized hypotheses for intervention, and evaluate change over time in a client's problems is described. This chapter also describes the use of the practitioner log, an adaptation of the client log. The practitioner log can be used in much the same way as a clinical record to monitor the delivery of services and for the same purposes as the client log. ■

Introduction
Types of Client Logs
Time Variations
    Preset Time Categories
    Open Time Categories
Target-Category Variations
    Exploratory Log
    Target Problem Log
    Interaction Log
    Evaluation Log

Putting Qualitative and Quantitative
    Information Together
Introducing Clients to Logs
Practitioner Logs
Maximizing and Verifying the Reliability
    and Validity of Logs
Summary

INTRODUCTION

One of the major tasks for the practitioner is to secure enough information about the client's life to adequately develop, implement, and evaluate an intervention program. We've suggested in previous chapters a number of ways of doing this, ranging from behavioral observation of specific behaviors, to using standardized questionnaires and individualized rating scales. In addition to these methods, all of which have slightly different focal points and uses, most practitioners elicit different types of qualitative information about the ongoing context in which a particular client's targets occur. The client log is a form of self-monitoring that will help you to obtain this type of information in a systematic, useful, and relevant manner, and it will help you with other assessment and evaluation tasks (Alter & Evans, 1990; Cormier

& Cormier, 1998; Schwartz & Goldiamond, 1975; Watson & Tharp, 1989).

Client logs (also called *client annotated records* and *critical incident recording*) serve four functions. First, they can help *pinpoint and define client problems* in a way that is sensitive to the unique perceptions and circumstances of individual clients. Second, they provide a way to explore and clarify the dynamic and unique contexts in which a client's problems occur. This can help you and the client *generate contextually sensitive individualized targets and interventive hypotheses.* Third, logs can incorporate some of the methods discussed in earlier chapters (e.g., self-monitoring of the frequency or duration of behaviors or ratings of individualized targets), and this information enhances the precision with which logs can be used to *evaluate change over time in a client's targets.* Finally, client logs can serve a *preventive/interventive function*—that is, to teach the client to focus on his or her unique situation in an orderly way that can enhance client functioning and promote better functioning in the future.

This chapter discusses different types of client logs and how they can be used to (a) pinpoint and define client problems, (b) generate contextually sensitive individualized intervention hypotheses, and (c) evaluate change over time in a client's targets. (We won't focus on the interventive function of logs because that is better left to a book on intervention strategies. Watson and Tharp [1989] provide an excellent discussion of how to use client logs for intervention, and Kopp [1988] provides an excellent review of the use of self-monitoring in general for intervention.) In addition, we'll give numerous examples of client logs and provide forms for client logs that you can use in your own practice. Finally, we'll discuss practitioner logs, an adaptation of client logs to the collection of information by the practitioner.

TYPES OF CLIENT LOGS

The client log is an organized journal, kept by the client, of events that are relevant to the target situation, focusing on the client's perception of the events or situations. The use of the client log is an attempt to help the client systematically and objectively take notes on those events to avoid any possible distortions of memory when presenting that information to the practitioner (e.g., Farmer & Nelson-Gray, 1990). Thus, logs are helpful in getting ongoing feedback about targets, as well as the contextual factors that may be inhibiting client growth or maintaining client problems.

All client logs use basically the same format. They involve a prepared form, which has listed across the top the types of information you want collected. The type of information that you list there would vary with the nature of the target. At a minimum it involves recording whether some incident occurred, when it occurred, and how the client responded to it. Figure 8.1 illustrates a general format for a log. However, client logs do differ in terms of *when* information is recorded, or *what* is recorded, as illustrated in Figure 8.2.

Time Variations

When you set up your plan for the client to use a log, you have two basic choices: using preset time periods, or letting the client establish the times to record, based on the client's evaluation of what incidents are critical.

Preset Time Categories. Establishing in advance regular periods of time for recording can mean one of two things: (a) You have some idea about when the target will occur, and you can specify that the client collect as much information as possible during that time; or (b) you need information about a whole range of client activities spread out over the entire day, and you want that information collected, to the extent possible, over regularly scheduled intervals.

The first option, focusing on one particular period of time, might occur when the client has narrowed down the occurrence of some target event to a particular time period. Let's say a client complains about family arguments during dinner and immediately before and after dinner. The client log then may cover the time period from 5:00 P.M. to 7:00 P.M. every night. You might then ask the client to keep a record

Client Name _____ Day and Date _____

Time	Client Records Important Event	Client Records Reaction to Event
____	_____	_____
	_____	_____
	_____	_____
____	_____	_____
	_____	_____
____	_____	_____
	_____	_____
	_____	_____
____	_____	_____
	_____	_____
____	_____	_____
	_____	_____

FIGURE 8.1   General format for client log.

Target Category

Time Dimension	Open: Any important event may be noted in the log	Specifically defined by practitioner and/or client
Times for recording in log are specifically set		
Open: Client should record in log whenever the event occurs		

FIGURE 8.2   Variations in client logs—problem categories (defined in advance or open) and time dimensions (preset or open).

of family arguments during those 2 hours. This information could be used to generate hypotheses about strategies to reduce these arguments (e.g., suppose that the arguments all centered on family finances). Also, the act of recording the arguments provides a record of their frequency each day, and this could be charted to provide a more precise quantitative basis for evaluating change (it might also be possible to record the duration of these arguments as part of this record).

The second option using preset time categories would be used to develop ideas about factors related to the client's target(s). You might ask the client to make an entry in his or her log about the events that occurred during that hour and his or her reaction to them. For example, a schoolteacher who wants to increase constructive student participation might be asked to record at the end of each class period the occurrences of satisfactory class participation and the events surrounding them. This record could be used to generate hypotheses about strategies to increase constructive class participation (e.g., suppose that most instances of constructive class participation occurred when the teacher asked students to think of examples of the material under discussion). The record also would indicate the frequency of constructive class participation, and this could be charted to provide a more precise quantitative basis for evaluating change. (It also might be possible to have the teacher record the duration of each occurrence or estimate each duration later on.)

With both types of preset logs, as with any other logs, it's best for the client to record as soon as possible after the event occurs. This way, events may be less distorted by memory. To increase the chance that the client will be able to do this, naturally occurring time prompts might be used (e.g., the end of a class period for a teacher), or some type of artificial reminder might be used (e.g., the client might set the alarm on a digital watch). Of course, recording immediately is no guarantee that events will not be distorted. In any case, if the client does forget to record at a particular time, encourage the client to fill in that part at a later time, even at the risk of the event not being

recorded as accurately as it might otherwise have been.

The main advantage of using preset time categories is that you probably will get a great deal of information. This is because the client is to record events that occur during those preset times even if he or she may not see them as critical. Thus, you and the client together will have the option of evaluating whether there may indeed have been something important related to the client's target during that period.

The disadvantage of preset categories is the flip side of the advantage. When the client records events every hour whether or not those events are "critical," you may get a good deal of material that is irrelevant, at least to the client's target.

Open Time Categories. The second time variation of a client log, using open time categories, is sometimes called *critical incident recording*. With this type of log, the client, with some advance guidance from you, makes a decision as events occur as to which events seem critical (i.e., are related to the problem). These events are then recorded as soon as possible after they occur. The period of time, of course, could vary between recording intervals. It may be once or twice a day, or it could be a dozen or more entries daily.

As an example of this type of log, a couple seeking help with their relationship could be asked to record events with each other that they found especially enjoyable and their responses to these events. This information then could be used to generate hypotheses about strategies to enhance the relationship (e.g., suppose that many of the enjoyable events involved their spending leisure time in mutually enjoyable activities). Such a record also would indicate the frequency of enjoyable events (per day or week), and this could be charted to provide a more precise quantitative basis for evaluating change. It also would be simple to have each partner rate his or her degree of satisfaction with each interaction using a simple individualized rating scale like the ones discussed in Chapter 6. These ratings would indicate which of the enjoyable interactions were most satisfying, providing further clues about how to enhance the relationship, and providing additional information that could be used to evaluate change over time. These ratings also could be averaged for each day and charted to provide a quantitative indicator of progress. Figure 8.3 illustrates a general form that could be used to record this type of information.

The main advantage of critical incident recording is that it deals only with data the client perceives as significantly related to the target. Thus, a large amount of information that may be irrelevant is omitted, and it may be possible to pinpoint those events affecting the continuation of the target.

The disadvantage of critical incident recording is that, because the client is screening out many activities and the time guidelines for recording are not precise, the recorded events may be distorted. At the least, they may not really be representative of critical incidents in the client's life. Of course, distortions or omissions could occur with any type of client log, but the lack of time guidelines may increase that

Client Name ____________ Day and Date ____________

Time	Client Records Important Event (Include Frequency or Duration Count)	Client's Reaction	Individualized Rating Scale

FIGURE 8.3 Log illustrating open time categories with IRS.

problem. It could be especially important, then, for the practitioner and client to go over in advance those events that should be recorded and those that reasonably could be omitted.

Target-Category Variations

Several types of target categories could be used to increase the specificity of what the client records. Each of these depends on the specific purpose of the client log. The first category, of course, would be more or less open, corresponding to the critical incident record, in which the client records whatever he or she views as essential. More specific target-category variations were proposed by Schwartz and Goldiamond (1975), who discuss three types of problem categories for client logs–the exploratory log, target problem log, and interaction log. We also discuss a fourth type of log, the evaluation log. All of the different types of logs can be viewed as adaptations or extensions of the general model illustrated in Figure 8.1.

Exploratory Log. The purpose of the exploratory log is to help clarify and define the target and to collect detailed information on the target to aid in assessment (Schwartz & Goldiamond, 1975). This is a beginning log, which is especially useful for pinpointing and defining problems and the circumstances surrounding their occurrence. It's a descriptive (rather than precisely analytic) log that can change over time to a more precise log once you have a clearer idea of what events are affecting the target. The exploratory log can be set up to record critical incidents, or it can use preset time categories, which you would determine based on the nature of the problem.

As an example of an exploratory log, Rose (1989, p. 101) reports asking clients to keep a diary of situations and whether they're dissatisfied or satisfied with their responses, in order to identify problematic situations and client strengths. Such a record could be used to generate hypotheses about how to intervene with individual clients. It also would indicate the frequency of situations (per day or week) in which clients were satisfied and dissatisfied with their responses, and this could be charted to provide a more precise quantitative basis for evaluating change. The client also could rate the degree of satisfaction with each recorded situation using a simple individualized rating scale. These ratings would indicate the situations in which the client was most satisfied, which might provide further clues about how to intervene, and these ratings also could be charted to provide a quantitative indicator of progress.

Forms for two types of exploratory logs are presented in Figures 8.4 and 8.5. Figure 8.4 presents a form for the most elementary exploratory log, the critical incident log. This log requires very little preset, specified information. Figure 8.5, suggested by Schwartz and Goldiamond (1975), presents a form for an exploratory log that has more preset categories. Of course, the time and event categories can be changed to fit the time and situation, and a column can be added for ratings from individualized rating scales. Finally, Figure 8.6, from Schwartz and Goldiamond (1975, pp. 166–167), presents an example of an exploratory log that is filled out (for other examples, see Alter & Evans, 1990, chap. 3, and Watson & Tharp, 1989, chap. 3).

Target Problem Log. The target problem log is used when the client and practitioner are unable to distinguish between the target, on the one hand, and other activities, situations, or events on the other. It's used when the conditions that are controlling or maintaining the target, say the antecedents and consequences, are not clear (Alter & Evans, 1990; Schwartz & Goldiamond, 1975; Watson & Tharp, 1989). The purpose here is to isolate those situations or events that occur at the same time as the target, before the target, and after the target. Figure 8.7 provides a form that can be used for a target problem log.

You might want to modify the categories of this form to be more explicit regarding a particular case. For example, in a case involving a client's anxiety about studying, instead of "events before problem," you might substitute "events that led you to think about studying,"

```
┌─────────────────────────────────────────────────────────────┐
│             CRITICAL INCIDENT RECORDING FORM                  │
│                                                               │
│   Client Name _____      Day and Date _____  │
│                                                               │
│       Time              Incident                Comment       │
│   _____     _____     _____  │
│                                                               │
│   _____     _____     _____  │
│                 _____     _____  │
│                 _____     _____  │
│                 _____     _____  │
│   _____     _____     _____  │
│                 _____     _____  │
│                 _____     _____  │
│                 _____     _____  │
│   _____     _____     _____  │
│                 _____     _____  │
│                 _____     _____  │
│                 _____     _____  │
│   _____     _____     _____  │
│                 _____     _____  │
│                 _____     _____  │
│                 _____     _____  │
│   _____     _____     _____  │
│                 _____     _____  │
└─────────────────────────────────────────────────────────────┘
```

FIGURE 8.4   Form for critical incident recording (without preset categories).

and so on. Thus, each form can be individualized to meet the unique needs of a particular client. For example, Gambrill (1977) suggests that a client log for problems in developing effective social skills could include categories focusing on instances of effective and ineffective behaviors (as defined by you and the client). The "reaction" category also could be used to record behaviors or responses that might have been more effective in that situation.

Interaction Log.   When the target is clearly an interpersonal one, you probably would want to obtain information on the activities of others that may be related to the client's target. This will allow you to examine interactions between the client and others that center on the identified target (Schwartz & Goldiamond, 1975). The interaction log will permit you to identify patterns or to develop an intervention plan focused on altering the dysfunctional elements in those patterns.

Figure 8.8 is a form that can be used for recording interaction information. The client should be instructed to fill in only those categories that are appropriate. For example, depending on who speaks first, one or another category might be left blank. If this does not apply, the client should just leave that space blank.

EXPLORATORY LOG

Client Name _____ Day and Date _____

Time	Place	Activity	Who Was There?	What You Wanted	What Happened	Your Reaction

FIGURE 8.5 Form for exploratory (descriptive) log.

EXPLORATORY LOG

Client Name __Peter Kotten__   Day and Date __April 22, 1994__

Time	Place	Activity	Who Was There?	What You Wanted	What Happened	Your Reaction
8:00 AM	Home	Eating breakfast	Wife and I	Eat; feel reasonably pleasant	She kept trying to talk to me	I got irritated and yelled at her
8:45 AM	In car	Driving to work	Just myself	Wanted to get over feeling bad and get to work relaxed	Driver cut in on me	Started honking and yelling at her
10:00 AM	Work	Completing a letter	Secretary and I	Get work done	She was not finished	Gave her a nasty look, but did not say anything

FIGURE 8.6 Partially completed exploratory log.

TARGET PROBLEM LOG

Client's Name _____

Day and Date _____

Time	Place	Activity	Who Was There?	Problem Behavior (What Happened)	Events Before Problem	Events After Problem	Other Events During Problem	Your Reaction

FIGURE 8.7   Form for target problem (analytic) log.

INTERACTION LOG

Client Name: _____

Day and Date _____

Time	Place	Who Was There?	What I Said	What They Said	What I Said	Other Events That Followed	Your Reaction

FIGURE 8.8 Form for interaction (analytic) log.

Evaluation Log. The types of logs discussed in this section can be extended to include frequency counts or individualized ratings of targets or other events, as illustrated earlier in this chapter. Other dimensions of target events, such as the duration of an event, also can be included. Extending logs in this way gives you a more precise quantitative basis for evaluating client change, and thus the name "evaluation" log.

The simple act of logging target events gives a good count of those events. Thus, without any additional effort, the client log provides information about the frequency of a target's occurrence.

It's also a relatively simple matter to include individualized rating scales in a log to have a client rate his or her feelings or thoughts about the recorded event. You can do this by adding one more category to any of the forms presented earlier in this chapter, that category being the client's score on an individualized rating scale designed to measure the client's feelings about the recorded event. For example, suppose your client is a mother who complains that she can't accomplish anything during the day and that she "just feels depressed all day." She could keep a critical incident log and score each entry on a 9-point scale from 1 ("not at all depressed"; "I can accomplish all I want to") to 9 ("extremely depressed"; "I can't

get anything done, I just sit and mope"). Figure 8.9 presents three hypothetical entries from her journal plus her own self-ratings. The ratings could be averaged each day and monitored over time, as could the daily frequency of critical incidents.

Figure 8.1 also can be used to illustrate a general model for an evaluation log. Frequency, duration, or ratings of target events from an evaluation log then can be dealt with and analyzed along the lines described in earlier chapters–including, for example, charting and comparing baseline and intervention periods.

PUTTING QUALITATIVE AND QUANTITATIVE INFORMATION TOGETHER

As we've mentioned earlier in this chapter, client logs can be combined with other measures to enhance the precision with which logs can be used to evaluate client change, and to generate contextually sensitive individualized interventive hypotheses (Alter & Evans, 1990; Nugent, 1991a; Reid, 1990; Reid & Davis, 1987). This can be done in different ways, but in each case it involves organizing the information in order to try to see the extent to which two events, behaviors, or targets go together (i.e., whether they're correlated over

| Client Name | Mrs. Olamana | Day and Date | Thursday, May 7, 1998 |
| | | | |

Time	Incident	Depression Scale Rating	Your Reaction
8 AM	Couldn't get baby to eat.	7	Damn! This is frustrating.
9 AM	Baby asleep, I'm watching TV.	2	I feel fine, relaxed.
10:30 AM	She's up again; wet the bed.	9	I don't think there's any way out. It's hopeless.

FIGURE 8.9 Hypothetical critical incident journal combined with IRS.

time). This is the idea of "concomitant variation" introduced in Chapter 4. If the events consistently seem to increase or decrease at the same time (i.e., they're positively correlated), or one consistently increases while the other decreases (i.e., they're negatively correlated), this provides important information to you about possible circumstances that influence a target. The fact that the two events are correlated doesn't necessarily mean one is causing the other, but it does give you enough information to suggest the need to examine the hypothesis that one *might* be causing the other.

Let's return to the example of your client, the mother who complains that she can't accomplish anything during the day and feels "depressed all day." As before, she could keep a critical incident log and rate each entry on a 9-point scale from 1 ("not at all depressed"; "I can accomplish all I want to") to 9 ("extremely depressed"; "I can't get anything done, I just sit and mope"). Figure 8.9 presents three hypothetical entries from her journal plus her own self-ratings. The incidents recorded in Figure 8.9 could be organized according to the ratings associated with the incidents, as illustrated in Figure 8.10, or they could be charted with notes about concomitant events, as illustrated in Figure 8.11 (this type of graph is sometimes called an "annotated chart"), to try to get some

idea about just what it is that makes the client depressed. This method provides excellent systematic feedback that examines the relationships between the occurrence of specific events, and problematic or positive changes in your client's way of thinking or feeling.

As another example, suppose that your client is a man who complains that he has very low feelings of self-esteem, but he can't pin down the things related to these feelings. Suppose that you ask the client to record one critical incident each day that makes him feel especially good about himself and one that makes him feel especially bad. Also, suppose you ask him to rate how each incident makes him feel on a 9-point scale ranging from 1 ("low" self-esteem) to 9 ("high" self-esteem).

The ratings for the two different types of incidents could be plotted, as illustrated in Figure 8.12. As the information on the chart suggests, the client's feelings of self-esteem appear to be related to on-the-job problems: either the pressure of work or the fear of criticism. To the extent that this possibility can be validated, it points to an important area of exploration for intervention. Conversely, his positive feelings of self-esteem seem to be associated with spending leisure time with friends and family, so the intervention might build on this as a way of increasing self-esteem. Therefore, the

Self-Ratings:		
1–3	4–6	7–9
Journal Entries		
1. Baby asleep; I'm watching TV.	1. _____	1. Couldn't get baby to eat.
2. _____	2. _____	2. She's up again; wet the bed.
3. _____	3. _____	3. _____

FIGURE 8.10   Categorizing events according to self-ratings.

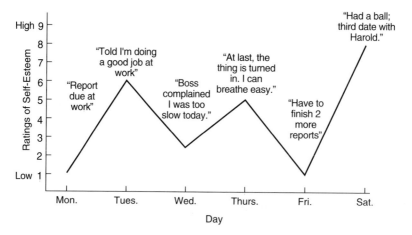

FIGURE 8.11 Example of a chart including ratings of self-esteem and data from a client log, as well as annotations of concomitant events.

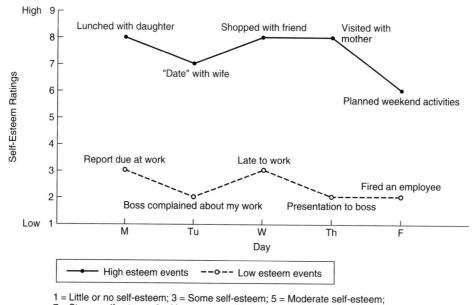

1 = Little or no self-esteem; 3 = Some self-esteem; 5 = Moderate self-esteem;
7 = Strong self-esteem; 9 = Very strong self-esteem

FIGURE 8.12 Self-esteem ratings of low and high self-esteem events.

annotation or logging on the graph combines the best of the qualitative narrative with the quantitative graphing. We don't need to drop the qualitative information from a log when we develop graphs, and indeed such annotations can make graphs more meaningful.

Again, we'd like to emphasize that when examining the relationship between qualitative and quantitative events, or between any events for that matter, it's important to remember that it's risky to assume that one variable causes another. For example, in the case of the depressed mother it might be that her depression is making it difficult for her to deal with her child, rather than vice versa. Perhaps other data, from the client log or from other sources, could shed light on this and lead to further suggestions for interventions.

INTRODUCING CLIENTS TO LOGS

When you introduce the client to the use of written logs, it may be a good idea to explain the logs as a way of helping the client record what happens to him or her, so that you can use the information to help plan and evaluate the intervention program. You might want to use a physician's notes as an example of why the log is needed. A physician keeps notes on the patient's complaint and situation in order to have a clear record that will suggest the etiology of the complaint and the progress toward its resolution.

One advantage of the log–and it seems reasonable to say this to the client–is that it's a more or less formal record of events that occur, but may be forgotten or somehow overlooked when the client meets with the practitioner. Many clients will respond quite positively to the idea that they're to keep track of important events in their own lives (Watson & Tharp, 1989).

With most clients, you will have to go over the log carefully in advance, demonstrate how it's to be used, and even fill in some of the information on the log using your own experiences as examples. You might demonstrate the interaction log, for example, by role-playing its completion with the client using the previous portion of the interview session as data for the log (clients receiving treatment in groups could role-play with one another [Rose, 1989, p. 101]). This way you can see whether the client understands what to do. In any case, be certain that you don't make the log too complicated, either in the information to be collected, or in the terminology that you use for the categories.

A most important condition for using client logs is to have forms available for the client to use. You can modify these forms to fit the needs of each client, but we don't suggest just telling the client to go out and fill out a notebook or journal "free-style." The prepared forms will structure the activity and make it seem more focused and more relevant.

Even when you prepare the forms for a client log, written logs assume that clients are literate, capable of writing and willing to write, and sufficiently disciplined to record the necessary information. When one or more of these assumptions are unreasonable for a client, other methods can be used. For example, clients can tape-record the information, although with some clients it will be necessary for you to practice with the client before recording can begin.

You probably will have to guide the client in the amount to write (or, when a tape recorder is used, how much to record). That is, you want to tell the client, with tact, that you don't want a complete "blow-by-blow" description of every event during the day, nor do you want a complete autobiography. Rather, you want to be clear that the recorded events should be related to the client's target(s), and should be recorded as succinctly as possible. You might suggest that the client summarize each event using only a line or two. You might even practice this with the client, using hypothetical situations. On the other hand, on the forms you do use, be sure that there's enough room between the lines for the client to write. There's nothing more frustrating for the client than trying to use a form that simply doesn't provide enough room, even for succinct statements.

When the client brings the logs in to you, you would want to go over them with the client. Schwartz and Goldiamond (1975) recommend that the practitioner, at least initially, read them aloud to the client. This is done so that the practitioner can serve as a model for how to deal with the information on the log. This is done also, in part, to reduce misunderstandings due to illegible handwriting, and because it allows the client to fill in additional details regarding the recorded events. The client may read the logs aloud to the practitioner if the client desires to do so. The session may cover the entire log, or concentrate on parts of it that seem especially critical or problematic.

Client logs are not for everyone. Indeed, even very motivated clients may tire of their use over time. Thus, you may get far more information from some clients in the baseline period than you will over a long intervention period. Many people will just tire of filling out these logs.

This is one reason that we recommend modification of logs into evaluation logs. If you are keeping track of the frequency or duration of each incident (counts), or are collecting information on an individualized rating scale for each incident, the longer form of the log may be modified over time so that the client simply counts each incident and/or rates it on an IRS, and the continuity of the measure from baseline through intervention is thereby maintained.

PRACTITIONER LOGS

Many practitioners take notes during or after talking with clients, and some even tape-record some sessions with clients. Practitioners can use some of the same types of logs used by clients to make recordings more systematic and productive, and these can be called "practitioner logs." In a way this isn't anything new; what we're talking about is similar to the systematic practice of clinical records that oftentimes are kept by practitioners (Kagle, 1983, 1984a, 1991; Reid, 1990; Reid & Davis, 1987). However, using a structured log-type record provides more focused and succinct information that is more easily analyzed, and it provides some control over practitioner bias by providing a structure for the information recorded (Reid, 1990; Reid & Davis, 1987).

Practitioner logs can serve the same functions as client logs. They can be used to (a) pinpoint and define client targets, (b) generate contextually sensitive, individualized, intervention hypotheses, and (c) evaluate change over time in a client's targets. In addition, practitioner logs can be used to monitor the services provided to clients.

Let's take an example of a practitioner log. Suppose that you are working to get the client to express his or her feelings to you. You might use the client's interaction log to identify circumstances that facilitate or impede achieving this objective. You could keep notes on your log indicating incidents when the client disclosed feelings, and the context in which this occurred (e.g., in response to a direct question by you, in the discussion of a particular area of client concern). (Another way to approach this would be to record "critical incidents" that seemed to elicit the expression of feelings.) The log you are keeping might provide clues about how to increase the expression of feelings (e.g., you need to make a request that the client express feelings). This log also would provide a record of the frequency with which the client expresses his or her feelings, and this frequency could be charted in order to monitor progress toward this objective. You also could record the quality of each self-disclosure using a simple individualized rating scale. These ratings might suggest areas in which the client is more or less able to disclose feelings, which might provide further clues about how to increase self-disclosure. These ratings also could be charted to provide an additional quantitative indicator of progress toward this intermediate goal.

Let's look at another example of a practitioner log. Suppose that you're leading an adolescent pregnancy prevention group composed of both boys and girls. As part of your assessment of the skills needed by these adolescents, and as part of your evaluation plan, you have mixed-gender dyads role-play stressful dating situations (e.g., being asked to spend the night with a date, being asked whether or not you have a birth control device) (e.g., Schinke et al., 1981). You could keep a log of these role plays for each adolescent (or perhaps audiotape or videotape and later record); on the logs you record the type of unreasonable request that is role-played and whether the adolescent is able to refuse the unreasonable request effectively. (A simple IRS also could be used to rate the effectiveness of the response.) This log could be used to generate individually tailored targets and intervention strategies. Also, a ratio of the number of effective refusals to the number of unreasonable requests could be constructed from the log for each client, and this quantitative index could be used to monitor progress for individual clients.

Practitioner logs also are useful for monitoring the delivery of services. In fact, this is a common use of logs (e.g., Kagle, 1983, 1984a, 1991; Seaberg, 1970; Videka-Sherman & Reid, 1982). For example, Kagle (1984a) provides an example of a "chronolog" to monitor the delivery of services (other such logs are discussed and illustrated in Kagle, 1991). This is just a log with a column to enter the (a) date of service, (b) time of service, (c) service activity, (d) person receiving the service, and (e) purpose and content of the service. An example of a chronolog adapted from Kagle is illustrated in Figure 8.13. The use of this general type of log is fairly widespread, and such information increasingly is being entered, stored, and organized using a computer (Mutschler, 1987; Mutschler & Hasenfeld, 1986).

As a practitioner you have extensive training in human behavior and intervention strategies, and you're intimately involved in the helping process with clients. This puts you in a unique position to observe and record information about the unique circumstances of your clients and about the services provided to them (Reid, 1990; Reid & Davis, 1987). Therefore, the use of practitioner logs can provide valuable information. However, you need to remember that your stake in the outcome may color your view of this process, and even more important, that the information available to you is limited to your firsthand observations of the client during a limited amount of time and in a restricted range of situations. Therefore, it's important to take steps with practitioner logs, as with all measures, to maximize the reliability and validity of the information collected.

MAXIMIZING AND VERIFYING THE RELIABILITY AND VALIDITY OF LOGS

Previous chapters discussed different factors that can influence the reliability and validity of client and practitioner reports of the frequency, duration, or intensity of client targets. We also discussed strategies for maximizing

Date	Time	Activity	With	Purpose/Content
7/29	9:00-9:15 a.m.	Phone call	Ms. M.	Scheduled a home visit and explained reason for visit.
7/30	3:00-5:00 p.m.	Home visit	Ms. M. and son	Discussed allegation of neglect with Ms. M. Talked with Ms. M. about her resources (food, employment). Assessed Ms. M.'s parenting knowledge, skills, and resources. Made arrangements for Ms. M. to apply for financial assistance. Scheduled another home visit.
8/6	3:00-5:00 p.m.	Home visit	Ms. M.	Followed up on financial assistance application. Worked with Ms. M. to enhance parenting skills. Worked with Ms. M. to increase social supports. Scheduled another home visit.

FIGURE 8.13   Example of a chronolog.

and verifying the reliability and validity of these reports. In particular, we emphasize the importance of obtaining and comparing information about client targets from multiple sources (e.g., clients, practitioners, relevant others, and independent observers), and using multiple measurement methods (e.g., observation of the frequency and duration of specific behaviors, ratings using individualized rating and standardized scales). These strategies also apply to client and practitioner logs, although logs do have some distinct features.

Client logs are useful because they capture a rich array of information about the client's perceptions of his or her targets and the unique circumstances under which these targets occur. Practitioner logs capture a rich array of information about a client from the unique perspective of a person who is highly trained and intimately involved in the helping process. However, the diversity and subjectivity of some of the information collected with logs has the potential to decrease the reliability and validity of the information. Therefore, it's especially important to use the strategies discussed in previous chapters to try to maximize the reliability and validity of the information collected with logs, and to verify the reliability and validity of this information by obtaining and comparing information from different sources and different measurement methods.

First and foremost, try at the outset to ensure that the information collected using logs is accurate. Explain to clients in a confident manner the importance of recording, and emphasize that accurate recording is essential to the success of the intervention. Gently impress on the client that the value of client logs depends almost completely on their accuracy, and be certain that the client doesn't think that he or she can "help" the program by being "over-generous" in reporting progress. Ensure that the information collected is relevant, the data collection task is not too taxing, and the measurement tasks are defined clearly. Make sure that the proper tools are available for recording (e.g., forms, tape recorder), and train, monitor, and retrain the client in the proper recording procedures. Make sure recording is done as soon as possible after the event to be re-

corded. Be sure you use the information that is collected; be encouraging, supportive, praising, and empathic of the client's recording efforts, but be careful you don't inadvertently encourage the client to report improvement when it doesn't occur.

A variety of strategies for verifying the reliability and validity of the frequency, duration, or intensity of a target were discussed in previous chapters. These strategies also can be applied to the information collected by logs. Try to verify the consistency with which different people observe the same events (i.e., interobserver reliability). Use of other observers in the client's home, making telephone calls, interviewing others in the client's environment about the events the client reports, and even comparing two independently prepared logs, all have been suggested by Schwartz and Goldiamond (1975) as methods of verifying the interobserver reliability of client logs. The reliability of practitioner logs can be verified by audiotaping or videotaping sessions with clients and having a supervisor, colleague, or in some cases a consultant review all or randomly selected parts of the recorded information; they even could independently construct a log with which the original log can be compared.

In general, the validity of the information collected by logs can be verified by comparing the information from logs to some standard (i.e., criterion validity) or to other measured variables with which it theoretically should or should not be associated (construct validity). For example, a man receiving help for verbally and emotionally abusing his wife might be asked to keep a log of abusive incidents and the circumstances under which they occur. His wife may be asked to keep a parallel log against which the husband's log could be compared (assuming the relative accuracy of the wife's information, and that these reports would not put the wife at further risk). The husband and wife also might be asked to each complete a standardized index of marital satisfaction on a regular basis, and changes in marital satisfaction and abuse could be compared over time, on the assumption that when abuse decreases, satisfaction will increase. Finally, one way to verify the validity of an interventive hypothesis generated by a log might be to implement the intervention suggested by the log and examine whether the expected change occurs.

Verifying the reliability and validity of logs is important, but what the client chooses to report and how it's reported is as important as "objective reality." Thus, both what the client does and doesn't report are topics for discussion in interviews. You and the client can decide on the meaning and utility of such information. Even if the client's data can't be checked objectively, this doesn't mean that the information automatically should be excluded from consideration. Simply discussing the decisions the client made to include or exclude certain occurrences can provide fruitful information for assessment and intervention.

SUMMARY

Client logs are journals kept by the client to record the unique qualitative contextual circumstances surrounding his or her targets, and to record quantitative dimensions of these targets. These logs can be set up to include preset (e.g., every hour) or open (e.g., critical incident) time categories, and can include any number of categories of information. Four types of logs—exploratory, target, interaction, and evaluation—can be used, and forms were provided for your use in practice. These logs can be used to pinpoint and define problems, generate individualized hypotheses for intervention, and evaluate change over time in a client's targets. The practitioner log is a variation of the client log that can be used for much the same purposes, although it also can be used to monitor the delivery of services. Finally, we discussed strategies for maximizing and verifying the reliability and validity of client and practitioner logs.

9

REACTIVITY AND NONREACTIVE MEASURES

PURPOSE: This chapter begins by describing reactivity as the way measurement procedures actually can produce changes in what is being measured. Then it presents a number of ways to minimize these effects. It proceeds by discussing the use of a wide range of unobtrusive measures, or measures that will not have a reactive effect. ■

Introduction
Reactivity of Measures
Sources of Reactivity
Overcoming Reactivity
Reactivity in Self-Monitoring
Guidelines for Using Reactivity
    in Self-Monitoring
Unobtrusive (Nonreactive) Measures

Archival Records
    Public Records
    Private Records
Behavior Products
Simple Observations
    Types of Simple Observations
Physical Traces
Summary

INTRODUCTION

A concern some practitioners express about single-system evaluation is that the evaluation will affect practice, presumably in some negative, or at least unpredictable, way. There's certainly a grain of truth to this concern. A client who knows that he or she will be observed by a practitioner, relevant other, or independent observer might behave or respond differently. Similarly, when a practitioner knows that his or her evaluations will be reviewed by peers, supervisors, administrators, or even clients, the records might be different from the way they would be otherwise. When a relevant other or

independent observer knows that his or her observations of a client will be reviewed by a practitioner, the observations might be different from the way they would be otherwise. As mentioned in Chapter 2, a target or event that changes as the result of being observed or otherwise measured is said to be "reactive."

The use of reactive measures makes it difficult to obtain a valid picture of client change, which in turn makes it difficult to determine accurately the effects of an intervention. A reactive measure may make an ineffective intervention appear effective, or an effective intervention appear ineffective. For example, suppose that a school social worker teaches a high school course on sexuality designed to reduce targeted sexual behaviors. Anonymous self-reports of the behaviors are collected weekly. There's a 3-week baseline period before the behaviors are discussed in class, followed by a 6-week program designed to reduce the behaviors. As shown in Figure 9.1, the hypothetical results suggest a reduction in the behaviors. One explanation for this is that the behaviors actually decreased; another is that the intervention made students feel guilty about engaging in the behaviors and reluctant to acknowledge and report them. Suppose in-

stead that the results in Figure 9.2 were obtained. One explanation for these results is that change did not occur; another is that the baseline rate was actually higher than reported because students initially underreported the behavior because they felt embarrassed, and so there was actually a decrease from baseline to intervention.

Reactivity makes it difficult to determine whether changes that do occur will be maintained when the evaluation plan is no longer in place. For example, when students are no longer asked questions about their sexual

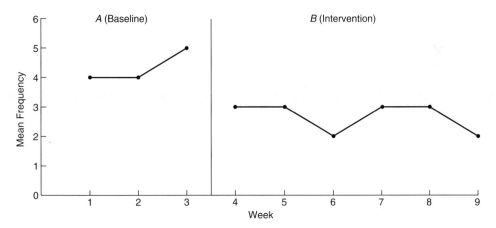

FIGURE 9.1   Mean frequency of targeted sexual behaviors.

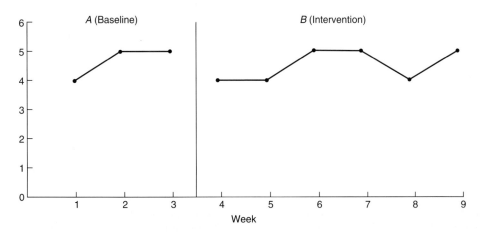

FIGURE 9.2   Mean frequency of targeted sexual behaviors.

behavior on a weekly basis they may be more likely to engage in the targeted behaviors because the behaviors are no longer called to their attention. However, it's also possible for reactive changes to persist after the observation ends. For example, simply asking students questions about their sexual behavior might cause them to reexamine and change their behavior.

Throughout the previous chapters we suggested a number of methods to minimize reactivity. Further, we don't mean to suggest that reactivity is a problem that occurs in all or even most evaluations. For example, in a review of observer reactivity, Foster and Cone (1986) found that only 34% of the behaviors studied appeared to be affected by the presence of an observer. Indeed, even when some reactivity does occur, it may not last long; that is, reactive effects tend to decrease over time. Thus, some of the inherent advantages of single-system evaluation, such as the collection of information on the client's target on a repeated basis over time, tend to minimize the significance of this problem. However, reactivity can occur, and it's difficult to predict the conditions under which it will occur. Therefore, methods that minimize reactivity are necessary to ensure the accurate measurement of client change and the accurate assessment of the effects of intervention.

REACTIVITY OF MEASURES

Fortunately some measurement methods are not reactive, and this chapter presents numerous nonreactive measures and ways they can be integrated into practice (see also Maisto & Maisto, 1983; Webb et al., 1981). First, however, some of the reasons for reactivity will be discussed, as well as methods to minimize reactivity, especially when clients are asked to monitor and record their own behavior.

Sources of Reactivity

Reactivity can occur for different reasons (Cook & Campbell, 1979; Rosenthal & Rosnow, 1991; Webb et al., 1981). An understanding of these reasons will help you minimize reactivity, and

it will help you evaluate evaluation strategies in terms of their potential reactivity.

Reactivity can occur because a client *adopts a role* that is inconsistent to some extent with his or her actual beliefs, feelings, or behaviors. This can happen when a client's behavior is influenced by his or her perceptions of the implicit or explicit goals, expectations, and behavior of the practitioner or other interested parties (e.g., family members). These sometimes are referred to as "demand characteristics" (Rosenthal & Rosnow, 1991). In response to these perceived goals, expectations, and behavior the client might adopt a "good client" role, acting in a way that is consistent with the implicit goals and expectations of interested parties (e.g., a client might present numerous problems when seeking help initially, but few problems after the initiation of an intervention). The client might instead adopt a "negativistic client" role, acting in a way that is inconsistent with these goals and expectations. Adoption of the "good client" role can make an intervention appear more successful than it really is, and adoption of the "negativistic client" role can have the opposite effect.

The fear of being evaluated and judged unfavorably can cause a client to behave in a way that makes him or her "look good." This fear is sometimes referred to as *evaluation apprehension* (Cook & Campbell, 1979) or the guinea pig effect (Webb et al., 1981). For example, suppose that you examine the effect of a family life education program on the contraceptive use of an adolescent girl (i.e., the rate of contraceptive use per number of occasions of intercourse). Several weeks of baseline information about contraceptive use is collected from the client prior to intervention. Suppose that the program makes the client more apprehensive about reporting incidents when contraception was not used, leading to overreports of contraceptive use and making it appear as if the rate of contraception increased. This would result in an inaccurate picture of change in contraceptive use, and it would make the intervention appear more effective than it is.

The frequency of measurement, in addition to measurement per se, also can influence reactivity. As the result of increasing familiarity with the measurement procedure or comfort with the presence of an observer, individuals may be less interested, motivated, or anxious during succeeding observations, or they may be more knowledgeable and skilled. The change in behavior resulting from repeated measurement is oftentimes referred to as a *testing effect*. In general, it's undesirable because it makes it difficult to get a picture of the target under conditions when it's not being measured, and it can make it difficult to determine the effect of an intervention. However, ironically perhaps, repeated measurement also can be used to reduce reactivity. That is, an observer might spend a period of time in a setting making observations prior to actual data collection, so that those being observed will become comfortable with the observer and will react less to being observed.

Client observations that are made by practitioners, relevant others, and independent observers also can be influenced by perceptions of implicit goals, expectations, or behaviors, or by evaluation apprehension. Observations made by practitioners might be influenced by agency or supervisor goals or expectations, or by apprehension about agency or supervisor oversight. Observations made by relevant others or independent observers might be influenced by the implicit goals, expectations, or behaviors of practitioners, or by apprehension about having their observations reviewed by practitioners or clients. Therefore, the observations of practitioners, relevant others, or independent observers might present an inaccurate picture of client change, and they might misrepresent the effects of interventions.

Characteristics of observers also can affect the behavior of those whom they observe. For example, the sex, age, ethnicity, and race of a practitioner, relevant other, or independent observer might influence client behavior, often subtly, sometimes dramatically. Likewise, *characteristics of clients,* such as those described for observers but also including characteristics of the problem and its severity, can influence observations made by a practitioner, relevant other, or independent observer. Similarly, *characteristics of those who oversee data collection* might influence those they supervise. For example,

supervisor characteristics or agency characteristics (e.g., secular vs. religious) might influence practitioner observations of a client, or practitioner characteristics might influence observations made by relevant others or independent observers.

Overcoming Reactivity

Behavior doesn't automatically change as the result of being observed or otherwise measured. As Rosenthal and Rosnow (1991) note, for people being observed to respond to implicit goals, expectations, or behaviors, they must be sensitive and receptive to these conditions, they must be motivated to respond to them, and they must be capable of responding to them. Potentially, reactivity can be short-circuited at any of these points.

There are several general ways to attempt to avoid reactivity. We discuss a number of these here, with a focus on use of the practitioner or relevant others as observers, and go into detail with some suggestions on how to deal with reactivity in self-monitoring in the following section.

First, it's probably obvious that the potential for reactive effects exists in many measures. Sometimes, they are difficult or impossible to avoid. In those situations, the best one can do, perhaps, is to be aware of the potential and to try to either use it constructively or at least account for it. (Some suggestions for doing this are offered in our discussion of reactivity in self-monitoring.)

A second possibility for overcoming reactive effects is to use measures that are valid and reliable (see Chapter 2). For example, if your measure has high test-retest reliability, it's stable, so that changes that do appear are less likely to be a result of changes in the measure itself rather than changes in the client. Similarly, if you're using direct observation to measure overt behaviors, using the training methods described in Chapter 5–by defining the behavior clearly and by regularly assessing the agreement between your primary observer and secondary observer(s)–you can be more confident that changes are not due to changes in the evaluation instrument.

Third, many of the problems of client-related reactivity can be overcome by the way you administer the measure and the type of instructions you give the client (e.g., encouraging the client to be as honest as possible when filling out a questionnaire). Many of these guidelines for administering a measure were described in previous chapters.

A fourth possibility is to attempt to use measures that are unobtrusive whenever possible. Unobtrusive measurement is done without the knowledge of the person being measured. When people are unaware that their behavior is being measured, they're less likely to react to the measurements. We discuss a range of unobtrusive measures later in this chapter.

A fifth possibility is to use multiple measures of a target (e.g., an unobtrusive and an obtrusive measure) or, multiple measures that are subject to different types of biases—for example, independent teacher and student reports of a student's school behavior. (There are several additional reasons for using multiple measures, and we discuss these in Chapter 10 on how to select a measure.)

In addition to the above general suggestions for overcoming reactivity, there are a number of ways to minimize reactivity when client behaviors are observed in the natural environment, and when the client knows that he or she is being observed (Barlow & Hersen, 1984, pp. 120–121; Foster & Cone, 1986, pp. 302–314; Kazdin, 1982). In general, though, these suggestions all involve having the observer try to be as inconspicuous and unobtrusive as possible:

1. The observer should avoid interacting with those to be observed before, during, and after the observations, and should minimize eye contact.

2. The observer's presence should be explained to those he or she will be observing in simple, matter-of-fact language, and then business as usual should proceed.

3. The observer should try to be positioned away from the ordinary flow of movement. The position should allow an unobstructed view of the entire area.

4. The observer's clothing and behavior should not be so different as to create unusual attention.

5. The observer should follow all formal and informal rules and regulations of the setting in which he or she is observing.

6. The observer should attempt to enter the setting during the least disruptive time—for example, before rather than during a class or group session.

7. The observer should spend a period of time in the setting immediately prior to data collection so that everyone in the setting will become accustomed to the observer's presence.

Of course, it probably goes without saying that none of the above actually guarantees that the measurement process will be nonreactive. We all know that the mere presence of someone else in our family, recreation, or work setting can change the "natural" pattern of activities. Nevertheless, the above suggestions were offered in the spirit of attempting to minimize those disruptions, even though they may never be eliminated completely.

Reactivity in Self-Monitoring

One of the most common measurement methods involves having clients observe and record their own behaviors. This is called self-monitoring, as discussed in Chapter 5. There's an extensive body of research evaluating the reliability, validity, utility, and, particularly, reactivity of self-monitoring (Bornstein et al., 1986; Kopp, 1988). Since many of the measurement strategies we describe in this book involve some form of self-monitoring, we discussed many of those concerns in the context of the specific measures. We also suggest going over at least one of the reviews of self-monitoring research that have appeared in the research (e.g., Bornstein et al., 1986; Kopp, 1988). However, because of the generality of this issue across situations, the reactivity of monitoring is reviewed briefly here.

Reactivity in self-monitoring has been observed using all types of research designs—

ranging from case studies to controlled group experimental designs—and in a wide range of target behaviors. On the other hand, a number of studies also have reported that self-monitoring did not in and of itself produce behavior changes. For example, a recent study showed that use of self-report standardized measures such as described in Chapter 7 was not reactive, in that it had no impact on dropout or outcome in psychodynamically oriented practice (Applegate, 1992). We believe it best to err on the conservative side and to be cautious in interpreting data—that is, presuming that reactivity may occur and concluding that it doesn't occur only when you have reasonable evidence. One obvious test of reactivity is to watch the baseline data to see if there are any systematic changes prior to intervention. If there are, you might conclude that reactive effects, or other uncontrolled effects, are present, and work from there, perhaps by extending the period of time during which you collect baseline data if this will not negatively affect your intervention.

One way of examining the possibility of reactivity in the measures you select for use in self-monitoring is to be aware of the factors that may control it. The following include some of these factors (Bornstein et al., 1986; Kopp, 1988; McFall, 1977b; Nelson, 1977):

1. *Motivation.* Higher motivation to change may lead to more reactive changes. Thus, you could expect more reactive changes in clients who seem highly motivated.

2. *Desired direction of the behavior.* Self-monitoring may lead positive behaviors to increase and negative behaviors to decrease.

3. *Practitioner instructions.* It may be that simply telling clients before intervention that their behaviors will or should change can produce reactive effects.

4. *Nature of the target.* Some studies have shown that verbal behavior is less reactive than motor behavior.

5. *Goals and feedback.* It appears that setting specific goals, being rewarded for progress, and getting feedback on performance increase reactive effects.

6. *Timing.* Recording prior to engaging in a target behavior (e.g., smoking, eating) seems to produce more reactivity than recording after engaging in the behavior.

7. *Nature of the recording instrument.* The more obtrusive the device used to record, the more reactivity seems to occur.

8. *Number of behaviors monitored.* The more behaviors that are self-monitored, the less likely it is that reactivity will occur (i.e., recording one behavior may lead to greater reactivity than recording two or three).

9. *Schedule of self-monitoring.* Recording behaviors intermittently seems to produce less reactivity than continuous recording.

It should be noted that the above factors that may affect reactivity in self-monitoring are only tentative conclusions. None has been demonstrated to affect reactivity in all cases. Yet there's enough consistency in these findings to lead to some suggestions for their utilization.

Guidelines for Using Reactivity in Self-Monitoring

You might actually want to use reactive effects to enhance your intervention program. That is, reactivity can be used in a positive sense, to add to the effects of your intervention (e.g., having a client self-monitor his or her caloric intake may lead to decreased caloric intake). This is a strategy that has been used in several studies (Bornstein et al., 1986; Kopp, 1988; McFall, 1977b; Nelson, 1977). The key here is to also use the factors described above to maximize the process.

By way of summary, we can suggest several tentative guidelines to help you use and evaluate reactive effects, either to increase or decrease reactivity. You must decide in a given case whether such changes are desirable. Because reactivity might be useful to you in some situations as a way of adding impetus to your planned intervention, we're including ways you can actually increase reactivity, in addition to ways you can decrease reactivity.

Increasing Reactivity

1. Have the client self-monitor positive behaviors that are to be increased or negative behaviors that are to be decreased.

2. Focus on motor behavior.

3. Focus on one or a very limited number of behaviors.

4. Record on a regular, systematic basis.

5. Make clear value statements about the desirability of change.

6. Set specific goals.

7. Give feedback on performance to your client.

8. Provide reinforcement for change.

9. Tell the client prior to intervention that his or her behaviors will or should change.

10. Have the client record prior to engaging in a target behavior.

11. Use a very intrusive recording device.

Decreasing or Avoiding Reactivity

1. Focus on verbal behavior.

2. Self-monitor multiple behaviors.

3. Record on an intermittent basis.

4. Use an unobtrusive measure.

5. Wait for baseline data to be stable before starting intervention (see Chapter 12).

6. Use reliability checks about which the client is unaware. Someone else in the natural environment, or the practitioner, can be asked to monitor the behaviors once in a while and the results can be compared. (This, of course, is not possible if the self-monitored behaviors, such as thoughts, are not observable to others.)

7. Compare the client's results with results on another measure presumably measuring the same phenomenon (e.g., the client's tally of the number of negative self-

references with his or her scores on an instrument designed to measure self-esteem).

8. Have independent observers collect data on the target prior to the client's self-recorded baseline and compare these two periods. (This, again, is not possible if the self-monitored behaviors are not observable to others.)

9. Compare the client's initial retrospective reports about the occurrence of the target in the recent past with the client's initial (baseline) self-monitoring.

In many of the above suggestions, the goal is to compare records obtained through self-monitoring with those obtained from other measurement methods. If undesirable reactivity appears to be high—thus producing inaccurate data—the practitioner can choose to change the measurement package or to engage in a miniprogram of intervention designed to help the client record more accurately.

Finally, there's some evidence that reactivity in self-monitoring may be more likely at the beginning of the recording program and may weaken over time (Kopp, 1988). Thus, in some circumstances, in the long run, reactivity may not be much of a problem at all. Still, it's probably wise at least to be aware of the possibility of the existence of reactive effects in self-monitoring, and to be very cautious in evaluating results obtained when self-monitoring is the only form of measurement used.

UNOBTRUSIVE (NONREACTIVE) MEASURES

Unobtrusive measures are measures that can be used without the knowledge of the person being measured. If a person (or organization for that matter) is not aware of evaluation, or at least of a particular form of measurement, there's no reason to believe that reactivity will occur. Consequently, we suggest that unobtrusive measures be considered as possibilities when you set out to measure your client's target. The remainder of the chapter presents a range of these unobtrusive (or nonreactive) measures for your use.

Unfortunately, many unobtrusive methods are indirect ways of measuring targets. In these instances they probably should serve as secondary sources of information when there is more direct evidence of changes in the client's target. However, in some instances, when the unobtrusive measure is a direct record of the targets (e.g., school grades or number of math problems finished correctly), it can serve as a primary measure.

The validity, reliability, directness, ease of use, accessibility, and relevance of these measures have to be estimated when you make your decision regarding whether to use them. As just one example, in deciding to use records that have been collected for other purposes as a measure of your target, it is important to determine that the records were collected consistently and in the same way across time, so that any changes in the records are not merely a result of changes in the way the records were being kept or some other irrelevant outside event.

Some unobtrusive measures have weaknesses that make their use as the sole or even primary data source open to question. We discuss some of these weaknesses in this chapter so that you can be aware of the pitfalls in some unobtrusive measures. Often, though, unobtrusive measures can be used in conjunction with other measures, and changes over time in the different measures can be charted and compared. For example, suppose that you're a school social worker charged with developing a schoolwide program to increase interaction among African American and white students. You might unobtrusively monitor the proportion of students sitting next to different-race students in the lunchroom or classroom. This measure would not capture the total amount of time spent together. Therefore, you might survey students weekly and ask them to report the total amount of time spent with different-race students. These self-reports would probably not be completely accurate, either. For example, upon implementation of the intervention there might be increased social pressure to interact with students of a different race, and this might lead to overreports of the amount of time spent (i.e., the intervention would appear effective even if it was not). However, if the changes in the different measures are comparable–for example, as shown in Figure 9.3–support is provided for the accuracy of the observed pattern of change.

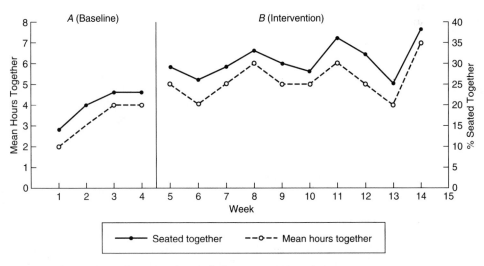

FIGURE 9.3   Interaction between white and African American students.

The type of unobtrusive measures we describe, in large part using the Webb et al. (1981) categories, are archival records, behavior products, simple observation, and physical traces.

Archival Records

If there's anything with which most helping professionals are familiar, it is records. Yet, while records are sometimes considered to be the professional's number one enemy, they can be extremely useful in helping measure the client's target. Archival records essentially refer to records that are kept for various purposes not necessarily related to your intervention program. But because these records are available from a variety of sources and can be useful, they comprise perhaps the most important form of unobtrusive measure. There are two basic types of archival records—public and private (Webb et al., 1981).

Public Records. There is a whole range of public records that could be considered as measures for evaluating the success of your interventions. For example, Webb et al. (1981) describe categories of records such as actuarial records (e.g., demographic records such as births, deaths, divorces, marriages), political and judicial records, government documents, and the mass media.

To some extent, we use a bit of license in calling all of these records "public." Not all may be available to everyone. Yet in the broadest sense, we refer to those measures that are truly public (open and available to every citizen), plus those that are collected by organizations and agencies that may not be widely available to all citizens, but are available to you as a helping professional (e.g., a school record). In essence we define public records as those that are usually maintained by organizations over periods of time for a variety of their own purposes, but may be used by you to measure the success of your intervention.

Many of these records are of particular value in analyzing changes over time in organizations, policies, or interventions aimed at groups or large collectives. Thus, if your inter-

vention efforts involve an attempt to change an agency's program policies, you have immediately available to you a whole range of data tapping important dimensions of possible interest—for example, measures of staff turnover, number of complaints, number or types of referral sources, productivity, characteristics of clients, time on the waiting list, number of premature terminations, case records, process recordings, and so on (e.g., see the many uses suggested in Tripodi & Harrington, 1979).

Let's say you design a program to increase the number of low-income clients coming to your agency. By simply inspecting the intake sheets of your agency, you will have excellent feedback regarding whether any changes did in fact take place. A chart documenting these changes might look like the one in Figure 9.4.

Similarly, you might want to use the functioning of the participants in your agency's programs as an overall outcome measure. You can do this by simply adding up individual data and using averages (Bloom, Butch, & Walker, 1979; Tripodi & Harrington, 1979).

Perhaps your goal is to decrease the occurrence of criminal acts among juvenile gang members who participate in your agency's program. You could use measures such as the average number of offenses per program participant; the proportion or number of those who are arrested or convicted, or who become recidivists; or the average length of stay in a correctional facility over some specified time period (Tripodi & Harrington, 1979). With all of these measures, though, it's important to be sure that the data are both valid and reliable. For example, program participants might simply be going into other neighborhoods to commit crimes. Or police, notified that a program is under way, may be more reluctant (or more willing) to arrest program participants. But if these obstacles can be overcome, your chart might look like Figure 9.5.

There are a host of other potential uses of public records, especially in the institutions and organizations in which most helping professionals work—hospitals, schools, clinics. These records can be used for evaluating not only the effects of programs aimed at changing agency policies, but also the effects of inter-

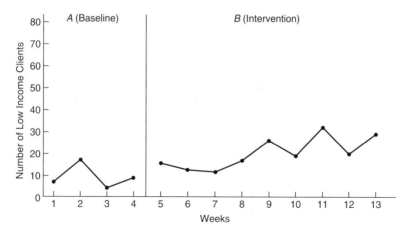

FIGURE 9.4   Number of low-income clients being seen at intake.

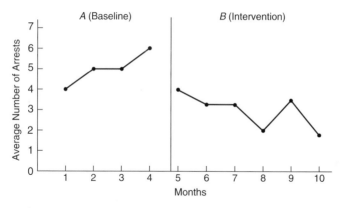

FIGURE 9.5   Average number of arrests per month of program participants.

vention programs on individuals. For example, Flaherty, Barry, and Swift (1978) illustrate the use of an unobtrusive measure–existing records of an early prevention project for high-risk children–to evaluate the development of interagency coordination.

Perhaps the best example of data available for other purposes that can be used to evaluate individual and program effect is school records. A whole range of data typically is collected in schools: academic grades, scores on standardized tests (IQ, achievement tests), attendance records, number of problems or pages finished correctly (don't forget the *cor-*

rectly part; it may be of little value to have 10 problems finished with the wrong answers, unless you're only building the client's motivation to spend time on the work). Of course, with data such as homework assignments, it's important to evaluate whether your client had roughly similar amounts and type of work over the days of the program so that any changes won't be purely a result of the teacher changing the assignment. (The teacher's cooperation might also be elicited to ensure consistency.)

You can use such data to evaluate changes in both groups or individuals. For example,

Figure 9.6 depicts the progress of a program intended to improve a student's attendance at school, while at the same time enhancing the learning conditions for the student at school. Figure 9.7 describes the results of a program intended to evaluate the practitioner's success in helping a whole class of low-income children turn in completed homework assignments every day.

A number of potential problems could arise with the use of public records. Many of these have been described by Flaherty et al. (1978), Cook and Campbell (1979), Webb et al. (1981), and Maisto and Maisto (1983). If you do use public records to evaluate an intervention program, it is important to assess the records you're using to determine whether these factors are present. If they are, you have to take them into account, especially in being particularly cautious in interpreting results.

At the most practical level, it is often difficult to determine what is available in the realm of public records. Once you do, you may have difficulty in obtaining access to the data; this could require a long process of negotiation with the organization. Then, if you do get ac-

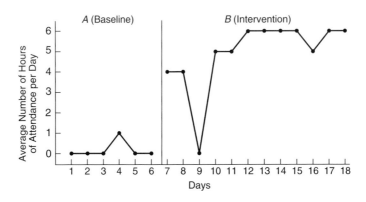

FIGURE 9.6 Average number of hours of attendance per day for Wilma.

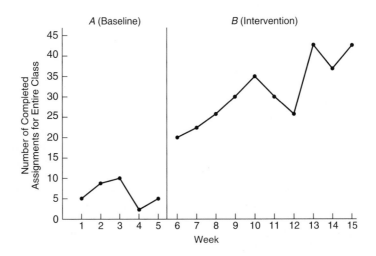

FIGURE 9.7 Number of assignments turned in per week in Ms. Jones's class of 25 students.

cess, you might be shocked to find that all the data weren't on hand in the first place.

A more important problem with public records—or any archival data—is that there may be systematic bias in their contents (Cook & Campbell, 1979). Definitions of what is to be collected may not have been adhered to or may have changed over time. Records may not be complete; the ones you do locate may not be an adequate representation of the rest. The records may not have been properly collected; for example, there may be suspicious regularities where the values entered remain the same for a long time, or there may be wide variability suggesting sloppy record-keeping procedures.

Finally, archival data are generally rather inflexible. You might want information by the week and it's only available by the month. You might need it broken down by race or other characteristics and it's not.

But, if you are to use archival data, you will have to be content with what you do find. The data are unobtrusive and can avoid many reactive effects. They particularly avoid the "guinea pig effect" of people knowing they're in a study; often, the data are collected well before a study or intervention program is undertaken, or they may have been collected for other purposes. Finally, records offer the advantage of allowing the evaluation of activities that otherwise might be lost (Flaherty et al., 1978). This is particularly so when evaluation was not perceived as necessary until after the fact.

Private Records.   Private records generally are much less available than public records, but they can be helpful to you in planning and evaluating intervention programs. Two key principles in use of private records, of course, are (a) obtaining the client's permission to examine them and (b) maintaining confidentiality about what you find.

The types of private records that Webb et al. (1981) describe are largely of value for other forms of research—for example, retrospective studies of the lives of important historical figures. They discuss use of autobiographies, diaries, and letters. Yet there are some implications of these materials for practice.

Let's say you're helping a family deal with a variety of stressful events including managing their finances. If this family is keeping a record of expenditures—checking account, budget book, shopping lists, and so on—you may be able to not only see how much money is spent over a given period of time, but also understand how the money is allocated (i.e., what proportion goes to food, activities, clothing). If the family is willing to keep ongoing records, you would have a good indication of changes from the preintervention to intervention periods.

Of course, using private records poses a problem in ascertaining their validity. (Political events reveal that this may be as much or more of a problem with public records.) Such records may be deliberately misrepresented or mistakenly distorted. Thus, one task for the practitioner is to try to evaluate whether the documents report accurate information and can be used as a measure for evaluating changes. In the event that they're unintentionally distorted, the practitioner can also help the client develop a more accurate system of keeping records.

Behavior Products

Behavior products are an important source of unobtrusive measures (see, e.g., Barlow, Hayes, & Nelson, 1984; Hayes, Barlow, & Nelson, 1998; Haynes & Wilson, 1979, pp. 140–144; and Nay, 1979, pp. 125, 126, 149–155). Behavior products essentially refer to the effects or results of behaviors rather than the behaviors themselves. That is, rather than directly monitoring the actual behavior of the client, you would monitor any temporary or permanent effect that can be seen as the result of a specifiable behavior. Ayllon and Azrin (1968) note that behavior products can be used when a more direct measure of the behavior might interfere with the behavior being observed, when it takes too much time to observe the behavior directly, or when the actual behavior itself is not available for measurement. Since the observer is not ordinarily present when behavior products are used (unless, of course, the observer happens to be the client), there's less chance for the measurement process to interfere with the natural occurrence of the behavior.

There are a number of advantages to using behavior products (Mann, 1976, p. 469; Nay, 1979, p. 125). First, a product readily lends itself to precise quantification. For example, the number of cigarettes smoked can be assessed by counting cigarette butts left in an ashtray. Second, the observer doesn't have to be present when a behavior is performed. For example, instead of watching a child litter his or her room, the observer can simply count how many articles weren't put away after the play period. Third, using behavior products generally doesn't disturb or interrupt the flow of the client's behavior. Even when the client is recording, he or she can carry out daily activities in an uninterrupted fashion, counting the product only at certain predefined times during the day (e.g., before going to bed). Finally, behavior products are relatively easy to implement, require little or no special equipment, and can easily be taught to the client or relevant others.

There are some problems with the use of behavior products, however (Nay, 1979, p. 126). First, the information is generally limited to "how many" or "how much," and controlling conditions cannot easily be evaluated. Second, many behaviors, as we define them (e.g., thoughts), don't leave products. Third, you have to be sure that the product really is a direct reflection of the behavior of concern and not other factors. This is especially true when more than one person is in the area where a product was left. For example, just because several toys are left out doesn't mean that Johnny left them out (watch out for his older brother). Finally, it may be that some behavior products are not sensitive to slight changes in the actual target behavior, so that these changes may not be noticed when only products are being monitored.

There are a number of behavior products that you could consider using. The number of cigarette butts in an ashtray is a good sign of the frequency of smoking. In a program to increase home safety practices for preschoolers you might unobtrusively observe the number of safety risks on a home visit (e.g., uncovered electrical outlets, accessible medicines, and

dangerous cleaning products). In a weight reduction program, the number of actual behaviors might be measured (e.g., how much or how fast one eats). But because this might prove not only inefficient but reactive, you might simply choose to monitor actual weight changes, the key product of eating behavior. (Of course, to the extent the client is aware of this monitoring, this would not be a totally unobtrusive measure.)

School settings and other settings involving children, including the home, provide a number of opportunities to use product measures. Completed assignments, children's workbooks, crayon writing on the wall, results on quizzes (a measure perhaps of studying behavior), and items not put away are examples of the range of behavior products available.

Other behavior products that could be considered relatively unobtrusive might be those involved in helping a family or a group on a ward in a hospital care for their own rooms—for example, items left on a floor, beds that are made, or other products of self-management programs. Similarly, if you were setting up a program to diminish litter in a low-income housing project, you might use a measure of the amount of litter in selected yards of the project as did Chapman and Risley (1974).

Let's assume you develop a token economy program on the psychiatric ward of a medical hospital. Rather than measuring the actual behaviors for which the tokens are earned, you might measure the behavior product—the number of tokens that the residents spend. This could be displayed as in Figure 9.8.

Simple Observations

The next category of unobtrusive measures—simple observation—is a variation on and an elaboration of several of the themes presented in earlier chapters. Specifically, simple observation refers to situations "in which the observer has no control over the behavior or sign in question, and plays an unobserved, passive and nonintrusive role in the research situation" (Webb et al., 1981, p. 197). In other words, the observer observes without the client being aware of it. Of course, once the target is ob-

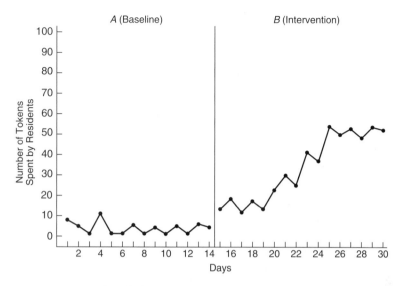

FIGURE 9.8   Number of tokens spent per day.

served, the remainder of the measurement procedure takes on all of the characteristics described in previous chapters. That is, the key difference here is who observes and how that person does it. A frequency count is treated as a frequency count no matter who does the counting.

Although simple observations do have the obvious advantage that while the practitioner or observer is observing, the client is not aware of it (e.g., through a transparent mirror or when students in a classroom or patients on a ward are engaged in some activity and don't notice the observer), there are problems inherent in this approach. The first one concerns problems arising from changes in the observer–either from growing bored with or becoming increasingly expert at the observations. Regular reliability checks as described in Chapter 5 would help to minimize that problem.

A second concern with simple observations is that they're limited to certain phenomena. Since the observer should generally be unnoticed (or, at least, should be observing in unnoticed ways), many of the observations may have to take place in public locations or private locations with special arrangements (one-way viewing mirrors, tape recorders, etc.).

Finally, there's a question of validity with regard to simple observations. Since sometimes one is looking for observable indicators that may be suggestive of other events (e.g., attitudes), it's important to be cautious in making interpretations. Simple observations are often best used as secondary sources of data or, perhaps, data that can be used to cross-validate other observations.

Types of Simple Observations.   The types of simple observations that you can use seem limited only by your imagination and creativity, not to mention the more practical consideration of having someone available to make the simple observations. But, in addition to just a count of some behavior or activity, four basic types of simple observations have been described (Webb et al., 1981).

The first type is the observation of physical signs that might be used to make inferences about attitudes or behaviors. Illustrations of these include changes in hairstyle or makeup, or wearing certain clothes or jewelry, exemplifying changes in style. An example of this would involve the client who complains about being unattractive to those of the other sex. The practitioner might set up a program to help the client learn to dress or groom more attractively, and use "physical signs" to evaluate success.

A second type of simple observation would be the analysis of expressive movements, including smiles, frowns, and gestures. Of course, when one is trying to infer attitudes, feelings, or behaviors from expressions and gestures, an obvious difficulty is in verifying the meaning of what is observed. This might be done by using other signs or other unobtrusive measures to validate the observations. In some circumstances—for example, with use of videotapes for feedback to clients—the practitioner might ask the client the meaning of some gestures that had been observed (but not necessarily the ones being measured to evaluate the program) to check the overall accuracy of inferences about the client's expressions or gestures. Since nonverbal communications tend to play a large part in interpersonal communications anyhow, their analysis for use as a simple observation simply means being more systematic in observing them. But analyzing and making inferences about others' nonverbal communication require understanding of the context and situation of gestures, and also the possible meaning for the sender and receiver.

A third category of simple observation is physical location analysis, examining the way the client uses his or her body in a given social space. This type of measure is commonly used in social psychological research on attitudes—for example, examining seating patterns as an index of interracial relations. But this type of measure also has promise as a secondary or proxy measure for therapeutic purposes. For example, the proximity of members of a family or group in their seating arrangements during sessions with the practitioner might be used to measure changes in their feelings about one another over time.

The fourth category of simple observation is the analysis of language behavior. The purpose of this is to analyze both the content and the expressiveness of the content in relation to time of day, presence of others, and location of the conversation. Thus, you might use tape recordings of interviews to keep track of changes in clients' feelings about themselves and/or oth-

ers. Then, by noting changes in both the frequency of the use of certain words (e.g., positive references to oneself) as well as qualitative or expressive changes in the use of those words, you would have a built-in measure of change over the course of the intervention program. Another example would be to structure family problem-solving activities and then to record these on videotape or observe them through a transparent mirror to be used as ongoing assessment and/or evaluation information.

Physical Traces

The last type of unobtrusive measure involves physical traces. Although there's considerable overlap between physical traces and behavior products, there are some differences. Physical traces refer to evidence left by an individual or group with no knowledge that it may be used for other (e.g., evaluation or research) purposes. Webb et al. (1981) distinguish between two types of trace measures—*erosion*, where the degree of wear on some object produces the measure, and *accretion*, measures of the deposit of some material. The distinction here is between materials *worn away* and materials *deposited*, with emphasis on the physical aspects of those effects. Physical trace measures generally require some degree of inference about the behaviors that produced them. Moreover, a good deal of rummaging around is often involved in order to discover trace measures. They, therefore, tend to be among the least-used measures, especially for single-system evaluation.

Erosion measures refer to the natural remnants of some individual's or group's activity that has selectively worn down certain objects. For example, if you're working in a nursing home, you might determine what the most popular activity in that home is by observing where the rugs were most worn. It might be in front of the television set or in front of the windows where people spend time looking out at the street. This could give you a possible measure for evaluating changes in the group's activities.

Other erosion measures might include decay and breakage (Nay, 1979). Active or aggressive physical activity can be inferred from the number of broken items (e.g., windows) in a school or on a ward. The frequency of repair, replacement, or cleaning of certain objects in a setting may be used as an indicator of frequency of usage.

One must be careful in using erosion measures to be sure that unrelated factors are not the reasons for observed changes. For example, a new janitor's zeal in cleaning may be responsible for changes in the patterns of use as detected by wear and tear on the floor. Similarly, it would help to know the amount of ordinary wear and tear on objects so that any excessive erosion or wear and tear can be related to target behaviors with more assurance (Nay, 1979).

The second category of physical traces is accretion measures. These are objects deposited by clients in a given setting or the ordinary debris left by client interaction with or consumption of material. In addition to some of the behavior products mentioned in an earlier section that may be viewed as accretion measures, such as cigarette butts, these measures often focus on analysis of remains or even rubbish. For example, Denzin (1970) pointed out that deposits of love letters in a waste basket could be used as a measure of troubled interaction patterns. Similarly, one could ask a spouse to count the number of beer bottles in the trash as a way of measuring the extent of the spouse's drinking problem.

Of course, reliability and validity concerns are as important in using physical traces as they are with other measures, and especially important when being used to make inferences about behaviors. For example, if you were to use the changing number of beer bottles in the trash per day as an indicator of the episodic nature of stress in the client's life, you would have to be certain that changes in the number of bottles simply don't reflect different patterns of throwing out the garbage, and represent only the client's drinking behavior.

SUMMARY

This chapter reviewed the nature of reactivity, changes that come about in a target due to the act of measurement. We discussed different sources of reactivity, and we suggested a number of ways of overcoming reactivity in general. We then focused on reactivity in self-monitoring and offered several guidelines for how to increase or decrease reactivity depending upon what is desirable in a given case.

The remainder of the chapter dealt with unobtrusive measures. Unobtrusive measures are measures that can be used to evaluate changes over time without interfering with or affecting the observed target simply by the act of measurement. In large part, these measures are most suited as secondary sources of data, although in certain instances, where they comprise direct evidence of changes, they may be suitable as primary measures. Four types of unobtrusive measures were described and examples presented of their potential use for practice: archival records (both public and private), physical traces (evidence left behind by the client), behavior products (rather than the actual behaviors themselves), and simple observations, where the observer doesn't play an active part in the client's interactions on the dimension being observed.

10 SELECTING A MEASURE

PURPOSE: This chapter briefly reviews all of the types of measures we've discussed in this book and then presents a framework to help you select measures in your practice. The use of multiple measures is strongly recommended, and guidelines for the selection and use of multiple measures are provided. ■

Introduction
Summary of Available Measurement Methods
Considerations in Deciding on a Measure
Characteristics of the Measure
Characteristics of the Target
Characteristics of the Practitioner and
    Practice Approach
Characteristics of the Client and
    Resources Available
An Exercise in Selecting Measures

Use of Multiple Measures
Why Multiple Measures?
    Changes Are Often Multidimensional
    Measures Often Do Not Correlate
    Multiple Measures Increase Confidence
Problems with Using Multiple Measures
The Measurement Package
Guidelines for Using Multiple Measures
Selecting a Measure
Summary

INTRODUCTION

We hope the chapters in this section have convinced you that there are ways to measure just about any target that you might encounter in practice. We hope also that we haven't overwhelmed you by offering so many options. Life would be so much easier if we could just point to one method and say: "Use it for everything; it always works." Unfortunately, both life and measurement just aren't that simple. Given that fact, and the fact that you probably would like to remain flexible about what you

measure, while at the same time having something other than guesswork to use in selecting measures, we'd like to present in this chapter some ideas on selecting appropriate measures for any given situation. These guidelines may not be as clear-cut as, say, a statistical test of significance, and they do require some creativity (the art of practice?) in evaluating the range of available measures and making a selection for each situation. But they also should provide some basis for helping you in that selection by describing some of the issues and criteria you would want to consider.

Summary of Available Measurement Methods

Before we get into the actual issues and guidelines, take a look at Table 10.1, which summarizes the measurement methods we've discussed and the guidelines for their use. (It might be a good idea for you to keep this summary handy as you contemplate which ones to choose.) The actual criteria for using each of these methods and the guidelines for using them were discussed in the chapter devoted to each.

CONSIDERATIONS IN DECIDING ON A MEASURE

Once you're familiar with the range of measures that are available and the indications for their use, there are still some other factors you would want to consider before you make your selection. We're going to describe several of these in the hope that it will help you be even more precise in your selections. These characteristics are not listed here in order of importance. In any given situation, any one of these characteristics might play the key role in your selection.

Characteristics of the Measure

In Chapter 2 we described a number of basic principles of measurement that are directly applicable in considering what measure to use. In essence, we noted that no measure is perfect or error free. But to the extent that a measure is intended to measure a certain characteristic, it should be influenced mainly by that characteristic and as little as possible by other factors. Thus, to briefly review some of the criteria we discussed, you want measures that are:

1. *Reliable.* Your measure must be consistent, giving similar results when it's used under similar conditions.

2. *Valid.* To the extent that it's possible to know this, you want to try to ensure that your measure measures what it's supposed to. We described a number of ways of assessing validity in Chapter 2.

3. *Sensitive to change.* If changes do occur in a target, you want to be sure that your measure will be able to pick them up. An insensitive measure, by definition, is one that won't indicate change even though actual changes have come about. Although we discussed this criterion largely in relation to standardized questionnaires (Chapter 7), it pertains to the use of any measure.

4. *Nonreactive.* Try to use measures that will do as little as possible to change the target simply by the act of measurement. If it seems your measure may produce some reactivity, use the guidelines in Chapter 9 to assess this and to use the reactivity to the benefit of the client.

5. *Direct.* To the extent possible, try to select a measure that most accurately represents (or actually is) the real target. The closer the measure approximates the real target, the more useful it will be. Indirect measures have their place, as we indicated in Chapter 2. But the more direct your measure, the more accurately you will be able to assess a situation.

6. *Easy to use.* Try to use measures that are easy enough to administer, score, and interpret so that they can be administered repeatedly.

7. *Accessible.* Try to use measures that are easy to obtain (e.g., not restricted to certain professions, not expensive).

8. *Relevant to intervention planning.* To the extent possible, use measures that will facilitate decisions about the presence of client targets, the factors affecting or maintaining the targets, the most effective intervention strategies for the targets, and, most important, the degree of improvement or deterioration in the target.

Characteristics of the Target

The nature of the target should be a major factor in deciding what measures to use. In Table 10.1, we review the wide range of measures

Table 10.1 Summary of available measurement methods.

Measure	Situations Where Best Used
Behavioral Observation	Use to measure overt or covert discrete target behaviors. Use direct observation to measure overt behaviors, and self-monitoring to measure overt or covert behaviors. • Use frequency recording when the goal is to increase or decrease the number of times a behavior occurs, and when the duration of the behavior is relatively constant and has a clear beginning and end. • Use duration recording when the goal is to increase or decrease the length of time a behavior occurs, or the length of time between events, and the behavior has a clear beginning and end. • Use interval recording when the goal is to increase or decrease the relative frequency or duration of behavior and frequency or duration recording is impractical (e.g., when the beginning and end of the behavior are difficult to discern or multiple clients or behaviors are observed simultaneously).
Individualized Rating Scales	Use to measure targets defined specifically for a given client, along relatively subjective dimensions (e.g., intensity, satisfaction, severity, importance). Use individualized self-report rating scales to elicit information from clients, and individualized observer rating scales to elicit information from practitioners, relevant others, or independent evaluators.
Standardized Questionnaires	Use to measure targets in terms of concepts with some general relevance to different clients, using a method that is standardized across clients, that often has demonstrated validity and reliability, and that lets you compare a client's data with relevant group norms. Use standardized self-report questionnaires to elicit information from clients, and standardized observer questionnaires to elicit information from practitioners, relevant others, or independent evaluators.
Logs	Use client logs to pinpoint and define client targets, to assemble a qualitative picture of events prior to, during, and after a target event, or to evaluate change in the frequency, duration, or intensity of self-monitored targets. • Use logs with preset time categories when you have some idea when a target occurs and you want data collected at regular intervals. • Use logs with open time categories when you need information about "critical incidents." • Use an exploratory log to pinpoint and define a target and to get information about the circumstances surrounding the target. • Use a target problem log when the target is defined, but information about the circumstances surrounding the target is unclear. • Use an interaction log to examine interactions between the client and others that centered on an identified target. • Use an evaluation log to measure change in the frequency, duration, or intensity of self-monitored targets. Use practitioner logs to pinpoint and define client targets, to assemble a qualitative picture of events prior to, during, and after a target event, to evaluate change in the frequency, duration, or intensity of client targets, and to monitor the provision of services.
Unobtrusive (Nonreactive) Measures	Use to measure change in client targets in a way that avoids changing the targets by measuring them. • Use archival records when relevant existing data are available and accessible. • Use behavior products or physical traces when a behavior has an observable temporary or permanent effect on the environment. • Use simple observations when unobtrusive observations are possible.

available so that you can fit one or more of these to a given target. It would make little sense under most conditions to select a measure that is valid and reliable but that doesn't accurately represent the desired outcome. This is perhaps the key—your measure should be a direct representation of the outcomes you hope to attain. If your goal is a change in a behavior, observe the behavior. If the goal is a change in perceptions, use a self-report measure of perceptions. *Make sure the measure you select is directly relevant to what you hope to accomplish.*

Characteristics of the Practitioner and Practice Approach

We haven't forgotten the important role that you play in selecting a measure. By this we mean not only your own preferences and choices, but also the intervention approaches you use.

First, we hope that your own comfort with a given measure won't be a major factor in selecting a measure. Not that comfort isn't important, but we believe that the main way of achieving comfort is by practice and experience. If your comfort were your only guideline, you'd stick only with what you already know and never try something new.

On the other hand, if everything else is equal, and you have a choice between two measures, each of which has similar characteristics and is equally relevant to the target, then go ahead and select whichever one you're more comfortable using. Indeed, the more comfortable you are with a given measure, the more you may induce confidence in others to use it.

Second, each measure you use should correspond to at least one component of your intervention, in the sense that the measured outcome is the direct target of at least one intervention. However, in considering the correspondence between measured targets and interventions, the entire configuration of targets and interventions for a case also should be considered. For example, intensive family preservation services designed to prevent the removal of a child from his or her home use multiple interrelated interventions (e.g., the provision of tangible, social, and emotional parenting resources and parent training), targeted at multiple interrelated short- and long-term outcomes (e.g., enhanced social supports, improved parenting skills, better parent–child relationships, elimination of maltreatment, continued parental custody) (e.g., Fraser, 1990; Pearson, 1990). Therefore, a measured target may be linked to more than one intervention (e.g., maltreatment may be reduced by the provision of resources and by parent training), and change in some targets may depend on change in other targets (e.g., continued parental custody may depend on reduced maltreatment and reduced maltreatment may depend on better social supports and parenting skills). Nevertheless, whenever possible, each target should be measured, and the measure of one target shouldn't be substituted for the measure of another target, because it's unlikely that one will represent perfectly the other (e.g., it's unlikely that a measure of parenting skills could substitute for a measure of the quality of parent–child relationships).

Finally, your theoretical orientation or approach to practice might play a part in your selection of measures. Thus, if a family comes to you with a problem involving anorexia nervosa (say, a teenage daughter who won't eat and is becoming dangerously thin), and your practice approach suggests that to affect anorexia nervosa you have to change family communication patterns (e.g., Minuchin, 1974), then it might be reasonable to select a measure of change in family communication patterns. Of course, this would not prevent you from also measuring the child's caloric intake or weight gain.

Characteristics of the Client and Resources Available

When it comes right down to it, you must select a measure that somebody is willing to use. In essence, our point is you have to consider who will be doing the observation and recording, and select measures that person will be willing to use. The measures should not be burdensome or irrelevant to the person(s) who will use them. (This may require a good deal of preparation of those persons on your part.)

They should be convenient and easy to use. Everything else being equal, try to select the easiest, most pleasant, least time-consuming measure. Make sure the rationale for and importance of the measure are clearly understood by the people who will use them. Select a measure that the person won't regard as silly or childish, or a waste of time.

An Exercise in Selecting Measures

If you're still having a problem with selecting measures, try the following exercise. Select a target that seems difficult to measure, and enumerate as many different practical methods for measuring it as possible. Suppose, for example, that you decide that the quality of the relationship between a parent and child would be difficult to capture. More specifically, suppose that you're faced with trying to enhance the quality of the relationship between a single mother and her adolescent son. Your task for this exercise is to devise as many practical ways as possible of measuring the quality of this relationship. Write them down before you read the rest of this section.

There are, in fact, a number of ways that the quality of the relationship between a parent and child can be measured, although of course no single measure can capture all aspects of the relationship that are of concern. The one or ones you choose may be determined by a combination of your negotiations with the client, that which appears most relevant to the case, or your theoretical orientation. Following are several ways that you can measure this target, corresponding to the chapters on measurement in this section of the book, and that also can serve as a focus for your intervention.

1. *Behavioral observations.* There are any number of different indicators that you, the client, or some other person (e.g., another family member, a teacher) could observe to measure the quality of the relationship (see Chapter 5). These might include, for example, the amount of time spent together, the amount of time necessary to resolve a disagreement, the number of arguments, the number of negative

statements the parent makes about the child, or vice versa. Furthermore, these observations could take place in the natural environment or in an analog setting, or they could be based on coded categories that you devise in conjunction with the client or using numerous existing coding schemes (e.g., Hersen & Bellack, 1988; Markman & Notarius, 1989; Mash, 1987; Shapiro & Kratochwill, 1988).

2. *Individualized rating scales.* You could work with the mother and the son to enumerate separate, individually tailored sets of targets relevant to the quality of the relationship, and to develop the most appropriate dimensions on which to rate the targets. Also, you could construct a scale for your own use that would include the targets you perceived as most important and the dimensions on which to rate these targets (see Chapter 6).

3. *Standardized questionnaires.* In Chapter 7 we described several standardized questionnaires that could be used to measure the quality of the relationship between a parent and child, and more generally the quality of family relationships. In fact, there are numerous standardized questionnaires devised specifically for measuring different aspects of the quality of the relationship between a parent and child and the quality of family relationships (e.g., Corcoran & Fischer, 1999a, 1999b; Fischer & Corcoran, 1994a, 1994b; Fredman & Sherman, 1987; Grotevant & Carlson, 1989; Hersen & Bellack, 1988; Jacob & Tennenbaum, 1988; Kestenbaum & Williams, 1988; McCubbin & Thompson, 1987; Touliatos et al., 1990). Moreover, the available measures include ones that are designed to obtain information from the perspective of parents, children, and practitioners.

4. *Logs.* The mother and son each could keep a log to record the unique qualitative circumstances surrounding aspects of their relationship, and to record quantitative dimensions of targets selected for in-

tervention, such as intensity and frequency. These could be used to pinpoint and define targets, generate individualized hypotheses for intervention, and quantify change over time in each client's targets. In addition, you could use a log in much the same way as a clinical record to monitor the delivery of your services and for the same purposes as the client log (see Chapter 8).

5. *Nonreactive measure(s)*. You could use public records (e.g., school records of the number of times the school contacted the mother about discipline problems with the son), or you could use simple observation and select some specific physical signs (e.g., proximity of the mother and son), expressive gestures (e.g., smiles or frowns), or language patterns (e.g., use of certain words). Other types of simple observations also could be used. For example, if one point of contention between the mother and son was the "messiness" of the son's room, when making home visits the practitioner could unobtrusively look into the son's room. If the room is too neat (e.g., everything perfectly in its place, etc.), then the mother may be putting too much stress on her son to behave. If the room is too messy (e.g., nothing in place, what the son might do if he didn't exercise any control whatsoever), then parental guidance may have broken down, which is a concern in this context. If the room is somewhat messy (e.g., what mother–son negotiate to be an acceptable degree of private sloppiness), then that is a positive in this context (see Chapter 9).

As mentioned before, in real practice, targets are rarely clearly defined and measures so obvious that you don't have to go through a process of creative thought to come up with measures. On the other hand, we believe it can be done. This is not an academic exercise with few real-world implications. Every time you're faced with a new problem or client, you have to go through a process such as the one we just described where you rule in or out one or more of the types of measures we described. Just for the sake of gaining experience, following the exercise on selecting measures you just completed, try to see how many of the measures described in this book really can be adapted to measure each of the targets on your list.

USE OF MULTIPLE MEASURES

Webb et al. (1981, p. 315) noted that in the selection of a measurement strategy, people often seek the single best measure. Instead, they and numerous other authors (e.g., Lambert et al., 1986; Shadish, 1986; Waskow & Parloff, 1975) propose, and we agree, that the best *set* of methods should be selected, with *best* defined as the set that lets you rule out the most important and likely threats to the validity of the results (e.g., observer's expectations, client's socially desirable responses) without requiring an unreasonable expenditure of resources. This can include the collection of information from multiple sources (e.g., a client's assessment of his or her depression and a relevant other's assessment of the client's depression), the use of multiple methods to measure the same target (e.g., a standardized self-report measure of depression and self-monitored depressive behaviors), and the measurement of multiple targets (e.g., depression and marital satisfaction). There are important reasons for using more than one measure with each client.

Why Multiple Measures?

At several points throughout this book, we have hinted at reasons for using multiple measures—for example, to provide a check on the reliability and validity of your measures, to balance and offset possible weaknesses inherent in individual measures, to provide information about internal and external changes, and so on. However, there are three other reasons that we haven't discussed.

Changes Are Often Multidimensional. Oftentimes there are unanticipated changes in different areas of functioning because of the complexity of human beings, organizations, and communities (Lambert et al., 1986). Different dimensions of the same target might respond differently to an intervention. For example, a client's self-reported feelings of depression might show improvement, but not the client's self-monitored depressive behavior. In addition, it's possible that an intervention program focused on one area may produce changes in other, related areas as well. For example, changing a parent's excessive drinking habits could easily affect the family atmosphere, communication, and activities. Therefore, the measurement of different areas of functioning can provide information about the breadth and generality of change and provide a more sensitive gauge of change.

Measures Often Do Not Correlate. Although the research findings vary on this, often different methods of measuring the same phenomenon are not highly correlated (e.g., Bostwick & Bostwick, 1987; Lambert et al., 1986). Therefore, in some cases there might not be much correlation over time among different methods used to measure the same target. This can happen for different reasons.

When different people observe a client, inconsistencies among observers over time can occur because they each observe the client in a different situation (e.g., a child might be observed by a teacher in a particular classroom, by his or her parents at home, and by the school social worker in a treatment group), and the client's behavior might change in different ways in different situations. Inconsistencies among observers over time also might result from legitimate differences of opinion among different involved parties (e.g., different members of a family can have legitimate differences of opinion about the degree of existing family cohesion, family conflict, or other dimensions of family functioning; social workers and clients can have legitimate differences of opinion about the adequacy of a client's parenting). Finally, in addition to inconsistencies among observers, inconsistencies can occur over time among measures of different dimensions of a target because these dimensions might change over time (e.g., behavioral indicators of family functioning, such as the amount of time spent together and the frequency of arguments, may have a more erratic pattern of change than the perceptions of family members concerning family functioning).

In essence, you can't assume that the degree of change registered by a single measure of a target, or as reported by a single person, gives you the whole picture. Often different measures place emphasis on different aspects of a target, and different people have access either to different samples of a client's behavior or to legitimate differences of opinion. The use of multiple measures and information collected from different sources is necessary to provide a comprehensive picture of a target and to ensure that if one measure is not sensitive to important areas of change, other measures will detect them.

Multiple Measures Increase Confidence. When you measure targets with multiple measures, and you measure multiple targets, you can get some idea about the validity of your measures by examining the interrelationships among the different measures. To explore the validity of your measures, first formulate hypotheses about how the different measures should be related (or correlated) over time and how individual measures fit in with the entire case situation. Next, begin your evaluation, and as you're going along examine the emerging patterns among the measures to see if they support your hypotheses.

If the bulk of your hypothesized relationships are supported by your evaluation results you can be more confident that you have an accurate picture of the actual change than if you measure a single target or if you measure given targets using a single method. If a measure doesn't change in a predicted fashion, then you can't be certain whether the measure is invalid or your hypotheses or theory about the measure is wrong, but you do know that you should be cautious about the interpretation of the results from the measure. However, the confidence placed in a particular measure should be judged in relation to the entire case situation (i.e., the results obtained with a single measure should be compared to the pattern of results obtained with all other relevant measures).

Problems with Using Multiple Measures

We want to be perfectly clear about this. We're not suggesting the use of multiple measures as a sort of "what the heck" approach ("What the heck, I might as well throw in more than one measure and see what I come up with."). Obviously, the more measures you use the greater your chance of finding "something." Instead, we hope your selection of measures will be grounded to the extent possible in a careful evaluation of possible relevant and important outcomes. In particular, it's important to select measures having different strengths and weaknesses (e.g., the use of several standardized self-report scales designed to measure the same target wouldn't provide much balance, because they probably would share many of the same potential biases).

Our recommendations to use multiple measures do contain some problems. One of these was alluded to above—the fact that changes are often inconsistent across measures and therefore difficult to evaluate coherently. Related to this is another major problem—trying to decide weightings for the measures (i.e., which are most important). If change doesn't occur in one but does in another, is it possible to conclude that intervention was effective?

Perhaps a partial solution to this problem lies primarily in the way clients rank their priorities. Change in measures of a client's major concerns might be weighted most heavily in evaluating success. Of course, if a client is involuntarily receiving some form of court-mandated intervention (e.g., for child maltreatment), measures of the court-mandated outcomes should be given a high priority, although client concerns also should be given important consideration. A second guideline might be to apply the principle that we discussed earlier about direct measurement: Changes that most directly represent changes in actual functioning should be given priority, and those that appear most removed from actual functioning receive lower priority in evaluating success.

Another problem with use of multiple measures is perhaps obvious—if you use more than

one measure, it will probably take more time and energy. Somebody has to do the measuring. We believe that the added time and energy involved in using multiple measures necessitate evaluating each circumstance individually. In some situations this might not be a problem. For example, you may use data that are already being collected for other purposes, say, from archival records. In other situations, the value of getting information using different methods or sources may outweigh any possible problems. At the least, to the extent that multiple measures are used, try to select those that don't overburden one person whether it would be because the tasks become tedious or boring, or simply are too time-consuming. Thus, it might be wise to have the client collect data using one measure, and someone else collect data using another.

Finally, sometimes with complex multidimensional interventions (e.g., the family preservation example discussed above) the correspondence between outcome measures and interventions can be relaxed. Remember, specific outcome measures should be linked directly to at least one intervention, although these links should be viewed within the entire configuration of interventions and outcomes.

The Measurement Package

One way of viewing all of the above is the need for developing a "measurement package" for every client and situation. The measurement package would be those measures that would be best suited to the specific target(s) involved in a given case, that would most adequately measure the changes expected to occur, and that would evaluate those changes from the points of view of those who are involved.

In this context, it might be helpful to distinguish between primary and secondary measures. The primary measure is the one closest to or the most direct expression of the target. It's also the one on which you would most expect change to occur. When use of more than one measure is not possible, this is the one measure you would select.

The secondary measure (or measures) would be less directly related to the specific target. It might be less direct, more general, more subjective. The secondary measure would be used to complement or supplement the primary measure. It would probably not be used as your sole source of data collection.

The measurement package, in addition to attempting to measure more than one dimension of a target, might also be constructed from the point of view of different people concerned with the target. Reviews of change measures in psychotherapy (Lambert, Christenson, & De-Julio, 1983; Waskow & Parloff, 1975) highlight this issue by categorizing measures on the basis of client measures, practitioner measures, relevant others' measures, and independent evaluators' measures.

We would suggest, when possible, to include at least two of these perspectives when selecting a measurement package. This will provide a broader perspective on the target, tap dimensions that might otherwise go unnoticed, add to the information that you will use in determining whether to change or terminate a program, and increase the validity of any observed changes, especially when independent reports agree.

Finally, it's important to select a measurement package in which the potential weaknesses inherent in individual measures are offset and balanced by other measures in the package (e.g., Shadish, 1986; Webb et al., 1981). For example, nonreactive measures might be selected to counterbalance reactive measures, information might be collected from relevant others to counterbalance the limited direct information available to you as the practitioner, general measures might be used to counterbalance the limited information elicited by specific measures, or individualized rating scales might be constructed and used to counterbalance the more general information elicited by standardized questionnaires.

A program of research conducted by Berlin (1980, 1983, 1985) and her colleagues (Berlin, Mann, & Grossman, 1991) concerning the effectiveness of cognitive interventions for alleviating depression in women provides a good example of the use of multiple measures. In various studies Berlin used observation by independent observers, self-monitoring, standardized questionnaires, and individualized rating scales. Information was obtained from clients, social workers, and independent observers. Various types of targets were measured, including intermediate outcomes and procedural objectives such as treatment tasks accomplished, quality of individual sessions, depression-related outcomes, and, of course, depression, the primary outcome of interest. Finally, Berlin used existing measures and measures constructed specifically for her evaluations.

Other programs of research also provide good illustrations of the use of multiple measures. These include the work of Schinke and his colleagues in the area of prevention (e.g., Blythe et al., 1981; Schinke et al., 1981; Schinke, Gordon, & Weston, 1990), the work of Rose and his colleagues in the area of group work (e.g., Rose, 1988, 1989), the work of Reid and his colleagues in the evaluation of task-centered treatment (e.g., Fortune, 1985; Reid, 1977, 1978), and the work of Reinherz and her colleagues in the evaluation of psychodynamic practice (e.g., Dean & Reinherz, 1986).

Although we don't want to overwhelm you with measures, one possibility you might want to consider is an adaptation of the Lazarus Patient's Therapy Session Report (Lazarus, 1971, pp. 253–271). After every session Lazarus administers a questionnaire to clients in which he requests information on a number of factors. These include the client's feelings about the session, subjects talked about in the session, what the client hoped to get out of the session, what problems or feelings the client was concerned about in that session, the client's feelings during the session, the client's feelings about coming to the session, the client's feelings about progress during the session, the client's perceptions of how the practitioner felt and how well the client was understood, and so on. This can be a particularly helpful source of evaluative feedback to the practitioner and can give both the practitioner and the client additional time to think about their relationship and discuss the problems they are working on at the next session.

You might want to use or adapt the Lazarus format or consider the abbreviated version shown in Figure 10.1 (adapted from Gottman & Leiblum, 1974). This format can be used in consultation with organizations or in other forms

---

Post-Session Report

_____   _____   _____
Client's Name   Practitioner's Name   Date

Please circle the number that comes closest to describing your feelings about the session you just completed.

1   2   3   4   5   6   7   8   9

Not productive   Moderately   Extremely
    at all   productive   productive

Please try to describe at least one positive and one negative incident, or a part of the discussion that occurred during the session, that might help explain your rating.

Positive incident

Negative incident

FIGURE 10.1   Post-session report form.

of intervention simply by changing the word *client* on the form.

Guidelines for Using Multiple Measures

Given the above considerations, we recommend the following guidelines for the construction of a measurement package (see also Hayes & Nelson, 1986; Lambert, Shapiro, & Bergin, 1986; Shadish, 1986):

1. Try to use more than one measure.

2. Try not to duplicate measures (e.g., two different self-report measures of depression) just for the sake of having multiple measures; select measures that use different measurement methods, that measure different targets, that measure different dimensions of the same target, or that are based on information obtained from different sources.

3. Try to include at least one direct measure, especially if an indirect measure is being used.

4. Try to select the most direct measures.

5. Try to include the observation of overt behaviors (actual functioning)–whether in the natural environment or in a contrived setting–whenever applicable.

6. Try to give priority to situation-specific measures rather than global measures (e.g., a measure of social anxiety related to a problem in heterosexual relationships, rather than a measure of general anxiety).

7. Try to include at least one nonreactive measure, especially if a reactive measure is being used.

8. Try not to overburden one person with all the measurement responsibilities.

9. Try to obtain measurement information from more than one person (e.g., client and relevant other).

10. Try to assess what type of change is more crucial in a given case, so that measurement can be geared toward assessing the most appropriate change.

11. Try to select measures that are tailored to the specific client, situation, and target.

12. Try to focus measurement resources on measuring the primary target(s) that brought the client to your attention.

SELECTING A MEASURE

Although we've covered numerous measures for numerous uses, you still need some way to begin to narrow down the field to help you make a selection for a given client. In Figure 10.2, we've provided a framework to help you begin that selection process.

The first thing you can do is evaluate a variety of characteristics that will help to provide some preliminary directions. These include, as we discussed earlier in this chapter, the nature of the target, your own preferences and practice orientation, the nature of the client, and the types of resources available. All of these can be evaluated regarding the ways in which they can aid or impede the collection of information on the target(s).

Next you can decide on the source or sources of information. As we discussed in this chapter, the source can be the client, you (the practitioner), a relevant other (such as a parent, spouse, teacher, or other caretaker), or an independent evaluator (e.g., a trained observer or a colleague of yours, such as another staff member).

Next, review the available measures. Based on your earlier decision about what sources of information would be most useful and feasible, you will begin to be able to narrow down the field. The client can provide information using self-monitoring of behaviors, individualized rating scales, standardized questionnaires, and logs. The practitioner, relevant others, and independent evaluators can use behavior observation, individualized rating scales, standardized questionnaires, logs, and nonreactive measures.

The next step is to evaluate the characteristics of the available measures. This should be done using the criteria discussed in Chapter 2: reliability, validity, directness, ease of use, accessibility, and relevance to intervention planning.

Finally, all that's left is for you to select your measurement package—not always a simple process, we admit, but a necessary one. Use the guidelines we presented in the previous section on use of multiple measures. Consider a primary and secondary source of information. Consider also collecting information from two sources and using two or more different types of measurement methods. Counterbalance the strengths and limitations of each measure so that you have measures that have different potential biases (e.g., biases likely to make a client look "good," and biases likely to make a client look "bad"). Putting this all together, we believe you will have a good chance of selecting a particularly useful measurement package to help you monitor and evaluate your practice.

SUMMARY

This chapter focused on helping you select the most appropriate measures to be used in any given case or situation. We first briefly reviewed the types of measures that we've discussed in this section of the book. Then we discussed the factors you should consider in deciding on a measure: characteristics of the measure itself, characteristics of the target, characteristics of the practitioner and practice approach, and characteristics of the client and available resources. The last section of the chapter recommended the use of more than one measure whenever possible, in essence, building the idea of a "measurement package" into your practice. The chapter concluded with a set of guidelines for using multiple measures and a framework for selecting a measure.

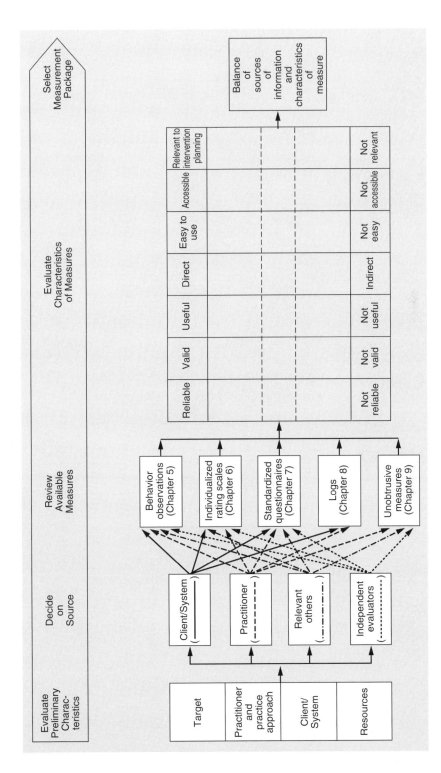

FIGURE 10.2 Framework for selecting a measure.

PART III

EVALUATION DESIGNS

Designs are planned arrangements for collecting data that can help you identify changes that have occurred in the target problem and determine what impact your service program had on those changes. As such, designs are logical tools emphasizing the "scientific" part of scientific practice. Different types of designs permit you to draw different conclusions, such as whether change in client problems occurred, and whether your interventions caused these observed changes.

Practitioners naturally establish *practice* designs in service programs; that is, they engage in orderly ways of introducing some interventions to see what effects they will have. *Evaluation designs* essentially are plans for data collection and analysis that are applicable to any service activities in which you might engage. By employing evaluation designs, especially single-system designs, you can use their logical power for identifying change and inferring causality in order to make your practice more effective. When such information is available on an ongoing basis with each case or situation, you will be able to modify the intervention so as to move more efficiently and, we hope, more effectively toward the goal.

The chapters in Part III discuss the variety of single-system designs that you can use in your practice. Chapter 11 begins with the basic principles of single-system design. Chapter 12 deals with baselining, the collection of information on target problems before intervention begins. Chapter 13 introduces the simplest and most basic evaluation designs in the context of the case study method to which they bear some historic relationship. Chapter 14 discusses designs that involve the planned introduction and removal of some intervention while observing changes in the target problem. Chapter 15 deals with multiple baseline and multiple target designs and other variations of these designs. Chapter 16 deals with changing intensity and successive intervention designs, and Chapter 17 with other complex and combined designs. These later chapters introduce some of the more rigorous single-system designs in part because each design serves essentially as a model to help you interpret changes that occur with whatever design you eventually use. However, in keeping with our focus on practical methods of evaluation we emphasize those which might be used in actual practice situations. The final chapter of Part III (Chapter 18) provides some suggestions on how to select a design for your particular case or situation. In each chapter, we provide a variety of illustrations to show you how practitioners, using a wide range of interventions and theoretical orientations, employ these designs to help them evaluate their practice. As you will see, there are many variations of each of the designs, and, in many instances, different designs are combined in one case to provide a more comprehensive evaluation. We hope this will convey the real flexibility and ultimate practicality of single-system designs.

BASIC PRINCIPLES OF SINGLE-SYSTEM DESIGNS

PURPOSE: This chapter presents an overview of single-system designs by briefly describing the basic principles underlying all of these evaluation approaches. There are four major purposes of these evaluation designs (Proctor, 1990): (a) to assess the case situation and to monitor changes in people and events over time; (b) to evaluate whether positive or negative changes have occurred in targeted events; (c) to evaluate whether the practitioner's interventions were causally linked with these changes—this is the question of the effectiveness of the intervention; and (d) to enable practitioners to compare effectiveness among interventions. The basic principles reviewed in this chapter will help you understand the ways in which single-system designs address these purposes. This chapter serves as a foundation for the rest of the chapters in this part of the book, to help you understand both the conclusions that can be derived from your own applications of single-system designs, and the conclusions that can be derived from others' practice evaluations. ■

Introduction

An Example Connecting Practice and Evaluation Designs

Purposes of Single-System Designs

Unique Characteristics of Single-System Designs

Comparison of Baseline and Intervention Periods

Intervention

Phases

   Types of Phases
   Length of Phases
   Adjacent–Nonadjacent Phases

Changes in Intervention

Complicating Factors

   Carryover
   Contrast
   Order of Presentation
   Incomplete Data
   Training Phase

Maintenance and Follow-Up Plans

Collaborative and Team Efforts

Causality in Single-System Designs

Criteria for Inferring Causality in Single-System Designs

   Design Validity
   Statistical Conclusion Validity: Did Change Occur?
   Internal Validity: Was Change Caused by Your Intervention?
   Construct Validity: Did You Implement Your Intervention and Measure Your Outcomes Accurately?

External Validity and Generalizability

Enhancing Generalizability

   Replication
   Probabilities
   Meta-Analysis

Overview of Single-System Designs

Summary

INTRODUCTION

In the larger sense, all practitioners design their practice; that is, they plan how they are going to deal with the client's problems, how they will establish and maintain a good working rapport, and the like. Within this overall "practice design," each message sent to the client is, in principle, a planned part of the whole. Similarly, we use the term *evaluation design* to describe how practitioners plan to evaluate progress and to evaluate the outcomes of cases: There is an overall plan for arranging to make suitable observations about baseline target events that will then be compared, according to logical rules, with the same target events after the intervention has been initiated. In this way, two key questions may be addressed: (1) Did the target problems or events change after the intervention began? and (2) What evidence is there that the intervention caused that change?

This chapter discusses the basic principles of single-system designs–that is, the assumptions and rules of logic for making planned comparisons of target events before, during, and after intervention–as a foundation for reading about the various types of designs in subsequent chapters. Some of these rules are presented as ideal types of designs in subsequent chapters. Some of these rules are presented as ideal types that we seek to approximate in practical situations that may not permit their full application. The fact that we cannot obtain laboratory-like controls in field situations does not mean that we lose the ability to evaluate changes in targets in highly useful ways. However, it is important to recognize how and to what degree we are violating these rules so that the interpretation of our results may be suitably modest.

All properly constructed single-system designs, from the most basic to the most elaborate, offer clear evidence with regard to the first key question concerning whether change occurred in the target after intervention. Some single-system designs–those we describe as more sophisticated or complex–also provide the logical basis to answer the second key question: whether our intervention *caused* these changes. We will introduce the logical bases for making this distinction between observing whether change occurred and being able to infer that we caused this change.

However, all single-system designs as approximate evaluation procedures are limited; they face complicating factors and threats to the design validity and generalizability of the results to new case situations. We will discuss these limitations so you will have a perspective on how to use single-system designs in an optimal way for practice evaluation. We conclude this chapter with a brief overview of the designs to be covered in succeeding chapters, and how they address these complications and threats.

AN EXAMPLE CONNECTING PRACTICE AND EVALUATION DESIGNS

Imagine a conventional case recording in which a practitioner summarizes the events in a case as they transpire, along with planning notes. The top half of Table 11.1 represents this practice design. A person comes to a social service agency as a result of feeling depressed; the practitioner takes a case history, collecting pertinent demographic and background information surrounding what appears to be the problem. These events are summarized in the first column of Table 11.1.

After the practitioner has made an initial assessment of the situation, he arranges to collect some more specific information to determine the scope and depth of the problem by asking the client to keep track of her happy and sad feelings and the events surrounding them in a log. The practitioner also asks her permission to obtain information from her employer on her job performance, and from her husband on whether she is eating adequately to maintain her health. This information will illuminate the context of her depressed and nondepressed feelings, as noted in the second column of Table 11.1.

The third and fourth columns represent the first intervention, which consists of trying, through rational conversation, to support

Table 11.1 Hypothetical example connecting practice and evaluation designs.*

	1	2	3	4	5	6
P R A C T I C E	The practitioner takes a case history.	He then arranges for the client to keep a log about her feelings when she is depressed, what came before and what were the consequences. Records of her work absences were also obtained, and her spouse rated her eating patterns.	Based on the initial information, the practitioner discusses the client's strengths and resources during the next session.	He continues this discussion into the next session as well. (The intention is to support the client's strengths by his focused attention.)	Not satisfied with client progress, the practitioner begins to train the client in assertiveness skills.	Assertiveness training continues until client data show it is having its desired effects on depression, job, and eating patterns. After consultation with the couple, the case is closed.

(Information gathering on the client's depressed feelings, work record, and eating patterns continues throughout these intervention periods.)

	1	2	3	4	5	6
E V A L U A T I O N	(Subjective frame of reference) Subjective reconstruction is made to establish a frame of reference for baseline data.	A (baseline) Baseline data are collected: Objective and systematic observations including self-reports, observer reports, and records that permit some tests of validity and reliability.	B (first intervention) The first intervention period.	The first intervention period continued.	C (second intervention) The second intervention period.	The second intervention period continued until termination. (The practitioner may decide to collect some follow-up data after a period of time to ensure that the desired goals have been maintained outside of treatment.)

(The same observations, self-reports, and data from records are collected throughout the intervention periods.)

*The upper half describes a *practice* design; the lower half describes an *evaluation* design. Reading the same segment of each half of the table shows the parallels between practice and evaluation.

(reinforce) client strengths while ignoring (extinguishing) client limitations so as to counteract her depressed state of mind. The practitioner continues to collect ongoing information from the client, the client's employer, and the client's husband throughout this time. He does not observe any important change in her feeling state, and so he decides to change his tactics.

In the fifth column, the practitioner begins a new intervention, trying to impart social skills to the client through assertiveness training so she will be able to solve her problems more directly. He begins to observe strong positive changes, as recorded on her logs, her employer work sheets, and her husband's reports, which appear to be resolving her presenting problem. So, after discussing this with the couple, he closes the case (sixth column).

Not many cases are as obliging as this one, but as an example, it serves to make our point on the parallels between practice and its evaluation. The bottom half of Table 11.1 represents an evaluation chart or graph, indicating how each of the practitioner's actions can be translated into evaluation design notations. These translations refer to the observation or intervention periods, and to their initiation, removal, and reinstatement. The notations A, B, C, and so on represent the symbols for different phases from which logical predictions may be made; these will be discussed in the chapters on specific designs.

The verbal case history is a subjective reconstruction of life events that simply establishes a frame of reference for the more objective baseline data, which will be used as the reference point against which new data from the intervention period are to be compared. The data collection continues throughout the service program in order for the client and practitioner to benefit from the logical comparisons that may be made with the information. Whatever the practitioner chooses to do first about the client problem constitutes the first intervention, and when it does not appear to be making any difference to the client's problem, the practitioner chooses to change the intervention. The data now inform the practitioner and client that the problem has

been significantly reduced, not merely in statistical ways, but in real-life behaviors as well, and so, the case is terminated.

This "textbook-perfect" case answers only the first question: Has some real improvement occurred in the client's problems? It cannot answer the second question: Did the practitioner's efforts help to cause that positive change? An answer to this latter question requires a more complex design, as we will discuss in later chapters. Our main point is that *whatever the practitioner does* can be summarized as notation in an evaluation design and subjected to logical analysis to answer the two fundamental questions on (1) the presence of change and (2) the causes of that change. These answers constitute a scientific evaluation of practice, and are a critical aspect of accountability, especially in these times of managed care.

PURPOSES OF SINGLE-SYSTEM DESIGNS

There are four main reasons for using single-system designs in every practice situation. These reasons constitute the linkages between practice and evaluation that make them one integral activity for the helping professions (Proctor, 1990). First, these designs encourage practitioners to *assess* the case as objectively as possible, and to *monitor* these changes in the client targets and/or situation over time. With the ongoing monitoring, you can make informed decisions that may help move events by successive approximation toward client goals—including changes in the intervention if this is indicated by the monitoring. *Assessing, monitoring, and adapting to change over time are the essence of sensitive practice and sensible evaluation.*

The second purpose of single-system designs is to *evaluate* whether changes actually have occurred in targeted events. This will involve some comparison of the initial status of the client and situation with some later status. This comparison depends on some more or less objective measurement of the targets over time, which is why we emphasize clear measurement procedures along with clearly defined targets. It is important to distinguish the evaluation of change from the next purpose of designs, inferring causality.

The third purpose of single-system designs builds on the second, but adds that the evaluation now concerns whether the practitioner's intervention could be *causally linked* to these observed changes. This added interest requires that the designs be logically strong enough to support the inferences of causality. Some single-system designs—generally the more rigorous or sophisticated ones—are logically capable of permitting causal inferences while others lack this quality. We discuss in detail the logical strengths and limitations of several designs in Chapters 13 through 17. They all have to do with the principle of concomitant variation, or, more specifically, the *principle of unlikely successive coincidences* (Jayaratne & Levy, 1979).

Briefly stated, these principles suggest that causation may be reasonably inferred the more observations we obtain on their joint appearances and/or their joint absences, given that one (the planned intervention or cause) precedes the other (the observed effect or change in the target). One such joint occurrence (e.g., introducing an intervention followed by a change in the problem) could perhaps happen by chance, but the more times these jointly occur, the less likely is their pairing to have occurred by accident. Rather, such a set of occurrences provides the basis for inferring causality (Jayaratne & Levy, 1979, p. 139), especially when the practitioner predicts the outcomes. For making causal inferences about whether the intervention produced the observed change, the practitioner generally needs a design more rigorous than the *A-B* design, which is not able to rule out the possibility that other events may have affected the problem. We discuss a number of more rigorous and sophisticated single-system designs in Chapters 14 through 17.

The fourth major purpose of single-system designs is to enable practitioners to *compare the effectiveness* of different interventions. All practitioners want to develop a repertoire of effective strategies but often find it difficult to do so because of the great variety of individual factors involved, such as client characteristics, the nature of an idiosyncratic problem in unique contexts, and chance happenings during the time spent with each client. However, by employing the more powerful evaluation designs, it becomes possible under some circumstances to compare specific practice techniques with one another in one client/situation. Thus, the practitioner can begin to develop a set of practice methods that are demonstrably more effective than others. While these are some of the most difficult outcomes to obtain using single-system designs, these individualized studies of the efficacy of different practice methods could lead to hypotheses that might be tested using powerful experimental/control group designs, so that what one practitioner knows to be likely about his or her intervention techniques might be extended to help other practitioners choose to explore these same methods. In this way, practice wisdom gets translated, through classical research methods, into a solid knowledge base for effective practice. Some of the single-system designs that allow comparison between interventions will be discussed in Chapters 15–17.

UNIQUE CHARACTERISTICS OF SINGLE-SYSTEM DESIGNS

There are a number of characteristics that make single-system designs different from other evaluation and research designs (although they share many common characteristics—see Table 1.1). We discuss these characteristics here, and refer back to them in all of the following chapters. Many of these distinctive characteristics of single-system designs enable you to look at causal relationships between the techniques you have used in practice and the changes you have observed in the client's problems or challenges.

We recognize that actual practice is often very complicated, where you may only see the client a few times, or where heavy caseloads make it difficult to devote as much time as one might like to any one case. Thus, many of the more sophisticated single-system designs may not be employed. (In such cases we believe that the basic *A-B* design should be used as a minimal attempt at evaluation.) Yet it is important to understand these design characteristics, not only to recognize them when you run across them in your reading, but to have them available when you do find you are able to evaluate your practice. Knowing these basic characteristics will help you to understand the strengths and weaknesses of whatever design you use.

Following, then, are the key characteristics of single-system designs.

Comparison of Baseline and Intervention Periods

The key distinguishing characteristic of single-system designs involves the planned comparison of a nonintervention (usually, a preintervention or baseline) period of observation with observations of the intervention period, or, in some cases, postintervention period. This is the "before, during, and after" comparison that is at the heart of evaluation; an intervention is implemented and compared to something else that lacks this intervention. Unlike classical experimental/control group designs in which the comparison is between groups, single-system designs involve a comparison between time periods for the same client or system. *The underlying assumption is that if the intervention had not occurred, the pattern of events observed during the baseline likely would have continued to occur as before.*

However, after the baseline, a planned intervention is implemented and has some impact on the target. The basic questions now are whether a change has occurred and whether the intervention can be inferred to have caused that change. The design has arranged events so that you can logically deduce answers to the first question and possibly to the second.

Whether a change has occurred between baseline and intervention periods is often easy to determine given several common features of single-system designs. First, the target event under study has to be clearly specified and measured in the same way during both baseline and intervention periods. (This was discussed in Part II.) Second, some method of reducing a number of problem events to a

comparative form and collecting information on them—the design proper—has to be developed. (This is discussed in Part III.) Third, a rule for comparing these forms (such as comparing the differences in the patterns between baseline and intervention periods) has to be implemented. (This is discussed in Parts III and IV.) Once these three steps are carried out, the comparison of data collected during the baseline period with data collected during the intervention period can be made. The comparison typically tells whether there are differences in the target between the two periods of time.

Intervention

Since the comparison between baseline and intervention periods is so crucial for single-system designs, it might be helpful to clarify at this point what we mean by the term *intervention*. As suggested in Chapter 1, it is important for the practitioner using single-system designs to be clear and precise in defining interventions. Sometimes this is more easily said than done. We often see practitioners having difficulty distinguishing between baseline and intervention periods. There are at least two major reasons for this.

The first is the assumption that just about everything the practitioner does is or should be helpful to the client. Therefore, the argument runs, how can one (or why should one) distinguish between distinct parts of the overall process—for example, between baseline and intervention?

The second reason is the fairly common problem that often interventions are defined or conceptualized so generally or so vaguely that the practitioner has trouble specifying its components and identifying when they are applied. For example, if you define your intervention as simply psychotherapy or casework or counseling or community change, you might have real trouble in specifying just where the assessment part of the process ends and the intervention begins.

At the broadest level, *intervention* is what the practitioner does in a planned way to affect or change a target problem. The intervention may be one technique, a combination of techniques put into a package, or a combination of packages that comprise an intervention program. For example, you may nod encouragingly as a hesitant teenager begins to tell his or her story; this might be described as one technique. But nodding encouragement is combined with attentive posture, good eye contact, and the like into a package termed *active listening*. Yet active listening may itself be combined with other packages of interventions to represent a programmatic intervention, such as described by the activities comprising task-centered practice (e.g., Reid, 1978).

Regardless of the relative complexity of the intervention technique, package, or program, it is the formal, planned, systematic nature of this intervention that distinguishes it from, say, a baseline or assessment period. This is not to say that a practitioner's contact with the client may not be helpful in the baseline period. It certainly may. But the intervention is planned in a formal sense, using the baseline and assessment information, to be *more* helpful than just the contact alone between the practitioner and client.

This conception also is not to deny the potentially strong effects that establishment of empathy, rapport, and respect—the relationship—can have on others (see Bohart & Greenberg, 1997, for reviews of research on the effectiveness of empathy as a crucial element in interpersonal helping). But the intervention used should go beyond that and build on that relationship or other possibly less specific effects of contact between practitioner and client. The assumption here is that the relationship *plus* the planned intervention should have a greater impact than just the relationship alone, accounting for differences between the baseline and intervention phases. Indeed, if you consider the relationship to be the heart of your approach to practice, you still might be able to differentiate between an assessment and baseline phase, where you might offer, for example, moderate levels of empathy, and an intervention phase, where you offer higher levels of empathy for therapeutic purposes (e.g., see the single-system design by Truax & Carkhuff, 1965, in which they experimentally

raised and lowered levels of empathy and warmth; also, see Nugent, 1992a).

At a more concrete level, intervention really reflects the notion of changes in the *practitioner's* behavior. Assume that we were able to measure the practitioner's intervention behavior. If during the baseline period no intervention behavior was present, and during the intervention period we detected the clear presence of behavior designed to change the client's problems, then we could say, at the least, that we were successful in identifying what that intervention was and distinguishing it from a period of nonintervention (say, the baseline). Conversely, of course, if no differences in practitioner behavior could be detected, we would have to conclude that the intervention really did not take place. For example, if trained observers are watching the practitioner (or viewing tapes, etc.), they can detect when more of some behavior is occurring and when less is occurring. This could be used to determine the presence or absence of "intervention behaviors." Nelsen (1985) makes the point that verifying the presence of the intervention (independent variable) as planned is crucial to both practice and its evaluation. Merely asserting that we are using a particular practice approach—for example, cognitive therapy—is not convincing unless we provide evidence that what we have done in fact represents what the relevant theorists define as the appropriate method of intervention.

There are a number of factors to consider in specifying your interventions (Blythe, Tripodi, & Briar, 1994; Blythe & Tripodi, 1989; Gresham, 1997; Nelsen, 1985; Tripodi, 1994). We call these *operational* features or *procedural* dimensions of the intervention. They include (a) the form of the intervention (e.g., the type of communication used, like asking questions or supplying information); (b) the content of the intervention (i.e., what specifically the client should be learning from the intervention, such as having the client's feelings discussed); (c) the dosage (i.e., how much and how often the intervention is applied); (d) the context in which the action takes place (e.g., a client may detect some disinterest in the practitioner's manner of asking questions, which colors how the client responds); (e) practitioner behaviors (i.e., what the practitioner is actually doing in order to achieve a particular objective); and (f) specification of involvement (i.e., clarification of the nature and extent of participation of key actors in a given intervention, including who, when, how often, and how long each are involved). These procedural dimensions can be summarized by developing practice prescriptions that describe as precisely as possible all the above in relation to particular clients or targets. This act of procedural specification then allows implementation monitoring (Chambers, Wedel, & Rodwell, 1992) to help ensure what is called *intervention integrity* (Gresham, 1997): Optimal implementation of the intervention as planned, in as thorough and detailed a fashion as the practice context allows.

We hope the above categories will not be viewed as attempts to dehumanize or overmechanize practice. Instead, they are presented as an attempt to help you clarify and operationalize the interventions you are constructing for a given client situation. We offer these suggestions not just so you will be able to use single-system designs, but so that you will be able to think as clearly and specifically as possible in all practice and evaluation situations (Rosen, 1993).

In essence, then, the intervention is the formally planned and systematically executed set of practitioner behaviors that are engaged in in order to change the target problem. To aid in precision, the practitioner might supply a specific description of those behaviors or techniques plus a specific rationale for engaging in those intervention behaviors—for example, why one technique or program was selected and others were not (see Blythe & Tripodi, 1989; Cormier & Cormier, 1998, chap. 11; Fischer, 1978b, chap. 2; Tripodi & Epstein, 1980, chap. 5, for a discussion of principles that can be used in the selection of intervention techniques). This intervention will be identified specifically enough so that it will be clear when the intervention actually began, how much or how often it was applied, and when it was not applied (withdrawn or terminated). Such specification will greatly enhance the practitioner's ability to draw comparisons between the baseline and intervention periods. (For more detailed discussion of procedures for developing and specifying interventions, see Thomas, 1984.)

In selecting your intervention, it is crucial—for both practice and evaluation purposes—that *your intervention is clearly related to your problem hypothesis and goals* so that the intervention can be expected logically (and perhaps theoretically and empirically) to have an impact on those goals. If your goal is to improve a client's self-esteem, the intervention should be geared toward changing self-esteem, rather than other, perhaps more readily accessible targets, such as "number of dates per month." Otherwise, the procedural specificity we are advocating could be a waste of time, since, because of the selection of inappropriate interventions, the target is unlikely to demonstrate change in your evaluation.

Phases

The first characteristic of single-system designs that must be discussed when making a comparison between baseline and intervention concerns *phases*—that is, the periods of time during which distinctive evaluation activities occur. Baseline is one phase in which, by definition, no planned intervention occurs, only planned observations of targeted problems and events. The intervention period is another phase in which some planned effort to affect the targeted problems, together with a planned observation of those problems, occurs.

Each of these phases is designated with a different letter; there are special variations to indicate when interventions are changed or when they are changed in intensity. However, it is difficult in the abstract to determine whether a different magnitude of the same intervention represents a new phase. Therefore, we present some notation that will enable you to distinguish between changes in the intensity or magnitude of one intervention and changes that constitute a completely different intervention.

Types of Phases.   In all designs, the letter *A* stands for the nonintervention or baseline phase. Letters of the alphabet following *A* typically are used to designate the intervention phases. In the most rigorous applications of single-system designs, each letter is supposed to stand for one distinctive intervention technique. For example, the first phase would be the baseline *(A)*; the second phase might be application of a single intervention technique, say, systematic desensitization *(B)*; and the third phase might be application of another separate technique, say, role-playing *(C)*. If the latter two techniques were combined in a fourth phase, it would be designated *BC*.

If only real practice were that uncomplicated! The fact of the matter is that in most sit-uations, practitioners do not have the luxury of applying only one technique per phase so that their different effects can be studied. Very few techniques are applied in isolation in real practice anyway, which can present problems for the practitioner and for the evaluator. The notation in Figure 11.1 is an attempt to distinguish among different types of phases, the changing of phases, and changing intensities across phases.

The top 3 rows of Figure 11.1 show distinctive phases, some of which contain only one technique. Others contain sets of distinct techniques combined and used at the same time

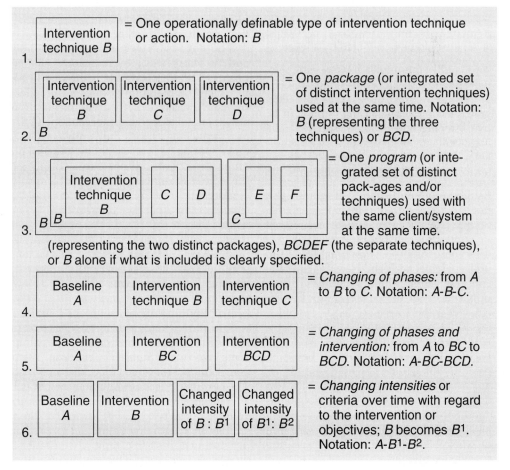

FIGURE 11.1 Notation for phases (rows 1–3), changing phases (rows 4–5), and changing intensities of the same intervention (row 6).

(the *package*) or integrated sets of distinct packages and perhaps techniques combined and used with a particular client (the *program*). A single letter can be used to designate a technique, a package, or a program, as long as it is understood that this letter may include one or two or more integrated practice techniques. Sets of letters, such as *BC* or *BCD*, may also be used to indicate packages or programs, with each letter designating a separate intervention technique or package.

Let's look at these options, using the example of a hypothetical family communications training seminar:

1. This family communications training seminar could be thought of in terms of its core *intervention technique* such as training in active listening (Gordon, 1970). As such, it would be designated by a letter, *B*.

2. This family communications training seminar might also be considered to be a *package* composed of separate but integrated techniques including training in active listening and problem solving training. It still may be designated by the single letter *B*, or by the set of letters *BC*, one letter for each of the specific techniques.

3. Family communication training also might be considered to be a *program*—that is, a set of packages and/or techniques integrated for work with one client like those named above, which are taught to both parents and children for optimal communication within a family. The set of packages for the *parents* might be designated by the letter *B*, or by the set of letters *BCD* (one letter for each of the techniques in the parent package), while the package for the children might be designated by the letter *C*, or by the set of letters *EF* (with one letter for each of the two techniques in the children's package). As another option, the entire program might be labeled *B*, given a detailed description of what this program includes (i.e., the specific techniques).

Regardless of whether the practitioner chooses to use the letter *B*, or the letters *BC* or *BCDEF*, each would designate family communication training as the intervention and would be shown on appropriate portions of the chart used in the evaluation process. The basic point is to be clear about how you designate a technique or a package or program of techniques and to be consistent in this usage.

To summarize, intervention may be thought of as a single *technique*, a *package* (a combination of two or more techniques), or a *program* (a combination of packages and/or techniques integrated in work with a given client or system). As described above, the intervention can be designated by a single overall letter (e.g., *B*) or by a separate letter for each of the components (e.g., *BCD* for a package comprised of three techniques). The key is to be clear in specifying just what the ingredients of the intervention are, no matter what the notation.

The next two rows of Figure 11.1 (rows 4 and 5) show ways of indicating change of phases. The simplest case is the one in row 4 in which the practitioner goes from collecting baseline measures, *A*, to a first intervention, *B*, and then to a second intervention, *C*. If the practitioner starts with the family communications training seminar as the first intervention, he or she might indicate this as *BC* to reflect the active listening and the problem-solving components (row 5). Then, if it becomes necessary to add a positive reinforcement component, *D*, he or she can do this easily by noting the new intervention as *BCD*. Likewise, if the practitioner starts out with the *BCD* intervention, but finds it is necessary to drop one component, *D*, he or she can indicate the new intervention as consisting only of *BC*.

The bottom row of Figure 11.1 indicates a way to show changes in the intensity or magnitude of the same intervention over time by using *superscript* numbers. Suppose a school counselor is working with a disruptive child. The counselor uses a 5-minute time-out period after each disruptive outburst, but this intervention doesn't work. The counselor then increases the length of the time-out to 10 minutes per outburst, and this rapidly diminishes the disruptive outbursts. This changing of the intensity of the same intervention from phase to phase is one type of changing intensity design. (Another type is changing the intensity of the objectives; both types are discussed in detail in Chapter 16.) Essentially the same intervention is used in each phase of a changing intensity design, but variations in what is expected of the client or what is done involving the intervention (e.g., giving longer than usual recesses for each major step in correct spelling) are made. The notation reflects these changing magnitudes of the same intervention by superscripts on the same letter—the B becomes B^1 the change in intensity from the first $B(B^1)$ to the second becomes B^2, and so on.

Length of Phases. The length of the baseline phase will be considered in detail in Chapter 12, but we can anticipate the discussion by noting that under most circumstances it is desirable to collect a sufficient number of data points to provide a clear and stable description of the target events at the time. This does not mean that stable data always have to be present. It only means that it is best to try and provide the opportunity for stable patterns to appear if they are going to do so. There will be variability in data, just as there is in life itself. Sometimes there will be larger social and biological cycles affecting events in the portions of time in which the practitioner is collecting data, such as the effects of seasonal unemployment or periods of wakefulness and sleeping. The practitioner must be sensitive to these factors in arriving at a clear picture of the client's situation that will be useful in understanding potential causal factors related to the problem and, therefore, affecting the development of an intervention program.

In addition to the phases being of sufficient length to permit the natural variability to appear as relatively stable patterns of events, the length of adjacent phases should be equal whenever possible. Equal length allows external and internal factors to influence behaviors in baseline and intervention phases equally, so that if differences do occur between the two phases, it will be more likely that these differences will be due to the planned intervention rather than the external events. The same principle holds when two or more intervention phases are being compared to one another. If they are of equal length, then some of the potential confounding factors for producing different results are equalized. Other problems, such as the effects of the order of presentation of the several interventions, continue; we will discuss these shortly.

There is an implicit conflict between two characteristics of phases—stability and equal length of phases to be compared. Both are desired, but they may set up contradictory forces, as when you are tempted to stop an intervention to make it the same length as the baseline, before the target problems have stabilized into a clear pattern of events. You also may be tempted to cut off baseline data before a clear picture of the problematic conditions has been obtained because you feel pressure to start the intervention, which may last for a long period of time. These are realistic dilemmas that practitioners face, and we have no perfect solution to suggest. At best we can recommend that reasonably clear and stable baseline data should be gathered if possible so as to have a sound basis for planning the intervention and for evaluating progress. Likewise, a clear and stable picture of change in the intervention phase probably is more important for practice than having an equal length of phases, even though this leaves the door open to alternative explanations regarding factors that may be producing the outcomes. In general, we recommend taking the option more useful for practice than for evaluation when there is a conflict. For example, you might choose stability over equal length of phases.

The main point for any phase, baseline or intervention, is to enable a clear and stable picture of the target problem to emerge. You should try to give enough time in the baseline phase to obtain an accurate picture of the target problem in order to plan an optimal course of action. Obviously, problems may arise. You may have to begin intervention quickly or else stand to lose the client; this produces a shorter baseline. On other occasions an intervention may be prematurely terminated, leaving an intervention phase shorter than the baseline. But, with everything else being equal, for good or perhaps ideal practice and certainly for the clearest evaluation, you should try to achieve both stability and equal length of phases.

Adjacent–Nonadjacent Phases. Consider an *A-B-C* design in which an initial baseline period, *A,* is followed by two distinct intervention periods, *B* and *C.* For logical comparisons, two phases to be compared should be adjacent–for example, *A-B* or *B-C*–rather than separated by an intervening phase, as in *A-C.* This is because with separated phases, the effects of events occurring in the intervening time, or the order among events, could produce the changes observed. If you want to compare the baseline with an intervention, *C,* then you would have to design a situation with this arrangement: *A-B-A-C.* In such a design a baseline is adjacent to each of the distinct interventions, *B* and *C.* However, you cannot compare the two interventions to *each other* because in the *A-B-A-C* design they are no longer adjacent. Obviously, the greater the separation between phases, the less clear their relationship becomes. With more complicated designs, however, it becomes possible to compare individual interventions with baselines and with other interventions (see Chapters 16 and 17).

The basic point about adjacent–nonadjacent phases is that for direct, logical comparison, phases should be adjacent. This means that the practitioner seeking a reasonably rigorous evaluation of several interventions employed with one client will have to arrange interventions and baseline periods carefully in order to make these determinations. We discuss designs that enable you to do this in Chapters 14 through 17.

Nonadjacent phases can, however, provide you with some hypotheses for future testing even though these phases don't offer the basis for direct logical comparison. That is, what *appears* to be true in a comparison of nonadjacent phases, may in fact turn out to be true when two interventions are compared with a more appropriate design, as discussed in subsequent chapters.

Changes in Intervention

One of the major strengths of single-system designs comes in the information they provide regarding the ongoing course of events related to target problems. With such information the practitioner and the client are in a position to take knowledgeable action in maintaining, changing, or terminating the intervention. As long as discrete interventions–individual techniques, packages, or programs–receive distinctive labels, the pattern and the content of interventions may be linked with outcomes of practice, and decisions about when to change the interventions may be empirically, theoretically, and practically grounded. When comparing two phases to ascertain the differences between them, you must know as clearly and unambiguously as possible what each phase contains.

Interventions might change between phases for several reasons. Some are related mainly to the information provided by your single-system design as you monitor progress:

1. The problem might be getting worse. Thus, you would want to change your intervention to forestall further deterioration.

2. The problem might be changing too slowly. Prior research, your own experience, or the client's feedback might indicate that positive change is not occurring at the desired or expected rate (if faster change is indeed realistic). Hence, you might need to adjust your intervention to hasten the pace of change.

3. Goals have been achieved. You therefore would want to make changes in your intervention as you move into a maintenance phase and, ultimately, as you terminate.

But, in addition to the feedback you receive from your single-system design, there are other reasons why your interventions might change. A number of these have been described by McMahon (1987). These include (a) practitioner "drift" or random fluctuations in the delivery of an intervention; (b) fatigue; (c) boredom; (d) the practitioner conveying his or her expectations; (e) motivation to hasten change; (f) the practitioner becoming more adept with a particular intervention over time; (g) pressure from colleagues or administrators; (h) changes in client variables, such as the client putting pressure on the practitioner to do things differently; and (i) lack of clarity or incompleteness of the interventive technique so that the technique implementation shifts over time.

Actually, the practitioner may not even be aware of some of these shifts. Thus, McMahon (1987) recommends using cues, prompts, videotapes of sessions, and role-playing of techniques to enhance awareness. Also, following clear procedural guides such as intervention manuals will help practitioners keep interventions focused. However, to the extent that the practitioner is aware of shifts in interventions, there are a number of ways these changes can be made. Each requires a different single-system design notation so that you can keep track of these changes in your design:

1. The first intervention may be changed in intensity; that is, more or less of it may be used. Or the criterion of what is acceptable performance may be changed; that is, more or less of the client's performance is now required to obtain the same intervention—for example, reinforcement. (These would use the notation of changing intensity, A-B^1-B^2.)

2. An entirely new intervention may be implemented, along with the old intervention (using notation such as A-B-BC).

3. An entirely new intervention may be implemented, in place of the old intervention, which is terminated (with the notation of A-B-C).

4. One intervention may be removed altogether with or without a substitution of other interventions (e.g., A-BC-B).

5. The first intervention may be continued without any changes (thus, the continuing notation of A-B).

In addition to these changes in single-system designs beyond the basic A-B design, various other kinds of changes frequently are made, such as the introduction of an intervention and its experimental removal as in the A-B-A-B design. Therefore, we must consider the terms used to describe these changes in design. In this book we will use the generic term *removal* to apply to any type of situation in which the original intervention is taken away. However, in the literature, you may note that two other terms–withdrawal and reversal–are frequently used (and confused). When the practitioner has taken an initial baseline and then initiated some intervention, a further change, called a *withdrawal,* may be made. This usually means the simple removal of the first intervention while continuing to collect data (given that a successful change in the target behavior has occurred) and an attempt to return to the original baseline condition (i.e., no intervention), so far as this is possible. The term *reversal* also is used, sometimes synonymously with withdrawal. More recent usage of the term *reversal* is that it involves removing an intervention and applying the same intervention in the removal phase (e.g., the second A phase in an A-B-A-B design) to a *different* (usually, alternative but incompatible) behavior after the first and successful intervention has occurred. Thus, withdrawal refers to complete removal, while reversal refers to removal and application of the intervention to an alternative behavior during the removal phase. The point of both types of removal is to compare changes in the target between the intervention phase and the no intervention, removal (withdrawal or reversal) phase (these terms are discussed in more detail in Chapter 14). Of course, following the removal phase, the intervention is reapplied to the original target behavior in both withdrawal and reversal designs.

In connection with changes of intervention and particularly removal, a distinction must be made between *reversible* and *irreversible changes.* Reversible changes are changes that disappear once the intervention is removed. Irreversible changes refer to changes that will not go away (or reverse) when an intervention is removed. Let's assume that a client has attended a series of assertiveness training sessions as part of his or her intervention. Is there any way we can remove this training from his or her thinking and behavior once it has been incorporated into his or her lifestyle? Presumably such learning experiences cannot easily be forgotten, so for practical purposes the impact of the intervention may not be removable for systematic study and comparison across phases. They are, in effect, irreversible. To the degree that any type of counseling, psychotherapy, education, or whatever is incorporated into a person's thinking and acting, it may be considered irreversible. The major way changes in intervention can be made in such situations is to add to the learning and identify changes in performance beyond the original performance. Reversible changes, for example, changes produced by giving chocolate candies for spelling difficult words correctly, can become irreversible ones, such as when a teacher moves away from candy and to verbal praise for good spelling and the child incorporates this pleasure in spelling correctly into his or her own standards of performance. (See the discussion of multiple baseline designs in Chapter 15 for ways of overcoming irreversibility in evaluating change.)

Although there are a number of possibilities for changing interventions, as we discussed above, there is one caution we'd like to add. If you are trying to determine just which one of your intervention techniques is really affecting the problem, it is important to change—add or remove—only one variable at a time as you move from phase to phase. If you change more than one variable—for example, removing two techniques and adding two more—your analysis would not allow you to determine which of the techniques or how much of each is having some effect on the problem (Barlow & Hersen, 1984). An everyday analogy would be spraining your ankle and then taking aspirins and using ice to ease the pain, finding this unsuccessful and switching to another pain killer plus an elastic bandage. If the pain eased, there would be no real way of knowing which components of your treatment really worked. While changing only one intervention component at a time is not always possible, and there also are other design questions to consider (which we discuss in subsequent chapters), we do want you to remember at this point that if you cannot change only one variable at a time as you move from phase to phase, you will have difficulty in interpreting what part of your program actually worked.

Complicating Factors

As single-system designs become more involved with changes from one intervention back to baseline or to other interventions, certain logical problems emerge that complicate their analysis. These complications all share the same effect of confusing any causal analysis because artifacts from the design itself might be involved in producing the effects. In fact, much of the discussion in this chapter—everything from length of phases to changes in intervention—could be interpreted as presenting threats to the internal validity of the evaluation. We return to this topic later on in this chapter. Following are some of these complicating factors and how one might attempt to overcome their effects.

Carryover. *Carryover* refers to a situation where the effects obtained in one phase appear to "carry over" into the next phase. The term *carryover* is generally used in the context of removal designs. Thus, if you attempted to remove a successful intervention to create a second baseline to determine whether your intervention was actually affecting the problem, and the problem stayed at that level despite the removal, carryover effects would pertain. In technical terms, it could be said that you were not able to retrieve the first baseline during the second baseline phase. Although this may indicate that the learning that was produced in the first intervention really was solid, or that it was irreversible as we suggested earlier, it does limit your ability to interpret whether or not your interventions were related to that positive outcome because you can't isolate the effects of the intervention you used. Indeed, carryover effects might also be produced by totally extraneous outside influences having some impact on the target problem. For example, a seasonal change—say, from cold to warm weather—might coincide with the end of a first intervention phase. Even with removal of the intervention, one could still not "retrieve the baseline" because positive changes might be related to, or reinforced by, the seasonal changes. Thus, carryover effects complicate your interpretation of your data.

Contrast. Even if you do return to a stable baseline condition before implementing a new intervention, it is possible that the client will observe a difference between the two interventions and react to this *contrast* rather than to the second treatment itself (Jayaratne & Levy, 1979, p. 228). For example, if a municipal judge was experimenting with the most appropriate level of traffic fines, first beginning with a 5-dollar fine and then trying a 50-dollar fine in a subsequent month, there might be a public outcry about the contrast and not about the need to have some system of fines. (See also the research of Kendall, Nay, & Jeffers, 1975.) Perhaps reducing the contrast between interventions (amount of traffic fines) might minimize this type of problem.

Order of Presentation. Another inevitable consequence of using several interventions is that one must come before the other, so the *order of presentation* of these interventions may itself be part of the causal impact. For example, if you implement an *A-B-C* or even an *A-B-A-C-A-D* design, you will not be able to detect whether part of the outcome was due to the order of the interventions, in that the effects of one intervention actually may build on the effects of a prior one. Nor will you be able to tell whether it would have been different had you implemented the interventions in a different order, for example *A-C-B* or *A-B-A-D-A-C*. Solutions to this problem are complex, but they could involve a randomized order of presentation so that no known bias in the order of presentations of the interventions will be acting on the client. On the other hand, a more sophisticated design may be used in which interventions are presented in deliberately counterbalanced sequences; we describe some possibilities for your use in Chapter 17.

Incomplete Data. There will be many occasions on which you will not have a continuous run of information in baseline and/or intervention periods. Unfortunately, some textbooks imply that clients always fit nicely into a neat 10-day baseline, followed immediately on the next day with the full-blown intervention. If so, fine. You have a nice *A-B* design. But some period of time often intrudes between the baseline and the intervention phases.

There are two types of situations in which this is likely to occur: when the data are incomplete for any reason—we take up this topic in this section—and when there is a training phase in the intervention period—discussed in the following section.

There are many possible reasons that the data may be incomplete. Examples would be if the client left town on a business trip; if the practitioner got sick; or if relatives came to visit the client, changing the context temporarily. In these kinds of situations we recommend that recording be continued, if possible. Depending on the situation, it may be necessary only to add a few more observations to make sure the former baseline pattern is continuing (see Figure 11.2a); or it may be necessary to do an entirely new baseline period if the gap in recording is lengthy (see Figure 11.2b). On some occasions, there may be stop-and-start baselining, in which case the practitioner must decide whether any of the baseline data are acceptable as a frame of reference (see Figure 11.2c). The overriding issue is to obtain some semblance of stable and typical data about the client's target situation.

When only a few data points need be added to the baseline (as in Figure 11.2a), then follow the instructions in Chapter 4 for presenting missing data on a chart by indicating the missing time units on the chart with dots rather than a solid line. When many data points are missed, then indicate that a new baseline has been established (A_2) with a new vertical construction line in dashes (as in Figure 11.2b). (A_2, with the 2 in subscripts, simply means the second baseline period, with no other changes implied.)

The most important point about incomplete data is how to use them as the baseline in the analysis that compares baseline with intervention data. Some analyses (discussed in Part IV) require that lines for analysis be drawn using all of the baseline data. If there are only a few gaps as indicated by dotted connecting lines, then use the entire baseline period as that frame of reference. If there are many gaps, and a new baseline period is taken, then use only the new baseline as the frame of reference for what happens during the intervention period. Or, you can analyze the data by using only the actual

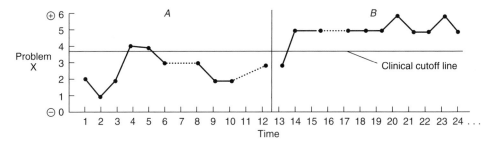

FIGURE 11.2a Hypothetical data showing a few missing data points in baseline and intervention. Analyze these data as if there were 12 baseline observations of which 2 are above a clinical cutoff line and 8 are below. Likewise, count 12 intervention observations of which 10 are above and 1 is below the cutoff line.

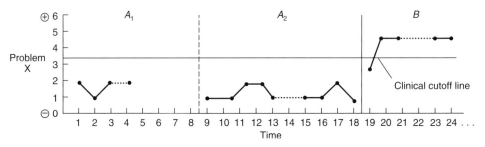

FIGURE 11.2b Hypothetical data showing a large gap in baseline A, requiring the establishment of a new baseline, A_2.

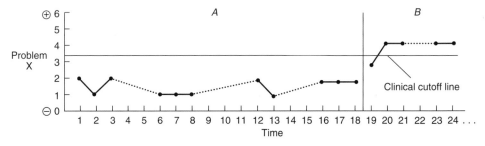

FIGURE 11.2c Hypothetical data showing stop and start baseline data that require the practitioner to decide if and when enough information is available to begin the intervention. The data can be analyzed using only the 11 actual data points in calculations of the proportion below the cutoff line (11/18); see Part IV.

collected data points, as in the case of Figure 11.2c, using 11 out of 18 baseline points.

Training Phase. The second very common situation in practice occurs when baseline data cannot be connected immediately with the intervention data because of a "training phase."

The practitioner wants to initiate some plan of action (intervention) after a stable baseline emerges, but because of the nature of that intervention, it is not likely to begin immediately due to the need to train someone (the client, a relevant other) in how to conduct the intervention. For example, the client may have to learn assertiveness skills over several workshop sessions before beginning to apply these skills in a work context. During the time that the client is learning these skills, there may be some effect on his or her behavior but not likely the full effect of this intervention. So recording likely will reflect this with no change in the target (Figure 11.3a), gradual changes in the target (see Figure 11.3b), or possibly irregular changes, as when some threshold must be reached before an effect occurs (see Figure 11.3c).

The basic question is how to analyze these training phase data relative to the comparison between baseline and intervention. The training

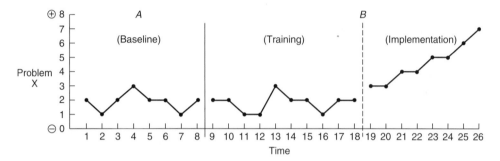

FIGURE 11.3a   Hypothetical data showing no change in target behavior during training phase.

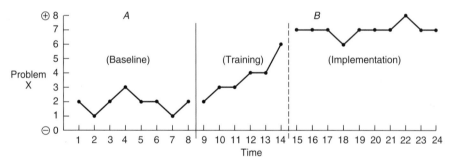

FIGURE 11.3b   Hypothetical data showing gradual changes in target behavior during a 6-week assertiveness training phase.

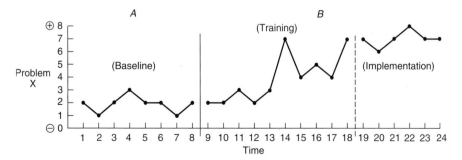

FIGURE 11.3c   Hypothetical data showing irregular changes in target behavior during a 10-week assertiveness training phase.

phase forces a separation between baseline and intervention, and thus violates the guideline involving the importance of having adjacent phases for analysis. We propose two solutions. The first is to continue to compare baseline against the combined training and intervention phases (as in Figures 11.3a, b, and c), and expect the obvious, that there may not be any major change during the training portion, although there may be some trend in a positive direction. If no change appears in an intervention phase that doesn't contain a training component, then the practitioner has to question whether this is due to the incomplete learning of the intervention or the intervention itself being ineffective. With a training phase, however, the practitioner should probably be willing to tolerate no change for a longer time than if the full intervention is applied and should have taken effect immediately. The dangers of interpreting data with training phases is that the combined training and intervention phases may exhibit some carryover effects. That is, it may be the special qualities of the training rather than the intervention itself that are, in part, causing the apparent changes in target behavior. For instance, being in a workshop on assertiveness training may itself be a stimulus for action.

The second possibility is to label separately the training and the intervention phases as B^1 and B^2 (as in Figure 11.4). An example would be when the practitioner has to train a parent in a child management program for 2 weeks before the parent actually uses it in an effort to change the child's behavior. In situations like this, one possibility is to use the following notation: A stands for baseline, B^1 for the training period, and B^2 for the period when the program is actually implemented. The rationale is that implementation period B^2 is largely a modification of B^1. This also allows you to determine whether any changes come about during the training period itself, and also whether the changes that occur during the implementation period exceed the changes in the training period. Presumably, in this illustration (Figure 11.4), because the training is a prior event necessary for the implementation of the program, whatever changes occur in B^2 could be a result of a combination of the training and the implementation. That is, the results from B^2 may be confounded because of possible carryover (or order of presentation effects) from B^1. However, if no changes had occurred in the B^1 phase, there would be more evidence that the changes may more likely be due to the intervention itself.

Maintenance and Follow-Up Plans

Implicit in many single-system designs is the apparent assumption that simply ending on an intervention phase will be sufficient to guaran-

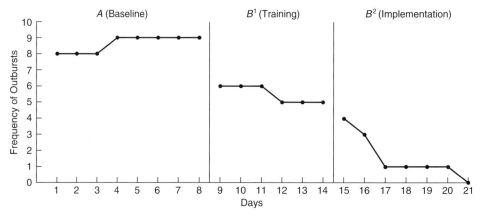

FIGURE 11.4 Chart illustrating phases for training and implementation as distinguished by changes in intensity.

tee that the positive effects of intervention will last forever. Of course, there is no guarantee of lasting effects of any service program. Thus, we strongly recommend the development of a *maintenance* or generalization plan to be added to all intervention plans as an attempt to ensure that the changes produced by your intervention program are lasting changes. Assuming just for the purposes of illustration that the B phase is the last intervention phase, we recommend several things for you to do to help ensure continuity of positive outcome. First, extend the B period to ensure that the problem has been changed to a satisfactory level. Second, conduct follow-ups on a periodic basis to ascertain how well this satisfaction level has been maintained. When it has not, or when it shows signs of slipping, then a "booster shot" of reinstituted intervention may help. Third, and most importantly, the last phase in your single-system design, following the successful completion of the intervention proper, should include a program to maintain and to transfer the changes to the client's natural environment after the intervention is completed (see Goldstein & Kanfer, 1979; Karoly & Steffen, 1980; Rzepnicki, 1991 for numerous examples of successful maintenance programs). Building in such a maintenance program is the essence of both good practice and good evaluation.

When you are developing a program to maintain and to transfer the effects of your intervention program to the natural environment, you actually have three options regarding your evaluation design. The first is to simply modify the intervention phase—B, for example—by fading out or changing the schedule of reinforcement or by seeing the client less frequently. You could then consider this maintenance phase as a B^2 phase with the original B phase becoming B^1 because you are modifying the intensity of the intervention. The second option is to continue your B-phase intervention and to add a new intervention to enhance the transfer process—for example, adding homework assignments to in-office role-playing. This would then be considered a new BC phase. The third option is to drop the B-phase intervention altogether after it has been successful and to add a completely new maintenance phase—for example, discontinu-

ing your work with a client being discharged from a hospital and beginning work with the family to maintain the changes. This would then add a separate C phase indicating a new intervention.

These three variations of maintenance and transfer programs are illustrated in Figure 11.5.

It still remains for you to be able to assess whether maintenance programs have worked and whether the target events have stayed unchanged after regular contact with the client has ended. Indeed, there are a number of new developments in single-system methodology that can aid in this analysis. Many of these developments, including some rather complicated procedures for assessing both generalization of specific targets from one situation to another and maintenance of target events, were described by Barrios and Hartmann (1988). Essentially, they consist of combinations of assessment probes and design strategies that could provide information on a number of technical points regarding change in the target over time.

But there remains no substitute for the good old-fashioned *follow-up* evaluation. Whether this is a single "probe" conducted once at some point following termination, or a series of reevaluations conducted at regular, predetermined intervals, we urge that you conduct follow-ups, preferably using the same measures that were used to evaluate change during the baseline and intervention periods. But even if this is not possible, we suggest, at the least, maintaining contact with the client—whether by telephone, mailed questionnaires, or in-person interviews—to inquire about whether changes have been maintained.

We believe that only after follow-up evaluation reveals that change has been maintained can the overall evaluation be considered complete. Not only that, maintaining contact with the client after termination, however minimal, is essential for practice purposes as well. It allows you to make yourself available in the event old problems reassert themselves or new problems arise, and, above all else, it shows that you care.

This discussion of maintaining intervention effects and transferring them to the client's natural environment is applicable to all single-system designs, especially those that end on an

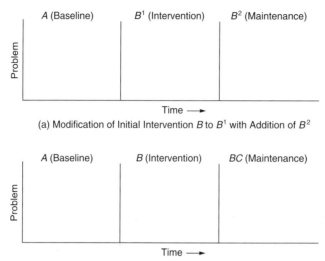

(a) Modification of Initial Intervention B to B^1 with Addition of B^2

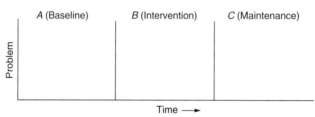

(b) Addition of Maintenance Program C to Intervention Program B Resulting in BC

(c) Dropping of Intervention B and Addition of Maintenance Program C

FIGURE 11.5   Three options for notation of maintenance and transfer programs.

intervention phase. It is also, we believe, an essential condition of good practice. We refer to this point on many subsequent occasions.

Collaborative and Team Efforts

Practitioners in agencies frequently find themselves in collaborative efforts with colleagues on behalf of a given client. In other circumstances, such team efforts are the rule, not the exception. Is there any way of teasing out the contributions of separate practitioners in these collaborative efforts, or is the collective intervention what is to be measured?

First, there is nothing wrong with measuring a collective effort. The intervention (B) can be viewed as a package of interventions taken as one. However, instead of there being several types of interventions conducted by one practitioner, in the team effort there may be one or more interventions conducted by two or more practitioners all at the same time period. Thus, one chart with one A-B design signifies results from the joint efforts of all concerned. For example, a client at a drug abuse center may undergo a number of experiences over the course of a 2-week period, such as a detoxification phase administered by one set of practitioners, an individual counseling procedure delivered by another practitioner, another intervention involving group counseling, possibly some job skills training, and so on. Different practitioners are involved in each of these phases.

The client's time is sorted carefully into a sequence of planned interventions to address the problems of addiction: (a) to be detoxified from the present state of addictiveness; (b) to gain understanding of the personal, family, and peer group factors that led to addiction in the past; (c) to gain skills in resisting these pressures in the present and future. With reference to goal c, there are a set of specific targets the client is learning, and measurement indicates the extent of that learning. However, what contributes to learning how to resist peer pressures to join in group drug use? Probably all of the experiences at the drug rehabilitation contribute in part. Is it possible to sort out the distinctive contribution of each?

If several interventions are being conducted concurrently–individual counseling, group counseling, and so on–then it would be difficult to sort out the unique contributions unless they are conducted at random times and, after each occasion, some measurement is taken of relevant variables. Then, this approximates the alternating intervention design (Chapter 17).

On the other hand, if the interventions are applied sequentially, then it might be possible to sort out the differential effects of each stage of the intervention, using one of the variations of successive intervention or changing intensity designs described in Chapter 16.

Another exploratory method might be to use a reverse log approach, where the practitioners each add a critical incident to a log on the client, indicating for a given class of problems–for example, "dealing with authority figures"–what happened before, during, and after a given episode. Then, in a team meeting, individual practitioners might attach numbers to the qualitative information, indicating whether the client was making very good or good progress, no change, or regression or strong regression, with regard to that target. By talking together when making these ratings, the practitioners could come to some understanding on a common frame of reference in assigning scores. Then, one could average the amount of progress made on a given target when the client was with one practitioner/situation, as contrasted with another practitioner/situation. These would be, admittedly, rough indicators, but if two practitioners were in one situation, there would be the possibility of a reliability

check. However, whether changes in the client are due to the method being used or to the practitioners' different personality fit with client, or both, could not be distinguished.

Another exploratory device would be to ask clients, at the end of each day, how much progress they felt they made during that day in each of the service situations. If the ratings are comparable to the reverse log, then one could compare how much constructive/destructive change client and specific practitioners observed in given situations. Averages for these changes also could be computed and compared with practitioner averages. Overall ratings of practitioner contributions to the client's problem solving also could be obtained from the client and compared to average ratings.

Finally, you could always conduct evaluations of your own work independent of whatever else goes on in the agency. Of course, it would be difficult or impossible to determine with a single A-B design the impact of your own work in a way that distinguishes it from all other agency efforts. On the other hand, even with use of an A-B design, changes in a target that seem to follow directly upon implementation of your intervention certainly can provide hypotheses for further investigation of the contributions of your own interventions in comparison to the contributions of others' work. And if a pattern of changes in several A-B designs across several clients emerges–for example, consistent changes in relation to implementation of your intervention–you have additional reason to suspect that your interventions are indeed adding substantially to the overall agency program. Use of some of the more rigorous designs described in subsequent chapters may then be used to investigate and perhaps further identify individual contributions to overall changes in clients' targets in the program.

CAUSALITY IN SINGLE-SYSTEM DESIGNS

In addition to being able to provide information about whether changes in the target have occurred between baseline and intervention, single-system designs also offer the possibility of making causal inferences—did the intervention produce the observed outcome? In this section we discuss some of the general principles related to these causal inferences, followed by a discussion of some of the threats to a conclusion that the intervention produced the changes; these "threats" are actually *alternative explanations* for a given set of results. These alternative explanations are threats to causal inferences and must be considered carefully in planning an evaluation. Following the discussion of causal inferences, the subsequent section discusses issues regarding generalizing the causal information obtained in one situation to other situations or clients.

Criteria for Inferring Causality in Single-System Designs

Discussions of causality have occupied philosophers of science from the beginnings of speculative thinking. We offer the following brief discussion of causation with this background in mind in an attempt to aid you in making reasonable inferences regarding the connection of your intervention to the observed changes in target problems. Several criteria that can be used to evaluate causal relationships in single-system designs are presented.

The first criterion for inferring causality is temporal arrangement, which means that the changes in the target problem must occur after the application of the intervention, not before. The charting of baseline and intervention data will quickly reveal whether this criterion is upheld. There probably will be some natural fluctuation during baseline in which the target problem may even move in a desired direction. However, over time, the typical pattern of the target probably will be portrayed by the baseline data pattern. With intervention, that pattern should change. As we discuss in Chapter 12, however, if baseline data appear to be improving in the absence of planned intervention, the effect of the service program might be hard to interpret.

The second criterion is the copresence of the application of the intervention and the desired change of target problems. This does not necessarily mean instantaneous change, since not all social-interpersonal behaviors and situations are that responsive. However, given a reasonable period of time (about the same length of time as the baseline period in many cases), changes should begin if you are to draw conclusions about the causal efficacy of the intervention. Frequently, the literature on a particular intervention will provide you with information on the time period you can expect before a given problem starts to change.

A third criterion suggests that if target problems change for the better in the absence of the intervention, something else is causally related to the outcome. If an intervention is removed before learning becomes irreversible, the target problem should show a decrease in desired performance. This is the basis for planned removal of an intervention and investigation of the concomitant change in the target problem.

The fourth criterion for making logical inferences about the causality of the intervention concerns the repeated copresence of the intervention and the manifestations of the desired change. Each time the first occurs the second should also be present. Given the natural variability of social events, we do not mean that this criterion demands perfect correlation, but rather that a clear pattern of continuing copresence is exhibited.

The fifth criterion brings in other possible influences to test whether they may be the actual cause of a given change in the target behavior. This criterion suggests the importance of attempting to determine whether there is any other continuously copresent factor that could be causally related to the outcome. If the desired change of the target event occurs in the presence of the intervention and with no other known influence, this becomes an additional source of information regarding causal inference.

The sixth criterion deals with consistency over time. The relationship of events—intervention and change in the target—should be maintained over time with no unexpected or unexplained fluctuation in that pattern.

The seventh and final criterion to be discussed here involves the conceptual and practical plausibility that the inference is grounded in scientific/professional knowledge—or at least isn't contrary to it—as well as being consistent with practical experience. This is a very broad criterion and perhaps is the starting point of the entire causal investigation, since you formulate your causal hypothesis on the basis of a review of the literature and conceptual-practical analysis of the situation when intervention plans are being made.

Having offered these seven criteria for making logical inferences about causality using single-system designs, we hasten to add that these do not provide absolute or certain grounds for making a causal inference. Social causality is a complex affair in which many apparently distant events may be intricately related in diverse ways. However, we offer these pragmatic criteria in the hope that you will be a little more prepared to back up your statements of effectiveness using single-system designs.

In summary, a way of viewing this discussion on criteria for inferring causality is to look for persistent *concomitant variation* between the intervention and the desired change in the target events. When these two—and only these two—events persistently covary (change together), you may have some basis for inferring causality, other things being equal. As mentioned previously, we might also think of these causal relationships in the context of the *principle of unlikely successive coincidences* (Jayaratne & Levy, 1979) in which a set of events occurs repeatedly, and while the first set might have happened by chance alone, with each succeeding pair of occurrences, it is increasingly unlikely that they are happening by coincidence, particularly if they were predicted to occur. This unlikeliness is another way of thinking about probability: The more unlikely some set of events is to happen by chance, the more likely it is to have occurred by design, specifically, by practice design. However, there are many other factors that have to be taken into consideration before excluding alternative explanations for why given outcomes occurred as they did, or before we can logically generalize from one situation to others. The next portion of this chapter covers these topics.

Design Validity. In Chapter 2, we discussed the term *validity*—or more accurately, measurement validity—as determining whether a measure actually was measuring what it was supposed to measure. But there are other uses of the word *validity* and they all refer to the design, and the way the design facilitates conclusions about causality. (The design also may facilitate conclusions about generalizability. This is called *external validity* and is discussed in the subsequent section.)

In this section, we focus on *design validity*: several ways in which characteristics of the design can affect conclusions that the intervention produced or caused any changes in the target. This is, of course, a key question for single-system designs. Indeed, the planned arrangements that comprise the designs are planned precisely to help us understand the effect of our interventions on target problems.

However, a number of factors affect our ability to draw conclusions about causality with single-system designs. We already have reviewed several of them in this chapter—differences among phases, differences in interventions, changing one variable at a time, and several complicating factors. In a sense, these can all raise questions about the validity of our causal inferences—are there other reasons than our intervention that would account for the results we obtained? Traditionally, these questions are called "threats to the validity of a design" because they can confound the conclusions about causality that we infer from our designs (Campbell & Stanley, 1963).

There are a number of other questions about alternative explanations for a given set of results—that is, other threats to the validity of research and evaluation designs in general, and single-system design in particular (Cook & Campbell, 1976, 1979; Kratochwill, 1978; Kratochwill & Levin, 1992; Shadish et al., 2002). One such question, or threat to the validity of a conclusion that involves the causality of our intervention, is that the observed change may have been brought about (caused) by factors other than the intervention; these factors are the alternative explanations for the findings, which thus become "threats" to our presumed interventive cause.

As context for the discussion that follows, we emphasize the point that *questions* these threats actually raise about how we designed the evaluation that produced our outcomes, rather than that there necessarily is an actual *threat* to our conclusions. When we think through the answers to these questions, we may discover that there is no threat to our conclusions because the design was strong enough to withstand the possible logical alternative answers for the results we obtained. In this case, we should look at these "threats" as questions to be answered so as to gain more confidence in our findings. But if we find that a threat is possible, given the design that we used, then we have to be less confident in our conclusion that the intervention caused the changes.

The most comprehensive discussion of these threats to the validity of designs is available in Shadish et al. (2002). They distinguish among three classes of threats affecting conclusions about causality: statistical conclusion validity (as well as external validity, discussed later in this chapter), internal validity, and construct validity. Since much of this material is concerned with classical research and not single-system designs, we will focus only on the threats that are pertinent to single-system designs, modifying the original concepts to fit this evaluation model wherever necessary. As you will see, there is some overlap among the threats in each area, although this categorization is probably more helpful than condensing all these threats into one category (e.g., simply considering them all threats to internal validity). We pose these validity issues as a series of questions.

Statistical Conclusion Validity: Did Change Occur?

Threats to statistical conclusion validity essentially refer to questions involving covariation between the independent variable (intervention) and the dependent variable (the target problem). Before knowing whether an independent variable caused changes in a dependent variable, it is important to know whether there are sufficient grounds to believe that the independent and dependent variables vary together as we discussed in the previous section on criteria for determining causality. Indeed, knowing whether two variables covary logically precedes decisions about causality. Most threats to statistical conclusion validity tend to make it more difficult to determine effectiveness by presenting obstacles that make it more difficult to detect change.

While some of the threats to statistical conclusion validity are related to the use of statistical tests (e.g., violations of assumptions underlying statistical tests, using an alpha value greater than .05, testing directional hypotheses, using the most powerful test of statistical significance), which we will discuss in Section IV, some of the threats can be controlled by design (Orme, 1991). These are listed below along with examples of each threat, all of which can make an intervention appear less effective.

Threats to Statistical Conclusion Validity

1. *Reliability of measures.* Measures that have low reliability make it difficult to detect true changes and may make an effective intervention appear ineffective.

   Example: Ryan used a measure of self-esteem with test-retest reliability of only .40. Although the client's self-esteem actually changed over time, Ryan couldn't tell with his measure whether the change was real or merely a reflection of an unstable measure.

2. *Reliability of intervention implementation.* The intervention may be implemented in different ways from occasion to occasion, or, if different practitioners are involved, from practitioner to practitioner. This decreases the chances of obtaining true differences and may make an effective intervention appear ineffective.

   Example: An agency administrator noticed that an intervention used widely in her agency did not appear effective when the results of the intervention were pooled for all practitioners using the intervention. She suspected that the reason for this was that practitioners were implementing the intervention in a variety of ways. In order to promote standardization, she and the practitioners produced a manual to describe specific steps of the intervention that all could follow.

3. *Random irrelevancies in the intervention setting.* Any random changes in the setting of the intervention including location, climate, time, and so on may affect scores on the outcome measure and make an effective intervention appear ineffective.

   Example: Because the agency was being refurbished, Irving was forced to change offices several times during the course of his intervention with the Trask family. These changes made the intervention appear less effective than before the disruptions.

4. *Number of observations.* The smaller the number of observations, the more difficult it is to detect the effect of an intervention.

Example: Terri was only able to collect two baseline observations and three intervention observations for her client. The small number of observations made it unclear as to whether substantial changes actually had occurred so that it was difficult to determine whether the intervention was effective.

Internal Validity: Was Change Caused by Your Intervention?

The best known of the major threats to design validity is internal validity. Of the three types of design validity, internal validity most specifically relates to questions about ascertaining whether the intervention caused the changes in the target problem. That is, once covariation can be assumed, the next task is to determine whether there are other characteristics of the design that could be affecting your ability to conclude that your intervention did in fact produce the observed changes. Internal validity requires evaluating whether a variety of *extraneous variables*–those outside of the intervention proper–could have influenced or produced observed changes.

In the list below, we review several common threats to the internal validity of single-system designs. The importance of these threats is that they pose certain risks in drawing conclusions about whether your intervention caused any observed changes, and we want to be sure you understand how their presence can affect those conclusions. It is important to point out that different designs contain different threats to internal validity; indeed, some of the more sophisticated designs actually can control many of these threats so that conclusions about causality can be made. In subsequent chapters in this part of the book, we describe the way certain designs do, in fact, control or minimize many of these threats.

Threats to Internal Validity

1. *History.* Did any other events occur during the time of the practitioner–client contacts that may be responsible for the particular outcome? Since single-system designs by definition extend over time, there is ample opportunity for such extraneous events to occur.

   Example: During the course of marital therapy, Andrew loses his job while Ann obtains a better position than she had before. Such events, though independent of the therapy, may have as much or more to do with the outcome than did the therapy.

2. *Maturation.* Did any psychological or physiological change occur within the client that might have affected the outcome during the time he or she was in a treatment situation?

   Example: Bobby was in a treatment program from the ages of 13 to 16. But when the program ended, it was impossible to tell if Bobby had simply matured as a teenager or if the program was effective.

3. *Testing.* Taking a test or filling out a questionnaire the first time may sensitize the client so that subsequent scores are influenced.

   Example: The staff of the agency filled out the evaluation questionnaire the first week, but most staff members couldn't help remembering what they said that first time so subsequent evaluations were biased by the first set of responses.

4. *Instrumentation.* Do changes in the measurement devices themselves or changes in the observers or in the way the measurement devices are used have an impact on the outcome?

   Example: Phyllis, a public health nurse, was involved in evaluating a home health program in which she interviewed elderly clients every 4 months for a 3-year period. About halfway through, Phyllis made plans to be married and was preoccupied with this coming event. She thought she had memorized the questionnaire, but in fact she forgot to ask blocks of questions, and coders of the data complained to her that they couldn't always make out which response she had circled on the sheets.

5. *Dropout.* Are the results of an intervention program distorted because clients drop out of treatment, leaving a different sample of persons being measured?

   Example: While studying the impact of relocation on nursing home patients, a researcher noticed that some patients were refusing to continue to participate in the research interview because they said that the questions made them very anxious and upset. This left the overall results dependent on only the remaining patients.

6. *Statistical regression or regression to the mean.* Statistically, extreme scores on an original test will tend to become less extreme upon retesting.

Example: Hank was tested in the vocational rehabilitation office and received one of the lowest scores ever recorded there, a fact that attracted some attention from the counselors who worked with him. However, because of a bus strike, Hank couldn't get to the center very often, and yet, upon retesting, he scored much better than he had before. Had Hank been receiving counseling during that period, it might have appeared as though the counseling produced the changes in score.

7. *Diffusion or imitation of intervention.* When intervention involves some type of informational program and when clients from different interventions or different practitioners communicate with each other about the program, clients may learn about information intended for others.

Example: Harvey was seeing a practitioner for help with his depression at the same time as his wife Jean was seeing a practitioner for help with anger management. Although their intervention programs were different, their discussions with each other led them each to try aspects of each other's program.

Construct Validity: Did You Implement Your Intervention and Measure Your Outcomes Accurately?

Construct validity in general refers to "confounding," as, for example, when two variables change at the same time so that results cannot be attributed unequivocally to one of them. (Don't confuse this use of "construct validity" as it affects *designs* with our use in Chapter 2 of the same term in regard to the validity of *measures*.) This occurs when the procedures intended to represent a particular cause or effect construct can be interpreted as other constructs. Thus, what one practitioner thinks is a causal relationship between two specific constructs is interpreted by another practitioner as a causal relationship between other constructs. So, intervention efforts (e.g., systemic family therapy) that seem to produce changes in a target could be confounded with other variables (e.g., the practitioner's warmth or attention). Ensuring construct validity means attempting to ensure that one's operations accurately reflect what is intended—one's constructs.

In the original work by Cook and Campbell (1979), most of the threats to construct validity

were viewed as threats to generalizability. However, we have divided up these threats, with some viewed as threats to making accurate causal statements, and others as threats to generalizability, listing the latter in the next section dealing with external validity.

The following list describes several of the key threats to construct validity as they affect conclusions about causality.

Threats to Construct Validity

---

1. *Mono-operation and mono-method bias.* Use of only one measure per target and/or one method of recording (especially when there is more than one target) lessens the ability to draw conclusions. Using more than one would enhance conclusions by examining the extent to which multiple measures or multiple recording methods coincide.

    Example: Gye used only one self-report scale to measure outcome, and even though it showed improvement, it was hard to tell if the changes had shown up in other areas of the client's functioning.

2. *Hypothesis guessing.* When clients try to "figure out" what the practitioner appears to want above and beyond what the practitioner has said, the client may change partly as a result of wanting to conform to this hypothesis rather than because of the actual intervention.

    Example: Even though the practitioner tried to clearly describe what he was trying to accomplish, Kyle kept thinking there was "something more" going on and his behavior began to change due to his own guessing and not the actual intervention program.

3. *Evaluation apprehension.* Many people are apprehensive about being evaluated and therefore present themselves to practitioners in ways that are not totally accurate.

    Example: Thelma was so concerned about filling out the questionnaire that she scored all her responses in ways that made her seem much less depressed than she actually was.

4. *Practitioner expectations.* When the client is able to perceive the practitioner's expectations, it is difficult to know whether observed changes are due to the actual intervention or the expectations of the practitioner.

    Example: The entire staff knew that the agency director's expectations were that the staff would work especially hard during the agency's evaluation, so many of the practitioners began to put in extra time at the agency.

5. *Interaction of interventions.* Whenever more than one intervention is used with the same client, it is difficult or impossible to tell which intervention affected the target.

Example: Kevin and Vikki, young parents of an abused child, were being aided by a series of parent skills training classes, followed by assertiveness training, and later by social effectiveness skills training. Communication between them seemed to have improved, and they were caring for their daughter more consistently. But at the end of intervention, the counselor wasn't able to pinpoint which of these treatments was most useful.

In Chapters 13 through 17 we discuss a number of single-system designs and will refer back to some of these threats to design validity in single-system designs with regard to what threats are especially relevant to what designs. At that time we will consider ways of overcoming these threats to the degree that this is possible. Often, the more complex designs attempt to reduce certain threats that the simpler ones cannot avoid. For example, the simple A-B design is always subject to the threat of history—something else occurring in the client's life that is external to the intervention but could affect the target problem. But with various experimental designs, when an intervention is removed and then later repeated, if the target problem also shows change (concomitant variation), then it is less likely that external events could be producing such a pattern.

EXTERNAL VALIDITY AND GENERALIZABILITY

One of the important services that classical research provides is the potential of cumulating its results and generalizing about one set of findings for application to new situations. However, single-system designs have been criticized for this very reason. Although something may be true of work with one client, it is very hard to prove that it likely will be true for some other clients, problems, or settings.

Therefore, the issue of external validity and generalizability is a vital one for both professional and practical reasons. Professionally, evaluation procedures such as single-system designs will not be adopted widely unless they can be shown to have the necessary practical and scientific credentials, including the capability to aid in generalizing results across clients and situations. In practice, professionals would find an intervention of little interest unless the efforts devoted to evaluating that intervention in one situation could demonstrate that the intervention was potentially useful in other situations.

External validity refers to the extent to which an effect of an intervention, and therefore the use of the intervention itself, can be generalized (Campbell & Stanley, 1963). There are two forms of external validity (Bracht & Glass, 1968). The first is called *population external validity,* and it refers to the extent to which results can be generalized to other populations or clients. The second is called *ecological external validity,* and it refers to the extent to which results can be generalized to other situations, settings, or environments outside of the context of the original study or evaluation. These, of course, are crucial questions, because if your interventions can be designed to be applicable to other clients and settings as revealed through your evaluations, it would make your practice more meaningful. Similarly, understanding principles of external validity will help you draw conclusions about generalizing the results of *others'* work to your own practice.

A key precondition for understanding external validity is the design validity of an evaluation in terms of its ability to generate statements about the causal effects of the intervention. This is because what we usually try to generalize is the *intervention* used in one or more instances to other clients or situations. Thus, it is important to be clear about whether it really was the intervention producing the changes—the key issue for design validity—before one begins considering the possibility of generalizing results.

The main issue for external validity and generalizability is the extent to which the clients, settings, problems, or practitioners are representative. If it can be said, for example, that the clients in study 2 are exactly like the clients in study 1, it would be reasonable to assume the results from study 1 could be generalized to some extent to the clients in study 2. In classical research, the method for dealing with representativeness is through the selection of a random sample from a population. This tends to ensure representativeness and hence generalizability.

But the situation is different with single-system designs. Here we typically are dealing with individuals, families, or small groups, none of which are selected randomly from some defined population. Even when a community is the focus of single-system design evaluation, it can rarely if ever be viewed as representative of some other community. Thus, the main threat to external validity from use of single-system designs is lack of *representativeness* of the client(s), situation(s), and/or problem(s) in a given evaluation, thereby placing restrictions on generalizing results to other people, situations, or problems.

There are several other types of specific threats related to external validity or generalizability. Most of these are derived from the work of Campbell and Stanley (1963), Kratochwill (1978), and Cook and Campbell (1979), and include some of the threats to construct validity as described by Cook & Campbell (1979). These threats are contained in the following list and concern the general question: *Can the results from a given single-system design be generalized to apply to different clients in different settings, and/or different practitioners?* Even more specifically, the concept of external validity poses the question: If you did the same thing under different circumstances, would you get the same results? In other words, each of the problems below limits generalizability from one single-system evaluation to another.

Threats to External Validity or Generalizability in Single-System Designs

---

1. *Interaction between the intervention and other variables.* Any intervention applied to new clients, in new settings, by new practitioners, will be different from the original intervention in varying degrees, thus reducing the likelihood of identical results.

Example: Esther's friend Louise was much taken with her tales of using self-monitoring with adolescent outpatients, so she tried to adapt the technique to youngsters in her school who were having problems related to hyperactivity. Even though she followed Esther's suggestions as closely as possible, the results did not come out as well as they did in the other setting.

2. *Practitioner effect.* The practitioner's style of practice influences outcomes, so different practitioners applying the same intervention may have different effects to some degree.

Example: Arnold had been substitute teaching on many occasions over several years in Marie's class and knew her course materials quite well. However, when he had to take over her class on a permanent basis because she resigned with a serious illness, he was surprised that he wasn't as effective in teaching her class as he had expected.

3. *Different dependent (target or outcome) variables.* There may be differences in how the target variables are conceptualized and operationalized in different studies, thus reducing the likelihood of identical results.

Example: Ernesto's community action group defined "neighborhood solidarity" in terms of its effectiveness in obtaining municipal services, defined as trash removal, rat control, and the expansion of bus service during early morning hours. While Juan used the same term, neighborhood solidarity, with a similar ethnic group, the meaning of the term had to do with the neighbors presenting a united front in the face of the school board's arbitrary removal of a locally popular principal.

4. *Interaction of history and intervention.* If extraneous events occur concurrently during the intervention, they may not be present at other times, thus reducing generalizability of the results of the original study.

Example: The first community mental health center opened amid the shock of recent suicides of several young unemployed men. It was forced to respond to the needs of persons facing socioeconomic pressures. However, when a new center opened in a nearby area, there was no similar popular recognition of this type of counseling, and considerably fewer persons went to the second center than to the first.

5. *Measurement differences.* To the extent that differences exist between two evaluations regarding how the same process and outcome

variables are measured, so too are the results likely to be different.

Example: The standardized scales used by Lee with his majority group clients were viewed by the several minority group members as being too offensive and asking questions that were too personal, so he had to devise ways of obtaining the same information in less obvious or offensive ways. The results continued to show considerable differences between majority and minority clients.

6. *Differences in clients.* The characteristics of the client—age, sex, ethnicity, social class, and so on—can affect the extent to which results can be generalized.

Example: Nick devised a counseling program that was very successful in decreasing dropouts in one school with mainly middle-class students. But when Nick tried to implement his program in a different school, one with largely low-income students, he found the dropout rate was hardly affected.

7. *Interaction between testing and intervention.* The effects of the early testing—for example, the baseline observations—could sensitize the client to the intervention so that generalization could be expected to occur only when subsequent clients are given the same tests prior to intervention.

Example: All members of an assertion training group met for 3 weeks and role-played several situations in which they were not being assertive. The formal intervention of assertion training started the fourth week, but by then all group members were highly sensitized to what to expect.

8. *Reactive effects to evaluation.* Simple awareness by clients that they are in a study could lead to changes in client performance.

Example: All employees at a public agency providing services to the elderly were participants in a study comparing their work with work performed by practitioners in a private agency. Knowing they were in the study, and knowing they had to do their best, the public agency practitioners put in extra time, clouding the issue as to whether their typical intervention efforts would produce similar results.

Enhancing Generalizability

The threats to external validity we described above are some of the major ones you should watch carefully in thinking about generalizability of results from one single-system evaluation to another. Because of these threats, and because generalizability is so highly related to representativeness—which is usually not present with single-system designs—it does appear as though external validity is one of the most important limitations of single-system designs.

On the other hand there are some possibilities for generalizing results from single-system evaluations. Thomas (1975), for example, suggests a number of these possibilities for generalizing such results:

1. When the variability between clients is known to be negligible so that replication would be redundant.
2. When one case in depth clearly exemplifies many.
3. When negative results from one case are sufficient to suggest the need for at least revision, and possibly even rejection, of the principles that generated the particular intervention.
4. When the behavior studied is very unusual and there is limited opportunity to study it.
5. When the practitioner wants to focus on a problem by defining questions and variables that may lead to more refined approaches.

Similarly, from a commonsense approach, you might try to generalize findings from one client to another based on how much alike their essential dimensions were. These dimensions include the particular target problems that would be operationally defined and empirically measured in the course of collecting baseline data. They also include other relevant features of the client that would be likely to influence how clients would respond to the same intervention by the same practitioner in the same setting. Among these features are demographic characteristics—age, sex, race, and the like—as well as pertinent individualizing factors—experiences with prior professional practitioners, level of self-esteem, and so on. In general, the more similar two clients are, the more likely the findings from one will apply to the intervention of the other.

Indeed, even though use of different interventions from one case to another is inevitable to some degree, practitioners seeking to extend results from one situation to another should attempt to make the interventions as similar as possible. This is equally true with the practitioner's style of practice, the target variables, and the measurement processes. Similarly, one should be sure that the client population and problems are similar—or differences accounted for—before attempting to generalize. However, differences will always remain, and, thus, threats to external validity are a continuing problem for all research, including that involving single-system evaluations.

Several other approaches to generalization of single-system designs have been developed. We briefly describe three of them here: replication, use of probabilities, and meta-analysis.

Replication. Even though representativeness is at the heart of generalizability, a second key to generalizability is in the *replication* of results. Replication essentially refers to successful repetition of results from one case, problem, setting, or situation to another. Replication as a method of generalizing results is especially pertinent because you may want to consider applying what you read in the literature to your own practice, or you may be thinking about generalizing your own work from one case to another.

Three types of replication that can lead to generalization of results in single-system evaluation have been described by Barlow and Hersen (1984). The first method is called *direct replication* (Sidman, 1960)—the most basic form of replication in single-system design—the repetition of a given intervention by the same practitioner. This is probably the most common form of replication (as we will see in our discussions of the other types—clinical and systematic replication), and therefore is a basic way of generalizing data from single-system designs.

Barlow and Hersen (1984) present several guidelines for direct replication that are ways in which a practitioner interested in extending results from one client to another may do so with greater confidence. First, the same practitioner working in the same setting should work with problems that are similar across clients,

such as a specific phobia. Second, client background characteristics should be as similar as possible to the case from which findings are to be generalized. A third guideline is that the intervention should be uniformly applied across clients until failure occurs. Intervention failure is not necessarily a troublesome event in single-system designs. It can be observed quickly during monitoring of data, and it prompts the practitioner to make rapid adjustments in the intervention and to test these adjustments for appropriate client change. If the additional interventions lead to success, they can be replicated further for their transferability. If they are not successful, the distinctive characteristics of that client can be studied to try to find out what elements may have caused these results, information that likewise can be used in replication studies. A fourth guideline suggests that one successful intervention and three successful replications may be sufficient to allow a practitioner to conclude the generalization was successful, but broad generalizability (to other settings, clients, or practitioners) cannot be claimed from such results. What is practical for persons working within agency settings to claim as generalizability from their work is hard to say definitively, but Barlow and Hersen's suggestion of one successful intervention, and three successful replications seems reasonable as a good beginning point.

The second, more sophisticated form of replication discussed by Barlow and Hersen (1984) is *clinical replication*—the repeating of an intervention *package* containing two or more distinct techniques that is applied by the same practitioner or group of practitioners to a series of clients in the same setting with multiple problems that generally cluster together. (Usually this problem cluster is given a label, such as "autism" or "hyperactivity," but opinions differ about the usefulness of such labels.) The guidelines for clinical replication are similar to the four guidelines for direct replication given above.

A series of common problems and interventions may be difficult to come by in some agencies because of the general heterogeneity of clients. Under these circumstances, it would be hard to develop a programmatic series of replications as required by this approach. On the other hand, where client problems remain fairly consistent, clinical replication—sometimes called field testing—is possible. Lovaas, Koegel, Simmons, and Long (1973) illustrate clinical replication in their work with autistic children, a problem composed of at least eight distinct factors that contribute to the syndrome, including mutism, deficiencies in social and self-help behavior, and severe affect isolation. Over a period of years and through direct replication, they tested treatments for each separate component, and the treatment package constructed from these early studies was administered to subsequent autistic children. Results and follow-up data that indicate the general utility of the treatment package, even though improvement wasn't even for all children, are presented by Lovaas et al. (1973). This fact prompted these researchers to continue looking for individual differences that impeded the treatment package.

Systematic replication is the third and most far-reaching approach discussed by Barlow and Hersen (1984). This is the attempt to replicate findings from a direct replication series, varying the setting, the practitioners, the problems, or any combination of these factors. This is obviously a more complex task and not one that a single practitioner is likely to undertake. However, we discuss this topic because collaborative efforts toward generalizing results of single-system designs may become more common.

Suppose that a practitioner working with a given client in a particular setting discovers that a technique called differential attention—briefly, reinforcing desired behaviors while ignoring others—appears to produce significant improvement. The practitioner repeats his or her work with other similar clients; this constitutes direct replication. Possibly, several colleagues of the practitioner learn about the technique and try it with their clients in the same institution with similar successful results (clinical replication). Suppose that the results of these separate studies are published, and other practitioners working with different clients in different settings become intrigued and try it with similar successful results. This would constitute an example of systematic replication.

In fact, this is approximately what did happen in a series of studies on differential attention; Barlow and Hersen (1984) document a large number of studies of differential attention

with different clients, settings, and practitioners, with initial results showing generally successful outcomes. In addition, equally useful negative results began to be reported with certain types of client problems (such as self-injurious behavior in children), thus setting limits on the usefulness of the technique. While Barlow and Hersen emphasize that practitioners should proceed with caution when applying differential attention to new situations, they also note that a solid beginning has been made in establishing the generalizability of this technique. This is one way in which the helping professions grow.

Probabilities. A different approach to generalization in single-system evaluations was proposed by Tripodi (1980). Basically, there is no agreement in the field on just how many successful replications are required before generalizability can be claimed. Tripodi suggests that statistical significance, using the binomial distribution, the two category probability distribution that is discussed in any standard text on statistics, can be used to determine the *number* of successful replications needed for evidence of generalization.

Tripodi (1980) discusses a number of assumptions that apply in using probabilities to assess generalizations, including similarity and specification of the following: Clients, interventions, administration of intervention, problems, a consistent criterion of success, and an expected probability of success with each client (e.g., a .50 probability of success; lower or higher probabilities can be used given the difficulty of the problem or the record of success with that problem based on previous research). Assuming, then, with no other evidence being available, an equal probability of success and failure (.50) for a given intervention, and using the standard .05 level of statistical significance, Tripodi (1980, p. 35) suggests that the estimated number of successes needed to achieve statistical significance can be determined by referring to a table of calculated probabilities such as can be found in many statistical texts (the tables are available in Chapter 19 in this book). Thus, as just one example, based on the .05 table in Chapter 19, 10 successes out of 12 tries at replication would be statistically significant. (To see this, in the .05

table in Chapter 19, first find .50 in the left-hand column, then 12 in the top row. The intersection of the two is 10.) With low numbers of replication attempts, six or fewer at the .05 level, all of the attempts would have to be successful to be statistically significant. Further, the greater the probability of success—that is, more than .50—the higher the number of successful replications needed for statistical significance. (For example, based on a review of the literature, the practitioner might be able to expect a higher probability of success for the intervention, say .75.) Thus, if any given proportion of successes meets or exceeds the critical value in the probability table and is statistically significant, it is likely that with a given margin of error (say, 5 out of 100 at the .05 level), the effect of chance can be ruled out and the replication and generalization can be considered successful.

Meta-Analysis. The last possibility for examining generalizability is through the relatively new development of the techniques of *meta-analysis*. Meta-analysis is a method for quantitatively comparing and analyzing the results of several studies. The data in the individual studies are converted to a common metric allowing easy comparison across studies. This common metric, called an effect size, allows an overall interpretation of whether the intervention periods of several single-system designs seem to have produced an effect on target problems beyond that which has occurred during several baseline periods. If so, this can be viewed as a kind of affirmation of generalizability.

While the literature of meta-analysis in general has exploded, with literally hundreds of studies and reviews available, the techniques only recently have been applied to single-system designs, and only a relatively few publications on that topic have appeared (e.g., Allison & Gorman, 1993; Corcoran, 1985; Faith, Allison, & Gorman, 1997; Gingerich, 1984; Holden et al., 1999; Jayaratne, Tripodi, & Talsma, 1988; Videka-Sherman, 1986; White, Rusch, Kazdin, & Hartmann, 1989). Indeed, meta-analytic techniques such as described below have been recommended for both analysis of the data in each single-system design as well as for cumulating results of several

single-system designs as a way of facilitating generalizability.

Unfortunately, there are a number of very serious issues regarding the use of meta-analysis, both in classical research and in single-system designs. Most of these issues are beyond the scope of this book (see Fischer, 1990, for a review of problems and issues with meta-analysis). However, since the use of meta-analysis is increasing, and it has been recommended by some authors as a way of examining generalization in single-system designs, we provide a brief introduction to the way meta-analysis can be used to examine generalizability of results of single-system evaluations.

Among several ways for accumulating results of studies for meta-analysis, the most widely used is called the effect size (ES). The effect size is simply a way of examining the magnitude of the effect of an intervention (how large it is) of one study or across a number of studies.

There are two commonly used methods for calculating ES (a number of other, more complicated formulas are described in Faith et al., 1997). The first (Glass, McGaw, & Smith, 1981) takes the mean of the control groups (or in single-system design terms, the baseline period, A) and subtracts it from the mean of the experimental group (in single-system design terms, the intervention period, B), and the results are divided by the standard deviation of the control group (baseline):

$$ES = \frac{M_B - M_A}{S_A}$$

where
$$B = \text{intervention period}$$
and
$$A = \text{baseline period}$$

The second formula is almost identical to the first except that the standard deviation in the denominator is actually the pooled standard deviation of both the baseline and intervention (or control and experimental group) periods.

We're not going to trouble you with too many of the technicalities of the calculations now, although we show you how to calculate an ES in Chapter 21, where we discuss statistical analysis of results from each single-system design. For now, we just illustrate how the process—and a conclusion about generalizability—works.

First, all the single-system design studies that focus on a particular intervention (that which you want to examine for generalization) are collected. Most types of single-system designs—from A-Bs to A-B-A-Bs to multiple baselines—can be used (White et al., 1989).

Second, using one of the two ES formulas described above, the overall ES for the set of studies is calculated. (If the number of studies is relatively small, say 10 or fewer, a correction factor, called K, devised by Hedges, 1981, can be used to correct for bias due to the small sample.) This ES hypothetically could run the gamut from −3.70 to +3.70, although the most commonly reported effect sizes are in the 0 to 1.5 range. Third, one should do as good a job as possible in evaluating the methodological adequacy of the included studies. For example, if it can be shown that the studies with the strongest designs support one conclusion about the overall impact of some intervention and the poorest studies support another, the meta-analytic reviewer might change his or her overall conclusion.

The final step in meta-analysis is to interpret the findings. This is done in two ways. First, the overall ES is interpreted. Since the ES is in effect a standardized score, it can be interpreted like a Z score as the mean difference between groups (baseline and intervention periods) in standard deviation units. Thus, an ES of +1 suggests the average client score in the intervention period was about one standard deviation above scores in the baseline period, an ES of .50 suggests the average client in the intervention period scored about one-half of a standard deviation above the scores in the baseline period, an ES of 0 suggests no difference in the scores of the average client between baseline and intervention, and a negative ES suggests scores in the intervention period actually deteriorated.

The second way of interpreting ES is to use any Z table to determine the percentile rank of the average client's intervention period scores above the baseline period. Thus, an ES of +1 (using the ES as a substitute for the Z score in the Z table) means the scores of the average client during the intervention period were above 84% of scores in the baseline, while an ES of .50 means the intervention period scores were above 69% of baseline scores. (A negative ES and a percentage below 50% again suggests a deterioration from baseline period scores.) The computer program that comes with this book, SINGWIN, can also do this for you.

So what does this actually tell you about the generalizability of a given intervention? What results of meta-analysis purport to show is that a given intervention may produce a certain magnitude of effect across several single-system designs. The larger the effect size, the greater the magnitude of the effect. Thus, one way of looking at this information is that the larger the effect size, the more that the intervention under study may be producing an effect across several studies. In other words, the effect size may be one way of looking at the possible generalization of an intervention across different situations, clients, and perhaps problems. Of course, as we mentioned earlier, deciding whether an intervention actually caused an observed outcome is a design issue rather than a statistical one. Nevertheless, meta-analysis may be one additional way of examining whether there is even some effect across studies before we decide whether it was our interventions that caused it.

As with all the guidelines for generalization discussed in this section, we urge extreme caution in interpreting the results of a meta-analysis. Apart from the fact that there are a number of issues regarding meta-analysis, there simply is no convincing (or at least agreed upon throughout the field) way to evaluate the significance (statistical, clinical, or social) of a given result. Knowing that, overall, a given intervention in several studies may have moved average scores in the intervention period to a point above 69% of the scores in a baseline may be interesting, and may indeed suggest some degree of generalizability of findings, but it has to be evaluated against a number of variables, including the time, effort, energy, and resources required to achieve such results.

In all, meta-analysis, along with the other methods described here, provides some ideas that can help in addressing the issue of generalizability in single-system designs. Used as rough guidelines, we believe all of these approaches help to advance the careful use of single-system designs to inform practice.

OVERVIEW OF SINGLE-SYSTEM DESIGNS

There are many ways to collect and analyze data in order to judge changes in target behavior and in order to decide whether the intervention can be inferred to be causally related to these changes. In this section, we preview the detailed discussions in the next set of chapters dealing with single-system designs. Each design is simply a systematic variation in observations and interventions with one or more targets. However, there are definable groupings among these designs that stem from the logical relationships among their components. In Figure 11.6 we illustrate the major features of the designs. In later chapters we will discuss details of their operation, their strengths and limitations, the appropriate uses for them in field settings, some variations on these basic designs, and how to discuss these designs with your clients.

The top row of Figure 11.6 includes case studies that involve only interventions–no baselines. There is, of course, careful observation going on during professional intervention, but there may or may not be systematic recording of changes. The missing baseline phase is indicated by dashed lines. The point is that there is no solid prior information with which to evaluate changes in targets. Even though you may add a new intervention, *C,* which can be compared to data collected during intervention phase *B,* we still lack a baseline for true comparison.

The second row illustrates the basic single-system design, termed the *A-B* design, *A* for baseline, *B* for intervention. This is the simplest design that provides more or less objective information on changes in the target. However, this basic design is subject to many alternative explanations for why the changes emerged as they did–these are the design validity threats described earlier in this chapter. There are some steps one can take to reduce these alternative explanations, and these are described in Chapter 13. We also discuss in Chapter 13 a variation of the *A-B* design, the repeated pretest-postest design.

The third row of Figure 11.6 shows the experimental designs. They are experimental in

the sense that you remove a successful intervention in order to study the effect of this manipulation on the target problem. If there is a concomitant variation with the presence and the absence of the intervention, then this provides the logical basis for inferring a causal link–that the intervention is likely causing some portion of the observed change. The *A-B-A, B-A-B,* and *A-B-A-B* designs are variations of experimental designs that involve removal of a successful intervention, and are powerful designs for drawing causal inferences. We discuss details of these designs, including practical and ethical issues about their use, in Chapter 14.

The next four designs, in row 4, all involve multiple targets analyzed at the same time. The first of these designs is called the *multiple baseline design.* It is important to note that you can compare the same intervention across different clients with the same problem and in the same setting, or, with different problems in the same client in one setting, or different settings with the same client involving the same problem. This is a versatile format, as we will see in Chapter 15.

Likewise, *multiple target designs* deal with different interventions addressed to different targets, but are viewed together so as to detect patterns of change among them. The multiple target design is just as susceptible to threats from alternative explanations as the basic single-system design, the *A-B,* but the multiple baseline design is able to remove some of these threats, as discussed in Chapter 15.

In Chapter 15, we also discuss *crossover designs,* in which two concurrent phase changes occur for different targets, using the same intervention but in reverse order from each other. This is indicated by target 1 receiving an *A-B* design, while target 2 receives a *B-A* design. If there are consistent effects–whenever the *B* is applied, the problem behavior changes–then this adds to the likelihood that *B* is causally related to target changes. The same conclusion can be drawn from a *BC* and *CB* arrangement, but the inference is weaker, since we lack a true baseline.

Also in Chapter 15 we describe the *constant-series design,* in which one target receives an *A-B* format, while another target receives either constant baseline observations or constant

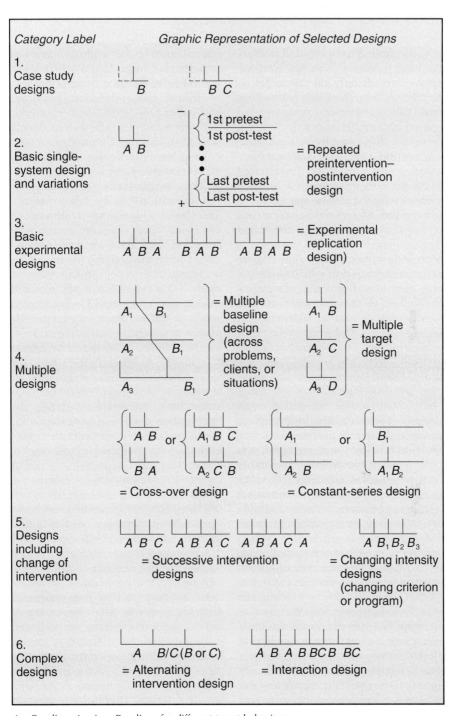

Category Label	Graphic Representation of Selected Designs

1. Case study designs

B $B\ C$

2. Basic single-system design and variations

$A\ B$

$\left\{ \begin{array}{l} \text{1st pretest} \\ \overline{\text{1st post-test}} \end{array} \right.$
•
•
•
$\left\{ \begin{array}{l} \text{Last pretest} \\ \overline{\text{Last post-test}} \end{array} \right.$

= Repeated preintervention–postintervention design

3. Basic experimental designs

$A\ B\ A$ $B\ A\ B$ $A\ B\ A\ B$

= Experimental replication design)

4. Multiple designs

$A_1\quad B_1$
$A_2\quad B_1$
$A_3\quad B_1$

= Multiple baseline design (across problems, clients, or situations)

$A_1\ B$
$A_2\ C$
$A_3\ D$

= Multiple target design

$\left\{ \begin{array}{l} A\ B \\ B\ A \end{array} \right.$ or $\left\{ \begin{array}{l} A_1\ B\ C \\ A_2\ C\ B \end{array} \right.$

= Cross-over design

$\left\{ \begin{array}{l} A_1 \\ A_2\ B \end{array} \right.$ or $\left\{ \begin{array}{l} B_1 \\ A_1\ B_2 \end{array} \right.$

= Constant-series design

5. Designs including change of intervention

$A\ B\ C$ $A\ B\ A\ C$ $A\ B\ A\ C\ A$

= Successive intervention designs

$A\ B_1\ B_2\ B_3$

= Changing intensity designs (changing criterion or program)

6. Complex designs

$A\quad B/C\ (B\text{ or }C)$

= Alternating intervention design

$A\ B\ A\ B\ BCB\ BC$

= Interaction design

A = Baseline; A_1, A_2 = Baselines for different target behaviors.
B = Discrete intervention plus observation; B^1, B^2 = Variations of same intervention.
BC, BCD = Concurrent presence of discrete interventions B, C, D.
L = Observation phase present; ⌐ = Observation phase absent.

FIGURE 11.6   Overview of categories of single-system designs.

intervention (the same *B* as in the *A-B* format). In the first case (constant baseline observations), if change occurs only on the target receiving the intervention, then this strengthens the inference that extraneous events are not causally related to target changes. It does not directly show that *B* is causally related, however. In the second case (constant intervention), if change occurs only when the different targets receive the same intervention, and not during the baseline in the *A-B* design, then this also strengthens the inference that extraneous factors are not causally related to the target changes.

The fifth row describes designs that involve changes in the intervention in which there is a true baseline. *Successive intervention designs* include any number of comparisons between baseline(s) and interventions in an attempt to enhance client outcome and perhaps begin to tease out which intervention appears more effective. Logically, these are weak designs for comparing the effectiveness of specific interventions, but the practitioner can get some valuable hints that might be tested with stronger designs. The successive intervention designs are discussed in Chapter 16.

Also in Chapter 16 are the *changing intensity designs,* in which either the criterion of what is adequate performance is changed (so as to move the client by successive approximations toward his or her objective), or the level or intensity of the intervention program changes (to facilitate the objective).

In the bottom row, we present complex designs, those involving combined interventions (either *alternating* or *simultaneous*) for the tentative information they provide on which is the stronger or preferred intervention. We also discuss the *interaction design* as the minimal logical form necessary to tease out the separate effects of two different interventions. These designs are discussed in Chapter 17.

We believe that the conceptualization of designs in this book offers a clear and practical way of categorizing the many different types of single-system designs. However, there are other ways to conceptualize them. In the event you run across these differences in the literature, we would like to provide you with a brief

introduction to the work of one set of authors in particular, indicating where in this book you will find the different designs discussed.

Barlow and colleagues (1984) and Hayes and colleagues (1998) seek to provide the underlying logic of single-system designs, as distinct from any specific form of a design, by discussing the within-series, between-series, and combined-series elements.

The within-series designs look at the changes within one set of data points over time. The simple within-series involves the following elements: First, a stable picture of events is recorded, and then an intervention is introduced while maintaining the recording. Finally, a comparison of the concomitant changes is made. (This refers essentially to the basic *A-B* design; see Chapter 13.) A complex within-series design involves coordinated changes of phases in which there is some underlying logic for the change. (This would be like an experimental *A-B-A-B* design; see Chapter 14.)

The between-series designs look at changes between two or more intervention conditions across time. There are two types: Alternating intervention designs involve the rapid and random alteration of interventions to get some information on which seems to work best for the client. The other type is less often used; it is called the simultaneous treatment design in which the client chooses which intervention he or she wishes (see Chapter 17). This may measure client preference, but not necessarily effectiveness (Barlow et al., 1984, p. 244).

Combined-series elements are best described by the familiar multiple baseline design in which a coordinated series of *A-B* designs are arranged so that phases change at different points in time depending on the effects of the interventions (see Chapter 15).

In the remaining chapters of this part of the book, we will be providing a variety of examples of each design. Some of these examples correspond directly to our descriptions of the way the designs should be implemented, but many of them involve either elaborations of these "ideal types," or implementation in actual practice where conditions impose some constraints on the design. You will also notice that, in most of the chapters, at least one illustration shows how the designs discussed in the chapter can be combined with designs described in other chapters. Finally, remember that our basic descriptions are of "pure" models for these designs; we hope that this will provide you with sufficient information to understand how deviations from the models affect your ability to draw conclusions. However, we do not want to discourage you from using your own variations. In fact, in Chapter 18, we provide some ideas for creative use of single-system designs.

SUMMARY

This chapter presented an overview of the characteristics of single-system designs, and some of the complications and threats to their design validity and their generalizability. Designs are used for one or both of two major purposes: to describe change in target problems, and/or to infer that intervention was causally related to that observed change. Some designs also can be used to compare two interventions with each other. Designs are the arrangements of observations made before, during, and/or after interventions through which these questions may be logically addressed.

This chapter also discussed the complex issues surrounding causality, the various alternative explanations that may be given for any evaluation outcome, and the issues regarding generalization of outcomes. Some single-system designs are stronger than others in reducing alternative explanations and in enhancing generalization. We concluded the chapter with an overview of single-system designs, each of which will be discussed in later chapters. However, we want to emphasize that the designs presented in this book are basically "ideal types" that are described to help you understand the variety of uses and conclusions that are available from single-system designs. In real practice, you may use some of these designs exactly as described in this book, or variations of them that specifically fit the needs of a particular case.

Essentially, all single-system designs begin with recording and then simply reflect the changes you make in your interventions in subsequent phases. This is in line with our emphasis in this book that practice guides evaluation, rather than the other way around.

BASELINING
Collecting Information
Before Intervention

PURPOSE: This chapter describes the key first phase of almost every single-system design—the baseline. We discuss the importance of baselines, types of baselines, and how to decide how long to continue baselines. We also discuss several issues related to collection of baseline information, including when baselines may not be necessary.   ■

Introduction
Purposes of the Baseline
Types of Baselines
How Long Should Baselining Continue?
Utility
Stability
Time
Summary of Length of Baselining
When Are Baselines Not Necessary?
Issues Regarding Baselining

Baselining Delays Intervention
    Does Baselining Actually Delay Intervention?
    Is Delaying Intervention Detrimental?
There Are Times When Baselines Are Impossible
Targets Often Shift during the Course
    of Intervention
People Won't Cooperate in Collecting
    Baseline Information
What If the Problem Improves during
    the Baseline?
Summary

INTRODUCTION

One of the most distinctive and helpful features of single-system evaluation involves collecting information on the target problem/situation before formal intervention actually begins. This is called *baselining*. The period of time over which this information is collected is called the *baseline.* The information or data you collect are called the *baserate,* which involves systematic collection of data on the client's problem–using the measures described in Part

II of this book–prior to the implementation of your formal intervention program. *The data you collect during baseline continue to be collected on the same target and in the same way throughout your intervention program.* They provide an important basis for monitoring and evaluating your effectiveness, since the baseline is almost always the first phase of your design. However, since baselining technically also could be defined as systematic collection of information on the target during *any* nonintervention period, a baseline phase could occur at any point in the overall process of contact with the client/system. (In subsequent chapters we discuss designs in which the baseline occurs in later phases of your design.)

This chapter discusses the purposes of collecting baseline data, describes how you actually go about doing it, discusses when you need baseline data and when you don't, gives several examples of baselines, and also discusses many of the issues involved in collecting baselines.

PURPOSES OF THE BASELINE

Why go through the trouble of collecting baseline information, especially if it has to be done in a more or less systematic, formal fashion? Won't this just be a nuisance for both the client and the practitioner? Can't you just intervene when you understand the problem? In fact, why go through all this recording business anyway?

As suggested in Chapter 4, there is one basic reason why recording–systematic measurement of target problems and the keeping of records on those observations–is necessary: It ultimately will help to enhance your effectiveness. The other purposes of, and our suggestions for, baselining flow from this basic principle.

In addition to the advantages of recording discussed in Chapter 4 and in the introduction to Part II, there are two key reasons why it is important to conduct baseline observations and to continue to record data throughout your intervention program. These reasons also directly relate to why baselining can help to enhance your effectiveness.

First, baseline information is crucial for *evaluation*. It serves as a basis for comparison with information collected during the intervention phase of your program. Thus, the baseline data–and by extension all of your recording–allow you to determine whether the target problem is changing in desired directions. In some situations you also can determine whether your program is actually producing the change (as opposed to other events or situations in the client's life). The basis for all this

is that the baseline represents what reasonably could be expected to continue to happen with the target problem over time unless something intervenes.

This reason for collecting baseline information is the one most directly related to enhancing your effectiveness. Collection of baseline information is an attempt to find out how often or how long a problem occurs (or, for that matter, whether it occurs at all) in its "natural" state of affairs and before you intervene. This is the basis for saying that single-system designs use clients as their "own control." The baseline functions as a sort of control (nonintervention) period. You will be able to monitor your progress once the intervention program has begun by comparing what is happening to the problem during intervention with what happened during the preintervention period. This allows you to evaluate whether there is progress, no change, or perhaps even a negative change (deterioration). This monitoring and comparison with the baseline provides crucial information as to whether the intervention program should be continued, modified, or even dropped altogether and a new program instituted.

Now you might argue that the occurrence of some problems and the success of some intervention programs are so clear-cut that you don't need to record data, let alone worry about a baseline. In some instances this might be true, and in a later section we describe when the collection of baseline data might be omitted. However, in many situations the baseline can provide invaluable information.

For example, suppose that the problem you are working on involves a conflict between a parent and child about the child cleaning up his or her room. You ask the parent to collect baseline data–for instance, the number of articles left out each night. Your baseline data reveal this to be an average of about 18 articles per day. You put that information on a chart such as Figure 12.1.

Let's say that you start an intervention program and, after 1 week, the parent concludes that it is not working and therefore not worth the effort. At least this might be the parent's

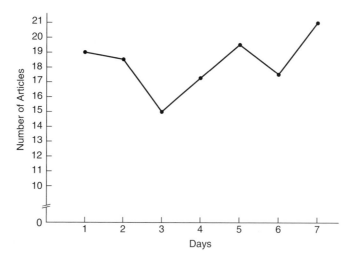

FIGURE 12.1   Number of articles left out each day during baseline.

conclusion without data available to compare the intervention program with the preintervention state of affairs. Once the parent tabulated the data collected, and plotted them on a chart, the pattern could look like the one in Figure 12.2. There were so many articles left out each day that a drop of only a few didn't look like much. However, there was in fact a drop—an average of about five articles less a day during the first week of intervention compared to the baseline. Encouraged by this and aided by the practitioner, the parent might continue or modify the program and look forward to an even greater drop in subsequent weeks.

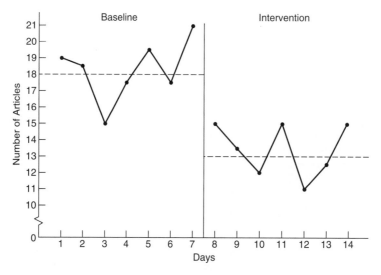

FIGURE 12.2   Number of articles left out each day during baseline and intervention.

The second basic reason for use of a baseline is that it provides crucial data for *assessment* purposes. The baseline data are not a substitute for a comprehensive assessment, but can provide especially important types of information as *part* of your assessment. When you are collecting baseline information, you are discovering a number of relevant facts about the client, problem, and situation. You may be finding out how often or for how long a problem occurs. You also may be discovering how often or for how long a positive behavior, thought, or feeling occurs so that your intervention program can build on that. You may be discovering where and when a problem occurs. Your baseline data might give you information on environmental factors that may be affecting a problem (e.g., events that precede it and perhaps elicit it or events that follow it and may reinforce it). Your baseline also may tell you how intensely the problem occurs (e.g., a client's self-evaluation of the intensity of his or her anxiety or the intensity of negative or positive thoughts).

All of this information is basic to your assessment of the case and situation. In the most obvious and important respect, the baseline information helps you decide on an intervention strategy designed specifically for the target of concern. This is because the problem will have been pinpointed, its controlling conditions (e.g., location and situation) noted, and its frequency, duration, and extent also clarified. Thus, you will be able to use this information to select an intervention program and specific techniques of intervention. This too is related to potentially enhancing your effectiveness, since the baseline information can help to provide a more accurate (better) assessment.

The baseline data, as part of the total assessment, help you to develop a *problem hypothesis,* a working hypothesis about factors that may be currently affecting or maintaining the problem. This hypothesis about the nature of the problem should be stated in terms relevant to developing your intervention program. Collecting baseline data makes this particularly feasible because the essence of the whole notion of baselining is observation or measurement of a problem as it occurs as well as

observation of the personal, interpersonal, and environmental factors affecting it.

As an example of this, let's say you are working in a school and a boy is referred to you for "disruptive behavior" in one of his classes—getting out of his seat without permission and talking out of turn. Without baselining the problem, you might have proceeded to begin an intervention program geared toward decreasing this behavior directly by, say, reinforcing him for sitting in his seat and not talking without permission. But a systematic period of baseline observations may have led to a totally different problem hypothesis. The baseline might have revealed that the problem really may have been a result of the child being bored in class, thereby leading to a totally different intervention, say, working with the teacher on developing more stimulating activities for the child.

The baseline data may provide assessment information that suggests an intervention program may not be necessary at all. Sometimes a client with a complaint about himself or herself or about someone else will realize after baselining that the problem is of less concern than was thought to be the case. The problem may not occur nearly as often as the client thought or may not be nearly as extensive. In some situations this may allow the practitioner and client to actually terminate their work, to lower the priority for that particular problem, or to free up time and energy for working on another problem.

TYPES OF BASELINES

There are basically two types of baselines. The first is the standard or typical *concurrent* or *prospective baseline.* This is the type most frequently discussed in the literature. Data are collected over time at the same time as other assessment activities are taking place. These data are gathered in a planned, systematic way over time and are an attempt to identify the naturally occurring level of the problem/situation during the time period prior to intervention. Much of the discussion in this book assumes use of a concurrent baseline.

The second type of baseline is the *reconstructed* or *retrospective baseline* (Bloom et al., 1979). Essentially, the reconstructed baseline is an attempt to *approximate* the naturally occurring level of the problem/situation by using the client's (or others') memories or recollections of the event or by using specific records of past events when they are available. The baseline is built on the basis of these "reconstructions" of the problematic event. This type of baseline can be used to supplement a concurrent baseline or as a substitute when concurrent baseline data cannot be gathered.

In supplementing a concurrent baseline, the reconstructed baseline simply provides additional information to give a clearer, longer-term perspective on the nature and occurrence of a problem. You may be able to use a client's memory of how often a problematic event occurred over the last few weeks to compare this with data collected using a concurrent baseline.

When you are using a reconstructed baseline as your only baseline (i.e., a concurrent baseline cannot be collected for one or more of the reasons described in Chapter 4 and other places in Part II), it will serve as a primary source of both assessment data and data for evaluating effectiveness. For example, you may be able to use agency records to develop a reconstructed baseline regarding the number of cases on the waiting list over the past few months with one type of agency program compared to the number of cases on the waiting list after you implement a new type of program.

There are two primary guidelines for use of a reconstructed or retrospective baseline when you are relying primarily on memory. The first is that a reconstructed baseline is best used when the problematic events represent relatively specific, identifiable events. This is because of the obvious difficulties in reproducing events from memory and the possible distortions this may produce. Therefore, events such as number of instances of physical abuse over the past 2 weeks, number of letters received, number of conversations initiated, number of dates, and so on, would be far more desirable to use in reconstructed baselines than events such as "feelings of inadequacy" over the past few months or "affectionate feelings I had in January."

The second guideline is that if the reconstructed baseline is based on memories, the memories used should be from the immediate past—the 2 weeks to a month immediately preceding the beginning of intervention. This presumably would be most helpful not only for assessment purposes, but also when comparing baseline with intervention periods for evaluation purposes. And it is also the period of time about which most people have the clearest memories.

Although the reconstructed baseline may not have the precision, nor perhaps the accuracy, of the concurrent baseline, when used judiciously and with the awareness of the possibility of distortions due to memory, it can serve as an important aid to practice. In agencies in which brief, crisis-oriented intervention is the norm, and/or in agencies in which contact with clients is limited to one or two instances, the reconstructed baseline might be the baseline of choice.

When a reconstructed baseline is based on archival records, the above guidelines need not apply. This is because those data already have been collected, and memory does not play any part in considerations of accuracy (see Chapter 9).

Figures 12.3 through 12.5 give examples of baselines. Figure 12.3 is a concurrent or prospective baseline collected over time while other assessment activities were being conducted, Figure 12.4 is a reconstructed or retrospective baseline based on the client's memories, and Figure 12.5 is a reconstructed baseline using archival records.

HOW LONG SHOULD BASELINING CONTINUE?

One of the most obvious issues you will have to face when collecting concurrent baseline data is how long you (or the client or another party) should continue baselining. That is, when should you stop baselining and begin the intervention period? Unfortunately, because single-system evaluation is not a fully developed science, there are no clear, readily verifiable answers to this question. However, we can suggest some rough guidelines.

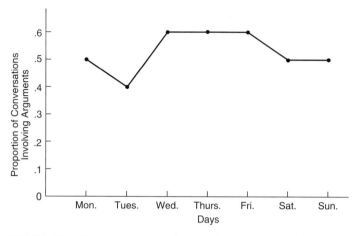

FIGURE 12.3   Concurrent (prospective) baseline: proportion of conversations involving arguments over 1 week.

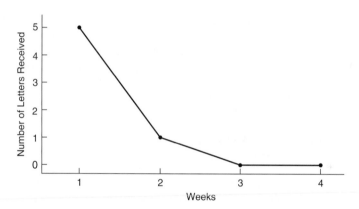

FIGURE 12.4   Reconstructed (retrospective) baseline based on memory: number of letters received over last month.

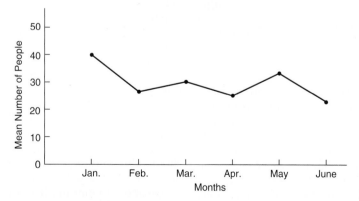

FIGURE 12.5   Reconstructed (retrospective) baseline using archival records: mean number of people kept on waiting list for more than a week.

Utility

The principal guideline is derived from the purposes of baselining—helping with both the assessment and the evaluation of progress. Hence, the first guideline is that the baseline should be collected for a period of time long enough to be *useful* in both of these endeavors. The baseline should not be imposed merely because it seems like the "scientific" thing to do and then not be used. The baseline period, then, shouldn't be so brief that it won't be of much help in assessing and evaluating your case/situation. Nor should the baseline period continue for too long to the point that additional data are not needed or become irrelevant.

If you're thinking that the above does not provide a very precise outline of exactly how much data are needed to be useful, you're right. But the principle of utility does help in the development of clearer guidelines.

Stability

The next guideline, and the one recommended by some of the more rigorous researchers, is that a baseline should be continued until it is "stable" (Barlow & Hersen, 1984). Although this too is a rather imprecise term, the idea here is that the baseline that presents a stable picture once it is graphed will be the baseline that is most useful. A stable baseline is one that does not contain obvious cycles or wide fluctuations in the data. Even more importantly, a stable baseline is one that allows you to be able to estimate what might happen to the target event in the future (Mann, 1976). That is, if your baseline is stable, you should be able to make a reasonable judgment as to what would likely happen to the problem later on if no intervention program were begun.

Stability in the baseline is important for at least two major reasons. First, if the pattern of the target problem is extremely variable and no real patterns can be detected in the variability, then the assessment becomes somewhat more difficult. It would be hard to determine what factors are affecting the changes in the target problem. Second, if the baseline is not stable, the practitioner will have difficulty in evaluating change once the intervention starts. This is because if the baseline is stable, you should be able to predict what is likely to happen to the target problem over time *without* the intervention program. Hence, the evaluation of change becomes more obvious. However, with an unstable baseline you can't predict future trends in the target problem, so even with an intervention program you couldn't be sure that the problem wouldn't have changed anyway.

Some basic principles for obtaining a stable baseline were described by Mann (1976). The first is that the longer you collect baseline data, the more likely it is that systematic changes or predictable patterns will become visible in the problem you are studying. Second, the more variation there is between points in the baseline, the longer the baseline you would need to achieve stability. Third, if variation between points on the baseline is relatively small, then a relatively short baseline will be all that is necessary to achieve stability. Fourth, following from the preceding, since an unstable baseline means that you can't predict future trends, you will need more data points in an unstable baseline to establish stability so that future trends *can* be predicted.

Barlow and Hersen (1984, pp. 73–79) have presented several baseline patterns that could occur in any set of data along with suggestions for how to handle those patterns. Figure 12.6 presents a few of the more basic patterns you are likely to encounter along with some suggestions on how to handle them in analyzing baseline data.

Figure 12.6a illustrates a stable baseline that is flat—that is, a baseline in which there are no apparent upward or downward directions in the data. This is the most desirable pattern for a baseline, not only because it is easy to predict the future pattern (the dotted lines) of the problem, but because it shows a relatively constant rate of occurrence of the problem. Therefore, any departure from this flat pattern would stand out, and a positive or negative change would be clear. Furthermore, if there is an absence of effects following introduction of intervention, this should also be clear; the steady state would just continue (Barlow & Hersen, 1984).

We should point out here that Figure 12.6a represents what might be called the "classic" stable baseline. Most writers on the subject (e.g.,

Barlow & Hersen, 1984) refer to this (the flat baseline with no upward or downward trend) as the only real stable baseline. However, we have added another dimension to the term stability—the notion of *predictability*. Thus, we maintain that several other baseline patterns (e.g., Figures 12.6b through 12.6d) also are stable or at least semistable because you still can predict

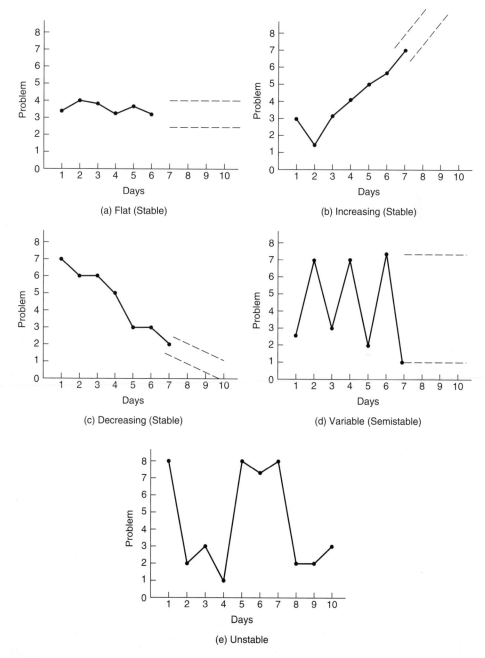

FIGURE 12.6   Patterns of stability in baseline data.

what would happen if the trend detected in the baseline phase continued unchanged. However, you should know that this view is not completely consistent with all other views on this issue and you might come across somewhat more limited ideas of what baseline stability means in the literature.

The charts in Figures 12.6b and 12.6c also show stable baselines because future trends can be predicted (dotted lines). However, these are also baselines with clear patterns or directions (trends) in them, one increasing and one decreasing. If the goal of intervention is to change the direction of the problem (e.g., to decrease the occurrence of a problem when the problem is increasing in the baseline, or vice versa), these baseline patterns are acceptable because any change in the direction of the problem can be noted easily. However, if the pattern in the baseline is already in the direction of improvement, an obvious problem of interpretation is involved. One possibility is to continue to collect baseline data until a flatter pattern (with less upward or downward direction) emerges. Another possibility is to implement intervention and then watch to see if the pattern continues at the same rate or decreases (suggesting possibly negative effects of intervention) or increases at an even higher rate, thus suggesting that intervention may have enhanced an effect that might have been occurring anyway.

Incidentally, any dramatic changes in the baseline pattern, especially in the desired direction, could indicate a reactive effect of recording. In such instances it would be desirable to extend the baseline if possible to see if this levels out with time.

A fourth pattern, the variable baseline, is commonly encountered in practice and is illustrated in Figure 12.6d. We consider this to be a semi-stable baseline because future direction of the problem can be plotted to some extent. But the variability (alternating high and low points) makes it difficult to draw any conclusions with a great deal of certainty. Thus, it might be best to attempt to extend this baseline also until a more stable pattern occurs. It would be even more desirable to try to assess the sources of variability, that is, to try to see if there are patterns in the target problem that can be related to identifiable factors. In this way the interven-

tion plan can focus on those factors apparently associated with the higher occurrence of the problem on certain days or at certain times.

The final baseline pattern, the unstable baseline, is shown in Figure 12.6e. This pattern is unstable because not only are the data extremely variable, but no patterns can be detected in the data and the future trend of the data is difficult to predict. Again, perhaps the best strategy for dealing with this kind of baseline information is to attempt to collect more data until the pattern somewhat stabilizes, although the strategies described previously also would be possible.

In several of the problematic situations described previously we have suggested extending the baseline until stability is achieved; however, there are other strategies for dealing with this problem. The two main ones involve (1) making alterations in the research design at subsequent phases in an attempt to evaluate the effects of the program (e.g., implementing intervention, withdrawing it, and reintroducing it), and (2) using some relatively simple statistics to try to increase the stability in the baseline data. These strategies, as well as the issues involved in their use, will be discussed in subsequent chapters in Part III as well as in Part IV.

We discussed the desirability of attaining a stable baseline almost as though it is possible to do so every time. However, there are a number of problems that may prevent you from extending a baseline to achieve stability. Two of the most common problems are: (1) you simply may not have the time to extend the baseline. (For example, the client may not be able or willing to stay involved in the program. If you are working in an institution, there may even be pressure to discharge the client.) And (2), even more importantly, there may be an ethical problem involved in withholding intervention for an extended period of time just to achieve a stable baseline. This second problem is especially true when the problem results in serious discomfort to the client or others (Barlow & Hersen, 1984).

In summary, you probably would be best off in trying to develop your own guidelines regarding a decision about how long a baseline should be extended to achieve stability. In some situations you may be able to apply the statistics we suggest in Chapter 19 to remove variability from the baseline data. In other situations you may not be able to find any satisfactory method of dealing with the instability, and you will just have to learn to live with it. In these situations any interpretation of changes found once intervention has begun should be done with awareness of the instability in the baseline pattern and with due caution.

Time

Another way of viewing the problem of how long to collect baseline data is to try to establish a basic guideline regarding number of baseline observations necessary and then to try to follow that guideline across most case situations. To that end we offer the following suggestions.

First, it appears that, as a very rough guideline, at least three observations are necessary to establish any sort of clear pattern during the baseline period (Hersen & Barlow, 1976). Thus, you would always want to make *at least* three observations during the baseline period. We emphasize that this is the minimum number of observations that would be necessary. In most situations three would probably be too few to be particularly helpful for either assessment or evaluation. The one exception to this rule would be when a clear pattern or direction of the problem is established during the baseline, and other practical considerations rule out the possibility of collecting more baseline data. This situation is illustrated in Figure 12.7.

In Figure 12.7a the problem seems to be occurring at a constant level, so a dramatic change, upward or downward, in the occurrence of the problem once intervention has begun might suggest that the three observations during baseline were sufficient. In Figure 12.7b the pattern is in the direction of the problem getting worse (e.g., an adolescent's rate of fighting increasing), so if intervention is begun after three observations and it reverses the direction, this would once again suggest that the three observations were sufficient.

A second suggestion regarding length of time is to try to achieve about 10 baseline points, if this is ethically and practically possible, because this number will be most useful for evaluation purposes. In particular, the validity of some of the simple statistical procedures we will suggest in Chapter 22 depends in part on having approximately 10 baseline observations. The greater the number of baseline points, the more likely it is that we will be able to detect a change if one actually occurs.

A third suggestion, which you can use if achieving 10 baseline points is not possible and which is perhaps the most practical guideline of all, especially when you are collecting data on a daily basis, is to aim for about 1 week of baseline data collection. These 7 days of data may have the practical advantage of being suited to weekly appointments or meetings. Also, 7 days often produces enough data to establish any direction in the baseline so that evaluations can be carried out. Seven days also gives a clear

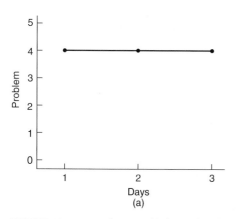
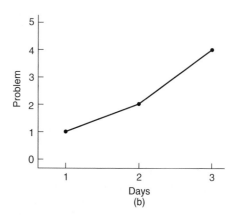

FIGURE 12.7 Two charts establishing a baseline pattern with only three observations.

picture of the typical pattern of occurrence of a problem over an entire week to aid in assessment. And finally, some of the statistical procedures discussed in Chapter 22 can be used with 7 baseline points, although this does impose some limitations on their validity.*

Summary of Length of Baselining

There are several ways to determine how long to collect baseline data. All of them should be guided by the principle of utility plus whatever realistic or ethical concerns may be present in a given case. It is desirable when possible to collect data until the baseline is relatively stable and also, if possible, for about 10 baseline points. However, what is most desirable may not always be possible, and in some situations it may be necessary to use even fewer baseline points, say, from 3 to 7. It is likely that the number of points necessary and possible will vary from case to case and situation to situation. Also, the type of recording method you use may affect the length of baseline. Some methods such as behavioral observations and individualized rating scales allow daily observations, thus facilitating relatively brief baselines. We hope the guidelines we have suggested will help you in making a decision in each case and situation.

WHEN ARE BASELINES NOT NECESSARY?

We've placed so much emphasis on collecting baseline data that you may be surprised to see that there are times when it may not be neces-

sary to do so. However, as we've said before, the purpose of recording is not to do recording for the sake of recording or to let the recording or research be the master of the practitioner. Instead, recording and single-system evaluation are important, we believe, only because they can help practice (and not hinder it). So what kinds of situations are there in which it may not be necessary to use a baseline?

The first situation is one in which there is simply no time to conduct a baseline, at least the standard type of baseline, concurrent with other assessment activities (observing the problem over time). Many crisis situations are typical of this condition. However, as we noted earlier, it does seem to be both practical and possible to use a reconstructed or retrospective baseline in situations such as this. For example, a reconstructed baseline developed by a practitioner and a client in a case of spouse abuse is displayed in Figure 12.8.

A second situation in which no baseline is necessary is one in which the problem situation presents an obvious danger to the client and/or his or her environment. Delaying intervention and collecting baseline data would therefore pose a clear threat to health and safety. Intervention in such a case must be begun immediately to attempt to avoid any further (or impending) harm to anyone involved. In situations such as these a reconstructed baseline might be possible. For example, if the problem involves a mother's complaint that her child doesn't pay attention to her warnings and dashes out into streets with heavy traffic, it might be possible to get the mother's estimate of how often the child does this. However, imagine how ridiculous (not to mention dan-

---

*A slightly more complicated guideline has been suggested by Gelfland and Hartmann (1975). They have proposed a formula for computing how many baseline data points are necessary. They suggest a minimum of 3 baseline points plus 1 additional point for each 10% of variability. This would be expressed as follows:

$$3 + 10\left(\frac{\text{highest} - \text{lowest rate}}{\text{highest rate}}\right)$$

To use Gelfland and Hartmann's example (1975, p. 232), let's say the purpose of the baseline is to determine how many homework problems Davy solves. Let's also say that the number of problems solved varies from 6 to 20 during the first 3 days of baseline. This would lead to the following computation:

$$3 + 10\left(\frac{20-6}{20}\right) = 3 + 10\left(\frac{14}{20}\right) = 3 + 10(.70) = 3 + 7 = 10$$

Thus, the baseline would consist of the first 3 days plus 7 additional days, or a total of 10.

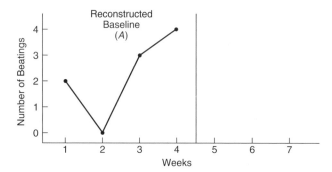

FIGURE 12.8   Reconstructed baseline showing wife's estimate of number of beatings per week in the month prior to contact with the practitioner. The notation *(A)* represents the reconstructed baseline events immediately prior to the onset of intervention.

gerous) it would be to delay intervention so that you could collect a concurrent baseline of how many times the child runs into the street over the next week.

In both of the above situations, the assumption that intervention can begin immediately, without the baseline, is based on the idea that the practitioner is, in fact, well prepared to do so. That is, he or she is familiar enough with the case/situation and effective techniques for dealing with it that little or no assessment time is necessary.

The final situation in which a baseline may not be necessary is when the problem with which you are concerned never occurs. Thus, your goal is to develop and then to increase the occurrence of some behavior, feeling, thought, organizational activity, or what have you. Obviously, if the problem never occurs (and your goal is to get it to occur presumably at some predetermined level), then a baseline would be a waste of time. If Marty never speaks or if the organization never admits African Americans, there is no need to spend time collecting information on rate of occurrence during baseline.

There may be one exception to the above guideline. It may be that you (or the client) only *think* the target problem never occurs, and that, in fact, it does occur but at very low frequencies or in somewhat disguised forms. Thus, a period of careful baseline observations may detect this occurrence, and the information would be particularly useful for designing an intervention program. It may require totally different intervention techniques to first de-

velop a behavior and then get it to increase than it would to simply get the already occurring target behavior to increase. Therefore, the task for the practitioner in such a situation is to make a decision on the basis of what would be most fruitful on a particular occasion. If the client reports absolutely no occurrence of the target problem, it is possible that going ahead and collecting baseline data would still yield some advantages for planning intervention. Of course, in such a situation it is important to present your rationale for collecting data in a way that won't insult the client by implying that he or she is not telling the truth in his or her initial report.

ISSUES REGARDING BASELINING

Baselining is a particularly valuable tool for helping to assess the client/situation and for helping to evaluate your effectiveness. Baseline data can be gathered, with few exceptions, no matter what method of intervention you are using and regardless of the level of intervention (i.e., whether you are dealing with individuals, families, groups, organizations, or communities).

However, despite the importance of the baseline period and in addition to some of the problems we described in previous chapters, there are some issues regarding baselining that bear discussion. Following, drawing especially on the work of Thomas (1978), are some of these issues.

Baselining Delays Intervention

There actually are two questions involved in considering this issue. The first is, Does baselining actually delay intervention? The second is, In situations in which baselining may delay intervention, is this detrimental?

Does Baselining Actually Delay Intervention? Regarding this first question, it would appear that in most cases and for several reasons, baselining should not delay the intervention program. First, baselining is not conducted outside of the context of the regular assessment. Baselining is conducted, at least in part, to help the assessment and to enhance the decision-making process regarding what intervention techniques to use. While assessment involves more than baselining, assessment and baselining are ordinarily concurrent events. The data collected are considered part of the general assessment data. Hence, under most conditions it is difficult to actually begin the intervention program before the baseline is completed, since a primary basis for selecting the intervention is the baserate information.

A second reason why baselining ordinarily should not delay intervention is that baselining usually does not take very long. As noted earlier in this chapter, a reliable baseline may be collected in as few as three data collection periods. Furthermore, the desired number of data points generally is only about 10. In rare situations in which the baseline data are extremely variable, collection of baseline data may be extended beyond these points.

It is important to note that in most instances in the literature the "points" for data collection refer to days. Thus, a typical baseline period might run from 3 to 12 days (i.e., 3 to 12 baseline points), and in many instances it might run approximately 1 week. It can be assumed that most practitioners have contact with their clients once or twice a week (in some instances, the contacts may be more frequent), and that in most cases at least 1 or 2 weeks are necessary before a systematic intervention program can be selected on the basis of the complete assessment. Therefore, not only is this period of time generally necessary for adequate intervention planning, but the period of time required for the baseline is often so short that the baseline per se hardly can be viewed as a major factor delaying the beginning of intervention.

There are some exceptions to this. As described earlier, there are some situations in which no baseline is necessary (although an equivalent amount of time might be necessary to complete the rest of the assessment). There also are situations in which the practitioner must engage in intervention immediately (e.g., emergencies), and for many of these a reconstructed baseline can be used for both assessment and evaluation purposes.

Is Delaying Intervention Detrimental? There are two conditions under which intervention *might* be delayed. Both of these in large part should be decisions that the practitioner and client make on the basis of their assessment. Both of these conditions might actually enhance the outcome of the case rather than harm it. The first condition has to do with lack of stability in the baseline. If, as noted previously, the baseline data are extremely variable, the practitioner and client might want to negotiate an extension of the baseline so that they will be better able to evaluate intervention effects. In this situation the decision to delay intervention is a deliberate one, since the delay will allow for a clearer evaluation of change. A decision such as this is made in the context of the total assessment, and if it is deemed that it would be more important to begin intervention immediately because of the needs of the case, then the decision should be to implement the intervention.

The second instance in which intervention might be delayed also involves a deliberate decision on the part of the practitioner and client. This is a situation in which more assessment information is necessary in order to select the appropriate intervention. As one example, it might be that the first week of baseline *hints* at a pattern that only another week of baseline data could uncover. The success of any intervention obviously depends on selecting the right intervention program. This selection must be grounded in and related to a thorough assessment. It would seem, therefore, that once again a delay caused by the need for better or clearer assessment information can only result in more, rather than less, effective intervention. In other words, the key to beginning an intervention without a baseline period or even a formal assessment period is that the practitioner is knowledgeable enough about precisely what intervention to use that he or she really doesn't need the baseline/assessment information in order to be effective.

There Are Times When Baselines Are Impossible

This statement certainly is often true, and situations in which baselines may be impossible were described earlier in this chapter. However, baseline information may be gathered and may be very useful in many situations in which it appears as though no baseline is necessary. The most common area in which this problem may occur is in emergency and crisis situations. For these we have recommended the reconstructed or retrospective baseline. While this is generally a cruder measure than the concurrent baseline, it can help both assessment and evaluation. Furthermore, the reconstructed baseline adds some degree of standardization to your practice so that comparable formats for all cases or situations are available as an aid to demonstrating your accountability.

Targets Often Shift during the Course of Intervention

A client's targets might change in important ways over time (Sorenson, Gorsuch, & Mintz, 1985). New targets might emerge; targets that were important initially might become less important; or targets might become more specific in nature. These changes might occur for different reasons (e.g., increased rapport between you and the client or relevant others, increased knowledge and awareness on the part of the respondent), but these changes need to be considered to get a complete and accurate picture of a client's targets. Therefore, just as assessment never really ends (you always are collecting information), you shouldn't just determine a client's targets once, and then have the same ones measured over time no matter what

else happens. You should periodically determine whether the targets have changed, and you should take such changes into account in the measurement of the targets. For example, if new targets emerge, these new targets should be measured and monitored over time.

For evaluation, it would be ideal if the initial set of targets identified for a client stayed the same. When different targets emerge over the course of a single-system evaluation, it becomes harder to determine change in targets and the reasons for any changes. For example, suppose that you use a design with a baseline phase followed by an intervention phase, using a specific set of targets elicited from the client at the beginning of baseline. You plan to have the client rate this set of targets on a regular basis during baseline and intervention, and then you'll compare the baseline and intervention ratings to determine change in the targets. If any new targets emerged during the course of intervention, you obviously wouldn't have ratings for them; this would make it difficult to determine the impact of the intervention on the new targets. Nevertheless, you shouldn't just ignore new targets, because you would end up with an incomplete and inaccurate picture of the client's targets.

Often in practice it is discovered that the original target is not appropriate for further work, that new or more urgent targets have emerged, or that the client is more willing to follow an intervention program focused on a problem that is different from the problem on which you currently are working (Thomas, 1978). With any of these conditions, unless the assumption is that intervention can be begun on the day the shifts (or desired shifts) are noted and that a period of adequate assessment and planning is not needed, it would seem the procedural guidelines would be the same as previously. Under most conditions, effective intervention requires thorough assessment and planning. In such situations, several strategies are possible: (a) You could continue to monitor the old target, continue that intervention, and begin baseline observations on the new problem; (b) you could continue to monitor the old target, but stop or delay the intervention while refocusing most of your attention on the new target (both recording and intervention);

(c) you could stop monitoring the old target but continue the intervention if resources are not stretched too thin; or (d) you could stop monitoring and stop the intervention with the old target because the new one seems a much higher priority, and refocus complete attention on the new problem, including recording and intervention.

People Won't Cooperate in Collecting Baseline Information

It is easy to see why some clients might be reluctant to collect baseline data. It might be seen as delaying efforts to resolve the problem, as being silly or childish, or as being busywork. In large part we view reluctance to baseline as a function of how you present it to the people whom you want to record. If you present baselining with confidence and clarity, if you explain that it is built into the overall assessment process as regularly as a medical person builds in the need to monitor blood pressure, and if you emphasize the overall importance of baselining to intervention planning and evaluation, then we believe that most of the battle already will be won. As you probably can tell, we believe that the recorder's commitment to collecting baseline data may largely be a reflection of your own commitment.

We don't mean to suggest that it is always a simple task to get people to cooperate, and when they don't, your job is to try to find out why and try to improve the situation. However, when baselining is explained as not necessitating any particular delay in problem solving, and when you carefully select one of the measures we described in Part II so the recorder will see its relevance and be willing to use it, baselining will become as common and comfortable in your practice as any other aspect of your approach.

What If the Problem Improves during the Baseline?

There are some circumstances during which you might either see some improvement in the problem during the baseline, or where the client claims there is improvement (even though the baseline data don't show it). Related to this is a more subtle issue: the concern among many practitioners that the very fact that they have made contact with the client and perhaps developed some rapport during the baseline may improve the problem compared to the prebaseline period, making it less likely to produce clear changes in the intervention period, since those changes already took place during the baseline.

It is important to acknowledge at the outset that there may indeed be observable changes during the baseline period, and/or changes between the prebaseline and baseline periods. Of course, the possibility always exists that the changes are due to reactivity, a topic we considered in detail in Chapter 9. We offered several suggestions for dealing with this problem there, including possibly extending the baseline (since the effects of reactivity often are short-lived).

Another way to evaluate this situation is to develop a reconstructed baseline for a period of a few weeks prior to the concurrent baseline as a way of comparing any differences between the two periods. This will produce at least a rough idea of the nature of those changes and what the practitioner has to do to enhance them during the actual intervention period.

But the essence of this whole issue as we see it lies in our definition of what intervention really means. In Chapter 11, we defined intervention as a formal, systematic, clearly defined and planned activity geared toward improving the problem/situation. At the heart of the definition is the distinction between accountable professional practice and what nonprofessionals may do to alleviate problems. It is our belief that, even if the problem does improve during the baseline due to rapport, effects of the relationship, or other nonspecific factors of professional–client contact, the professional can and must go beyond these effects in producing changes due to his or her intervention program. In other words, the very nature of professional intervention—its identification as a formal program to change a problem/situation—means that it generally should build on and go beyond the relationship between the practitioner and client. We know that in some cases, the relationship may be all we can offer to the client, and it may even be sufficient (see Bohart & Greenberg, 1997, for a recent review of research on empathy). But the huge array of intervention technologies available to the helping professions and the considerable research on this topic (see, e.g., Acierno, Hersen, & Ammerman, 1994; Chambless et al., 1996; Chambless et al., 1998; Fischer, 1993; Fraser et al., 1997; Nathan & Gorman, 1998; Pikoff, 1996; Reid, 1997a; Roth & Fonagy, 1996; Thyer & Wodarski, 1998; Wodarski & Thyer, 1998; Woody & Sanderson, 1998) strongly suggest that we, as professionals, should be able to demonstrate that our interventions have a clear effect over and above that which might be accomplished during an assessment/baseline and even rapport building phase of contact with the client.

SUMMARY

This chapter has presented basic principles and procedures of baselining. We first described the two basic purposes of baselining as helping you in your assessment of the case/situation and aiding you in evaluating the outcome. We briefly discussed the two major types of baselines, concurrent/prospective and reconstructed/retrospective, and the differences in their use. The next section discussed issues regarding how long baselining should be continued and the principles for deciding this, which involve utility, stability, and selecting a period of time using several guidelines. We also discussed the situations in which baselines may not be necessary. The chapter concluded with a review of some of the basic issues involving baselining.

FROM THE CASE STUDY TO THE BASIC SINGLE-SYSTEM DESIGN: *A-B*

PURPOSE: This chapter discusses basic designs, from the traditional case study, which draws its subjective conclusions from simultaneous observation and intervention, to the first, basic single-system design, the *A-B* design. The *A-B* design has a clear baseline and intervention phase to make a more or less objective determination as to whether a change has occurred in the target problem. We recommend that, at a minimum, this basic *A-B* design be used with every case/situation. ■

Introduction
Case Studies or Predesigns

Design *A:* Observation Only $\boxed{A}$ - - - -

Design (*B*): Intervention Only $\boxed{\;\;(B)}$

Design *B:* The Case Study (Simultaneous Intervention and Observation) $\boxed{\;\;B}$

Design *B-C:* Changes in the Case Study $\boxed{\;\;B\;|\;C}$
  Strengths of the Case Study Method
  Limitations of the Case Study Method
  Recommendations Regarding Case Study Methods
  Case Illustrations
  Introducing the Client to the Case Study

Design *A-B:* The Basic Single-System Design $\boxed{A\;|\;B}$
Strengths of the *A-B* Design
Limitations of the *A-B* Design
Recommendations Regarding the *A-B* Design
Case Illustrations
Aggregating *A-B* Designs
An Elaboration of the *A-B* Design: The Repeated Preintervention–Postintervention Design
Introducing the Client to the Basic Single-System Design
Summary

INTRODUCTION

All single-system designs are constructed from two basic elements arranged in different ways for different purposes. One or more intervention periods are usually combined with one or more baselines (nonintervention periods) in order to develop conclusions about changes in the target problem and, possibly, the effects of the intervention on that problem. In this and the following four chapters, we describe a number of designs and the strengths and limitations they exhibit. We also give our recommendations for the use of each design, as well as some suggestions for presenting them to clients.

Chapter 13 discusses three topics, the first of which is case studies. These are not formal evaluation designs. They do not permit planned comparisons between phases of service. We discuss them because they are both historically important as precursors to true evaluation designs, and because they are still commonly used as if they provided objective information. We label case studies as "predesigns," meaning that they may contain one or another of the basic elements of a true evaluation design, but they do not integrate all of the vital elements.

The second topic in Chapter 13 involves the basic single-system design, the *A-B* design, which we believe is a major evaluation tool for helping professionals because it permits a logical comparison of an intervention with a nonintervention period for the same client or client-system. This is the minimal arrangement of components that allows for a more or less objective assessment of the client situation before and during (or after) intervention. With the *A-B* design, we can determine whether there was a difference between the *A* and the *B* sets of data.

A third topic of Chapter 13 deals with a recent elaboration of the *A-B* design. Our reason for introducing this new and useful way of analyzing certain kinds of data is to emphasize that the *A-B* design is very flexible and can be extended in creative ways to meet the needs of practice situations.

In Chapters 14 through 17, we take the same basic *A* and *B* components arranged in different ways to represent the more complex and rigorous designs from which you can obtain information that will permit you to infer not only whether there was a difference between baseline and intervention periods, but also whether the intervention was causally linked with the outcome.

One last introductory word: We describe a large number of cases, adapted from the literature and also from our practice and students' practice, using various designs to illustrate the basic principles. Almost none of them will be "textbook perfect" because they are taken from real practice. These cases serve an important function, showing how these principles may be creatively adapted to fit particular practice circumstances. Where possible, we note the ways in which deviations from some of the principles described in Chapter 11 could affect conclusions or interpretations of the data.

CASE STUDIES OR PREDESIGNS

Design *A:* Observation Only $\boxed{A}$ ____

Design (*B*): Intervention Only ____ (B)

Within the category of case study designs we can distinguish those observations and immediate interventions from true designs that offer planned comparisons needed to make logical deductions about changes in target problems. Let's begin with the situation in which only observations are made; we label this Design *A*, meaning that only measurement or observation has taken place, with no intervention as such following. For example, a person may be admitted to a psychiatric hospital simply for observation. A child may be monitored after a traumatic event (e.g., the death of a parent). Therefore, this predesign may provide useful information about the need for intervention, especially if careful measurement procedures are used.

In addition, helping professionals may come in contact with persons seeking information. The intake interview may clarify enough for the would-be client to enable him or her to carry on without further services, even though the practitioner thought additional services might be useful. What is essentially information collection for the practitioner may be the stimulus for personal action on the part of the client, a point to which we will return shortly.

We can identify another variation of case study designs in which only intervention occurs. We will describe this as Design (*B*), meaning an intervention or (*B*) phase that did not include concurrent observation or measurement. The most typical occasion for this would be in an emergency situation in which, for example, a bleeding person prompts a passerby to deliver first aid. This is not a pure case, for first aid properly given involves a quick survey of the entire situation, first, so as not to hurt the victim in one place while trying to help in another, and second, so as not to overlook other needs. However, this can be done very quickly, so the major emphasis is on immediate, temporary relief until medical help can be summoned.

Some forms of clinical intervention may also involve immediate assessment and immediate action, such as when a shy, unassertive client, who is having difficulty getting deserved promotions, tries to tell the therapist what she sees as the substantive problem, and the therapist begins to address her problem as expressed in metacommunication terms, that is, the way she sounds—too unassertive, too passive in a situation calling for more assertive behavior. Again, as with good first aid, there is some quick assessment of the situation, although it may be based more on what the theory says people *should* be like than on relevant background characteristics. For example, some regional ways of speaking involve slow, soft speech that might easily be interpreted as unassertive behavior upon first hearing them.

We want to emphasize the limitations of these A and (B) formats, since they tend to underlie a natural inclination of beginners to ask questions without real purpose or to "do something" without understanding what needs to be done, in what order, and by whom. The examples used for Design A do not involve simply asking questions for the sake of asking questions; such questioning ordinarily is well planned, although the plan is not necessarily visible to the persons being questioned. Likewise, taking immediate action against some visible wound may divert attention from more lethal problems that are less visible. For these parallel reasons we will take a strong stand that the basic single-system design, the A-B, with its planned attention both to measured observations and intervention is the minimum basis of scientific practice. A careful baseline and a clear intervention are the minimum components of good service.

Basically, these observation-only and intervention-only formats quickly merge into the next type of design, the case study, labeled B, in which there is some degree of simultaneous intervention and observational assessment.

Design B: The Case Study (Simultaneous Intervention and Observation) $\boxed{B}$

By case study we mean the simultaneous intervention and observation (recording) performed by a helping professional. This is labeled B and should be distinguished from the (B) situation in which, in principle, intervention occurs without formal observations. An important variation occurs when the practitioner uses two or more interventions at the same time, BC, each with its own distinctive intervention but sharing a common observational assessment.

Barlow and Hersen (1984) suggest that historically the case study was a means by which practitioners communicated their successes on a case to their colleagues. From these communications, "schools" of practice were formed in a tradition that dates back at least as far as the days of Hippocrates, who first described his cases—successes as well as failures. Freud, for example, presented cases to illustrate his theory, although he went far beyond these cases to conceptually reconstruct the dynamics involved. The case study method dominated clinical practice for the first half of this century and is still widely used in agencies as tools for continuing development of staff.

The core of the case study method is a careful study of the presenting condition viewed within whatever context is deemed appropriate. For the psychoanalyst the context is the client's symbolic reconstruction of perceived relationships and events. For some social workers and community psychologists the context may be the relationship of the individual client to his or her physical and social environments. Whatever standardization emerges through study of the case comes from the theoretical perspective under which it is constructed.

However, this has sometimes led to the parochial reasoning that practitioners are obliged to see and to treat the kinds of factors that a given theory considers important to the relative exclusion of those to which the theory does not attribute causal force. In short, the case study method could be an invitation to biased perceptions if the practitioner is not absolutely scrupulous about the openness with which he or she views clients and their problems. This is a difficult balancing act. Further, the case study does not allow systematic comparison between a nonintervention and intervention period. Thus, the case study method has a mixed reputation among practitioners and researchers.

Design *B-C:*
Changes in the Case Study ⌊__⌋*B*⌊*C*

One important extension of the case study is the addition of other interventions in a separate phase. Because the case study (in contrast to the intervention-only format) includes observational assessments, the *B-C* "design" has two consecutive sets of observational data. This permits the practitioner to make some additional judgments about changes in the client from phase to phase beyond those possible in the more limited case study, since he or she has two sets of data points. This still does not permit the practitioner to have a baseline or nonintervention comparison, although if, after the first intervention, there doesn't appear to be much change in the client, the *B* period is sometimes used as if it were a baseline period. However, if the client seems to have made progress (or has deteriorated), it is difficult to use a *B-C* format to make judgments about change or factors possibly affecting that change in the target problem because of possible order effects as described in Chapter 11, and, again, because there is no baseline or nonintervention period.

Sometimes practitioners use, in effect, a *B-C-D-E-F . . .* format, changing the intervention program during each contact with the client. The more changes that appear, the more difficult it is to sort out what is happening, since not enough time is usually given for the problem to stabilize during any one phase, and the more difficult it is to know what are possible causal factors. At this point applying design principles to practice may not benefit the practitioner, because the picture becomes somewhat confused.

Strengths of the Case Study Method. On the positive side, writers such as Barlow and Hersen (1984), Browning and Stover (1971), Lazarus and Davison (1971), and Kazdin

(1992), although in slightly different contexts, make the following types of observations. First, the case study "method" can foster clinical speculation and innovation because it is easily administered in just about any situation. Second, this method can cast light (or doubt) on a theoretical assumption or prediction by giving immediate feedback through testing that idea in practice. Third, the case study method can help to develop or to refine technical skills by close connection between practice techniques and their evaluation. Fourth, case studies permit the investigation of rare phenomena without having to collect large amounts of data from many persons. Fifth, case studies may be transitional experiences for some practitioners; the subjective information purposely collected in these approaches represents an introduction and perhaps a stimulus to use of more rigorous single-system designs. The hunches they generate and subjectively test are the same hunches that may be put to more exacting investigation.

Limitations of the Case Study Method. The case study method has a number of weaknesses and limitations. First, frequently several techniques are administered at the same time, making it difficult for the practitioner to tease out the active ingredients so as to benefit the next phase of intervention—using just the most effective intervention—and to be of use for future case situations. Second, the practitioner is often casual in specifying problems and in measuring those problems to see if changes occur. This leads to a strong bias in favor of interpreting events in terms of how a theory predicts the events will turn out. There is little independence in making observations that are the basis of the data. Third, there is typically little validity or reliability-checking in case studies, making it difficult for others to use the same procedures in the same way. The case study method doesn't provide any impetus to challenge desired outcomes for alternative explanations as to why they turned out as they did. Fourth, case studies are rarely systematic, nor do they follow clear guidelines regarding measurement, design, or analysis. From the point of view of the canons of logic, case study methods are grossly lacking in power to make causal inferences, and there are few solid benchmarks even to indicate whether change occurred. Primarily, this is because baseline/intervention comparisons are not used in case studies.

Recommendations Regarding Case Study Methods. There is no question but that the case study method is a weak evaluation design if one considers it an evaluation design at all. As a practice design it may be fruitfully used in developing testable ideas in clinical as well as community practice. However, testable ideas also can be developed in the designs we will soon describe, so we suggest that if the case study method is used at all, it should be used as a temporary device until you are able to identify specific problems and set up clear measurement procedures for them. By making use of the suggestions offered in this book, we think that it is fully possible to do the specifying and measuring almost immediately. Therefore, we recommend leaving the case study approaches as methods of last resort (as during an emergency situation) or as very temporary approaches.

Case Illustrations. The first illustration is adapted from the case records of a family service agency dealing with people in the armed services and their families:

Mrs. D. came into the office greatly upset because she hadn't heard from her son in over 2 months. He is in the army, stationed in Germany for the past 9 months. He had established a pattern of writing a letter home each week until about 2 months ago when letters stopped. Mrs. D. has written a dozen imploring letters asking her son to write to her. She has not called him due to the expense (and also because she is intimidated by the thought of long-distance overseas calls). Her medical problems (ulcers) are acting up because of this situation, and she was told by a friend that we might do something to help. I told her that I would look into the situation and call her back soon. After Mrs. D. left, I confirmed her information about her son's location in Germany and sent a cable to the base commander. I received a return cable from the chief medical officer informing me that Private D. was injured in a serious auto accident 2 months ago. The medical officer requested that I inform the family that their son was now out of danger and was recuperating. I cabled back to set up a long-distance telephone call

between mother and son and then called Mrs. D. with this information.

In this type of situation, one in which there would likely be contact with the client (Mrs. D.) only once or twice, there is little time to collect much information. The practitioner's task is quite clear: to find out the information and then to transmit it sensitively to the mother while helping her to make further contact with the son. These activities and goals are quite specific; either they were achieved or not. The measured target behavior—numbers of letters written for a period of time—initially could only be reconstructed from the conversation with the client. This target behavior was later reconfirmed by the medical officer, a reliability check of sorts. Thus, even with a case study with very limited information, it is possible to make certain types of evaluations (Bloom et al., 1979). Figure 13.1 presents these data as an example of a reconstructed baseline, turning this basically simple case study into a somewhat more developed *A-B* design. This case is also an illustration of one way of dealing with limited-contact cases, as we discuss further in Chapter 18.

A second example of a case study illustrates a common practice phenomenon, *changing the intervention* (Design *B-C*). Tenants in a public housing project organized an informal committee to appeal to the city to repair the apartment complex and to have better garbage pickup and pest control. A social work student was interning at this housing project and aided the neighbors in organizing their thoughts and presenting them to the Department of Housing at City Hall (phase *B*). Individual tenants made brief speeches about the conditions of their apartments or the problems they faced with garbage and pests. These presentations did not appreciably affect services, so after a period of time the committee met to consider stronger measures. At the suggestion of the student they took pictures of the apartments and the grounds and invited the mayor and his deputies to join them at a press conference they were going to call, in which they would display the pictures and have the tenants tell their stories to the local television station and newspapers (phase *C*). The mayor called the

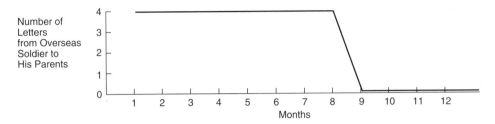

FIGURE 13.1   Reconstructed baseline data for the Mrs. D case. (Adapted from "Evaluation of Single Interventions" by M. Bloom, P. Butch, and D. Walker, 1979, *Journal of Social Service Research, 2,* pp. 301–310.)

Department of Housing, and they met with the committee in a special meeting *before* the scheduled press conference. Concrete actions that met many of the tenants' demands followed from that session.

In this situation the action component took priority over any formal measurement process. However, one might argue that the photographs constitute a "before" picture that could have been compared with photographs of the same places "after" the city took action. Note that there were two relatively discrete actions, a *B* and a *C* intervention, to use our formal terms. The first was the tenant groups making individual presentations to the Department of Housing, and the second was a concerted effort to influence the city services by a tenant group going through the mass media. It apparently seemed superfluous at first to the tenants and the student to collect objective information for evaluation. Yet it was apparently the existence of this information (such as the pictures) together with the ability to act collectively on this information (through the mass media) that started some reaction to their requests. Clear information is needed for effective and accountable services.

Introducing the Client to the Case Study. How might you tell the client or another participant in a case study that you are going to make simultaneous observational assessments along with the intervention? The question is raised at this early stage of discussion about evaluation designs because the ethical implications are fully present throughout our discus-sions of single-system designs (as well as throughout all of research). Clients have the right to know what is going to happen to them, whether information is going to be collected, and how it is going to be used (see Chapter 25 on the Client's Bill of Rights.) As soon as observational assessments or measurements are made and records are kept, the client has a right to know about it.

In addition to the ethical reasons, most clients expect that what they say and the context of their lives will be carefully examined in order to enable the practitioner to help. Clients may not know the exact form of these data, nor how they are collected, but they generally recognize that effective service requires good information. They may also know that such information possibly could be used against them in situations in which case records may be used by public officials under certain legal conditions. So it is important for you to clarify the existence of information collection and its specific use. How can this be done?

We make some recommendations here for introducing the case study to the client that will also be useful in presenting other designs, but each design will require some special discussion concerning its particular format. We add to these recommendations at each stage. To begin with, we suggest four types of statements to be made, each with its own individual expression for the particular circumstances of the client or situation, including when the client/system is a family, a group, a neighborhood, or any of the various receivers of professional services. Sometimes persons other than clients are involved in collecting data. These other persons—say, relevant others—also could be called "mediators" or "recorders" (any person other than the client who collects data on the problem).

1. *"I want to understand your situation so I can be helpful to you.* You (the client or the mediator) know the situation very well, but I have to ask questions until I understand what is happening and how you feel about it."

2. *"I need clear facts in order to be most helpful.* Even though the situation may be clear to you (the client or the mediator), it may not be clear to others who are involved. So I am going to be asking factual questions, such as how many or how often, in order to get as clear a picture of the situation as possible. It is similar to a medical person using a thermometer to get the facts about your temperature, even though you are sure you have a fever. Some of the questions I will be asking will be like a social thermometer in order to get the facts about your personal or social situation."

3. *"I will share these facts with you continuously,* both to check them with you and to keep you informed about the basis of my suggestions for you. Please tell me if I am wrong about anything."

4. *"I will build my plans for helping you based on these facts, and I will also modify these plans as the factual information changes over time.* I will be gathering information throughout the time we are together because this is how I'll know if we are moving in the right directions. It will also help us in knowing when our work together isn't needed anymore—that is, when you have resolved the problems that brought you here."

DESIGN A-B: THE BASIC SINGLE-SYSTEM DESIGN $\boxed{A \mid B}$

The *A-B* design is often seen as the foundation of single-system designs (Kratochwill, 1978)

because of the basic distinction between, and the combining of, a baseline observation period, *A*, and an intervention period, *B*. The *A-B* design and single-system designs in general are fundamentally different from the case study in a number of important ways. Single-system designs involve planned use of a formal evaluation design, clear measurement rules, explicit analytic procedures, and clear identification of an intervention program, including when intervention starts and when it is completed. Single-system designs, in contrast to case studies, are generally more systematic and rigorous in the observation of events and in the analysis of the resulting data. Intervention is ordinarily not undertaken in single-system designs until baseline observations are made, and then this information is used as part of the ongoing process of evaluating practice.

The assumption underlying the *A-B* design is that the problems observed during baseline will likely continue in the same pattern if no changes are made in the system of forces acting on these problems. However, the intervention is a planned change seeking to modify the problematic events in a desired direction. Thus, the practitioner can compare the extent to which the problem occurs after the intervention with the pattern of problematic events existing before the intervention. The *A-B* design can clearly indicate whether any changes in problematic behaviors occurred. Certain analyses (to be discussed in Part IV) can determine whether such changes in patterns of events could have happened by chance alone. This becomes important information in practice decisions on whether to continue or to modify the intervention as we will discuss later. (Other designs discussed in subsequent chapters will also look at the possibility of making a judgment that the intervention actually produced the change.)

The *A* phase of the *A-B* design refers to the nonintervention/observation period, which we described as the baseline phase in Chapter 12. This A phase can take many forms, depending on the theory of or approach to practice being used and the nature of the events being observed, using the measures described in Part II of this book. All of the study or assessment methods used in this phase share one attribute:

They seek to obtain information without changing the events in the process–that is, without being reactive (see Chapter 9). This goal is attained only to a degree as we discuss near the end of this chapter. However, in principle, just about all theories of practice attempt to obtain accurate information about the client and problem–the assessment proper–in order to take knowledgeable action.

The *B* phase of the *A-B* design refers to an intervention period along with the continued collection of data. These data are collected on the same targets and with the same measures as used in the *A* phase. We have stated previously that the single-system design is theory free, in the sense that any intervention may be evaluated within the workings of the design. The more specific the intervention, the more clearly it is evaluated. That is why we urge practitioners to be clear and specific about defining what interventions are employed. However, we are not suggesting that you get so minutely quantitative as to lose sight of the conceptual entity you are seeking to influence. "Family therapy" is awfully broad and nebulous as an intervention when the target is, say, communication problems between a teenager and a stepparent. Both the nature of the target and more specific interventions must be identified in order to really affect the specific target as well as to have an evaluation of the process that makes any sense to the practitioner. For example, persisting arguments over expenditures of money might be one target under consideration, and hours stayed out on weekends might be another. The intervention method might be limited to Parent Effectiveness Training (Gordon, 1970) in this case or more specific kinds of communication training in others. In short, be as specific in stating what the intervention is as you are in defining the problem.

Interventions may differ in scope and still be encompassed by the single-system design. It may be that one specific event has to be altered, such as training the nursing home staff to refer to Mrs. Willowby by her name and to have discussions with her about the setting and current events as subtle reality prompters for an elderly person showing signs of memory loss. Or the intervention can involve rearranging an entire social context, such as when Mr.

Axton was admitted to the long-term-care facility after a stroke left him paralyzed on the right side.

The process of helping involves the development of an intervention plan based on sound information about the client. Plans for measurement related to the success or failure of that intervention plan should be closely related to it. There must be agreement between the intervention plan and the outcomes selected for measurement; the various types of observations and measures taken must relate to the targeted conditions in the case and to the interventions used to modify those targets. That is, there should be a logical and reasonable relationship among the target problem, the measures, and the intervention. The *A-B* design provides time for the practitioner to think through carefully what the problems appear to be and what specific interventions may be selected to deal with them.

Strengths of the *A-B* Design

This basic single-system design is widely applicable to most types of problems and settings as well as to all levels of intervention (i.e., from individuals to communities). It is the "work horse" of practice evaluation for reasons that are not hard to identify. Foremost among these is that *A-B* designs can reveal clearly whether there has been a change in target events, providing both monitoring and evaluation information. This is vital information that can lead to a number of practitioner reactions; *monitoring* of ongoing events lets the practitioner know whether to continue a given intervention or whether to modify it one way or another, including termination. As an *evaluation* device, the *A-B* design provides information to the practitioner and to the client about outcome, and also provides information to the agency and to society at large. This evaluation function has some limitations as we shall see, but any other more rigorous evaluation designs begin with these *A-B* characteristics.

As part of its systematic observations, the *A-B* design also can be helpful in the study or assessment phase of interacting with clients as we noted in Chapters 11 and 12. One impetus that evaluation has on practice may be to seek more operational understanding of the presenting problems, not only to be able to measure them, but because greater specificity means greater clarity in developing relevant intervention plans. Further, we strongly recommend that the basic *A-B* design be elaborated upon by adding maintenance and follow-up phases, as is illustrated in some of the subsequent case studies, to be certain the improvements obtained in the *B* phase do not disappear over time.

The *A-B* design is the simplest logical structure permitting a planned comparison between the two key elements of the evaluation, the nonintervention period and the intervention period. Differences that emerge between the baseline and the events during and after intervention provide a very tentative look at possible causal factors. A key question is whether the intervention caused the observed change. Unfortunately, this basic design cannot exclude a number of logical alternatives that could account for the observed results. These alternative explanations have been discussed in Chapter 11, but the point here is that obtaining such empirical results may prompt you to ask other questions that can be answered better by more rigorous designs. Not only can the practitioner using the *A-B* design flexibly adapt to new events emerging during intervention, but he or she can use other designs that consist of additions to the *A-B* arrangement that will begin to answer causal questions. Whether you add a whole new interventive phase, *C,* to the *A-B* design, or whether you begin another set of observations and interventions on a different problem to see whether this problem might be a controlling influence on the first problem, the comparison between baseline and intervention is the underlying theme.

Limitations of the *A-B* Design

In some ways the limitations of this basic single-system design are the converse of its strengths. Most important is that the *A-B* design can provide clear information only on changes in the problem between baseline and intervention; it appears to, but does not necessarily, provide strong evidence about whether the intervention *caused* the observed change. This is an important point, so let's examine it more closely. It is easy to assume that if there is one different event (the intervention) introduced into a stable set of events (the baseline condition of the target problem), then the different event caused the observed change. This, in fact, may very well be so, particularly when that different event was part of a planned program and when all other alternative explanations can absolutely be ruled out. However, to twist an old saying, people tend to accept any apparent cause in the hand rather than look for alternative causes in the bush. Scientists tend to beat the bush for alternative explanations to be certain that they possess valid causal information. The *A-B* design does not permit control of many alternative explanations for why the results occurred as they did. If Mrs. Willowby begins to regain her memory for persons, places, and time, we would like to infer that this was caused by the reality orientation program the staff engaged in. However, the *A-B* design doesn't exclude the fact that there may also have been a simultaneous change in her diet or other activities that may have had something to do with her improved cognitive functioning. With any *A-B* design, an event outside the intervention, even a change in season, that occurs at the same time as the intervention, could be responsible for observed changes. The classes of alternative explanations for results of interventions were summarized in Chapter 11; each applies directly to the *A-B* design.

Thus, we can't automatically assume the changes were due to our efforts. The *A-B* design is very simple. In essence, all that it clearly reveals is that there has been a change in a given problem. If the intervention program is complex–that is, if it contains several techniques at the same time–the *A-B* design doesn't permit us to know which one or which combinations were more influential. Also, when focused only on a single problem, this design may not provide enough information on the event in question or on the related events that may be changing to provide a clear picture of the client/problem configuration. This is the reason why in Chapter 10 we suggested multiple measures of problems so as to capture a broad or holistic view of the significant dimensions of the client/situation. No one evaluation nor any finite set of evaluations can fully express the complexity of human lives. However, obtaining meaningful data on one event can lead the practitioner to think that he or she has a strong hold on the full picture, which may lead to a false sense of security.

A fundamental limitation on any design that has a baseline concerns the question of whether intervention has already begun once the practitioner begins to ask questions of the client. Hasn't there been an effect on the client already by his or her simply coming to someone for help? Won't the client think he or she is being "treated" when the practitioner asks pertinent questions? And won't the relationship inevitably have some effect on client functioning?

It is true that there may be detectable differences in the client's feelings, thoughts, or behaviors when he or she first comes to the practitioner. However, if we keep our focus on the client's specific problems rather than on nonrelated or nonspecific factors, then we may have another picture. The most important consideration is whether the target problem changes, and this requires a baseline perspective that may or may not be independent of talking with the practitioner. The client may feel better or more relieved to be in contact with a professional helper, and this even may be reflected in other situations, but whether this contact has fundamentally affected the target problem is the real issue. Moreover, the nonspecific effects of the baseline contacts probably will diminish over time as the novelty wears off and the hard work of solving problems emerges as the main task. Thus, as we noted in Chapter 12, the main issue is not whether there has been a change in the problem when comparing the reconstructed level of the problem prior to baseline with the baseline data. Rather, the key question is whether the level of the problem that *is* occurring during the baseline can be reduced further in the intervention period after a formal intervention plan is implemented. In other words, has the goal been attained and the problem removed?

Recommendations Regarding the *A-B* Design

There is a tendency among some practitioners and researchers to play down the *A-B* design because it doesn't permit the functional analyses about causality that more complex designs do permit. However, we take a strong stand with this key single-system design because it is basic, because it is fully within the reach of every practitioner with every client and problem, and because it provides a great deal of vital information to the practitioner.

In particular, the *A-B* design is most adaptable to the almost infinite variety of circumstances in which practitioners find themselves as a way of clearly indicating whether change in target problems has occurred. If used in addition to stimulate use of more rigorous designs that can tease out causal relationships, then the *A-B* design will have made a very important contribution. In comparison to the case study methods that easily fall into self-fulfilling prophecies, this key single-system design provides the basic foundation and the fundamental building block for a large array of logical ways of inferring causal efficacy of the intervention. We therefore recommend its use as the basic single-system design for practice.

Case Illustrations

The first illustration of an *A-B* design comes from a student case reported by Dean and Reinherz (1986) involving the treatment of depression in a dying patient using a psychoanalytic approach as intervention. The 53-year-old client was a patient on an oncology ward, and was receiving palliative care during the last stages of advanced metastatic ovarian cancer. The student chose supportive therapy to reduce the client's depression, to aid her in the process of "letting go," and to help her complete unfinished family business (finding a guardian for her 13-year-old daughter).

The data on depressive behavior in Figure 13.2 were collected from the student's process notes indicating the frequency of depressive behavior. Specifically, these included a content analysis of the process notes involving

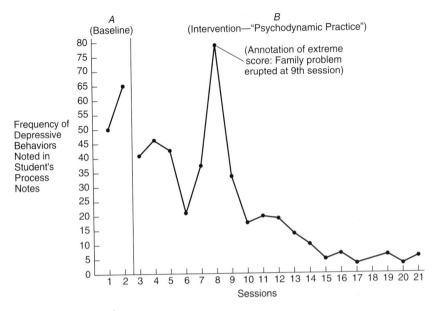

FIGURE 13.2   Frequency of depressive behavior of dying cancer patient.
(Adapted from "Psychodynamic Practice and Single-System Design: The Odd
Couple" by R. G. Dean and H. Reinherz, 1986, *Journal of Social Work
Education, 22*, p. 76.)

"statements of affect, statements reflecting actions taken, and recorded expressions of affect" (Dean and Reinherz, 1986, p. 76). The
authors note that the student made a reliability check of this content analysis in which another clinician reviewed 10% of the interviews; the interrater reliability showed 82%
agreement.

In the original article, Dean and Reinherz
also present parallel charts from the physician's and nurse's observations of the client's
level of depression. Apparently, a four-step rating scale was used, but details are not provided. There are clear parallels among the
three charts (the student social worker's, the
physician's, and the nurse's), including the annotated upsurge around the ninth session,
when a family problem erupted (the patient's
older son disagreed with his mother regarding
custody for the younger sister). Other charts
with similar results were reported dealing with
the frequency of "letting-go" behavior and
"comfort-with-death" statements indicating improvements according to the psychodynamic
frame of reference the student was using. (This

convergence of measures provides evidence of
"triangulation," i.e., agreement among several
measures such that the evidence that real
change occurred is bolstered.)

This study (and others presented by Dean
and Reinherz) are noteworthy for several
reasons. First, the student not only learned to
conduct good practice according to the psychodynamic model, but also was able to demonstrate the successful outcome of this case using
reasonable and accessible empirical evidence.
There are some limitations in this study, such
as the fact that only a brief baseline was obtained and the measures used were of unknown reliability and validity (with the exception noted above). Furthermore, since care
was provided by a variety of helping professionals, it is very difficult to distinguish the
unique contributions of any one practitioner.
(It might have been possible to address some
of these problems. For example, the student
might have reconstructed a baseline by using
the medical and psychiatric records to see
whether others had noted depressive expressions and behaviors.)

However, far more important is the fact that the student creatively adapted the evaluation model to the exigencies of the case situation. A baseline provides a reference point, and it is to some extent a judgment call to know when the point for comparison is reached, especially when a client's health is rapidly deteriorating. Any measurement tool has to be adapted to the client's capability and to the tolerance of the situation. Even though an *A-B* design cannot sort out the unique contributions of different members of a helping team, it can provide information on critical changes taking place. Thus, as we have stressed throughout this book, a creative adaptation to achieve some empirical evaluation of practice is an excellent beginning. We trust that once you have mastered the basic designs and procedures, you will go on to try more rigorous variations.

It is also important to note that this is one of many case examples we provide in this book of the usefulness of single-system designs involving interventions from a variety of different theoretical orientations. Just a few of many interesting examples in the literature, supporting this broad utility and refuting the myth that single-system designs are useful only in behavior modification, include Broxmeyer's (1978) psychodynamic analysis of an acting-out youth, Nelsen's (1978) use of an *A-B* design with a communication theory perspective, and Haynes's (1977) use of single-system designs within an ego psychology model. Tolson (1977) also presents studies involving the task-centered casework perspective; McCullough (1984) presents plans for the use of single-system designs in applied cognitive psychology; while Kolko and Milan (1983) use the existential approach in a study of paradoxical instructions. These examples support our claim that single-system designs are theory free–that is, that this evaluation methodology can be employed by a practitioner to test the interventions derived from almost any practice theory.

A most creative use of single-system designs was reported by Vera (1990). In this report, Vera used single-system designs to evaluate changes resulting from two divorce adjustment groups. A total of 11 clients in two groups were provided 10 weeks of semistructured treatment involving three components: (a) education,

(b) support, and (c) therapy. A number of measures were utilized, including the Generalized Contentment Scale, the Index of Self-Esteem, and the Index of Peer Relations. (All of these standardized measures are described in Chapter 7; they were developed by Hudson [1992] and each has excellent reliability and validity.) The author defined improvement in divorce adjustment as a positive change in the Index of Well-Being, a composite score obtained by averaging the scores of each client on the three scales noted above with lower scores equaling greater improvement. (This combining of scores is not a practice we can necessarily recommend, since this combination is of unknown reliability and validity.)

Although Vera states that she conducted a multiple baseline design in comparing the two groups, data in the article are presented on each of the 11 clients in a separate chart. Two of these charts were selected and adapted for presentation here, one for a client described as improved (Figure 13.3a) and one for a client described as having little or no improvement (Figure 13.3b).

As can be seen in Figure 13.3a, this client appeared to show a dramatic change from the baseline in which the client obviously was deteriorating to a dramatic turnaround and improvement during the intervention period. This improvement was generally maintained in the follow-up, although there is a slight trend in a negative direction. The second client, as shown in Figure 13.3b, shows almost no improvement, with data in both the intervention and follow-up phases closely paralleling the baseline.

A very interesting addition to this study was the fact that Vera also collected qualitative data from the screening interview and from information elicited in the group meetings. These data mainly focused on factors that could delay adjustment to divorce such as presence or absence of support, multiple losses, other life events, and so on. When these data were applied to these two cases, it was found that the client who improved had only one of these factors, while the client who did not improve had five, the most of all 11 clients. The addition of these qualitative data is an excellent example of concomitant variation, the idea that we can use single-system designs to compare

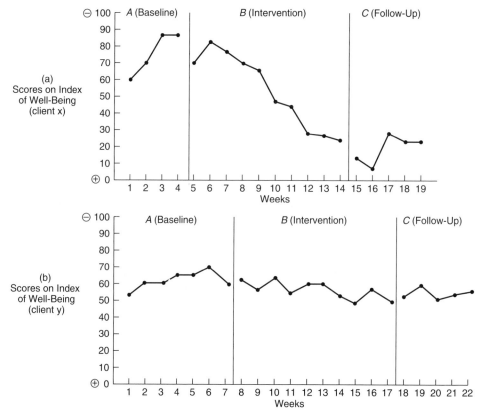

FIGURE 13.3   Changes in adjustment to divorce. Lower scores = more positive adjustment. (Adapted from "Effects of Divorce Groups on Individual Adjustment: A Multiple Methodology Approach" by M. I. Vera, 1990, *Social Work Research and Abstracts, 26,* pp. 10–20.)

changes in the measures we are using with changes that occur at the same time outside of the intervention proper to examine their potential effects on overall change.

The inclusion of the follow-up period, and the use of standardized measures, a group intervention program, and qualitative measures make this an excellent example for showing the potentials of single-system design. The relatively short length of the baseline for at least the first client (4 data points or 4 weeks) does impose some limitations on conclusions that can be drawn. But it should be pointed out, as noted in Chapter 7, that when using standardized measures as the only measure, there are some built-in limitations, since they typically are administered only once per week. Thus, it

is reasonable to assume that Vera did not think it wise or practical to delay beginning her intervention period only because of the use of standardized measures.

A recent evaluation illustrated the use of single-system procedures in an *A-B* design using systemic, brief, problem-solving therapy (Slonim-Nevo & Vosler, 1991). The client was a 41-year-old woman who sought help because of constant jealousy over the relationship that her husband had with his first wife. A 9-point individualized self-rating scale was used to assess the intensity of the obsession, with baseline ratings ranging between 7 and 8 (higher scores indicating more intense obsession). The client and practitioner agreed that resolution would be achieved when the problem was between a 2 and a 4 on the scale. The intervention plan involved use of paradoxical interventions, including reframing to define the attacks of jealousy as a mechanism to pursue "normal" fighting and to enable the couple to enjoy the process of making up. A prescription for three jealousy attacks per week was also given (prescribing the symptom).

As can be seen from the chart in Figure 13.4, in a brief time the ratings of jealousy had dropped to the point of satisfaction of the client, and stayed at the same level at a 6-month follow-up.

While the baseline in this case was rather short (three points) so that a clear trend could not be discerned, this case shows the flexibility and potential for use of single-system designs in brief, nonbehavioral practice.

King, Winett, and Lovett (1986) combine classical research designs with a single-system design to measure the effect of training in coping skills among women from dual-earner families. Two interventions were used to aid coping skills in a study involving four groups: (a) a time-management training program and (b) a social support group, as well as (c) a combina-

tion of interventions 1 and 2, along with (d) a fourth group acting as a delayed-treatment control. That is, this fourth group waited for 4 weeks (after the study was finished), and then they were offered the combined program. Three months after the conclusion of the study, there was a telephone follow-up interview.

At baseline, there was no significant difference among the four groups on the target behavior, the mean number of minutes members of the group spent in high priority activities (i.e., whatever was pleasing to the individual involved, averaged over all of the individuals in a group). King et al. (1986) are mainly concerned with the experimental/control group design, but since they also use an *A-B* design, we can use this case to illustrate the blending of both classical and single-system designs.

Figure 13.5 shows data adapted from the King et al. (1986) study. Notice the pattern of changes in the four groups during intervention, *B*, and what happens at follow-up. The control group continues its poor baseline pattern during the *B* phase, but after receiving the delayed intervention, does well at follow-up, comparing favorably with the other three groups. If it had continued to do poorly, this would have cast doubt on the intervention program. It is unfortunate that the baseline was so short in this study, since that adds severe limitations to the analysis of change. On the other hand, the addition of the control group, the lack of change for that group in the intervention period, and then the dramatic improvement in the follow-up period after intervention is applied add considerable weight to the notion that the intervention produced the observed changes.

Another example of an *A-B* design is provided by McSweeny's (1978) study of the effects of charging 20 cents for local directory assistance for telephone callers in Cincinnati. This study has several interesting variations that we wish to call to your attention. First, the time span extended over a 14-year period. Second, a million callers were involved in the *A-B* study, all treated as a single system of persons involved in using or not using directory assistance. Third, parallel data were presented on long-distance directory-assistance calls for which additional charges were not made.

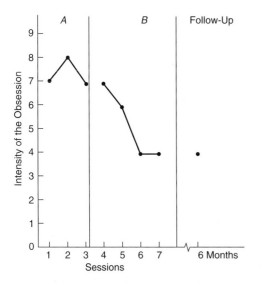

FIGURE 13.4   Design using a brief paradoxical therapy for jealousy. (Adapted from "The Use of Single-System Design with Systemic Brief Problem-Solving Therapy" by V. Slonim-Nevo and N. R. Vosler, 1991, *Families in Society, 72,* pp. 38–44.)

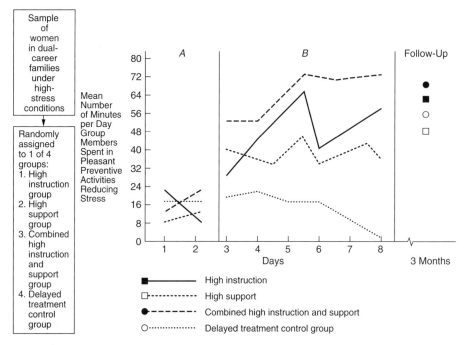

FIGURE 13.5   Combined experimental-control group design using an *A-B-Follow-Up* design. (Adapted from "Enhancing Coping Behaviors in At-Risk Populations: The Effects of Time-Management Instruction and Social Support in Women from Dual-Earner Families" by A. C. King, R. A. Winett, and S. B. Lovett, 1986, *Behavior Therapy, 17,* pp. 57–66.)

McSweeny's graph of these data indicate a remarkable drop–some 60,000 fewer calls per day after the charge was introduced. Since the long-distance directory-assistance calls continue on their preintervention trend while the local directory-assistance calls drop, the author has, in effect, two *A-B* designs whose joint pattern provides a very tentative logical basis for making a causal inference, a point to which we will return in Chapter 15. But we point to this study as an example of *A-B* designs aggregating the responses of large numbers of people (cf. Campbell, 1969).

In each of these examples of *A-B* designs, a baseline period was identified using various types of measures. Then an intervention period was begun, again varying in the number and type of specific actions taken to affect the behavior, feelings, activities, or thoughts of the clients or target persons. Data ranging from one person to a large aggregated group of per-

sons (the million people who potentially might use the local directory-assistance service in Cincinnati) were used in making comparisons between baseline and intervention. Changes were observed in each example, and some observations were made about presumed causality. However, to be more conservative in the use of these evaluation tools, we would have to caution that the safest interpretation is that changes clearly did occur, but that conclusions about causality (why did the changes occur?) cannot be made unequivocally without use of more powerful designs. Yet for practitioners and decision makers these kinds of data are often used as the basis for policy or program changes. This is a risk that should be understood clearly. If such data are used as the basis of continuing hypotheses that will be tested in further action, then this may be a satisfactory solution until stronger tests may be conducted.

Aggregating *A-B* Designs

It is possible to develop causal clues by aggregating the results of several *A-B* designs. One illustration that expands on the basic *A-B* design is shown by the work of Levy and Bavendam (1995) in the field of women's health issues, a woefully neglected area of study. They present five individual cases concerning theory-guided pamphlets developed to enable women's self-care regarding urologic problems (a frequent-urgency syndrome). All cases involve an *A-B* design, and thus no causal inferences on the individual cases can be made with regard to the effectiveness of the treatment. Three of the five cases appear to have successful results, while two showed no change, although one of these showed a reduction in feelings of urgency.

What can we learn from the aggregate of cases, as contrasted to individual cases? Levy and Bavendam (1995, p. 436) suggest that we have "...useful clues for further intervention design and development. In particular, this type of intensive research permits the investigation of possible factors operating for subjects for whom change was not as evident." It turns out that two women who reported no change in frequency stated in the exit interview that they did not follow the major recommendation in the pamphlet. So, while pamphlets may be useful for some clients, others may need a more intense intervention. The next step is to tease out who needs intensive discussions and who will benefit fully by a well-written pamphlet.

Jensen (1994) presents a study of psychosocial treatment of depression in nine women, using *A-B* designs, not a multiple baseline design as the author suggests, based on the fact that she used randomly assigned 3-, 4-, or 5-week baselines. Her methods of assignment and implementation of intervention do not fit the technical definition of multiple baseline designs, as we describe in Chapter 15. Therefore, each design has to be considered individually. Yet, since they all concern a common problem (depression), the author rightly seeks to find whatever pattern there is beyond the outcomes of the separate cases. In general, all nine clients with moderate to severe depression scores in baseline change to mild or asymptomatic levels by the end of the 11- to 13-week contact time.

As Jensen suggests, it may be possible to build on these findings (that are in conformity with prior research she describes) to scale down or add to the intervention such that positive changes occur. When a change occurs, we know we have (or have lost) a major component of the intervention that may be a possible cause of the results. (Clearer answers to this question require more powerful designs, which we will discuss in Chapters 14, 15, and 16.)

An Elaboration of the *A-B* Design: The Repeated Preintervention–Postintervention Design

An interesting variation of the *A-B* design, suggested by Thyer and Curtis (1983), is termed the *repeated preintervention–postintervention design*. (In the original reference, this design was called the *repeated pretest-posttest design*.) In this design, measures are taken on the client's targeted behaviors immediately before and immediately after *each* treatment session, as opposed to any other temporal arrangement such as on a daily basis. This design is to be used only with targets that may be expected to change immediately following an intervention session, such as in the case described below, the desensitization of phobias. Since only the amount of time of the session separates the before and after measures, Thyer and Curtis (1983) assert that threats to internal validity are somewhat reduced. Presumably, each treatment session should show the client's behavior improving from before to after the treatment period. There should also be progressive improvement on the sets of data between sessions.

An example on the lugubrious side may help to clarify this design. Thyer and Curtis (1983) present a case of a 26-year-old woman who developed an extreme fear of frogs brought on by a traumatic incident in which she suddenly ran over a group of frogs as she was mowing the lawn, spewing bloody pieces all over. In the spirit of the regular *A-B* design, the practitioner took a preintervention measure, consisting of a series of measures of anxiety relating to how close a frog was moved toward her. So, for example, measures of anxiety were taken when the frog was 15 feet away from the client; again, when the frog was 10 feet away; and so on, until the client touched the frog. As can be seen in the top of Figure 13.6, the client was more anxious the closer the frog was brought to her before her treatment session began (blank circles and squares on the chart). Anxiety was measured in two ways. The practitioner had the client rate her anxiety level using an individualized rating scale called subjective units of disturbance scale

(SUDS) (Wolpe, 1973); they also measured her pulse rate.

A treatment session was given involving regular desensitization methods (Thyer, 1983). Then immediately after this treatment, the practitioner had the client again measure her anxiety to a frog at gradually decreasing distances to her. The graphs of Figure 13.6

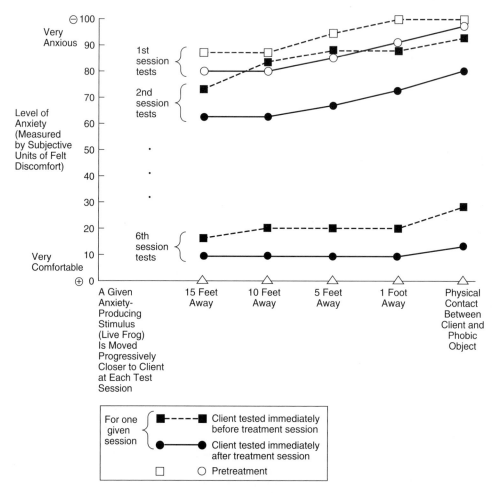

FIGURE 13.6   The repeated preintervention–postintervention design. This chart depicts patterns of client responses to one specific target immediately before and immediately after a given treatment session. A trend toward improvement is seen both in the before and the after pattern within each session. There is also consecutive improvement across sessions. (Hypothetical data adapted from "The Repeated Pretest-Posttest Single-Subject Experiment: A New Design for Empirical Clinical Practice" by B. A. Thyer and C. G. Curtis, 1983, *Journal of Behavior Therapy and Experimental Psychiatry, 14,* pp. 311–315.)

represent the pairs of data before and after each session—hence the label of a repeated preintervention–postintervention design.

Over the six sessions of the treatment contract, the SUDS for close contact with the frog was greatly reduced—that is, her subjective experience of anxiety was lowered. Her pulse rate was lower and steadier, reflecting an inner calm rather than her former anxious state. A telephone follow-up 5 months later revealed satisfactory maintenance of these improvements and the absence of any other functional limitation in her behavior.

Several observations can be made about this case example. First, in its measurement strategy, this design bears some similarity to the alternating intervention design described in Chapter 17. However, since the alternating intervention design compares *two interventions* and the repeated preinterventions–postinterventions design doesn't have that purpose, dealing with only one intervention, it appears to be a closer relative of the *A-B* design. Second, patterns of data are being compared (the before-and-after of a given session pattern, plus the patterns of these pairs of changes over the six treatment sessions). Tests of statistical significance (such as described in Chapter 22) would not likely be used in such a case. There is a broad consistency in positive changes seen within each of the six sessions and across the six sessions (even though the client sometimes seems to backtrack a little despite the fact she had progressed in the prior session). Such qualitative comparisons of patterns would ordinarily be analyzed by visual methods (see Chapter 20), or visual methods combined with descriptive statistics (see Chapter 21).

The same design could be used with targets that had only one measure before and after a given session. So long as there was a measurable drop within each session, and the decreasing problem behavior was maintained over all of the sessions, one could draw conclusions about the nature of the change in the target condition. The first before-session measure would constitute the primary baseline, and each before-session measure would be a comparison point for the after-session measure. Rather than obtaining a number of baseline data points,

what one obtains in this design is one true baseline data point (the initial treatment session), and then comparison points are obtained in each succeeding session. The logical basis for inferring that a real difference in before and after measures has occurred rests with the before-and-after data for each session, along with the pairs of session data across consecutive treatment sessions. These changes would constitute an example of "unlikely successive coincidences." Logically, such changes are unlikely to happen by chance alone, thus adding to the inference that these positive outcomes possibly were caused, in part, by the intervention. We discuss other designs in the following chapters that deal with such inferences about the practitioner's role in causing the observed outcomes. But, for the time being, recognize that this repeated preintervention–postintervention design is logically somewhat more powerful than the basic *A-B* design.

Because of the experimental (in the sense of "new") nature of this design, and its restricted usage (only to those situations where the target is likely to be changed appreciably within each treatment session), we will forgo our usual format of identifying strengths, limitations, and recommendations of a design, and simply recommend consideration of this new approach to evaluation of practice situations. We believe that this design is important for two other reasons. First, it illustrates the flexibility of even the most basic single-system designs. And second, it introduces a kind of analysis by observable patterns that is a variation on the typical methods of visual analysis, and thus may be more satisfying to those who seek holistic measures to bolster their analyses.

Citing the work of Thyer and Curtis (1983) that we just described as a model for their measurement procedures, Secret and Bloom (1994) made use of a modified version of the *A-B* design to evaluate a self-help approach with a phobic child who had been deathly afraid of dogs for several years. Because it was not possible for the practitioner to be with the child during times when she was staying with a babysitter who had a large dog—and no other alternatives were feasible for the parents—the practitioner arranged for the 9-year-old child to help herself learn to master the phobia by means of a contextual therapy model (Zane, 1978)–a kind of combined cognitive, affective, and environmental approach.

The practitioner helped the little girl to identify a hierarchy of seven specific dog fears, from being in the same room with a dog, to having a dog jump on her. Baseline measures consisted of the child's rating of all seven of these fears each day for a week when she was at the babysitter's home. Data show high levels of fear for the three most stressful items, and a middle level of fear for the other four, less stressful items.

The intervention consisted of the child's making statements to herself regarding the following: (1) to be aware of her fears by rating them, (2) to stay with the dog as long as she could, even though she was afraid, and (3) to tell herself that she was doing well, even though she was afraid. Data show a drop to zero of the middle-level fear items, and rapid changes to zero of the most stressful items (except for having a dog jump on the little girl). These dramatic changes took place within six intervention sessions. (The babysitting arrangement was canceled at that time because of a change in the mother's employment status.) These data are graphed in Figure 13.7. Follow-ups (taking the child back to the sitter's house and its large dog, and observing the child's behavior) at one month, four months, and one year later showed consistent positive results.

We are naturally curious about these rapid improvements, even though the authors point to other rapid improvements in the literature (e.g.,

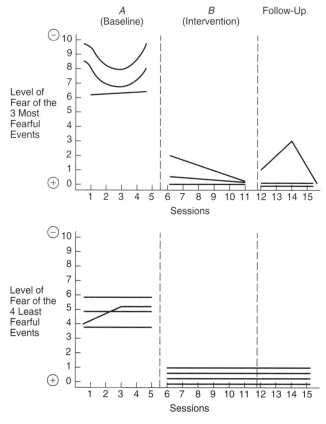

FIGURE 13.7 Profile analysis of a child's pattern of dog phobia as measured by the Dog Rating Scale. (Adapted from Secret & Bloom, 1994, with simplified graphed data.)

MacDonald, 1975). The child was eager to get over the phobia, and perhaps received unintended modeling when she observed the sitter's son grooming the dog. Yet, her prior phobic reactions were extreme and long lasting. The authors assert that the internal pattern of changes may supply a different form of logical basis for inferring causality. That pattern is maintained in baseline, during intervention, and in the several follow-ups. They describe this approach as a profile analysis, building on the earlier work of Thyer and Curtis (1983), who used another form of profile analysis, as described previously. In this case, a set of phobic items are viewed as a group that would logically change at about the same rate. In this way, we can see several nuances of the same target change all at once.

This case illustration shows how practitioners use ideas taken from the literature to develop innovative forms of practice and evaluation.

Introducing the Client to the Basic Single-System Design

Earlier in this chapter, we presented some basic points on introducing the notion of evaluation to clients or others involved in the problem/situation. We now want to add to that discussion the unique aspects of the *A-B* design that clients and others should understand. In addition to stating that you want to understand the client's situation clearly, that you need clear

facts to be most helpful, and that you will share your understanding of these facts with the client, we suggested that you indicate that fact gathering helps the practitioner to build a plan of action and modify it as needed.

Beginning with this last point we recommend that, for the *A-B* design, you add that, "some portion of the fact gathering will continue throughout our contacts together, not only while we're trying to assess the situation, but even during the intervention period in order to have, as it were, a continuing record of the pulse of the situation." Tell the participants that knowing exactly how much progress is being made or is not being made helps you decide what steps to take and what steps may need changing over time.

In addition, depending on how you practice, it may be useful to *train the client* to be aware of these clear indicators of the problem or of goal attainment so that he or she can continue the monitoring after intervention is terminated: "If you (the client or mediator) are aware of an emerging problem, you might be able to handle it before it gets too serious. So part of my (the practitioner's) job will be to help you monitor your own situation so as to be on the lookout for growing problems."

On all occasions be ready, willing, and able to share progress reports and answer questions about how you are using these data for monitoring and evaluation.

SUMMARY

This chapter introduced several arrangements for evaluating work with clients, from observation only, *A*, to intervention only, (*B*), to the case study, *B*, in which intervention and observational assessment occur simultaneously. We also discussed variations on the case study, as when additional interventions are joined to the first intervention, *B-C*. The strengths, limitations, and recommendations regarding case studies were presented along with some guidelines for introducing the idea of evaluation to clients.

In essence, however, the focus of this chapter has been on the *A-B* design, the basic single-system design, with its many potentials for service to nearly all practitioners in almost all conceivable situations. This design, the first of the planned arrangement of baseline and intervention phases, clearly provides information on whether the client target problems changed. This can lead to the formulation of other hypotheses regarding causal elements that can be tested with other designs. We noted the strengths and limitations of the *A-B* design, and concluded with our strong recommendation that this be the minimum design used with every case or situation. We also presented an elaboration of the *A-B* design, the repeated preintervention–postintervention design showing how it might be used creatively in special contexts.

THE EXPERIMENTAL SINGLE-SYSTEM DESIGNS:
A-B-A, A-B-A-B, B-A-B

PURPOSE: This chapter introduces a set of single-system designs that add a form of experimental control to the evaluation, in which an intervention is introduced and then removed in order to study causal effects. These designs are among the most powerful of the single-system approaches, but they raise difficult ethical and practical issues. Thus, the aim of this chapter is to provide an understanding of their strengths and limitations so that you can make wise choices regarding their use. ■

Introduction
Why Would a Practitioner Use an
   Experimental Design?
When Should an Intervention
   Be Removed?
Basic Experimental Designs
Experimental Removal of Intervention
   Design: A-B-A $\boxed{A \mid B \mid A}$
   Strengths of the A-B-A Design
   Limitations of the A-B-A Design
   Recommendations Regarding the
      A-B-A Design
   Case Illustrations
   Introducing the Client to the
      A-B-A Design
Experimental Replication
   Design: A-B-A-B $\boxed{A \mid B \mid A \mid B}$
   Strengths of the A-B-A-B Design
   Limitations of the A-B-A-B Design

Recommendations Regarding the A-B-A-B
      Design
   Case Illustrations
   Introducing the Client to the A-B-A-B Design
Experimental Repeat of Intervention
   Design: B-A-B $\boxed{B \mid A \mid B}$
   Strengths of the B-A-B Design
   Limitations of the B-A-B Design
   Recommendations Regarding the B-A-B Design
   Case Illustrations
   Introducing the Client to the B-A-B Design
Summary

INTRODUCTION

The notation of evaluation designs used in this book illustrates how complex designs are additive versions of more elementary ones. In Chapter 13 we discussed the basic components of evaluation designs–the *A* phase, involving observation or data collection only, and the *B* phase, introducing some intervention while continuing the data collection. We then combined these phases in a certain order, *A-B,* so as to benefit from the logical possibility of comparing a before picture with the events during and after the intervention. In the present chapter, and in those to follow, we continue to add *A* phases and *B* phases (or other interventions–*C, D,* etc.) in various orders and arrangements to benefit from other logical possibilities in understanding causal relationships. Such understanding is at the heart of effective practice because it contributes to our knowledge about what interventions work with what problems.

We suggested earlier that practitioners interacting with clients generate designs naturally in the course of assessing the problems and strengths in the clients' situations, making plans aimed at helping clients attain their goals and then observing during the intervention period what effects the services seem to be having on them. By abstracting and generalizing from these common experiences it is possible to identify types of evaluation designs with various logical strengths and limitations derived from the properties of the designs themselves.

However, the group of designs discussed in this chapter appears to have a somewhat different origin from some of the other designs, stemming more from the experimental laboratory than from the clinic or the community action center. The emphasis of the laboratory is on experimental control over as many factors as possible in determining causal relationships among events. In the everyday world the practitioner often does not have such control over clients or events, and indeed, this control may be counterproductive when the practitioner seeks to have clients assert effective control over their own lives. However, if we are to understand causal relationships in order to make effective practice decisions, at times we may need to use some of the evaluation designs that provide this relatively rigorous information.

Consider this commonplace situation: A client has come for assistance, receives it, and the service is terminated when the problem is apparently resolved. Occasionally, the practitioner makes a further contact to ask how things are going. If all is well, that's fine. If not, perhaps a social or psychological booster shot (more *B*) is given, or possibly a new intervention (*C*) is implemented, until the practitioner and client are once again content with a stable problem resolution. We submit that this informal follow-up, with or without booster shots, is the basis of the following evaluation designs insofar as they ask the question: What happens after the (first) intervention is terminated? This question implies not only an interest in whether target events change, but whether the intervention produced stable changes, and, ultimately and most critically, what caused those changes. Causal knowledge is fundamentally useful in effective practice with a given client and also when working with other, similar clients.

We have labeled each of the designs in this chapter as "experimental." But don't emphasize this label too strongly, as all designs imply some degree of experimental arrangement of events in nature. What we wish to stress here is that by design a practitioner may wish to terminate an intervention *and* return to the nonintervention/observation period as a planned way of understanding the causal efficacy of the intervention. The underlying assumption is that if some event (the problem) changes with the introduction of a new condition (the intervention) and then changes back to its original state upon removal of that condition, then that condition may logically be inferred to be causally related to that change.

As a whole, these designs are called *experimental removal* designs. The essence of experimental removal designs is the search for patterns in the data that correspond to changes in the phases of the design. Once the data are collected and charted, you can examine them to see if there are changes that are related to the onset and removal of intervention, and conversely, to the beginning and end of non-intervention (the baseline periods). The fact that changes in these patterns of data do correspond to the specific phases of the design provides the basic evidence for inferring causality. You can actually examine the data to see the ways in which your intervention did or did not affect the problem all along, from the initial contact with the client to the very last contact. In Chapter 11, we call this the "principle of unlikely successive coincidences," in that if the problem is seen to change in a positive direction only during the intervention periods, and reassert itself only during the nonintervention periods, this covariation is unlikely to be a coincidence; hence, a causal inference seems reasonable.

The question is, under what conditions is it appropriate to purchase the causal knowledge at the price of having to remove a successful intervention? Answers to this question are presented in this chapter in the form of a series of designs, together with a discussion of their strengths and limitations.

Why Would a Practitioner Use an Experimental Design?

The introduction of an intervention and then its removal after it has achieved some level of desired change are not typical procedures among practitioners, although widely used in laboratory studies. Why then would you ever want to remove a successful intervention, and is it ethical to do so? The major answer to this question is that you would remove an intervention when it becomes important to know whether what you did appeared to cause the target problem to change, and when such removal would not have a serious negative effect on both overall problem resolution and client feelings, behaviors, and interactions with others. And as always, in all practice situations, when you believe a procedure violates your personal or professional ethics, we urge you to consider other options.

There are a number of occasions when causal information would be most helpful, and possibly essential to obtain. For example, if you worked in a large institution that had numerous clients with the same set of presenting problems, it would be useful to develop the technology—that is, the techniques of practice—that would reliably produce effective outcomes. What technology is building for this institutional setting is also useful information for the professions at large; it clarifies the scope and limitations of given techniques with certain classes of clients. Helping professions develop skills and show themselves accountable to the extent that effective technology is generated.

Another reason for needing causal information is that individual practitioners learn an array of approaches and techniques in their educational programs. While they can perform these intervention methods, they may not know with which methods they are most adept. Therefore, by demonstrating the functional link between interventions and outcomes in specific cases, you can learn how you can serve clients more effectively—by using tools with which you are most skilled and by learning more about those with which you are not.

An additional reason for wanting to provide causal information has to do with the motivations of the users of the design. Let's say you have trained a rather dubious nursing staff to implement a particular intervention with their patients on their ward. They go along with the program but don't really feel committed to participating. What could be more motivating to a person than to show through the power of one of these designs the causal relationships between their intervention and positive changes in the problem? Once we can clearly establish for people—clients or relevant others—that what they are doing really *is* having a desired effect, we will have gone a long way toward encouraging their participation in the program.

When Should an Intervention Be Removed?

Some of the terms discussed in Chapter 11 are particularly applicable to experimental designs. These are *withdrawal* and *reversal,* the two types of removal procedures. With both types the removal procedures constitute a new phase following the intervention phase; the new phase is labeled A (remember, we are trying to "reconstitute" the baseline) or A_2 to distinguish it from A_1, the first baseline. *With-*

drawal refers simply to not applying (or removing) the intervention altogether, in the hope of returning to the original baseline (nonintervention) conditions. *Reversal* refers to removing the intervention from the original target problem (say, e.g., crying), but applying it to another target problem. The second target problem can be either a polar opposite of the original (e.g., laughing—one can't laugh and cry at the same time), or it could be any other target problem; at the same time, except for continuing to record, the original target problem (the crying) is ignored. The advantage of the reversal design is that intervention can be continued, but is simply applied to a different problem. With both removal designs, though, the goal is to see whether the target problem changes toward its preintervention state when intervention is removed; if it does, then you are demonstrating "experimental control" over the problem, that is, providing evidence of a causal relationship between application of the intervention and changes in the problem.

There are some intervention procedures that are obviously more difficult to remove than others. We described these as *irreversible* in Chapter 11. For those that are impossible to remove—for example, instructions to the client that cannot be reversed—you will have to consider other than an experimental design (e.g., multiple baseline designs, which we will discuss in the next chapter). For other interventions—for example, techniques where the client already has been given instructions on what to do and/or already has begun practicing—you may, first, just ask the client not to practice what he or she has been taught, and/or second, discontinue your instruction, help, and support with regard to that specific technique. In these situations, even though the client may remember the instructions, simply not practicing them may be a sufficient removal. In fact, treating all cases as a practice "experiment" as we suggested in Chapter 1 allows you to explore the potentialities and limitations of any practice and evaluation procedures. What doesn't work need not be used.

Of course, the mere fact that you remove and then reinstate your intervention, obtaining clear sequential changes across the problem, does not *prove* that it was your specific techniques affecting the problem. It is still possible that some subtle (or not so subtle) alteration in other influences (e.g., the differential way you or others such as mediators attend to the client concurrent with each phase) also may be producing the change. That is, sequential changes in the problem according to whether you apply or remove your intervention does not prove that the techniques themselves are causing the change. This is so even though it may be, in fact, some part of the intervention proper that is producing the changes. However, we are speaking here about inferences and degree of inferences. When your clear and specific interventions are chosen for the very reason that they are likely to affect the problem, then the probability that the causal inference is correct is increased. In the final result, however, as we suggested in Chapter 11, the conclusion about ultimate causality may have to await the results of several replications, thereby increasing both internal and external validity.

Actually, there are two types of removal designs. The first, and the one we've discussed most extensively, is the *planned* removal. This is where the practitioner plans to remove and then reimplement intervention in order to look for a causal relationship.

The second type of removal design might be called accidental or *unplanned* removal. In cases such as these, for one reason or another (e.g., illness or vacation), the intervention plan cannot be implemented for a brief period. If you are lucky, or if you have informed participants in advance, the recorder will continue to collect data. This will give you a built-in removal period in that you will be able to have a fairly systematic look at what happens to the problem during this unplanned removal period. Then, the intervention can be reimplemented, if needed.

However, even if data are not being collected during the removal period, you may be able to get some notion of changes in the target when the intervention is not being applied. This can be through feedback from the client (reconstructing his or her impressions of what happened) or through reviewing the data once recording begins again.

In both of the above cases we recommended that you use this information as though it were a removal, but with caution, since the unplanned nature of the removal may make the information difficult to compare with earlier phases. At any rate, the unplanned removal may give you not only information that allows you very tentatively to infer causality (did the problem change during the unplanned removal and change again once intervention was reimplemented?), but also information about what may be helpful in planning subsequent phases of intervention and termination.

But the question remains: When should an intervention be removed? Actually such removal is multidetermined, by environmental factors such as time limitations imposed by the treatment setting; the limits of resources available; the finite patience and cooperation of the staff (especially those in institutional settings); predictions from the literature as to when an intervention would be likely to have an effect on a given problem; and most importantly, the degree of harm that may befall a client or others in such a setting (Barlow & Hersen, 1984). In particular, *if it seems likely that some degree of harm may come to the client or to others by removing an intervention program, this would be a major sign that removal would not be appropriate* and that other designs (e.g., multiple baseline designs discussed in Chapter 15) should be substituted (see also Chapter 25 on ethics in single-system designs).

Additional considerations regarding removal of an intervention are related to the design itself. We have discussed some of these issues in Chapter 11 on phases and length of phases, but it bears repeating that the major factor regarding determining when to change phases (including intervention phases) is the semblance of stability in the data. There is no easy formula for what constitutes stability of data. However, when it appears as though some stability in the data in the intervention phase suggests the intervention has begun to have a positive effect, say for at least 3 consecutive data points, then you might consider the possibility of removing the intervention to examine causal effects. It's also a good idea to try to remember to keep the first intervention period as short as possible when you are considering a removal. This will give the changes less time to become irreversible, a point to which

we will return later in this chapter in the discussion of carryover effects. Finally we also recommend using some simple methods of analysis (discussed in Part IV) to get an approximation of when the set of intervention data are different, visually and/or statistically, from the baseline data and to determine that the pattern of data points in the intervention phase does not vary irregularly. Then, at that point, you can make the decision about removing the intervention.

BASIC EXPERIMENTAL DESIGNS

Experimental Removal of Intervention Design: A-B-A $\quad$ |A|B|A|

The first two phases of the *A-B-A* design are exactly like those of the *A-B* design discussed in Chapter 13. The logical comparison that is possible in the *A-B* design is possible also between these two phases (*A* and *B*) in the *A-B-A* design. In the present design, however, the practitioner decides to return to baseline conditions, the second *A* phase in the *A-B-A*. Now two adjacent comparisons are possible–between the first baseline and the intervention, and between the intervention and the second baseline. The underlying assumption is that if the intervention is really the causal ingredient, then by removing it the target should return to the way it was before that intervention. An ideal example is a dark room (baseline condition), the turning on of a light switch (intervention creating light), followed by the turning off of the light switch (return to a dark room). Of course, it is not as simple as this to "turn off" human behaviors following an intervention, a point to which we return shortly.

The critical feature of the *A-B-A* design is the second *A,* which changes a basic *A-B* design (A_2) into an experiment. The experiment consists of testing whether the introduction of the intervention is likely to have caused changes in the observed target behavior. The clearest way to test this idea with a given set of client and environmental factors is to take away the successful intervention and to see whether the target changes as it would if the cause of the improved behavior (the intervention) were removed. The second *A* is, in a sense, analogous to a follow-up, but differs in that the second *A* is obtained while the practitioner still has contact with the client, while follow-up occurs after termination. The practitioner then can choose to terminate or go into a second intervention phase, which then constitutes another experimental design which will be discussed shortly.

As always, it may be necessary to move into a maintenance phase with the successful *A-B-A* design. This is a halfway stage between an *A-B-A-B* and the *A-B-A* design. It requires the practitioner to return to a service phase in the sense of teaching the client new skills–namely, to maintain the successful activities identified in the *B* phase.

An example of the withdrawal *A-B-A* is given in the classic experiment by Ayllon (1963) in which a psychiatric patient hospitalized 9 years had collected large numbers of towels and stored them in her room. There had been several unsuccessful attempts to change this behavior, which was viewed by many staff members as reflecting an unconscious need for love and security. Ayllon began his work by taking a baseline count of the number of towels in the patient's room when she wasn't there. Then, the intervention was to have the staff people give her towels–between 7 and 60 a day–to reach a satiation point. This was achieved in several weeks when she had 625 towels hoarded in her room. At that point in the intervention period she herself started to take towels out of her room. The researcher returned to baseline conditions–the usual allotment of towels dispensed in the regular way was reinstituted–and data showed that the patient went to an average of 1.5 towels in her room per week. This rate was maintained during a year of follow-up observations, contrary to predictions from the psychiatric staff at the hospital.

The *A-B-A* design raises an important question, that of maintenance of interventive effect. Presumably, the *B* phase of this design saw the client attain some stable and desired form of behavior. (In the case of the satiated patient the turning point was when she began to remove towels herself rather than hoarding them as she had for 9 years.) Therefore, removing the intervention can show whether the client's performance was learned (i.e., whether it became a relatively stable part of the client's behaviors). With the hoarding patient, the learning appears to have been effective.

Strengths of the A-B-A Design.   The added comparisons derived from the removal of the intervention offer stronger bases of inferring causality than in the basic single-system design, the *A-B*. The practitioner now has two points of logical comparison as contrasted to one in the *A-B* design. Given the fact that the successful intervention is purposely removed in order to observe its effects–namely, whether the target problems also change in the direction they were before intervention–this provides an experimental manipulation of the independent variable in order to identify causal factors.

Moreover, if the practitioner replicates this design with other client problems, the effect is cumulative with regard to causal inferences. To clarify this point, suppose that more than one target problem for a given client increases upon intervention and decreases upon its removal. For each separate target event the intervention appears to be causally involved. However, this inference receives added weight when the set of interrelated predictions are supported, since it is increasingly unlikely that every target in the set would have changed in that same direction by chance alone. A network or system of results provides more information than the sum of its constituent results, since new predictions can be derived more readily from a network of events than from a single event.

Limitations of the A-B-A Design.   The major limitation of the *A-B-A* design stems from the practice concern about ending contact on a nonintervention phase, having removed the successful intervention. If the intervention is in fact a causal factor, then presumably the target problem has returned to near the preintervention level (the baseline phase), which is to say, to some problematic level that led the client to seek help (or receive it) in the first place. (The exception to this statement occurs with techniques such as satiation, as discussed above, or when the intervention produces irreversible changes.) Regardless of how much information is obtained about causality, helping professionals would have a very difficult time accepting this design if it violated the most basic axiom of helping: Do no harm. Returning a client to a problematic state after having resolved that state may appear to practitioners to be doing harm.

However, all interventions end, and one might consider the termination period of intervention in general to be a type of *A* phase, as long as follow-up observations are made. Therefore, one approach to having an *A-B-A* design without this ethical and practice concern is to use an *A-B* design and have an extended follow-up analogous to the second *A* phase. That is, the second *A* phase can be viewed as simply follow-up with continual monitoring of the problem. Then, intervention can be reimplemented if necessary.

There are also alternative explanations (described in Chapter 11) that are especially pertinent to this design. For example, consider sequential confounding–events in the final observation period may not be the same as in the first observation period, since there may be carryover from the intervening period. Carryover is an important problem for all multistage intervention programs. As we discussed above, it is difficult to reinstate any given set of social forces, and in the case of irreversible events such as new learned behaviors, it may be impossible to reinstate even a similar set of forces. Generally speaking, what people learn cannot always be removed simply by ceasing to teach that piece of information or skill. Solutions to this dilemma require use of more sophisticated designs as discussed in subsequent chapters, wherein variations of intervention are deliberately counterbalanced so that carryover effects of particular arrangements are controlled in the design. (We will discuss further effects of carryover in relation to the next design, the *A-B-A-B*.)

Another practical limitation of the *A-B-A* design is in communicating it to the client. How do you tell a client that you are removing the intervention after attaining the desired goal? We will discuss this issue in the section on introducing the client to this design, but we note it here because use of this design could take on the flavor of having a client as a "guinea pig" in

an experiment. Moreover, the recipient of services, at least on the surface, may not appear to stand to benefit directly or obviously from the removal of the intervention.

Recommendations Regarding the A-B-A Design. We do not recommend this design for most practice situations and refer the user to any of the other single-system designs discussed in this and later chapters that can accomplish the same logical analysis as this one but that do not have such a steep price to pay for attaining this logical advantage. If this design were used with a client on one part of his or her problems while maintaining contact because of others, then the *A-B-A* design might be used within a cluster of other designs (see Kirchner et al., 1980, who employ an *A-B-A* design within an overall multiple baseline design, a study that is discussed in more detail in Chapter 15).

Also, for situations in which the case terminates after an *A-B* design, it would be good practice (and good evaluation) to have follow-up observations on a planned basis to assess whether the intervention was sustained after contact with the practitioner. However, in general, since there are other ways of obtaining the kind of information the *A-B-A* design offers, we cannot recommend it under ordinary circumstances.

Case Illustrations. In a recent report, Ludwig and Geller (1999) present one study from the literature on organizational behavior in a series of investigations on the promotion of safe driving among pizza deliverers, using a rare *A-B-A* design with a non-equivalent control group. As these authors note, the pizza delivery business is a dangerous occupation, with a driving accident rate three times the national average. This is probably due to the fact that the majority of pizza drivers are inexperienced drivers (ages 16 to 25), driving at the riskiest time periods (between 5 P.M. and 2 A.M.) who are compensated with commissions based on the frequency of pizzas deliveries.

Ludwig and Geller (1999) distinguished between the target of an intervention and the agent of change. Most of the time, researchers are the intervention agents, but in this study, the agents of change were the pizza deliverers themselves, and they also were the targets of change. Prior research by these authors showed that the driving behavior of pizza deliverers could be dramatically improved by a driving safety awareness program, using seat belts, and making a personal commitment to buckle-up. Other research suggested that response generalization could occur, that is, an improvement in another area would occur similar to the targeted behavior.

In the current study, the pizza deliverers were involved in promoting a community safe-driving practice (i.e., the use of seat belts) being sponsored by their store. In fact, the pizza drivers were the actual target of intervention, and in addition, their use of turn signals also was studied as a non-targeted but related safe-driving practice. Using two stores in one community, one experimental (A), the other a control (B), the experimental group was enlisted as agents in a community-wide safety belt program, while the control group did not participate in the community program. Trained observers unobtrusively watched pizza deliverers in both groups, with a 10-week baseline period, followed by six weeks of training at store A, and then six more weeks of follow-up observation. There was a 5-week break, and another seven weeks of follow-up observation.

Although the pizza deliverers were the main target of intervention, there was also a bona-fide community intervention program, such as radio announcements, safety belt reminder cards on the top of each box of pizza sold, with a system of vouchers good for a free pizza for those customers spotted with the safety belt reminder card in their cars.

The results on 7,843 vehicular observations collected during this study show several important outcomes: First, there was a very high (approximately 92% average) interrater reliability on checks for use of seat belts and turn signals by pizza deliverers. These observations noted a substantial increase in seat belt use for the experimental group (from 57% to 75%, with a follow-up measure of 74% usage), while the control group did not show such a change. Second, data on the response generalization to use of turn signals was interesting. Again, the experimental group increased from 41% at baseline to 76% after intervention (and 73% at follow-up). The control group showed a slight decrease in turn signal usage during the same time period, supporting the response generalization hypothesis. There was also a telephone survey of people using pizza services–this was a university town–and there was a slightly favorable response to the community project and the involvement of the pizza store in it, which gives rise to some statements about the cost-effectiveness of such preventive programs.

Figure 14.1 shows a simplified version of both *A-B-A* designs, on seat belt use and use of turn signals, for experimental and control groups, over a 10-month period. Since the targets did not return to original baseline (*A*) levels in the second baseline period (A_2) these designs also can be viewed as *A-B* designs with follow-up. These designs offer an example of an intervention on one target that appears to have generalized to a related target, while at the same time showing continuation of the improvement. This study also illustrates the ways in which single-system designs and classical research–the non-equivalent control group design–can work together to develop answers to socially significant problems.

Another report of a practical application of the *A-B-A* design by Altus, Welsh, Miller, and Merrill (1993), focused on the effect of contingent reinforcement on an educational program for new members of a consumer cooperative. These new participants in a university housing cooperative were required to complete a standard 14-week educational program, consisting of lessons on the history of cooperatives, and on local co-op rules and procedures. A baseline of 4 weeks indicated low levels of new members completing the lesson's study guides. So, a 5-week dual intervention was introduced, in which members received a $2 rent reduction for completing the study guide at 90% or greater accuracy, and lesser reductions for 80% to 89%, and 70% to 79%; they also received a $2 fine for failing to complete the lesson or scoring below 70%. This intervention was removed on the 10th week for 5 weeks.

Thus far, the results are clear: With no contingencies provided (A_1 and A_2), the percentage

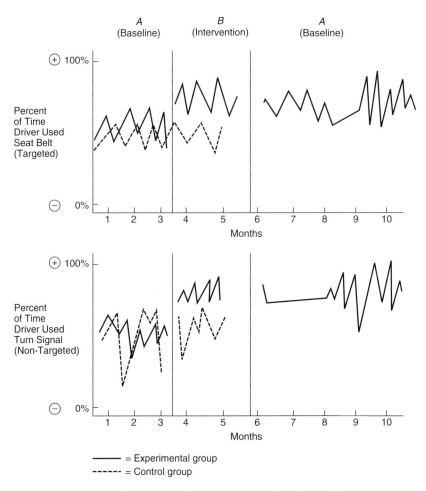

FIGURE 14.1   Percent of time pizza drivers in experimental and control groups used seat belts (targeted) and turn signals (non-targeted) during a safe driving campaign. (Adapted from Ludwig & Geller, 1999.)

of new members completing the lesson study guides is very low; with an intervention of credits and fines that is managed by the researcher (*B*), the rate of completion of the study guides is very high. New members scored slightly higher on the current period's study lesson than old members did on the same test, suggesting that new members were rapidly prepared to the level of old members in a short time period. (See Figure 14.2.)

But in the real world, researchers do not impose experimental conditions beyond the life of the study. So the question arises, can a member-managed intervention of the same credits and fines continue to motivate new members of the cooperative to attain high levels of study of its philosophy, history, and procedures? The data show that such a member-managed intervention was successful in producing a highly informed membership, even 9 years after the conclusion of this study. As Altus et al. (1993) note, this educational program is a simple, inexpensive, and sustainable way of providing cooperative members with the tools they need to maintain a democratic setting. In terms of this book, we note that this *A-B-A* eval-

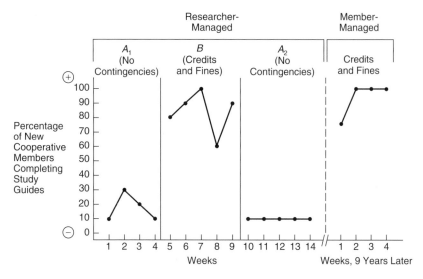

FIGURE 14.2   Percentage of new housing cooperative members completing study guides on the philosophy and procedures of cooperatives. (Adapted from Altus, Welsh, Miller, & Merrill, 1993.)

uation supplied the experimental results sufficient for members to base their own continuation of the intervention program indefinitely.

Another *A-B-A* design was employed by McNees, Egli, Marshall, Schnelle, and Risley (1976) in a study designed to prevent shoplifting, possibly the single most common crime in the United States. The study itself involved identifying baseline rates for shoplifting at a department store and then having an intervention of signs posted strategically notifying people that shoplifting was a crime, and that it would be a punishable offense. Data show that these signs were successful in reducing shoplifting while not affecting sales rates. The signs then were removed, and shoplifting returned to its previous levels. These authors conducted a second study along similar lines in which items thought to be high theft risks were publicly identified as such. Using the same design, it was found that this approach reduced shoplifting to nearly zero without affecting sales.

The removal of the intervention in this situation was not viewed as harmful to the system, although it might have been useful to leave the public notices posted even if it wasn't feasible to specially tag each high-risk item given the high turnover of items at the department store. However, this study suggests that the *A-B-A* design may be employed in creative ways that are useful and provide clear accountability for the methods involved.

A fascinating case recently was reported and showed the creative use of single-system designs with four clients infected with AIDS (Orgnero & Rodway, 1991). The intervention approach was based on Heimler's Social Functioning (HSF) method. HSF is a psychosocial approach that is particularly useful with AIDS patients. It is used in crisis interventions, in caring for the terminally ill, and in teaching stress management. It focuses on both internal and external sources of distress and addresses the major aspects of a person's being (social, physical, emotional, and spiritual). All clients were in great physical, mental, and emotional distress.

Two measures were used. The first was the Heimler Scale of Social Functioning, a standardized measure that produces a Coping Index that ranges from 0.0 to 2.5, with higher scores indicating poorer coping. The scores for each client were charted and tests of statistical significance, all of which are described in Part IV of this book, were used. In all cases, the results showed statistically significant (positive) changes in the clients' coping scores. One of these charts, showing a statistical test called the two-standard-deviation band approach (described in earlier editions of this book but now revised as discussed in Chapter 22 and in Orme & Cox, 2000), has been adapted in Figure 14.3 (with this approach, two consecutive points outside of the band indicate statistical significance).

The second measure was an individualized self-rating scale adapted for each client. The scores on those scales generally supported the results on the Heimler Scale of Social Functioning.

With all clients, an *A-B-A* design was used. In every case, the intervention effects were maintained in the second *A* phase, suggesting that the changes had stabilized or become irreversible, and that the second *A* phase was serving best as a follow-up period (rather than an experimental manipulation).

This report is of particular interest for many reasons: First, it deals with AIDS, an enormous social and health problem that is still currently

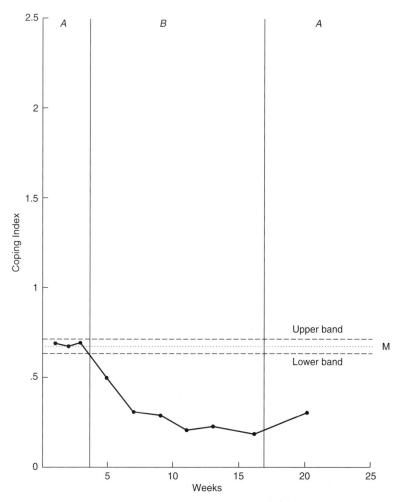

FIGURE 14.3 *A-B-A* design showing impact of HFS intervention with AIDS patient using two-standard-deviation band approach. (Adapted from "AIDS and Social Work Treatment: A Single-System Analysis" by M. I. Orgnero and M. R. Rodway, 1991, *Health and Social Work, 16*, pp. 123–141.)

underserved; second, it illustrates single-system designs used with a broad-based psychosocial intervention (HSF); third, it is one of the few published reports using an *A-B-A* design; and fourth, this report in one article illustrates use of several of the procedures discussed in this book.

Introducing the Client to the A-B-A Design.
Frankly, introducing clients to an experimental procedure is one of the major problems of these designs. It is difficult to explain to a client or relevant other who expects help why successful service is being removed. There are several basic approaches to this problem. First, if someone other than the client is collecting data, or if the data are collected routinely apart from the service program (such as school grades, etc.), then the practitioner can simply not tell the client. While this is a pure form of experimental procedure in which the reactive effects of data collection are minimized, you may have to make a judgment as to how ethical and/or suitable this strategy would be with each case or situation. For example, this may be most suitable with clients who may not be active participants in planning (such as very young infants or institutionalized persons with limited capacities) when approval of guardians can be secured.

The second approach involves telling participants. For example, you could say, "*You have been doing well so far* (in achieving your goals). *Let's keep recording to see how it continues to go, but let's not do x* (the intervention or service program). *This way we'll be able to see how you do without x* (the service program)."

A third approach combines the first two approaches. For example, if parents are involved in helping their child perform some desired activity, then the parents can be informed about the change in phases (such as the withdrawal of reinforcement). The child is not told, and the parents continue to collect data as before.

A fourth approach is linked to the next design (one that ends on an intervention phase). That is, you can introduce the idea of removal of intervention but raise the possibility of returning to intervention if needed. "This part of the service plan is a trial run in preparation for the time when we end treatment. However, we need to know whether you're ready for stopping treatment by seeing how you handle problems on your own. We will keep track of events just as we did before in order to determine how well the treatment has worked."

Experimental Replication Design: *A-B-A-B* $\boxed{A\,|\,B\,|\,A\,|\,B}$

The *A-B-A-B* design is a very important single-system design, for excellent reasons as we shall see. It is a design of many names. Campbell and Stanley (1963) refer to it as an "equivalent time-sample design," while Glass, Willson, and Gottman (1975) refer to it as the "operant" design because of its close association with operant behavioral psychology. Leitenberg (1973) uses this design in his discussion of reversal and withdrawal types of designs. We use the label *experimental replication* to emphasize the distinctive features of the *A-B-A-B*–namely, that the first two phases are repeated in the second two phases. We also want to emphasize its experimental nature in the planned replication, a fact that may limit its employment.

Each adjacent comparison can reveal differences in the data, which then may be related to the differences in the experiences involved. In the first comparison, between initial baseline and initial intervention as in an *A-B* design, the practitioner observes the changes occurring. A clear and apparently stable difference between A_1 and B_1 sets the stage for asking the causality question, What part did the intervention play in these results? This also would apply, by the way, to deterioration as well as improvement effects. (The *subscripts* indicate which of the phases is being considered; for example A_1 refers to the first baseline, A_2 to the second baseline, and so forth; other than the order of presentation, there are no differences between A_1 and A_2 or B_1 and B_2 phases.) If B_1 is determined to be a stable pattern of events, a third change, removal of the intervention, provides the first experimentally manipulated source of evidence that the intervention may be causally related to observed changes. Assuming the second baseline data return to, or return nearly to, their initial state, this lends logical support to the experimental evidence that the intervention was indeed functionally linked with the change. Thus far we have an *A-B-A* design. Now, by adding a final intervention period (B_2), we add a second experimentally manipulated source of evidence regarding the causal nature of the intervention. By purposely manipulating the intervention, we have provided a strong basis for the inference of causality. By planning and observing these three instances of concomitant variation—A_1-B_1, B_1-A_2, A_2-B_2—we see the distinction between a change in target behaviors that happened by planned intervention in contrast to nature's random ways. In a word, we see evidence that the practitioner probably has helped cause the resulting change in target events.

We discussed previously the point that single-system designs are often additive—that is, that the strengths and characteristics of simpler designs such as A-B and A-B-A appear in the more complex designs, although their drawbacks (which may be overcome by the more complex designs) do not necessarily reappear. This fact will simplify the discussion here, but we want to remind you of these previous discussions.

One of the more important additions of the A-B-A-B design is that it terminates on an intervention phase that is professionally more acceptable than the A-B-A design, even though both involve removal of intervention in the course of service. Positive changes are supposed to occur from A_1 to B_1 and from A_2 to B_2, while changes from B_1 to A_2 should show a reduction of effect or decreasing change. This pattern of expected changes is part of the logical pattern that gives this design its strength. We believe that this also provides the design with some protection from several threats to internal validity. Specifically, we believe that the A-B-A-B designs (and to a lesser extent the A-B-A and the B-A-B designs) are usually relatively safe from alternative explanations due to: changing events occurring outside the immediate practice context ("history"), events occurring within the client ("maturation"), extreme scores naturally becoming less extreme over time ("regression to the mean"), and changes brought about by the very act of testing itself. In each case it appears that the alternation of interventions and removal of interventions (and the parallel changes in target behaviors) lessen the possibility that these other extraneous factors could have influenced the data, particularly in short time periods.

Strengths of the A-B-A-B Design. Replication is a very strong source of support with regard to causal efficacy of the intervention. It is as if one were generalizing through replication what happened in the first part of the intervention to apply to what happened in the second part, although there might be differences expected because of the cumulation of influences and the more easily learned behaviors the second time around.

By ending on a service phase this design meets some practice and social criteria of ethical suitability and sensitivity lacking in the A-B-A design. Empirically, the practitioner–client relationship terminates at a point at which it has attained its goals twice, suggesting that learning has occurred. Logically, the removal and reintroduction of the intervention provides a strong basis for asserting control over the target problem when the predicted pattern of data emerges. Of course, as with all other designs, we recommend use of maintenance and follow-up phases once the changes in the final B phase are well established and stable.

The A-B-A-B design also begins to provide the kind of information about functional relationships between variables that is also at the heart of classical experimental/control group designs. This is a knowledge-building function rather than simply a knowledge-using function. Practitioners using this type of design are in a good position to report their findings to the profession in order to help others choose specific interventions for specific types of clients so that they will be likely to obtain defined classes of outcomes. This is a very strong scientific contribution to the knowledge base of all professions, stemming from the work of practitioners in the field under ordinary practice conditions.

Moreover, for the practitioner himself or herself, this experimental design will help to build a repertoire of effective intervention techniques. We believe it is of major value for practitioners to know what interventions produce what types of effects given the background and skills of the unique practitioner.

For others involved in the experimental situation, such as parents or staff persons who are mediators participating in the intervention programs, there is the added benefit that they can see how their specific efforts are contributing to the client's behavior. This reinforces the mediator's behavior (Tharp & Wetzel, 1969), and thus ensures more cooperation with the intervention program. Designs such as this one, that can reinforce the all-important direct mediators or implementers of an intervention program, are very important considerations in planning interventions.

Limitations of the A-B-A-B Design. There are several problems involved in using this design. First, it is somewhat more cumbersome and more time-consuming than the basic *A-B* design. There has to be more control over the situation than many practitioners may have in order to be able to institute the replication part of the design. In addition, the issue of removing a successful intervention (B_1) once it has been attained is a problem here as it was with the *A-B-A* design, although less so, since the intention clearly is to return to intervention after A_2. Should the client drop out before the B_2 phase is started, the practitioner would be left with an *A-B-A* design with its attendant problems.

It also is difficult to juggle the length of phases of the *A-B-A-B* design. As discussed in Chapter 11, in an ideal situation each phase should be of equal length, but in practice this is rarely possible. We recommend in such cases—in which other things are equal and in which phases cannot all be the same length—that B_2 be the longest phase and A_2 be the shortest. This means that the removal period would be minimized and the last intervention period extended for as long as possible to ensure that the problem stays changed.

But what if the B_1 phase doesn't show any change? Does this destroy the whole design? In effect, it makes the B_1 phase equal to A_1. It would not be wise simply to repeat the *B* intervention again, so a new intervention, *C*, could be added to form a new design, *A-B-C*. The fact that *B* does not seem to have an impact is important information so that the practitioner does not lose for having tried it and moved to a modified design. Again, single-system designs are very flexible and take into

account such occurrences; this is a great plus in the overall aim of being sensitive to the unique events in a case.

Another problem that experimental designs such as the *A-B-A-B* are subject to is carryover effects. Carryover effects, as we defined them in Chapter 11, simply are the inability to retrieve the original baseline (A_1) levels of the problem in a subsequent baseline (A_2). Thus, as an example, if a problem is occurring, say, at a rate of 14 occurrences per hour in the first baseline (A_1), and your intervention reduces this to a rate of 5 occurrences during B_1, carryover effects would be present if, in the second baseline phase (A_2), when the intervention is withdrawn, the problem does not return to, or close to, its original level (say, staying in A_2 at a level of 5 to 8 occurrences per hour). Figure 14.4 describes two hypothetical *A-B-A-B* designs, one with and one without carryover effects.

It is not always clear why carryover effects appear (Barlow & Hersen, 1984). It may be that instructions were irreversible, that the changes in phases just happened to coincide with some external factor, that the absence of changes (carryover) is only temporary, or other reasons that you simply may not know at the time. It also may be that the problem simply has been resolved, or is well on the way toward being resolved, and the new behavior is simply well learned. To the extent that this is true (e.g., the problem has reached some stable, desired level) this may be an obvious advantage for the practitioner who then could turn the second baseline phase (A_2) into a maintenance and termination phase. Thus, from a practical point of view, presence of carryover effects may be advantageous.

On the other hand, carryover effects can pose problems. It is not always clear when we do or do not have carryover effects. There is a fuzzy area in which the problem does not quite reach its original level but clearly does move in that direction. In our example (Figure 14.4a) this fuzzy area would be roughly between three to five occurrences per day. In situations like this your guide should be both *stability* (does the problem stabilize at a given level with the absence of intervention?) and *directionality* (is there a clear trend away from the

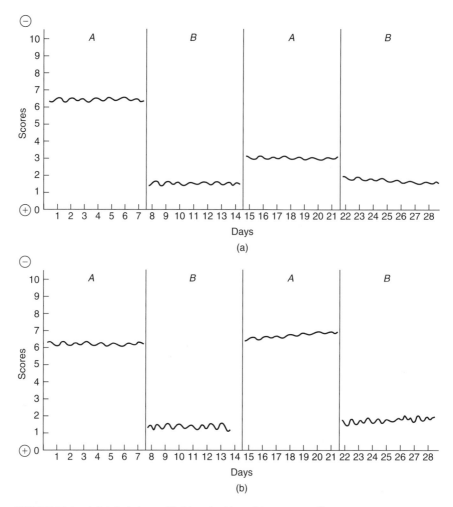

FIGURE 14.4   *A-B-A-B* designs with (a) and without (b) carryover effects.

intervention phase level and toward the original baseline level?). If these two conditions do not pertain and you cannot make a relatively clear judgment as to whether the problem really has moved in the direction of the first baseline, then carryover effects probably have occurred.

But why should you care? Given the obvious practice advantages of carryover effects, do they really make a difference? The answer to this question depends on the purpose of your design. If you are really attempting to establish *why* the problem changed and whether

your techniques affected it, these carryover effects make it unclear as to the extent to which you can claim the intervention program produced the changes that were observed.

One way of preventing carryover effects is to keep the phases, especially B_1, relatively short. This way, carryover effects have less opportunity to appear; that is, it is easier to retrieve the first baseline in phase A_2 if the first intervention phase (B_1) is relatively short. This is because the newly learned behaviors have less time to become irreversible or be part of a permanent change in the target. If they do appear and you want to maintain your *A-B-A-B* design, you could extend the second *A* phase (removal) to see whether the problem eventually does move toward its original level without intervention. In situations in which you are not certain how to interpret the data (the fuzzy area), be sure to interpret with caution. Finally, you can always turn the second *A* phase into a maintenance and termination phase as we suggested above and be very happy with the fact that the problem *has* changed for the better.

Another possible limitation of the *A-B-A-B* design is the effect on colleagues or other workers of removing a successful intervention. As we mentioned before, it can be highly motivating when people see how their efforts are affecting a problem. However, you may run into the problem of other staff persons complaining about bearing the brunt of a client's problematic behavior. Thus, when the second baseline is implemented, all they see is that they have to go back to dealing with a problem that already has been reduced. Our suggestion is to prepare the staff for the removal period, explaining its purpose and eliciting their cooperation in advance. Of course, as we noted above, due to possible carryover effects, the problem in the A_2 phase often doesn't attain the same level as in the A_1 phase, presenting staff with a less difficult task than they had to cope with during the preintervention period.

A final problem with the *A-B-A-B* design is analogous to problems in classical experimental designs. In single-system and group experimental designs, the problem may change when intervention is applied and removed (or, in a group design, in comparison with a control group), but there is no guarantee that your specific intervention techniques brought about the changes. They very well may have. But change also could be due to different ways of relating to clients during intervention and nonintervention periods, to different amounts of attention or enthusiasm, and so on. In classical experiments, this problem is addressed by adding more groups to the experiment—for example, an attention-placebo group, and/or an alternative intervention group, and/or by comparing practitioners' levels of interpersonal skills across groups. The problem is much

trickier with single-system designs. It can be addressed somewhat by the designs we describe in Chapter 17 that can compare alternative approaches. But the problem of not being clear about what part of the intervention was responsible for the changes is perhaps best addressed in single-system designs by replication, using strategies described in Chapter 11. When a similar intervention produces similar results across numerous instances with different practitioners and clients, you can have more confidence in a conclusion that the formal intervention itself (i.e., the techniques) was responsible for the observed changes.

As with other single-system designs, we are concerned that successful intervention effects are maintained and transferred to the client's natural environment. Sufficient time and energy should be devoted to this task by being sure to build in a maintenance phase at the end of the B_2 phase. (Goldstein & Kanfer, 1979; Karoly & Steffen, 1980; Rzepnicki, 1991).

Recommendations Regarding the A-B-A-B Design. The experimental replication design is a very strong tool that makes many demands on the client as well as on the practitioner. If it is necessary to know or to demonstrate to others whether an intervention is in fact a controlling influence before further interventions are carried out, then this design would be very useful. It also has many secondary benefits, such as seeing whether a client has attained a stable, desired level of the problem while a relationship still exists with the helping professional. If the client maintains the desired level of the problem during the second *B* period, then this can be the basis for terminating work on that target event. If not, then the practice structure is already set up to continue working on that target event until it can be stably and independently maintained. Likewise, mediators can see evidence of the impact of their work, a strong reinforcing factor.

Thus, we view the *A-B-A-B* design as a very powerful method, perhaps too powerful for some practice purposes, but useful in many contexts. Where there is need for causal information, this is a highly recommended design. You must decide whether it is worth the extra effort and time–from both client and yourself– to use the *A-B-A-B* design.

Case Illustrations. Jason and Brackshaw (1999) used an *A-B-A-B* design to demonstrate the effectiveness of an intervention to reduce a child's excessive TV watching (averaging over 4 hours a day) *and* to reduce that child's excessive weight (this 11-year-old child was 5 feet 3 inches and weighed 172 pounds). These authors cite considerable evidence about the harmful effects of excessive TV watching in young children–such as an inverse relationship between school performance and excessive TV watching. There also are empirical relationships between obesity in youngsters and future health problems. Furthermore, there is evidence that a couch potato pattern of watching TV may be linked to the increasing rates of obesity.

Jason and Brackshaw (1999, p. 148) present a study of one child, an 11-year-old Latina referred from a health clinic because, as her mother described her, she was "totally controlled by the TV." The authors devised an ingenious device in which the child was able to earn TV viewing time in exchange for an equal amount of time riding a stationary bicycle. The family agreed to participate in this project and recorded data over the next 130 days, including a reliability check by an independent adult recording the child's TV viewing time. There was 100% interrater reliability.

We have reconstructed the graph showing this classic *A-B-A-B* design, with follow-up (see Figure 14.5). The first baseline (A_1) of one-week duration simply observed the child's ordinary number of hours of TV watching, which varied between 4 and 6 hours a day. Then the first intervention was implemented (B_1) over seven days in which the child had to earn TV viewing time with an equivalent number of minutes on the exercise bike. The results are a dramatic reduction of hours viewing TV, to between zero and 2 hours of watching. Then the second baseline (A_2) is introduced for a two-week period, which shows the child going back to slightly less than the old rate of TV viewing. Then the second intervention (B_2) over the next 30 days shows a relatively consistent pattern of viewing, 1 hour or less per day. Note that this intervention is continued for a relatively long period of time in which the child has probably learned the lesson intended. Seven weeks later, the child shows that she has maintained that low level of TV viewing in follow-up. The child also said that she wanted to lose weight and came to enjoy the intervention. In fact, the child lost 20

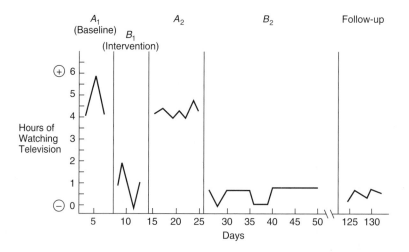

FIGURE 14.5   Television watching over different phases of an *A-B-A-B* design. (Adapted from Jason & Brackshaw, 1999.)

pounds by follow-up, and the 20 pound loss was maintained a year later as reported by the parents. In the newly freed up time, she turned to other activities such as playing with friends, which probably accounted for the maintenance of the low TV viewing, even after the intervention was removed. Thus, this design was able to document not only the socially significant changes in the target, but the probable causal effects of this simple intervention.

We make the point throughout these examples that real-life illustrations are more complex than hypothetical illustrations that might be constructed to clarify the principles of evaluation. Thus, in this case as in many of our examples, certain of the principles in Chapters 11 and 12, such as length of baseline, stability of target event, and unequal length of phases, were not implemented in an optimal way. This is part of the reality of practice. Rather than negate the value of each evaluation, it does present limitations regarding the certainty one can use in interpreting causal relationships. Thus, as a general guideline, we suggest that with each variation from the "ideal design," you simply use more caution in interpreting results.

A report by Brigham, Meier, and Goodner (1995) used the *A-B-A-B* design in a primary prevention effort to determine whether it was possible to increase designated drivers (DDs) so as to reduce alcohol-related accidents, a significant social and public health problem. Young drivers (and probably relatively recent drinkers) are disproportionately represented among persons driving while intoxicated (DWI). So, Brigham et al. conducted an informal survey of local drinking establishments and found that few people participated in designating one member of their party who would not drink with the others so as to be able to drive them home safely. A local bar agreed to participate in the study; this bar had a long-standing designated driver program in which a person identified himself or herself as the DD and could get free coffee or soft drinks.

First, a team of observers sitting by the bar would be signaled by the bartender that someone had come forward as a designated driver. Two observers had to agree on the identity of this person—an interobserver reliability check— especially when this DD left the bar with his or her friends, in order to verify that this person was in fact the designated driver. These observations were made for three consecutive weekends (Friday and Saturday nights, from 8:30 P.M. to 1:00 A.M.) to represent the baseline rate of DDs.

The intervention consisted of three large wall posters and placards placed on the tables announcing the program: "Designated drivers, tell your server who you are, your drinks are on us! Free [brand name drinks X, Y, Z] or other nonalcoholic beers & wines, mixed drinks & coffee." The intervention lasted four weekends until the authors saw considerable improvement and some stability in the data.

Then the second baseline period began by the removal of the posters and placards, at which time the number of self-identified designated drivers returned to baseline levels. A second intervention period repeated the conditions of the first, and a similar increase in DDs occurred, but with somewhat less stability over 7 weekends.

The results, shown in Figure 14.6, indicate the success of the intervention. However, the question might be raised as to whether having a designated driver encourages the others to drink more heavily than they might otherwise have done. The authors present a brief report suggesting that increased drinking occurs in less than 5% of respondents from another study. In general, this study illustrates the very practical advantages of a fairly sophisticated single-system design applied to a common problem using a simple, everyday intervention.

Pigott, Fantuzzo, and Clement (1986) present the results of a study showing the effectiveness of a reciprocal peer-tutoring intervention in increasing the arithmetic performance of underachieving fifth-grade students. Mixed ethnic groups of boys and girls were involved in teams to help one another improve their achievements on daily 7-minute arithmetic drills.

As indicated in Figure 14.7, adapted from data presented by Pigott et al. (1986), baseline data (A_1) were collected by the teacher's aide on the number of accurately completed arithmetic problems for the entire class. Three different classes were involved, and procedures were the same in each classroom, with drill sessions occurring at the same time of the day

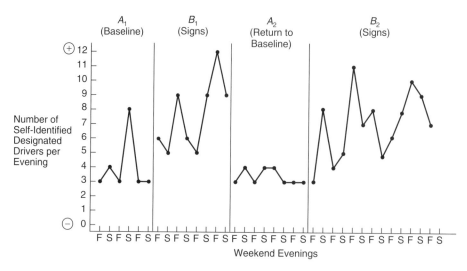

FIGURE 14.6   Number of self-identified designated drivers per evening at a college campus bar. (Adapted from Brigham, Meier, and Goodner, 1995.)

each day. Each class had a special experimental team of underachieving students. Figure 14.7 shows both the changes within the experimental teams over time, and how these special teams compared to their normally achieving classmates, an important added feature in this study because this makes for a built-in quasi-experimental control group for comparison purposes.

The intervention (B_1) consisted of reciprocal peer tutoring and a group contingency plan. Peer tutoring involved each member of a four-person team being trained to take parts such as "coach" (giving instructions to the team), "scorekeeper" and "referee" (both independently counting the number of correct scores by team members–a reliability check), and "manager" (determining the team's score and comparing it with the team goal, and providing the team reward–"we WON!"). The group contingency aspect involved reinforcing the "we-ness" of the team effort. The regular student–teacher interactions and feedback were, in addition, constant throughout the study. The first intervention (B_1) period results indicate that two of the three classes show strong improvements in performance roughly equivalent to ordinary class members, while the third shows a trend toward improvement.

The second baseline (A_2) involved a return to individual work on the arithmetic drills; all three peer teams show declines from the previous intervention level. The second intervention phase (B_2) indicates that the target teams equal or exceed their normally achieving classmates' performance in all three classes. A maintenance phase indicates that the special teams are continuing to perform well, and in a 12-week follow-up period, the overall gains are holding; in fact, the special teams at follow-up appear to be doing about as well as their classmates.

Sociometric information collected also suggested that such team efforts may be useful in attaining other objectives, such as the reduction of racial and ethnic tensions. There also was no reduction of social status of the target students relative to nontreated students in the classes. The authors note that future research will have to be directed toward teasing out which factors of the peer-tutoring project are the active ingredients in attaining these kinds of results. This illustrates the way in which one function of single-system designs is to generate hypotheses that may be tested with classical, experimental/control group designs.

Our next example of an *A-B-A-B* design involves a combined experimental and qualitative analysis of a cognitive-behavioral intervention for anger (Nugent, 1991a). The client,

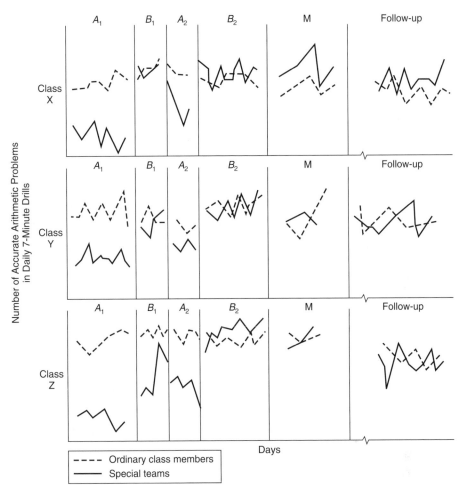

FIGURE 14.7   An *A-B-A-B* design on reciprocal peer tutoring. (Data adapted from "The Effects of Reciprocal Peer Tutoring and Group Contingencies on the Academic Performance of Elementary School Children" by H. E. Pigott, J. W. Fantuzzo, and P. W. Clement, 1986, *Journal of Applied Behavior Analysis, 19,* pp. 93–98.)

Diane, a 28-year-old married woman, was concerned about her own severe angry "blowups" in which she verbally abused her husband and children. In the initial interview, the therapist developed a reconstructed or retrospective baseline over the past week; the client expressed so much distress that a concurrent baseline was deemed unwise. The intervention consisted primarily of a "triple-column technique," in which the client, whenever she feels angry, lists in a notebook her automatic thoughts, evaluates them for distorted patterns,

and substitutes rational responses. The first intervention phase (B_1) lasted 10 days. Following this, a removal phase was initiated, but the client became concerned over an increase in the frequency and intensity of her outbursts. Thus, the removal phase was limited to only 4 days. The removal phase (A_2) was followed by a 7-week B_2 phase. At the end of it, the client and her husband were referred to a marriage therapist for work on their relationship.

At the same time as the above procedures were occurring, the therapist obtained qualitative results including open-ended interviews with the client, an open-ended telephone interview with the client's husband, plus a follow-up telephone interview and questionnaire 5 months after the treatment was completed.

As can be seen from Figure 14.8, there appears to have been a clear diminishing in angry outbursts over time. The author also applied a very sophisticated statistical analysis (a time-series regression model) to these data that showed the changes also were statistically significant. The qualitative information provided by the client and her husband supported the quantitative results reported on the chart. The qualitative report also revealed that the client had substantially changed the intervention to be more suitable to her own style. Thus, while both qualitative and quantitative information supported the success of the overall process, some question remains as to the mechanisms by which the intervention, as modified by the client, affected the change.

The Nugent (1991a) report illustrates a number of the points made in this and previous chapters. First, quantitative and qualitative analyses can work hand in hand. Second, single-system designs can be very flexible. In this case, the design and intervention were modified to meet this client's needs. Third, even without optimal conditions (in this case, a

retrospective baseline and unequal length of phases), conclusions about effectiveness, and some inferences about causality still can be made. In this case, the conclusions are bolstered by the use of a wide variety of information, plus application of statistical analysis to the results to confirm that results likely were not due to chance.

Austin, Alvero, and Olson (1998) used a variation of the *A-B-A-B* design that is applicable to situations when completely different participants are involved in a study and yet when the effects of the intervention can be clearly viewed. Austin et al. conducted their study at a restaurant in which the hostesses ordinarily said "goodbye" and opened the door for exiting patrons. The target of this intervention was safety belt usage, recognizing the important preventive service that these devices provide. The researchers obtained consent for the hostesses to add to their usual farewell remarks "Don't forget to buckle up."

Figure 14.9 shows a reconstructed graph of this demonstration project. The initial baseline was relatively long (27 days, representing evenings from Thursday through Sunday). Two consecutive 1-hour sessions were conducted each evening—one with the experimental safety remark, the other without it. There were also two reliability checks: The first, in-

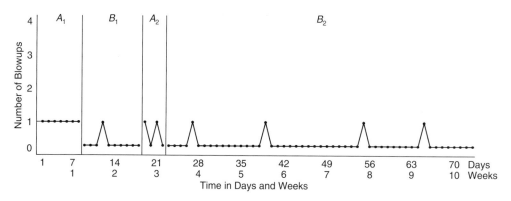

FIGURE 14.8   Results of a cognitive-behavioral intervention with anger. (Data adapted from "An Experimental and Qualitative Analysis of a Cognitive-Behavioral Intervention for Anger" by W. R. Nugent, 1991, *Social Work Research & Abstracts, 27*, pp. 3–8.)

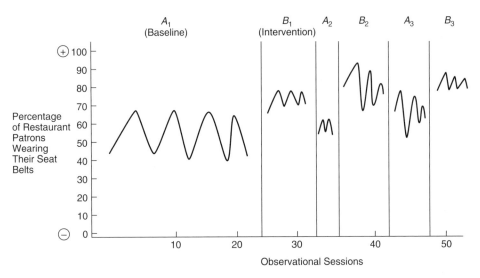

FIGURE 14.9   An extended experimental replication design (*A-B-A-B*) showing the percentage of restaurant patrons who used their seat belts after being prompted by the restaurant hostess as they left. (Adapted from Austin, Alvero, & Olson, 1998.)

volving an independent observer during 20% of the sessions, considered whether or not the safety message was in fact given by hostesses. The results showed an average delivery of the prompt at 92%. (Sometimes the hostesses were busy with other tasks, and could not deliver the message.)

The second reliability check considered whether or not patrons in fact buckled up after leaving the restaurant. Another independent observer check during 20% of the sessions showed there was 97% agreement on safety belt use. These two reliability checks show great sensitivity to the points in the study where slippage might occur in reduction leading to an overall meaning of the study.

After the long baseline, the authors use relatively short periods of intervention and return to baseline, for reasons not explained in the article. However, in each case, the introduction of the intervention (B_1, B_2, B_3) shows higher levels of usage, while the returns to baseline (A_2, A_3) show a pattern similar to the initial baseline (A_1). Average seat belt use across baselines is about 57%, while usage increased to about 77% during prompting conditions. Since we can as-

sume that most of the customers over this period of time were different, the slight differences in seat belt usage in the three intervention periods may not be particularly significant. However, what is of practical significance is the fact that the manager of the restaurant was so impressed with the results that he continued the safety prompt after the study ended.

Why was the design A-B-A-B-A-B used, rather than a simpler A-B-A-B design? We infer that the evaluators wanted to be doubly sure of their results, since different customers were involved, and the return to baseline and new intervention periods were relatively brief. This study lacks a long-term follow-up which would have been interesting to see if the intervention continued to have its positive effects on different customers. Overall, this study illustrates a very simple intervention evaluated by an easily implemented but rigorous single-system design applied to a highly significant social issue: saving lives.

Our final example is based on the work of Miltenberger and his colleagues who have conducted a series of studies employing single-system designs with such problems as treatment of motor tics in children, stuttering, finger sucking, the prevention of sexual abuse in adults who are developmentally disabled, among others. We have chosen a complex study of the treatment of hair pulling and hair manipulation by a developmentally disabled young adult who also has cerebral palsy, to illustrate how single-system designs can help fine tune a treatment process (Rapp et al., 2000). The design in this study may be described with the horrendous title of *A-B-A-B-C-A-D-E-F-A-F-D-F.* However, don't let this complex label hide the fact that this is an elaborated *A-B-A-B* design with several variations employed as the practitioners were getting ever closer to their goal.

Chronic hair pulling (trichotillomania) produces noticeable hair loss and is presumed to be associated with some experience of gratification. There are few studies with successful treatment outcomes; Rapp et al. employ a behavioral model suggesting that this habit is automatically reinforced, and hence, repeated. This is seen as especially true of individuals who are developmentally disabled.

The exact process of treatment is well beyond our needs for this evaluation example, but interested readers are invited to study the process in the original article. Briefly, the client in this situation was a young woman who was severely developmentally disabled with mild cerebral palsy affecting one side of her body, so that she could manipulate her hair only with her right hand. She had been doing this since early childhood. All sessions took place in her home when her mother was present. We will discuss only the living room activities, although treatment was also conducted in her bedroom.

Data were recorded by videotaping 10 minute segments and then breaking them down second by second to observe the percentage of time she was observed pulling or manipulating her hair. The practitioners used four discrete interventions, interspersed with returns to baseline or other interventions. These interventions consisted of wrist weights (2.5 and 5 pound), and a golf glove—both of which were selected as having been effective previously in clinical settings; and a response

interruption (RI) plus differential reinforcement of other behaviors (by the clinicians [DRO] in one case, and with the mother [DRO-M], in another). Other objects were placed within the client's reach to manipulate instead of pulling her hair.

Social validity data were collected as well–photographs of the client's scalp–that were rated by 15 graduate students in psychology. Also, the acceptability of treatment was assessed by asking the mother about her feelings about the treatment program.

Results of the client's hair pulling are indicated in Figure 14.10. What we observe is a relatively high baseline for hair pulling (mean = 7.6% of the time); a very high baseline for hair manipulation (approximately 50% of the time) was also reported but is not shown here. Both hair pulling and manipulation were reduced to nearly zero with the first two new interventions–at least for a short time until the young woman learns how to negate the intervention. Then, with the last interventions, RI + DRO and later, RI + DRO-M, the behavior goes to near zero, returns in a brief baseline, and then remains at zero (see Figure 14.10).

The authors interpret these results to indicate that the hair pulling behavior was essentially suppressed, mainly through using a combination of RI and DRO. Methods that worked in the clinic (weights, gloves) were not as effective in the home setting. The last methods used (differential reinforcement) were transferred to the mother to continue (F).

The authors were aware of various limitations of this study, such as the absence of long-term follow-ups, the possibility of confounding outcomes by the treatment-ordering effects (a baseline did not proceed the first use of RI + DRO), and others. However, the strengths of this investigation illustrate how single-system designs can be used to track the process of practice, and ultimately to identify likely sources of change as implemented by practitioners.

Introducing the Client to the A-B-A-B Design. This design is complicated and sometimes difficult to explain to clients, mediators, or others involved in the service program. Some of the

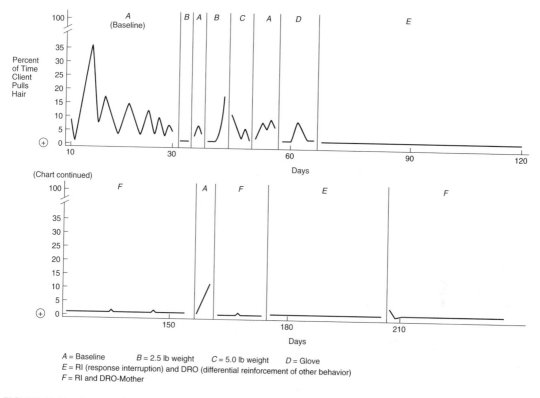

A = Baseline   *B* = 2.5 lb weight   *C* = 5.0 lb weight   *D* = Glove
E = RI (response interruption) and DRO (differential reinforcement of other behavior)
F = RI and DRO-Mother

FIGURE 14.10   Percent of time client engaged in hair pulling at home in living room. (Adapted from Rapp et al., 2000.)

approaches that we recommend for use with the *A-B-A* design apply here, except that you can emphasize that the client will end up on an intervention phase so as to make sure that the service program has been an overall success. We also recommend that you alert the client that part of the final intervention phase may be used to help the client maintain improved behavior after the intervention is over. This is a service required in any intervention, but the repetitive nature of the *A-B-A-B* design provides ideal conditions for making plans for the maintenance phase. Following are some comments you could use to introduce these ideas:

"*An important part of service is to discover whether what we have done together is sufficient to last when you are on your own. Therefore, we are going to stop the treatment part of our contacts for a*

short period of time (A_2) *during which we will continue to collect information about y* (the target). *Then we will return to the treatment* (or some variation of it) *until we are certain that you can handle these types of problems on your own.*

"*This means that as part of our final services to you, we will talk about* (and practice) *how you can continue to solve the types of problems we have been discussing on your own*" (producing an *A-B-A-B-M* design).

Experimental Repeat of Intervention Design: *B-A-B* $\boxed{B\,|\,A\,|\,B}$

Because of the unusual characteristics of the *B-A-B* design it might be helpful to begin with an example (L. Z. Bloom, 1980). Andre spent the first year of college struggling with courses that required term papers, not because he didn't know the material, but because he always seemed to be procrastinating and writing the papers at the last minute. They never turned out very well. At the start of his sophomore year he attended a voluntary two-session workshop on the reduction of writing anxiety. At the first session the instructor spoke with each participant, encouraged everyone to share his or her particular writing problems (others were procrastinators like Andre), and then suggested some methods to reduce the problems. For Andre the instructor suggested a firmer scheduling of his time, the marking out of times of the day when he was most alert, and the locating of private places where he could think and write undisturbed. She asked Andre to keep track of the number of minutes spent actually thinking and writing as compared to the total number of minutes set aside for this task. He spoke with the instructor a few days later to make sure he was collecting data correctly.

In the interval between sessions Andre was on his own again. The suggestions worked for a while, but it was easy to fall back into his familiar bad habits, although he did manage to keep track of the time spent actually writing, as the instructor had asked. When he returned to the final workshop session, he recognized that he hadn't made much progress. The instructor reviewed his efforts and suggested a renewed version of the same advice–public posting of his time schedule and visibly checking off when he was on or off that schedule. This time it worked and stayed that way (L. Z. Bloom, 1980).

This example is typical of many situations in which, for various reasons, the intervention (B) begins at once, followed by an interval during which no intervention is explicitly present (A), followed by another intervention period (B).

The anxiety-reduction workshop is not a perfect example of the B-A-B design because there was no guarantee that participants would reach a level of competence in the first B period before that intervention was removed. However, the workshop presents an example of a fairly common situation in which we begin with an intervention that achieves some stable level of desired behavior before it is removed. During the removal period when no intervention is applied, the behavior presumably falls

to a less desired level, and then when the practitioner reinstates the intervention, the target behavior once again reaches the objectives set for it. The design finishes with a service phase just like the A-B-A-B design.

While the absence of a true preintervention baseline means that the practitioner loses his or her opportunity for systematic comparisons with an initial baseline, as is possible in the A-B-A-B design, there are still a number of important comparisons that can be made: The first intervention may be compared with the baseline period, and the baseline period may be compared with the second intervention period. We offer the label of this design–the experimental repeat of intervention (there is no general agreement about how it should be identified other than by the letters B-A-B)–to emphasize the point that the intervention has been conducted successfully when the practitioner decides to remove the intervention, establish a baseline period, and then reimplement the intervention to determine whether the intervention is really affecting the problem. This is like having a basic single-system design, A-B, but with prior knowledge of how the client may react to the intervention that will be introduced. If the problem occurs again during the A phase, but the client returns to the same level of the target event in the second intervention phase as exhibited in the first intervention phase, then you can assume, other things being equal, that the planned interventions are likely related to the observed changes in the problem.

As mentioned in earlier sections, it would be wise in any design that ends in a service phase to include, or add as a separate phase, a program that will maintain the gains achieved through intervention.

Strengths of the B-A-B Design.   The major strength of this design stems from your ability to use it when you must begin intervention without a preliminary baseline phase–for example, in crisis situations or when delaying intervention might be harmful–and still establish whether the intervention appears to be affecting the problem. As with other experimental designs you purposely remove a successful intervention to observe the changes in target behaviors and then reinstate the intervention according to plan. If the data vary in accordance with that practice hypothesis, then there is a stronger basis for causal inference.

The other strength of the *B-A-B* design, in contrast to the *A-B-A* design, which has the same number of logical comparisons, is that the *B-A-B* design ends on a service phase, thus fulfilling professional demands that work with the client be sensitively terminated when the target problems have been resolved. This design permits crisis intervention to begin immediately while still not losing the opportunity for an experimental design in the sense that we have been using this term for single-system designs.

Limitations of the B-A-B Design.

A major limitation of this design, which is shared with the other removal designs, is the question of ethical suitability of removing a successful intervention—unless it is an accidental or unplanned removal—in order to test the functional connection between the intervention itself and the outcome. Such a design requires considerable control over the situation and the cooperation of others in accepting the removal of a successful intervention while some nonintervention (and likely problematic) condition ensues.

Another limitation, at least in terms of logical inferences, is that the lack of the initial baseline sharply reduces the logical comparisons that can be made. Lacking an initial baseline, this design may disguise an initial training phase with its partial or incomplete achievement of desired behavior change.

Recommendations Regarding the B-A-B Design.

We recommend this design almost to the degree that we would recommend the more powerful *A-B-A-B* design. When no initial baseline can be conducted and situations occur permitting and benefiting from the logical analysis that removal designs can offer, then this design can be quite useful. It also is useful in contexts such as crisis intervention or other dangerous situations for clients when there isn't time for a full-blown initial baseline. Thus, while the *B-A-B* design has its limitations stemming from lack of the initial baseline, it is a strong design and well worth considering on

a selective basis. It might also be worth considering a *B-A-B-A* design where the second baseline permits the planned observation of the staying power of the *B* intervention. Finally, it may be possible, even in crisis situations, to add a reconstructed baseline as a first phase, thereby allowing an additional baseline-intervention comparison to enhance causal inferences.

Case Illustrations.

An interesting example of the *B-A-B* design with group data comes from the field of preventive dentistry (McDonald & Budd, 1983). A community dental unit (instructors and students) went to a local grade school to instruct young children in proper ways to brush their teeth. At the same time, they used red-dye disclosing tablets to measure how effective a given brushing had been in removing plaque. A period of months intervened during which time the school children were left to their natural environment regarding dental health. The parents of the children were given disclosing tablets to be used on randomly assigned days. A second instructional session was then held to clarify and reinforce earlier instruction, as well as to obtain another set of data on how well children were following the brushing instructions. Figure 14.11 presents data collected in this project.

It can be observed from the data that most children attained the dental health criterion level during the first instructional phase, suggesting that they understood how to brush their teeth properly. The long middle period of the study showed that, initially, students were strongly influenced by the presence of the disclosing tablets, but over time they became less aware of or less pressured by them and their scores dropped. Finally, the second intervention showed that these students could easily regain their criterion performance. This suggests the usefulness of an ongoing reminder, or booster shot.

The final example of a *B-A-B* design involves the unfortunate suicide of a popular high school student one weekend, which was the stimulus for a crisis intervention team to come to the student's high school the following Monday morning. The crisis team led discussions about the event among students and

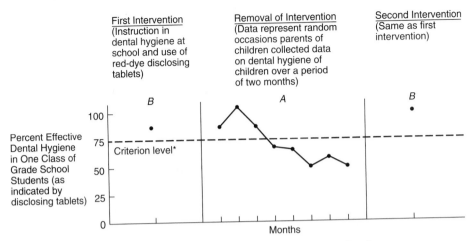

First Intervention
(Instruction in
dental hygiene at
school and use of
red-dye disclosing
tablets)

Removal of Intervention
(Data represent random
occasions parents of
children collected data
on dental hygiene of
children over a period
of two months)

Second Intervention
(Same as first
intervention)

*Criterion level normatively defined as the lowest acceptable level of effective dental hygiene that promotes desired incidences of dental health.

FIGURE 14.11   Illustration of a *B-A-B* design in preventive dentistry. (Adapted from McDonald and Budd, 1983.)

teachers, in both large and small groups. Participants voiced feelings of distress, sadness, and anger over the suicide, and asked what could have been done to prevent it. The crisis team recommended that everyone at the school learn the danger signs of suicide—such as suicide talk or previous attempts, personality or behavior changes for no apparent reason, and various forms of depressed behavior that occur nearly every day for at least 2 weeks. The team instituted an early-warning system whereby a student or teacher could turn in a confidential note to the school health team describing a person's danger signs. The notes had to be signed in order to be considered valid—that is, not practical jokes—but were to be kept confidential by the health team who would follow up on the leads individually and privately.

Records were kept of the numbers of signed notes received and acted upon. The notes were taken as a sign of shared concern for fellow students, and were thus encouraged by the crisis team in the first week they were at the school. They had intended to spend at least 2 weeks there, but another emergency occurred—a fire in a nursing home that required relocation of survivors and meetings with them and their families—that took the team away for 2 weeks.

This constituted an unplanned removal phase. When they returned to the school, they resumed their group discussions. The early-warning note system was maintained throughout this time, and continued throughout the school year. Figure 14.12 presents the data from this project.

As part of their service program, the crisis team set up support groups among students and teachers that became the main thrust of the maintenance phase (C) of this report—where the clients (students and teachers) were trained to help themselves after the crisis team left. Figure 14.12 shows the initial crisis intervention phase, B_1, then a baseline phase when they were suddenly called to serve another group, and a return to the intervention phase, B_2, plus a maintenance phase.

Introducing the Client to the B-A-B Design.
First, we suggest you review previous introductions (in this chapter and Chapter 13). In addition, there are some aspects directly related to the unique features of this design. On the one hand it may be easier to discuss the evaluation component of a project in which the practitioner has already achieved a successful intervention. If the entire project is described before the first intervention, then the same directions

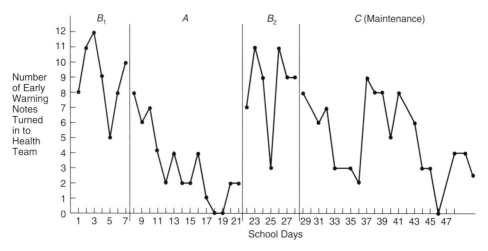

FIGURE 14.12   Crisis intervention at a high school regarding a student suicide, illustrating a *B-A-B* design plus maintenance phase.

applicable to the other experimental designs hold here too. On the other hand, clients may raise questions regarding the *B-A-B* design such as, why change anything? Or why rock the boat? Our suggested responses to these types of statements are as follows: "*I am as pleased as you are about the positive changes in the problem* (or the positive steps toward achievement of the goal), *and I want to make sure that we can keep this level of achievement going after the service program is over. Therefore, I would like to have a trial run by removing the treatment and still continuing to collect information about how well you are doing with these types of problems. If the problem returns to bothersome levels, we can start the treatment once again and that will be the last part of the service program. We want to make sure you can handle these problems on your own in the future.*"

SUMMARY

We have described three experimental designs, all of which involve the removal of a successful intervention (i.e., one in which observations of target behaviors appear to be clearly moving toward desired levels) followed by a baseline period in order to test the potential causality of the intervention's effect on the target behavior. Variations on this return to baseline make up the three designs: *A-B-A, A-B-A-B, B-A-B*. Because of the successively unlikely occurrence that such variations in the target problem could have happened by chance, we have the basis for inferring a causal influence on the part of the planned intervention. This means that not only is the pattern of change documented, but control over that change is to some extent documented as well. This is the basis for a functional analysis of the events in question. This is a very powerful set of designs that you should consider carefully, evaluating each design for its own strengths and limitations.

We also discussed the difficulties in using such designs, such as practical problems (there could be carryover effects from one phase to the next phase), ethical considerations (is it right to stop a successful intervention in order to satisfy an interest in understanding causality?), and collegial problems (who wants to work with a troublesome client, especially after the problem appears to be resolved?). Thus, with logical power come social dilemmas regarding practicality.

15

MULTIPLE DESIGNS FOR SINGLE SYSTEMS
Baselines, Targets, Crossovers, and Series

PURPOSE: This chapter deals with single-system designs that involve multiple elements, specifically multiple baselines and multiple targets, and certain variations of these two. Multiple-baseline designs can be used with more than one problem, client, or setting. Multiple-baseline designs also can be used as an alternative to the experimental designs when there are practical limitations (such as carryover effects), or ethical concerns (such as removing a successful intervention for a serious problem), or problems in staff cooperation (who would have to handle the return to the problematic behavior phase). Multiple-target designs are helpful in generating meaningful patterns among behaviors. Crossover and constant-series designs offer some interesting and practical variations on the other multiple designs. Overall, the four designs discussed in this chapter are very accessible for ordinary use by practitioners. ■

Introduction

Multiple-Baseline Designs: Across Problems, Clients, or Settings

x	A	B
y	A	B
z	A	B

Strengths of the Multiple-Baseline Design

Limitations of the Multiple-Baseline Design

Recommendations Regarding the Multiple-Baseline Design

Case Illustrations

Across Problems

Across Clients

Across Settings

Introducing the Client to the Multiple-Baseline Design

Multiple-Target Designs

x	A	B
y	A	C
z	A	D

Case Illustration

Strengths of the Multiple-Target Design

Limitations of the Multiple-Target Design

Recommendations Regarding the Multiple-Target Design

Introducing the Client to the
  Multiple-Target Design
Variations on Multiple Designs
Crossover Designs

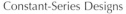

Constant-Series Designs

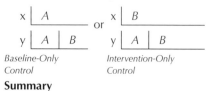

Baseline-Only   *Intervention-Only*
Control   *Control*
Summary

INTRODUCTION

There are several relatively powerful single-system designs that involve working with several target problems, several clients, or several settings at the same time, while holding the other two of the three elements constant. (That is, if we work with several problems, then we work with only one client in one setting.) With the multiple-baseline design in particular, the practitioner can make some logical inferences about possible causal effects of the intervention without removing the intervention. Thus, the multiple-baseline design can serve as an alternative to the experimental designs discussed in Chapter 14. Moreover, the designs discussed in this chapter emphasize a fact that practitioners have always faced, that client problems and goals often come in multiples. One way to represent this practical state of affairs in design terms is by way of multiple-baseline designs, so as to identify patterns of change and the possible causal relationship between interventions and outcomes.

The designs discussed in this chapter may appear in some ways more complicated than those discussed earlier. However, we want to emphasize that this complexity exists mainly in the initial presentation of the designs because they are different from the ones we've already examined. Once you understand the underlying arrangement of baselines and interventions, we hope you will recognize that these are quite easy to use in ordinary practice.

MULTIPLE-BASELINE DESIGNS: ACROSS PROBLEMS, CLIENTS, OR SETTINGS

Multiple-baseline designs have three elements that may be varied: target problems, clients, and the settings in which the client(s) and problem(s) exist. When one element (say, two or more of a client's problems) is studied, the other elements have to be kept constant (one client in one setting). These three patterns are illustrated in Figure 15.1. While there are different elements examined in each of the three cases, the same basic pattern of analysis is used. In this section, we introduce this basic pattern.

Multiple-baseline designs exhibit the following characteristics: There are two or more different target problems, clients, or settings on which baseline information is collected (indicated by the x, y, and z in the figure at the beginning of this section). As soon as a stable pattern of baseline data is obtained on all of the targets, then an intervention (B) is introduced only to the first target. The second and third baselines are continued. If a desired change occurs in the first target while no obvious change occurs in the second and third, then the same intervention, B, is applied to the second target, while the third baseline is continued. Again, if

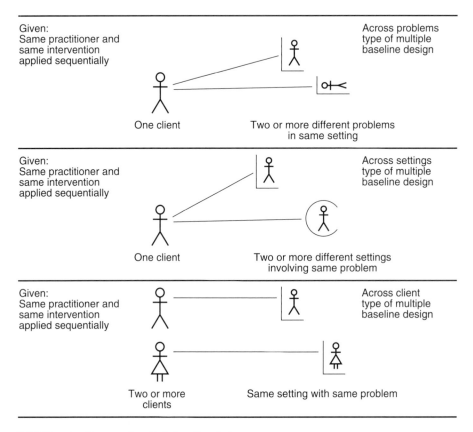

Given:
Same practitioner and
same intervention
applied sequentially

Across problems
type of multiple
baseline design

One client

Two or more different problems
in same setting

Given:
Same practitioner and
same intervention
applied sequentially

Across settings
type of multiple
baseline design

One client

Two or more different settings
involving same problem

Given:
Same practitioner and
same intervention
applied sequentially

Across client
type of multiple
baseline design

Two or more
clients

Same setting with same problem

FIGURE 15.1   Patterns of multiple-baseline design components across
problems/goals, client/systems, and situations.

a desired change occurs in the second target
(and the first target continues to maintain its desired changes), then the same intervention, *B*, is
applied to the third target. If a desired change
occurs in the third target, while the first and second targets maintain their desired changes,
then we have the basic multiple-baseline pattern that permits us to note that desired changes
occurred when, and only when, the specific intervention occurred on a sequential basis. This
becomes the basis for inferring causality, that
the intervention likely was a primary cause related to the observed outcomes in the several
targets, viewed sequentially. This basic pattern
holds whether the targets are two or more client
problems, two or more different clients, or two
or more different settings, as indicated in Figure
15.1. The essence of the inference of causality
is that the *changes occurred in sequence,* only after

introduction of the intervention. Thus, once
again, the "principle of unlikely successive coincidences" would permit the argument that
there may be a causal relationship between implementation of the intervention and changes
in the target.

Some special issues affect the different types
of multiple-baseline designs. One concerns the
number of targets used. Opinions differ. Hypothetically, two targets would be sufficient to
demonstrate sequential change involving the
same intervention. However, some writers recommend three targets at a minimum (Barlow &
Hersen, 1984), while others suggest four or
more (Kazdin & Kopel, 1975). Greater numbers of targets, each changing when and only
when an intervention is applied to it, make it increasingly unlikely that these planned changes
are happening by chance alone.

Obviously, the more targets that are required for the use of a multiple-baseline design, the less likely it is that some practitioners will use the design. So we offer our standard caution: The consensus on minimum numbers of target problems is three. If you use only two targets, then consider the findings merely suggestive. If you can handle more than three, then you have much stronger evidence of causality.

It is important to add that any two targets may be treated in sequence as the basis of a multiple baseline design. For example, consider a practitioner with four targets. If targets 2 and 3 changed when an intervention was applied to target 1, there would be a serious problem if only the first three targets were being observed. However, as long as target 4 did not change, the practitioner can still try for a multiple baseline with the first and fourth targets only. The second and third targets become simple *A-B* designs, which, when viewed in tandem with the other targets, may also be suggestive about the pattern of problems facing the client.

Another topic with regard to multiple-baseline designs concerns how long a successful intervention should be continued on the first target before applying that same intervention to a second target. Again, opinions differ, but a consensus suggests that at least three sessions or observations are needed to indicate a stable improvement in the first target and no major change in the second. A larger number would be preferable for reasons similar to those discussed in Chapter 12 on length of baseline.

The versatility of multiple-baseline designs is remarkable. The logic of the design states that two or more targets in the same system and context are needed for sequential treatment as the basis of inferring causality for that intervention. Thus, we may use two or more different clients as targets, or two or more different problems from the same client as targets, or two or more different settings involving the same client and problem. We illustrate each of these variations briefly now, and then go into greater detail later.

The first type of multiple-baseline design is *across problems,* and involves one client (or client/system) with two or more problems (the different baselines) in one setting. As an exam-

ple of a multiple-baseline design across problems, Jacobson (1979) used this design in work with couples showing severely distressed marital relationships. Taking one couple as an example (Jacobson discusses six cases), the process first involved a 2-week baseline period consisting of an assessment and use of a modified version of the Spouse Observation Checklist (Weiss, Hops, & Patterson, 1973), data on which were phoned in at the end of each day. (Figure 15.2 summarizes about 14 baseline data points by averaging each week's data and recording these average points.) At the initial intervention session (the third week), the couple was presented with an analysis of their marital problems and a rationale for the treatment they were about to receive. Each session began with an analysis of the data the clients had supplied during the previous meetings.

The first intervention consisted of instructing the clients to increase the intimate behaviors desired by the spouses and to decrease those activities designated as undesirable. Four weeks of this intervention did not produce any desired changes, so the practitioner added a second intervention (problem-solving training) on the seventh week, at which time substantial improvements were made. After 3 weeks of stable, desired behavior on the first target problem, with no significant change in the baseline of the second target problem, the practitioner introduced the problem-solving training plus instructions for the second problem (husband's positive communications to his wife). A major improvement is recorded, while the first target problem continues at a generally high level of performance. Jacobson notes that this design cannot tease out the influences of problem solving alone because it may be confounded (at least in the first baseline) with the first intervention (instructions) and in both baselines with relationship skills and other communications; this is left to future research. However, this is an interesting example of a multiple-baseline design with two separate intervention phases in one of the baselines, and an overall effect that appears to show that some part of the intervention was probably related to the changes across two problems.

The second type of multiple-baseline design is *across settings,* in which one client (or

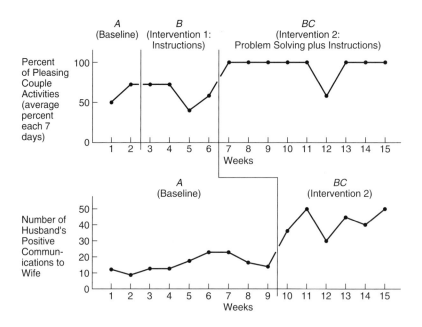

FIGURE 15.2   Case illustration of a multiple-baseline design across problem behaviors for a married couple. (Data adapted from "Increasing Positive Behavior in Severely Distressed Marital Relationships: The Effects of Problem-Solving Training" by N. S. Jacobson, 1979, *Behavior Therapy, 10*, p. 318.)

client-system) has one problem exhibited in two or more settings (the different baselines). A study that used different settings for the same intervention with the same client/system was conducted by Kirchner et al. (1980). They studied the effects of a helicopter patrol on rates of home burglaries in two high-density crime areas (see Figure 15.3). An interesting feature of this study is that they employed an *A-B-A* model within the multiple-baseline design: Not only did they take an initial baseline and then introduce an intervention, but they also removed that intervention to return to the initial baseline conditions, thereby adding an experimental dimension to their design. This occurred because they had only one helicopter to use for two areas. We focus here mainly on the multiple baseline design across settings, however. The mean figure per day, comparing *A* to *B* in both baselines, indicates that the helicopter patrol seems to be exerting some controlling influence over home burglaries. However, in addition, we can observe that the impact of the patrol in one area did not influence rates of bur-

glaries in the other. This is an important piece of information that only a comparison of multiple elements (as in this type of design) can reveal, and it is a basic condition for the proper use of the multiple-baseline design.

The third type of multiple baseline is *across clients* or *client-systems*, in which the same practitioner applies the same intervention sequentially to two or more persons/groups who exhibit the same problems in the same setting. A study by Switzer, Deal, and Bailey (1977) illustrates this type of design. The amount of stealing among second graders in a school was controlled by using group contingencies, but not by antitheft lectures. The three classes are the client/system in this study, and the common problem is theft. Figure 15.4 shows a reconstruction of the data and indicates that for two classes, the antitheft lectures did not have the desired impact; in fact, the mean rate of theft increased slightly. However, group contingencies—in which the whole class was rewarded with: (a) extra free time for no thefts, (b) their normal time if stolen things were returned, or

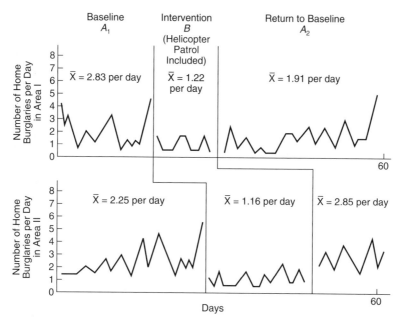

FIGURE 15.3   Illustration of multiple-baseline design across settings: The number of home burglaries in two high-density crime areas in which a helicopter patrol was added and removed as the intervention. (Data reconstructed from "The Applicability of a Helicopter Patrol Procedure to Diverse Areas: A Cost-Benefit Evaluation" by R. E. Kirchner, J. F. Schnelle, M. Domash, L. Larson, A. Carr, and M. P. P. McNees, 1980, *Journal of Applied Behavior Analysis, 13,* p. 145.)

(c) loss of free time if stolen things were not returned–did appear to produce success. Having observed the lack of effect of the antitheft lectures on the first two classes, the researchers did not bother to try them with the third class. Rather, the clearcut success of group contingencies on the first two classes was applied directly to the third group, showing once again the flexibility of the single-system design in using feedback from client data.

These three cases illustrate the three types of multiple-baseline designs. We next consider the strengths and limitations of these designs and our recommendations regarding their use. Then we present a number of case examples to illustrate the underlying patterns as well as the variations these designs can include.

Strengths of the Multiple-Baseline Design

To summarize some of the points mentioned in the previous examples, it is clear that this de-sign is quite adaptable to changes in either problems/goals, clients/systems, or settings. Indeed, when clients present multiple problems, this design represents one way of dealing with them in a planned fashion whereby you might cluster those with high priority for immediate action, and then in sequence deal with others later, and still obtain considerable insight into whether your interventions were responsible for the changes observed. This assumes that the *same* intervention can be applied to different problems, or in different settings, or to different clients (with the same problem).

Likewise, there are few designs in the single-system spectrum that permit practitioners to compare interventions across settings such as is possible with the multiple-baseline design. This has important implications if you wish to test the hypothesis that a given conceptual behavior pattern (e.g., unassertiveness) is exhibited consistently across different situations. Thus, this design may be especially helpful to those seeking to test implications from conceptual models.

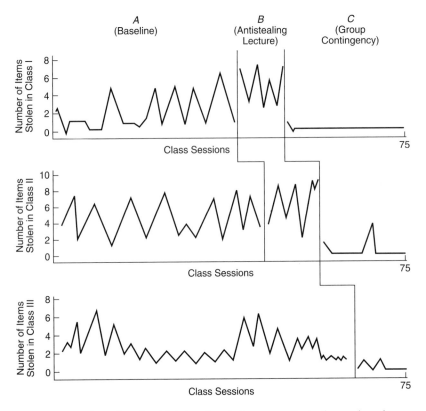

FIGURE 15.4 Illustration of multiple-baseline design across clients: the number of thefts among three classes of second graders before and after two interventions. (Adapted from "The Reduction of Stealing in Second Graders Using a Group Contingency" by E. B. Switzer, T. E. Deal, and J. S. Bailey, 1977, *Journal of Applied Behavior Analysis, 10,* p. 270.)

More important for practice and evaluation purposes, though, is the generalizability of our interventions across settings and locations.

The multiple-baseline design may be the design of choice when problems of carryover or irreversibility of effects are present or when the first intervention cannot be removed so that you can't use experimental (removal) designs. This is because with removal designs you stay with the same problem, client, and setting so that carryover or irreversibility may limit any conclusions that could be drawn from the removal. On the other hand, since multiple-baseline designs use *different* problems, clients, or settings, standard carryover or irreversibility effects are not as germane; this is because you are switching domains (problems, clients, settings) rather than removing the in-

tervention and staying with the same domain. (However, it is also possible to have carryover effects over clients, problems, and/or settings, a point to which we return below.)

We have also suggested the usefulness of this design *in place of* the experimental designs that remove a successful intervention in order to test whether that intervention is causally linked to observed changes. With the multiple-baseline design, if the first target changes while the others remain more or less unchanged, then this tells you that not only has the first target changed, but the change is limited to that target even when other events are present and are part of the total intervention effort. This focused demonstration of control over desired targets is at the heart of the multiple-baseline design. That is, the controlled application of the intervention and the predicted sequential effect become the basis for an inference that the practitioner's efforts are causally related to the observed change.

It may be argued that using the multiple-baseline procedure also is a way of testing the generalizability of the intervention. If the problems are similar and the settings are similar, then sequential application of the same intervention to different clients offers some basis for inferring that the intervention is generalizable, assuming there is no contact among recipients of the service that would constitute contamination of the data. In a similar way, it is possible to generalize an intervention across problems and situations as well.

Finally, this design is relatively easy to implement with most cases or situations. This was demonstrated by the Rinn and Vernon (1975) study in a community mental health center in which simply making salary increases contingent on use of multiple baselines and other evaluation tools with all clients dramatically increased use of multiple baselines with virtually all clients.

Limitations of the Multiple-Baseline Design

Many times it is hard to arrange life in neat packages such as are demanded in principle by the multiple-baseline designs. Yet practitioners have to develop a set of priorities, because they cannot work on every problem at the same time. Therefore, while practice is complex, the multiple-baseline design seems ready-made for such complexity because it allows you to sort out targets and deal with them one at a time while collecting baseline data on the others.

Within the design itself, some special problems emerge. You are required to obtain stable baselines from two or more targets. It is easily conceivable that one or another of those targets may resist presenting a nice, neat, stable baseline. What should you do with the other problems in the meantime? We suggest that you go to work on those targets that have stabilized using the multiple-baseline design. For the unstable ones, you can continue to search for a stable baseline and do a simple *A-B* design. Linking these "unruly" targets with the

overall multiple-baseline design might provide other insights as to the relationships among the several target events. (We will discuss more of this with regard to the next design.)

There is yet another problem when several targets are identified and one is dealt with in sequence before the others: the issue of *order of intervention*. This is more of a problem with multiple baselines across problems, because there may be an unknown effect of the order of intervention on the overall outcome of the service program. One answer would be to deal with target problems in some random order, but that would be unsatisfying to most practitioners. The other option is to vary the order across different clients and to try to compare differences among outcomes. However, this is very tenuous, since so many other considerations affect outcomes. When the problems in a set are all of equal difficulty, a random selection (or just flipping a coin) among targets would be quite possible.

A third problem with use of multiple-baseline designs is that the same intervention is required to be used across all problems, clients, and situations. This is because the main purpose of the multiple baseline is to produce a causal statement about the effects of a specific intervention. Sometimes, this presents a problem for the practitioner who would like to study the causal effects of his or her interventions using a multiple-baseline design, but who is faced, for example, with one client who has two different problems calling for two separate interventions. While we ordinarily recommend using the same intervention whenever possible in order to get as clear a picture of causality as possible, in situations such as this, we can offer—very tentatively—the following suggestion. If you must use different interventions but would like to also use the multiple baseline design, then go ahead. However, be aware that even if the problems do change sequentially and only after your intervention is applied, you will not be able to conclude that your specific interventions had an effect. The best you can conclude is that something in your program (your interventions, your attention, your personal style, and so on) produced the changes in the problem, a somewhat less precise conclusion than using only one intervention allows. Of course, it is important to note that it is always difficult to conclude that only your techniques produced the change and not some other uncontrolled influence—for example, changes in the way you attend to the client. This is even true for experimental removal designs. However, there probably is a sounder basis for inferring causality when you implement the same intervention as opposed to using two or more different interventions on different problems.

A fourth problem with multiple baselines, and perhaps the key problem, has to do with the possibility that changes associated with introduction of the first intervention with the first baseline may show up in the other baselines as well. This is another variation on the theme of carryover effects. Stated another way, the problems (or baselines) may not be independent. That is, the changes introduced in one baseline become general (across the baselines) rather than specific (occurring in only one baseline at a time, sequentially). Hence, it is said that the baselines are "dependent." Since the main purpose of the multiple baseline is to attempt to rule out the effects of "history" and other related threats to design validity described in Chapter 11, this would more or less invalidate the use of the multiple baseline to make causal inferences (what *produced* the changes?).

In line with Kazdin and Kopel (1975), we have three recommendations for this situation. First, try your best to use problems, clients, or settings that are as independent as possible. Try to select problems, clients, or settings that appear to be relatively distinct from each other so that changes in one don't produce changes in the other. While it is not always possible to tell whether problems, clients, or situations are distinct from each other just by looking at the baseline data, at the least you can try to choose two baselines that don't vary consistently with each other (as one goes up, the other consistently goes up or down). This is less of a concern when dealing with multiple baselines across clients because the problems of two or more clients would be less likely to affect each other than two problems of the same client (with some exceptions such as spouses, siblings, etc.).

Second, try to use as many baselines as possible—three or four rather than just two.

The more baselines you use, the greater the chance you have of finding at least two in which the changes introduced into the first don't generalize to the second. If at least two targets show the predicted effects of sequential changes, then the logic of the multiple baseline is applicable to those targets. Indeed, even if none of the changes generalizes to other baselines, the more baselines you use, the more solid is the evidence for inferring causality.

The third and last recommendation, as a sort of last resort, is to consider using an experimental removal on one of the baselines such as in the Kirchner et al. (1980) study discussed earlier. We suggest this only when the previous recommendations fail or are impossible, and when it is crucial to determine whether your techniques are really affecting the problem. We recognize that you may be using a multiple-baseline design precisely because you do not want to use a removal and that this recommendation would be a problem under those circumstances. Nevertheless, it is an option.

Recommendations Regarding the Multiple-Baseline Design

If given the choice of removing a successful intervention (as in the experimental designs described in Chapter 14) or applying the same interventions to several targets in sequence as in multiple-baseline designs, then the choice may be dictated by ethical and practical considerations. The multiple-baseline design provides a relatively strong basis for logical inference of causality and is highly flexible in its use in field settings. For example, it would be possible, as illustrated by the Kirchner et al. (1980) study, to incorporate other designs within the multiple-baseline program (they used an *A-B-A* design as part of their program). The multiple-baseline design does require considerable planning and control of the situation. This suggests that if you specifically consider the alternative of multiple-baseline designs as you are specifying goals and formulating intervention plans, you will increase your chances of using this strong and ethically sound method of evaluating practice. We urge its careful consideration for both practice and ethical reasons, but also because of its potential contribution to conceptualization and empirical knowledge building as you attempt to grasp the whole picture of a given client/system.

Case Illustrations

Across Problems. A recent case illustrates the use of a multiple-baseline design across three problems. The case involved a woman who was being seen for pervasive ritualistic behavior that interfered with all aspects of her functioning (Cooper, 1990). The practitioner had seen the client for 3 years, once or twice a week, using psychodynamic psychotherapy. While the practitioner saw a number of gains from this treatment, she was having no impact on the client's ritualizing behavior. The practitioner, therefore, decided to implement a behavioral treatment that included modeling, exposure, and response prevention techniques.

The practitioner asked the client to do self-monitoring of the frequency of three of the ritualized behaviors: number of twists, presses, and clicks of her makeup case each morning; minutes spent rinsing in the shower; and percentage of times counting her belongings.

As can be seen in Figure 15.5, the intervention program on these three rituals was completed in 8 weeks. With the three problems, the changes occurred only after the intervention began on each. (Note that because the baselines were started at different times and at different intervals, the standard chart was not possible. However, by examining the dates of each chart, you can still see that the changes in the targets occurred in sequence.) This sequencing of effects lends credence to Cooper's (1990) conclusion that the intervention appears related to the change in each behavior. Although the author does not provide data on

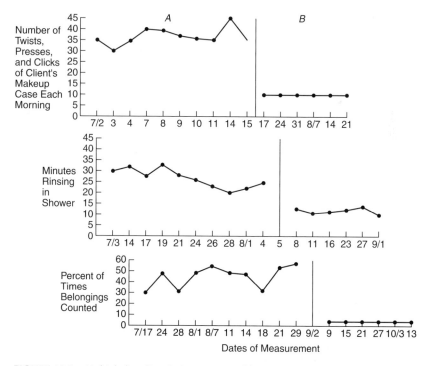

FIGURE 15.5 Multiple-baseline design across problems: treatment of an obsessive-compulsive disorder with modeling, exposure, and response-prevention. (Note time intervals are not drawn equally.) (Adapted from "Treatment of a Client with Obsessive-Compulsive Disorder" by M. Cooper, 1990, *Social Work Research & Abstracts, 26,* pp. 26–32.)

what happens to the problem in each baseline after intervention begins with the subsequent problem, she does state that by the 6-month follow-up, 46 of 54 rituals were gone, apparently including the 3 in this report.

This case had two other interesting dimensions. First, in addition to visually analyzing the data on the clients, the author used the celeration line, which we describe in Chapter 21, to statistically analyze the results. With all three problems, the results were statistically significant.

The second fascinating aspect was the impact this case apparently had on the author. Being able to help her client reclaim her life in only 2 months, after 3 years of unsuccessful psychotherapy, profoundly affected the author, opening up new treatment possibilities for all clients. The author states that her practice is now far more innovative and eclectic.

Hall, Schlesinger, and Dineen (1997) conducted a replication of a study by Bates (1980) on the effectiveness of a social skills training package (that is, a set of interventions all delivered at one time) for developmentally disabled adults. They used a multiple-baseline design across four targeted skills that these people had to learn. These four skills include: introduction and making small talk, asking for help, differing with others, and handling criticism.

What is particularly interesting about this study is that the authors used three criteria to evaluate the effectiveness of the intervention package. One was a role-play exercise that tested materials covered in the training program. A second criterion involved other role situations for which there was no direct training. "Being trained" means that the participants were trained to respond appropriately in two situations per skill. "Not trained" means two other situations per skill, tested after the training phase was over, were used to observe response generalization. All training was conducted either at an empty cafeteria or in an interviewing room at an inner-city community college (group #1; reported here) or at a university mental retardation center (group #2; not reported here).

The third criterion of effectiveness was an *in vivo* assessment, that is, a real life situation at a new location (a local store). This represents a practical criterion of evaluation, one that is too rarely used in the evaluation literature. It is, in many ways, the most difficult and yet most meaningful of criterion measures. Let's examine the Hall, Schlesinger, and Dineen (1997) procedures, displayed in Figure 15.6.

First, they plotted group means of the four participants on all four target skills, using the mean scores of two trained raters for increased reliability. (The authors also note that all individual behavior changes were similar to group changes.) They use the following notation: Circles represent situations used in training; squares represent situations not used in training; and triangles represent *in vivo* tests. Note in Figure 15.6 that the trained and untrained situations were identical at the initial baseline testing, since no training had been given for either. Stable rates appear in the first 2 weeks of baseline measurement, so the group training package begins with the first skill (making small talk), which improves over the next week. Meanwhile, the baselines remain the same in all of the other skill areas. In week 2, the same intervention is applied to the second skill area, which likewise improves while the remaining baselines stay the same. And so on throughout the four-step multiple baseline.

By the end of the fourth week of intervention, the group means are above the baseline rates for tested situations and for situations not tested in training (that is, generalization occurred, but at a lower level of response than to trained situations). Most interesting are the follow-up results of the *in vivo* tests—these are new tests of the generalization of learning—which are below both tested and untested situations, except in the skill area of handling criticisms where the *in vivo* data are close to the tested situations and above the untested situations. These findings have to be viewed in light of the fact that follow-up took place very close to the intervention period and may not have been a true test of the lasting effects of the intervention, nor its generalization to new settings.

The authors do not report statistical significance on their results, but assuming that there was general improvement in social skills after training, this improvement appears to be limited to trained situations and to a lesser degree to similar but not trained situations. There were no baseline evaluations made of the *in*

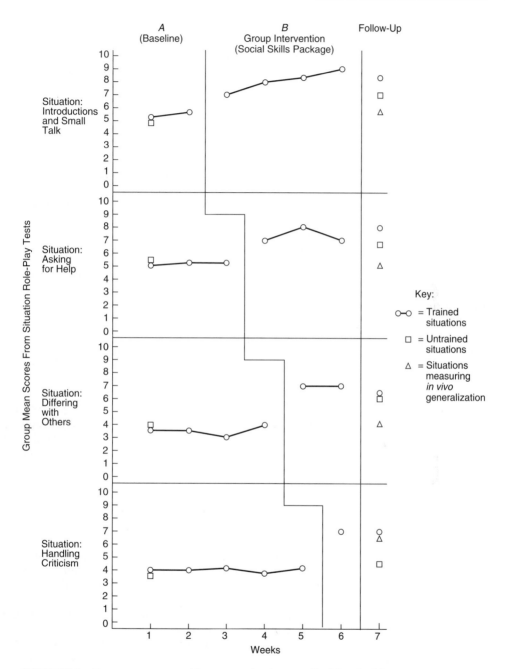

FIGURE 15.6   Group mean scores of four-person developmentally delayed adults from situational role-play tests. (Adapted from Hall et al., 1997.)

vivo situations, so it is hard to interpret those results. However, the training appears not to be effective in three out of four *in vivo* situations, where it ultimately has to be effective if these

developmentally delayed adults are to "make it" in the real world. The authors conclude that ". . . the treatment package was effective in improving social skills, but not powerful enough to effect significant changes in other settings" (Hall et al., 1997, p. 187). Teasing out this important result means that the next studies in this area can build on prior knowledge and construct their training program to address *in vivo* situations more specifically. This is a good example of how single-system evaluation can have a role in knowledge development.

Across Clients. In a recent report, Jung and Jason (1998) used a multiple-baseline design to present a culturally sensitive promotive intervention. This intervention involved training Asian American immigrants in interviewing skills that would increase their probability of success in job hunting, while not changing their ethnic values. These authors point out that there are a number of incompatible values in self-presentation between the Asian and American perspectives, such as demonstrating deference as a sign of respect for others (versus being appropriately assertive on one's own behalf). Such courteous behavior may be interpreted as passive or unmotivated in Western culture, while assertiveness in a first meeting situation may be seen as impolite in Asian culture. So, the training task was to emphasize that Asian values should not be abandoned in many settings (home, ethnic community), but could be modified in Western job application settings so as to optimize chances of getting a job for which the individual was well qualified.

Three Asian American volunteers participated in the study, which consisted of sequential training on: 1) social greeting skills, 2) verbal assertiveness, 3) work independence but also social compatibility with team members, and 4) determination to be successful based on previous accomplishments. Data were collected during twelve simulated interviews over a 6-day period to assess the baseline and post-intervention skills on these four skills. The interviews were videotaped and evaluated by four trained volunteer observers. There was 75% agreement on videotape ratings and 95% agreement between two observers of the actual four interview skill dimensions. (There were also other ratings, but we will focus on the taped interviews, except for the important note that several social validity measures were used,

including one in which household members were also interviewed with regard to possible adverse effects of this training in Westernized customs. No adverse effects at home were noted.)

Figure 15.7 presents an approximation of one participant's experience in the job training, as representative of the others as well. The results are typical of multiple baseline designs, with three exceptions. First, instead of one client with multiple problems, this design used a small group of clients with multiple target problems. Second, the initial target on two of four behaviors showed some improvement during baseline, but after intervention, there was an abrupt increase in performance for all behaviors and participants. Third, there was some improvement in the second skill–verbal assertiveness–at the time when the first intervention was introduced, although this mainly was continuation of an earlier trend in the baseline of verbal assertiveness. However, on average, there was a clear improvement with the group of three clients on all behaviors.

The data show clear improvement in the four behavioral aspects of Westernized job interviewing skills. Some of the four proved more difficult to attain high levels of expression than others. Expressing social skills reached nearly 100% levels, and verbal assertiveness reached about 75% expression. However, working independently yet being a team player and expressing determination to be successful based on previous work accomplished did improve as compared to baseline, but were still at about only the 50% level of expression. In addition, because all targets showed improvement mainly after intervention was begun, and because the intervention was the same across all targets, this multiple-baseline design allows the inference that the intervention, social skills training, probably was responsible for the changes.

A 1-month follow-up indicated that all of the trainees had looked for jobs, and one had a job offer, while another was forming a family business with relatives. One limitation of this study is that the follow-up was too brief a time period for adequate assessment of the overall effects. However, the implications of this study are important for helping professionals in dealing

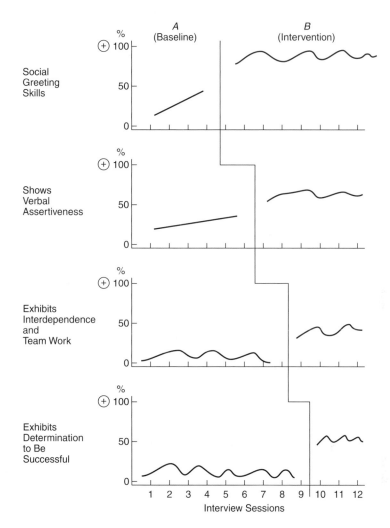

FIGURE 15.7   Percent of occurrences of four types of interview skills used by Asian-American job seekers as part of a job-training program. (Adapted from Jung & Jason, 1998.)

with diversity and adaptation, without damaging either the individual's ethnic culture or his or her opportunities within the dominant culture.

A very interesting example of the use of a multiple-baseline design with three clients with similar problems in a single setting was described by Kolko and Milan (1983). The clients were one female and two male adolescents referred to a private counseling center by a county juvenile court. All three had school-related problems in common, including tardi-ness and academic problems. The problems were conceptualized by the practitioner as a type of "resistance," and for the intervention, the practitioner selected the techniques of re-framing combined with paradoxical instruc-tion. The reframing component was designed to induce or maximize opposition, while the paradoxical instruction—sometimes called "pre-scribing the symptom"—directed the clients to maintain their truancy and tardiness problem behaviors. The primary outcome measures were archival records–class attendance and academic grades–thus minimizing reactivity. The reliability for observing class attendance/absence was over .89 for all clients.

Figure 15.8 is an adaptation of the original multiple baseline report of Kolko and Milan (1983). As can be seen from the data, in all three cases, attendance improved only after the introduction of the intervention and appears to be relatively well maintained at follow-up. Although the first baseline was rather short (two points), the length of the second and third baselines was adequate. This and the clear sequencing of effects all support the causal relationship between application of the intervention and change in the problem. In all three cases, grades also improved following the implementation of intervention, and parents and teachers indicated that there was improvement in other areas as well.

Perhaps the most interesting part of this case is that single-system design procedures were used with an intervention from a phenomenological perspective, one that is often viewed as, if not unresearchable, difficult to study. This case, along with many others in this book, provides additional validation of our notion that single-system designs can be used with interventions from any theoretical system.

Barone, Greene, and Lutzker (1986) present a report on home safety with families being treated for child abuse and neglect. Their study involves a multiple-baseline design across families. They note that over 90% of all injuries, and more than half of the fatalities among children under 5 years of age, occur in the home. There are approximately 4 million home accidents a year involving children. Because children who are abused or neglected are at high risk, the authors experimented with a Home Safety Education package to help in reducing hazards in the home. (An audio slide show was presented on several occasions at the beginning of the intervention period indicating the hazards and how

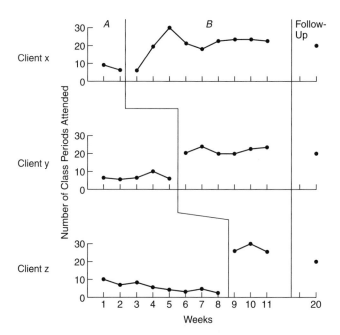

FIGURE 15.8   Multiple-baseline design across clients: application of reframing and paradoxical instruction to academic problems. (Adapted from "Reframing and Paradoxical Instruction to Overcome 'Resistance' in the Treatment of Delinquent Youths: A Multiple Baseline Analysis" by D. J. Kolko and M. A. Milan, 1983, *Journal of Consulting and Clinical Psychology, 51,* pp. 655–660.)

to control them.) The results of their work are shown in Figure 15.9 adapted from their report to emphasize two of the three reported cases.

After the baseline (8 days for one family and 18 days for the other), the intervention was administered, the Home Safety Education package, which involved the slide show, instruction and check-ups. As soon as a stable and acceptable level of target behavior was observed in the first family, intervention was begun with the second. With both families, a kind of maintenance phase, involving unannounced follow-up checks, was also implemented. We describe this as a maintenance function, rather than a simple follow-up, because the service team was still in a treatment relationship with the clients. The data indicate a concomitant reduction of hazardous household conditions with the presence of the Home Safety Education package,

although family Y reduced fewer hazardous materials than did family X.

Several points can be made about the clients in Figure 15.9. First, the scale of total hazardous items differs between the two charts because the Y family always had a much lower rate than the X family; this is indicated on the chart by the break marks above 40 items for the Y family. Second, notice that there is an asterisk on each chart, indicating the point in the service process when unannounced check-ups were instituted (at about 17 days for family X and 35 days for family Y). These check-up data represent discrete probes—that is, they are not linked together as are the baseline and intervention data points—as in the ordinary presentation of follow-up data. However, these data also might be considered a kind of maintenance phase, since the presence of the practitioners at these

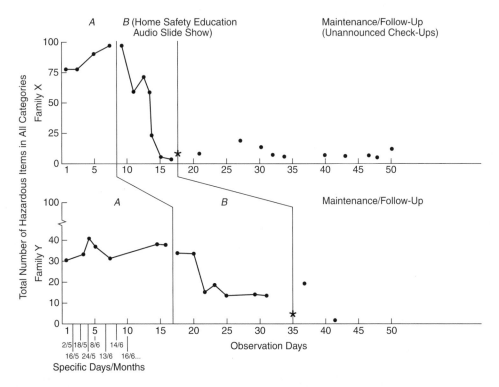

FIGURE 15.9 Multiple-baseline design across family units to study a home safety education program for abusive/neglectful families. (Data adapted from "Home Safety with Families Being Treated for Child Abuse and Neglect" by V. J. Barone, B. F. Greene, and J. R. Lutzker, 1986, *Behavior Modification, 10,* pp. 93–114.)

unannounced check-ups involved an intervention. Note, too, how the time line is indicated, using both the days and months, and the number of observations. Both are useful–the days might indicate some cycles related to social patterns, while the numbers of observations will be used in the analysis of these data.

We want to raise one ethical point in connection with the study by Barone et al. (1986) regarding the length of baseline in connection with cases of suspected child abuse and neglect. Presumably the families involved in this study were known to the protective care practitioners so that baselines of 8 and 18 days were not an immediate risk to the children involved. However, in some cases, a baseline may need to be greatly shortened or eliminated altogether if the events of the case involve risk to participants.

Rolider and Van Houten (1988) conducted a multiple-baseline design with a removal component that shows how several single-system designs can be integrated. Three young boys were sucking their thumbs at an age when this might lead to dental problems, and so a behavioral program was undertaken to eliminate daytime thumbsucking. Examine Figure 15.10, which uses notation from the original article, to follow what happened in this study.

First, a baseline was taken sampling the times the boys had their thumbs in their mouths. Then, in multiple-baseline fashion, the intervention was applied to the first boy while the others were uninterrupted. This intervention (B_1) involved restraining the thumbsucking by having absorbent cotton taped over the thumb, plus other aversive social contingencies (loss of television time if seen thumbsucking, etc.). When a stable desired rate had been reached with the first boy, the same procedure was started with the second, while monitoring of the third boy continued. When stable desired behaviors were attained in the second boy, and continued in the first, the removal part of the design was implemented with the first two boys (i.e., there was a return to baseline), while the third received the intervention (B_1). Note in Figure 15.10 that thumbsucking for the first two boys rose to nearly the heights where the boys had started.

Then, the intervention B_2 was reinstated with the first two boys, while it also was present in the third boy, all of whom showed nearly perfect behavior (no thumbsucking). Next, a new intervention (C) was introduced to the third child (finger-tip bandages plus the social contingencies). When the desired behavior continued with the less drastic intervention (C), it was substituted first in the second boy, and then in the first, like a multiple baseline in reverse (starting from the bottom up). This was followed by a third intervention phase (D) that involved no physical restraints on the boys' fingers, but did continue the social contingencies. This served as a sort of maintenance phase. Finally, the treatment was terminated, but with follow-up observations at 2, 4, and 6 months after the cases were closed. After implementation of intervention C, the children completely eliminated thumbsucking from their behaviors.

This series of phases could also have been annotated as follows, using just the first boy as an example: A_1 = baseline; BC, with B = restraining and C = social contingencies; A_2; CD, with C = social contingencies and D = bandages; and C in the last phase = social contingencies. The chart then would be

$$\lfloor A_1 \mid BC \mid A_2 \mid CD \mid C \rfloor$$

Since social contingencies were present in all intervention phases, it would be difficult to isolate the exact cause of change (although there were no apparent differential effects of B, C, or D). However, it does appear that the intervention in general is causally related to the change.

Besa (1994) used narrative therapy (NT) with six families exhibiting parent–child conflicts, and empirically evaluated the outcomes employing a variation of a multiple-baseline design. The baseline condition takes place "in the initial session [when] a parent is trained in how to take baseline measurements of the target behavior. . . . The baseline period was operationally defined as the initial period that showed no declining rate of problem behavior"–that is, it was a stable problem behavior (pp. 310–311).

The intervention period (B) reflects the unique meaning of narrative therapy (White, 1989), an eclectic approach that opposes the labeling and pathologizing of people, and looks

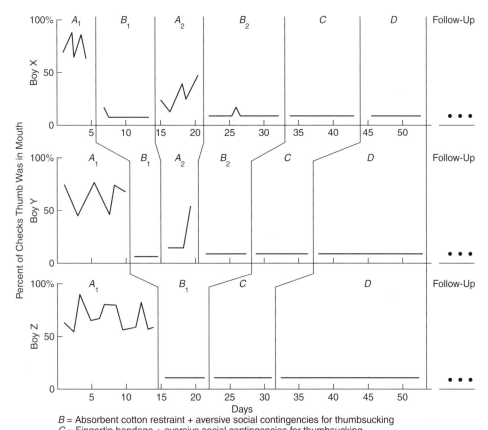

FIGURE 15.10   Multiple-baseline design across clients involving thumbsucking. (Data adapted from "The Use of Response Prevention to Eliminate Daytime Thumbsucking" by A. Rolider and R. Van Houten, 1988, *Child and Family Behavior Therapy, 10,* pp. 135–142.)

for "healthy exceptions" on which to base an intervention. For example, rather than saying that a person is "schizophrenic," the NT practitioner asks the client how schizophrenia pushes him or her around, thus externalizing the problem and taking the blame off the person and family by asking how the problem has influenced their lives. Then they can develop new (healthy) stories about themselves, rather than repeating the old (pathological) stories (pp. 311–314). The targeted outcomes are defined in measurable terms, such as "not doing chores, arguing, attention seeking instead of doing homework," and the like (p. 311). Between-session tasks are

assigned, often as a behavioral contract, to initiate some "unique [and healthy] outcome" (p. 323). Besa also employs a 1-month follow-up in which the parents again measure the target behavior over a 3-day period.

The interventions apparently were done with two families in a time period, permitting a "time-lagged baseline" to be used (see Figure 15.11). This is not the same as a true multiple baseline, because clients and settings and problems were all different, unless one were willing to grant that the targets were functionally similar (e.g., arguments in one family, swearing in another) and the setting was the therapist's

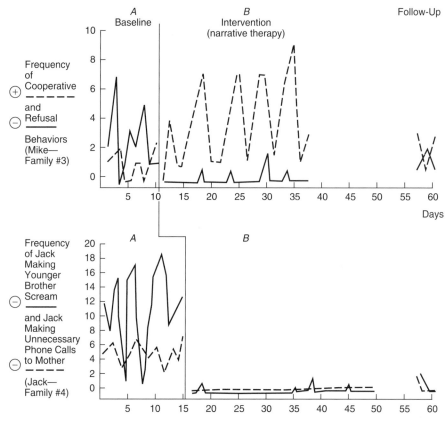

FIGURE 15.11 Clinical data on the children of two families who received narrative therapy. (Adapted from Besa, 1994.)

office rather than the separate homes of the families. Hence, this design probably would resemble most closely a multiple baseline across clients. Besa asserts that, "The results suggest that NT produced the reductions in parent/child conflicts especially" (p. 323), obvious in the three negative behaviors. We would agree only to the extent that these data present the basis for a strong hypothesis that requires more structured testing. But such structure often doesn't appear in field settings, and so this leaves us with an interesting hypothesis that others may use to guide their practice–carefully. It also leaves us with a very interesting example of a practice-based adaptation of a sophisticated single-system design, one that may be difficult to classify, but does

reflect the practitioner's reality and attempt to evaluate practice.

Across Settings. Fox, Hopkins, and Anger (1987) report a longitudinal study involving a token economy promoting safety performance in open-pit mining, using a variation of a multiple-baseline design. Mining is a very hazardous occupation, with 500 people killed and 40,000 injured in 1985 alone (National Safety Council, 1986). So when one token economy program was begun in 1972 at the Shirley Basin Mine (Wyoming) that appeared (with an *A-B* design) to show substantial results, a second program was begun at the Navajo Mine (Arizona) in 1975, thus permitting a quasi–multiple-baseline design to be employed. We call this a "quasi–multiple baseline design" because it violates one of the principles of a multiple baseline across settings, thereby confounding conclusions. In this case, while there were two settings and one problem, the client-system involved different (rather than the same) workers at the two mines. But these data do illustrate how single-system designs can be adapted to work with large numbers of people.

Baseline data were taken from official records of deaths and injuries, given standard work and the ordinary but extensive safety training conditions. A token economy was devised whereby individual workers were given a specified number of trading stamps with each monthly paycheck if they had not suffered a lost-time injury during that time period. There were also group awards of the same type if workers in one unit all had avoided such lost-time injuries. Safety suggestions were further

rewarded with trading stamps. However, if a worker did lose time because of an injury, he or she would not get the trading stamps for a given period of months, depending on the extent of the injury. Likewise, stamps were lost for damage to equipment and failure to report an injury. Bonuses initially were given to people who hadn't had injuries in the previous 2 years. Stamps could be redeemed at nearby stores for any of hundreds of items.

Figure 15.12 shows the results of this enormous project involving between 500 and 1,000 people over a period of 13 years. The left side of the charts indicates numbers of injuries (solid line), decreasing in the baseline for the Shirley Basin Mine and increasing in the baseline for the Navajo Mine; the right side of the chart indicates the costs related to those injuries (dashed line). The authors also report a cost-effectiveness measure, the ratio of dollars saved

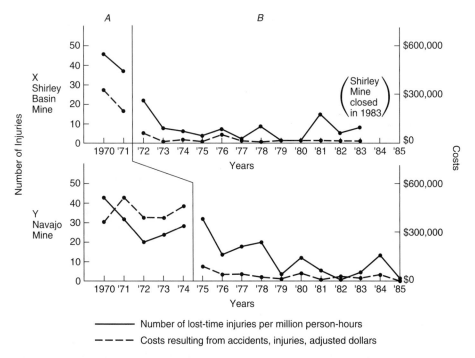

FIGURE 15.12   A quasi–multiple-baseline design showing data on injuries and on costs related to mining accidents. (Data adapted from "The Long-Term Effects of a Token Economy on Safety Performance in Open-Pit Mining" by D. K. Fox, B. L. Hopkins, and W. K. Anger, 1987, *Journal of Applied Behavioral Analysis, 20*, pp. 215–224.)

by the reduction in costs of accidents and injuries, to dollars spent on the token economies. These ratios ranged from a low of 12.9:1 to a high of 27.8:1 in favor of the token economy program. (These figures mean that, for example, there would be a savings of $12.90 for every dollar invested in the token economy.)

Knapczyk (1988) used a multiple-baseline design across settings in his work with two young teenagers who were exhibiting aggressive behaviors in several school settings. The teenagers were in special education programs but were mainstreamed in several classes as well. Analysis of their aggressive behaviors showed that these behaviors tended to occur when the youngsters tried to initiate social interactions but were rebuffed in various ways by their classmates. Knapczyk carefully operationalized the interactional event that led to aggression and then worked out alternative social behaviors that could be used to replace the aggressive ones.

Baseline data consisted of the same observations that had been used to identify when aggressive behaviors occurred. The intervention involved modeling and rehearsal of social skills relevant to each of the three specified settings—the special class, the shop class, and a gym class. As indicated in Figure 15.13, displaying these data for one of these youngsters, in textbook-perfect fashion, problematic behaviors continued in a given setting until the intervention was administered specific to that setting. After the intervention, a clear reduction in the problem behavior was seen and generally was maintained during the follow-up period. The author noted that these findings support other research reports about the need for social skills training for special-education students to fulfill the purpose of mainstreaming these youths. In many instances, improved social performance is necessary to have them effectively integrated into the regular educational setting.

Cushing and Kennedy (1997) provide evidence regarding the effectiveness of peer tutoring for the tutor, while other studies have looked at the effects on the person tutored. They show, using a multiple-baseline design, that academic engagement, assignment completion, grading, and perceived classroom participation all are improved in students without disabilities who provided peer support for students with moderate to severe disabilities. In Figure 15.14, one tutor (Louie) is followed over a period of 25 days in different academic settings as he tutors another student (Leila). As the first part of the multiple baseline demands, a baseline condition (Louie working alone) is observed in English class for 12 days, while this same baseline continues in both science and social studies classes without any significant change. When an increase in Louie's participating in English class is observed in the intervention phase in the first baseline, then the same intervention (tutoring Leila in another subject, science) takes place as we observe changes in Louie's percentage of time academically engaged in science class, where his participation is much improved. Meanwhile, the baseline continues in the third area, social studies, until improved and stable data appear in the science class. Then, the same intervention is introduced, where Louie tutors Leila in social studies, where again, an improvement in Louie's participation is clear. This study shows the creative use of a sophisticated single-system design applied to a very common, everyday situation in many schools.

Brothers, Krantz, and McClannahan (1994) use an *A-B-C* with follow-up design within a multiple-baseline design across settings to study how to increase participation in recycling waste paper at a child development institute. This study is set against a backdrop of efforts to preserve the environment, rather than continuing to burden landfills with paper products that do not biodegrade (even after 25 years of burial).

A baseline period of 10 working days established the weight of paper trash in three settings: the administrative, office, and instructional areas of the institute. Then, the first intervention for staff in all three settings began with the announcement (in their paychecks) that a centrally located recycling container would be available (in approximately the center of the building) the next work day. Since this information was available to all staff, it constitutes a common intervention, *B*. The results showed some increase in recycling at levels that became reasonably stable.

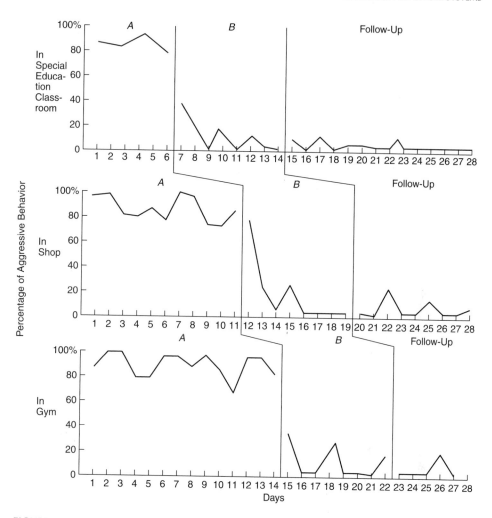

FIGURE 15.13   A multiple-baseline design in which the aggressive behavior of one client was modified in three different school settings. (Adapted from "Reducing Aggressive Behaviors in Special and Regular Class Settings by Training Alternative Social Responses" by D. R. Knapczyck, 1988, *Behavior Disorders, 14,* pp. 27–39.)

A third intervention, *C,* was introduced 10 working days later in the *administrative* area by means of another memo in the paychecks of these workers (privacy and exclusiveness of intervention *C*) informing them that there would be local (desktop) containers in their area for recycling. This produced a stronger increase in recycling in the administrative area, while recycling levels remained more or less constant in the other two areas. Another 10 days later, a memo was sent to workers in the *office* area informing them that a local container would be available in their area (another *C* intervention); again, the data show in increase in recycling among office workers, while the same level of recycling continued as before with workers in the instructional area. In yet another 10 working days, a memo was sent to workers in the *instructional* area informing them that local containers would be available, and again, increased

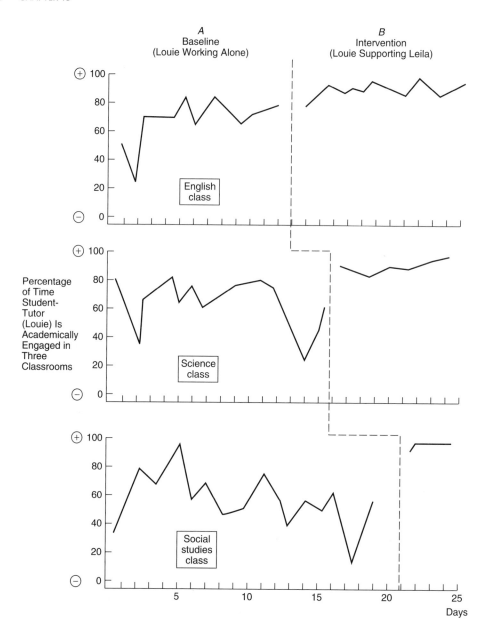

FIGURE 15.14 Percentage of time a student-tutor (Louie) is academically engaged in three classrooms when working alone or supporting (tutoring) another student (Leila). (Adapted from Cushing and Kennedy, 1997.)

rates of recycling appear. The changes in recycling occurred in sequential fashion, only after intervention *C* was applied (see Figure 15.15).

Four follow-ups were conducted at 1-, 2-, 3-, and 7-month periods, which indicated that recycling was continuing at very high levels (between 84% and 98%) among all three work settings. This study provides the logical basis for asserting that desktop containers are a low-cost, highly successful way to attain recycling objectives and to maintain them over the long run. Thus, the multiple-baseline design

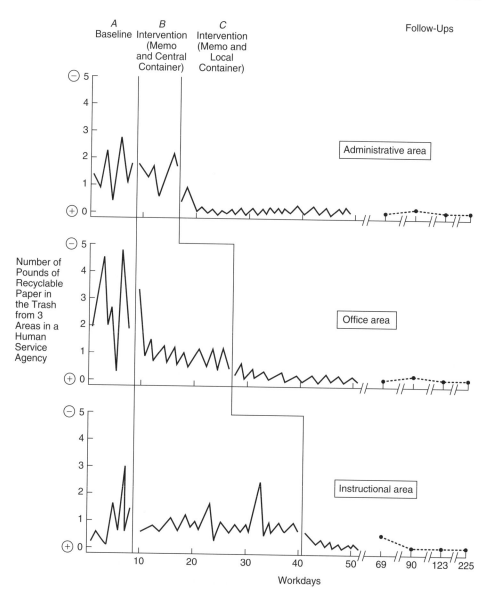

FIGURE 15.15   Number of pounds of recyclable paper in the trash from three areas in a human service agency. (Adapted from Brothers, Krantz, & McClannahan, 1994.)

provided a fairly objective basis for making office decisions that are environment-friendly.

Introducing the Client to the Multiple-Baseline Design

We are happy to report that introductions to this design are often easier than introductions to ex-perimental designs. In the case of multiple-baseline designs, you say what you would ordinarily say in "partializing" a problem—setting priorities among a set of tasks to be accomplished. "*In looking over the set of problems you have presented and as we have discussed them, it seems the best strategy is to work on the problem of x first, and see how we're doing before we start on the next problem. Once the first problem seems to be doing okay, then we'll start work on y, since this seems to be the order of their importance to you."*

Then, in describing the baseline (as in earlier "introduction" sections), you would go on to discuss the intervention and achieving some stability in this phase before going on to the next problem. *"We'll be using a B approach to deal with the first problem, and I would like you to help collect information about it both before we start working on it and during the time that intervention is going on. This way we'll know the extent of the changes in the problem. Also, continuing to collect information until we have finished with all of the problems will tell us whether a problem stayed fixed once we completed work on it."*

For each of the tasks in sequence, you can use these words, or words to this effect. If you plan on using other designs, such as the experimental removal design within the multiple-baseline procedure, then these variations can be introduced to the client as discussed in Chapter 14.

MULTIPLE-TARGET DESIGNS

x	A	B
y	A	C
z	A	D

Multiple target designs are sets of two or more simultaneous *A-B* designs involving different targets and, usually, but not necessarily, different interventions that are presumed to be dealing with conceptually related problems. By viewing the patterns of changes between or among the *A-B* designs, you may be able to generate some practice hypotheses. For example, does the pattern of events in the baseline periods suggest priorities for intervention plans? Let's see what this might look like in practice.

Case Illustration

It will be useful to begin with an example of this design, which we believe to be widely used in practice, although not with sufficient awareness of how useful a tool is at hand. In this illustration the practitioner was a psychiatric social worker employed at an outpatient department

of a university medical school's psychiatric clinic. Each chart on the client, shown in Figure 15.16, can be interpreted independently as an *A-B* design—the pedophiliac fantasies, the feelings of depression, and the frequency of social contacts with peers (Bloom & Block, 1977). Each has its own unique intervention.

Notice some important patterns among these three charts, which are arranged so that the same time units appear in parallel. The one time during the baseline when the client had contacts with peers her own age was in or near the major low points of the other two charts when viewed together. When one chart was low (problematic behavior) and the other high (nonproblematic behavior), no social contact was made. Let's look at the intervention period to test this pattern hypothesis. Again, the lowest points of both the other charts (the pedophiliac fantasies and the feelings of depression charts) occur first before a period of time begins when the patient has frequent contacts with her peers. Is this a meaningful pattern or just an accident?

We suggest that this type of multiple target analysis can generate meaningful patterns, but not as logical bases for establishing causal relationships. Rather, these patterns of concomitant variation among two or more different baselines generate *practice hypotheses* to be tested in the next steps of practice. For example, the data from these three charts suggest that the order of practice would be to reduce the psychological distress (pedophiliac fantasies and feelings of depression) before the desired social behavior can be expected to occur. This is counter to another hypothesis that the practitioner might have followed: If the client could only make social contacts, then her self-defeating thoughts and feelings might be reduced. However, the patterns of baseline data among the three charts do not appear to support this order of events nor the practice strategy based on it.

Should you depend on these patterns to make critical practice decisions? Probably not on an unequivocal or sole basis. But as tentative empirical evidence, it is a first approximation for a practice strategy. Certainly, conceptual or theoretical practice guides also may be used. However, if they run counter to the im-

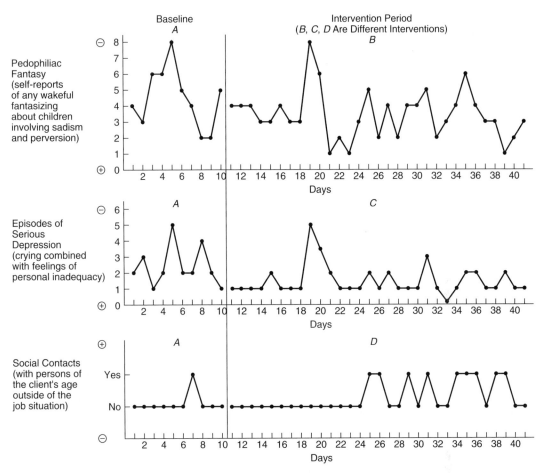

FIGURE 15.16   Illustration of a multiple target design. (Note that the charts are drawn so events occurring in the same time periods can be compared.) (Adapted from "Evaluating One's Own Effectiveness and Efficiency" by M. Bloom and S. R. Block, 1977, *Social Work, 22,* pp. 130–136.)

mediate empirical evidence, then you should be very cautious about adopting either the theory or the tentative empirical patterns.

Strengths of the Multiple-Target Design

The simplicity of this design is appealing. As a set of *A-B* designs applied to different targets typically with different interventions, each separate design can stand by itself. In addition, by positioning the charts of the several *A-B* de-

signs so that the data for the same time points are matching (as in Figure 15.15), you might be able to observe patterns across different events as well as within each given event. Sometimes a theory might predict a configuration of events in advance, in which case you are aided in looking for that configuration (cf. Campbell & Fiske, 1959). But even when no conceptual pattern has been predicted, visually inspecting the several charts at the same time may unearth patterns not previously suspected. These patterns are to be taken as hypotheses for further testing, not as established facts. This approach may be one operational definition of "practice insight"–that is, an intuitive grasping of diverse pieces of information to form one integrated view of the client. This also may be the way concepts are formed–abstractions from varied instances of behavior.

Limitations of the Multiple-Target Design

There are many logical, sound designs that can provide clear information not only on change, but also on the basis for causal inference, so that the choice to use the multiple-target design, which lacks these strengths–because the changes are not planned to occur on a sequential or staggered basis as with the multiple-baseline design–must be well founded. In fact, use of the multiple-target design really implies less a decision in advance than a comparison of patterns of data from three *A-B* designs after the fact. We make some recommendations shortly about when the best use of this design might be made.

In addition to problems regarding causality, there are some other problems regarding the use of the multiple target design. What if, for example, there is progress on one target event and not on the others? This breaks down the predicted pattern about what causal factors were involved. We do not necessarily view this as a limitation. It is as important to know what is not the case as it is to know what is the case. Such a state of affairs (when no patterns of events appear to make sense) is sufficient to drive the practitioner back to the beginning to seek to understand the situation. However, it is far better to learn what you do not know than to be deceived (by yourself) into thinking you have some understanding when you have little.

Recommendations Regarding the Multiple-Target Design

We recommend that those who make use of only the basic single-system design (*A-B*) as their approach to evaluation also consider using this additive design. It requires no more effort than goes into monitoring each separate component and may offer some good oppor-

tunities to form and test some systematic hunches about the nature of the entire case or sets of cases. Until the logic of the pattern of changes is explicated, we don't recommend reliance on this design as a tool of ultimate evaluation. However, it can be useful as an initial tool that will lead to more rigorous testing. Since so many clients are troubled by multiple problems, this multiple-target design commends itself as one method of grappling with complex situations.

As an exploratory tool with rare cases, it might be very useful to try to find some patterns that are linked with available knowledge bases. The common features of an uncommon circumstance might suggest ways to approach finding these patterns. Also, for common problems in which you believe you know the likely course of events, the multiple-target design may be a useful shorthand for keeping track of events without getting into an elaborate design.

Introducing the Client to the Multiple-Target Design

Simply use the suggestions given for the *A-B* design; the added advantages of looking for patterns is "free," although you may wish to share these insights with your clients to check them out. For example, you might say, "*I notice that just before you do* (some problematic act), *from the charts it looks like X and Y occur–for example, low levels of X and high frequencies of Y. This suggests a pattern to be on the lookout for. What do you think?*"

Depending on your guiding theory of practice, it may be possible to give the observed pattern a label. For instance, feeling depressed and frustrated may be preceded by an exchange with a client's boss and spouse, both of whom make unfair demands on the client's time. A label for this pattern might be unassertiveness and might be helpful in focusing practice activities.

VARIATIONS ON MULTIPLE DESIGNS

Two types of newly developed designs could be viewed as variations of the "multiple" designs we have discussed. These are crossover and constant-series designs. Each type of design offers some unique advantages, although neither has the explanatory capacity of the multiple-baseline design.

Crossover Designs

x	A	B		x	A	B	C
y	B	A	or	y	A	C	B

Every basic design in the single-system universe can be modified to fit different practice contexts. These modifications will change the logical basis for inferring causality, but may be necessary because of the nature of the presenting circumstances. In this section and the following section, we discuss some variations partly for their own sake, but also in part to stimulate creative thinking about single-system designs.

Some important variations on the multiple-target designs have been suggested by Barlow et al. (1984) (see also Hayes et al., 1986). They are called crossover designs, in which two concurrent interventions (typically, the same intervention for both targets) take place, each on a separate target but in reverse order for one client. One type of crossover design would involve two *A-B* designs for one client, performed concurrently, but in an *A-B* order for one target and a *B-A* order for the other. Then, if changes occur when and only when the intervention is applied, we have some, but a limited, basis for inferring causality. For the *A-B* designs, it is necessary to replicate the interventions on these targets, or to add more targets, as a basis for inferring causality, since clients may respond to some intervention because of its novelty in spite of the varied order of presentation (Barlow et al., 1984).

Suppose that a neighborhood association is trying to cut down on litter in the streets, while at the same time trying to encourage recycling of paper, glass, and metals. Because of limited personnel, the officers of the association propose to take one problem at a time, beginning with the litter problem. They devise an information package that identifies the scope of the problem, indicates the costs in managing the problem, and proposes some simple steps in reducing the problem. They decide to measure the amount of litter on the neighborhood streets and also the number of people sorting their trash for recycling on garbage pickup days. When the litter campaign gets under way, they begin their measurement of both problems and note some sizable reductions in littering, while there is no effect on recycling. Then they send out a similar package on recycling, and continue to monitor results on both measures. Thus, they have used an *A-B* design for the recycling problem and a *B-A* design for the littering problem. If positive change is observed when and only when the same intervention is applied to each target, then there is somewhat stronger evidence of causality than with two separate *A-B* designs.

Another type of crossover design involves two different interventions presented concurrently but in reverse order, such as in an *A-B-C* and an *A-C-B* order. When consistent changes occur, such as improvements associated with *B* and no changes with *C,* then, "the likelihood of that effect is increased beyond that of the component simple phase changes were they not synchronized" (Barlow et al., 1984, p. 265). Barlow et al. provide an example drawn from the educational research field. A school wishes to test the differences between two methods of teaching, one using programmed texts, the other employing conventional texts. The programmed text comes in two versions, for math and for English, and so by random choice, the programmed text in English is used for a month while the regular text in math is used. Then the next month, the process is reversed, and the regular text is used in English, while a programmed text is used in math. The students are tested frequently on what they are learning in these courses. If the programmed text proves superior to the regular texts in both math and English, regardless of when they were introduced to the same set of students, then there is greater likelihood of establishing the effectiveness of this intervention than would have been attainable by two separate *B-C* comparisons.

The major requirements of the crossover designs are having two concurrent phase changes with the same interventions presented in reverse order (*A* to *B, B* to *A;* or *B* to *C, C* to *B,* etc.). These phases must be in the same setting, with the same length of phases. In this way, various threats to the internal validity of the findings are kept equivalent for each target of intervention. Crossovers like this can be added to any situation involving two targets when the same intervention can be used with each. It is a way of strengthening the *A-B* comparisons with no extra effort except careful planning of when each phase is to occur. (We discuss in Chapter 16 other ways in which rearrangement of phases can add inferences about causality.)

Constant-Series Designs

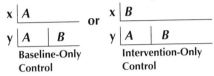

Baseline-Only Control   Intervention-Only Control

This variation of the multiple-target design also was suggested by Barlow et al. (1984). One form of the constant-series design involves the fact that practitioners frequently assess or measure target problems without taking corrective action. Rather than waste this information, the practitioner can combine this situation with a simple *A-B* design to demonstrate that while the *A-B* shows predicted changes, the other target (*A*-only) remains about the same. This is termed a *baseline-only control*.

Another form of the constant-series design involves the situation in which intervention (*B*-only) is required immediately and continuously on one target, while another target permits the regular *A-B* design. Rather than waste this information, the practitioner can combine this situation with a simple *A-B* design to demonstrate that while the constant intervention shows continuous improvement, the *A-B*

design (with the same intervention) shows variations in the target depending on whether the intervention is being applied. This is termed an *intervention-only control.*

Barlow et al. (1984) suggest that these constant-series designs would be much stronger if an *A-B-A-B* design were used in conjunction with a constant baseline or a constant intervention as described above. But, if the experimental design were employed, there would be little need to use the constant-series design, since the point is to provide some basis for inferring causality, which is much better done using the stronger experimental design.

In general, the constant-series designs provide some evidence about the causal efficacy of the intervention by observing it to be associated with changes in the target when present, and with no changes in the target when it is not present. They are not logically strong designs but provide enhanced confidence for using the results from the basic *A-B* design, with little additional effort. As Barlow et al. (1984) point out, if a practitioner were to do a baseline-only control on one target, an intervention-only control on another target, and a basic *A-B* design on the third, all with equivalent results (such as positive change occurring when and only when the *B* was presented), then a set of separate weak (but nonintrusive) designs are combined into a single pattern that adds to the meaningfulness of the overall results. It is difficult to indicate precisely how strong such a composite would be, but this combination would exhibit a kind of concomitant variation that is the basis for the logical strength of multiple-baseline designs.

SUMMARY

Several types of relatively powerful designs seem to parallel practice activities very closely, and thus provide you a relatively easy way to evaluate your own practice. This chapter presented several of these designs, all of which include multiple elements: multiple baselines across problems, clients, or situations; multiple-target designs that involve two or more different targets and their different interventions; and two variations of these designs, the crossover and the constant-series designs. Common to them all is the emphasis on patterns of outcomes.

Multiple baselines involve obtaining a stable baseline on two or preferably more targets (problems, clients, or situations) and then introducing an intervention to the first target while recording baseline information on the others. After a desired level of change has stabilized in the first target, the same intervention is applied to the second, and so on. This logically demonstrates control over the targets and shows that change occurs only when the intervention is employed. This is a powerful single-system design with the added advantage (over experimental designs of Chapter 14) that no removal of intervention is necessary. It is possible to use a variety of other single-system designs within the multiple baseline design, increasing its flexibility and utility.

Multiple-target designs are conjoint *A-B* designs that are analyzed for patterns among them that can serve as the basis for practice hypotheses, but not logical inferences of causality as such. This is a vital service for practitioners and can be employed in a wide variety of situations.

Crossover and constant-series designs are variations of multiple-target designs that, through different arrangements and comparison of phases, allow slightly stronger causal inferences than do multiple-target designs.

Any design beyond the basic *A-B* adds requirements, and the designs described in this chapter are no exception. However, we have stressed how close these designs are to what practitioners ordinarily do, and thus recommend their use whenever possible.

CHANGING INTENSITY DESIGNS AND SUCCESSIVE INTERVENTION DESIGNS

PURPOSE: This chapter presents several designs that involve successive changes in the interventions, in the intensity of the interventions, or in the intensity of the outcomes. These designs build upon those discussed previously, but they have some distinctive features relevant to a wide variety of practice situations, and they require separate explanation for their appropriate use. ■

Introduction

Changing Intensity Designs:
A-B^1-B^2-B^3 | A | B^1 | B^2 | B^3 |

Changing Criterion Design

Changing Program Design

Characteristics of Changing Intensity Designs

Strengths of Changing Intensity Designs
Limitations of Changing Intensity Designs
Recommendations Regarding Changing Intensity Designs
Case Illustrations
Introducing the Client to Changing Intensity Designs

Successive Intervention Designs: *A-B-C, A-B-A-C, A-B-A-C-A*

The *A-B-C* Design | A | B | C |

The *A-B-A-C* Design | A | B | A | C |

The *A-B-A-C-A* Design | A | B | A | C | A |

Strengths of the A-B-A-C-A Design
Limitations of the A-B-A-C-A Design
Recommendations Regarding the A-B-A-C-A Design
Case Illustrations
Introducing the Client to the A-B-A-C-A Design

Extensions of the Successive Intervention Design

Summary

INTRODUCTION

Practitioners often use different interventions over the course of a case. These different interventions may reflect new problems that have arisen since the last contact or may reflect new ideas that occurred to the practitioner about the case/situation. It is important that single-system designs capture these changes in intervention or in the intensity of intervention.

Yet this is also a problem because changes in interventions are difficult to assess logically (Thomas, 1978). Was it the last intervention that caused the change, or the cumulative impact of the past several sessions, or the order of presentation, or what? The designs discussed in this chapter may help to provide some guidelines for changing interventions as well as some bases for making determinations about changes in target problems.

CHANGING INTENSITY DESIGNS: $A\text{-}B^1\text{-}B^2\text{-}B^3$

| A | B^1 | B^2 | B^3 |

An important extension of the *A-B* design is the *changing intensity design.* There are two types of changing intensity designs—the *changing criterion* design and the *changing program* design. We describe each of these separately in the following sections.

Changing Criterion Design

The first type of changing intensity design is the changing criterion design in which the *criteria* or requirements of the client's performance are increased (or decreased) in a stepwise progression in order to attain a given objective. First, a baseline period, *A,* is followed by an intervention period, *B.* Presumably some change occurs in the desired direction; however, the change is not at the desired

level. The practitioner has many options as to what to do next, including, in the changing criterion design, retaining the same intervention but requiring a higher level of performance for a given consequence to occur. These second and subsequent intervention periods would be distinguished from the first by *superscripts:* The first *B* period becomes B^1, followed by B^2, B^3, and so on. (Remember, superscripts are different from subscripts: The former denote change in intensity, the latter denote only what order a given phase has in a sequence of phases.) The changing criterion design thus permits the practitioner to move in graduated steps toward a terminal goal—for example, setting a series of sequential, intermediate objectives that the client can attain at progressively higher performance levels on the way toward achieving the final goal.

Let's use as an illustration of this procedure the efforts of a small human service agency to document its effectiveness, a necessary effort to maintain its status in receiving United Fund moneys. The United Fund adopted a policy that member agencies had to document a certain minimum level of verified successful case outcomes, and gave each agency a year's time in which to provide this documentation. Quarterly installments of funds were made contingent on showing progress over preceding quarters. Figure 16.1 shows that the agency in question made satisfactory progress, with an increase in percentage of successful case outcomes each quarter, thereby qualifying them for funds each quarter.

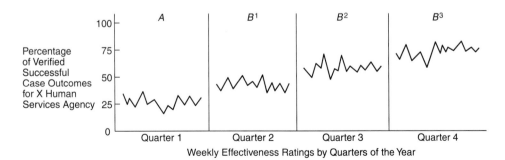

FIGURE 16.1 Changing criterion design illustrated by rising levels of agency performance required in order that it receive a quarterly allotment of United Fund support.

Changing Program Design

The second type of changing intensity design involves changing the intervention *program* (rather than the criterion or client's performance) by increasing or decreasing in a stepwise progression the intensity or amount of intervention activities required to produce a given outcome. First, a baseline period, *A,* is followed by an intervention period, *B.* Some change may occur in the desired direction; however, the change does not reach the desired level. Again, the practitioner has many options as to what to do next, one of which involves changing the intensity of the intervention by progressive steps. That is, in subsequent phases, you would modify the original intervention by providing progressively more or less of it, although the objectives and goals remain the same. More of the intervention would be offered if the terminal goal had not been reached (e.g., more varied or more intense reinforcement, increasing the number of sessions or meetings per week, etc.). Less of the intervention would be offered if the goal *had* been reached and you wanted to reduce your participation gradually before termination (e.g., changing to an intermittent reinforcement schedule, reducing the number of practitioner-client contacts, etc.). Just as in the changing criterion design, these second and subsequent intervention periods would be distinguished from the first by superscripts, with

the first intervention period becoming B^1, followed by B^2, B^3, and so on.

For example, consider this situation: Wes, a 7-year-old boy, was giving his parents such a hard time that they were at their wits' end. Among several complaints, the clinical psychologist and the parents agreed to focus first on what appeared to be the most disturbing of his behaviors: tantrums. The psychologist thought that a time-out procedure might be the fastest way of eliminating the tantrums. A measurement plan was established using both frequency and duration of tantrums as the target. Unfortunately, the first intervention phase–using 10-minute time-outs in the parents' bedroom–had only a negligible impact on Wes, as can be seen in Figure 16.2. The second intervention (B^2) used 15-minute time-outs, and progress was clearly evident; but the tantrum behavior appeared to stabilize at an unacceptable level. The practitioner and the parents then decided to intensify the intervention (B^3) to 20-minute time-outs, and within the week, the problem had receded to an acceptable level and Wes himself seemed more cheery and upbeat.

Characteristics of Changing Intensity Designs

Strengths of Changing Intensity Designs. Both the changing criterion and the changing program designs exhibit their controlling im-

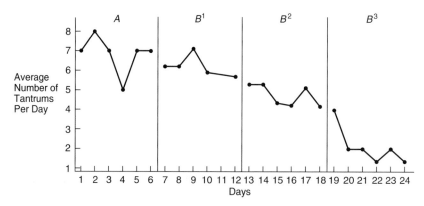

FIGURE 16.2 Changing program design illustrating increases in the intensity of the intervention (time out: B^1 = 10 minutes, B^2 = 15 minutes, B^3 = 20 minutes).

pact on the target problem by the successive progression of changes toward a desired outcome, linked with stepwise changes in either the criterion of performance expected of the client (in the changing criterion design) or changes in the intervention program in response to the client's performance (in the changing program design). Both types of changing intensity designs are flexible; such changes can be planned, or they can be made on an ad hoc basis as the situation warrants. Changing intensity designs are simpler than multiple baseline designs in that they do not require two or more independent targets in order to study change and causality; however, the sequential changes in one target present similar–though less powerful–types of information. Unlike experimental designs, changing intensity designs do not remove interventions in demonstrating change. Thus, they are not subject to some of the ethical and practical problems that the more powerful experimental designs produce.

The changing criterion design sets intermediate objectives on the way toward some terminal goal, and, therefore, each step on the way may be viewed as the client reaching a subgoal. This may be very motivating for some clients.

The changing program design is relatively easy to use and offers precise control over the intervention program, making successive changes in the intensity of the intervention in response to feedback from monitoring the target. This may be useful in the cost/benefit sense of knowing the optimal balance of obtaining some desired outcome for a given amount of intervention.

Overall, the core idea of changing intensity designs is that a stepwise progression of either objectives or interventions is systematically built into the design. This contributes considerable structure and direction to practice, and yet may be very motivating for the client as well.

Limitations of Changing Intensity Designs.
Both the changing criterion and the changing program designs are limited to situations in which you can shape behaviors and events gradually over time to produce desired results. You must make sure that the initial baseline is

sufficiently stable so that sequential changes are not already occurring. Moreover, for the most precise information, each step should be restabilized before going on to the next step; this requires close monitoring, and thus makes this design relatively labor-intensive. However, we realize that this "restabilization" may not always be possible, since the changes in these designs are a response to changes, or lack of sufficient changes, in the target.

Changing intensity designs are not good designs for establishing causality. Despite the fact that you can assess change as occurring at the same time as the program or the criterion is changing, factors such as carryover and order effects across the phases or even history (changes in the target problem as a result of some other event in the client's situation) make it difficult to interpret causal effects clearly.

In addition, it is not clear how much change should be required between each step. Too big a change may produce problems in attaining the goal, while too small a change may have little meaning to the client. You have to experiment with changes during the course of the intervention. The best guide is probably to examine the stability of the change. If you have not reached the terminal goal and the intermediate change or lack of change seems stable, then this would be the point at which you would change the criterion or the program.

Recommendations Regarding Changing Intensity Designs.
Overall, the limitations of this design probably reflect its relatively recent addition to the family of evaluation designs. We expect that its flexibility and versatility will commend it to practitioners, and that their experiences will further clarify the strengths and limitations of these designs.

Using these designs, you are required to be able to control graded sequences of the program or the performance criteria needed to obtain a given goal. However, being able to specify intermediate steps simplifies practice when the terminal goal is difficult to reach. Changing intensity designs are to be used under the same conditions as *A-B* designs, but they reflect the realities of practice in which practitioners wish (or need) to make changes in program or performance criteria as they go along. In addition, changing program designs, in particular, can be used to keep track systematically of changes in the client as you gradually reduce or fade out your participation prior to termination. These designs are therefore highly practical and practice oriented, even though they are not powerful tools for causal analysis. They require minimal sophistication and rigor and can be used in a wide variety of settings and circumstances. We recommend their consideration as an extension of the basic single-system design.

Case Illustrations. The first illustration shows a changing criterion design used with chronic back pain as the target. Chronic back pain is a persistent problem for large numbers of people, many of whom typically react to the post-treatment pain with self-disabling behaviors, such as slow, guarded walking, which is believed (incorrectly) will be helpful in reducing the pain. Geiger, Todd, Clark, Miller, and Kori (1992) conducted a rigorously controlled study on the use of feedback and contingent reinforcement to improve walking behavior in persons with chronic back pain. The dependent variable was rate of walking, chosen because it "(a) is incompatible with common self-protective debilitating pain behavior . . . , (b) can be accurately measured, (c) has been used by a number of researchers . . . , and (d) is of obvious importance in everyday activities" (Geiger et al., 1992, p. 180).

Geiger et al. (1992) also used a self-rating scale on pain and recording of medications taken. (Most of the clients came to the hospital on medications, but all medications were eventually eliminated as part of the general treatment, independent of the study.) Fifteen participants at a chronic pain clinic agreed to take part in the study in which a clever reinforcement system was constructed (involving tokens that could be exchanged for a state-operated lottery ticket, a relaxation tape, biofeedback cards, or a gourmet dinner). Points would be rewarded for given walking speeds relative to each client's starting rate. "The initial criterion for each client was the average of his/her two highest baseline rates plus 5%. Criteria for successive steps in the changing criterion design were similarly determined" (Geiger et al., 1992,

p. 180). Some of these experimental clients used only contingent reinforcement, while others began with either no reinforcement, or noncontingent reinforcement, but later moved to contingent reinforcement. Each of these experimental participants showed generally the same pattern of results, when the contingent reinforcement was applied (see Figure 16.3).

A five-person comparison group involving no reinforcements and noncontingent reinforcements also was used, thus combining a classical research design with a single-system design. Reliability checks were taken (interobserver ratings of walking speed), which produced agreements between 99% and 100%.

Baseline was established for each client, beginning with either a no-reinforcement condition, or a noncontingent condition. The pattern shown in Figure 16.3 is typical of all of the experimental clients. The baseline showed the characteristic guarded pace, with contingent reinforcements leading to increased rates. The overall results showed a positive direct correlation between walking speed and contingent reinforcement plus feedback. Each new criterion was met, except in the last criterion in one experimental client. Average self-ratings on pain were collected over a baseline of four sessions, and a final treatment pattern over the last four sessions. Geiger et al. (1992, p. 184) report the average decrease in reported pain was 36% for experimental clients, and 13% for comparison clients.

Overall, this study shows that it is possible to rigorously control a study of chronic lower back pain and walking, using a relatively simple, practical, and inexpensive method of providing contingent reinforcement (and the feedback on how well one is doing). The changing criteria were reasonable steps—that is, clients were medically able to meet them if they counteracted their (falsely) self-protecting behaviors and walked more rapidly. And the method of arriving at the new criterion is clear and applicable across clients.

Burley, Gutkin, and Naumann (1994) use a changing criterion design in the context of assessing the efficacy of an academic hearing peer tutor for a profoundly hearing-impaired student. The person being tutored was a hearing-impaired 13-year-old sixth-grade girl who ex-

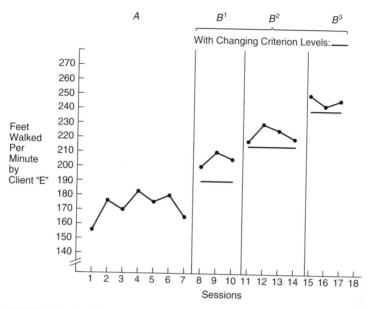

FIGURE 16.3 Walking rates for one experimental client ("E") using no-reinforcement baseline in a changing criterion design. (Adapted from Geiger, Todd, Clark, Muller, & Kori, 1992.)

hibited considerable difficulty in acquiring math skills; otherwise, she was doing satisfactorily in a mainstreamed classroom environment. The tutor was a 12-year-old sixth-grader who had no hearing impairment and had exhibited above-average skills in mathematics, and average skills in other areas. We should also note that this school had many hearing-impaired students, so the tutor had some minimal skills in sign language and finger spelling prior to this study. Both participants were described as "average students overall with minimal social and cognitive delays" (p. 416).

The teacher of the tutored student identified several related math objectives—adding fractions with different denominators, subtracting fractions with the same denominators, subtracting fractions with different denominators, and converting mixed numbers to fractions. These were chosen as required in her current work and yet beyond what she had presently mastered. The objectives were to be addressed sequentially; thus, this design is not completely the same as a changing criterion design (one goal with changes in its subgoals or objectives), but it is functionally equivalent. The tutor was tutored

by the first evaluator on some basic math signs, such as for plus, and minus, but that was the extent of the directing of the tutor, other than suggesting the tutor use visual strategies.

Baseline consisted of 10 written math items per objective, where inclusion as targets required the learner to miss 60% or more on any one objective. Peer tutoring sessions lasted about 20 minutes and occurred just prior to the beginning of the school day, with a total of 19 post-baseline sessions. The tutoring session was well-structured: Each session began with the tutor presenting 10 written math problems and giving the learner 10 minutes to complete each worksheet. No math problem was repeated throughout the study. The tutor would check answers against the evaluator's answer sheet, and would communicate with the learner about errors on these problems, or, if time permitted, she would communicate with the learner about problems she had solved correctly, and/or they would play a game together. A sign language interpreter was present in the room during each session, but played no role at all in the tutoring (except to show the tutor a few more math signs, such as divide).

The results, shown in Figure 16.4, indicate that the learner succeeded in reaching the criterion of mastery—when a score of 70% correct or better was obtained for 3 consecutive days on a given target—for each of the four selected objectives. (Although there was only one baseline point, in effect this one point could be seen as the cumulative effect on these math objectives up to that time in the semester.) Indeed, it looks as if the learner was able to make rapid strides once attention was turned to a new learning objective, building on previous related skills. For the evaluators, this was also a demonstration that a youngster with normal hearing could successfully tutor a profoundly hearing-impaired youngster. As in other peer tutoring situations, not only did the learner learn math from the experience, but the tutor became more fluent in fingerspelling and signing, and both enjoyed the experience (although the tutor

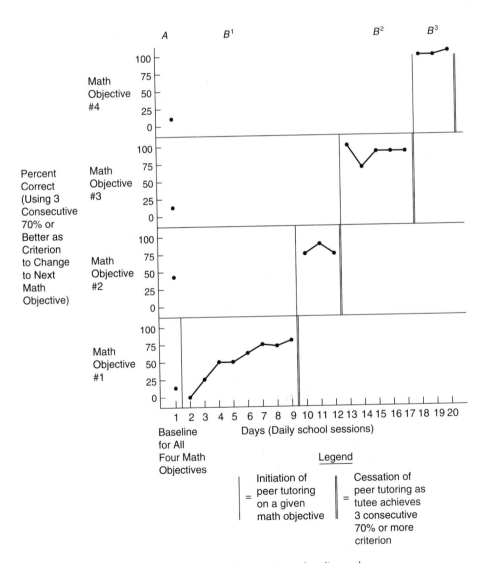

FIGURE 16.4   Percent correct of each math objective during baseline and intervention, using a changing criterion design. (Adapted from Burley, Gutkin, & Naumann, 1994.)

experienced some frustration when the student did not seem to grasp some concepts–an experience all teachers will have). Further study is needed on whether this kind of interaction enhances the status and social interaction of hearing-impaired students with nonimpaired students. In general, Burley et al. (1994, p. 418) recommend the changing criterion design as especially useful in such school contexts where instructional objectives change rapidly in a stepwise progression, and where it would fit better in the ecology of teaching, as compared to removal designs like the *A-B-A-B,* or the more time-consuming multiple baseline designs.

A study by Pinkston, Linsk, and Young (1988) on home-based behavioral family treatment of the impaired elderly employs a design similar to changing intensity designs. In this study, the changes are progressively added distinct tasks. The changes in tasks may be seen as roughly equivalent to changes in the interventions, making this study equivalent to a changing program design. Data from one of their cases are adapted in Figure 16.5. The case involves an effort to help an impaired elderly man keep himself clean by engaging in several identified cleaning tasks. Baseline data show a low rate of personal cleanliness.

The intervention involved a graded sequence of personal care instigations carried out by the wife of this 66-year-old man in their own home. First (B^1), she was directed to bring him a warm wet washcloth while he was still in bed. She talked to him in a soothing manner when she washed and dried his face and hands. The second stage of this intervention (B^2) involved helping him to bathe weekly. The third stage of the intervention (B^3) consisted of the wife prompting him to wash his own face and hands in the bathroom as well as to take a bath weekly. A maintenance period followed these graded interventions, after which the program was terminated when a reasonably stable and desired degree of cleanliness was attained. Follow-up calls over the next year indicated that he was able to maintain this degree of personal cleanliness.

A study by Taggart, Taggart, and Siedentop (1986) employed a changing criterion design to measure the effects of a home-based physical activity program to help physically inactive children. Using instruments developed earlier, the authors measured such factors as cardiorespiratory endurance, abdominal strength, lower back strength, and the like, and selected the least able students, who were invited to participate with their parents in the study.

The outcome measure was the number of activity points accumulated by each participant each week, derived from a number of physical activities (running, bicycling, rope skipping, etc.), each with its specific point values. Trainers (doctoral students in physical education) instructed cooperating families individually on how to contract with their child, how to monitor each activity, and how to

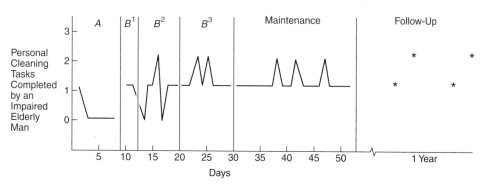

FIGURE 16.5 Changing program design involving behavioral family treatment of an elderly person. (Adapted from "Home-Based Behavioral Family Treatment of the Impaired Elderly" by E. M. Pinkston, N. L. Linsk, and R. N. Young, 1989, *Behavior Therapy, 19,* pp. 331–344.)

provide the reinforcers when the child meets the agreed upon weekly criterion of physical activity. Various reinforcers were used, but parents were encouraged to fade out extrinsic rewards in favor of intrinsic ones.

The goals of the intervention program involved stepwise change in the weekly criterion rate for a given target behavior. Figure 16.6 shows data adapted from the study, in which a baseline mean of activity points is compared with changing (increasing) criteria that would enable the child to obtain his or her agreed-upon reward. In this case, the child showed a baseline rate of 160 activity points. Then, following the principle of progressive overload—that in order to achieve fitness gains, there has to be a systematic increase in effort expended to a level above the one to which that individual had become accustomed—the criterion was raised each week to a level slightly above the previous week. Note that one week showed a drop in activity level, so the criterion is adjusted accordingly to make achieving the new level within reasonable grasp.

In the entire study group of 12 families and their children, 88% of the established criteria were achieved, allowing at least the hypothesis that the change in the children's behavior may, in part, have been caused by the reward system established by the family contingent on the achievement of the criterion level of physical activity. This type of research has much potential significance for physically inactive children and their parents.

Watson-Perczel, Lutzker, Greene, and McGimpsey (1988) present a study of families adjudicated for child neglect. The focus of their study was an attempt to help the families clean up their homes, which were extremely and dangerously dirty. Homes were often infested with freely roaming bugs; excrement and rubbish were frequently present in various rooms; and the children were invariably poorly clothed and sent to school unclean.

Into these difficult circumstances ventured the practitioners, who (among many activities and goals) attempted to instruct the clients on how to clean their homes. First, the practitioners established rapport with the families, including identifying private areas with the clients that would not be measured. Then the team used a data-collection system referred to as the

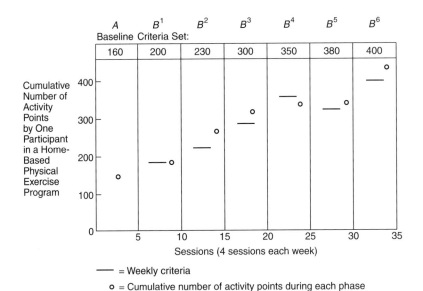

FIGURE 16.6 Graph showing effects of a home-based activity program on one child, employing a changing criterion design. (Adapted from "Effects of a Home-Based Activity Program: A Study with Low-Fitness Elementary School Children" by A. C. Taggart, J. Taggart, and D. Siedentop, 1986, *Behavior Modification, 10*, pp. 487–507.)

Checklist for Living Environments to Assess Neglect (CLEAN). Each room that was to be cleaned was assessed by areas and functions, thus establishing a reliable tool to measure cleanliness across clients.

The intervention was the teaching in stages of effective cleaning methods. Sequentially increasing activities and responsibilities were publicly assigned, along with training on how to perform them. In terms of this text, we would describe these increasing duties and training elements as changing intensities of the intervention program.

Figure 16.7 is adapted from data presented in the text of the study by Watson-Perczel et al. (1988). Note that two rooms in one client's home are identified for cleaning and receive the same intervention staggered over an 11-day period. This constitutes a multiple baseline design on top of the changing intensity design. A third room (representing several others not subject to this same cleaning effort) shows somewhat less change over the period of the study (although the initial levels were higher so that there was less room for improvement), suggesting that generalization to

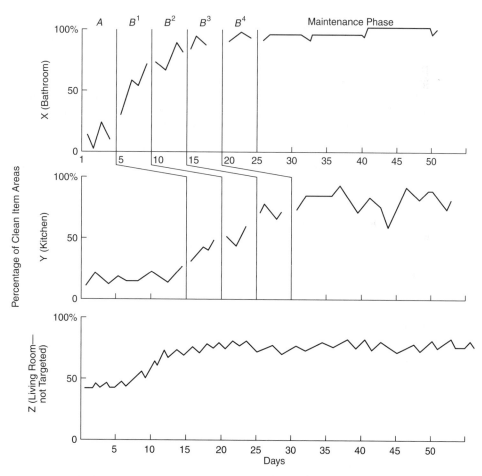

FIGURE 16.7   Illustration of a changing program design (with a multiple-baseline design superimposed) with each *B* phase involving a change in cleaning methods. (Adapted from "Assessment and Modification of Home Cleanliness among Families Adjudicated for Child Neglect" by M. Watson-Perczel, J. R. Lutzker, R. Greene, and B. J. McGimpsey, 1988, *Behavior Modification, 12*, pp. 57–81.)

other parts of the house may not be taking place.

Martella, Leonard, Marchand-Martella, and Agran (1993) present a study of the effects of a self-monitoring program for reducing the frequency of negative self- or other-statements and increasing positive ones in a student with mild mental retardation who was enrolled in a self-contained classroom at a middle school. The student's negative statements—"I'm so stupid," "I'm going to kill you," "I hate this f–ing calculator," and so forth–had isolated him from his classmates. Self-monitoring involves independent recording with a cue, as distinguished from self-recording in which some cue, like a beeper, is given. As such, self-monitoring requires considerable training so that the student can identify both positive and negative statements. He was to record only his negative statements; the trainer also rated his positive ones.

Interestingly, two reinforcement menus were used differentially in this study. One involved "small" reinforcers (25 cents or less); the others were "large" reinforcers (more than 25 cents). The student was trained to recognize among his verbalizations those statements that were either negative or positive, and to record their occurrence on a chart. This study targeted negative statements, and assessed positive ones "to determine the collateral effects of training" (Martella et al., 1993, p. 80). Reliability was ascertained by two raters who were trained in recognizing negative and positive statements; interobserver reliability for negative and positive statements averaged 96% to 99% over the two periods of the study.

Criterion levels were set by identifying the average frequency of negative statements at baseline, and then the criterion was decreased by 25% in each of four intervention phases. Prior to each intervention phase, the trainer would inform the student of the maximum number of negative statements he could say that corresponded with the criterion level of that phase, and the trainer would mark on the student's chart where this number was. Baseline frequency was 16, so phase B^1 criterion was 12; phase B^2 was 8; phase B^3 was 4; and phase B^4 was 0.

In addition, the student was asked to indicate what he was going to earn from the rein-

forcement menus. If the student's count of negative statements was in agreement with the trainer (at 80% agreement or higher), he could receive a small reinforcement. If the student agreed with the trainer's indications of negative statements and the number of these negative statements was at the criterion level for four consecutive sessions, then he was allowed to receive a large reinforcement. After successful results were obtained in self-monitoring, the trainer began a partial withdrawal of the training components over three phases, beginning with the large reinforcer, and ending in removal of even the small reinforcer, at which time natural social reinforcers (pleasant fellow-student interactions) may have taken over from the tangible artificial ones.

Results are presented in Figure 16.8. We will show only one of the two periods in which the study took place, which also means we will not display the multiple baseline aspect of the study. However, similar results occurred in both periods. (There are two baselines: The first, A, was a concurrent baseline, but the second baseline, $\bar{A}$, was constructed artificially from the average of the first baseline. This is one way of constructing a practical but objective baseline against which to make comparison.)

While the results are gratifying, the authors are careful to mention limitations of the study, including not disaggregating the possible factors influencing the changes in behavior–reinforcements, self-monitoring, and the like. We would further note that calling attention to negative statements, rather than accentuating the positive ones, may have prolonged the negative. As the authors note, we don't have clear evidence about what caused the increase in positive statements, which may have been the critical factor in reuniting this student with his classmates.

Introducing the Client to Changing Intensity Designs. In addition to the previously described introductions to each design, the present design requires further explanation about the changing intensities of the program or criteria for acceptable performance. (In interpreting results of these designs, we must keep in mind that it is possible that the clients' knowledge of their own performance will aid them in

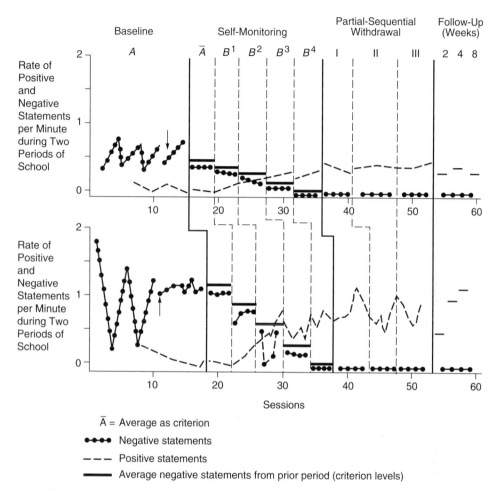

FIGURE 16.8   The rate of positive and negative self- and other-statements for an adolescent student with mild mental retardation across two school periods. The arrows indicate when pretraining began. The horizontal bars in the self-monitoring period are the sequential criterion levels. (Adapted from Martella et al., 1993.)

surpassing their record, or perhaps knowledge of their nearness to the goal also could be a stimulus.) However, it is conceivable that there are situations in which the client cannot be told about the changing intensities. For example, a severely disturbed youth (diagnosed as schizophrenic) was being aided in stretching out the intervals between outbursts in his classroom by means of a token reward given to him if he was able to control himself until a preset alarm clock rang. Unknown to him the practitioner was increasing the intervals between rings.

Assuming that it is possible to inform clients about the changes in program or per-

formance criteria level, we suggest the following wording: "*Helping you solve your problem will be like climbing the steps of a ladder; each rung will move you closer to your goal. Your goal is G, and so we will arrange that if you accomplish O (the objective or a portion of that goal), then you can have R (the client's preferred reinforcement). Each time you move closer to that goal, we will provide this reward, and then we'll talk about what it will take to get that reward the next time.*"

Similar introductions can be made for the changing program design. We suggest the following wording: "*Helping you solve your problem will be like climbing the steps of a ladder; each rung will move you closer to your goal. I* (the practitioner) *will change the intervention* (increasing it or decreasing it according to the goal that the client and practitioner are seeking) *at each step of the way to your goal."*

SUCCESSIVE INTERVENTION DESIGNS: *A-B-C, A-B-A-C, A-B-A-C-A*

The successive intervention designs consist of a series of designs that employ different intervention methods, each applied one after the other in separate phases. Some of these are among the most commonly used of all designs, because in actual practice, it is often very difficult to apply just one intervention method or program and achieve effectiveness. Usually there is some need for changes in or additions to the intervention, either in new interventions or introduction of a maintenance program. Another reason why successive intervention designs are frequently used is that feedback from the data may indicate that a given intervention program is not working satisfactorily. Thus, changes in intervention programs are frequent, and our discussion of these successive intervention designs attempts to point out some of the logical possibilities and limitations of such formats.

Successive intervention designs can be planned in advance for more systematic comparisons between phases and to test the effects of a maintenance program. A much more common use in everyday practice is when immediate feedback suggests the need for modifications in an intervention. The changes are made and you simply note on the chart with a new phase when the changes began. There is a wide variety of successive intervention designs you might construct, some involving removals (return to baseline) between phases and others involving additions or complete changes in intervention, all depending on the needs of the particular case or situation. We will briefly introduce you to some of the major representa-

tives of this group of designs and to the logical possibilities for conclusions drawn from each design. Remember, though, that these *are* merely examples, since successive intervention designs can be any combination of phases that is necessary for a given case. We begin with the simplest one, the *A-B-C* design.

The *A-B-C* Design | A | B | C |

The *A-B-C* design can be described as an extension of the *A-B* design, but with the addition of a new intervention, *C.* (The last phase could just as well be called *BC* if intervention *B* was continued and intervention *C* is added to it.) Comparisons can be made between the baseline and the first intervention. However, there is some logical difficulty in comparing the baseline with the second intervention, since an intervening event, *B,* has occurred, and we cannot distinguish the effects of *C* from the cumulative and ordered effects of *B* and *C.* If data from the *B* phase indicate a stable, positive change as compared to *A,* then observing clear changes after *C* provides a hint of causal factors but does not offer a clear basis for making a claim about causality because the phases are nonadjacent. We will soon describe more completely why the apparent change in the target from phases *B* to *C* is not an adequate basis for detecting causal relationships.

Of course, this design could be continued with subsequent phases, each designating a new intervention—for example, *A-B-C-D-E.* Similarly, this design or variations of it could be used both to add and combine phases—for example, when one does not want to completely eliminate a prior intervention. An example of this might be an *A-B-C-CD* design. However, these additions and combinations make it even more difficult to draw conclusions about causality because of order and carry-over effects.

Practitioners might consider using the *A-B-C* design or elaborations of it as an economic way to test some practice ideas, recognizing that it does not provide the basis for inferring causality. If time and conditions do not permit the removal of one intervention and a return to baseline before the introduction of another, and if circumstances do not permit changing the intensity of the intervention as discussed earlier in this chapter, then it may be appropriate to employ the *A-B-C* design. But this design is most commonly used in practice to simply reflect changes in interventions based on monitoring changes in the client's progress (or lack of progress) toward a goal.

Another common situation in which the *A-B-C* design may be used is when *C* is a maintenance phase. That is, when the intervention *B* has been successful but a completely new intervention is needed to teach the client to use *B* without the aid of the practitioner, then phase *C* is properly employed to develop maintenance of the successful effects from phase *B*. Phase *C* tests the impact and the stability of maintenance training. A maintenance phase is a very useful and important addition to any *A-B* design.

The *A-B-A-C* Design | A | B | A | C |

The *A-B-A-C* design represents a large improvement over the *A-B-C* design because of the return to baseline before moving to the second intervention, *C*. This is a weak form of an experimental design (see Chapter 14), but rather than give it this label, we prefer to emphasize its limitations in providing causal knowledge by describing it, and the next design, as an experimental, successive intervention design. With an *A-B-A-C* design we can determine the full effects of the *B* phase by comparing it with the first and second baseline periods, since the second *A* phase is implemented because the *B* phase shows positive change. But we would need a third baseline to determine the full effect of intervention *C,* as we illustrate in the next section. It is important to note that because of the economy of an *A-B-A-C* design (two interventions are tested with one baseline before each intervention), you may be deceived into thinking that you are *comparing* two different interventions, *B* and *C,* when in fact you are experimentally examining only one, the *B* phase, and are raising some questions about the other, the *C* phase, that cannot logically or fully be answered within the context of this design. In short, we must carefully distinguish between what is required for determining the effects of one intervention and what is required for comparing the effects of two different interventions. We will return to this point shortly, as the next successive intervention design is introduced.

The *A-B-A-C* design may be employed in situations similar to those discussed in connection with the *A-B-C* design, but when you also want to have a stronger picture of the effects of the *B* phase. This is a very economical way of looking at two interventions, even though we emphasize that this design doesn't provide the logical basis for comparing the two interventions for their relative effect on the target problem.

A very appropriate use of the *A-B-A-C* design would be to have *C* be a maintenance phase to teach the client how to maintain the level of effect reached in the *B* phase. In such situations the last phase also could include a reinstatement of the *B* phase plus the additional training for a maintenance phase, *C.* It would be more appropriate to use the notation *A-B-A-BC* to indicate this particular form of the design.

A-B-A-C-A Design | A | B | A | C | A |

This form of the successive intervention design builds on the preceding designs but adds some important factors due to the return to the baseline after the second intervention. Let's examine it in detail. After the initial baseline, an intervention, *B,* is introduced, presumably to the point at which the problem is showing a positive change from the baseline, although the terminal goal will not have been reached. The first intervention is then removed, employing the same logic as discussed in the experimental designs chapter (Chapter 14), which is to have a basis for determining whether or not the intervention was likely causally linked with the observed change. Let's presume that the second baseline shows a return to near the original level, thus supporting the inference that *B* was causally linked with the observed change in the target. Next, a new intervention, *C,* is introduced, and after its positive and stable effects have been observed, it too is removed to produce a third baseline in order to provide a basis for determining the causal linkage of *C* to the outcome. Apart from the need to evaluate the effects of two separate interventions, a major reason for implementing a *new* intervention in the *C* phase is that, although changes in the *B* phase were positive, they had not achieved the terminal goal; hence, the need to employ a new intervention.

With this design, you would know about the effects of two separate interventions, *B* and *C,* each with its first and second baselines. The temptation again is to view such an *A-B-A-C-A* design as a direct comparison between the *B* and the *C* interventions; however, it is not totally appropriate to make this comparison. With the *A-B-A-C-A* design, you cannot really compare the contrasting or relative effects of *B* and *C,* because *B* and *C* are not adjacent to each other, as is required for such a comparison (as described in Chapter 11). Other reasons for this limitation on comparing the relative effects of *B* and *C* are that there may be some additive impact of the two interventions or the order of presentation may have something to do with the outcome. If you want to clarify the relative effects of the interventions, you must use an interaction design (discussed in Chapter 17).

However, the *A-B-A-C-A* design does provide some hints about the two different interventions that can be followed up later with a more sophisticated design since it is useful to be able to study the separate effects of two interventions on a given target. We discuss the *A-B-A-C-A* design more fully below as a representative of successive intervention designs.

Strengths of the* A-B-A-C-A *Design. As with other experimental designs, this design presents a basis for making causal inferences. However, it goes beyond some of the previously described experimental designs by providing information on two different interventions for one client. By returning to the baseline on each occasion after each intervention has been made, you have a clear, logical picture of their separate effects. This is an economic feature of this design, enabling you to do a test of two interventions (individual techniques, packages, or programs) with the same client.

This design presents you with other important information, namely, two apparently successful interventions in connection with the one client. It also presents some choices as to what to do with this information. For example, you may wish to combine interventions, *BC,* to observe their joint effect. Or, based on your observations, you may wish to return to the apparently more successful intervention of the two before moving into a termination and maintenance phase.

There is another value in the use of the *A-B-A-C-A* design: You are aided in developing knowledge of effective intervention techniques for your repertoire. Also with the *A-B-A-C-A* design, other persons who are involved in the different interventions can observe the impact of their contributions, and thereby be reinforced and encouraged to continue their contributions.

Limitations of the* A-B-A-C-A *Design. As we have stressed, the temptation with this design is to compare results obtained from the *B* and *C* interventions. However, logically this cannot be done, as explained previously, because of other influences such as carryover effects, lack of adjacent phases of the two interventions, and order-of-presentation effects that may confound the picture. This design is not capable of sorting out these influences.

It may be difficult to convince a client to change from one already established, successful intervention to another intervention, although you can point out that the problem has not been completely resolved yet nor the final goal attained and that you would like to try a new intervention to achieve better results. If the client asks why you didn't try the new intervention first, you may say that you had to test out the simpler approach before considering the more involved one. You also may point out that the intervention previously tried may be the more efficient one.

The end phase is based on observation alone rather than on intervention. This presents some practical problems should undesirable patterns of data appear (if the pattern remains positive, the final *A* phase can function as a follow-up phase). Presumably you could continue with another intervention—this is the point of successive intervention designs—but it will require additional explanations to the client as to why you changed from a successful *B* phase to another intervention that ended with less successful data appearing in the third baseline period. You have to expect some of these negative turns of events with the successive intervention designs, and these will always require explanation to a client who may be less than pleased.

While order effects tend to be a problem with the successive intervention design, some of the principles of this design, combined with the principles underlying the experimental removal designs described in Chapter 14, can be used to study, and rule out, order effects.

Let's say, in the development of a successful technique or technique package, you were to conduct an evaluation resulting in the pattern shown in Figure 16.9. The way to check out the possibility of order effects is simply to reverse the order of the two interventions *B* and *C* with

another client with a similar problem. This could produce a chart such as the one represented in Figure 16.10, tentatively validating the notion of the greater effectiveness of *C* over *B*. Thus, an *A-B-A-C-A* design becomes an *A-C-A-B-A* design with the second client. This is similar to the rearrangement of phases described in Chapter 15 regarding crossover designs. The main difference is that the rearrangement of phases in crossover designs occurs simultaneously, while the suggestion here is to reverse the order of the interventions with a subsequent client.

Recommendations Regarding the* A-B-A-C-A *Design. When the final observation phase (third baseline) of this design is analogous to a follow-up phase in which the client simply is watched carefully after two successful

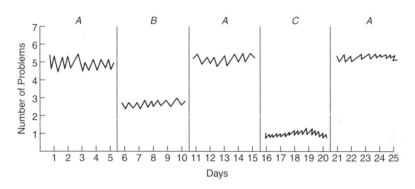

FIGURE 16.9   Hypothetical data to illustrate problem of order effects.

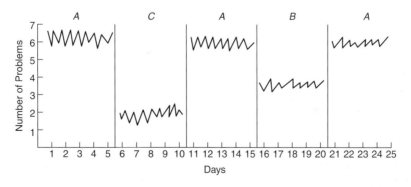

FIGURE 16.10   Hypothetical data illustrating how to study order effects (in comparison with Figure 16.9).

intervention phases, there is much to commend in the *A-B-A-C-A* design. It is an extension of the *A-B-A-B* type of experimental design, which offers economy and power in looking for possible causal effects, even though it has limits on comparing relative effects of the interventions involved. We recommend this design in the same way we recommend the other experimental designs, particularly the *A-B-A-B* design, with the additional value that it allows the fairly common practice situation of use of two separate interventions with one client. It should be used when information on the functional relationships between interventions and outcomes is required. The *A-B-A-C-A* design is particularly useful when the first intervention, *B,* has not produced a strong enough change and the second intervention, *C,* is introduced in an attempt to reach the client's goal. The design requires a fair amount of control over the situation, and this may present some difficulties in some settings.

Case Illustrations. Lloyd, Eberhardt, and Drake (1996) conducted a series of studies on cooperative learning with eighth- to eleventh-graders, using at one point, an *A-B-C-B-C* design—a kind of successive intervention design with removal of some interventions—so as to compare the effects of group and individual reinforcement contingencies in the context of group study. There has been a good deal of study of cooperative learning situations, where small groups of students work together to learn some topic. However, Lloyd et al. extended this type of study further by also comparing individual and group contingent reinforcements on average scores. (They also examined low-scoring individuals to study the effect of group study, but we will not discuss this part of their work.)

The particulars of the study that we feature here are these: Seventeen students in a first-year Spanish class in high school were given daily 10-item vocabulary quizzes. Baseline data (*A*) were plotted on the number of correct answers under the condition of individual study (in any way the individual chose) with no contingencies for however they performed. Then, group study was introduced; this consisted of two groups composed of

equal numbers of high- to low-scoring students, all of whom studied together one day for the quiz on the next day, for the same amount of time (7 minutes) as in the individual study condition.

The *B* intervention consisted of two factors: (1) group study and (2) individual reinforcements for 9 or 10 correct answers; individual students would receive small tangible rewards, a pencil or candy, and public recognition. The *C* intervention consisted of a different set of factors: (1) group study and (2) group reinforcements, in which all members of a group would receive some reward based on the average performance of the group of 9 correct answers or higher, or else to members of both groups if both mean scores were 9 or 10.

Independently, Lloyd et al. also collected anonymous survey information from participating students that served as social validation for the main part of the study. Students were asked about their preferences regarding both the individual and group contingencies, or none at all.

Figure 16.11 shows 31 successive quizzes and the average number of correct answers. Not shown here are the ranges of scores for each quiz, but they generally followed the average group scores. Overall, the results suggest that group study improved average spelling scores, but that group study and group contingencies improved average spelling scores the most, and had some positive effect on the ranges of scores. However, Lloyd et al. (1996, p. 198) note that students with low baseline rates appear to be least likely to benefit from group study. These findings support the general trends in the literature.

We note that this design is a successive intervention design, except that instead of a return to baseline, there is experimental manipulation of two interventions. Thus, this design provides a strong hint about the differential effects of the *B* and *C* interventions, but it does not provide a full logical determination of their separate effects. For a full logical analysis, we would need an interaction design as described in Chapter 17. Yet, important information was obtained in this classroom procedure where there were limits on how many removals might be ethically employed. In this case, the removal

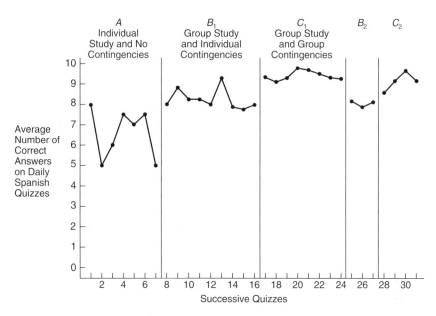

FIGURE 16.11   Average number of correct answers during three conditions of study plus reinforcement. (Adapted from Lloyd, Eberhardt, & Drake, 1996.)

phase actually was just a change to another intervention to allow the opportunity for the experimental study of the effects of group versus individual reinforcement.

Maag, Rutherford, and DiGangi (1992) conducted what they called a multiple treatment design related to on-task and academic productivity of learning-disabled students. However, because they were explicitly testing a theory and added components as directed by the theory, we would like to interpret this as a theory-guided variation on the successive intervention designs. Instead of the conventional addition of distinctive interventions, the Maag et al. study examines the effects of a theory-directed addition of components for one group of participants.

Learning theory applied to education has led to consideration of self-management training (Thoresen & Mahoney, 1974). Self-monitoring has been identified as the major component of self-management training. Self-monitoring is itself composed of two elements—self-observation and self-recording; that is, a student must first become aware of his or her own behavior, and then be able to record the presence or absence of the targeted response (Maag et al., 1992,

p. 157). In addition, contingent reinforcement, well established as able to increase performance, may be connected to self-management training. The authors point out that there has been little research on the differential efficacy of self-observation and self-recording as they influence reactivity, that is, how self-observing and self-recording influence self-monitoring, particularly with regard to educational goals such as having learning disabled students be on-task and solving math problems. Thus, this study involves three separate interventions: self-observation (B), self-recording (C), and contingent reinforcement (D).

In addition, behavior change studies often ignore the social context. So, a question of the *social validity* of the change (Kazdin, 1977) is raised: Do the changes in behavior make any difference in how the person functions in society? To answer this question, Maag et al. (1992) obtained information on the performance of non-learning disabled peers' functioning on the target variables, which thus provides a measure of ordinary student functioning in that school society. Then, the performance of learning disabled students can be compared against this norm of performance to assess the social validity of the intervention, as well as the sheer amount of observed change.

Six learning disabled children in elementary school were studied, along with random nondisabled students from the same grades who were observed at the same time as the target children. Reliability checks (interobserver reports) were conducted and found to be at high levels. With regard to self-observation, a teacher's aide, who ordinarily circulated around the room, would touch the students on the shoulder as a relatively unobtrusive cue to have the students ask themselves, "Am I working on the assignment?" With regard to a unit of self-observing and self-recording, the children were prompted to indicate their behavior in an age-appropriate manner (the younger children checked off a smiling face if on-task, or a frowning face if not; older children checked in columns labeled on-task and off-task). Contingent reinforcement came in the form of praise when the students had improved over the previous session's performance or (in phase 2 of contingent reinforcement) if the students had improved in successively increasing rates over the previous session's level—a kind of changing intensity design feature—of the goals they and their teacher set collaboratively. Follow-up observations were also collected one week after the last intervention terminated.

Illustrative results are presented in Figure 16.12. Maag et al. (1992, p. 161) report "Distinct and substantial changes in both on-task

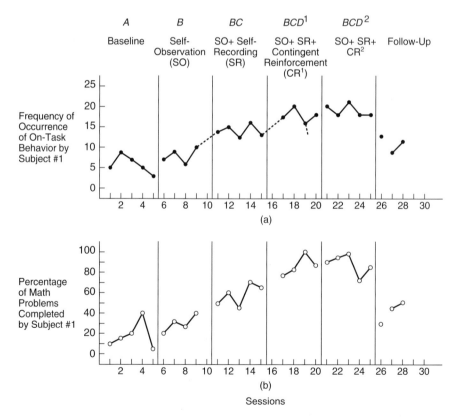

FIGURE 16.12   The frequency of occurrence of on-task behavior and the percentage of math problems completed by subject #1, a learning-disabled student (missed sessions are indicated simply by not recording on a particular day). (Adapted from Maag, Rutherford, & DiGangi, 1992.)

behavior and academic productivity occurred for each student with the implementation of three out of the four experimental conditions: self-observing and self-recording (as one unit), and the two phases of self-observation, self-recording, and contingent reinforcement." When self-observation alone was used, it did not influence either on-task or academic behavior. Maag et al. (1992, p. 168) note that the largest gains in academic productivity occurred during the phase of contingent reinforcement plus goal setting. There were individual variations in response to these progressive interventions, depending in part on the level at which students began, and their cognitive characteristics. Of course, as with all successive intervention designs, it is difficult to conclude just what was the most relevant factor in producing the results due to order and carryover effects, and the simple cumulative effects of multiple interventions.

Miller, Miller, Wheeler, and Selinger (1989) employed an A-B-A-BC^1-BC^2-FU design actually combining a successive intervention and changing program design. The design was used to study whether a cognitive behavior modification program used with institutionalized "behaviorally disordered" students would both increase academic performance and decrease inappropriate classroom behaviors. One client, a highly aggressive 11-year-old youth with an IQ of 73 (full-scale Wexler Intelligence Scale for Children, Revised, WISC-R) was aided in his arithmetic. Ordinarily, he would refuse to do the work, cry, and make defeatist statements ("I can't do this," "This is too hard") (see Figure 16.13).

The first baseline (A_1) consisted of measurement of his level of subtraction skills. Four days of daily problem sets indicated a stable (zero) level. (While this is a brief baseline, it was consistent with the youth's prior grade pattern for mathematics in general.) The first intervention B consisted of a self-instructional method for working subtraction problems. The student was trained in this procedure for 4 days until he performed at 90% accuracy without prompts from the practitioner. The B phase lasted for 8 days, including the training period.

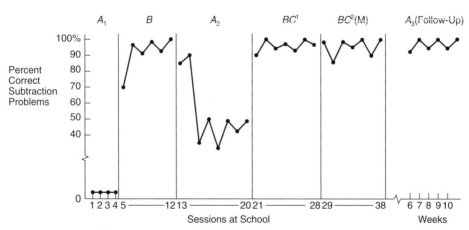

B = Self-instruction taught by the practitioner

C = Self-monitoring taught by the practitioner

M = Maintenance phase, a fade-out of the practitioner's role; back to regular classroom instruction

FIGURE 16.13 An illustration of a successive intervention design with maintenance and follow-up phases. (Adapted from "Can a Single-Classroom Treatment Approach Change Academic Performance and Behavioral Characteristics in Severely Behaviorally Disordered Adolescents: An Experimental Inquiry" by M. Miller, S. R. Miller, J. Wheeler, and J. Selinger, 1989, *Behavioral Disorders, 14,* pp. 215–225.)

A return to baseline, A_2, was accomplished by using the same kind of daily problem sets without the self-instructional tools. There were also some new but similar problem sets, so that this baseline, A_2, was not exactly like A_1. Eight days were taken in A_2, longer than expected because of what was termed "erratic performance" of the youth. (We would not necessarily interpret this A_2 behavior as erratic; it looks from the data as if it was possible that the youth was simply continuing to use his new self-instructional tool for several more days into A_2, even without the reinforcement of the experimenter's attention.)

Likewise, there was a modification in the second intervention, which we would identify as BC; self-monitoring, C, was added to the self-instruction of B. This phase took 8 days. When a stable level of performance was achieved, the practitioner began to reduce her involvement with the student, and to turn the learning situation back to the regular classroom with the standardized arithmetic problem sets and ordinary teacher feedback. This phase is described by the authors as fading; we consider this a BC^2 phase with the first BC phase becoming BC^1. It may also be considered a maintenance phase, because the youth was aided to function in a regular environment, rather than in the special experimental one. Follow-up over a 5-week period indicated that the student was maintaining his new skill. This design illustrates a combined successive intervention and changing program design.

Introducing the Client to the* A-B-A-C-A Design. The *A-B-A-C-A* design and the variations of the successive intervention designs presented here are perhaps a little more difficult to present than some of the earlier designs because of their two or more different interventions. Presumably the first intervention was partially successful, and therefore you are in the position of saying something like the following:

I am pleased that this (first) intervention has worked as well as it has, but I believe that there is more to be accomplished, and so I am suggesting another intervention that will approach the problem from a different angle. My hope is that we can make even more gains using this second approach, which,

based on how you handled the first intervention, now offers greater promise of being more effective.

To do this I will remove the first intervention but continue to collect information about how you are handling the problem/situation. Then, shortly, we can put the new information into effect and watch the very same behaviors as we have before to see whether they improve more than they did in the previous effort. If by chance they do not, then we can always go back and pick up on that first intervention again. However, in the long run it will be better, I believe, to try this second intervention. How does that sound to you?

Extensions of the Successive Intervention Design

There are three designs that we want to call to your attention that extend the principles of these successive intervention designs while permitting you to isolate the most effective component of an intervention package. The first is the *multiple-component design* that contrasts two or more interventions with or without a formal baseline. The second is an *additive* or *construction design* that adds components to an initial intervention. The third is a *differentiating* or *strip design* that subtracts components from an initial intervention package (see Jayaratne & Levy, 1979; Thomas, 1975). The eventual result of this additive or differentiating process is to end up with what *appears* to be the most effective intervention for a given client. We emphasize the word *appears* because all of these methods are in fact shortcuts to a logically more rigorous design to be discussed in the next chapter. The major value of these shortcut methods is their immediate feedback to the practitioner because they permit a rapid and approximate testing of the relative effectiveness of two interventions with a given client. In addition, these designs are useful in the general process of technique building and knowledge development for professional practice as they are used to identify components of practice that lead to more effective results.

The *multiple-component design* (Thyer, 1993) combines elements of the experimental replication and successive intervention designs. It can be used with or without baseline phases, although eliminating baseline phases, of course, limits its potential for logical inferences regarding causality. The purpose of this design is to attempt to compare the relative effectiveness of two different interventions.

The basic approach to the multiple-component design is to use the basic model of the experimental replication design (A-B-A-B), but to substitute different interventions for a "quick and dirty" comparison.

Use of such a design was described by Underwood et al. (as cited in Thyer, 1993). This design involved intervention with a severely developmentally disabled youth who engaged in high levels of self-injurious behavior during which he would strike his hand or face with his fist. The practitioner, a graduate student in social work, found two promising interventions in the literature, and he implemented them in a way that is similar to an experimental replication design. However, because of the severe level of the target problem, the practitioner chose not to use a baseline period.

The first intervention, called *interruption, B_1,* was implemented as a first phase. After five sessions and little change in the problem (frequency of actual or attempted self-injurious behavior), the second intervention, interruption plus differential reinforcement, BC_1, was implemented with a gradual decrease in the target.

The second phase lasted 15 sessions. The third phase consisted of removal of BC and reimplementation of the original intervention, B_2. This lasted eight sessions with very little change in the frequency of self-injurious behaviors. The fourth phase was a reimplementation of the combined intervention, BC_2; during this phase, the problem dropped to its lowest frequency. These data are presented in Figure 16.14.

In this example, the two B phases functioned almost as baseline phases in the experimental replication design, suggesting the possibility that the BC intervention had more potential in reducing the frequency of the target problem. Of course, the absence of baseline phases, the problem of order effects, and the presence of carryover effects in the third phase all present complicating factors. But this design was a good example of creative use of single-system designs to deal quickly, and through use of literature-based interventions, with a very serious problem.

The *additive* or *construction design* can be described by the following notation A-B-A-C-A-BC-$(\ )$. In this design, intervention B is attempted first, followed by a removal (A_2). Presumably, the practitioner is not satisfied with results obtained with B, so he or she tries

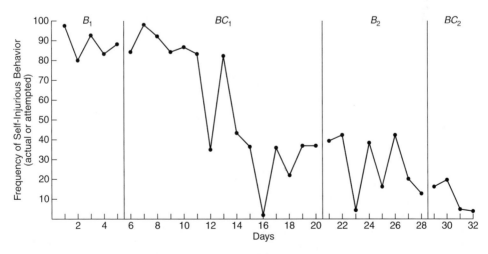

FIGURE 16.14 A multiple-component design applied to a problem of self-injurious behavior. (Adapted from "Single-System Research Designs" by B. A. Thyer, 1993, in R. M. Grinell, Ed., *Social Work Research and Evaluation* [4th ed., 94–117], Itaska, IL: Peacock.)

a new intervention, *C*. Following a third removal, A_3, the practitioner then combines the *B* and *C* phases to see if this combination appears to be more effective than the previous interventions. The final phase, indicated by the parentheses, ( ), indicates selection of the apparently most effective combination, *B*, *C*, or *BC*. (Of course, because all of these phases are not adjacent, these comparisons must be approximate.) Follow-up would be necessary to test empirically whether the choice among *B*, *C*, or *BC* did indeed lead to successful change. A much less rigorous variation of this design, with conclusions therefore more speculative, would be to drop the removal phases. This results in an *A-B-C-BC-( )* design, a perhaps more realistic attempt to develop hypotheses for future testing.

The *differentiating* or *strip design* is described by the following notation: *A-BC-A-B-A-C-( )*. In the strip design, the practitioner begins with a combined intervention, *BC*, but then attempts to ferret out the apparently most effective component of the intervention. He or she does this by applying each of the components (*B* and *C*) separately, and by then ending up with the apparently most effective component (*B*, *C*, or

BC). Again, because intervention phases are not adjacent, comparison across all interventions can only be approximate. It should be noted that by beginning with the combined intervention, *BC*, there might be a cumulative impact of an initially strong program that could exceed the impact of the separate ingredients. A follow-up should be conducted to test whether the choice among *B*, *C*, or *BC* did result in successful change. Of course, with these designs, because of the successive administration of several interventions or components of interventions, order effects cannot be ruled out. As with the construction design, it also would be possible to drop the removal phases, resulting in a design that is more realistic for practice but less rigorous, *A-BC-B-C-( )*.

By adding or subtracting intervention components within the context of returning to baseline, you can tentatively consider the impact of these separate actions in relation to one another. It is important to note that these short-cut designs do not provide a fully rigorous analysis of the relative effectiveness of components in an intervention package. (The following chapter will discuss a design that does allow such an analysis, the Interaction Design.)

SUMMARY

This chapter presented two major types of designs as illustrations of the numerous possibilities of designs that involve change, either in the intensity of the service program or the client's goals, or in having successive, discrete interventions introduced. Although they are extensions of the basic *A-B* design, they make important contributions in their own right.

Changing intensity designs vary in two ways. First, they may involve increasing (or decreasing) the criterion level of desired performance, and second, they may involve changing the intensity of the program itself. In either case the same intervention program is being used, but either the programs or the objectives are modified by degrees in order to move the client by successive approximation toward his or her goal.

Successive intervention designs come in many forms, from the simple *A-B-C* design to the more elaborate *A-B-A-C-A* design and extensions of the *A-B-A-C-A* design such as the multiple component, additive, and differentiating designs. These designs reflect the very common occurrence of using more than one intervention (technique, package, or program) in practice. While appearing to test two (or more) interventions, in fact these designs only offer hints as to their differential impact. For this, more complex designs are required, and it is to these designs that we turn in the next chapter.

17 COMPLEX AND COMBINED DESIGNS

PURPOSE: This chapter considers several ways of trying to sort out the differential effects of specific interventions. The complex designs considered here are extensions of previously discussed designs that enable you to compare or distinguish between the effects of two interventions. They are among the most rigorous of single-system designs, and, correspondingly, are more difficult to undertake than designs considered previously. ■

Introduction
Alternating Intervention Design: *A-B/C-(B or C)*

A	B/C (randomized alternation of *B* and *C*)	*B* or *C* (apparently most effective intervention)

Strengths of the Alternating Intervention Design
Limitations of the Alternating Intervention Design
Recommendations Regarding the Alternating Intervention Design
Case Illustrations

Introducing the Client to the Alternating Intervention Design
Interaction Design: *A-B-A-B-BC-B-BC*

A_1	B_1	A_2	B_2	BC_1	B_3	BC_2

Strengths of the Interaction Design
Limitations of the Interaction Design
Recommendations Regarding the Interaction Design
Case Illustrations
Introducing the Client to the Interaction Design
Summary

INTRODUCTION

The preceding chapters have brought you to the point of making clear identification of changes in target problems between baseline and intervention and of building the logical basis for inferring causality. The task of this chapter is to provide some basic information about designs to help you parcel out the effects of distinctive interventions. We present two designs (and variations on their themes) that will move you to the point of being able to make these determinations, at first approximately, and then with stronger evidence.

We speak of variations on the theme of the designs presented previously. In fact, each variation is fully a design in its own right. We call them variations to emphasize certain characteristics shared with other designs previously discussed and to illustrate how the designs discussed in this chapter basically are extensions of those discussed earlier. Since some of the designs described in this chapter require a large degree of control that is absent from most practice situations, these designs are rarely used in everyday practice. However, there are specific indications for their appropriate use, and each does illustrate a model for interpreting causal effects. Therefore, we provide an introduction to the basic principles related to these complex formats—the alternating intervention and the interaction designs.

ALTERNATING INTERVENTION DESIGN: *A-B/C-(B* OR *C)*

A	*B/C* (randomized alternation of *B* and *C*)	*B* or *C* (apparently most effective intervention)

What do you do when you have two or more interventions that might work with a given problem, when you want to compare them relatively quickly, and when you are unable or unwilling to use a removal design? There actually are a number of designs that can accomplish this task. At the most general level, these can be called *multi-element designs* (Ulman & Sulzer-Azarof, 1975). Multi-element designs compare the effects of two or more interventions and/or other variables (e.g., two or more practitioners or locations for applying the interventions) on one target problem. There are a variety of types of multi-element designs such as the multiple-schedule design, concurrent-schedule design, and simultaneous-treatment design (see Barlow et al., 1984; Barlow & Hersen, 1984; Hayes et al., 1998; and Kazdin & Hartmann, 1978). There are subtle differences among all of those designs, although they all tend to be rather complicated. Hence, there are relatively few reports of their application in typical practice settings. Because of this, we cannot recommend most of them for everyday practice. Instead, we refer the reader who would like to pursue use of those designs to the references cited above.

One multi-element design, however—the *alternating intervention design* (Barlow & Hayes, 1979)—though similar in many respects to other multi-element designs, does appear to be both feasible for use in practice, and relevant to a common but critical practice problem. That problem involves trying to decide what intervention to use with a given problem when two or more interventions (or two variations of one intervention) appear equally feasible. When you are faced with this situation, the alternating intervention design appears to be the design of choice.

The essence of the alternating intervention design is the fairly rapid alternation of two (and sometimes three) interventions so that their effects can be compared quickly with each other. Based on this comparison, the apparently most effective intervention is selected for continuing use.

There generally are three phases in the alternating intervention design (plus a maintenance and follow-up phase). The first phase is the baseline period during which preintervention observations of the target problems are taken as usual. Let's assume that based on these observations, you decide that there are two interventions that would be good choices for working with that problem, but that it is not clear just which one would be better, given the particular client and situation.

In the second phase of this design, you implement both of these interventions, rapidly alternating them in a *counterbalanced* fashion. Counterbalancing refers to presenting each a roughly equal number of times but in such a way that the effects of the order of presentation are ruled out. (We describe how to do this below.) The results of this alternation of interventions are appraised, and the intervention that appears to be more effective in the second phase is then selected and applied by itself to the problem in the third phase, we hope to a successful conclusion. This results in an *A-B/C-(B* or *C)* design with the last phase comprised of the *B* or *C* intervention that appears more effective.

The only real trick in using the alternating intervention design is to counterbalance the two interventions, and, actually, this does not have to be too big a chore. The goal here is to present the interventions an approximately equal number of times, but varying the order in such a way that the order of presentation does not affect the results. In other words, if you were applying two interventions, you would not want to apply one for 3 weeks, and the other one for the following 3 weeks. Obviously, the overall results would be confounded by such an ordering. What you are trying to accomplish is for intervention 1 to be followed as often as possible by intervention 2, *and* vice versa.

So how do you do this? Simple. Just flip a coin! Consider intervention 1 as heads and intervention 2 as tails and then flip a coin to see which comes first each time you plan to administer an intervention. All you have to add to that is the restriction that no intervention will be applied more than a certain number of times in a row. That is, if heads comes up three times in a row, then you might automatically apply the "tails" intervention next. As a general guideline (there are no real, scientifically derived standards as of yet), we would suggest three times as the maximum for each intervention to be applied consecutively before the next intervention is applied.

Just as an illustration of this design, let's say that an unemployed client comes to see you complaining that she has tremendous anxiety about job interviews. She is so worried about them that she is unwilling to undertake any. Let's say that you determine that she does have adequate skills for the interviews but that the anxiety keeps her from exercising those skills. Assume you develop an 11-point individualized rating scale to measure the anxiety, do a 1-week baseline, and decide to try the technique of systematic desensitization, a technique for overcoming maladaptive anxiety. But assume also you are not sure whether to do traditional desensitization or to add a new variation, coping self-statements (e.g., "I can make it"; "This

interview won't be so bad") to the relaxation procedure. You decide to use an alternating intervention design in which in one session you would use desensitization without coping skills and in one session you would use desensitization with coping skills. By flipping a coin, you get the pattern displayed in Table 17.1. The application of these interventions produces the results illustrated in Figure 17.1. Based on these results, in the final phase you implement desensitization with coping self-statements.

Strengths of the Alternating Intervention Design

The alternating intervention design actually allows two sets of comparisons. The first, and the most important because of its uniqueness with this design, is the comparison between two interventions. This has been discussed previously. The second comparison is between baseline and intervention periods. While the conclusions that can be generated from this comparison are probably no greater than one can conclude from an *A-B* design, the alternating intervention design does allow this baseline-to-intervention comparison. In this case, the comparison is between the *A* phase and the *B/C* phase, and then the *B/C* phase with the final phase, since they are adjacent.

Another major advantage of this design is its flexibility. Not only can two interventions be compared, but several other types of comparisons are possible. As the case example earlier illustrated, it is possible to examine two variations of one technique to determine which variation would be best for a particular client or even two completely different techniques. It is also possible to examine time variations in application of an intervention (three sessions a week versus one session a week, or morning applications of a technique versus afternoon

Table 17.1 Counterbalanced order of desensitization with and without coping statements.

				Alternation Phase (Determined by flipping a coin)					
Day 8	9	10	11	12	13	14	15	16	17
With coping	Without coping	Without coping	With coping	Without coping	With coping	With coping	Without coping	With coping	Without coping

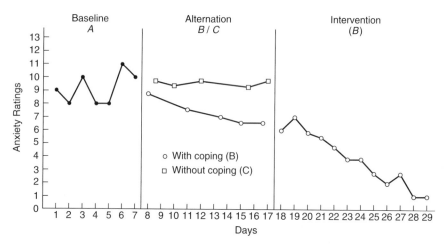

FIGURE 17.1   Illustration of alternating intervention design using systematic desensitization with and without coping self-statements.

applications), or to examine the use of more than one practitioner applying the same intervention. For example, a teacher at a university elementary school was having trouble with the child of a visiting professor from overseas. The young child simply did not follow her instructions. The principal was sensitive to cultural differences and suggested asking a second teacher (a male) of the same grade level to alternate with the first teacher in order to test out the idea that the child might do better with a male teacher. For a week the two teachers alternated including the child in their classes, and they recorded the number of "following instructions" behaviors. In this way they were able to determine in which class the child seemed to exhibit better self-control, enabling

him to gain greater benefits from the year at the foreign school.

Of course, the more variations that are examined, the more complicated the counterbalancing. Thus, for example, in Table 17.2 (from Kazdin & Hartmann, 1978, p. 915), we see an example of counterbalancing involving two interventions, two practitioners, and two time periods.

Finally, a major advantage of the alternating intervention design is that it does not require a removal, and therefore might be more acceptable than experimental removal designs in many settings. Indeed, many practitioners often attempt to compare interventions to determine which is most effective, but may do so in a haphazard and unsystematic way. The al-

Table 17.2 Administration of the two interventions (I_1 and I_2), balanced across practitioners (P_1 and P_2) and time periods (T_1 and T_2). (From "The Simultaneous Treatment Design" by A. E. Kazdin and D. P. Hartmann, 1978, *Behavior Therapy, 9*, p. 915.)

			Days				
Time Period	1	2	3	4	5	6	. . . n
T_1	$I_1\ P_1$	$I_1\ P_2$	$I_2\ P_1$	$I_2\ P_2$	$I_1\ P_2$	$I_1\ P_1$	
T_2	$I_2\ P_2$	$I_2\ P_1$	$I_1\ P_2$	$I_1\ P_1$	$I_2\ P_1$	$I_2\ P_2$	

ternating intervention design simply allows a feasible structure and overall plan for making such comparisons so that results are more reliable. In fact, because the interventions are counterbalanced, order effects (sequential confounding), which could be expected to show up in nonsystematic comparisons, can to some extent be ruled out.

Limitations of the Alternating Intervention Design

The alternating intervention design does not clearly rule out contrast effects–that is, differences arising due to the client's awareness of two different conditions being applied. Indeed, most material on the subject (e.g., Barlow & Hayes, 1979) states that in the alternating intervention design, it is crucial for the client to be *able* to discriminate between the two applications of the interventions. To the extent that differential results are produced, this is all well and good. But if the results are produced *because* of the client's awareness of the differences rather than the interventions themselves, the conclusions are obviously confounded.

Similarly, there may be a possibility of both order and carryover effects using an alternating intervention design. Although this is to some extent limited by the rapid alternation and counterbalancing as we mentioned above, one cannot be completely sure that order and carryover effects are not present.

Another problem relates to external validity (see Chapter 11). That is, the extent to which the eventually selected intervention in one alternating intervention design can be applied *by itself* (without the alternating process or the other intervention) to another, even similar problem needs to be evaluated on an empirical basis each time.

Another problem with the alternating intervention design is that if the practitioner is not able or willing to continue to alternate interventions or other conditions until the differences become clear, this design is not feasible. In fact, even more importantly, if the interventions you plan to evaluate are not likely to produce fairly rapid, observable changes under such alternating conditions, then the alternating intervention design should not be used.

Finally, there is some problem with the visual interpretation of these data. How much of a difference is "enough"? There really are no clear answers for that question. It is possible for some of the statistics we suggest in Part IV to shed some light on this issue by doing a separate, simple statistical analysis on each intervention in the second phase in comparison to the baseline to see if one reaches statistical significance. In addition, it is possible to use more sophisticated data analysis techniques such as randomization tests (Holden et al., 1999; Onghena, 1992), although typically these require advanced statistical skills and computers (Van Damme & Onghena, 1992).

Recommendations Regarding the Alternating Intervention Design

When the practice task is to compare two or more interventions or intervention variations, and removal phases are impractical or impossible, the alternating intervention design is the design of choice. Moreover, this design may be used when there is difficulty in achieving a good or stable baseline, since the main comparison is between interventions. Further, we recommend this design for comparing two interventions involving two different practitioners. However, the limitations just described do suggest that this design be used with caution. For example, it may be hard to distinguish the effects of one intervention from another, leaving you unsure of what to do next. Further, if causal linkages are to be examined, we suggest that removal or multiple baseline designs be utilized, or the more complicated designs described in the next section. Of course, if a quick, approximate answer to the question–"Which of the following interventions seems to be most effective with this client?"–is needed, the alternating intervention design can be quite useful.

Case Illustrations

In a recent report, Kastner et al. (2000) studied the effects of Ritalin delivered to six fourth- and fifth-grade boys diagnosed with Attention Deficit-Hyperactivity Disorder, Combined Type (ADHD-CT). While the use of Ritalin for this disorder is controversial, the question posed by this study is a focused one: whether Ritalin given 45 minutes to 1 hour before testing the boys' reading skills was better or worse than giving it 3 to 4 hours before the testing. To determine the probable most effective time scheduling of the drug in a relatively short period of time (number of testing sessions), the relatively rare alternating intervention design was used.

All of the tests of the 1-hour versus the 3- or 4-hour sequencing were done in a random sequence, with the provision that a maximum of three continuous occurrences of any particular condition would be allowed (as suggested earlier in this chapter). The basis for making an alternation was mastery of the reading passage by a given youngster. The passages to be read were also sequenced from easier to more difficult. The next randomly ordered condition (either the 1-hour or the 3- or 4-hour interval after administration of the drug) began at the next intervention session. (The fewer trials needed to master the material, the better.)

As seen in Figure 17.2, the graph portrays a reconstructed version of one of the six graphs for the subjects in this study. Note that the data points indicate *cumulatively* the number of trials it took the boys to master the reading passage. On the bottom line we observe the number of passages mastered (rather than time units per se). The two conditions, identified here as short interval and extended interval, are presented as two conditions compared in the same phase against each other. In all six cases, the short interval–which was considered optimal–had better effects than the extended interval. In the one representative example we present here, the pattern shows that it takes more trials to master a passage when the drug is given 3 to 4 hours before the testing than when the drug is 1 hour before the testing period.

An important part of this study was the independent verification of the more efficacious condition. The six boys differed by degree in this independent verification, but in general, even with an independent observer verifying the number of trials to mastery, the short in-

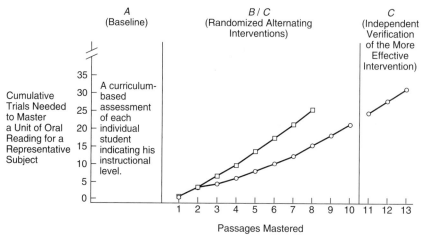

B = o—o—o = Short interval between taking medication and number of trials needed to master a unit of oral reading (45 minutes to 1 hour after ingestion; this is considered the optimal condition).

C = □—□—□ = Extended interval (3 to 4 hours after ingestion; this is considered non-optimal).

FIGURE 17.2   An alternating intervention design involving randomized short or extended intervals of time after ingestion of Ritalin before a child is able to master a unit of oral reading. (Adapted from Kastner et al., 2000.)

terval had lower cumulative trials to mastery than did the extended trials conducted during the main part of the evaluation.

Linton and Singh (1984) reported on the effects of two training procedures for teaching sign language to hearing-impaired developmentally disabled adults. Using the alternating intervention design, they combined a technique called positive practice overcorrection (repeating the right answer five times) with positive reinforcement, or used the overcorrection procedure alone. (The authors used a no-training control technique as well, but we will adapt their data to illustrate the alternating intervention part of their study.) Reliability of ratings of accuracy of the clients' signs was acceptable for two independent raters.

Figure 17.3 presents some data adapted from the Linton and Singh study on one client. A training phase is visible the first 5 days of the intervention period (*B/C*), although not identified as such by the authors; learning to sign takes practice. However, once the client caught on, he first showed more successful signing with the overcorrection technique alone. Overcorrection plus positive reinforcement appear to have confused the client at first. However, in time, the combined overcorrection technique plus positive reinforcement clearly became the stronger conditions producing more words signed correctly. Thus, this combination was

the method of choice in the second intervention period, labeled *B* in the chart.

While it might appear obvious that the combination of methods would be better than the one alone, this was not the case immediately. There was a training period in which the client had to learn the skill and perhaps another training period in which the client came to appreciate the additional reinforcement given on top of producing a correct sign.

The following example of an alternating intervention design illustrates that practitioners may combine evaluation and research in one project, to the advantage of both. Maheady, Mallette, Harper, and Sacca (1991) tested a teaching innovation (called Heads Together [HT]) against the common instructional approach (the whole group approach [WG]) with a difficult, unruly class. The common whole group approach involves the teacher asking a general question to the class, and then calling on volunteers to answer, which tends to encourage the high-achieving students and discourage the low-achieving ones. The Heads Together approach involves arranging students in heterogeneous groups of four, with one high-achieving student, two average-achieving students, and one low-achieving student, who number themselves 1 to 4 and sit together. The teacher asks a question, allows a short time for the four-member groups to put their heads

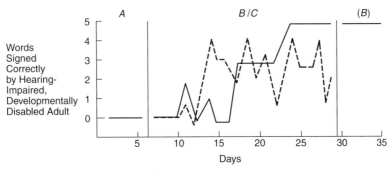

FIGURE 17.3 Alternating intervention design using positive practice overcorrection and overcorrection alone. (Adapted from "Aquisition of Sign Language Using Positive Practice Overcorrection" by J. M. Linton and N. N. Singh, 1984, *Behavior Modification, 8,* pp. 553–566.)

together to come up with the best answer—thus ensuring that everyone on the team knows the answer. Thus, when the teacher asks "How many Number ____s (1, 2, 3, or 4) know the answer?" that member of the team, who can be high-, average-, or low-achieving, raises his or her hand. The teacher also asks other teams with the same number if they agree with that answer or want to correct it. Each team receives points for correct answers, and individual scores are also recorded. Team membership remained the same throughout the project.

Ordinarily, the teacher would conduct a social studies unit four times a week of about 30 minutes in length. For this study, she conducted this unit twice a week, once in the morning and once in the afternoon, so that the randomized alternation between the whole group and the Heads Together methods could be compared. Baseline measures were taken during the ordinary whole group method, and then the alternating interventions were used.

Figure 17.4 presents the results on the percentage of correct answers on social studies quizzes. Maheady et al. (1991, p. 29) point out that, in the baseline condition, about one-third of the class had failing averages, while two students earned A grades. In the alternating phase (B/C), the class averages were plotted separately, with students always performing better in the Heads Together method. In the last phase (B), the HT method is used all of the time, with similar results. Maheady et al. (1991, p. 29) point to the important fact that no student had a failing grade under the HT conditions, and six students earned A grades. These practitioners also studied on-task behavior with the alternating intervention format and found a similar pattern favoring the HT conditions, except that when HT was used alone in the third phase, there was no improvement in on-task behaviors. The experimenters suggest that team enthusiasm (congratulating one another) may have accounted for the off-task behavior; they

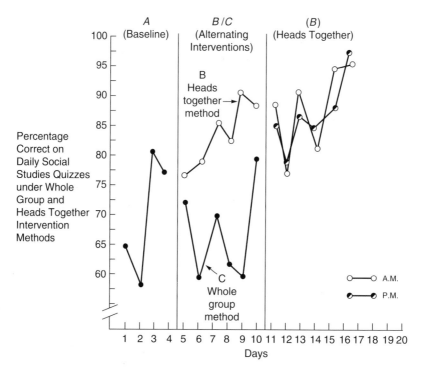

FIGURE 17.4 The mean percentage correct on daily social studies quizzes under alternating intervention design. (Adapted from Maheady, Mallette, Harper, & Sacca, 1991.)

propose to reconsider their measurement procedure to take account of this side effect of the HT method. The results are encouraging in the face of current educational challenges–changing demographics of the schools, rapidly enlarging knowledge base, and exhortations to improve learning for everyone. By forming heterogeneous learning groups and encouraging peer-teaching of teammates who then respond in a teacher-questioning format, Maheady et al., (1991) seem to be moving toward a very useful innovation.

Introducing the Client to the Alternating Intervention Design

The basic similarity of the alternating intervention design to other designs means that you can use the material in previous introductions to help you begin your discussion of this design. However, for the unique element of this design, the fact that more than one intervention will be used in the same phase, we suggest the following: "*I am going to suggest that we try two approaches to help resolve your problem. We know that each will be of some help, but I can't tell without trying each which is the more effective one. Once we get some ideas about how well each method works, we'll use the better one. This will require that we continue to keep accurate records of how you are doing.*"

Let's say, however, that the techniques you use in one intervention contradict the techniques in another intervention. More explicitly, if what you tell the client in the instructions in one intervention seems nonreversible, you might try the following, once you actually get into the alternation of the interventions: "*I know that with our other approach, I suggested you do (X). Now what I'd like you to do is specifically not do (X). We will then see which way is better. When we start this next approach, be sure to specifically not do (X).*"

INTERACTION DESIGN: *A-B-A-B-BC-B-BC*

| A_1 | B_1 | A_2 | B_2 | BC_1 | B_3 | BC_2 |

The major concern of the interaction design is to sort out the differential effects of multiple interventions by comparing adjacent interventions in a logically controlled manner. We have discussed in previous chapters how the separate effects of two discrete interventions can be determined for one target, and we noted at that time that further design phases would be necessary in order to determine the differential or relative effect of these two interventions. For example, we considered the *A-B-A-C-A* design as representative of successive intervention designs. Although the second and third returns to the baseline enabled the practitioner to determine the *separate* effects of *B* and *C*, it was not possible to make a logical comparison of the *relative* effectiveness of *B* and *C*. Without overcomplicating this point, we would like to present a strategy for studying such interactions.

The interaction design, designated as *A-B-A-B-BC-B-BC,* may be the minimal arrangement of elements from which you can determine the interactive effects of two interventions. This means they would be studied separately and in combination by comparing differences in the adjacent *B* and *BC* phases (Barlow & Hersen, 1984). After first conducting a standard *A-B-A-B* sequence, you then add in the next phase a new intervention, *C,* to the earlier intervention, *B.* Then, the subsequent return to *B* and reintroduction of the combined *BC* would allow for analysis of the additive and controlling effects of the first intervention, *B,* and the combined intervention, *BC* (Barlow & Hersen, 1984).

This is the most complex of the designs we present in this book, and so we will explain why it technically appears to be the minimal arrangement for making interaction comparisons among interventions with the same client or target. The components are familiar. First of all there are the repeated baseline and intervention phases as in an *A-B-A-B* design. This provides the kinds of causal information on the *B* intervention that we recognize from the experimental replication design. In addition, there is a set of four phases, *B-BC-B-BC* (overlapping the first *A-B-A-B* set), in which two types of interventions are alternated. (You will recognize this set of phases as comparable to the multiple-component design discussed in Chapter 16.) These two types bear a special relationship to each other, with the *B* phase being a component of the *BC* phase package. Since the causal influence of the *B* phase has been assessed in the first *A-B-A-B* segment of the interaction design, the adjacent comparisons of the *B* with *BC* permit analysis of the additional effects of the *C* component of *BC*. The second *B* intervention, B_2, functions as if it were the baseline for the *BC* intervention, and it too requires a removal (the third *B* intervention or B_3) for a definitive analysis of the effects of the second *BC* intervention, BC_2. This design allows determination of the contributions *C* makes toward the effects obtained by *BC*, after separately analyzing the effects of *B* in the first four phases. Thus, this design allows the analysis of separate and additive effects of the interventions.

There are several possible variations of the interaction design. Two important variations involve combining the principles of the interaction design with those of the differentiating (strip) and additive (construction) designs discussed in Chapter 16. These combinations would provide a more convincing demonstration of which of the components is most effective than use of the more approximate strip/construction methods described in Chapter 16.

The first variation would be the *interaction/strip* design: *A-BC-A-BC-B-BC-( )*. With this design, you would begin with a baseline and then introduce a package of interventions, *BC*. The practitioner would determine the causal impact of *BC* by using an experimental design (similar to the *A-B-A-B*) in the first four phases. Then, taking this intervention of known effects, *BC*, you could differentiate between its components by stripping down the package to one intervention, *B*. By again experimentally manipulating this intervention, *BC-B-BC*, you not only can compare the effects of *BC* and *B* (because they are adjacent), but will understand the extent to which the intervention *C* contributed to the overall effects of *BC*. Then, the last step is to use what appears to be the most effective component, indicated by the parentheses. If you wanted, in addition, to do a separate comparison of the *B* and *C* interventions, the entire process would be viewed as follows: *A-BC-A-BC-B-BC-B-C-B-( )*.

The second variation is the *interaction/additive* design: *A-B-A-B-BC-B-BC-B-( )* (tech-

nically, the last *B* phase may not be necessary, since the *B* was manipulated earlier in *A-B-A* fashion). We have provided the basic logical analysis of the additive (or construction) design in the earlier discussion of the general interaction design. It does bear repeating, however, that at the conclusion of the use of this design you have the basis for analyzing not only the causal effects of *B* and *BC*, but the comparative effects as well, thereby ending up with the most effective component.

These variations of interaction designs provide the soundest logical basis for making complex comparisons. You might want to compare the differences between these designs and the strip/construction, successive intervention designs in Chapter 16. The interaction design variations are rather long and fierce looking until they are broken down into their component elements and the reasons are understood regarding why they are put together as they are. We also want to emphasize that this is the way interventions often are combined in actual practice: Some techniques may be combined into a package or program, and then some are partialed out as experience reveals them to be less effective. Or, from a simple beginning that doesn't seem to be making the desired impact on the client's problems, you add other intervention components to make a new package. The interaction design in its additive or differentiating forms is simply a flow from the kind of thinking that went into the less complex designs as we move toward asking more demanding questions: What is the comparative effect of each of the interventions (or intervention packages) I have used?

Strengths of the Interaction Design

This powerful design (and its variations) is able to show change in target problems, to provide the basis for logically inferring whether the intervention had any causal relationship with that outcome, and to locate the differential effects of each element in the intervention process (the components or the combinations). This type of design also encourages practitioners to try out multiple interventions with some hope of sorting out what effects each may have. It also may be useful in testing conceptual ideas derived from practice theory. In short, the strengths of this interaction design are like those of the previously described *A-B-A-B* designs, plus the interaction design has the capacity to make a powerful differentiating or component analysis.

Limitations of the Interaction Design

It is obvious that the *A-B-A-B-BC-B-BC* design (and its variations) is complex and would require a good deal of time and control to perform adequately. As such it requires considerable dedication to pursue this design, as more immediate practical interests might be served by a simpler design. In addition, these designs also involve the same problems as any standard removal design, compounded by the successive alternations.

Recommendations Regarding the Interaction Design

Interaction designs tend to require considerable control over variables, time, and energy. It would seem on the face of it that they only would be used in limited situations, such as studies of the effects of drugs or other practice efforts within institutions in which a fair degree of control is possible. However, given the power of these designs, keep them in mind as possible designs to use when you need knowledge of the differential effects of interventions. (We will provide one illustration outside of a highly controlled environment to illustrate its possibilities.)

For present purposes, introducing the interaction design has another value, that of illustrating the logical extensions of the many design principles illustrated throughout this part of the book. If you understand the logic behind this design, then you should be able to use and analyze any single-system design, because all of these designs are made up of one or another of the logical principles illustrated in this interaction design.

Another value of interaction designs is that they can aid in the never-ending process of technique building (Fischer, 1978b). Interaction designs show great potential for helping to isolate the effective components of our practice. It is the rare practitioner who does not continually add or subtract different intervention components from his or her overall intervention plan, based on some standard as to what works and what doesn't. Interaction designs give us the potential for being systematic in that effort, for clearly and carefully identifying those components of practice that work or don't work with a variety of clients and problems/situations. This is the heart of professional practice, and the process of technique building—systematically identifying effective components of our practice—is one of the ways we can all add to the cumulative growth of professional knowledge.

Case Illustrations

We first will present a disguised version of one actual case in which a graduate social work student used a variation of the interaction design. A family agency ran a summer camp for emotionally frail youngsters. In one section of the camp, a group of eight boys ranging from 8 to 10 years old was under the guidance of a team of social workers who took turns with different aspects of their care and tending. The boys soon called themselves the "Ferrets," a very apt name, as these youngsters spent the better part of most days fighting with one another, crying, or clinging to the counselors.

One counselor, Greg, decided to attempt some group activities that would reduce the fighting and bickering that were threatening to the youngsters and frustrating to the staff. The camp defined fighting as hitting or throwing things at another camper, and the staff was required to record incidents of such behavior as a matter of routine work. All staff members used the same criteria regarding fighting, which made record keeping easy.

Greg used a psychodynamic model to conceptualize the events in this group. The model involved a consideration of latency-age boys having weak, incomplete egos with narcissistic, libidinal functioning and impulsivity. These factors, combined with thin emotional insulation and an inadequate protection against overstimulation, resulted in a propensity to fight.

The boys chose to play team baseball, but they possessed neither the skill nor the cooperative ability to handle this sport, and it probably would have led to more frustration and fighting. In the context of ordinary summer activities at the camp, Greg made some plans involving what he termed, "mock athletic experiences"— that is, those that would resemble athletics and thus appeal to these young boys, but would be harmless and would teach them some of the rules of sharing and cooperation (see Figure 17.5).

Baseline (A) data collection involved measures of fighting during ordinary camp activities such as eating, swimming, arts and crafts, game time, quiet time, and so on. Greg was with the boys almost daily (with relief time supplied by his team colleagues). Greg introduced a "powder-puff volleyball game" in which a large, soft ball was to be kept in the air by the group as a whole for 1 minute at a time for the "team" to get a point. They would record their scores each day, playing against their former high score. This is termed B, the intervention. Greg and the staff continued to collect data on fighting behavior among group members. He noticed some reduction of fighting and a little more friendly interaction, but it did not appear clinically or socially meaningful.

Greg was due for a relief period in which he went home for a week. His colleague took over all of the activities, except that the colleague did not know about the powder-puff volleyball, so this activity was removed. Because fighting was recorded as usual by the staff, this period constitutes a return to baseline, A_2 (although it makes a possibly unwarranted assumption that the counselors are interchangeable).

Greg returned, noted that the fighting had returned to its former high levels, and so he reinstituted the powder-puff volleyball game, B_2. Again the rates of fighting inched downward, but not very fast nor enough to be of practical importance. Greg decided to add a campfire discussion each evening, at which time he led the boys in thinking about the day's activities, especially about how they were getting along with one another. This constitutes a C intervention, and since it took place each day along with powder-puff volleyball, the set of interventions may be described as BC. Greg noticed a much sharper reduction in fighting, and was quite pleased with himself as he went to the counselors' Fourth of July picnic. There he promptly got a bad case of poison ivy, which put him in the camp infirmary for nearly a week.

During his absence, his team colleagues took over the group, and Greg urged them to continue the powder-puff volleyball; the boys had learned the rules by now and were pretty much doing it on their own. The campfire discussions were, however, postponed until Greg returned.

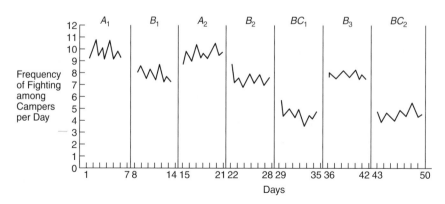

FIGURE 17.5 Reconstruction of camp data on the "Ferrets," illustrating an interaction design (from a disguised student case).

This period of time might be considered as a B_3 phase; fighting activity was recorded as usual.

When Greg returned, he saw that the fighting had once again increased, and so he reinstituted the campfire discussion as well as the powder-puff volleyball, BC_2. He was pleased with the results, although he noted that as the boys prepared to leave for home, they once again broke into fights and crying bouts, just as they had on arrival. He attributed this to the stress of leaving, but recognized that the therapeutic gains were probably only temporary. Unfortunately, he did not attempt any follow-up, although he did report to the family agency his results that appeared to differentially control the problem behaviors in the camp setting. His main consolation was that the agency was going to consider using his new game and the discussion method in their ongoing afterschool programs. (See Figure 17.4 for a reconstruction of these camp data; Greene, personal communication, 1986.)

A variation of an interaction design was used to explore multiple interventions. Stock and Milan (1993) used this design to understand the effects of various interventions on improving dietary practices of three elderly persons at an independent living facility. Each of these individuals had a strong medical need to eat healthful foods; none was in fact following these directives. The dining room was decorated like a fine restaurant, with linen table cloths, fresh flowers, and a menu with four choices in each of the four courses—appetizers, entrees, vegetables, and desserts.

We have changed the notation of this design to conform to the practices suggested in this book. Note that Stock and Milan have a B-A-B design in the first three phases, but it fails to produce any changes in the behavior of the three clients, probably because the initial B phase had been long in existence at the living facility, and it wasn't recognized by the clients as anything new, that is, "an intervention."

The first condition (B) involved menus already in place at the facility in which there were prompts for the healthful foods—a heart was placed by those items that were low-cholesterol and calorie-modified; the names of these dishes were intended to sound appealing. The data show fairly low percentages of healthy choices by the three targeted clients.

The second condition (A) was the removal of these prompts, which constitutes a baseline situation for this study. Note there is no deterioration in healthy choices at this time, and indeed, one client (client #2) seems to improve in her healthy choices. The third condition was a brief reinstatement of the first condition (B_2). The data show little change from the baseline levels.

A fourth condition—various kinds of enhanced prompts, feedback, and social reinforcement—is termed C because it was quite different from B, even though it was based on B. The fifth condition was the introduction of a lottery, in which residents (including the three target individuals) would win prizes through healthy food choices. Let us term this condition D, and since it is taking place concurrently with C, is indicated as CD.

A sixth condition, E, is added, and it, too, takes place concurrently with C and D. This involves having residents (including the three target clients) serve as confederates in helping to make healthy food choices. This addition combined with the prior intervention to form a CDE intervention.

Next, the authors systematically remove components to study their effects. In the seventh condition, component E is removed, leaving the CD unit. Then, in the eighth condition, the D is removed, leaving the C unit. Finally, in the ninth condition, C is removed and B is reinstated.

The results presented in Figure 17.6 are simpler to describe than was the design. Prompts and no prompts produced equally low percentages of healthy food choices—the three target residents were simply ignoring hearts on menus or their absence. However, the enhanced prompts, feedback, and social reinforcement had a strong positive effect on the residents, but the lottery and acting as a confederate generally had little additional effect. Finally, the removal of all of these enhanced prompts and a return to only hearts on menus led to a return to low choices of healthy foods,

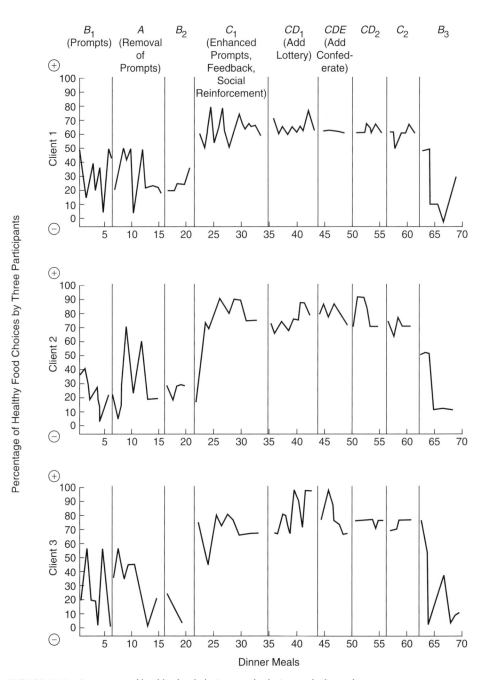

FIGURE 17.6 Percentage of healthy food choices made during each dinner by three participants (Amy, Beth, Carl) at an independent living facility during nine experimental conditions of the study. (Adapted from Stock & Milan, 1993.)

suggesting that the experience did not leave any lasting impressions on the three clients.

From these results, the authors can sort out apparently effective from less effective interventions, and recognize the likelihood that enhanced prompts will be necessary on a continuing basis to stabilize healthy food choices in these three target residents who responded in a relatively similar manner across all conditions.

Does this design provide any basis for causal inference? In addition to the inferences that indeed can be made from the designs tracking each individual's progress (based on the removals and additions and subtractions of interventions), when we find three separate individuals responding in relatively similar ways, we can begin to formulate an even stronger causal hypothesis that would need further empirical testing. This is like having three simultaneous replications in one study. It is also like a multiple target design with removal and successive interventions.

Introducing the Client to the Interaction Design

We recommend that you use as an introduction the approaches given previously with the *A-B-A-B, A-B-A-C-A,* and alternating intervention designs, especially the suggestions about trying different approaches to find better ways to solve the client's problem. We could locate little evidence that this design has been used often in the applied area. Indeed, chances are that with such a long or extended service program, you won't be in a position to give the client a full overview even in the unlikely circumstance that you had planned an interaction design. Again, we suggest that you use whatever introductions described previously fit the circumstances.

SUMMARY

This chapter has dealt with some complex extensions of previously discussed designs that are intended to provide either quick, approximate information about the differential effects of the components of intervention or logically sound information on the same topic using an elaborate design.

The alternating intervention design, *A-B/C-(B* or *C)* begins from a baseline, followed by an intervention phase in which two or more interventions are randomly alternated, possibly with more than one practitioner involved. Based on your evaluation of how each intervention went, you try the "best" one and evaluate it in the regular way. This is a fast and economic approach to looking at multiple interventions to determine the most effective one.

The interaction design is a very powerful logical design but a cumbersome one as well. The *A-B-A-B-BC-B-BC* design is the minimum arrangement for full logical determination of the additive and separate effects of multiple interventions, and it illustrates many of the logical principles of design we have been discussing in this book.

There are other complex designs, but these essentially have been used mainly in laboratory settings and not in field settings. However, the important point is that you should feel free to be creative in constructing a design as long as your interpretation of results follows the basic principles of the design that we have described.

18 SELECTING A DESIGN

PURPOSE: This chapter provides some specific guidelines for selecting a design most suited to your needs. It also provides a discussion of one of the most important components of effective practice and evaluation: creativity in use of single-system designs. We also discuss the use of single-system designs in minimal-contact situations and in managed care. The final section of the chapter discusses some pertinent issues related to your use of single-system designs. ■

Introduction
Framework for Selecting a Design
Needed: A Design for All Seasons
Creativity in Single-System Designs:
    Making Your Own Designs
Evaluation in Minimal-Contact Situations
Baseline Approximations
Intervention Data
Involving the Client in Evaluation

Dichotomous Data
Single-System Designs in Managed Care:
    The Stretch Design
Trouble-Shooting: "Okay, I Understand
    Everything That You Said, But My Case
    Is Different."
Summary

INTRODUCTION

Having come this far in the book you must be wondering how you will ever sort out all of the possible designs and their infinite variations. In this chapter we present a set of general guidelines to assist you in selecting a design–or a group of designs–that most closely fits your needs. No single set of guidelines can determine exactly which design is the "best" one for a given situation. You must be willing to consider these suggestions based on your own practice wisdom. However, as points of departure, these guidelines may be useful when adjusted to the realities at hand.

FRAMEWORK FOR SELECTING A DESIGN

By asking five questions, you can be guided to one or a cluster of related designs through which you can evaluate your practice. Figure 18.1 represents these questions as a flow

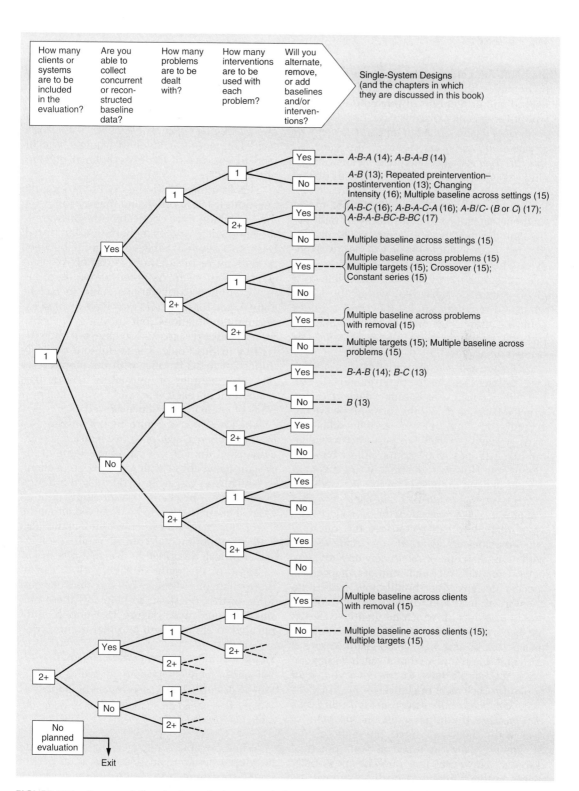

FIGURE 18.1 Framework for selecting a single-system design.

diagram; the guiding questions are framed as dichotomies that branch off and ultimately lead to one or a cluster of related designs that will fit the specifics of your case.

1. *Do you wish to conduct an evaluation of your services at all, and if yes, then with how many distinct clients or systems?* The possible answers include "Yes, with one client," "Yes, with two or more clients," and "No, I don't want to use systematic evaluation with this client." The more-than-one category refers primarily to multiple baseline designs that will compare clients. For the most part a single client will be involved, even when there are different individuals in that system. Each evaluation will relate to a given system or subsystem within the larger whole (in a family study, the child's grades could be monitored on one chart, while the parents' communication patterns could be studied on another).

2. *Are you able to collect* initial *baseline data?* A "yes" answer includes the determination to collect either concurrent baseline data or reconstructed baseline data if the former type are not accessible. A "no" answer leads to other designs; it may be possible to perform an evaluation even though you cannot collect baseline data at first. However, the bulk of single-system designs depend on having an initial baseline.

3. *Do you plan to intervene with one or more than one problem at the present time?* (If you change your mind, you can reconsider this question when it comes up again.) If you decide to deal with more than one problem concurrently, you have (eventually) a small number of possible specific designs. We should note that some choices will lead you to unnamed endpoints—that is, to points for which no identified design has been presented in this book. This merely means that no one has staked claim to such a design; it doesn't mean that no such design can exist. You simply have to construct your own design for such a set of choices.

4. *How many interventions are to be used with each problem?* If you have just one problem to deal with, then you have the bulk of the designs we have discussed at your potential disposal. However, this question potentially places further limitations on the eventual designs that might be relevant to your needs. You can choose to use either one intervention or

two (or more) interventions for a given problem. (This may involve other practitioners working with you.)

5. *Do you plan to alternate new baselines and/or new interventions after completing the first intervention?* This question involves whether you intend to use any of the experimental or complex designs.

This framework is to be used by asking the questions listed in order, and then by following the branching lines connecting the answers to the end, where one or more designs are listed. In some cases you will have to choose between designs by reconsidering the distinctive characteristics of each. As noted above there are many unfilled slots; designs could in fact be constructed for them and may have been in experimental situations, but they are not common practice designs and so have not been described in this book. It is useful and critically important to be familiar with the literature to pick up examples of unusual or new designs (many emerge each year) and to stimulate new ways of evaluating practice as well.

The lower tier of Figure 18.1, involving two or more clients, has only two entries specifically listed. In fact, you could use some of the designs listed above with more than one client, in which case we suggest you look at a design listed in the "one client" tier and apply it for all cases. The main point to be observed about the lower tier is that these conditions could also lead to experimental/control group designs, such as those described by Kazdin (1992).

Some of the paths in Figure 18.1 lead to more than one design. We therefore suggest some further questions to help sort these out, since it would make Figure 18.1 unduly complicated to embed them into that framework.

Will one or more interventions be added?

Will one or more observations be used?

Will single or combined interventions be employed?

Will the design end on an intervention or on an observation (baseline) phase?

When possible, we suggest that you attempt to select a design in advance—that is, as part of your assessment prior to the point at which intervention actually begins. This is possible in many "controlled" practice situations and in some "less controlled" practice situations. However, again, because of the complexity of practice, it may not be possible in each and every case. In fact, in real practice you will probably modify your design as you go, changing phases and adding or subtracting interventions as the practice needs change. For example, one of our students was using an *A-B* design for a smoking-reduction program. One of the measures he was using, in addition to frequency of smoking, was an individualized rating scale dealing with the client's anxiety. The student found that as the smoking decreased the client's anxiety went up, thus leading the student to institute a technique for decreasing anxiety (relaxation). As a result the design became an *A-B-BC* design, with *B* being the smoking reduction program and *C* being the relaxation training.

NEEDED: A DESIGN
FOR ALL SEASONS

There are many variations of single-system designs as we have seen, each with its own strengths as well as limitations. Our students have told us that, as they are busy practitioners, all this information is sometimes more than they want to know or have time to digest when they are facing a client. What they want is a basic model, a point of departure that will fit most of the problems they might face every day in the field. When some complex problems emerge, they will then go "back to the books" to find an evaluation procedure commensurate with that task.

Unfortunately, there is no such thing as a design for all seasons. However, we can recommend what we call an all-purpose single-system design that incorporates the basic features of this evaluation approach and yet permits the addition of other features when needed. Another way of viewing this design is as a sort of summary of much of the material presented in Part III of this book.

It should come as no surprise that we recommend the basic single-system design, *A-B*, as our all-purpose design. This combination of elements—a more or less objective baseline that is compared to some clearly specified intervention addressed to an operationally defined target problem/goal—seems to us to be the rock-bottom, simplest, most easily performed, and yet reasonably helpful combination for identifying change and pointing the way to additional analysis of possible causal factors.

In short, we believe that this all-purpose design can be a beginning point, not an end point, for evaluating practice. We are under few illusions about the state of perfection of single-system designs, including this basic design. However, we believe that it is a quantum leap to the *A-B* design from the subjective or intuitive approaches to evaluating practice commonly used. There are many differences between the *A-B* design and its relatives, including the experimental designs, the multiple baselines and complex designs, and the like, but these differences are more a matter of degree than of kind. Moreover, we have emphasized throughout the book that single-system designs are highly flexible and adaptable to current circumstances in a case. This means that you can add other intervention or baseline phases to the basic *A-B*, as portrayed in Figure 18.2, and thereby increase the information from the design.

In fact, we believe that once you sample the delights of using the basic design, you will be drawn to other designs as needed, because the knowledge of how well (or poorly) the intervention is progressing is a highly potent reinforcer. *The fundamental step in becoming an accountable professional is to start evaluating with the A-B design.*

CREATIVITY IN
SINGLE-SYSTEM DESIGNS:
MAKING YOUR OWN DESIGNS

We believe that you should feel free to construct your own practice designs. We do not make this recommendation lightly. In this book we have offered a variety of the most basic and practical designs that we think will be sufficient for most of the situations you will face. However, we recognize that client and case situations are nothing if not variable and unpredictable, so this section on creativity may be useful to all practitioners on occasion.

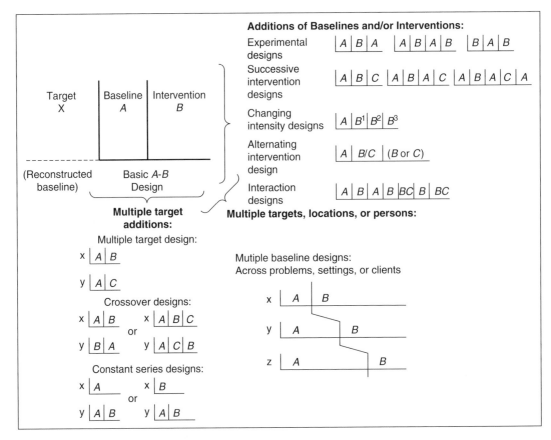

FIGURE 18.2   Possible additions to the all-purpose design, *A-B*.

To suggest that you can "make up" your own design is not to remove the responsibility that comes from constructing a logical structure. You must still know what you are doing and why. Indeed, the designs we presented in this book can be thought of largely as models (or "ideal" types), not the final word on designs but illustrations of some basic possibilities and principles of design construction. Examining the basic designs carefully should be sufficient background for you to understand and to apply the guidelines presented below. However, the foreground of evaluation deals with people in social and cultural settings. You must be sensitive to what is feasible as well as to what is desirable in any evaluation context. An oppressed family may have to spend most of its available energies in holding itself together and therefore may not be able to cooperate fully in an evaluation plan; in such a case, you will have to arrange data-collection methods that are less burdensome to the family, even though such methods may be second best as empirical evaluation sources.

Thus, flexibility and sensitivity are the major dimensions of creativity in single-system designs. Consider the following guidelines for developing your own designs:

1. Obtain the original baseline conditions, if at all possible, with clear, direct measures that are culturally and socially sensitive to the people involved.

2. Plan your interventions with your clients with the same clarity and with the same sensitivity to the personal, social, and cultural structures and forces at work. Be able to define the components of your

intervention plan. While it is preferable in an evaluation sense to use just one specific intervention at a time, systems-oriented practice theory suggests the value of attending to a network of inter-related and interacting factors. The compromise between these two demands is to be clear about the interacting components, so hunches can be formed as to which seems to be the more effective (as in the alternating intervention design).

3. If progress is not occurring toward the client's goals, consider what intervention components you have, and those you have not yet employed, and speculate about other combinations. By having these interventions operationally defined it is possible to think through various combinations.

4. Let your practice observations (based on the best available information) be your guide to action, and let the evaluation design follow from those decisions. Recognize you can add As, Bs, Cs, and Ds . . . ad infinitum. For every combination, however, you must be responsible for the answers to questions such as
   a. Will changes from previous interventions be apparent or carry over? (Should you have a return to baseline to make these changes clear, or will change appear even with a new intervention?)
   b. Will your choices of designs make clear the likely causal patterns among factors?
   c. Are you sensitive enough to the client to conclude the program with a stable desired goal attained within the social and cultural definitions of what your client sees as desirable?

5. While you may distinguish minor variations in emphasis or variations in technique as distinctive interventions, it may be helpful to stand back and look at your interventions more globally in order to see whether some more basic pattern is at work, such as A-B or A-B-A-C. This will help you to interpret your design. Look

for designs within designs. You may have an overall game plan, but on some specific topic you may conduct what is in effect an experiment within the larger service program. Interpret these internal or sub-system designs independently, and then apply their overall outcome as part of the larger design. At all times be imaginative, but be responsible for your designs.

EVALUATION IN MINIMAL-CONTACT SITUATIONS

There are many situations in which practitioners have only brief contacts with clients such that conventional single-system evaluation methods *appear* to be unusable. For example, crises usually require rapid interventions and often referral to other agencies for additional services. Short-term services as in acute hospitals or drug rehabilitation centers are given to clients in a brief time period crowded with many types of activities and personnel. Hot lines have almost no sustained contact with callers—little background information, little follow-up. There are many other situations in which practitioners have minimal contact with clients, even in settings that are presumably organized for longer services—for example, where contacts require "first aid" skills or provision of concrete services. But there are a number of options for addressing these situations, characterized here as a "minimal-contact situation" (MCS).

First, let us review the steps in the conventional practice and evaluation process in order to understand the kinds of adaptations that must be undertaken in an MCS. Ordinarily, you will make contact with a client, establish rapport, and begin to collect information about the presenting problem. When formally collected as systematic measurement, this information represents baseline data. Such information is collected until you believe that a clear and stable picture of the problems and strengths of the client or the situation has emerged. Then, continuing these same data-collection methods, you plan an intervention and monitor its progress until you see some clear and stable positive change. At this time, further analysis occurs in order to make the decision to terminate services. Then you begin a maintenance phase in order to transfer the service effects to the client's natural environment when you will no longer be in the picture. Likewise, follow-up contacts may be undertaken to ascertain whether the service effects are holding up.

Minimal contact still means that some presenting problem or challenge is known; otherwise, considerations of service delivery or evaluation are meaningless. If a person comes in for apparent assistance with some unspecific problem that never becomes clear, the practitioner essentially is helpless to make constructive changes in that situation—unless clarifying the lack of a problem is the issue at hand. In the latter case, the presenting problem is to define the problem—or possibly the lack of a real problem. In general, minimal-contact services do address specified problems. Often, these problems are quite specific, concrete, and time limited. Frequently, clients in MCSs do not want associations with the practitioner to be longer than necessary to deal with the specific focal problem.

Thus, all you are "given" in an MCS is the fact of an existing problem, without any dimensions of the problem; you may never know about the events leading up to the crisis, and you may never learn about what happens to the clients after they leave the office. The core of minimal-contact services is the here-and-now problem, with the client generally seeking "while-you-wait" services. Minimal-contact services are, with good reason, difficult to evaluate objectively using conventional single-system design methods.

However, it is possible to adapt these conventional single-system evaluation methods to the MCS to obtain some minimal evaluations. We grant that minimal evaluations are not the first choice in objective assessment, but rather should be used when there are few other choices available. Not only can each evaluation provide you feedback on that particular case, but comparison of outcomes across cases—using a standardized format such as the *A-B* design—can provide information across all your cases and for the agency as a whole. And using the same format across all cases—even MCSs

where you may be stretching the design a bit—keeps you in the habit of systematic evaluation.

Let us describe a variety of minimal-evaluation methods. Essential ingredients for minimal evaluations are some kind of baseline data together with some kind of equivalent intervention data, such that comparison between them can permit you to make some type of estimate of change.

Baseline Approximations

There are several ways to approximate baseline data under conditions of minimal contact. First, you can use *reconstructed* or *retrospective baseline data* derived from information the client supplies even within the MCS. For example, take the case introduced in Chapter 13 of the distraught parent who tells the Red Cross worker that she hasn't heard from her son for over a month. A soldier stationed in Germany, he had written her faithfully for the previous 6 months. Probing might reveal that the son had been in the habit of writing about once a week during that time, at least to send postcards or other souvenirs weekly (Bloom et al., 1979). This conversation permitted the reconstruction of a baseline against which to compare the effects of the service that reestablished contact between parent and son, who in fact had been in an automobile accident. What the reconstruction of the baseline did in this case was to establish the existence of a problem, as contrasted to some minor lapse in writing home, and thus the need for immediate help rather than waiting until possibly clogged mail could be delivered.

As another example, based on an actual case of one of the author's students, a woman came to a community mental health center reporting that she was being abused by her spouse. The practitioner and the woman decided that reconciliation with the spouse would be impossible, and that the woman would have to go to the local shelter. After two contacts with the client, a place at the shelter became available. The practitioner arranged for the woman's admission, where she stayed for 2 weeks until a bond against further harassment by the spouse was obtained and a permanent placement arranged. Based on a reconstructed baseline of instances of abuse, and concurrent and follow-up recording, the chart for the case looked like the one displayed in Figure 18.3.

A second kind of approximate baseline can be described as *inferred baseline data* derived from parallel information known about other clients or people living in like situations. For example, a person applying for emergency food relief recently had come to town from out of state. His funds had soon been exhausted before he was able to find work. From current censuses at the public welfare agency, it is clear that many people are in a like circumstance. You thus would be justified in presuming a baseline of fiscal need, pending additional investigation, while emergency services and aid are provided.

A third kind of comparison point is a *known end state* that can be compared with a currently unknown present state. For example, a pregnant woman comes to a homeless shelter obviously undernourished. In these circumstances, it is not possible to engage in a lengthy psychosocial and medical history, but because of the known requirements of good nutrition for pregnant women, services may be evaluated to the extent that they are able to provide her with appropriate levels and types of food.

Intervention Data

Given these approximate baseline data or comparison points, you would provide services as appropriate to the situation, and repeat the information-gathering method or its equiv-

alent. In the case of the overseas soldier who was not writing home weekly, a telephone contact was established and was equivalent to the weekly written communiques. For the unemployed man, receiving financial and in-kind aid at the level presumed adequate by that state fulfilled the demand for success during the intervention period. For the pregnant woman, the provision of nutritious food also could be said to be a successful intervention as compared to norms of nutrition.

How successful are these helping actions? There are several ways to count the level or degree of success of help provided. First, one might use an agencywide "batting average," the number of fulfilled needs (e.g., reestablished contact between mother and son; adequate food and shelter for the unemployed man and the pregnant woman, etc.) compared to all of the presenting cases for a given period of time. For example, if the Red Cross saw 10 emergency cases like that of the distraught parent each week, and was able to come to a successful resolution of 8 of these situations, then the agency batting average for that week would be .80. Such averages themselves could be averaged over a yearly fiscal period for agency accountability rates.

In the individual case, depending on the problem and how it's measured, you might be able to establish a goal and then simply note whether it was achieved. Or, if the measure involves some count, you might be able to indicate on a chart whether the problem has increased or decreased. Or, you might employ

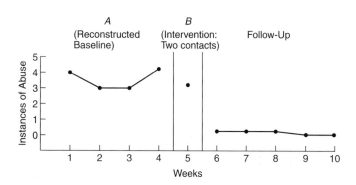

FIGURE 18.3 Illustration of brief contact design with instances of spousal abuse as the problem.

the *Goal Attainment Scale* strategy, described in Chapter 3, of presuming that there is in any given situation an "expected" level of success, along with several degrees above and below this expected level. So the case of the distraught parent might have been further specified as follows (or words to this effect, according to the content of the situation):

1. Least favorable outcome thought likely
2. Less than expected success
3. Expected level of success
4. More than expected success
5. Most favorable outcome thought likely

The Red Cross worker expected that she would be able to find out through channels whether there was a problem with the soldier in Germany and, thus, to reestablish communications. What she did not expect was that the soldier was in an accident and that she had to make extra arrangements through the hospital where he was staying to reestablish connections with his mother. This might constitute a rating of "more than expected success." Or had there been no medical problem, but merely a lapse of writing, the practitioner might have set up a more reliable means of communication between parent and son, such as persuading the son to send home letters once a week. This solution might also have constituted a rating of "more than expected success." Had the practitioner asked the mother what an ideal communication would be in her opinion, and if the mother had reported her difficulty in getting through the international telephone system to call her son when she didn't receive weekly letters, then an intervention that taught the mother the necessary skills to master international calling might have been accorded "most favorable outcome" status. The numbers associated with given outcomes might then be combined over a practitioner's caseload to give a rating of favorable solutions overall. Individual cases that did not meet agency or practitioner averages might be reconsidered in case conferences to see how services might have been improved.

Another form of evaluation that could be used in some MCSs would be the *brief exit questionnaire* that asks clients one or two questions about the services provided, to better help clients in the future. Comparative questions could be posed, although this may require a level of sophistication that is inappropriate for some settings or types of clients. For example, one might ask:

1. How helpful or unhelpful was the service you just now received from the practitioner?
   a. Very helpful
   b. Helpful
   c. Neither helpful nor unhelpful
   d. Unhelpful
   e. Very unhelpful
2. How much of the main problem you came with has been solved (or fixed)?
   a. None of the main problem I came with has been solved (or fixed).
   b. Little of my main problem has been solved (fixed).
   c. Some of my main problem has been solved (fixed).
   d. Most of my main problem has been solved (fixed).
   e. All of my main problem has been solved (fixed).

This kind of user survey does not provide a totally objective basis for judging the effectiveness of service, but it does provide an otherwise unattainable subjective impression from the client. Of course, how much of the response will be social acquiescence and how much will reflect real change is difficult to say. Such data might best be used as a description of user responses, and correlated with other types of approximate outcome measures as described here.

A variation of this exit survey would be a *follow-up survey* or contact by the original practitioner, who would ask essentially how the situation had gone since the brief contact occurred. Ethically, the practitioner should inform the client that such follow-up contacts will be made, with the client's permission. The purpose of the follow-up is to assess the services provided, and to offer additional services as needed. This information will assist the agency to improve its services as well (by trying to expand services that have been helpful and change those that have not worked well).

Involving the Client in Evaluation

Another issue related to minimal contact is whether to involve the clients in their own evaluation. Frequently, MCSs don't easily permit the mutuality and cooperativeness of extended service work and evaluation. However, clients should be informed that some form of evaluation is being conducted as quality assurance for the agency and as a protection for the client. Also, sometimes, taking part in the approximate evaluation provides another tool that clients can take with them as they seek to solve problems on their own after the agency contact. Thus, whether or how you involve minimal contact clients with the evaluation process depends on the context itself.

You must be prepared to take on the full evaluation role, based on whatever information can be obtained during the brief contacts. Aids like recording devices would be helpful (e.g., in a content analysis of the conversation to establish the number of times anxiety was expressed at the initial meeting, as compared with the number of times at the final meeting). But, essentially, conventional means of identifying the state of the presenting problem should be used, and then the same or equivalent method should be repeated at the end of the contacts—or, if possible, in a follow-up contact. Once this before/after approximation has been made, the choices of using a one/zero batting average approach, a modified Goal Attainment Scaling approach, or one of the other approaches can be made.

Dichotomous Data

Single-system designs also can be used when the problem is dichotomous, involving simply whether some event occurred. This is a common occurrence with minimal-contact cases with recording simply keeping track of the occurrence of some event on a "yes" or "no" basis. The case described earlier involving the soldier who suddenly stopped writing his mother from Germany (because he had been involved in a serious auto accident) is an instance of this dichotomous analysis, with minimal contact with the client. Figure 18.4 illustrates the intervention and the subsequent outcome wherein the soldier was reunited with his mother by telephone and resumed his letterwriting.

This example of the soldier brings up another important part of minimal-contact evaluation, the setting of practice goals or objectives whose attainment can be clearly identified. In the case of the soldier, the goal was reunion with the mother in some form, by telephone if not letter. This was attained and the case resolved for all practical purposes. In fact, Bloom et al. (1979) identified a "batting average" of successes on a sample of minimal contact cases: The number of cases of success present in the sample compared to the total number of cases in the sample. In short, practical criterion goals can be used to determine when minimal contact cases have been resolved successfully. Many examples come to mind: If clients come in for emergency fuel rations, then whether they obtain satisfaction regarding their heating

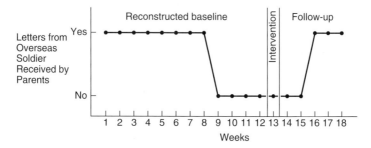

FIGURE 18.4   Illustration of dichotomous problem—number of letters received.

problems is a practical criterion of success or nonsuccess. If a traveler gets useful aid for his or her travels, then this is a criterion for success or nonsuccess. If an information agency makes an appropriate referral to a service agency and the client follows up, then the information agency function has been accomplished successfully.

SINGLE-SYSTEM DESIGNS IN MANAGED CARE: THE STRETCH DESIGN

Managed care is imposing a wide array of demands on the helping professions (discussed in Chapter 25; see also Corcoran & Vandiver, 1996). Some of these new policies may reduce financial costs for various social and health services, which is generally desirable when such costs have been rising precipitously. However, these same managed care demands also will reduce services for persons in justifiable need and with preventable problems, which is very undesirable because short-term savings will lead to long-term social and financial costs in the same or related areas, as well as an unacceptable level of human misery. These are policy issues beyond the range of this book, but we have to be realistic in adapting good practice to the demands of the managed care philosophy. This includes having the evaluation tools available that can be produced in less time but with a reasonable amount of rigor, so as to provide documentable answers regarding the outcomes of services, regarding both intermediate objectives and long-term outcomes.

We believe that most of the material covered in this book can be of considerable help in documenting intervention outcomes. Yet, we also recognize that, under some circumstances, practitioners may need even briefer methods of more or less objective evaluation. For this purpose, we introduce a method we call *stretch single-system evaluations*. We will present the basic method, and then we will apply it to some of the other advanced designs we have discussed.

Imagine an ideal single-system design, with a nice clear target and regular measures over, say, 20 sessions, once a week for five months. Clearly, this may soon become a distant memory for many practitioners in this era of managed care in which the pressures for accountable outcomes within 8 to 12 sessions, or even fewer, is more commonplace than a "leisurely" five-month contact. Question: How to obtain (or approximate) the evaluation strengths of a longer period of client-practitioner contact (say, 20 sessions or more) within the managed care time-limited context (say, just 10 sessions)?

Consider the following scenarios: First, the traditional 20-session arrangement, followed by the stretch single-system evaluation within 10 sessions. Both are *A-B* designs, with no training, maintenance, booster, or follow-up phases, to keep the example simple.

Conventional Single-System Design

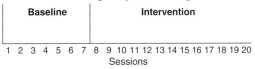

Stretch Single-System Design

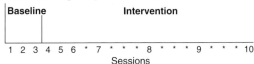

In place of the traditional 20 paid sessions, we now have 10 paid sessions, but stretched out over 20 time units. The asterisks represent periods of time the client does not receive professional interventive services, but which are used to continue data collection. The length of these noninterventive periods increases from 1 to 4 units over the course of intervention. There are a total of 10 such "non-interventive" units, which, along with the 10 service units totals 20 units in which the practitioner is monitoring the service. In emergencies, sessions could be held, and in some cases, sanctioned by managed care rules.

Strictly speaking, this is a suggestion for a lean single-system design of 3 baseline units (#1, #2, #3) and 3 service units (#4, #5, #6) along with 4 other contact times (#7, #8, #9, and #10) that can serve either as (a) more service periods, (b) maintenance training, (c) "booster shots" if needed, or (d) follow-up. The total period of time is the same 20 time units of the traditional practice evaluation; however, the actual paid contact time is just 10 time units. The ability to fine-tune practice–as either service, maintenance, booster shot, or follow-up–may be an especially important advantage of the stretch method. Clients are fully informed of this arrangement and the responsibility that it implies for their own contributions to achieving their outcomes. They will be "on their own" for longer periods of time during the intervention process, even though monitoring will continue during this period. Clients could call in data during the weeks when there are no intervention services given, or they could bring in recorded data on forms on which they and the practitioner have agreed.

We recognize this stretch evaluation procedure will not be useful when continuous services and monitoring are needed for certain conditions, but since no client can be forever served and monitored, the practitioner has to begin thinking in terms of experiences in self-maintenance, and for this, the stretch evaluation may be useful.

We can expand this stretch evaluation to other single-system designs, such as the multiple baseline across problems in one client, where the baseline period itself may need to have "non-contacts" while targeted data are still collected. For example, consider the following pattern where there are stretched periods in both baseline and intervention phases, but where an intervention occurs following the change from *A* to *B* phases.

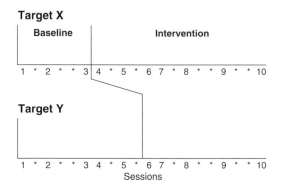

Target X

| Baseline | Intervention |

1 * 2 * * 3 4 * 5 * 6 7 * 8 * * 9 * * 10

Target Y

1 * 2 * * 3 4 * 5 * 6 7 * 8 * * 9 * * 10
Sessions

In this illustration, there are 6 units of baseline data for Target X, and 10 units of baseline data

for Target Y. Other patterns of noninterventive data gathering can be considered, as relevant to the content of the service.

Clearly, this stretch evaluation is even more approximate than the traditional single-system design, and requires case situations where valid and reliable data may be collected in the nonintervention units. However, this stretch approach does offer clients greater participation in their own service program (and especially in training for self-maintenance), so there may be some benefits from this externally imposed time-and-service constriction from managed care.

TROUBLE-SHOOTING: "OKAY, I UNDERSTAND EVERYTHING THAT YOU SAID, BUT MY CASE IS DIFFERENT."

Every case *is* different. The main point we have been making regarding understanding single-system designs as evaluation tools is to be able to connect them to practice. That is, we have described some of the methodological concepts and principles of evaluation and have endeavored to connect these abstractions to actual cases that appeared in the literature or that were conducted by our students. Let's look more closely at some tough cases and think through how the basic designs might be applied to complex human situations.

Case 1. "I only see my clients one or two times, and I am so busy rushing through what I have to get accomplished that I don't have any time for the luxuries of evaluation."

Response to Case 1. Ouch! That is a tough situation. But let's think about what is possible in these kinds of cases. What basic aspects of single-system design are applicable?

Clearly this practitioner is doing something, which sounds like an intervention, *B*. So far, so good. But with one or two client contacts, it doesn't sound too promising for any kind of experimental removal, or even the addition of a new intervention.

On the other hand, the practitioner has already said she has no time for a baseline, but we can ask whether she does a rapid assessment of the presenting problems as the basis of her intervention (B). If so, she may have enough information to do at least a reconstructed baseline, indicated by the notation (A). This is not the strongest design in the world, but certainly a rough basis for identifying changes that may be occurring. What any practitioner needs in cases of brief contact is some verbal or archival description of the problem in enough detail to make a sensible and sensitive plan of intervention. In some cases, perhaps not all, this would be enough information to reconstruct a baseline.

In other cases, there may be an obvious criterion of success so that all the practitioner needs to know is that the client is not presently successful (at the first interview situation), but that by the end of this contact, the problem may be resolved according to that criterion of success. If so, this too would be the basis of evaluation.

Case 2. "I'm part of a team of workers dealing with a bunch of clients who are seen individually and in various kinds of groups. I work there part of the week, and so I don't even have continuing contact with clients. Old clients leave, and an equal number of new clients come in. How am I supposed to evaluate in this three-ring circus?"

Response to Case 2. This is another tough set of questions. Let's look at them one at a time. The team versus individual worker contribution is difficult only if you have to sort out the two for some accountability reason. If your final outcome is the resolution of client problems, then it doesn't matter who does it, so long at it is accomplished. But if you need to demonstrate your particular contribution to the team effort, that's more difficult. (We discussed several approximate ways of doing this in Chapter 11 under the heading, Collaborative and Team Efforts.)

You can look at the evaluation issue as being one of whether you supply information to others who do the major hands-on part, or whether others supply information to you for the same purpose. If you supply information primarily, then evaluate whether all of the needed information is made available to the direct-contact

part of the team in time. You get a kind of batting average: required information presented in either a timely fashion or not. If you receive information from others primarily to make direct contact with the client regarding problem-solving issues, then evaluate in the conventional way whether these issues have been resolved, plus whether you had the relevant information in a timely fashion. (This is a polite way of saying evaluate as usual, but note whether everyone did his or her part. Your personal record should probably include only those situations where all of the essential information was available.)

Another way of looking at this problem is to think about it in terms of applying one of the designs in this book to your piece of the problem. If you are working with a client on a particular problem, and other people in your agency are working with the client as well—even on the same problem—you can still get some feedback on your contribution. All it takes is some recording of the problem, and keeping track of when you start your intervention. This will produce an A-B design, and if the problem starts to change only after you begin your intervention, you may begin to suspect that your intervention is crucial. If you go so far as to add a removal phase and then reinstitute the intervention (an A-B-A-B design), if the target problem changes in relation to these phases, you can be pretty sure your intervention is having an impact, no matter what everyone else is doing.

The next point in case 2 was evaluating part-time versus full-time work. It may be difficult to do both practice and evaluation part-time, but what happens in part-time practice? Does someone else cover for you, or do you space the meetings to fit the times you can be there? Is it possible to do the same with evaluation? For example, what about public records (such as teachers' grade books or employers' absenteeism records)? Can the clients keep records in between times? Given your answers to these kinds of questions, can you come up with a design that accommodates these features?

The last point, about clients moving through a system, can be answered more clearly. Think about what evaluation options are available to you, and ask what designs might be used. For example, should you evaluate the progress of the entire group? If so, what baseline will you consider? Unless there are good records available, this might be problematic, as reconstructing baselines from memory is risky.

What about beginning with the new clients and running thorough evaluations on them? In time, as older clients leave, you will have full sets of data on the entire group. This also gives you a chance to do some trial evaluations to see what kinds of measurement systems work best.

Remember that there are distinctive measures of individual-level and group-level phenomena, and consider measuring both. For example, is there any measure of the morale of the clients (or staff) as a whole at different periods of time? This would be a group-level measure. Parallel measures of individual satisfaction could be obtained to compare the individual's score against the norms of the group. Changes in both group and individual scores make interesting reading because they hint at differential effectiveness with each individual and a comparison of how fast an individual is making progress relative to the group.

Case 3. "Nothing ever happens in my cases. The kind of services my agency supplies are just supportive, keeping an eye on clients just in case there is an emergency; then some other agency comes in and does the work."

Response to Case 3. If we may be so bold, we'd like to suggest you have things upside down. Your clear target is to maintain the status quo (perhaps some sort of adequate or reasonably healthy and happy living for clients). What you have to look out for are signs of change, especially deterioration. So what kinds of targets would these "no-changes" be? And by what means could you indicate states of health and healthy functioning? In short, we believe that your evaluation task is essentially the same as described above, but you will be monitoring current levels of adequate or productive functioning.

While we are talking about monitoring current levels of positive functioning, let us note that evaluation of primary prevention usually involves study of health and healthy functioning, and the attainment of desired new states of

healthy functioning. So remember that "targets" can refer to both problems and desired goals.

Case 4. "My client is so vague about everything that it is impossible to nail down what is troubling him. Every meeting there is a long list of new complaints, but none of them are very specific. I spend all my time getting clear about the details of one week's experiences until it is time to quit, and then I wait for a whole new set next week."

Response to Case 4. You appear to have a case of wandering targets. It is related to the doorknob syndrome, when the client, about to leave with hand on the doorknob says, "Oh, by the way, this happened to me last week," and a whole new problem suddenly appears in an untimely fashion. That is a difficult but common malady, and the only thing we can suggest (if pointing out this pattern to the client and trying to get some focus doesn't work) is to look for patterns among the diverse instances. This is where the kinds of notation from single-system designs may be helpful. Start keeping track as if each instance were the label of a category, and then group the categories as best you can. Once you have a few categories, deal with them in some order of the client's priorities. This is where the client can begin to do some sorting among issues as well. Perhaps the need for training in problem-solving may itself be an underlying issue.

Case 5. "I would love to evaluate my cases, but they drop out prematurely. Is there anything I can do about this?"

Response to Case 5. This is a difficult problem, but we believe that the major issue lies in the practice area, not in the evaluation realm. If this is true of a large proportion of your caseload, and those of others in your agency, then it looks as if some institutional structures may be interfering with continuity in service. If it is mainly *your* clients that are dropping out of treatment, then use whatever data you have on whatever clients you had, and go over them in detail with a colleague or your supervisor. This is an opportunity to examine your own methods in detail. It very well may be chance, or the type of difficult problems with which you work, but it might also be that you need to brush up on certain techniques, enhance communication of interpersonal skills, and so on.

Case 6.   "I was going along quite well with my client. I figured out what targets to deal with and was in the middle of the baseline period, when the client tells me that the problem has changed. Do I have to start all over again? What do I do with the old problem?"

Response to Case 6.   Yes, you do have to start all over with a genuine new problem—if you are certain that it is new and not simply a variation on the original problem. Don't be surprised that problems change; that is just part of life when one is under varied stresses. But we do have to be sensitive to genuine changes in problems.

What do you do with the old target and all that work you went through to gather baseline data? First, don't throw away any data. The original problem may return, and you have some solid baseline data ready to go. Second, if the original problem is important enough in its own right, then continue monitoring it as if you were closing out a target upon completion of your work with that part of the client's problems. You also have the choice of monitoring and intervening with both problems at the same time. Also, sometimes baselining reveals that no real problem exists on one of the targets—and that in itself is vital information. The same is true with problems that change in the middle of the baseline. It is important to document that some important developments took place. You might check to see how and why the problem happened to disappear before your contributions were needed. Does the client have some resources and skills that can be put to work with other problems?

Case 7.   "I am a little embarrassed to admit this, but the great problem I thought I had identified in the first session turned out by session 3 not to be the problem at all. In the meantime, I had the client involved in baselining for three weeks. What do I do about this first problem?"

Response to Case 7.   Maybe nothing. If you did the best you could to identify a problem at the first session, and started baselining, then that may be exactly what was appropriate at the time given the information you had. If, by the third session, you learn new information, and the target now shifts to another problem entirely, then start baselining that new problem and drop the first—if it really is not a problem.

Don't be embarrassed about making a judgment with the best available information at the time and then finding new information that produces a change in judgment. Be embarrassed only if you don't change when you have new information indicating change is necessary.

Case 8.   "I am taking a class at school where I am learning about these single-system designs, but when I go to my practicum, my field instructor doesn't believe in evaluation and won't support me in this. I am caught between a rock and a hard place. What am I supposed to do?"

Response to Case 8.   Alas, there are still some good practitioners out in the field who are not convinced that evaluation is a vital and necessary part of good practice. While we personally hope that these people see the light—or at least bow to the collective wisdom of accrediting bodies that mandate that students know how to evaluate their own practice in field settings—we appreciate your situation.

There are several things you might do. First, inform your advisor about these limitations on your education, and perhaps your school can apply some needed pressure. Second, failing this, try to link up with some colleagues whose agencies do permit them to evaluate their practice. You could share a case, or even better, consider attempting to be a teacher yourself to convey these skills to a cooperative practitioner at that other agency who might be willing to evaluate his or her own case. Both methods will give you the hands-on experience you need. A third method is to conduct a single-system evaluation on yourself—identify something you would like to do more or less of; read the literature on how to do this while you are keeping a baseline; then intervene and maintain the measurement of the targeted behavior; and analyze the results. This way, you get to be both client and practitioner, and you might gain a useful perspective on evaluation that you might not see in any other way.

Case 9. "My client won't permit me to do any evaluation. Period. What am I supposed to do now?"

Response to Case 9. We wonder why the client has refused so strongly? He or she may have been "burned" by other evaluation or research experiences, but if you have tried your best to show how monitoring and evaluation will help you to provide better services, and the client still refuses, then by all means agree that you will not do any evaluation involving this client.

However, this doesn't mean that you won't do whatever good practice calls for, and part of good practice requires that you know what the problems are that require service, and how your interventions are affecting them. Consider the full range of unobtrusive and nonreactive measures—those that truly do not involve the client in participating in any evaluation process. Your evaluations are then part of case records only, as tools to guide practice interventions.

We believe that this suggestion for unobtrusive evaluation, without the client's participation or knowledge, fulfills the ethical obligations of good practice since evaluation is vital for the conduct of effective practice. However, if you feel that this indirect evaluation violates your agreement with the client, then you have several final options: (a) do not do any evaluation whatsoever (although we hope that having gotten this far in this text, it may be hard for you ever to go back again to practice without thinking about clear identification of targets and monitoring their changes); (b) terminate the case because you cannot practice without knowing exactly what the problem is or how well your intervention is working; or (c) transfer the case to a practitioner who is willing to work under these limiting restrictions.

Case 10. "My client just loves this evaluation business. She is the kind of person who makes lists and is well organized, and when I asked her to keep track of several targets, she constructed checklists and completed them exactly as we discussed. Now I have tons of data and I don't know what to do with them all. And the client wants to do more tracking of targets!"

Response to Case 10. Sometimes clients are very helpful in evaluation because they find the activity itself useful to them. However, we find ourselves without a great deal of sympathy—and maybe even some envy—for your plight of having "tons of data." Assuming that you have three, four, five, or more targets, this still amounts mainly to putting five dots in appropriate places on graph paper for each time unit, and then keeping up to date about the analysis (see Part IV). If this gives you an accurate picture of changes in the client's condition, then that is a very small price to pay in terms of time and effort. So enjoy!

SUMMARY

This chapter provided specific guidelines by which you can select a design or a group of designs most suited to your client's needs. Recognizing that each situation is unique, we also note that there are common issues in most situations that can be described by a set of questions:

How many clients are to be included in the evaluation?

Are you able to collect baseline data?

How many problems are to be dealt with?

How many interventions are to be used with each problem?

Will you alternate or add baselines and/or interventions?

By using this set of questions as described in this chapter, we believe you will be able to make a wise selection of a design or from a group of related designs.

As soon as you begin to use single-system designs with real clients, you will discover the necessity of being creative and adaptive; we provided some basic suggestions on the use of creativity with single-system designs. We encourage you to use the basic principles as best you can—only be responsible for dealing with the common problems people face in using single-system designs. We hope our answers provide helpful points of departure for your own creative solutions.

Single-system designs have great potential for use across the full range of contacts—from minimal to long term—with clients. They can be adapted to the types of problems just about any agency typically sees. They also have the flexibility to be adapted by practitioners to meet the needs of just about any case or situation.

PART IV

ANALYZING YOUR RESULTS

At this point in the practice process you've measured the client's targets and have used a design with which to collect these data. The next task is to analyze the data in order to make a decision regarding the next steps in practice.

In Part IV we discuss a number of ways to analyze these data. All of them are relatively easy to understand and to use, although they demand varying degrees of effort, and they require different kinds of assumptions to use them most appropriately.

Chapter 19 begins with an introduction to some of the basic issues, problems, and tools of analysis, including the distinctions among statistical, practical, and theoretical significance. It also defines the concepts of effort, effectiveness, and efficiency that are occasionally confused as practice is analyzed. Also introduced are a number of issues in the analysis of time-series data and some basic tools that will help you compute most of the statistics we discuss in this section.

Chapter 20 presents the topic of visual analysis. Visual analysis involves simply looking at the data and finding discontinuities and other patterns that aid in the interpretation of the results, and this chapter offers a number of aids in making such judgments.

Chapter 21 describes four different types of descriptive statistics that are useful for summarizing patterns of raw data, for supplementing visual analysis, and for computing and interpreting some of the tests of statistical significance discussed in Chapter 22. These four types of descriptive statistics include (a) measures of central tendency (mean, trimmed mean, median), (b) measures of variability (standard deviation, range, trimmed range), (c) measures of trend (celeration line, regression line, slope), and (d) measures of effect size (Δ-index and g-index). The different conditions under which these statistics should and shouldn't be used are described.

Chapter 22 presents several different approaches to determining statistical significance: (a) the proportion/frequency approach, (b) the X-Moving Range-Chart (three-standard-deviation-band approach), (c) chi-square, (d) t-test, and in the Appendix, (e) the randomization test and (f) time-series analysis. Each approach has its strengths and limitations, and the conditions under which the particular tests should and shouldn't be used are described.

In Chapter 23, we describe the personal computer program that comes with this book, SINGWIN. This program will compute virtually all of the statistics described in this section, and will do so with far more speed and accuracy than any of the hand calculations will allow.

In Chapter 24, we present a series of flow diagrams to aid you in selecting the analytic procedure that will be most appropriate for a given set of data.

19 BASIC PRINCIPLES OF ANALYSIS

PURPOSE: This chapter introduces the general concepts and rules for analyzing a set of data to determine whether a significant change has taken place. The chapter discusses a number of issues that you must understand in order to analyze your results appropriately, and provides a number of tools—including the introduction to a personal computer program—that will help you analyze your results. ■

Introduction

Distinguishing Effort, Effectiveness, and Efficiency

Effort, Effectiveness, and Efficiency in Single-System Designs

Significance—Practical, Statistical, and Theoretical

Practical Significance

Statistical Significance

Power

Theoretical Significance

Comparing and Aligning the Three Types of Significance

Evaluating Goal Achievement

Goal Determination

Social Validation

Goal-Attainment Scaling

Target Complaints

Visual Analysis

Statistics

Issues in Analysis of Data

How Long Should Information Be Collected?

When Should You Change Interventions?

Training Phases, Maintenance Phases, and Follow-Ups

Computer Analysis of Data for Single-System Designs

SINGWIN: A Personal Computer Program for the Analysis of Single-System Design Data

The Issue of Autocorrelation

The Debate over Autocorrelation

Computational Steps in Testing for Autocorrelation

Computer Procedures in Testing for Autocorrelation

Tools in Analysis of Data

The Transformation of Autocorrelated Data

Moving Average Transformation

First Differences Transformation

Computing and Graphing Transformed Data with SINGWIN

Probability Tables for Use in Single-System Designs

Data Showing Apparent Improvement

Reading the Table

Data Showing Apparent Deterioration

Computing Probabilities with SINGWIN

Summary

INTRODUCTION

By this point in the helping process, you've obtained some more or less objective data, as well as many subjective impressions, about the client. The task now is to analyze these data–that is, to look at them, perhaps to rearrange them in particular ways, and to perform additional operations on them as needed–to arrive at a conclusion about the data and the events in real life to which these data refer. In this chapter we discuss the basic concepts and procedures in this analytic process.

As in the problem-solving process itself, analysis begins with a question or challenge: What do these data tell us about X? This question directs you to look at the data in certain ways that will subsequently answer that question. What form will the answers take? If you're trying to reduce a client's depression, then you should look for evidence that depression has been lowered, as well as seek evidence that no new problems have emerged. The more clearly you can formulate your first questions regarding the data, the more readily will the answers be forthcoming. However, you also may find new questions emerging as you interpret portions of the data. Question formation is a dynamic process that continues as long as new questions are raised by previous analyses of data.

Once a question is raised, the next step is to arrange the data to provide answers. The next four chapters will present major ways of doing this, from simple visual inspection of changes in the data, to simple procedures for testing logical and statistical conclusions concerning the data. The rationale and utility of each of these methods is presented.

Underlying these procedures are some basic ideas that are useful for each of them. These are the ideas that form the basis of principles of analysis for single-system design: How can practitioners distinguish the effort they put into helping a client from the effect of that effort and the efficiency by which it's delivered? What is pragmatically significant change? What is statistically significant change? What is theoretically significant change? What if these three don't coincide? How can you be as alert to significant deterioration as to improvement?

We also discuss some topics both as issues and as tools to be used in the analysis of data. These topics include consideration of autocorrelation, the transformation of autocorrelated data, and the use of probability tables.

DISTINGUISHING EFFORT, EFFECTIVENESS, AND EFFICIENCY

In analyzing what the service program has meant for a client, some practitioners point to the fact that they have worked hard on behalf of their clients, made many visits, written many reports, and so forth. This is very meaningful to those who are on the front lines delivering services, but it may carry less weight with those who either receive the services or who underwrite the programs. These latter two groups of people are more concerned with the effectiveness of these interventions and how efficiently they were delivered. We can clarify these terms–effort, effectiveness, and efficiency–by reference to the single-system design model in Figure 19.1. As we'll see, effectiveness and efficiency require some form of evaluated outcome, and efficiency also requires a comparison between outcome and effort expended.

Effort refers to the work that goes into a service program. It's summarized in Figure 19.1 as the intervention–the range of activities that makes up the helping program. Measures of effort may include the amount of time spent with a client or with others. Effort may involve the amount of money provided during a given period of time. Sometimes agencies count the mileage practitioners travel or how far clients are transported for services. The intervention period on the chart indicates only a telescoped version of the efforts expended. For example, training each partner in a marriage to do more of what the other spouse thinks is good and to do less of what that spouse thinks is not good requires considerable teaching and role-playing time and effort. The phrase *reciprocal reinforcement* summarizes these efforts. It requires additional analysis to attach cost figures to the various efforts that go into any given intervention.

Baseline–*A*	Intervention(s)–*B* (*C,D...*)
(Preintervention phase)	(The independent variable) Intervention: Generally guided by previous research and/or by some practice theory chosen by practitioners. Interventions should be specified clearly and linked to specific targets.

Target		**Data**	**Monitoring and Analysis**
(The dependent variable) The target is derived from client problems and goals; it is operationally defined, and is represented by some scale showing its magnitude at each unit of time. The set of targets represents the client's problems/goals.	Target Scale	Data are recorded at the intersections of a time unit and a measured value of the target. The same measurement procedure is used in the baseline and in the intervention phase.	Comparisons are made about the target before and during short intervention, and possibly at follow-up. Monitoring is an ongoing comparison during intervention and is used as corrective feedback for practice. Analysis compares the final outcome with original objectives.

Time Line

FIGURE 19.1   Schematic presentation of the evaluation process in single-system designs.

Effectiveness refers to changes that come about in a target event. Effectiveness also refers to the impact or outcome–seen either in a positive or negative sense–that the service program has on achieving the goals of intervention. Part IV is directed primarily at describing how to determine effectiveness. In Figure 19.1, effectiveness is based on a comparison of a target during a period before, during, and after some intervention(s) relative to the intervention goals. Obviously, effectiveness requires effort to be expended. However, the focus is on the outcome of service, particularly the observation and analysis of observable client changes, in relation to specific practitioner actions and other extraneous influences. Thus, effectiveness is a complicated affair requiring careful attention. We return to this point shortly.

Efficiency refers to how much effectiveness was attained given how much effort and how much time. Time and effort are costs to society to provide help; effectiveness is a benefit, both to the individuals involved and to society indirectly. Thus, efficiency is a ratio that compares costs and benefits. In Figure 19.1 efficiency would be indicated by looking at the number of time units and the measures of effort related to the determination of effectiveness. It costs so much (in personal or material resources) to obtain so much outcome. Efficiency in organizational terms refers to optimizing this combination, achieving the best outcomes for the least costs.

Effort, Effectiveness, and Efficiency in Single-System Designs

Figure 19.1 casts the chart in the form of a practice hypothesis, and the various analytic procedures to be discussed in Part IV are ways of interpreting these results against defined criteria. We consider several categories of criteria (in Chapters 20, 21, and 22) against which observed results can be compared; they form a continuum from the relatively simple visual approaches to the relatively complex statistical ones, but they are all quite manageable by practitioners without mathematical backgrounds or inclinations. The basic questions the chart poses are the following: Did the target problems change significantly from what they had been at the baseline period? And is there a logical basis for inferring that the intervention was causally involved in these outcomes?

The causality question–was your intervention responsible for the observed changes?–is primarily a design issue and was discussed in Part III. The other question, however–was there a significant change in the target problem?–is a question that can be resolved through a variety of analytic methods, including visual inspection of patterns of change in the data and the use of statistics. We use the word *analysis* as the generic term to cover the ways in which the issue of the significance of change gets addressed. Although there is overlap between the two questions–is the change significant and did my interventions cause it?—there are some clear differences as well. For example, a statistically significant change means the change probably is "real"; it did not occur by chance. But statistical significance says nothing about what *caused* the change. This is a question for the designs to answer; it may or may not have been your interventions. However, the use of the analytic procedures described in Part IV does provide part of the foundation for undertaking a further causal analysis based on the variety of designs described in Part III.

In this chapter, then, to prepare you for use of the analytic procedures in subsequent chapters, we discuss some basic principles of analysis, those concepts and rules that will help you determine whether or not change occurred in the targets of your intervention.

SIGNIFICANCE—PRACTICAL, STATISTICAL, AND THEORETICAL

A key concept in the analysis of data concerns the significance of observed changes in the data from baseline to intervention periods and to other variations as described in the chapters on design. Given that life itself is a continuous series of changes, are the changes observed in the practice situation meaningful or not? The answer to this question implies another question: Meaningful to whom? There are three broad categories of answers, each with several subtypes. The broad classes will be called practical, statistical, and theoretical significance.

Practical Significance

Even if there's improvement in a target from one phase (e.g., baseline) to another (e.g., intervention), you can't conclude necessarily that the change was sufficient. Such a conclusion requires evidence of what is known variously as "practical significance," "clinical significance," or "social validation" (e.g., Jacobson, 1988; Jayaratne, 1990, and the commentary that accompanies Jayaratne's chapter), but all include the idea that somebody—especially the client—believes that there has been *meaningful change* in the problem. We'll use the term *prac-*

tical significance because it seems to us the most comprehensive of the available terms for this concept.

There are different methods for determining practical significance, but each one involves the comparison of a client's functioning against some standard, and a determination of whether a discrepancy exists between the level of functioning and the standard. For example, the problems of a psychiatric patient may be sufficiently resolved to warrant deinstitutionalization, with appropriate medication and outpatient services, but the patient's behavior may still be inappropriate by community standards. A student's classroom behavior may show improvement over the course of intervention, but the student's teacher may still view the behavior as problematic. Even after losing a certain amount of weight, a client may decide that he or she is overweight based on his or her personal standards.

There are different types of personal and social standards that can be used to determine practical significance, depending on the target of intervention, including a comparison of a client's functioning with: (a) the average functioning of a nonproblematic peer group; (b) the average functioning of a peer group that exhibits exemplary behavior; (c) the subjective impression of the client or relevant others; (d) the expectations from theories of development or psychopathology; (e) the cultural norms or values of relevant groups; or (f) the intervention goals set by the practitioner and/or the client. Therefore, it may be appropriate to think of practical significance with a variety of terms—practical, social, clinical, personal—depending on the targeted intervention, but we will use the term *practical significance* to encompass all of these.

Criteria and procedures for determining practical significance are not as well developed as some other procedures—for example, those for determining statistical significance (to be discussed next). Moreover, the selection and application of criteria for determining practical significance often involve personal values, and sometimes personal values that are in conflict (e.g., husband and wife, parent and child). Therefore, the criteria for determining practical significance may require a process of discussion and negotiation among different involved parties in much the same way that targets for intervention are selected. Nevertheless, such standards are necessary as a basis for making decisions concerning the course of intervention.

Statistical Significance

Any analysis involves comparisons between two or more events in connection with some valued state of affairs, such as a client's goal. For example, sets of data collected before an intervention are compared with sets of data collected during and after intervention; thus, analysis involves two sets of facts and one set of values. If we don't have any independent value or criterion to analyze these differences (such as a criterion score necessary to gain admission to school, maintaining weight within a desired range, scoring in the normal range of a standardized scale measuring depression), then we have to find our valued reference point within our sets of data. For example, with an *A-B* design where we have intervened in phase *B* to improve a client's condition as compared to the baseline *A,* in part the valued objective is built into the design. The analysis directs us to compare the intervention data with the baseline data according to some procedure, to determine whether the client's condition has improved.

Unfortunately, various haphazard or chance factors can cause a target to appear to change over time (e.g., imperfect reliability in the measurement of a target, inconsistency in the implementation of baseline or intervention activities, events in a client's life). Therefore, it's necessary to decide whether there's a systematic difference in a target under different conditions or whether the observed difference is just due to haphazard or chance factors. Some researchers have asserted that systematic differences between conditions should be so obvious that visual inspection is sufficient to "analyze" the data (e.g., Parsonson & Baer, 1986). Others have argued that tests of statistical significance should be used to analyze single-system data (e.g., Edgington, 1987; Gibson & Ottenbacher, 1988). Currently there's considerable debate about the relative merits of visual and statistical analysis.

We believe that visual analysis is very important, and we discuss it in the next chapter. We also believe that tests of statistical significance have merit. Tests of statistical significance can be used to provide the weight of standardized rules to a conclusion that an observed change is significant. They also can be used to tease out subtle effects, given enough observations. Statistics also can be used, as we describe, to take account of problems such as autocorrelated data. In short, the use of statistics can help to increase the precision of our conclusions.

It is important to note that, although tests of statistical significance can provide a basis for deciding whether there's a systematic difference in a target under different conditions, they don't indicate what caused the difference. It might be that the intervention caused the difference, but as discussed Chapter 11, there are are other possible explanations for such a difference. The plausibility of these alternative explanations depends on the type of design used and the pattern of the results obtained.

When tests of statistical significance are used to decide whether there's a systematic difference in a target between conditions, the following steps are used, and these steps are illustrated in Figure 19.2:

1. State what you hope to find (e.g., the mean number of parent–child conflicts is less during intervention than during baseline). Statisticians call this the *research* hypothesis, but because of our focus on evaluation we'll call it the *evaluation* hypothesis.

2. State the opposite of what you hope to find (e.g., the mean number of parent–child conflicts during intervention is the same or greater than the mean number of conflicts during baseline). It traditionally is stated this way to put the burden of "proof" on the intervention/evaluation. Statisticians refer to this as the *null hypothesis*. Paradoxically, this is the hypothesis that is tested. If the null hypothesis is rejected, your evaluation hypothesis is supported because it's the opposite of the null hypothesis.

3. Collect your evaluation data.

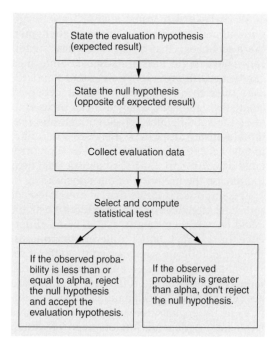

FIGURE 19.2   Process in determining statistical significance.

4. Select and compute the appropriate statistical test. (We discuss the selection and computation of statistical tests in Chapter 22.) This test will tell you how likely it is to get a difference between conditions as large or larger than the one you actually got if the null hypothesis is true. Statisticians call this the *observed probability*.

5. If the observed probability is equal to or less than some small value selected before you conduct your test, typically .05 (and referred to as *alpha*), reject the null hypothesis and accept your evaluation hypothesis. Alpha also is known as the *level of significance,* and tells us how probable it is that we are incorrectly rejecting the null hypothesis (if alpha is .05, then larger values would include .06, .10, .25, etc., and smaller values would include .04, .01, or .001). If the null hypothesis is rejected, this means the outcome was statistically significant.

6. If the observed probability is greater than alpha (i.e., greater than .01, .05, .10, or whatever value you select), do not reject the null hypothesis.

Tests of statistical significance are used to make decisions, and with these or any other procedures, including visual analysis, there's always some chance that the decision will be wrong. The different types of incorrect and correct decisions are illustrated in Figure 19.3, and as shown in this figure there are two types of possible decision errors. First, you might conclude that a difference exists when it really doesn't, that is, you reject the null hypothesis when it shouldn't be rejected. This is called a Type I error by statisticians. The probability of making a Type I error is determined by your alpha level. Second, you might conclude that a difference doesn't exist when it really does, that is, you don't reject the null hypothesis when it should be rejected. This is called a Type II error by statisticians, sometimes signified as *beta*. As practitioners and evaluators, we are concerned about avoiding Type II errors because we want to correctly reject the null hypothesis when we should (when it is false), that is, find an effect of our intervention when there really is one. The probability of doing so is called *power*.

Power.   Power is the probability of finding an effect of our intervention when there really is an effect. In single-system design terms, this is the probability that you'll correctly detect a difference between phases if there is one. Obviously, you want this probability to be large, and there are numerous strategies you can use to increase power (Cohen, 1988; Orme, 1991); some of those strategies are somewhat technical and beyond the scope of this book (see Allison, Silverstein, & Gorman, 1997, for a review of these strategies).

Other strategies for increasing power are somewhat impractical. For example, one of the main reasons we are concerned about power in single-system designs is that power is, in part, a function of sample size, or, in single-system design terms, it is a function of the number of data points over time. Thus, one of the most important ways of increasing power is to try to collect as many observations as is possible, practical, and consistent with good practice. (There actually are numer-

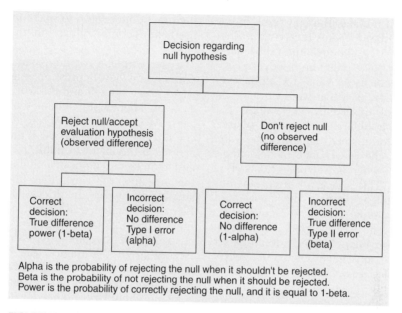

FIGURE 19.3   Outcomes of decisions concerning the null hypothesis.

ous tables available to help you determine the number of data points you need to achieve a given level of power–say, .80–which allows only a 20% probability of making a Type II error. See Allison et al., 1997, for a review of those tables.)

We will indicate the number of observations that is best in Chapter 22. However, given the costs involved in collecting more observations, especially in this era of managed care, we think you may be better off to consider one of the following strategies. Remember that the idea here is to increase your chances of detecting a real difference between phases.

1. Implement your intervention as consistently and accurately as possible, practical, and consistent with good practice.

2. Increase the strength of your intervention as much as possible, practical, and consistent with good practice.

3. Use the most reliable and valid outcome measures that are possible, practical, and consistent with good practice, and collect outcome measures in a consistent and careful fashion.

4. Test directional (one-tailed) hypotheses. These are hypotheses that predict the direction of a relationship (positive or negative). This will increase your chance of detecting an existing difference between phases, but only if the difference is as predicted (e.g., a better outcome during intervention than baseline).

5. Use the most powerful test of statistical significance permitted by the assumptions of your data. Some statistical tests are better than others at detecting differences between phases. We'll have more to say about this in Chapter 22, when we discuss specific tests.

6. Increase alpha (e.g., use .10 instead of .05). Increasing alpha in order to increase the chance of detecting an existing difference is very controversial and requires some brief comments here. There is a long history and very strong scientific convention of using the .05 level (Cowles & Davis, 1982). Also, very importantly, increasing alpha increases the chance that you'll conclude there is a difference when there isn't (Type I error). This is an

important mistake. It might result in current and future clients receiving an ineffective service, although upon subsequent use the mistake might be discovered.

Why not use a value for alpha even lower than .05, if that would reduce the chance of mistakenly concluding that there is a difference between phases? Well, unfortunately, the lower the value of alpha, the less chance of detecting a difference when one actually exists (Type II error). This also is an important mistake. It might result in the intervention being abandoned and consequently the mistake left undiscovered, the current client receiving unneeded additional services, and subsequent clients not receiving an effective service.

Ideally single-system designs should be undertaken that minimize the chance of either of these mistakes, and we've discussed strategies for doing this that don't involve increasing alpha. Unfortunately, sometimes these other strategies, even in combination, are impractical, insufficient, or at odds with good practice. In any case, in these situations we don't believe that you should blindly adhere to the .05 convention at the cost of having very little chance of detecting an effective intervention. In these situations you might consider setting alpha greater than .05, say perhaps .10, although this is something that you should do as a last resort, and something that you should decide before analyzing your data.

Theoretical Significance

A third kind of significance related to changes in client behavior or changes in the environment is called theoretical significance (Bloom, 1987). The practitioner conceptualizes and plans his or her intervention with certain expectations in mind based on the theory employed. That is, the theory describes a future pattern of events, given certain initial causes. The practitioner seeks to use this theory as a guide to what is to be expected in the given case, and translates the general causal suggestions into specific events with a client. Briefly,

the practitioner seeks to make the theoretical prediction come to pass in the life of the client.

For example, a cognitive-behavioral practitioner might view depression as a kind of mental set about oneself and the world, along with associated behaviors fulfilling these mental images (McCullough, 1984). According to this cognitive-behavioral theory, if the practitioner can teach the client to think in a certain way and to do certain kinds of activities that change this negative self-view, then the depression should disappear. In McCullough's (1984) therapy system derived from this theory, there are two training stages: one involving cognitive changes, and the other, behavioral changes. According to the theory, the client should begin at one level of depressive functioning (i.e., during baseline), and eventually the depression should be reduced when the client comes to understand certain aspects of his or her depression (during intervention). However, after a subsequent intervention involving the learning of behavioral skills, the client should be doing demonstrably better than under either of the other two situations. Predicted changes in depression based on McCullough's therapy system are visually represented in Figure 19.4. Follow-ups (McCullough suggests 2-year follow-ups) should show that clients have maintained their successful resolution of the depression.

Given this theory with its clear expectations of the patterns that are likely to occur, there are several possible outcomes. First, it might be that the client performs just as the theory predicts, in which case we can say that the results exhibit theoretical significance. (Note that nothing is said about the specific degrees of change; theoretical significance generally deals in ordinal statements, as contrasted with interval or ratio statements.)

On the other hand, it may be that the client's depression lifts, but not in the way predicted by the theory. For example, suppose clients receiving McCullough's therapy got completely better (statistically and practically) during the first (cognitive) intervention. That would be fine (statistically and practically) for this one client, but it would not help you, the

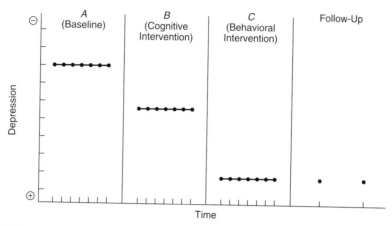

FIGURE 19.4   Change in depression predicted by McCullough's (1984) therapy system.

practitioner, to have a working theory that could be applied to other clients. The success would be a mystery in that your theory did not lead you to expect these results in the way they came about. Theoretical significance would not be achieved.

There's a third logical possibility. If the client did not improve during the first intervention, then you have several options as dictated by the theory: You might continue with the cognitive phase to see if it eventually gains some positive change, but might intensify the intervention to see if this could bring about the expected changes. Or you might consider other theories that might be better suited to this client's situation. Perhaps a straightforward behavioral model might be needed on grounds that the client may not have the cognitive sophistication or perseverance to understand or use the cognitive tools alone. In this case, you begin again with a new set of theoretical expectations derived from the behavioral model.

Unfortunately, theories are often vague about predicted patterns of change, and especially about specific stages of such changes. It's often possible to draw on the "practice wisdom" of experienced practitioners who have some sense of the likely course of events from the perspective of a given theory. (Indeed, we should press our theorists and our teachers of practice theories to provide the specific expec-

tations so that we might benefit more fully from their guidance.) However, when it's not possible to obtain an expected pattern from a given theory–that is, when we have no way of testing theoretical significance–we should turn to the other two forms of significance in a given case.

Comparing and Aligning the Three Types of Significance

Practical, statistical, and theoretical significance are important for scientific practice regardless of whether the intervention is with individuals, groups, organizations, or communities. However, they are independent ideas. One may have attained practical significance, but neither statistical nor theoretical significance, or vice versa. For example, it may be that a former psychiatric patient underwent a statistically significant change in the level of his bizarre behavior, as he was expected to do according to the theory used by his clinicians. But he may not yet be acting within an acceptable range of behaviors in his local public library. Likewise, he may be exhibiting some very significant behavior as far as practical matters are concerned–for example, he has not made a second attempt on his own life since having therapy–but statistically and theoretically speaking, we might want to monitor him for a longer period of time, since the nonsuicidal behavior so far exhibited could have occurred by chance alone, and our theory directs us to be aware of novel stresses for which he may not be prepared.

Although independent, these three forms of significance have important implications for one another. We view theoretical and statistical significance as tools for better understanding what is occurring in the client's life, compared to the collective wisdom about what might be expected regarding the client's type of problem. Practical significance, which is probably the most commonly used form of significance among the three, should be viewed as the "bottom line" we must achieve to validate our helping roles in society.

As a scientific practitioner, you try to align all three forms of significance. You must achieve practical results, resolve the problems clients come in with, and not create new social disturbances in so doing. But in order to build a repertoire of effective intervention methods, rather than reinvent the wheel with each new client, you must seek to demonstrate solid statistical improvements that are unlikely to have happened by chance alone. You also must seek to understand why these results happened as they did; that is, you must seek theoretical significance. With the three combined, you approximate the ideals of the scientific practitioner—sensitive (practical significance) and effective (statistical and theoretical significance) helping. To paraphrase Kant, having statistical and theoretical significance without the practical is hollow, but having practical significance without the other two is blind. All are needed for scientific practice, since they address different but important and complementary issues.

EVALUATING GOAL ACHIEVEMENT

Assuming that your intervention has been proceeding more or less smoothly and your monitoring of data shows that your intervention is achieving positive results, at some point you will want to evaluate whether your objectives and goals have been met. There are several ways of doing this, and, in fact, most of these

ways can be integrated into a comprehensive evaluation package (Gingerich, 1983).

Goal Determination

If your objectives and goals have been stated in clear, operational terms regarding the client's performance, you simply may be able to check whether the client's performance or activities actually meet the stated goals using whatever measurement system you have selected. If they do, you know you have arrived. For example, if the client's goal was to maintain his weight at 145 pounds for at least 3 weeks, once he has accomplished that, you will know your goals were achieved.

Social Validation

There are times when you may want to use a method to evaluate goal achievement that is not part of your basic measurement system, but that can add information to the overall evaluation. When you compare your client's functioning with others' or use others' judgments, we call this social validation. In essence, you are using social criteria to add to your overall evaluative impressions.

Two types of social validation were described by Kazdin (1977). The first is called *social comparison,* in which peers of the client who are comparable demographically, but don't exhibit the target problem, serve as the criterion against which the client's performance is evaluated. Thus, if the client's performance appears to be within the "typical range" of this normative comparison group, the change has received social validation.

The second approach is called *subjective evaluation.* This involves judgments by experts of how important the client's observed change is. These are qualitative judgments commonly involving overall improvement of the client. The "experts" could be anyone with expertise in the problem area—other practitioners or caretakers such as teachers, physicians, or nurses.

Both methods of social validation involve some hazard in the evaluation process: The judgments may be flawed due to limited knowledge of the client's performance or conditions prior to the intervention, or the norm groups may not be appropriate or the comparisons biased in some way. Thus, we are only suggesting social validation as supplements to the other methods described here.

Goal-Attainment Scaling

The methods of GAS, described in Chapter 3, are another way of evaluating overall goal achievement, since they are designed to do just that.

Target Complaints

An individualized rating scale, based on target complaints, such as the ones described in Chapter 6, can be used to aid in evaluating overall goal achievement. If you have not used an IRS as one of your basic tools for a given client, you may establish one to be used only at the end of the intervention to supplement your other data. This allows clients or relevant others to evaluate success based on their own impressions. You can use one of the formats described in Chapter 6, or a simple checklist such as the one illustrated in Figure 19.5. With slight modification, this form also can be used to obtain the client's impressions of success.

Visual Analysis

Probably the most basic analytic method of single-system designs is to do a visual analysis—a comparison of the data you are collecting on your charts during the intervention phase with the data you collected during the baseline period. This provides you with ongoing feedback in evaluating goal achievement. We describe visual analysis in detail in Chapter 20.

One variation of visual analysis is the *aim-star technique* (White, 1977). This procedure essentially synthesizes the practice of goal determination as discussed above with the process of visual analysis. If the goal has been clearly identified in advance, you simply draw a star on your standard chart at the level of performance that you have targeted for the client at about the time that you expect the client to reach that

level (as illustrated in Figure 19.6). You could even use a series of stars on the chart to correspond to your objectives, with each corresponding to successively greater achievements. While it may be difficult to be precise about exactly when the client will reach that point, having it plotted on the chart in advance establishes a clear goal toward which you and the client can work, and also adds to the client's motivation as he or she begins to approach that goal.

Statistics

As we suggested in Chapter 3, and as one variation of the material to be discussed in subsequent chapters, you can use statistics to help you evaluate your goals. We said that in the absence of other clear guidelines, you can establish goals that indicate success when statistical significance is reached. This approach tends to integrate both practical and statistical significance in that your goals are pre-established by recourse to statistics. A range of practical, easy-to-compute statistics are reviewed in Chapters 21 and 22.

Much of the rest of the book discusses how to use some of these procedures for evaluating goal attainment, but first we provide an overview of issues in the analysis of data and the use of personal computers for conducting some of these analytic tasks.

ISSUES IN ANALYSIS OF DATA

How Long Should Information Be Collected?

This is a question parallel to the one asked in Chapter 12: How long should baselining continue? In that chapter we offered a number of suggestions, some of which gave no answers about the exact number of observations you need to make. We have some additional guidelines to provide at this point, and we provide more specific answers when we discuss particular statistical tests in Chapter 22, because the exact number of observations is related to the statistical test used.

In general, as we indicated earlier in our discussion of power, the more information

Your Name _____

Date _____

Name of Person You're Evaluating _____

Level of Improvement

Compared to the first time I evaluated this person, the problem is now:

Problem	Much Worse	Worse	Same	Improved	Very Much Improved
1. _____	____	____	____	____	____
2. _____	____	____	____	____	____
3. _____	____	____	____	____	____
4. _____	____	____	____	____	____

FIGURE 19.5 Checklist for evaluating outcome.

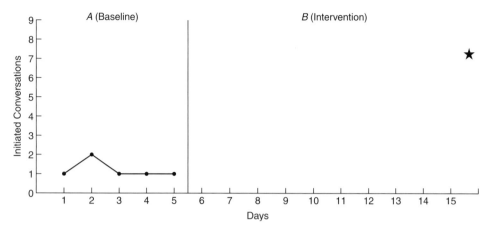

FIGURE 19.6   Illustration of "aim-star" technique.

you have (i.e., the more observations you make), the better your chances of accurately detecting a real difference between phases. However, if there is a large difference in the level of the target between phases it will be easier for you to detect accurately, and you won't need to collect as many observations. Therefore, the more powerful the intervention effect, the easier it will be to detect accurately, and the fewer the observations you will need. On the other hand, smaller differences between phases require more information to accurately determine whether any observed differences are real, or simply due to chance fluctuations over time. To detect subtle intervention effects you will need more information. In short, if you don't collect enough information you might miss a difference between phases, and hence an intervention effect (Cohen, 1988; Orme, 1991).

One way to decide whether you have enough information is to wait until practical, statistical, and theoretical significance converge. Obviously you should collect data throughout the intervention period in order to know how well the client is progressing toward his or her goals. However, practitioners collect enormous amounts of subjective impressions along with a handful of empirically defined and collected information. There may be an overpowering temptation to stop the rigorous data collection when you feel that the goals

have been obtained based on subjective impressions. We don't oppose this application of practice wisdom, but we would like to offer a suggestion to make it less idiosyncratic. Based on the discussion of statistical, practical, and theoretical significance, we suggest that formal measurement of outcomes end when these tests of significance are aligned—that is, when statistical, practical, and theoretical significance have been attained. In this way we can provide a more or less objective foundation for what essentially are subjective judgments about whether target events lie within an acceptable range, to the client, practitioner, and/or others. In general, information is collected as long as it contributes to the attainment and maintenance of intervention goals. If further information is needed for the maintenance phase or for follow-up, then of course such information should be collected, as it was during the intervention phase.

When statistical, practical, and theoretical significance are not in alignment, it's likely that further monitoring of the intervention, and perhaps a change in the intervention, is needed. The lack of practical significance means that further steps are necessary in the successive approximation toward a goal of satisfying psychological and/or social functioning. The lack of statistical significance means the absence of empirical force to demonstrate successful outcomes. The lack of theoretical significance means we have no clear conceptual framework from which to interpret the data.

If there's some doubt about the lasting quality of the outcome, it's wise to continue monitoring. This judgment may be made based on expectations derived from reviewing the literature, from other experiences with similar targets, or from a knowledge of the client's background. It's also possible to make this judgment by examining the whole set of target events for a given client; if one target has improved sufficiently, it may be necessary to continue observing it until the others among the cluster of targets also improve sufficiently. It also may be reassuring to clients to note that they can maintain successful accomplishments while they're working to resolve other concerns. This use of stable data should be shared with clients.

Using the procedure to be discussed in Chapter 22 of estimating efficiency by means of projecting the trends of current interventive efforts, you can make a rough prediction of how long it will take to arrive at statistical significance, at least given current trends. Then, based on client needs and agency resources, you can decide whether to continue the intervention. How that decision is made depends on the practitioner and the agency involved.

All things considered, collecting information, although it does carry a price tag, may be one of the cheapest investments in practice. If intervention is to continue, then we would suggest that evaluation—at least, of the major aspects of the client's situation—be continued as well.

When Should You Change Interventions?

This is a basic question for practice. It presumes that the problems and strengths of the client are being monitored, and that you are asking not only to evaluate the data collected, but also to translate these evaluations into decisions for possible changes in the intervention. There are eight logical combinations of the presence or absence of practical, statistical, and theoretical significance that can help you come to some decision, as depicted in Figure 19.7.

The first case is when all three forms of significance are present. This happy state of affairs should give clear direction for practice decisions, as the theory tells us what to expect to happen, the statistical analysis informs us that this has happened, and the practical meaning is clear that these are changes appropriate to

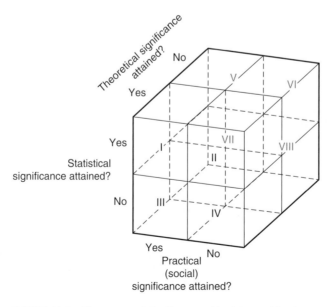

FIGURE 19.7 Three types of significance with eight combinations.

function adequately in society. In the best of all possible worlds, you probably would be well advised to continue with the intervention until this alignment of information informs you that the client's objectives have been attained.

The next three cases are when only two of the three forms of significance are present. For example, suppose practical and statistical significance have been attained, but not theoretical; then you would be well advised to continue until client objectives have been attained. You should recognize that what has happened here may not support your guiding theory of practice, which means that you should consider what unique factors might explain this, or think about how the theory might be strengthened to incorporate the events of this case. Or you might wish to consider new theories that better explain the outcomes. A single case is not enough to discard a well-developed theory, but as information accumulates over many cases, we probably should be prepared to seek stronger theories as needed.

In the situation in which there's practical and theoretical significance, but not statistical, you should look to see if there is a trend in the data. As will be seen in Chapter 22, it's possible in some cases to project how long it will take, given the present state of affairs in a case, for that case to show statistically significant results. If there's a clear positive trend, and success is predicted without considerable expenditure of time and effort, then consider completing the case by attaining statistical significance along with the other two. If there's no clear trend, or if the data appear to be deteriorating, then you might want to check the evidence for the other forms of significance again, as this would be an inconsistent pattern.

The last of this set of three cases would be when there's statistical and theoretical significance, but no practical outcomes. This pattern strongly suggests that the intervention be continued longer, as matters are moving in the right direction according to both theory and analysis of current data. It may be that this pattern suggests strengthening the intervention to attain the desired practical effect along with the other two forms of significance.

The next three cases occur when there's only one form of significance. For example,

when practical significance alone is present, we're under great temptation to make decisions on this sole piece of information. This practical significance is very important, but it may be superficial so that once you terminate, the problems may reappear. Stronger certainty would come either when you had expected this improvement to occur early (a part of the expectations from your theory), or when the magnitude of change could not have happened by chance alone (statistical significance). However, if you had to choose one form of significance that you could not do without, then practical significance would probably be it.

If you've obtained statistically significant improvement alone, this is an indication that you're probably on the right path, although without theoretical significance you may not know what particular path it is. If you're moving in the right direction, though, you should probably continue the intervention until practical significance is achieved.

If you obtain theoretical significance only, then your theory probably will already tell you to keep on with the intervention, because this is not the end of the expectation. Such information may tide you over during rough parts of cases. For example, behavioral theory suggests that clients may react at first with a sharp rise in problematic behaviors when reinforcement for those behaviors is purposively removed and the problematic behaviors ignored. Obviously there would be no practical or statistical significance in that situation, but it could be anticipated because of the theory.

The final case is where there are no forms of significance present, even after some considerable interventive efforts. Then the message is very clear that you should consider rapidly changing the intervention. Included in this situation would be sudden negative changes. You should be annotating any extreme data points, and when several come in short order, this may be enough information to make major changes in the intervention.

Thus, the various patterns among the three forms of significance can be used to suggest approaches to the intervention. The general point is that this is what we mean by feedback from the evaluation to practice. You can use practical, statistical, and theoretical guidelines as part of the basis for making decisions about practice.

Training Phases, Maintenance Phases, and Follow-Ups

Throughout this book, we've made the point that single-system designs use some special phases in the problem-solving process. Here, we link our discussions of training, maintenance, and follow-up phases with analysis—how these distinctive parts of evaluation fit into our analysis and decision making on a case.

During the *training phase* the client will often not perform immediately at the highest levels because he or she has to learn how and what to do, and learning takes time and practice. So analysis of the training phase requires that we look for trends in the right direction, given enough time for the client to learn whatever is needed to achieve the desired outcome. If the client's target behavior shows no sign of improvement, or is getting worse, then double-check to make sure that the intervention is in fact being used as intended. If it is, then consider changing the intervention in some way—making it stronger if you're convinced by available evidence that this is the appropriate intervention for this case, or changing to something new if you're not so convinced. If the client's target behavior is moving in the right direction with reasonable speed, then be reassured and continue the intervention as planned.

Events in the *maintenance phase* tell you something quite different. In this case, you've attained a stable pattern of success in achieving the client's objectives, but you wish to ensure that this learning will be transferred to the natural environment. So the maintenance phase contains those new learning experiences to ensure the transfer of effects. Maintenance is part of the intervention in general, even though it's not the intervention per se. Thus, you should continue regular observations of the target behavior. However, because you're introducing something new, you should expect some variation in the pattern achieved in the regular intervention phase. If this occurs, you can look for a new steady state indicating that the client

can handle the problem on his or her own, and then terminate. If, however, there's a sharp deterioration in the target event, then you may have caused a problem rather than solved one. First, double-check with the client about extraneous events that may be influencing this deterioration. If such events don't appear to be present, then monitor the maintenance intervention to see if it appears to be having an iatrogenic effect (harm caused by the practitioner). If the problems are severe, you probably should drop the maintenance activities and go back to the intervention to regain the stable, desired level of behaviors. Once that has been reachieved, you can try a new maintenance activity, or terminate while the target problem is in a desired state.

Follow-ups are probably the cheapest form of insurance the practitioner has that his or her interventions are effective. They can help answer several important questions:

1. Does the impact of the service maintain itself after the end of the intervention program? Is the client independently controlling his or her own fate?

2. Have there been major modifications in the events under study, suggesting a need for a "booster shot" (cf. McDonald & Budd, 1983)?

3. Has the client incorporated the intervention experience as a way of dealing with new problems?

On a carefully planned basis you should make contact and reassess the client's functioning on the target problems, using the same form of measurement of the target events that you used throughout the baseline and intervention periods, if possible. One method of conducting follow-ups is to select the times with progressively increasing intervals—for example, 1 month, 3 months, 6 months, and then a year following termination. Or you can select the times to make those contacts using a table of random numbers (found in many statistics texts). Random selection of the exact time for follow-ups increases the chance that the selected times will provide a representative picture of the client's functioning; it also makes the follow-up assessments more comparable to data collected prior to follow-up. However you select follow-up times, though, you don't necessarily have to tell the client exactly when you plan to reassess his or her functioning, but only that you would like to check back several times for some months to see how things are going.

Be prepared for a possibly ambivalent response on occasion, because you represent a time in the former client's life that may be difficult and embarrassing for that client—and your presence may perhaps be an unhappy reminder. However, you're also showing continuing interest and availability, which should be reassuring to the former client. We suggest you accept whatever follow-up is acceptable to the client, even if it's a brief telephone call on how the client is doing on the former target behaviors. These follow-ups become "reconstructed" follow-up data, similar to reconstructed baseline data. Use them cautiously to provide a broad perspective on the persistence of results without clear detail. But do try to use them.

We would recommend a minimum of three follow-up contacts, if possible. Two follow-ups might give you a rough estimate of whether there was a trend during follow-up, but three observations would be even better because they would give you an estimate of whether there was a stable trend or a changing trend (e.g., increasing functioning followed by decreasing functioning). Also, if you do only one or two follow-ups it might be that you just catch the client at a particularly good or bad time, whereas three (or more) follow-ups increase the chances that the follow-up data provide a representative picture of the client's functioning.

Another consideration in determining the number and schedule of follow-ups is the nature of the target. For example, problems might be associated with a particular day of the week (e.g., "blue Mondays," caused by starting the work week), time of the month (e.g., shortage of money and resulting tensions prior to receiving monthly checks), or time of the year (e.g., holidays or personal anniversaries). Such patterns should be considered in determining the schedule of follow-ups.

COMPUTER ANALYSIS OF DATA FOR SINGLE-SYSTEM DESIGNS

Personal computers can increase the speed, efficiency, and accuracy with which single-system data are analyzed. Personal computers also increase the range of statistical procedures that can be used because they can do certain mathematical procedures that would be too cumbersome to do by hand or with a calculator (autocorrelation and some tests of statistical significance come to mind). However, the use of personal computers to analyze single-system data requires an investment of time and money, especially initially. On the other hand, the cost of personal computers is decreasing, their power is increasing, computer programs are becoming more and more user-friendly, and computers are increasingly available to practitioners in the workplace (Patterson, 2000). Therefore, personal computers can be important tools for the analysis of single-system data.

You could use a wide variety of personal computer programs to compute particular statistics for the analysis of single-system design data. There are several broad categories of such programs.

First, there are commercial programs designed primarily for the analysis of group designs. These programs compute some of the statistics we discuss in this book. They include SPSS and SAS, two programs widely used by human service professionals and other social science researchers.

Second, any search of the Internet for shareware programs will turn up a number of diverse personal computer programs that will compute some relevant statistics and charts (not to mention a lot of other software). These programs are distributed free or for a small fee, but you're obliged to pay a registration fee if you decide to use them.

Third, spreadsheet programs such as Microsoft Excel can compute some relevant statistics and line charts. An interesting feature of these programs is that they can be customized to compute statistics for the analysis of single-system designs (e.g., Alter & Evans, 1990; Bronson & Blythe, 1987; Orme & Cox, 2001; Patterson, 2000).

Finally, there are some programs designed for specific limited types of analysis of single-system design data. For example, Crosbie (1993, 1995) developed a personal computer program named ITSACORR designed specifically to conduct time-series analyses of single-system data. Van Damme and Onghena (Onghena & Edginton, 1994; Onghena & Van Damme, 1994) developed SCRT, a personal computer program designed specifically to conduct randomization tests for single-system designs. Other specific programs have been discussed in Franklin, Allison, and Gorman (1997).

Many of the programs mentioned above are very useful and sophisticated computer programs, but most of the things they do are not relevant to the analysis of single-system designs, or they just don't do some of the things needed in the analysis of single-system design data. Also, some, but not all, of these programs are quite expensive. In any case, personal computer–based data analysis is a rapidly growing area, so you should look for current developments in such journals as *Computers in Human Services, Social Science Computer Review,* and *Computers in Psychiatry/Psychology;* in reference books such as *Personal Computer Applications in the Social Services* (Patterson, 2000), *Computer Use in Psychology: A Directory of Software* (Stoloff & Couch, 1992); on the Web in such places as "CUSSnet" **http://www.uta.edu/cussn/cussn.html**), Computers in Mental Health (**http://www.ex.ac.uk/cimh/welcome.htm**), and New Technology in the Human Services (**http://www.fz.hse.nl/causa/swbib/sw_keyw.htm**); and in software review sections of professional journals.

SINGWIN: A Personal Computer Program for the Analysis of Single-System Design Data

We are pleased to include with this book what we think is the most comprehensive program for the analysis of single-system design data. This program is named SINGWIN, and it is a Windows-based program designed by Charles Auerbach, David Schnall, and Heidi Heft LaPorte specifically for this book.

SINGWIN computes most of the statistics we discuss, and generates most of the graphs and charts. Furthermore, as you'll see in Chapter 23, SINGWIN is a program that we think you'll find very user friendly and it only will take a small investment of your time to learn. It's menu-driven, and we believe that after a small amount of practice you won't even need the instructions provided in Chapter 23. Also, SINGWIN requires only a very basic personal computer.

All computer programs—no matter how carefully constructed, tested, and explained—pose problems and questions for users. Also, most computer programs grow over time to encompass new features. To address these issues, you can go to the web page for this book: **http://www.ablongman.com/bloom**. There is a button marked "Technical Support." You also can request technical support for SINGWIN by sending e-mail to *singwin@ymail.yu.edu*. Finally, the other website for this book, **http://utcmhsrc.csw.utk.edu/evaluatingpractice/**, includes sections detailing Frequently Asked Questions concerning SINGWIN.

THE ISSUE OF AUTOCORRELATION

All statistical tests require certain assumptions. The violation of assumptions can result in the detection of a difference between phases when a difference doesn't really exist (Type I error), or the failure to detect a difference when it really does exist (Type II error) (e.g., Crosbie, 1987; Kenny & Judd, 1986; Toothaker, Banz, Noble, Camp, & Davis, 1983). Furthermore, when the number of observations is small, as it often is in practice, the consequences of violating many of these assumptions are exacerbated.

One of the most troublesome assumptions underlying many statistical tests as applied to the analysis of single-system designs is the assumption that the observations are independent. *Independence* essentially means that one observation can't be predicted from other observations. For example, if a client's behavior at one time predicts other behavior, the observations would not be independent. Or if two or more clients shared a common environment or history—for example, a husband and wife or clients hospitalized on the same ward—the observations of the different clients might not be independent (Kenny & Judd, 1986).

When observations are not independent they're said to be dependent, or correlated. Of particular importance to the analysis of single-system design data is the correlation of adjacent observations within a series of observations made over time. This type of dependency is known as *serial dependency*, and is quantified by a type of correlation known as an *autocorrelation*.

When there are three or more observations in a phase, more than one autocorrelation can be computed. It might be that values for a variable are dependent on the immediately preceding values, the values before that, or the values before that, and so on. The temporal distance between two observations is known as a *lag*, so a lag 1 autocorrelation indicates the extent to which the values of a variable are dependent upon immediately preceding values, a lag 2 autocorrelation indicates the extent to which they're dependent upon the values before that, and so on. Data can be autocorrelated at a particular lag (e.g., lag 2) but not at another lag (e.g., lag 1) and *an autocorrelation of any lag can invalidate tests of statistical significance that assume that the observations are independent.* The total number of possible autocorrelations for a series of observations is the number of observations, minus 1. However, typically the lag 1 autocorrelation is considered the most important, especially when small numbers of observations are involved.

The Debate over Autocorrelation

There's ample reason to believe that autocorrelation can increase Type I or Type II errors (depending on whether observations are positively or negatively correlated and whether they're correlated within or between phases).

However, there's considerable debate about the extent to which single-system design data are autocorrelated, and this issue is far from settled (Busk & Marascuilo, 1988; Huitema, 1985, 1988; Matyas & Greenwood, 1991, 1997; Sharpley & Alavosius, 1988; Wampold, 1988). In fact, one argument is that the issue is not at all whether the autocorrelation is significant but the effect any autocorrelation has on the use of statistics. Sharpley and Alavosius (1988) have shown that even low levels of autocorrelation—statistically significant or not—can distort the data in traditional statistics, leading to Type I or Type II errors. Thus, an autocorrelation of .1 will inflate traditional statistics (such as the t and F tests and, presumably, many of the statistics we present in this book) above their correct value by 110%, an autocorrelation of .2 by 122%, of .3 by 136%, of .4 by 153 %, of .5 by 173%, of .6 by 200%, of .7 by 238%, of .8 by 300%, and of .9 by 435%. The presence of autocorrelation really can produce distortion in your ability to understand the statistical significance of your data, and we urge you to consider this point whether or not the autocorrelation you compute is statistically significant.

We believe that the issue is broader and more complex than the general question—"are single-system design data autocorrelated?"—would imply. Each data set—like each client—is different. We also believe it is safest to err on the side of caution. Therefore, we present methods for detecting autocorrelation and for transforming autocorrelated data into a form suitable for statistical analyses. Thus, we will make this an issue you can explore for yourself with each data set.

Unfortunately you can't necessarily see autocorrelation in a set of data (Kratochwill, 1978). Other aspects of time-series data, such as stability, variability, and overlap, are easier to discern through visual inspection. Thus, as we discuss in Chapter 20, autocorrelation can complicate visual as well as statistical analysis. Fortunately, there are statistical procedures to detect autocorrelation, and we describe these procedures below.

If there's reason to believe that data are autocorrelated, or that other assumptions are violated, you have a couple of different options. First, sometimes it's possible to use another statistical procedure that relies on less stringent assumptions. We describe different statistical tests in Chapter 22. A second option is to transform the data so the required assumptions are met. For example, transformations can be used to remove autocorrelation from a set of observations. We describe several such transformations below.

Computational Steps in Testing for Autocorrelation

Since the publication of earlier editions of this book, there has been considerable research conducted by Huitema and his colleagues concerning how best to compute autocorrelation and test it for statistical significance with the relatively small number of observations typically available in single-system designs (Huitema & McKean, 1994a,b,c, 1996; Huitema, McKean, & Zhao, 1996). The traditional method of computing autocorrelation is known as r_K and the traditional method of testing it for statistical significance is known as Bartlett's test (r_K was significant, i.e., autocorrelated, if it was greater than $2/\sqrt{n}$). These methods were developed based on the assumption of a large number of observations, and recent research indicates that they are often inaccurate regarding the number of observations typically available in single-system designs (e.g., Huitema & McKean, 1991, 1994a,b). Our reading of the recent autocorrelation literature, and

consultation with Huitema, leads us to recommend a new version of the autocorrelation that Huitema and McKean label r_{F2} (1994a,b), and a new test of statistical significance that Huitema and McKean label t_{F2} (1994b).

Let's take a hypothetical example and illustrate how to compute the r_{F2} autocorrelation and test it for statistical significance using t_{F2}. Suppose that you're working with a parent and child to increase the number of daily positive contacts. Eight days of baseline data are collected (see Figure 19.8), and these data are listed in Step 1 of Exhibit 19.1. In this exhibit the computational steps are identified on the left side of the page and are illustrated with data from our example on the right side of the page (pages 535–536). (Note that if all scores within a phase are the same, the data within that phase won't be autocorrelated, and you can move on to the procedures described in Chapters 21 and 22.)

Our example only includes baseline data. Other phases also should be tested for autocorrelation because serial dependency in any phase can lead to incorrect conclusions. However, in general, autocorrelations should be computed separately for separate phases, because differences between phases can produce misleading estimates of the degree of autocorrelation (Gorsuch, 1983; Huitema, 1985, 1988;

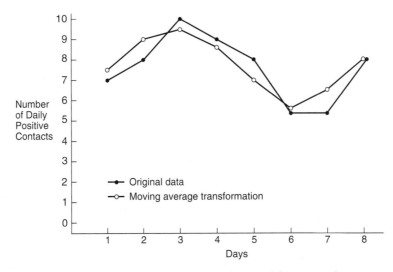

FIGURE 19.8 Data set for analyzing autocorrelation (Exhibit 19.1) and moving average transformations (Exhibit 19.3).

EXHIBIT 19.1   Calculating Autocorrelation.

Steps for Computing and Testing a Lag I Autocorrelation	*Data from Figure 19.8*
1. Record observed scores, *s,* for one phase only.	$s_1 = 7$ $s_2 = 8$ $s_3 = 10$ $s_4 = 9$ $s_5 = 8$ $s_6 = 5$ $s_7 = 5$ $s_8 = 8$
2. Sum the observed scores, $\sum_s$	$\sum_s = 60$
3. Divide the sum of the scores by the number of scores used to compute the sum, *N.* This gives the mean, M	$M = \dfrac{60}{8} = 7.5$
4. Following is the computational formula for the autocorrelation, r_{F2} (Huitema & McKean, 1994, p. 332): $\left[\dfrac{[(.5)(s_1 - M)^2 + (.5)(s_n - M)^2] + [(s_1 - M)(s_2 - M) + \cdots + (s_{n-1} - M)(s_n - M)]}{(s_1 - M)^2 + (s_2 - M)^2 + \cdots + (s_n - M)^2} \right]\left[1 + \dfrac{5}{N-1} \right]$	
5. Compute the term in brackets on the left of the top row of the autocorrelation formula. This states that: (1) the mean is subtracted from the first score, then this value is squared and multiplied by .5; (2) the mean is subtracted from the last score, then this value is squared and multiplied by .5; and (3) the values from 1 and 2 are summed.	$(.5)(s_1 - M)^2 = (.5)(7 - 7.5)^2 = .125$ $(.5)(s_8 - M)^2 = (.5)(8 - 7.5)^2 = .125$ $.125 + .125 = .25$
6a. Compute the term in brackets on the right of the top row of the autocorrelation formula using this and the next step. This step states that you subtract the mean from each score. (Be careful with negative numbers: $109 - 95 = +14$, but $60 - 95 = -35$.)	$s_1 - M = 7 - 7.5 = -.5$ $s_2 - M = 8 - 7.5 = +.5$ $s_3 - M = 10 - 7.5 = +2.5$ $s_4 - M = 9 - 7.5 = +1.5$ $s_5 - M = 8 - 7.5 = +.5$ $s_6 - M = 5 - 7.5 = -2.5$ $s_7 - M = 5 - 7.5 = -2.5$ $s_8 - M = 8 - 7.5 = +.5$
6b. Using numbers from 6a, multiply the first score minus the mean, by the second score minus the mean. Then, this product is added to the product of the second score minus the mean times the third score minus the mean . . . , over all such pairs of scores. This sum is the term in brackets on the left of the top row of the autocorrelation formula.	$(-.5)(+.5) = -.25$ $(+.5)(+2.5) = +1.25$ $(+2.5)(+1.5) = +3.75$ $(+1.5)(+.5) = +.75$ $(+.5)(-2.5) = -1.25$ $(-2.5)(-2.5) = +6.25$ $(-2.5)(+.5) = \underline{-1.25}$ 9.25

(continued)

EXHIBIT 19.1 (Continued)

Steps for Computing and Testing a Lag I Autocorrelation	Data from Figure 19.8
7. Compute the bottom row of the autocorrelation formula. This states that the first score minus the mean of the scores is squared and added to the second score minus the mean and squared, and this is followed across all the other scores. This gives the value for the bottom row of the auto-correlation formula.	$(7 - 7.5)^2 = (-.5)^2 = .25$ $(8 - 7.5)^2 = (+.5)^2 = .25$ $(10 - 7.5)^2 = (+2.5)^2 = 6.25$ $(9 - 7.5)^2 = (+1.5)^2 = 2.25$ $(8 - 7.5)^2 = (+.5)^2 = .25$ $(5 - 7.5)^2 = (-2.5)^2 = 6.25$ $(5 - 7.5)^2 = (-2.5)^2 = 6.25$ $(8 - 7.5)^2 = (+.5)^2 = \underline{.25}$ 22
8. Compute the term in brackets on the right of the autocorrelation formula. This states that you divide 5 by the number of observations minus 1, and then you add 1 to this value.	$1 + \dfrac{5}{N - 1} =$ $1 + \dfrac{5}{8 - 1} = 1.71$
9. Compute r_{F2} using data from steps, 5, 6(b), 7, and 8.	$r_{F2} = \left(\dfrac{.25 + 9.25}{22}\right)(1.71) = .74$

Remember that an autocorrelation of 0 indicates no lag 1 autocorrelation, an autocorrelation of 1 indicates perfect positive lag 1 autocorrelation, and an autocorrelation of –1 indicates perfect negative autocorrelation.

10. The following steps show how to test whether an autocorrelation is statistically significant (i.e., whether it is possible to reject the null hypothesis that the lag 1 autocorrelation equals 0; if the results are statistically significant, the data *are* autocorrelated, i.e., not independent, and the null hypothesis is rejected). The computational formula for the test statistic, t_{F2}, is (Huitema & McKean, 1994b, p. 332):

$$t_{F2} = \cfrac{r_{F2}}{\sqrt{\left[1 + \dfrac{5}{N-1}\right]^2}\left[1 - \cfrac{[(.5)(s_1 - M)^2 + (.5)(s_n - M)^2] + [(s_1 - M)(s_2 - M) + \cdots + s_{n-1} - M(s_n - M)]^2}{\dfrac{(s_1 - M)^2 + (s_2 - M)^2 + \cdots + (s_n - M)^2}{N + 1}}\right]}}$$

11. Plug the correct numbers into the formula and compute t_{F2}, the statistic used to test whether an autocorrelation is statistically significant. (Table 19.1 provides some common square roots to make your calculations a little easier.)	$t_{F2} = \dfrac{.74}{\sqrt{\left[1 + \dfrac{5}{8-1}\right]^2\left[\dfrac{1 - (.43)^2}{8 + 1}\right]}}$ $t_{F2} = \dfrac{.74}{\sqrt{[1.71]^2\,[.09]}}$ $t_{F2} = \dfrac{.74}{\sqrt{.26}}$ $t_{F2} = \dfrac{.74}{.51}$ $t_{F2} = 1.45$
12. If t_{F2} is equal to or greater than the absolute value (i.e., ignoring whether it is + or −) of the critical value of t with $N + 5$ degrees of freedom (see Exhibit 19.2 where N of $8 + 5 = 13$), the data are autocorrelated.	In this case the absolute value of t_{F2} (i.e., 1.45) is *not* greater than the critical value of 2.14. So, the null hypothesis that the lag 1 autocorrelation equals 0 cannot be rejected (i.e., the results are not significant; they do not support the hypothesis that the data are autocorrelated). However, this does not necessarily mean that the data are not autocorrelated–the number of observations may be too small to allow the detection of the autocorrelation.

TABLE 19.1 Common square roots used in computing autocorrelation.

$\sqrt{1} = 1.00$	$\sqrt{11} = 3.32$	$\sqrt{21} = 4.58$	$\sqrt{55} = 7.42$
$\sqrt{2} = 1.41$	$\sqrt{12} = 3.46$	$\sqrt{22} = 4.69$	$\sqrt{60} = 7.75$
$\sqrt{3} = 1.73$	$\sqrt{13} = 3.61$	$\sqrt{23} = 4.80$	$\sqrt{65} = 8.06$
$\sqrt{4} = 2.00$	$\sqrt{14} = 3.74$	$\sqrt{24} = 4.90$	$\sqrt{70} = 8.37$
$\sqrt{5} = 2.24$	$\sqrt{15} = 3.87$	$\sqrt{25} = 5.00$	$\sqrt{75} = 8.66$
$\sqrt{6} = 2.45$	$\sqrt{16} = 4.00$	$\sqrt{30} = 5.48$	$\sqrt{80} = 8.94$
$\sqrt{7} = 2.65$	$\sqrt{17} = 4.12$	$\sqrt{35} = 5.92$	$\sqrt{85} = 9.22$
$\sqrt{8} = 2.83$	$\sqrt{18} = 4.24$	$\sqrt{40} = 6.32$	$\sqrt{90} = 9.49$
$\sqrt{9} = 3.00$	$\sqrt{19} = 4.36$	$\sqrt{45} = 6.71$	$\sqrt{95} = 9.75$
$\sqrt{10} = 3.16$	$\sqrt{20} = 4.47$	$\sqrt{50} = 7.07$	$\sqrt{100} = 10.0$

EXHIBIT 19.2 Number of observations (N) and critical values of t for testing autocorrelation ($p < .05$, two-tailed).*

N (df)	t	N (df)	t	N (df)	t	N (df)	t
3 (8)	2.29	9 (14)	2.13	15 (20)	2.06	21 (26)	2.04
4 (9)	2.24	10 (15)	2.11	16 (21)	2.06	22 (27)	2.03
5 (10)	2.21	11 (16)	2.10	17 (22)	2.05	23 (28)	2.03
6 (11)	2.18	12 (17)	2.09	18 (23)	2.05	24 (29)	2.02
7 (12)	2.16	13 (18)	2.08	19 (24)	2.04	25 (30)	2.02
8 (13)	2.14	14 (19)	2.07	20 (25)	2.04	26 (31)	2.02

Note: The numbers in parentheses refer to the results of N + 5 (see Exhibit 19.1, step 12).

Huitema & McKean, 1996). (Also, you should note that when there's a trend in a set of scores–that is, they are systematically increasing or decreasing–the method outlined above for computing an autocorrelation can produce an inaccurate autocorrelation; Huitema, 1988; Huitema & McKean, 1996.)

If you find that r_{F2} is not significantly different from zero–that is, the data don't appear to be autocorrelated–you could proceed to use the statistics described in subsequent chapters with increased confidence that the data aren't autocorrelated. However, only relatively large autocorrelations are likely to be detected with the relatively small number of observations in most single-system designs, so the failure to detect an autocorrelation may not fully justify the conclusion that the data are not autocorrelated (cf. DeCarlo & Tryon, 1993; Huitema & McKean, 1991; Matyas & Greenwood, 1991; Suen & Ary, 1987). The reason for this is that some statistical tests are not very sensitive with small numbers of observations. Our suggestion is to interpret the autocorrelation test results with caution when the number of observations is very small. In fact, with six or fewer observations, you could treat the data as though they were autocorrelated just to be on the safe side.

What do you do if the data are autocorrelated? First you could refrain from using tests of statistical significance at all. Thus, you would simply be satisfied with visual inspection of the data, as we describe in Chapter 20, and perhaps supplement this visual inspection with some of the descriptive statistics that we describe in Chapter 21. However, you should be aware of the fact that precisely because of autocorrelation, even your visual analysis will be somewhat suspect, and again, you should interpret these data cautiously (Matyas & Greenwood, 1990). In other words, what looks like a "significant" change may really be just a function of the autocorrelation in the data.

Second, you could use tests of statistical significance that don't assume the absence of autocorrelation. We briefly discuss two such approaches in Chapter 22.

Third, you could go ahead and compute tests of statistical significance that assume the absence of autocorrelation, but use them as rougher guides than you would ordinarily because autocorrelation may have introduced errors in the eventual statistical result.

Fourth, you could try to transform the data to remove the autocorrelation. In a subsequent section we suggest methods of transforming autocorrelated data. However, we want to add a word of caution: If you do transform the data, you will be losing many of the original characteristics of those data. This may be necessary in using some analytic procedures, but you have to be careful in interpreting results because your transformation may have affected the basic character of the data.

Computer Procedures in Testing for Autocorrelation

Here's how use SINGWIN to compute and test an autocorrelation for statistical significance. As you will see, this is a much easier method than hand calculation.

1. Start SINGWIN (see "Starting SING-WIN" in the SINGWIN User's Guide, Chapter 23).
2. Open the "ex19-1.dbf" file (containing the Exhibit 19.1 data) that comes with SING-WIN (see "Opening the Existing File").

3. Follow the steps outlined in the section entitled "Computing and Testing Autocorrelation."

TOOLS IN ANALYSIS OF DATA

The Transformation of Autocorrelated Data

Transformations of autocorrelated data can reduce or remove this autocorrelation by mathematical means, making it possible to use certain statistical tests and even facilitating visual analysis. There are two general types of transformation that can rather easily be used—the *first differences transformation* and the *moving average transformation* (cf. Gottman & Leiblum, 1974). In deciding which procedure to use, we suggest the following guidelines: (a) if the data appear to have a linear trend, then use the first differences transformation; (b) if the data appear to be fluctuating wildly, then use a moving average transformation—this is also called *smoothing* the data. (Smoothing also can be used if the first differences transformation doesn't succeed in removing the autocorrelation from the data.)

Moving Average Transformation. When the data are widely fluctuating within a phase, you can smooth the data by using the moving average transformation. All you're doing here is plotting the means for adjacent pairs of data points. The computations for the moving average transformation, using the data from Exhibit 19.1 for illustrative purposes (though they are not wildly fluctuating), are shown in Exhibit 19.3. Note that in this example the moving average transformation not only did not remove the autocorrelation, but it actually increased it (the data were not wildly fluctuating in the first place). In such a case, procedures that do not assume that observations are independent, or more sophisticated transformations, may be needed.

First Differences Transformation. The data from an example of a target problem of "satisfying time spent together" are shown in Figure 19.9 as original data (top line). These data clearly show a linear trend (moving upward).

EXHIBIT 19.3 Calculating a moving average transformation.

Steps for Computing a Moving Average Transformation	Data from Exhibit 19.1
1. Record observed scores, s.	$s_1 = 7$ $s_2 = 8$ $s_3 = 10$ $s_4 = 9$ $s_5 = 8$ $s_6 = 5$ $s_7 = 5$ $s_8 = 8$
2. Compute the average for successive pairs of data points until all data are accounted for.	$\dfrac{7+8}{2} = 7.5$ $\dfrac{8+10}{2} = 9$ $\dfrac{10+9}{2} = 9.5$ $\dfrac{9+8}{2} = 8.5$ $\dfrac{8+5}{2} = 6.5$ $\dfrac{5+5}{2} = 5$ $\dfrac{5+8}{2} = 6.5$ $\dfrac{8}{1} = 8$
3. Compute the autocorrelation using the transformed data, and test it for statistical significance using steps 2–12 from Exhibit 19.1.	$r_{F2} = .93$ $t_{F2} = 4.72$ $df = N + 5 = 13$ The autocorrelation is significant so these data *are* autocorrelated.* *Critical value in Exhibit 19.2 $= 2.14$
4. Graph the transformed data.	See Figure 19.8 (the "moving averages" data set)

5. Other combinations of data may be averaged, such as groups of three or more data points, and other types of averages may be used (e.g., medians).

6. Once baseline data are transformed, you must transform the data in the intervention phase as well. This transformation is done as described above.

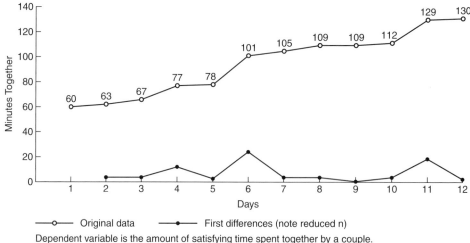

FIGURE 19.9   Example of first difference transformation with negative numbers.

As we noted earlier, special procedures beyond the scope of this book are needed to accurately compute an autocorrelation for data showing a trend, and so it is not even appropriate to compute r_{F2} for these data ($r_{F2} = 1.34$ in this case, clearly beyond the theoretical upper bound, that is, 1, of the autocorrelation). The steps for transforming these data using a first differences transformation are shown in Exhibit 19.4. As shown in Figure 19.9, though, while the first difference transformation appears graphically to be successful in removing this trend (bottom line), the autocorrelation for these transformed data is statistically significant, meaning the data still are autocorrelated ($r_{F2} = -.49$, $t_{F2} = 3.5$, df$[N + 5] = 16$; $p < .05$). Therefore, as suggested in Exhibit 19.4, another transformation can be attempted (of course, the transformed data in Figure 19.9 could be used, but with great caution in interpreting them).

Computing and Graphing Transformed Data with SINGWIN

Here's how to use SINGWIN to transform data using the moving average or first difference transformation and how to graph and compute statistics based on the transformed data.

1. Start SINGWIN (see "Starting SING-WIN" in the SINGWIN User's Guide, Chapter 23).

2. Open the "ex-19-1.dbf" (containing the Exhibit 19.1 data) or "fig19-9.dbf" (containing the Figure 19.9 data) file that comes with SINGWIN (see "Opening an Existing File").

3. Read the section entitled "Creating a Line Chart" to make sure that you know how to create a basic line chart of untransformed data.

4. Follow the steps outlined in the section entitled "Creating Charts of Transformed Data" to get line charts of moving average or first difference transformed data.

5. Follow the steps outlined in the section entitled "Computing Transformations" to transform and save data using either the moving average or first difference transformation, and to then manipulate these transformed data in various ways (e.g., compute and test autocorrelation or other statistics, create graphs).

Probability Tables for Use in Single-System Designs

When we use probability tables to aid our analysis of single-system design data, we use some simple but powerful tools to determine whether a set of outcome events could have happened by chance alone, given the nature of the baseline events. As far as you are

EXHIBIT 19.4   Calculating first differences transformation.

Steps for Computing First Differences Transformation	Data from Figure 19.9
1. Record observed scores, *s*.	$s_1 = 60$ $s_2 = 63$ $s_3 = 67$ $s_4 = 77$ $s_5 = 78$ $s_6 = 101$ $s_7 = 105$ $s_8 = 109$ $s_9 = 109$ $s_{10} = 112$ $s_{11} = 129$ $s_{12} = 130$
2. Subtract the second score from the first, the third from the second, and so on until all scores are accounted for. Note that there are 11, not 12, difference scores. (If the data are in a decreasing direction, do a transformation in the same way, but add a constant (say, 10) to each score to remove the minus signs in graphing the data.)	$63 - 60 = 3$ $67 - 63 = 4$ $77 - 67 = 10$ $78 - 77 = 1$ $101 - 78 = 23$ $105 - 101 = 4$ $109 - 105 = 4$ $109 - 109 = 0$ $112 - 109 = 3$ $129 - 112 = 17$ $130 - 129 = 1$
3. Compute the autocorrelation using the transformed data, and test it for statistical significance using steps 2–12 from Exhibit 19.1.	$r_{F2} = -.49$ $t_{F2} = -3.547$ The autocorrelation is significant so these data still are autocorrelated (t_{F2} is greater than the critical value of 2.10 in Exhibit 19.2).
4a. Graph the transformed data.	See Figure 19.9 (bottom line)
4b. If the transformed data contain negative numbers, add a constant to each value that will make all the numbers positive.	See Figure 19.10

5. If the transformed data are still autocorrelated, the first differences transformation may be repeated, or a second differences transformation may be used (subtracting data two points away from each other) before trying a moving average transformation. For each transformation, use the new *n* and test each transformation to see if the data are autocorrelated.

6. Once baseline data are transformed, you must also transform the intervention data just as you did with the baseline data and graph these data.

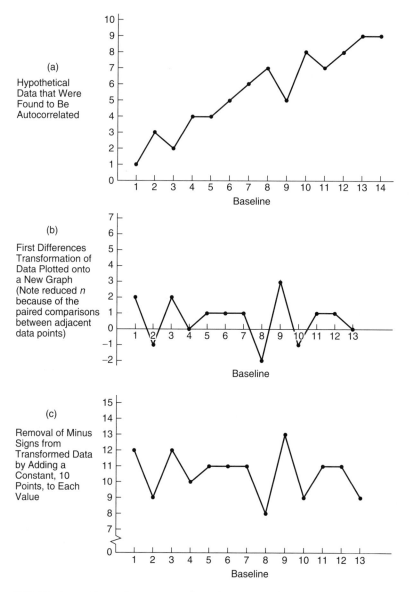

(a)

Hypothetical Data that Were Found to Be Autocorrelated

(b)

First Differences Transformation of Data Plotted onto a New Graph (Note reduced *n* because of the paired comparisons between adjacent data points)

(c)

Removal of Minus Signs from Transformed Data by Adding a Constant, 10 Points, to Each Value

FIGURE 19.10 Charts illustrating transformed data.

concerned, most of the statistical work has been done and is presented in table form for easy and ready use. Tables 19.2, 19.3, and 19.4 (from Bloom, 1975) will be used in conjunction with the proportion/frequency approach (described in Chapter 22). They also can be used as part of the Probability Method for determining

generalizability of single-system designs as described in Chapter 11. It will be helpful to discuss these tables in general here so that their specific application with these analytic approaches will be more understandable.

Probability tables summarize a large number of mathematical operations, each of which tells us how likely it is that some set of events occurred given certain conditions. These conditions are built into the structure of the tables and involve the proportion of specified events during the baseline and the number (or frequency) of observations made during intervention. Let's examine the tables more closely.

Each table is constructed identically, except that different levels of statistical significance are represented. Table 19.2 presents those combinations of proportions and numbers of events that indicate whether some particular set of observed events is or is not likely to have happened by chance alone at the .05 level. This means that there are 5 times out of 100 when chance factors could have caused a given rare set of outcomes. (As in rolling dice, some combinations of numbers like 7 are more likely to occur because there are more combinations to form 7 on the dice than there are to form 2 or 12.) For example, a sudden, marked improvement in a client's functioning that was observed to have been very poor for a long period of time (before intervention) is a desired but probabilistically unlikely event. We assume that a client's behavior will tend to stay about the same as the stable baseline picture has described it, other things being equal. But "other things" are not equal. The intervention purposely attempts to influence events in a certain direction; researchers refer to this as a directional, or one-tailed, test. Thus, when a statistically unlikely event occurs, the statistical notation $p < .05$ can be used. This means the probability is 5 or fewer times in 100 that the observed set of events could have happened by chance alone.

The one-tailed test and the tables (19.2, 19.3, and 19.4) assume that you're expecting the client problem to change in a positive direction. If you aren't sure whether the client's problem will change in a positive or negative direction, this is called a nondirectional, or a two-tailed, test. The same tables can be used to test the significance of nondirectional tests by doubling the significance level. If the .05 level of significance table is used (Table 19.2), then the nondirectional test would be examined using the same numbers in the table, but for statistical significance at the .10 level. The .01 table becomes .02, and the .001 table becomes .002.

The potential significance level of both the positive and the negative directions are added together in the nondirectional, or two-tailed, test.

Rare occurrences demand our attention, particularly when we appear to have some part in producing this unusually desired or undesired state of affairs. Note that probability statements don't assert causality; they merely state that such and such an observation is likely or unlikely to occur by chance and therefore focuses our attention. Causality is to be inferred largely from the evaluation design employed, as we discussed in Part III.

The other tables, 19.3 and 19.4, present the same information as Table 19.2 except that they indicate probability levels at the .01 and the .001 levels, respectively. That is, with Table 19.3 the cell entries indicate the number of intervention events that could not have happened by chance alone except one or fewer times in a hundred, or with Table 19.4, one or fewer times in a thousand. These are lower levels of significance (greater significance, indicating that the events are even more rare); for their levels of significance they permit fewer opportunities for chance factors to be related to any given outcome. A practitioner would want to achieve these lower levels of significance when life-threatening issues were at stake or when very important outcomes were under consideration. No law demands any given level of statistical significance; exploratory research is occasionally presented at the .10 level of significance so as not to miss potentially useful interventions that are not yet clearly defined or enacted. The .05 level is generally considered satisfactory for most research purposes, and we use it for the basic level in our single-system evaluation work as well.

One other feature to note in these tables relates to our discussion of power earlier in this chapter. In all of the probability tables, you will soon be able to see that the larger the number of data points, the "easier" it will be to find statistical significance.

Each of the tables has the same title but with different levels of statistical significance indicated. Let's examine the brief instructions printed at the top of all three tables, as they indicate the way the tables are to be used. We'll use Table 19.2 as an example. This table shows

TABLE 19.2 The .05 table for analyzing client data.

Brief Instructions: This table shows the *number* of observations of a specified type (e.g., desired behaviors) during the *intervention period* that are necessary to represent a significant increase at the .05 level of statistical significance as compared to the *proportion* of like observations during the *baseline period*. The steps in using the table are as follows:

1. Identify the proportion of observations in the desired zone in the baseline in the left-hand column (divide number of specified baseline events by *total* number of baseline events). Use "conservative rule" as needed.

2. Identify the total number of observations in the intervention period in the top row of table. Use "conservative rule" as needed.

3. Compare the total number of specified observations in the intervention period with the number at the intersection of the correct column and row. If the observed number is equal or greater than the number at the intersection, then the comparison is statistically significant at the .05 level.

Proportion of specified observations in the desired zone in the baseline period	Total Number of Observations in Intervention Period																												
	4	6	8	10	12	14	16	18	20	24	28	32	36	40	44	48	52	56	60	64	68	72	76	80	84	88	92	96	100
.05	2	2	3	3	3	3	3	4	4	4	4	5	5	5	6	6	6	7	7	7	8	8	8	8	9	9	9	10	10
.10	3	3	3	4	4	4	5	5	5	6	7	7	8	8	9	9	10	10	11	12	12	13	13	14	14	15	15	16	16
1/8	3	3	4	4	5	5	5	6	6	7	8	8	9	10	10	11	12	12	13	14	14	15	15	16	17	17	18	19	19
.15	3	3	4	4	5	5	6	6	7	8	8	9	10	11	12	12	13	14	15	15	16	17	18	18	19	20	21	21	22
1/6	3	4	4	5	5	6	6	7	7	8	9	10	11	12	13	13	14	15	16	17	18	18	19	20	21	22	22	23	24
.20	3	4	5	5	6	6	7	8	8	9	10	11	12	13	14	15	16	17	18	19	20	21	22	23	24	25	26	27	28
.25	4	4	5	6	7	7	8	9	9	11	12	13	14	16	17	18	19	20	22	23	24	25	26	27	29	30	31	32	33
.30	4	5	6	6	7	8	9	10	10	12	13	15	16	18	19	21	22	24	25	26	28	29	30	32	33	35	36	37	39

	4	5	6	7	8	9	10	11	13	15	16	18	19	21	22	24	26	27	29	30	32	33	35	36	38	39	41	42
1/3	4	5	6	7	8	9	10	11	13	15	16	18	19	21	22	24	26	27	29	30	32	33	35	36	38	39	41	42
.35	4	5	6	7	8	9	11	12	13	15	17	18	20	22	23	25	27	28	30	31	33	35	36	38	39	41	42	44
3/8	4	5	6	7	8	9	11	12	14	16	18	19	21	23	25	26	28	30	31	33	35	36	38	40	42	43	45	47
.40	4	5	6	8	9	10	12	13	15	16	18	20	22	24	26	28	29	31	33	35	37	38	40	42	44	46	47	49
.45	4	6	7	8	9	10	13	14	16	18	20	22	24	26	28	30	32	34	36	38	40	42	44	46	48	50	52	54
.50	—	6	7	9	9	11	13	15	17	19	22	24	26	28	31	33	35	37	40	42	44	46	48	51	53	55	57	59
.55	—	6	8	9	10	12	14	16	18	21	23	26	28	31	33	35	38	40	43	45	48	50	52	55	57	59	62	64
.60	—	6	8	10	11	13	15	17	19	22	25	27	30	33	35	38	41	43	46	48	51	54	56	59	61	64	66	69
5/8	—	—	8	10	11	14	16	17	20	23	25	28	31	34	36	39	42	45	47	50	53	55	58	61	63	66	69	71
.65	—	—	8	10	11	14	16	17	20	23	26	29	32	35	38	40	43	46	49	52	54	57	60	63	65	68	71	74
2/3	—	—	8	10	12	15	16	18	21	24	27	30	32	35	38	41	44	47	50	53	55	58	61	64	67	70	72	75
.70	—	—	—	10	12	15	17	18	21	24	28	31	34	37	40	43	46	49	52	55	58	61	64	67	70	73	75	78
.75	—	—	—	—	12	16	17	19	22	26	29	32	35	39	42	45	48	51	55	58	61	64	67	70	74	77	80	83
.80	—	—	—	—	—	16	18	20	23	27	30	34	37	40	44	47	51	54	57	61	64	67	71	74	77	81	84	87
5/6	—	—	—	—	—	—	18	20	24	27	31	34	38	42	45	49	52	56	59	63	66	69	73	76	80	83	87	90
.85	—	—	—	—	—	—	—	20	24	28	31	34	38	42	46	49	53	56	60	63	67	70	74	78	81	85	88	92
7/8	—	—	—	—	—	—	—	—	24	28	32	36	39	43	47	50	54	57	61	65	68	72	76	79	83	86	90	94
.90	—	—	—	—	—	—	—	—	24	28	32	36	40	44	47	51	54	58	62	66	69	73	77	80	84	88	91	95
.95	—	—	—	—	—	—	—	—	—	—	—	—	—	—	—	52	56	60	64	68	72	76	79	83	87	91	95	99

*Tables of the Cumulative Binomial Probability Distribution—By the staff of the Harvard Computational Laboratory, Harvard University Press, 1955. This table constructed under the direction of Dr. James Norton, Jr., Indiana University–Purdue University at Indianapolis, 1973.

(This table is reproduced by permission of the author and the publisher from the Paradox of Helping: Introduction to the Philosophy of Scientific Practice by Martin Bloom [New York: John Wiley and Sons, 1975].)

TABLE 19.3 The .01 table for analyzing client data.

Brief Instructions: This table shows the *number* of observations of a specified type (e.g., desired behaviors) during the *intervention period* that are necessary to represent a significant increase at the .01 level of statistical significance as compared to the *proportion* of like observations during the *baseline period.* The steps in using the table are as follows:

1. Identify the proportion of observations in the desired zone in the baseline in the left-hand column (divide number of specified baseline events by *total* number of baseline events. Use "conservative rule" as needed.
2. Identify the total number of observations in the intervention period in the top row of table. Use "conservative rule" as needed.
3. Compare the total number of specified observations in the intervention period with the number at the intersection of the correct column and row. If the observed number is equal to or greater than the number at the intersection number, then the comparison is statistically significant at the .01 level.

Total Number of Observations in Intervention Period

Proportion of specified observations in the desired zone in the baseline period	4	6	8	10	12	14	16	18	20	24	28	32	36	40	44	48	52	56	60	64	68	72	76	80	84	88	92	96	100
.05	3	3	3	4	4	4	4	5	5	5	6	6	6	7	7	7	8	8	8	—	9	9	10	10	—	11	11	—	12
.10	3	4	4	5	5	5	6	6	7	7	8	9	9	10	11	11	12	12	13	13	14	15	15	16	16	17	17	18	19
1/8	3	4	5	5	6	6	6	7	7	8	9	10	11	11	12	13	14	14	15	16	16	17	18	18	19	20	20	21	22
.15	4	4	5	5	6	7	7	8	8	9	10	11	12	13	14	14	15	16	17	18	18	19	20	21	22	22	23	24	25
1/6	4	4	5	6	6	7	8	8	9	10	11	12	13	14	14	15	16	17	18	19	20	21	22	23	23	24	25	26	27
.20	4	5	6	6	7	8	8	9	9	11	12	13	14	15	16	17	18	20	21	22	23	24	25	26	27	28	29	30	31
.25	4	5	6	7	8	9	9	10	11	12	14	15	16	18	19	20	22	23	24	25	27	28	29	30	32	33	34	35	36
.30	4	6	7	8	8	9	10	11	12	14	15	17	18	20	21	23	25	26	27	29	30	32	33	35	36	38	39	40	42

1/3	—	—	—	6	7	8	9	10	11	12	13	15	16	18	20	21	23	25	26	28	30	31	33	34	36	38	39	41	42	44	46
.35	—	—	—	6	7	8	9	10	11	12	13	15	17	19	20	22	24	26	27	29	31	32	34	36	37	39	41	42	44	46	47
3/8	—	—	—	6	7	8	9	11	12	13	14	16	18	19	21	23	25	27	29	31	32	34	36	38	39	41	43	45	46	48	50
.40	—	—	—	6	7	9	10	11	12	13	14	16	18	20	22	24	26	28	30	32	34	36	38	40	41	43	45	47	49	51	53
.45	—	—	—	6	8	9	10	12	13	14	15	17	20	22	24	26	28	31	33	35	37	39	41	43	45	47	49	51	54	56	58
.50	—	—	—	—	8	10	11	12	14	15	16	19	21	24	26	28	31	33	35	38	40	42	45	47	49	51	54	56	58	60	63
.55	—	—	—	—	8	10	11	13	14	16	17	20	22	25	28	30	33	35	38	40	43	45	48	50	53	55	58	60	63	65	67
.60	—	—	—	—	—	10	12	13	15	16	18	21	24	26	29	32	35	37	40	43	46	48	51	54	56	59	62	64	67	70	71
5/8	—	—	—	—	—	10	12	14	15	17	18	21	24	27	30	33	36	39	41	44	47	50	53	55	58	61	64	66	69	72	73
.65	—	—	—	—	—	—	12	14	15	17	19	22	25	28	31	34	37	40	43	45	48	51	54	57	60	63	65	68	71	74	75
2/3	—	—	—	—	—	—	12	14	16	17	19	22	25	28	31	34	37	40	43	46	49	52	55	58	61	64	67	70	73	75	78
.70	—	—	—	—	—	—	—	14	16	18	19	23	26	29	32	35	38	42	45	48	51	54	57	60	63	66	69	72	75	78	81
.75	—	—	—	—	—	—	—	—	—	18	20	23	27	30	34	37	40	44	47	50	53	57	60	63	66	70	73	76	79	82	86
.80	—	—	—	—	—	—	—	—	—	—	—	24	28	31	35	38	42	45	49	52	56	59	63	66	69	73	76	80	83	86	90
5/6	—	—	—	—	—	—	—	—	—	—	—	—	28	32	36	39	43	46	50	54	57	61	64	68	71	75	78	82	85	89	92
.85	—	—	—	—	—	—	—	—	—	—	—	—	—	32	36	40	43	47	51	54	58	61	65	69	72	76	79	83	87	90	94
7/8	—	—	—	—	—	—	—	—	—	—	—	—	—	—	—	36	40	44	48	51	55	59	62	66	70	74	77	81	85	88	92	96
.90	—	—	—	—	—	—	—	—	—	—	—	—	—	—	—	—	44	48	52	56	60	63	67	71	75	79	82	86	90	94	97
.95	—	—	—	—	—	—	—	—	—	—	—	—	—	—	—	—	—	—	—	—	—	—	—	—	—	—	—	—	92	96	100

*Tables of the Cumulative Binomial Probability Distribution—By the staff of the Harvard Computational Laboratory. Harvard University Press, 1955. This table constructed under the direction of Dr. James Norton, Jr., Indiana University–Purdue University at Indianapolis, 1973.

TABLE 19.4 The .001 table for analyzing client data.

Brief Instructions: This table shows the *number* of observations of a specified type (e.g., desired behaviors) during the *intervention period* that are necessary to represent a significant increase at the .001 level of statistical significance as compared to the *proportion* of like observations during the *baseline period*. The steps in using the table are as follows:

1. Identify the proportion of observations in the desired zone in the baseline in the left-hand column (divide number of specified baseline events by *total* number of baseline events). Use "conservative rule" as needed.
2. Identify the total number of observations in the intervention period in the top row of table. Use "conservative rule" as needed.
3. Compare the total number of specified observations in the intervention period with the number at the intersection of the correct column and row. If the observed number is equal to or greater than the number at the intersection, then the comparison is statistically significant at the .001 level.

Proportion of specified observations in the desired zone in the baseline period	\[Total Number of Observations in Intervention Period\] 4	6	8	10	12	14	16	18	20	24	28	32	36	40	44	48	52	56	60	64	68	72	76	80	84	88	92	96	100
.05	3	4	4	5	5	5	5	6	6	6	7	7	8	8	9	9	10	10	10	11	11	11	12	12	12	13	13	14	14
.10	4	5	5	6	6	7	7	8	8	9	10	10	12	12	12	13	14	14	15	16	16	17	18	18	19	19	20	21	21
1/8	4	5	6	6	7	7	8	8	9	10	11	12	12	13	14	15	16	17	17	18	19	20	20	21	22	23	23	24	25
.15	4	5	6	7	7	8	9	9	10	11	12	13	14	15	16	17	18	18	19	20	21	22	23	24	25	25	26	27	28
1/6	4	5	6	7	8	8	9	10	10	11	12	14	15	16	17	18	19	20	21	22	23	24	25	25	26	27	28	29	30
.20	—	6	7	7	8	9	10	10	11	12	14	15	16	17	19	20	21	22	23	24	26	27	28	29	30	31	32	33	34
.25	—	6	7	8	9	10	11	12	12	14	16	17	19	20	21	23	24	26	27	28	30	31	32	34	35	36	37	39	40
.30	—	6	8	9	10	11	12	13	14	15	17	19	21	22	24	26	27	29	30	32	34	35	37	38	40	41	43	44	46

p																														
1/3	—	—	—	8	9	10	11	12	13	14	16	18	20	22	24	26	27	29	31	33	34	36	38	39	41	43	44	46	48	49
.35	—	—	—	8	9	10	12	13	14	15	17	19	21	23	25	26	28	30	32	34	35	37	39	41	42	44	46	48	49	51
3/8	—	—	—	8	9	11	12	13	14	15	17	20	22	24	26	28	30	31	33	35	37	39	41	43	45	46	48	50	52	54
.40	—	—	—	8	10	11	12	13	15	16	18	21	22	25	27	29	31	33	35	37	39	41	43	45	47	49	51	52	54	56
.45	—	—	—	—	10	12	13	14	16	17	19	22	24	26	29	31	33	35	38	40	42	44	46	49	51	53	55	57	59	61
.50	—	—	—	—	10	12	13	15	17	18	20	24	26	28	31	33	36	38	40	43	45	48	50	52	55	57	59	62	64	66
.55	—	—	—	—	—	12	14	15	17	20	22	24	26	30	33	36	38	40	43	46	48	51	53	56	59	61	64	66	69	71
.60	—	—	—	—	—	—	14	16	18	20	22	25	27	31	34	38	40	43	45	48	51	54	57	59	62	65	68	70	73	76
5/8	—	—	—	—	—	—	—	16	18	20	23	26	29	32	35	38	41	44	47	50	52	55	58	61	64	67	70	72	75	78
.65	—	—	—	—	—	—	—	—	18	20	23	26	29	33	36	39	42	45	48	51	54	57	60	63	66	69	71	74	77	80
2/3	—	—	—	—	—	—	—	—	18	20	23	27	30	33	36	39	42	46	49	52	55	58	61	64	67	70	73	76	79	82
.70	—	—	—	—	—	—	—	—	—	20	24	27	31	34	37	40	44	47	50	53	56	60	63	66	69	72	75	78	81	84
.75	—	—	—	—	—	—	—	—	—	—	—	28	32	35	39	42	45	49	52	55	59	62	65	69	72	75	79	82	85	89
.80	—	—	—	—	—	—	—	—	—	—	—	—	32	36	40	43	47	50	54	58	61	65	68	72	75	79	82	85	89	92
5/6	—	—	—	—	—	—	—	—	—	—	—	—	—	—	40	44	48	51	55	59	62	66	70	73	77	80	84	88	91	95
.85	—	—	—	—	—	—	—	—	—	—	—	—	—	—	—	44	48	52	56	59	63	67	70	74	78	81	85	89	92	96
7/8	—	—	—	—	—	—	—	—	—	—	—	—	—	—	—	—	—	52	56	60	64	68	71	75	79	83	86	90	94	97
.90	—	—	—	—	—	—	—	—	—	—	—	—	—	—	—	—	—	—	—	—	—	—	72	76	80	84	88	91	95	99
.95	—	—	—	—	—	—	—	—	—	—	—	—	—	—	—	—	—	—	—	—	—	—	—	—	—	—	—	—	—	—

*Tables of the Cumulative Binomial Probability Distribution—By the staff of the Harvard Computational Laboratory, Harvard University Press, 1955. This table constructed under the direction of Dr. James Norton, Jr., Indiana University–Purdue University at Indianapolis, 1973.

(This table is reproduced by permission of the author and the publisher from the *Paradox of Helping: Introduction to the Philosophy of Scientific Practice* by Martin Bloom [New York: John Wiley and Sons, 1975].)

the number of *observations* of a specified type (e.g., desired behavior) during the intervention period that are necessary to represent a significant increase at the .05 level over the *proportion* during the *baseline period*. This means that to use the table you must find, first, in the left-hand column, the proportion of observations of specified events during the baseline period that are in a desired zone, and second, in the row at the top of the table, the total number of observations in the *intervention period*. (We explain this in more detail later, especially about how you construct a "desired zone.") Then, third, by looking at the cell entry at the intersection of these two terms, you have the statistical answer. All three tables follow the same instructions and are constructed the same way; the only differences are the level of significance.

A given cell entry—say, the intersection of proportion .30 and number 36, which is 16—means that that number or higher numbers (17, 18, 19 . . .) would be adequate to represent a statistically significant change at the .05 level for Table 19.2. If the intervention period provides evidence that 16 or more observations of the target event were in a desired zone, then that would be statistically significant under the conditions specified (proportion equals .30 in the baseline with 36 observations during the intervention period). Each different combination of proportion and number has a different cell entry to specify how many such observations are needed for statistically significant results. Intersections where there are no numbers (indicated by a horizontal hatch mark) indicate that we don't have enough information to determine statistical significance; we need to continue collecting data (the proportion of observations in the desired zone in the baseline was already too high given a relatively low number of intervention points).

The use of these tables with the proportion/frequency approach to statistical significance that we describe in Chapter 22 also offers some degree of control for the potential problem of varying length of baseline and intervention periods. The tables require a higher number of observations in the "desired zone" as the number of intervention points increase, but along the lines of our discussion on power, the *percentage* of observations in the desired

zone needed to achieve significance actually decreases.

Data Showing Apparent Improvement. At this point we must distinguish between two broad classes of events, one in which the intervention data seem to be moving in a desired direction (improvement) and another in which the intervention data seem to be moving in an undesired direction (deterioration). Obviously, either may happen in practice situations, and our analysis must be able to deal with both. Let's discuss the improvement situation. The top row of the tables indicates the total number of observations in the given intervention period. Note that not all numbers are presented in the tables. When you have a number that is not listed in the tables, we recommend that you use the next *higher* number. This recommendation makes it harder to obtain statistical significance, so if statistical significance is achieved with the higher number, then it would have been achieved with a lower number as well. We call this the *conservative rule*. Since analysis of single-system design data generally is approximate, it appears safer to use a more conservative estimation of statistical significance. Let's look at a specific example.

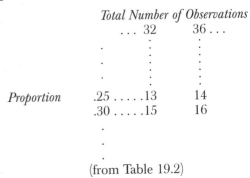

	Total Number of Observations	
	. . . 32	36 . . .
	.	.
	.	.
	.	.
	.	.
Proportion	.25 13	14
	.30 15	16
	.	
	.	
	.	

(from Table 19.2)

Suppose that you have intervened on 33 occasions and have determined that the baseline proportion of observations in the desired zone is rounded off to 26%, or .26. (We describe in detail how to construct desired zones and determine what this proportion is in Chapter 22 in the context of the proportion/frequency approach. Basically, it simply involves determining whether the goal is for the target event to increase or decrease to establish which direction is "desired," drawing a boundary line, which extends through the intervention period, and then comparing the number of baseline observations in that desired zone with the total number of baseline observations to determine the proportion of observations in the desired zone in the baseline period.) Suppose further that 14 of the observations in the intervention period were in the desired zone (which can be defined in different ways by different analytic procedures, as we see shortly in Chapters 20, 21, and 22). Is this set of events a statistically likely or unlikely state of affairs? The conservative rule must be applied to both the number of interventions used (since Table 19.2 doesn't show 33 units) and to the proportion of specified baseline events (since Table 19.2 doesn't show .26 either). Let's say that you detect some general trend toward improvement in the client's behavior. Therefore, you use the next higher number and proportion in order to make a conservative estimate of what the actual number and proportion would show with regard to this situation. Let's look closely at adjacent numbers and proportions to see why this may be important. Had we used 32 rather than 36 as our number in the intervention period, and .25 rather than .30 as our baseline proportion, we could have claimed a statistically significant difference between baseline and intervention with fewer observations in the desired zone (13 rather than 16). Likewise, had we used either a lower proportion or a lower number rather than higher ones, we still could have claimed statistical significance with fewer interventions in the desired zone.

Reading the Table. Now it's time to read the table for the answer to our question: Is the observed change statistically significant? Recall that we said that you had observed 14 occasions when the client's behavior was in the desired zone during intervention, and that we were using the conservative rule, adjusting the baseline proportion to .30 and the number of observations during intervention to 36. Table 19.2 shows that 16 observations (the cell where the proportion of .30 and the number of observations of 36 intersect) of the specified (desired) type are needed for statistical significance. Since you obtained only 14, it's clear that there

is not statistical significance at the .05 level. However, if you had 60 observations in the intervention period, using the .30 proportion in the baseline, you would have needed 25 observations in the desired zone for the data to be statistically significant. Twenty-five obviously is more than the 16 required with 36 observations, but 25 out of 60 is a lower *percentage* than 16 out of 36; this is how power works.

Let's continue the example and imagine that you had observed 19 instances of desired behavior in the intervention period (with the same adjusted proportion of .30 and the adjusted number 36). According to Table 19.2 this is statistically significant at the .05 level. However, this also means that we could look further at the other tables to see whether it's significant at other levels as well (although, technically, one should specify the significance level in advance and stop there if it is achieved). Looking at the same adjusted number and proportion in Table 19.3 we find that 18 occurrences are needed for statistical significance at the .01 level, so the data are significant at this level. However, Table 19.4 shows that under these same conditions, 21 events are needed in the desired zone in the intervention period for significance at the .001 level, so we did not succeed in attaining statistical significance at the .001 level. Thus, in our example we would say that the observed client outcomes reached the .01 level of statistical significance.

Data Showing Apparent Deterioration. We must also be on the lookout for negative changes or deterioration. The same basic ideas can be used for deterioration as well. However, you can identify the events in this case in an *undesired* zone and complete the analysis as before. To continue our first example, suppose 14 out of 33 observations were in the desired zone in the intervention period with a baseline proportion of observations of .30 (as above). We determined earlier that this number did not demonstrate statistically significant improvement. We noted that you subjectively judged that there was a trend in a positive direction. However, since there was a large number of observations in the *undesired* zone in the intervention period, you also should check for significant deterioration.

There are 19 times out of 33 interventions when events fell into the undesired zone. To interpret these possibly deteriorating findings conservatively, you should go to the next *smaller* number and proportion, thus making it easier to indicate that deterioration occurred. The conservative rule is applied in this way (using the next smaller number and proportion) because of ethical concerns over deterioration and the need to be especially vigilant in detecting it. Let's illustrate this point.

In our example of 33 interventions with a proportion of .30 in the desired zone in the baseline (we used the conservative rule to raise this from the actual .26), we can determine the proportion of *undesired* baseline observations by simply subtracting the proportion of observations in the desired zone in the baseline (originally .26) from 1.00; this leaves us with a baseline proportion of .74 in the undesired zone. (Or you simply could count the number of baseline observations in the undesired zone and divide by the total number of baseline observations.) Then, in Table 19.2, we would look at the number 32 and the proportion .70 to locate the lowest number indicating possible deterioration. That intersection shows 28, meaning 28 or more observations in the undesired zone would indicate statistically significant deterioration. Since only 19 such events fell in the undesired zone in our example, it's not statistically significant deterioration. Of course, a substantial number of observations in the undesired zone–even when they are not *statistically* significant–raises serious questions, sufficient to call for a review of the intervention being used.

However, suppose that the number of observations in the undesired zone of the intervention period in this example was 28. How would we read the table for assessing the statistical significance of deterioration? Strictly speaking, these tables are constructed for testing a one-directional hypothesis (whether there is improvement in the target event). The .05 level of significance refers to findings related only to improvement. We can use the same tables to assess deterioration as well, but we have to double the .05 level to determine deterioration. The .05 table becomes .10, .01 becomes .02, and .001 becomes .002. Thus, when a statistically significant *deterioration* is found on the .05-level table, we must assume that the table is being used for testing a two-tailed, nondirectional hypothesis, as we discussed previously, and assign the probability of .10 as indicating how likely it is that deterioration occurred by chance alone. That is to say, we double the probability level of a given table when we indicate that statistically significant deterioration has been achieved. Thus, this .10 level might be taken as tentative evidence of deterioration.

Computing Probabilities with SINGWIN

Here's how to use SINGWIN to compute probabilities.

1. Start SINGWIN (see "Starting SING-WIN" in the SINGWIN User's Guide, Chapter 23).

2. Follow the steps outlined in the section entitled "Computing a Proportion/Frequency Approach," and enter the following: # Baseline Points = 12; # Baseline Successes = 2; # of Intervention Points = 12; # of Intervention Successes = 5.

SUMMARY

In this chapter we've presented some distinctions that are important in the analysis of data. We've explained effort (the amount of work performed), effectiveness (the results of the work), and efficiency (the comparison of results and efforts expended). These terms can help you understand that accountability is not simply a matter of raising effectiveness levels; accountability must also exhibit an optimal ratio of effort expended for the effectiveness obtained.

We also discussed practical, statistical, and theoretical significance. The first refers to social and personal criteria of acceptable behaviors in various social settings, the second relates to mathematical rules, and the third involves theoretical expectations. Sometimes they coincide, but not necessarily; they are independent concepts of equal importance for scientific practice. However, we want you to understand the implications of the several combinations of significance that we discussed early in this chapter.

We presented guidelines for determining the number of observations in a phase and for determining when to change an intervention. We also discussed the use of follow-ups in single-system designs, suggesting that follow-ups be used to obtain vital information on the lasting quality of your services.

We introduced the issue of autocorrelation, noting that it can be a very serious problem for rigorous evaluation. We showed how to test for the presence of autocorrelated data, and we discussed what to do about it. The latter included a presentation on how to transform auto-correlated data into data that are usable by the several analytic techniques to which we turn in succeeding chapters. We showed how to test for autocorrelation and how to transform autocorrelated data using simple hand computations and using an easy-to-use personal computer program, SINGWIN, that comes with this book. Finally, we presented a discussion of probability tables that can be used with some analytic procedures, and we showed how SINGWIN could be used in place of these tables if you prefer.

VISUAL ANALYSIS OF SINGLE-SYSTEM DESIGN DATA

PURPOSE: This chapter describes the most basic method of analyzing data from single-system designs: visual inspection of patterns in the data. After presenting some definitions of visual patterns, we'll describe the major patterns and their implications for evaluation as well as the limitations of visual inspection. ■

Introduction   **Interpreting Ambiguous Patterns**
Definition of Terms   Guidelines for Interpretation
Basic Patterns and Implications   **Problems of Visual Inspection**
Interpreting Several Patterns Simultaneously   **Creating a Chart with SINGWIN**
Visual Inspection of Raw Data   **Summary**

INTRODUCTION

This chapter discusses the visual analysis of single-system design data–simply looking at the data and finding discontinuities and other patterns that aid in the interpretation of the results. This method is notably flexible and easy to use, and it draws its major strength from the pictorial nature of the data and the practical considerations related to them. For example, suppose that an AIDS patient took less than 10% of his daily requirement of the drug AZT before intervention during a baseline period, and then 100% during implementation of an intervention designed to increase compliance. The graphed results would provide strong visual evidence for improvement in compliance with the AZT regimen. Such "common sense" analysis could be treated mathematically, and

very likely these results would indicate a statistically significant difference between baseline and intervention phases. But if the results are so obvious from visual inspection, why go further? As we'll see, there are circumstances that lead to problems with visual analysis, and under these circumstances, the statistical approaches that are discussed in the next two chapters can prove useful. However, a careful visual inspection of the data should be a starting point for all of the other methods of analysis discussed in Part IV.

DEFINITION OF TERMS

There are several properties of data appearing in graphs that require careful definition. Although the ideas are simple, many terms have been used (sometimes in conflicting ways) to describe them. Let's begin by looking at a graph that presents data as simply as possible. Figure 20.1 shows a set of data as if they fell along straight lines. Of course, sometimes data do, in fact, appear along a straight line, but most of the time in real practice the data will vary. To view the data in a simple form, we draw a horizontal line through a set of data that best represents their average magnitude; we call this the mean line. The mean is computed by adding all of the values, and dividing this total by the number of data points. (We return shortly to data that vary, and in Chapter 21 we'll show you how to compute another type of average, the median.)

First look at the mean line in the baseline period of Figure 20.1a. The first property of graphed data to be considered is *level*, which refers to the magnitude of the variable as indicated by the data at any point. When the data are increasing or decreasing, as in Figure 20.1b during the intervention period, the final magnitude or level is determined at the point at which the intervention ends. (However, one could examine the magnitude of the data at any point in the baseline or intervention phase to determine the level of the data at that point.) A *change in level* between the baseline and the intervention phase is called a *discontinuity*. A major discontinuity (major change in level between baseline and intervention phases) is an important indicator of change in the target, and is consistent with the hypothesis that the

intervention may have produced that change. These differences in levels are indicated in Figure 20.1a and b by arrows.

A second property of graphed data concerns *stability,* defined as clear predictability from a prior period to a later one (note, however, that the literature often refers to stable data only as flat data; see Chapter 12 regarding baselines). Figure 20.2 provides some illustrations of this. Figure 20.2a shows a mean line that is projected (by a dashed line) into the intervention period. Figure 20.2b shows a trend line; even though it's increasing in magnitude, it's still predictable. If the baseline data cannot be represented adequately by a line–for example, if baseline data are highly irregular– then the baseline is not stable, because no clear prediction can be made as to the direction that intervention data will take.

A third property of graphed data concerns *trends* in the data–that is, directionality of the data. Data may show an increasing trend, a decreasing trend, no trend (flat data), or a pattern that varies irregularly. Furthermore, trends can occur both within a given phase (sometimes called *slope*) or across phases (sometimes called *drift*). Figure 20.3 illustrates different patterns of trends. Note that for a trend across phases to exist, the slope within each phase must be in the same direction as in Figure 20.3d, whether or not the angle of the slope is the same.

A fourth property of graphed data concerns whether there's *improvement, deterioration,* or *no change* from one phase to the next. Depending

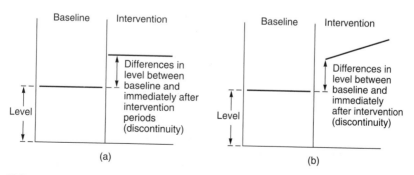

FIGURE 20.1   Illustration of levels of data and differences between levels in baseline and intervention periods.

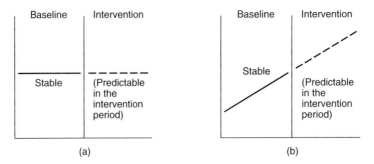

FIGURE 20.2 Illustrations of stability of data between baseline and intervention periods.

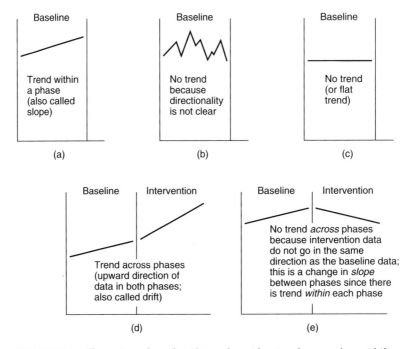

FIGURE 20.3 Illustrations of trends within a phase (slope) and across phases (drift).

on how the target problem is defined–for example, if more of the target is desirable or if less of the target is desirable–trend and level combine to indicate improvement or deterioration. Figure 20.4 illustrates this property.

Figure 20.4a and b show exactly the same pattern of data, but the definition of desired and undesired levels of behavior are reversed, producing the overall pattern of improvement and deterioration, respectively. Figure 20.4c shows a situation in which some middle zone is desired, such as a client trying to maintain a desired weight level; again, the definition of improvement depends on the definition of target events. Figure 20.4d illustrates yet another variation in which some minimum level of acceptable performance is defined, such as in weight requirements for making a wrestling team. The direction of data in itself doesn't define improvement or deterioration; it's the nature of

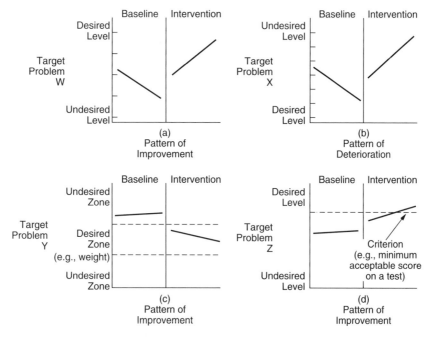

FIGURE 20.4   Illustrations of patterns of improvements and of deterioration, depending on defined levels or zones of desired events.

the target that generates these labels. This is where client and societal values are directly related to the evaluation of practice outcomes.

BASIC PATTERNS AND IMPLICATIONS

Now we can construct a figure that shows basic, but simplified, patterns in single-system design data from which change–improvement or deterioration–can be inferred. Figure 20.5 presents nine basic patterns, each with three subtypes (X, Y, and Z)–27 patterns in all–that will illustrate the large bulk of data patterns that you are likely to encounter. All of the data are simplified as straight-line data in order to clarify the patterns and their implications. The top three patterns assume that the baseline data are flat and at a midlevel of magnitude. (Obviously, other levels could be used, but the same patterns would be present.) The middle three patterns involve an increasing baseline, while the bottom three patterns show a decreasing baseline.

In a like manner we've assumed that intervention periods show data that are either increasing (X), staying the same (Y), or decreasing (Z). In this way we can economically present 27 combinations of baseline and intervention events. More important, we can suggest the predominant interpretation of each of the various patterns of data. Figure 20.5 has been constructed by varying level, discontinuities (changes in level between phases), trends within a phase (slope), and trends across phases (drift). In order to emphasize whether one, two, or three changes are occurring, we indicate the interpretation by corresponding degrees–for example, "improvement," "strong improvement," or "very strong improvement." Note also that we've arbitrarily designated (by pluses and minuses on the vertical axis) "up" as improvement and "down" as deterioration.

Figures 20.5a, b, and c begin with a flat baseline, and then, depending on whether there's a change in level and a change in the trend between phases, they indicate degrees of improvement or deterioration. Also noted are

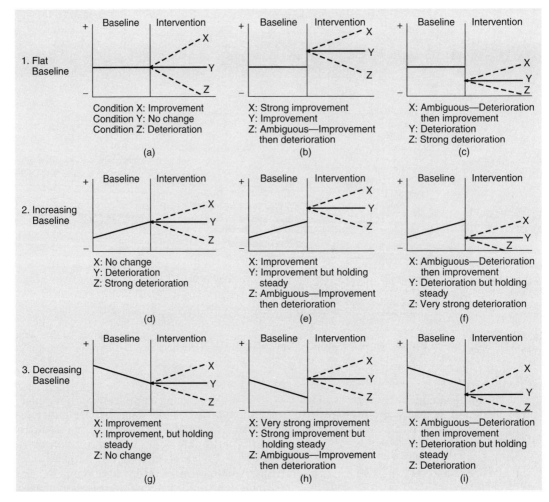

FIGURE 20.5 Basic patterns in data from simplified single-system designs. (This figure assumes the desired level or zone is up as indicated by +.)

some ambiguous situations in which, after an initial improvement (based on a change in level), the data begin to show deterioration (see Figure 20.5b, condition Z); in the same manner, after an initial deterioration in the target the data begin to change in the direction of improvement (as in Figure 20.5c, condition X), which is another ambiguous situation. In ambiguous situations we suggest you continue the intervention phase (when conditions are improving) if possible to see whether the trend continues. However, when an initial improvement shows signs of deteriorating, you should act before the deterioration gets out of hand.

This could involve changing the intervention or increasing the intensity of the current intervention.

Figures 20.5d, e, and f begin with an increasing slope during baseline. Assuming that the high end of the vertical axis represents a desired level of events, then changes that take place between baseline and intervention must include consideration of the trend as well as the level. The condition Y in these three patterns is a flat line and represents an improvement or deterioration (depending on baseline conditions) that is holding steady. That is, after the initial change from baseline to intervention there's no slope. For some conditions, such as in work with a terminally ill person, "holding one's own" (a flat line) may be a major accomplishment. However, in other cases there's an element of ambiguity in this steady state that may require you to reconsider whether the intervention is powerful enough at this time.

In Figure 20.5d, condition X, there's an interesting point to be made: Even though there's a trend that continues in a desired direction from the baseline and through the intervention period (drift), the general pattern is one of no change, since that same increasing pattern was present during the baseline period. It's only when, in addition to the drift, there's a change in level, or in the *angle* of the slope (clearly increasing or decreasing in the intervention period), that such a pattern becomes an improvement or a deterioration, depending on baseline circumstances.

In the last set of three patterns, Figures 20.5g, h, and i, the baseline exhibits a decreasing or worsening trend. Thus, any change toward improvement or holding steady may qualify as a desired change if the level also holds steady or improves. Very strong improvement is possible under the terms described in Figure 20.5h, condition X, just as very strong deterioration is possible in Figure 20.5f, condition Z. Both of these patterns involve changes in level and slope.

There are many other aspects of graphs that could be used as aids in interpretation, but if we were to illustrate every one, we would need to present hundreds of patterns, and that would defeat the purpose of this chapter. However, we'll mention some other variations in data that may have an impact on interpretation. First, consider the starting level of the baseline data. Under certain conditions, such as when using a depression scale, a very high starting score limits the amount of upward change. In this case an upward change would be a negative change or signify deterioration because the higher the score, the more depressed the person could be said to be.

On the other hand, consider the timing of the changes in intervention. Either the target events change immediately after the intervention, or they change gradually after some delay as illustrated in Figure 20.6. There may be a period of time during which the client is trained to perform the intervention, such as training in free association or in thought stopping. Little change would be expected during the training part of intervention; however, you may be "counting" this time in evaluating the intervention. As discussed in Chapter 11, our advice is to continue monitoring the intervention after the training, or to make the training phase separate.

Another pattern of data that sometimes may be important concerns the stability of the observed change. For example, there may be an initial impact, perhaps due to the novelty of the intervention (the "honeymoon" period), but once the intervention becomes routine, the impact returns to the original level, as illustrated in Figure 20.7. Stopping the intervention too soon would have missed this important point. You would be wise to take action soon after an initially successful intervention begins to deteriorate. This situation might call for another intervention or a stronger intensity of the first intervention.

By using averages portrayed as mean or trend lines in baseline and intervention, we

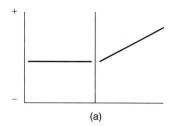

(a)

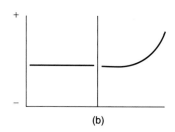

(b)

FIGURE 20.6   Illustrations of immediate (a) and delayed (b) effects of intervention.

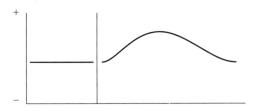

FIGURE 20.7   Illustration of an unstable data change.

hide another obvious characteristic of graphs that should be considered—*variability* in data. In baselines, stability usually refers to data falling within a relatively narrow, predictable range. The more variability in baseline data, as illustrated in Figure 20.8b, the more caution you must use in interpreting changes during intervention. More control was exhibited over the target problem in Figure 20.8b than in Figure 20.8a relative to the starting conditions at their baselines, but it's clear that the baseline in Figure 20.8b was less stable.

A final pattern of data that might emerge is a *cycle*. Identification of such cycles can provide clues concerning the origins of problems, which might in turn suggest interventions. For example, there might be changes in a target associated with a particular day of the week (e.g., "blue Mondays," caused by starting the work week), time of the month (e.g., shortage of money and resulting tensions prior to receiving monthly checks), or time of the year (e.g., seasonal affective disorders). Similarly, there might be changes in a target associated with holidays, or personal anniversaries. Therefore, in addition to labeling time periods with sequential numbers, it also can

be useful to label them with days of the week and dates.

Interpreting Several Patterns Simultaneously

There are many times when you may be called upon to interpret the patterns of more than one graph at the same time. Just think about any multiple target design as only one example. We would like to offer some introductory ideas on this topic.

There are three general patterns of simultaneous graphing that can be used to make overall sense of changes in the several targets you are addressing:

1. *Alignments* exist when all of the graphs that are being considered together have essentially the same pattern of improvement, no change, or deterioration. Obviously, we are interested in improvement, but simultaneous patterns of no change or deterioration also inform you as to needed changes in intervention, as we shall see. We suggest this notation: + + +, 000, and − − − to indicate such alignment among three graphs for a single client/system, where the pluses indicate improvement, the zeroes no change, and the minuses deterioration.

2. *Dominance* exists when a majority of the graphs being considered together show a common pattern, either of improvement, no change, or deterioration. These would be represented as + + 0, + + −, 0 0 +,

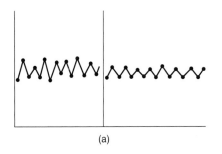

(a)

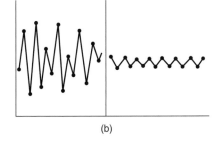

(b)

FIGURE 20.8   Illustrations of variability in data.

$0\ 0-,\ --+,\ --0.$ (When four or even numbers of graphs are used, this principle can be adapted in terms of the importance of the respective targets, as discussed below.)

3. *Disagreement* would exist when no pattern among graphs appears. These would be represented as $+0-$. (Again, adaptation to this principle has to be made for even numbers of graphs.)

Ordinarily, we seek alignment in improvements among however many graphs are being monitored simultaneously. However, there are exceptions, such as being content with the most optimal expected pattern of no change in a terminally ill patient, or a steady state of positive functioning on targets we are tracking but don't want to change. (The latter would constitute a check for "symptom substitution" phenomena.)

When we get a pattern of dominance, we have to introduce another element into this discussion, the relative importance of each target. If one target is of overwhelming importance, then this weighting may be more important than alignment or dominance on other targets. This is a subjective weighting and should be made before considering the patterns of relationship among graphs. When two out of three are important, and the third less so, then there is still a dominant trend. When the three are such that two targets are still of less importance than the strong third target, then we have in effect a pattern of disagreement.

Another consideration is the internal pattern. The $+$, 0, and $-$ patterns permit us to distinguish findings that are "one step" or "two steps" discrepant. The pattern $++0$ shows two positives and one neutral result, one step apart, while the pattern $++-$ shows two positives and one negative result, two steps apart in the sense of the meaning of the results. (To clarify "two steps apart," visualize $+$ as 3, 0 as 2, and $-$ as 1. Therefore, $++-$ can be seen as two steps apart.) The two-step pattern $++-$ suggests that the negative graph may not be conceptually or practically related to events in the two positive graphs, and the entire service plan should be reconsidered. In general, any two-

step discrepancy suggests reconsideration of the overall plan.

When these one- or two-step arrangements are combined with weightings, we suggest that the important successful graphs become the central focus of revised practice plans, and new targets or interventions be considered. The successful graphs become a known entity, and new service ideas can be introduced (new targets and methods) with reference to building on this success, expanding it into new aspects of the client situation.

To illustrate these simultaneous patterns, let's reconsider Figure 20.5. Look at the middle column of graphs b, e, and h. The three Xs on these graphs each show improvement over baseline, and would be indicated as $+++$ for this discussion of simultaneous analysis of data. Likewise, the three Ys show improvement, while the Zs end in a deteriorating pattern as compared with baseline. Thus the Zs would be indicated as $---$.

Next, consider the left column graphs a, d, and g, with reference to the X, Y, and Z patterns. (a)X, (d)Y, and (g)Z show positive change, deterioration, and no change. If these three graphs represented one client's situation, it would indicate disagreement, and would suggest the need for reconsideration of the service plan (possibly using the one successful graph as the anchoring point for building a new approach to intervention).

In general, to identify and comprehend the configuration of outcomes on multiple targets, you must reduce each graph to its simplest pattern (such as those indicated by straight lines on Figure 20.5). If there are major differences in the importance or weighting of each target, include this in how you think about patterns of results. Assuming relatively equally important targets, then use the notation for alignment, dominance, or disagreement, and make the next service plans accordingly.

Another way of thinking about analyzing the results of several graphs simultaneously is to simplify several patterns by combining them. In some areas of evaluation, this, in a sense, is already done for you. For example, a standardized scale usually combines items tapping into a common domain. These items are analyzed as being statistically related to each other to justify being put into a single scale. In a similar way, we have suggested choosing targets from one client/system, representing important domains of that system. Each target that is graphed may be interpreted in its own right. But we have stressed that it is the combination of targets that represents the whole client/system. There are no standard ways to form these combinations of targets. Some designs, such as the multiple baseline design, make the decision for you in showing interrelationships. But when multiple targets are used, we are left with the dilemma of how to put all of the information we gather together: Overall, how well is this client/system progressing?

One way to combine targeted materials is simply to add them together, as in the following student case situation. A 7-year-old child was having serious problems at home with his mother and stepfather. He refused to do chores or be cooperative in any way. At school, he also was not completing assigned tasks, and he was throwing tantrums at the slightest provocation. The practitioner developed interventions with these various targeted behaviors, and chose to use a 5-point scale with each. In order to provide feedback for the child (and parents), the student used individual charts but presented the family with a composite chart—the simple sum of the individual graphs. There was some progress on two of the three graphs, but less on the third. But the simple additive graph showed overall success, and served to encourage the child to gain control over his behavior. The practitioner thought that this sim-plified graph succeeded in conveying important information to the clients that discussions of specific, individual charts could not do.

VISUAL INSPECTION OF RAW DATA

The eye tends to complete visual gestalts. That is, there's a tendency to find patterns among objects appearing in the same visual space. For example, the headlights, grill, and bumper on some cars appear to be smiling faces, and moving clouds appear to take the shape of animals.

Batches of data points on evaluation graphs also often appear to be taking a particular direction, such as upward or steady. In the preceding discussion we simplified the set of data points into straight lines, some horizontal, and others with upward or downward trend. When we introduced data in Figure 20.8, their variability made them somewhat harder to interpret, especially if we hadn't drawn lines between adjacent points. Even so, it's sometimes difficult to find the dominant direction of a set of data points.

For example, in Figure 20.9 both graphs have the same mean line (indicated by the horizontal dashed lines) but differences in variability. In order to convey this difference in variability, often it's better to draw and connect the actual data points instead of drawing straight lines to indicate means or trends.

When there is an increasing or decreasing trend in the data, a mean (horizontal) line will be misleading, as illustrated in Figure 20.10a.

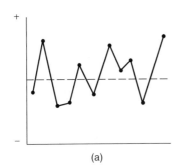

(a)

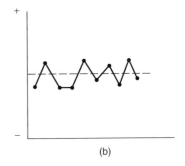

(b)

FIGURE 20.9   Illustrations of mean lines drawn on baseline data that differ in variability.

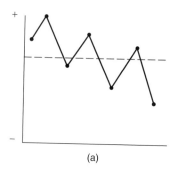
(a)

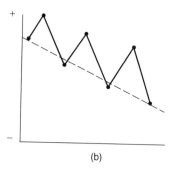
(b)

FIGURE 20.10   Illustrations of a mean line (a) and a trend line (b) with the same target event data.

Rather, what is needed is a line that follows the general trend of the data themselves as illustrated in Figure 20.10b. In Chapter 21 we describe different ways to construct trend lines.

Another way in which sets of data are viewed is by looking for typical patterns. For example, in Figure 20.11 a set of data has been collected during one period of time, and although these data are quite variable, they still represent the levels of behavior that the client can exhibit. Therefore, we can ask, what is typical about this set of events? "Typical" events can be defined in different ways. For example, one way would be as data varying within some set distance around the mean. Since one standard deviation above and below the mean in a normal curve contains about two-thirds of all the data falling under that curve, we could define as typical an area in which two-thirds of the data points fall, and then areas above and below that line as either desired or undesired, depending on the nature of the target. This approach is used with the proportion/frequency statistic, described in Chapter 22. Or, to be even more rigorous, we could establish a broader zone, say plus or minus three standard deviations, which would encompass some 99.7% of all scores. Scores outside of that zone, then, could be seen as (extremely) desired or undesired (as with the 3-standard deviation band approach discussed in Chapter 22). The important point about typical events is that

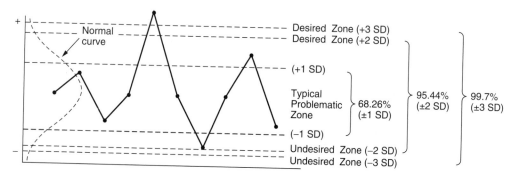

FIGURE 20.11   Illustration of data points in which the "typical" pattern has been indicated by the pair of dashed lines representing an approximation of a zone one standard deviation above and below the mean of these data. A normal curve is indicated by a dotted curve to show the "typical" or middle zone where about two-thirds of the data are likely to fall (i.e., ± 1 SD). The external dashed lines equal a rarer situation, ± 3 SD (99.7% of the data), representing the desired and undesired zones.

you would expect them to continue in their typical pattern over time unless something intervenes to change them, such as an intervention program.

INTERPRETING AMBIGUOUS PATTERNS

If only the world of visual analysis of patterns presented in Figure 20.5 were as clear as we have depicted it. In that figure, we illustrated some 27 different patterns of data, most of which can result in relatively clear conclusions about changes between baseline and intervention periods.

But, as with our presentation of basic designs in Part III, these patterns essentially are ideal types, presented to show you optimally clear and basic patterns to help you understand key characteristics of single-system design data.

But what is intended as optimally clear and basic for a textbook does not necessarily always reflect real-life practice. In fact, if you look closely at Figure 20.5, you will see several patterns that we have called *ambiguous*. It is an unfortunate, but frequently true, aspect of practice that the data patterns produced in real-life single-system evaluations often are ambiguous, and the resulting implications from such a visual analysis are often unclear (see also Rubin & Knox, 1996, for a discussion of this problem).

This all-too-common result of ambiguous patterns is one of the reasons we recommend supplementing your visual analysis with statistical analysis. Ambiguous and/or wildly fluctuating patterns of data can be transformed, if need be, as we described in Chapter 19, so that underlying patterns can be more clearly revealed. Moreover, even when the patterns are not wildly fluctuating so that transformations are not necessary, the use of the statistics we recommend in the next two chapters can provide clear guidelines for making decisions in a number of ways, from when to change interventions to evaluations of overall effectiveness.

But the use of statistics to some extent still does not directly address the issue of finding

the best use and interpretation of an ambiguous data pattern.

Figure 20.12 presents several ambiguous patterns, building on those presented in Figure 20.5. In Figure 20.12a, we see a wildly fluctuating baseline leading to a problem in understanding the meaning and consistency of the targeted event as well as in knowing when to stop the baseline and move to the intervention period.

Figure 20.12b illustrates the ambiguous pattern of apparent initial improvement followed by deterioration, leading to the problem of trying to recapture that initial improvement while not wanting to terminate while the target event is deteriorating. The opposite problem is illustrated in Figure 20.12c, deterioration then improvement, leaving the practitioner to wonder whether the improvement is temporary or a possible result of concomitant variation with factors other than the intervention.

Figures 20.12d and e show multiple variations in the intervention phase leading to ambiguous patterns. In Figure d, there is a pattern of improvement then deterioration then improvement while Figure e shows the reverse pattern, deterioration then improvement then deterioration. Both sets of patterns leave the practitioner wondering whether a termination date is possible, whether changes are only temporary, and how to assess the real meaning of the changes.

Finally, an all-too-common pattern in real practice is the one portrayed in Figure 20.12f, wildly fluctuating data in the intervention period, to the point that the practitioner cannot make an informed judgment one way or another.

Guidelines for Interpretation

In many places in this book, we've mentioned the fact that some of the procedures associated with single-system design evaluations are approximate, that is, the best we can do under the complicated circumstances of practice, but often less than perfection. There are few situations of single-system design evaluation, though, where the term "approximate" rings more true than when the data pattern and,

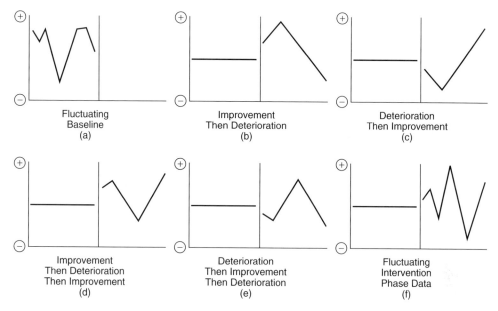

FIGURE 20.12   Examples of ambiguous data patterns.

hence, the visual analysis, is ambiguous. So our first, admittedly less than satisfactory, guideline for dealing with an ambiguous pattern is this: Do the best you can. We've discussed this principle of utility elsewhere in the book; in this context, we mean to try to understand even small patterns–or trends–in the data; consider concomitant variation or events in the life of the client or client/system outside of the intervention as possible explanations for ambiguous patterns; and attempt to piece together all the evidence as systematically as possible.

Utility also implies added discussions with the client(s) about what the data mean and working together on what seems to be working and what doesn't. The client may have ideas about what is going on that may clarify ambiguous results. Indeed, variability might be due to inconsistencies in service or inconsistencies in how a client completes homework assignments. This effort to enhance communication will give the client a closer connection to, and sense of control over, the entire intervention process; this also is good practice for self-maintenance later.

Second, when the pattern is ambiguous and the potential decision you have to make on the basis of those data is particularly crucial, you might want to consider extending the phase with the ambiguous pattern to achieve more stable results, as we suggested in Chapter 12 with regard to unstable baselines. Of course, we recognize that some practice situations don't allow an extension of time, but other situations may permit a trade-off between the time available and the need to have a clearer pattern of results.

Third, with a consistently ambiguous data pattern, you might want to consider changing your intervention to see whether that change will produce a clearer, and, one hopes, positive, pattern.

Fourth, when ambiguous patterns are present, we suggest you pay even more attention than you might otherwise to issues of practical significance that we described in the previous chapter. In this context, consultations with the client and relevant others can help you make a decision that may cut through the ambiguous pattern to get at the heart of the matter: Are the changes meaningful to the people affected?

Fifth, as we discussed in Chapter 10, we urge you to use more than one measure. Ambiguous patterns on the charted measures suggest a perfect reason for use of more than one measure: The additional measure(s) may reveal a pattern of changes that is clearer than the one you charted. Thus, a synthesis of results from several measures may produce a clearer pattern and allow greater confidence in your decision to continue with the same intervention, to change intervention, or to begin termination procedures.

Sixth, we discussed in Chapter 2 some of the consequences of the way measures are used. Well, these consequences could include ambiguous data patterns. For example, inconsistencies in how measurements are taken (when, how, and where measurements are collected, as well as who collected the measurements) could produce considerable variability in the data resulting in ambiguous patterns. Further, variability that leads to ambiguous patterns could result from using an unreliable measure, even if it is used consistently.

Seventh, you would also want to consider what we described in the previous chapter as theoretical significance. There may be sufficient information in the body of knowledge you used to inform your practice selections to provide some hypotheses as to what the ambiguous patterns might mean, or even as to whether you might expect such an ambiguous result to be a predictable phase of the intervention. For example, a key part of treatment of problems associated with borderline personality from a psychodynamic perspective is setting limits (Corcoran & Keeper, 1992). It follows then that a persistent problem in therapy would be some gains followed by a testing of those limits and temporary regression. Thus, the data would show an ambiguous pattern that actually involves the predictable ups and downs of the therapeutic process.

And finally, of course, as we mentioned earlier in this section, ambiguous data patterns provide an optimal reason for adding a statistical procedure to your overall analysis of change.

Individually, and as a package, these several suggestions can help you overcome a great deal of the interpretation difficulties that could result from ambiguous data patterns. But ambiguity isn't the only problem that could occur in visual analysis. In the following section, we describe several additional problems in visual analysis, whether or not the pattern is ambiguous.

PROBLEMS OF VISUAL INSPECTION

Any graphic method depends on the care with which data points are graphed. Therefore, we recommend that graph paper (or, if possible, computer-generated graphs, as illustrated with the CASS program in Chapters 4 and 7) and SINGWIN in this part of the book be used to aid evaluation, not only for keeping straight which columns and rows are to be used for a given target event, but also for comparing data across several target events at the same time. Even with graph paper, though, there are problems in interpreting visual representations of data (e.g., DeProspero & Cohen, 1979; Gibson & Ottenbacher, 1988; Jones, Vaught, & Weinrott, 1978; Matyas & Greenwood, 1990).

One problem relates to how data are represented on graphs. Consider Figures 20.13a and b in which the same data are presented with different intervals on the vertical and horizontal axes. In Figure 20.13a the sharp valleys and peaks don't suggest that stable behaviors have been achieved during baseline; they also make interpretation of intervention data difficult. However, in Figure 20.13b the softened curves produced by using larger intervals with exactly the same data disguise these differences. Which graph is accurate? They are both accurate but for different purposes. If you wish to show the minute variations in behavior, then small intervals are preferable both on the vertical axis and on the horizontal axis (the time line). When large variations in behavior are expected, larger intervals may be useful to present the data in perspective. You should try to keep the intervals on both axes approximately the same so that no distortions are artificially produced. Imagine the distortions in presentation if the intervals on the horizontal axis in

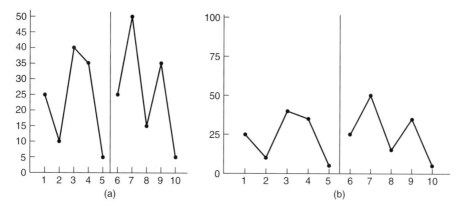

FIGURE 20.13 Illustrations of the same data points presented on charts with different intervals showing the exaggerated or softened effect that charting alone will produce.

Figure 20.13a were used with the intervals on the vertical axis in Figure 20.13b.

Autocorrelation, as discussed in Chapter 19, is another potential problem in the visual analysis of graphed data. Autocorrelation can bias visual judgments in the same way it can bias judgments based on conventional statistical tests (Gorsuch, 1983; Jones et al., 1978; Matyas & Greenwood, 1990). It can make differences between phases appear larger or smaller than they really are, depending on the nature of the autocorrelation (e.g., whether it's positive or negative). And it is also very likely that visual inspection of a set of data cannot reveal the underlying autocorrelation. Thus, observed changes may actually have been quite predictable because of the autocorrelation. Therefore, you cannot assume that even some clear visual patterns will lead to error-free interpretations. Visual analysis is a tentative evaluation approach. It is useful for making quick and approximate judgments, but when the data relate to important content or when there is any doubt about the clarity of the data, nonvisual (i.e., statistical) methods should be employed in the analysis.

There are other problems associated with visual inspection. When there are complex patterns, such as a bimodal pattern (two separate peaks) within a set of data, it is often diffi-

cult to interpret such information by simple inspection. The patterns themselves are important. Do high periods (of desired performance) come early or late in the set of data? Even more complicated is the interpretation of extremely variable data. It is difficult to make a judgment as to whether any change at all took place across phases with variable data since the variability can make it difficult to judge the level of the data. In general, when such problems arise, we recommend that you use one of the statistical procedures presented in the next two chapters to aid in your analysis of the data.

Another problem emerges when two or more persons (including the client as well as other helping professionals) are involved in the interpretation of visual patterns of data. A person's expectations, to say nothing about the person's values and biases, about the client's behavior may influence his or her interpretation. That is, what may appear to be major change to one observer may be considered as insignificant by another. Without clearcut rules for analysis—which is what statistical procedures provide—there's considerable leeway in interpreting data as supporting one's practice hypotheses.

In all, then, visual inspection of data should be considered a very useful beginning, especially for *monitoring* ongoing events, because rapid feedback permits you to correct obvious problems. But unless the patterns are very clear, with sufficient numbers of observations and with stable baseline data, other methods of analysis, discussed in the next two chapters, also should be employed. Also, the possibility of autocorrelation is always present with data; it requires special techniques, such as the transformations described in Chapter 19, so that distortions can be minimized.

CREATING A CHART WITH SINGWIN

Here's how to use SINGWIN to create a chart.

1. Start SINGWIN (see "Starting SINGWIN" in the SINGWIN User's Guide, Chapter 23).

2. Create and open a new file, or open an existing file (see "Creating a New File" and "Opening an Existing File").

3. Follow the steps outlined in the section entitled "Creating a Line Chart."

SUMMARY

Visual inspection of data for obvious changes in pattern is easy and should be done in all cases, especially when you seek quick, approximate information that will be used rapidly in formulating ongoing practice hypotheses. We've presented some basic patterns of data simplified as mean and trend lines to draw out these implications more clearly. We've distinguished three attributes of graphed data in particular—the level of the data, the trend or directionality of data within one phase (slope), and the trend or directionality of data across phases (drift). When baseline phases are compared to intervention phases using these three attributes, we can indicate general patterns of improvement, strong improvement, or very strong improvement (depending on the number of attributes affected), or we can indicate the same three patterns of deterioration, depending on the definition of desired or undesired events.

It's difficult to interpret data when they're variable or autocorrelated. Therefore, visual analysis contains inherent risks. It may be advisable to supplement the visual analysis with some of the simple statistical analyses we describe in the next two chapters.

21 DESCRIPTIVE STATISTICS

PURPOSE: Raw data sometimes are difficult to interpret because of their variability. This chapter reviews simple descriptive statistics that you can use to aid in your visual analysis by summarizing patterns of observations within phases in order to examine changes across phases. Four different categories of descriptive statistics are discussed and illustrated: measures of central tendency, variability, trend, and effect size. These statistics can supplement the visual analysis procedures described in Chapter 20, and many are necessary for the tests of statistical significance described in Chapter 22. ■

Introduction
Measures of Central Tendency
Median
Mean
Measures of Variation
Range
Standard Deviation
Computing and Graphing Measures of Central Tendency and Variation with SINGWIN
Measures of Trend
Celeration Line

Creating A Celeration Line Chart with SINGWIN
Measures of Effect Size
Δ-Index
g-Index
Computing Effect Size with SINGWIN
Additional Issues Regarding Effect Size
Optimal Uses and Cautions for Specific Descriptive Statistics
Summary

INTRODUCTION

Raw data frequently are difficult to interpret because of their variability. In Chapter 20 we illustrated the usefulness of summarizing and describing a series of data points by computing the mean of the data points, and then superimposing a mean line on the graphed data. The mean is only one of several descriptive statistics that can summarize a series of scores with a single, easily understood number or line. The mean and other descriptive statistics that we discuss in this chapter are useful because they aid in the visual analysis of data, and because most of these statistics are used in the tests of statistical significance that we describe in the next chapter.

Four categories of descriptive statistics are useful for summarizing single-system data: measures of central tendency, variability, trend, and effect size.

MEASURES OF CENTRAL TENDENCY

Often you'll want to identify the typical value in a series of scores, and then superimpose a line representing the typical value on the graphed data (e.g., a mean line). Typical values are called measures of central tendency. The median and the mean are the two measures of central tendency most applicable to single-system data.

Median

The median (Md) is the value above and below which 50% of a set of scores fall, when the scores are ordered from the lowest to highest value. The middle score is the median. Note that a variable must be measured at an ordinal or interval level of measurement before it makes sense to order its values, and so the median should not be used when a variable is measured at the nominal level of measurement (e.g., in diagnostic classification).

Computation of the median can be illustrated using data from a study reported by Allison, Gripton, and Rodway (1983), in which pal-

liative care was provided to terminal cancer patients who were referred for "dysfunctional reactive emotions." Palliative care "implies alleviation of distressing or painful symptoms associated with physical deterioration and infirmity" and "combines empathic care and professional understanding directed towards the physical, emotional, and spiritual needs of both patient and family" (p. 29). One outcome examined by Allison et al. was the frequency of daily crying episodes, and these data are illustrated in Figure 21.1. These data are for a 74-year-old middle-class married woman. This woman was lucid and alert, not bedridden, and had family and friends who were attentive to her. However, her continuous crying episodes were disruptive to the client and to her caregivers.

The median is computed using the steps shown in Exhibit 21.1.

An advantage of the median is that it has a commonsense interpretation as a typical value. Another advantage is that it is not influenced by *outliers* (that is, values that are very different from the typical value). (As a very rough guide, we can consider as an outlier any score that is more than two standard deviations above or below the mean score.) For example, suppose that during baseline there was one day that the client had 13 crying episodes, so the baseline scores, ordered from lowest to highest, were 0,

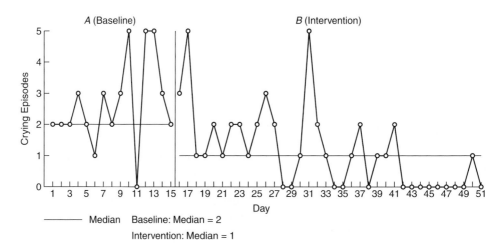

FIGURE 21.1 Daily frequency of crying: medians (Md).

EXHIBIT 21.1   Calculating the Median.

Steps for Computing the Median (Md)	*Baseline Data from Figure 21.1*
1. Order the observed scores from smallest to largest and number these scores from 1 through *n*, where *n* is the total number of scores.	s n 0 (1) 1 (2) 2 (3) 2 (4) 3 (5) 2 (6) 2 (7) 2 (8) 3 (9) 3 (10) 3 (11) 3 (12) 5 (13) 5 (14) 5 (15)
2. Locate the middle position of the ordered scores. The actual score in this position is the median.	$= (n + 1) \times .50$ $= (15 + 1) \times .50$ $= 8$ Median (Md) $= 2$ (actual score in position 8)

3. When there's an even number of scores, there isn't a single number that divides the set of scores. In this case the median is the average of the two midmost values. For example, if the scores are 2, 3, 5, and 6, the middle position is between 3 and 5, and the median is:

$$\frac{3 + 5}{2} = 4$$

1, 2, 2, 2, 2, 2, 2, 3, 3, 3, 3, 5, 5, 13. In this case the median would still be 2. Therefore, the median provides an especially useful measure of central tendency when there are outliers.

Mean

The mean (M), as discussed in Chapters 19 and 20, Is simply the sum of a set of values, divided by the number of values summed. The baseline and intervention means for the Allison et al. data are illustrated in Figure 21.2, and Exhibit 21.2 shows how the mean is computed.

The major advantage of the mean (which is used with variables measured at the interval or ratio level) over the median is that the mean takes into account the numerical value of every score, not just the rank order of the scores. In

this sense the mean uses more of the available information to determine the typical value.

The fact that the mean takes account of the numerical value of every score is a drawback when there are outliers—that is, extreme scores in a set of scores. For example, suppose again that during baseline there was one day that the client had 13 crying episodes, so the baseline scores, ordered from lowest to highest, were 0, 1, 2, 2, 2, 2, 2, 2, 3, 3, 3, 3, 5, 5, and 13 (the outlier). In this case the mean equals 3.20, in contrast to a mean of 2.67 when the last score is 5 instead of 13. The mean, then, is pulled toward and distorted by outliers.

A variation of the mean, the *trimmed mean* (tM) is useful when there are outliers (Rosenthal & Rosnow, 1991). A trimmed mean is computed by excluding a certain percentage of

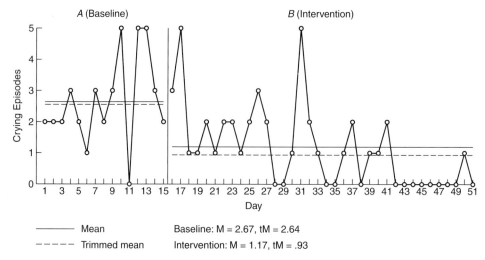

FIGURE 21.2 Daily frequency of crying: means (M) and trimmed means (tM).

EXHIBIT 21.2 Calculating the Mean.

Steps for Computing the Mean (M)	Baseline Data from Figure 21.1
1. Record observed scores, s.	$s_1 = 2$ $s_2 = 2$ $s_3 = 2$ $s_4 = 3$ $s_5 = 2$ $s_6 = 1$ $s_7 = 3$ $s_8 = 2$ $s_9 = 3$ $s_{10} = 5$ $s_{11} = 0$ $s_{12} = 5$ $s_{13} = 5$ $s_{14} = 3$ $s_{15} = 2$
2. Sum the observed scores, $$\Sigma_s$$	$\Sigma_s = 40$
3. Divide the sum of the observed scores by the number of scores used to obtain the sum. This gives the mean, M	Mean (M) $= \dfrac{40}{15} = 2.67$

the highest and lowest values (e.g., 10%), and then computing the mean based on the remaining values. The 10% trimmed means (excluding 10% of the total from the highest and 10% of the total from the lowest scores) for baseline and intervention are illustrated in Figure 21.2 for the Allison et al. data, and Exhibit 21.3 shows how they are computed.

Notice in Figure 21.2 that the 10% trimmed mean for the baseline is virtually identical to the untrimmed mean because of the limited extent of extreme values. However, the discrepancy between the trimmed and untrimmed means for the intervention phase is a little

greater, in large part because of the two days on which there were five crying episodes.

Trimmed means protect against distortions created by outliers, as do medians. However, trimmed means have the advantage over medians in that they make greater use of the information available in a set of numbers. Therefore, in general, trimmed means are preferable to medians as measures of central tendency, unless the number of available observations is so small as to preclude trimming some number of extreme observations. However, if all of the scores tend to cluster (i.e., there are no outliers), the mean is preferable to the trimmed mean as

EXHIBIT 21.3 Calculating the Trimmed Mean.

Steps for Computing the 10 Percent Trimmed Mean	*Baseline Data from Figure 21.1*
1. Record observed scores, *s*, ordered from the smallest to the largest.	s n 0 (1) 1 (2) 2 (3) 2 (4) 2 (5) 2 (6) 2 (7) 2 (8) 3 (9) 3 (10) 3 (11) 3 (12) 5 (13) 5 (14) 5 (15)
2. Determine how many scores are 10% of the total (*n*)	$= .10 \times n$ $= .10 \times 15$ $= 1.5$ or 2, rounded to the nearest whole number
3. Exclude 10% of the total from the lowest scores (in this example score 0 and 1) and 10% of the total from the highest scores (in this example 5 and 5). Compute the mean using this "trimmed" set of 11 scores.	10% of lowest scores (2) = 0, 1 10% of highest scores (2) = 5, 5
4. Divide sum of remaining scores by the number of remaining scores (11).	10% Trimmed Mean (tM) $= \frac{29}{11} = 2.64$

a measure of central tendency because it takes the most information into account.

MEASURES OF VARIATION

Measures of central tendency indicate the typical value of a set of scores, but it's also necessary to have a measure of variation to fully describe a set of scores. When a measure of central tendency is reported it should always be accompanied by an appropriate measure of variation. For example, suppose that in the Allison et al. (1983) study the number of crying episodes was 2 every day during baseline. The baseline median would be the same as it was originally, 2, but this hypothetical data and original data are different in a way that isn't captured by the median. In one case all of the scores were the same (i.e., there was no variation, or "dispersion," "spread," or "variety" as it's sometimes called), and in the other case there were days during which 0, 1, 2, 3, or 5 crying episodes occurred (i.e., there was quite a bit of variation). Therefore, to fully describe a set of scores, a measure of variation is needed, in addition to a measure of central tendency; the range and the standard deviation are the two measures of variability most applicable to single-system data.

A measure of variability is important for the comprehensive description of a set of scores, but variability is also important because the more variability there is within a phase, the more difficult it is to detect differences between phases. For example, suppose that Allison et al. had observed 3 crying episodes each and every day during baseline and 1 each and every day during intervention. You could be a lot more certain about the change from baseline to intervention in this hypothetical situation than in the actual situation illustrated in Figure 21.2. Unfortunately, variability within a phase can be caused by a variety of things, including changes in a client's life situation over which little control can be exercised. However, variability within phases can be reduced in several ways: By increasing the reliability with which the outcomes are measured and intervention and baseline phases are implemented, by increasing the similarity of clients when comparisons are made across clients (e.g., mul-

tiple baseline across clients design), and by decreasing irrelevancies (such as extraneous variables) in the setting in which a single-system evaluation is implemented (Orme, 1991).

Range

The range (R) is the difference between the highest and the lowest value in a set of scores, and it's the simplest measure of variation. The range for the Allison et al. baseline and intervention phases is 5, because during each phase the highest value is 5 and the lowest is 0 (i.e., $5 - 0 = 5$). A more useful way to express the range is simply to say that the scores range from 0 to 5, because this indicates that the range is 5 and it also indicates the lowest and the highest values (e.g., values that range from 25 to 30 also have a range of 5).

The range depends completely on the most extreme values in a set of scores. If these extreme values are uncharacteristic of the majority of the scores (e.g., they're outliers) the range won't provide an accurate picture of the variation in a set of scores. To continue our example, suppose that during baseline there was one day that the client had 13 crying episodes so the baseline scores, ordered from lowest to highest, were 0, 1, 2, 2, 2, 2, 2, 2, 3, 3, 3, 3, 5, 5, and 13. This outlier would change the range to 13 ($13 - 0 = 13$), instead of the original 5.

A variation of the range, *the trimmed range* (tR), is useful when there are outliers (Rosenthal & Rosnow, 1991). A trimmed range is computed by excluding a certain percentage of the highest and lowest values. For example, a commonly computed trimmed range known as the *interquartile range* (Q) takes into account the middle 50% of the values in a set of scores. Exhibit 21.4 shows how the interquartile range is computed.

The interquartile range, or the range if appropriate (no outliers), can be represented by lines superimposed on the graphed data. Such range lines provide a picture of changes in variability from one phase to another. This is illustrated in Figure 21.3 for the Allison et al. data.

Range lines are useful for more than portraying changes in variability from one phase to another. They're also useful for portraying changes in the "typical" state of a target from

EXHIBIT 21.4 Calculating the Interquartile Range.

Steps for Computing the Interquartile Range (Q)	*Baseline Data from Figure 21.1*
1. Order observed scores from smallest to largest and number these scores from 1 through *n*, where *n* is the total number of scores.	s n 0 (1) 1 (2) 2 (3) 2 (4) 2 (5) 2 (6) 2 (7) 2 (8) 3 (9) 3 (10) 3 (11) 3 (12) 5 (13) 5 (14) 5 (15)
2. Locate the upper position of the interquartile range ("upper hinge") by multiplying the total number of scores (*n* = 15) by .75. The actual score in the resulting position is the upper end of the interquartile range.	upper position = 15 × .75 = 11.25 (or 11) actual score = 3
3. Locate the lower position of the interquartile range ("lower hinge") by multiplying the total number of scores (*n* = 15) by .25. The actual score in the resulting position is the lower end of the interquartile range. Q is the difference between the upper and lower hinge.	lower position = 15 × .25 = 3.75 (or 4) actual score = 2 interquartile range (Q) = 2 *to* 3, or 1

one phase to another. For example, "typical" might be defined by the interquartile range (or, as we discuss in the next chapter, it might be defined as the area where two-thirds of the scores fall). Typical then is taken to be the middle 50% of the values in a set of scores. Thus, as illustrated in Figure 21.3 for the Allison et al. data, during baseline the typical number of crying episodes was 2 to 3, but during intervention the typical number was 0 through 2.

Standard Deviation

Like the median, the range and the trimmed range don't take into account the numerical value of all of the scores, so they don't make use of all available information to determine variability. The standard deviation (SD) does take

account of the numerical values of the scores. The standard deviation, simply put, tells us the average amount by which the scores in a given distribution deviate from the mean of the distribution. The SD is important not only because it is used in a variety of other statistics, but because knowing the SD tells us the exact percentage of scores above and below the mean (if the scores are distributed normally).

The steps used to compute the standard deviation for the Allison et al. baseline data are shown in Exhibit 21.5.

Values indicating one standard deviation above the mean (e.g., $2.67 + 1.45 = 4.12$, for baseline) and one standard deviation below the mean (e.g., $2.67 - 1.45 = 1.22$, for baseline) can be computed and represented by lines superimposed on the graphed data. (In the same

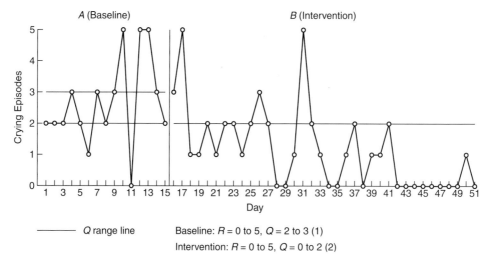

FIGURE 21.3 Daily frequency of crying: interquartile range lines (Q).

way, ± 3 standard deviation bands can be computed, a point we will illustrate in detail in Chapter 22 as the basis for one of the statistics discussed there.) This is illustrated in Figure 21.4 for the Allison et al. data.

Lines representing one or more standard deviations above and below the mean provide a picture of changes in variability from one phase to another, and they're also useful for portraying changes in the "typical" state of a target from one phase to another. If the scores for a phase are normally distributed (i.e., they have a "bell-shaped" distribution with the mean, the mode, and the median all about the same), 68% of the scores will fall between one standard deviation above the mean and one standard deviation below the mean, and 95% will fall between about 2 standard deviations above the mean and about 2 standard deviations below the mean. Thus, as illustrated in Figure 21.4 for the Allison et al. data, during baseline the "typical" (i.e., one SD above to one SD below the mean) number of crying episodes during baseline ranged from 1.22 to 4.12, and during intervention from 0 (actually $-.15$, but a negative number of crying episodes doesn't make sense) to 2.49 crying episodes.

COMPUTING AND GRAPHING MEASURES OF CENTRAL TENDENCY AND VARIATION WITH SINGWIN

Here's how to use SINGWIN to compute all of the measures of central tendency and variation that we just discussed and illustrated, as well as many of the band graphs.

1. Start SINGWIN (see "Starting SING-WIN" in the SINGWIN User's Guide, Chapter 23).
2. Open the "allison.dbf" file (containing the "Allison" data) that comes with SING-WIN (see "Opening an Existing File").
3. Follow the steps outlined in the section entitled "Computing Measures of Central Tendency and Variability" to get the values of these statistics.
4. Follow the steps outlined in the section entitled "Getting Two Standard Deviation Bands" to get values (but not graphs) for these bands.
5. Follow the steps outlined in the section entitled "Band Graphs" to get one and two standard deviation band graphs and interquartile range band graphs.

EXHIBIT 21.5   Calculating the Standard Deviation.

Steps for Computing the Standard Deviation	*Data from Figure 21.1*
1. Record observed scores, s.	$s_1 = 2$ $s_2 = 2$ $s_3 = 2$ $s_4 = 3$ $s_5 = 2$ $s_6 = 1$ $s_7 = 3$ $s_8 = 2$ $s_9 = 3$ $s_{10} = 5$ $s_{11} = 0$ $s_{12} = 5$ $s_{13} = 5$ $s_{14} = 3$ $s_{15} = 2$
2. Sum the observed scores, $$\Sigma_s$$	$\Sigma_s = 40$
3. Divide the sum of the observed scores by the number of scores used to obtain the sum. This gives the mean, M	$\text{Mean} = M = \dfrac{40}{15} = 2.67$
4. Compute $$(s - M)$$ for all scores. These are called "deviation scores," because they indicate the extent to which each score deviates from the mean.	$2 - 2.67 = -.67$ $2 - 2.67 = -.67$ $2 - 2.67 = -.67$ $3 - 2.67 = +.33$ $2 - 2.67 = -.67$ $1 - 2.67 = -1.67$ $3 - 2.67 = +.33$ $2 - 2.67 = -.67$ $3 - 2.67 = +.33$ $5 - 2.67 = +2.33$ $0 - 2.67 = -2.67$ $5 - 2.67 = +2.33$ $5 - 2.67 = +2.33$ $3 - 2.67 = +.33$ $2 - 2.67 = -.67$

(*continued*)

MEASURES OF TREND

When a target is increasing or decreasing systematically over time–that is, when there's a trend–neither the mean nor the median provides an accurate summary of the target. For example, consider the hypothetical data illustrated in Figure 21.5. The baseline and intervention means are both 5, which seemingly suggests no difference between baseline and intervention. However, there's a clear difference between baseline and intervention; during baseline the number of crying episodes steadily increased, and after the implementation of the intervention the number steadily decreased.

A trend can be summarized by a line superimposed on graphed data in much the same way as a mean or a median line. A line used to summarize a trend usually is called a *trend line*. The steeper the trend line, the greater the amount of change over time. For example, Figure 21.6 illustrates three different baseline and intervention trend lines representing different amounts of change over time. Notice that the steeper the incline of the line, the greater the change over time. Also, notice that when the trend line is flat it indicates that there's no change over time, and in this case the trend line corresponds to the mean line.

The steepness of a trend line (i.e., amount of change over time) can be summarized by a measure called a *slope*, symbolized by the letter *b*. This term was used also in Chapter 20 to describe directionality of data within a phase. But slope has additional meaning in analyzing data. A slope indicates the average amount of change

EXHIBIT 21.5   (Continued).

Steps for Computing the Standard Deviation	Data from Figure 21.1
5. Square each of these "deviation scores" $(s - M)^2$	$(-.67)^2 = .45$ $(-.67)^2 = .45$ $(-.67)^2 = .45$ $(+.33)^2 = .11$ $(-.67)^2 = .45$ $(-1.67)^2 = 2.79$ $(+.33)^2 = .11$ $(-.67)^2 = .45$ $(+.33)^2 = .11$ $(+2.33)^2 = 5.43$ $(-2.67)^2 = 7.13$ $(+2.33)^2 = 5.43$ $(+2.33)^2 = 5.43$ $(+.33)^2 = .11$ $(-.67)^2 = .45$
6. Sum the squared "deviation scores" $\sum(s - M)^2$	29.35
7. Find $n - 1$, where n is the number of scores.	$15 - 1 = 14$
8. Compute formula for the standard deviation, SD. Divide the squared deviation scores (step 6) by $n - 1$ (step 7) and find the square root.	$\sqrt{\dfrac{\sum (s - \bar{x})^2}{n-1}} =$ $\sqrt{29.35/14} =$ $\sqrt{2.10} = 1.45$

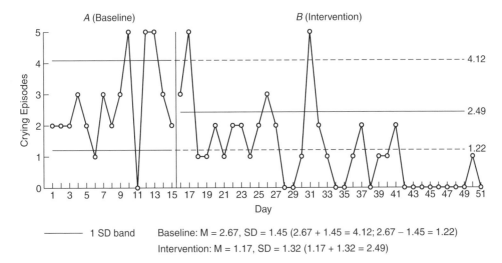

FIGURE 21.4   Daily frequency of crying: one standard deviation (SD) bands.

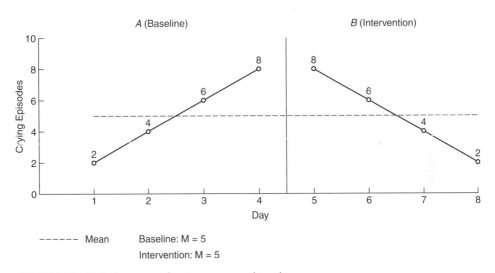

FIGURE 21.5   Daily frequency of crying: means and trends.

from one time to the next. In the data illustrated in Figure 21.5, there's an increase of 2 crying episodes per day during baseline (i.e., 2, 4, 6, 8), and so the slope equals + 2. During intervention there's a decrease of 2 crying episodes per day, and so the slope equals −2. In Figure 21.6 trend lines having slopes of 0 (no trend), 1 (modest trend), and 2 (steep trend) are illustrated for the baseline phase, and trend lines having slopes of 0 (no trend), −1 (modest trend), and −2 (steep trend) are illustrated for

the intervention phase. Therefore, as illustrated in Figure 21.6, the larger the absolute value of the slope (i.e., ignoring whether it's positive or negative), the steeper the incline of the line. The closer the value of the slope is to 0, the less the trend, and when the slope equals 0 it indicates that there's no trend present in the scores.

If there's no trend (i.e., slope = 0), it's reasonable to compute a measure of central tendency (i.e., mean, trimmed mean, or median) to describe the general pattern of the data. If

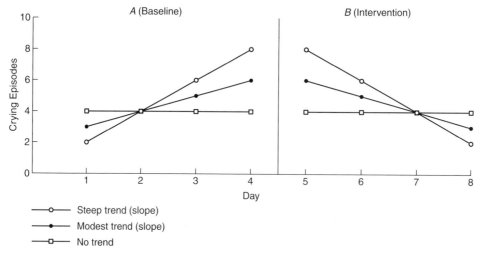

FIGURE 21.6   Daily frequency of crying: no trend, modest trend, steep trend.

there's a trend, a trend line should be constructed and used to describe the general pattern of the data.

We suggest you always compute a trend line prior to computing a measure of central tendency to see whether a trend exists. One way to construct a trend line is to draw the line that appears to best summarize the trend in the scores. However, in most data sets the scores don't fall exactly along a straight line, in which case this "eyeball" method isn't very precise, and the chances are that no two people would end up drawing exactly the same line (cf. Mosteller, Siegel, Trapido, & Youtz, 1985). For example, as we show below, there's a decreasing trend in the number of crying episodes during the intervention phase for the data illustrated in Figure 21.1. However, it would be difficult to visually determine the best trend line, and different people would probably end up drawing the trend line in different ways. Therefore, we'll describe a method that can be used to determine the line that best summarizes the trend in a target: the *celeration line* technique.

Celeration Line

One of the simplest ways to determine a trend line is to use a procedure called the semiaverage (Neiswanger, 1956; Parsonson & Baer,

1978) or the celeration line approach (Gingerich & Feyerherm, 1979; White, 1977). This approach was proposed in the first edition of this book as the basis for a particular test of statistical significance based on the binomial distribution, but more recent evidence suggests that it is not useful for that purpose (Crosbie, 1987). However, it *is* useful to describe a trend line within or across phases. And the celeration line is discussed again in Chapter 22 as a way of facilitating the chi-square (χ^2) test of significance.

Essentially, a celeration line is a line connecting the midpoints of the first and second halves of a phase. Depending on the pattern of data in the two halves of the phase, the line may be accelerating or decelerating; hence the general label *celeration line*.

The celeration line may be constructed in two ways. Both use exactly the same methods in the baseline phase as is described below. But one method develops an entirely new celeration line in the intervention phase; then, patterns of trend can be compared between the two phases. The second method simply extends the celeration line from the baseline construction through the intervention period. This method allows for making a prediction about the trend in the intervention phase based on the observed trend in the baseline. There is some degree of predictive validity for this use of the celeration line (White, 1977). It is recommended to have at least 9 to 11 baseline points for the best predictive validity, but for clinical purposes, it appears as though some confidence can be placed in predictions based on as few as 7 points (White, 1977).

Gingerich and Feyerherm (1979) suggest the simplified procedure outlined and illustrated in Exhibit 21.6 and Figure 21.7 for constructing a celeration line for a baseline, but this procedure can be used for any phase. Also, Exhibit 21.7 takes the celeration line a step further and shows how to compute its slope, and hence quantify the average amount of change over time within a phase. The celeration lines for baseline and intervention are illustrated in Figure 21.8.

Several conclusions can be drawn from the chart in Figure 21.8. First, using the two separate celeration lines, it can be seen that there are different patterns of trend in the A and B phases, with the trend accelerating in the A phase and decelerating (in a positive direction) in the B phase.

Second, it can be seen from the extension of the baseline celeration line into the B phase that the "natural course of events" predicts a continuing upward trend in the frequency of crying episodes, so that a decrease in this pattern would go against the prediction made from the nonintervention (A) phase, suggesting the possible impact of some new or external event (the intervention).

And third, as shown in Figure 21.8, the baseline slope equals .14, and this indicates that on the average there's an *increase* of .14 crying episodes per day during baseline. As is also shown in Figure 21.8, the intervention slope equals −.08, and this indicates that on the average there's a .08 *decrease* in the number of crying episodes per day during intervention.

When there aren't outliers within either half of the phase, it's best to compute the celeration line using means, as we illustrate in Exhibit 21.7. However, when there are outliers within either half of the phase, it's better to use trimmed means (when there are enough scores in each half of the phase) or medians (when there are few scores in each half of the phase).

When there's a trend in a set of scores, the method outlined in Chapter 19 for computing

an autocorrelation can produce an inaccurate autocorrelation (Huitema, 1988; Huitema & McKean, 2000). You can determine whether there is a trend by a visual examination of the data, although a visual examination probably will detect only strong trends, or by computing a celeration line (or a regression line, as described below). If there is no trend, the celeration line will be flat.

Lines representing trends can be constructed using different methods. The celeration line method is one approach. With a large enough number of observations, a variation of the celeration line can be used in which the data are divided into thirds, instead of halves (Franklin, Gorman, Beasley, & Allison, 1997). A regression line is another method, and one that typically is taught in introductory statistics courses, albeit as applied to group data.

A regression line can provide a more precise, though fairly similar, representation of trend than a celeration line. While the step-by-step calculations for a regression analysis can be enumerated and computed by hand, for all practical purposes this should be done using a preprogrammed calculator or a computer. Our computer program, SINGWIN, will easily do this for you. You might also note that there are many inexpensive calculators on the market that come with simple built-in regression programs, most spreadsheet programs (e.g., Microsoft Excel) compute and graph regression lines, and virtually all computer statistical packages designed for the analysis of group data compute a regression analysis.

Creating a Celeration Line Chart With SINGWIN.   Here's how to use SINGWIN to create a celeration line chart.

1. Start SINGWIN (see "Starting SINGWIN" in the SINGWIN User's Guide, Chapter 23).

2. Open the "allison.dbf" file (containing the "Allison" data) that comes with SINGWIN (see "Opening an Existing File").

3. Follow the steps outlined in the section entitled "Creating a Celeration Line Chart."

EXHIBIT 21.6   Calculating the Celeration Line.

Steps for Computing the Celeration Line	*Baseline Data from Figure 21.1*
1. Record observed scores, *s*.	$s_1 = 2$ $s_2 = 2$ $s_3 = 2$ $s_4 = 3$ $s_5 = 2$ $s_6 = 1$ $s_7 = 3$ $s_8 = 2$ $s_9 = 3$ $s_{10} = 5$ $s_{11} = 0$ $s_{12} = 5$ $s_{13} = 5$ $s_{14} = 3$ $s_{15} = 2$
2. Divide the scores for the phase (e.g., baseline) in half (Figure 21.7a) and then divide these halves in half by drawing dashed vertical lines on the chart at these points (Figure 21.7b). (For even numbers draw the line between data points; for odd numbers draw the line through the mid point.)	$s_1 = 2$ $s_2 = 2$ $s_3 = 2$ $s_4 = 3$ $s_5 = 2$ $s_6 = 1$ $s_7 = 3$ $s_8 = 2$ $s_9 = 3$ $s_{10} = 5$ $s_{11} = 0$ $s_{12} = 5$ $s_{13} = 5$ $s_{14} = 3$ $s_{15} = 2$
3a. Determine the mean level of events for the first half of the phase by adding the scores for that half and dividing by the number of scores in that half. (With an odd number of points in a phase, omit the middle number from calculation of the mean for each half. However, be sure to include any points on the 1/4 and 3/4 lines.)	$\sum_{s_1-s_7}^{\text{mean}_1} = 2$ 2 2 3 2 1 $\underline{3}$ 15 $\dfrac{15}{7} = 2.14$

(*continued*)

EXHIBIT 21.6   (Continued).

Steps for Computing the Celeration Line	Baseline Data from Figure 21.1
3b. Determine the mean level of events for the second half of the phase by adding the scores for that half and dividing by the number of scores in that half.	$\sum_{s_9-s_{15}}^{\text{mean}_2} = \begin{array}{r} 3 \\ 5 \\ 0 \\ 5 \\ 5 \\ 3 \\ 2 \\ \hline 23 \end{array}$ $\dfrac{23}{7} = 3.29$
4. Draw a hatch mark on the 1/4 and the 3/4 lines where the mean level of events occurs (Figure 21.7c), and draw a line connecting these two intersections (Figure 21.7d). This line represents the pattern of behavior observed during the baseline phase and, by extension, what likely will continue to occur in the future if conditions don't change. This is called the celeration line, accelerating when there's a trend in an upward direction and decelerating when there's a downward trend.	
5. Extend this celeration line into the intervention period (Figure 21.7e). This is a projection line representing the estimate of what events would ordinarily look like (the prediction) if the baseline pattern were to continue and if there were no intervention.	
6. As an alternative to step 5, you can calculate the celeration line for the intervention phase by using the same procedures as in steps 1–4 above.	
7. Compute the slope (b) of the celeration line by subtracting the mean of the first half of the baseline phase from the mean of the second half of the phase, and dividing this by the number of scores between the 1/4 and 3/4 marks, including the ¾ mark, but not including the 1/4 mark.	Baseline slope $= \dfrac{3.29 - 2.14}{8} = .14$ Intervention slope $= \dfrac{.44 - 1.88}{18} = -.08$

MEASURES OF EFFECT SIZE

Computing and graphing central tendency, variation, and trend within a phase, and then visually comparing these measures across phases provides a useful basis for determining changes from one phase to the next. However, there are more numerically precise ways to compare the amount of change from one phase to another, and these are called measures of effect size (ES).

In Chapter 11, we discussed the use of meta-analysis as one way of looking at the generalizability of findings from a group of studies. However, we didn't describe precisely how to conduct a meta-analysis or how to calculate its key indicator—the effect size (ES).

In this section, then, we present a little of the nuts and bolts of meta-analysis, and particularly, how the effect size can be used as one way of analyzing data from single-system designs.

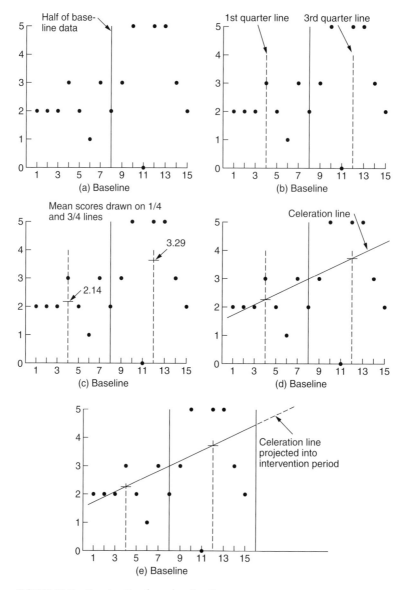

FIGURE 21.7 Constructing the celeration line.

As you may recall from Chapter 11, meta-analysis is a method for aggregating and statistically analyzing the results of several studies. It does this largely by developing a common metric (or statistic) that allows the results of individual studies to be compared across studies and across outcome measures. The most widely used "common metric" is the *effect size* used to estimate the magnitude of effect (i.e., the

magnitude of the difference between one group and another). This presumably is related–given the strength of the internal validity of a study–to the interventions being used.

But this effect size has an additional value. It actually can be used to characterize the data in a given study. In the case of single-system designs, the effect size can be used to estimate the magnitude of the difference between a baseline

EXHIBIT 21.7   Calculating the Δ-index.

Steps for Computing the Δ-index	*Data from Figure 21.9*	
1. Record observed scores, s, for baseline and intervention periods.	*Baseline (A)* $s_1 = 2$ $s_2 = 5$ $s_3 = 7$ $s_4 = 3$ $s_5 = 3$ $s_6 = 6$ $s_7 = 5$ $s_8 = 8$ $s_9 = 3$ $s_{10} = 3$	*Intervention (B)* $s_{11} = 7$ $s_{12} = 8$ $s_{13} = 8$ $s_{14} = 9$ $s_{15} = 8$ $s_{16} = 4$ $s_{17} = 4$ $s_{18} = 8$ $s_{19} = 8$ $s_{20} = 8$
2. Sum these scores ($\sum_s$).	45	72
3. Divide the sum by the number of scores, n, to obtain the sum. This gives the mean, M.	$\frac{45}{10} = 4.5$	$\frac{72}{10} = 7.2$
4. Compute the standard deviation, SD, for the baseline scores. Begin by computing (S – M).	$2 - 4.4 = -2.5$ $5 - 4.5 = .5$ $7 - 4.5 = 2.5$ $3 - 4.5 = -1.5$ $3 - 4.5 = -1.5$ $6 - 4.5 = 1.5$ $5 - 4.5 = .5$ $8 - 4.5 = 3.5$ $3 - 4.5 = -1.5$ $3 - 4.5 = -1.5$	
5. Square each of these results.	$(-2.5)^2 = 6.25$ $(.5)^2 = .25$ $(2.5)^2 = 6.25$ $(-1.5)^2 = 2.25$ $(-1.5)^2 = 2.25$ $(1.5)^2 = 2.25$ $(.5)^2 = .25$ $(-1.5)^2 = 2.25$ $(-1.5)^2 = 2.25$	
6. Sum these amounts ($\sum$).	36.5	

(continued)

and intervention phase, and it is for that purpose that we discuss the use of effect sizes here.

As we mentioned in Chapter 11, there are relatively few references available regarding use of meta-analysis for data from single-system designs (Allison & Gorman, 1993; Corcoran, 1985; Faith et al., 1997; Gingerich, 1984; Jayaratne et al., 1988; Videka-Sherman, 1986; White et al.,

EXHIBIT 21.7 (Continued).

Steps for Computing the Δ-index	Data from Figure 21.9
7. Find $n - 1$, where $n =$ the number of scores.	$10 - 1 = 9$
8. Compute the formula for the standard deviation, SD. (Note that Table 19.1 on common square roots may be used as an approximation if needed.)	$\sqrt{\dfrac{\Sigma(S-M)^2}{n-1}}\sqrt{\dfrac{36.5}{9}}=\sqrt{4.05}=2.01$
9. Complete the Δ-index formula.	$\dfrac{M_B - M_A}{S_A}$ $M_B = 7.2$ $M_A = 4.5$ $S_A = 2.01$ $\dfrac{7.2-4.5}{2.01}=\dfrac{2.7}{2.01}=1.34$

10. Interpret ES on table of Z scores (Table 21.1).	ES (Z) of 1.34 is equivalent to a percentile of .9099 or .91 (area in larger portion of curve; positive effect). This means:
	a. The client's score on the outcome measure in the intervention period is 1.34 SDs above the score in the baseline period;
	b. There was an improvement of approximately 41% over the average score in the baseline period.
	  .9099
	  $-$.5000
	  .4099 or 41%

1989; for an illustration of the use of meta-analysis to analyze single-system data, see Holden et al., 1999). Most of these articles are concerned with aggregating data from several studies rather than focusing on the analysis of data within one study. To make this even more complicated, several different procedures have been recommended for calculating the ES in single-system designs.

In line with the overall purpose of this book and the other statistics described in this chapter, we describe two procedures and mention a third that seem most practical for you to compute, noting some of the problems and issues. The two procedures are called the Δ(delta)-index, and the *g*-index.

Δ-Index

This ES uses the same formula described in Chapter 11 for computing the ES (Glass et al., 1981):

$$ES = \frac{M_B - M_A}{S_A}$$

where M_B refers to the mean of the intervention period (B) and M_A refers to the mean of the baseline period (A).

The Δ-index is perhaps the easiest of the basic ES formulas to calculate. What this formula tells us simply is to find the mean of all the scores on a particular outcome measure for

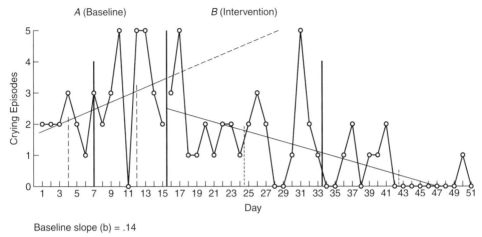

FIGURE 21.8   Daily frequency of crying: celeration lines.

the baseline period, and subtract that from the mean of all the scores on the same measures in the intervention period. Then, all you have to do is divide this figure by the standard deviation of the scores in the baseline period (using the formula for computing the standard deviation shown earlier in this chapter in Exhibit 21.5).

The steps for calculating Δ are illustrated in Exhibit 21.7 using the data from Figure 21.9.

The basic Δ-index is rather straightforward and relatively easy to compute. (For a simple

correction that will make a very small adjustment in your ES and that can be used with less than 20 data points in each phase, and for a suggestion on how to account for change over time using gain scores, see Corcoran, 1985.) But, you might ask, what does it mean?

The effect size is a little different from the other procedures we've described in this chapter. The ES essentially tells you how different the scores in the intervention phase were from the scores in the baseline phase (the magnitude

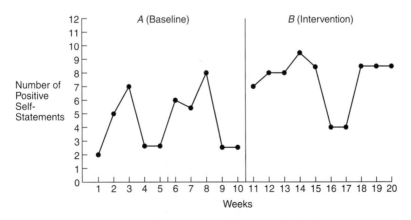

FIGURE 21.9   Data illustrating changes from baseline to intervention for effect size analysis.

of the effect). But it does not tell you whether these differences were statistically significant or due to chance (ways of doing this are described in Chapter 22).

There are three ways to interpret this ES. The first is simply to get an idea of how big a difference there is between the baseline and intervention phases. The larger the ES, the larger the magnitude of the effect. (Cohen, 1977, suggested as a rough guide that an ES of .2 could be considered small, an ES of .5 medium, and an ES of .8 a large effect. In a review of some 300 meta-analyses, Lipsey & Wilson, 1993, basically confirmed Cohen's suggestions in that the distribution of actual effect sizes more or less conformed to Cohen's criteria.) If the desired direction of change from baseline to intervention is upward (higher scores mean positive change), then a positive effect size means there is a positive difference between the baseline and intervention period with the larger the ES, the greater the difference.

If the desired zone is in a negative direction (where lower scores mean positive change), then a negative ES still means there is a positive difference between baseline and intervention.

A second way to interpret the meaning of the ES is in terms of basic assumptions about this procedure. A key assumption is that the scores are normally distributed, and while this

may be a very tentative assumption for single-system design scores, it does allow use of a Z table to interpret scores. Thus, one interpretation of the meaning of the ES is as the standardized mean difference between the two phases, or the mean difference in standard deviation units. Thus, an ES of +1 suggests the scores in the intervention period on the outcome measure are one standard deviation above the scores in the baseline phase.

A third interpretation, related to this, is to examine in a table of Z scores the percentile difference between the baseline and intervention scores. Substituting the ES for the Z (or standard score) in the excerpted Z table (Table 21.1) allows you to estimate the extent to which the client improved in average performance in the intervention period over baseline period.

Thus, if the ES is .00, it shows no difference between the baseline and intervention phases. An ES of +1.00 suggests an improvement of about 34% (.8413 − .5000 = .3413 on the Z table) in the intervention phase over average performance in the baseline phase. If the ES is −1.0 (with negative scores being undesirable), it suggests that performance in the intervention phase was about 34% *less* than in the baseline phase (.5000 − .1587 = .3413 on the Z table).

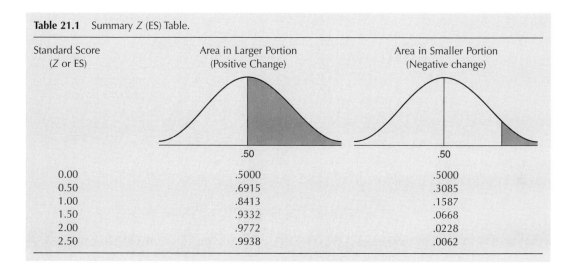

Table 21.1   Summary Z (ES) Table.

Standard Score (Z or ES)	Area in Larger Portion (Positive Change)	Area in Smaller Portion (Negative change)
	.50	.50
0.00	.5000	.5000
0.50	.6915	.3085
1.00	.8413	.1587
1.50	.9332	.0668
2.00	.9772	.0228
2.50	.9938	.0062

Overall, then, the effect size is a useful index for determining just how large a change has occurred between baseline and intervention phases. It is up to you and the client to determine whether this magnitude of effect really has clinical or social significance—that is, whether it is meaningful. You can even compare the ES obtained with a given client with reported effects in the literature using the same type of intervention, and use this information to help you make a decision about continuing, changing, or terminating the intervention.

The *d*-index is a variation of the Δ-index that is interpreted in virtually the same ways as the Δ-index. However, the *d*-index is somewhat more precise, especially when there is a small number of baseline observations, because it uses the pooled standard deviation (basically an average) from baseline and intervention. The pooled standard deviation is slightly more complex to compute, though. Steps for computing it can be found in the second edition of this book or in other references (e.g., Cohen, 1988; Hedges & Olkin, 1985). Also, as noted below, SINGWIN computes the *d*-index.

g-Index

When there's a trend in either phase, the Δ and *d* effect size may not be appropriate. However, the *g*-index (Cohen, 1988, p. 147) can be used to provide a rough index of ES when there's a trend, and we discuss this measure because it's simple to use and understand. Also it can be used in conjunction with the celeration line technique discussed in this chapter, and with the proportion/frequency test of statistical significance that we discuss in the next chapter.

The *g*-index can be used with the celeration line technique in the following manner (and it also can be used with a mean or median line in the absence of a trend). When the appropriate trend line is used to summarize a set of baseline scores, about half of the scores will be above the trend line and half below. If the scores above the trend line are scores that are better than average, then one intervention goal would be to increase the proportion of scores that are higher than the baseline average. (If

lower scores indicate a more desirable state of affairs, then scores below the trend line are better than average, and the goal would be to increase the proportion of scores that are lower than the baseline average.)

The *proportion of baseline* scores above the trend line is determined by dividing the number of scores above the line by the total number of *baseline* scores. The *proportion of intervention* scores above the baseline trend line is determined by extending the baseline trend line into the intervention phase, determining the number of intervention scores above this line, and dividing the number of scores above the line by the total number of *intervention* scores. If there's no systematic difference between the baseline and intervention phases, the proportion of *intervention* scores above the extended trend line will be the same as the proportion of *baseline* scores above the trend line. Therefore, the *g*-index is computed using the following formula:

$$P_B - P_A$$

where: P_B = the *proportion* of intervention scores in the desired zone of the *extended* baseline trend line (i.e., in the intervention phase) *minus*

P_A = the *proportion* of baseline scores in the desired zone of the baseline trend line

Let's illustrate the *g*-index using an example in which an acting-out teenager is being monitored by serving hours of volunteer work at the library he has vandalized. He has not been working the 5 hours a week as required, so the probation officer has instituted an arrangement whereby he must sign in at the library for the required number of hours before he can get permission to be with his friends. Several different patterns of results are shown in Figures 21.8, 21.10, and 21.11 (remember, the "desired zone" can be above *or* below the mean or trend line; you and the client determine that based on the nature of the target).

Figure 21.8 illustrates a situation in which the baseline scores are best summarized using a trend line calculated using the celeration line method. In this example the proportion of baseline scores below the baseline trend line (i.e., in the desirable direction) is .40 (i.e., 6/15)

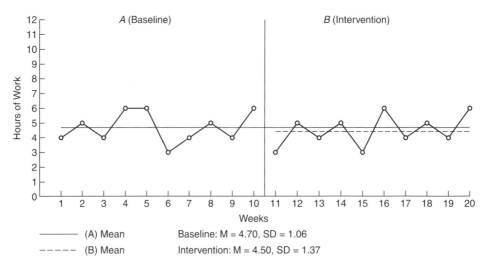

FIGURE 21.10 Hours of completed volunteer work.

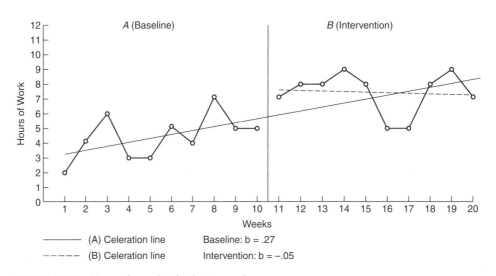

FIGURE 21.11 Hours of completed volunteer work.

and the proportion of intervention scores below the extended baseline trend line is .97 (i.e., 35/36). Therefore, the g-index in this example is .57 (i.e., .97 − .40 = .57).

Figure 21.10 illustrates a situation in which it's reasonable to summarize the baseline scores using a mean line (just a trend line with the slope equal to 0). In this example the proportion of baseline scores above the extended

baseline mean line, that is, in the intervention phase, is .50 (i.e., 5/10), and the proportion of scores above the baseline mean is also .50 (i.e., 5/10). Therefore, the g-index in this example is 0 (i.e., .50 − .50 = 0). (Notice that the baseline and intervention means are virtually identical in this case.)

Figure 21.11 illustrates a situation in which it's reasonable to summarize the baseline scores using a trend line (calculated by the celeration line method described earlier). In this example the proportion of baseline scores above the baseline trend line is .40 (i.e., 4/10), and the proportion of scores above the extended baseline trend line in the intervention phase is .70 (i.e., 7/10). Therefore, the g-index in this example is .30 (i.e., .70 − .40 = .30). (Notice that the baseline and intervention slopes—.27 versus −.05—are noticeably different in this case.)

As with the Δ-index, there are two basic features of the g-index to consider. The first is its size, irrespective of whether it's positive or negative. The larger the g-index, the larger the magnitude of the effect. The sign of the g-index (positive or negative) also is important because it indicates whether the client improved or deteriorated from baseline to intervention. *Whether your desirable zone is above or below the extended line, a positive g-index indicates improvement and a negative g-index indicates deterioration.*

The g-index, unlike the Δ-index, doesn't take the numerical values of the scores into account; it considers only whether scores are above (or below) a mean or trend line. Therefore, although the g-index can be applied when there isn't a trend in either phase, we recommend the Δ-index in this situation because it takes more information into account and therefore provides a more precise measure of ES. However, when there's a trend, we recommend the g-index because it can take the trend into account.

Computing Effect Size With SINGWIN.
Here's how to use SINGWIN to compute delta and the d-index and to determine percentage improvement.

1. Start SINGWIN (see "Starting SINGWIN" in the SINGWIN User's Guide, Chapter 23).

2. Open the "ex21-9.dbf" file (containing the data from Exhibit 21.9) (see "Opening an Existing File").

3. Follow the steps outlined in the section entitled "Computing Effect Size."

Additional Issues Regarding Effect Size

A major issue with the use of the effect size—as with any other statistic—is the issue of causality. Statistics do not demonstrate causality. You need a rigorous design to do that. Thus, with ES, you're not demonstrating that the intervention *caused* the difference between the baseline and intervention phases. The ES tells you how large the difference is between baseline and intervention phases, but not why that difference occurred. Again, only an analysis of design factors, possible threats to design validity, and your own logic will allow you to develop a conclusion about why the changes came about.

A second issue with the Δ-index is that it's based on these assumptions: (a) there is no trend in the data and that the differences between phases can be represented by differences between the means of the two phases; and (b) the scores are independent, that is not autocorrelated. If the data are positively autocorrelated within phases, these indexes will overestimate the size of the effect. If the data are negatively autocorrelated within phases, these indexes will underestimate the size of the effect. One way to handle these problems is to transform the data to remove the trend and autocorrelation, as discussed in Chapter 19, and then compute the ES using the transformed data. A much simpler way to handle trend is just to use the g-index. (Other more versatile and complex methods for computing effect sizes for autocorrelated data and/or data that evidence a trend are discussed in Faith et al., 1997. Of course, if trend and/or autocorrelation do exist and you decide to go ahead and calculate an ES using Δ anyhow, be sure to interpret it with caution.)

A third issue is that the use of the ES is most appropriate with *A-B* designs. However, if you're using a more complicated design such as a multiple baseline or *A-B-A-B*, you could average the ESs from different *A-B* comparisons (although you shouldn't do this if there are different patterns among baseline phases or among intervention phases). This will give you an estimate of the overall ES for the entire design, a rough idea as to the magnitude of effect for all the intervention periods compared to all the baseline periods.

A fourth issue is that to some extent you have control over the size of the difference between phases, and hence the size of the ES (Orme, 1991). For one thing, a stronger intervention can produce a larger difference between baseline and intervention phases. For example, you might meet with an abusive parent daily or once a month. Moreover, the sessions can consist of 15 minutes of casual discussion about parenting skills, or a full hour of intensive instruction, feedback, and role-play. For another thing, a more valid and sensitive outcome measure can produce a larger difference between baseline and intervention phases than a less valid or less sensitive measure. In particular, differences between intervention and baseline phases will be decreased by outcome measures that result in either *ceiling* (place a limit on measuring how much) or *floor* (place a limit on measuring how little) effects (e.g., a knowledge measure that measures neither how little nor how much a client knows) or by outcome measures that use gross scale units (e.g., improvement/no improvement). Finally, carrying out the activities for a phase as planned can produce a larger difference between baseline and intervention. For example, during intervention, practitioners or clients might not implement the planned activities that are necessary for the success of the intervention, or during baseline they might engage in unplanned activities that lead to improvement (e.g., a client gets help elsewhere or a practitioner provides services).

A fifth issue is that the size of an ES depends on the size of the difference between phases, relative to the variability within phases. Therefore, the ability to detect differences between phases is increased by a reduction in variability within phases. Another way to think about this is that variability within conditions is "noise" that makes it more difficult to "hear" or detect existing differences between conditions; reducing this noise makes it easier to detect these differences. Therefore, to increase the ES you can increase the valid differences *between* phases (e.g., by increasing the strength of intervention, the validity with which phases are implemented, or the validity with which outcomes are measured), and you can reduce the variability *within* phases (e.g., by increasing the reliability with which outcomes are measured and interventions implemented, increasing the similarity of clients when comparisons are made across clients, and by decreasing irrelevancies such as the simultaneous occurrence of other events in the setting in which a single-system evaluation is implemented).

A sixth issue (or perhaps we should say advantage) is that we have illustrated in this section the use of the ES to estimate the magnitude of the effect within a single study. But the same principles and exactly the same calculations apply when using the ES as a basis for a meta-analysis of several studies as we suggested in Chapter 11 (e.g., Jayaratne et al., 1988). Thus, all that would be missing to complete a meta-analysis for assessing generalizability among several studies would be to calculate the average ES for all the studies combined, for all similar outcome measures across all the studies, or both.

Finally, and perhaps most importantly, the ES and meta-analysis procedures we've described are relatively new to the world of single-system designs. Some of the underlying principles have yet to be worked out and there are numerous issues associated with their use (e.g., Allison & Gorman, 1993; Corcoran, 1985; Faith et al., 1997; Fischer, 1990; Gingerich, 1984; Videka-Sherman, 1986; White et al., 1989). Since ES analysis has only rarely been used with single-system designs, these cautions apply even more so with regard to the applications discussed in this book. Thus, we urge their use only within a framework of cautious interpretation and integration with the other methods of analysis—visual, theoretical, and statistical—described in this book.

OPTIMAL USES AND CAUTIONS FOR SPECIFIC DESCRIPTIVE STATISTICS

Different descriptive statistics are appropriate under different circumstances. Therefore, it's important to understand which statistic is appropriate under which set of circumstances. This is a complex question about which we provide an overview in Chapter 24, but here we want to summarize the optimum uses for each statistic discussed in this chapter (where each is especially appropriate) and what particular cautions to be aware of (where each procedure has its limitations).

Measures of central tendency (mean, trimmed mean, median) should be used to represent the single value that best represents the "typical" score within a phase, and a horizontal line representing this value should be superimposed on the graphed data. Measures of central tendency should not be used when the data points exhibit a trend. The mean is most appropriate when there are no outliers. The trimmed mean is most appropriate when there are outliers, and when there's a sufficient number of scores within a phase to trim perhaps 10% of the highest and lowest scores and still have enough scores to compute the mean. The median is most appropriate when there are outliers, and when trimming 10% of the highest and lowest scores would not leave enough scores to compute a mean.

Measures of variability (standard deviation, range, trimmed range) should be used in conjunction with the appropriate measure of central tendency to represent the upper and lower boundaries within a phase of zones (e.g., desired and undesired) in which "typical" values are found, and horizontal lines representing the upper and lower boundaries of these zones should be superimposed on the graphed data. A standard deviation should be computed when there are no outliers. When there are outliers, compute a trimmed range, such as the interquartile range. It's possible to use measures of variability to compute "typical" zones around trend lines (Morley & Adams, 1991), although we only described the use of these statistics to determine such zones when there's no trend within a phase.

Linear trend lines (e.g., celeration or regression lines) should be used to represent the average amount of change over time within a phase when the data are increasing or de-

creasing over time, and straight lines representing this change can be superimposed on the graphed data. These lines should trend upward if the data are increasing, or downward if the data are decreasing. The slope of these lines should be computed to quantify the average amount of change over time. A celeration line (or regression line) can be computed if there are no outliers. When there are outliers, you could compute a celeration line based on trimmed means (when there are enough scores in each half of the phase) or medians (when there are few scores in each half of the phase). Linear trend lines, the only ones we discussed, should not be used when there's reason to believe that a trend doesn't fall along a relatively straight line (i.e., curved or curvilinear trends).

If there is any possibility of a trend, we recommend that you compute a celeration line before computing measures of central tendency. If the celeration is flat, then decide on the most appropriate measure of central tendency and variability. For example, results shown in Figure 21.8 suggest that the measures of central tendency and variability that we've illustrated using these data do not provide the best representation of the Allison et al. data.

If a trend is detected, the procedure in Chapter 19 for computing an autocorrelation does not provide an accurate estimate of autocorrelation. Currently there are no good practical ways to compute an accurate estimate of autocorrelation when data evidence a trend given the number of observations usually available with single-system designs.

Measures of effect size (e.g., Δ-index, *d*-index, and *g*-index) should be used to describe the size of the difference between two phases, and as a basis for conducting meta-analyses. The Δ-index or *d*-index should be used when there is no trend in either of the phases being compared, with the *d*-index preferred with a smaller number of baseline points. The *g*-index can be used in conjunction with the appropriate trend line when there's a trend. None of the effect sizes should be used when data are autocorrelated, unless the data are first transformed.

SUMMARY

Raw data are sometimes difficult to interpret because of their variability. Descriptive statistics can summarize patterns of data, making the visual analysis of data easier. Descriptive statistics also are important because they are necessary components of the tests of statistical significance that we discuss in the next chapter. Therefore, this chapter presented simple descriptive statistics that you can use to summarize central tendency, variability, and trend within a phase, in order to make comparisons between phases. Traditional measures of central tendency and variability were presented (e.g., mean, median, standard deviation, range), but newer methods that provide better summaries of data with outliers were emphasized (e.g., trimmed means and trimmed ranges). Measures of trend (celeration line, regression line) were described for use when data are increasing or decreasing over time. Also, measures of the magnitude of change from one phase to another—that is, measures of effect size—were presented.

The accurate description of a set of scores requires different categories of descriptive statistics (e.g., a measure of central tendency and a measure of variability). Therefore, the purposes of the different categories of descriptive statistics and the circumstances under which they should and shouldn't be used were described. In addition, for each category of descriptive statistics (e.g., measures of central tendency), the considerations involved in the selection of a particular statistic (e.g., median or trimmed mean) were detailed. However, there are circumstances where the single best measure of central tendency (e.g., median or trimmed mean), variability (standard deviation or trimmed range), trend (e.g., celeration line computed with or without outliers), or ES (Δ- or g-index) won't be clearcut. In these circumstances we urge you to compute and compare multiple measures and interpret your data with due caution when different seemingly appropriate measures lead to different conclusions.

Finally, step-by-step hand/calculator computations for the statistics were described and illustrated. Also, the steps needed to calculate these statistics using the personal computer program SINGWIN were briefly introduced.

22 TESTS OF STATISTICAL SIGNIFICANCE FOR SINGLE-SYSTEM DESIGNS

PURPOSE: This chapter discusses several different tests to determine statistical significance of the data in your single-system design: (a) the proportion/frequency approach, (b) the three-standard-deviation-band approach (X-Moving Range-Chart), (c) the chi-square, and (d) the *t*-test. Each approach has its strengths and limitations, and the conditions under which the particular tests should be used are described. ■

Introduction
Proportion/Frequency Approach
Computing Proportion/Frequency with SINGWIN
Other Uses of the Proportion/Frequency Approach
Considerations in Using the Proportion/Frequency
  Approach
**Three-Standard-Deviation-Band Approach
  (X-Moving Range-Chart)**
Computing the X-Moving Range-Chart (X-mR-
  chart) with SINGWIN
Considerations in Using the X-mR-Chart
Additional Uses of SPC Charts

Chi-Square
Computing Chi-Square with SINGWIN
Considerations in Using Chi-Square
***t*-Test**
Computing the *t*-test with SINGWIN
Considerations in Using the *t*-test
**General Considerations in Using Tests
  of Statistical Significance**
**Optimal Uses and Cautions for Specific
  Analytic Procedures**
Summary

INTRODUCTION

This chapter presents several relatively practical statistical methods that you can use in your analysis of data: (a) the proportion/frequency test, (b) the three-standard-deviation-band test

(X-mR-chart), (c) the chi-square, and (d) the *t*-test.

As you will see, there are some special conditions under which one or another of the analytic approaches might be most suitable–or unsuitable. Each has desirable and undesirable

595

aspects. However, the selected tests cover a broad range of situations, and they can be computed using either a simple calculator or the personal computer program that comes with this book, SINGWIN. In Chapter 24 we present a framework to help you decide which one to use under what conditions, including the visual approach discussed in Chapter 20 and the descriptive statistics covered in Chapter 21.

The tests presented in this chapter are not the only tests of statistical significance available for analyzing single-system design data (e.g., Franklin et al., 1997; Kazdin, 1984; Kratochwill & Levin, 1992; Krishef, 1991; Suen & Ary, 1989), and different tests were excluded for different reasons. Tests were excluded if they required a sophisticated knowledge of statistics, if they required accessibility to expensive or difficult-to-use computer programs, if they were limited to use in atypical situations, or if existing evidence suggested they were invalid.

Some of the notable methods we haven't discussed include analysis of variance, complex variations of time-series analysis (Glass et al., 1975; Gottman, 1981; Hartmann et al., 1980; Nurius, 1983; Suen & Ary, 1989), and randomization tests (Edgington, 1984, 1987; Marascuilo & Busk, 1988; Onghena, 1992; Wampold & Worsham, 1986; Holden et al., 1999, present a case illustration of a single-system design using random assignment of treatment conditions to times, a prerequisite for statistical randomization tests.). These are available for your use, although they require more detailed knowledge of statistics and in some cases accessibility to relatively expensive computer programs. We briefly describe the conditions for use of time-series analyses and randomization tests at the end of this chapter.

The proportion/frequency test, the three-standard-deviation-band test, and the chi-square all can be computed by hand or using SINGWIN. The *t*-test can be computed by hand, and the computational steps can be found in any introductory statistics text. However, we show how to compute the *t*-test more easily using SINGWIN.

PROPORTION/FREQUENCY APPROACH

The proportion/frequency approach to the analysis of single-system designs is a procedure that compares a "typical" pattern of events during baseline with a typical pattern during intervention, using the binomial distribution tables discussed in Chapter 19 (Bloom, 1975). Since this approach assumes the data are independent or not autocorrelated, you should use the test for autocorrelation presented in Chapter 19 before you use the proportion/frequency approach. In addition, this approach hinges on the meaning of *typical*, so we must define how this term is used.

In ordinary conversations, we have little difficulty using the word *typical* to mean representative of some set or class of events. You might ask, "What is Bill typically like?" The answer is an abstraction, generalizing from a large number of instances about what is most similar to them all (or to put it another way, the least dissimilar from them all). The measures of central tendency, discussed in Chapter 21, are one way of characterizing typical events. However, it's too limiting to refer simply to the central tendency of some set of events because it doesn't take into account the variability of such events. A "zone" of behavior constructed around a measure of central tendency, such as the mean, provides a more comprehensive characterization of the "typical" set of events. This method is similar to discussions of the normal curve that is bisected by its mean. The area under the normal curve has known properties that will be very helpful to our analysis. For example, one standard deviation above and below the mean includes about two-thirds of the area under that curve. Two standard deviations above and below the mean includes about 95% of that area.

Thus, if we wish to say that what is true of two-thirds of all cases that fall under a normal curve could be used to define what is typical of some behavior, then we can describe "typical" in fairly precise terms. However, there's nothing absolute about this—any set of limits can be used when it applies to some specific data. An example of this would be when some normative criterion level of behavior or performance is known, such as "normal" ranges of affect versus depressed levels of affect. In like manner, some variables are dichotomous, such as absent or present from school, did or did not have sexual intercourse, and so on. These also can be graphed with the appropriate zones indicated (see Figure 22.1).

Figure 22.1a shows a trichotomy in which a typical middle zone is identified (by a simple procedure described below) by means of an empirical representation of the typical problematic behaviors. The extremely undesired zone has no upper limit—whatever is beyond the typical is extremely undesired. The desired zone is less than the typical amount of problematic behaviors. Obviously, it probably would be best not to have tantrums, but relatively speaking, if intervention were able to change the pattern of events anywhere below the typical range of problematic behaviors, there would be some value attached in practical terms. We also would be able to determine whether such a change was statistically significant.

Figure 22.1b shows the instance where there's a preset norm of desired behavior, and even though the baseline pattern of events could have been trichotomized, it would have been irrelevant to the objectives of the achievement test. The third instance, Figure 22.1c, shows a dichotomy in which the zones are represented graphically. Now let's turn to an example to illustrate the proportion/frequency approach and its various applications.

First, suppose we're interested in the client census of an agency over a period of time in order to justify its continued support by the local United Fund. One set of relevant observations would be the number of clients who come to the agency and who stay in treatment until they and the practitioners agree on termination. Otherwise, they would be counted as premature terminators or dropouts. For any given month the percentage of dropouts would be computed by dividing the number of dropouts by the number of initial applicants, and multiplying this result by 100. (For simplicity, let's disregard length of service, and so on.) Figure 22.2 shows the baseline data for the previous year. Ordinarily, you would test for autocorrelation using the procedures outlined in Chapter 19. Let's assume the baseline data are not autocorrelated, or are transformed if they were autocorrelated, and then continue with the following steps.

Second, a "typical zone" is identified in the baseline data. This zone represents the typical presenting situation—in this case, the percentage of clients who typically stay in treatment until planned termination rather than dropping out. Sometimes the percentage drops sharply; this is extremely undesirable from the point of view of the agency. Other times the census is very high—many people stay in treatment until the planned end—a good state of affairs from the perspective of the agency. But the middle zone represents what is typically the case. To find this typical zone follow the procedures described in Exhibit 22.1.

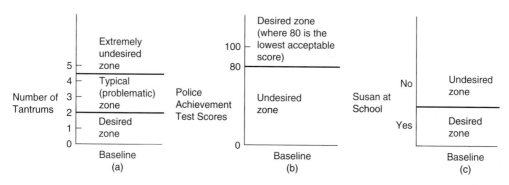

FIGURE 22.1   Illustrations of desired zones on graph.

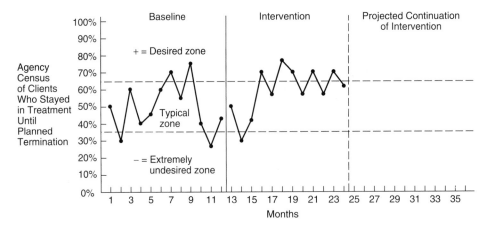

FIGURE 22.2 Illustration of the proportion/frequency approach together with an excerpt from Table 19.2 to indicate level of statistical significance attained.

Third, an intervention program begins while the same data are collected as in baseline. In our example, the agency administrators implement a program designed to increase the satisfaction and motivation of clients to stay in treatment until an agreed-upon termination is reached.

Fourth, a comparison is made between baseline and intervention following the steps in Exhibit 22.2.

Computing Proportion/Frequency with SINGWIN

You also can use SINGWIN to compute the proportion/frequency approach. It's easy. Just follow these steps:

1. Start SINGWIN (see "Starting SING-WIN" in the SINGWIN User's Guide, Chapter 23).

2. Follow the steps outlined in the section entitled "Computing a Proportion/

Frequency Approach" and enter the following: # Baseline Points = 12; # Baseline Successes = 2; # of Intervention Points = 12; # of Intervention Successes = 5.

Other Uses of the Proportion/Frequency Approach

Suppose that only 4 months appeared in the desired zone in the example in Figure 22.2. This would not be statistically significant at the .05 level, but what does this tell you? You can either give up on this intervention as leading to nonsignificant results, modify the intervention and attempt to make it stronger, or leave it alone (especially if no untoward side effects have emerged from the intervention over the year) if there's a trend in the right direction. Four out of 12 times seems like it might be a trend. However, with the proportion/frequency approach, you can make a crude guess as to how long it would take be-

EXHIBIT 22.1   Calculating Zones.

1. Count the number of baseline data points. Figure 22.2 shows 12 months (i.e., 12 data points) of baseline data.

2. Divide the number of baseline data points by 3 and multiply the dividend by 2. This gives two-thirds of the baseline data. In our example, 12 divided by 3 is 4, and 4 times 2 is 8. This means we must find the middle zone with about 8 data points in it.

3. To find the approximate middle two-thirds of the baseline data, draw a band enclosing the number of baseline points closest to the middle zone as determined in step 2. (The number of baseline points has nothing to do with the *scores* of those points. You just want to include 8 points.) Indicate this middle zone by drawing dashed horizontal lines between data points (as shown in Figure 22.2) which enclose the typical zone (8 points). Be careful not to draw a line on top of any data point; you won't know which side of the zones it lies in. This typical zone, then, encompasses about two-thirds of all the baseline data.

4. Leave at least 1 data point above and below the middle two-thirds projection lines, if possible, for computational reasons. This will be used to calculate the proportions of certain events in the baseline period. If this is not possible, use the "conservative" rule. This means that since there's no zero proportion on Tables 19.2, 19.3, or 19.4, one would use the next available proportion as the closest approximation, namely, .05.

5. Label each zone according to the nature of the target problem. In Figure 22.2, having a higher percentage of clients stay in treatment until a planned termination is desirable, so the upper part of the chart becomes the desired zone; a low percentage of clients staying in treatment is undesirable, so the lower part of the chart becomes the undesired zone.

fore this trend reached a statistically significant level.

This procedure also can be used as a form of *efficiency* estimation. It assumes that the set of events occurring in the first intervention period is the best guess as to what will tend to be repeated in a second or subsequent intervention period. Therefore, simply project the same number of events in the desired zone in the first intervention period, then check the tables in Chapter 19. For Figure 22.2, project another 5 out of 12 months in the desired zone for the next 12 months. This would make a total of 10 months in the desired zone out of a total of 24 months. Checking Table 19.4, we observe that 8 or more events of the desired type are needed for significance at the .05 level. This means that if the first intervention conditions are repeated in a second intervention, it's a reasonable guess that if the intervention is continued for another 12 months, statistical significance will be obtained. These are some big "ifs," but it's a basis for making a

crude estimate, where ordinarily we have very little objective basis on which to proceed.

Considerations in Using the Proportion/Frequency Approach

One of the major limitations of the proportion/frequency approach is that it can lead to inaccurate conclusions when the data are autocorrelated. Therefore, this approach should not be used when there's reason to believe that the data are autocorrelated, unless the transformations described in Chapter 19 are successful in removing the autocorrelation.

The number of required observations for use of the proportion/frequency approach depends primarily on the size of the difference that you want to detect between the two phases. In general, the larger the number of data points per phase, the more likely you are to detect an existing difference between phases; the larger the number of data points, the smaller the difference you'll be able to detect (this, again, is a

EXHIBIT 22.2 Determining Significance with the Proportion/Frequency Approach.

1. Determine how many times during the *baseline* period the target was in the desired zone. Looking at Figure 22.2, the target was in the desired zone twice in the 12-month period.

2. Find the proportion of events in the desired zone during baseline. In our example, this means dividing the total number of observations in the baseline, 12, into the number of observations in the desired zone, 2. Two divided by 12 is .1667, or 1/6. Tables 19.2, 19.3, and 19.4 all show the fraction 1/6 in the proportion column, so we don't even have to do the division to find the proportion; see the excerpt from Table 19.4 in Figure 22.2.

3. Determine how many time units are in the intervention period under consideration. In our example there are 12 months of intervention. Locate this number on the top row of Table 19.2. The Number of Interventions row stands for the total number of data points during the intervention period.

4. Determine whether there's a statistically significant difference between baseline and intervention by using the tables. In our illustration we would enter the body of Table 19.2 at the intersection of the proportion (step 2 above, 1/6) and the number of intervention units (step 3 above, 12). The number shown is 5, which means the number of observations in the desired zone during the intervention period that are necessary to represent a significant increase at the .05 level over the proportion of like events during the baseline period. Looking at Figure 22.2, we note that the intervention period contained five desired events (5 months that showed percentages above the typical pattern of clients who stayed until a mutually accepted termination). Therefore, we conclude that there was a statistically significant change in this target problem at the .05 level. This means that such a set of events could not have occurred by chance alone except 5 or fewer times in 100, a sufficiently rare event to say that its occurrence is statistically significant. If there had been 7 months in the desired zones, we could check the other tables (Tables 19.3 and 19.4) in order to see whether the data reached these significance levels. Using the same number (12) and proportion (1/6, or .167), we observe a 6 in Table 19.3 and an 8 in Table 19.4, which means that the 7-month instance is significant at the .01 level, but not at the .001 level.

reflection of statistical power). As discussed in Chapter 21, this effect size can be quantified using the *g*-index. For the example we used to illustrate the proportion/frequency approach, the *g*-index is computed by subtracting the proportion of baseline intervention observations in the desired zone from the proportion of intervention observations in the desired zone (i.e., $5/12 - 2/12 = .25$). If you use at least eight observations per phase, you will have a reasonable chance of detecting a moderate effect size (i.e., $g = .40$). If you want to have a reasonable chance of detecting a somewhat smaller effect size (i.e., $g = .30$), you probably would need at least 16 observations per phase (Orme, 1991).

THREE-STANDARD-DEVIATION-BAND APPROACH (X-MOVING RANGE-CHART)

A number of methods that are adaptable for analysis of single-system design data were first described by Shewhart (1931). These methods originally were developed for evaluation in industrial quality control, and are known more generally as "statistical process control charts" or simply "control charts" (Orme & Cox, 2001). Statistical process control charts date back to the 1920s, and they are at the heart of "statistical process control" (SPC), a large and versatile body of industrial quality control techniques (e.g., Doty, 1996; Ostle et al., 1996; Wheeler & Chambers, 1992). In previous editions of this book, we described a method known as the two-standard-deviation band (or Shewhart chart), based on Shewhart's (1931) work as adapted by Gottman and Leiblum (1974). However, we have discovered that there is a better method for constructing and interpreting this chart than the method described in earlier editions of this book. For reasons that we hope will be clear when we describe how it is constructed, both the Gottman and Leiblum version and the new version presented below are known in the SPC literature as an *X-Moving Range-Chart* (X-mR-chart) (Doty, 1996; Pitt, 1994; Wheeler & Chambers, 1992). We also call it the *three-standard-deviation-band approach.*

The X-mR-chart can be used in a number of ways. It can be used to determine whether there is a statistically significant difference between an individual data point and the mean of a series of data points (i.e., an abrupt change from the mean). The X-mR-chart can be used to detect change from one phase to the next. For example, it can be used to determine whether a data point during intervention is significantly different than the baseline mean. The X-mR-chart also can be used to detect change within a phase (e.g., Pfadt et al., 1992; Pfadt & Wheeler, 1995). For example, in prevention programs, the occurrence of large abrupt changes (e.g., excessive weight loss or gain) may signal the need to modify the prevention process. Or, the identification of a large abrupt relapse after successful implementation of an intervention may signal a need for "booster shots." In addition, the identification of a large abrupt change for better or worse can stimulate a search for the cause of such outcomes, which then can be incorporated into the intervention or prevention process (e.g., an increase in caregiver satisfaction associated with increased social support). Also, in observation-only designs, it is necessary to determine if some large abrupt change for the worse occurs (e.g., postpartum depression), which then may require intervention. Finally, in comparing data across phases, and in deciding when to change phases, it is important to determine if there are large abrupt changes within a phase that would make it difficult to make comparisons across different phases.

In brief, to construct and use the X-mR-chart to test the significance of change from the baseline to the intervention phase (i.e., from the *A* phase to the *B* phase), the mean level of a set of baseline data is identified and plotted. Then, three standard deviation levels are identified and plotted above and below the mean line (a specialized version of the standard deviation is used that is computed differently from the commonly used method described in Chapter 21). These baseline standard deviation bands then are extended into the intervention phase, and if one observation during the intervention phase

falls outside of the three standard deviation bands, there has been a statistically significant change in the mean (Doty, 1996; Pitt, 1994; Wheeler & Chambers, 1992).

If the underlying distribution of the outcome variable is normal, there is a 99.73% probability that any one data point will fall between these limits, and there is a .27% chance that any one data point will fall outside of these limits (i.e., alpha = .0027). The basic idea of the X-mR-chart is that plus or minus three standard deviations represents about 99.7% of the scores under a normal curve. (You can see a rough approximation of this graphically in Chapter 20, Figure 20.11). Scores that move outside of that band are very rare, probabilistically speaking. With such a rigorous criterion, you can be confident that any change detected probably is not due to chance.

Let's use the example of a weight loss program with an 8-week retrospective baseline and an 8-week intervention program. Baseline data and the steps for computing the elements of the X-mR-chart are described in Exhibit 22.3. The x-mR-chart is shown in Figure 22.3.

This example illustrates both the use and a limitation of this approach. In this illustration, one data point fell below the lower three-standard-deviation-band at week 12, indicating a statistically significant weight loss. However, the next week the observation moved back inside the three standard deviation band. Obviously the practitioner's work was not done after week 12, and the intervention needed to be extended or intensified beyond that time. The result may be significant, at that point, but not lasting, although in this example, the weight did, once again, drop below the lower band and remain there for three weeks.

Computing the X-Moving Range-Chart (X-mR-chart) with SINGWIN

Here's how to use SINGWIN (see Chapter 23) to compute the X-mR-chart.

1. Start SINGWIN (see "Starting SING-WIN" in the SINGWIN User's Guide, Chapter 23).

EXHIBIT 22.3 **Calculating the X-moving range-chart (x-mR-chart).**

Steps for Computing the X-mR-Chart	Baseline Data from Figure 22.3
1. Record observed baseline scores.	$s_1 = 119$ $s_2 = 122$ $s_3 = 120$ $s_4 = 118$ $s_5 = 118$ $s_6 = 117$ $s_7 = 118$ $s_8 = 119$
2. Sum the observed scores. $\sum_s$	$\sum_s = 47$
3. Divide the sum of the observed scores by the number of scores used to obtain the sum. This gives the mean, M	M = 951/8 = 118.88
4. Compute the range (R) of each two adjacent data points and treat all numbers as positive. (Note that there will be one fewer range value than data points.)	$s_2 - s_1 = 122 - 119 = 3$ $s_3 - s_2 = 120 - 122 = 2$ $s_4 - s_3 = 118 - 120 = 2$ $s_5 - s_4 = 118 - 118 = 0$ $s_6 - s_5 = 117 - 118 = 1$ $s_7 - s_6 = 118 - 117 = 1$ $s_8 - s_7 = 119 - 118 = 1$
5. Sum the ranges. $\sum_R$	$\sum_R = 10$
6. Divide the sum of the ranges by the number of scores minus one. This gives the mean range, $\bar{R}$	$\bar{R} = 10/7 = 1.43$
7. Divide the mean range by 1.128, a correction factor, to get the standard deviation. SD	$SD = \dfrac{1.43}{1.128} = 1.27$
8. Multiply the standard deviation by 3.	$3 \times 1.27 = 3.81$

(continued)

EXHIBIT 22.3   (Continued).

Steps for Computing the X-mR-Chart	*Baseline Data from Figure 22.3*
9. To get the upper band *add* the three standard deviations to the mean.	upper = M + 3SD = 118.88 + 3.81 = 122.69
10. To get the lower band *subtract* the three standard deviations from the mean.	lower = M − 3SD = 118.88 − 3.81 = 115.07
11. We could also label one area of the chart as the desired zone and one as the undesired zone, depending on the nature of the target problem (the direction in which we want the problem to change). In Figure 22.3, because we want the weight to decrease, the lower band is the desired zone.	

12. If the band drops below the horizontal axis of the chart, you could add a constant, say, of 10, to all figures including each score, the mean, and the standard deviation. Replot all these points higher on the chart, and do the same for the intervention period. Then proceed with the analysis.

13. If one data point goes beyond a band in the desired direction in the intervention phase, the results show improvement that is statistically significant at the .05 level (actually .0027). If one data point goes beyond the band in the undesired direction in the intervention phase, the results show deterioration that is statistically significant at less than the .05 level (.0027).

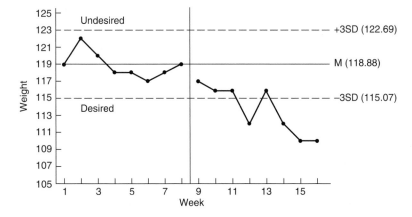

FIGURE 22.3   Pounds of weight over 16 weeks.

2. Open the "fig22-3.dbf" file (containing the Figure 22.3 data) that comes with SING-WIN (see "Opening an Existing File").

3. Follow the steps outlined in the section entitled "Computing XmR."

Considerations in Using the X-mR-Chart

The three-standard-deviation-band approach or X-mR-chart is a relatively simple procedure that can be used with just about any number of data points although, as with all statistical tests, the more observations, the better. However, there may be a slight advantage over other approaches when there are fewer baseline points or when the baseline data are fluctuating and it is difficult to find a stable pattern. This is because a reduced reliability in estimating the "true" level of the baseline is countered somewhat by the large bandwidth (three standard deviations) outside of which the target must occur in order for the change to be considered significant.

There are some limitations to the use of the three-standard-deviation-band approach. One potential limitation of the X-mR-chart, and SPC charts more generally, is the criterion used to determine change. With the use of the three-standard-deviation rule, alpha is set to .0027, two-tailed. Data points outside of the three standard-deviation bands command attention because they are so unlikely. However, the probability of correctly detecting a change (i.e., statistical power) is limited by this low alpha value. Less stringent decision criteria (e.g., the use of two standard-deviation bands) might be useful (Blumenthal, 1993; Carey & Lloyd, 1995), especially when using SPC charts for practice evaluation, but when the three-standard-deviation rule is used, the X-mR-chart will work well even when there is autocorrelation and the outcomes are distributed in different ways (e.g., something other than a normal distribution) (e.g., Wheeler & Chambers, 1992).

There are four situations in which the X-mR-chart should not be used, or should be used with caution. First, the X-mR-chart should only

be used with an interval level outcome variable. Second, the X-mR-chart should not be used, or used only with caution, when there are trends, especially pronounced trends, in the data. This is because the X-mR-chart is used to detect a change in the mean, like the *t*-test, for example. Imagine an increasing trend in the baseline phase and a decreasing trend in the intervention phase (as in Chapter 20, Figure 20.3[e]). The mean would be the same, and you wouldn't detect a statistical change though there actually was a dramatic change. Similarly, a rapidly increasing or decreasing baseline could be predictive of intervention phase data that could move beyond the boundaries even of the three-standard-deviation band, not because of intervention, but because of changes that already had begun in the baseline (i.e., trend across phases or drift).

There are two very rough ways to determine the presence of trend (in addition to those described in Chapter 21). The first is just to examine the data visually. If the baseline data look as though there is clear directionality (increasing or decreasing) in the data (trend) to the extent that this directionality looks as though the trend would have continued to increase or decrease in the next phase (without actual changes due to intervention), you can assume trend. The second method is to use a pencil to lightly draw on your chart a straight line from the first baseline point to the last. If two-thirds or more of the baseline points touch or cluster around that line, *and* the same conditions pertain as in the visual assessment described earlier in this paragraph, you can be certain pronounced trend is present.

The third limitation in using the X-mR-chart has to do with autocorrelation. While we believe this approach can be reliably used when the data are autocorrelated, we also believe it should be used with caution if the data are autocorrelated. This is because there is some disagreement about the extent to which autocorrelation distorts conclusions drawn from SPC charts (Wheeler & Chambers, 1992). When in doubt, you can test the data for autocorrelation using the procedure described in Chapter 19; if the data are autocorrelated, you can transform them to remove the autocorrelation using the methods described in Chapter 19.

Fourth and finally, when there is a large discrepancy between the number of baseline points and the number of intervention points (typically, the intervention period is longer), the X-mR-chart should be used with caution. This is because the greater passage of time for the intervention period may lead to a drift outside of the band that is due more to time than to the presumed effects of the intervention. Of course, the use of the three-standard-deviation bands makes such a nonmeaningful drift relatively unlikely.

Additional Uses of SPC Charts

Although we described a number of limitations of the X-mR-chart, there actually are other SPC Charts that can be used to overcome these disadvantages, for example, when trend is present (Doty, 1996) or when the data are autocorrelated (e.g., Atlienza, Tang, & Ang, 1998; Liu & Tang, 1996). Similarly, when the outcome variable is dichotomous–for example, whether group members attend group meetings, anorectic clients skip meals, clinic clients keep appointment, children attend school– other SPC charts can be used. One easily constructed SPC chart for use with dichotomous outcomes is the proportion-chart or p-chart, the steps for which are described in Orme & Cox (2001).

Finally, there are a number of software packages that run SPC charts (Orme & Cox, 2001). Among these, SPC XL (**http://www. sigmazone.com/SPC_XL/spc_xl.html**) seems particularly attractive because of its low price and the fact that it works with Microsoft Excel, which provides extensive graphics capabilities and the ability to export results easily to word processor packages such as Microsoft Word. Also, SPSS produces SPC charts. The control chart function in SPSS is available under the Graph submenu, and it allows you to choose from among several categories of SPC charts. Another option is to construct spreadsheets (for example, Zimmerman & Icenogle, 1999). Orme and Cox (2001) have developed Excel spreadsheets to enter data; calculate CL, UCL, and

LCL; and dynamically display an SPC chart. Thus far, they have developed spreadsheets for the X-mR-chart, X̄-R-chart, R-chart, p-chart, and c-chart. These spreadsheets are available without charge at **http://utcmhsrc.csw.utk.edu/ evaluatingpractice/course%20materials.htm**.

As noted above, the X-mR-chart is just one member of a large family of SPC charts (e.g., Doty, 1996; Orme & Cox, 2001; Ostle et al., 1996; Wheeler & Chambers, 1992). Indeed, the SPC literature is vast, dating back to Shewhart's 1931 work, and so entering this literature can be daunting. In addition to the literature cited above, one especially useful starting place for the interested reader is the web page of the American Society for Quality (ASQ) (http://www.asqc.org). Among other features, this site provides a glossary, a searchable database of relevant articles, and a catalog of books. Also, the *Journal of Quality Control,* published by the ASQ, and the journal *Technometrics,* published jointly by the ASQ and the American Statistical Association, are good sources for SPC and related topics.

CHI-SQUARE

One of the most familiar statistics to most helping professionals is the chi-square (χ^2). Chi-square is a nonparametric or distribution-free statistic. It has very few assumptions that constrain its use, although it does assume that the data are independent, so it should be used only with caution if your data are autocorrelated (and not transformed). But, chi-square is a well-known procedure, relatively easy to compute. Its strengths and capabilities are better established than the two statistics described so far in this chapter.

The chi-square is used to determine whether there is a significant difference between the expected and observed frequencies in different categories. Therefore, it is necessary to have some system for establishing those frequencies, since we generally are faced with raw scores in the data we collect with our clients.

To develop frequencies, therefore, we can use any of the methods for determining desired and undesired zones described earlier.

For purposes of illustration we will use the celeration line, described in Chapter 21. All we have to do is decide which is the positive or desired direction and which is the negative or undesired direction in a celeration line (similar to the way we do with the proportion/frequency or three-standard-deviation band approaches). That is, if we want a target to increase, then the area *above* the celeration line is considered the desired or positive zone. If the goal is for the target to decrease, then the area *below* the celeration line is the desired or positive zone.

We are using the celeration line mainly for illustrative purposes. We recognize that research on the celeration line has shown its use as a method for determining statistical significance using a different statistical test to be questionable (Crosbie, 1987). However, in this case, the celeration line is not the heart of the statistic; it is used only to establish categories for the chi-square test.

The chi-square is very easy to compute by hand. (It also can be computed by your SINGWIN computer program, as we illustrate below.) It provides a reliable method for conventional statistical testing of the hypothesis that the differences between the expected and observed frequencies of baseline and intervention periods will be statistically significant. The data in Exhibit 22.4, illustrating how to calculate chi-square, will be based on the same chart used for the calculation of the effect size, Δ, in Chapter 21 (reproduced in Figure 22.4).

Since all of your data will be in the same configuration as the information in Exhibit 22.4—that is, in a 2 × 2 cross-tabulation—your calculations can proceed in exactly the same way as those in the illustration. As can be seen from the results, the difference between the baseline and intervention was not significant, suggesting the need to extend or intensify the intervention, or perhaps to change the intervention completely in an effort to provide a more powerful effect.

Computing Chi-Square with SINGWIN

Here's how to use SINGWIN to compute chi-square.

1. Start SINGWIN (see "Starting SING-WIN" in the SINGWIN User's Guide, Chapter 23).

2. Open the "fig22-4.dbf" file (containing the figure 22.4 data) that comes with SINGWIN (see "Opening an Existing File").

3. Follow the steps outlined in the section entitled "Computing Chi-Square."

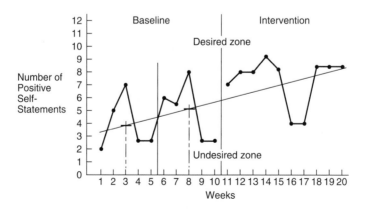

FIGURE 22.4 Data illustrating a celeration line for chi-square analysis in Exhibit 22.4.

EXHIBIT 22.4   Calculating Chi-Square.

Calculation of Chi-Square Using Celeration Line Data

1. Calculate celeration line using procedure described in Chapter 21, Exhibit 21.6	See Figure 22.4.
2. Determine desired and undesired zones.	In Figure 22.4, because the goal is to increase positive self-statements, points above the line are considered the desired zone and points below the line are considered undesired zone.

3. Count the points in the desired (positive) and undesired (negative) zones for the baseline and intervention periods.	Baseline
	  Desired zone = 5 points above line
	  Undesired zone = 5 points below line
	Intervention
	  Desired zone = 8 points above line
	  Undesired zone = 2 points below line

4. Place the points in a two-way table (cross-tabulation) with the rows representing the phase and the columns representing the outcome. These are called the observed frequencies.

	Desired (+)	Undesired (−)
BL	5	5
Inter.	8	2

5. Determine the expected frequencies.
   (a) Determine column totals: $5 + 8 = 13$ and $5 + 2 = 7$.
   (b) Determine row totals: $5 + 5 = 10$ and $8 + 2 = 10$.
   (c) Determine grand total: add the two row totals.
   (d) For each cell, multiply row by column totals and divide by grand total. Insert in cells. These are the expected frequencies.

	Desired (+)	Undesired (−)	
BL	6.5 5	3.5 5	10
Inter.	6.5 8	3.5 2	10
	13	7	20

(+)	(−)
$\dfrac{10 \times 13}{20} = 6.5$	$\dfrac{10 \times 7}{20} = 3.5$
$\dfrac{10 \times 13}{20} = 6.5$	$\dfrac{10 \times 7}{20} = 3.5$

(*continued*)

EXHIBIT 22.4 (Continued)

Calculation of Chi-Square Using Celeration Line Data	

6. Subtract the expected frequency from the observed frequency in each cell.	(+) $5 - 6.5 = -1.5$ $8 - 6.5 = 1.5$ (−) $5 - 3.5 = 1.5$ $2 - 3.5 = -1.5$
7. Square each of these results.	(+) (−) $-1.5^2 = 2.25$ $1.5^2 = 2.25$ $1.5^2 = 2.25$ $-1.5^2 = 2.25$

8. Complete the chi-square formula
$$\chi^2 = \sum \frac{(O - E)^2}{E}$$
by dividing each product from Step 7 by its expected frequency.

	Desired (+)	Undesired (−)
BL	$\frac{2.25}{6.5} = .346$	$\frac{2.25}{3.5} = .642$
Inter.	$\frac{2.25}{6.5} = .346$	$\frac{2.25}{3.5} = .642$

9. Sum these figures. This is your chi-square.

.346
.346
.642
.642
1.976 or 1.98

10. Check the following table to see if the chi-square is significant (all 2 × 2 tables have 1 degree of freedom). If your calculated value is the same or higher than the given χ^2 value below, it is statistically significant at that probability level:

$\chi^2 = 1.98$
Not significant

Probability

	.10	.05	.02	.01	.001
χ^2	2.706	3.841	5.412	6.635	10.827

Considerations in Using Chi-Square

The chi-square is a fairly simple method to calculate that is based on well-established statistical principles. Because of its construction and long tradition of use, in general it may be a more reliable statistic to use than either the proportion/frequency approach or the three-standard-deviation-band procedure. However, its use in this context, with single-system designs, is relatively unexplored, and future research may place serious constraints on its value.

There are a few technical considerations that limit the use of chi-square. It does assume the data are independent (not autocorrelated). The chi-square also requires an adequate sample size with expected frequencies in at least three of the four cells greater than five. The cell frequency in our example was really only borderline appropriate. (For smaller samples, the Fisher Exact Probability Test is more appropriate. The steps for calculating this test are available in most statistics texts, and SINGWIN reports the obtained probabilities for this test.) Further, the chi-square test is only a two-tailed test—that is, we can only tell whether the baseline and intervention periods differed from each other in terms of expected versus observed frequency of desired and undesired scores. We are not testing the hypothesis that the intervention period will have more scores in the desired zone than the baseline period. It is up to us to look at those data and make the judgment as to which seems to be the more desirable pattern once we know whether the data are statistically significant.

t-TEST

The proportion/frequency approach, the three-standard-deviation-band approach, and the chi-square are procedures for determining statistical significance that can be computed easily by hand or using a simple calculator. There are several other procedures that for all practical purposes require a computer and a little more statistical sophistication, but we think that you will find them practical and useful. We'll describe one of these approaches, the *t*-test, in this section.

Under some circumstances the *t*-test can be used to test whether there's a statistically significant difference between the mean score in one phase and the mean score in another phase. The *t*-test can be computed by hand or using a simple calculator, and the steps for this are described in almost any elementary statistics text. It also can be computed easily using SING-WIN. Let's illustrate how to compute the *t*-test using data from the case of "Benny" reported by Kolko and Milan (1983). These data are illustrated in Figure 22.5, along with the phase means and standard deviations, and the actual values of the scores (these data were estimated from Kolko and Milan's graphed data).

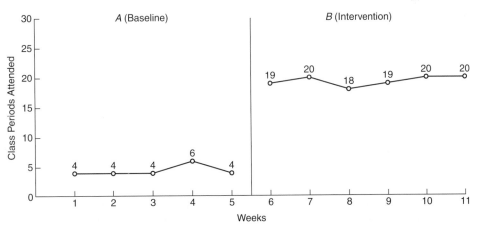

Baseline: M = 4.40, SD = .89

Intervention: M = 19.33, SD = .82

FIGURE 22.5 Number of class periods attended.

Computing the *t*-test with SINGWIN

Here's how to use SINGWIN to compute the *t*-test.

1. Start SINGWIN (see "Starting SING-WIN" in the SINGWIN User's Guide, Chapter 23).
2. Open the "benny.dbf" file. The instructions for entering this file are contained in Chapter 23 in the section entitled "Creating a New File."
3. Follow the steps outlined in the section entitled "Computing a *t*-Test."

Considerations in Using the *t*-test

The *t*-test shouldn't be used with autocorrelated data (Kenny & Judd, 1986; Toothaker et al., 1983), at least not without transformation of the data to remove the autocorrelation. Also, if there's a trend within either phase, the mean will not provide an accurate summary of the data within the phase, as discussed and illustrated in Chapter 21, and so the *t*-test shouldn't be used to test for a difference between phase means when there's a trend in either phase. Also, the *t*-test assumes that the observations within each phase are normally distributed (i.e., have a "bell-shaped" distribution with the mean, mode, and median values about the same) and the variability within each phase is the same. While these assumptions are difficult to test, the violation of these assumptions is not particularly problematic unless the number of observations is small and/or the number of observations in different phases is quite different (e.g., the larger number of observations divided by the smaller number of observations is greater than 1.5). (The "Unequal Variances" *t*-test in SINGWIN should be used if there's reason to believe that the standard deviations are unequal, with a very rough guide being one variance or standard deviation more than twice as large as the other, but otherwise the "Equal Variances" *t*-test in SINGWIN should be used.)

The number of required observations for use of the *t*-test depends primarily on the size of the difference between the two phases that you want to be able to detect. In general, the larger the number of data points per phase, the more likely you are to detect an existing difference between phases, and the larger the number of data points, the smaller the difference you'll be able to detect. As discussed in Chapter 21, this effect size can be quantified using the Δ-index. We recommend that you have at least six observations per phase, and if you do this, it will give you a reasonable chance of detecting a large effect size (i.e., $\Delta = 1.50$). If you want to have a reasonable chance of detecting a somewhat smaller effect size (i.e., $\Delta = 1.00$), you will need at least 13 observations per phase (Orme, 1991).

GENERAL CONSIDERATIONS IN USING TESTS OF STATISTICAL SIGNIFICANCE

In this chapter we described tests of statistical significance for single-system designs that we think cover a broad range of typical situations, and that we think can be used with basic statistical and personal computer skills. They are to be used in the spirit of practical evaluation: attempting to get some feedback that is as precise as possible given the available time and energy in order to guide your decision making. We haven't discussed all available methods, and the methods we've discussed are accurate under some circumstances and inaccurate under other circumstances, as are all statistical methods.

For just about all of the statistics discussed in this chapter there is a variety of common issues. One of the most important is the issue of autocorrelation. The procedures may be weakened in direct proportion to the degree of autocorrelation in the data, as we described in Chapter 19. Therefore, we suggest that you test your data for autocorrelation, and transform the data if necessary. However, remember that there's a chance that you won't detect autocorrelation as significant even when it exists, especially when a small number of observations are used. Therefore, since any degree of autocorrelation can distort the results of statistics, tests that assume the absence of autocorrelation should be used and interpreted with considerable caution.

Another important issue to consider in the use of tests of statistical significance is the number of available observations. We've provided some very tentative suggestions for several of the tests. However, in general, the larger the number of data points per phase, the more likely you are to detect existing intervention effects, and the larger the number of data points, the smaller the intervention effect you'll be able to detect (the concept of power again). Therefore, decisions based on small numbers of observations should be made with considerable caution and recognition of their potential fallibility, and especially their potential insensitivity to detecting existing differences between phases.

Fortunately, increasing the number of data points is not the only way to increase the sensitivity of statistical tests to intervention effects (e.g., Lipsey, 1990; Orme, 1991). We can summarize some of these here. You can use directional (or one-tailed) tests of hypotheses as opposed to nondirectional (or two-tailed tests) where appropriate, to increase sensitivity. You can use more valid and reliable outcome measures, and implement interventions in the most reliable, valid, and powerful way possible. To the extent it is practical, we suggest you try to equalize the number of data points in the different phases being compared. You can pool different phases and then make comparisons based on these pooled phases (e.g., combine the data points from two separate baseline phases, assuming the pattern of data is the same in each, and compare these pooled baseline data to data from an intervention phase). However, we realize this may not be feasible or desirable in most practical situations since the original form of the data is lost. Thus, there are a number of things that you should consider to increase the chances that your statistical tests will be sufficiently sensitive to detect existing intervention effects.

The statistical tests described in this chapter can be used in a variety of ways. We've placed major emphasis here on determining whether a change is statistically significant. However, as we suggested in Chapter 3, there are other ways you can use statistics to help you make judgments about goal achievement. For example, you can set up your typical zone of behavior for the proportion frequency approach or three-standard-deviation-band before intervention starts, with your goal simply being a statistically significant change in the problem. Then, when the change reaches the point designated in advance, you've reached both your goal and statistical significance. This can be a big help in setting goals when other criteria are not available.

Most of the procedures here were designed to compare two phases, such as a baseline and an intervention phase. However, there are some other possibilities for their use that you may want to consider. For example, you can extend the three-standard-deviation bands or proportion/frequency zones into the second A phase in an A-B-A-B design. This then can be used as an approximate guideline for when to stop the removal and reimplement intervention (e.g., when the problem drops out of the statistically significant range comparing, as always, adjacent phases). Similarly, for the multiple-baseline design you can use statistics to determine when to start intervention with the next target. Thus, when the previous target reaches statistical significance (even if more intervention is needed to achieve practical significance), you can begin intervention on the next target. Also, if your design consists of an A phase followed by several intervention phases (e.g., A-B-BC-BCD), all of the intervention phases could be combined into one data set and then the baseline data could be compared with the combined set of intervention data. Just keep in mind that for these purposes, particularly, the standards for use of the statistics we've described are not well established for single-system designs, so don't try to interpret those uses in absolute terms.

Given the nature of the statistics presented in this chapter, and particularly the use of statistics noted in the previous paragraph, we urge that the statistics be taken largely as rough working guides to help you in making your decisions. Putting together the patterns you detect through visual analysis, descriptive statistics, and tests of statistical significance is simply a good (but not perfect) way of trying to provide as much information as possible in the quest for informed decision making.

OPTIMAL USES AND CAUTIONS FOR SPECIFIC ANALYTIC PROCEDURES

Different statistical tests are appropriate under different circumstances. Therefore, it's important to understand which method of analysis is appropriate under which set of circumstances. This is a complex question that we discuss in more detail in Chapter 24, but here we want to summarize what we see as the optimum uses for each procedure discussed in this chapter (where each is especially appropriate) and what particular cautions to be aware of (where each procedure has its limitations).

The *proportion/frequency* approach can be used to compare data from two conditions (e.g., baseline and intervention) when the outcome is measured continuously on an interval scale (i.e., actual scores that can take on any value) or dichotomously; in the case of a dichotomous outcome variable you simply label which half is the preferred portion of the dichotomy and use that as the desired zone for computational purposes. (This produces a "desired" and "undesired" zone, which basically are all you need; they are predetermined without figuring out the middle or typical zone. This is pretty much the way any clinical cutoff point is predetermined.) An important use of the proportion/frequency approach is in making estimates regarding efficiency—that is, in predicting how long it likely will take, based on existing information, for present patterns in the intervention data to become statistically significant. The proportion/frequency approach should not be used when there's a trend within phases or when the data are autocorrelated (unless the data are suitably transformed). (The issue of trend is less important when the direction of baseline data is toward undesired behavior because a reversal of this pattern would be statistically and practically significant.) The proportion/frequency approach also is particularly useful when the intervention phase is longer than the baseline phase. This is because the use of the tables (from Chapter 19) requires an increasing number of intervention points in the desired zone as the number of intervention points increases; this controls somewhat for the differences in number of points between the phases.

The *X-mR-chart three-standard-deviation-band approach* can be used to determine whether there is a statistically significant difference between an individual data point and the mean of a series of data points, and so it can be used to detect change from one phase to the next or to detect change within a phase. The X-mR-chart should only be used with interval level outcome variables; it should not be used when there is a pronounced trend in the data, and it can be used, but with caution, when data are autocorrelated or when the number of intervention points *greatly* exceeds the number of baseline points.

The *chi-square* statistic is sort of a bridge between the first two statistics and the *t*-test, and is easily calculated by hand or by computer. Because it is a nonparametric or distribution-free statistic, the chi-square has less rigorous assumptions than the *t*-test. However, the chi-square does assume independence, so there should be caution in its use if the data are autocorrelated. Since the chi-square does not take the actual values of the outcome variable into account, it may be less sensitive to intervention effects than the *t*-test, though it probably has greater flexibility. And because the chi-square has not been used extensively with data from single-system designs, future research will have to be conducted to determine its validity in the context of single-system designs.

The *t*-test can be used to compare data from two conditions when the outcome is measured continuously, when the variability within phases is approximately equal (although this is not as important when the number of observations in different phases is approximately equal), and when the distribution of scores within phases is approximately normal (although this is not as important when the number of observations is relatively large). The *t*-test should not be used when there's a trend within phases or when the data are autocorrelated (unless the data are suitably transformed). If these conditions are met, the *t*-test will be more sensitive to existing intervention effects than the proportion/frequency approach, the three-standard-deviation-band approach or the chi-square because the t-test takes the actual values of the outcome variable into account, not just whether the outcome value is above or below some given value.

The *randomization* tests we mentioned in the Introduction (e.g., Onghena, 1992) can be used to compare data from two conditions when the outcome is measured continuously on an interval-level measure, when there's no trend within phases, and when treatment times are randomly assigned to treatments. Autocorrelation is not of concern with this test, and unlike the t-test, it does not require equal variability in different phases or a normal distribution of the outcome variable within phases. Of course, there are relatively few single-system designs that use ran-

domization, so this procedure has rather limited utility (see Holden et al., 1999, for an exception to this generalization).

The *time-series analysis* also mentioned in the Introduction (e.g., Gottman, 1981) can be used to compare data from two conditions when the outcome is measured continuously on an interval-level measure. Time-series analysis is optimally applied when the data are presumed to be autocorrelated, or when you assume they're autocorrelated and don't wish to transform them so that you can use some other analytic procedure. Also, time-series analysis is useful for comparing changes in trends across phases. However, time-series analyses generally require very large baselines and use of a specialized computer program.

SUMMARY

This chapter presented the computational steps for three simple analytic procedures—the proportion/frequency approach, the three-standard-deviation-band approach (X-Moving Range-Chart), and the chi-square. It also provided instructions for computing a t-test. Initially, even these procedures may appear to require lots of hard mathematics. However, when you go over each, one step at a time, and become familiar with what is actually required, the analytic procedures become more feasible. For the first three tests, both hand and computer calculations are presented, while for the t-test, only computer calculation were described (see also Chapter 23).

Each of the procedures described has its own strengths and limitations, which you must understand in order to use it wisely. This will require some practice, but the directions for optimal uses and cautions are short and easy to use. A little practice will make them both familiar and comfortable. Familiarity with these procedures and their optimal uses and limitations will provide the basis for the suggestions in Chapter 24 for making a selection among these analytic procedures. We want to emphasize that in the context of single-system designs, most of these procedures are approximate. They should be used holistically for decision making, in concert with the other criteria described in Chapter 19.

23

COMPUTER ANALYSIS OF SINGLE-SYSTEM DESIGN DATA
SINGWIN User's Guide

PURPOSE: This chapter shows you how to use SINGWIN, a personal computer program for the analysis of single-system design data. The CD-ROM for this program is included with this book, and the Appendix at the end of this chapter shows you how to install it. ■

Chapter Overview
Starting SINGWIN
Exiting SINGWIN
Getting the Big Picture
File Menu
Statistics Menu
Graphs Menu
Reports Menu
Using Specific Procedures
Files
   Creating a New File
   Opening an Existing File
   Copying a File
   Copying a File Using a New Name
   Deleting a File
Graphs
   Creating a Basic Line Chart
   Creating Other Types of Basic Line Charts
   Creating Charts of Transformed Data

Creating Band Graphs
Creating a Celeration Line Chart
Statistics
   Computing and Testing Autocorrelation
   Computing Transformations
   Computing Measures of Central Tendency and
    Variability
   Computing Standard-Deviation Bands
   Computing Effect Size
   Computing a Proportion/Frequency Approach
   Computing the X-Moving Range-Chart (Three-
    Standard-Deviation-Band Approach)
   Computing a Chi-Square
   Computing a t-Test
Generating Reports
Appendix: Installing SINGWIN
Summary

We are very pleased to include with this book a comprehensive program for the analysis of single-system design data. This program is named SINGWIN, and it is a Windows-based personal computer program designed by Charles Auerbach, David Schnall, and Heidi Heft Laporte specifically for this book.

SINGWIN computes most of the statistics that we discuss, and generates most of the graphs and charts. Furthermore, as you'll see in this chapter, SINGWIN is a program that we think you'll find very user-friendly, and it only will take a small investment of your time to learn. It's menu-driven, and we believe that after a small amount of practice you won't even need the instructions provided in this chapter. Also, SINGWIN requires only a very basic personal computer by the standards of today (although SINGWIN will work on most computers with Windows 95 or 98, we recommend Windows ME or newer).

All computer programs, no matter how carefully constructed, tested, and explained, pose problems and questions for users. Also, most computer programs grow over time to encompass new features. To address these issues, you can contact the developers of SINGWIN on the World Wide Web by first accessing the web page for this book: **http://www.ablongman.com/bloom.** Once there, just click on the "Technical Support" button. You can request technical support for SINGWIN at this site, or you can e-mail *singwin@ymail.yu.edu.* You can also go to **http://utcmhsrc.csw.utk.edu/ evaluatingpractice/** for Frequently Asked Questions about SINGWIN.

CHAPTER OVERVIEW

This chapter is organized into three sections. First, we show you how to start and then exit the program. Second, we give you an overview of the program and its organization and features. Finally, we show you very specifically how to use SINGWIN for the tasks we described in Chapters 19 through 22. *Before you do any of this, however, you have to install SINGWIN. Installation instructions are included in an Appendix at the end of this chapter.*

We assume that you know very little about computers, and we apologize in advance if this isn't the case. There are a few things that you need to know at the outset, but if you've used Windows before, or you have used CASS or CAAP from Chapters 4 and 7, you probably already know these.

Before starting, first be sure to familiarize yourself with the basic operations of your computer (e.g., location of your A drive, "Enter" key, Ctrl key, and ←↑→↓ keys). In particular, find out what version of Windows is installed on your computer.

Also, you'll need to know the following terms to install and use this software:

- **"Click"** means use your mouse to move the arrow you see on your screen to a certain word or place on the screen, and then click the *left* mouse button once.

- **"Right-click"** means use your mouse to move the arrow you see on your screen to a certain word or place on the screen, and then click the *right* mouse button once.

- **"Double-click"** means use your mouse to move the arrow you see on your screen to a certain word or place on the screen, and then click the *left* mouse button *twice quickly.*

STARTING SINGWIN

Single
Statistics

▶ Double-click the "Single Statistics" icon.

▶ Double-click the "SINGWIN" icon in the "Single Statistics" window.

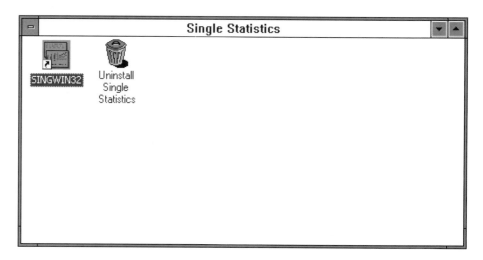

Double-click the SINGWIN32 icon on your desktop. A blank screen with a menu bar appears. This is the "Main Menu." You can click any of these items and menus will be displayed. Next we'll give you an overview of each of these menus, and then we'll give you more detailed instructions for using selected options listed on these menus.

EXITING SINGWIN

If at any time in the exercises we describe below you want to exit the program, here's how you do it.

► Click "File" and "Exit Program."

► Click "Yes" in response to the question "Are you certain?"

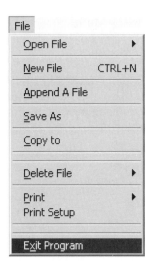

GETTING THE BIG PICTURE

Before showing you how to use SINGWIN to construct graphs, compute statistics, and do other fun things, we want to give you an overview of the organization and capabilities of SINGWIN. To do this we'll illustrate and briefly describe each of the menus around which SINGWIN is organized.

File Menu

► Click "File."

Use this menu to manage your files. For example, you need to enter data, or open an existing file before you can use SINGWIN to compute statistics, graph data, or do much of anything. You also might want to change an existing file, save a file under a different name or in a different location, copy a file, or delete a file, and you use this menu to carry out these tasks. You can click on "Print" to print graphs and statistics. Finally, and these are somewhat different tasks, use the "File" menu to configure your printer (we don't think you'll need to do this, though) and exit the program.

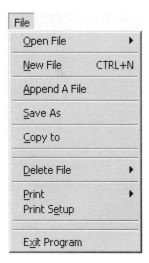

SINGWIN USER'S GUIDE

Statistics Menu

▶ Click "Statistics."

Use this menu to get descriptive and inferential statistics. Also, use it to transform data using either the moving average or first differences transformation.

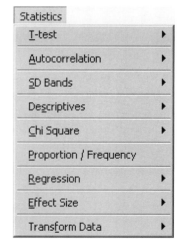

Graphs Menu

▶ Click "Graphs."

Use this menu to graph your raw and transformed data and to superimpose trend lines (e.g., celeration and regression) and descriptive statistics (e.g., means and standard deviation bands) on your graphs.

Reports Menu

▶ Click "Reports."

Use this menu to generate a printed report of basic baseline or intervention information, including raw data and descriptive statistics.

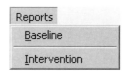

USING SPECIFIC PROCEDURES

Now that you have a general idea about what you can do with SINGWIN, we'll show you specifically how to accomplish these tasks. The vast majority of what you'll want to do can be accomplished using three of the menus listed on the "Main Menu": "File," "Statistics," and "Graphs." The "Reports" menu is useful, and we'll describe and illustrate it, but you won't need it for the majority of what you want to achieve.

Please note that some of the caluclations presented in earlier chapters may differ slightly from results obtained with SINGWIN. This is due to differences in the number of decimal places between hand calculations and SINGWIN.

There are two basic things you need to know how to do before you do anything else (in addition to knowing how to enter and exit SINGWIN): (1) create and enter data into a new file and (2) open an existing file (either one that you create or one that comes with SINGWIN). These are the first tasks we show you how to do in the following section. After you know how to do these two tasks you can skip ahead to the section on graphs or the one on statistics. However, in the following section on files we also show you how to edit an existing file, copy a file, copy a file using a new name, and delete a file. You can come back to these file management tasks when you need them.

After explaining and illustrating how to use files, we next turn to graphs. The most basic graph is the line chart, and we first show you how to use SINGWIN to create these. After you know how to do this you can skip around in this section and examine how to create charts of transformed data (e.g., moving average), band graphs (e.g., two-standard-deviation-band graphs) or celeration line charts.

After explaining and illustrating how to create graphs, we do the same with statistics. We start this section off by showing you how to compute and test an autocorrelation and then go on to other procedures, but you can try the procedures in this section in any order you like.

Finally, we explain and illustrate how to select cases and generate reports.

Files

In this section we first show you how to create and enter data into a new file and then how to open an existing file. These are the two basic file management tasks you need to know. Then, we show you how to edit an existing file, copy a file, copy a file using a new name, and delete a file.

Creating a New File.   You have to enter your data into a file in order to use them. Here's how you do this.

▶ Click "File" and "New File CTRL+N." (When you see CTRL+ some letter it means that instead of using the menu for that function, when you're in the "Main Menu" screen, you can hold the control key (Ctrl) and press that letter to do the same thing.)

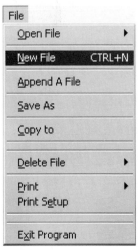

A file "dialog" box appears in which you enter the name of your new file, and in which you can view the names of existing files.

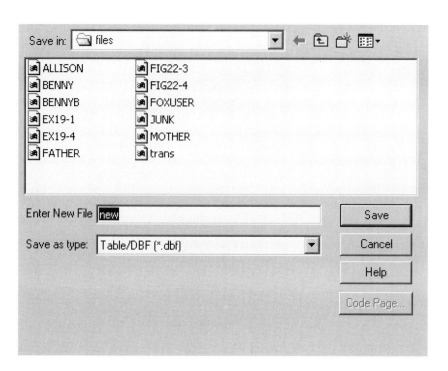

Here's how to use this dialog box.

▶ Click "Cancel" if at any time you want to exit to the "Main Menu" without completing the task.

▶ New file names are entered in the space to the right of the title "Enter New File" (the file will be saved as "new.dbf" unless you put another name in its place).

▶ Names of existing files are listed above where you enter the name of a new file.

▶ The location of existing files is shown next to "Save in:" (e.g., these files are located on your "C" (or hard) drive in the "files" directory).

▶ If you want to change the location of the file to another drive/location click (▼) on the right side of "Save in:", then click the down arrow (▼) to find and highlight the drive/location (e.g., the "A" drive if you want to save your files on a "floppy" disk in your "A" drive), and click. We suggest that you save your files on a floppy disk if you're not using SINGWIN on your own computer. If you do this, remember to change the drive to "A" when you look for them later.

▶ Let's enter the data for "Benny" from Kolko and Milan (1983; see Figure 22.5), and name our file "benny" (all files need to have a 1 to 8 character name followed by ".dbf"). Type **benny.dbf** (notice that "benny.dbf" will replace "new.dbf"). Finally, click "Save."

The data entry screen will appear.

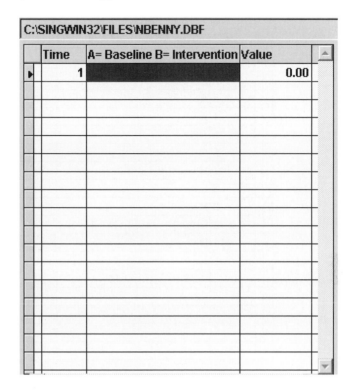

C:\SINGWIN32\FILES\NBENNY.DBF

	Time	A= Baseline B= Intervention	Value	
▶	1		0.00	

Following is a description of what the menus at the top of this screen do.

▶ Click "Add" to add a time period.

▶ Click "Data" and then "Delete Data" to delete a highlighted line of data (click a line to highlight it).

▶ Click "Data" and then "Insert Data" to insert a new time period immediately after the time period that is highlighted.

Here's how to enter the "Benny" data. (Use the arrow keys on your keyboard (←↑→↓) to move around in this screen. If you make a mistake, just go to it and type over it.)

▶ Click "Add Data" until you have 11 time periods (the number of weeks in the "Benny" design).

▶ Enter **A** in the "Baseline/Intervention" column for the first 5 time periods (i.e., 5 weeks of baseline data). Enter **B** in the remaining 6 time periods (i.e., 6 weeks of intervention data).

▶ Enter the data for each time period in the "Value" column. (You can use CTRL-A to start a time period.)

Here's what the data entry screen looks like after you've entered the "Benny" data.

	Time	A= Baseline B= Intervention	Value
	1	A	4.00
	2	A	4.00
	3	A	4.00
	4	A	6.00
	5	A	4.00
	6	B	19.00
	7	B	20.00
	8	B	18.00
	9	B	19.00
	10	B	20.00
▶	11	B	20.00

C:\SINGWIN32\FILES\NBENNY.DBF

▶ Click the "X" in the upper right-hand corner of the file when you're finished entering and checking your data. Your file will be saved automatically and you'll be returned to the "Main Menu."

Opening an Existing File. Before you can use SINGWIN to create graphs, compute statistics, or do almost anything, you need to open the file you want to use. Here's an example of how to do this.

▶ Click "File." Then, move the arrow to "Open File" and "File." Click "File."

▶ Double-click "BENNY" to get the "Benny" file (or single-click, then click "Open"). (Click "Cancel" if at any time you want to exit to the "Main Menu" without doing any of this.)

(The location of the drive on which the "BENNY" file is located ["C" in this case] is listed under "Look in:." If you want to change the location of the file to another drive/location, click ▼ on the right side of the "Look in:" box, click [▼] to find and highlight the drive/location [e.g., the "A" drive if you want to open or save your files on a "floppy" disk in your "A" drive], and click. We suggest that you save your files on a floppy disk if you're not using SINGWIN on your own computer. If you do this, remember to change the drive to "A" when you look for your files later.)

The screen with your data (shown previously when we showed you how to create a new file) will appear and you can edit away using the same methods used to enter your data originally. (Note that the name of the file, "Benny" in this case, will be in the lower left corner of your screen. This is how you'll know that a file is open.) For now, click the "X" in the upper right corner of the file to close it. You're now ready to create graphs, compute statistics, and have fun.

Copying a File.   There are times when you'll want to copy a file from one location to another (e.g., "C" drive to "A" drive). There also are times when you'll want to copy a file under a new name. For example, when you transform data, as described below, a new file containing the transformed data is created and assigned a name automatically (i.e., "trans.dbf"). If you don't copy this file under a new name, every time you transform data this file will be erased and replaced automatically with the new transformed data. Here's an example of how to copy a file under a new name or to a new location.

▶ Click "File" then "Copy to."

▶ Click the name of the file (e.g., BENNY.DBF) you want to save under a different name or to a new location. This will insert that file name in the "Enter" box. (Click "Cancel" if at any time you want to exit to the "Main Menu" without doing any of this.)

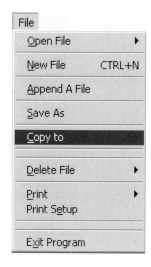

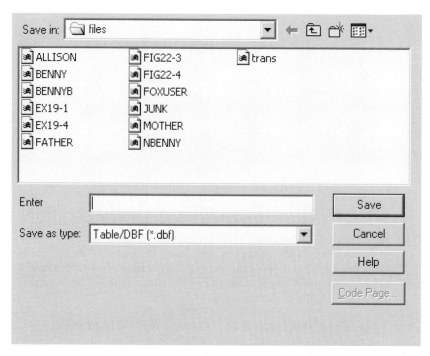

If you want to change the location of the file to another drive/location click the down arrow (▼) on the right side of the "Save in:" box, then click the down (▼) arrow to find and highlight the drive/location (e.g., the "A" drive if you want to save your files on a "floppy" disk in your "A" drive), and click.

▶ Click "Save" and you'll be returned to the "Main Menu."

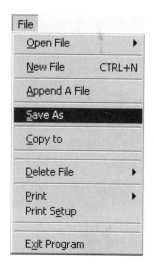

SINGWIN USER'S GUIDE

Copying a File Using a New Name. There are times when you want to retain an existing file but also save it as another file with a new name (e.g., to add or change data without changing the original file). Here's an example of how to do it.

▶ Open the "BENNY" file.

▶ Click "File" then "Save As."

Type the new file name (e.g., **nbenny**). This new name will replace "new" in the space next to "Enter New File" (you also can save this new file in a new location [e.g., a disk in the "A" drive] by changing the drive location, as shown previously). Click the "Save" button and you'll be returned to the "Main Menu." For now, click the "X" in the upper right corner of the file to close it.

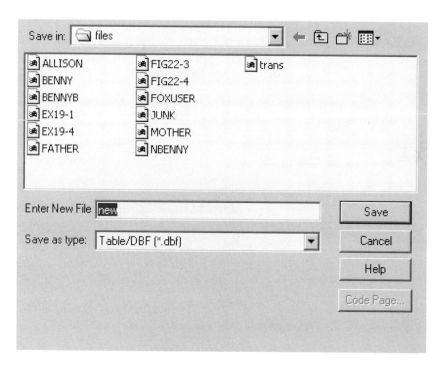

Deleting a File. There are times when you want to delete a file (e.g., to do some "house cleaning"). Here's an example of how to do it.

- ▶ Click "File." Then move the arrow to "Delete File" and "Behavior File" (i.e., any file but a chart file).
- ▶ Double-click the name of the file you want to delete from the dialog box listing your files (not shown) and you'll be returned to the "Main Menu."

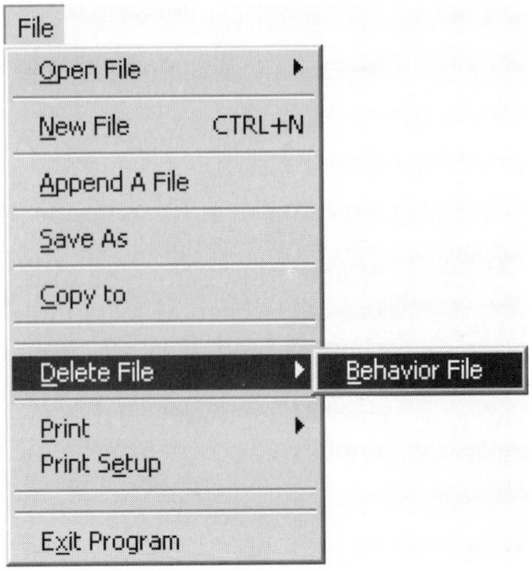

Graphs

In this section we'll show you how to create line charts, transformed data charts, band graph charts, and celeration line charts. Read the first section on creating a line chart, and then you can skip around in this section any way you like.

You might note that SINGWIN also creates overlay charts, bar graphs, regression plots, and scatter plots. We don't discuss these latter graphs, but these are used easily enough if you understand and have a need to use these graphs.

Creating a Basic Line Chart. A line chart is the starting (and sometimes ending) point for your analysis of single-system design data. Here's an example of how to create one.

- ▶ Open the "Benny" file.
- ▶ Click "Graphs." Then, move the arrow to "Line Chart" and "Baseline-Intervention." Click "Baseline-Intervention."

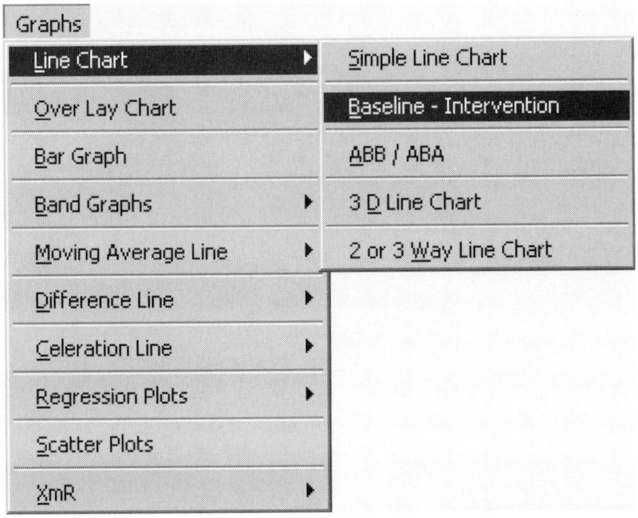

A very basic line chart appears, although it's difficult to interpret because it doesn't yet have the axis labeled or a vertical line separating the different phases. The interpretation of this graph will be clearer after we show you how to put this information on the graph.

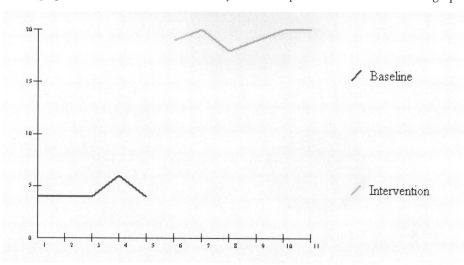

The "Edit Graphs" menu above the chart (not shown) can be used to enhance the appearance of this graph. Here's an example of how to do it.

▶ Click "Edit Graphs," then move the cursor to "Titles" and "Main Title" and click on "Main Title."

▶ When the computer responds "Enter a Graph Title," do just that, then press the "Enter" key (we entered **"Benny"** with the quotation marks, although the quotation marks aren't necessary).

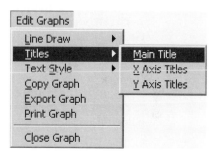

▶ Click "Edit Graphs," then move the cursor to "Titles" and "X Axis Titles." Click on "X Axis Titles." Then, when the computer responds "Enter X Axis Title," do just that, then press the "Enter" key (we entered **Weeks**).

▶ Click "Edit Graphs," then move the cursor to "Titles" and "Y Axis Titles." Click "Y Axis Titles." Then, when the computer responds "Enter Y Axis Title," do just that, then press the "Enter" key (we entered **Classes Attended**).

▶ Click "Edit Graphs," then move the cursor to "Line Draw" and "Draw Line." Click "Draw Line" to enter a vertical line separating the baseline and intervention phases (you can insert multiple lines if you have multiple phases). When the computer responds "Enter X Axis Starting Point" enter the last baseline (or whatever phase) time period (e.g., 5 in this case) and press the "Enter" key. A vertical line will be drawn between the time point you indicated and the next time point.

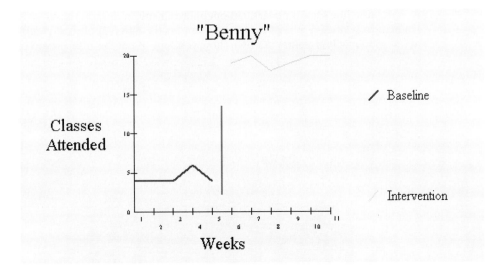

Click "Edit Graphs" and "Print Graph" if you want to print this graph, or click the "X" in the upper right corner of the graph to exit to the "Main Menu." You also can copy it to another computer program if you want to include it, for example, in a text document. Here is how to incorporate a graph into a Microsoft Word document.

Create your graph. Click "Edit Graphs" then "Copy Graph." Then, open your Word document and put your cursor where you want to insert the graph. Then, click "Edit" and then "Paste."

Creating Other Types of Basic Line Charts.   Following is a brief description of the "Simple Line Chart," "ABB/ABA," and "3D Line Chart" options, and a more detailed description of the "2 or 3 Way Line Chart" option:

- The "Simple Line Chart" option creates a line chart for a single phase.
- The "ABB/ABA" option creates a line chart for a three-phase design. If you select this option the program will ask you to enter the lower and upper range (i.e., time period) for each of the three series (i.e., phases.)

Series 1 Lower Range	0 Upper Range	0
Series 2 Lower Range	0 Upper Range	0
Series 3 Lower Range	0 Upper Range	0

- The "3D Line Chart" option creates a three-dimensional version of the line chart. We prefer the two-dimensional version, but you might like the three-dimensional one. Try it if you like.
- The "2 or 3 Way Line Chart" option lets you combine two or three files with the same number of baseline and intervention time points to create a single line chart with two or three different outcomes charted. This kind of chart lets you examine how different sources see the same outcome (e.g., interrater reliability) or how different outcomes or different measures of the same outcome covary over time. Let's take an example of this.

In Chapter 7 (see Figure 7.1) we gave an example of a mother and father who both completed a scale measuring their child's behavior problems. Both the mother and father completed the scale daily. An *A-B* design was used, with 7 baseline measurements and 21 intervention measurements. The data from the mother and father come with this program and they are in files named, respectively, "mother.dbf" and "father.dbf."

▶ Click "Graphs." Then move the arrow to "Line Chart" and "2 or 3 Way Line Chart." Click "2 or 3 Way Line Chart."

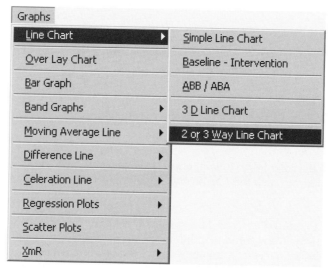

The "Multi Way Line Charts" dialog box appears. You need to move the two (or three) files you want to combine from the list on the left side of this box to a list on the right. To move a file you click it and then press ▶. Use this procedure to move the MOTHER.DBF and FATHER.DBF files from the left to the right.

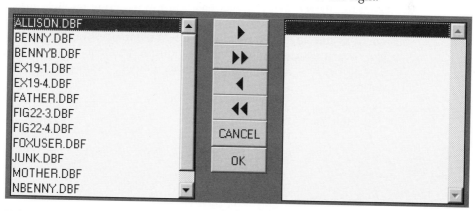

When you have moved your files from the left to the right, click "OK." If you like you can add a chart title, axis titles, and a vertical line separating phases using the procedures shown above for the simple line chart.

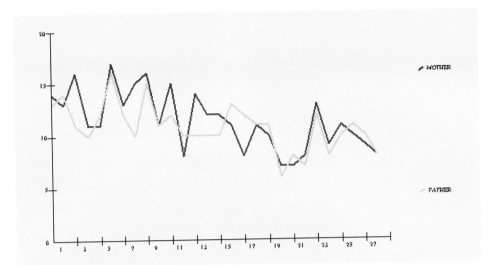

As described previously, click "Edit Graphs" and "Print" if you want to print this graph, or click the "X" in the upper right corner of the graph to exit to the "Main Menu."

Creating Charts of Transformed Data. In Chapter 19 we discussed the use of the moving average and first difference transformation as methods to remove autocorrelation so you could compute statistics that assume data are not autocorrelated. Also, we discussed how the moving average transformation could be used to "smooth" data and make visual analysis easier. SINGWIN will compute these transformations and chart them. Also, as we'll describe later when we discuss the "Statistics" menu, SINGWIN will let you save these transformed data and manipulate them in various ways (e.g., compute autocorrelations and descriptive statistics using the transformed data).

Here's how to create a chart of data transformed using the first differences transformation. The moving average transformation is so similar that you'll be able to do this yourself after you see how to do the first differences transformation. To do this for intervention data, just select that option from the menu shown below. (Note that the "by Time Period" option lets you specify a range of time points to include in the transformation.)

▶ Open the "ALLISON" file, which comes with the program (this data set is described in Chapter 21, Figure 21.1).

▶ Click "Graphs." Then, move the arrow to "Difference Line" and "Baseline Only." Click "Baseline Only."

▶ Press the "Enter" key in response to the "Enter a Constant" box.

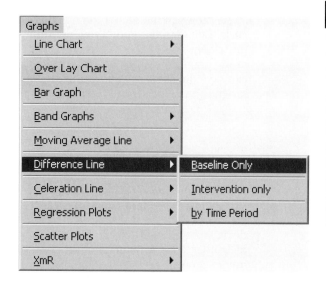

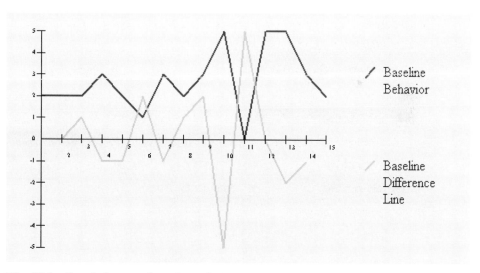

The "Edit Graphs" menu (not shown) above the chart can be used to enhance the appearance of this graph (e.g., add titles and a line separating baseline and intervention phases). To do this use the same methods described above for the line chart.

SINGWIN USER'S GUIDE

As shown in the section on creating a line chart, click "Edit Graphs" and "Print" if you want to print this graph, or click the "X" in the upper right corner of the graph to exit to the "Main Menu." (You also can save the chart or export it to another computer program by selecting the requisite menu option.)

Creating Band Graphs.   In Chapter 21 we showed you how to create one- and two-standard-deviation- and interquartile-band graphs. Here's an example of how to create a two-standard-deviation band graph for baseline data. To create one-standard-deviation- and interquartile-range-band graphs, and to get each of these three types of band graphs for intervention data, just select the appropriate option from the menus shown below. (Note that the "by Time Period" option lets you specify a range of time points to include in the creation of the band graph.)

▶ Open the "BENNY" file.

▶ Click "Graphs." Then, move the arrow to "Band Graphs," "Two Standard Deviations," and "Baseline Only." Click "Baseline Only."

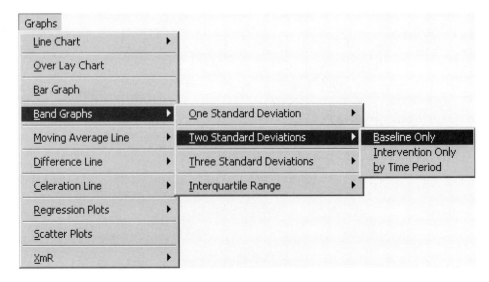

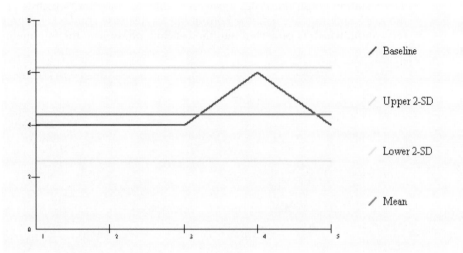

The "Edit Graphs" menu (not shown) above the chart can be used to enhance the appearance of this graph (e.g., add titles and a line separating baseline and intervention phases). To do this use the same methods described above for the line chart.

As shown in the section on creating a line chart, click "Edit Graphs" and "Print" if you want to print this graph, or click the "X" in the upper right corner of the graph to exit to the "Main Menu." (You also can copy the chart to another computer program by selecting the requisite menu option.)

Creating a Celeration Line Chart.   A celeration line chart gives you a good idea of whether there is a linear (i.e., straight line) trend within a phase, and whether the trend is increasing or decreasing. This is important for the visual analysis of your data (e.g., comparing trends in different phases) and for determining the appropriateness of using various descriptive statistics to summarize your data (e.g., the mean is not appropriate when there is a trend). Here's an example of how to construct a celeration line chart.

▶ Open the "BENNY" file.

▶ Click "Graphs." Then, move the arrow to "Celeration Line" and "Baseline-Intervention." Click "Baseline-Intervention."

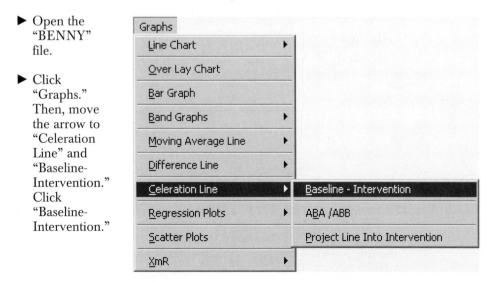

The resulting graph illustrates a celeration line for baseline, which is projected into the intervention phase (i.e., the bottom line in this case), and a celeration line for intervention, which is projected into the baseline phase (i.e., the top line in this case).

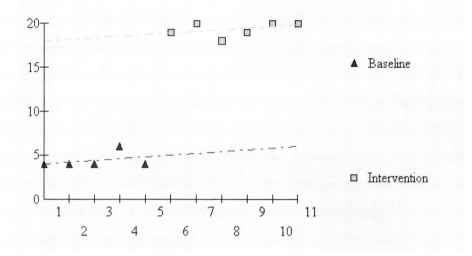

The "Edit Graphs" menu (not shown) above the chart can be used to enhance the appearance of this graph (e.g., add titles and a line separating baseline and intervention phases). To do this use the same methods described above for the line chart.

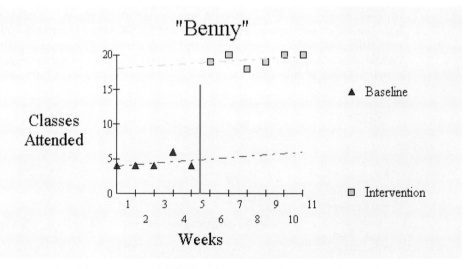

As shown in the section on creating a line chart, click "Edit Graphs" and "Print" if you want to print this graph, or click the "X" in the upper right corner of the graph to exit to the "Main Menu." (You also can copy the chart to another computer program by selecting the requisite menu option.)

Following is a brief description of the other "Celeration Line" options:

- The "ABA/ABB" option creates a celeration line chart for a three-phase design. If you select this option the program will ask you to enter the lower and upper range (i.e., time period) for each of the three series (i.e., phases).

```
Series 1 Lower Range    0 Upper Range    0
Series 2 Lower Range    0 Upper Range    0
Series 3 Lower Range    0 Upper Range    0
```

- The "Project Line Into Intervention" option is used when you have only baseline data and you want to estimate (project) what will occur during intervention from what did occur during baseline. Here's an example of how to do this.

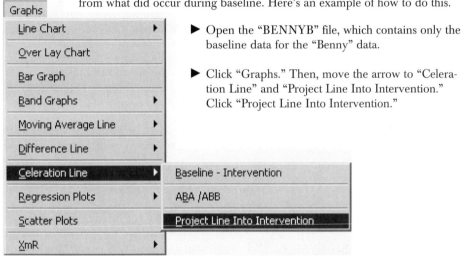

▶ Open the "BENNYB" file, which contains only the baseline data for the "Benny" data.

▶ Click "Graphs." Then, move the arrow to "Celeration Line" and "Project Line Into Intervention." Click "Project Line Into Intervention."

The resulting graph illustrates a celeration line for baseline, which is projected into the intervention phase. In this example there are five baseline observations; the celeration line is based on these first five observations, and the celeration line is projected into the next five time periods.

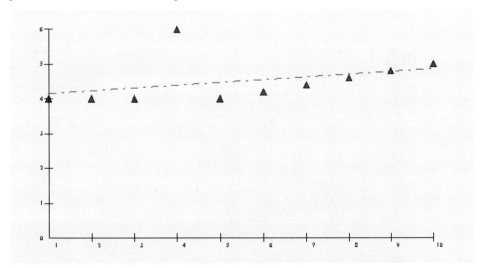

The "Edit Graphs" menu (not shown) above the chart can be used to enhance the appearance of this graph (e.g., add titles and a line separating baseline and intervention phases). To do this, use the same methods described above for the line chart.

Statistics

In this section we'll show you how to compute autocorrelation, transformations, measures of central tendency and variability, effect size, the proportion/frequency approach, the three-standard-deviation-band approach, the chi-square test, and the *t*-test. You can skip around in this section any way you like.

Computing and Testing Autocorrelation. Throughout Chapters 19 through 22 we discussed the importance of autocorrelation. Here's an example of how to compute one for baseline data. To compute one for intervention data, just select that option from the menu shown below. (Note that the "by Time Period" option lets you specify a range of time points to include in the computation of the autocorrelation.)

▶ Open the "BENNY" file.

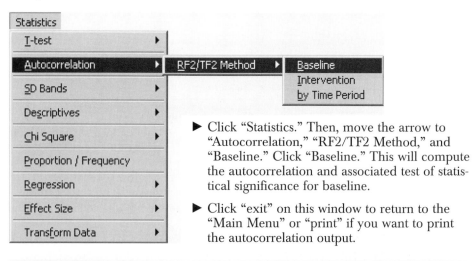

▶ Click "Statistics." Then, move the arrow to "Autocorrelation," "RF2/TF2 Method," and "Baseline." Click "Baseline." This will compute the autocorrelation and associated test of statistical significance for baseline.

▶ Click "exit" on this window to return to the "Main Menu" or "print" if you want to print the autocorrelation output.

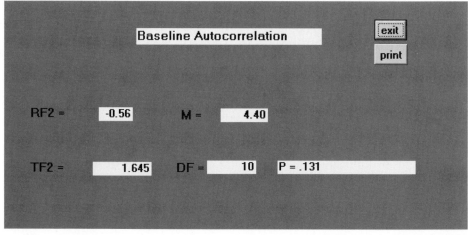

Computing Transformations. In Chapter 19 we discussed the use of the moving average and first differences transformation as methods to remove autocorrelation so you could compute statistics that assume data are not autocorrelated. Also, we discussed how the moving average transformation could be used to "smooth" data and make visual analysis easier. Finally, in the previous "Graphs" section we showed how SINGWIN would compute and graph these two transformations; if all you want is a graph of your transformed data, use the procedure we describe in the preceding "Graphs" section.

Use the procedure we describe next if you want to compute these transformations, obtain the autocorrelation for the transformed data, and automatically save the transformed data in a new file which you then can use–for example, to create charts of the transformed data or to compute a new set of descriptive statistics.

Here's how to do all of this using a moving average transformation for baseline data. The first differences transformation is so similar that you'll be able to do this yourself after you see how to do the moving average transformation (the only difference is the computer will ask you to "Enter a constant or press 'enter' to ignore," and you should press the "Enter" key in response). Also, to do this for intervention data just select that option from the menu shown below. (Note that the "by Time Period" option lets you specify a range of time points to transform.)

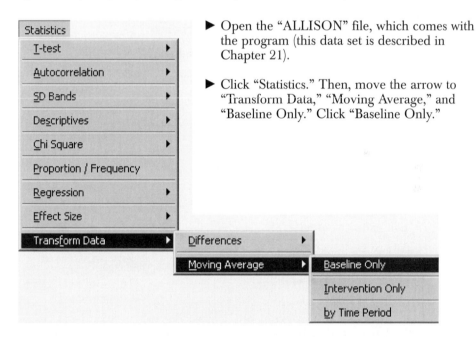

▶ Open the "ALLISON" file, which comes with the program (this data set is described in Chapter 21).

▶ Click "Statistics." Then, move the arrow to "Transform Data," "Moving Average," and "Baseline Only." Click "Baseline Only."

A "Baseline Autocorrelation" window (not shown) will appear automatically. Click "Exit" on this window to return to the "Main Menu" or "Print" if you want to print the autocorrelation output.

SINGWIN automatically has saved the transformed (baseline) and the untransformed (intervention) data in a new file named "TRANS.DBF." Therefore, you can open this new file and go ahead and construct a new line chart, celeration chart, descriptive statistics, or whatever you like using this new file.

Each time you transform data the "TRANS.DBF" file will be overwritten by the latest data. Therefore, if you want to save a particular file of transformed data, you have to save this file under another file name or in a different location. To do this use the "Copy to" option on the "File" menu, a procedure we described above in the "Files" section.

After saving the "TRANS.DBF" file under a new name it's possible to transform the data again. For example you could transform the phase(s) that was not transformed (intervention in this case) using the moving average or first differences transformation. You then could save this file under a new name and use it.

Computing Measures of Central Tendency and Variability. In Chapter 21 we showed how descriptive statistics could be used to get a clearer picture of your raw data. Here's how to compute all of the measures of central tendency and variability we discussed in that chapter for baseline. To compute these for intervention data just select that option from the menu shown below. (Note that the "by Time Period" option lets you specify a range of time points to include in the computation of the descriptive statistics.)

► Open the "BENNY" file.

► Click "Statistics." Then, move the arrow to "Descriptives" and "Baseline." Click "Baseline." (Note that in the "Descriptive Statistics" window for the "BENNY" file the 25th and 75th percentile are the same because all but one of the baseline scores were 4.)

► Click "Exit" on this window to return to the "Main Menu" or "Print" if you want to print the descriptive statistics output.

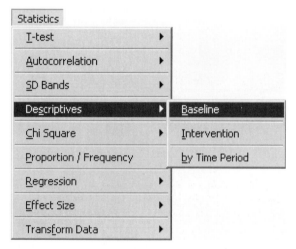

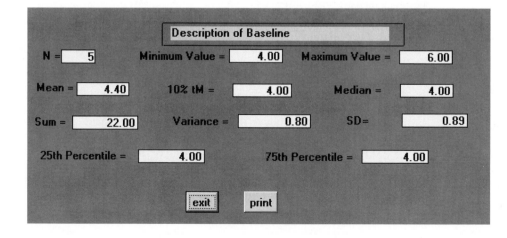

Computing Standard-Deviation Bands. You could use the mean and standard deviation from the "Descriptive Statistics" option above to hand-calculate two- or three-standard-deviation bands, but the computer can do it for you. Here's an example of how to do it for baseline. To compute these for intervention data, just select that option from the menu shown below. (Note that the "by Time Point" option lets you specify a range of time points to include in the transformation.)

▶ Open the "ALLISON" file.

▶ Click "Statistics." Then, move the arrow to "SD Bands" and "Baseline." Click "Baseline."

▶ Once you have the baseline standard-deviation band calculated by SINGWIN, just plot the results on your chart.

▶ Click "Exit" on this window to return to the "Main Menu."

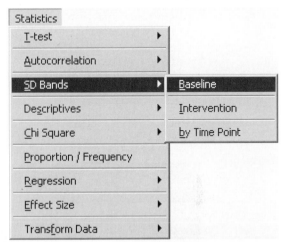

Baseline SD Bands		
Mean = 2.67		SD = 1.4475

	Lower Band	Upper Band
1-SD	1.2192	4.1142
2-SD	-0.2283	5.5617
3-SD	-1.6758	7.0091

Computing Effect Size. In Chapter 21 we explained how to quantify the size of an effect using an "effect size." Here's an example of how to compute the "delta index," comparing baseline and intervention. To compute the "*d*-index" just select that option from the menu shown below. (Note that the "by Time Period" option lets you specify a range of time points to include in computation of the effect size.) SINGWIN will not compute the "*g*-index" yet, but watch for updates on our web page.

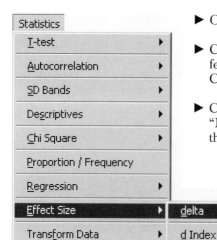

▶ Open the "BENNY" file.

▶ Click "Statistics." Then, move the arrow to "Effect Size," "delta," and "Baseline-Intervention." Click "Baseline-Intervention."

▶ Click "exit" on this window to return to the "Main Menu," or "print" if you want to print the effect size information.

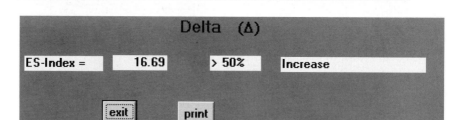

Computing a Proportion/Frequency Approach. There is some degree of judgment involved in determining desirable and undesirable zones for the proportion/frequency approach. Therefore, the proportion/frequency approach requires some hand computations, as described in Chapter 22, to determine the following:

- Desirable and undesirable zones
- Number of baseline points
- Number of baseline successes (baseline points in the desired zone)
- Number of intervention successes (intervention points in the desired zone)

After you determine the above, click "Statistics" and move the arrow to "Proportion/Frequency." Click "Proportion/Frequency."

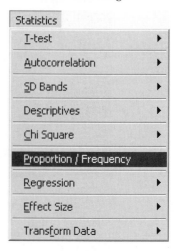

The "Proportion/Frequency" window will appear.

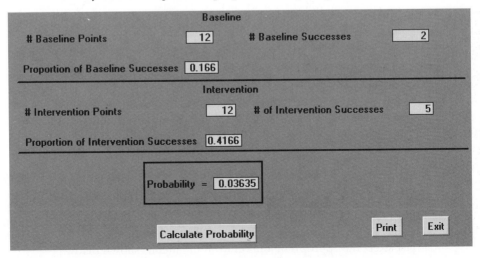

▶ Enter the number of baseline points and press the "Tab" key.

▶ Enter the number of baseline successes (points in the desired zone) and press the "Tab" key twice.

▶ Enter the total number of intervention points and press the "Tab" key.

▶ Enter the number of intervention successes (points in the desired zone) and press the "Tab" key twice.

▶ Click "Calculate Probability." The proportion of successes (baseline successes) and the probability value (one-tailed) will appear. If the probability is .05 or less (as in the display below, .03635), the results are statistically significant.

▶ Click "Exit" when you're finished and you'll be returned to the "Main Menu," or "Print" if you want to print the proportion/frequency information.

Computing the X-Moving Range-Chart (Three-Standard-Deviation-Band Approach). In Chapter 22 we explained the use of the three-standard-deviation-band approach. Here's an example of how to construct this chart.

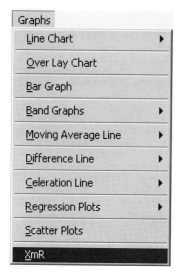

▶ Open the "FIG22-3.DBF" file (containing the Figure 22.3 data).

▶ Click "Graphs." Then, move the arrow to "XmR" and click on it.

Here's what you get after you use the "Edit Graphs" menu to add labels, as described above for the line chart. (Using statistical process control language, UCL stands for "upper control limit" and LCL stands for "lower control limit," which corresponds to the upper and lower three-standard-deviation bands.)

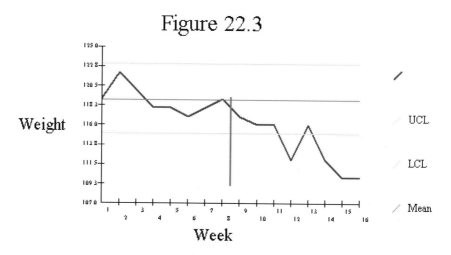

Figure 22.3

As you can see, since there were several observations outside of the three-standard-deviation band (or control limits) in the desired direction; therefore, these data were not significant.

Computing a Chi-Square.   In Chapter 22 we explained the use of chi-square using the region above (+) or below (–) a baseline celeration, mean, or median line to define a desirable zone. Here's an example of how to compute a chi-square test using the points above the baseline celeration line to define the desirable zone. To use points above (+) or below (–) the baseline mean or median to define a desirable zone, just select the appropriate option from the menus shown below.

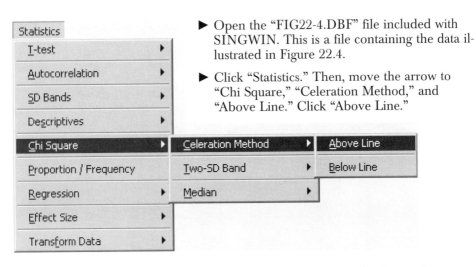

▶ Open the "FIG22-4.DBF" file included with SINGWIN. This is a file containing the data illustrated in Figure 22.4.

▶ Click "Statistics." Then, move the arrow to "Chi Square," "Celeration Method," and "Above Line." Click "Above Line."

You can enter a title if you like (we entered "Figure 22.4.Data"). The results are statistically significant if $p = .05$ or less. In the following example, $p = .160$; therefore, these results are not statistically significant. (Note that the following screen also presents results for Fisher's exact test, a more appropriate procedure when the numbers of cases in the cells are less than 5.) Then, click "exit" on this window to return to the "Main Menu" or "print" if you want to print the chi-square output.

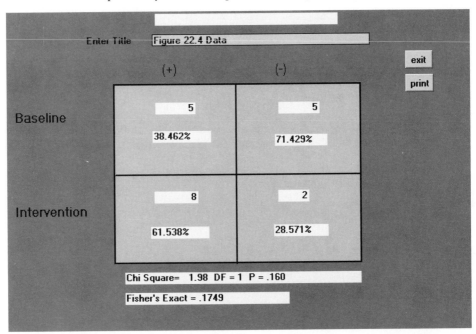

In this example neither the probability value of .160 for the chi-square test, nor the probability value of .1749 for Fisher's Exact test, is less than the standard alpha value of .05. Thus, there is not support for the evaluation hypothesis that the number of intervention successes is greater than the number of baseline successes.

Computing a t-Test. In Chapter 22 we explained the use of the *t*-test. Here's an example of how to compute one.

▶ Open the "BENNY" file.

▶ Click "Statistics." Then, move the arrow to "T-test" and "Intervention-Baseline." (Note that the "by Time Periods" option lets you specify a range of time points to include in the computations.) Click "Intervention-Baseline."

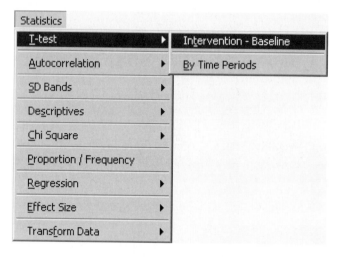

As with the other procedures, if *p* is less than .05, the results are significant. (See chapter 22, page 610, for guidelines on the use of the Equal or Unequal Variance approach.) In the *t*-test window, *p* = .000 means the results *are* significant at a very low level of significance.

▶ Click "exit" on this window to return to the "Main Menu," or "print" if you want to print the *t*-test information. You also can enter a title for this output, if you like.

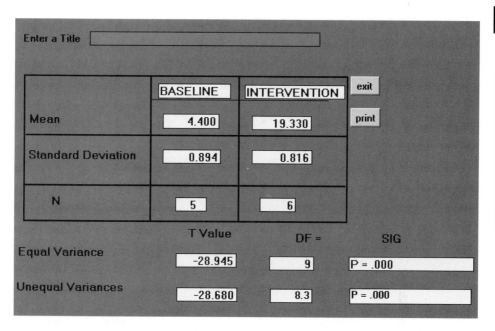

Generating Reports

You can generate a printed report of baseline or intervention data using the "Reports" menu. This lists the data for the selected phase. It also includes the phase mean and standard deviation, and the autocorrelation and information concerning its test of statistical significance.

▶ Open the "BENNY" file.

▶ Click "Reports" and "Baseline."

A window will appear requesting a title information for the report output. Enter whatever you like here (e.g., **Benny Baseline Data**) and press the "Enter" key.

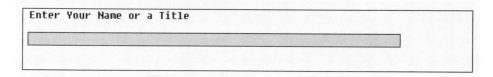

A print "dialog" box (not shown) will appear. Click "OK" to print the report.

SINGWIN USER'S GUIDE

■ APPENDIX: INSTALLING SINGWIN

Before starting, first be sure to familiarize yourself with the basic operations of your computer (e.g., location of your C drive, "Enter" key, Ctrl key, and ←↑→↓ keys).

Also, you'll need to know the following terms to install and use this software:

- **"Click"** means use your mouse to move the arrow you see on your screen to a certain word or place on the screen, and then click the *left* mouse button once.
- **"Right-click"** means use your mouse to move the arrow you see on your screen to a certain word or place on the screen, and then click the *right* mouse button once.
- **"Double-click"** means use your mouse to move the arrow you see on your screen to a certain word or place on the screen, and then click the *left* mouse button *twice quickly*.

▶ Insert the CD in your CD drive and wait until the following appears. Then click "Install SINGWIN."

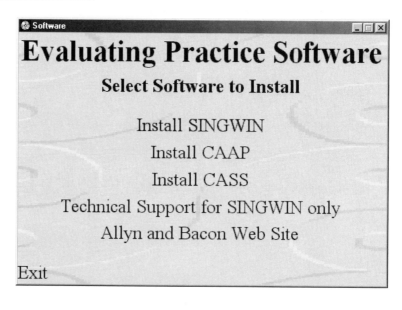

SINGWIN USER'S GUIDE

▶ Click "Next" on each of the following three informational windows.

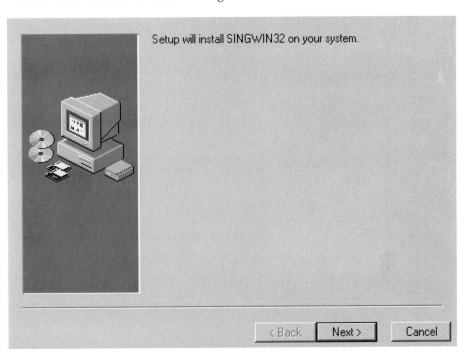

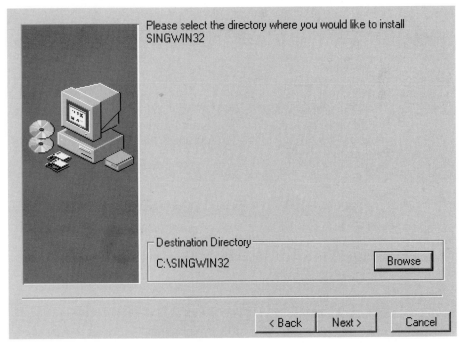

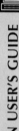

SINGWIN USER'S GUIDE

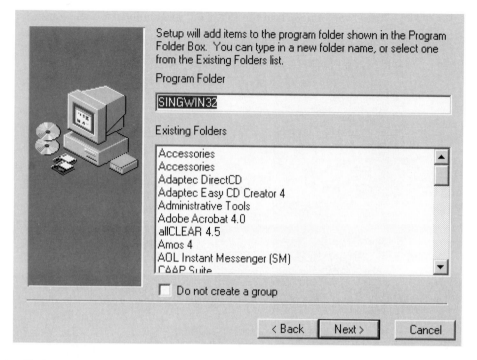

Setup will add items to the program folder shown in the Program Folder Box. You can type in a new folder name, or select one from the Existing Folders list.

Program Folder

SINGWIN32

Existing Folders

Accessories
Accessories
Adaptec DirectCD
Adaptec Easy CD Creator 4
Administrative Tools
Adobe Acrobat 4.0
allCLEAR 4.5
Amos 4
AOL Instant Messenger (SM)
CAAP Suite

☐ Do not create a group

< Back   Next >   Cancel

▶ Click "OK."

SINGWIN32 was successfully installed.

OK

▶ Move the cursor to "SINGWIN32" (the 32 refers to the 32-bit version of SINGWIN). Hold the left mouse button down; drag this icon to your desktop area; and release the mouse button. Click the "X" in the upper right corner of this window.

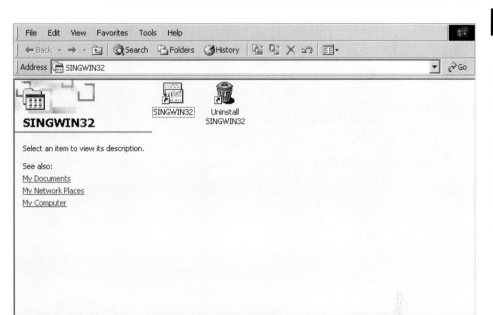

▶ Click "Exit."

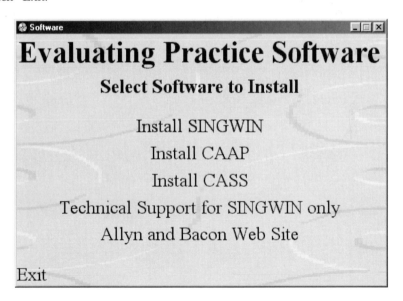

▶ Double-click the "SING 32" icon to start SINGWIN.

SUMMARY

This chapter has covered the use of SINGWIN, the computer program for statistical analysis of single-system data that comes with this book. We showed you (in the Appendix) how to load this program, how to create files, and then how to generate graphs and calculate just about all of the statistics described in Chapters 19, 21, and 22. We realize that, for many people, use of the computer for statistical analysis can be frightening at first. But we hope you will find that, with a little practice, you will be able to master this program. We hope that you will be delighted with the speed, efficiency, and accuracy of these computer calculations, especially in comparison to the often dreary and time-consuming tasks of hand calculation.

SELECTING A PROCEDURE FOR ANALYZING DATA

PURPOSE: This chapter presents guidelines for selecting among general analytic strategies (e.g., visual analysis, visual analysis supplemented with descriptive statistics, tests of statistical significance) and step-by-step considerations for selecting specific analytic methods (e.g., mean or median, X-Moving Range-Chart, proportion/frequency approach, etc.). The limitations of these guidelines are discussed, including additional considerations that need to be taken into account. ■

Introduction
Framework for Selecting a Procedure for
   Analyzing Data
Other Statistical Considerations

Nonstatistical Considerations
Limitations
Summary

INTRODUCTION

There are many considerations and decisions involved in selecting a procedure for analyzing single-system evaluation data. In Chapters 20, 21, and 22 we suggested three general strategies: visual analysis, visual analysis supplemented with descriptive statistics, and tests of statistical significance. For each general strategy we suggested more specific methods. This chapter presents a framework and step-by-step guidelines that summarize and simplify the process of selecting a general strategy and the specific analytic methods most appropriate for particular circumstances. However, we caution you that these are *general* guidelines–there may be overriding considerations for going directly

to one or another form of analysis not suggested by this framework.

FRAMEWORK FOR SELECTING A PROCEDURE FOR ANALYZING DATA

We recommend that you first consider visual analysis of the data. Look for obvious discontinuities between baseline and intervention periods. If there's a marked and obvious visible change in level or slope across phases (see Chapter 20), consider two questions. First, does this particular discontinuity fit your plans? That is, is this the kind of change you wanted to achieve? Did your practice hypothesis call for increasing or decreasing the target events as they occurred? Second, and perhaps more important, do these results provide a direction for practice without further analysis or investigation of other factors? If you can answer yes to these two questions, then we recommend that you proceed directly to the use of these data by means of visual analysis and not bother to do further analysis, unless there's need for more rigorous documentation of the outcomes for reasons other than the practice itself.

Raw data are sometimes difficult to interpret because of their variability. Descriptive statistics can summarize patterns of data, making the visual analysis of data easier. Therefore, if you have doubts about the answers to the questions concerning visual analysis, consider supplementing your visual analysis with descriptive statistics, as discussed in Chapter 21 (e.g., a mean line bracketed by two standard-deviation bands).

Figure 24.1 provides a step-by-step series of considerations involved in selecting the most appropriate statistics for describing overall patterns within phases, which then can be used to make comparisons across phases. For example, suppose that for a set of baseline data you don't have any reason to believe there's a trend; you want to determine a typical value

for the phase (i.e., a measure of central tendency); you have an interval level outcome measure; and there are no outliers. In this situation you would compute a mean and superimpose it on the graphed baseline data. Also, as discussed in Chapter 21, we recommend that a measure of central tendency always be accompanied by a measure of variability. In the situation just described the most appropriate measure of variability would be the standard deviation (i.e., no trend, interval-level outcome measure, no outliers), and so you would compute the standard deviation and construct a one- or two-standard-deviation band around the mean. This same step-by-step decision process would be followed for other phases in the design (e.g., intervention), and changes across phases would be assessed visually with the aid of the descriptive statistics superimposed on the graphs.

Computing and graphing central tendency, variation, or trend within a phase, and then visually comparing these summary measures across phases provide a useful basis for determining changes from one phase to the next. However, there are more precise ways to describe the amount of change from one phase to another (and also to supplement tests of statistical significance, discussed below). These

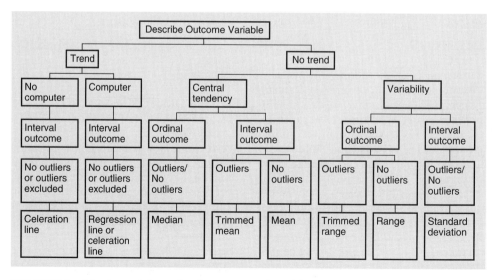

FIGURE 24.1 Selecting statistics to describe an outcome variable.

methods of describing changes are called measures of effect size (ES). Two measures of ES were discussed in Chapter 21, and the steps involved in their selection are illustrated in Figure 24.2. For example, suppose you want to compare a baseline and intervention phase, you don't have any reason to believe there's a trend in either phase, and you don't believe the data in either phase are autocorrelated (or you've transformed the data to remove the autocorrelation). Furthermore, you have an interval-level outcome measure, and there are no outliers, or the outliers have been identified and excluded from consideration. In this situation you would compute the Δ-index (or the d-index) as discussed in Chapter 21. If there is a trend, with or without outliers, you would compute the g-index.

As discussed in Chapter 19, various haphazard or chance factors can cause a target to seem to change over time (e.g., imperfect reliability in the measurement of a target, inconsistency in the implementation of baseline or intervention activities, events in a client's life).

Therefore, when possible and practical, tests of statistical significance should be used to decide whether there's a systematic difference in a target under different conditions or whether the observed difference is due to haphazard or chance factors. Measures of ES as in Figure 24.2 then can be used to quantify the amount of change.

Figure 24.3 provides a step-by-step series of considerations involved in selecting the most appropriate test of statistical significance for a particular situation. For example, suppose again that you want to compare a baseline and intervention phase, you don't have any reason to believe there's a trend in either phase, and you don't believe the data in either phase are autocorrelated, r_k (or you've transformed the data to remove the autocorrelation). Moreover, you have a computer available (of course, all of these procedures are calculated easily by computer using SINGWIN), and you are willing to use SINGWIN or some comparable program; you have an interval-level outcome measure; and you selected the treatment time based on practice considerations (i.e., nonrandom assignment of treatment time). In this situation you would use the t-test to determine whether there was a statistically significant difference between baseline and intervention. If there is no trend from one phase to the next, the t-test is more powerful than the chi-square test for detecting change (so the t-test can detect a smaller change with the same number of observations or the same change with a smaller number of observations). The chi-square test really shouldn't be used in this situation. If there is a trend in either phase, the t-test shouldn't be used, but the chi-square test will work.

As a way of summarizing the main categories of analytic procedures, Figure 24.4 suggests a progression from visual analysis as a first step through tests of statistical significance.

OTHER STATISTICAL CONSIDERATIONS

The factors outlined in Figures 24.1, 24.2, and 24.3 are primary considerations involved in

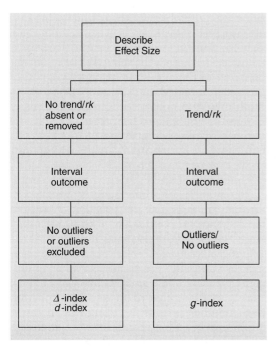

FIGURE 24.2 Selecting an effect size statistic.

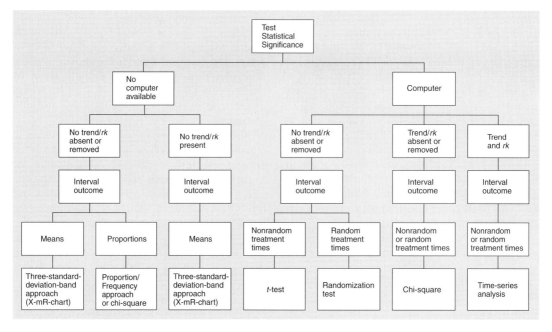

FIGURE 24.3   Selecting a test of statistical significance.

the selection and use of the analytic procedures discussed in this book, but they are not the only factors. Two additional considerations involve the assumptions required by the recommended tests of statistical significance (but not noted in Figure 24.3) and the number of required observations.

All statistical tests are based on certain assumptions. The violation of assumptions can result in the detection of a difference between phases when a difference really doesn't exist (a Type I error) or the failure to detect a difference when it really does exist (a Type II error) (e.g., Crosbie, 1987; Kenny & Judd, 1986; Toothaker et al., 1983). Some of these assumptions are explicitly or implicitly considered in Figures 24.1, 24.2, and 24.3 (e.g., the absence of autocorrelation), but some are not. For example, as discussed in Chapter 22, the *t*-test assumes that the observations within each phase are normally distributed (i.e., have a bell-shaped distribution) and that the variability within each phase is the same. We have not detailed all of the assumptions underlying all of the recommended statistics, not because we think they're unimportant, but because many of these are difficult to test, especially with the number of observations typical of single-system designs. Furthermore, other assumptions are not seriously problematic when violated to a limited extent.

The number of observations is another factor that can influence the selection of particular statistics. For example, with a relatively large number of observations, the standard deviation will provide a relatively accurate measure of variability given an interval-level outcome measure and a small number of outliers. With a small number of observations and/or a large number of outliers, the trimmed range might provide a better indicator of variability. The Δ-index, which is based on means and standard deviations, also probably won't be influenced much by a small number of outliers

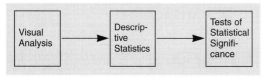

FIGURE 24.4   Summary of analytic procedures.

when the number of observations is relatively large, but this won't necessarily be the case when the number of observations is relatively small and/or the number of outliers is large. Finally, the number of observations suggested for different statistical tests is described in Chapter 22. However, as a general rule you should remember that statistical analyses and visual analysis will be prone to a considerable amount of error when there are only a few observations on which to base decisions. It's difficult to make accurate decisions based on small amounts of information using any analytic technique.

NONSTATISTICAL CONSIDERATIONS

Visual analysis and the methods outlined in Figures 24.1, 24.2, and 24.3 help to determine whether there are systematic differences between baseline and intervention phases. However, this isn't sufficient, as discussed in Chapter 19. With any analytic methods you should assess whether the obtained results are practically and theoretically significant. If only one or the other type of significance is present, then you must decide whether this is sufficient to use as a basis for the next practice decisions

If the context of the situation is serious and potentially life threatening, you will probably want to have as rigorous an analysis of the data as possible. For example, suppose a suicidal patient has been seen in therapy for 4 months, and the daily monitoring of suicidal thoughts has shown great reduction in such thoughts. Moreover, the client has increased his social activities, which has led him to become involved in a self-help group. A visual analysis of the charted data shows a sharp decline in undesirable behaviors and thoughts. Is this enough? The literature on suicidal behavior may inform you to watch out for occasional depressive bursts that could be suicidal. Therefore, it might be wise to continue monitoring the client regardless of the improved results and to use more stringent statistical criteria (e.g., set alpha equal to .01 instead of .05).

Information from measured outcomes is only a part of the client information available to you, and all of this information should be taken into consideration in evaluating change. To continue the example of the suicidal client, perhaps his former wife is moving back to town in several weeks, and in spite of his dramatic improvement to date, this new event might impose a stress that is beyond his coping abilities. Such information should be taken into consideration in evaluating the adequacy of change.

LIMITATIONS

Oftentimes it will be difficult to determine with certainty whether data have certain characteristics. For example, it may be difficult to determine whether there's a trend, whether data are autocorrelated, whether a measure is best considered ordinal or interval, or whether there are outliers. When this happens, we suggest that you try multiple analytic procedures, if possible. For example, if you suspect that an observation is an outlier with undue influence on your results, you might try the analysis with and without the observation. If you suspect a trend in the data, you might compute statistics appropriate for data with a trend (e.g., a celeration line) and statistics appropriate for data without a trend (e.g., a mean line). In any case, if these multiple analyses yield substantially the same conclusions, you can be more confident in your conclusions. If they're in disagreement, rely on the procedure most likely to fit the characteristics of the data, or simply view your results as tentative and perhaps requiring more information.

As is apparent from Figures 24.1, 24.2, and 24.3 there are circumstances that are not covered in our recommendations, and the statistics discussed in this book are not the only ones available for the analysis of single-system design data (e.g., Franklin et al., 1997; Kazdin, 1984; Krishef, 1991; Morley & Adams, 1989, 1991; Onghena, 1992; Suen & Ary, 1989). For example, it's possible to use measures of variability to compute "typical" zones around trend lines (Morley & Adams, 1991); we described the use of these statistics only to determine such zones when there's little or no trend within a phase (i.e., measures of central tendency bracketed by indicators of variability). However, we've tried to provide recommendations that cover many, if not most, situations you will encounter. We've also tried to recommend approaches that are rela- tively practical, even though some of the procedures we recommend are easier to understand and apply than others. You might want to consult the other references we provided under some circumstances.

SUMMARY

This chapter presented general guidelines for selecting among general strategies (e.g., visual analysis, visual analysis supplemented with descriptive statistics, tests of statistical significance) and step-by-step considerations for selecting specific analytic methods. We suggested putting together the patterns you detect through visual analysis, descriptive statistics, and tests of statistical significance as a good (but not perfect) way of trying to provide as much information as possible in the quest for informed decision making.

The guidelines presented in this chapter may be helpful in the majority of cases, but the guidelines should be viewed as a point of departure and not a command, because there are limitations in any such framework. First, visual and statistical strategies are not the only considerations involved in determining the existence of change. Practical and theoretical significance also are important, as discussed in Chapter 19, and it's your right and responsibility to make the decision about how to use the data in the context of accountability to the client and to society at large. Second, sometimes it will be difficult to determine particular characteristics of the data with certainty (e.g., whether they are autocorrelated), and consequently multiple procedures might be necessary or the decision simply must be viewed with caution. Finally, there are circumstances not covered in Chapters 19 through 22, and hence not covered in our recommendations. In some circumstances you might have to turn to other sources, and in some circumstances there are no procedures ideally suited to the conditions at hand.

PART V

THE CHALLENGE OF SINGLE-SYSTEM DESIGNS

The most challenging aspect of single-system designs is to try to encourage large numbers of practitioners to use these simple evaluative procedures to improve their practice. To do this, practitioners also must convince clients that it is in their best interests to cooperate in generating objective information on the topics that bring them to helping professionals. In addition, agency administrators will have to see the usefulness of having the means to plan the allocations of staff workloads and to demonstrate accountability to various funding groups.

In this revolution of accountability, students and teachers have been our most helpful allies. They generally have recognized the challenge we have been describing, and have been receptive to the methods we propose—although not without critical questioning, which has stimulated us to sharpen our presentation. In this final chapter of the book, we hope to continue this dialogue, and to encourage all of these users to experiment with these ideas aimed at making practice effective, efficient, and sensitive to the varied needs of our many clients.

25 NOT FOR PRACTITIONERS ALONE
Evaluation for Clients, Administrators, Educators, and Students

PURPOSE: This chapter reviews a number of issues and recent criticisms of single-system evaluation. We first discuss the use of single-system designs in managed care and primary prevention. We then discuss evaluation from the perspective of clients, administrators, educators, and students, not so much referring to how it is done—this is discussed in the preceding chapters—but rather referring to why and under what conditions. We also present a working draft of a code of ethics for the evaluation of practice. ■

Introduction
Special Application of Single-System Designs
Managed Care and Single-System Designs
Using Single-System Designs in Primary
  Prevention
Recent Criticisms of Single-System Evaluation
The First Set of Criticisms: Single-System
  Evaluation and Practice
The Second Set of Criticisms: Research and
  Evaluation Issues
The Third Set of Criticisms: Ethical Issues
  in Single-System Designs
The Fourth Set of Criticisms: Meta-Issues in
  Philosophy, Politics, and Socioeconomics
The Fifth Set of Criticisms: Technological Issues

For the Client
Questions about Evaluation
How Can Recording Help the Client
  (and the Practitioner)?
Ethical Considerations in Using
  Single-System Designs
A Model Consent Form
For the Administrator
Evaluation: Do I Have a Choice?
Staff Development
Staff Cooperation and Deployment
Examples of Evaluation in Agency Settings
For Educators and Students
Summary

INTRODUCTION

This is the age of accountability, especially for human service professions. Scarce resources and numerous options for spending those that are available mean that the human service professions have to have a strong basis for their requests from the public treasury. This book has been directed primarily at helping professionals, the people who will actually use these evaluation procedures in working with clients. The goal is to enable those practitioners to know how well the intervention is going both during and after the service period so that the intervention may be made more effective, more efficient, and less costly in psychological, social, and financial terms.

However, there are other audiences to whom this book is directed and other issues that have to be considered. It is directed to those who must understand the purpose of evaluating practice and the ethical issues that surround these practices. In this chapter, we address a variety of special issues as they affect clients, administrators, teachers, and students.

First, we will discuss some special applications of single-system designs. Then, we will discuss some of the recent criticisms of single-system designs and, in some cases, of evaluation itself, and provide our perspective on these criticisms. We then will address the remainder of this chapter to our several constituent groups.

SPECIAL APPLICATIONS OF SINGLE-SYSTEM DESIGNS

Although most of this book has discussed use of single-system designs in "typical" intervention situations—with individuals, couples, families, groups, organizations, and communities—there are two important applications that are not quite so typical: the use of single-system designs in managed care and primary prevention, the topics of this section.

Managed Care and Single-System Designs

Managed care refers to a system of policies and procedures for connecting the quality and quantity of client care to public fiscal accountability, in what amounts to a kind of grand cost–benefit analysis and external control system. (That is, the direct practice worker no longer has full control over the nature and extent of services that will be paid for under the existing financial plan.) With the rapid increase in costs of health, education, and welfare, social critics are exploring ways to contain and reduce costs, while attaining equivalent or improved outcomes, by having a presumably disinterested party examine the proposed intervention goals and methods in light of the best available practice information so as to determine what is allowable under these general guidelines. In principle, this is a laudable social goal; the devil is in the details (Strom-Gottfried, 1997; Corcoran & Vandiver, 1996).

While managed care is being discussed widely in the applied social sciences, there are relatively few discussions of the role of practice evaluation–the topic of this book–and its potential role under an external accountability system. Nevertheless, evaluation procedures are integral to managed care. All managed care systems include quality assurance reviews to assess the extent to which the service provided approximates some desired form of practice. Similarly, managed care relies on utilization reviews–retrospective, concurrent, and prospective–comparing services against a set of criteria to determine the necessity and appropriateness of those services. (We, of course, recognize that there are numerous other forces that influence decisions in managed care systems, including political and economic forces that are beyond the scope of this book.) Therefore, we offer the following *tentative* assessment and suggestions, in light of the rapidly changing array of methods and populations being covered by managed care.

First, the emergence of managed care reflects events in the larger society, and is a reality that helping professionals have to address. It is written into law (P.L. 97-248); it is included in private third-party payers and corporate benefit programs; and it is becoming part of the normative thinking in society and many of its professional associations (Corcoran & Gingerich, 1994, p. 328; Strom-Gottfried, 1997).

Second, a distinction must be made between review processes that take place before services are rendered–called *managed care reviews*–and those that occur during or after services–called *quality assurance reviews (QARs)* (Corcoran & Gingerich, 1994; Tischler, 1990). Both involve a review process that examines the proposed and delivered services with regard to their necessity, duration, quality, and outcome, while also considering best-practice knowledge, quality of care, and reduction of unnecessary costs. Corcoran and Gingerich (1994, p. 329) note that "Concrete and specific short- and long-term [intervention objectives and goals] are required, as well as evidence of observable changes (Osman & Shueman, 1988)."

Third, the philosophy and procedures for single-system designs, in general, offer individual practitioners and whole agencies a specific and useful means of attaining the highest professional standards of evaluated practice while at the same time enabling them to provide almost all of the required information for peer reviews and managed care. All of the steps we propose in this book would be useful in achieving this dual goal of quality interventions and cost-effectiveness. While the managed care and quality assurance reviews do introduce a fiscal dimension to social services, the procedures suggested for single-system designs also introduce client preferences and professional decisions, which both embody values underlying the helping process. These values are part of the choices made in identifying clients' short-term objectives and long-term goals, in the choice of methods used to attain them, in clients' comfort and satisfaction given in feedback on the helping process itself, and in societal satisfaction on effective problem resolution.

Fourth, some single-system methods provide a way to project efficiency estimates–how long it would take, under existing patterns of success, for the client to attain stable and satisfactory outcomes, and at what costs in terms of professional time and energy. It may be that this systematic thinking will need to be incorporated into the basic evaluation plans for social services.

In the following section, we will elaborate on the parallels between the demands likely to emerge from the managed care/quality assurance review perspectives and the enhanced perspective on evaluation that results from single-system designs and that fulfills these demands while maintaining professional standards.

Typical Demands of a Managed Care or Quality Assurance Review (based on a current review of these systems-in-change)	**Expanded Single-System Evaluation** (enhanced to clarify procedures that are likely to match external systems review)
1. Definition of the presenting problems and the context of these problems that may require changes and amelioration.	1. Operational definitions of target behaviors, which may need to be expanded to include the context in which each target exists. This is similar to a social-ecological perspective of looking at the person in the environment, and measuring both person and environmental factors because either or both may be used as targets of intervention. Consideration may also be given to preventive interventions, as part of a long-term cost–benefit analysis.
2. Normative information will be needed on the types of interventions that have been used, their ranges of success with these kinds of problems, and the realistic goals that can be set in this regard.	2. Evaluated practice is routinely based on the best available information, and future practice may need to document this best usage. Access to information databases and retrieval and printing of abstracts may become one form of such documentation of best available information for both treatment and primary prevention services. The setting of goals and objectives continues to be part of the client–practitioner process, so that

3. Based on preliminary assessments of the client's full situation, a categorical match will be conducted by an external reviewer, who will then indicate the average time that is needed with the standard or validated methods in regard to a given condition. The practitioner has to decide whether to accept this interpretation or to provide further information on extenuating circumstances that require the provision of more or less time and/or covered services.

In addition to outcome measures, managed care thinking also will require something new in single-system designs: a continuing concern for the quality of care, including client satisfaction, and how well the intervention conforms to standard expectations for best treatment.

4. The external reviewer may be involved to some degree in observing the monitoring of changes in the targeted behaviors. This may be done by reviewing charts as described in this book, or practice evaluation forms, or computer assisted case-recording methods (Corcoran & Gingerich, 1994).

appropriate values are incorporated into the service program.

3. The baseline for the target and for relevant factors in the context may be used as the basis for considering extenuating circumstances. While each case is going to be different, there are still basic similarities to cases in the literature from which we can expect likely outcomes. It may be possible to take baseline data, make a projection of the likely course of events if some intervention is not undertaken, and then connect some financial estimates of the cost of the continuing or escalating problem. This will require social agencies to begin analyzing their records based on their own experiences in serving a given range of cases.

Then, if there is any service being conducted, a worker could make an efficiency estimate as described in Chapter 22 of this book. This would say how long (and thus, at what cost) a given program of intervention has to be continued before statistically significant results are projected, given current rates of change. It may be necessary to expand this efficiency estimate by adding the clinical or practical significance of such changes, since this represents another way to view social costs.

The considerations of client satisfaction and service expectations for best treatment may require additional data (on client satisfaction) and more explicit operationalization of actual interventions used to match "best treatment" models. With regard to client satisfaction, it should be simply a matter of selecting some mutually agreeable satisfaction measure, and gathering data periodically—rather than gathering data continuously (which may be reactive and counterproductive).

4. The monitoring of the progress of practice is a step ahead of the managed care/quality assurance review process. Single-system designs may have to be clearer in specifying the immediate and intermediate objectives on the path toward some long-term goal. Then, part of the charting and monitoring can be a cooperative process with the reviewer, probably on a random review basis showing where the client is vis-a-vis a particular objective in a series of objectives toward the goal. With appropriate charting, the practitioner would be ready at any time to convey progress toward objectives, and to record mitigating circumstances if any (as in annotations on the chart). This approach requires that evaluators work with reviewers to reach agreement as to what constitutes the evidence they need.

5. Extensions, when needed, are based on further evidence that the problem has changed or the circumstances in which it exists have changed, so that more time and services are needed to achieve a predictable objective. It is also possible that changing events may mean that less time and services are needed.

6. There will likely be some record-keeping system of both process measures and outcome measures, as part of the payment for covered services.

5. The notion of a predictable objective allows for more accurate efficiency estimates. Agencies should keep track of the accuracy of their efficiency estimates and how closely practitioners succeed in achieving predicted goals in projected times. These rates of accurate efficiency estimates can be added to other information when practitioners request extensions, and so forth.

6. The nature of this final accounting system is still to be determined, but evaluators should be prepared to influence the final form by making it compatible with the range and depth of their single-system designs. That is, everything that we propose be done using good practice and with good single-system evaluation should be usable in any final accounting form. Moreover, as Strom-Gottried (1997, p. 14) points out with regard to social work cases, "Many clients have complex and long-standing difficulties that are intricately related to environmental conditions, oppression, and poverty. Regardless of the worker's skills, resources, and motivation, some problems will prove difficult and time-consuming to remediate. How can we promote efficiency and effectiveness, yet also assure that workers and clients are not set up for failure by trying to meet unrealistic performance standards with insufficient time and resources? How can we assume that performance targets are used responsively and not as justification for further reduction in services and funding?"

Using Single-System Designs in Primary Prevention

Primary prevention is the third helping modality (along with *treatment* of, or *intervention* with, existing problems or conditions, and *rehabilitation* of persons or groups involved in those treatments or interventions); it presents some special considerations for using single-system evaluations that we discuss and illustrate in this section. Primary prevention may be defined as the *coordinated actions* seeking to *prevent* predictable problems, *protect* existing states of health and healthy functioning, and *promote* desired objectives (Bloom, 1996). It is because the specific predicted preventable problem has not yet occurred, and the at-risk individual or group is functioning relatively well with regard to that predicted untoward condition, that we can speak of taking preventive actions. It is this

no-problem-yet status that sometimes makes it difficult for evaluators to figure out how to measure process and outcome in prevention, especially over a long period of time. The same issues emerge when evaluating the promotion of desired objectives and the protection of existing states of health and healthy functioning.

However, in principle, primary prevention may be evaluated in exactly the same way as any other treatment or rehabilitation concern, as long as specific targets are identified, and repeated measures are employed with relevant designs. Instead of measuring problem behaviors or events, primary preventers often measure strengths in persons or environments that keep the problem from happening or that promote the emergence of dysfunctional or undesirable behaviors or events. For example, in the study by Fox, Hopkins, and Anger (1987) described in Chapter 15, the reduction of accidents in open-pit mining was arranged by promoting safe behavior in individual workers and in teams of workers. King, Winett, and Lovett (1986) trained women from dual-earner families in coping skills to deal with the multiple stresses in their lives. And Mayer and colleagues (1986) used positive health-oriented signs to promote choice of healthy (i.e., low-fat) dishes at a cafeteria. Other examples of the evaluation of primary prevention projects using single-system designs include: Thyer and Geller's (1987) promotion of seat belt use, Pigott et al.'s (1986) use of peer tutoring to increase arithmetic performance, and McDonald and Budd's (1983) study in preventive dentistry.

On the other hand, some primary prevention projects have to address undesired behaviors, such as the study by McNees et al. (1976) on posting shoplifting warning signs so as to reduce this most common of crimes. It would be difficult to construct a commercial situation reinforcing honest behavior without raising the possibility of dishonest (shoplifting) behavior. This primary prevention example is probably more the exception than the rule. (Even in evaluating conventional problem behavior, we recommend measuring desired behaviors rather than emphasizing undesired ones.)

Let's illustrate a single-system design with a primary prevention situation. Suppose a school nurse and social worker team formed a group with 10th-, 11th-, and 12th-grade female students who were being treated for sexually transmitted diseases (STDs) at the school-based health clinic (cf. Dryfoos, 1994). The common problem involved the immediate treatment condition (STDs), but the service team was aware of some related long-term concerns as well. These young women were at high risk for school dropout, unwanted pregnancies, and limited future career options. The service team addressed the immediate STD problems first, and then arranged to deal with these longer-term risky behaviors. First, the service team redefined them as positive targets antithetical to the negative terms:

1. A preventable problem: The negative term, "dropout," was redefined; the target would be to help the young women to stay in school, which is the antithetical and positive goal regarding dropout.

2. A protectable situation: The negative risk of their becoming unintentionally pregnant was redefined in its antithetical form; the protective goal consists of maintaining their existing states of health and their self-desired nonpregnancy.

3. A promotable concern: The negative risk of limited future career options was redefined; the promotive concern would be to enhance the potential of these young women so as to have some high-quality career options instead of dead-end, low-paying jobs.

Taking these changes of negative-to-positive goals, let us suggest some operational measures for each and see how these would be charted in a primary prevention project. We will employ the distinctions between ultimate goals and intermediate objectives (or subgoals) discussed in Chapter 3, because some primary prevention work involves long periods of time. It may be difficult to stay connected in a longitudinal project, but intermediary objectives that are on the path toward the long-term goal should be valuable and worth attaining in their own right, as well as being a logical step toward the desired long-term goal.

School Dropout: Attendance is the logical antithetical measure with regard to the prevention of dropout. If there is need for rapid feedback to the social worker on nonattendance, then daily data may be necessary; once a stable pattern of attendance is obtained, then weekly or longer attendance records may be used. Daily attendance is an obvious intermediate objective to the long-term goal of a satisfactory attendance rate. However, mere attendance does not tell us how much the student has learned, and, conceptually, we would like to see students not only attend school, but also learn something. Grades in the basic subjects constitute a rough but available indicator of learning. So, by combining attendance with grades, we have an operational definition of a positive concept (perhaps "educational engagement") that is antithetical to school dropout. Note that, in effect, we measure the nonoccurrence of the risky condition (dropout) by measuring in detail the opposite positive conditions (attendance and passing grades). Dropout could occur for other than academic reasons, such as traumatic social events or pressures, but these would appear as annotations on our charts. Such dropouts would not "count" in a kind of batting-average approach with the group of high school women in our STD treatment example. We would count only the academic successes, that is, the number of students with both good attendance rates and passing grades, divided by the total number of students in the STD group, to give the rate of success in this part of the project.

Pregnancy: Protecting the existing state of health and nonpregnant status at this time are other clear objectives antithetical to unwanted teen pregnancy. We'll focus on the pregnancy issue for this discussion. Nonpregnancy can be attained in two ways–abstinence, and the proper use of birth control methods–but we are emphasizing the goal of not being pregnant during the person's time as a high school student. So, a monthly self-report of one's nonpregnant status would be adequate. This self-report on such a personal topic is a delicate issue, but we see this as representing a kind of self-monitoring intervention that enables the young woman to demonstrate control over her own life in this area, and for which she would receive whatever program reinforcements are present, such as tokens exchangeable for scholarship funds for college or technical school.

Long-Term Career: Any long-term goal such as obtaining a job that pays a livable wage and that the worker enjoys is difficult to evaluate because it is an ultimate, long-term goal that may occur only years after high school. However, there are clearly some intermediate steps that are necessary toward attaining the ultimate goal, and primary prevention/single-system designs can provide evaluation of the attained merit of these intermediate objectives. For young women to begin to enter high-quality life career options of their own choice, it would be necessary to obtain: (1) the requisite education (measured by mastery of relevant courses at school, as identified by the academic counselors), (2) the requisite skills (measured by achievement of relevant work or volunteer experiences, such as working for a nonprofit

organization, or volunteering to help older clients at a nursing home, etc.), and (3) the requisite level of self-efficacy, or the belief that one can succeed in accomplishing the specific course of actions involved (Bandura, 1986), as measured by paper-and-pencil tests or reports by teachers.

Figure 25.1 shows the charts used in this example. As with charting methods discussed earlier in this book, there are some criteria for each set, such as acceptable attendance rates, and grades adequate to pass and graduate. Sometimes multiple charts are used for one target condition; at other times, one chart will do. Thus, the same basic procedures for single-system designs in treatment/intervention and rehabilitation may be applied in primary prevention work, given a clear conceptual analysis and construction of targets.

RECENT CRITICISMS OF SINGLE-SYSTEM EVALUATION

A number of thoughtful scholars, researchers, teachers, and practitioners have offered criticisms of single-system designs and the evaluation approach they embody (Heineman-Pieper, 1994; Laird, 1994; Nelsen, 1994; Sherman & Reid, 1994; Tyson, 1994; Wakefield & Kirk, 1996; 1997; Witkin, 1997; and others). We have tried to deal with these issues in writing the fourth edition of this text, but we thought it might be helpful to draw together many of these criticisms so that we could address them directly, and let the readers be the judge. We count ourselves among the critics of single-system designs in the sense that we have added and subtracted to this edition, according to our sense of the best available thinking on these evaluation methods. But we appreciate these outside critics–however painful their criticisms may be–calling attention to our mistakes and our misinterpretations, because we have been, are, and probably will be wrong in the future on some of these points–although, we would argue, not on all of them. So, critics keep us honest, and we want to share these criticisms and responses with the readers (see also Cone, 2001, for an extensive discussion of the issues involved in evaluating outcomes).

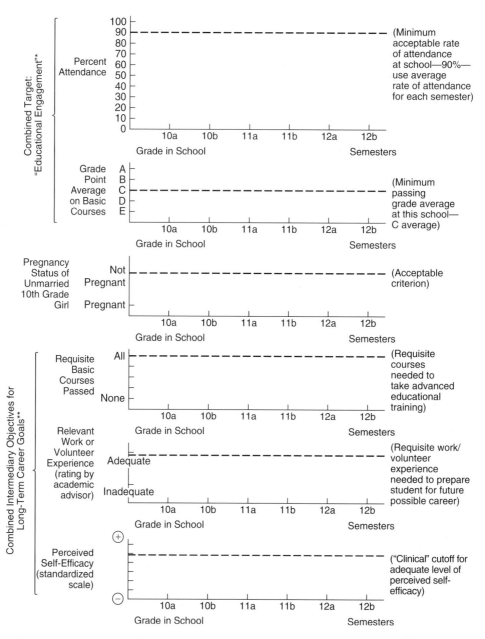

FIGURE 25.1 Components of preventive, protective, and promotive evaluation objective for one 10th-grade girl in an STD intervention group, viewed over a 3-year period.

*"Success" = joint occurrence of at-or-above minimal attendance and C or better grade average for each semester period.

**"Success" = joint occurrence of: (1) passing all requisite basic courses, (2) obtaining relevant work or volunteer experiences, and (3) having a perceived self-efficacy at or above the "clinical" cutoff mark.

We propose to sort out the array of critical comments into five sections relating single-system designs and the evaluation methods to: (1) practice; (2) research; (3) ethical issues; (4) philosophical, political, and socioeconomic issues—we'll term these the meta-issues for short; and (5) technological issues. Of course, we recognize that there may be overlap among categories. We believe that readers who might use single-system designs in their own practice should read the practice (#1) and ethical issues (#3) at least, while research students who are studying or using single-system designs would also profit from looking at the research (#2) and the technological (#5) issues. We would suggest that the meta-issues (#4) might be most interesting to persons concerned with the larger philosophical-political-social contexts in which evaluation is practiced, because we will discuss topics on ideology, paradigms, managed care, and sociocultural and feminist issues.

We will discuss specific issues within these five sets by stating the criticisms in italics, followed by our response.

The First Set of Criticisms: Single-System Evaluation and Practice

1. *Evaluation interferes with practice, because the efforts required by evaluation take too much time and effort away from practice itself.* This criticism has a grain of truth: It does take time to learn how to do single-system evaluations, but like any professional educational component, once learned and practiced, they become second nature. As with the learning of new intervention techniques, one cannot attain complete comfort without considerable practice. Similarly, during the process of conducting practice with a client, a group of clients, or a system, the practitioner indeed may have to take time away from the specific actions that constitute methods that change persons and environments to do other things that support these specific practice actions. Included among these supportive measures would be thinking about the meaning of events to the client and relevant others, about specific targets, about interventions that are likely to have a direct impact on those targets, about monitoring how these interventions

are going, and about deciding whether and when to terminate services, and so forth. As we discussed in detail in Chapter 1, these are some of the component steps of evaluation, and thus are simply a part of good practice. Not doing evaluation—that is, not performing the actions described above—would constitute a very strange kind of practice. Engaging in good active listening skills, sociocultural sensitivity, good ethical behavior, and so forth all take time away from specific practice actions in a narrow sense of the term—and yet no one complains about these components of good practice as taking time away from practice. We submit that evaluation components are exactly like these other components of good practice. Evaluation, good communication skills, cultural sensitivities, and ethical considerations are different ways to describe aspects of good practice.

2. *Evaluation imposes too rigid requirements that force practitioners to do things (such as having long baselines when the client needs immediate service) that they would not do if they weren't doing evaluation.* This criticism is misdirected. The practitioner and client have to agree that the idea of evaluation feedback will be useful in the context of service, and then they have to consider the best way to achieve this useful component of practice. (We discuss this later as part of our suggested Client Consent Form.) There are ways of evaluating practice by beginning with service if this is needed, such as the *B-A-B* design; it is possible to begin an intervention using reconstructed baseline data if necessary; and it is always possible to drop evaluation, before or during baseline, if it proves to be harmful in any significant way to the client. One always has to balance the benefits from evaluation against the costs of doing the evaluation. We have tried to point out the flexibility in designs and methods so as to offer practitioners lots of choices in proposing and using single-system designs. We have challenged practitioners to be creative as well as sensitive in doing evaluation. But we recognize that there could be occasions when evaluation may not be helpful or may be actually harmful, and, thus, in these situations, evaluation should not be used.

3. *Evaluation doesn't add anything to practice that good practitioners don't already do.* The sense

of this criticism is that evaluation is unnecessary because good practitioners already have a sense of how matters are proceeding, and merely applying numbers to this sensitivity is unnecessary. This is partly true; good practitioners do think about clear problem definitions and clear modes of intervention directly related to resolving these problems, and they do have some understanding of how the client is changing over time. We think using some evaluation tools may help make these good practitioners even more informed and supply them with more crisp and objective information on which to make better decisions. However, students have to learn how to be good practitioners, and perhaps these evaluation methods might be jump-starts to progress to the stage of high-level practice where clear problem definitions, clear modes of intervention, and the like become second nature. And, as we discussed earlier, managed care may demand objective methods of accountability, even from experienced practitioners. We have made the point that single-system design methods are also highly sensitive to the practice context, and able to provide more objective accountability as well.

4. *The goals of evaluation often interfere with the goals of practice.* This is a persistent misperception that is related to another point we will discuss shortly: that evaluation, a knowledge-using enterprise, is different from research, a knowledge-building activity. The goal of evaluation is to facilitate the goals and objectives of practice. The components of, and steps in, evaluation are also the components and steps in good practice, as we presented them in the Prologue and in Chapter 1.

The Second Set of Criticisms: Research and Evaluation Issues

1. *Evaluation in practice is just another way to conduct research on practice.* This criticism is intended to show that the actual nitty-gritty practices of doing evaluation impose research-like restrictions that interfere with good practice. It is true that evaluation uses many of the same tools and methods as research (such as interobserver reliability, objective counting of target behaviors, statistical formulas in arriving at

probability statements, etc.), but this criticism neglects the strong differences that distinguish evaluation from research.

Research is logically separate from practice, frequently with different goals from practice (e.g., building knowledge for the sake of knowledge), and is bound by the strict requirements of its constituent logical models, including such factors as random assignments, experimental and control groups, pre-identified goals, unchanging interventions, subjects who typically are not consulted about goals, methods, or roles, and so forth.

Evaluation, on the other hand, especially single-system evaluation, has goals compatible with practice; it is intended to facilitate practice, and its underlying model demands the incorporation of client and community values, client participation in the formation of practice goals and objectives to the extent possible, a flexible logical structure that permits additions and subtractions of interventions during the service period, multidimensional contextual analyses, and so forth. All of these features that characterize the basic ingredients of research and evaluation are essentially different from each other. Evaluation is not research; research is not evaluation.

However, there are many occasions when researchers use time-series methods to conduct research per se, in part because time-series methods are able to access factors that classical research cannot on some occasions. To take only one example, in Chapter 16, we described a study by Martella and colleagues (1993) on self-monitoring in helping a student decrease the frequency of negative self- and other-statements, while increasing positive ones, in a classroom. These researchers used a combined changing criterion design and multiple-baseline design to study whether their methods—self-monitoring combined with differential token reinforcements—would achieve positive results. While the results were clearly positive—the young man did decrease using negative statements and did increase using positive ones—the primary objective of this project was to study self-monitoring in order to contribute new or extended knowledge on this topic to the psychological literature. The secondary objective was to help the student in question, but any student could have served the researchers' purpose. They were careful to be sensitive to the student's abilities, and presumably received permission for the study from his parents. It probably would have been difficult to assemble a large number of developmentally disabled persons, randomly divide them into experimental and control groups, train the experimental subjects to suitable levels of competence on self-monitoring, and then engage large numbers of monitors to implement and collect reliable data. It was enough to study one person with great care and create strong time-series designs to get published in a journal that offers knowledge to other practitioners about self-monitoring. We accept (gladly) these kinds of pure knowledge-building projects, but we expect that few practitioners will organize their evaluations of practice primarily to build generalized knowledge as did Martella et al. Our book—and single-system designs in general—focuses on evaluation and the benefits of rapid feedback for stimulating good practice.

2. *Conducting an evaluation takes practitioner time and energy away from the client, who then does not get the full benefit of the services.* Apart from the fact that the entire focus of the evaluation is on and for the client, this criticism in part turns on the meaning of the word "client": whether that is only the one person sitting before you now, or whether it is the collective sense of client. We believe that "client" means both the individual(s) before the practitioner now and also all of the individuals and groups the practitioner ever will see. Feedback from single-system designs is intended primarily to enhance practice with the immediate client/system. Practitioners should fully and directly serve the specific client before them, but they also should learn from this experience in order to serve other clients better. We believe that it is fully ethical and essentially incumbent on practitioners to learn as much as possible about their intervention methods with different categories of client problems, so as to be able to progress in their effectiveness with similar cases. When the opportunity presents itself, it may be useful for practitioners to understand what is causing what, rather than simply determining that some desirable change has occurred. This is a kind of repertoire-of-practice-

building aspect of evaluation, and it is different from the classical research approach, even though it may lead to shared knowledge of effective methods under certain circumstances. We wish more practitioners would share their practice wisdom in this way. The current client has likely benefited from prior evaluated practices, and future clients we hope also will benefit. Clients would not wish to consult with practitioners who did not learn from their practice experiences. Single-system designs provide one set of methods of developing a repertoire of effective interventions under certain conditions.

The Third Set of Criticisms: Ethical Issues in Single-System Designs

1. *Single-system designs violate the basic code of ethics of helping professionals by diverting their attention to evaluation rather than their attending exclusively to practice.* This chapter will include an extensive discussion of ethical issues, but we want to explore here some of the implications of the message of the Hippocratic oath: Help if you can, but if not, do no harm. All of practice is predicated on the belief that performing certain methods in sensitive but systematic ways likely will help. We believe that the evaluation components added to whatever practice model the practitioner is employing will contribute to performing those methods in a sensitive and systematic way. This is the essence of the ethical code—help if you can. We also have argued that *not* using evaluation components may lead to ethical concerns (Bloom & Klein, 1994)

The second part of the ethical code, do no harm, is also part of the safety features in the single-system methodology: Clients are involved in the formulation of problems and goals, values to be considered, methods to be employed, interpretation of the data, and application of data to the next stages in client service wherever this is feasible. At each of these points, clients might break off engaging in the evaluation components because of perceived or anticipated harms. We believe that doing so will lead to a less sensitive and effective service, but clients can exert this control over evaluation so as to limit harm.

Even more to the point, it may be a violation of professional ethics *not* to evaluate. As just one example, the Code of Ethics of the National Association of Social Workers, adopted by the NASW Delegate Assembly on August 15, 1996, specifically states that social workers should monitor and evaluate the implementation of programs and practice interventions.

2. *Single-system designs do not help practitioners to prevent extreme cases of mortality (such as fatal child abuse).* This criticism is valid. Yet, we would argue that both research and practice share the inability of single-system designs to address adequately this kind of issue. However, it may be that if single-system evaluation were being conducted on, say, an abusive parent, it might seem to that parent that a more or less public spotlight is trained on his or her behaviors with regard to fundamental targets (the health and well-being of the child) on an ongoing basis; then the behaviors may not progress to the point of abuse or neglect. Does this make evaluation a kind of intervention? In the case of the abusive parent, it may be so; we are saying: "Here is what we are officially observing in your behavior vis-a-vis your child." To any client, we are saying: "Here is what we agreed to observe in your behavior and the environment vis-a-vis your problem or goal." In general, this further suggests that evaluation components are one part of good practice.

3. *Single-system designs cannot be used to study interventions in major social problems, such as poverty, unemployment, or discrimination.* This is to some extent true, strictly speaking. We can't hide behind the small numbers that are commonly found in most single-system designs. However, remember that the "client" can be a system of any number, such as the millions of callers in a Cincinnati telephone system project (McSweeny, 1978), or the hundreds in an open-pit mining project (Fox et al., 1987). Yet, this criticism is right on the mark. There are very few single-system design studies, or any kind of studies for that matter, on demonstration projects to prevent poverty, to protect existing states of healthy employment, or to promote tolerance among masses of citizens.

However, we can point to single-system evaluations of small pieces of the larger issues, such as the King et al. (1986) study to enhance coping behaviors in women who were in dual-earner families; Levy and Bavandan's (1995)

study promoting health care in women; the McNees et al. (1976) study to prevent shoplifting; the Jason, Billows, Schnopp-Wyatt, and King (1996) study on reducing illegal sales of cigarettes to minors; the Altus et al. (1993) study on evaluating an ongoing consumer co-operative over a nine-year period; the Brigham et al. (1995) project to increase "designated drivers" so as to reduce alcohol-related accidents; and the Brothers et al. (1994) effort to evaluate a recycling project. These are all instances where major social concerns were addressed, using single-system design methods, focusing on specific representatives of the larger group that is involved. These successful instances should be considered as the foundation for ideas for addressing larger numbers of persons with similar problems. Indeed, Miringoff, Miringoff, and Opdycke (1996) created a time-series model for an index on social health (measuring 16 leading indicators including infant mortality, child abuse, teenage suicide, high school dropout, adult unemployment, poverty in the over-65 age group, etc.). While this is not a single-system design as such, it does illustrate the use of this kind of methodology with regard to understanding more clearly the nature of these social problems.

The Fourth Set of Criticisms: Meta-Issues in Philosophy, Politics, and Socioeconomics

1. *Single-system designs and evaluation are part of the larger philosophy of science enterprise termed postpositivism (Reid, 1997b) and are heir to its flawed assumptions and methods.*

The naturalistic, heuristic, constructivist critics of single-system designs have long lists of arguments against neo-positivist approaches, including single-system designs. Readers will find the hard-hitting discussions by Heineman-Pieper (1994), Tyson (1994), and others (see various authors in Sherman & Reid, 1994) to be most interesting. Rather than address every criticism, we will select representative ones.

The experimental method, including ". . . the modified form in which it is applied to single-subject studies" (Heineman-Pieper, 1994, p. 72) is said to involve prospective rather than retrospective studies, operational definitions, data gathering by structured instruments, and the like, which are best applied to closed systems or "nonhuman subjects." These methods are said to be imposed on the clients and thereby change them in unacceptable ways that damage the helping process. We would agree that there are costs for any intervention into another person's (client's) life situation that change that situation to some degree; the question is whether the intervention (and the evaluation) are worth the price. We believe that more or less objective feedback of monitored interventions, as well as the interventions themselves, are well worth that cost.

Critics suggest that single-system designs are "interventionist" because ". . . they involve manipulation of the treatment process" that introduces "nontherapeutic motives and experiences into the treatment relationship, and therefore, always reduce the quality of the service being offered" (Heineman-Pieper, 1994, p. 73). We simply disagree. We suggest that good evaluation *adds* to the quality of the service being offered by documenting significant changes and thus supporting client change efforts far beyond just talking about change—even within a trusting relationship. No practice ideology has a monopoly on what is "good service" and who best offers it. The proof is in the reality.

Critics argue that positivist researchers (presumably including those who use single-system designs) believe their work is confirmed by Hanson's (1969, p. 74) wonderful phrase, "immaculate perceptions," using immutable formulas and numbers, while striving for absolute confirmation and total objectivity. As readers of this book will recognize, the discussion of single-system designs in the previous pages is anything but absolute, immutable, unchanging, and immaculate. Single-system designs are approximate, highly flexible, and constantly changing to fit the needs of client and practitioner.

Critics argue that the findings from single-system designs are paper-thin (rather than the "thick" knowledge of qualitative naturalistic studies), stripped of the context of real life, which leads to avoiding the role of advocate for some valued position (while remaining loyal to the "value-free" position of the positivist), and thus are a "handmaiden to the status quo." (Heineman-Pieper, 1994, p.82). In contrast to these critical remarks, the single-system designs we have been discussing involve value decisions of client and practitioner throughout, where targets are representatives of the global but unmeasurable whole, and where the set of targets may represent a "thick" understanding of the client's situation. (We call attention to the Secret and Bloom, 1994, paper for a truly multifaceted view of a typical clinical problem.) As Tyson (1994, p. 102) notes, "all data collection strategies are heuristics that give priority to one form of accuracy but sacrifice another. . . ." We have argued that single-system designs seek to balance the priorities of successful client outcome and objectivity. Losing either one while gaining the other is a mistake no ethical practitioner should ever make.

2a. *Single-system designs reflect the dominance of a positivist research establishment with its emphasis on unattainable objectivity and its selection of simplistic targets of study rather than the meaningful understanding of the whole situation—in short, the futile aping of the quantitative model and the neglect of qualitative methods.*

2b. *Single-system designs reflect the soft fuzzy thinking of qualitative methods, with its kindly efforts of deep understanding of the entire world of the objects of study at the price of losing objectivity and perspective, and its neglect of quantitative research, which is the basis of modern science.*

Rather than get involved in the seemingly endless debates on the nature of contemporary applied social science (see, for example, our discussion in Chapter 1 as well as the Letters in the September 1997 issue of *Social Work Research*), we would only reply that single-system designs reflect a joint origin in both qualitative and quantitative perspectives, and that we believe single-system designs contain the best of both perspectives. With qualitative methods, single-system designs are vitally concerned with the unique characteristics of the client's situation. Discussions with the client with regard to problems and/or goals, alternative methods and likely costs and benefits, and involvement in the process and outcome of the study as these affect practitioners' interventions and client outcomes are all the hallmarks of single-system designs in common with some forms of qualitative research. With quantitative methods, single-system designs share the concern for objectivity, for replicability, and for using a scientific language that communicates with all qualified persons so that our knowledge of effective ways of helping can expand and be used by other helping professionals.

We find it significant that single-system designs often are the subject of criticism by scientific positions that are, theoretically, diametrically opposed to each other. This suggests to us the folly of being too much convinced by one's own rhetoric about the truth and rightness of one's own ways, and the inconceivable stupidity of others (who disagree).

3. *Managed care will be making significant demands on practitioner accountability that will be detrimental to professional practice. Single-system evaluation is a too-willing accomplice of managed care, and is tarred by the same brush.*

Managed care is a reality that we have to address, whether we want to or not, as it will likely grow to dominate many of the service areas where helping professionals are at work. Although, at this time, "managed care" is a broad label without a fixed meaning, it appears likely that some form of accountability will be involved. We certainly have no complaint about accountability, and we are happy, in this specific sense, to be an accomplice to the accountability movement because we believe that this will lead to greater openness and rigor in the evaluation of professional practice, to the benefit of clients, practitioners, and the payers of these services. This does not mean that we are silent about the abuses of managed care that are surfacing all about us. Rather, we hope that the incorporation of accountable methods by all practitioners might forestall an imposed set of standard methods and demanded outcomes that are difficult to achieve in any human service situation. We believe it is possible to demonstrate more or less objective outcomes and effective methods without having third-party nonprofessionals determining what practitioners can and cannot do in the actual context of service.

4. *There has never been any scientific evidence that the use of single-system designs helps in enhancing practice outcome (as distinct from the issue in which single-system designs document change and* *inferred causes of the change in a given case situation). Moreover, most graduates still are not using single-system design methods, after two decades of inclusion in educational curricula.*

Our goal in explicating single-system designs and methods is to explicate single-system designs and methods. We assert (and cite ample literature and our own experiences) that these methods can help us document significant positive client changes, and in the case of using advanced designs, that we also can infer the causality of these changes. We also have illustrated a number of other ways that practice can be enhanced from the use of single-system evaluations–from the way we identify problems and goals to our recording of outcomes. These are different tasks than scientifically demonstrating that using single-system design methods versus not using them will lead practitioners to better outcomes in practice. (Recent studies by Faul, McMurty, and Hudson, 2001, and Slonim-Nevo and Anson, 1998, do suggest, though, that adding evaluation procedures to an intervention can positively affect client outcomes beyond the effects of the intervention alone.) The latter is a research question, and a good one, but it is not the one we address, or need to address in this book, so long as we can demonstrate hundreds of times with many different targets in many different fields that the outcome of practice efforts is significantly positive, and (when suitable designs are used) that what we did is likely to be one cause of that improvement. This, in itself, is an important task and one that involves a great deal of effort, and we make no apologies for not covering other (research) tasks in this book.

5. *Single-system evaluators have been largely silent with regard to ethnic, gender, and other issues regarding oppressed persons.* In one sense, this is a justified criticism in that few studies have been conducted specifically on such topics–primarily because single-system design is an evaluation method, not a research tool per se. Classical research methods, such as in Fischer, Dulaney, Fazio, Hudak, and Zivotofsky's (1976) study of sexism in social work, Bloom's (1983) review of primary prevention studies regarding minorities, or Hamilton and Orme's (1990) work on racial differences on parenting

measures, may be better suited to this task. However, people of different ethnic backgrounds, genders, and other social characteristics have been clients and their problems or challenges have been evaluated, as this book amply demonstrates.

However, it is important to continue to work to ensure that there is no systematic bias in the use of single-system designs against people with any particular social characteristic. The goal of social and cultural competence—sensitivity to and knowledge of our clients' (and colleagues') characteristics and differences—are the same for use of single-system designs as they are for all of practice. However, there can be many places where such biases may emerge, such as in formulation of target problems or challenges. For example, if a woman is being seen by a practitioner with regard to her depressed feelings and actions, it is possible that a biased practitioner may direct attention to the woman alone as the source of her own problems, rather than exploring what part her social and cultural training and roles may play in her depression. Once a target is identified, intervention plans to address it may further continue the bias. If the woman is seen as the predominant source of her depression, then treatments will likely be addressed to the woman alone, as contrasted with making adaptive changes in her social and cultural settings. The choice of who is to collect data, and how these data are interpreted, may yet continue the bias. If the client's husband is involved in data collection, and if, in fact, he is part of the social environment creating the depressive context, then there will be bias in the data collection and ultimately its interpretation. All of these systematic errors in evaluation may be totally unintended and invisible to the practitioner who would claim to be free of such biases (Broverman, Broverman, Clarkson, Rosenkrantz, & Vogel, 1970). Yet, it is one of the ironies of the helping professions that we, as self-consciously open-minded persons, may be displaying unknown biases—until critics help us to see ourselves and our discriminatory actions in a clearer light. Thus, the admonition to be sensitive to one's own biases is as central to the use of single-system designs as it is in every

other realm of professional service. We believe that sharing the problem identification and other aspects of intervention with the client is one of the best ways to avoid the worst of these biases. Listening carefully to critics of single-system evaluation is another way of checking ourselves against unintended biases.

The Fifth Set of Criticisms: Technological Issues

1. *There are some technological problems that strike at the very heart of single-system designs and their evaluation process. They either make these designs impossibly difficult to do on a routine basis (e.g., autocorrelation), or they challenge the logical meaning of data analysis and interpretation (for instance, definitions of significance, and methods of analyzing data).* These technological issues, such as autocorrelation (discussed in Chapter 19), the meaning of significance (also discussed in Chapter 19), and the methods of analyses (discussed in Chapter 20 through 24), are real and do represent important concerns regarding single-system design because they call attention to possible methodological issues that may limit the usefulness of such evaluation forms, or else they offer new ideas that force us to change how we have considered some basic topics. Whenever possible, we take a conservative position, call attention to the issues, and caution users that future study may lead to different suggestions for evaluating practice. With regard to new ideas, we approach them cautiously and offer them on an experimental basis. The main point we want to make with regard to such new ideas is that they may prove fruitful or not, and we hope to respond accordingly. The discerning reader of these several editions of *Evaluating Practice* will notice some absences and changes in our discussion of these topics, as technical knowledge has grown, shifted, or retreated. We cannot promise the reader "truth" in these matters, only the best of present-day thinking as it applies to single-system designs. While negotiating the challenges of autocorrelation and methods of analysis may be time-consuming, we have offered advances in time-saving methods through the use of computer programs and the

CD that comes with this book. In the end, it is a choice of balancing the costs of obtaining and analyzing valuable data against the benefits of knowing what we are doing and how well the interventions are succeeding.

We now turn to discussion of a number of other issues—in particular, ethical issues. We address these by posing a series of questions, addressed to the various groups for whom this book was written.

FOR THE CLIENT

Questions about Evaluation

What shall I expect from evaluation? What are my rights? My responsibilities? What problems and possible advantages may I expect if I cooperate with the evaluation of my own situation?

Evaluation is not new to practitioners; it has always been a part of professional helping, but often was largely a subjective judgment rather than a more or less objective procedure. Evaluation has moved from a global, poorly defined process to a more specific and empirically oriented set of procedures. It has become incorporated into the helping process as a vital adjunct to the intervention itself. However, this addition is not without costs. It often is time-consuming to collect information about one's feelings, thoughts, and behaviors, as well as those of others. Is this effort worth the costs?

We believe that it is worth the price, and that clients get more than their fair share for energies expended on behalf of evaluation. First, accountability is a pressure obliging practitioners to demonstrate their competent performance of the role that society has assigned them. After all, the helping professional often is given enormous prerogatives and independence of function, so accountability is one way of making a quality-control check. Most practitioners are convinced that they have knowledge and skills that can be helpful in resolving psychosocial problems. That they are asked to demonstrate this is sometimes embarrassing for them, but it is not more nor less than the

ethics of their professions demand. It also may be embarrassing when the client participates in an evaluation because it opens up the practitioner's work to scrutiny. But this is misplaced embarrassment, since *the fundamental objective of helping is to help, and the fundamental objective of evaluation is to improve that helping.* The professional presumably is trained to try a variety of methods to attain the client's objectives if the first method does not work. Thus, accountability is a pressure to ensure competency in helping; it is a fair demand, and no party to it should feel embarrassed by results, since this is the information needed to achieve the mutual goal of client and practitioner—helping to solve the client's problems.

A second reason that evaluation is worth its weight in effort to the client is that the client is directly a party to the evaluation. The client is as biased in favor of desired outcomes as the practitioner. Therefore, more or less objective evaluation is a method of protecting one from one's self. The attempt to achieve objectivity may prevent premature stopping of intervention, and may help terminate a fruitless process. The point is that we have more or less independent confirmation of hopes (or doubts), and this is the information that we can use to make decisions with regard to intervention. For a little bit of time and effort in collecting or participating in data collection, clients can have a more or less objective basis for making vital decisions in regard to their own lives.

How Can Recording Help the Client (and the Practitioner)?

There is a myth (not supported by actual research; see Campbell, 1988, 1990; Mutschler, 1979, 1984) that clients will resist recording their own problems or strengths. What the myth may really point to is the fact that practitioners may be uncomfortable about asking clients to do recording. In this section we emphasize how recording can help the client and the practitioner in addition to those benefits described in Chapter 4.

First, recording can describe the actual scope of the problem. This is protection against natural tendencies to exaggerate or to minimize. If clients are prepared to share information with practitioners at all, then sharing accurate information should be acceptable, especially if the practitioner can convince the client (and himself or herself) of the utility of collecting data. Demonstrate how these data will be used. Let the client have a real part in the intervention, and the data will become real to the client.

Second, recording helps clients be aware of their behavior. Benjamin Franklin wrote in his *Autobiography and Other Writings* that for many years he kept track of his tendencies toward being disorderly, intemperant, not silent, and so on. He kept track of these tendencies by putting down a dot for each time he exhibited one of these behaviors. He expressed surprise at how many little dots there were. However, he also wrote that it gave him much pleasure to reduce the number of those dots. Awareness can be a motivating factor.

Third, this awareness leads to another important phenomenon for clients. By getting used to thinking about a behavior, one becomes used to thinking about its impact before it happens. This is something similar to anticipatory feedback. The charting of a set of behaviors often indicates the ripple effects of one event. The awareness of this (as pointed out by the practitioner) may be helpful to the client's understanding and self-control.

Fourth, recording can be a significant step in a client's independence from professional intervention. Keeping track of events can make the intervention briefer by helping the practitioner aid the client more clearly and directly. After the program of service is over, the client might profit by keeping track of events as a way of maintaining self-awareness of problems and strengths. It is important that clients be encouraged to chart strengths so as to accentuate the positive. Recording encourages honesty with one's self and with others. As long as the operations for measurement are precise and reasonably objective, recording presents life as it actually appears, without a sugar coating; thus the problems will not be exaggerated either.

Ethical Considerations in Using Single-System Designs

Ethical questions naturally arise as increasing numbers of people learn about single-system designs and use them in many different contexts. Each choice you make regarding what kinds of practice and what forms of evaluation to use involve ethical decisions that may not always be obvious to the people involved. In this section, we continue our exploration of ethical principles that may be helpful in a variety of service contexts. We recognize that our statements may be controversial—they represent only our opinions—but we offer them as a beginning point for the discussions that may ultimately provide clear ethical guidelines for the helping professions.

First, though, we must emphasize that we view evaluation as an intrinsic part of practice so that the ethical guidelines of practice apply (when applicable) to evaluation. However, many professional codes of conduct largely involve the conduct of the professional with regard to the practitioner role: responsibilities to clients, to colleagues, and to the employing agency, as well as to the profession and society. Frequently, little is said about research and evaluation. (We noted earlier in this chapter the recent NASW Code of Ethics revision that mandates evaluation of practice interventions.) Thus, to supplement professional, practice-oriented codes of ethics, we offer 11 ethical statements focusing on evaluation in the context of practice on the grounds that for practice to be ethically conducted, evaluation must be integral to it. As ethical principles, these statements are guidelines for identifying the social and personal benefits and risks associated with the application of single-system designs for practice purposes. They generally are constructed like a formula for estimating how to maximize the benefits and minimize the risks in making a decision about whether to evaluate and how to evaluate.

1. *Provide demonstrable help.* As we noted earlier, the Hippocratic oath begins with the basic idea of providing help to clients. The original statement that has been the

basis of so much of our ethical thinking in the helping professions is translated in this form:

As to diseases, make a habit of two things—to help, or at least to do no harm. (From *The Epidemics,* as quoted by Veatch, 1981, p. 22)

Our suggestion for a first ethical principle for evaluating practice likewise begins with the statement to offer help, but to do so in the context of *demonstrable* help. The demonstration must be objective, for, as Demosthenes noted: "Nothing is so easy as to deceive as one's self; for what we wish, that we readily believe." Demonstrated help involves several components: (a) the accurate identification of the presenting problems and potentials in the client situation, (b) corroboration of the extent to which help is in fact offered as intended for these identified concerns, and (c) documentation of ongoing changes and final outcomes relative to the client's goals and the social context. This first principle restates our basic belief that practice and evaluation are intricately related; caring practice and scientific practice necessarily mean *evaluated* practice.

2. *Demonstrate that no harm is done.* The Hippocratic oath continues that if one cannot help, then at least one should do no harm. Our suggestion for evaluating practice extends this principle to situations in which you are providing service on the assumption that you are helping. Because of the complexity of human behavior and circumstances, it is often difficult to tell whether a change in the client situation has occurred, and especially whether what you did affected that change. In some client situations, holding one's own is about the best outcome attainable, and slower-than-expected deterioration may be a positive result as well.

Systematic evaluation can provide information on whether there is deterioration from the initial state before intervention began. Thus, the meaning of doing no harm has to be clarified for a given client and situation. Because of practitioner bias or blindness, intended or not, there is always a danger that problems in the case may not be observed. Systematic evaluation is a key way that the trend toward harm becomes visible and subject to change.

There is an extended sense of doing no harm when scientific practice is viewed from a systems perspective. Clearly, you would not want to do anything that leaves the client damaged. Neither would you want to perform an action that helps the client at a comparable or greater expense to others, either those directly related to the case, or to the public at large. Thus, "do no harm" must be extended to include the client and affected others.

When there is a conflict between doing good for the client and doing significant harm to some other, the general principle of doing no significant harm to anyone takes precedence over doing good for someone. Other means of serving the client must be found that will approximate the joint goals of helping and doing no harm. Evaluation follows the general practice ethics in such situations (cf. Reamer, 1982), but offers a way to specify the extent of the changes that might be involved in order to think more clearly about ethical decisions that would thereby be involved.

The concept of equivalent or comparable harm can be considered in the sense of a zero-sum versus a nonzero-sum situation. In the former or closed system, what one party gains, the other party loses. For example, a child cannot be both left at home with an abusive family and removed from that home. It is an ethical decision to weigh the potential good to the child (to be removed from an abusive situation) versus the potential harm to the family (for being denied ordinary parental rights).

In the nonzero-sum situation, what one party gains is not gained at the expense of the other party. For example, it would be conceivable that the harm of removing a child may be very destructive to the parents over the long run, so this dilemma becomes a stimulus to innovative thinking, such as having a third party live with the family for a period of time, or having the whole family move into a protective/training setting where staff could model appropriate parenting while safeguarding the child.

In general, the serious consideration of not doing significant harm may stimulate innovative practice—and careful documentation. Society demands strong evidence in such situations, and the helping professions can use evaluation to test their innovative practices.

3. Because evaluation is intrinsic to good practice, the practitioner should *involve clients in the consideration of evaluation of their situation* while coming to agreement on the overall practice relationship. This principle states that clients should be guaranteed informed consent regarding the objectives and methods of practice, which include the evaluation of that practice. Focusing on the evaluation aspect, there are some pros and cons of introducing systematic evaluation in any particular situation. The pros (such as having more or less objective information as feedback to guide the practitioner toward helping the client achieve his or her goal) and cons (such as the time and energy needed to obtain the information and interpret it) should be considered with the client, as far as practical, before entering into the task.

The practitioner's obligation is to discuss what service will entail with (and perhaps even without) evaluation, and what information will or will not be available, accordingly. If the clients, or their guardians, are not able to participate in such a consideration, then some objective review panel or ombudsman should be consulted, in the same way that a supervisor or a medical review committee double-checks a practitioner's specific practices.

4. *Involve the client in the identification of the specific problem or objective and in the data collection process as much as possible.* This principle emerges from the value stance of the helping professions, that client participation in the definition of the situation for which professional help is being received is part of the client's right to self-determination. Participating in the helping process is critical to most practice methods; it also is important to most single-system designs. Practitioners must respect the client's values as expressed in the definition of the problems to be resolved and the goals or objectives to be attained. This does not mean that you cannot add objectives that reflect the values of significant others.

Baseline and intervention data may be directly or indirectly intrusive in the lives of clients and others, and should be collected only as long as needed to gain a clear perspective on the client situation. This perspective is to be used as a basis for planning the intervention and as a basis for determining when to change interventions and to terminate practice.

For some clients, involvement in their own data collection may be a burden; for others, it will constitute another aid to problem resolution itself. Some clients cannot or will not provide accurate information. Thus, this principle emphasizes that there is no one right way for involving clients in data collection, no automatic inclusion or exclusion of the client in the evaluation process. The prior guidelines of doing demonstrable helping and doing no harm may be applied in this situation of involving clients in the evaluation to the extent possible.

5. *Evaluation should intrude as little as possible on the intervention process,* while still being capable of collecting useful and usable information. Scientific practice includes both intervention services and the monitoring of the progress and the outcome of these services. However, monitoring activities may sometimes interfere with the delivery of services (Thomas, 1978). In such cases, there is no question but that the service side of practice takes precedence over the evaluation side of practice.

However, such interference must be nontrivial before evaluation is to be removed from practice because, on balance, information that evaluation provides can be vital to practice. For example, a client was asked to keep track of her developmentally challenged child's behaviors in putting on his clothes in the correct order. This took some time and energy for an already frustrated mother, but she soon realized that the child was dressing correctly the great majority of the time, and hence realized that the source of her frustrations was in some other area. She might never have realized this without going through the effort of measuring the child's behavior. The removal of evaluation from practice means a reduction in useful and usable information for practice, and not simply the elimination of a luxury accessory.

6. *Stop evaluation whenever it is painful or harmful to the client, physically, psychologically, or socially,* without prejudice to the services offered. Clients have the right to understand that they are being evaluated as part of being served, and that the evaluation may help you to offer more effective services. However, if at any time in the practice process–including before evaluation is to begin–the client finds the prospect or the reality of evaluation to be severely problematic, then it is incumbent upon you to find other ways of evaluating that do not so burden the client.

This principle does not mean that all evaluation will be removed, since evaluation is essential to the conduct of practice. Rather, this principle emphasizes that evaluation shall not injure the client because of the evaluation process itself. (Obviously, a corresponding practice principle emphasizes that practice shall not injure the client because of the practice process itself; cf. Stuart, 1970.) Unobtrusive and nonreactive forms of evaluation may be feasible and unoffensive to the client (see Chapter 9).

7. *Confidentiality* with regard to the data resulting from evaluation of the client/ situation must be maintained to the extent possible given organizational guidelines. Clear limits should be preset with the client's knowledge regarding who has access to information emerging from evaluation. The data should be shared with the client to the extent possible. There may be contraindications to such sharing that emerge during the time of service. For instance, one contraindication would be where shared data may exaggerate the process of deterioration.

Data may be shared with other helping professionals involved with the case, but only in the context of professional helping. For example, case conferences frequently involve a group of professionals discussing the current events of agency cases on an ongoing basis, so as to benefit from the collective thinking on client problems and available evaluation data.

Confidentiality is not an absolute; clients have to be apprised of this fact. Case records may be subpoenaed by courts when there may be life-threatening circumstances involving persons affected by the client's behaviors (cf. *Tarasoff v. Regents of University of California* [17 Cal. 3rd 425, 1976]; Kopels & Kagle, 1993; Wilson, 1983).

Data may be used for research reports, provided no identifying information on individual clients is present. However, this raises a special risk in which practitioners make evaluation choices for the sake of the research data rather than what is appropriate for practice. A student of one of the authors reported that she changed a successful intervention because she wanted to use an experimental design; her teacher may have contributed to this misguided enthusiasm for evaluation by urging students to come up with a strong design. Since the facts of the case did not call for such a change, the student and the teacher may have been acting beyond ethical bounds.

8. *Balance the costs and benefits of evaluating practice.* Practice itself involves a compli-

cated assessment of the costs and benefits of various actions in the client situation. There may be occasions when you would not perform some rational action because the costs are too high or the benefits too low. But most of the time, a projected favorable cost–benefit ratio helps to shape interventive actions.

Likewise, with the evaluation of practice, every action has a cost and some have personal and social benefits. Evaluation requires the likelihood that there will be a favorable balance, with the benefits from monitoring change and assessing outcome outweighing the costs in client energy, tolerance, money, and agency resources. This principle requires that you be able to assign weights, at least figuratively, to these categories, reflecting the individual client situation.

It sometimes is useful to predict the length of services necessary to achieve a statistically significant outcome (see Chapter 22), which could be useful in practitioner and agency planning. Achieving the projected statistical significance would still have to be aligned with achieving practical and theoretical significance (see Chapter 19).

9. *Evaluation should proceed only in the context of sensitivity to and respect for the client's individuality, particularly ethnicity, race, income level, sexual orientation, and gender.* Most helping professionals are aware of the need to be respectful of the client's individuality. But evaluation adds a completely new component to how one interacts with one's client(s). Use of questionnaires or other data-gathering devices may be viewed with suspicion by members of some groups. Some people may be reluctant to provide this information, particularly if they are of a different gender or ethnic group than the practitioner, or members of oppressed minority groups. Of course, there is no substitute for empathy and sensitivity on the part of the practitioner. It is your job to be concerned about how clients perceive these evaluation efforts, to include them as

much as possible in planning them, and to do whatever you can to ensure that your efforts at evaluation will not be used in oppressive ways or even be perceived in those ways.

10. *Evaluation is theory-neutral and value-tinged. Any conceptual guideline may have its implications evaluated, but every strategic choice stemming from that guideline has value implications.* This statement sums up our position that single-system designs can be used with any theory of practice, as long as the targets and interventions can be clearly and accurately identified. Theories project some vision of the future, and under some conditions, predictions of that future can be tested with single-system designs, and also with classical group designs. However, every practice decision is, in effect, subjected to evaluation on a formal or informal basis. Because value questions can be raised about every professional helping action, it becomes useful to have clear evidence about the trend of events and the outcome of actions, using more or less objective measures. Thus, evaluation provides the evidence for values. You evaluate your practice not only for factual information, but to supply evidence about the values involved in your helping actions.

11. *A Client Bill of Rights is an intrinsic part of a code of ethics for evaluating practice.* The following rights are the minimum:

1. Clients have the right to know what the *problem* is (from the perspective of the practitioner) in clear language that they can understand.
2. Clients have the right to participate in selecting *goals* and *objectives* of their intervention.
3. Clients have the right to know specifically what is going to happen during the *intervention process*—who is supposed to do what to whom and under what conditions?
4. Clients have the right to know how long the intervention is likely to last (*time dimensions*).

5. Clients have the right to know *alternative methods* of dealing with their problems, and what the probability is that the one(s) selected will lead to successful resolution of the difficulties.

6. Clients have the right to know how much the intervention will *cost* them. If they do not directly pay fees, it is equally a right to know the value of the services being provided.

7. Clients have the right to know what *records* will be kept and who will have access to them.

8. Clients have the right to know in advance about conditions regarding the *termination* of services.

9. Clients have the right to take increasing *control* over their own lives, so far as they are able, or to know (or have a guardian know) why this is not so.

10. Clients have the right to have all professional interventions systematically *evaluated* and to be a part of and informed about the *evaluation* of their own situations, so that they may profit from and make decisions based on these data.

11. Clients have the right to the most *effective interventions* available, based on the practitioner's review of the most current and relevant research and other literature.

A Model Consent Form

Exhibit 25.1 provides a model consent form for use in evaluation with single-system designs. It may require variations added to reflect special service situations. But, at least, these are the categories that you should closely consider. We again want to emphasize that *separate* consent for evaluation is not necessary since we view evaluation as just one component of overall practice. Thus, consent in this context is for practice to proceed and *includes* consent for evaluation.

FOR THE ADMINISTRATOR

Do I have a choice whether to evaluate? How can I get my staff to cooperate? How can I convincingly present information to funding agencies? What about the image of our agency?

We have presented an optimistic picture of single-system evaluation, not omitting the difficulties, but accentuating the potentials. However, there is another side of evaluation, one that the administrator has to face. It is to this special set of issues that we now turn, for evaluation is difficult for many reasons totally separate from the evaluation task itself.

Evaluation: Do I Have a Choice?

No. The question really is what kind of evaluation you will choose for your agency, not whether you can choose to evaluate at all. Even privately funded institutions are subjected to various kinds of overt and covert pressure in this age of accountability, and public or quasi-public agencies have numerous pressures that are, at the core, evaluative in nature.

There are many forms of evaluation. The general label "program evaluation" is given to those attempts to view the complex workings of an organization or some component (program) of an organization relative to some set of stated objectives. The evaluation of social, educational, and welfare agencies is a special subcategory in program evaluation because of the factors studied—human satisfactions, feelings, understandings, and actions. No matter how difficult the task of evaluating these intangibles is, there is considerable pressure to present *some* evaluation. Formal program evaluation—as represented by the classical experimental, control-group designs—is a difficult, expensive enterprise, but it can present very powerful data. We offer single-systems designs as an alternative, or more accurately as a complement, to the classical program evaluations (see also Hasenfeld & Patti, 1989).

Most program evaluation is conducted in ways that produce grouped data. This is a very efficient way of summarizing the typical pattern among a number of clients, but the problem is that this also hides individual differences. The failures tend to offset the successes, suggesting that nothing significant happened. However, in fact, many significant events may have occurred. If a means were available for identifying individual outcomes, then it may

EXHIBIT 25.1 Model consent form.

Client Consent Form

Preamble: This is a statement of intent for services to be rendered to_____
(client) by_____ (practitioner) beginning on_____(date).

1. The following are targets to which we will devote our cooperative efforts: (state problem or objectives as relevant)
    A. Problem: _____ Objective: _____
    B. Problem: _____ Objective: _____ etc.

2. The overall goals of service are:
    A. _____ B. _____ etc.

3. While it is difficult to know exactly how long it will take to deal effectively with these targets of service, problems like these generally take about _____ weeks.
   (Or we can agree in advance to work together for a set period of time, and in this time accomplish all we can do. Let us agree that we will work together exactly _____ weeks, and re-evaluate our timing then.)

4a. The task of the practitioner is to provide guidance in thinking about alternative approaches to solutions of these problems. Several possible alternatives have been suggested, including:
    A. _____ B. _____ etc.

4b. We (client and practitioner) have decided that _____approach is most likely to be helpful with the least negative side effects.

4c. The practitioner will be implementing the following interventive activities:
    A. _____ B. _____ C. _____

4d. The client will be doing the following tasks/activities as part of the intervention:
    A. _____ B. _____ C. _____

5a. In considering how to monitor ongoing events in this situation, and to evaluate the outcome, the practitioner is to suggest some methods of evaluation. Several possible alternatives have been suggested, including:
    A. _____ B. _____ etc.

5b. We (client and practitioner) have considered the options and have decided that _____ is most likely to be helpful in understanding the changes in events.

6. In these evaluation methods, it is understood that
    A. _____(name party) will give
    B. _____(specified types of information such as measures used) to
    C. _____(name of receiver of information) on
    D. _____(date information is due), which will then be analyzed and interpreted by the practitioner (and shared, as appropriate, with the client and relevant others).

7. The costs or fees involved in this service are set by the agency. The total fees are as follows: _____
   (break down fees, as relevant). (The client is expected to pay the fee after each visit; if the client is unable to do so, please discuss this matter with the practitioner. If the client is not directly paying for the fees, then the above information may be useful to know regarding the financial aspects of this service.)

8. Several kinds of records will be kept:
   First, a service record in which the practitioner indicates summaries of client contacts.
   Second, agency records are kept related to fiscal matters for this case and the entire caseload of the agency.
   Third, information is kept monitoring the progress of the case, and whether or not case objectives are attained. Clients may be requested to participate in providing some of these data, which will be used to monitor progress and assess the outcome of practice.

9. Access to the records on this case will be restricted to
    a. agency personnel (for case management/collective thinking, and for fiscal matters)
    b. research personnel (for collective analysis–no individual names will be identified)
    c. outside legal authorities (only when the case records are subpoenaed)

10. Special requests regarding the practice and evaluation of this situation as made by the client, and agreed to by the practitioner:
    A. _____ B. _____ etc.

Client's Signature _____ Practitioner's Signature_____ Date _____ be shown that some cases were "successful." It would also have to be admitted that there were some cases of failure—and a number of individuals who did not make any changes at all. This is important information because it directs us to take differential action—learn what went wrong (as far as possible) and try to correct for this in new cases, or in present cases before the deterioration becomes serious and irreversible. For the middle group of persons who do not change appreciably, the attempt can be made to change events to turn this situation around.

Single-system designs can supply administrators with this type of information about individual clients. Indeed, several types of information, as listed below, would be available to administrators through the use of single-system designs:

1. Data on clients, including specific types of client problems and strengths, seen at their agency

2. Data on how specific practitioners succeed with selected types of problems

3. Data on how individual practitioners are succeeding in general (overall caseload performance)

4. Data on how the set of practitioners is performing (agency "batting average")

These types of data have an internal and an external face. Internally they supply information for the relevant parties. For example, as explained above, information on client performance can be a big boost to client morale and motivation to continue treatment. But for the practitioner, information on his or her performance is a double-edged sword. If it tells the practitioner of successes, all well and good; if it reveals less than satisfactory performance, then this becomes pressure to change. One type of change is attacking the evaluation system (as we discuss shortly), but the other type of change is accepting the information as reasonably valid and looking for ways of benefiting from its suggestions. Perhaps a given practitioner does not work well with specific types of problems; he or she can transfer a case with such problems before becoming too deeply in-

volved. On the other hand, this same practitioner also could get some special supervision in working with these types of problems. The point is that information can produce a crisis that can serve as an opportunity for positive change or as simply a burden or negative part of one's work load. More on this shortly.

The external face of these types of data refers to how evaluators of that information react to it. Practitioners react to clients' data in ways that keep the movement of the cases flowing toward desired goals. Supervisors in agencies keep supplies and supports flowing toward practitioners based on their individualized performance record. This could include merit bonuses for those doing particularly well (Rehr, 1989; Rinn & Vernon, 1975) and extra supervision or additional training for those not doing well. The point is not to make evaluation a punitive device for the staff, but rather to have it be an opportunity for advancement along a variety of fronts. Over time, probably all practitioners need some additional support for difficult types of case problems. Most practitioners probably would benefit from demonstrated successes with certain types of cases.

Obviously, external evaluators of agency functioning are an important audience to consider when choosing how the performance of an agency is going to be evaluated. We submit that the face validity of single-system designs may be very persuasive to board members who may not be versed in the use of more complicated research and statistical procedures. Explanations of how specific client problems and strengths were targeted for measurement before, during, and after intervention with given results would go far in making the evaluation process intelligible to decision makers. With this method, summary scores such as agency batting averages would become more meaningful. There would be positive pictures to present through individual analysis, even though there would also be negative ones. Moving agency practice in the direction of successful methods suggests both goals and promise for succeeding years.

Even for sophisticated reviewers of agency programs, single-system designs offer important advantages. Through the use of more powerful designs within this group, practitioners can offer strong evidence for showing that their interventions really did bring about changes in their clients' problems. In addition, the range of cases to be evaluated likely will be much more extensive with single-system designs, as most, if not all, practitioners can take part in doing evaluations of their own cases. Certainly the costs are lower when practitioners incorporate and use evaluation information within their own practices rather than waiting for control-group designs (and these are only group averages, not individual changes) to report back to the agency. Indeed, the involvement of practitioners in evaluation is a strong point in an agency's favor showing its willingness to respond to the immediate feedback such data provide.

Staff Development

Evaluation of a practitioner's own practice is an important addition to staff development, because it has not been until rather recently that practitioners have had courses that conveyed information on single-system designs. As students in field placements come to agencies ready and able to evaluate their own practice, it may be somewhat embarrassing if no one is able to provide this type of guidance. (Indeed, the students may do the teaching in these cases.) However, workshops in single-system designs for supervisors and practitioners are immediately rewarding, as practitioners may quickly and relatively easily apply the basic principles to their own practices—although they too must work at learning these principles.

It would be helpful to have a staff member who is well trained in these methods to act as consultant to the rest of the staff in these training phases. Questions always arise as to how to specify targets, how to chart particular events, and the like, and it is useful to have some resident expert—someone well trained in the procedures who can act as a catalyst to the other members of the staff, a consultant on particular problems, and an interpreter for boards and the public. It also would be helpful to have an assistant, perhaps a part-time student, who could do the routine analyses of the data and be helpful in other ways in the mechanical parts of the evaluation process. Neither of

these two positions is essential for the most part, but such support systems do make evaluation easier.

An important contribution to the integration of research and practice in agencies is a book by Reid (1987) that is addressed to both practitioners and administrators; it spells out how a research and/or evaluation program can be integrated into human service agencies. While the practical suggestions presented by Reid are too numerous to detail here (they did, after all, require an entire book), briefly noting some of the topics might illustrate how they can be used to integrate ideas presented here into workable strategies for conducting successful evaluation programs in agencies while simultaneously providing services to clients.

Reid (1987) illustrates how to synthesize evaluation activities into daily job responsibilities. He has suggestions about actually making evaluation enjoyable(!), avoiding some of the common organizational and practice pitfalls in conducting evaluations, and strategies for involving staff in evaluation programs. He also offers a checklist of the key points that need to be addressed to complete evaluations successfully. While not all of the suggestions in Reid's book are focused on single-system designs, the basic principles can be applied to virtually any type of research or evaluation activity in an agency to facilitate accountable, scientific practice.

Staff Cooperation and Deployment

If an administrator is convinced of the value of single-system designs in the workings of his or her agency, then the next major step is to gain the cooperation of the staff in making evaluation an integral part of agency practice. This requires careful explanation not only about how to evaluate, but about what evaluation will mean for the practitioners themselves (their salary, promotion, or even tenure at the agency). Concerning the question of how to evaluate, it is relatively easy to bring in consultants and workshops to the agency or to have some or all practitioners attend classes at nearby colleges and universities.

The other side of the coin, how evaluation will affect a practitioner's job, is a question that has to be answered carefully. We suggest that case evaluation be separated from merit rewards up to a point, because of the enormous range of forces that may be acting on clients and that are out of the control of practitioners. Everyone will run into such difficult cases sooner or later. However, there is a point in attempting to increase the effectiveness of practitioners—for the good of clients and society at large.

Earlier we referred to the work of Rinn and Vernon (1975), who report on a program to set up incentives (annual salary increases) for practitioners to engage in systematic evaluation of their practice at a community mental health center. Such record-keeping systems were monitored, and salary increments were tied to the practitioners' performance. The results: Both merit raises and use of evaluation procedures (including multiple-baseline designs for each client) increased. Note that the administrators were not connecting salary with *successful* performance, but rather they were connecting it only with the *use* of evaluation procedures believed by the agency to facilitate successful practice. We believe that this is a feasible solution for both practitioner and administrator, since use of a single-system design approach is likely to result in more effective practice as ongoing feedback corrects intervention efforts.

For practitioners who can show success, even if the success is only with particular cases or with particular problem events, there may be an additional system of rewards and benefits. It is important to a professional—as with all people—that he or she be given due recognition.

Single-system designs provide the basis for clear and specific recognition on several counts: first, just for their use; second, for the success itself; and third, for the sake of learning what went right and what can be conveyed to colleagues in and beyond the agency so that they can benefit from the successful experience. The ethical guidelines of all the helping professions direct their practitioners to contribute to the development of their discipline through communication of effective work.

One major advantage for both administrators and the whole organization is that single-system designs can be used to monitor not only an individual practitioner's practice, but also to monitor practice throughout the whole agency. This can be done most readily when similar instruments are used throughout the agency, thus allowing the cumulation of information across all practitioners (Benbenishty, 1989).

An example of this combination of single-system designs and the group approach to monitoring and evaluation was provided by Benbenishty (1988) in monitoring task-oriented interventions in an agency in Israel. Each of the practitioners in the agency used a single-system design with each family in his or her caseload. In addition, the data from each practitioner were aggregated to develop a database that described the monitoring and evaluation efforts of the entire agency. Thus, not only could practitioners compare their own results with the overall record of all practitioners in the agency, but the agency itself has a database for sharing with consumers, its board, and funding bodies.

Another example of this aggregation of data from individual practitioners involves the work done at the Lutheran Social Services of Wisconsin and Upper Michigan (William R. Benedict, personal communication, 1986). This agency, mentioned in Chapters 3 and 4 with regard to use of the Goal Attainment Scaling (GAS) and the Problem-Oriented Record (POR), routinely aggregates individual outcome data from the GAS across all agency practitioners. These data then become part of the basis for quality assurance reviews, leading to an evaluation of improvements from prior audits as well as identification of areas of concern.

These two forms of cumulating results across practitioners provide excellent models of accountable organizational practice. They not only can highlight an agency's strengths, but they can point to areas of practice that might need bolstering in subsequent years.

Examples of Evaluation in Agency Settings

A number of agencies across the United States are using a variety of different methods to evaluate their services. The methods used by a sampling of these agencies are summarized here to illustrate the range of evaluation procedures and the ways they can be applied.

A study of social workers' use of single-system evaluation in a traditional, psychodynamically oriented family agency setting was conducted by Mutschler (1979, 1984). She trained a small group of six experienced social workers to identify treatment goals using a variety of standardized measures, and to monitor their specific interventions to gain feedback on the progress toward goal attainment. A 6-month training period consisted of biweekly meetings in which 15 single-system evaluation procedures were discussed. The social workers eventually selected a portion of these for their actual use, including the Target Problem Measure, which we call an individualized rating scale (Battle et al., 1966), Goal Attainment Scaling (Kiresuk & Sherman, 1968), and Global Ratings of Improvement or Deterioration, in which both clients and practitioners rated overall perceived changes during and at the end of treatment.

The six social workers were to use these procedures throughout the 1-year evaluation phase, with each practitioner working with four randomly assigned clients. Four months after the project ended, follow-up questionnaires were employed to see, in part, whether the social workers had continued to use any of these evaluation tools.

Mutschler found that the social workers did indeed continue use of evaluation procedures for the full 2-year project but tended to use the briefest, and those perceived as most relevant, forms of evaluation. The initially negative or neutral attitudes of experienced practitioners were changed through involvement in the development and application of the measures they were to use. This was particularly true of the single-system designs (which emphasized achievement of service outcomes) rather than control-group designs (which emphasized studies of differential effectiveness of treatments). Mutschler also emphasized the need for changes in the organizational context that encourage evaluation as a part of practice.

Fanshel, Masters, Finch, and Grundy (1989) report on a sophisticated, computer-based, management information system (MIS) in an agency offering preventive services to families with children at risk for placement in foster care.

Each month, the social work associate (a specially trained paraprofessional) completed a form about the previous, mutually agreed-on problems that the clients and their social workers had identified. Problems were considered either open or resolved, and the amount of time spent working on the case during that month was documented. These monthly reports were consolidated on a larger time-series data file, enabling the agency to determine which kinds of problems got solved and which did not.

The authors discovered that the highest percentage of problems reported resolved—at 57%—were in a category called adult income and employment, which involved restoring families to public assistance eligibility after their status had been canceled for various reasons. Child educational and vocational training problems were resolved at a rate of 49%, while adult social relations problems were the least likely to be resolved—at 25%. Knowing these agency figures presumably gave direction for plans to strengthen specific interventive methods.

It also is possible to analyze individual cases with this management information system. Knowing the likelihood of resolution for a given category, practitioners could calculate the probabilities for resolving the problems presented in a given case. These probabilities are the added likelihoods of each problem category. Then the actual number of problems resolved could be compared with the expected number to indicate whether the practitioner had done better or less well than expected (compared to agency norms). These are some of the uses that emerged from this MIS program. (See also Grasso et al., 1989; Mutschler, 1989; and Schuerman, 1989, for other agency uses of computers and expert systems as aids to practice.)

In Chapter 3 we discussed the report by Whittaker et al. (1988) on multiple indicators of success in residential youth care and treatment. Routinely collected data on individual youths, their families, and community factors from intake through community follow-up, are used to track multiple indicators of success at the different stages of the placement process. For example, the authors were interested to know whether there would be other partial indicators of success during the treatment process, such as decreases in violent acting-out behaviors. The routinely collected data made it possible to answer these questions, and to visualize multiple indicators of success in the context of their service program.

The Lutheran Social Services Agency of Wisconsin and Upper Michigan, as described in the previous section, also has been using a large number of routine standardized forms that describe the process and outcome of their cases (William R. Benedict, 1986, personal communication). This agency uses case records, service plans, and evaluations of service effectiveness using Goal Attainment Scaling as part of its quarterly clinical audit and uses this information as part of quality assurance reviews. Case records are reviewed to ascertain compliance with agency standards and formats in each area of service delivery. All cases are evaluated to ensure that a goal-oriented service plan has been established. And every case is evaluated using GAS with a goal of reaching at least a score of 50 on the level of success scale (the mid-point or expected level of success). These results are even charted on standardized forms used by each practitioner with each case.

These examples reflect the range of ways in which agencies have been getting involved in evaluation of their practices on routine bases. This kind of information can be used to evaluate how well the agency as a whole is doing, and where it needs to make further efforts toward improvement of services. The key term in all this is *routine* evaluation, undertaking systematic measurement of what is done and how well it is working as an ordinary part of agency life. Aided by computers for the management of large bodies of such information, it is now possible to know up to the minute how well the agency is doing and what more needs to be done. This is clearly a beginning picture of the future of scientific practice.

FOR EDUCATORS AND STUDENTS

Educators: Do I know enough about this type of evaluation method to teach it? What about classical research? Does teaching single-system de-

signs mean ignoring other types of designs? Is this just a fad?

Students: Can I really learn enough of this type of evaluation to use it on my own? I have "math anxiety"; can I get through a course on single-system designs?

We and several of our colleagues have taught single-system designs in various undergraduate and graduate programs across the country for a number of years, and we feel very close to the questions raised above on behalf of educators and students. In this section we try to respond to these questions based on our own experiences.

Does anyone know enough about anything to justify teaching it? The answer is relative. We may never know "enough," but as long as we have substantial knowledge of the particular topic and a well-rounded background of which the topic is a part, we may know enough to teach a course. To put it more positively, there is no better way to learn than by teaching. We hope this book can serve as one of the inputs for a course on single-system designs.

We often hear a concern that single-system designs may replace classical research. This is unlikely, however, since both serve different functions and, as we noted in Chapter 1, address different questions. There will always be a need for classical research designs and the supporting statistical procedures. Single-system designs are special forms of evaluation designs particularly appropriate for applied uses by nonresearchers who have been trained in their implementation. These single-system designs are practice oriented; they supply rapid feedback on the course of clinical and social system events, and they evaluate differences in outcomes between nonintervention periods and intervention periods. This is applied information, and it is acknowledged as an approximation of the experimental, control group design. The latter (classical) research is to some extent a more specialized discipline, and most professional educational programs do not give equal educational experience in research and in practice. Therefore, it is unrealistic to expect less than fully prepared practitioners to engage in classical research, except for the rare individual who seeks out special training and support, or when the practitioner takes part in a supporting role. What we are suggesting, in addition to all of the other benefits, is a way to encourage you to directly experience the pleasures of evaluation in the hopes of enticing you to take more advanced courses in classical designs and statistics.

Is the single-system design merely a fad? We prefer to consider it more a part of a paradigm shift (Fischer, 1981; 1993). Practitioners have long experienced the frustration of trying to apply classical research models to their own situations in the field and coming away empty-handed. Even when research teams are brought in, their services are often too remote from everyday problems in the agency to be perceived as of much use. Their often ponderous reports are long in coming, heavy in language, and low in applicability to this or that client here and now. Therefore, there is a search for new ways of solving the problem. Certain ideas are suggested and tentatively found to be useful. Others expand on the ideas and procedures, and soon textbooks that communicate the knowledge on a broad scale are written. This is pretty much a description of the field of single-system designs, with one exception: Single-system (or time-series) designs have been around in a variety of forms for over 100 years, and they have been heavily used by some social sciences such as economics and by the physical sciences and in agriculture, from whence many evaluation procedures were derived. We therefore conclude that single-system designs are no fad, but, rather, they represent a fundamental groundswell rebelling against the misapplication of complex research models to direct practices. However, we may be biased. Our final comment on this point is: Watch the professional literature; the literature on this topic has expanded enormously in recent years, and this is one way of distinguishing between a fad and a legitimate new development.

Students have a special right to be heard. They are the ones who ultimately are asked to experiment with new evaluation and practice procedures. Is it possible to learn enough about single-system designs in one or two classes to be competent in their use? We firmly believe that it is. This is not to say that all of the nuances of this approach, especially at first, will be digested completely—is anything ever so fully and finally learned? But the basic procedures, as described in this book, are relatively clear and are, we believe, relatively simple. We know from our own experiences that we can teach these procedures to typical classes of students in a regular semester. However, we recommend an additional semester for actual practice of these evaluation skills. Most importantly, we recommend that the skills not lie dormant in a practice and/or evaluation class; they should be integrated with and tried in field experiences and with the expectations and criteria for competent performance in general.

Single-system designs make heavy use of elementary logic (such as concomitant variation as the basis for inferences of causality) and thus far have placed comparatively little emphasis on advanced statistics. Although it may not even be necessary, one basic course in elementary statistics usually will supply all the information needed, at least for the time being. However, the logic of practice designs (Chapter 11) is a form of mathematical reasoning, and if you have mastered that chapter, as just one example, you have reason to doubt the self-stereotyping many students perpetuate—that is, that they have trouble with math or logic ("math anxiety").

Mathematics is often a rather abstract subject, exquisite in its formal characteristics and logical power, but unlike many other aspects of the knowledge of the helping professions. However, when students are directly working with clients and observe the usefulness of applying numbers to target events, we cannot help but believe that we will make many converts to this practical application of "numbers." To master a task (especially when putting in considerable effort) is the surest way of developing a committed user. This is one of the basic assumptions of this book: That using single-system designs will lead to more effective practice, and that many of the tasks associated with it, including a small amount of numerical calculations, will add to the delight of accomplishment.

In fact, single-system designs pose a powerful challenge to students (and faculty and practitioners): the challenge of keeping up to date and attempting to master new knowledge and new technology to the point where you can make a reasoned decision about how helpful it is to your work. Much of the material in this book is part of the challenge: learning about the ways computers can help us in managing our practice, learning the skills of analysis of data, integrating new knowledge with old, and evaluating it all as to its utility and importance. These are all hallmarks of the new breed of scientific practitioners. We, in fact, believe that these multiple challenges are ethical prerequisites for effective practice. Indeed, the evidence for the notion that mastery of the knowledge in this book will enhance your practice is in your hands.

SUMMARY

The utility of single-system designs in the end result really depends on what you want to make of them. There are times when their application is difficult or time-consuming or their appropriateness is even somewhat unclear. Yet we believe the advantages of single-system designs far outweigh the potential disadvantages.

In this chapter, we reviewed a number of ethical and other issues pertinent to clients, administrators, students, and educators. Out of all this, we hope we have convinced you if not to adopt single-system evaluations lock, stock, and barrel, then to give them a try and to decide after your own experience with evaluating your practice whether the endeavor is indeed worthwhile. We hope—no, we predict—that it will be.

REFERENCES

ACIERNO, R., HERSEN, M., & AMMERMAN, R. T. (1994). Overview of the issues in prescriptive treatments. In M. Hersen & R. T. Ammerman (Eds.), *Handbook of prescriptive treatment* (pp. 3–30). New York: Plenum.

ADAY, L. A. (1989). *Designing and conducting health surveys.* San Francisco: Jossey-Bass.

ALBERT, R. (1986). *Law and social work practices.* New York: Springer.

ALBERTI, R. E., & EMMONS, M. L. (1974). *Your perfect right: A guide to assertive behavior.* San Luis Obispo, CA: Impact Press.

ALESSI, G. (1988). Direct observation methods for emotional/behavioral problems. In E. S. Shapiro & T. R. Kratochwill (Eds.), *Behavioral assessment in schools: Conceptual foundations and practical applications* (chap. 2). New York: Guilford Press.

ALEXANDER, J. E., ROBBINS, M. S., & SEXTON, T. L. (2000). Family-based interventions with older, at-risk youth: From promise to proof of practice. *Journal of Primary Prevention, 21,* 185–205.

ALLEN, K. E., HART, B., BUELL, J. S., HARRIS, F. R., & WOLF, M. M. (1964). Effects of social reinforcement on isolated behavior of a nursery school child. *Child Development, 35,* 511–518.

ALLISON, D. B., FRANKLIN, R. D., & HESHKA, S. (1992). Reflections on visual inspection, response guided experimentation, and Type I error rate in single-case designs. *Journal of Experimental Education, 61*(1), 45–51.

ALLISON, D. B., & GORMAN, B. S. (1993). Calculating effect sizes for meta-analysis: The case of the single case. *Behavioral Research and Therapy, 31,* 621–631.

ALLISON, D. B., SILVERSTEIN, J. M., & GORMAN, B. S. (1997). Power, sample size estimation, and early stopping rules. In R. D. Franklin, D. B. Allison, & B. S. Gorman (Eds.), *Design and analysis of single-case research* (pp. 245–277). Mahwah, NJ: Lawrence Erlbaum.

ALLISON, H., GRIPTON, J., & RODWAY, M. (1983). Social work services as a component of palliative care with terminal cancer patients. *Social Work in Health Care, 8,* 29–44.

ALTER, C., & EGAN, M. (1997). Logic modeling: A tool for teaching critical thinking in social work practice. *Journal of Social Work Education, 33*(1), 85–102.

ALTER, C., & EVANS, W. (1990). *Evaluating your practice: A guide to self-assessment.* New York: Springer.

ALTER, C., & MURTY, S. (1997). Logic modeling: A tool for teaching practice evaluation. *Journal of Social Work Education, 33*(1), 103–117.

ALTUS, D. E., WELSH, T. M., MILLER, I. K., & MERRILL, M. H. (1993). Efficacy and maintenance of an education program for a consumer cooperative. *Journal of Applied Behavior Analysis, 26*(3), 403–404.

AMERICAN PSYCHIATRIC ASSOCIATION. (1980). *Diagnostic and statistical manual of mental disorders* (3rd ed.). Washington, DC: Author.

AMERICAN PSYCHIATRIC ASSOCIATION. (1994). *Diagnostic and statistical manual of mental disorders* (4th ed., rev.). Washington, DC: Author.

AMERICAN PSYCHIATRIC ASSOCIATION. (2000). *Diagnostic and statistical manual of mental disorders* (4th ed., text revision). Washington, DC: A.P.A.

AMERICAN PSYCHOLOGICAL ASSOCIATION. (1967). Standards for educational and psychological tests and manuals. In D. N. Jackson & S. Messick (Eds.), *Problems in human assessment* (pp. 169–189). New York: McGraw-Hill.

AMERICAN PSYCHOLOGICAL ASSOCIATION. (1974). *Standards for educational and psychological tests.* Washington, DC: Author.

AMERICAN PSYCHOLOGICAL ASSOCIATION, AMERICAN EDUCATIONAL RESEARCH ASSOCIATION, & NATIONAL COUNCIL ON MEASUREMENT IN EDUCATION. (1985). *Standards for educational and psychological testing.* Washington, DC: American Psychological Association.

ANASTASI, A. (1976). *Psychological testing* (4th ed.). New York: Macmillan.

ANASTASI, A. (1988). *Psychological testing* (6th ed.). New York: Macmillan.

ANDERSON, H., & GOOLISHIAN, H. (1988). Human systems as linguistic systems: Preliminary and evolving ideas about the implications for clinical theory. *Family Process, 27,* 371–393.

ANDERSON, J. D. (1987). Integrating research and practice in social work with groups. *Social Work with Groups, 9,* 111–124.

ANDRULIS, R. S. (1977). *Adult assessment.* Springfield, IL: Chas. C Thomas.

ANESKO, K. M., SCHOIOCK, G., RAMIREZ, R., & LEVINE, F. M. (1987). The homework problem checklist: Assessing children's homework difficulties. *Behavioral Assessment, 9,* 179–185.

APPLEGATE, J. S. (1992). The impact of subjective measures on nonbehavioral practice research: Outcome vs. process. *Families in Society, 73,* 100–108.

ARKAVA, M. L., & SNOW, M. (1978). *Psychological tests and social work.* Springfield, IL: Chas. C Thomas.

ATIENZA, O. O., TANG, L. C., & ANG, B. W. (1998). A SPC procedure for detecting level shifts of autocorrelated processes. *Technometrics, 40,* 340–351.

ATTKISSON, C. C., HARGREAVES, W. A., HOROWITZ, M. J., & SORENSEN, J. E. (EDS.). (1978). *Evaluation of human services programs.* New York: Academic Press.

AUERBACH, A. H. (1983). Assessment of psychotherapy outcome from the viewpoint of expert observer. In M. J. Lambert, E. R. Christensen, & S. S. DeJulio (Eds.), *The assessment of psychotherapy outcome* (pp. 537–568). New York: Wiley.

AUSTIN, J., ALVERO, A. M., & OLSON, R. (1998). Prompting patron safety belt use at a restaurant. *Journal of Applied Behavior Analysis, 31,* 655–657.

AYLLON, T. (1963). Intensive treatment of psychotic behavior by stimulus satiation and food reinforcement. *Behavior Research and Therapy, 1,* 53–61.

AYLLON, T., & AZRIN, N. (1968). *The token economy: A motivational system for therapy and rehabilitation.* Englewood Cliffs, NJ: Prentice Hall.

BABBIE, E. (1990). *Survey research methods* (2nd ed.). Belmont, CA: Wadsworth.

BABBIE, E. (1998). *The practice of social research* (8th ed.). Belmont, CA: Wadsworth.

BAILEY, K. D. (1978). *Methods of social research.* New York: Free Press.

BAILEY, K. D. (1982). *Methods of social research* (2nd ed.). New York: Free Press.

BALASSONE, M. L. (1991). A research methodology for the development of risk assessment tools in social work practice. *Social Work Research and Abstracts, 27,* 16–23.

BALES, R., COHEN, S., & WILLIAMSON, S. (1979). *SYMLOG: A System for the Multiple Level Observations of Groups.* New York: Free Press.

BANDURA, A. (1969). *Principles of behavior modification.* New York: Holt, Rinehart, & Winston.

BANDURA, A. (1986). *Social foundations of thought and action: A social cognitive theory.* Englewood Cliffs, NJ: Prentice-Hall.

BARBER, B. (1990). *Social studies of science.* New Brunswick, NJ: Transaction.

BARKLEY, R. A. (1988). Child behavior rating scales and checklists. In M. Rutter, A. H. Tuma, & I. S. Lann (Eds.), *Assessment and diagnosis in child psychopathology* (chap. 5). New York: Guilford Press.

BARLOW, D. (ED.). (1993). *Clinical handbook of psychological disorders: A step by step manual.* (2nd ed.).

BARLOW, D. H. (ED.). (1988). *Behavioral assessment of adult disorders* (2nd ed.). New York: Guilford Press.

BARLOW, D. H., & HAYES, S. C. (1979). Alternating treatment design: One strategy for comparing the effects of two treatments in a single subject. *Journal of Applied Behavior Analysis, 12,* 199–210.

BARLOW, D. H., HAYES, S. C., & NELSON, R. O. (1984). *The scientist practitioner: Research and accountability in clinical and educational settings.* New York: Pergamon Press.

BARLOW, D. H., & HERSEN, M. (1973). Single-case experimental designs: Uses in applied clinical research. *Archives of General Psychiatry, 29,* 319–325.

BARLOW, D. H., & HERSEN, M. (1984). *Single case experimental designs: Strategies for studying behavior change* (2nd ed.). New York: Pergamon Press.

BARONE, V. J., GREENE, B. F., & LUTZKER, J. R. (1986). Home safety with families being treated for child abuse and neglect. *Behavior Modification, 10,* 93–114.

BARRIOS, B., & HARTMANN, D. P. (1986). The contributions of traditional assessment: Concepts, issues, and methodologies. In R. O. Nelson & S. C. Hayes (Eds.), *Conceptual foundations of behavioral assessment* (chap. 3). New York: Guilford Press.

BARRIOS, B. A. (1984). Single-subject strategies for examining joint effects: A critical evaluation. *Behavioral Assessment, 6,* 103–120.

BARRIOS, B. A., & HARTMANN, D. P. (1988). Recent developments in single subject methodology: Methods for analysing generalization, maintenance, and multicomponent treatments. In M. Hersen, R. M. Eisler, & P. M. Miller (Eds.), *Progress in behavior modification* (Vol. 22, pp. 11–47). New York: Academic Press.

BARTH, R. P. (1984). Professional self-change projects: Bridging the clinical-research and classroom-agency gaps. *Journal of Social Work Education, 20,* 13–19.

BASKIN, D. (ED.). (1990). *Computer applications in psychiatry and psychology.* New York: Brunner/Mazel.

BATES, P. (1980). The effectiveness of interpersonal skills training on the social skills acquisition of moderately and mildly retarded adults. *Journal of Applied Behavior Analysis, 13,* 237–248.

BATTLE, C. C., IMBER, S. D., HOEHN-SARIC, R., STONE, A. R., NASH, E. R., & FRANK, J. D. (1966). Target complaints as criteria of improvement. *American Journal of Psychotherapy, 20,* 184–192.

BEAUCHAMP, T. L., FADEN, R. R., WALLACE, R. J., JR., & WALTER, L. (EDS.). (1982). *Ethical issues in social science research.* Baltimore: Johns Hopkins University Press.

BECK, A. T. (1976). *Cognitive therapy and emotional disorder.* New York: International Universities Press.

BECK, A. T., WARD, C. H., MENDELSON, M., MOCK, J., & ERBAUGH, J. (1961). An inventory for measuring depression. *Archives of General Psychiatry, 4,* 561–571.

BECK, D. F., & JONES, M. A. (1973). *Progress on family problems.* New York: Family Service Association of America.

BEIDEL, D. C. (1988). Goal attainment scaling. In M. Hersen & A. S. Bellack (Eds.), *Dictionary of behavioral assessment techniques* (pp. 238–241). New York: Pergamon Press.

BELLACK, A. S., & HERSEN, M. (1977). Self-report inventories in behavioral assessment. In J. D. Done & R. P. Hawkins (Eds.), *Behavioral assessment* (pp. 52–76). New York: Brunner/Mazel.

BELLACK, A. S., & HERSEN, M. (EDS.). (1988). *Behavioral assessment: A practical handbook* (3rd ed.). New York: Pergamon Press.

BENBENISHTY, R. (1988). Assessment of task-oriented family interventions with families in Israel. *Journal of Social Service Research, 11,* 19–43.

BENBENISHTY, R. (1989). Combining the single-system and group approaches to evaluate treatment effectiveness on the agency level. *Journal of Social Service Research, 12,* 31–47.

BENBENISHTY, R., & BEN-ZAKEN, A. (1988). Computer-aided process of monitoring task-centered family interventions. *Social Work Research and Abstracts, 24,* 7–9.

BENEDICT, W. (1978). *Evalutreat: A unified approach to program evaluation and direct service delivery.* Stoughton, WI: Lutheran Social Services of Wisconsin and Upper Michigan.

BENJAMIN, L. W. (1965). A special Latin square for the use of each subject "as his own control." *Psychometrika, 3,* 499–513.

BENTLEY, K. J. (1990). An evaluation of family-based intervention using single-system research. *British Journal of Social Work, 20,* 101–116.

BERCIER, J. M. (1987). *Modifying a child's hyperactive behavior through positive reinforcement.* Unpublished student paper, Louisiana State University.

BERGIN, A. E. (1971). The evaluation of therapeutic outcomes. In S. L. Garfield & A. E. Bergin (Eds.), *Handbook of psychotherapy and behavior change: An empirical analysis* (pp. 217–270). New York: Wiley.

BERGIN, A. E. (1978). The evaluation of therapeutic outcomes. In S. L. Garfield & A. E. Bergin (Eds.), *Handbook of psychotherapy and behavior change: An empirical analysis* (2nd ed., pp. 139–190). New York: Wiley.

BERLIN, S. B. (1980). Cognitive-behavioral intervention for problems of self-criticism among women. *Social Work Research and Abstracts, 16,* 19–28.

BERLIN, S. B. (1983). Single-case evaluation: Another version. *Social Work Research and Abstracts, 19,* 3–11.

BERLIN, S. B. (1985). Maintaining reduced levels of self-criticism through relapse-prevention treatment. *Social Work Research and Abstracts, 21,* 21–33.

BERLIN, S. B., MANN, K. B., & GROSSMAN, S. F. (1991). Task analysis of cognitive therapy for depression. *Social Work Research and Abstacts, 27,* 3–11.

BESA, D. (1994). Evaluating narrative family therapy using single-system research design. *Research on Social Work Practice, 4*(3), 309–325.

BILLINGSLEY, F., WHITE, O. R., & MUNSON, R. (1980). Procedural reliability: A rationale and an example. *Behavior Assessment, 3,* 229–243.

BIRCH, H. G., & GUSSOW, J. D. (1970). *Disadvantaged children: Health, nutrition, and school failure.* New York: Harcourt, Brace, Jovanovich.

BIRD, H. R., CANINO, G., RUBIO-STIPEC, M., & RIBERA, J. C. (1987). Further measures of the psychometric properties of the Children's Global Assessment Scale. *Archives of General Psychiatry, 44,* 821–824.

BLEIBERG, J., GARMOE, W., CEDERQUIST, J., REEVES, D., & LUX, W. (1993). Effects of dexedrine on performance consistency following brain injury: A double-blind placebo crossover case study. *Neuropsychiatry, Neuropsychology, and Behavioral Neurology, 6*(4), 245–248.

BLOCH, S., BOND, G., QUALLS, B., YALOM, I., & ZIMMERMAN, E. (1977). Outcome in psychotherapy evaluated by independent judges. *British Journal of Psychiatry, 131,* 410–414.

BLOOM, L. Z. (1980). Teaching anxious writers: Implications and applications of research. *Composition and Teaching, 2,* 47–60.

BLOOM, L. Z., COBURN, K., & PEARLMAN, J. (1975). *The new assertive woman.* New York: Delacorte Press.

BLOOM, M. (1975). *The paradox of helping: Introduction to the philosophy of scientific practice.* New York: Wiley.

BLOOM, M. (ED.). (1980). *Life span development: Bases for preventive and interventive helping.* New York: Macmillan.

BLOOM, M. (1983). Prevention/promotion with minorities. *Journal of Primary Prevention, 3*(4), 224–234.

BLOOM, M. (1986). *The experience of research.* New York: Macmillan.

BLOOM, M. (1987). Theoretical significance. In N. Gottlieb (Ed.), *Perspectives on direct practice evaluation,* (Monograph No. 5). Seattle: School of Social Work, University of Washington.

BLOOM, M. (1990). *Introduction to the drama of social work.* Itasca, IL: Peacock.

BLOOM, M. (1996). *Primary prevention practices.* Thousand Oaks, CA: Sage.

BLOOM, M. (1999). Single-system evaluation. In I. Shaw & J. Lishman (Eds.), *Evaluation and social work practice.* Thousand Oaks, CA: Sage.

BLOOM, M., & BLOCK, S. R. (1977). Evaluating one's own effectiveness and efficiency. *Social Work, 22,* 130–136.

BLOOM, M., BUTCH, P., & WALKER, D. (1979). Evaluation of single interventions. *Journal of Social Service Research, 2,* 301–310.

BLOOM, M., & FISCHER, J. (1982). *Evaluating practice: Guidelines for the accountable professional.* Englewood Cliffs, NJ: Prentice Hall.

BLOOM, M., FISCHER, J., & ORME, J. G. (1995). *Evaluating Practice: Guidelines for the accountable professional.* (2nd ed.). Boston: Allyn & Bacon.

BLOOM, M., & KLEIN, W. (1994). Is there an ethical responsibility to use practice methods with the best empirical evidence of effectiveness? Yes. In H. Hudson & P. Nurius (Eds.), *Controversial issues in social work research* (100–105). Boston: Allyn & Bacon.

BLOOM, M., & ORME, J. G. (1993). Ethics and single-system design. *Journal of Social Service Research, 18,* 161–180.

BLUMENTHAL, D. (1993). Total quality management and physicians' clinical decisions. *JAMA, 269,* 2775–2778.

BLYTHE, B., TRIPODI, T., AND BRIAR, S. (1994). *Direct practice research in human service agencies.* New York: Columbia University Press.

BLYTHE, B. J. (1983). *An examination of practice evaluation among social workers.* Unpublished doctoral dissertation, University of Washington, School of Social Work.

BLYTHE, B. J. (1989). *Evolution and future development of clinical research utilization in agency settings.* Paper presented at the Boysville of Michigan and Wayne State University, School of Social Work, conference on Research Utilization, Detroit.

BLYTHE, B. J., & BRIAR, S. (1985A). Agency support for evaluating the outcomes of social work service. *Administration in Social Work, 9,* 25–36.

BLYTHE, B. J., & BRIAR, S. (1985B). Developing empirically based models of practice. *Social Work, 30,* 483–488.

BLYTHE, B. J., GILCHRIST, L. D., & SCHINKE, S. P. (1981). Pregnancy-prevention groups for adolescents, *Social Work, 26,* 503–504.

BLYTHE, B. J., & TRIPODI, T. (1989). *Measurement in direct practice.* Newbury Park, CA: Sage.

BOHART, A. C., & GREENBERG, L. (EDS.). (1997). *Empathy reconsidered: New directions in psychotherapy.* Washington, DC: American Psychological Association.

BOND, G. R., BLOCH, S., & YALOM, I. D. (1979). The evaluation of a "target problem" approach to outcome measurement. *Psychotherapy: Theory, Research and Practice, 11,* 48–54.

BORENSTEIN, M., & COHEN, J. (1988). *Statistical power analysis: A computer program.* Hillsdale, NJ: Erlebaum.

BORNSTEIN, P. H., HAMILTON, S. B., & BORNSTEIN, T. (1986). Self-monitoring procedures. In A. R. Ciminero, K. S. Calhoun, & H. E. Adams (Eds.), *Handbook of behavioral assessment* (2nd ed., 176–222). New York: Wiley.

BOSTWICK, N. K., & BOSTWICK, G. J., JR. (1987). Intersource consensus and outcome evaluation. In N. Gottlieb (Ed.), *Perspectives on direct practice evaluation* (chap. 6). Seattle: University of Washington, School of Social Work.

BRACHT, G. H., & GLASS, G. V. (1968). The external validity of experiments. *American Educational Research Journal, 5,* 437–474.

BRADBURN, N. M., SUDMAN, S., ET AL. (1979). *Improving interview method and questionnaire design: Response effects of threatening questions in survey research.* San Francisco: Jossey-Bass.

BRAGER, G., & SPECHT, H. (1973). *Community organizing.* New York: Columbia University Press.

BRIAR, S. (1973). Effective social work intervention in direct practice: Implications for education. In S. Briar et al. (Eds.), *Facing the challenge.* New York: Council on Social Work Education.

BRIAR, S. (1989). *Integration of practice and research: Past, present, and future.* Paper presented at the Boysville of Michigan and Wayne State University, School of Social Work, Conference on Research Utilization, Detroit.

BRIGHAM, T. A., MEIER, S. M., & GOODNER, V. (1995). Increasing designated driving with a program of prompts and incentives. *Journal of Applied Behavior Analysis, 28*(1), 83–84.

BRONSON, D. E. (1985). *Computer-assisted practice evaluation using Lotus 1-2-3.* Amherst: State University of New York, School of Social Work.

BRONSON, D. E., & BLYTHE, B. J. (1987). Computer support for single-case evaluation of practice. *Social Work Research and Abstracts, 23,* 10–13.

BROTHERS, K. J., KRANTZ, P. J., & McCLANNAHAN, L. E. (1994). Office paper recycling: A function of container proximity. *Journal of Applied Behavior Analysis, 27*(1), 153–160.

BROVERMAN, I., BROVERMAN, D., CLARKSON, F., ROSENKRANTZ, P., & VOGEL, S. (1970). Sex-role stereotypes and clinical judgments of mental health. *Journal of Consulting and Clinical Psychology, 34,* 1–7.

BROWN, J. A., & BROWN, C. S. (1977). *Systematic counseling: A guide for the practitioner.* Champaign, IL: Research Press.

BROWNING, R. M., & STOVER, D. O. (1971). *Behavior modification in child treatment: An experimental and clinical approach.* Chicago: Aldine & Atherton.

BROXMEYER, N. (1978). Practitioner-research in treating a borderline child. *Social Work Research and Abstracts, 14,* 5–10.

BRUGHA, T. S. (1989). Social psychiatry. In C. Thompson (Ed.), *The instruments of psychiatric research* (chap. 11). New York: Wiley.

BURLEY, S., GUTKIN, T., & NAUMANN, W. (1994). Assessing the efficacy of an academic hearing peer tutor for a profoundly deaf student. *American Annals of the Deaf, 139*(4), 415–419.

BUROS, O. K. (ED.). (1978). *The eighth mental measurements yearbook* (Vols. 1–2). Highland Park, NJ: Gryphon Press.

BURRILL, G. C. (1976). The problem-oriented log in social casework. *Social Work, 21,* 67–68.

BUSK, P. L., & MARASCUILO, L. A. (1988). Autocorrelation in single-subject research: A counter-argument to the myth of no autocorrelation. *Behavioral Assessment, 10,* 229–242.

BUSK, P. L., & MARASCUILO, L. A. (1992). Statistical analysis in single-case research: Issues, procedures, and recommendations, with applications to multiple behaviors. In T. R. Kratochwill & F. R. Levin (Eds.), *Single-case research design and analysis: New directions for psychology and education* (pp. 159–185). Hillsdale, NJ: Lawrence Erlbaum.

BUTCHER, J. N. (ED.). (1987). *Computerized psychological assessment: A practitioner's guide.* New York: Basic Books.

CABOT, R. C. (1931). Treatment in social casework and the need of criteria and of tests of its success or failure. *Proceedings of the National Conference of Social Work.*

CALLAHAN, N. M., & REDMON, W. K. (1987). Effects of problem-based scheduling on patient waiting and staff utilization of time in a pediatric clinic. *Journal of Applied Behavior Analysis, 20,* 2.

CAMPBELL, D. T. (1969). Reforms as experiments. *American Psychologist, 24,* 409–429.

CAMPBELL, D. T., & FISKE, D. W. (1959). Convergent and discriminant validation by the multitrait-multimethod matrix. *Psychological Bulletin, 56,* 81–105.

CAMPBELL, D. T., & STANLEY, J. C. (1963). *Experimental and quasi-experimental designs for research.* Chicago: Rand McNally.

CAMPBELL, D. T., & STANLEY, J. C. (1966). *Experimental and quasi-experimental designs for research.* Chicago: Rand McNally.

CAMPBELL, J. A. (1988). Client acceptance of single-system evaluation procedures. *Social Work Research and Abstracts, 24,* 21–22.

CAMPBELL, J. A. (1990). Ability of practitioners to estimate client acceptance of single-subject evaluation procedures. *Social Work, 35,* 9–14.

CANDY, J., BALFOUR, F. H. G., CAWLEY, R. H., HILDEBRAND, H. P., MALAN, D. H., MARKS, I. M., & WILSON,

J. (1972). A feasibility study for a controlled trial of formal psychotherapy. *Psychological Medicine, 2,* 345–362.

CANTRIL, H. (1965). *The pattern of human concerns.* New Brunswick, NJ: Rutgers University Press.

CARDENAS, J., & FIRST, J. M. (1985). Children at risk. *Educational Leadership, 43,* 4–9.

CAREY, R., & LLOYD, R. C. (1995). *Measuring quality improvement in healthcare: A guide to statistical process control applications.* Quality Resources: New York.

CASSELL, J. (1982). Does risk-benefit analysis apply to moral evaluation of social research? In T. L. Beauchamp, R. R. Faden, R. J. Wallace, Jr., & L. Walter (Eds.), *Ethical issues in social science research.* Baltimore: Johns Hopkins University Press.

CAUTELA, J. R. (1977). *Behavior analysis forms for clinical intervention.* Champaign, IL: Research Press.

CAUTELA, J. R., & UPPER, D. (1975). The process of individual behavior therapy. In M. Hersen, R. M. Eisler, & P. N. Miller (Eds.), *Progress in behavior modification* (Vol. 1, pp. 276–306). New York: Academic Press.

CHAMBERS, D. E., WEDEL, K. R., & RODWELL, M. K. (1992). *Evaluating social programs.* Boston: Allyn & Bacon.

CHAMBLESS, D. L., ET AL. (1996). An update on empirically validated theories. *The Clinical Psychologist, 49,* 5–18.

CHAMBLESS, D. L., ET AL. (1998). Update on empirically validated theories, II. *The Clinical Psychologist, 51,* 3–16.

CHAPMAN, C., & RISLEY, T. R. (1974). Anti-litter procedures in an urban high-density area. *Journal of Applied Behavior Analysis, 7,* 377–384.

CHASSAN, J. B. (1979). *Research design in clinical psychology and psychiatry* (2nd ed.). New York: Irvington Press.

CHEUNG, P. P. L., & HUDSON, W. W. (1982). Assessing marital discord in social work practice: A revalidation of the index of marital satisfaction. *Journal of Social Service Research, 5,* 101–118.

CHIU, L. H. (1988). Measures of self-esteem for school-age children. *Journal of Counseling and development, 66,* 298–301.

CIARLO, J. A., BROWN, T. R., EDWARDS, D. W., KIRESUK, T. J., & NEWMAN, F. L. (1986). *Assessing mental health treatment outcome measurement techniques.* (DHHS Publication No. ADM86–1301). Rockville, MD: National Institute of Mental Health.

CICCHETTI, D. V., & SHOWALTER, D. (1990). A computer program for calculating subject-by-subject kappa or weighted kappa coefficients. *Educational and Psychological Measurement, 50,* 153–158.

CICCHETTI, D. V., & SPARROW, S. S. (1981). Developing criteria for establishing interrater reliability of specific items: Applications to assessment of adaptive behavior. American *Journal of Mental Deficiency, 86,* 127–137.

CIMINERO, A. R., CALHOUN, K. S., & ADAMS, H. E. (1977). Self-monitoring procedures. In A. R. Ciminero, K. S. Calhoun, & H. E. Adams (Eds.), *Handbook of behavioral assessment* (pp. 195–232). New York: Wiley.

CLARK, D. A., BECK, A. T., & ALFORD, B. A. (1999). *Scientific foundations of cognitive therapy and the therapy of depression.* New York: Wiley.

COATES, T. J., & THORESEN, C. E. (1978). Using generalizability theory in behavioral observation. *Behavior Therapy, 9,* 605–613.

CODDINGTON, R. D. (1972). Significance of life events as etiologic factors in diseases of children: 2. Study of normal population. *Journal of Psychosomatic Research, 16,* 205–213.

COHEN, B-Z. (1987). The ethics of social work supervision revisited. *Social Work, 32,* 194–196.

COHEN, J. (1960). A coefficient of agreement for nominal scales. *Educational and Psychological Measurement, 20,* 37–46.

COHEN, J. (1977). *Statistical power analysis for the behavioral sciences* (Rev. ed.). New York: Academic Press.

COHEN, J. (1988). *Statistical power analysis for the behavioral sciences* (2nd ed.). Hillsdale, NJ: Erlbaum.

COHEN, L. H., SARGENT, M. M., & SECHREST, L. B. (1986). Use of psychotherapy research by professional psychologists. *American Psychologist, 41,* 198–206.

COMBS-ORME, T. D. (1990). Ethics and personal values in the practice of maternal and child health social work. In T. Combs-Orme (Ed.), *Social work practice in maternal and child health.* New York: Springer.

COMBS-ORME, T. D., & ORME, J. G. (1986). Reliability of self-reported child abuse and neglect in a general population survey. *Social Work Research and Abstracts, 22,* 19–21.

COMPTON, B. R., & GALAWAY, B. (1979). *Social work processes.* Homewood, IL: Dorsey Press.

COMREY, A. L., BACKER, T. E., & GLASSER, E. M. (1973). *A sourcebook for mental health measures.* Los Angeles: Human Interaction Research Institute.

CONE, J. D. (1977). The relevance of reliability and validity for behavioral assessment. *Behavior Therapy, 8,* 411–426.

CONE, J. D. (2001). *Evaluating Outcomes: Empirical Tools for Effective Practice.* Washington, DC: American Psychological Association.

CONOLEY, J. C., & KRAMER, J. J. (1989). *The 10th mental measurements yearbook.* Lincoln, NE: Buros Institute of Mental Measurements.

CONOLEY, J. C., & KRAMER, J. J. (1995). *The 12th mental measurements yearbook.* Lincoln, NE: Buros Institute of Mental Measurements.

CONTE, J. R., & LEVY, R. L. (1979). *Problems and issues in implementing the clinical-research model of practice in educational and clinical settings.* Paper presented at the meeting of the Council on Social Work Education, Boston.

COOPER, M. (1990). Treatment of a client with obsessive-compulsive disorder. *Social Work Research and Abstracts, 26,* 26–36.

COOK, T. D., & CAMPBELL, D. T. (1976). The design and conduct of quasi-experiments and true experiments in field settings. In M. Dunnette (Ed.), *Handbook of industrial and organizational psychology* (pp. 223–326). Chicago: Rand McNally.

COOK, T. D., & CAMPBELL, D. T. (1979). *Quasi-experimentation: Design and analysis issues for field settings.* Chicago: Rand McNally.

COOPER, M. (1990). Treatment of a client with obsessive-compulsive disorder. *Social Work Research and Abstracts, 26,* 26–36.

CORCORAN, K., & FISCHER, J. (1987). *Measures for clinical practice.* New York: Free Press.

CORCORAN, K., & FISCHER, J. (2000A). *Measures for clinical practice: A sourcebook. Vol. 1. Couples, families and children* (3rd ed). New York: Free Press.

CORCORAN, K., & FISCHER, J. (2000B). *Measures for clinical practice: A sourcebook. Vol. 2. Adults* (3rd ed). New York: Free Press.

CORCORAN, K., & GINGERICH, W. J. (1994). Practice evaluation in the context of managed care: Case-recording methods for quality assurance reviews. *Research on Social Work Practice, 4*(3), 326–327.

CORCORAN, K., & KEEPER, C. (1992). Psychodynamic treatment for persons with borderline personality disorders. In K. Corcoran (Ed.), *Structuring change: Effective practice for common client problems* (pp. 255–271). Chicago: Lyceum.

CORCORAN, K., & VANDIVER, V. (1996). *Maneuvering the maze of managed care: Skills for mental health practitioners.* New York: Free Press.

CORCORAN, K. J. (1985). Aggregating the idiographic data of single-subject research. *Social Work Research and Abstracts, 21*, 9–12.

CORDRAY, D. S. (1986). Quasi-experimental analysis: A mixture of methods and judgment. In W. M. K. Trochim (Ed.), *Advances in quasi-experimental design and analysis.* San Francisco: Jossey-Bass.

CORMIER, W., & CORMIER, S. (1991). *Interviewing strategies for helpers: A guide to assessment, treatment and evaluation* (3rd ed.). Monterey, CA: Brooks/Cole.

CORMIER, S., & CORMIER, W. (1998). *Interviewing strategies for helpers: Fundamental skills and cognitive behavioral interventions* (3rd ed.). Pacific Grove, CA: Brooks/Cole.

COULTON, C. J., & SOLOMON, P. L. (1977). Measuring outcomes of intervention. *Social Work Research and Abstracts, 13*, 3–9.

COUNCIL ON SOCIAL WORK EDUCATION, COMMISSION ON ACCREDITATION. (1984). *Handbook of accreditation standards and procedures.* Washington, DC: Author.

COUNCIL ON SOCIAL WORK EDUCATION. COMMISSION ON ACCREDITATION. (1994). *Handbook of accreditation: Standards and procedures, revised.* New York: Author.

COWGER, C. D. (1994). Assessing client strengths: Clinical assessment for client empowerment. *Social Work, 39*, 262–268.

COWLES, M., & DAVIS, C. (1982). On the origins of the .05 level of statistical significance. *American Psychologist, 37*, 553–558.

CRONBACH, L. J. (1983). *Designing evaluations of educational and social programs.* San Francisco: Jossey-Bass.

CROSBIE, J. (1987). The inability of the binomial test to control Type I error with single-subject data. *Behavioral Assessment, 9*, 141–150.

CROSBIE, J. (1993). Interrupted time-series analysis with brief single-subject data. *Journal of Consulting and Clinical Psychology, 61*(6), 966–974.

CROSBIE, J. (1995). Interrupted time-series analysis with short series: Why it is problematic, how it can be improved. In J. M. Gottman (Ed.), *The analysis of change* (pp. 361–395). Mahwah, NJ: Lawrence Erlbaum.

CROSBIE, J., & SHARPLEY, C. F. (1989A). DMITSA–A simplified interrupted time-series analysis program. *Behavior Research Methods, Instruments, and Computers, 21*, 639–642.

CROSBIE, J., & SHARPLEY, C. F. (1989B). *DMITSA: A statistical program for analyzing data from interrupted time-series.* Victoria, Australia: Behavioural Computing.

CROSBIE, J., & SHARPLEY, C. F. (1991). *DMITSA 2.0: A statistical program for analysing data from interrupted time-series.* Clayton, Australia: Monash University.

CROSS, D., SHEEHAN, P. W., & KAHN, J. A. (1980). Alternative advice and counsel in psychotherapy. *Journal of Consulting and Clinical Psychology, 48*, 615–625.

CROSS, D. G., SHEEHAN, P. W., & KAHN, J. A. (1982). Short- and long-term follow-up of clients receiving insight-oriented therapy and behavior therapy. *Journal of Consulting and Clinical Psychology, 50*, 103–112.

CUSHING, L. S., & KENNEDY, C. H. (1997). Academic effects of providing peer support in general education classrooms on students without disabilities. *Journal of Applied Behavior Analysis, 30*(1), 139–151.

DARLINGTON, R. B. (1990). *Regression and linear models.* New York: McGraw-Hill.

DASBERG, H. H., VAN DER KLEIJN, E., GUELEN, P. J. R., & VAN PRAAG, H. M. (1974). Plasma concentrations of diazepam and of its metabolite N-desmethyldiazepam in relation to anxiolytic effect. *Clinical Pharmacology and Therapeutics, 15*, 473–483.

DAVIDSON, C. V., & DAVIDSON, R. H. (1983). The significant other as data source and data problem in psychotherapy outcome research. In M. J. Lambert, E. R. Christensen, & S. S. DeJulio (Eds.), *The assessment of psychotherapy outcome* (pp. 569–602). New York: Wiley.

DAVIS, L. E., & PROCTOR, E. K. (1989). *Race, gender and class: Guidelines for practice with individuals, families, and groups.* Englewood Cliffs, NJ: Prentice Hall.

DEAN, R. G., & REINHERZ, H. (1986). Psychodynamic practice and single system design: The odd couple. *Journal of Social Work Education, 22*, 71–81.

DeCARLO, L. T., & TRYON, W. W. (1993). Estimating and testing autocorrelation with small samples: A comparison of the C-statistic to a modified estimator. *Behaviour Research & Therapy, 31*, 781–788.

DENZIN, H. K. (1970). *The research act: A theoretical introduction to sociological methods.* Chicago: Aldine.

DEPROSPERO, A., & COHEN, S. (1979). Inconsistent visual analyses of intrasubject data. *Journal of Applied Behavior Analysis, 12*, 573–579.

DeRICCO, D. A., & NIEMANN, J. E. (1980). *In vivo* effects of peer modeling on drinking rate. *Journal of Applied Behavior Analysis, 13*, 149–152.

DeVELLIS, R. F. (1991). *Scale development: Theory and applications.* Newbury Park, CA: Sage.

DOBSON, K. S., & CRAIG, K. D. (EDS.). (1998). *Best Practice: Developing and Promoting Empirically Supported Interventions.* Newbury Park, CA: Sage.

DOLAN, M. M., & VOURLEKIS, B. S. (1983). A field project: Single subject design in a public social service agency. *Journal of Social Service Research, 6*, 29–43.

D'ONOFRIO, C. N. (1989). The use of self-reports on sensitive behaviors in health program evaluation. In M. T. Braverman (Ed.), *Evaluating health promotion programs* (chap. 5). San Francisco: Jossey-Bass.

DOTY, L. A. (1996). *Statistical process control* (2nd ed.). New York: Industrial Press.

DRYFOOS, J. (1994). *Full-service schools: A revolution in health and social services for children, youth, and families.* San Francisco: Jossey-Bass.

EDGINGTON, E. S. (1984). Statistics and single case analysis. In M. Hersen et al. (Eds.), *Program in behavior modification* (pp. 83–119). New York: Academic Press.

EDGINGTON, E. S. (1987). *Randomization tests* (2nd ed.). New York: Marcell Dekker.

EDGINGTON, E. S. (1995). *Randomization tests,* (3rd ed.). New York: Marcel Dekker.

EDLESON, J. L., MILLER, D. M., STONE, G. W., & CHAPMAN, D. G. (1985). Group treatment for men who batter. *Social Work Research and Abstracts, 21,* 18–21.

ENDICOTT, J., SPITZER, R., FLEISS, J., & COHEN, J. (1976). Global Assessment Scale: A procedure for measuring overall severity of psychiatric disturbance. *Archives of General Psychiatry, 33,* 766–771.

EPSTEIN, I., & TRIPODI, T. (1977). *Research techniques for program planning, monitoring and evaluation.* New York: Columbia University Press.

EPSTEIN, L. H. (1976). Psychophysiological measurement in assessment. In M. Hersen & A. S. Bellack (Eds.), *Behavioral assessment: A practical handbook* (pp. 207–232). New York: Pergamon Press.

EPSTEIN, S. (1983). Aggregation and beyond: Some basic issues on the prediction of behavior. *Journal of Personality, 51,* 360–392.

EVANS, I. M. (1986). Response structure and the triple response-mode concept. In R. O. Nelson & S. C. Hayes (Eds.), *Conceptual foundations of behavioral assessment* (chap. 5). New York: Guilford Press.

FAITH, M. S., ALLISON, D. B., & GORMAN, B. S. (1997). Meta-analysis of single-case research. In R. D. Franklin, D. B. Allison, & B. S. Gorman (Eds.), *Design and analysis of single-case research* (pp. 245–277). Mahwah, NJ: Lawrence Erlbaum.

FANSHEL, D., MASTERS, P. A., FINCH, S. J., & GRUNDY, J. F. (1989). *Strategies for the analysis of data bases in social service systems.* Paper presented at the Boysville of Michigan and Wayne State University, School of Social Work, conference on Research Utilization, Detroit.

FARMER, R., & NELSON-GRAY, R. O. (1990). The accuracy of counting versus estimating event frequency in behavioral assessment: The effects of behavior frequency, number of behaviors monitored, and time delay. *Behavior Assessment, 12,* 425–442.

FAUL, A. C., MCMURTY, S. L., & HUDSON, W. W. (2001). Can empirical clinical practice techniques improve social work outcomes? *Research on Social Work Practice, 11,* 277–299.

FELDMAN, R. A., CAPLINGER, T. E., & WODARSKI, J. S. (1983). *The St. Louis conundrum: The effective treatment of antisocial youths.* Englewood Cliffs: Prentice Hall.

FERGUSON, K. L., & RODWAY, M. R. (1994). Cognitive behavioral treatment of perfectionism: Initial evaluation studies. *Research on Social Work Practice, 4*(3), 283–308.

FERRON, J., & ONGHENA, P. (1996). The power of randomization tests for single-case phased designs. *Journal of Experimental Education, 64*(3), 231–239.

FERRON, J., & WARE, W. (1994). Using randomization tests with responsive single-case designs. *Behaviour Research and Therapy, 23*(7), 787–791.

FERRON, J., & WARE, W. (1995). Analyzing single-case data: The power of randomization tests. *The Journal of Experimental Education, 63,* 167–178.

FICKLING, J. A. (1993). *The construction and testing of a measure of parental knowledge of home-based injury risks to preschool children.* Unpublished doctoral dissertation. University of Maryland, Baltimore.

FISCHER, J. (1976). *Effectiveness of social casework.* Springfield, IL: Chas. C Thomas.

FISCHER, J. (1978A). Does anything work? *Journal of Social Service Research, 1,* 215–243.

FISCHER, J. (1978B). *Effective casework practice: An eclectic approach.* New York: McGraw-Hill.

FISCHER, J. (1981). The social work revolution. *Social Work, 26,* 199–207.

FISCHER, J. (1986). Eclectic Casework. In J. C. Norcross (Ed.), *Handbook of eclectic psychotherapy* (pp. 320–352). New York: Brunner/Mazel.

FISCHER, J. (1990). Problems and issues in meta-analysis. In L. Videka-Sherman & W. J. Reid (Eds.), *Advances in clinical social work research.* Silver Spring, MD: National Association of Social Workers Press.

FISCHER, J. (1993). Empirically-based practice: The end of ideology? *Journal of Social Service Research, 18,* 19–64.

FISCHER, J., & CORCORAN, K. (1994A). *Measures for clinical practice: A sourcebook: Vol. 1. Couples, families, children* (2nd ed.). New York: Free Press.

FISCHER, J., & CORCORAN, K. (1994B). *Measures for clinical practice: A sourcebook: Vol. 2. Adults* (2nd ed.). New York: Free Press.

FISCHER, J., DULANEY, D. D., FAZIO, R. T., HUDAK, M. T., & ZIVOTOFSKY, E. (1976). Are social workers sexists? *Social Work, 21,* 428–433.

FISCHER, J., & GOCHROS, H. L. (1975). *Planned behavior change: Behavior modification in social work.* New York: Free Press.

FLAHERTY, E. W., BARRY, E., & SWIFT, M. (1978). Use of an unobtrusive measure for the evaluation of interagency coordination. *Evaluation Quarterly, 2,* 261–173.

FLEISS, J. L. (1981). *Statistical methods for rates and proportions* (2nd ed.). New York: Wiley.

FLEISS, J. L. (1986). *The design and analysis of clinical experiments.* New York: Wiley.

FONAGY, P., & MORAN, G. S. (1990). Studies of the efficacy of child psychoanalysis. *Journal of Consulting and Clinical Psychology, 58*(6), 684–695.

FORD, D. H., & URBAN, H. B. (1998). *Contemporary models of psychotherapy: A comparative analysis.* (2nd ed.). New York: Wiley.

FORTUNE, A. E. (ED.). (1985). *Task-centered practice with families and groups.* New York: Springer.

FOSTER, S. L., & CONE, J. D. (1986). Design and use of direct observation procedures. In A. R. Ciminero, K. S. Calhoun, & H. E. Adams (Eds.), *Handbook of behavioral assessment* (2nd ed., chap. 9). New York: Wiley.

FOWLER, D. R., FINKELSTEIN, A., PENK, W., BELL, W., & ITZIG, B. (1987). An automated problem-rating interview: The DPRI. In J. Butcher (Ed.), *Computerized psychological assessment: A practitioner's guide.* New York: Basic Books.

FOX, D. K., HOPKINS, B. L., & ANGER, W. K. (1987). The long-term effects of a token economy on safety performance in open-pit mining. *Journal of Applied Behavioral Analysis, 20,* 215–224.

Foxx, R. M., & Rubinoff, A. (1979). Behavioral treatment of caffeinism: Reducing excessive coffee drinking. *Journal of Applied Behavior Analysis, 12,* 335–344.

Frankl, V. E. (1962). *Man's search for meaning: An introduction to logotherapy.* Boston: Beacon Press.

Franklin, B. (1961). *Autobiography and other writings.* New York: Signet.

Franklin, R. D., Allison, D. B., & Gorman, B. S. (Eds.). (1997). *Design and analysis of single-case research.* Mahwah, NJ: Lawrence Erlbaum.

Franklin, R. D., Gorman, B. S., Beasley, T. M., & Allison, D. B. (1997). Graphical display and visual analysis. In R. D. Franklin, D. B. Allison, & B. S. Gorman (Eds.), *Design and analysis of single-case research* (pp. 119–158). Mahwah, NJ: Lawrence Erlbaum.

Fraser, M. (1990). Program outcome measures. In Y. T. Yuan & M. Rivest (Eds.), *Preserving families: Evaluation resources for practitioners and policymakers* (chap. 5). Newbury Park, CA: Sage.

Fraser, M. W., Nelson, K. E., & Rivard, J. C. (1997). Effectiveness of family preservation services. *Social Work Research, 21,* 138–153.

Fredman, N., & Sherman, R. (1987). *Handbook of measurements for marriage and family therapy.* New York: Brunner/Mazel.

Friedan, B. (1993). *The fountains of age.* New York: Simon & Schuster.

Furey, W., & Forehand, R. (1983). The Daily Child Behavior Checklist. *Journal of Behavioral Assessment, 5,* 83–95.

Gable, R. K. (1986). *Instrument development in the affective domain.* Boston: Kluwer/Nijhoff.

Gambrill, E., & Butterfield, W. (1988). Computers as practice and research tools. *Social Work Research and Abstracts, 24,* 4–6.

Gambrill, E. B. (1977). *Behavior modification: Handbook of assessment, intervention, and evaluation.* San Francisco: Jossey-Bass.

Garb, H. N. (1989). Clinical judgment, clinical training, and professional experience. *Psychological Bulletin, 105,* 387–396.

Garfield, S. L., & Bergin, A. E. (Eds.). (1978). *Handbook of psychotherapy and behavior change* (2nd ed.). New York: Wiley.

Garfield, S. L., & Bergin, A. E. (Eds.). (1986). *Handbook of Psychotherapy and Behavior Change* (3rd ed.). New York: Wiley.

Garlington, W. K., & DeRicco, D. A. (1977). The effect of modelling on drinking rate. *Journal of Applied Behavior Analysis, 10,* 207–211.

Geiger, G., Todd, D. D., Clark, H. B., Miller, R. P., & Kori, S. H. (1992). The effects of feedback and contingent reinforcement on the exercise behavior of chronic pain patients. *Pain, 49,* 179–185.

Geismar, L., & Krisberg, J. (1967). *The forgotten neighborhood.* Metuchen, NJ: Scarecrow Press.

Gelfand, D. M., & Hartmann, D. P. (1975). *Child behavior analysis and therapy.* New York: Pergamon Press.

Geller, E. S. (1990). Preventing injuries and deaths from vehicle crashes: Encouraging belts and discouraging booze. In J. Edwards, R. S. Tinsdale, L. Heath, & E. J. Posavac (Eds.), *Social influence processes and prevention.* New York: Plenum Press.

George, J. T., & Hopkins, B. L. (1989). Multiple effects of performance-contingent pay for waitpersons. *Journal of Applied Behavior Analysis, 22,* 131–141.

Germaine, C. B., & Bloom, M. (1999). *Human behavior in the social environment: An ecological view* (2nd ed.). New York: Columbia University Press.

Gettinger, M. (1988). Analogue assessment: Evaluating academic abilities. In E. S. Shapiro & T. R. Kratochwill (Eds.), *Behavioral assessment in schools: Conceptual foundations and practical applications* (chap. 7). New York: Guilford Press.

Gibbs, L. E. (1991). *Scientific Reasoning for Social Workers: Bridging the Gap Between Research and Practice.* New York: Merril/Macmillan.

Gibson, G., & Ottenbacher. K. (1988). Characteristics influencing the visual analysis of single-subject data: An empirical analysis. *Journal of Applied Behavioral Science, 24,* 298–314.

Gillespie, D. F. (1987). Ethical issues in research. In A. Minahan et al. (Eds.), *Encyclopedia of social work* (18th ed.). Silver Spring, MD: National Association of Social Workers Press.

Gillespie, D. F., & Seaberg, J. R. (1977). Individual Problem Rating: A proposed scale. *Administration in Mental Health, 5,* 21–29.

Gilligan, C. (1982). *In a different voice: Psychological theory and women's development.* Cambridge, MA: Harvard University Press.

Gingerich, W. (1979). Procedure for evaluating clinical practice. *Health and Social Work, 4,* 104–130.

Gingerich, W., & Feyerherm, W. (1979). The celeration line technique for assessing client change. *Journal of Social Service Research, 3,* 99–113.

Gingerich, W. J. (1983). Significance testing in single-case research. In A. Rosenblatt & D. Waldfogel (Eds.), *Handbook of clinical social work* (pp. 694–720). San Francisco: Jossey-Bass.

Gingerich, W. J. (1984). Meta-analysis of applied time-series data. *Journal of Applied Behavioral Science, 20,* 71–79.

Gingerich, W. J., Schirtzinger, J., & Hoffman, D. L. (1991). *My Assistant: Design and development of a computer-assisted case management system.* Paper presented at the HUSITA-2 conference. New Brunswick, NJ.

Giuli, C. A., & Hudson, W. W. (1977). *Assessing parent-child relationship disorders in clinical practice.* Mimeograph. Honolulu, University of Hawaii, School of Social Work.

Glass, G. V., McGaw, B., & Smith, M. L. (1981). *Meta-analysis in social research.* Beverly Hills, CA: Sage.

Glass, G. V., Willson, V. L., & Gottman, J. M. (1975). *Design and analysis of time-series experiments.* Boulder: Colorado Associated University Press.

Goldfried, M. R. (1977). Behavioral assessment in perspective. In J. D. Cone & R. P. Hawkins (Eds.), *Behavioral assessment* (pp. 3–22). New York: Brunner/Mazel.

Goldfried, M. R., & Linehan, M. M. (1977). Basic issues in behavioral assessment. In A. R. Ciminero, K. S. Calhoun, & H. E. Adams (Eds.), *Handbook of behavioral assessment* (pp. 15–46). New York: Wiley.

GOLDSTEIN, A. P., & KANFER, F. H. (1979). *Maximizing treatment gains: Transfer enhancement in psychotherapy.* New York: Academic Press.

GOMEZ, E., ZURCHER, L. A., FARRIS, B. E., & BECKER, R. E. (1985). A study of psychosocial casework with Chicanos. *Social Work, 30,* 477–482.

GORDON, T. (1970). *Parent effectiveness training.* New York: Wyden.

GORDON, V. C., & LEDRAY, L. E. (1985). Depression in women: The challenge of treatment and prevention. *Journal of Psychosocial Nursing, 23,* 26–34.

GORMAN, B. S., & ALLISON, D. B. (1997). Statistical alternatives for single-case designs. In R. D. Franklin, D. B. Allison, & B. S. Gorman (Eds.), *Design and analysis of single-case research* (pp. 159–214). Mahwah, NJ: Lawrence Erlbaum.

GORSUCH, R. L. (1983). Three methods of analyzing limited time-series (N of 1) data. *Behavioral Assessment, 5,* 141–154.

GOTTMAN, J. M. (1973). N-of-one and N-of-two research in psychotherapy. *Psychological Bulletin, 80,* 93–105.

GOTTMAN, J. M. (1981). *Time-series analysis: A comprehensive introduction for social scientists.* New York: Cambridge University Press.

GOTTMAN, J. M., & GLASS, G. V. (1978). Analysis of interrupted time-series experiments. In T. R. Kratochwill (Ed.), *Single subject research: Strategies for evaluating change* (pp. 197–235). New York: Academic Press.

GOTTMAN, J. M., & LEIBLUM, S. R. (1974). *How to do psychotherapy and how to evaluate it.* New York: Holt, Rinehart, & Winston.

GOTTMAN, J. M., & NOTARIUS, C. (1978). Sequential analysis of observational data using Markov Chains. In T. R. Kratochwill (Ed.), *Single subject research: Strategies for evaluating change* (pp. 237–285). New York: Academic Press.

GRANT, R., & MALETZKY, B. (1972). Application of the Weed system to psychiatric records. *Psychiatry in Medicine, 3,* 119–120.

GRASSO, A. J., EPSTEIN, I., & TRIPODI, T. (1989). Agency-based research utilization in a residential child care setting. *Administration in Social Work, 12,* 61–80.

GREEN, G. R., LINSK, N. L., & PINKSTON, E. M. (1986). Modification of verbal behavior of the mentally impaired elderly by their spouses. *Journal of Applied Behavior Analysis, 19,* 329–336.

GREENWOOD, K. M., & MATYAS, T. A. (1990). Problems with the application of interrupted time series analysis for brief single-subject data. *Behavioral Assessment, 12,* 355–370.

GREIST, J. H., KLEIN, M. H., & VAN CURA, L. J. (1973). A computer interview for psychiatric patient target symptoms. *Archives of General Psychiatry, 29,* 247–253.

GRESHAM, F. M. (1997). Treatment integrity in single-subject research. In R. D. Franklin, D. B. Allison, & B. S. Gorman (Eds.), *Design and analysis of single case research.* Mahwah, NJ: Lawrence Erlbaum.

GROHOL, J. M. (2000). *The Insider's Guide to Mental Health Resources Online.* New York: Guilford Press.

GROTEVANT, H. D., & CARLSON, C. I. (EDS.). (1989). *Family assessment: A guide to methods and measures.* New York: Guilford Press.

GUBA, E. G., & LINCOLN, S. (1989). *Fourth generation evaluation.* Newbury Park, CA: Sage.

GURIN, G., VEROFF, J., & FELD, S. (1960). *Americans view their mental health.* New York: Basic Books.

HALE, R. L., & STEAGALL, J. W. (1990). *Business MYSTAT: Statistical applications.* Cambridge, MA: Course Technology.

HALE, R. L., & STEAGALL, J. W. (1992). *Business MYSTAT: Statistical applications, DOS edition.* Cambridge, MA: Course Technology.

HALL, J. A., SCHLESINGER, D. J., & DINEEN, J. P. (1997). Social skills training in groups with developmentally disabled adults. *Research on Social Work Practice, 7(2),* 187–201.

HAMILTON, M. (1967). Development of a rating scale for primary depressive illness. *British Journal of Social and Clinical Psychology, 6,* 278–296.

HAMILTON, M. A. (1960). A rating scale for depression. *Journal of Neurology, Neurosurgery, and Psychiatry, 23,* 56–62.

HAMILTON, M. A., & ORME, J. G. (1990). Examining the construct validity of three parenting knowledge measures using LISREL. *Social Service Review, 64,* 121–143.

HAMMILL, D. D., BROWN, L., & BRYANT, B. R. (1989). *A consumer's guide to tests in print.* Austin, TX: Pro-Ed.

HANSON, N. (1969). Logical positivism and the interpretation of scientific theories. In P. A. B. Achinstein (Ed.), *The legacy of logical positivism.* Baltimore: Johns Hopkins University Press.

HANTULA, D. A. (1995). Disciplined decision making in an interdisciplinary environment: Some implications for clinical applications of statistical process control. *Journal of Applied Behavior Analysis, 28,* 371–377.

HARGREAVES, W. A., ATTKISSON, C. C., & OCHBERG, F. M. (1977). Outcome measurement instruments for use in community mental health program evaluation. In W. A. Hargreaves, C. C. Attkisson, & J. E. Sorensen (Eds.), *Resource materials for community mental health program evaluation.* Rockville, MD: U.S. Department of Health , Education, and Welfare.

HARROP, J. W., & VELICER, W. F. (1985). A comparison of alternative approaches to the analysis of interrupted time-series. *Multivariate Behavioral Research, 20,* 27–44.

HARTMANN, D. P., GOTTMAN, J. M., JONES, R. R., WILLIAM, G., KAZDIN, A. E., & VAUGHT, R. (1980). Interrupted time-series analysis and its application to behavioral data. *Journal of Applied Behavior Analysis, 13,* 543–560.

HARVARD GRAPHICS 3.0: USER'S MANUAL. (1991). Mountain View, CA: Software Publishing.

HASENFIELD, Y., & PATTI, R. (1989). *The utilization of research in administrative practice.* Paper presented at the Boysville of America and Wayne State University, School of Social Work, conference on Research Utilization, Detroit.

HAWKINS, R. P. (1986). Selection of target behaviors. In R. O. Nelson & S. C. Hayes (Eds.), *Conceptual foundations of behavioral assessment.* New York: Guilford Press.

HAYES, S. C., BARLOW, D. H., & NELSON, R. O. (1998). *The scientist practitioner: Research and accountability in clinical and educational settings* (3rd ed.). Boston: Allyn & Bacon.

HAYES, S. C., & NELSON, R. O. (1986). Assessing the effect of therapeutic interventions. In R. O. Nelson & S. C. Hayes (Eds.), *Conceptual foundations of behavioral assessment* (chap. 12). New York: Guilford Press.

HAYES, S. C., NELSON, R. O., & JARRETT, R. B. (1986). Evaluating the quality of behavioral assessment. In R. O. Nelson & S. C. Hayes (Eds.), *Conceptual foundations of behavioral assessment* (chap. 13). New York: Guilford Press.

HAYNES, J. (1977, MARCH). *An evaluation of psychosocial casework using the single-subject design: First findings.* Paper presented at the meeting of the Council on Social Work Education, Phoenix, AZ.

HAYNES, S. N. (1978). *Principles of behavioral assessment.* New York: Gardner.

HAYNES, S. N., & WILSON, C. C. (1979). *Behavioral assessment.* San Francisco: Jossey-Bass.

HAYS, R. D., & HAYASHI, T. (1990). Beyond internal consistency reliability: Rationale and user's guide for multitrait analysis program on the microcomputer. *Behavior Research Methods, Instruments, and Computers, 22,* 167–175.

HEDGES, L. V. (1981). Distribution theory for Glass' estimators of effect size and related estimators. *Journal of Educational Statistics, 6,* 107–128.

HEDGES, L. V., & OLKIN, I. (1985). *Statistical methods for meta-analysis.* New York: Academic Press.

HEINEMAN, M. B. (1981). The obsolete scientific imperative in social work research and practice. *Social Service Review, 57,* 371–397.

HEINEMAN-PIEPER, M. B. (1985). The future of social work research. *Social Work Research and Abstracts, 21,* 3–11.

HEINEMAN-PIEPER, M. (1994). Science, not scientism: The robustness of naturalistic clinical research. In E. Sherman & W. J. Reid (Eds.), *Research in social work* (pp. 71–88). New York: Columbia University Press.

HELMTADTER, G. C. (1964). *Principles of psychological measurement.* New York: Appleton-Century-Crofts.

HEMPHILL, J. (1956). *Group Dimensions: A Manual for Their Measurement.* Columbus, OH: Monographs of the Bureau of Business Research, Ohio State University.

HEPWORTH, D. H., & LARSEN, J. (1990). *Direct social work practice: Theory and skills* (3rd ed.). Chicago: Dorsey Press.

HERSEN, M. (1973). Self-assessment of fear. *Behavior Therapy, 4,* 241–257.

HERSEN, M., & BARLOW, D. H. (1976). *Single Case experimental designs: Strategies for studying behavior change.* New York: Pergamon Press.

HERSEN, M., & BELLACK, A. S. (1976). A multiple baseline analysis of social-skills training in chronic schizophrenics. *Journal of Applied Behavior Analysis, 9,* 239–246.

HERSEN, M., & BELLACK, A. S. (EDS.). (1988). *Dictionary of behavioral assessment techniques.* Elmsford, NY: Pergamon Press.

HESBACHER, P. T., RICKELS, K., & WEISE, C. (1968). Target symptoms: A promising improvement criterion in psychiatric drug research. *Archives of General Psychiatry, 18,* 595–600.

HIGGONBOTHAM, H. N., WEST, S. G., & FORSYTH, D. R. (1988). *Psychotherapy and behavior change: Socialcultural and methodological perspectives.* New York: Pergamon Press.

HILL, W. (1977). Hill Interaction Matrix (HIM): The Conceptual Framework, Derived Rating Scaled and Updates Bibliography. *Small Group Behavior, 8,* 251–268.

HOFFMAN, L. (1990). Constructing realities: An art of lenses. *Family Process, 29,* 1–12.

HOGARTY, G. E. (1989). Meta-analysis of the effects of practice with the chronically mentally ill: A critique and reappraisal of the literature. *Social Work, 34,* 363–373.

HOLDEN, G., BEARISON, D. J., ROLE, D. L., ROSENBERG, G., & FISHMAN, M. (1999). Evaluating the effects of a virtual environment (STARBRIGHT World) with hospitalized children. *Research on Social Work Practice, 9,* 365–382.

HOLMES, T. H., & RAHE, R. H. (1967). The social readjustment rating scale. *Journal of Psychosomatic Research, 11,* 213–218.

HOPKINS, B. L. (1995). Applied behavior analysis and statistical process control? *Journal of Applied Behavior Analysis, 28,* 379–386.

HOWE, M. W. (1974). Casework self-evaluation: A single-subject approach. *Social Service Review, 48,* 1–23.

HUDSON, W. W. (1976). *Guidelines for social work practice with families and individuals.* Mimeograph. Honolulu, University of Hawaii, School of Social Work.

HUDSON, W. W. (1977A, June). Elementary techniques for assessment single-client/single-worker interactions. *Social Service Review, 51,* 311–326.

HUDSON, W. W. (1977B). *A measurement package for clinical workers.* Paper presented at the meeting of the Council on Social Work Education, Phoenix, AZ.

HUDSON, W. W. (1978A). First axioms of treatment. *Social Work, 23,* 65–66.

HUDSON, W. W. (1978B). Research training in professional social work education: Issues and problems. *Social Service Review, 52,* 116–121.

HUDSON, W. W. (1981). Development and use of indexes and scales. In R. Grinnell (Ed.), *Social work research and evaluation.* Itasca, IL: Peacock.

HUDSON, W. W. (1982A). Behavioral mismeasurement. *Social Work Research and Abstracts, 18,* 37–38.

HUDSON, W. W. (1982B). *The clinical measurement package: A field manual.* Homewood, IL: Dorsey Press.

HUDSON, W. W. (1990A). *Computer assisted social services.* Tempe, AZ: WALMYR.

HUDSON, W. W. (1990B). Computer-based clinical practice: Present status and future possibilities. In L. Videka-Sherman & W. H. Reid (Eds.), *Advances in clinical social work research* (pp. 105–117). Silver Spring, MD: National Association of Social Workers Press.

HUDSON, W. W. (1992). *The WALMYR assessment scales scoring manual.* Tempe, AZ: WALMYR.

HUDSON, W. W. (1996A). *Computer assisted social services.* Tallahassee, FL: WALMYR.

HUDSON, W. W. (1996B). *Computer assisted assessment package.* Tallahassee, FL: WALMYR.

HUDSON, W. W. (1996C). *A statistical package for the personal computer: SPPC for Win95.* Tempe, AZ: WALMYR.

HUDSON, W. W., ACKLIN, J. D., & BARTOSH, J. (1980). Assessing discord in family relationships. *Social Work Research and Abstracts, 16,* 21–29.

HUDSON, W. W., & FAUL, A. C. (1998). *The clinical measurement package: A field manual* (2nd ed.). Tallahassee, FL: WALMYR.

HUDSON, W. W., & GLISSON, D. H. (1976). Assessment of marital discord in social work practice. *Social Service Review, 50,* 293–311.

HUDSON, W. W., HARRISON, D. F., & CROSSUP, P. C. (1981). A short form scale to measure sexual discord in dyadic relationships. *Journal of Sex Research, 17,* 157–174.

HUDSON, W. W., & HUDSON, K. L. (1990). *Statistical package for the personal computer.* Tempe, AZ: WALMYR.

HUDSON, W. W., & McMURTRY, S. L. (1997). Comprehensive assessment in social work practice. *Research on Social Work Practice, 7*(1), 79–98.

HUDSON, W. W., & PROCTOR, E. K. (1976A). *The assessment of depressive affect in clinical practice.* Mimeograph. Honolulu, University of Hawaii, School of Social Work.

HUDSON, W. W., & PROCTOR, E. K. (1976B). *A short-form scale for measuring self-esteem.* Mimeograph. Honolulu, University of Hawaii, School of Social Work.

HUDSON, W. W., WUNG, B., & BORGES, M. (1980). Parent-child relationship disorders. *Journal of Social Service Research, 3,* 283–294.

HUITEMA, B., & GIRMAN, S. (1978, MAY). *The statistical structure of behavior modification data.* Paper presented at the convention of the Midwest Association of Behavior Analysis, Chicago.

HUITEMA, B. E. (1985). Autocorrelation in applied behavior analysis: A myth. *Behavioral Assessment, 7,* 107–118.

HUITEMA, B. E. (1986). Statistical analysis and single-subject designs: Some misunderstandings. In A. Poling & R. W. Fuqua (Eds.), *Research methods in applied behavior analysis: Issues and advances* (pp. 209–232). New York: Plenum Press.

HUITEMA, B. E. (1988). Autocorrelation: 10 years of confusion. *Behavioral Assessment, 10,* 253–294.

HUITEMA, B. E., & McKEAN, J. W. (1991). Autocorrelation estimation and inference with small samples. *Psychological Bulletin, 110,* 291–304.

HUITEMA, B. E., & McKEAN, J. W. (1994A). Two reduced-bias autocorrelation estimators: r_{F1}, and r_{F2}. *Perceptual and Motor Skills, 78,* 323–330.

HUITEMA, B. E., & McKEAN, J. W. (1994B). Tests of H_0: $\rho_1 = 0$ for autocorrelation estimators r_{F1}, and r_{F2}. *Perceptual and Motor Skills, 78,* 331–336.

HUITEMA, B. E., & McKEAN, J. W. (1994C). Reduced bias autocorrelation estimation: Three jackknife methods. *Educational and Psychological Measurement, 54*(3), 654–665.

HUITEMA, B. E., & McKEAN, J. W. (1996). Tests for the jackknife autocorrelation estimator r_{Q2}. *Educational and Psychological Measurement, 56*(2), 232–240.

HUITEMA, B. E., & McKEAN, J. W. (1998). Irrelevant autocorrelation in least-squares intervention models. *Psychological Methods.*

HUITEMA, B. E., McKEAN, J. W., & ZHAO, J. (1996). A Simple, effective alternative to the Durbin-Watson Test for O.L.S. Intervention Models. *Journal of Educational and Behavioral Statistics, 21*(4), 390–404.

HUITEMA, B. E., & McKEAN, J. W. (2000). A simple and powerful test for autocorrelated errors in OLS intervention models. *Psychological Reports, 87*(1), 3–20.

HUNTER, J. E., & SCHMIDT, F. L. (1990). *Methods of meta-analysis.* Newbury Park, CA: Sage.

HURST, W., & WALKER, H. K. (EDS.). (1972). *The problem-oriented system.* New York: Medcom.

ISAAC, S., & MICHAEL, W. B. (1971). *Handbook in research and evaluation.* San Diego: EDITS.

IVANOFF, A., BLYTHE, B. J., & BRIAR, S. (1987). The empirical clinical practice debate. *Social Casework, 68,* 290–298.

JACOB, T., & SEILHAMER, R. A. (1985). Adaptation of the Areas of Change Questionnaire for parent-child relationship assessment. *American Journal of Family Therapy, 13,* 28–38.

JACOB, T., & TENNENBAUM, D. L. (1988). *Family assessment: Rationale, methods, and future directions.* New York: Plenum Press.

JACOBS, C. J. (1989). Childhood injury prevention: A new role for child welfare? *Social Work, 34,* 377–378.

JACOBSON, N. S. (1979). Increasing positive behavior in severely distressed marital relationships: The effects of problem-solving training. *Behavior Therapy, 10,* 311–326.

JACOBSON, N. S. (ED.). (1988). *Defining clinically significant change. Behavioral Assessment* (special issue), 10.

JANOSKY, J. E., AL-SHBOUL, Q. M., & PELLITIERI, T. R. (1995). Validation of the use of a nonparametric smoother for the examination of data from a single-subject design. *Behavior Modification, 19*(3), 307–324.

JASON, L. A., & BRACKSHAW, E. (1999). Access to TV contingent on physical activity: Effects on reducing TV-viewing and body-weight. *Journal of Behavior Therapy and Experimental Psychiatry, 30:* 145–151.

JASON, L., BILLOWS, W., SCHNOPP-WYATT, D., & KING, C. (1996). Reducing the illegal sales of cigarettes to minors: Analysis of alternative reinforcement schedules. *Journal of Applied Behavior Analysis, 29*(3), 333–344.

JAYARATNE, S. (1977). Single-subject and group designs in treatment evaluation. *Social Work Research and Abstracts, 13,* 35–42.

JAYARATNE, S. (1978). Analytic procedures for single-subject designs. *Social Work Research and abstracts, 14,* 30–40.

JAYARATNE, S. (1982). Jayaratne replies. *Social Work Research and Abstracts, 18,* 38–39.

JAYARATNE, S. (1990). Clinical significance: Problems and new developments. In L. Videka-Sherman & W. J. Reid (Eds.), *Advances in clinical social work research* (pp. 271–285). Silver Spring, MD: National Association of Social Workers Press.

JAYARATNE, S., & DANIELS, W. (1981). Measurement cross-validation using replication procedures within single-case designs. *Social Work Research and Abstracts, 17,* 4–10.

JAYARATNE, S., & LEVY, R. L. (1979). *Empirical clinical practice.* New York: Columbia University Press.

JAYARATNE, S., TRIPODI, T., & TALSMA, E. (1988). *The comparative analysis and aggregation of single-case data. Journal of Applied Behavioral Science, 24,* 119–128.

JENSEN, C. (1994). Psychosocial treatment of depression in women: Nine single-subject evaluations. *Research on Social Work Practice, 4*(3), 267–282.

JOHNSON, M. (1976). An approach to feminist therapy. *Psychotherapy: Theory, Research and Practice, 13,* 72–76.

JOHNSON, S. M., & BOLSTAD, O. D. (1973). Methodological issues in naturalistic observation: Some problems and solutions for field research. In L. A. Hammerlynck, L. C. Handy, & E. J. Mash (Eds.), *Behavior change:*

Methodology, concepts, and practice. Champaign, IL: Research Press.

JONES, R. R., REID, J. B., & PATTERSON, G. R. (1975). Naturalistic observation in clinical assessment. In P. McReynolds (Ed.), *Advances in psychological assessment* (Vol. 3, pp. 329–366). New York: Wiley.

JONES, R. R., VAUGHT, R. S., & WEINROTT, M. (1977). Time-series analysis in operant research. *Journal of Applied Behavior Analysis, 10,* 151–166.

JONES, R. R., VAUGHT, R. S., & WEINROTT, M. (1978). Effects of serial dependency on the agreement between visual and statistical inference. *Journal of Applied and Behavior Analysis, 11,* 277–283.

JUDD, C. M. (1987). Combining process and outcome evaluation. In M. M. Mark & R. L. Shotland (Eds.), *Multiple methods in program evaluation* (pp. 23–42). San Francisco: Jossey-Bass.

JUDD, C. M., & KENNY, D. A. (1981). *Estimating the effects of social interventions.* New York: Cambridge University Press.

JUDD, C. M., SMITH, E. R., & KIDDER, L. H. (1991). *Research methods in social relations* (6th ed.). New York: Holt, Rinehart, & Winston.

JUNG, R. S., & JASON, L. A. (1998). Job interview social skills training for Asian-American immigrants. *Journal of Human Behavior in the Social Environment, 1*(4), 11–25.

KAGLE, J. D. (1983). The contemporary social work record. *Social Work, 28,* 149–153.

KAGLE, J. D. (1984A). Restoring the clinical record. *Social Work, 29,* 46–50.

KAGLE, J. D. (1984B). *Social work records.* Homewood, IL: Dorsey Press.

KAGLE, J. D. (1991). *Social work records* (2nd ed.). Homewood, IL: Dorsey Press.

KALLMAN, W. M., & FEUERSTEIN, M. (1977). Psychophysiological procedures. In A. R. Ciminero, K. S. Calhoun, & H. E. Adams (Eds.), *Handbook of behavioral assessment* (pp. 329–366). New York: Wiley.

KALLMAN, W. M., & FEUERSTEIN, M. J. (1986). Psychophysiological procedures. In A. R. Ciminero, K. S. Calhoun, & H. E. Adams (Eds.), *Handbook of behavioral assessment* (2nd ed., chap. 10). New York: Wiley.

KAMPHAS, R. W., & FRICK, P. J. (1996). *Clinical Assessment of Child and Adolescent Personality and Behavior.* Boston: Allyn & Bacon.

KANE, R. A. (1974). Look to the record. *Social Work, 17,* 412–419.

KANFER, F. H. (1975). Self-management methods. In F. H. Kanfer & A. P. Goldstein (Eds.), *Helping people change* (pp. 309–356). New York: Pergamon Press.

KAPLAN, R. M., & SACCUZZO, D. P. (1982). *Psychological testing: Principles, applications, and issues.* Monterey, CA: Brooks/Cole.

KAROLY, P., & STEFFEN, J. J. (EDS.). (1980). *Improving the long-term effects of psychotherapy.* New York: Gardner.

KASTNER, J. W., TINGSTROM, D. H., & EDWARDS, R. P. (2000). The utility of reading to read with boys with ADHD-CT administered at two different intervals post methylphenidate ingestion. *Psychology in the Schools, 37*(4), 367–377.

KATZER, J., COOK, K. H., & CROUCH, W. W. (1978). *Evaluating information.* Reading, MA: Addison Wesley.

KAZDIN, A. E. (1975). *Behavior modification in applied settings.* Homewood, IL: Dorsey Press.

KAZDIN, A. E. (1976). Statistical analysis for single-case experimental designs. In M. Hersen & D. H. Barlow (Eds.), *Single case experimental designs: Strategies for studying behavior change.* New York: Pergamon Press.

KAZDIN, A. E. (1977). *Assessing the clinical or applied importance of behavior change through social validation. Behavior Modification, 1,* 427–452.

KAZDIN, A. E. (1980). *Research design in clinical psychology.* New York: Harper & Row.

KAZDIN, A. E. (1982). Observer effects: Reactivity of direct observation. In D. P. Hartmann (Ed.), *Using observers to study behavior: New Directions for methodology of social and behavioral science* (pp. 5–19). San Francisco: Jossey-Bass.

KAZDIN, A. E. (1984). Statistical analyses for single-case experimental designs. In D. H. Barlow & M. Hersen (Eds.), *Single case experimental designs: Strategies for studying behavior change* (2nd ed.). New York: Pergamon Press.

KAZDIN, A. E. (1992). *Research design in clinical psychology* (2nd ed.) New York: Macmillan.

KAZDIN, A. E., & HARTMANN, D. P. (1978). The simultaneous treatment design. *Behavior Therapy, 9,* 912–922.

KAZDIN, A. E., & KOPEL, S. A. (1975). On resolving ambiguities of the multiple-baseline design: Problems and recommendations. *Behavior Therapy, 6,* 601–608.

KAZI, M. A. F., & WILSON, J. T. (1996). Applying single-case evaluation methodology in a British social work agency. *Research on Social Work Practice, 6*(1), 5–26.

KELLERMAN, H., & BURRY, A. (1997). *Handbook of Psychodiagnostic Testing.* Boston: Allyn & Bacon.

KELMAN, H. C. (1982). Ethical issues in different social science methods. In T. L. Beauchamp, R. R. Faden, R. J. Wallace, Jr., & L. Walter (Eds.), *Ethical issues in social science research.* Baltimore: Johns Hopkins University Press.

KENDALL, P. C., NAY, W. R., & JEFFERS, J. (1975). Time out duration and contrast effects: A systematic evaluation of a successive-treatment design. *Behavior Therapy, 6,* 609–615.

KENNEDY, M. M. (1979). Generalizing from single case studies. *Evaluation Quarterly, 3,* 661–668.

KENNY, D. A., & JUDD, C. M. (1986). Consequences of violating the independence assumption in analysis of variance. *Psychological Bulletin, 99,* 422–431.

KENT, R. N., & FOSTER, S. L. (1977). Direct observational procedures: Methodological issues in naturalistic settings. In A. R. Ciminero, K. S. Calhoun, & H. E. Adams (Eds.), *Handbook of behavioral assessment* (pp. 279–328). New York: Wiley.

KERLINGER, F. N. (1979). *Behavioral research: A conceptual approach.* New York: Holt, Rinehart, & Winston.

KERLINGER, F. N. (1986). *Foundations of behavioral research* (3rd ed.). New York: Holt, Rinehart, & Winston.

KESTENBAUM, C. J., & WILLIAMS, D. T. (EDS.). (1988). *Handbook of clinical assessment of children and adolescents.* Austin, TX: Pro-Ed.

KEYSER, D. J., & SWEETLAND, R. C. (EDS.). (1984–1991). *Test critiques* (Vols. 1–8). Austin, TX: Pro-Ed.

KIDDER, L. H., & JUDD, C. M. (1986). *Research methods in social relations* (5th ed.). New York: Holt, Rinehart, & Winston.

KIMMEL, A. J. (1988). *Ethics and values in applied social research.* Newbury Park, CA: Sage.

KING, A. C., WINETT, R. A., & LOVETT, S. B. (1986). Enhancing coping behaviors in at-risk populations: The effects of time-management instruction and social support in women from dual-earner families. *Behavior Therapy, 17,* 57–66.

KIRCHNER, R. E., SCHNELLE, J. F., DOMASH, M., LARSON, L., CARR, A., & MCNEES, M. P. P. (1980). The applicability of a helicopter patrol procedure to diverse areas: A cost-benefit evaluation. *Journal of Applied Behavior Analysis, 13,* 143–148.

KIRESUK, T. J., & GARWICK, G. (1979). Basic goal attainment scaling procedures. In G. R. Compton & R. Gallaway (Eds.), *Social work process* (Rev. ed., pp. 412–420). Homewood, IL: Dorsey Press.

KIRESUK, T. J., & LUND, S. H. (1977). Goal attainment scaling: Research evaluation and utilization. In H. C. Schulberg & F. Baker (Eds.), *Program evaluation in the health fields* (Vol. 2). New York: Behavioral Publications.

KIRESUK, T. J., & LUND, S. H. (1978). Goal attainment scaling. In C. C. Attkisson, W. A. Hargreave, M. I. Horowitz, & S. E. Sorenson (Eds.), *Evaluation of human service programs.* New York: Academic Press.

KIRESUK, T. J., & SHERMAN, R. E. (1968). Goal attainment scaling: A general method for evaluating comprehensive community mental health programs. *Community Mental Health Journal, 4,* 443–453.

KIRESUK, T. J., & SHERMAN, R. E. (1977). A reply to the critique of goal attainment scaling. *Social Work Research and Abstracts, 13,* 9–11.

KIRESUK, T. J., SMITH, A., & CARDILLO, J. E. (EDS.). (1993). *Goal Attainment Scaling: Applications, Theory and Measurement.* New York: Erlbaum.

KIRK, S. A. (1990). Research utilization: The substructure of belief. In L. Videka-Sherman & W. J. Reid (Eds.), *Advances in clinical social work research.* Silver Spring, MD: National Association of Social Workers Press.

KLEIN, W. C., & BLOOM, M. (1995). Practice wisdom. *Social Work, 40,* 799–807.

KLONOFF, H., & COX, B. (1975). A problem-oriented system approach to analysis of treatment outcome. *American Journal of Psychiatry, 132,* 836–841.

KNAPCZYK, D. R. (1988). Reducing aggressive behaviors in special and regular class settings by training alternative social responses. *Behavior Disorders, 14,* 27–39.

KNOX, D. (1975). *Dr. Knox's marital exercise book.* New York: David McKay.

KOHLBERG, L. (1983). *The psychology of moral development.* New York: Harper & Row.

KOLKO, D. J., & MILAN, M. A. (1983). Reframing and paradoxical instruction to overcome "resistance" in the treatment of delinquent youths: A multiple baseline analysis. *Journal of Consulting and Clinical Psychology, 51,* 655–660.

KOPELS, S., & KAGLE, J. D. (1993). Do social workers have a duty to warn? *Social Services Review, 67,* 101–126.

KOPP, J. (1988). Self-monitoring: A literature review of research and practice. *Social Work Research and Abstracts, 24,* 8–20.

KRATOCHWILL, T. R. (ED.). (1978). *Single subject research: Strategies for evaluating change.* New York: Academic Press.

KRATOCHWILL, T. R., & LEVIN, J. R. (EDS.). (1992). *Single-case research design and analysis: New directions for psychology and education.* Hillsdale, NJ: Erlbaum.

KRATOCHWILL, T. R., & PIERSEL, W. C. (1983). Time-series research: Contributions to empirical clinical practice. *Behavioral Assessment, 5,* 165–176.

KRISHEF, C. H. (1991). *Fundamental approaches to single subject design and analysis.* Melbourne, FL: Krieger.

KRUG, S. E. (1988). *Psychware sourcebook: 1988–1989* (3rd ed.). Kansas City, MO: Test Corporation of America.

KRUG, S. E. (1993). *Psychware sourcebook* (4th ed.). Kansas City, MO: Test Corporation of America.

LABAW, P. (1985). *Advanced questionnaire design.* Cambridge, MA: Abt Books.

LAIRD, J. (1994). "Thick description" revisited: Family therapist as anthropologist-constructivist. In E. Sherman & W. J. Reid (Eds.), *Qualitative research in social work* (pp. 175–189). New York: Columbia University Press.

LAKE, D. G., MILES, M. B., & EARLE, R. B., JR. (1973). *Measuring human behavior: Tools for the assessment of social functioning.* New York: Teachers College Press.

LAMBERT, M. J., CHRISTENSEN, E. R., & DEJULIO, S. S. (EDS.). (1983). *The assessment of psychotherapy outcome.* New York: Wiley.

LAMBERT, M. J., HATCH, D. R., KINGSTON, M. D., & EDWARDS, B. C. (1986). Zung, Beck, and Hamilton Rating Scales as measures of treatment outcome: A meta-analytic comparison. *Journal of Consulting and Clinical Psychology, 54,* 54–59.

LAMBERT, M. J., SHAPIRO, D. A., & BERGIN, A. E. (1986). The effectiveness of psychotherapy. In S. L. Garfield & A. E. Bergin (Eds.), *Handbook of psychotherapy and behavior change* (pp. 157–212). New York: Wiley.

LANG, N. C. (1994). Integrating the data processing of qualitative research and social work practice to advance the practitioner as knowledge builder: Tools for knowing and doing. In E. Sherman & W. J. Reid (Eds.), *Qualitative research in social work.* (pp. 265–278). New York: Columbia University Press.

LANG, P. J. (1968). Fear reduction and fear behavior: Problems in treating a construct. In J. M. Shlien (Ed.), *Research in psychotherapy* (Vol. 3, pp. 90–101). Washington, DC: American Psychological Association.

LANG, P. J. (1977). Physiological assessment of anxiety and fear. In J. D. Cone and R. P. Hawkins (Eds.), *New directions in clinical psychology* (pp. 178–195). New York: Brunner/Mazel.

LAZARUS, A. A. (1971). *Behavior therapy and beyond.* New York: McGraw-Hill.

LAZARUS, A. A., & DAVISON, G. C. (1971). Clinical innovation in research and practice. In A. E. Bergin & S. L. Garfield (Eds.), *Handbook of psychotherapy and behavior change: An empirical analysis* (2nd ed., pp. 196–213). New York: Wiley.

LEITENBERG, H. (1973). The use of single-case methodology in psychotherapy research. *Journal of abnormal Psychology, 82,* 87–101.

LEVI, J. (1981). The log as a tool for research and therapy. *Social Work, 26,* 333.

LEVI, L., & ANDERSON, L. (1975). *Psychosocial stress: Population, environment, and the quality of life.* Holliswood, NY: Spectrum Press.

LEVITT, J. L., & MARSH, J. L. (1980). *A collection of short form repeated measurement instruments suitable for practice.* Mimeograph. Chicago, University of Chicago, School of Social Service Administration.

LEVITT, J. L., & REID, W. J. (1981). Rapid-assessment instruments for practice. *Social Work Research and Abstracts, 17,* 13–19.

LEVY, R. L., & BAVENDAM, T. G. (1995). Promoting women's urologic self-care: Five single-case replications. *Research on Social Work Practice, 5*(4), 430–441.

LEYDON, J. (1984). Depression in the dying: A psychosocial approach. *In Evaluating practice through single-system design.* Unpublished master's research report. Boston, Simons College, School of Social Work.

LIBERMAN, B. L., FRANK, J. D., HOEHN-SARIC, R., STONE, A. R., IMBER, S. D., & PANDE, S. K. (1972). Patterns of change in treated psychoneurotic patients: A five-year follow-up investigation of the systematic preparation of patients for psychotherapy. *Journal of Consulting and Clinical Psychology, 38,* 36–41.

LIBERMAN, R. P., & SMITH, V. (1972). A multiple baseline study of systematic desensitization in a patient with multiple phobias. *Behavior Therapy, 3,* 597–603.

LIEBERMAN, M., YALOM, L., & MILES, M. (1973). *Encounter Groups: First Facts.* San Francisco: Jossey-Bass.

LIEBERMAN, M. A., SOLOW, N., BOND, G. R., & REIBSTEIN, J. (1979). The psychotherapeutic impact of women's consciousness-raising groups. *Archives of General Psychiatry, 36,* 161–168.

LIEFF, J. D. (1987). *Computer applications in psychiatry.* Washington, DC: American Psychiatric Press.

LIGHT, R. J., SINGER, J. D., & WILLETT, J. B. (1990). *By design: Planning research on higher education.* Cambridge, MA: Harvard University Press.

LINDSLEY, O. R. (1968). *Training parents and teachers to precisely manage children's behavior.* Mimeograph. University of Kansas, School of Education.

LINTON, J. M., & SINGH, N. N. (1984). Acquisition of sign language using positive practice overcorrection. *Behavior Modification, 8,* 553–566.

LIPSEY, M. W. (1990). *Design sensitivity: Statistical power for experimental research.* Newbury Park, CA: Sage.

LIPSEY, M. W., & WILSON, D. B. (1993). The efficacy of psychological, educational, and behavioral treatment. *American Psychologist, 48,* 1181–1209.

LIU, R. Y., & TANG, J. (1996). Control charts for dependent and independent measurements based on bootstrap methods. *Journal of the American Statistical Association 91*(436), 1694–1700.

LLOYD, J. W., EBERHARDT, M. J., & DRAKE, G. P., JR. (1996). Group versus individual reinforcement contingencies within the context of group study conditions. *Journal of Applied Behavior Analysis, 29*(2), 189–200.

LOEWENBERG, F., & DOLGOFF, R. (1988). *Ethical decision for social work practice* (3rd ed.). Itasca, IL: Peacock.

LOEWENBERG, F. M., & DOLGOFF, R. (1996). *Ethical decisions for social work practice* (5th ed.). Itasca, IL: F. E. Peacock.

LOHMAN, L. S. (1976). *Identification of unsafe driving reactions and related counter measures.* Monograph published by the Highway Safety Research Center, University of North Carolina.

LONETTO, R., & TEMPLER, D. I. (1983). The nature of death anxiety. In C. D. Spielberger & J. N. Butcher (Eds.), *Advances in personality assessment* (Vol. 3). Hillsdale, NJ: Erlebaum.

LOVAAS, O. I., KOEGEL, R., SIMMONS, J. Q., & LONG, J. D. (1973). Some generalization and follow-up measures on autistic children in behavior therapy. *Journal of Applied Behavior Analysis, 5,* 131–166.

LUDWIG, T. D., & GELLER, E. S. (1999). Behavior change among agents of a community safety program: Pizza deliverers advocate community safety belt use. *Journal of Organizational Behavior Management, 19*(2), 3–24.

MCCUBBIN, H. I., & THOMPSON, A. I. (EDS.). (1987). *Family assessment inventories for research and practice.* Madison: University of Wisconsin, Madison.

MCCUBBIN, H. I., THOMPSON, A. I., & MCCUBBIN, M. A. (1996). *Family assessment: Resilience, coping and adaptation. Inventories for research and practice.* Madison: University of Wisconsin Press.

MCCULLOUGH, J. P. (1984). The need for new single-case design structure in applied cognitive psychology. *Psychotherapy, 31,* 389–400.

MCDONALD, M. R., & BUDD, K. S. (1983). "Booster shots" following didactic parent training: Effects of follow-up using a graphic feedback and instructions. *Behavior Modification, 7,* 211–223.

MCDOWELL, I., & NEWELL, C. (1996). *Measuring health: A guide to rating scales and questionnaires.* New York: Oxford University Press.

MCFALL, R. M. (1977A). Analogue methods in behavioral assessment: Issues and prospects. In J. D. Cone & R. P. Hawkins (Eds.), *Behavioral assessment: New directions in clinical psychology* (pp. 152–177). New York: Brunner/Mazel.

MCFALL, R. M. (1977B). Parameters of self-monitoring. In R. B. Stuart (Ed.), *Behavioral self-management: Strategies, techniques, and outcomes* (pp. 196–214). New York: Brunner/Mazel.

MACKLIN, E. (1982). The problem of adequate disclosure in social science research. In T. L. Beauchamp, R. R. Faden, R. J. Wallace, Jr., & L. Walter (Eds.), *Ethical issues in social science research.* Baltimore: Johns Hopkins University Press.

MCMAHON, P. M. (1987). Shifts in intervention procedures: A problem in evaluating human service interventions. *Social Work Research and Abstracts, 23,* 13–16.

MCNEES, M. P., EGLI, D. S., MARSHALL, R. S., SCHNELLE, J. F., & RISLEY, T. R. (1976). Shoplifting prevention: Providing information through signs. *Journal of Applied Behavior Analysis, 9,* 399–405.

MCREYNOLDS, P. (ED.). (1968). *Advances in psychological assessment* (Vol. 1). Palo Alto, CA: Science & Behavior Books.

McReynolds, P. (Ed.). (1971). *Advances in psychological assessment* (Vol. 2). Palo Alto, CA: Science & Behavior Books.

McReynolds, P. (Ed.). (1975). *Advances in psychological assessment* (Vol. 3). Palo Alto, CA: Science & Behavior Books.

McReynolds, P. (Ed.). (1977). *Advances in psychological assessment* (Vol. 4). Palo Alto, CA: Science & Behavior Books.

McSweeny, A. J. (1978). Effects of response cost on the behavior of a million persons: Charging for directory assistance in Cincinnati. *Journal of Applied Behavior Analysis, 11,* 47–51.

Maag, J. W., Rutherford, R. B., Jr., & DiGangi, S. A. (1992). Effects of self-monitoring and contingent reinforcements on-task behavior and academic productivity of learning-disabled students: A social validation study. *Psychology in the Schools, 29,* 157–172.

MacDonald, M. (1975). Multiple impact therapy in a child's dog phobia. *Journal of Behavior Therapy and Experimental Psychiatry, 6,* 317–322.

Mager, R. F. (1972). *Goal analysis.* Belmont, CA: Fearon.

Magura, S., & Moses, B. S. (1987). *Outcome measures for child welfare services.* Washington, DC: Child Welfare League of America.

Magura, S., Moses, B. S., & Jones, M. A. (1987). *Assessing risk and measuring change in families: The Family Risk Scales.* Washington, DC: Child Welfare League of America.

Maheady, K., Mallette, B., Harper, G. F., & Sacca, K. (1991). Heads together: A peer-mediated option for improving the academic achievement of heterogeneous learning groups. *Remedial and Special Education, 12*(2), 25–33.

Mahoney, M. J. (1978). Experimental methods and outcome evaluation. *Journal of Consulting and Clinical Psychology, 46,* 660–672.

Maisto, S. A., & Maisto, C. A. (1983). Institutional measures of treatment outcome. In M. J. Lambert, E. R. Christenson, & S. S. DeJulio (Eds.), *The assessment of Psychotherapy outcome* (pp. 603–625). New York: Wiley.

Malcolm, D. S. (1989). A BASIC program for exploratory data analysis. *Behavior Research Methods, Instruments, and Computers, 21,* 463–464.

Malcolm, R., Sturgis, E. T., Anton, R. F., & Williams, L. (1989). Computer-assisted diagnosis of alcoholism. *Computers in Human Services, 5,* 163–170.

Mann, R. A. (1976). Assessment of behavioral excesses in children. In M. Hersen & A. S. Bellack (Eds.), *Behavioral assessment: A practical handbook* (pp. 459–492). New York: Pergamon Press.

Marafiote, R. A. (1985). *The custody of children: A behavioral assessment model.* New York: Plenum Press.

Marascuilo, L. A., & Busk, P. L. (1988). Combining statistics for multiple-baseline, AB and replicated ABAB designs across subjects, *Behavioral Assessment, 10,* 1–28.

Mark, M. M. (1986). Validity typologies and the logic and practice of quasi-experimentation. In W. M. K. Trochim (Ed.), *Advances in quasi-experimental design and analysis* (pp. 47–66). San Francisco: Jossey-Bass.

Markman, H. J., & Notarius, C. I. (1989). Coding marital interaction [Special issue]. *Behavioral Assessment, 11.*

Marsh, J. C., & Shibano, M. (1984). Issues in the statistical analysis of clinical time-series data. *Social Work Research and Abstracts, 20,* 7–12.

Martella, R. C., Leonard, I. J., Marchand-Martella, N. E., & Agran, M. (1993). Self-monitoring negative statements. *Journal of Behavioral Education, 3*(1), 77–86.

Martens, W. M., & Holmstrup, E. (1974). Problem-oriented recording. *Social Casework, 55,* 554–561.

Martin, G., & Pear, J. (1978). *Behavior modification: What it is and how to do it.* Englewood Cliffs, NJ: Prentice Hall.

Mash, E. J. (1987). Behavioral assessment of child and family disorders [Special issue]. *Behavioral Assessment, 9.*

Mash, E. J., & Barkely, R. A. (Eds.). (1999). *Treatment of Childhood Disorders* (2nd ed.). New York: Guilford.

Mash, E. J., & Terdal, L. G. (Eds.). (1988). *Behavioral assessment of childhood disorders* (2nd ed.). New York: Guilford Press.

Maslow, A. H. (1968). *Toward a psychology of being* (2nd ed.). Princeton, NJ: Van Nostrand.

Masterson, J. (1972). *Treatment of the borderline adolescent.* New York: Wiley.

Mattaini, M. A. (1993). *More than a thousand words: Graphics for clinical practice.* Washington, DC: National Association of Social Workers Press.

Matyas, T. A., & Greenwood, K. M. (1990). Visual analysis of single-case time-series: Effects of variability, serial dependence and magnitude of intervention effect. *Journal of Applied Behavior Analysis, 23,* 341–351.

Matyas, T. A., & Greenwood, K. M. (1991). Problems in the estimation of autocorrelation in brief time-series and some implications for behavioral data. *Behavioral Assessment, 13,* 137–158.

Matyas, T. A., & Greenwood, K. M. (1997). Serial dependency in single-case time series. In R. D. Franklin, D. B. Allison, & B. S. Gorman (Eds.), *Design and analysis of single-case research* (pp. 215–243). Mahwah, NJ: Lawrence Erlbaum.

Mawhinney, T. C. (1988). *Organizational behavior management and statistical process control: Theory, technology and research.* Binghamton, NY: Haworth Press.

May, P. R. A. (1968). *Treatment of schizophrenia.* New York: Science House.

May, R. B., Masson, M. E. J., & Hunter, M. A. (1989). Randomization tests: Viable alternatives to normal curve tests. *Behavior Research Methods, Instruments, and Computers, 21,* 482–483.

Mayer, J. A., Heins, J. M., Vogel, J. M., Morrison, D. C., Lankester, L. D., & Jacobs, A. L. (1986). Promoting low-fat entree choices in a public cafeteria. *Journal of Applied Behavior Analysis, 19,* 397–402.

Mayer, J. E., & Timms, N. (1969). *The client speaks: Working class impressions of casework.* London: Routledge.

Mehm, J. G., & Knutson, J. F. (1987). A comparison of event and interval strategies for observational data analysis and assessments of observer agreement. *Behavioral Assessment, 9,* 151–168.

Meichenbaum, D. (1985). *Stress inoculation training.* Boston: Allyn & Bacon.

Millar, A., Hatry, H., & Koss, M. (1977). *Monitoring the outcomes of social services: Vol. 2. A review of past research and test activities.* Washington, DC: Urban Institute.

MILLER, D. C. (1977). *Handbook of research design and social measurement* (3rd ed.). New York: David McKay.

MILLER, G. A., GALANTER, E., & PRIBRAM, K. H. (1960). *Plans and the structure of behavior.* New York: Holt, Rinehart, & Winston.

MILLER, M., MILLER, S. R., WHEELER, J., & SELINGER, J. (1989). Can a single-classroom treatment approach change academic performance and behavioral characteristics in severely behaviorally disordered adolescents: An experimental inquiry. *Behavioral Disorders, 14,* 215–225.

MILLSTEIN, S. G., & IRWIN, C. E., JR. (1983). Acceptability of computer-acquired sexual histories in adolescent girls. *Journal of Pediatrics, 103,* 815–819.

MILNER, J. S. (1986). *The Child Abuse Potential Inventory: Manual* (2nd ed.). Webster, NC: Psytec.

MILNER, J. S., GOLD, R. G., & WIMBERLEY, R. C. (1986). Prediction and explanation of child abuse: Cross-validation of the Child Abuse Potential Inventory. *Journal of Consulting and Clinical Psychology, 54,* 865–866.

MINTZ, J. (1972). What is "success" in psychotherapy? *Journal of Abnormal Psychology, 80,* 11–19.

MINTZ, J., & KIESLER, D. J. (1982). Individualized measures of psychotherapy outcome. In P. C. Kendall & J. N. Butcher (Eds.), *Handbook of research methods in clinical psychology* (pp. 491–534). New York: Wiley.

MINTZ, J., LUBORSKY, L., & CHRISTOPH, P. (1979). Measuring the outcomes of psychotherapy: Findings of the Penn Psychotherapy Project. *Journal of Consulting and Clinical Psychology, 47,* 319–334.

MINUCHIN, S. (1974). *Families and family therapy.* Cambridge, MA: Harvard University Press.

MIRINGOFF, M. L., MIRINGOFF, M. L., & OPDYCKE, S. (1996). Monitoring the nation's social performance: The index of social health. In E. F. Zigler, S. L. Kagan, & N. W. Hall (Eds.), *Children, families, and government: Preparing for the twenty-first century.* New York: Cambridge University Press.

MONETTE, D. R., SULLIVAN, T. J., & DEJONG, C. R. (1990). *Applied social research: Tool for the human services* (2nd ed.). Fort Worth, TX: Holt, Rinehart, & Winston.

MOOS, R. H. (1987). *The social climate scales: A user's guide.* Palo Alto, CA: Consulting Psychologists Press.

MOOS, R. H. (1988). Assessing the program environment: Implications for program evaluation and design. In K. J. Conrad & C. Roberts-Gray (Eds.), *Evaluating program environments* (chap. 2). San Francisco: Jossey-Bass.

MOOS, R. H. (1990). Conceptual and empirical approaches to developing family-based assessment procedures: Solving the case of the family environment scale. *Family Process, 29,* 199–208.

MOOS, R. H. (1974). *Evaluating treatment environments: A social ecological approach.* New York: Wiley.

MOOS, R. H. (1975A). Assessment and impact of social climate. In P. McReynolds (Ed.). *Advances in psychological assessment* (Vol. 3). San Francisco: Jossey-Bass.

MOOS, R. H. (1975B). *Evaluating correctional and community settings.* New York: Wiley.

MOOS, R. H. (1979). *Evaluating educational environments.* San Francisco: Jossey-Bass.

MORAN, P. W., & LAMBERT, M. J. (1983). A review of current assessment tools for monitoring changes in depression. In M. J. Lambert, E. R. Christensen, & S. S. DeJulio (Eds.), *The assessment of psychotherapy outcome* (pp. 263–303). New York: Wiley.

MORELAND, K. L. (1987). Computerized psychological assessment: What's available. In J. N. Butcher (Ed.), *Computerized psychological assessment: A practitioner's guide.* New York: Basic Books.

MORLEY, S., & ADAMS, M. (1989). Some simple statistical tests for exploring single-case time-series data. *British Journal of Clinical Psychology, 28,* 1–18.

MORLEY, S., & ADAMS, M. (1991). Graphical analysis of single-case time series data. *British Journal of Clinical Psychology, 30,* 97–115.

MORRISON, J. K. (ED.). (1979). *A consumer approach to community psychology.* Chicago: Nelson-Hall.

MORRISON, J. K., LIBOW, J. A., SMITH, F. J., & BECKER, R. R. (1978). Comparative effectiveness of directive vs. nondirective group therapist style on client problem resolution. *Journal of Clinical Psychology, 34,* 186–187.

MORROW-BRADLEY, C., & ELLIOTT, R. (1986). Use of psychotherapy research by professional psychologists. *American Psychologist, 41,* 198–206.

MOSTELLER, F., SIEGEL, A. F., TRAPIDO, E., & YOUTZ, C. (1985). Fitting straight lines by eye. In D. C. Hoaglin, F. Mosteller, & J. W. Tukey (Eds.), *Exploring data tables, trends, and shapes (chap. 6).* New York: Wiley.

MUTSCHLER, E. (1979). Using single-case evaluation procedures in a family and children's service agency: Integration of practice and research. *Journal of Social Service Research, 3,* 115–134.

MUTSCHLER, E. (1984). Evaluating practice: A study of research utilization by practitioners. *Social Work Research and Abstracts, 29,* 332–337.

MUTSCHLER, E. (1987). Computer utilization. In *Encyclopedia of social work* (18th ed.). Silver Spring, MD: National Association of Social Workers Press.

MUTSCHLER, E. (1989). *Evolution and future practice uses of computers in human service agencies.* Paper presented at the Boysville of Michigan and Wayne State University, School of Social Work, conference on Research Utilization, Detroit.

MUTSCHLER, E., & HASENFELD, Y. (1986). Integrated information systems for social work practice. *Social Work, 31,* 345–349.

MUTSCHLER, E., & ROSEN, A. (1979). Evaluation of treatment outcome by client and social worker. In *The social welfare forum.* New York: Columbia University Press.

MYERS, L. L., & THYER, B. A. (1997). Should social work clients have the right to effective treatment? *Social Work, 42,* 288–298.

NACHIMAS, D., & NACHIMAS, C. (1976). *Research methods in the social sciences.* New York: St. Martin's Press.

NATHAN, P. E., & GORMAN, J. M. (EDS.). (1998). *Treatments that work.* New York: Oxford University Press.

NATIONAL ASSOCIATION OF SOCIAL WORKERS. (1980). *Code of ethics.* Silver Spring, MD: Author.

NATIONAL SAFETY COUNCIL. (1986). *Accident facts.* Chicago: National Safety Council.

NAY, W. (1977). Analogue measures. In A. R. Ciminero, K. S. Calhoun, & H. E. Adams (Eds.), *Handbook of behavioral assessment* (pp. 233–277). New York: Wiley.

NAY, W. (1979). *Multimethod clinical assessment,* New York: Gardner Press.

NAY, W. R. (1986). Analogue measures. In A. R. Ciminero, K. S. Calhoun, & H. E. Adams (Eds.), *Handbook of behavioral assessment* (2nd ed., chap. 8). New York: Wiley.

NEISWANGER, W. E. (1956). *Elementary statistical methods as applied to business and economic data* (Rev. ed.). New York: Macmillan.

NELSEN, J. C. (1978). Use of communication theory in single-subject research. *Social Work Research and Abstracts, 14,* 12–19.

NELSEN, J. C. (1981). Issues in single-subject research for nonbehaviorists. *Social Work Research and Abstracts, 17,* 31–37.

NELSEN, J. C. (1984). Intermediate treatment goals as variables in single-case research. *Social Work Research and Abstracts, 20,* 9–10.

NELSEN, J. C. (1985). Verifying the independent variable in single-subject research. *Social Work Research and Abstracts, 21,* 3–8.

NELSEN, J. C. (1994). Ethics, gender, and ethnicity in single-case research and evaluation. *Journal of Social Service Research, 18*(3/4), 139–152.

NELSON, R. O. (1977). Methodological issues in assessment via self-monitoring. In J. D. Cone & R. P. Hawkins (Eds.), *Behavior assessment: New directions in clinical psychology* (pp. 217–240). New York: Brunner/Mazel.

NEWMAN, F. L. (1983). Therapist's evaluation of psychotherapy. In M. J. Lambert, E. R. Christensen, & S. S. DeJulio (Eds.), *The assessment of psychotherapy outcome* (pp. 498–536). New York: Wiley.

NEWMANN, J. P. (1987). Gender differences in vulnerability to depression. *Social Service Review, 61,* 447–468.

NEWMAN, M. G., CONSOLI, A., & TAYLOR, C. B. (1997). Computers in assessment and cognitive behavioral treatment of clinical disorders: Anxiety as a case in point. *Behavior Therapy, 28,* 211–235.

NORUSIS, M. J. (1991). *SPSS/PC+studentware plus.* Chicago: SPSS.

NUGENT, W. R. (1987). Information gain through integrated research approaches. *Social Service Review, 61,* 337–364.

NUGENT, W. R. (1988). A vector model of single case design data and its use in analyzing large single case design replication series. *Journal of Social Service Research, 12,* 49–82.

NUGENT, W. R. (1991A). An experimental and qualitative analysis of a cognitive-behavioral intervention for anger. *Social Work Research and Abstracts, 27,* 3–8.

NUGENT, W. R. (1991B). A mathematical model for analyzing single subject design replication series. *Journal of Social Service Research, 15,* 93–129.

NUGENT, W. R. (1992A). The affective impact of a clinical social worker's interviewing style: A series of single-case experiments. *Research on Social Work Practice, 2,* 6–27.

NUGENT, W. R. (1992B). Psychometric characteristics of self-anchored scales in clinical application. *Journal of Social Service Research, 15,* 137–152.

NUGENT, W. R. (1993). A validity study of a self-anchored scale for measuring self-esteem. *Research on Social Work Practice, 3,* 276–287.

NUGENT, W. R., SIEPPERT, J. D., & HUDSON, W. W. (2001). *Practice Evaluation for the 21st Century.* Belmont, CA: Brooks/Cole.

NUNNALLY, J. C. (1978). *Psychometric theory* (2nd ed.). New York: McGraw-Hill.

NURIUS, P. S. (1983). Use of time-series analysis in the evaluation of change due to intervention. *Journal of Applied Behavioral Science, 19,* 215–228.

NURIUS, P. S., & HUDSON, W. W. (1988). Computers and social diagnosis: The client's perspective. *Computers in Human Services, 5,* 21–36.

NURIUS, P. S., & HUDSON, W. W. (1993). *Human services: Practice, evaluation & computers.* Pacific Grove, CA: Brooks/Cole.

O'BRIEN, F., AZRIN, N. H., & HENSON, K. (1969). Increased communication of chronic mental patients by reinforcement and by response priming. *Journal of Applied Behavior Analysis, 2,* 23–29.

OGLES, B. M., & MASTERS, K. S. (1996). *Assessing Outcome in Clinical Practice.* Boston: Allyn & Bacon.

O'LEARY, K. D. (ED.). (1987). *Assessment of martial discord: An integration for research and clinical practice.* Hillsdale, NJ: Erlebaum.

ONGHENA, P. (1992). Randomization tests for extensions and variations of *ABAB* single-case experimental designs: A rejoinder. *Behavioral Assessment, 14,* 153–172.

ONGHENA, P., & EDGINGTON, E. S. (1994). Randomization tests for restricted alternating treatments designs. *Behaviour Research and Therapy, 32*(7), 783–786.

ONGHENA, P., & VAN DAMME, G. (1994). SCRT 1.1: Single-case randomization tests. *Behavior Research Methods, Instruments, & Computers, 26,* 369.

ORENSTEIN, A., & PHILLIPS, W. R. (1978). *Understanding social research: An introduction.* Boston: Allyn & Bacon.

ORGNERO, M. I., & RODWAY, M. R. (1991). AIDS and social work treatment: A single-system analysis. *Health and Social Work, 16,* 123–141.

ORME, J. G., & COX, M. E. (2001). Analyzing single-subject design data using statistical process control charts. *Social Work Research, 25,* 115–127.

ORME, J. G. (1991). Statistical conclusion validity and single-system designs. *Social Service Review, 65,* 468–491.

ORME, J. G., GILLESPIE, D. F., & FORTUNE, A. E. (1983). Two-dimensional summary scores derived from ratings of individualized client problems. *Social Work Research and Abstracts, 19,* 30–32.

ORME, J. G., & GILLESPIE, D. F. (1981). Target complaints as an individualized outcome measure. *International Journal of Behavioral Social Work and Abstracts, 1,* 199–203.

OSMAN, S., & SHUEMAN, S. A. (1988). A guide to the peer review process for clinicians. *Social Work, 33,* 345–348.

OSTERLIND, S. J. (1989). *Constructing test items.* Hingham, MA: Kluwer Academic Publishers.

OSTLE, B., TURNER, K. V., JR., HICKS, C. R., & McEL-RATH, G. W. (1996). *Engineering statistics.* Belmont, CA: Duxbury Press.

OSTROM, C. W., JR. (1990). *Time series analysis: Regression techniques* (2nd ed.). Newbury Park, CA: Sage.

PAGE, T. J., & IWATA, B. A. (1986). Interobserver agreement: History, theory, and current methods. In A. Poling & R. W. Fuqua (Eds.), *Research methods in applied behavior analysis: Issues and advances* (chap. 6). New York: Plenum Press.

PARSONSON, B. S., & BAER, D. M. (1978). The analysis and presentation of graphic data. In T. R. Kratochwill (Ed.). *Single subject research: Strategies for evaluating change* (pp. 101–165). New York: Academic Press.

PARSONSON, B. S., & BAER, D. M. (1986). The graphic analysis of data. In A. Poling & R. W. Fuqua (Eds.), *Research methods in applied behavior analysis: Issues and advances* (pp. 157–186). New York: Plenum Press.

PATIENCE, W. (1990). MicroCAT testing system version 3.0. *Journal of Educational Measurement, 27,* 82–88.

PATTERSON, D. A. (2000). *Personal computer applications in the social services.* Boston: Allyn & Bacon.

PATTERSON, D. A., & BASHAM, R. E. (in press). A data visualization procedure for the evaluation of group treatment outcomes across units of analysis. *Small Group Research.*

PATTON, M. Q. (1990). *Qualitative evaluation and research methods* (2nd ed.). Newbury Park, CA: Sage.

PEARSON, C. L. (1990). Service inputs and outputs. In Y. T. Yuan & M. Rivest (Eds.), *Preserving families: Evaluation resources for practitioners and policymakers* (chap. 4). Newbury Park, CA: Sage.

PECORA, P. J., ET AL. (1995). *Evaluating Family-Based Services.* Hawthorne, N.Y.: Aldine de Gruyter.

PEDHAZUR, E. J., & SCHMELKIN, L. P. (1991). *Design, measurement, and statistics.* Hillsdale, NJ: Erlebaum.

PEHM, L. P. (1976). Assessment of depression. In M. Hersen & A. S. Bellack (Eds.), *Behavioral assessment: A practical handbook* (pp. 233–260). New York: Pergamon Press.

PFADT, A., COHEN, I. L., SUDHALTER, V., ROMANCZYK, R. G., & WHEELER, D. J. (1992). Applying statistical process control to clinical data: An illustration. *Journal of Applied Behavior Analysis, 25,* 551–560.

PFADT, A. & WHEELER, D. J. (1995). Using statistical process control to make data-based clinical decisions. *Journal of Applied Behavior Analysis, 28,* 349–370.

PIGOTT, H. E., FANTUZZO, J. W., & CLEMENT, P. W. (1986). The effects of reciprocal peer tutoring and group contingencies on the academic performance of elementary school children. *Journal of Applied Behavior Analysis, 19,* 93–98.

PIKOFF, H. B. (1996). *Treatment effectiveness handbook: A reference guide to the key research reviews in mental health and substance abuse.* Buffalo, NY: Data for Decisions.

PINDYCK, R. S., & RUBINFELD, D. L. (1991). *Econometric models and econometric forecasts* (3rd ed.). New York: McGraw-Hill.

PINKSTON, E. M., & LINSK, N. L. (1984). *Care of the elderly: A family approach.* Elmsford, NY: Pergamon Press.

PINKSTON, E. M., LINSK, N. L., & YOUNG, R. N. (1988). Home-based behavioral family treatment of the impaired elderly. *Behavior Therapy, 19,* 331–344.

PITT, H. (1994). *SPC for the rest of us: A personal path to statistical process control.* Reading, MA: Addison Wesley.

POLANSKY, N., CHALMERS, M. A., BUTTENWEISSER, E., & WILLIAMS, D. P. (1981). *Damaged parents—An anatomy of child neglect.* Chicago: University of Chicago Press.

POLSTER, R. A., & COLLINS, D. (1988). Measuring variables by direct observations. In R. M. Grinnell, Jr. (Ed.). *Social work research and evaluation* (3rd ed., chap. 8). Itasca, IL: Peacock.

POSAVAC, E. J. (1995). Statistical process control in the practice of program evaluation. *Evaluation Practice, 6*(2), 121–130.

PROCIDANO, M. E., & HELLER, K. (1983). Measures of perceived social support from friends and from family: Three validation studies. *American Journal of Community Psychology, 11,* 1–24.

PROCTOR, E. K. (1990). Evaluating clinical practice: Issues of purpose and design. *Social Work Research and Abstracts, 26,* 32–40.

QUATROCHI-TUBIN, S., & JASON, L. A. (1980). Enhancing social interactions and activity among the elderly through stimulus control. *Journal of Applied Behavior Analysis, 13,* 159–163.

QUERA, V. (1990). A generalized technique to estimate frequency and duration in time sampling. *Behavioral Assessment, 12,* 409–424.

RADIN, N. (1979). Assessing the effectiveness of school social workers. *Social Work, 24,* 132–137.

RANDALL, R. B. (1972). Errors frequently made in using the problem-oriented system. In J. W. Hurst & H. K. Walker (Eds.), *The problem-oriented system* (pp. 67–71). New York: Medcom.

RANKIN, E. D., & MARSH, J. C. (1985). Effects of missing data on the statistical analysis of clinical time series. *Social Work Research and Abstracts, 21,* 13–16.

RAPP, J. T., MILTENBERGER, R. G., GALENSKY, T. L., ELLINGSON, S. A., STRICKER, J., GARLINGHOUSE, M., & LONG, E. S. (2000). Treatment of hair pulling and hair manipulation maintained by digital-tactile stimulation. *Behavior Therapy, 31,* 381–393.

REAMER, F. G. (1982). *Ethical dilemmas in social services.* New York: Columbia University Press.

REAMER, F. G. (1987). Ethics committees in social work. *Social Work, 32,* 188–192.

REAMER, F. G. (1995). *Social work values and ethics.* New York: Columbia University Press.

REESE, E. P. (1966). *Analysis of human operant behavior.* Dubuque, IA: Wm. C. Brown.

REHR, H. (1989). *Practice uses of accountability systems in health care settings: Social work and administrative perspectives.* Paper presented at the Boysville of Michigan and Wayne State University, School of Social Work, conference on Research Utilization, Detroit.

REICHARDT, C. S., & GOLLOB, H. F. (1987). Taking uncertainty into account when estimating effects. In M. M. Mark & R. L. Shotland (Eds.), *Multiple methods in program evaluation* (pp. 7–22). San Francisco: Jossey-Bass.

REID, D. H. (1987). *Developing a research program in human service agencies.* Springfield, IL: Chas. C Thomas.

REID, J. B., BALDWIN, D. V., PATTERSON, G. R., & DISHION, T. J. (1988). Observations in the assessment of childhood disorders. In M. Rutter, A. H. Tuma, & I. S.

Lann (Eds.), *Assessment and diagnosis in child psychopathology* (chap. 6). New York: Guilford Press.

REID, T. R. (1987, FEBRUARY 28). Can New Mexico's population lose 35,000 pounds by spring? *The Washington Post*, p. 43.

REID, W. J. (1977). Process and outcome in the treatment of family problems. In W. J. Reid & L. Epstein (Eds.), *Task-centered practice* (chap. 4). New York: Columbia University Press.

REID, W. J. (1978). *The task-centered system.* New York: Columbia University Press.

REID, W. J. (1990). Change-process research: A new paradigm? In L. Videka-Sherman & W. J. Reid (Eds.), *Advances in clinical social work research* (pp. 130–148). Silver Spring, MD: National Association of Social Workers Press.

REID, W. J. (1997A). Evaluating the dodo's verdict: Do all interventions have equal outcomes? *Research on Social Work Practice, 21,* 5–16.

REID, W. J. (1997B). Is neo-positivism a suitable epistemological framework for HOSE courses? Yes. In M. Bloom & W. C. Klein (Eds.), *Controversial issues in human behavior in the social environment* (pp. 2–7). Boston: Allyn & Bacon.

REID, W. J., & DAVIS, I. P. (1987). Qualitative methods in single-case research. In N. Gottlieb (Ed.), *Perspectives on direct practice evaluation* (chap. 4). Seattle: University of Washington, School of Social Work.

REID, W. J., & HANRAHAN, P. (1982). Recent evaluations of social work: Grounds for optimism. *Social Work, 27,* 328–340.

REID, W. J., & HANRAHAN, P. (1988). Measuring implementation of social treatment. In K. J. Conrad & C. Roberts-Gray (Eds.), *Evaluating program environments* (chap. 6). San Francisco: Jossey-Bass.

REID, W. J., & SMITH, A. D. (1989). *Research in social work* (2nd ed.). New York: Columbia University Press.

RENNE, C. M., & CREER, T. L. (1976). Training children with asthma to use inhalation therapy equipment. *Journal of Applied Behavior Analysis, 9,* 1–11.

REPP, A. C., HARMAN, M. L., FELCE, D., VAN ACKER, R., & KARSH, K. G. (1989). Conducting behavioral assessments on computer-collected data. *Behavioral Assessment, 11,* 249–268.

RICHEY, C. A., BLYTHE, B. J., & BERLIN, S. B. (1987). Do social workers evaluate their practice? *Social Work Research and Abstracts, 23,* 14–20.

RICKERT, V. I., SOTTOLANO, D. C., PARRISH, J. M., RILEY, A. W., HUNT, F. M., & PELCO, L. E. (1988). Training parents to become better behavior managers: The need for a competency-based approach. *Behavior Modification, 12,* 475–496.

RINN, R. C., & VERNON, J. C. (1975). Process evaluation of outpatient treatment in a community mental health center. *Journal of Behavior Therapy and Experimental Psychiatry, 6,* 5–11.

ROBINSON, J. P., & SHAVER, P. R. (1973). *Measures of social psychological attitudes* (Rev. ed.). Ann Arbor: University of Michigan, Institute for Social Research.

ROLIDER, A., & VAN HOUTEN, R. (1988). The use of response prevention to eliminate daytime thumbsucking. *Child and Family Behavior Therapy, 10,* 135–142.

ROSE, S., & TOLMAN, R. (1985). Evaluation of client outcomes in groups. In M. Sundel et al. (Eds.), *Individual change through small groups.* New York: Free Press.

ROSE, S. D. (1988). Practice experiments for doctoral dissertations: Research training and knowledge building. *Journal of Social Work Education, 24,* 115–122.

ROSE, S. D. (1989). *Working with adults in groups: Integrating cognitive-behavioral and small group strategies.* San Francisco: Jossey-Bass.

ROSEN, A. (1992). Facilitating clinical decision making and evaluation. *Families in Society: The Journal of Contemporary Human Services, 73,* 522–532.

ROSEN, A. (1993). Systematic planned practice. *Social Service Review, 67,* 84–100.

ROSEN, A., & PROCTOR, E. K. (1981). Distinctions between treatment outcomes and their implications for treatment evaluation. *Journal of Consulting and Clinical Psychology, 49,* 418–425.

ROSEN, D., & ZYTOWSKI, D. G. (1977). An individualized, problem-oriented self-report of change as a follow-up of a university counseling service. *Journal of Counseling Psychology, 24,* 437–439.

ROSENTHAL, R. (1991). *Meta-analytic procedures for social research* (Rev. ed.). Newbury Park, CA: Sage.

ROSENTHAL, R., & ROSNOW, R. L. (1991). *Essentials of behavioral research: Methods and data analysis* (2nd. ed.). New York: McGraw-Hill.

ROTH, A., & FONAGY, P. (1996). *What works for whom? A critical review of the psychotherapy research.* New York: Guilford.

RUBIN, A., & BABBIE, E. (1997). *Research methods for social work* (3rd ed.). Belmont, CA: Wadsworth.

RUBIN, A., & KNOX, K. S. (1996). Data analysis problems in single-case evaluation: Issues for research on social work practice. *Research on Social Work Practice, 6*(1), 40–65.

RUCKDESCHEL, R. A., & FARRIS, B. E. (1981). Assessing practice: A critical look at the single-case design. *Social Casework, 62,* 413–419.

RUGH, J. D., GABLE, R. S., & LEMKE, R. R. (1986). Instrumentation for behavioral assessment. In A. R. Ciminero, K. S. Calhoun, & H. E. Adams (Eds.), *Handbook of behavioral assessment* (2nd ed., chap. 4). New York: Wiley.

RUGH, J. D., & SCHWITZGEBEL, R. L. (1977). Instrumentation for behavioral assessment. In A. R. Ciminero, K. S. Calhoun, & H. E. Adams (Eds.), *Handbook of behavioral assessment* (pp. 79–116). New York: Wiley.

RUTTER, M., TUMA, A. H., & LANN, I. S. (EDS.). (1988). *Assessment and diagnosis in child psychopathology.* New York: Guilford Press.

RYBACK, R. S. (1974). *The problem-oriented record in psychiatry and mental health care.* New York: Grune & Stratton.

RZEPNICKI, T. L. (1985). Task-centered in foster care services: Working with families who have children in placement. In A. E. Fortune (Ed.). *Task-centered practice with families and groups* (chap. 10). New York: Springer.

RZEPNICKI, T. L. (1991). Enhancing the durability of the intervention gains: A challenge for the 1990's. *Social Service Review, 65,* 92–111.

SAINATO, D. M., MAHEADY, L., & SHOOK, G. L. (1986). The effects of a classroom manager role on the social interaction patterns and social status of withdrawn kindergarten students. *Journal of Applied Behavior Analysis, 19,* 187–195.

SALEEBEY, D. (ED.). (1992). *The strengths perspective in social work practice.* New York: Longman.

SALEEBEY, D. (1997). Is it feasible to teach HBSE from a strengths perspective, in contrast to one emphasizing limitations or weaknesses? (Yes). In M. Bloom & W. C. Klein (Eds.), *Controversial issues in human behavior in the social environment* (pp. 16–23). Boston: Allyn & Bacon.

SANDERS, R. M. (1978). *How to plot data: A manual for students, researchers, and teachers of the behavioral sciences.* Lawrence, KS: H & H Enterprises.

SANDERSON, W. C., & WOODY, S. (1995). Manuals for empirically validated treatments. *The Clinical Psychologist, 48,* 7–11.

SATIR, V. (1972). *Peoplemaking.* Palto Alto, CA: Science & Behavior Books.

SAWIN, K. J., & HARRIGAN, M. (1994). *Measures of family functioning for research and practice.* New York: Springer.

SCHINKE, S. P., BLYTHE, B. J., & GILCHRIST, L. D. (1981). Cognitive-behavioral prevention of adolescent pregnancy. *Journal of Counseling Psychology, 28,* 451–454.

SCHINKE, S. P., GORDON, A. N., & WESTON, R. E. (1990). Self-instruction to prevent HIV infection among African-American and Hispanic-American adolescents. *Journal of Consulting and Clinical Psychology, 58,* 432–436.

SCHLESINGER, H. J., MUMFORD, E., GLASS, G. V., PATRICK, C., & SHARFSTEIN, S. (1983). Mental health treatment and medical care utilization in a fee-for-service system: Outpatient mental health treatment following the onset of chronic disease. *American Journal of Public Health, 73,* 422–429.

SCHÖN, D. (1983). *The reflective practitioner: How professionals think in action.* New York: Basic Books.

SCHUERMAN, J. R. (1989). *Expert system and ordinary research as sources for practice guidance.* Paper presented at the Boysville of Michigan and Wayne State University, School of Social Work, Conference on Research Utilization, Detroit.

SCHUTTE, N. S., & MALOUFF, J. M. (1995). *Sourcebook of adult assessment strategies.* New York: Plenum.

SCHWARTZ, A., & GOLDIAMOND, I. (1975). *Social casework: A behavioral approach.* New York: Columbia University Press.

SCRIVEN, M. (1967). The methodology of evaluation. In R. W. Tyler, R. M. Gagne, & M. Scriven (Eds.), *Perspectives on curriculum evaluation, A.E.R.A.* (Monograph Series on Curriculum Evaluation, No. 1). Chicago: Rand McNally.

SEABERG, J. R. (1965). Case recording by code. *Social Work, 10,* 92–98.

SEABERG, J. R. (1970). Systematized recording: A follow-up. *Social Work, 15,* 32–41.

SEABERG, J. R. (1981). IPR-2: A revised measure of outcome. *Social Work Research and Abstracts, 17,* 45–46.

SEABERG, J. R. (1988). Child well-being scales: A critique. *Social Work Research and Abstracts, 24,* 9–16.

SEABERG, J. R., & GILLESPIE, D. F. (1977). Goal Attainment Scaling: A critique. *Social Work Research and Abstracts, 13,* 4–9.

SECRET, M., & BLOOM, M. (1994). Evaluating a self-help approach to helping a phobic child: A profile analysis. *Research on Social Work Practice, 4*(3), 338–348.

SEDERER, L. I., & DICKEY, B. (1996). *Outcomes Assessment in Clinical Practice.* Baltimore: Williams & Wilkins.

SELIGMAN, L. (1999). *Selecting Effective Treatments: A Comprehensive, Systematic Guide for Treating Mental Disorders* (Rev. ed.). San Francisco: Jossey-Bass.

SELLTIZ, C., WRIGHTSMAN, L. J., & COOK, S. W. (1976). *Research methods in social relations* (3rd ed.). New York: Holt, Rinehart, & Winston.

SHADISH, W. R. (1986). Planned critical multiplism: Some elaborations. *Behavioral Assessment, 8,* 75–103.

SHAFFER, D., GOULD, M. S., BRASIC, J., AMBROSINI, P., FISHER, P., BIRD, H., & ALUWAHLIA, S. (1983). A Children's Global Assessment Scale (CGAS). *Archives of General Psychiatry, 40,* 1228–1231.

SHAPIRO, E. S., & KRATOCHWILL, T. R. (1988). Analogue assessment: Methods for assessing emotional and behavioral problems. In E. S. Shapiro & T. R. Kratochwill (Eds.), *Behavioral assessment in schools: Conceptual foundations and practical applications* (chap. 2). New York: Guilford Press.

SHARPLEY, C. F. (1986). Fallibility in the visual assessment of behavioural interventions: Time-series statistics to analyze time-series data. *Behaviour Change, 3,* 26–33.

SHARPLEY, C. F. (1987). Time-series analysis of behavioural data: An update. *Behaviour Change, 4,* 40–45.

SHARPLEY, C. F., & ALAVOSIUS, M. P. (1988). Autocorrelation in behavioural data: An alternative perspective. *Behavioural Assessment, 10,* 243–251.

SHEAFOR, B. W., HOREJSI, G. R., & HOREJSI, G. A. (1991). *Techniques and guidelines for social work practice* (2nd ed.). Boston: Allyn & Bacon.

SHERMAN, E., & REID, W. J. (EDS.). (1994). *Qualitative research in social work.* New York: Columbia University Press.

SHEWHART, W. A. (1931). *Economic control of quality of manufactured products.* New York: Van Nostrand Reinhold.

SIDERIDIS, G. D., & GREENWOOD, C. R. (1996). Evaluating treatment effects in single-subject behavioral experiments using quality-control charts. *Journal of Behavioral Education, 6*(2), 203–211.

SIDMAN, M. (1960). *Tactics of scientific research: Evaluating experimental data in psychology.* New York: Basic Books.

SIEGEL, D. H. (1984). Defining empirically based practice. *Social Work, 29,* 325–331.

SIEGEL, D. H. (1985). Effective teaching of empirically based practice. *Social Work Research and Abstracts, 21,* 40–48.

SIEGEL, D. H. (1990). Computer-based clinical practice: An asset or pie in the sky? In L. Videka-Sherman & W. J. Reid (Eds.), *Advances in clinical social work research* (pp. 118–122). Silver Spring, MD: National Association of Social Workers Press.

SIEGEL, S., & CASTELLAN, N. J., JR. (1988). *Nonparametric statistics for the behavioral sciences* (2nd ed.). New York: McGraw-Hill.

SILBERGELD, S., ET AL. (1995). Assessment of environment-theory systems: The group atmosphere scale. *Journal of Consulting and Clinical Psychology, 43*, 460–469.

SIMON, R. L. (1987). The impact of training for empirically based practice. *Journal of Social Work Education, 23*, 24–30.

SIRLES, E. A. (1982). Client-counselor agreement on problem and change. *Social Casework, 63*, 348–353.

SISCO, C. B., & PEARSON, C. L. (1994). Prevalence of alcoholism and drug abuse among female AFDC recipients. *Health and Social Work, 19*, 75–77.

SISSON, L. A., BABEO, T. J., & VAN HASSELT, V. B. (1988). Group training to increase social behaviors in young multihandicapped children. *Behavior Modification, 12*, 497–524.

SJOBERG, G. (ED.). (1967). *Ethics, politics, and social research.* Cambridge, MA: Schenkman.

SLAUGHTER, D. T., & EPPS, E. G. (1987). The work environment and student achievement of Black-American children and youth. *Journal of Negro Education, 56*, 3–20.

SLONIM-NEVO, V., & ANSON, Y. (1998). Evaluating practice: Does it improve outcome? *Social Work Research, 22*, 66–74.

SLONIM-NEVO, V., & VOSLER, N. R. (1991). The use of single-system design with systemic brief problem-solving therapy. *Families in Society, 72*, 38–44.

SMITH, D. (1976). Goal Attainment Scaling as an adjunct to counseling. *Journal of Counseling Psychology, 28*, 22–27.

SMITH, K. (1983). Tests of significance: Some frequent misunderstandings. *American Journal of Orthopsychiatry, 53*, 315–321.

SORENSON, R. L., GORSUCH, R. L., & MINTZ, J. (1985). Moving targets: Patients' changing complaints during psychotherapy. *Journal of Consulting and Clinical Psychology, 53*, 49–54.

SOWERS, J.-A., VERDI, M., BOURBEAU, P., & SHEEHAN, M. (1985). Teaching job independence and flexibility to mentally retarded students through the use of a self-control package. *Journal of Applied Behavior Analysis, 18*, 81–85.

SPIELBERGER, C. D. (1983). *Manual for the State-Trait Anxiety Inventory* (Rev. ed.). Palo Alto, CA: Consulting Psychologists Press.

STAAT, H., VAN LEEUWEN, E., & WIT, A. (2000). A longitudinal study of informational interventions to save energy in an office building. *Journal of Applied Behavior Analysis, 33*, 101–104.

STARK, L. J., COLLINS, F. L., JR., OSNES, P. G., & STOKES, T. F. (1986). Using reinforcement and cueing to increase healthy food choices in preschoolers. *Journal of Applied Behavior Analysis, 19*, 367–369.

STATISTICAL ANALYSIS SYSTEM INSTITUTE. (1990). *SAS introductory guide for personal computers.* Cary, NC: Author.

STEWART, N. R., WINBORN, B. B., JOHNSON, R. G., BURKS, H. M., & ENGELKES, J. R. (1978). *Systematic counseling.* Englewood Cliffs, NJ: Prentice Hall.

STOCK, L. Z., & MILAN, M. A. (1993). Improving dietary practices of elderly individuals: The power of prompting, feedback, and social reinforcement. *Journal of Behavior Analysis, 26*(3), 379–387.

STOLOFF, M. L., & COUCH, J. V. (1988). *Computer use in psychology: A directory of software* (2nd ed.). Washington, DC: American Psychological Association.

STOLOFF, M. L., & COUCH, J. V. (1992). *Computer use in psychology: A directory of software* (3rd ed.). Washington, DC: American Psychological Association.

STONE, M., LEWIS, C., & BECK, A. (1994). The structure of Yalom's Curative Factors Scale, *International Journal of Group Psychothereapy, 44*, 239–245.

STRAYHORN, J. M. (1977). *Talking it out.* Champaign, IL: Research Press.

STREINER, D. L., & NORMAN, G. R. (1989). *Health measurement scales: A practical guide to their development and use.* Oxford: Oxford University Press.

STROM-GOTTFRIED, K. (1997). The implications of managed care for social work education. *Journal of Social Work Education, 33*(1), 7–18.

STRUBE, M. J. (1989). A general program for the calculation of the kappa-coefficient. *Behavior Research Methods, Instruments, and Computers, 21*, 643–644.

STUART, R. (1970). *Trick or treatment: How and when psychotherapy fails.* Champaign, IL: Research Press.

SUDMAN, S., & BRADBURN, N. M. (1982). *Asking questions.* San Francisco: Jossey-Bass.

SUEN, H. K. (1988). Agreement, reliability, accuracy, and validity: Toward a clarification. *Behavioral Assessment, 10*, 343–366.

SUEN, H. K., & ARY, D. (1987). Application of statistical power in assessing autocorrelation. *Behavioral Assessment, 9*, 125–130.

SUEN, H. K., & ARY, D. (1989). *Analyzing quantitative behavioral observation data.* Hillsdale, NJ: Erlebaum.

SUEN, H. K., ARY, D., & ARY, R. M. (1986). A note on the relationship among eight indices of interobserver agreement. *Behavioral Assessment, 8*, 301–303.

SUNDEL, M., & SUNDEL, S. S. (1975). *Behavioral modification in the human services.* New York: Wiley.

SUZUKI, L. A., MELLER, P. J., & PONTEROTTO, J. G. (EDS.). (1996). *Handbook of Multicultural Assessment: Clinical, Psychological and Educational Applications.* San Francisco: Josey-Bass.

SWITZER, E. B., DEAL, T. E., & BAILEY, J. S. (1977). The reduction of stealing in second graders using a group contingency. *Journal of Applied Behavior Analysis, 10*, 267–272.

SYSTAT. (1990A). *Business MYSTAT: An instructional business version of SYSTAT for IBM-PC/compatibles.* Evanston, IL: Author.

SYSTAT. (1990B). *MYSTAT: An instructional version of SYSTAT for IBM-PC/compatibles.* Evanston, IL: Author.

TAGGART, A. C., TAGGART, J., & SIEDENTOP, D. (1986). Effects of a home-based activity program: A study with low fitness elementary school children. *Behavior Modification, 10*, 487–507.

THARP, R. G., & WETZEL, R. J. (1969). *Behavior modification in the natural environment.* New York: Academic Press.

THOMAS, E. J. (ED.). (1974). *Behavior modification procedure: A sourcebook.* Chicago: Aldine.

THOMAS, E. J. (1975). Uses of research methods in interpersonal practice. In N. A. Polansky (Ed.). *Social work research* (Rev. ed., pp. 254–283). Chicago: University of Chicago Press.

THOMAS, E. J. (1978). Research and service in single-case experimentation: Conflicts and choices. *Social Work Research and Abstracts, 14,* 20–31.

THOMAS, E. J. (1984). *Designing interventions for the helping professions.* Beverly Hills, CA: Sage.

THOMAS, E. J., BASTIEN, J., STUEBE, D. R., BRONSON, D. E., & YAFFE, J. (1987). Assessing procedural descriptiveness: Rationale and illustrative study. *Behavioral Assessment, 9,* 43–56.

THOMPSON, C. (ED.). (1989A). Affective disorders. In C. Thompson (Ed.). *The instruments of psychiatric research* (chap. 4). New York: Wiley.

THOMPSON, C. (ED.). (1989B). *The instruments of psychiatric research.* New York: Wiley.

THOMPSON, C. (1989C). Introduction. In C. Thompson (Ed.). *The instruments of psychiatric research* (chap. 1). New York: Wiley.

THOMPSON, J. R., & KORONACKI, J. (1993). *Statistical process control for quality improvement.* New York: Chapman & Hall.

THORNDIKE, R. L., & HAGEN, E. (1969). *Measurement and evaluation in psychology and education* (3rd ed.). New York: Wiley.

THYER, B., & GELLER, S. (1987). The "buckle-up" dashboard sticker: An effective environmental intervention for safety belt promotion. *Environment and Behavior, 19,* 484–494.

THYER, B. A. (1983). Treating anxiety disorders with exposure therapy. *Social Casework, 64,* 77–82.

THYER, B. A. (1993). Single-system research designs. In R. M. Grinnel, Jr. (Ed.). *Social work research and evaluation* (4th ed., pp. 94–117). Itasca, IL: Peacock.

THYER, B. A., & CURTIS, G. C. (1983). The repeated pretest-posttest single-subject experiment: A new design for empirical clinical practice. *Journal of Behavior Therapy and Experimental Psychiatry, 14,* 311–315.

THYER, B. A., & WODARSKI, J. S. (EDS.). (1988). *Handbook of Empirical Social Work Practice: Mental Disorders.* New York: Wiley.

THORESEN, C. E., & MAHONEY, M. J. (1974). *Behavioral Self-Control.* New York: Holt.

TISCHLER, G. L. (1990). Utilization management and the quality of care. *Hospital and Community Psychiatry, 41,* 1099–1102.

TOLSON, E. R. (1977). Alleviating marital communication problems. In W. J. Reid & L. Epstein (Eds.), *Task centered practice* (pp. 100–112). New York: Columbia University Press.

TOOTHAKER, L. E., BANZ, M., NOBLE, C., CAMP, J., & DAVIS, D. (1983). N = 1 designs: The failure of ANOVA-based tests. *Journal of Educational Statistics, 8,* 289–309.

TOULIATOS, J., PERLMUTTER, B. F., & STRAUS, M. A. (EDS.). (1990). *Handbook of family measurement techniques,* Newbury Park, CA: Sage.

TRIPODI, T. (1980). Replication in clinical experimentation. *Social Work Research and Abstracts, 16,* 35.

TRIPODI, T. (1994). *A primer on single-subject design for clinical social workers.* Washington, DC: National Association of Social Workers Press.

TRIPODI, T., & EPSTEIN, I. (1980). *Research techniques for clinical social workers.* New York: Columbia University Press.

TRIPODI, T., & HARRINGTON, J. (1979). Uses of time-series designs for formative program evaluation. *Journal of Social Service Research, 3,* 67–78.

TRUAX, C. B., & CARKHUFF, R. R. (1965). Experimental manipulation of therapeutic conditions. *Journal of Consulting Psychology, 29,* 119–124.

TYMCHUK, A. J. (1981). Ethical decision making and psychological treatment. *Journal of Psychiatric Treatment and Evaluation, 3,* 507–513.

TYMCHUK, A. J. (1982). Strategies for resolving value dilemmas. *American Behavioral Scientist, 26,* 159–175.

TYSON, K. (1994). Heuristic guidelines for naturalistic qualitative evaluations of child treatment. In E. Sherman & W. J. Reid (Eds.), *Qualitative research in social work* (pp. 89–112). New York: Columbia University Press.

ULMAN, J. D., & SULZER-AZAROF, B. (1975). Multielement baseline design in educational research. In E. Ramp & G. Semb (Eds.), *Behavior analysis: Areas of research and application.* Englewood Cliffs, NJ: Prentice Hall.

U.S. DEPARTMENT OF HEALTH AND HUMAN SERVICES. (1981). *Regulation is for the protection of human subjects.* Washington, DC: U. S. Government Printing Office.

VANCE, H. B. (1997). (ED.). *Psychological Assessment of Children. Best Practices for School and Clinical Settings.* (2nd ed.). New York: Wiley.

VAN DAMME, G., & ONGHENA, P. (1992). *Single-case randomization tests.* Department of Psychology, Center for Mathematical Psychology and Psychological Methodology, Tiensestraat, 102, B-300 Leuven, Belgium.

VAN DEN BRINK, W. P., & VAN DEN BRINK, W. G. J. (1989). A comparison of the power of the *t* test, Wilcoxon's test, and the approximate permutation test for the two-sample location problem. *British Journal of Mathematical Statistical Psychology, 42,* 183–189.

VAN RIEZEN, H. V., & SEGAL, M. (1988). *Comparative evaluation of rating scales for clinical psychopharmacology.* New York: Elsevier.

VEATCH, R. M. (1981). *Theory of medical ethics.* New York: Basic Books.

VELICER, W. F., & HARROP, J. W. (1983). The reliability and accuracy of the time-series model identification. *Evaluation Review, 7,* 551–560.

VERA, M. I. (1990). Effects of divorce groups on individual adjustment: A multiple methodology approach. *Social Work Research and Abstracts, 26,* 11–20.

VERNON, R., & LYNCH, D. (2000). *Social Work and the Web.* Belmont, CA: Wadsworth.

VIDEKA-SHERMAN, L. (1986). Alternative approaches to aggregating the results of single-subject studies. *Social Work Research and Abstracts, 22,* 22–23.

VIDEKA-SHERMAN, L. (1988). Meta-analysis of research on social work practice in mental health. *Social Work, 33,* 325–338.

VIDEKA-SHERMAN, L., & REID, W. J. (1982). The structured clinical record: A clinical education tool. *The Clinical Supervisor, 3,* 45–62.

WAINER, H., & BRAUN, H. I. (EDS.). (1988). *Test validity.* Hillsdale, NJ: Erlbaum.

WAKEFIELD, J. C. (1988). Psychotherapy, distributive justice, and social work: Part 1. Distributive justice as a conceptual framework for social work. *Social Service Review, 62,* 187–216.

WAKEFIELD, J. C., & KIRK, S. A. (1996). Unscientific thinking about scientific practice: Evaluating the scientist-practitioner model. *Social Work Research, 20,* 83–95.

WAKEFIELD, J. C., & KIRK, S. A. (1997). Science, dogma, and the scientist-practitioner model. *Social Work Research, 21*(3), 129–208.

WALLS, R. T., WERNER, T. J., BACON, A., & ZANE, T. (1977). Behavior checklists. In J. D. Cone & R. P. Hawkins (Eds.), *Behavioral assessment* (pp. 77–146). New York: Brunner/Mazel.

WAMPOLD, B. E. (ED.). (1988). The autocorrelation debate [Special issue]. *Behavioral Assessment, 10.*

WAMPOLD, B. E., & WORSHAM, N. L. (1986). Randomization tests for multiple-baseline designs. *Behavioral Assessment, 8,* 135–144.

WARWICK, D. P. (1982). Types of harm in social research. In T. L. Beauchamp, R. R. Faden, R. J. Wallace, Jr., & L. Walter (Eds.), *Ethical issues in social science research.* Baltimore: Johns Hopkins University Press.

WASKOW, I. E., & PARLOFF, M. B. (EDS.). (1975). *Psychotherapy change measures.* Rockville, MD: National Institute of Mental Health.

WATSON, D. L., & THARP, R. G. (1989). Self-directed behavior: *Self-modification for personal adjustment* (5th ed.). Belmont, CA: Brooks/Cole.

WATSON-PERCZEL, M., LUTZKER, J. R., GREENE, B. F., & MCGIMPSEY, B. J. (1988). Assessment and modification of home cleanliness among families adjudicated for child neglect. *Behavior Modification, 12,* 57–81.

WEBB, E. J., CAMPBELL, D. T., SCHWARTZ, R. D., & SECHREST, L. (1966). *Unobtrusive measures: Nonreactive research in the social sciences.* Chicago: Rand McNally.

WEBB, E. J., CAMPBELL, D. T., SCHWARTZ, R. D., SECHREST, L., & GROVE, J. B. (1981). *Nonreactive measures in the social sciences* (2nd ed.). Boston: Houghton Mifflin.

WEED, L. L. (1968). Medical records that guide and teach. *New England Journal of Medicine, 278,* 593–599, 652–657.

WEED, L. L. (1969). *Medical records, medical education, and patient care: The problem-oriented record as a basic tool.* Cleveland: Case Western Reserve University Press.

WEED, L. L. (1972). Questions often asked about the problem-oriented record: Does it guarantee quality? In J. W. Hurst & H. K. Walker (Eds.), *The problem-oriented system* (pp. 51–56). New York: Medcom.

WEISS, C. (1972). *Evaluative research.* Englewood Cliffs, NJ: Prentice Hall.

WEISS, R. L., HOPS, H., & PATTERSON, G. R. (1973). A framework for conceptualizing marital conflict, a technology for altering it, some data for evaluating it. In L. A. Hamerlynck, L. C. Handy, & E. J. Mash (Eds.), *Behavior change: Methodology, concepts, and practice.* Champaign, IL: Research Press.

WEISSMAN, M. M. (1990). *Social Adjustment Scale: References to publications using the various versions of the scale and information on translations.* Unpublished manuscript, Columbia University, College of Physicians and Surgeons.

WEISSMAN, M. M., & BOTHWELL, S. (1976). Assessment of social adjustment by patient self-report. *Archives of General Psychiatry, 33,* 1111–1115.

WEISSMAN, M. M., PRUSOFF, B. A., THOMPSON, W. D., HARDING, P. S., & MYERS, J. K. (1978). A social adjustment by self-report in a community sample and in psychiatric outpatients. *Journal of Nervous and Mental Disease, 166,* 317–326.

WELLS, C. C., & MASCH, M. K. (1986). *Social work ethics day to day: Guidelines for professional practice.* New York: Longman.

WETHERILL, G. B., & BROWN, D. W. (1991). *Statistical process control: Theory and practice.* London: Chapman & Hall.

WETZLER, S. (ED.). (1989). *Measuring mental illness: Psychometric assessment for clinicians.* Washington, DC: American Psychiatric Press.

WETZLER, S., & VAN PRAAG, H. M. (1989). Assessment of depression. In S. Wetzler (Ed.). *Measuring mental illness: Psychometric assessment for clinicians* (chap. 4). Washington, DC: American Psychiatric Press.

WHEELER, D. J., & CHAMBER, D. S. (1992). *Understanding statistical process control (2nd ed.).* Knoxville, TN: SPC Press.

WHITE, D. M., RUSCH, F. R., KAZDIN, A. E., & HARTMANN, D. P. (1989). Applications of metaanalysis in individual-subject research. *Behavioral assessment, 11,* 281–296.

WHITE, L., TURSKY, B., & SCHWARTZ, G. E. (EDS.). (1985). *Placebo: Theory, research, and mechanisms.* New York: Guilford Press.

WHITE, M. (1989). *Literate means to therapeutic ends.* Adelaide, Australia: Dulwich Centre.

WHITE, O. R. (1974). *The "split middle"–A "quickie" method of trend estimation.* University of Washington, Experimental Educational Unit, Child Development and Mental Retardation Center.

WHITE, O. R. (1977). Data-based instruction: Evaluating educational progress. In J. D. Cone & R. P. Hawkins (Eds.), *Behavioral assessment: New directions in clinical psychology.* New York: Brunner/Mazel.

WHITEMAN, M., FANSHEI, D., & GRUNDY, J. F. (1987). Cognitive-behavioral interventions aimed at anger of parents at risk of child abuse. *Social Work, 32,* 469–474.

WHITTAKER, J. K., OVERSTREET, E. J., GRASSO, A., TRIPODI, T., & BOYLAN, F. (1988). Multiple indicators of success in residential youth care and treatment. *American Journal of Orthopsychiatry, 58,* 143–148.

WILLSON, V. L., & PUTNAM, R. R. (1982). A metaanalysis of pretest sensitization effects in experimental design. *American Educational Research Journal, 19,* 249–258.

WILSON, S. J. (1978). *Confidentiality in social work: Issues and principles.* New York: Free Press.

WILSON, S. J. (1983). Confidentiality. In A. Rosenblatt & D. Waldfogel (Eds.), *Handbook of clinical social work.* San Francisco: Jossey-Bass.

WINETT, R. A., LECKLITER, I. N., CHINN, D. E., STAHL, B., & LOVE, S. Q. (1985). Effects of television modeling on residential energy conservation. *Journal of Applied Behavior Analysis, 18,* 33–44.

WITKIN, S. L. (1997). Another visit to empirical practice land. *Social Work Research, 21*(3), 205–207.

WITKIN, S. L., & GOTTSCHALK, S. (1988). Alternative criteria for theory evaluation. *Social Service Review, 12,* 83–98.

WITKIN, S. L., & HARRISON, D. F. (1979). Single-case designs in marital research and therapy. *Journal of Social Service Research, 3,* 51–66.

WITTENBORN, J. R. (1984). Observer ratings. In M. Hersen, L. Michelson, & A. S. Bellack (Eds.), *Issues in psychotherapy research* (chap. 4). New York: Plenum Press.

WOLF, M. M. (1978). Social validity: The case for subjective measurement or how applied behavior analysis is finding its heart. *Journal of Applied Behavior Analysis, 11,* 203–214.

WOLPE, J. (1969). *The practice of behavior therapy.* New York: Pergamon Press.

WOLPE, J. (1973). *The practice of behavior therapy* (2nd ed.). New York: Pergamon Press.

WODARSKI, J. S., & THYER, B. A. (EDS.). (1998). *Handbook of Empirical Practice. Social Problems and Practice Issues.* New York: Wiley.

WOODY, S. R., & SANDERSON, W. C. (1998). Manual for Empirically Supported Treatments: 1998 Update. *The Clinical Psychologist, 51,* 17–21.

WOOD, K. H. (1979, SEPTEMBER). *Integration of practice and research: Proposal for an experiment.* Paper presented at the Western Regional Workshop on Integrating Practice and Research, Council on Social Work Education, Berkeley.

WOODARD, C. A., ET AL. (1978). The role of Goal Attainment Scaling in evaluating family therapy outcome. *American Journal of Orthopsychiatry, 48,* 464–476.

YAFFE, J., & GOTTHOFFER, D. (2000). *A Quick Guide to the Internet for Social Workers.* Boston: Allyn & Bacon.

YALOM, I. D., BLOCH, S., BOND, G., ZIMMERMAN, E., & QUALLS, B. (1978). Alcoholics in interactional group therapy: An outcome study. *Archives of General Psychiatry, 35,* 419–425.

YEATON, W. H., & SECHREST, L. (1981). Critical dimensions in the choice and maintenance of successful treatments: Strength, integrity and effectiveness. *Journal of Consulting and Clinical Psychology, 49,* 156–168.

YU, D., & MARTIN, B. L. (1987). Low-cost procedures to conserve a public sport environment. *Behavior Modification, 11,* 241–250.

ZANE, M. D. (1978). Contextual analysis and treatment of phobic behavior as it changes. *American Journal of Psychotherapy, 32,* 338–355.

ZARIT, S. H., REEVER, K. E., & BACH-PETERSON, J. (1980). Relatives of the impaired elderly: Correlates of feelings of burden. *Gerontology, 20,* 649–655.

ZELANZNY, G. (1985). *Say it with charts.* Homewood, IL: Dow Jones-Irwin.

ZIMMERMAN, J. (1975). If it's what's inside that counts, why not count it? Self-recording of feelings and treatment by "self-implosion." *Psychological Record, 15,* 3–16.

ZIMMERMAN, S. M., & ICENOGLE, M. L. (1999). *Statistical quality control using EXCEL.* Milwaukee: ASQ Quality Press.

ZURAVIN, S., ORME, J. G., & HEGAR, R. (1994). Predicting the severity of child abuse injury using ordinal probit regression. *Social Work Research, 18,* 161–180.

NAME INDEX

A

Abell, N., 234
Acierno, R., 42, 379
Adams, M., 593, 655
Aday, L. A., 200, 261
Agran, M., 468–469
Alavosius, M. P., 533
Albert, R., 122, 226
Alessi, G., 186
Alexander, J. F., 18
Alford, B. A., 10
Allison, D. B., 358, 520–521, 581, 586, 592
Allison, H., 570–571, 574–578
Alter, C., 127, 277, 282, 288, 532
Altus, D. E., 407–409
Alvero, A. M., 28, 420–421
American Psychiatric Association, 257
American Psychological Association, 59, 64, 73
Ammerman, R. T., 42, 379
Anastasi, A., 64, 73, 75, 76, 77, 79, 80, 81, 217
Anderson, L., 199
Andrulis, R. S., 71
Anesko, K. M., 219, 260
Ang, B. W., 605
Anger, W. K., 446–448, 663
Anton, R. F., 138
Applegate, J. S., 254
Arthur, G., 256
Ary, D., 177, 186, 537, 596, 655
Ary, R. M., 177
Asberg, M., 255
Atienza, O. O., 605
Attkisson, C. C., 255
Auerbach, A. H., 261

B

Babbie, E., 200, 215, 261
Bach-Peterson, J., 222
Baer, D. M., 519, 580
Bailey, J. S., 432–434
Bailey, K. D., 202
Balassone, M. E., 74
Bales, R. F., 192
Banz, M., 532
Barkely, R. A., 42
Barlow, D. H., 8l, 82, 300, 307, 340, 356, 357, 362, 370, 371, 372, 373, 382, 383, 404, 413, 430, 453, 456, 482, 485, 489
Barone, V. J., 442–444
Barrios, B., 345
Barry, E., 305
Baskin, D., 137
Battle, C. C., 195, 198, 199, 207, 685
Bavandan, T. G., 395, 670
Beasley, T. M., 581
Beck, A., 10, 77, 83, 255
Becker, R. R., 198
Beidel, D. C., 102
Bell, W., 88
Bellack, A. S., 84, 179, 213, 224, 316
Benbenishty, R., 106, 127, 137, 263, 684
Benedict, W. R., 103, 136, 684, 686
Bentley, K. J., 37
Ben-Zaken, A., 127

Auerbach, C., 532, 615
Austin, J., 28, 420–421
Ayllon, T., 307, 405
Azrin, N., 307

Bergin, A. E., 46, 83, 197, 261, 321
Berlin, S. B., 190, 202, 207, 320
Besa, D., 444–446
Billows, W., 670
Bird, H. R., 254, 258
Bloch, S. R., 199, 207, 452–453
Bloom, L. Z., 423–424
Bloom, M., 9, 12, 38, 41, 43, 195, 197, 226, 261, 304, 368, 384, 385, 397–399, 502–506, 522, 542, 545, 547, 549, 452–453, 596, 663, 669, 671, 672
Blumenthal, D., 604
Blythe, B. J., 127, 190, 320, 333, 334, 532
Bohart, A. C., 38, 333, 379
Bond, G. R., 199, 207
Bornstein, P. H., 165, 166, 175, 300, 301
Bornstein, T., 165
Bostwick, G. J., Jr., 254, 259, 261, 318
Bostwick, N. K., 254, 259, 261, 318
Bothwell, S., 215, 260
Boylan, F., 106
Bracht, G. H., 353
Brackshaw, E., 27, 416–417
Bradburn, N. M., 200, 261
Brager, G., 92
Braun, H. I., 75
Briar, S., 333
Brigham, T. A., 417–418, 670
Brody, E. M., 260
Bronson, D. E., 127, 532
Brothers, K. J., 448–451, 670
Broverman, D., 673
Broverman, I., 673

Brown, L., 213
Bryant, B. R., 213
Brown, C. S., 88, 99, 100, 108, 179
Brown, J. A., 88, 99, 100, 108, 179
Brown, T. R., 212, 255
Browning, R. M., 383
Broxmeyer, N., 391
Budd, K. S., 425–426, 530, 664
Burdock, E. I., 255, 260
Burley, S., 462–465
Burrill, G. C., 134
Busk, P. L., 533, 596
Butch, P., 304, 385
Butcher, J. N., 138, 263, 264
Buttenweisser, E., 60

C

Camp, J., 532
Campbell, D. T., 43, 44, 45, 74,
 75, 76, 134, 298, 306, 307,
 349, 350, 352, 353, 354, 394,
 411, 453, 674
Canino, G., 254
Caplinger, T. E., 186
Cardenas, J., 80
Carey, R., 604
Carhuff, R. R., 333
Carlson, C. I., 84, 213, 224, 316
Castellan, N. J., Jr., 68
Cautela, J. R., 88, 198
Chalmers, M. A., 60
Chambers, D. E., 334
Chambers, D. S., 600, 601, 604, 605
Chambless, D. L., 42, 379
Chapman, C., 308
Chapman, D. G., 37
Chassan, J. B., 44, 45
Childers, B., 256
Chiu, L. H., 216
Christensen, E. R., 320
Christoph, P., 199
Ciarlo, J. A., 212, 213, 254, 255,
 256, 259, 260
Cicchetti, D. V., 189
Clark, D. A., 10
Clark, H. B., 462–463
Clarkson, F., 673
Clement, P. W., 417–419
Coddington, R. D., 80
Cohen, J., 189, 254, 520, 527, 588,
 589
Cohen, L. H., 46
Cohen, S., 192, 566
Collins, D., 170
Combs-Orme, T. D., 61

Cone, J. D., 42, 43, 165, 169, 170,
 172, 175, 176, 177, 181, 183,
 185, 186, 189, 298, 300, 665
Conners, C. K., 260
Conoley, J. C., 137, 212, 213, 217,
 263
Consoli, A., 137
Cook, T. D., 43, 44, 45, 74, 134,
 298, 306, 307, 349, 350, 352,
 354
Cooper, M., 437–438
Corcoran, K., 36, 84, 97, 137, 212,
 213, 229, 263, 316, 358, 506,
 566, 586, 587, 592, 660, 661,
 662
Cormier, S., 277–278, 334
Cormier, W., 277–278, 334
Couch, J. V., 137
Coulton, C. J., 203, 204
Council on Social Work
 Education, 36
Cowger, C. D., 7
Cowles, M., 521
Cox, B., 199, 207
Cox, M. E., 600, 605
Craig, K. D., 42
Crosbie, J., 532, 580, 606, 654
Cross, D., 199
Crouch, J. V., 263
Csapo, K. G., 256
Curtis, C. G., 395–396, 397, 399
Cushing, L. S., 448, 450

D

Dalaney, D. D., 672
Daniels, W., 74
Dasberg, H. H., 199
Davidson, C. V., 259
Davidson, R. H., 259
Davis, C., 521
Davis, D., 532
Davis, I. P., 288, 292, 293
Davis, L. E., 80
Davison, G. C., 383
Deal, T. E., 432–434
Dean, R. G., 37, 320, 389–390
DeCarlo, L. T., 537
DeJong, C. R., 261
DeJulio, S. S., 320
Denzin, H. K., 311
DeProspero, A., 566
DeVellis, R. F., 261
DiGangi, S. A., 475–477
Dill-Standiford, T. J., 256
Dineen, J. P., 438–440

Dobson, K. S., 42
Dolgoff, R. 20
D'Onofrio, C. N., 80
Doty, L. A., 600, 601, 605
Drake, G. P., Jr., 474–475
Dryfoos, J., 664

E

Eberhardt, M. J., 474–475
Edgington, E. S., 519, 596
Edleson, J. L., 37
Edwards, B. C., 77, 216
Edwards, D. W., 212, 255
Edwards, R. P., 28
Egli, D. S., 409
Elliott, R., 46
Ellsworth, R. B., 255, 256
Endicott, J., 254
Epps, E. G., 80
Epstein, I., 263, 334
Erbaugh, J., 77
Evens, W., 127, 277, 282, 288, 532

F

Faith, M. S., 358, 586, 592
Fanshel, D., 190, 685
Fantuzzo, J. W., 417–419
Farmer, R., 124, 278
Faul, A. C., 161, 224, 229, 250, 672
Fazio, R. T., 672
Felce, D., 175
Feld, S., 83
Feldman, R. A., 186
Feuerstein, M. J., 56, 179, 197
Feyerherm, W., 580, 581
Fickling, J. A., 76
Finch, S. J., 685
Finkelstein, A., 88
First, J. M., 80
Firth-Cozens, J. A., 256
Fischer, J., 38, 41, 42, 46, 84, 94,
 97, 119, 121, 131, 172, 174,
 195, 212, 213, 229, 316, 334,
 358, 379, 491, 592, 672, 687
Fiske, D. W., 44, 75, 76, 453
Flaherty, E. W., 305, 306, 307
Fleiss, J. L., 68, 189, 219, 221, 254
Fonagy, P., 42, 370
Ford, D. H., 10
Forehand, R., 219
Fortune, A., 130, 207, 320
Foster, L., 256
Foster, S. L., 165, 169, 170, 172,
 175, 176, 177, 181, 183, 185,
 186, 189, 256, 298, 300

Fowler, D. R., 88
Fox, D. K., 446–448, 663, 670
Frankl, V., 10
Franklin, B., 675
Franklin, R. D., 532, 581, 596, 655
Fraser, M. W., 42, 315, 379
Fredman, N., 84, 224, 316
Friedan, B., 7
Furey, W., 219

G

Gable, R. K., 202, 204, 261
Gable, R. S., 56
Gambrill, E. B., 101, 108, 168, 169, 170, 186, 283
Garfield, S. L., 46
Garner, J. W., 236, 242, 243
Garwick, G., 102–104
Geiger, G., 462–463
Gelfand, D. M., 123, 374
Geller, E. S., 406–408, 664
Germain, C., 9
Gettinger, M., 190
Gibbs, L. E., 43
Gibson, G., 519, 566
Gilchrist, L. D., 190
Gillespie, D. F., 105, 195, 207
Gilligan, C., 80
Gingerich, W. J., 36, 137, 200, 203, 263, 358, 524, 580, 581, 586, 592, 660, 661, 662
Glass, G. V., 353, 358, 411, 586
Gochros, H., 119, 121, 131, 172, 174
Gold, R. G., 74
Goldfried, M. R., 82
Goldiamond, I., 121, 278, 282, 283, 291, 294
Goldstein, A. P., 345, 415
Goodner, V., 417–418
Gordon, A. N., 320
Gordon, T., 334, 387
Gordon, V. C., 40
Gorman, D. R., 255
Gorman, B. S., 358, 520, 581, 586, 592
Gorman, J. M., 42, 379
Gorsuch, R. L., 377, 534, 567
Gotthoffer, D., 138
Gottman, J. M., 83, 93–94, 99, 100, 320, 411, 538, 600–601, 613
Gottschalk, S., 38
Goyette, C. H., 260
Grant, R., 134
Grasso, A., 106, 263, 685

Greenberg, L., 38, 333, 379
Greene, B. F., 442–444
Greene, R., 466–467, 491–493
Greenwood, K. M., 533, 537, 538, 566, 567
Gresham, F. M., 333, 334
Gripton, J., 570
Grohol, J. M., 138, 263
Grossman, S. F., 320
Grotevant, H. D., 84, 213, 224, 316
Grove, J. B., 76
Grundy, J. F., 190, 685
Guelen, P. J. R., 199
Gurin, G., 83
Gutkin, T., 462–465

H

Hakerem, G., 255, 260
Hall, J. A., 438–440
Hamilton, M. A., 77, 255, 672
Hamilton, S. B., 165
Hammill, D. D., 213
Hanrahan, P., 46, 130
Hanson, N., 671
Hardesty, A. S., 255, 260
Harding, P. S., 215
Hargreaves, W. A., 255, 260
Harman, M. L., 175
Harper, G. F., 487–489
Harrigan, M., 84, 212, 213, 224
Harrington, J., 304
Hartmann, D. P., 123, 345, 358, 374, 482, 484
Hasenfeld, Y., 293, 680
Hatch, D. R., 77, 216
Hayaski, T., 262
Hayes, S. C., 74, 77, 175, 222, 307, 321, 362, 453, 482, 485
Haynes, J., 391
Haynes, S. N., 169, 179, 184, 307
Hays, R. D., 262
Hedges, L. V., 359, 589
Heineman-Pieper, M., 48, 665, 670, 671
Heller, K., 222
Hemphill, J., 262
Hersch, E. L., 256
Hersen, M., 42, 81, 82, 84, 179, 213, 224, 300, 316, 340, 356, 357, 370, 371, 372, 373, 379, 382, 383, 404, 413, 430, 482, 489
Hesbacher, P. T., 199
Hill, W., 263
Hogarty, G. E., 46

Holmes, T. H., 80
Holmstrup, E., 134
Hopkins, B. L., 446–448, 663
Hops, H., 431
Horejsi, G. A., 134
Horejsi, G. R., 134
Hudak, M. T., 672
Hudson, W. W., 49, 61, 66, 71, 74, 77, 84, 94, 127, 137, 138, 161, 218, 224, 229, 232–234, 235–250, 263, 264, 391, 531, 672

Huitema, B. E., 533, 534–537, 581

I

Icenogle, M. L., 605
Irwin, C. E., Jr., 138, 264
Iwata, B. A., 177, 189

J

Jacob, T., 84, 213, 222, 224, 316
Jacobs, C. J., 98
Jacobson, N. S., 431–432, 518
Jarrett, R. B., 74
Jason, L. A., 27, 416–417, 440–441, 670
Jayarante, S., 43, 51, 74, 331, 341, 349, 358, 478, 518, 586, 592
Jeffers, J., 341
Jensen, C., 395
Johnson, M., 199
Jones, M. A., 74, 83, 256
Jones, R. R., 566, 567
Judd, C. M., 200, 207, 261, 532, 533, 610, 654
Jung, R. S., 440–441

K

Kagle, J. D., 102, 122, 134, 292, 293, 678
Kahn, J. A., 199
Kallman, W. M., 56, 179, 197
Kalman, M. A., 256
Kane, R. A., 134, 136
Kanfer, F. H., 345, 415
Karoly, P., 345, 415
Karsh, K. G., 175
Kastner, J. W., 28, 485–487
Kazdin, A. E., 179, 180, 183, 185, 186, 254, 256, 300, 358, 383, 430, 436, 475, 482, 484, 498, 524, 596, 655
Keeper, C., 566
Kendall, P. C., 260, 341

Kennedy, C. H., 448, 450
Kenny, D. A., 532, 533, 610, 654
Kerlinger, F. N., 261
Kestenbaum, C. J., 84, 224
Keyser, D. J., 213, 217
Kidder, L. H., 200, 207
Kiesler, D. J., 102, 195, 198, 204
King, A. C., 393–394, 664, 670
King, C., 670
Kingston, M. D., 77, 216
Kirchner, R. E., 406, 432–433, 436
Kiresuk, T. J., 102–104, 212, 255, 685
Kirk, S. A., 46, 665
Klein, W. C., 12, 669
Klonoff, H., 199, 207
Knapczyck, D. R., 448–449
Knox, K. S., 564
Koegel, R., 356
Kohlberg, L., 80
Kolko, D. J., 37, 391, 441–442, 609, 620
Kopel, S. A., 430, 436, 678
Kopp, J., 165, 166, 175, 278, 300, 301, 302
Kori, S. H., 462–463
Kovacs, M., 255
Kramer, J. J., 137, 212, 213, 217, 263
Krantz, P. J., 448–451
Kratochwill, T. R., 190, 191, 316, 349, 354, 386, 533, 596
Krishef, C. H., 596, 655
Kroeker, D., 256
Krug, S. E., 137, 263

L
Labaw, P., 261
Laird, J., 48, 665
Lambert, M. J., 77, 83, 197, 216, 222, 254, 259, 261, 317, 318, 320, 321
Lang, N. C., 50
Lann, I. S., 260
Laporte, H. H., 532, 615
Lawton, M. P., 260
Lazarus, A. A., 320, 383
Leary, K. D., 190
Ledray, L. E., 40
Leiblum, S. S., 83, 93–94, 99, 100, 320, 538, 600–601
Leitenberg, H., 411
Lemke, R. R., 56
Leonard, I. J., 468–469
Levi, L., 199
Levin, J. R., 349, 596

Levine, F. M., 219, 260
Levitt, J. L., 213, 224
Levy, R. L., 331, 341, 349, 395, 478, 670
Liberman, B. L., 198
Libow, J. A., 198
Lieberman, L. A, 199
Lieberman, M., 262
Light, J. R., 202
Linn, B. S., 260
Linn, M. W., 260
Linsk, N. L., 168, 180, 465
Linton, J. M., 487
Lipsey, M. W., 74, 77, 588
Liu, R. Y., 605
Lloyd, R. C., 604
Lloyd, J. W., 474–475
Loewenberg, F., 20
Lonetto, R., 97
Long, J. D., 356
Lovaas, O. I., 356, 357
Lovett, S. B., 393–394, 664
Luborsky, L., 199
Lugwig, T. D., 406–408
Lutzker, J. R., 442–444, 466–467
Lyerly, S. B., 255
Lynch, D., 138

M
Maag, J. W., 475–477
MacDonald, M., 399
Mager, R. F., 97, 99
Magura, S., 74, 256
Maheady, K., 487–489
Mahoney, M. J., 475
Maisto, C. A., 298, 306
Maisto, S. A., 298, 306
Malcolm, R., 138, 264
Maletzky, B., 134
Mallette, B., 487–489
Malouff, J. M., 212, 213, 224
Mann, R. A., 308, 320, 370
Marafiote, R. A., 176
Marascuilo, L. A., 533, 596
Marchand-Martella, N. E., 468–469
Markman, H. J., 179, 191, 316
Marshall, R. S., 409
Martella, R. C., 468–469, 668–669
Martens, W. M., 134
Mash, E. J., 42, 190, 316
Maslow, A., 8
Masters, P. A., 685
Matyas, T. A., 533, 537, 538, 566, 567
Mayer, J. A., 664
Mayer, J. E., 83

McClannahan, L. E., 448–451
McCubbin, H. I., 84, 224, 316
McCullough, J. P., 37, 391, 522–523
McDonald, M. R., 425–426, 530, 664
McDowell, I., 224, 260
McFall, R. M., 301
McGaw, B., 358
McGimpsey, B. J., 466–467
McKean, J. W., 534–537, 581
McKeon, J. J., 255, 260
McMahon, P. M., 40, 338, 339
McMurty, S. L., 672
McNees, M. P., 409, 664, 670
McSweeny, A. J., 393–394, 670
Meichenbaum, D., 10
Meier, S. M., 417–418
Mendelson, M., 77
Merrill, M. H., 407–409
Milan, M. A., 37, 391, 441–442, 493–495, 609, 620
Miles, M., 262
Miller, D. M., 37
Miller, I. K., 407–409
Miller, M., 477–478
Miller, R. P., 462–463
Miller, S. R., 477–478
Millstein, S. G., 138, 264
Milner, J. S., 74
Miltenberger, R. G., 421–422
Mintz, J., 102, 195, 198, 199, 204, 377
Minuchin, S., 315
Miringoff, M. L., 670
Mock, J., 77
Monette, D. R., 261
Montgomery, S. A., 255
Moos, R. H., 212
Moran, P. W., 77
Moreland, K. L., 138, 263
Morley, S., 593, 655
Morrison, J. K., 198, 199
Morrow-Bradley, C., 46
Moses, B. S., 74, 256
Mosteller, F., 137, 580
Mutschler, E., 199, 293, 674, 685
Myers, J. K., 215
Myers, L. L., 42

N
Nathan, P. E., 42, 379
Naumann, W., 462–465
Nay, W. R., 165, 172, 190, 307, 308, 310, 341
Neiswanger, W. E., 580

Nelsen, J. C., 37, 40, 333, 391, 665
Nelson, K. E., 42
Nelson, R. O., 74, 301, 307, 321
Nelson-Gray, R. O., 124, 278
Newell, C., 224, 260
Newman, F. L., 212, 254, 255, 263
Newman, M. G., 137
Newmann, J. P., 80
Noble, C., 532
Norman, G. R., 66, 202, 261
Norton, J., Jr., 545, 547, 549
Notarius, C. I., 179, 191, 316
Nugent, W. R., 43, 137, 161, 198,
    199, 288, 333, 418–420
Nunnally, J. C., 64, 202
Nurius, P. S., 127, 137, 138, 161,
    218, 263, 264

O
Ochberg, F. M., 255
Olkin I., 589
Olson, R., 28, 420–421
Onghena, P., 485, 596, 655
Opdycke, S., 670
Orgnero, M. I., 409–410
Orme, J. G., 61, 207, 226, 350,
    520, 527, 574, 592, 600, 605,
    610, 672
Osman, S., 661
Osterlind, S. J., 261
Ostle, B., 600, 605
Ottenbacher, K., 519, 566
Overall, J. E., 255
Overstreet, E. J., 106

P
Page, T. J., 177, 189
Parloff, M. B., 197, 317, 320
Parsonson, B. S., 519, 580
Patience, W., 262
Patterson, D. A., 137, 263, 531,
    532
Patterson, G. R., 431
Patti, R., 680
Pearson, C. L., 71, 315
Penk, W., 88
Perlmutter, B. F., 84
Perris, C., 255
Pfadt, A., 600
Pigott, H. E., 417–419, 664
Pikoff, H. B., 42, 379
Pinkston, E. M., 168, 180, 465
Pitt, H., 600
Polansky, N., 60
Polster, R. A., 70
Procidano, M. E., 222

Proctor, E. K., 80, 222, 327, 330
Prusoff, B. A., 215

Q
Qualls, B., 199, 207
Quera, V., 186

R
Rahe, R. H., 80
Ramirez, R., 219, 260
Rapp, J. T., 421–422
Raskin, A., 255, 260
Reamer, F. G., 20, 676
Reatig, N., 255, 260
Reever, K. E., 222
Rehr, H., 682
Reibstein, J., 199
Reid, W. J., 42, 46, 48, 130, 198,
    199, 213, 224, 254, 259, 261,
    288, 292, 293, 320, 333, 379,
    665, 670, 683
Reinherz, H., 37, 320, 389–390
Repp, A. C., 175
Ribera, J. C., 254
Rickels, K., 199
Rinn, R. C., 435, 682, 684
Risley, T. R., 308, 409
Rivard, J. C., 42
Robbins, M. S., 18
Rodway, M. R., 409–410, 570
Rodwell, M. K., 334
Rolider, A., 444–445
Rorer, L., 256
Rose, S. D., 173, 183, 190, 192,
    282, 291, 320
Rosen, A., 98, 199, 334
Rosen, D., 199, 207
Rosenkrantz, P., 673
Rosenthal, R., 298, 299, 571, 574
Rosnow, R. L., 298, 299, 571, 574
Roth, A., 42, 379
Rubin, A., 215, 261, 564
Rubio-Stipeo, M., 254
Rugh, J. D., 56, 174, 179, 197
Rusch, F. R., 358
Rutherford, R. B., Jr., 475–477
Rutter, M., 260
Ryback, R. S., 134
Rzepnicki, T. L., 132, 345, 415

S
Sacca, K., 487–489
Saleebey, D., 7
Sanders, R. M., 127
Sanderson, W. C., 42, 379
Sargent, M. M., 46

Sawin, K. J., 84, 212, 213, 224
Schalling, D., 255
Schinke, S. P., 190, 320
Schlessinger, D. J., 438–440
Schnall, D., 532, 615
Schnelle, J. F., 409
Schnopp-Wyatt, D., 670
Schoiock, G., 219, 260
Schön, D., 38
Schuerman, J. R., 685
Schulterbrandt, J. G., 255, 260
Schutte, N. S., 212, 213, 224
Schwartz, A., 121, 278, 282, 283,
    291, 294
Schwartz, R. D., 76
Seaberg, J. R., 105, 195, 293
Sechrest, L. B., 46, 76
Secret, M., 397–399, 671
Sedvall, G., 255
Segal, M., 212, 213, 254, 255, 259,
    260
Seilhamer, R. A., 222
Seligman, L., 42
Selinger, J., 477–478
Sexton, T. L., 18
Shadish, W. R., 317, 320, 321
Shapiro, D. A., 83, 197, 254, 256,
    261, 321
Shapiro, E. S., 190, 191, 316
Sharpley, C. F., 533
Sheafor, B. W., 134
Sheehan, P. W., 199
Sherman, E., 48, 665, 670
Sherman, R., 84, 102, 224, 316, 685
Shewhart, W. A., 600
Shueman, S. A., 661
Siedentop, D., 465–466
Siegel, A. F., 580
Siegel, D. H., 138, 263
Siegel, S., 68
Sieppert, J. D., 137, 161
Silverstein, J. M., 520
Simmons, J. Q., 356
Singer, J. D., 202
Singh, N. N., 487
Sirles, E. A., 199
Sisco, C. B., 71
Slaughter, D. T., 80
Slonim-Nevo, V., 37, 392–393
Smith, A. D., 254, 259, 261
Smith, E. R., 200
Smith, F. J., 198
Smith, M. L., 358
Solomon, P. L., 203, 204
Solow, N., 199
Sorenson, R. L., 377

Sparrow, S. S., 189
Specht, H., 92
Spitzer, R., 254
Staat, H., 27
Stanley, J. C., 45, 134, 349, 353, 354, 411
Steffen, J. J., 345, 415
Stiles, W. B., 256
Stock, L. Z., 493–495
Stoloff, M. L., 137, 263
Stone, G. W., 37
Stone, M., 262
Stover, D. O., 383
Straus, M. A., 84
Streiner, D. L., 66, 202, 261
Strom-Gottfried, K., 660, 663
Stuart, R., 678
Sturgis, E. T., 138
Sudman, S., 200, 261
Suen, H. K., 177, 186, 189, 537, 596, 665
Sullivan, T. J., 261
Sulzer-Azarof, B., 482
Sundel, M., 88, 92
Sundel, S. S., 88, 92
Sweetland, R. C., 213, 217
Swift, M., 305
Switzer, E. B., 432–434

T
Taggart, A. C., 465–466
Taggart, J., 465–466
Talsma, E., 51, 358
Tang, L. C., 605
Taylor, C. B., 137
Templer, D. I., 97
Tennenbaum, D. L., 84, 213, 224, 316
Tharp, R. G., 278, 282, 291, 413
Thomas, E. J., 198, 334, 355, 375, 377, 459, 478, 677
Thompson, A. I., 84, 224, 316
Thompson, C., 212, 213, 216, 254, 255, 256, 260
Thompson, W. D., 215
Thorensen, C. E., 475
Thyer, B. A., 42, 379, 395–396, 397, 399, 478–479, 664
Timms, N., 83
Tingstrom, D. H., 28
Tischler, G. L., 661
Todd, D. D., 462–463
Tolman, R., 192
Tolson, E. R., 391

Toothaker, L. E., 532, 610, 654
Touliatos, J., 94, 213, 216, 224, 316
Trapido, E., 580
Tripodi, T., 51, 106, 263, 304, 333, 334, 357, 358
Truax, C. B., 333
Tryon, W. W., 537
Tuma, A. H., 260
Tyson, K., 48, 665, 670, 671

U
Ulman, J. D., 482
Ulrich, R. F., 260
Upper, D., 198
Urban, H. B., 10

V
Van Acker, R., 175
Van Damme, G., 485, 532
van der Kleijn, E., 199
Vandiver, V., 506, 660
Van Houten, R., 444–445
van Leeuwen, E., 27
van Praag, H. M., 199, 216
van Riezen, H. V., 212, 213, 254, 255, 259, 260
Vaught, R. S., 566
Veatch, R. M., 676
Vera, M. I., 391–392
Vernon, J. C., 435, 682, 684
Vernon, N., 138
Veroff, J., 83
Videka-Sherman, L., 46, 293, 358, 586, 592
Vogel, S., 673
Vosler, N. R., 37, 392–393

W
Wainer, H., 75
Wakefield, J. C., 665
Walker, D., 304, 385
Wampold, B. E., 533, 596
Ward, C. H., 77
Waskow, I. E., 197, 317, 320
Watson, D. L., 78, 282, 291
Watson-Perczel, M., 466–467
Webb, E. J., 76, 298, 304, 306, 307, 308, 309–310, 317, 320
Wedel, K. R., 334
Weed, L. L., 134
Weinrott, M., 566
Weise, C., 199
Weiss, C., 43
Weiss, R. L., 431

Weissman, A., 255
Weissman, M. M., 215, 260
Welsh, T. M., 407–409
Weston, R. E., 320
Wetzel, R. J., 413
Wetzler, S., 212, 213, 216
Wheeler, D. J., 600, 601, 604, 605
Wheeler, J., 477–478
White, D. M., 358, 359, 586, 592
White, M., 444
White, O. R., 444, 580, 581
Whiteman, M., 190
Whittaker, J. K., 106, 685
Wilcox, L. W., 260
Willett, J. B., 202
Williams, D. P., 60
Williams, D. T., 84, 224
Williams, L., 138
Williamson, S., 192
Willson, V. L., 411
Wilson, C. C., 88, 307
Wilson, D. B., 588
Wilson, S. J., 122, 678
Wimberley, R. S., 74
Winett, R. A., 393–394, 664
Wit, A., 27
Witkin, S. L., 38, 665
Wittenborn, J. R., 254, 259, 261
Wodarski, J. S., 42, 186, 379
Wolf, M. M., 199
Wolpe, J., 396
Wood, K. H., 42
Woody, S. R., 42, 379
Worsham, N. L., 596

Y
Yaffe, J., 138
Yalom, I. D., 199, 207
Yalom, L., 262
Young, R. N., 465
Youtz, C., 580

Z
Zane, M. D., 398
Zarit, S. H., 222
Zelanzny, G., 127
Zhao, J., 534
Zimmerman, E., 199, 207
Zimmerman, S. M., 605
Zivotofsky, E., 672
Zubin, J., 255
Zubin, S., 260
Zytowski, D. G., 199, 207

SUBJECT INDEX

A

A (indicating baseline),
334–335, 381–382
(*A*) (indicating reconstructed
baseline), 335
A-B designs, 386–399
Abscissa (horizontal axis), 127
Accessibility, 84
Accountability, professional,
41–42, 51
Additive and controlling effects
of intervention, 478–480
Additive or construction design,
A-B-A-C-A-BC-( ), 479
Administration, 225–228
of questionnaires, 225–229
of scales, examples, 232–249
of standardized measures,
225–229
use of evaluation in, 680–686
Agency use of single-system
procedures, 684–686
staff cooperation and
deployment, 683–684
staff development, 683
Aim-star technique, 525, 527
Alignment of graphs, in
multiple-target design,
560
Alignment of three types of
significance, 523–524
All-purpose evaluation design,
A-B, 499
additions to, 499–501

All-purpose measurement
procedure, 499
Alpha levels, 522–521
Alternating intervention design,
A-B/C- (*B* or *C*),
482–489
case illustration, 485–489
introducing clients to, 489
limitations of, 485
recommendations regarding,
485
strengths of, 483–485
Alternative explanation of
outcomes, 43, 401–402
Analogues, 189–191
audiotape or videotape, 190
enactments, 191
measures, 191
paper and pencil, 190
role-playing, 190–191
Analysis, 513–656
basic principles of, 513–533
change interventions, based
on analysis, 528–530
computer analysis of single-
system design data,
531–532, 614–650
of data, in case illustration,
24–27, 40
descriptive statistics for,
569–594
effectiveness, 516–518
efficiency, 516–518
effort, 516–518

how long should data be
collected?, 525–528
in maintenance phase,
530–531
overview, 516, 517
selecting a procedure for
analysis,, 651–656
significance, 518–524
comparing forms of,
523–524
practical form of, 516–517
statistical form of, 519–522
theoretical form of,
522–523
tests of statistical significance
for, 595–613
in training phase, 530–531
visual, 554–568
Analytic procedures, 651–656
Analyzing and using results in
case illustration, 22–24
Anchors, in individualized
rating scales, 199–201,
203–207
Annotation of data on charts,
126–127, 290
Archival records, 304–307
private, 307
public, 304–307
Assessment:
of client situation, 13–15
inevitable changes in, 15–16
preliminary, 118
role of baseline in, 367

The Assistant (program for recording behaviors), 175
Autocorrelation, (r_{F2}), 532–540
  computational steps in testing for, 534–538
  debate over, 533–534
  definition of, 532
  detection of, 532–533
  problems in, 532–533
  transformation of autocorrelated data, 538–542

B
B (indicating intervention), 335
Baselines and baselining, 39, 364–379
  archival data, used in, 368
  assessment purposes in, 367
  assumptions underlying, 331–332
  in case illustration, 21
  changes in, 378–379
  collecting and charting, 368–370
  comparing baseline and intervention periods, 332
  concurrent or typical, 367, 369
  conditions when unnecessary, 374–375
  definition of, 36, 364
  delay of intervention, 376–377
  illustrated on charts, 366, 369, 371, 373, 375
  impossible to obtain, 377–378
  inferred baseline data, 368, 369
  issues in, 375–379
  length of, 368–369, 374
  number of observations needed, 373–374
  patterns of, 371
  problem hypotheses, 367
  problems in, 372–373, 376–379
  prospective, 367, 369

purposes of, 365–367
  reconstructed or retrospective, 368, 369
  stability, 370–373, 377–378
    patterns of, 371–372
  time, 373–374
  types of, 367–368
  uncooperative persons in, 378
  used in evaluation, 365
  utility, 370
Baselining (*see* Baselines and baselining)
Baserate, definition of, 364
Batting average (agency norm of successful intervention), 682
B, C,. . . . (indicating distinct interventions), 335
BC, BCD, etc. (indicating combined interventions), 335–336
Behavior:
  accurate observations of, 175–176
  analog situations for measuring, 189–191
  definition of, 165
  group, recording of, 191–193
  guidelines for, 166–168
  instruments for recording, 173–175
  interobserver reliability, 189
  methods of recording, 179–189
    duration recording, 183–185
    frequency recording, 179–183
    interval recording, 185–189
  observation, 163–193
    reliability of, 176–177
    validity of, 176–177, 178–179
  rates, 172–173
  sampling, 168–173
    continuous, 169
    samples (noncontinuous), 169–173

Beta, 521
Bimodal pattern of data, 567
Booster shots in single-system designs, 401, 530
Brief contacts, evaluations for, 501–506
  baseline approximations in, 502–503
  client involvement in, 505
  dichotomous data in, 505–506
  intervention data for, 503–504
Brief exit questionnaires, 504

C
CAAP (Computer Assisted Assessment Package), 139, 267–276
  user's guide, 267–276
Campbell Collaboration (listing of outcome studies), 42
Carryover effects, 340
Case illustrations:
  abused children and home safety, 442–444
  aggressive behavior in school, 448–449
  Angela, student at senior center, 95
  angry blowups, 418–420
  Attention Deficit-Hyperactivity Disorder and drugs, 485–487
  back pain (chronic) and walking, 462–463
  Barbara, student with developmentally disabled child, 95–96
  behaviorally disoriented adolescent and math problems, 477–478
  burdens of elder care and teenage daughter, 222–224
  cooperative learning in older school children, 474–475
  coping skills among women in dual-earner families, 393–394

depressed woman, example connecting practice and evaluation, 328–330

designated drivers, 417–418

dietary improvements in elderly clients, 493–495

divorce adjustment cases, 391–392

dog phobia, 398–399

Douglas, student at residential center for disturbed adolescents, 195–196

dying cancer patient, 389–391

elderly man (impaired) and family aide for bathing, 465

emotionally disturbed boys at summer camp, the "Ferrets," 491–493

exercise combined with access to TV in obese child, 416–417

exercise with physically inactive children, 465–466

Francis, student at alcohol recovery center, 96

fear of frogs, 395–397

George, student in a research class, 96

related to goals and objectives, 108–112

hair pulling client, 421–423

hearing-impaired student and peer tutor, 462–465

interviewing skills training for Asian Americans, 440–441

Irene, student in rural mental health center, 96–97

Jack, student at hospital for mentally ill, 97

jealous woman, treatment of, 391–392

learning-disabled children and self-monitoring, 475–477

mining safety and green stamps as token reinforcer, 446–448

Mrs. Abbott and the Roaring Nineties Club, 3–31

Mrs. D, uncommunicative son overseas, 384–385

neglected children and dirty homes, 466–467

obsessive-compulsive disorder, treatment of, 437–438

parent–child conflicts, with narrative therapy, 444–446

paradoxical instructions for academic problems, 441–442

pedophiliac fantasies in socially isolated client, 452–453

peer tutoring, 417–419, 448, 449

preventive dentistry, 425

recycling paper trash, 448–451

safety belt encouragement in restaurant, 420–421

self-esteem problems, 289–290

self-monitoring program for negative self or other statements, 468–469

social skills training of developmentally disabled adults, 438–440

student suicide and crisis intervention, 425–426

STD and a 10th-grade girl, 664–666

successful outcomes of a small agency, 459

teaching sign language to hearing-impaired adults, 487

team as teaching unit, educational innovation, 487–489

telephone study in Cincinnati, 393–394

temper tantrums, 460

thumbsucking and dental problems, 444–445

Case notes, from computer, 148–149

Case study method (or case study design), 381–386

case illustrations, 384

components of, 381–382

history of, 382–383

introducing clients to, 385–386

limitations of, 382

problems with and limitations of, 383–384

recommendations of, 384

strengths of, 383

CASS (Computer Assisted Social Services) computer program, 52, 139–162

Causality, 347–353

in *A-B-A* designs, 401–402, 404

in *A-B-A-B* designs, 401–402, 412

in *A-B-A-B-BC-B-BC* designs, 489–491

in *A-B-A-C* designs, 471

in *B-A-B* designs, 401–402, 424

did change occur, 350

criteria for inferring, 348–349

design validity, 349–350

inferences regarding, 349–350

in multiple baseline designs, 430

threats to, 350–355

Cautions, in use of analytic procedures, 653–656

Celeration line, 580–581

in determining trend line, 580

limitations in use of, 581

steps in construction of, 580, 584

Central tendency, measures of, 570–574

Change:
in level of data, 555–557
multidimensional, 321–322
sensitivity of measures to, 313
Changing criterion design (*see*
Changing intensity
design)
Changing intensity design
(A-B^1-B^2-B^3), 458–470
case illustrations, 462–468
changing criterion type, 459
changing program type, 460
introducing client to,
468–470
limitations of, 461
recommendations regarding,
461–462
strengths of, 460–461
Changing program design (*see*
Changing intensity
design)
Changing the intervention,
338–340, 384–385
Chart (or graph):
computer programs for,
139–162
cumulative data, 132
definition of, 36
shared with clients, 127
steps in, 126–134
charting the targets, 126–134
Checklists:
in data collection, 123
of problems, 89–91
Children's Global Assessment
Schedule (CGAS), 258
Chi-square, test of statistical
significance, 605–609
calculating, 607–608
cautions in using, 606, 609
computing with SINGWN,
606
Classical research, brief
overview, 43–48
compared with single-system
designs, 43–46
Client Bill of Rights, 24
Client concerns, specifying
problems and potentials,
88–97

Client logs: 277–295
use in assessment, 277–278
client involvement in,
280–282, 291–292
combined with other
measures, 278, 288–291
critical incident log, 280–282
definition of, 277–278
evaluation function of, 278
evaluation log, 288
exploratory log, 282, 284–285
general model of, 278, 279
interaction log, 283, 287
introducing clients to,
291–292
practitioner log, 292–293
problem-category variations,
279
reliability with regard to,
293–295
target problem log, 282–283
time variations types,
278–282
uses of, 278
validity with regard to,
293–295
Client records, getting from
computer, 145–147
Client samples, 171
Client self-report questionnaire,
213
Client/system, definition of, 36
Clinical cutting score (or
clinical cutoff), 80, 113
Clinical measurement package,
229–254
Clinical (or practical)
significance, 516–517
Cochrane Collaboration (listing
of outcome studies), 42
Codes, in measurement,
179–181
Collaborative efforts in single-
system design, 121–123
Collections of standardized
measures, 254, 255–256,
257, 258, 259, 260
Combined designs, 481–495
Comparison groups (*see* Control
groups)

Comparison between classical
research and SSD,
43–48
Comparison of intervention,
logical bases for,
347–353
Complex designs, 481–495
Computational steps:
celeration line, 582–583
Δ-index (delta index), 585
interquartile range, 575
mean, 572
median, 571
standard deviation, 577–578
trimmed mean, 573
**Computer analysis of single-
system design data,**
using SINGWIN,
614–650
user's guide, 614–650
**Computer Assisted
Assessment Package**
(CAAP), 139–140
**Computer Assisted Social
Services** (CASS),
139–162
copyright notice, 160
guidelines for use of,
139–162
legal notices regarding, 160
training materials for, 161
Computer-generated steps:
autocorrelation (with
SINGWIN), 538
celeration line charts (with
SINGWIN), 581
central tendency and
variability (with
SINGWIN), 576
chi-square (with SINGWIN),
606
client disk, creating, 142–147
computer assisted social
services (CASS),
139–162
effect size (with SINGWIN),
591
evaluating personal
problems, 147–150
new file, 142–147

printing client scores, 273–276
proportion/frequency approach (with SINGWIN), 598
X-mR-Chart (with SINGWIN), 601, 604
Computerized recording of caseload, 137–162
advantages and disadvantages of, 137–138
Concepts, 38
Conceptualization:
as basis for measurement, 13, 38
of the presenting problem, 8–10
principles of, 57–85
Concomitant variation, in experimental designs, 131, 178
Concurrent baseline, 367
Concurrent schedule design, 482
Confidentiality, 678
Consent forms, 681
Conservative rule, use in probability tables, 550
Consistency of measures, 64
Constant series design, 456
Construct validity, 74–75
Construction or additive design, A-B-A-C-A-BC-( ), 479
Context, in evaluating practice, 51–53, 80
Continuous recording, 169
Contract, in single-system designs, 19
Contrast effects, 341
Contrast group (see Control group)
Control group (comparison or contrast group), 44, 365, 415
Cooperation in recording, 121–123
Core practice skills, 38
Correlation, 65, 74, 131

Cost-benefit (effectiveness) analysis, 506–507, 678–679
Costs in research and evaluation, 45
Countability of behavior, 93
Counterbalanced intervention, 483
Creating a new client record, 142–147
Creativity in single-system designs, 499–501
Crisis intervention (minimal contact situation), 501–502
Criterion level of performance, 100–101, 557–560
Criterion validity, 73–74
Critical incident recording, 288
Critical thinking, 501–502, 507–511
Criticism of single-system designs, 48–50, 665–674
ethical issues, 669–670
meta-issues in philosophy, poilitics, and socioeconomics, 670–673
practice issues, 667–668
research and evaluation issues, 668–669
technological issues, 673–674
Crossover designs, 455–456
Cumulative charting, 131–132
Cutting score (clinical cutoff), 80, 113
Cycle, 560

D
Data, analysis of, 515–553
Data collection:
of baseline information, 126
charting, 126–132
how long?, 525–528
how many targets?, 125–126
how often?, 124–125
phases, 132–134
presentation of, 127–132
standardized recording procedures, 126
when?, 123–124

where?, 123–124
who should collect?, 118–121
Decision making, in case illustration, 29–30, 40
Definitions:
conceptual, 38–39
operational, 38–39
Delayed intervention, 559
Δ-index (delta index), 585–589
calculating, 585–586
Dependent variable in single-system designs, 517
Dereification, 94
Descriptive statistics, 569–594
case illustration, 26
cautions, in use of, 592–593
measures of central tendency, 570–574
mean, 571–574
median, 570–571
measures of effect size, 581–592
Δ-index (delta index), 585–589
g-index, 589–591
issues regarding, 591–592
measures of trend, 576–581
celeration line, 580–584
trend line, 578
measures of variation, 574–576
range, 574–575
standard deviation, 575–576
optimal use, 592–593
using SINGWIN, 576, 581, 591
Design for all seasons, 499
Designs (see Evaluation designs)
Deterioration in client behavior, 551–552
Developing a working theory, 8–10
Diagrams:
of experimental/control group designs, 47
of single-system designs, 47
Dichotomous problem situations, 505
Differences in level of data, 555

Differentiating or strip design [*A-BC-A-B-A-C-*( )], 480
Directness of measures, 81–83, 165
Disagreement, in pattern of results, 561
Discontinuity in levels of data, 554–557
Dispersion (*see* Measures)
Do-it-yourself-questionnaires, 260–261
Dominance, in patterns of results, 557–560
Drift:
  change in practitioner's intervention, 338
  trend of data across phases, 556
Drop-outs, premature, 664–665
Duration:
  definition of, 165
  measures of, 183–184
  recording, 183–184
  reliability, 184–185
  sample form regarding, 184

E

Ease of use of single-system designs, 84
Educators and single-system designs, 686–688
Effect size (ES), 358–359, 581–586
Effectiveness, 46, 517, 672
Efficiency, 517, 660–663
  use in proportion/frequency approach, 599–600
Effort, 516
Elabortion of the *A-B* design, 395–399
Electromechanical measuring devices, 56
Empathy, 38
EMPIRICIST (direct observation of behaviors, using computer programs), 168
Equivalent time-sample design, 411

Errors, decision, 521
ES (*see* Effect size)
Ethical considerations in single-system design, 675–680
  Client Bill of Rights, 679–680
  model client consent form, 680–681
  ethical review of case, 11–12
  suggested ethical principles, 675–680
Ethical context:
  of practice, 8–10
  for using results, 22–24
Ethical design, in practice plans, 19–20
Evaluation:
  for administrators, 680–686
  in agency settings, 684–686
  clients, 674
  compared to monitoring, 36
  compared to research, 44–46, 48–50
  definition, 36
  design, 21–22, 40, 328–330
  educators and students, 686–688
  of goal achievement, 524–529
  as practice, 41–43
  for practitioners, 40–41
  overview, 51–54
  role of baseline in, 365
  schematic presentation of, 47, 329, 517
Evaluation designs, 325–512
  A (observation only), 381–382
  A-B, 386–399
    aggregating *A-B* designs, 395
    assumptions of, 381–382
    the basic single-system design, 386–387
    case illustrations, 389–394
    elaboration of the *A-B* design, 395–399
    introducing client to, 399
    limitations of, 388–389

  recommendations regarding, 389
  strengths of, 387–388
  A-B-A (experimental removal of intervention design), 404–411
    case illustrations, 406–411
    introducing client to, 411
    limitations of, 405–406
    recommendations regarding, 406
    strengths of, 405
  A-B-A-B (experimental replication design), 411–423
    case illustrations, 416–422
    introducing client to, 422–423
    limitations of, 413–415
    recommendations regarding, 415–416
    strengths of, 412–413
  A-B-A-B-BC-B-BC (interaction design), 489–495
    case illustrations, 491–495
    introducing client to, 495
    limitations of, 491
    recommendations regarding, 491
    strengths of, 490–491
  A-B-A-B-BC-B-BC-B-( ) (interaction/additive design), 490
  A-B-A-C (successive intervention design), 471
  A-B-A-C-A (successive intervention design), 471–480
    case illustration, 474–478
    extensions of, 478–480
    introducing client to, 478
    limitations of, 472–473
    recommendations regarding, 473–474
    strengths of, 472
  A-B-A-C-A-BC-( ) (additive or constructive design), 479–480

A-B^1-B^2-B^3 (changing intensity design), 458–470
case illustrations, 462–468
changing criterion type, 459
changing program type, 460
introducing client to, 468–470
limitations of, 461
recommendations regarding, 461–462
strengths of, 460–461
A-B-C (successive intervention design), 470–471
A-B/C-$(B$ or $C)$ (alternating intervention design), 481–489
case illustration, 485–489
introducing clients to, 489
limitations of, 485
recommendations regarding, 485
strengths of, 483–485
A-BC-A-B-A-C-( ) (differenting or strip design), 480
A-BC-A-BC-B-BC-( ) (interaction or strip design), 490
(B) intervention only, 382–383
B-A-B (experimental repeat of intervention design), 423–427
case illustrations, 425–427
introducing client to, 426–427
limitations of, 425
recommendations regarding, 425
strengths of, 424–425
B-C (design changes in case study), 383
case study method, 381–386
basic components of, 381–382

case illustrations, 384
introducing client to, 385–386
history of, 382–383
limitations of, 383–384
recommendations regarding, 384
strengths of, 383
constant-series designs, 456
crossover designs, 455–456
definition of, 325
multiple baseline designs, 429–452
case illustrations, 437–451
combined with other evaluation designs, 432–433
introducing clients to, 451–452
limitations of, 435–436
patterns of components in, 430
strengths of, 433–435
types of, 431–433
multiple target designs, 452–454
case illustration, 452–453
introducing clients to, 454
limitations of, 454
recommendations regarding, 454
strengths of, 453–454
Evaluation logs, 288
Event sampling, 168–169
Exit questionnaires, 504
Experimental designs, 400–427
Experimental group designs and single-system designs, 43–48
Experimental removal of intervention design $(A$-B-$A)$, 404–411
Experimental repeat of intervention design $(B$-A-$B)$, 423–427
Experimental replication design $(A$-B-A-$B)$, 411–423
Experimental single-system designs, 400–427

Experimenter bias, 83
Exploratory logs, 282
forms for, 283–289
External validity, 353–359
enhancing, 355–356
threats to, 354–355

F
Face validity, 71
Facts in evaluation, 40
Feedback, in single-system designs, 44
Figure of basic patterns of data for visual analysis, 558
Files, on SINGWIN computer program:
copying, 623–624
creating, 619
creating charts (or graphs), 626
deleting, 626
editing/viewing, 619–626
file menu, 617
renaming, 625
First aid services, 501–502
First difference transformation, 538–540
computational steps, 541–542
computer steps, 540
Fit the method to the client, 215
Flow diagram for evaluating practice, 4–5, 53
Follow-up, 530–531
Form for post-session report, 321
Formulas:
autocorrelation, 535–537
celeration line, 582–583
chi-square, 607–608
Δ-index (delta index), 585–586
first-differences transformation, 541
g-index, 589
interquartile range, 575
mean, 572
median, 571
moving average transformation, 539

Formulas: *(continued)*
  number of baseline data
    points, 374
  proportion/frequency, 599
  reliability measures, 182
  reverse-scoring procedures,
    250–251
  standard deviation, 577–578
  trimmed mean, 573
  three-standard-deviation-
    band approach (X-mR-
    chart), 602–603
Framework of questions for
    selecting a single-system
    design, 497
Framework for selecting a
    procedure for analyzing
    data, 651–656
Freeze technique, group
    measure, 192
Frequency, definition of, 165
Frequency measures, 179–183
  reliability in, 181–182
  sample forms for, 181, 182
Fuzzy concepts, 38, 98

G
Generalizability, 355–359
  by meta-analysis, 358–359
  by probability, 357–358
  by replication, 356–357
g-index, 589–591
Global Assessment of
    Functioning Scale
    (GAF), 257
Global Assessment–Geriatric
    Subjects (GAGS), 259
Goal Attainment Scaling (GAS),
    102–105
  criticism of, 105
  guide to, 102–104
Goals and objectives:
  case illustrations of, 109–112
  client goals and objectives,
    98
  compared with results, 27–29
  components of, 99–101
  defined, 98–99
  evaluating achievement,
    524–525

goal statements:
  under what conditions?,
    101
  to what extent?, 100–101
  who?, 99
  will do what?, 99–100
  for groups, 105–107
  indicators of success,
    multiple, 106–107
  objectives, defined, 98–99
  overview of procedures to
    identify problems and
    goals, 115
  problems in setting goals:
    anticipating impediments,
      108
    anticipating negative
      outcomes, 107
    who sets the goals?,
      107–108
  specifying, 97–102, 115
  statistics in, 101–102, 113–114
  ultimate, 98
Goals and problems, specifying
    targets of intervention,
    86–115
Graphs (*see* Charts)
Group-level measures, 105–107
Groups, setting goals in,
    105–107
Guide for selecting:
  analytic procedures, 651–656
  designs, 496–514
  measurement procedures,
    312–323

H
History, alternative explanations
    of outcomes, 351,
    412–413
Homework, by clients, 195–196
Homogeneity, defined, 67–68
Horizontal axis (abscissa), 127
Human subjects review
    committee, 44
Hypotheses:
  in case illustration, 28–29
  in practice, 20, 367
  in single-system designs, 51,
    74–75, 318, 352, 367, 519

I
Identifying goals and
    objectives, 8
Identifying problems and
    strengths, 7–8
Idiographic evaluation design,
    37
Immediate intervention effects,
    559
Improvement in data on client
    functioning, 557–560
Incomplete data, 341–342
Independence, 533–534
Independent data collectors, 120
Independent variable
    (intervention), 517
Indexes (also called scales):
  of Alcohol Involvement
    (IAI), 236
  of Brother Relations (IBR),
    247
  of Child's Attitude toward
    Father (CAF), 246
  of Child's Attitude toward
    Mother (CAM), 245
  of Clinical Anxiety (ICA),
    235
  of Clinical Stress (ICS), 234
  construction of, 199–209
  of Family Relations (IFR),
    249
  Generalized Contentment
    Scale (GCS), 232
  interpretations of, 251–253
  limitations of, 253–254
  of Marital Satisfaction (IMS),
    77–78, 238
  Non-Physical Abuse of
    Partner Scale (NPAPS),
    242
  observer rating scales, 197
  of Parental Attitudes (IPA),
    244
  of Partner Abuse Scale: Non-
    Physical (PASNP), 240
  of Partner Abuse Scale:
    Physical (PASPH), 241
  of Peer Relations (IPR), 237
  of Physical Abuse of Partner
    Scale (PAPS), 243

of Self-Esteem (ISE), 233
self-rating scales, 197
of Sexual Satisfaction (ISS), 239
of Sister Relations (ISR), 248
standardized scales, available, 254–261
  computer use, 263–264
  constructing and using, 199–210
  for groups, 262–263
  for others, 257–261
  for practitioners, 254–257
  for self, 261–262
  uses of, 196–199
Indicators of problems, 61–62, 107
Indirect measures, 81–84
Individualized Rating Scales:
anchors for use in, 203–207
constructing and using, 199–209
dimensions to be rated, 200–202
response categories, number of equidistant, 202–203
use of, 196–199
who, when, where to collect data for, 207–209
Inferences of causality (*see* Causality)
Information for Practice, 137
Informed consent, 24
Instruments, 173–175
examples of, 174–175
principles for selecting, 174
for recording behavior, 173–174
Integrating research, evaluation, and practice, 35–56
Intensive research design, 37
Interaction/additive design [*A-B-B-B-BC-B-BC-( )*], 490
Interaction design (*A-B-A-B-BC-B-BC*), 489–495
case illustrations, 491–495
introducing client to, 495
limitations of, 491

recommendations regarding, 491
strengths of, 490–491
Interaction log, 283
Interaction/strip design [*A-BC-A-BC-B-BC-( )*], 490
Internal validity, 351
Interpretation of data, 564–566
Interquartile range (*Q*), 575–576
Interresponse interval recording, 183–184
Interval level of measurement, 59, 165
recording, 185–189
  forms for, 187, 188
  reliability in, 187–189
Intervention, 36, 68–96, 332–334
change, when to, 338–340, 528–530
choice of, 332–334
clear relationship between intervention and problem/goal, 334
compared to baseline, 39
defined, 36
influenced by evaluation, 528–530
irreversible, 339–340
noted as X, 134
operational versus procedural, 333–334
planning, 332–334
reversible, 339–340
when to be removed, 402–404
Introducing client to specific design (*see specific single-system design*)
IRS (*see* Individualized Rating Scales)
Interventions, selection of, 17–19

K
K (corrective factor), 359
Kappa (measure of agreement), 68
Knowledge-building, 50
Knowledge-using, 50

Known end-state data for approximate baseline, 503

L
Lag, 533
Latency recording, 183–185
Length of baseline, 368–369
Level of data (magnitude of data), 555
Level of probability (0.05, 0.01, 0.001), tables for, 544–549
Limitations of guide for guide for selecting analytic procedure, 655–656
Limitations of research and evaluation designs, 46
Logs, 277–295
use in assessment, 277–278
client involvement in, 280–282, 291–292
combined with other measures, 278, 288–291
critical incident log, 280–282
definition of, 277–278
evaluation function of, 278
evaluation log, 288
exploratory log, 282, 284–285
general model of, 278, 279
interaction log, 283, 287
introducing clients to, 291–292
practitioner log, 292–293
problem-category variations, 279
reliability with regard to, 293–295
target problem log, 282–283
time variations types, 278–282
uses of, 278
validity with regard to, 293–295

M
Maintenance phase, 530–531
Managed care, single-system designs evaluation in, 506–507, 660–663

Mean (M), 571–574
Mean line, defined, 578
  examples, 578–580
Measurability of behavior,
  61–62, 94
Measurement, 58–85
  advantages of, 59–60
  all-purpose procedure, 197
  can everything be
    measured?, 61–62
  characteristics of, 62–69
  of client problems, 60–61
  definition as first step in,
    60–61
    conceptual definition, 60
    nominal definition (*see*
      Conceptual definition)
    operational definition, 61
  definition of, 58
  error, 63
    random measurement
      errors, 63
    systematic measurement
      errors, 63
  factors influencing choice of
    measures, 81–84
  factors influencing reliability
    and validity, 79–81
  indicators, 61–62
  levels of, 58–59
    interval level, 59
    nominal level, 58–59
    ordinal level, 59
    ratio level, 59
  package, 319–320
  plan, 116–138
  principles, of, 57–85
  of problems or potentials, 58
  and recording plan, steps in,
    41–42, 118–126
  relationship between validity
    and reliability, 79
    reliability issues, 63–70
    validity issues, 70–79
  repeated, 44 (*see also* Time
    series design)
  selecting methods of, 118,
    312–326
  steps in developing a
    recording plan, 118–126

who collects the data?,
  118–123
Measures:
  central tendency, 570–577
  characteristics:
    of clients, 315–316
    of measures, 313
    of practitioners, 315
    of targets, 313, 315
  confidence in using multiple
    measures, 318
  correlations between, 318
  direct, 81–83, 313
  effect size (ES), 581–592
  guidelines for using multiple
    measures, 317–319
  indirect, 81–84
  linear trends, 593
  measurement package,
    319–329
  multiple, 317–319,
    321–322
  nonreactive, 296–311
  primary, 319
  problems using multiple
    measures, 319
  proxy, 62
  reactivity of, 296–311
  repeated, 39
  secondary, 319–329
  selecting, 322
  sensitivity to change, 77
  situations where best used,
    314
  standardized, 211–266
  summary of, 314
  trends in, 576–581
  unobtrusive, 302–311
  variations in, 574–576
Median (Md), 570–571
Meta-analysis, 358–359,
  581–592
Minimum contact situations,
  evaluation designs for,
  501–506
Missing data, charting, 129–130
Model consent form, 681
Monitoring, definition of, 36
Monitoring intervention
  progress, 39, 40, 44, 136

Moving average transformation,
  538–540
Multidimensional measures,
  213
Multi-element designs, 482–483
Multiple-baseline designs,
  429–452
  case illustrations, 437–451
  across clients, 429, 432–433
  introducing client to,
    451–459
  limitations of, 435–436
  number of targets in, 430
  patterns of, 430
  across problems, 429, 431
  recommendations regarding,
    436–437
  across situations (settings),
    429, 431–432
  strengths of, 433–435
Multiple-component design,
  478–480
Multiple measures, 317–322
  guidelines for use of,
    321–327
  problems in using, 319
Multiple-schedule design, 482
Multiple-target design, 452–454
  case illustrations, 452–453
  introducing client to, 454
  limitations of, 454
  recommendations regarding,
    454
  strengths of, 453–454

N
N = 1 research (evaluation)
  designs, 37
Naturalistic research, 48
Negative numbers,
  transformed, 542
Negative outcomes or results,
  551–552, 557–558
Nominal level of measurement,
  58–59
Nonintervention (*see* Baseline)
Nonreactivity (*see* Reactivity;
  Unobtrusive measures)
Nonstatistical considerations in
  monitoring, 655

Normal curve and the proportion/frequency approach, 563
Notations for phases, 335
Null hypothesis, 519–521

O

Objectives:
  components of, 99–101
  definition of, 98–99
  extent, 100–101
  versus goals, 98
  indicators, 99
  outcome, 98–99
  specifying, 97–98, 99–101
  using statistics in, 101–102
Observation:
  accuracy of, 175–176
  methods of, 179–181
  reliability and validity in, 176–179
Obstacles to research and evaluation, 668–669
On-line help, 151
Operational definition of client problem or goal, 61, 87, 95–97
Operational dimension of the intervention, 333
Order of intervention:
  presentation, 341
  problems in, 340–344
Ordinal level of measurement, 59
Ordinate (vertical axis), 129
Other (than client or practitioner) as data collector, 120–121
Outcomes, in goal statements, 97–99
Outliers, definition of, 570
Own control, in single-system design, 365

P

Package of techniques, 319–320
Patterns in visual analysis, 557–560
  ambiguous patterns, 564
  chart showing basic patterns, 558
  interpreting several patterns simultaneously, 560–562
Performance, measurement of goal attainment, 102–105
Phases of the intervention program, baseline and intervention, 132–134, 334–338
  adjacent/nonadjacent, 338
  changes in intervention, 338–340
  complications in, 340–432
    carryover, 340
    contrast, 341
    incomplete data, 341–342
    order of presentation, 341
  definition of, 39, 132
  follow-up, 344–346
  length of, 337
  maintenance, 344–346
  notation, 114–115, 335
  shown on charts, 342, 343, 344
  training, 342–344
  types of, 39, 334–338
Physical traces, in unobtrusive measures, 310–311
Post-session reports (*see* Follow-up)
Power (to detect a difference between phases if there is one), 520–522
Practical, statistical, and theoretical significance, 518–523
Practice:
  approaches (practice designs), 39
  decisions, 40
  design, 17–19, 39–40
  as evaluation, 20, 41–43
  hypotheses, 51, 75, 452
  insight, 454
Practitioner:
  characteristics of, 120, 315
  as data collector, 39–40, 120
  definition of, 36
  scientific, definition of, 41–42
Predesigns, 381–386
Preliminary assessment, 88–92
Prevention, evaluated by single-system designs, 663–666
Primary measure, 319
Primary prevention, and single-system evaluation, 663–666
Principles:
  of analysis, 515–553
  of conceptualization and measurement, 57–85
  of single-system design, 327–363
Probability, computing, 540–552
Probability tables, for single-system designs, 540–552
  0.05 table, 544–545
  0.01 table, 546–547
  0.001 table, 548–549
  reading tables, 551
    for apparent improvement, 550–551
    for apparent deterioration, 551–552
  use in proportion/frequency approach, 540–552
Problem(s):
  characteristics of, 87
  as defined by clients, 87–89
  examples of, 95–97
  number to record, 125–126
  prioritizing, 91–92
  specifying, 88–92
Problem checklist, forms for, 89, 90, 91
Problem construction and formulation, 92–95
Problem evaluation, 117–137
Problem hypotheses, role of baseline in, 365–367
Problem identification, preliminary steps in, 88–92
Problem-oriented record (POR), 134–137
Problem prioritization, 91–92

Problems and goals, specifying
   targets of intervention,
   86–115
Problems and strengths,
   redefined, 16
Problem selection, 89–91
Problems of visual inspection,
   566–568
Problem-solving process, 37, 42
Problem survey, 88–89
Procedural dimension of
   intervention, 333
Program, as set of techniques or
   packages, 335
Progress, role of baseline
   in determining,
   136–137
Proportion/frequency
   approach:
   computing with SINGWIN,
      598
   efficiency estimation,
      598–599
   limitations of, 599
   steps in using, 599
   strengths in, 596–598
Prospects of research and
   evaluation, 46
Proxy measures, 83
Psychoanalytic case using
   single-system design,
   389–391

Q
Q (interquartile range), 574–575
Qualitative information, 48–50
Quantitative vs. qualitative
   research and evaluation,
   48–50
Quality assurance review
   (QAR), 661
Quantitative information,
   48–50
Quantitative research, 48–50
Questionnaires:
   do-it-yourself types, 261–262
   standardized, 211–266
Questions regarding single-
   system designs, and
   answers to, 507–511

R
r_{F2} (autocorrelation), 532–540
   computation steps for testing
      for, 534–537
   computer steps for testing
      for, 538
Random measurement error,
   63
Range, 574–575
Rapid assessment instruments,
   213–214
Rapport-building, 3, 6–7
Rates, 172–173
   computing, 172–173
   illustrations, 173
Rating scales, 194–210
   construction of, 199–207
   example of, 195–196
   use of, 196–199
Ratio level of measurement, 59
**Reactivity and nonreactive
   (unobtrusive)
   measures,** 296–311
   in archival records, 304–307
   in behavioral products,
      307–308
   causes or sources of,
      298–299
   decreasing or avoiding,
      299–300
   definition of, 296–298
   guidelines for using in self-
      monitoring, 301–302
   overcoming, 299–300
   in physical traces, 310–311
   in private records, 307
   in public records, 304–307
   in self-monitoring, 300–301
   in simple observations,
      308–310
   types of measures, 304–311
   unobtrusive measures,
      302–311
Reconstructing baselines, 368,
   369
Recording:
   as anxiety-producing,
      118–120
   client nonparticipation,
      118–120
   continuous, 124–125, 132,
      169
   forms for, 181, 182, 184, 187,
      188
   in groups, 191–193
   as help to clients, 365–367
   instruments, 173–175
      principles for selecting,
         174
   interruptions, 377–378
   plans for, 116–137
   in public as embarrassing,
      174–175
   not resisted by clients,
      674–675
   samples of, 168,
      169–172
   spot-checks, 170
   time samples, 169–171
Recording plan:
   advantages of a systematic,
      117–118
   developing a, 116–138
   steps in developing:
      begin collecting baseline
         information, 126
      decide how often to collect
         data,124–125
      decide on number of
         targets to record,
         125–126
      decide when and where
         to collect data,
         123–124
      decide who should collect
         data, 118–123
      enhancing cooperation for,
         121–123
      select a method of
         measurement, 118
      standardize recording
         procedures, 126
Records, in nonreactive
   measures, 304–308
Reference books for tests and
   measures, 265–266
Reification, 94
Relationship, 39
Relevant others as data
   collectors, 120–121

Reliability:
accessibility of measure, 84
administrative procedures,
    63–65, 79–80
alternative-forms, 66–67
of behavioral measures,
    166–168
choosing among measures of,
    70
definition of, 63–64
directness, 81–84
    direct measures, 81
    indirect measures, 82–83
ease of use, 84
of frequency measures, 177
high (acceptable level),
    defined, 70
    coefficient alpha, or
        Cronbach's Alpha or
        KR-20, 67–68
    internal-consistency
        reliability, 67–68
    split-half reliability, 67
homogeneity, 67
independent observations,
    64, 68
internal consistency form,
    67–68
    coefficient alpha reliability,
        or Cronbach's Alpha or
        KR-20, 67
    split-half reliability, 67
inter-observer (inter-rater), 68
for interval measures,
    175–176
Kappa, 68
levels of acceptable, 70
moving averages, 219
population factors, in, 80–81
of questionnaires, 218–221
in reactive measures, 303
relationship to validity, 79
relevance to intervention
    planning, 84
sameness of observations, 64,
    68
stability of a measure, 65
standard error or
    measurement (SEM)
    form, 68–70

test–retest form, 65–66
for time-sampling measures,
    65–66
Removal design, 401–402
    accidental, 403
    planned, 403
Removal of intervention, when
    not required, 338–340
Repeated measures, 39
Repeated pretest–posttest
    design, 395–397
Replication, 356–357
    clinical, 356
    direct, 356
    systematic, 357
Reports:
    to agency, 30
    to community, 30
    to the profession, 31
Representativeness of sampling,
    170
Research:
    classical, as compared to
        single-system designs, 47
    distinguished from
        evaluation, 48–50
    as practice, 41–43
    steps in, 47
Response bias, 227
Response set, 227
Retrospective baseline data,
    502–503
Reversal procedure, 403
Reverse scoring, 250–251
Rights of clients, 679–680
Role of client, in reactivity,
    298–299

S
Samples:
    client, 171
    rates, 172–173
    recording, 173–174
    situation (or setting), 172
    time, 169–171
Sampling, 168–173
Scales (see Indexes)
Scientific practice, components:
    ethical choices, 1–2
    evaluation component, 2

practice component, 1
practice theory, 1
practitioner, 2
Scientific practice, schematic
    figure describing, 2
Scientific practitioner,
    definition of, 41–42
Scoring the Clinical
    Measurement Package,
    250–253
    computational method,
        250–251
    computer method, 267–276
Secondary measure, 319–320
Selecting analytic procedure,
    651–656
    in case illustration, 27
    framework for selecting a
        procedure, 651–653
    limitations, 655–656
    nonstatistical considerations,
        655
    other statistical
        considerations,
        653–655
Selecting design, 496–512
    creativity in making your
        own designs, 499–501
    design for all seasons, 499
    framework for, involving five
        questions, 496–499
    minimal contact situations,
        evaluation designs for,
        501–506
    steps in, 497
Selecting efficient size statistic,
    653–655
Selecting measure, 312–326
    characteristics involved in the
        decision for:
        client and available
            resources, 315–316
        measure, 313
        practitioner, 315
        target, 313, 315
    considerations in, 313–316,
        323
    an exercise in, 316–317
    the measurement package,
        319–321

Selecting a measure (continued)
multiple measures, 317–319
guidelines for using, 321–322
problems in using, 319
summary of, 314, 323
Selecting a test of statistical significance, 654–655
Self-anchored scales (see Individualized Rating Scales)
Self-monitoring, 165
Self-report measures, 277–295
Semiaverage approach to data analysis (see Celeration line, in determining trend line)
Sensitivity:
to change, 75
to client life experiences and culture, 80–81
Serially dependent data (see Autocorrelation)
Shewhart Chart (two-standard-deviation-band approach) (see Three-standard-deviation-band approach)
Short-term intevention (see Minimal contact situations)
Significance:
practical (or clinical or social), 518–519
statistical, 519–520
theoretical, 522–525
Simultaneous interpretation of several patterns of data, 452–454
Simultaneous treatment design, 482
Single-case experimental design, 37
Single-case study design, 37
Single-N research, 37
Single-organism research, 37
Single-system evaluations:
advantages, 50–51
analysis of data, 40

baseline and intervention phases, 39
basic characteristics of, 37–41
compared to classical research, 48–50
decision making, 40–41
developing your own, 499–501
disadvantages of (see Criticism of single-system design)
evaluation designs, 40
integrating evaluation and practice, 41
integrating different evaluation designs, 496–499, 500
measuring targets, by operational definitions, 38–39
practice designs, 39–40
purpose of, 37, 41–43
repeated measures, 39
specifying targets, problems or objectives/goals, 38
Single-system designs,
principles of, 327–363
causality in, 347–353
criteria in inferring, 348–349
changes in intervention, 338–340
characteristics of, 331–347
baseline period, 332
intervention period, 332–334
collaborative and team efforts in, 346–347
complications in, 340–344
carryover, 340
contrast, 341
incomplete data, 341–342
order of presentation, 341
training phase, 342–344
construct validity, 352–353
definition, 37
design validity, 349–350
example of, 328–330
external validity and generalizability, 353–359

enhancing through, 355–359
threats to, 354–355
internal validity, 351–352
maintenance and follow-up plans, 344–346
booster shot, 345
overview of, 360–363
diagram of designs, 361
phases in, 334–338
adjacent/nonadjacent, 338
changes of, 338–340
length of, 337
notation for, 335
purposes of, 330–331
statistical conclusion validity, 350
threats to, 350–351
SINGWIN (computer program), 522, 540, 552, 614–650
exiting, 616–617
files:
creating new, 619
copying, 623–624
copying using a new name, 625
deleting, 626
editing/viewing, 619–626
opening, 622–623
graphs (or charts):
creating band graphs, 632–633
creating basic line chart, 626
creating celeration line chart, 633
creating charts of transformed data, 630
creating other types of basic line charts, 628–631
installing, 646–649
menus:
file, 617
graphs, 619
reports, 619
statistics, 618
overview of, 615–618
reports generated by, 645

starting SINGWIN, 616
statistics:
    computing and testing
        autocorrelation, 636
    computing chi-square,
        642–644
    computing effect size, 596,
        639–640
    computing measures of
        central tendency and
        variability, 638–639
    computing proportion/
        frequency approach,
        640–641
    computing
        transformations,
        637–638
    computing *t*-test, 644
    computing X-moving
        range-chart (three-
        standard-deviation-band
        approach), 642
Situation samples, 172
Slope (trend of data within
    given phase), 555
SOAP (acronym for monitoring
    progress in case), 136
Social desirability response, 227
Social validation (significance),
    524–525
    social comparison form,
        524–525
    subjective evaluation form,
        524
Sociocultural sensitivity in
    evaluation, 80–81
Specification of problem, 38,
    88–95
    checklists for, 89, 90, 91
    clarifying, 92–93
    countability, 93
    definitions (conceptual,
        operational), 91
    dereification in, 94
    increases and decreases in,
        94
    measurability, 94–95
    prioritizing, 91–92
    problems in, 94
    verifying sources in, 93–94

Square root, table of, 537
Stability:
    of change of intervention,
        555–557
    of data, 555–557
    of measures, 65–66
Stable baselines, problems in,
    543–545
Staff cooperation, in use of
    single-system designs,
    683–684
Staff development, role of single-
    system designs in, 683
Standard deviation, 575–576,
    577–578
Standard error of measurement
    (SEM), defined, 68–70
Standard treatment group (*see*
    Control group)
Standardized measures (*see*
    Standardized
    questionnaires)
Standardized questionnaires,
    211–276
    accessibility for obtaining
        instrument, 224–225
    accuracy, maximizing,
        225–227
    administering, 225, 227–228
    advantages of, 214–216
    cautions in use of, 214–216
    Children's Global
        Assessment Schedule
        (CGAS), 258
    computer management of,
        263–264, 267–276
    defining principles of, six
        characteristics, 212–214
    directness of measures,
        216–218
    do-it-yourself, 261–262
    ease of use, 224
    frequency of administration,
        228
    Global Assessment–Geriatric
        Subjects (GAGS), 259
    for independent observers,
        257–261
    other names for scales or
        indexes, 212

    outline for evaluating, 217
    for practitioners, 254–257
    problems with, 253–254
    purpose of, 216
    Rapid Assessment
        Instruments (RAI),
        213–214
    relevance to intervention
        planning, 218
    reliability of, 213, 218–221
    selecting, 216
    self-report types of, 228–229
    sources of locating, 265–266
    timing of administration, 228
    use in groups, 262–263
    validity of, 213, 221–224
    WALMYR Assessment
        Scales, 229–254
        interpreting scores of,
            251–253
        overview of, 230–231
        scoring procedures for,
            250–251
Statistical conclusion validity,
    350–351
Statistical, practical, and
    theoretical significance,
    518–519
Statistics, descriptive, 569–594
    cautions, in use of, 592–593
    measures of central tendency,
        570–574
        mean, 571–574
        median, 570–571
    measures of effect size,
        581–592
        Δ-index (delta index),
            585–589, 593
        d-index, 589, 593
        g-index, 589–591
        issues regarding,
            591–592
    measures of trend, 576–581
        celeration line, 580–584
        trend line, 578
    measures of variation,
        574–576
        range, 574–575
        standard deviation,
            575–576

Statistical significance, tests of, 26–27, 595–613
Strengths of clients and/or environments, 88, 91
Stretch *A-B* design, 506–507
Strip or differentiating design [*A-BC-A-B-A-C-*( )], 480
Subscales, 213
Subscripts, 411
Success, indicators of, in example, 107
Successive coincidence, principle of, 349
Successive intervention design (*A-B-C; A-B-A-C; A-B-A-C-A*):
  case illustration, 474–478
  extensions of, 478–480
    additive or construction design, 478, 479–480
    differentiating or strip design, 478, 480
    multiple-component design, 478–479
  introducing client to, 478
  limitations of, 472–473
  recommendations regarding, 473–474
  strengths of, 472
Superscript numbers, 336
Systematic measurement error, 63

T
Tables of probability, use in single-system designs, 544–549
Table of square roots, 537
Targets:
  basic characteristics in single-system designs, 36, 87
  checklist of problems and strengths, 88–91
  complaint scale, 525
  defined, 36, 87
  guidelines for becoming specific regarding, 92–95
    clarity, 92–93
    countability, 93
    dereifying, 94

increasing strengths, decreasing problems, 94
  measurability, 94–95
  verifying sources, 93
prioritizing, 91–92
selecting, 89–91
specification of, 87, 88
starting where client is, 88–89
steps in identifying, 88–95
Target problem log, 282–283
  forms for, 283
Task (service) analysis, with computer, 149
Team evaluation and collaborative efforts in evaluation, 346–347
  teasing out individual contributions, 347
Techniques, as defining phases, 335–336
Tests of statistical significance, 595–613
chi-square approach, 605–609
  considerations in using, 606–609
  general considerations in using, 610–613
  cautions in using, 612–613
proportion/frequency approach, 596–600
  considerations in use of, 599–600
  efficiency estimation use, 598–599
  tables for, 544–549
  zones in, 597–598
statistical process control charts (SPC), 600–601
  considerations in using, 610
three-standard-deviation-band-approach (X-moving range-chart), 600–605
t-test, 609–610
X-moving range-chart (X-mR-chart), 600–605
  additional uses for, 605

considerations in using, 604–605
Theoretical context for using results, 22–24
Theoretical orientation of practitioner, related to practice approach, 37–38
Theoretical significance, 522–523
Theory-free aspect of single-system designs, 37, 51
Thermometer, psychological, 200
Thick description, 48
Threats to validity:
  construct validity, 352–353
  different variables, 350
  diffusion, 352
  dropout, 351, 664–666
  guessing, 352
  history, 351
  instrumentation, 351
  interaction, 353
  internal validity, 351
  maturation, 351
  number of observations, 350
  practitioner effect, 352
  reliability of measures, 350
  statistical conclusion validity, 350–351
  statistical regression, 351–352
  testing, 351
Three-standard-deviation-band approach (X-moving range-chart), 600–605
  calculating, 602–603
  computing (with SINGWIN), 601, 604
  considerations in using, 604–605
Time sampling measures, 169–172
  client-recorded, 170–171
  with continuous recording, 169
  sample form, 171
Time-series analysis, 37
Time-series design, 37
Time variations, 278–282

open time type of log,
280–282
present time type of log,
278–280
Timing of change in
intervention, 338–340
Training, of observer, 167
Training phase, 530–531
Transformation of autocorrelated
data, 538–541
computations for, 539, 541
computer steps for, 540
Treatment (*see* Intervention)
Trend line, definition of, 578
Trends in data, 556–557, 558,
576–580
measures of trend, 576–581
Trimmed mean, 571–574
Trimmed range, 574–575
Trouble-shooting issues on
difficult case situations,
507–511
Three-standard-deviation-band
approach (X-mR-chart),
600–605
computational steps for,
602–603
computer steps for (with
SINGWIN), 601, 604
considerations in using,
604–605
t-test, 609–610
cautions with, 612–613
computing with SINGWIN,
610
considerations in using, 610
Type I and Type II decision
errors, 520–521
Typical patterns of problematic
events, 597–598

U
Ultimate goals, 98
Undesired zone in
proportion/frequency
approach, 113
Unidimensional measures, 213
Units of analysis, 38, 61
Unlikely successive coincidence
principle, 349

Unmeasurable problems, 61–62
Unobtrusive measures, 302–311
archival records, 304–311
behavioral products, 307–308
physical traces, 310–311
private records, 307
public records, 304–307
simple observation, 308–310
Unreliable observations, 71–73
Unstable baselines, 555–557
Utility:
in baselining, 370
of research and evaluation
findings, 45

V
Validity:
accessibility of a measure, 84
administrative procedures,
79–80
in baselining, 374
of behavioral measures,
177–179
choosing among measures of,
78–79
concurrent, 73–74
construct, 74–75
content, 71–73
random error, 72
systematic error, 72
convergent, 75–76
criterion-related (empirical),
73–74
definition of, 70–71
design, 349–350
discriminant validity, 75
discriminative, 75–76
ease of use, 84
empirical, 73–74
face, 71
faith, 71
Individualized Rating Scales,
196–199
internal, 351–352
known groups or
discriminant, 73–74
population factors in, 80–81
predictive, 74
of questionnaires, 221–224
in reactive measures, 75

reactivity, as threat to, 76–77
relationship to reliability, 79
relevance to intervention
planning, 84
sensitivity to change, 77
and single-system designs, 51
social, 80
statistical conclusions,
350–351
threats to, 74–78
Values in research and
evaluation, 45, 80
Variability of data in visual
analysis, 560–564
Variation, measures of, 574–576
Verifying sources, 93
Vertical axis (ordinate), 129
Visual analysis of single-
system design data,
554–568
definition of terms,
554–557
angle of slope, 559
change in level of data,
555–556
cycle pattern of data, 560
delayed (or honeymoon
period) changes, 559
deterioration, 555–556
discontinuity, 555
drift, 556
improvement, 555–556
level, 555
slope, 556
patterns of visual change,
557–562
diagram of basic patterns,
558
stability, 555
trends, 555
simultaneous interpretations of
patterns of data, 560–562
alignment, 560
disagreement, 561
dominance, 560–561
visual inspection of raw data,
562–568
ambiguous patterns, 564
guidelines for, 564–566
problems in, 566–568

W

WALMYR Assessment Scales
(WAS), 229–254
cautions in using,
253–254
interpretations of,
251–253
Wandering changes of
intervention, 509
Withdrawal of intervention,
402–404

World Wide Web Resources for
Social Workers, 137
Working theory:
developing, 8–10
use in recognizing events,
10–11

X

X-mR-chart (*see* Three-
standard-deviation-
band approach)

Z

Z (standard score), 588
Zones (or levels):
of desired behavior, 597
of extremely undesired
behavior, 597
of typical problem behavior,
597